WORLD RESOURCES

1994-95

WORLD RESOURCES

1994-95

A Report by
The World Resources Institute

in collaboration with

The United Nations
Environment Programme

and

The United Nations
Development Programme

Financial support was also provided by the Swedish
International Development Authority for database
activities and by the World Bank and the Netherlands
Ministry for Foreign Affairs for distribution

New York   Oxford
Oxford University Press
1994

The cover shows a Dogon woman drawing
water from a well on Mali's Gondo Plain.
The dusty harmattan winds from the Sahara,
which occur during January and February,
are a harbinger of the rainy season.
Photo by José Azel.

The World Resources Institute, The United Nations Environment Programme, and the United Nations Development
Programme gratefully credit or acknowledge permission to
reprint from the following sources:

Part I: Figure 3.1 and Table 3.2, United Nations Statistical
Division.

Part II: Figures 4.2 and 5.1, Don Carrick, DLC Designs; Fig-
ures 4.3, 4.7, 4.8, 4.14, and Table 4.1, Food Research Institute;
Box 5.3, Tables 1 and 2, Reprinted from *World Development*,
Vol. 16, No. 10 (1988), B. Bowander, S.S.R. Prasad, and
N.V.M. Unni, "Dynamics of Fuelwood Prices in India,"
pp. 1221 and 1218, respectively, with kind permission from
Elsevier Science Ltd., The Boulevard, Langford Lane,
Kidlington 0X5 1GB, U.K.

Part III: Figure 6.6, World Food Programme; Figure 6.9 and
Table 6.2, International Service for National Agricultural Research (the Netherlands).

Printed in the United States of America on recycled paper.

Oxford University Press

Oxford New York Toronto
Delhi Bombay Calcutta Madras Karachi
Kuala Lumpur Singapore Hong Kong Tokyo
Nairobi Dar es Salaam Cape Town
Melbourne Auckland

and associated companies in
Berlin Ibadan

ISBN 0-19-521044-1
ISBN (PBK) 0-19-521045-X
Library of Congress Cataloging Number: 86-659504
ISSN 0887-0403

World Resources is a biennial publication of the World Resources
Institute, 1709 New York, Ave., N.W., Washington, DC, 20006

Printing (last digit): 9 8 7 6 5 4 3 2 1

Contents

Preface

The *World Resources* series is published to meet the critical need for accessible, accurate information on environment and development. Wise management of natural resources and protection of the global environment are essential to achieve sustainable economic development and hence to alleviate poverty, improve the human condition, and preserve the biological systems on which all life depends.

Publication of *World Resources 1994–95*, the sixth in the series, reflects an ongoing collaborative effort of the United Nations Environment Programme (UNEP), the United Nations Development Programme (UNDP), and the World Resources Institute (WRI) to produce and disseminate the most objective and up-to-date report of conditions and trends in the world's natural resources and in the global environment.

This volume has a special focus on people and the environment, in support of the 1994 United Nations International Conference on Population and Development. Part I consists of three special chapters that highlight different aspects of people and the environment: natural resource consumption trends and their environmental consequences; the complex interactions among population growth, environmental degradation, and other factors; and the special and indeed essential role of women in sustainable development. Additional material pertinent to these topics is found throughout the volume. Part II continues the tradition of examining in each volume a particular region in more detail. In this case, it provides an overview of the environmental and natural resource issues faced by the world's two most populous nations, China and India, as they develop. Part III reports on basic conditions and trends, key issues, major problems and efforts to resolve them, and recent developments in each of the major resource categories, from agriculture to water resources to atmosphere and climate. Supporting data, as well as the core data tables from the World Resources Database, are found in Part IV.

Additional information and data can be found in the *Environmental Data Report*, published by UNEP in cooperation with WRI and the U.K. Department of the Environment, and in the forthcoming *Human Development Report 1994*, published by UNDP.

In an effort to make an expanded set of data accessible to policymakers, scholars, and nongovernmental organizations, WRI also publishes the *World Resources Database*—expanded to include additional countries, variables, and where possible a 20-year data set—on diskette.

The audience for the *World Resources* series has steadily expanded, with English, Spanish, French, Arabic, German, Japanese, and Chinese editions now in print. With this volume, an Indian edition, in English but printed in New Dehli, is planned to be added. A *Teacher's Guide to World Resources* is also available to make the series accessible and useful to teachers and students.

WRI, UNEP, and UNDP share the conviction that the *World Resources* series can best contribute to management of the world's natural resources and to a broadened awareness of environmental concerns by providing an independent perspective on these critical global issues. Accordingly, while both UNEP and UNDP have provided essential information, invaluable critical advice, and in some instances direct editorial collaboration, final responsibility for substance and editorial content of the series remains with WRI.

We commend the *World Resources* staff for its efforts in assembling and analyzing this unique collection of information on natural resources and the global environment and in producing the volume in a timely fashion. The Editorial Advisory Board, chaired by Dr. M.S. Swaminathan, provided active advice and support at all stages of the project.

We wish to thank the Compton Foundation, Inc., and Mrs. Louisa Duemling for support of the special focus chapters; the World Bank and the Netherlands Ministry of Foreign Affairs for assistance in distribution of the report, the Inter-American Development Bank and the African Development Bank for support of the Spanish and French editions, respectively, and the Swedish International Development Authority and the U.S. Environmental Protection Agency for support to expand and strengthen the *World Resources* Database.

Jonathan Lash
President
World Resources Institute

Elizabeth Dowdeswell
Executive Director
United Nations
Environment Programme

James Gustave Speth
Administrator
United Nations
Development Programme

Acknowledgments

World Resources 1994–95 is the product of a unique international collaboration involving many institutions and individuals. Without their advice, support, information, and hard work, this volume could not have been produced.

We are especially grateful for the advice and assistance of our many colleagues at the World Resources Institute (WRI), the United Nations Environment Programme (UNEP), and the United Nations Development Programme (UNDP). Their advice on the selection of material to be covered and their diligent review of manuscript drafts and data tables, often under time pressure, have been invaluable.

Institutions

We wish to recognize and thank the many other institutions that have contributed data, reviews, and encouragement to this project. They include:

The Carbon Dioxide Information Analysis Center **(CDIAC)**
The Congress of the United States, Office of Technology Assessment **(OTA)**
Development Alternatives with Women for a New Era **(DAWN)**
The Food and Agriculture Organization of the United Nations **(FAO)**
The Global Environmental Monitoring System of UNEP **(GEMS)**
The International Labour Organisation **(ILO)**
The International Institute for Environment and Development **(IIED)**
The International Food Policy Research Institute **(IFPRI)**
The Monitoring and Assessment Research Centre **(MARC)**
The National Aeronautics and Space Administration **(NASA)**
The National Oceanic and Atmospheric Administration **(NOAA)**
The Natural Resources Defense Council **(NRDC)**
The Organisation for Economic Co-operation and Development **(OECD)**
The Organization of American States **(OAS)**
The Oxford Committee for Famine Relief **(OXFAM)**
The United Nations Children's Fund **(UNICEF)**
The United Nations Educational, Scientific, and Cultural Organization **(UNESCO)**
The United Nations Population Division
The United Nations Statistical Division **(UNSTAT)**
The United States Agency for International Development **(U.S. AID)**
The World Bank
The World Conservation Monitoring Centre **(WCMC)**
The World Conservation Union **(IUCN)**
The World Health Organization **(WHO)**

Individuals

Many indviduals contributed to the development of this volume by providing expert advice, data, or careful review of manuscripts. While final responsibility for the chapters rests with the *World Resources* staff, the contributions of these colleagues are reflected throughout the book. Special thanks to Luis Gómez-Echeverri, manager of UNDP's Environmental and Natural Resources Group; to Danielle Mitchell, who coordinated access to pertinent UNEP experts in Nairobi; and to Pete Peterson and Ann Willcocks at MARC. We also thank our authors, who performed diligently and then endured patiently our numerous queries and often substantial editorial changes. The primary authors are listed at the end of each chapter. Reviewers, consultants, and major sources for each chapter include:

Natural Resource Consumption David Berry, U.S. Bureau of Mines; Peter D. Blair, Energy and Materials Program, OTA; Fred Campano, United Nations, Projections and Perspective Studies Branch; Stephen D. Casler, Allegheny College; Robert Gramlich, WRI; Lawrence Klein, University of Pennsylvania; Grecia Matos, U.S. Bureau of Mines; S. Murthy, Indira Gandhi Institute of Development Research; M. Panda, Indira Gandhi Institute of Development Research; Vikas Parekh, U.S. Bureau of Mines; Kirit Parikh, Indira Gandhi Institute of Development Research; Jyoti Parikh, Indira Gandhi Institute of Development Research; Don Rogich, U.S. Bureau of Mines, Janusz Szyrmer, University of Pennsylvania; Gu Weiwen, Drexel University.

Population and the Environment H. Abaza, UNEP; Varonique Arthaud, ILO; G. del Bigio, UNESCO; Eduard Bos, World Bank; Farid El Boustani, UNESCO; Sarah Burns, WRI; Kevin Cleaver, World Bank; Maria Concepción Cruz, World Bank; Robert Engelman, Population Action International; Leo Goldstone, UNDP; Bhakta Gubhaju, U.N. Population Division/DESD; Paul Harrison, U.N. Consultant; Carl Haub, Population Reference Bureau; Larry Heligman, U.N. Population Division; Carole Jolly, National Research Council; Gareth Jones, UNICEF; Sofi Lawrence, ILO; Nyein Nyein Lwin, UNICEF; Thomas Merrick, World Bank; Carrie Meyer, George Mason University; Stephen Mink, World Bank; Laura Mourino, UNDP; D. Okpala, UNEP; Mercedes de Onis, WHO; Robert Repetto, WRI; Joe Schamie, U.N. Population Division; William Seltzer, U.N. Statistical Division; Ann Thrupp, WRI; Carol Torel, WHO; Barbara Torrey, National Research Council; Richard Turnage, U.S. Bureau of the Census; Greg Watters, WHO; M. Gordon Wol-

man, Johns Hopkins University; Elizabeth Zell, Centers for Disease Control.

Women and Sustainable Development Peggy Antrobus, DAWN; Essma Ben-Hamida, Enda Inter-Arabe; Janet Brown, WRI; Beatrice Edwards, OAS Environmental Education Program; Don Edwards, Panos Institute; Louise Fortman, University of California at Berkeley; Jill Gay; Irene Guijt, IIED; John Hammock, OXFAM America; Cynthia Helms, WRI Board of Directors; Ana Isla, Women for a Just & Healthy Planet; Rachael Kyte, Women's Environment Development Office; Augusta Molnar, World Bank; Rosalie Norem, U.S. AID; Robert Repetto, WRI; Diane Rocheleau, Clark University; Irene Tinker, University of California at Berkeley; Marisol Tovarias, CODEFF; Joanne Vanek, UNSTAT; Mary Beth Weinberger, U.N. Population Division; Sally Yudelman, International Center for Research on Women.

China Robert N. Anderson, World Bank; Franklin Cardy, UNEP; R. Christ, UNEP; Paul Faeth, WRI; Qu Geping, National Environmental Protection Agency, China; Arthur Holcombe, UNDP; J. Hurtubia, UNEP; Zhang Kunmin, National Environmental Protection Agency, China; Gordon MacKenzie, UNEP; Terry S. Mast, WRI; David Melville, World Wide Fund for Nature; Nick Menzies, Ford Foundation; Carrie Meyer, George Mason University; Christopher Muller, U.S. Bureau of Land Management; Doug Murray, Lingnan Foundation; Jim Nickum, East-West Center; R. Orthofer, UNEP; Walter Parham, The Bishop Museum, Honolulu; P.J. Peterson, MARC, London; Lester Ross, Chadbourne and Parke, New York; Stapleton Roy, U.S. Ambassador to China; Boris Rozanou, UNEP; Scott Rozelle, Stanford University; Milton Russell, University of Tennessee and Oak Ridge National Laboratory; Vaclav Smil, University of Manitoba; Kirk Smith, East-West Center; Jinhua Zhang, UNEP.

The author wishes to gratefully acknowledge the National Committee on U.S.-China Relations, and especially the committee's Douglas Murray, for arranging a research and fact-gathering trip to China in September 1992. We also thank our hosts, especially Professor Qu Geping, formerly administrator of the National Environmental Protection Agency (NEPA) and now chairman of the Environmental Protection Committee of the National People's Congress; Zhang Kunmin, deputy administrator of NEPA; Xia Kunbao, director of NEPA's foreign affairs office; Zhou Zejiang; director of the science and technology office of the Nanjing Research Institute of Environmental Sciences; Shi Zhenhua, deputy director of the Jiangsu Environmental Protection Bureau; Lu Fukuan, director of the Shanghai Environmental Protection Bureau; Wu Boren, deputy director of the Guangdong Environmental Protection Bureau; and the many other NEPA officials, officials at other ministries and commissions, and provincial environmental officials who were kind enough to meet with us during this visit.

India Yinka Adebayo, UNEP; Ruth Alsop, Ford Foundation; A. Ayoub, UNEP; Amitabna Bhattacharya, UNDP; Bob Blake, WRI; Thomas A. Blinkhorn, World Bank; B. Bowonder, Center for Energy, Environment and Technology, Administrative Staff College of India at Hyderabad; Jeffrey Y. Campbell, Ford Foundation; Uttam Dabholkar, UNEP; Gunvant Desai, International Food Policy Research Institute; Daryl Ditz, WRI; Habib El-Habib, UNEP; Paul Faeth, WRI; Madhav Gadgil, Indian Institute of Science; H. Gopalan, UNEP; N. Htun, United Nations; Yateen Joshi, Tata Energy Research Institute (TERI); S.V.S. Juneja; T.N. Khoshoo, TERI; Carrie Meyer, George Mason University; K.P. Nyati, Confederation of Indian Industry; Mary Paden, WRI; Mark Poffenberger, University of California at Berkeley; Robert Repetto, WRI; K.M. Sarma, UNEP; Samar Singh, World Wildlife Fund; C.S. Sinha, TERI; Mark Svendsen, IFPRI; M.S. Swaminathan, M.S. Swaminathan Research Foundation; V. Vandeweerd, UNEP.

Food and Agriculture Sultan Ahmad, World Bank; Nikos Alexandratos, FAO; J.R. Anderson, International Service for National Agricultural Research (the Netherlands); Janos Ay, FAO; A. Curti, FAO; Paul Faeth, WRI; Nina Fedoroff, Carnegie Institution of Washington; Stephen Gasteyer, Applied Research Institute of Jerusalem; Kenton Miller, WRI; Luther Val Giddings, U.S. Department of Agriculture; Peter Hazel, IFPRI; Robert Horsch, Monsanto; P.G. Pardey, International Service for National Agricultural Research; Francesco Pariboni, FAO Statistics Division; David Pimentel, Cornell University; D.S. Prasada Rao, University of New England (Australia); Roel R. Ravanera, Agrarian Reform and Rural Development; Johannes Roseboom, International Service for National Agricultural Research; Neil Schaller, Wallace Institute for Alternative Agriculture; James Tarrant, U.S. AID; Ann Thrupp, WRI; Gary Toenniessen, Rockefeller Foundation; Joachim von Braun, IFPRI; Friedrich M. von Mallinckrodt, UNDP; B. Waiyaki, UNEP; John Westra, WRI; S. Zarqa, FAO.

Forests and Rangelands Barry Adams, Alberta Forestry Land and Wildlife; Tom Bartlett, Colorado State University; Thadis Box, College of Agriculture and Home Economics, New Mexico State University; Ing. Victor Sosa Cedilo, Departmento de Inventorios Forestales, RONA, UNEP; Harold Dregne, International Center for Arid & Semi-Arid Land Studies; Paul Faeth, WRI; Philip M. Fearnside, Department of Ecology, National Institute for Research in Amazonas, Brazil; Curtis Flather, Rocky Mountain Forest and Range Experiment Station, U.S. Forest Service; Lawrence Ford, U.S. AID; Jerry Holechek, Department of Animal & Range Sciences, New Mexico State University; Lynn Huntsinger, University of California at Berkeley; Nelson Hutabarat, Embassy of Indonesia; Nels Johnson, WRI; Steve Johnson, Native Ecosystems; Alex Korotkov, Economic Commission for Europe (ECE), FAO Agriculture and Timber Division; T. Maukonen, UNEP; C.H. Murray, FAO; T.J. Peck, ECE, FAO Agriculture and Timber Division; L.R. Rittenhouse, Colorado State University; K.D. Singh, FAO.

Biodiversity Francoise Burhenne-Guilmin, IUCN Environmental Law Centre; Arthur H. Campeau, Ambassador for Environment/Department of External Affairs and International Trade, Canada; John Caldwell, WCMC; John Carr, Conservation International; David Downes, Center for International Environmental Law; Brian Groombridge, WCMC; Lee Hannah, Conservation International; Jerry Harrison, WCMC; Nathalie Johnson, World Bank; Tim Johnson, WCMC; Kenton Miller, WRI; Walter Reid, WRI; Vincente Sanchez, Embassy of Chile; Nigel Sizer, WRI; Thomas Stone, The Woods Hole Research Center; Dan Tunstall, WRI; Hamdallah Zedan, UNEP.

Energy Yinka Adebayo, UNEP; Christian Averous, OECD; Deborah Bleviss, International Institute for Energy Conservation; William Chandler, Battelle Pacific Northwest Laboratories; Joy Dunkerley, OTA; Howard Geller, American Counsel for an Energy-Efficient Economy; Taka Hiraishi, UNEP; Gerald Houck, U.S. Bureau of Mines; Steven Karekezi, African Energy Policy Research Network; Anatoly Konevsky, UNSTAT; Keith Kozloff, WRI; Jim MacKenzie, WRI; Tse Pui-Kwan, U.S. Bureau of Mines; Kevin Rackstraw, American Wind Energy Association; Michael Schomberg, World Energy Council; Kirk Smith, East-West Center; Gordon Talisford, UNSTAT.

Water Vaughn Anthony, Northeast Fisheries Service; Christian Averous, OECD; Bob Beardsley, Woods Hole Oceanographic Institution; Ken Brink, Woods Hole Oceanographic Institution; Adele Chrispoldi, FAO; Francis Christie, Imariba; Uttam Dabholkar, UNEP; Arthur Dahl, UNEP; S. Garcia, Fishery and Resources Environment Division; Peter H. Gleick, Pacific Institute; Habib El Habr, UNEP; Lee Kimball, Consultant; Pamela Mace, NOAA, National Marine Fisheries Service (NMFS); Gordon B. Munro, University of British Columbia; Richard Neal, NOAA, NMFS; John B. Pearce, NOAA, NMFS; Guilio Pontecorvo, Columbia University; Walter Rast, UNEP; Manuel Vegas, Consultant; Michael Weber, NOAA, NMFS; Harold Weeks, Oregon Department of Fish and Wildlife; John Wise, Consultant; Ivan Zrajevskij, UNEP.

Atmosphere and Climate Christian Averous, OECD; Tom Boden, CDIAC; C. Boelke, GEMS; Uttam Dabholkar, UNEP; Paul Faeth, WRI; Jim Hansen, NASA Goddard Institute for Space Studies; John Harte, University of California at Berkeley; Andreas Kahnert, Economic Commission for Europe, FAO Agriculture and Timber Division; Charles Keeling, Scripps Institute of Oceanography; M.A.K. Khalil, Oregon Graduate Institute of Science and Technology; Dan Lashof, NRDC; Jim MacKenzie, WRI; Michael McElroy, Harvard University; Irving Mintzer, Center for Global Change, University of Maryland, College Park; R. Orthofer, UNEP; Ann Willcocks, MARC.

Industry Peter Nohr Anderson, UNEP; Matthew Arnold, Management Institute for Environment and Business; Stephen Barg, International Institute for Sustainable Development, Canada; Robert P. Bringer, 3M Corporation; Richard Denison, Environmental Defense Fund; Harry Fatkin, Polaroid Corporation; Joel Hirschhorn, Hirschhorn & Associates; Howard Klee, Amoco Corporation; Joel Makower, Tilden Press; David Sarokin, U.S. Environmental Protection Agency; Bruce Smart, WRI; W. Ross Stevens, III, E.I. DuPont de Nemours & Company.

International Institutions H. Abaza, UNEP; Nancy Alexander, Bread for the World; Antonio Donini, U.N. Executive Office of the Secretary General; Lee Kimball, Consultant; Adnan Z. Amin, OPDIAA; Lauren Looney, United Nations Information Center; Anni Lukacs, IUCN Environmental Law Centre; Maria Marotta, Oceans and Coastal Areas Programme, UNEP; Gareth Porter, Environmental and Energy Study Service; Glenn Prickett, NRDC; Kathryn Sessions, U.N. Association of the U.S.A.; Allen D. Putney, IUCN; Richard Tarasofsky, IUCN Environmental Law Centre; Geraldine Velandria, U.N. *Chronicle*; Frederick von Bolhuis, World Bank; Ann Willcocks, MARC; Maurice Williams, Overseas Development Council.

National and Local Policies and Institutions Dorm Adzobu, Consultant; Albert Adriaanse, Ministry of Housing, Physical Planning and Environment (the Netherlands); Walter Arensberg, WRI; Patrizio Civili, U.N. Executive Office of the Secretary General and Administrative Committee on Coordination; John Dixon, World Bank; Guillermo Espinoza G., Comisión Nacional del Medio Ambiente; Ronald Flippi, Consultant; Michael J. Furst, Consultant; Carlos Linares, WRI; Spike Millington, U.S. AID; Kirk Talbott, WRI; Hans van Zijst, Royal Netherlands Embassy.

Basic Economic Indicators Sultan Ahmad, World Bank; Boris Blazic-Metznr, World Bank; Betty Dow, World Bank; Alan Heston, University of Pennsylvania; Tranjit Kaur, World Bank; Asieh Kehyari, World Bank; Lawrence Klein, University of Pennsylvania; Farhad Mehran, ILO; D.S. Prasada Rao, University of New England (Australia); Dale Rothman, WRI; David Sieslikowski, World Bank; Bevin Stein, OECD; Dan Tunstall, WRI.

Land Cover and Settlements Rob Birch, American Automobile Manufacturers Association; Judith Hinds, Population Action International; Jonas Rabinovitch, UNDP.

Production Staff

A talented team of copyeditors, factcheckers, proofreaders, production editors, and desktop publishing experts accomplished the enormous task of preparing this volume for the printer. We thank them for their dedication, hard work, and high professional standards. In addition to the *World Resources* staff, they include:

Additional Fact Checking and Research
Rob Gramlich, Lisa Bryant, Kara Page

Copyeditors　Constance Buchanan, Michael Edington

Proofreaders　Evelyn Harris, Trish Weisman, Arthur Haupt

Manuscript Processing　Kathryn Solee

Additional Graphics Production
James Mangani

Index　Julie Phillips

Desktop Production　Susanne Kamalieh

Mechanical Production
EPI, Rockville, MD

We are especially grateful to WRI Librarian Sue Terry for assisting us with research and materials.

It has been a privilege to work with so many outstanding individuals throughout the world in producing *World Resources 1994–95*.

Allen L. Hammond
Editor-in-Chief

Introduction

This volume focuses on a closely linked set of issues related to people and the environment. Two of the three special lead chapters look at problems associated with the interaction between human populations and natural resources: those caused by taking resources from the environment or putting waste products into the environment (natural resource consumption), and those associated with the sheer growth in human populations. The third chapter focuses on an issue that intersects the previous two: the role of women in sustainable development.

These issues—natural resource consumption, the environmental impact of population growth, and women's role in sustainable development—are complex and controversial. Chapter 1 concludes that consumption and its environmental impact is not simply a function of life styles or the scale of industrial activity, although both are important factors; geographic patterns of production, terms of trade, level of technology, and the extremes of wealth and poverty also play a role. A careful examination of natural resource consumption patterns reveals some surprising differences from the conventional wisdom: it is renewable resources that are most in danger of depletion, not nonrenewable resources; the industrial countries as a group are the source of the majority of the natural re-

sources that they consume (petroleum and a few other commodities are major exceptions); and export of manufactured goods from developing countries to industrial countries is growing much more rapidly than the export of raw materials. On the other hand, the chapter also confirms and documents that, on a per capita basis, consumption in the industrial countries is far greater than in developing countries; that natural resource consumption among industrial countries has had by far the greatest impact on global environmental problems such as changes to the Earth's atmosphere; and that poverty and the inability to meet basic needs often compels the use of natural resources in ways that can lead to their degradation.

Chapter 2 concludes that the environmental impact of population growth depends on many factors other than the size of populations, especially social factors. It matters, for example, whether population growth takes place in rural or in urban areas, what level of human capital (as indicated by education levels and health) the population attains, and how rapidly growth occurs (either through natural increase or migration). A number of case studies (two in developing countries, one in an industrial country) show that such factors as poverty or wealth, government policies regarding natural resource management, land tenure

Introduction

and land use planning, and overall economic circumstances play a major role in determining whether population growth leads to environmental degradation and what form that degradation takes. This chapter, too, takes note of the close links between resource degradation, poverty, and further population growth.

One critical factor in both alleviating poverty and in finding development paths that are environmentally sustainable is the role of women. Chapter 3 points out that women in developing countries are often primary managers of natural resources on a local level, in addition to providing food, health care, child rearing, and a wide range of subsistence work for their families; that women often face an unusual number of barriers that inhibit their contributions to their societies; and that elevating the education, legal rights, economic opportunities, and cultural status of women is critical to the achievement of sustainable development. In fact, the record shows that development projects that do not include women as participants and that are not designed with women's needs in mind often fail. And the evidence is quite clear that investments in the education and health care of women—as well as in increasing access to family planning services—are among the most important factors in slowing population growth.

All three special chapters in the first section support the idea that environmental and developmental issues are intimately connected. All three also identify many opportunities for both industrial and developing countries to adopt policies that would help to further sustainable development.

In addition to these special chapters, this volume of *World Resources* contains a number of other features of particular note.

It offers two reports on regional environmental conditions, trends, and issues in Asia: one on China, the other on India. The chapters, like the countries themselves, are large and diverse, yet still of necessity omit many important issues. Nonetheless, what emerges is a sense that China is developing with enormous economic momentum and yet faces equally immense environmental problems that, if not addressed, could slow development or leave the country and its people environmentally impoverished. India has a wealth of natural resources, but poverty and the rate of growth of its population, as well as increasing industrialization, are straining those resources and increasing the risk of serious degradation.

The inclusion for the first time of a chapter on international policies and institutions acknowledges that we may be at the dawn of a new era of international environmental governance. Issues such as climate change clearly are global in nature and require global institutions for their management, including new mechanisms for financing the new strategies. The Global Environment Facility, examined in this chapter, is one attempt to forge such an institution.

While the world community grapples with the development of effective international policies and institutions, the work to move towards sustainable develop-

ment must still be done largely at the national and local levels. The chapter on national and local policies and institutions describes how the Netherlands is breaking new ground in trying to understand what sustainability really means for a national economy. Meanwhile, many developing nations are trying to identify environmental and resource priorities and devise strategies to deal with their most serious problems.

Questions about policies and institutions range well beyond these two chapters; indeed, they permeate much of this volume. For example, the chapter on water discusses the crisis of global fishery resources, a classic problem of the global commons and the difficulties of creating institutions to sustainably manage such resources. The chapter on biodiversity assesses the current status of the biodiversity convention.

This edition of *World Resources* also recognizes the environmental impact of industrial activity by including a new chapter devoted solely to those issues. In industrialized countries the adoption of cleaner processes is now recognized by many companies as a cost-effective practice. A key question is whether the momentum towards industrial transformation can continue to build.

Another issue of overriding importance is the relationship between the industrialized and developing countries, and particularly the willingness of industrialized countries to support sustainable development in the developing countries. For example, the chapter on food and agriculture includes a discussion on current developments in the area of agricultural biotechnology. This field holds much promise for the future of agriculture, yet there is uncertainty about whether the benefits will be monopolized by industrialized countries or shared with developing countries, and if so, how. Access to modern technologies and practices—including energy conservation practices—emerges as a theme in the examination of energy options and trends in developing countries in the "Energy" chapter.

This volume continues the tradition of presenting the latest data on environmental conditions and trends. A new United Nations assessment of tropical forests is discussed in the chapter on forests and rangelands. The latest figures on greenhouse gas emissions are presented in the chapter on atmosphere and climate, together with the results of a new assessment of air pollution in 20 of the world's megacities. The atmosphere chapter also provides an updated assessment of the complexities of climate change science.

In addition to the updated core data presented in every issue, the data chapters present a wealth of new information to help give context to the global debate. These new data sets include, among others, data comparing national wealth using purchasing power instead of currency exchange rates, data on the flow of trade between North and South, the status of megacities, the value of agricultural production, the status of natural habitat, the value of mineral reserves, the large lakes of the world, and the budgets of international organizations.

1. Natural Resource Consumption

Consumption, especially of natural resources, is the focus of much current discussion. People living in industrialized countries—collectively known as the North—constitute a small fraction of the Earth's human population, yet at present, they consume a large share of the world's natural resources. From the perspective of developing countries—the South—such consumption not only deprives them of resources needed for future development but also contributes disproportionately to the world's environmental degradation. These issues are controversial and complex.

THE RESOURCE CONSUMPTION ISSUE

Consumption in the North includes a wide variety of goods and services associated with a consumer culture, while in the South it focuses primarily on basic needs. If consumption patterns differ from North to South, they also differ significantly from commodity to commodity. Industrialized countries are the largest consumers of energy, which is integral to the lifestyle of most countries of the North. Developing countries, however, consume the most wood and wood prod-

ucts, primarily as fuelwood and charcoal, and clear most of the forestland, primarily for agriculture. Patterns differ over time as well: in past centuries, industrialized countries cleared their forests; and in the next century, developing countries will become the largest users of energy.

The environmental consequences of natural resource consumption are often borne by people other than those to whom the benefits of that consumption accrue (1). The North has had a greater impact on the global commons than the South has had, by dominating the marine fisheries of the open ocean, many of which are now endangered, and contributing a larger share of industrial chemicals now degrading the Earth's stratospheric ozone shield. Northern consumption of fossil fuel has contributed disproportionately to the buildup of carbon dioxide in the atmosphere and hence to the threat of global climatic change (2).

Consumption of metal, fiber, and food produced for the world market (dominated by the North) causes primarily local, not global, environmental degradation. As a group, the industrialized countries are the largest producers and consumers of most such materials and thus face the largest potential environmental impact. However, because of less efficient methods and technologies and fewer effective controls in the South, degradation is often relatively more severe there.

The environmental problems caused by natural resource consumption may be compounded when the people of the South claim their rightful share of the Earth's natural resources and their countries become industrialized. In recent decades, consumption of most natural resources has grown faster in the South than in the North, although most per capita consumption levels are still far below those in the North (3).

Nonetheless, the North's patterns of resource consumption are not environmentally sustainable even today, either for the region itself or as a model for the world. Stabilizing atmospheric concentrations of long-lived greenhouse gases such as carbon dioxide, for example, would require immediate 60 percent reductions in current emissions from human activity worldwide, and equity would suggest that such reductions should occur in those countries—primarily in the North—that have per capita emission levels well above the world average (4). Maintaining current emission levels, even with no growth, means eventually doubling and then quadrupling the atmospheric level of greenhouse gases, with the potential of committing the world to centuries of global warming, major change in precipitation patterns, and significant sea level rise (5).

Virtually all industrialized countries continue to release to the environment a massive quantity of toxic material—heavy metals, hazardous chemicals, and acidic gases. (See Chapter 12, "Industry.") If such emissions continue, toxic material will accumulate in the environment and eventually reach levels that could degrade forests and other ecosystems, pose health hazards to humans, and overwhelm natural cycles such as those that maintain the Earth's protective stratospheric ozone layer. Altering the natural resource consumption patterns that drive these problems is likely to require either far more efficient and less polluting technology or significant change in lifestyles, or both.

The South, too, has some unsustainable patterns of consumption that directly threaten the livelihood of people who depend on natural resources and that potentially foreclose their availability to future generations. In specific areas, freshwater resources, soils, forests, and habitats that support biodiversity are becoming severely depleted or degraded. Often, losses are a direct result of the struggle of severely impoverished people to earn a subsistence living by supplementing inadequate income with locally available natural resources in an unplanned manner. Achieving more sustainable resource consumption patterns will thus require development that alleviates poverty. Moreover, the urban areas and industrializing regions of the South are increasingly replicating the environmental problems associated with Northern resource consumption patterns—air and water pollution, release of toxic material to the environment, and solid-waste disposal—even though per capita resource consumption remains relatively low.

The pattern of natural resource commodity consumption and its environmental consequences is closely associated with the pattern of economic relationships between North and South. Over the past two decades, most natural resource commodity prices have declined in real terms (adjusted for inflation), intensifying economic pressure on countries of the South, for whom such commodities constitute a principal export. At the same time, natural resource commodities have become less important to the economies of most Northern countries, whose primary exports are high-value manufactured goods and services. The result is an unequal distribution of the benefits derived from use of the Earth's natural resources.

In recent decades, a number of developing countries have experienced more rapid economic growth than industrialized countries. In part, such growth reflects an increasing transfer of basic production to the South and the expansion of manufacturing in many developing countries. Thus, there has been an increasing shift in the South-to-North trade from raw natural resource commodities such as roundwood to lumber products, from copper ore to refined copper or even copper wire, from cotton lint to textiles, and from hides to shoes and other leather products. Such shifts reflect the process of development: they create additional economic value and employment in the South, although they may also increase the environmental burden.

Even if such shifts are taken into account, altering patterns of natural resource consumption and addressing their environmental consequences in the South as well as in the North may require significant change in the economic relationships between the two regions. Change could be crucial if underlying problems such as poverty and a more equitable division of the Earth's resources are to be addressed.

This chapter will examine patterns of natural resource consumption in industrialized and developing countries and the extent to which they act as a barrier or potential barrier to economic and human development. It will examine consumption trends and the environmental implications of current resource production and consumption for a number of specific resources and explore in a preliminary way the resource content of trade between North and South. Two case studies will examine in greater detail aspects of natural resource consumption in the United States and India, seeking to illustrate the complexity of resource consumption issues and the difficulty of altering current patterns. Policy measures for altering natural resource consumption in ways that could reduce its environmental and developmental impact are briefly considered. The chapter will thus attempt to provide a factual base for broader discussion of natural resource consumption issues.

Social and Historical Patterns

The background to this discussion includes a long history of economic relationship between Northern and Southern countries in which the latter's natural resources, often under the direct control of Northern governments or private entities, were exploited for

Northern consumption. European colonies in Africa and Asia, U.S. commercial activity in Latin America, and Japanese activity in Asia are well-documented examples (6) (7) (8) (9) (10). Colonial relationships enriched the North and often severely degraded the natural resource base of the South.

There is also a pattern of Northern consumption that may appear self-indulgent to Southern countries still struggling to meet basic human needs for many of their people. In the United States, for example, residential homeowners spend about $7.5 billion a year to care for their lawns, despite the fact that runoff from lawn chemicals contributes to municipal water pollution, grass clippings to solid-waste disposal problems, and exhaust from lawnmowers to urban air pollution (11) (12). Northern families spend about $9 billion a year on video games for their children (13). In 1989–91, by comparison, U.S. foreign development aid of all kinds totaled $10.1 billion and that of Japan $9.7 billion. (See Chapter 15, "Basic Economic Indicators," Table 15.2.)

There is enormous economic disparity between North and South. Per capita gross domestic product (GDP) and gross national product (GNP) are not reliable measures of natural resource consumption, but they do indicate the gap between North and South. Based on purchasing power parity, average 1991 GDP per capita is $18,988 for countries in the Organisation for Economic Co-operation and Development (OECD), compared with just $2,377 for developing countries. Disparity is often larger than the averages suggest. For the United States and India—the two countries used here as case studies—the 1991 per capita GDP based on purchasing power is $22,130 and $1,150, respectively. Based on currency exchange rates, appropriate for commodities moving in international trade, the gap between North and South is larger still, with average GDPs of $21,215 and $836, respectively. (See Table 15.1 and Technical Note 15.1.)

Even though many developing economies have been growing more rapidly than industrial economies in recent decades in percentage terms, the absolute size of the gap between rich and poor (on a per capita GNP basis) continues to widen. (See Figure 1.1.) Such disparities—in income and in access to resources and technology—between North and South cannot be ignored in a discussion of resource consumption.

NATURAL RESOURCE CONSUMPTION AND DEVELOPMENT

Nonrenewable resources, by definition, are finite. Hence the frequently expressed concern that high levels of consumption will lead to resource depletion and to physical shortages that might limit growth or development opportunity. Evidence suggests, however, that the world is not yet running out of most nonrenewable resources and is not likely to, at least in the next few decades. By a number of measures, reserves of energy and of subsoil minerals are more abundant, and real world prices for such commodities are generally lower today than 20 years ago, despite rising global consumption. Moreover, new technology is increasingly making possible substitutes for many traditional natu-

Figure 1.1 Trends in Gross National Product Per Capita, 1970–92

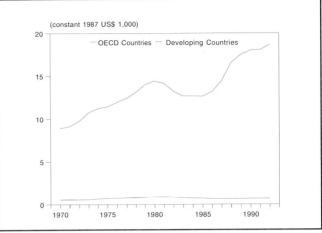

Sources:
1. The World Bank, *The World Tables, 1993*, on diskette (The World Bank, Washington, D.C., 1993).
2. United Nations (U.N.) Population Division, *Interpolated National Populations, 1950–2025, 1992 Revision*, on diskette (U.N., New York, 1993).

ral resource-based materials. Technology development is also yielding to more efficient means of providing light, motive power, and other energy-related services. Such changes are paving the way to economies less dependent on natural resources. When shortages do emerge, experience and economic theory suggest that prices will rise, accelerating technological change and substitution.

Renewable resources, in contrast, are often thought to be indefinitely renewable. Yet some are location-specific or depend on finite resources such as land. As natural systems are asked to supply more and more and to absorb ever more waste and pollution, degradation of their productive capacity and even the possibility of ecosystem collapse cannot be ruled out. In many areas, exploitation of both biological and physical resources already exceeds the regenerative ability of natural systems. Thus not only are many renewable resources increasingly scarce, but damage to the underlying systems that sustain or renew them threatens the near-term economic and human development of many nations.

Nonrenewable Resources

For minerals, economists distinguish between the resource base (all known resources) and reserves (that portion of a resource that can be produced at a profit at current prices). A traditional measure of the abundance of nonrenewable resources is the reserve-to-production ratio or reserve life index, which expresses the number of years of production at current annual rates that proven reserves will sustain. Since new resources are continually discovered and new process technologies increase the portion of those that can be economically recovered, estimates of reserves are continually adjusted. Nonetheless, the reserve-to-production ratio provides a snapshot of the perceived abundance of a mineral at a given time; changes in the ratio over time measure whether perceived abundance is increasing or decreasing.

A comparison of the world reserve-to-production ratios for nine major metals and for the three major fossil fuels shows that the ratio varies from about 20 years (for zinc, lead, and mercury) to well over 100 years (for iron, aluminum, and coal). Petroleum reserves constitute a 40-year supply at current production levels. (See Chapter 21, "Energy and Materials," Tables 21.4 and 21.5.) For most minerals, ratios generally increased over the 1970–90 period, despite rising consumption (14) (15). In many instances—were there incentive to undertake the drilling needed to establish additional reserves—reserve figures could be higher (16).

An alternative measure of resource abundance is provided by trends in supply and demand as measured by world commodity prices. Commodity prices are far more volatile measures than reserves, because they reflect a wide variety of market forces and (for oil) cartel actions, but the (inflation-adjusted) trend for major subsoil resources confirms that, in economic terms, they are less "scarce" than they were 20 years ago. (See Chapter 15, "Basic Economic Indicators," Table 15.4.)

An additional and critical factor for many nonrenewable resources is the prospect of substitution. In long-distance communication systems, copper is increasingly being replaced by optical fibers made of glass. Advanced plastics and composite materials are reducing the amount of iron and steel used in automobiles and the amount of aluminum used in airplanes. Increasing sophistication in the design of materials at a molecular level implies the ability to develop entirely new methods of meeting human needs and to engineer around any shortages of many minerals. Generally, this trend may imply that less and less of the economic value of final products will be attributable to raw materials. More efficient methods of converting fuel into electricity—from gas turbine/combined-cycle technologies to fuel cells—promise to reduce the energy needed to meet a given level of demand for power. In the next century, alternative technologies such as biomass, solar, wind, and nuclear may be able to supply a significant fraction of energy needs, reducing pressure on fossil fuel resources.

Deliberate policies could restrict demand still further or create more sustainable sources of supply. Recycling, for example, has already substantially reduced primary consumption of iron and aluminum in the United States. The use of "demand management" techniques in the U.S. utility sector, including regulatory provisions that reward utilities for investing in the energy efficiency of their customers, is considerably reducing the demand for electricity. Energy tax policies have successfully restrained demand for petrol in Europe. Similar measures may soon be seen in some parts of the developing world, where there are increasingly strong economic incentives for energy efficiency in the industrializing sectors. (See Chapter 9, "Energy," Chapter 4, "China," and Chapter 5, "India.")

Even without more resource-sparing policies, however, the cumulative effect of increasing reserves, more competition among suppliers, and technology trends that create substitutes suggests that global shortages of most nonrenewable resources are unlikely to check development in the early decades of the next century. Local shortfalls may occur, however, and the advanced technology that creates substitutes is largely under the control of the North. It is also clear that current rates of use of most nonrenewable resources are not indefinitely sustainable. Depletion of these resources today may limit opportunity for future generations.

Renewable Resources

Some renewable natural resources have identifiable economic value, but most of the biological and physical systems that sustain them lie outside the economic system. Thus economists assign a value to a stand of timber or to the annual fish catch or even to a quantity of water, but not to the ecosystems or hydrological systems that produce and renew these resources. Other renewable natural resources such as sunlight, air, and a diversity of plants and animals are traditionally taken for granted as "free goods" of nature, which, along with the corresponding lack of price signals, may contribute to a lack of awareness of impending shortages. Yet it is the world's renewable resources—and the resource base from which they stem—that are most in danger of being severely degraded and depleted in some regions.

Clean Air

In a recent survey of 20 of the world's largest cities, air pollution at levels that exceed World Health Organization guidelines was widespread (17). All cities surveyed exceed the guidelines for at least one air pollutant, and 14 exceed the guidelines for two pollutants. (See Chapter 12, "Atmosphere and Climate," Conditions and Trends.) Suspended particulate matter is the most prevalent form of pollution, often in combination with high concentrations of sulfur dioxide—a mix that is particularly hazardous to health. As urban areas expand, the number of people and sources of pollution threaten to outstrip even determined regulatory efforts. In developing countries, where urban areas are growing at 4 percent per year or more, the technical infrastructure for emission controls often lags behind growth, and enforcement is lax. Clean air may become an increasingly rare resource for a large fraction of the Earth's population.

Clean Water

In urban areas of the developing world, at least 170 million people lack access to clean water for drinking, cooking, and washing; in rural areas, more than 855 million lack clean water (18). Water supplies are contaminated by disease-bearing human waste and, in some regions, by toxic chemicals and heavy metals that are hard to remove from drinking water with standard purification techniques. Use of polluted water spreads diseases that kill millions and sicken more than one billion each year; according to the *World Development Report 1992*, water pollution is the most serious environmental problem facing developing countries because of its direct effect on human welfare and economic growth (19). Sewage and water treatment technologies are widely available but capital intensive. In addition, the capacity of rivers to support aquatic life and of coastal fisheries to maintain their productivity is threatened by pollution, loss of oxygen associated with the decomposition of pollutants, and algal blooms stimulated by nutrient runoff from areas of intensive fertilizer application. With surface waters increasingly polluted, many people have turned to groundwater sources, which in some places is drawing down aquifers faster than they can be replenished. Although opportunities exist to use and reuse water more efficiently, there is no substitute for water; new sources of supply (such as desalinization) tend to be expensive and energy intensive.

Fertile Soil

The Global Assessment of Soil Degradation study conducted for the United Nations Environment Programme found that in recent decades, nearly 11 percent of the Earth's fertile soil has been so eroded, chemically altered, or physically compacted as to damage its original biotic function (its ability to process nutrients into a form usable by plants); about 3 percent of soil has been degraded virtually to the point where it can no longer perform that function (20). In some regions, significant soil degradation is widespread—in Central America and Mexico, for example—affecting 25 percent of vegetated land. In some instances, loss of productivity has been made up by increasing the input of fertilizer, but yields are still lower than they would have been had soil degradation not occurred (21). The continued loss of soil fertility, combined with rapidly rising populations in most of the developing world, poses the threat of insufficient food, fiber, and fuelwood supplies in the future. More intensive cultivation, higher- yielding crop varieties, and novel (even synthetic) sources of food from biotechnology may ultimately substitute for losses in soil fertility and shortages of arable land. (See Chapter 6, "Food and Agriculture.") But substitutions could come at a high social cost, for example, reducing agricultural employment and food security for the poorest segments of developing societies (22).

Biodiversity and Ecosystem Services

Life depends on a number of ecosystem "services" that are largely taken for granted. These services include microbial recycling of soil nutrients, flood prevention and erosion control in watersheds, maintenance of the world's stocks of plants and animals, and replenishment of atmospheric oxygen. Yet with ecosystems increasingly degraded or converted for human use, their ability to provide services or to support healthy, diverse communities of plants and animals is becoming more and more jeopardized. In particular, loss of biodiversity appears to be accelerating. Scientists estimate that 4 to 8 percent of tropical forest species may face extinction over the next 25 years (23). One expert believes that just under half of the world's 250,000 flowering plant species occur only in areas that will be largely deforested or otherwise disturbed over the next three dec-

ades (24). Tropical forestland, a particularly rich habitat, was converted to other uses at an estimated 15.4 million hectares (about 0.8 percent) per year during the 1980s (25). (See Chapter 7, "Forests and Rangelands," Conditions and Trends.) Wetlands are also under ever-growing pressure. Although no reliable figures are available, damage to coral reefs appears to be on the rise. Despite stepped-up efforts to create wildlife and nature preserves, germ plasm banks, and genetically managed zoo populations, pressure on habitats is a serious threat to the Earth's genetic heritage and to the ecosystems in which diversity flourishes.

Both nonrenewable and renewable resources are critical to development. But while local shortages of specific nonrenewable resources—and some renewables such as fish or lumber—can often be compensated for through imports, similar shortages of fresh air, freshwater, and viable ecosystems generally cannot. Shortages of renewable resources and depletion of the resource base that supplies them can thus impede both near-term development and long-term sustainability. Emerging shortages and their impact on development are concentrated especially, but not exclusively, in developing countries.

NATURAL RESOURCE CONSUMPTION AND ENVIRONMENTAL DEGRADATION

Natural resource consumption patterns vary widely. To gain some insight into these patterns and their environmental consequences, it is helpful to examine the trends in production and consumption of some representative resources, both renewable and nonrenewable. The following sections feature quantitative global estimates of where a number of pertinent resources originate and where they are initially used (primary consumption). The analysis does not take into account value-added manufacture, export, and final consumption of goods and services containing natural resources in countries other than those where primary consumption occurs. The estimates may thus under- or overstate true consumption. Consumption and production data are presented as five-year averages in weight units. For this discussion, the industrialized world refers to OECD countries. All other countries, including China, are considered developing countries, except for the former centrally planned or transition countries of Eastern and Central Europe and the former Soviet Union.

Fossil Fuels

Fossil fuels have long been in the forefront of discussions about resource use. Access to and control over these resources, especially petroleum, have played a prominent role in military engagements; significant upheaval in the world economy followed the two "oil shocks" of 1973–75 and 1979–81; and, most recently, the potential impact on the Earth's climate of the burning of fossil fuels has raised new concern (26) (27).

Worldwide, consumption of fossil fuel has risen. (See Figures 1.2A and 1.3.) The industrialized world's share has declined to less than 50 percent of the world total. Meanwhile, consumption has risen dramatically in developing countries (by a factor of 4 over 30 years) and substantially in the former planned economies (by

Figure 1.2 Fossil Fuel Trends, Five-Year Averages, 1961–90

A. Consumption

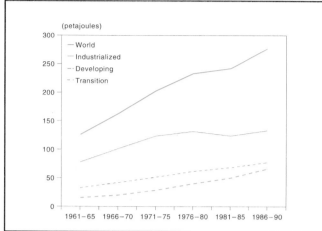

B. Production

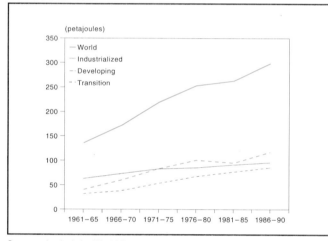

Source: Analysis by World Resources Institute (1993) based on data from United Nations Statistical Division (UNSTAT), *U.N. Energy Tape* (UNSTAT, New York, 1992).

Figure 1.3 World Share in Fossil Fuel Consumption, Average 1986–90

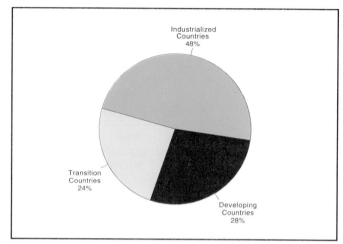

Source: Analysis by World Resources Institute (1993) based on data from United Nations Statistical Division (UNSTAT), *U.N. Energy Tape* (UNSTAT, New York, 1992).

Table 1.1 Fossil Fuel Consumption
(gigajoules/person)

Classification	1961–65	1966–70	1971–75	1976–80	1981–85	1986–90
Industrialized	115.82	142.53	165.70	169.52	153.81	160.06
Developing	7.37	8.26	10.34	12.91	14.53	17.28

Source: Analysis by World Resources Institute (1993) based on data from United Nations Statistical Division (UNSTAT), *U.N. Energy Tape* (UNSTAT, New York, 1992).

a factor of 2.4). Since the first oil shock, per capita consumption has declined moderately in industrialized countries but has risen rapidly in developing countries; industrial per capita levels are still very high (by a factor of 9) relative to those of the developing world. (See Table 1.1.)

Similar patterns hold for the production of fossil fuels among the three country clssifications. (See Figure 1.2B.) Production has been larger than consumption in developing and centrally planned countries; the reverse is true for industrialized countries. The difference between per capita production and consumption in the industrialized world has narrowed somewhat since 1970.

An extraordinarily wide range of environmental degradation is associated with fossil fuel production, transport, and use. Local effects include land degradation from strip-mining of coal and the disposal of deep-coal mine tailings, and from oil and gas production and transport in fragile environments; freshwater pollution from acid mine drainage, oil refinery operations, and improper disposal of used petroleum products; marine pollution from oil spilled or deliberately flushed out of tankers; and air pollution from fossil fuel combustion (sulfur dioxide and particulates), refinery operations (toxic emissions), coal combustion (dust and soot), and industrial and automobile fuels (urban smog). Regional effects include acid precipitation, primarily from coal and oil combustion, with its impact on monuments; buildings; forests and other vegetation; soil; and lakes. In addition, there is the potential global impact of climate change driven by greenhouse gases such as carbon dioxide, a product of all fossil fuel combustion, and methane emitted during the production, transport, and use of natural gas.

On a per capita basis, industrialized countries clearly contribute a disproportionate share of the impact of fossil fuel consumption on the global commons. Local effects accrue primarily in the country in which a fuel is consumed (most coal is consumed where it is mined). Acid precipitation, however, crosses national boundaries.

Metals and Minerals

Consumption patterns for aluminum and copper—examined here to illustrate the general case of metals and other nonenergy minerals—are similar to those for fossil fuel. Overall, the major regions have expanded their use of aluminum and copper, with consumption growing most rapidly in developing countries (ninefold

Figure 1.4 Metal Trends, Five-Year Averages, 1961–90

A. Aluminum Consumption

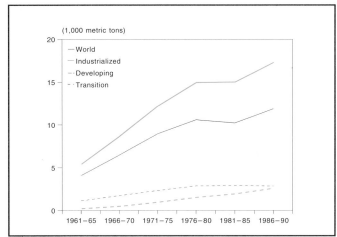

B. Bauxite Production

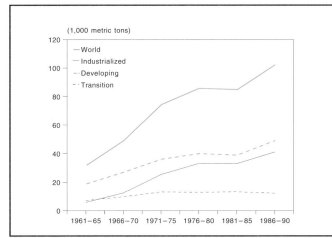

Sources:
Analysis by World Resources Institute (1993) based on data from:
1. World Bureau of Metal Statistics, *World Metal Statistics Yearbook, 1992* (World Bureau of Metal Statistics, Ware, U.K., 1992).
2. Metallgesellschaft Aktiengesellschaft, *Metallstatistik 1961–71* and *Metallstatistik 1970–80* (Metallgesellschaft A.G., Frankfurt, Germany, 1972 and 1981).

Figure 1.5 World Share in Aluminum Consumption, Average 1986–90

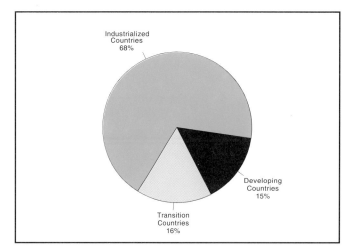

Sources:
Analysis by World Resources Institute (1993) based on data from:
1. World Bureau of Metal Statistics, *World Metal Statistics Yearbook, 1992* (World Bureau of Metal Statistics, Ware, U.K., 1992).
2. Metallgesellschaft Aktiengesellschaft, *Metallstatistik 1961–71* and *Metallstatistik 1970–80* (Metallgesellschaft A.G., Frankfurt, Germany, 1972 and 1981).

Table 1.2 Aluminum Consumption

(metric tons/100 people)

Classification	1961–65	1966–70	1971–75	1976–80	1981–85	1986–90
Industrialized	5.99	9.00	11.89	13.50	12.56	14.13
Developing	0.13	0.23	0.37	0.51	0.58	0.69

Sources:
Analysis by World Resources Institute (1993) based on data from:
1. World Bureau of Metal Statistics, *World Metal Statistics Yearbook, 1992* (World Bureau of Metal Statistics, Ware, U.K., 1992).
2. Metallgesellschaft Aktiengesellschaft, *Metallstatistik 1961–71* and *Metallstatistik 1970–80* (Metallgesellschaft A.G., Frankfurt, Germany, 1972 and 1981).

growth for aluminum and fivefold for copper over 30 years). (See Figures 1.4A and 1.6A.) The industrialized world's share of global consumption has consequently been declining, although per capita consumption in that region is still much higher (by a factor of 20 for aluminum and 17 for copper) than in the developing world. (See Figures 1.5 and 1.7 and Tables 1.2 and 1.3.)

The story is quite different on the production side. Production of bauxite (the primary aluminum ore) has risen sharply in the industrialized world, which is approaching the share produced by the developing world. (See Figure 1.4B.) The latter's share of copper production has risen slightly. (See Figure 1.6B.)

Extraction, refining, dispersive use, and the disposal of metals and industrial minerals may cause significant local environmental problems. Mining can degrade land, creating quarries, vast open pits, and a huge amount of solid waste. During 1991, for example, more than 1,000 million metric tons of copper ore were dug up to obtain 9 million metric tons of metal (28). Air pollution includes dust from mining, acidic gases from smelting and refining, and carbon dioxide from cement production. Fine particles of toxic trace metals—which accumulate in soil and aquatic ecosystems and in animal and human food chains—are often dispersed during mining and refining operations; larger quantities are deliberately or inadvertantly dispersed during use. (See Chapter 12, "Industry.") Leaching from tailings or abandoned mines and the disposal of chemicals used in refining are significant sources of water pollution in mining regions. Improper use of minerals, for example in asbestos insulation, lead plumbing and gasoline additives, and lead- and chromium-based paints, can threaten human health.

A careful accounting of the environmental impacts from mineral consumption remains to be done. Preliminary studies suggest that use of heavy metals has left a significant, toxic legacy in the soil, ecosystems, and food chains of many industrial countries. The impact of the initial extraction of minerals falls on the producer states, both developing and industrialized; the

Figure 1.6 Copper Trends, Five-Year Averages, 1961–90

A. Consumption

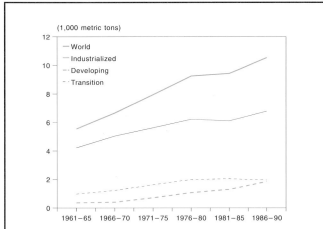

(1,000 metric tons)

B. Production

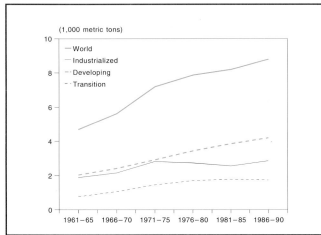

(1,000 metric tons)

Sources:
Analysis by World Resources Institute (1993) based on data from:
1. World Bureau of Metal Statistics, *World Metal Statistics Yearbook, 1992* (World Bureau of Metal Statistics, Ware, U.K., 1992).
2. Metallgesellschaft Aktiengesellschaft, *Metallstatistik 1961–71* and *Metallstatistik 1970–80* (Metallgesellschaft A.G., Frankfurt, Germany, 1972 and 1981).

Figure 1.7 World Share in Copper Consumption, Average 1986–90

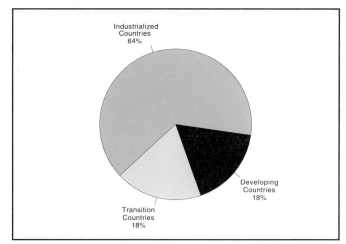

Sources:
Analysis by World Resources Institute (1993) based on data from:
1. World Bureau of Metal Statistics, *World Metal Statistics Yearbook, 1992* (World Bureau of Metal Statistics, Ware, U.K., 1992).
2. Metallgesellschaft Aktiengesellschaft, *Metallstatistik 1961–71* and *Metallstatistik 1970–80* (Metallgesellschaft A.G., Frankfurt, Germany, 1972 and 1981).

Table 1.3 Copper Consumption
(metric tons/1,000 people)

Classification	1961–65	1966–70	1971–75	1976–80	1981–85	1986–90
Industrialized	6.17	7.00	7.46	7.90	7.50	8.06
Developing	0.17	0.17	0.26	0.34	0.38	0.48

Sources:
Analysis by World Resources Institute (1993) based on data from:
1. World Bureau of Metal Statistics, *World Metal Statistics Yearbook, 1992* (World Bureau of Metal Statistics, Ware, U.K., 1992).
2. Metallgesellschaft Aktiengesellschaft, *Metallstatistik 1961–71* and *Metallstatistik 1970–80* (Metallgesellschaft A.G., Frankfurt, Germany, 1972 and 1981).

primary benefit from their use accrues to the consumer states, still overwhelmingly the industrial countries.

Forest Products

Forests, extremely diverse biological communities, produce a range of products including firewood and charcoal, lumber, paper, and crops such as coffee, oil palm, and rubber. The most common forest product in developing countries is firewood, the major source of cooking and heating fuel in most rural communities and in many major urban areas. Traditional fuels, largely firewood and brush, supply about 52 percent of all energy required in sub-Saharan Africa. (See Chapter 21, "Energy and Materials," Table 21.2.) Charcoal produced from forests is also a major domestic energy source and in countries such as Brazil, an important industrial fuel. Industrialized countries also use large amounts of wood as fuel, especially in the paper industry, but the

most common wood products in the region are lumber, paper, and other industrial manufactures.

With careful planning of growth and harvesting, wood and other forest products are, in principle, renewable resources. But achieving renewability takes time—often decades, sometimes centuries. Without careful management, pressure for short-term exploitation can lead to tree removal, soil degradation, and conversion of woodland to other uses—a process more akin to mining than to sustainable harvesting.

Roundwood refers to any wood felled or harvested from trees, regardless of its final use. Globally, roundwood consumption has nearly doubled over 30 years, but the share of world consumption has fallen in transition and industrialized countries and risen in developing ones. (See Figure 1.8A.) Global per capita consumption has grown slightly, with the level in industrialized countries remaining approximately 2.5 times that of developing countries. (See Table 1.4.)

Production of roundwood has risen in all sectors of the world economy, but most rapidly in developing countries. (See Figure 1.8B.) Generally speaking, each region appears to consume its own production, although there are significant local exceptions. Japan, for

Table 1.4 Roundwood Consumption
(cubic meters/person)

Classification	1961–65	1966–70	1971–75	1976–80	1981–85	1986–90
Industrialized	1.10	1.60	1.14	1.17	1.17	1.29
Developing	0.43	0.44	0.44	0.46	0.48	0.48

Source: Analysis by World Resources Institute (1993) based on data from Food and Agriculture Organization of the United Nations (FAO), *Agrostat PC*, on diskette (FAO, Rome, 1992).

example, imported about 60 percent of the roundwood it consumed in 1991, over 20 percent of which came, until recently, from the state of Sabah in eastern Malaysia (29) (30) (31). Relatively little roundwood is exported—the developing region presently exports less than 2 percent of its production, and the industrial region imports little more than 3 percent of its consumption. Value-added exports of processed wood such as lumber, panels and veneers, pulp and paper, and furniture account for the bulk of wood-related trade; there is significant South-to-North trade in such products, particularly to Japan.

Consumption of forest resources can lead to environmental problems as well as loss of critical habitat and species. The severity of these problems depends on the method and extent of exploitation. In many parts of Asia and Africa, for example, fuelwood consumption exceeds supply, contributing to deforestation and devegetation. The demand for fuelwood and leaves and foliage used as cattle fodder is estimated to be six times the sustainable yield of India's forests. (See Chapter 5, "India.") And the urban demand for firewood has contributed to severe shortages around most cities in Africa (32).

Logging for timber, which in principle can be sustainable, is often not. Clearcutting, as practiced in North America, and similarly destructive methods in many tropical forests have destroyed habitat, contributed to the erosion of underlying soil and the degradation of watersheds, exacerbated flooding, and, in some cases, led to severe deforestation. (See Chapter 7, "Forests and Rangelands.") The Food and Agriculture Organization of the United Nations estimates that the area in tree plantations, a growing source of the world's lumber and paper, increased by almost 18 million hectares during the 1980s (33). But tree plantations, although they may mitigate erosion, do not support the same level of biodiversity as natural forests. Pulp and paper mills are a significant source of water pollution. Paper is the largest component of municipal solid waste in most industrial countries, constituting more than one third of such waste in the United States (34).

Cultivating tree crops other than lumber, such as coffee trees and oil palms, can also cause environmental degradation. Clearing forest for plantations frequently leads to erosion, and heavy pesticide use on coffee and oil palm plantations may result in water pollution (35).

Traditional agricultural practices (shifting cultivation) have little environmental impact on forestland when population density is low and fallow periods are long. As population increases and fallow periods de-

Figure 1.8 Roundwood Trends, Five-Year Averages, 1961–90

A. Consumption

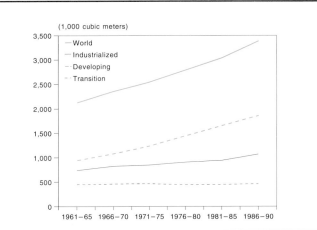

B. Production

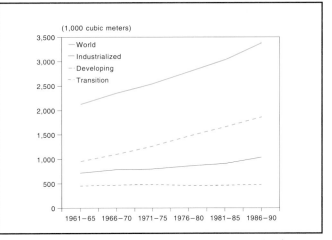

Source: Analysis by World Resources Institute (1993) based on data from Food and Agriculture Organization of the United Nations (FAO), *Agrostat PC*, on diskette (FAO, Rome, 1992).

crease, however, shifting cultivation can degrade forestland and even lead to its permanent conversion to agriculture.

Agricultural Products

Forests take a long time, decades or more, to regrow. In contrast to wood, agricultural products such as grain, meat, and fiber can be renewed roughly every year. Beef and veal consumption trends are reported here because there are approximately 1.3 billion cattle in the world, and more than half of the grain consumed in industrialized countries and in some developing countries is fed to livestock. (See Chapter 18, "Food and Agriculture," Table 18.3.) A considerable portion of cropping activity is thus attributable to meat consumption. Of agricultural fibers, cotton—grown in over 60 countries and the principal crop on 2.5 percent of the world's cultivated land—is discussed here (36).

World consumption of beef and veal has risen steadily over the past 30 years. (See Figure 1.9A.) Consumption per capita is approximately six times higher in

Figure 1.9 Beef and Veal Trends, Five-Year Averages, 1961–90

A. Consumption

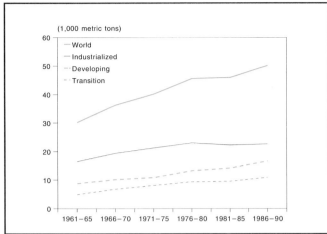

B. Production

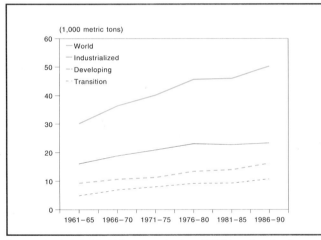

Source: Analysis by World Resources Institute (1993) based on data from Food and Agriculture Organization of the United Nations (FAO), *Agrostat PC*, on diskette (FAO, Rome, 1992).

Figure 1.10 World Share in Beef and Veal Consumption, Average 1986–90

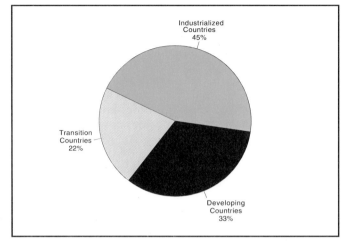

Source: Analysis by World Resources Institute (1993) based on data from Food and Agriculture Organization of the United Nations (FAO), *Agrostat PC*, on diskette (FAO, Rome, 1992).

Table 1.5 Beef and Veal Consumption
(kilograms/person)

Classification	1961–65	1966–70	1971–75	1976–80	1981–85	1986–90
Industrialized	24.53	27.37	28.59	29.65	27.69	27.17
Developing	3.98	4.06	3.84	4.21	4.05	4.29

Source: Analysis by World Resources Institute (1993) based on data from Food and Agriculture Organization of the United Nations (FAO), *Agrostat PC*, on diskette (FAO, Rome, 1992).

industrialized countries than in developing countries, but the share of world consumption is rising in the latter while falling in the former. (See Table 1.5 and Figure 1.10.) The consumption share in transition economies has also been rising, along with production activity. (See Figure 1.9B.) There is a near balance between production and consumption in all three economic regions.

The world's livestock population is growing much faster than its human population, diverting resources that could be used to grow grain for human consumption. A wide range of environmental problems are associated with raising livestock and with leather processing. Overgrazing contributes to soil degradation and devegetation; in arid lands, overgrazing can lead to desertification. In Latin America, converting land for pasture has significantly hastened forest loss. On feedlots in some industrialized countries, manure disposal and water pollution are problems. In developing countries, chemicals used to tan hides are often dumped into streams, where they become a major source of water pollution.

Cotton lint consumption and production are generally balanced in each of the three main regions. (See Figures 1.11A and B.) Industrialized countries import, on balance, from developing countries, but this pattern has been changing. The shares traded by each of these two regions have fallen substantially in recent years. The share of world consumption appears to be growing in developing areas and falling in industrialized areas, although it should be noted that textile production has been shifting to developing countries, so that industrialized country consumption of fiber in manufactured form may be rising. (See Figure 1.12.) Per capita consumption is growing slightly in the industrialized and developing countries. For the former, this trend follows an initial fall in the 1960s. (See Table 1.6.)

Cotton is also the cause of a number of local environmental problems, most of which stem from the extremely heavy use of pesticides. In India, for example, 56 percent of all pesticides used in the country is applied to cotton (37), a pattern similar to that in many other cotton-growing countries. Contamination by pesticides and herbicides is a problem in the soil, water, and food chain of many cotton-growing countries, and their overuse can devastate local ecosystems (38). Clearing land for cotton has contributed to deforestation and severe erosion in Central America. Diverting water to irrigate cotton was a major cause of the de-

Figure 1.11 Cotton Trends, Five-Year Averages, 1961–90

A. Consumption

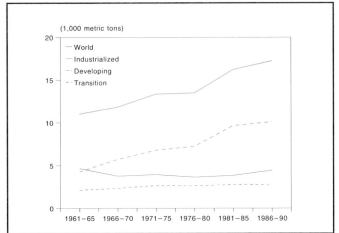

B. Production

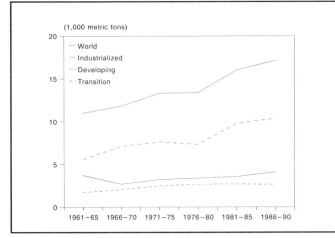

Source: Analysis by World Resources Institute (1993) based on data from Food and Agriculture Organization of the United Nations (FAO), *Agrostat PC*, on diskette (FAO, Rome, 1992).

struction of the Aral Sea in the former Soviet Union (39). Unless care is taken, processing cotton lint into textiles can be a health hazard to workers, causing brown lung disease. The chemicals used to bleach and dye fabric are a major source of water pollution in some countries. And concern is growing about pesticide and herbicide residue in cotton fiber and seed products, including cooking oil and animal feed (40).

TRADE PATTERNS AND TRENDS IN NATURAL RESOURCES

An overview of global supply and demand patterns can be obtained from world trade matrices, showing the value in current U.S. dollars of exports and imports, for commodity classifications, by groups of countries. The trade patterns shown differ somewhat from those based on the volume or weight of the resources in question. Commodities are not treated individually but rather are grouped by standard international trade classifications. (See Table 1.7 and Chapter 15, "Basic Economic Indicators," Table 15.5.)

Figure 1.12 World Share in Cotton Consumption, Average 1986–90

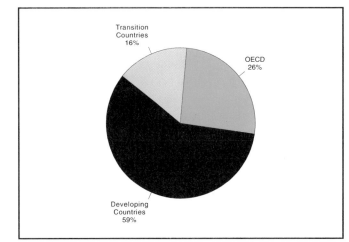

Source: Analysis by World Resources Institute (1993) based on data from Food and Agriculture Organization of the United Nations (FAO), *Agrostat PC*, on diskette (FAO, Rome, 1992).

Table 1.6 Cotton Consumption
(kilograms/person)

Classification	1961–65	1966–70	1971–75	1976–80	1981–85	1986–90
Industrialized	6.91	5.32	5.30	4.70	4.77	5.35
Developing	1.93	2.29	2.40	2.29	2.76	2.60

Source: Analysis by World Resources Institute (1993) based on data from Food and Agriculture Organization of the United Nations (FAO), *Agrostat PC*, on diskette (FAO, Rome, 1992).

World Trade Patterns

The tables illustrate that OECD countries today acquire about 73 percent of the value of their agricultural imports from one another. Developing countries send about 66 percent of their total agricultural exports to industrial countries, but these commodities amount to only about one quarter of the North's total agricultural imports, a consequence, in part, of trade barriers. The share of Northern agricultural imports coming from Southern countries has, in fact, been declining. Developing countries also trade among themselves in agricultural goods, but this trade represents a much smaller share of their total exports than is the case for trading among industrialized countries.

Industrial raw material is also traded on a large scale within the industrialized world. Seventy percent of the North's imports comes from the North; only 25 percent comes from the South, though this constitutes about 65 percent of Southern exports of industrial raw materials. The share of the North's industrial raw material coming from the South has fluctuated but is now at its lowest level in almost 30 years; the share of Southern exports sent to the North has also declined somewhat. In contrast, the former planned economies have, on average, been shipping a growing proportion (65 percent in 1990) of their exports to industrial countries, even though the total amount is small compared to that from developing countries. (See Chapter 15, "Basic Economic Indicators," Table 15.5.)

Table 1.7 World Trade Matrices, 1990[a]

Agriculture, Food and Beverages[b]

	Imports			
Exports	OECD	Developing	Transition	Total
OECD	157,672	39,084	8,317	205,074
Developing	54,810	18,722	9,011	82,544
Transition	4,852	1,217	3,062	9,132
Total	217,334	59,025	20,391	296,750

Industrial Raw Material and Edible Oils[c]

	Imports			
Exports	OECD	Developing	Transition	Total
OECD	98,837	22,808	2,193	123,839
Developing	34,267	17,369	1,525	53,162
Transition	5,561	1,257	1,741	8,560
Total	138,665	41,436	5,459	185,560

Mineral Fuels[d]

	Imports			
Exports	OECD	Developing	Transition	Total
OECD	91,392	11,233	1,106	103,732
Developing	159,721	39,850	2,320	201,891
Transition	20,833	2,499	6,301	29,634
Total	271,946	53,583	9,727	335,257

Manufactures[e]

	Imports			
Exports	OECD	Developing	Transition	Total
OECD	1,578,007	377,995	41,688	1,997,690
Developing	278,812	143,390	5,969	428,172
Transition	26,936	12,600	33,709	73,244
Total	1,883,755	533,984	81,366	2,499,105

Source: United Nations (U.N.) Macroeconomic and Social Policy Analysis Division, unpublished data (U.N., New York, 1993).
Notes: a. These tabulations are in millions of current U.S. dollars and therefore are not free of inflation effects. The diagonal entries in the matrices would be 0 for individual countries, but for groups of countries, as here, they indicate intratrade, that is, trade among the countries in the respective groups. b. Standard International Trade Commodities (SITC) 0 and 1. c. SITC 2 and 4. d. SITC 3. e. SITC 5–9. For additional information, see Chapter 15, "Basic Economic Indicators," Table 15.5.

The mineral fuel category of merchandise trade provides an extreme case of delivery of a primary, nonrenewable item from developing to industrialized countries. For decades, oil-exporting developing nations have shipped a fair amount of mineral fuel to industrialized countries, but by 1990, the volume and value had risen. Nearly three fourths of Southern exports in this category were sent to OECD countries. In 1990, the exports of transitional countries (mainly from the former Soviet Union) were also sent, on a large scale, to OECD countries. This pattern had started earlier but was reinforced by much-reduced trade within transitional countries as Russia sought hard currency earnings. About 60 percent of the North's imports of mineral fuel by value came from the South in 1990, compared with about 34 percent from North-North trade.

More than 60 percent of all world trade in manufactured products takes place among the OECD countries. They have a surplus in trade with developing countries; a fairly steady fraction of their exports over the last three decades, about 20 percent, flows to developing countries. This pattern is the reverse of the surplus of industrial raw material exports from developing to industrialized countries. An important trend, however, is that Southern exports of manufac-

tured goods to the North are growing rapidly, while exports of industrial raw material to the North and imports of manufactured goods from the North are not. (See Chapter 15, "Basic Economic Indicators," Table 15.5.)

Consumption Patterns

A more detailed analysis of world trade in natural resource-based commodities has been carried out by the United Nations Conference on Trade and Development (UNCTAD) (41). Because of data difficulties, the analysis excluded China, Viet Nam, and North Korea as well as the transition countries. It provides an overview of consumption trends from 1965 to 1988 for several groups of commodities—domestic and imported raw material and semiprocessed or semimanufactured goods such as steel bars, copper wire, cotton yarn, leather shoes, and plywood. The analysis considers a wide range of nonfood agricultural commodities and nonferrous minerals and metals as well as steel and wood (by volume, the two most widely used commodities). Because the analysis was based on consumption volume rather than weight or value (as in the earlier analyses) and because of a somewhat different regional mix of countries, the trends cannot be directly compared with those mentioned earlier.

The UNCTAD analysis shows that the volume of many agricultural commodities consumed in the North generally declined or remained steady between 1965 and 1988. Natural rubber was an exception, showing significant growth. Consumption of most nonferrous minerals and metals generally increased—aluminum, nickel, and phosphate rock spectacularly so—while consumption of manganese, tin, and tungsten declined. Steel consumption showed net growth over the period but has been in decline since 1968. Wood consumption has risen fairly steadily.

In developing countries, the pattern is one of net increases in the consumption of nearly all commodities studied. The volume of agricultural materials more than doubled, led by increases in the use of natural rubber and wool. Consumption of nonferrous minerals and metals rose even more, led by nickel, tungsten, aluminum, and phosphate rock. Steel use climbed fourfold and wood consumption nearly doubled.

Trade Pattern Implications

Trade patterns are complex and continuously changing. A degree of specialization does occur, with a significant share of raw material from the South going to the North and manufactured goods processed in the North returning to the South. As noted earlier, the terms of trade in this South-North-South cycle are generally unfavorable to the South. Yet generalizations can be misleading. For many natural resource commodities, for example, the largest supplier to the North is the North itself, although the pattern varies by country. Moreover, a significant portion of the South's natural resource exports is now in the form of processed or semimanufactured goods, with more of the value-added retained in developing countries; trade in manufactured goods from South to North is also growing rapidly.

Figure 1.13 U.S. Material Consumption Trends, 1900–89

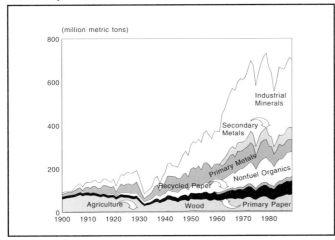

Source: U.S. Bureau of Mines, "Materials and the Economy," *Minerals Today* (April 1993), p. 15.

Figure 1.14 U.S. Material Intensity Trends

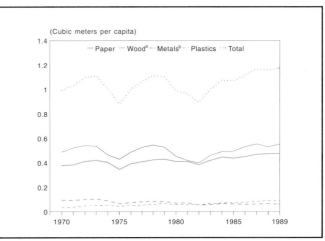

Source: U.S. Bureau of Mines, "Materials and the Economy," *Minerals Today* (April 1993), p. 16.
Notes:
a. Wood covers lumber, plywood, veneer, and other forestry products.
b. Metals include primary and secondary.

RESOURCE CONSUMPTION PATTERNS AND IMPLICATIONS: UNITED STATES

Historical Pattern

The U.S. economy consumes an enormous quantity of material. Apparent consumption, defined as domestic production plus recycling and imports and less exports, is the basis of the analysis reported here. In 1989, a total of about 4.5 billion metric tons of natural resources was consumed in the United States—about 18 metric tons per person. Construction material (stone, sand, and gravel) accounted for 1.8 billion metric tons of the total, energy fuel for another 1.7 billion metric tons, and food (meats and grains) for about 317 million metric tons (42). Consumption in 1989 also included 317 million metric tons of industrial minerals, 109 million metric tons of metal, 157 million metric tons of forestry products, 107 million metric tons of nonrenewable organic material such as asphalt and chemicals, and 6.7 million metric tons of natural fiber (43).

The historical pattern for some of those materials contains several features of note. (See Figure 1.13.) Wood use has risen in the last decade after remaining relatively constant for the previous 20 years; paper use has been increasing since 1900. A decline in primary-metal consumption over the last few decades reflects increasing recycling and production from scrap (secondary metal), while an increase in consumption of nonfuel organic material reflects the rising use of plastic, synthetic fiber in textiles and carpets, synthetic rubber, and petrochemical products. Industrial minerals such as fertilizer and mineral feedstock for the chemical industry have been used in relatively constant amounts since 1960 (44).

The intensity of natural resource consumption—measured either per capita or per unit of U.S. GNP—is declining for some commodities but not for all. Materials exhibiting the strongest current growth, such as plastic and paper, weigh much less than most of the metal and industrial minerals they are displacing. Thus, per capita consumption of forestry products,

metal, and plastic—measured by weight—has been declining over the past 20 years, but per capita consumption measured by volume has been expanding slowly. (See Figure 1.14.) According to the U.S. Bureau of Mines, these trends reflect the growing use of more highly engineered and generally lighter material, packaging material, and paper, among other factors. Over the last decade, for example, the United States has used more plastic on a volume basis than all metals combined (45). The rising volume of material consumption may partially explain the growing volume of postconsumer waste, despite reduced per capita consumption of primary metal.

Consumption Expenditure by Income Group

The U.S. Bureau of Labor Statistics compiles expenditure data based on consumer surveys. Although still highly aggregated, such data provide some insight into consumption patterns of different income groups for natural resources or natural resource-based products and services. The 1990 data given here are reported by five income groups representing quintiles of income—the highest through the lowest 20 percent. The data are for "consumer units" roughly corresponding to families or households.

The self-reported pretax income of these groups ranges from $5,637 for the lowest quintile to $76,660 for the highest quintile; the lowest-income groups report expenditures that exceed their income—significantly so for the poorest—reflecting underreporting of income. For that reason, expenditures are compared here with total expeditures, not with income. Expenditure figures for each group are given for five natural resource-dependent categories: food consumption (both total and the percentage consumed away from home), housing (including shelter and household equipment and supplies), utilities (such as fuel, electricity, and water consumed in the home), transportation (includ-

Table 1.8 U.S. Consumption Expenditure by Income Group, 1990

(in U.S. dollars)

Income Group	Total Expenditure	Food	Food Consumed Away from Home (percent)	Housing and House Operations	Utilities	Transportation	Clothing
Lowest 20 %	12,908	2,401	33	3,226	1,214	2,041	667
Second 20 %	17,924	3,113	34	4,308	1,558	3,238	961
Third 20 %	24,673	3,859	40	5,772	1,844	4,610	1,335
Fourth 20 %	34,247	5,256	42	7,834	2,076	6,463	1,958
Highest 20 %	55,411	7,127	51	13,961	2,658	9,624	3,391

Source: Analysis by World Resources Institute (1993) based on data from U.S. Bureau of Labor Statistics, *Consumer Expenditures in 1990* (U.S. Department of Labor, Washington, D.C., 1991).
Note: Data are for consumer units, roughly corresponding to families or households.

ing vehicle purchases, gasoline, and factors such as air travel and public transportation), and clothing. Total expenditures include these and others not given here. (See Table 1.8.)

The lowest-income group spends relatively more on food and housing than on anything else—19 and 25 percent, respectively, of their total expenditure. Food expenditures increase with income, yet constitute smaller percentages of income in each higher-income group, accounting for only 13 percent in the highest. Expenditure for food eaten outside the home becomes a higher proportion of total food spending as incomes rise, approximately equaling the cost of food eaten within the home for the highest-income group. The type of food purchased varies also: the poorest group spends twice as much on meat as on cereal and bread, a ratio that declines to 1.6 for the wealthiest group.

Expenditures for housing and transportation are significant for all income groups. As a percentage of total expenditures, consumption in these areas is roughly constant across income groups—varying only between 23 and 25 percent for housing and between 16 and 19 percent for transportation. Energy expenditures for home heating and electricity and for other utilities such as water and sewage rises with income, but less sharply, accounting for only about 5 percent of total expenditures in the highest-income group as compared

with 9 percent for the lowest. Clothing expenditure as a percentage of total expenditures varies only slightly across income groups.

The top two income groups, 40 percent of the population, consume more than half of the resources, as measured by their expenditure share: utilities 51 percent; food 57 percent; housing 62 percent; transportation 62 percent; and clothing 64 percent. (See Table 1.8.)

Domestic and Imported Resources

Natural resource consumption in the United States is relatively high compared with average world consumption. (See Table 1.9.) The ratio of U.S. per capita consumption to the world average varies from 1.5 for cement to 6.9 for plastic. Comparisons with consumption in developing countries would show even larger ratios. (See Box 1.1.)

With a few exceptions (notably petroleum), most of the natural resources consumed in the United States are from domestic sources. (See Table 1.9.) For many mineral and metal commodities, the United States provides 85 percent or more of its raw material requirements. The major exceptions are bauxite (for aluminum) and potash, which are largely imported, and petroleum and iron ore, which are imported in significant quantity. Imports of these commodities come from industrial and transition countries as well as

Table 1.9 U.S. and World Consumption of Selected Ores and Commodities, 1990

Ore/Commodity	U.S. Apparent Consumption (million metric tons)	Domestic Production[a] (percent)	World Production (million metric tons)	Per Capita Consumption U.S./World
Petroleum feedstocks[b] (quadrillion BTU)	1.3	62.3	4.1	6.7
Bauxite	12.0	5.0	109.6	2.3
Phosphate[c]	5.3	100.0	48.6	2.3
Salt	40.6	90.9	183.5	4.7
Potash[d]	5.5	31.4	29.3	4.0
Industrial sand and gravel	24.8	100.0	120.8	4.4
Iron ore	76.9	73.4	919.3	1.8
Plastic from petroleum feedstocks	25.4	See petro. feedstocks	78.3	6.9
Fibers from petroleum feedstocks	3.9	See petro. feedstocks	13.2	6.3
Aluminum[e]	5.3	See bauxite	18.0	6.2
Copper[f]	2.2	97.4	10.5	4.4
Iron and steel[g]	97.7	88.1	770.6	2.7
Nitrogen	14.9	84.9	97.1	3.3
Cement	81.3	86.0	1,152.8	1.5

Source: Analysis by U.S. Bureau of Mines (1993) based on data from:
1. United States Bureau of Mines (USBM), *1990 Minerals Yearbook* (USBM, Washington, D.C., 1993).
2. United States Department of Energy (DOE), *Annual Energy Review, 1991* (DOE, Washington, D.C., 1992).
3. Donald G. Rogich and staff, "Material Use, Economic Growth, and the Environment," paper presented at the International Recycling Congress, Geneva, Switzerland, January 1993.
Notes: a. Domestic production stated as a percent of apparent consumption. b. Ratio of U.S. per capita consumption and world per capita consumption includes petroleum and natural gas used for plastics and fibers from feedstocks. These amounts were assumed using 45.7 percent of total petroleum chemical feedstock consumption. Percent for domestic sources uses a weighted average of 22.2 percent natural gas and 77.8 percent petroleum. c. Phosphate-phosphorous pentoxide content of fertilizer. d. Potassium oxide content. e. World production is from primary sources only. f. World production is refined copper. g. World production is for raw steel.

Box 1.1 U.S. and Indian Consumption Compared

The United States has a higher standard of living than India and a more developed industrial economy. This difference is reflected in the natural resource consumption of the two countries. The United States consumes nearly 3 times as much iron ore as India, 4.6 times as much steel, 3.6 times as much coal, 12 times as much petroleum, 3 times as many head of cattle and sheep, and 1.7 times as much roundwood (by volume). (See Table 1.)

The United States has less than one third the population of India, so per capita consumption differences are significantly larger. In particular, U.S. consumption of all sources of fossil energy is so large that per capita emissions of carbon dioxide, a principal greenhouse gas, are 19 times those of India. (See Chapter 11, "Atmosphere and Climate," Figure 11.2.)

Neither India nor the United States is entirely self-sufficient in natural resources.

Both import a significant fraction of the nickel, potash (a key fertilizer ingredient), and petroleum they consume. In addition, the United States imports most of its bauxite and a considerable share of its iron ore. India exports more iron ore than it consumes. The United States exports significant quantities (compared with its consumption) of aluminum and copper, smaller quantities of nickel, iron ore, phosphate rock, potash, coal, and roundwood.

Table 1 Natural Resource Consumption, United States and India, 1991

(1,000 metric tons except where noted)

Resource	U.S. Consumption	Indian Consumption	U.S./India Per Capita Ratio	Exports (percent of consumption) U.S.	India	Imports (percent of consumption) U.S.	India
Aluminum	4,137	420	33.7	42.6	0.0	36.0	2.4
Bauxite	12,835	4,648	9.4	0.5	3.2	95.9	1.2
Copper	2,057	157	44.8	39.0	0.0	24.9	12.9
Iron Ore	64,810	25,384	8.7	20.5	124.1	6.2	0.0
Crude Steel	93,325	20,300	15.7	6.2	0.4	15.3	10.6
Nickel	137	15	31.2	26.9	0.0	96.5	100.0
Phosphate rock	40,177	2,381	57.6	12.6	0.0	1.4	76.4
Potash	5,612	1,043	18.4	11.1	0.0	80.7	100.0
Coal	672,036	184,992	12.4	12.7	0.0	0.5	2.9
Petroleum	666,032	53,294	42.7	0.9	0.0	43.6	45.0
Natural Gas (terajoules)	21,387,719	397,250	183.9	0.7	0.0	9.0	0.0
Beef and Veal (head)	35,989	11,758	10.5	0.9	0.3	5.4	0.0
Roundwood (1,000 cm^3)	468,003	281,045	5.7	6.4	0.0	0.5	0.5
Pulpwood (1,000 cm^3)	136,377	1,208	385.7	8.6	0.0	1.0	0.0

Sources: Analysis by World Resources Institute (1993) based on data from:
1. U.S. Bureau of Mines (USBM), *1991 Minerals Yearbook,* Vol. 3, Asia and Pacific Region (USBM, Washington, D.C., 1993).
2. USBM, *Mineral Commodity Summaries, 1993* (USBM, Washington, D.C., 1993).
3. United Nations Statistical Division, *1991 Energy Statistics Yearbook* (U.N., New York, 1993).
4. Food and Agriculture Organization of the United Nations (FAO), *1991 Forest Products Yearbook* (FAO, Rome, 1993).
5. FAO, *1991 Production Yearbook* (FAO, Rome, 1993).
6. FAO, *1991 Trade Yearbook* (FAO, Rome 1993).

Note: Most consumption figures are given in weight, but some are in volume, energy, or other units. For consistency, these data are from U.N. sources and may differ somewhat from national figures for both the United States and India used elsewhere in this chapter. The data do not include exports or imports of national resources incorporated into manufactured goods.

from developing countries. The United States is a net exporter of wood (but not of paper), coal, and grain.

The Distribution of Environmental Impacts

The predominantly domestic base for U.S. natural resource consumption creates local environmental impacts primarily within the United States. However, non-U.S. regions that export natural resources or natural resource-based products to the United States may also experience significant local environmental impact. In addition, there may be indirect or displacement effects of U.S. consumption, such as higher world oil prices due to large U.S. imports and hence, additional coal or fuelwood consumption in developing countries.

The global environmental impact of U.S. natural resource consumption presents a different picture. The United States is the world's leading producer of greenhouse gas emissions, which may result in global warming, and it plays a significant role in degrading the global commons. (See Chapter 11, "Atmosphere and Climate.") Heavy fossil fuel consumption in the

United States is not only the source of most U.S. greenhouse gas emissions but also a cause of acid precipitation in Canada. Thus, a more detailed examination of the structure of fossil fuel-based energy use in the United States is warranted.

U.S. fossil fuel consumption and carbon dioxide emissions for the 1970s and 1980s were calculated for this case study for 85 sectors of the economy using input-output analysis. (See Box 1.2.) Data for imports were also calculated and combined to give estimates of total demand. The results were used to extrapolate direct and indirect sector-by-sector energy use and carbon dioxide emissions to the year 2000, assuming no major changes in technology or economic structure.

The analysis shows that a number of sectors of the U.S. economy share major responsibility for carbon dioxide emissions. Primary energy industries provide fuel and convert it to more convenient forms such as gasoline and electricity, but they are not the only major sources of carbon dioxide emissions. Many of their customers who use energy directly, or who use other

Box 1.2   U.S. Sector Analysis Method

The analysis of carbon dioxide emissions is based on a series of 85-sector input-output (interindustry) tables for 1972, 1977, 1982, and 1987. These tables show how much of each sector's output is used in producing every other sector's output, that is, intermediate deliveries for further processing. The tables are combined with a bill of final demand, which describes how much of each sector's output is direct contributions to GNP—for example, as deliveries to consumers, as exports, or for public sector use. The final demand is added to the amount delivered as input for other sectors to get values for the total demand for nationally produced goods and services.

These data were first used to calculate how much fossil energy was consumed and how much carbon dioxide was emitted by each sector of the economy during the years in question. Secondly, they were used to extrapolate final demand, sector by sector, in the United States from 1990 to 2000. These results, in turn, allow estimates of U.S. carbon dioxide emissions, in total and by sector, for the year 2000, on the basis of the technology and industry patterns that prevailed in the mid-1980s. Technological progress will certainly be made during this period (mid-1980s to 2000), some of which will help reduce carbon dioxide emissions; thus, the esti-

mates could be interpreted as a worst-case scenario.

Trends in final demand were established for each year (1972, 1977, 1982, and 1987), then extrapolated, either linearly or exponentially (semi-log linearly) to 1990 and to 2000. The number of British thermal units (BTUs) in each sector's final demand were estimated in order to derive both direct and indirect quantities. Finally, each sector's final demand was converted from dollars to BTUs before the tonnage of carbon dioxide associated with each sector's BTUs in final demand was computed.

goods and services that require energy, are responsible for a large share of U.S. emissions. (See Table 1.10.)

The wholesale and retail trade sector, construction, and transportation are large sources of carbon dioxide emissions, but significant contributions also come from medical, educational, and other nonprofit organizations, motor vehicle production, food manufacturing, and eating and drinking establishments.

These are large sectors, in some cases energy-intensive ones, so their presence at the top of the list is not surprising. But it is a reminder that food, shopping malls and other stores, and even the nonprofit sector, also contribute in a major way to global pollution.

Among sectors not directly responsible for large carbon dioxide emissions are many of those concerned with natural resource production. These include livestock production (although other agricultural production, including the supply of feed for livestock and

dairy farming, are important carbon dioxide producers), and forestry (although the manufacture of paper and allied products is a large source of carbon dioxide emissions).

How might carbon dioxide emissions change in the near future in response to the technologies and policies of the 1990s? Between 1972 and 1987, U.S. emissions grew at a rate of 1.8 percent per annum, according to calculations based on the analysis reported above. In this same period, total demand grew by 2.6 percent per annum. This model suggests that carbon dioxide emissions expand at a rate slightly below that of total demand. Extrapolation of the model from 1990 to the year 2000 points to real growth in total demand of only 1.8 percent annually, in part because of the 1990–91 recession, and corresponding growth of carbon dioxide emissions of about 1.4 percent annually over the decade. Thus, it appears that although the growth of carbon dioxide emissions may slow naturally, it will not stabilize of its own accord in the near term.

Implications

Relative to GNP or population, U.S. consumption is expanding for some natural resource commodities, such as paper and plastic, and declining for others, such as primary metal. Domestic resources supply a large portion of that consumption for many raw materials and commodities. Nonetheless, U.S. consumption remains high, relative to world levels. It is therefore incumbent upon the United States to take a leadership role in seeking technologies and policies to use natural resources more efficiently and to minimize the environmental consequences of such use.

Of particular importance are global environmental problems such as emissions of greenhouse gases that can cause global warming. Here, the United States, as the world's largest consumer of fossil fuels, has a special responsibility. Yet, because many sectors of the U.S. economy are major contributors (directly and indirectly) to carbon dioxide emissions, significant changes in U.S. emissions would require widespread adjustments. And while this analysis suggests that the

Table 1.10   Top 10 U.S. Economic Sectors by Carbon Dioxide Emissions, 1990

(million metric tons)

Sector	Emissions	Fossil Fuel Emissions (percentage of total)
Private utilities (electric, gas, water)	1,949	39.76%
Petroleum refining and related industries	671	13.69%
Wholesale and retail trade	251	5.13%
New construction	227	4.63%
Coal mining	208	4.25%
Transportation and warehousing	187	3.82%
Health, education, social service, and nonprofit organizations	158	3.21%
Food and related products	138	2.83%
Motor vehicles and equipment	124	2.52%
Eating and drinking establishments	65	1.32%

Source: Analysis by University of Pennsylvania (1993) based on data from:
1. Citibank, *CITIBASE Citibank Economic Database*, on diskette (Citibank, New York, 1993).
2. *Economic Report of the President*, 1990 and 1993 editions, (U.S. Government Printing Office, Washington, D.C., 1990 and 1993).
3. United States Bureau of the Census, *Statistical Abstract of the United States, 1992* (U.S. Government Printing Office, Washington, D.C., 1992).
4. Bureau of Economic Analysis, *Benchmark Input-Output Accounts for the U.S. Economy (1972, 1977, 1982, and 1987 benchmarks), Survey of Current Business* (U.S. Department of Commerce, Washington, D.C.).
Note: Direct and indirect emissions are based on estimates of total demand for fossil fuel only. Data were scaled to correspond to independent estimates of total U.S. CO_2 emissions.

Box 1.3 Analytical Method and Data for India

The National Accounts Statistics (NAS) for India, published annually by the Central Statistical Organization, provide private consumption expenditure data for the entire Indian population. However, these data are available only at the aggregate level and do not help investigate distribution of consumption by income group.

Several standard sources of data on consumption distribution across classes in India were used in the analysis. The first is from household surveys carried out by the National Sample Survey Organization, the latest of which is for 1987–88. Next are two surveys carried out by the National Council of Applied Economic Research: a market information survey of households

that provides consumption distribution data for several durable and nondurable goods, and a survey looking at consumption distribution for specific fuels such as electricity, coal, gas, and firewood. The last source of data is a series of surveys carried out by the Indian commissioner for textile products.

Data compiled from all of these sources give consumption distributions corresponding to the sectors of an input-output table. The shares of consumption by different income groups thus obtained were applied to total consumption expenditure levels as estimated in the input-output table to generate consumption vectors for different classes. This procedure was adopted because absolute consumption levels from

various sources differ, as a result of sampling and nonsampling survey errors and different time periods covered.

While consumption distribution figures in the NAS data relate to household groups defined by per capita total consumption expenditure, in the other sources, groups are defined by per capita income. To reconcile different sources, the assumption was made that the ranking of households by income and consumption expenditure is the same. Rural and urban population was also reclassified into three income groups each. Per capita expenditure levels for the reclassified groups were obtained using linear interpolation from the original data sources.

growth of carbon dioxide emissions may slow naturally, it will not cease in the near term without specific policy efforts.

Even stabilizing U.S. emissions at 1990 levels, while an important near term goal, is not enough; if sustainability is to be achieved, far more must be done.

RESOURCE CONSUMPTION PATTERNS AND IMPLICATIONS: INDIA

The consumption of natural resources and its environmental implications differ widely among various groups in India. Consumption patterns were analyzed for different income groups in both rural and urban India. The environmental implications of these patterns are discussed by examining the relative magnitude of resources required, directly and indirectly, to support the consumption of persons belonging to different income groups.

Resources are needed in the production of a refrigerator, for example, directly in the manufacturing process, indirectly in the steel and concrete used to build the refrigerator factory and in the energy to ship the refrigerator to market. Such direct and indirect uses represent the ultimate demand of particular consumption patterns on society's total available resources.

As in the case study of the United States, direct and indirect resource use of different income groups in Indian society was calculated by means of input-output analysis. The latest such table available for India for 1989–90 includes 60 sectors of the economy. Accordingly, this fiscal year is used as the basis for an analysis of consumption pattern differences by sector. (See Box 1.3.)

Income Distribution

In 1989–90, the top income group, constituting about 1.5 percent of the total Indian population, had a household income above 56,000 rupees (Rs 16.6 = U.S.$1 in 1989–90). (See Table 1.11.) The average household income of this group is estimated to be about Rs 90,000, or about Rs 25,700 on a per capita basis (assuming an average household size of 3.5 for this income class);

based on purchasing power parity, this was equivalent to U.S. $6,181 per year in 1990. This standard of living is high in India, but it falls well below the average income of the United States, which was about $19,309 per person in 1990. (See Box 1.4.)

This relative measure places the condition of India's poor in its proper perspective. In 1989–90, about 59 percent of the Indian population (495 million people) had an annual household income of less than Rs 12,500. (See Table 1.11.) With an average family size of about five, this large group had a per capita annual income of less than Rs 2,500 (about $601 per annum based on purchasing power parity). Most of this group, which includes landless persons, isolated tribal groups, and urban slum dwellers in search of jobs, do not even meet their basic minimum food, clothing, and shelter needs. Outside the economic mainstream, they depend on their environment—particularly the resources of common property such as forests, ponds, and rivers—to meet many of their survival needs including food, fuel, and fodder. This dependence on the environment among the poorest group is an important feature of the consumption patterns within India.

Consumption Expenditures by Income Group

For the analysis, the Indian population was placed into six income groups—the top 10 percent, the middle 40 percent, and the bottom 50 percent, separately for rural and urban dwellers. The urban population ac-

Table 1.11 Income Distribution in India

Income per year (Rupees/Household)	Rural	Urban	Total
	(percent of population)		
Up to 12,500	67.34	37.14	58.84
12,501–25,000	23.89	34.76	26.95
25,001–40,000	7.07	17.89	10.11
40,001–56,000	1.16	6.46	2.66
Above 56,000	0.54	3.75	1.44
All classes	100.00	100.00	100.00

Source: S.L. Rao, ed., *Consumer Market Demographics in India* (NCAER, New Delhi, 1993).

Box 1.4 Consumption Potential: India and Western Countries Compared

A widely held view is that India, because it is large and heavily populated, has an upper-income groups whose lifestyle is comparable to that of a Western country such as Belgium. This perception of a Belgium-within-India even has a name, Belindia. Do the data justify this view?

The highest-income group in India, 1.5 percent of its population, constitutes about 12 million people, roughly comparable to Belgium's total population of 10 million. The standard of living of this tiny group is high by Indian standards, but it represents a per capita purchasing power of only U.S.$6,181, about 35 percent that of the average Belgian (about $17,510) and below the per capita expenditure of the lowest 20 percent of the U.S. population.

Cultural differences between India and Western countries and differences in consumption patterns may account for the perception of Belindia. In India, servants and part-time household help earn low wages and often substitute for appliances; many households employ domestic help. Jewelry (usually possessed by women) is often preferred as an investment to bank deposits or stocks. Elaborate marriage and funeral ceremonies are socially mandated, once-in-a-lifetime events whose financing can force families to sell land or other possessions and can even drive them into bankruptcy. On the other hand, automobiles, large houses or apartments, a multitude of appliances, and other everyday features of the typical Western lifestyle are still uncommon in India. Thus, even among its elite, Indian cultural patterns imply a much lower consumption of natural resources than do the energy—and material goods—intensive pattern of most Western societies.

---

counts for 39.6 percent of total consumption of all goods and services in India, while the rural population accounts for 60.4 percent. In absolute terms (measured in rupees), per capita consumption in rural areas is about one half that of urban areas.

Consumption distribution within urban areas is more unequal than within rural areas. Measured in rupees, the lowest-income group's per capita consumption is about 15 percent of that of the highest income group for urban areas, about 25 percent for rural areas.

Food and Clothing

Disparities in consumption between income groups are relatively low for food crops and higher for animal products, processed food, and textiles. (See Figures 1.15A and B.) For example, individuals in the lowest rural group consume about one tenth as much milk and meat as individuals in the urban top income group. The poor do not purchase but rather collect such items as forest fruit, fuelwood, and fish from village commons; they also graze animals in common pasture or woodland. Survey data typically underestimate the consumption of common property resources. The low figures for some essential items may thus only mean that part of actual consumption is consumption of common property resources that are not reflected in survey data.

Durable Goods, Energy, Transport

For durable goods, energy and transport, the disparities between distribution and consumption are relatively high between income groups. (See Figures 1.16 A and B, and 1.17 A and B.) For many such commodities, the per capita consumption of the lowest-income rural group is almost negligible compared with that of the highest-income urban group. Disparities are greatest for transport services, where the share of the top two income groups in both rural and urban areas (one half of the population) accounts for as much as 85 percent of total private expenditure on transport services; this indicates the relative isolation of the lowest-income group or its dependence on mass transport. Consumption by the highest-income group of electricity, petroleum products, and machine-based household appliances—products that have global environmental impact—is about 75 percent of the total consumption for these commodities in India. Disparities in consumption of energy, transport, and durable goods are the result of negligible or low consumption by the poor.

Direct and Indirect Use of Resources

When indirect consumption of resources required to produce consumer goods is also taken into account, the disparities between income groups grow, particularly for consumption of energy and minerals. (See Ta-

---

Table 1.12 Direct and Indirect Per Capita Consumption in India, 1989–90 (Rupees/Annum)

Commodities	Rural Bottom 50%	Rural Mid 40%	Rural Top 10%	Urban Bottom 50%	Urban Mid 40%	Urban Top 10%
Sugarcane	52.71	99.17	183.20	53.84	93.58	149.83
Cotton	50.21	65.48	70.43	60.70	105.62	213.99
Coal and lignite	21.51	37.27	80.63	40.40	94.27	237.79
Crude petroleum and natural gas	39.85	66.29	138.95	76.00	185.84	496.93
Iron ore	0.22	0.40	0.97	0.36	0.93	2.57
Other metallic minerals	1.27	2.47	6.07	2.30	6.13	16.29
Cement	2.42	4.21	11.81	3.56	8.13	28.52
Iron and steel	25.76	47.14	114.17	42.04	109.58	306.28
Electricity, gas and water supply	81.05	136.36	264.63	150.11	346.35	830.90
All commodities	3,170.99	5,636.45	11,586.79	4,926.13	11,110.65	28,128.77
Population (in millions)	303.3	242.6	60.7	102.3	81.8	20.5
Percentage of population	37.4	29.9	7.5	12.6	10.1	2.5

Source: Analysis by the Indira Gandhi Institute for Development Research, Bombay, 1993.

ble 1.12.) For minerals such as coal, iron ore, and crude petroleum, the resources required to support consumption by the lowest rural income group are only 8 to 10 percent of what is needed for the highest urban income group on a per capita basis.

While consumption differences between income groups are not high for essential items such as food and clothing, they are substantial for other commodities and the resources required to produce them. Consumption by upper-income groups (50 percent of the population) account for a large portion of the country's use of energy, minerals, and chemicals and, hence, a large portion of the global environmental impact such as emissions of carbon dioxide—as well as much of the local air and water pollution caused by industrial processes. By international standards, per capita consumption is modest, well below average consumption in industrialized countries. Wide disparity between income groups largely reflects the virtual absence of consumption of nonfood items (other than clothing) by the poor. This inability to purchase market goods is a concern, because it drives the poor to meet their basic needs by relying primarily on the environment.

The Environmental Effects of Poverty

Poor people who cannot meet their subsistence needs through purchase are forced to use common property or private resources such as forests for food and fuel, pastures for fodder, and ponds and rivers for water. Though Indians have depended on such resources for millenia, the pattern of use has recently been modified by two major forces. Population growth has increased the pressure on natural resources, in some cases to the point of destruction. At the same time, natural resources are being used by higher-income urban dwellers in new ways. These two trends have hurt the poor.

Household tap water is available to 35 percent of urban households and only 18 percent of rural households in India (46). Other residents share a community water tap or use wells, ponds, and rivers. Overuse of water resources by the poor, driven by population pressure, has resulted in some contamination and, where demand exceeds supply, exhaustion. Urban populations are also making growing use of rivers to dispose of untreated sewage and industrial effluent. The result is that the health of those dependent on untreated sources of water is increasingly at risk.

Those who can afford it buy cleaner commercial fuels—such as kerosene, liquified petroleum gas, or electricity—for cooking. The poor, however, must gather biofuel—wood, crop residue, and animal dung—from the local environment and risk the health effects of cooking with it, which include respiratory disease, anemia, and cancer. Women and children are the most exposed to risk.

As populations increase, the requirement for fuel may exceed the sustainable natural supply, leading to the gradual shrinkage of woodlands and the expenditure of more time and effort to collect fuel. At the same time, the urban or village need for wood in construction puts an additional demand on the same resource; those who can pay for wood are often supplied with

Figure 1.15 Indian Per Capita Consumption, Food and Clothing, 1989–90

A. Urban

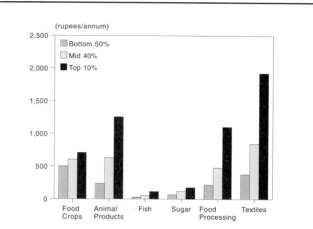

B. Rural

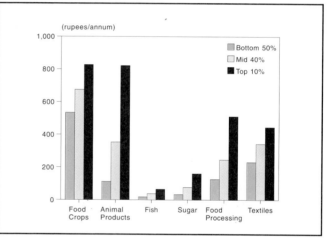

Source: Analysis by the Indira Gandhi Institute of Development Research, Bombay, 1993.

chainsaws and trucks, technologies that make large-scale wood removal easy and are not available to the poor. Commercial markets for wood and paper products support the creation of contract woodlots, but planted forests do not supply the variety of nontimber resources on which the poor depend and may divert land and water that was formerly available for use by the poor. Commercial demands for crop residue and animal dung—as feedstock or as fuel for gasifiers and biogas generators—also deprive the poor of fuel.

Sanitation services are available to only 37 percent of urban and 8 percent of rural households in India (47). Human waste, disposed of in open or common spaces, can spread pathogens through the air, in water supplies, and by direct contact. Waste-related health hazards increase as populations grow and affect the urban and rural poor most severely.

The poor are both agents and victims of environmental degradation. They suffer most directly the consequences of degradation, whether caused by their own actions or by consumption (direct and indirect) on the part of higher-income groups. Moreover, the

Figure 1.16 Indian Per Capita Consumption, Durables, 1989–90

A. Urban

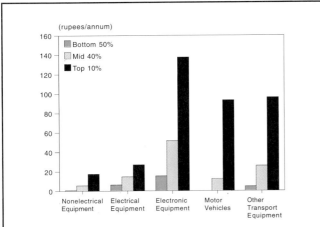

B. Rural

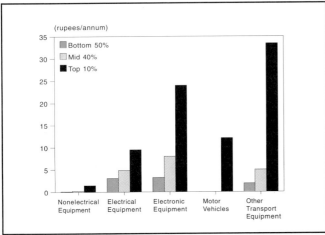

Source: Analysis by the Indira Gandhi Institute of Development Research, Bombay, 1993.

Figure 1.17 Indian Per Capita Consumption, Energy and Transport, 1989–90

A. Urban

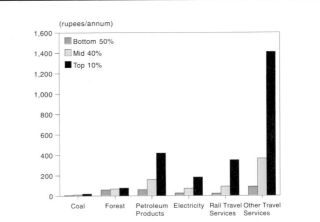

B. Rural

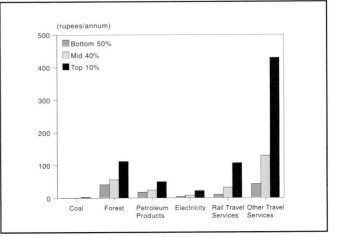

Source: Analysis by the Indira Gandhi Institute of Development Research, Bombay, 1993.

poor often have no alternative when the environmental resources they depend on are degraded—the environment is an integral and irreplaceable aspect of their life support system. Undependable food supplies, unsafe drinking water, polluted air, and unsanitary conditions contribute significantly to reduced life expectancy and high child mortality. These conditions, in turn, contribute to population growth as the poor make fertility decisions to compensate. Children are valuable—they gather fuel, collect drinking water, and care for aging relatives. But because many children die, it is necessary to have many. The result is a vicious cycle: a larger population leads to more poverty and more pressure on the environment.

Implications

The consumption patterns discussed above largely drive natural resource production and use in India. With the exception of iron ore and a few other commodities, most of the natural resources produced in India are also consumed within India. (See Box 1.1.) The environmental consequences of consumption patterns

include industrial pollution, a growing problem in India, that could be alleviated, in part, by more efficient processes to reduce effluents and conserve energy and materials. Without greater efficiency, local pollution may worsen as consumption rises along with urban populations and incomes. More efficient use of energy and coal to generate electricity could also keep Indian contributions to the global buildup of greenhouse gases to a minimum. On a per capita basis, however, current levels of consumption and pollution are far lower than in industrial countries.

A far more difficult—and from a global perspective, possibly more critical—problem is the vicious cycle of poverty, population growth, resource degradation, and more poverty. In addition to human degradation, this cycle degrades and threatens to exhaust renewable resources on which local populations depend. Thus, development and environmental goals are inextricably linked: development that alleviates poverty is essential, if renewable resources—especially from common property—and sustainable livelihoods for a large fraction of the population are to be preserved in nations such as India. Consequently, policies that accelerate development can play a vital environmental role, if they are properly designed.

POLICY IMPLICATIONS

Agenda 21, adopted at the 1992 United Nations Conference on Environment and Development (UNCED) in Rio de Janeiro, contains the following explicit objectives regarding consumption:

■ *All countries should strive to promote sustainable consumption patterns;*
■ *Developed countries should take the lead in achieving sustainable patterns;*
■ *Developing countries should seek to achieve sustainable consumption patterns in their development process, guaranteeing the provision of basic needs for the poor, while avoiding those unsustainable patterns, particularly in industrialized countries, generally recognized as unduly hazardous to the environment, inefficient and wasteful, in their development processes. This requires enhanced technological and other assistance from industrialized countries.*

The environmental and developmental impact of natural resource consumption makes many present consumption practices unsustainable. Industrialized countries need to consider how to reduce consumption and increase the efficiency of natural resource use. Most importantly, however, they need to mitigate significantly their impact on the global commons, exemplified by the buildup of greenhouse gases from the consumption of fossil fuel. In the Climate Convention signed at UNCED, industrialized countries made tentative commitments to stabilize emissions of greenhouse gases at 1990 levels; this is an important first step. But even if these commitments are fulfilled, the North will still be far from a sustainable consumption pattern on fossil fuel, and the region's potential impact on the global climate will continue to rise.

Developing countries would also benefit from more efficient use of natural resources. Even though per capita consumption is far lower than in industrialized countries, their large and growing populations suggest that total natural resource use and related pollution problems will become significant both locally and globally. Most important, however, developing countries need to protect their endangered renewable-resource base, which will mean accelerating and targeting development in ways that can alleviate poverty and enabling poor people to meet their basic needs in ways that do not degrade water, soil, or forest resources or reduce biodiversity.

Governments around the world could adopt a number of policies to help reduce pollution and environmental degradation caused by natural resource extraction, production and use, as well as to safeguard the natural systems that support renewable resources. Many of these policies would also help to improve economic efficiency and promote more sustainable patterns of natural resource consumption in both industrialized and developing countries. Although the underlying principles are widely endorsed, few such policies have been effectively implemented and many remain politically controversial.

Using the Price Mechanism

Because individuals and companies alike respond to price signals, governments have long used taxes and subsidies as economic policy levers. The same means can be used to encourage more efficient use of resources and to reduce environmental pressure from resource consumption. If the environmental costs of human economic activity were more adequately reflected in the prices paid for goods and services, for example, then companies and ultimately consumers would have an economic incentive to adjust their behavior so as to reduce pollution and waste. Twenty years ago, the OECD agreed on this principle, called polluter pays, as a means of incorporating environmental externalities into the economic system in a way that does not give unfair advantage to the industries of one country over another. Though the idea of pollution and other green taxes is gaining attention, the polluter pays principle has never been systematically implemented in industrialized countries, and it remains controversial in many developing countries.

European countries have long used high taxes on petrol to restrain demand. More recently, taxes on the carbon content of all forms of fossil fuel have been proposed as a means of curbing growth in emissions of carbon dioxide (48). One proposal in the United States calls for taxes of $30 per ton of carbon, and some analyses have suggested still higher taxes to hold U.S. emissions at 1990 levels. The extent to which a carbon tax would affect economic growth is a controversial question. Virtually all studies suggest that if the revenues were used to lower other taxes, a carbon tax could promote, rather than hinder, economic growth (49). However, if imposed unilaterally, this kind of tax could alter a nation's economic competitiveness so that international cooperation may be required for such a policy to be implemented.

Taxes have been used or are being considered for many environmental purposes, among them reducing various forms of pollution, municipal solid waste, and congestion on urban highways, as well as encouraging recycling of materials. If such taxes were revenue-neutral (revenues used to reduce other taxes), they could encourage both environmental protection and economic growth by shifting the tax burden away from more desirable economic activities such as work (income taxes), employment (social security taxes), savings, and investment (50).

Removing Subsidies That Encourage Unsustainable Use

Production of natural resource-related commodities is often subsidized in both industrialized and developing countries. Water supplied by public agencies for irrigation in the United States, for example, is 85 to 90 percent subsidized, on average (51). The practice is widespread: the United States also subsidizes timber production and cattle grazing on public lands, Canada subsidizes the hydroelectricity and timber production, Germany subsidizes the production of coal. Such countries as Indonesia, the Philippines, and Papua New Guinea, in effect, support timber production by failing to charge concession holders an adequate royalty. India subsidizes irrigation water and electricity production. Russia and most Central and Eastern European countries support energy production. Agriculture is also subsidized in many countries, for example, through price supports in the United States and Europe and pesticide subsidies in the Philippines (52).

Such subsidies encourage wasteful use of resources, often creating or exacerbating environmental problems. This is the result that underpricing energy has had throughout the former Soviet Union. Salinization from overirrigation is a major cause of land degradation in India and in some areas of the United States. Heavy use of coal in Germany has been a major contributor to air pollution and acid rain.

Eliminating or reducing such subsidies would confer both economic and environmental advantages and, just as with environmental taxes, send more appropriate price signals to businesses and consumers alike. It would reduce waste and pollution and ensure more efficient consumption of natural resources. It would free up fiscal resources that could be used to upgrade production and reduce pollution, diversify the economy, alleviate poverty, or support development in other ways. Of course, the elimination of subsidies, by weeding out inefficient or marginal enterprises, could raise unemployment. In developing countries, it could also have a serious impact on the livelihood of the poor. What is called for is the careful targeting of subsidies where they are most needed.

Measuring Consumption Costs Accurately

Accounting schemes that more accurately measure the environmental costs of economic activity at all levels could also help increase the efficiency of natural resource use and reduce related environmental impacts. For example, adjusting national accounts to include the costs of natural resource depletion or degradation might lead to more appropriate policies and resource management strategies (53). At the level of the individual company, full-cost accounting would make management aware of the environmental cost of pollution and raw material use and encourage more responsible behavior. Frank Popoff, the chairman and chief executive officer of Dow Chemical Company, has called for industry to voluntarily adopt full-cost accounting in its own operations, suggesting that this could be "the most important step down the path to sustainable development" (54). More widespread information about the environmental implications of individual consumption patterns might prove effective in reducing wasteful consumption, especially among the most wealthy segments of industrial society, and in encouraging the adoption of more sustainable lifestyles.

Development That Can Reduce Poverty

Much has been written about policies that could significantly aid development in the South, particularly the alleviation of poverty (55) (56). These include targeting "human-capital" investments in health care and education for the poorest segments of society, adopting legal reforms to extend land tenure and other

rights to the rural poor and to legitimize the informal economies among the urban poor, and enhancing the status of women while increasing their participation in development. (See Chapter 3, "Women and Sustainable Development.")

More general efforts could be made to encourage economic growth and provide employment in developing countries. One possible—and highly controversial—policy lever is to reduce trade barriers in industrialized countries for goods imported from developing countries. This would likely increase Northern consumption of natural resources from the South, it might exacerbate local environmental problems in the South, and it would have an economic and social impact in the North. Yet such a policy could also powerfully stimulate development and reduce the overall environmental consequences of present consumption patterns in both North and South.

Japan, the United States, and the industrialized countries of Europe maintain barriers against most agricultural imports and significant subsidies for their own agricultural exports. These protectionist policies support a system of high-input, intensive agriculture that has major environmental and developmental impacts. The problems include pesticide and fertilizer runoff (a major source of water pollution), excessive soil erosion, and loss of biological diversity.

Agricultural protectionism imposes a heavy price on both industrial and developing countries. Within the OECD, for example, it costs domestic consumers and taxpayers an estimated $150 billion annually, more than double what farmers in OECD countries gain (57). Trade barriers prevent market development and job creation among low-cost producers, perpetuating poverty, subsistence agriculture, and their environmental effects in developing countries. Lower world food prices also depress export income in developing countries and elsewhere, inhibiting needed investment in domestic agriculture.

Removal or substantial reduction of such protection would expand agricultural trade. Global liberalization of trade could increase income in developing countries by as much as $60 billion per year, reducing poverty and natural resource degradation (58). Often the poorest segments in the developing world have not benefited from expanded agricultural trade; efforts must be made to ensure that in the future they do. There must also be a means of ensuring that expanded export production in the South is sustainable and does not simply transfer environmental problems from North to South. For example, pesticides are not yet as heavily used in developing as in industrial countries, but they are often applied in the South without adequate consideration of their effect on human health. (See Chapter 6, "Food and Agriculture.")

The Multi-Fibre Agreement and other trade barriers restrict imports of textiles, clothing, footwear, and other relatively labor-intensive products from developing countries that are low-cost producers and thus have a comparative advantage in the world market. These, like agricultural trade barriers, have the effect of lowering income in developing countries and raising consumer prices in industrialized countries. In the 1980s, for example, U.S. consumers paid about $18 billion per year in excess cost just for clothing and textiles (59). Removing such trade barriers could increase employment, promote economic diversification in developing countries, and lower consumer costs in industrialized countries. It would require efforts to offset employment dislocation in the North and potential additional environmental problems in the South.

International Agreements

Regulation is still an essential policy mechanism for controlling pollution and other forms of environmental degradation in virtually every country. In dealing with global environmental problems, however, international agreements that harmonize approaches and ensure joint action play a critical role. The Vienna Convention and the subsequent Montreal Protocol on Substances that Deplete the Ozone Layer—which, as amended, requires industrial countries to phase out production of chlorofluorcarbons (CFCs) by 1996— serve as successful prototypes of such agreements. Global CFC emissions are already beginning to decline. The climate and biodiversity conventions signed at UNCED in 1992, just coming into force, still require implementing agreements. (See Chapter 11, "Atmosphere and Climate," and Chapter 8, "Biodiversity.") Agreements will not be easy to achieve and enforce, but they have the potential to alter unsustainable patterns of natural resource consumption, restraining growth in fossil fuel consumption, for example, or channeling use of renewable resources into more sustainable patterns.

Additional international agreements or novel institutional arrangements may be needed to facilitate access to new technologies. At present, most technology development occurs in the North, increasingly in the private sector. Yet greater and more rapid access to technology, as well as policies that encourage development of new technology, are critical to enabling both the South and the North to make more efficient use of natural resources (60). Biotechnology provides one example. Using biotechnology and other techniques to enhance agricultural productivity on existing agricultural land will be essential to protect habitats critical to biodiversity from being converted to farmland. But finding ways to make the biotechnology developed by

Northern corporations available to international agricultural research centers for adaptation and application in the South could require novel licensing approaches. (See Chapter 6, "Food and Agriculture.")

Other kinds of international agreements can be used to protect natural resource commodities or to promote more sustainable production methods. One recent example is the international ban on trade in ivory, which has reduced the slaughter of elephants while causing some difficulty for countries that already manage their elephant herds sustainably. Proposals to reduce or halt consumption of other such endangered commodities, likely to be controversial, may also be proposed.

CONCLUSION

The world now faces a unique set of challenges related to sustainable resource use. On the one hand, it must find the means to foster development that interrupts the vicious cycle of poverty, population growth, and renewable resource degradation seen in many developing countries. On the other hand, it must also gather the will to adopt policies that alter unsustainable and environmentally damaging patterns of consumption in all countries, but especially industrial ones, which collectively have a huge impact on the global environment. Policy options exist for reducing pollution, for preventing the exhaustion of resources, and for shifting resource consumption to more sustainable patterns. Getting such policies accepted and implemented will not be easy, but are actions that are nonetheless essential for achieving a sustainable future.

This chapter is the product of a joint research effort organized and supported by the United Nations Development Programme (UNDP) and the World Resources Institute (WRI). Contributors include Lawrence Klein, Benjamin Franklin Professor of Economics (emeritus) at the University of Pennsylvania; Kirit Parikh, director of the Indira Gandhi Institute of Development Research in Bombay; Jyoti Parikh, Senior Professor at the Indira Gandhi Institute of Development Research; and Allen Hammond of the World Resources staff. Luis Gómez-Echeverri, manager of UNDP's Environmental and Natural Resources Group, played an important role in organizing and planning the chapter. The authors acknowledge with gratitude data provided by the U.S. Bureau of Mines. As with all World Resources materials, WRI assumes responsibility for the final form of the chapter.

References and Notes

1. Jyoti and Kirit Parikh, Subir Gokarin, *et al.*, "Consumption Patterns: The Driving Force of Environmental Stress," Indira Gandhi Institute of Development Research Discussion Paper No. 59, Indira Gandhi Institute of Development Research, Bombay, 1991, pp. 1–3.

2. World Resources Institute in collaboration with the United Nations Environment Programme and the United Nations Development Programme, *World Resources 1992–93* (Oxford University Press, New York, 1992), p. 206.

3. U. Hoffmann and D. Zivkovic, "Demand Growth for Industrial Raw Materials and its

Determinants: An Analysis for the Period 1965–1988," United Nations Conference on Trade and Development Discussion Paper No. 50, Geneva, 1992, pp. 33–43.

4. J.T. Houghton, G.J. Jenkins, and J.J. Ephraums, eds., *Climate Change: The IPCC Scientific Assessment* (Cambridge University Press, Cambridge, U.K., 1990), Appendix I.

5. S. Manabe and R.J. Stouffer, "Century-Scale Effects of Increased Atmospheric CO2 on the Ocean-Atmosphere System," *Nature*, Vol. 364, No. 6434 (1993), pp. 215–217.

6. J.T. Thom, "Deforestation and Desertification in Twentieth-Century Arid Sahelien Af-

rica," and C. L. Goucher, "The Impact of German Colonial Rule on the Forests of Togo," in *World Deforestation in the Twentieth Century*, John Richards and Richard Tucker, eds. (Duke University Press, Durham, North Carolina, 1988), pp. 61–66 and 73–75.

7. M. Gadgil and R. Guha, *This Fissured Land* (Oxford University Press, Delhi, 1992), pp. 113–214.

8. P. Evans, *Dependent Development: The Alliance of Multinational, State, and Local Capital in Brazil* (Princeton University Press, Princeton, New Jersey, 1979), pp. 55–83.

9. S. D. Krasner, *Defending the National Interest: Raw Materials Investments and U.S. Foreign Policy* (Princeton University Press, Princeton, New Jersey, 1978), pp. 155–177.

10. Philip Hurst, *Rainforest Politics: Ecological Destruction in South-East Asia* (Zed Books, London, 1990), pp. 245–251.

11. *The National Gardening Survey* (The National Gardening Association, Burlington, Vermont, June 1993), p. 27.

12. U.S. Environmental Protection Agency (EPA), *Lawn Care Pesticides White Paper* (EPA, Washington, D.C., February 1993), pp. 1–2.

13. Andrew Pollack, "Sega Takes Aim at Disney's World," *New York Times* (July 4, 1993), p. 6, sec. F.

14. World Resources Institute (WRI), *World Resources Database* on diskette (World Resources Institute, Washington, D.C., 1992).

15. David Berry, Program Manager, Material Use Patterns, U.S. Bureau of Mines, Washington, D.C., 1993 (personal communication).

16. George Miller, President, Mining Association of Canada, Ottawa, 1993 (personal communication).

17. United Nations Environment Programme and the World Health Organization, *Urban Air Pollution in Megacities of the World* (Blackwell, Oxford, U.K., 1992), p. 45.

18. The World Bank, *World Development Report, 1992* (Oxford University Press, New York, 1992), p. 47.

19. *Ibid.*, pp. 45–46 and 48.

20. *Op. cit.* 2, pp. 111–117.

21. *Op. cit.* 2, pp. 111–117.

22. Paul Kennedy, *Preparing for the 21st Century* (Random House, New York, 1993), pp. 65–81.

23. W.V. Reid, "How Many Species Will There Be?" in *Tropical Deforestation and Species Extinction*, T. Whitmore and J. Sayer, eds., (Chapman and Hall, London, 1992), p. 63.

24. P.H. Raven, "Biological Resources and Global Stability," in *Evolution and Coadaptation in Biotic Communities*, S. Kawano, J.H. Connell, and T. Hidaka, eds., (University of Tokyo Press, Tokyo, 1988), pp. 17–18.

25. Food and Agriculture Organization of the United Nations (FAO), *Forest Resources Assessment, 1990: Tropical Countries* (FAO, Rome, 1993), p. ix.

26. Daniel Yergin, *The Prize: The Epic Quest for Oil, Money and Power* (Simon and Schuster, New York, 1991), pp. 13–14.

27. The National Academy of Sciences, National Academy of Engineering, and Institute of Medicine, *Policy Implications of Greenhouse Warming: Mitigation, Adaption and the Science Base* (National Academy Press, Washington, D.C., 1992), pp. 4–6.

28. H. Linneman, H. Kox, C. Vandertak, *et al.*, *Preliminary Conditions for International Commodity-Related Environmental Agreements*, research project on international commodity-related agreements (Free University, Amsterdam, 1993), pp. 77–80.

29. Food and Agriculture Organization of the United Nations (FAO), *Agrostat PC* (FAO, Rome, 1993).

30. "Malaysian Log Ban Could Reduce Japanese Imports," *Jakarta Post* (May 14, 1993), p. 8.

31. Food and Agriculture Organization of the United Nations (FAO), *FAO Yearbook: Forest Products, 1991* (FAO, Rome, 1993), pp. 3 and 9.

32. M. Bhagavan, "The Woodfuel Crisis in the SADCC Countries," *Ambio*, Vol. 13, No. 1 (1984), p. 25.

33. K.D. Singh, "The 1990 Tropical Forest Resources Assessment," *Unasylva*, Vol. 44, No. 174 (1993), p. 18.

34. U.S. Environmental Protection Agency (U.S. EPA) *Characterization of Municipal Solid Waste in the United States: 1990 Update* (U.S. EPA, Washington, D.C., 1990), p. 12.

35. *Op. cit.* 28, pp. 83, 88, and 95.

36. *Op. cit.* 28, p. 117

37. *Op. cit.* 28, p. 117.

38. R.G. Williams, *Export Agriculture and the Crisis in Central America* (University of North Carolina Press, Chapel Hill, North Carolina, 1986), pp. 48–51.

39. "Official Report of the Government Committee on Aral Sea Regions," *Meteorology and Hydrology*, Vol. 9 (1988), World Resources Institute in collaboration with the United Nations Environment Programme and the United Nations Development Programme, cited in *World Resources, 1990–91* (Oxford University Press, New York, 1990), p. 171.

40. Christoo Vasillikiotis, "Cotton," *Ecology Center Terrain*, Vol. 22, No. 5 (1992), p. 2.

41. *Op. cit.* 3.

42. World Resources Institute calculations.

43. Donald G. Rogich, "United States and Global Material Use Patterns," paper presented at the ASM International Conference on Materials and Global Environment, Washington, D.C., September, 1993.

44. U.S. Bureau of Mines, "Minerals and the Economy," *Minerals Today* (April 1993), pp. 14–18.

45. *Ibid.*

46. National Sample Survey Organization, *Sarvekshana: Journal of the National Sample Survey Organization* (Government of India Department of Statistics, New Delhi, April–June 1990).

47. *Ibid.*

48. Roger C. Dower and Mary Beth Zimmerman, *The Right Climate for Carbon Taxes: Creating Economic Incentives to Protect the Atmosphere* (World Resources Institute, Washington, D.C., 1992).

49. Robert Repetto, Roger C. Dower, Robin Jenkins, *et al.*, *Green Fees: How a Tax Shift Can Work for the Environment and the Economy* (World Resources Institute, Washington, D.C., 1992), pp. 57–58, 60–61, and 69.

50. *Ibid.*, pp. 71 and 83–84.

51. Robert Repetto, *Skimming the Water: Rent-Seeking and the Performance of Public Irrigation Systems* (World Resources Institute, Washington, D.C., 1992), p. 15.

52. Paul Faeth, ed., *Agricultural Policy and Sustainability: Case Studies from India, Chile, the Philippines and the United States* (World Resources Institute, Washington, D.C., 1993), pp. 8–10.

53. Robert Repetto, W. Magrath, M. Wells, *et al.*, *Wasting Assets: Natural Resources in the National Income Accounts* (World Resources Institute, Washington, D.C., 1989), pp. v and 6–11.

54. Frank Popoff and David T. Buzzelli, "Full-Cost Accounting," *Chemical and Engineering News*, Vol. 71, No. 2 (January 11, 1993), p. 8.

55. United Nations Development Programme, *Human Development Report, 1992* (Oxford University Press, New York, 1993), pp. 7–8.

56. The World Bank, *World Development Report, 1990* (Oxford University Press, New York, 1990), p. 4.

57. David Blandford, "The Costs of Agricultural Protection and the Difference Free Trade Would Make," in *Agricultural Protectionism in the Industrialized World*, Fred H. Sanderson, ed. (Resources for the Future, Washington, D.C., 1990), pp. 407–409.

58. A. Salazar, P. Brandao, and W. Martin, "Implications of Agricultural Trade Liberalization for the Developing Countries," The World Bank Policy Research Working Papers, The World Bank, Washington, D.C., 1993, pp. 22 and 38.

59. The World Bank, *World Development Report, 1987* (Oxford University Press, New York, 1987), p. 151.

60. George Heaton, Robert Repetto, and Rodney Sobin, *Transforming Technology: An Agenda for Environmentally Sustainable Growth in the 21st Century* (World Resources Institute, Washington, D.C., 1991).

2. Population and the Environment

Over the next 30 years, global population is projected to grow by nearly two thirds, from the current 5.5 billion to 8.5 billion. Though this is considered a projection, substantial growth is inevitable because of the relatively large percentage of young people in today's population. This provides a built-in momentum for further population growth, even as the number of children per family declines. Of the 8.5 billion people, about 7.1 billion will live in developing countries, primarily in urban areas. Population in industrialized countries, now 1.2 billion, is projected to rise only to 1.4 billion by the year 2025, with virtually all of that growth occurring in the United States (1).

Longer-term growth depends on the course of fertility decline in developing countries, which in turn depends on the effectiveness of family planning programs, progress in reducing poverty and elevating the status of women, and many other factors. But a reasonable estimate is that global population will continue to grow, reaching 10 billion in the year 2050 (2).

What does this historically unprecedented increase mean in human terms? Can the world feed twice as many people? Can it improve the diet of impoverished people in developing countries? Can its cities absorb several billion people and improve health, housing, and services? Or will the stress of population growth overwhelm our capacity to adapt, leading to a downward spiral of scarcity and conflict?

Equally significant, what does a doubling of world population suggest for the global environment? Must forests inevitably be destroyed under the pressures of rapidly increasing food demand? Do twice as many people mean twice as much pollution and energy consumption? Or will rising aspirations and living standards in developing countries cause environmental stress to increase much faster than population growth? Could the world in 2050 provide a comfortable standard of living for 10 billion people without inflicting possibly irreversible environmental damage?

These questions are the latest points of contention in a debate that has continued for several hundred years. During this debate, two facts have become clear.

First, population growth does have a significant impact on the environment, but the relationship is not straightforward. Many other factors—government policies, the legal system, access to capital and technology, the efficiency of industrial production, inequity in the distribution of land and resources, poverty in the South and conspicuous consumption in the North—may work separately or together to buffer or increase humankind's impact on the environment. The potential for reducing the effect of population growth depends largely on altering factors such as these that compound the environmental impact of human activity.

Second, human ingenuity is an extraordinary resource, with the potential to mitigate the environmental effect of population growth by finding ways to use resources more efficiently and to limit environmental pollution.

The general picture is clear: the increase in population will affect resources and the environment in many significant ways. Population growth will heighten demand for food, energy, water, health care, sanitation, and housing, for example. What is much less clear is how the demand for such goods and services will be met and the effect this will have on the environment.

A critical challenge for government is how to devise policies that mitigate the environmental and resource effects of population growth and that encourage a slowing in the rate of population growth. Poverty reduction, elevating the status of women, and effective family planning are important components of any strategy. But countries differ too much from one another—for example, in availability of resources, rate of population growth, and social structure—to make sweeping policy proposals useful in specific contexts.

One significant aspect of population growth is frontier expansion, a process that has largely ended in industrialized countries but continues in many parts of the developing world. Today much more is known about the consequences of expansion, including the loss of biodiversity and the release of gases into the atmosphere from deforestation, both of which are significant at the local level and potentially at the global level.

A second important trend is rapidly increasing population in coastal areas, environments that are easily damaged by development.

This chapter includes three case studies: two deal with frontier expansion in the Philippines and Costa Rica and one with population growth in coastal areas of the United States. These studies shed some light on the connections between population and environmental degradation, but many related issues—the impact of population growth on the urban environment, on health, and on the status of women, to name just a few—are only briefly mentioned. Much more work needs to be done to develop our understanding of the complex relationship between population, resources, and environment. The 1994 United Nations conference on population and development will provide heightened attention to the issue. (See Box 2.1.)

POPULATION TRENDS AND PROJECTIONS

How many people inhabit the Earth is an important factor in determining the impact of human activity on the environment. Also important are the rate population increases, how people are distributed geographically, and the investment in health and education—

Box 2.1 The United Nations 1994 Conference on Population

Population issues will receive special attention at the United Nations in 1994, culminating with the Cairo International Conference on Population and Development in September. Most of the international community and many nongovernmental organizations (NGOs) have participated in preparatory meetings for the conference. Many countries have formed ad hoc national committees that typically include representatives from government departments and agencies, NGOs, and universities. The principal task of each committee has been to prepare a national report on population, without the help of international experts, to be submitted to the conference (1).

Delegates will be considering the so-called Cairo Document, which is expected to include action-oriented recommendations to address the population and development challenges of the next few decades. Dr. Nafis Sadik, head of the U.N. Fund for Population Activities and secretary-general of the conference, has suggested a set of goals to be attained by the year 2015. These include reducing the infant death rate from the current 62 to 12 per 1,000 live births; lowering the maternal mortality rate to 30

per 100,000 women; extending life expectancy to 75 years in all countries; giving all pregnant women access to prenatal services; entitling all school-age children to complete their primary education; enabling contraception to reach 71 percent of the population; and making family planning information and services universally accessible (2).

Financing is expected to be a key issue at the conference. Sadik is asking donor countries to allocate 4 percent of their official development assistance to population activity—more than double the current level (3). Other issues expected to require special attention include reproductive health, international migration, and the elimination of unsafe abortions (4).

The conference will also examine the relationships between environmental degradation, demographic factors, and sustainable development. Discussions before the conference will focus on specific regions where population pressure and poverty appear to be hastening environmental degradation. Issues receiving special attention include deforestation in Central America; desertification in Africa; coastal and marine degradation in the Bay

of Bengal; forested upland areas of Nepal, the Philippines, Thailand, and Indonesia; and the environmental problems of small island states in the South Pacific (5).

References and Notes

1. "National Activities: Preparing for Cairo," *ICPD 94: Newsletter of the International Conference on Population and Development*, No. 7 (United Nations Population Fund, New York, June 1993), p. 4.
2. "Investing Directly in People," *ICPD 94: Newsletter of the International Conference on Population and Development*, No. 7 (United Nations Population Fund, New York, June 1993), p. 6.
3. *Ibid.*, p. 1.
4. "The Outcome of Prepcom II: Putting Population at the Centre of the Development Debate," *ICPD 94: Newsletter of the International Conference on Population and Development*, No. 7 (United Nations Population Fund, New York, June 1993), p. 1.
5. "Round Tables Address Critical Issues," *ICPD 94: Newsletter of the International Conference on Population and Development*, No. 7 (United Nations Population Fund, New York, August 1993), p. 6.

that is, the "human capital" represented by these numbers. (See Human Capital Formation, below.)

The rate of population growth matters because of the human ability to adapt to changing conditions. If population grows slowly, human behavior, institutions, and technology will likely adapt fast enough to accommodate the growth. If population grows quickly, more stress is put on environmental resources, physical infrastructure, and governments. It is thus likely that different accommodations are made under conditions of rapid population growth than under slow growth.

Where people live is equally important, because location influences aspirations, values, behavior, consumption patterns, and other factors. Location also helps determine the type of environmental impact that human activity has. The world's most rapid demographic change is occurring in urban areas: while global population is likely to double between now and 2050, the combined effects of rural-to-urban migration and natural increase mean that urban population is likely to triple.

Population Growth

Today the world is experiencing the most rapid increase in human population ever seen. (See Figure 2.1.) Each year from now until well into the 21st Century, more than 90 million people will be added to the world total. A useful gauge is the number of years required to add each billion. In 1950, world population stood at 2.5 billion. By just 1975, the total was 4 billion, and only 12 years later, 5 billion. The sixth, seventh, and eighth billion will arrive spaced only 10 or 11 years apart. The world population growth rate is not expected to stabilize for 40 or 50 more years (3).

This rapid growth has two causes: improved health conditions worldwide, which brought down the death rate, and an expanding population base (a population of 2 billion growing at 2 percent per year will add 40 million people each year; a population of 5 billion growing at 2 percent will add 100 million).

The declining death rate is one of the major accomplishments of human civilization. The timing and speed of this change, however, have varied widely. In the industrialized world, advances in public health and medicine came slowly; life expectancy rose gradually as new ways to improve health conditions were developed. In 1800, life expectancy at birth was about 35 years. By 1900, it had risen to about 50 years, a 15-year increase that took an entire century to achieve (4). By 1950, the industrialized world enjoyed a life expectancy of 66, an increase of 16 years in a half century. Today, that has risen to 75 (5).

Change came more rapidly to developing countries. By 1950, life expectancy had risen to about 40 years. Today, it stands at 62, an increase of more than half a year every 12 months (6). Much of this increase was caused by the rapid adoption of health measures learned in industrialized nations over a period of centuries.

The death rate dropped as life expectancy rose and global population growth began climbing to a record level. Worldwide, the growth rate peaked at 2 percent per year in the late 1960s. But the experience of developing and industrialized countries has been dramati-

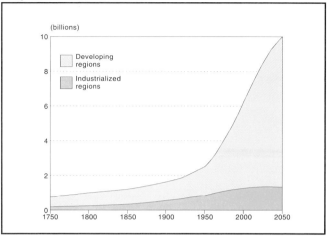

Figure 2.1 Trends and Projections in World Population Growth, 1750–2050

Sources:
1. United Nations (U.N.) Population Division, *Long-Range World Population Projections: Two Centuries of World Population Growth, 1950–2150* (U.N., New York, 1992), p. 22.
2. Carl Haub, Director of International Education, Population Reference Bureau, Washington, D.C., 1993 (personal communication).

cally different. Given the protracted time frame of the increase in life expectancy in industrialized countries, the annual population growth rate rarely climbed above 1 percent. As the death rate slowly dropped, society changed and the birth rate fell slowly, too. In developing countries, the growth rate accelerated after World War II as the death rate dropped (7).

The world growth rate of 2 percent in the late 1960s was the historic peak. By the early 1970s, high birth rates in some developing countries began a gradual downward trend in response to improving social and economic conditions and family planning programs.

Currently, the industrialized world has a low birth rate, having completed the demographic transition to urban populations with small families. Growth is only about 0.4 percent per year, most of it in only one country, the United States. Some countries in Europe are already seeing a new phenomenon, population decline due to a low birth rate rather than emigration. Even in the republics of the former Soviet Union, birth rates have tumbled. In the largest two, Russia and Ukraine, population is now declining.

The developing world, whose 4.3 billion people account for 75 percent of global population, now supplies about 95 percent of the annual population increase. Although the growth rate in the developing world stands at 2 percent per year, down from the late 1960s high-water mark, its population is projected to rise to 8.7 billion by the middle of the next century from a current total of 4.3 billion (8) (9).

Population Projections

Population projections are based on the assumption that, in the long term, the birth rate will come down in countries where it is high today and that life expectancy will rise where it is low. It is important to stress that this is an assumption about future behavior, which cannot always be predicted. Moreover, projec-

Figure 2.2 Long-Range Population Projections, 1990–2150

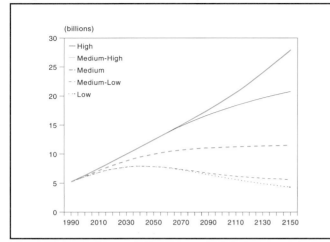

Source: United Nations (U.N.) Population Division, *Long-Range World Population Projections: Two Centuries of Population Growth, 1950–2150* (U.N., New York, 1992), p. 14.

Note: Variations in population projections depend primarily on different assumptions about fertility trends. The low projection assumes fertility will stabilize at 1.7 children, the medium projection assumes stabilization at 2.06, and the high projection assumes stabilization at 2.5 children. (See *World Resources 1992–93*, p. 80.)

tions can vary dramatically when underlying assumptions change. (See Figure 2.2.)

In population projections, an important variable is the time at which a country's fertility rate drops to the replacement level of two children per woman. In a newly industrialized country such as South Korea, the rate has already dropped below the replacement level. In a group of developing countries that includes Brazil, Colombia, and Argentina, the fertility rate has dropped to less than 3 children per woman, but not to replacement. Another group, among them India, Turkey, and Ecuador, experienced a fertility decline to about 4 children per woman, but further decline has been uneven. A final group of countries, including Uganda, Nigeria, and Syria, has shown either very little or no birth rate reduction (10). (See Chapter 16, "Population and Human Development," Table 16.2.)

Typically, population projections assume that the replacement level will be reached in all countries of Africa in about 2045–2050. For other countries, the date varies from as early as 2010 to 2050. In India, for example, U.N. projections assume that replacement will be reached by 2025–2030 (11) (12).

The track record of projections is actually rather good, at least at the world level. As the projection period becomes longer, however, deviation from the "medium" scenario (which asssumes a world population of 10 billion in 2050 that rises to a stabilized size at 11.5 billion a century later) is likely to grow. Projections are much less reliable for smaller geographic areas such as regions or countries, and global projections can mask important changes in the outlook for regions.

Regional Trends

In recent years, fertility has decreased more rapidly than projected in Latin America but has remained higher than projected in South Asia.

Today, Asia has the largest population and the widest range in birth rates. China recently reported a drop below the replacement level in 1992, sooner than expected. South Asia's total fertility rate has dropped to 4.3, but its future course is in doubt. In India, fertility decline leveled off in the early 1980s at about 4 children per woman. In Bangladesh, a recent survey recorded that country's first drop in the birth rate, to a total fertility rate of 4.7 children per woman from about 7 in 1970–75. Pakistan shows very little evidence of decline (13).

In Southeast Asia, a total fertility rate of 3.4 signals real progress, particularly in Indonesia and Thailand where the rates are 3.1 and 2.2, respectively. In Western Asia, fertility remains high in most Arab states. The regional total fertility rate is 4.7. A successful family planning program in Turkey, which has about half the region's population, makes it an exception (14).

In sub-Saharan Africa, fertility decline has only begun to appear, and then only in certain countries. The region's total fertility rate stood at 6.7 in 1960 and was still at 6.4 in the early 1990s. Initial fertility declines in Zimbabwe, Kenya, Cameroon, and other nations of the region suggest a trend that may continue, but the future remains uncertain. If fertility does not decline as projected by the United Nations or if it levels off above the replacement rate, Africa's population could be much larger than current projections. In North Africa, where government policies to lower the birth rate have been in effect for years, the total fertility rate stands at 4.7; fertility decreases have been slow but steady (15).

In Latin America, whose overall fertility rate of 3.1 is about the same as Asia's, fertility decline has been generally uniform. The region's largest country, Brazil, now has a total fertility rate of 2.8; the second largest country, Mexico, has reduced its rate to 3.2. Replacement level fertility, however, has proven elusive. No country in the region (excluding the Caribbean) has achieved the two-child family yet. (See Chapter 16, "Population and Human Development," Table 16.2.) Replacement level fertility is not projected to occur until 2045–2050, the same as Africa (16) (17).

Migration

Assumptions about migration do not affect global population projections but can have a considerable effect on projections for individual countries. International migration is on the rise even as press reports increasingly describe most industrialized countries as having a closed-door policy. Despite signs of growing resentment toward immigrants in many industrialized countries, perceived economic opportunity elsewhere remains a strong incentive for migration. Moreover, many industrialized countries, with less-than-replacement fertility and aging populations, are also likely to need new people to fill their labor forces. Thus the issue of migration from poorer countries with an excess labor force to richer countries with an aging population will continue to be an important one in many regions of the world.

Germany has experienced a heavy influx of asylum seekers since the collapse of communism in Eastern

Europe. Even before unification with East Germany, immigration totaled about 1 million in 1989 (18) (19). In the United States, immigration is now approaching the peak levels of the early 20th Century. In FY92, for example, 810,635 immigrants, refugees, and asylum seekers were granted legal residence, the largest number since 1914 (20). This number was supplemented by an uncertain number of illegal immigrants, estimated by the U.S. Census Bureau at 200,000 annually.

In sub-Saharan Africa, free migration has always been a tradition, although much of it is seasonal. In the late 1980s, there were about 35 million international migrants in the region, fully half of the world total. Countries such as Côte d'Ivoire, Nigeria, South Africa, Zimbabwe, and Zambia are common destinations (21).

Within South Asia and North Africa, there is a pattern of workers migrating to oil-rich Middle East nations. In East Asia, the Philippines provides a significant portion of all the intraregional immigrant laborers and a growing number of the illegal immigrants in Japan. There is also continuing migration from Bangladesh into India (22).

Given relative population growth rates and incomes, migration pressure appears likely to be strong from North Africa into southern Europe, from Latin America into the United States, from East and Southeast Asia into North America and possibly Japan, and from the southern tier of former Soviet republics into Russia (23).

Migration also occurs within countries. In the United States, there has been continuing migration in recent decades to coastal areas of the Pacific and the Gulf of Mexico; more than 50 percent of the U.S. population now lives within 70 kilometers of a coastal area. In China, there are growing migration pressures from the arid and relatively poor interior to the economically booming coastal provinces. But by far the most dramatic internal migration pattern—found in nearly every country—is migration from rural to urban areas.

Urbanization

The world's population is urbanizing much faster than it is growing. There are several reasons: declining resource availability per capita, shrinking economic opportunities in rural areas, and opportunities and services available in urban areas. In virtually every country, per capita consumption of goods and services is higher in urban areas than in rural communities.

Just how fast fertility drops and life expectancy rises will depend in part on how fast the world urbanizes. When people move into urban areas, they gain job opportunities, their income increases, their family size declines, and they live longer. Their access to health and education facilities improves, providing a higher level of human capital than in rural areas. Education not only enhances knowledge, it also raises expectations. This is true for people who are born in urban areas and also for people who migrate to cities from rural areas, since they tend to adopt urban behavior patterns.

Urban populations exhibit consumption patterns that are unlike those of rural populations and that have a different kind of environmental impact. City residents, for example, tend to consume more indus-

trial goods and energy-intensive services, at least in developing countries. (See Chapter 1, "Natural Resource Consumption.") Urban populations everywhere create concentrated air and water pollution and solid waste.

Today, populations in the industrialized world are about three-fourths urban, compared with about one third in the developing world. Again, global numbers conceal wide regional differences. Latin America, for example, is already as urbanized as Europe. By the year 2005, half of the world's people will live in an urban area; by the year 2025, that number will be about two out of three (24). This is an enormous change from the past, when the world was essentially agrarian.

The rate of urbanization is not just a product of migration; it is also a result of the birth rate among the urban population. In the industrialized world, migration was a gradual process; from 1875 to 1900, the annual rate of urban growth was 2.8 percent (25). In the developing world, urban populations have grown at an annual rate of about 4 percent from 1975 to 1990. Such rapid urbanization places enormous strain on developing countries to provide the infrastructure necessary to support their populations. By 2025, 4 billion people in developing countries will be classified as urban—equivalent to the world's total population in 1975 (26).

HUMAN CAPITAL FORMATION

Human capital is one of the most important factors in determining a population's productivity, behavior, and values. Human capital is the result of investment in education and health. Such investment increases people's options, raises their productivity at work, and changes their behavior at home. Health investments are reflected in the increasing life expectancy and the decreasing morbidity of the population of most countries. Educational investment is measured by either formal attainment levels (number of those who have finished secondary school or beyond) which increase slowly, or by the number of total school enrollments, which have increased very rapidly in many developing countries. Demographers are particularly interested in the connection between women's education and fertility rates.

Education Trends

Progress in women's education remains slow in many countries, which has profoundly negative consequences for development. (See Chapter 3, "Women and Sustainable Development.") In industrialized countries, 95 percent of females are enrolled in secondary grades, and in some areas the rate of enrollment at this level equals or exceeds that for males. But developing countries, except for Latin America, lag considerably behind on this measure. (See Figures 2.3. and 2.4.)

In Africa, which has the world's highest fertility, U.N. estimates show that secondary enrollment rates have stagnated since the mid-1980s, perpetuating a cycle of high birth rates and poor education. An expanding population requires constantly increasing education expenditures, a difficult burden for struggling African economies. It is noteworthy that the gap between male and female education rates has remained nearly

Figure 2.3 Secondary Enrollment Rates

A. Latin America, 1975–90

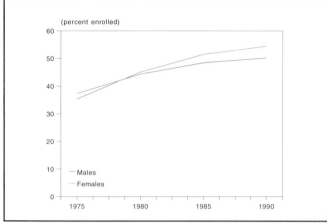

B. Asia, 1975–90

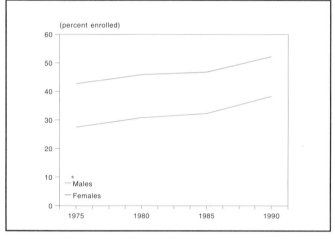

C. Africa, 1975–90

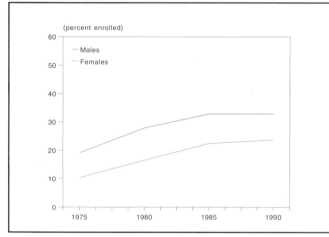

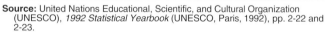

Source: United Nations Educational, Scientific, and Cultural Organization (UNESCO), *1992 Statistical Yearbook* (UNESCO, Paris, 1992), pp. 2-22 and 2-23.

constant. In Asia, the most recent trend is more encouraging. An upturn can be observed since 1985, although, once again, the male-female gap is unchanged.

The experience in Latin America is different from that in Africa and Asia. Here, female secondary enroll-

ment is more than 50 percent; in fact, the enrollment rate for females has long been higher than that for males. It is probably no coincidence that Latin America also records the lowest overall fertility rate of any developing region (27).

Education and Fertility

There is a significant relationship between the education of women and fertility; for the most part, the total fertility rate declines as educational levels rise. The connection is most pronounced among those who have completed primary school and had some secondary instruction. Typically, the association is more apparent in urban than in rural areas, presumably because higher education is more accessible in cities. The extent of the association between education and fertility rate is not constant, however, because schooling is but one aspect of human development (28). Both Asia and Latin America have roughly the same average fertility rate, despite significant differences in school enrollment. China's strict population program lowers the fertility rate in Asia more than its educational level might suggest. In Arab countries, social factors that encourage large families keep fertility high despite major strides in female education. With extremely low rates of female enrollment and high fertility levels, Africa is only beginning the demographic and educational transitions.

Education, by improving job opportunities and increasing the incentive for smaller families, is linked to the use of contraception. Rates of contraceptive use are extremely low for women with no schooling, even in countries where total use is rather high. (See Figure 2.5.) Secondary school education produces the highest level of use. Moreover, women with higher education also delay marriage and the start of childbearing (29). Informal education can also promote the use of contraception. People learn informally on the job, in adult education classes, or through the media, which has become a powerful source of education about new ways of life for people who cannot afford formal education.

Given today's trends in both health and educational investment, future populations are likely to have considerably more human capital than current or past populations. Simple extrapolations of the total size of future populations may miss one of the most important trends: those populations will be qualitatively different because of better health and education.

HUMAN IMPACT ON THE ENVIRONMENT: A LONG-TERM PERSPECTIVE

Humans have had an extraordinary impact on the global environment over the past several centuries. Yet, because environmental conditions in the past are little known, it is difficult to estimate rates of anthropogenic change. Furthermore, natural variations in climate, vegetation, and land forms over the past 20,000 years make it hard to know the extent to which environmental change is a product of human activity. Even today, knowledge is limited in many areas. Estimates of the number of Earth's species, for example, vary from a few million to at least 30 million (30).

Figure 2.4 Percent of Females Enrolled in Secondary School

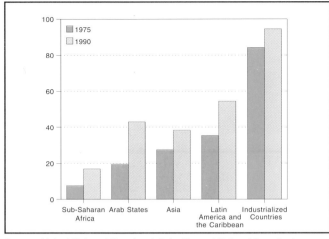

Source: United Nations Educational, Scientific, and Cultural Organization (UNESCO), *1992 Statistical Yearbook* (UNESCO, Paris, 1992), pp. 2-22 and 2-23.

Figure 2.5 Percent of Women Who Practice Contraception, Late 1980s and Early 1990s

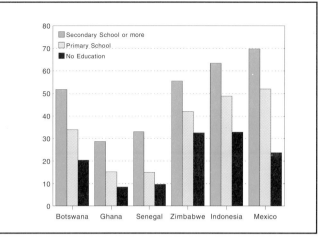

Source: Naomi Rutenberg, Mohamed Ayad, Luis Hernando Ochoa, *et al.*, "Knowledge and Use of Contraception," Demographic and Health Surveys, Comparative Studies No. 6, Institute for Resource Development/Macro International, Columbia, Maryland, 1991, Table 5.3, p. 19.

Of the many human-induced changes that have occurred over the past several centuries, two are especially noteworthy: habitat alteration and pollution.

Habitat Alteration

The global landscape has changed profoundly over the past several centuries, succumbing to the axes, saws, and ploughs of a growing world population. With human settlement expanding, forests have been cleared to grow crops, wetlands have been drained, and grasslands have been irrigated. For example, it is estimated that the continental United States contained about 89 million hectares of wetlands in 1780. By the 1980s, that area had shrunk to about 42 million hectares, or just 53 percent of the 1780 total. Most of this loss came from agricultural conversion. In important farm states such as Illinois, for example, wetlands declined from an estimated 3.3 million hectares in the 1780s to roughly 500,000 hectares in the 1980s (31).

The most dramatic change in global land use has been the expansion of cropland and the reduction of forestland. From 1700 to 1980, it is estimated, forest- and woodland declined globally from roughly 6.2 billion hectares to 5.1 billion hectares, or nearly 20 percent. Over the same period, cropland increased from about 270 million hectares to about 1.5 billion hectares, or about 460 percent. Meanwhile, grassland and pasture declined in some regions and increased in others, with the net result that the global total (about 6.8 billion hectares) stayed about the same (32).

Deforestation and agricultural expansion occurred earlier in Europe and North America than in Latin America and Africa. In North America roughly 72 million hectares of forestland was cleared from 1700 to 1920, with forest cover essentially stable from 1920 to 1980. (See Figure 2.6.) Globally, however, the pace of change has accelerated, with more cropland expansion occurring in the 30-year span from 1950 to 1980 than in the 150-year span from 1700 to 1850 (33).

Frontier expansion was an important safety valve for growing populations in the 19th Century. The settlement of the American West is a well-known example; parts of Asia and Africa also experienced periods of frontier expansion. Frontier expansion is largely over in industrialized countries but is continuing in many regions of the developing world. Meanwhile, the political context of this phenomenon has changed: the environmental implications of frontier expansion are now carefully studied and debated. And in many cases, the areas of easiest access with the best cropland potential are now settled, so that any further expansion will encroach on the marginal areas—the tropical forests, steep hillsides, and semiarid regions—that have relatively fragile resources.

Cropland expansion has been accompanied by a widespread increase in productivity and intensity of land use. In the 20th Century, agriculture became a science of seeds, inputs, and growing conditions, all designed to increase yields. Technology and infrastructure played important roles in this development: machines became more efficient at grinding grain and pumping water, while canals and roads vastly improved the transportation of goods. Emerging world commodity markets, particularly for goods such as cotton, tea, bananas, coffee, sugar, and beef, contributed significantly to forest conversion (34).

In recent years, rapidly growing populations in developing countries have increased demand for basic commodities such as fuelwood. Some 2 billion people rely on fuelwood for cooking and heating, yet in many developing countries demand is far greater than supply. In many areas of Western and sub-Saharan Africa, fuelwood consumption is running 30 to 200 percent ahead of the average increase in the stock of trees (35).

Soil Degradation

The expansion of global agriculture has taken a heavy toll on soil health. Soil productivity depends on its or-

Figure 2.6 Long-Term Trends in Forest and Cropland Area and Population Growth in the United States and Canada, 1700–1980

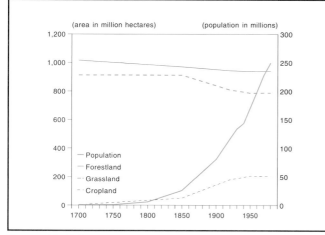

Source: John F. Richards, "Land Transformation," in *The Earth as Transformed by Human Action*, B.L. Turner, William C. Clark, Robert W. Kates, *et al.*, eds. (Cambridge University Press, Cambridge, 1990), p. 164.

ganic matter, soil humus. It is estimated that agricultural activity has reduced the world supply of organic carbon in soil humus by about 15 percent of its original pre-agricultural stock. Carbon loss occurred at a rate of roughly 300 million metric tons per year over the past 300 years, but within the past 50 years the rate rose to as much as 760 million metric tons per year (36).

It is estimated that since World War II, 1.2 billion hectares, or about 10.5 percent of the world's vegetated land, has suffered at least moderate soil degradation as a result of human activity. This is a vast area, roughly the size of China and India combined. If lightly degraded soil is included, the total affected area rises to about 17 percent of global vegetated land.

The most widespread degradation has occurred in Asia, where about 450 million hectares are at least moderately degraded, and Africa, where moderate or worse degradation affects 320 million hectares.

For the world as a whole, the principal causes of soil degradation since World War II are overgrazing, deforestation, and agricultural activities. (See *World Resources 1992–93*, pp. 111–118.)

Pollution

The disposal of human waste directly affects the quality of freshwater resources. Contaminated drinking water, in turn, transmits diseases such as diarrhea, typhoid, and cholera. These diseases were widespread during the late 19th and early 20th centuries in Europe and North America, where they ranked among the leading causes of death and illness (37).

New York City shows how population growth affects pollutant load. From 1880 to 1980, the metropolitan region's population grew by a factor of five, from roughly 3 million to roughly 15.2 million. Estimated waterborne discharges of organic carbon, nitrogen, and phosphorus from human waste rose in direct proportion to population growth. By 1980, about 68 percent of the organic carbon and about 19 percent of the

nitrogen and phosphorus were being removed by sewage treatment (38).

In the 20th Century, other factors, particularly industrial pollution and large-scale agriculture, began to have a major impact on freshwater quality. By 1951, a study of the Raritan River found that municipal loads were equivalent to a population of 220,000 people, but discharges from industrial plants were equivalent to the effluent of 450,000 people. New consumer goods also had a powerful impact on water quality. In the New York City region, for example, detergents with phosphates were not introduced until the 1950s. Yet by 1980, these detergents were adding 18,000 tons of phosphorus to the region's surface water; this is substantially more than the total phosphorus load that comes from human waste (39).

Population-related waterborne diseases have been largely eliminated in industrialized countries but continue to be a significant problem in developing countries. It is estimated that in developing countries, diarrheal diseases were killing about 2.9 million children annually in the early 1990s and 1 million adults and children over 5 annually in the mid-1980s (40) (41).

Energy Consumption and Greenhouse Gases

From 1850 to 1990, the consumption of commercial energy (from coal, oil, gas, nuclear power, and hydropower) increased more than 100-fold, while use of biomass energy (fuelwood, crop waste, and dung) roughly tripled (42). (See Figure 2.7.)

The combustion of fossil fuels (coal, oil, and gas) emits carbon dioxide (CO_2) into the atmosphere. CO_2 constitutes the largest source of greenhouse gases, which trap infrared radiation that would otherwise escape into the atmosphere. Since the Industrial Revolution, atmospheric concentrations of CO_2 have increased by about 25 percent. Emissions from fossil fuel use alone have increased 3.6 times since 1950 (43).

Worldwide consumption of fossil fuel from 1860 to 1949 resulted in the release of an estimated 187 billion metric tons of CO_2 (44). Over the past four decades, fossil fuel use has accelerated, creating an additional 559 billion metric tons of CO_2. From 1950 to 1989, the United States was the largest emitter, followed by the European Community and the former Soviet Union (45). Land use change, including deforestation for agricultural purposes, is responsible for an additional estimated 220 billion metric tons of CO_2 since 1860 (46).

FRONTIER MIGRATION

As this brief historical perspective suggests, in many cases, habitat alteration and pollution are closely related to population. But the total environmental impact of human activity is not simply a function of population. Other factors such as per capita consumption, the environmental impact of particular technologies, government policy, and legal constraints can all significantly affect the environment.

The situation facing industrialized and developing countries differs in some respects. In many developing countries, rapid population growth accompanies heavy dependence on natural resources—forestland, cropland, grassland, and fisheries—for development, while a high share of total economic activity is devoted to agricultural production (47). In many, perhaps most, developing countries, stocks of natural resources are being used faster than the rate of natural replenishment. And many developing countries, particularly those where more than 50 percent of the population depends on agriculture for a livelihood, are faced with a growing shortage of cropland. In the developing world during the 1980s, the amount of arable land per capita declined by 1.9 percent annually (48).

Farmers, often unable to invest in conservation measures, are forced to overuse their land. As a result, cropland productivity declines and land may eventually be abandoned. It is estimated that 70,000 square kilometers of farmland is abandoned every year because the soil is exhausted, while productivity on another 200,000 square kilometers declines (49).

Land scarcity is made worse in many countries by unequal distribution of landholdings. Combining such conditions with sluggish rural economic growth and few opportunities for rural employment off the farm, forces many people to move to cities, coastal areas, or unsettled frontiers. Moving to unsettled frontiers can set off a process of habitat destruction with profound environmental consequences.

Frontier migration is discussed in the following case studies which illustrate the complicated relationship between population growth and environmental degradation. In both the Philippines and Costa Rica, land-tenure policies and narrowly conceived macro-economic policies adopted in response to the debt crisis of the early 1980s combined with rapid population growth to intensify environmental stress.

The Philippines

The Philippines has a relatively large population—estimated at 62.4 million in 1990—occupying a land base of about 300,000 square kilometers. With over 200 people per square kilometer, the Philippines is one of the most densely populated countries in the world.

The population is expanding rapidly. Growth averaged 2.8 percent annually from 1950 to 1985, and declined to 2.5 percent between 1985 and 1990—still higher than in countries such as India, Indonesia, and Malaysia. The population growth rate in the Philippines is expected to decline to about 2 percent by the end of the decade. Such rapid growth is putting great pressure on the economy to generate employment. During the 1990s, about 4.4 million new jobs must be created every year just to keep pace with young people entering the job market (50).

Population pressure is also intense in upland areas, where, by 1985, an estimated 17.5 million people lived (32 percent of the total population). About 11 million people, or 63 percent of the population, lived in forested areas. In 1985, about 70 percent of the upland population were migrants from lowland areas. (See Table 2.1.) Primarily because of this continual migration, the upland population growth rate rose to about 4 percent annually between 1980 and 1985. By 1987, upland areas accounted for 30 percent of total cultivated area

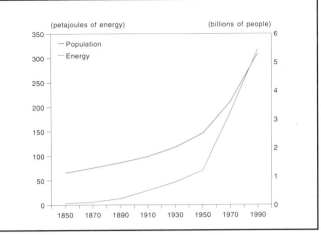

Figure 2.7 Growth of World Population and Commercial Energy Use, 1850–1990

Source: Adapted from figures compiled by John Holdren in "Population and the Energy Problem," *Population and Environment*, Vol. 12, No. 3 (Spring 1991), p. 245.

in the Philippines, a threefold increase in less than three decades (51).

Causes of the Upland Migration

Many factors contribute to the movement of people to upland areas. These include the following:

■ Downturns in economic growth. During the 1970s, the predominant flow of migrants was toward the cities. By far the most popular destination was Manila, which has absorbed more than one million people during the decade and more than half of all migrants who moved from one region to another. Migrants were pulled by Manila's employment opportunities and pushed by other factors, such as the government's aggressive program against illegal forest occupants in 1976 (52).

The pattern changed considerably during the 1980–85 period, when the Philippines went through an economic crisis provoked by a combination of domestic economic policy, excessive bank lending, and external shock. To obtain stabilization loans from the International Monetary Fund, the government imposed sharp measures to control inflation and government spending. The shock treatment hit the poor especially hard, driving unemployment up and real wages down. With employment opportunities in Manila sharply reduced, migration to upland areas increased significantly (53).

The collapse of the sugar industry in the western Visaya islands—a result of falling commodity prices—plus reduced incomes for rice and corn farmers in the Cagayan region also contributed to the massive migration to upland sites. By 1985, about 17.5 million people—roughly one third of the total population—were living in upland areas (54).

■ Limited access to land and inequitable land distribution. With the arable lowlands fully cultivated by the mid-1970s, growing numbers of people found their access to agricultural land limited. Moreover, this resource was inequitably distributed: in 1980, just 3.4 percent of farms occupied 26 percent of agricultural land, often the country's most productive. In many

Table 2.1 Interregional Migrants in the Philippines

Year	Net Migrants (thousands)[a]			
	1960–70[b]	1970–75	1975–80	1980–85
Lowland[c]				
Urban[d]	207	621	1,023	1,391
Rural	-547	-792	-1,850	-3,395
Total lowland	**-340**	**-171**	**-827**	**-2,004**
Upland[e]				
Urban	83	186	541	785
Rural	384	275	822	1,761
Total upland	**467**	**461**	**1,363**	**2,546**
Unclassified[f]				
(upland and lowland)	-127	-256	-536	-542

Source: Maria Concepcion Cruz, Carrie A. Meyer, Robert Repetto, *et al., Population Growth, Poverty, and Environmental Stress: Frontier Migration in the Philippines and Costa Rica* (World Resources Institute, Washington, D.C., 1992), p. 37.
Notes: a. Net of in- and out-migrants for the particular period. Migrants are defined as persons 10 years and older moving residence during a specified time period. b. Migration figures for this period are adapted from Peter C. Smith, "The Changing Character of Interregional Migration in the Philippines," *Philippine Geographical Journal*, Vol. 20, No. 4 (1977), pp. 146–162. c. Lowland is land with less than 18% slope or nonupland as classified by Department of Environment and Natural Resources (DENR). It excludes flatland in identified mountain zones. d. Census-defined classification of *urban* and *rural* is based on Philippine national population census (1960–80) and national Barangay Census (1985). e. Upland has 18% slope or higher, as officially classified by DENR. It includes municipalities with 75% or more of land area classified as upland. f. These are rural municipalities with less than 75% of land area classified as upland. Of the 542,000 out-migrants in 1980–85, 67% were short-distance movers (within province) leaving lowland rural areas for nearby upland sites.

cases, small farmers sold their holdings to larger land-owners; much of the land was then resold or leased to multinational corporate exporters of crops such as bananas, pineapples, and coconuts (55).

The combination of land concentration and population growth contributed to a large increase in landless workers. From 1975 to 1980, the percentage of landless farm workers in the agricultural labor force grew from 40 to 56 percent. Over 60 percent of landless workers were employed on sugar and coconut farms at less than subsistence wages. A close connection existed between landlessness and upland migration; between 1980 and 1983, more than 60 percent of all upland migrants were landless (56).

■ Widespread poverty. Poverty is a severe problem in the Philippines, but it is most serious in rural areas. In 1985, about 28 percent of the population had incomes below the subsistence level; about two thirds of those people lived in rural areas (57).

Population growth rates are particularly high among the rural poor; rural women average 7 births while urban women average 3.8 births. Family-planning services tend to favor urban residents; contraceptives are used by about 27 percent of rural women, about half the rate of their urban counterparts (58).

■ Resettlement programs. Government-sponsored resettlement schemes also brought about 200,000 families into upland areas in the 1960s and 1970s. But road building and other support programs attracted resettlement migrants, and eventually 1.3 million migrants occupied forestland that became accessible through the resettlement programs (59).

■ Timber policies. Government timber policies contributed to the upland migration. Timber licenses were awarded for a period of 25 years, well short of the time needed for forests to regenerate, so timber operators were given an incentive to log the forests and then leave. Migrants also provided a source of cheap labor for logging operations.

The result was a network of roads and logged land that was much easier for migrants to clear for cultivation. By 1985, more than 62 percent of the total upland population resided in timber concession areas (60).

Environmental Impact

The upland migration has exacted a heavy environmental toll in the Philippines. Cultivated upland areas increased from 582,000 hectares in 1960 to over 3.9 million hectares in 1987. (See Table 2.2.) Soil erosion was estimated at about 122 to 210 tons per hectare annually for newly established pasture, compared with less than 2 tons per hectare for land under forest cover. Forest cover declined from 50 percent of the national territory in 1970 to less than 21 percent in 1987 (61).

Many upland sites reached a population density of 300 persons per square kilometer in the 1980s; these areas typically suffered a high rate of deforestation and soil loss. Greater density tended to increase cropping frequency, eventually leading to soil erosion and declining yields, and to shorten the fallow period when land was taken out of production. Many indigenous shifting cultivators were forced to move to higher and steeper slopes and to shorten fallow periods, which exacerbated soil erosion in the uplands (62).

Other factors continue to play a role in the loss of forest cover in the Philippine uplands. Demand for fuelwood is large and growing. Total consumption of fuelwood in 1985 was estimated at 28.5 million cubic meters, about the same as the volume of wood lost to deforestation and nearly eight times more than commercially harvested wood. Population growth is expected to increase demand in the 1990s, perhaps to 55 million cubic meters annually—about 6 percent of the nation's entire volume of timber—by the year 2000 (63).

Commercial logging, 10 million cubic meters annually in the 1970s, has fallen to less than half that level because many remaining stands are immature, degraded, or commercially insignificant. Logging is often the beginning of deforestation, as it enables small farmers to convert degraded forest to farmland (64) (65).

Thus in the Philippines, a dense and rapidly growing population, fully developed arable lowlands, inequitable distribution of landholdings, an economic downturn that reduced urban opportunities and increased unemployment, and government forestry policy all contributed to large-scale migration to the uplands, wide loss of forest cover, and soil erosion.

Costa Rica

Costa Rica's population is growing rapidly, about 2.6 percent per year. In 1990, over one third of Costa Ricans were under 15 years of age, so that population growth will continue to have considerable momentum for several more decades. The current population, estimated at 3 million in 1990, may double to 6 million before stabilizing in the middle of the next century.

Table 2.2 Lowland and Upland Cropped Area in the Philippines

Land Type	Area (thousand hectares)				Annual Rate of Change (%)		
	1960	1971	1980	1987	1960–71	1971–80	1980–87
Lowland cropped	5,581	6,424	7,760	8,845	1.3	2.1	1.9
Upland cropped	582	1,283	2,349	3,927	7.5	7.0	7.6
Total	**6,163**	**7,707**	**10,109**	**12,772**	**2.1**	**3.1**	**3.4**

Source: Maria Concepcion Cruz, Carrie A. Meyer, Robert Repetto, *et al.*, *Population Growth, Poverty, and Environmental Stress: Frontier Migration in the Philippines and Costa Rica* (World Resources Institute, Washington, D.C., 1992), p. 23.

Over half of Costa Rica's population occupies just 6 percent of its land area, the San José metropolitan area and its periphery in the fertile Central Valley. Whereas 72 percent of the land in the metropolitan area was devoted to agriculture in the early 1970s, by the mid-1980s only 46 percent was crop- or pastureland. In the outlying districts, the percentage of land devoted to farming and grazing also dropped slightly over this period, from 61 percent to 57 percent. The pressure to convert land for agriculture in rural areas seems considerable, yet less than 20 percent of Costa Rica's land is considered suitable for annual or perennial crops (66).

Like many other developing countries, Costa Rica experienced a severe economic recession as a result of the 1979 oil price shocks, the 1980 increase in world interest rates, and the lending cutbacks that precipitated a debt crisis in the early 1980s. In 1981 and 1982, real wages, after rising steadily since the mid-1970s, dropped by 30 percent. Unemployment, under 5 percent in 1980, more than doubled and was particularly severe in urban areas. The number of people below the poverty line rose from 600,000 to 900,000, with most of the increase occurring in cities. In 1981, inflation reached triple digits, Costa Rica's currency was devalued over 400 percent, and the government stopped paying interest on its external debt (67).

The recession was short-lived. To renew financial relations with multilateral agencies, the government imposed a shock treatment that included cuts in public services and a 28 percent reduction in the size of the government. The measures reduced inflation to an annual rate of 10 to 15 percent and revived exports (68).

Although brief, the recession nevertheless was so severe that it changed migration patterns within Costa Rica and put new pressures on fragile land.

During the 1970s, several factors—greater opportunity in urban areas, a depressed agricultural sector, and the exhaustion of poor soil—created a strong flow of migrants toward urban areas, primarily the capital city of San José (69). (See Table 2.3.) The industrial sector employed twice as much labor in 1975 as in 1964 (70). Meanwhile, lack of opportunity in rural areas helped push people towards San José. Though cattle ranching expanded rapidly during the 1970s, it required relatively little labor. Rural out-migration was particularly strong in the cattle-producing regions of the country and in districts with poor soil (71).

In 1981–82, with the San José economy badly weakened, migrants moved out of the city. In rural districts with good land, population increased 51 percent from 1973 to 1984. (See Table 2.4.) But pressure also increased on marginal land: over this same period, population grew nearly 27 percent on land classified as poor and 16 percent on land classified as very poor (72).

In addition to population pressure and the economic downturn, agriculture and land management policies played an important role in the clearing and use of marginal land. For example, at the time Costa Rican law gave ownership rights to anyone who cleared and held land for one year. Squatters had to wait 10 years to claim legal title to the land, but they could sell the "improvements" made in the first year to cattle ranchers or speculators, who then qualified for title immediately. The law encouraged the poor and landless to clear marginal public and private land, sell it, and then move on to repeat the process.

Landless migrants could also apply to the Agrarian Development Institute (IDA) to obtain unused private land under the 1961 land reform law. Most IDA land was poor and in remote areas, and migrants who obtained it often sold it illegally (73).

The environmental damage of these combined pressures has been considerable. A 1982 study estimated that squatters and IDA settlers were responsible for as much as one half of illegal deforestation (74). From 1970 to 1989, an estimated 2.2 billion metric tons of soil eroded in Costa Rica, about one third on pastureland.

Most of the deforestation in Costa Rica was caused by the demand for pastureland rather than for timber. The demand for pastureland, in turn, can be largely attributed to government policies to promote the beef export industry. For example, the government provided subsidized credit to ranchers and allowed high delinquency rates, which encouraged ranching that would not otherwise have been profitable (75).

By 1984, over half of Costa Rica's agricultural land—1.6 million hectares—was in pasture, yet land use studies indicated that about two thirds of that land was not suited for pasture and should have remained forest.

In the Costa Rican case, population pressure in the fertile Central Valley, a severe economic downturn, and agriculture and land management policies led to the clearing and use of marginal land and subsequent widespread deforestation and soil erosion.

COASTAL DEVELOPMENT

Coastal populations are swelling around the world, putting pressure on oceans, wetlands, and coastal biodiversity. Coastal urban populations are expected to increase globally, with the most dramatic increases expected in Asia, Africa, and South America. (See Chapter 22, "Water," Table 22.6.)

2 Population and the Environment

Table 2.3 Net Migrants and Net Migration Rates in Costa Rica by Land Use Classification

	1968–73		1978–84	
Regions	Net Migrants	Migration Rate[a] (%)	Net Migrants	Migration Rate (%)
Metropolitan areas	32,876	6.9	-1,942	-0.3
San José periphery	10,328	3.1	14,011	3.0
Rural dense areas	-2,797	-6.0	-1,298	-2.5
Rural nondense land quality:				
Good	5,654	4.5	6,859	3.6
Poor	-12,405	-4.6	-4,367	-1.3
Very poor	-33,658	-9.3	-13,263[b]	-3.1

Source: Maria Concepcion Cruz, Carrie A. Meyer, Robert Repetto, et al., *Population Growth, Poverty, and Environmental Stress: Frontier Migration in the Philippines and Costa Rica* (World Resources Institute, Washington, D.C., 1992), p. 62.
Note: Rural dense areas include five districts with population density greater than 28 persons per square kilometer.

Table 2.4 Population 5 Years or Older in Costa Rica by Land Use Capacity

Regions	1973	1984	Population Increase 1973–84 (%)
Metropolitan areas	476,953	623,422	30.7
San José periphery	334,926	469,293	40.1
Rural dense areas	46,548	52,316	12.4
Rural nondense land quality:			
Good	125,041	188,815	51.0
Poor	267,052	338,700	26.8
Very poor	362,321	421,441	16.3
Total	**1,612,841**	**2,093,987**	**29.8**

Source: Maria Concepcion Cruz, Carrie A. Meyer, Robert Repetto, *et al.*, *Population Growth, Poverty, and Environmental Stress: Frontier Migration in the Philippines and Costa Rica* (World Resources Institute, Washington, D.C., 1992), p. 65.

Even in areas such as the United States where population growth is relatively slow, there is considerable migration toward coasts. As the U.S. population gets older and the number of retired people rises, the movement toward coastal regions on the Gulf of Mexico and the Pacific is likely to accelerate.

Between 1960 and 1990, population in the 772 coastal counties of the United States expanded by almost 41 million (43 percent), slightly more than did the U.S. population as a whole. Growth was fastest in the coastal areas of the Pacific and the Gulf, nearly doubling over this period. By 1991, about 34 million people lived along the Pacific coast and about 16 million lived in counties bordering the Gulf (76).

Helped along by a growing tourist industry, the economic boom in coastal areas was greater than population movements suggested. Between 1970 and 1989, almost half of all U.S. building construction occurred in coastal regions, even though they represent only 11 percent of the nation's total land area. Florida and California outpaced other coastal states in all types of construction, including residential. (See Figure 2.8.)

Rapid coastal development in the states bordering the Gulf of Mexico took a heavy toll on coastal wetlands, which are an important habitat for wildlife and marine species. From the 1950s through the 1980s, roughly 8,000 hectares of this land was lost annually in the contiguous United States, with the heaviest losses in Louisiana, Florida, and Texas. By the early 1980s, new state and federal wetland protection laws had largely stemmed the losses, but population growth will continue to put pressure on coastal habitat (77).

The environmental impact of rapidly increasing population was partially checked by massive federal spending. Since the enactment of the 1972 Clean Water Act, more than $75 billion has been invested in municipal wastewater treatment. As a result, concentrations of lead, DDT, and polychlorinated biphenals in coastal fish, shellfish, and sediments are decreasing. Eutrophication (nutrient enrichment) has declined as a result of improved treatment processes and phosphate detergent bans.

But many problems remain, especially in urban bays and estuaries. A 1990 federal report found that all coastal states except Hawaii reported at least some impairment of designated uses of estuaries. About 37 percent of commercial shellfish beds in estuaries are closed or subject to harvest restrictions, often because of pollution from sewage treatment plants, septic systems, and urban runoff (78).

Population growth will continue to threaten fragile coastal areas. Between 1988 and 2010, the population of almost one third of the coastal counties in the southeastern United States is projected to increase by 35 to 75 percent. The trend will be most pronounced in eastern Florida, where the coastal population per shoreline mile is expected to go up nearly 30 percent. Much of this growth will take place in retirement-oriented communities. Florida's projected population of 19 million in 2010 is more than triple the 1960 figure (79).

Changing Policy Environment

The development of U.S. coastal areas was relatively uncontrolled. Many communities sprawled across landscapes. Coastal wetlands were filled for housing developments, their waters directed into channels.

Many local governments favored development and overlooked master land-use plans in making decisions on zoning, building permits, and public works projects. In Florida's metropolitan Dade County, which includes Miami, county commissioners developed a master plan requiring every new residential development to be part of a well-planned community with a complete system of sewers. As early as 1961, there was a sewer plan for the entire county, but it was not followed until the mid- to late 1960s. The county continued to allow septic tanks and the kind of urban sprawl that the master plan regarded as undesirable (80).

On many environmental issues in Dade County, however, private conservation groups had political clout. In the early 1960s, for example, a small conservation group called the Safe Progress Association was instrumental in defeating a proposal for a port and oil refinery in Biscayne Bay. The group maintained that Biscayne Bay was a poorly flushed salt lagoon, easily harmed by industrial pollution, that pollution was likely if the port and refinery were built, and that a clean environment was important for the growth of the county's retirement community and tourism (81).

A decade later, Dade County still had no clear land use policy for the south Biscayne Bay region, especially with respect to bay front development or maximum population density. The issue came to a head in the early 1970s over a proposal to build a new town with as many as 250,000 people along 3 kilometers of bay front property. Local conservationists protested the proposal. The plan, ultimately approved by the county, limited population to 51,000 and excluded all development along the bay except for a marina. By the mid-1970s, there was much stronger public support for controlling growth and keeping development from exceeding the carrying capacity of natural systems (82).

The massive growth of the 1970s and 1980s finally led the state to adopt a comprehensive growth management system in 1984–86. It required development to proceed on a "pay as you grow" basis, which meant building infrastructure to support new development. The state government also attempted to combat urban sprawl, developing policies that promoted redevelopment and the use of existing urban infrastructure (83).

The management system also contained provisions to end coastal development in unsuitable areas, including a ban on urban development along coasts likely to be under water within 30 years. The state has attempted to limit development in high hazard coastal areas and barrier islands and has led in acquiring environmentally sensitive lands. In 1990, the state legislature committed $300 million annually for 10 years for land acquisition (84).

Barrier Islands

Barrier islands, the long, narrow spits of beach that lie along much of the east coast, are attractive sites for retirees and vacation-home owners looking for waterfront property. By 1980, half of the 280 coastal barriers along the Atlantic and Gulf coasts were at least partially developed, 70 heavily so (85).

Over the past few decades, however, both scientific researchers and political activists have drawn attention to the fact that shores are fragile, in many cases changing land forms that cannot be easily controlled. They are constantly exposed to wind, waves, and tides, and periodically to severe flooding and damage from hurricanes and other storms. Furthermore, engineering controls are often counterproductive or have unintended consequences.

Ignoring these hazards, developers began in the 1950s to build new homes on barrier islands, with the help of billions of dollars in taxpayer subsidies for the construction of bridges, causeways, and sewage treatment plants. When developments were destroyed by natural disasters, they have often been rebuilt with the help of federally subsidized flood insurance.

This pattern of development and redevelopment was expensive; between 1978 and 1987, for example, about $1 billion was paid to rebuild areas that had been previously rebuilt (86).

By 1982, the U.S. Congress agreed to cut off federal subsidies on undeveloped barrier islands. The new law, which applied to 186 undeveloped barrier areas, barred federal spending for flood insurance, U.S.

Figure 2.8 Ten U.S. States Leading in Coastal Residential Construction, 1970–89

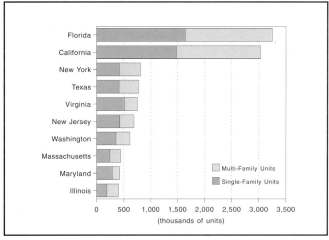

Source: Thomas J. Culliton, John J. McDonough, Davida A. Remer, *et al.*, *Building Along America's Coasts: 20 Years of Building Permits, 1970–89* (U.S. National Oceanic and Atmospheric Administration, Rockville, Maryland, 1992), pp. 11, 17, 22, and 27–49.

Army Corps of Engineers development projects, housing loans, and assistance for the construction of sewer systems, highways, water supply systems, airports, bridges, and jetties. The law does not bar private development, but the withdrawal of federal subsidies makes private development much more difficult. A study of 157 units in the system found that between 1982 and 1989, major development had occurred on only 10 of the units (87).

The Chesapeake Bay

The Chesapeake Bay lies in the heavily populated mid-Atlantic region of the United States. The region is home to several large cities, including Baltimore, Maryland; Washington, D.C.; and Richmond, Virginia. The District of Columbia and the states of Maryland, Virginia, and Pennsylvania have most of the land and water affecting the bay. The bay itself is about 300 kilometers long and from 6 to 50 kilometers wide. Its watershed is about 20 times larger, stretching north into Pennsylvania and New York and west into Virginia and West Virginia. The Chesapeake Bay watershed includes nearly 50 rivers (88).

The bay is shallow, with an average depth of less than 7 meters (89). As a result, winds can affect normal water volume by as much as 10 to 20 percent. Tides send a charge of water up the length of the bay twice a day. The upper reaches are freshwater and the mouth is saltwater. Salinity in the middle of the bay varies considerably, increasing during droughts and declining in wet periods. Wet years can virtually double the amount of nutrients washed off the land (90) (91) (92).

The Chesapeake Bay is an extremely productive ecosystem. Its waters support a major commercial fishery, producing about 45 million kilograms of seafood annually during the 1980s, more than half the nation's blue crab catch, and 90 percent of its soft crabs. The shallow water allows sunlight to penetrate and produce vast meadows of grass, which provide food for wildlife and habitat for fish and shellfish. The bay also has about 200,000 hectares of tidal marshland, another important wildlife and fish habitat and food source (93).

Industry, agriculture, infrastructure, and residential development all contribute pollutants to the bay. Population-related sources of pollution include:

■ Sediment. A hectare of land cleared for construction can flush 100 times more sediment into the bay than well-managed farmland (94). Sediment clouds the water, reducing the amount of sunlight that reaches submerged grass, and covers gravel bottoms that are important habitats for spawning fish (95).

■ Lawns and golf courses. The proportion of the watershed in turf, such as home lawns and golf courses, is increasing rapidly and fertilizers and pesticides are applied liberally (96). More than 10 percent of Maryland's land surface is covered with turf.

■ Stormwater runoff. Rain in urban and residential areas flushes into the watershed large amounts of nitrogen, phosphorus, and organic matter from leaves, grass clippings, and garbage (97).

■ Septic tanks. Most of the watershed's residents are connected to sewage treatment plants, but a significant number use septic tanks—about 250,000 households in Maryland, more than 1 million in Pennsylvania, and about 660,000 in Virginia. Septic tanks can introduce bacteria to soil and waterways and discharge nitrogen into groundwater. The use of tanks encourages sprawl on large lots that use open space inefficiently (98).

■ Sewage sludge. Conventional sewage treatment produces vast amounts of sludge, which is often reused as fertilizer and can add nitrogen and phosphorus runoff to the watershed (99).

■ Recreational boating. Boating, an ever more popular sport on the bay, is not a major polluter, but it does contribute oil and toxic metals to the water (100).

■ Airborne pollution. Emissions from individual automobiles are down, but this gain has been offset by increases in the number of cars and vehicle kilometers traveled. Between 1952 and 1986, population rose 50 percent, while vehicular pollutants rose by more than 250 percent. Total vehicle kilometers traveled increased by 31 percent in Maryland and 40 percent in Virginia in the last decade (101).

Though some river systems in the watershed have become less polluted, the bay itself is still affected by both sewage and land runoff. Agricultural pollution appears to have peaked, but population growth continues to put pressure on the bay environment.

Over the past several decades, Maryland, Virginia, and Pennsylvania have enacted laws to reduce pollution in the bay watershed. For example, all three have established sediment control programs. Studies, however, indicate that many construction sites do not fully comply with the regulations (102).

In the late 1980s, all three bay states and Washington, D.C., banned the use of phosphate in laundry detergent. This change almost immediately reduced phosphorus discharges into the bay by 30 to 50 percent (103). It also substantially improved water quality in the Potomac and Patuxent rivers, two of the bay's largest tributaries. Reducing nitrogen pollution is more diffi-

cult. Maryland recently began an ambitious effort to remove nitrogen from the Patuxent River.

All three states have committed to a 40 percent reduction in phosphorus and nitrogen discharges by the year 2000. The phosphorus target may be reached before then, but achieving the 40 percent target for nitrogen may require some expensive technical changes in sewage treatment plants (104).

In the mid-1980s, Maryland enacted the Chesapeake Bay Critical Area Protection Law, which limits development in areas within 1,000 feet of tidal waters or 1,000 feet from the landward side of tidal wetlands. To reduce shoreline development, the law requires that any new water-dependent land use be practiced in existing developments (105). But the region continues to be characterized by sprawling development that consumes more open space per person, requires more infrastructure, and increases both the distances traveled by vehicles and the pollution they produce. The pattern could be altered to favor dense, clustered development, but as yet there is little political support for such change. In short, the environmental impact of demographic pressure in the region is exacerbated by land use policies and infrastructure development.

CONCLUSION

The effect of population on the environment is a fundamental issue in both the industrialized and the developing world.

In industrialized countries, the population-environment connection is magnified by affluence and high per capita consumption. In developing countries, the impact per person may be less significant than the impact of rapid growth and large-scale migration.

The population-environment connection is particularly significant in cases of uncontrolled migration into environmentally sensitive areas. Governments often encourage such movement through policies that are not conventionally thought of as demographic. Subsidies by the U.S. Government, for instance, played a large role in the rapid development of coastal barrier islands, even though those are poor candidates for human occupation. In the Philippines, government subsidies for timber development hastened migration into forest areas.

Similarly, infrastructure development can promote population movement. In the United States, road building is a critical part of the sprawling development and reliance on automobiles that has characterized growth for many decades. In developing countries, facing widespread poverty and landlessness, road building in previously inaccessible areas will stimulate large-scale spontaneous migration into surrounding forestland and a conversion of that land to agriculture. Human proximity to roads tends to increase deforestation (106).

Effective land-use controls could reduce the environmental impact of new arrivals, but in many cases controls are not in place. In the Chesapeake Bay region, growth during the next few decades will result in land being used at three times the 1950 rate (107). In many developing countries, newcomers are without secure title to the land and thus have little incentive to treat it with care. Farmers with secure titles tend to convert less land to agriculture and invest in long-term conservation measures (108).

Governments in the developing world have few easy solutions for dealing with rapid population growth, migration, and resource degradation. And the situation is not likely to improve. In the 1990s, about 42 million people will enter the global labor force each year, about 39 million of them in developing countries that are already heavily burdened by unemployment and underemployment (109).

Job creation is essential, especially in rural agricultural areas with high poverty, unemployment, and landlessness. Poverty, by reducing incentives for long-term resource management, can further the degradation of forestland and soil. Environmental degradation, in turn, lessens the labor productivity of the poor and the productivity of the natural resources they manage (110).

In some circumstances, poverty imposes short time horizons, as the discussion of squatter laws in Costa Rica suggests. To meet present income needs, poor farmers tend to favor rapid resource extraction and short-term production strategies such as overgrazing pastureland (111). Poverty also hinders the transition to slower population growth. (See Chapter 3, "Women and Sustainable Development.")

All of these factors interact in complex ways that vary from country to country and community to community. Population policies cannot be confined to family planning because they are affected by other factors. Tenurial policy is both environmental and population policy when it encourages uncontrolled land use in frontier areas. Economic policy that depresses wages also has significant demographic consequences. An ineffective family planning program becomes, in effect, resource policy because it has massive long-term environmental ramifications (112).

The best argument for family planning and environmental protection is that both are critical to sustainable development. While population pressure certainly contributes to environmental degradation, many other factors may worsen the impact. Government policymakers should look for ways to reduce population growth and devise policies that minimize the environmental effect of current population growth.

This chapter was written primarily by Robert Livernash, World Resources staff member. The section on demography was adapted from a paper by Carl Haub, director of information and education at the Population Reference Bureau (PRB) in Washington, D.C., and Barbara Boyle Torrey, former president of PRB now at the National Research Council in Washington, D.C. The case studies on the Philippines and Costa Rica were adapted from a 1992 WRI study entitled Population Growth, Poverty, and Environmental Stress: Frontier Migration in the Philippines and Costa Rica, *by Maria Concepcion Cruz, Carrie A. Meyer, Robert Repetto, and Richard Woodward.*

References and Notes

1. United Nations (U.N.) Population Division, *World Population Prospects: The 1992 Revision* (U.N., New York, 1993), p. 153.
2. United Nations (U.N.), *Long-Range World Population Projections: Two Centuries of Population Growth, 1950–2150* (U.N., New York, 1992), p. 14.
3. *Op. cit.* 1, p. 284.
4. Carl Haub, Demographer, Population Reference Bureau, Washington, D.C., 1993 (personal communication).
5. *Op. cit.* 1, pp. 228–229.
6. *Op. cit.* 1, pp. 228–229.
7. *Op. cit.* 1, pp. 160–167, 192–197, and 204–209.
8. Population Reference Bureau (PRB), *1993 World Population Data Sheet* (PRB, Washington, D.C., 1993).
9. *Op. cit.* 1, pp. 152–153.
10. *Op. cit.* 8.
11. *Op. cit.* 2, pp. 6–8.
12. *Op. cit.* 1, pp. 216–221.
13. *Op. cit.* 1, pp. 218–219.
14. *Op. cit.* 1, pp. 218–219.
15. *Op. cit.* 1, pp. 216–217, 296, and 348.
16. *Op. cit.* 1, pp. 220–221.
17. *Op. cit.* 2, p. 8.
18. Sharon S. Russell and Michael S. Teitelbaum, *International Migration and International Trade* (The World Bank, Washington, D.C., 1992), p. 11.
19. Franz-Josef Kemper, "New Trends in Mass Migration in Germany," in *Mass Migrations in Europe: The Legacy and the Future*, Russell King, ed. (Belhaven, London, 1993), p. 257.
20. U.S. Immigration and Naturalization Service (INS), *Statistical Yearbook of the Immigration and Naturalization Service* (INS, Washington, D.C., forthcoming).
21. *Op. cit.* 18, pp. 18–21.
22. *Op. cit.* 18, pp. 24–27.
23. *Op. cit.* 18, pp. 15–17 and 26–27.
24. United Nations (U.N.) Population Division, *Urban and Rural Areas, 1950–2025 (The 1992 Revision)*, on diskette (U.N., New York, 1993).
25. *Op. cit.* 4.
26. United Nations (U.N.) Population Division, *World Urbanization Prospects, 1950–2010 (The 1992 Revision)*, on diskette (U.N., New York, 1993).
27. United Nations Educational, Scientific and Cultural Organization (UNESCO), *Statistical Yearbook, 1992* (UNESCO, Paris, 1992), pp. 2-22–2-23.
28. Susan H. Cochrane, "The Effects of Education, Health, and Social Security on Fertility in Developing Countries," World Bank Working Paper No. S93, The World Bank, Washington, D.C., 1988, pp. 2–4.
29. Naomi Rutenberg, Mohamed Ayad, Luis Hernando Ochoa, *et al.*, "Knowledge and Use of Contraception," Demographic and Health Surveys, Comparative Studies No. 6, Institute for Resource Development/Macro International, Columbia, Maryland, 1991, pp. 11–12.
30. Peter H. Raven, "Biological Resources and Global Stability," in *Evolution and Coadaptation in Biotic Communities*, S. Kawano, J.H. Connell, and T. Hidaka, eds. (University of Tokyo Press, Tokyo, 1988), p. 16.
31. Thomas E. Dahl, *Wetlands Losses in the United States: 1780's to 1980's* (U.S. Department of Interior, Washington, D.C., 1990), pp. 6 and 9.
32. John F. Richards, "Land Transformation," in *The Earth as Transformed by Human Action*, B.L. Turner, William C. Clark, Robert W. Kates, *et al.*, eds. (Cambridge University Press, Cambridge, 1990), pp. 163–164.
33. *Ibid.*
34. Michael Williams, "Forests," in *The Earth As Transformed by Human Action*, B.L. Turner, William C. Clark, Robert W. Kates, *et al.*, eds. (Cambridge University Press, Cambridge, 1990), pp. 188 and 191–192.
35. *Ibid.*, p. 194.
36. Boris G. Rozanov, Viktor Targulian, and D.S. Orlov, "Soils," in *The Earth as Transformed by Human Action*, B.L. Turner, William C. Clark, Robert W. Kates, *et al.*, eds. (Cambridge University Press, Cambridge, 1990), p. 213.
37. Harry E. Schwarz, Jacque Emel, William J. Dickens, *et al.*, "Water Quality and Flows," in *The Earth as Transformed by Human Action*, B.L. Turner, William C. Clark, Robert W. Kates, *et al.*, eds. (Cambridge University Press, Cambridge, 1990), p. 254.
38. Joel A. Tarr and Robert U. Ayres, "The Hudson-Raritan Basin," in *The Earth as Transformed by Human Action*, B.L. Turner, William C. Clark, Robert W. Kates, *et al.*, eds. (Cambridge University Press, Cambridge, 1990), p. 631.
39. *Ibid.*, pp. 630–631.

40. Barbara Vobejda, "Child Deaths from Disease on Decline Worldwide," *Washington Post* (December 21, 1993), p. A1.

41. Alan D. Lopez, "Causes of Death: An Assessment of Global Patterns of Mortality around 1985," *World Health Statistics Quarterly*, Vol. 43, No. 2 (1990), p. 98.

42. John P. Holdren, "Population and the Energy Problem," *Population and Environment*, Vol. 12, No. 3 (1991), pp. 244–245.

43. Carbon Dioxide Information Analysis Center (CDIAC), Oak Ridge National Laboratory, *Trends '91: A Compendium of Data on Global Change* (CDIAC, Oak Ridge, Tennessee, 1991), pp. 1–15 and 389.

44. Susan Subak and William C. Clark, "Accounts for Greenhouse Gases: Towards the Design of Fair Assessments," in *Usable Knowledge for Managing Climate Change*, William C. Clark, ed. (Stockholm Environmental Institute, Stockholm, 1990), p. 73.

45. *Op. cit.* 43, pp. 389, 401, 429, and 433.

46. *Op. cit.* 44.

47. United Nations Economic and Social Council, "Recommendations of the Expert Group Meeting on Population, Environment, and Development: Report of the Secretary-General of the Conference," report prepared for the International Conference on Environment and Development, New York, August, 1993.

48. *Ibid.*

49. *Ibid.*

50. Maria Concepcion Cruz, Carrie A. Meyer, Robert Repetto, *et al.*, *Population Growth, Poverty, and Environmental Stress: Frontier Migration in the Philippines and Costa Rica* (World Resources Institute, Washington, D.C., 1992), pp. 15–16.

51. *Ibid.*, pp. 18–21 and 23.

52. *Ibid.*, p. 39.

53. *Ibid.*, pp. 29–33 and 39–42.

54. *Ibid.*, pp. 18 and 42.

55. *Ibid.*, pp. 22 and 25–27.

56. *Ibid.*, p. 27.

57. *Ibid.*, p. 26.

58. *Ibid.*, pp. 15–18 and 25.

59. *Ibid.*, p. 28.

60. *Ibid.*, pp. 28–29.

61. *Ibid.*, pp. 23–25.

62. *Ibid.*, pp. 21–22.

63. *Ibid.*, p. 24.

64. Wilfrido D. Cruz and Robert Repetto, *The Environmental Effects of Stabilization and Structural Adjustment Programs: The Philippines Case* (World Resources Institute, Washington, D.C., 1992), pp. 20–21.

65. *Op. cit.* 50, pp. 24–25.

66. *Op. cit.* 50, pp. 45–47.

67. *Op. cit.* 50, pp. 3, 6, and 56–58.

68. *Op. cit.* 50, p. 57.

69. *Op. cit.* 50, pp. 60–61.

70. Carlos Araya Pochet, "Crisis e Historia Económica y Social en Costa Rica, 1970–1982," in *Costa Rica Hoy: La Crisis y Sus Perspectivas*, J. Rovira Mas, ed. (Editorial Universidad Estatal a Distancia, San José, Costa Rica, 1983), p. 23.

71. *Op. cit.* 50, p. 61.

72. *Op. cit.* 50, pp. 64–65.

73. *Op. cit.* 50, pp. 52–54.

74. Gary Hartshorn, Lynne Hartshorn, Agustín Atmella, *et al.*, *Costa Rica: Country Environmental Profile* (Tropical Science Center, San José, Costa Rica, 1982), p. 30.

75. *Op. cit.* 50, p. 49.

76. "Coastal Living: For Majority of U.S., It's Home," *Population Today*, Vol. 21, No. 7/8 (July/August 1993), p. 4.

77. Walter V. Reid and Mark C. Trexler, *Drowning the National Heritage: Climate Change and U.S. Coastal Biodiversity* (World Resources Institute, Washington, D.C., 1991), p. 8.

78. Committee on Wastewater Management for Coastal Urban Areas, National Research Council, *Managing Wastewater in Coastal Urban Areas* (National Academy of Sciences, Washington, D.C., 1993), pp. 32–33.

79. Thomas J. Culliton, Maureen A. Warren, Timothy R. Goodspeed, *et al.*, "50 Years of Population Change along the Nation's Coasts," report prepared by the U.S. Department of Commerce, National Oceanic and Atmospheric Administration, Rockville, Maryland, 1990, pp. 15–19.

80. Luther J. Carter, *The Florida Experience: Land and Water Policy in a Growth State* (Resources for the Future, Washington, D.C., 1974), p. 156.

81. *Ibid.*, pp. 158–159.

82. *Ibid.*, pp. 167, 171, and 183.

83. John M. DeGrove, *Planning and Growth Management in the States* (Lincoln Institute for Land Policy, Cambridge, Massachusetts, 1992), pp. 13–18.

84. *Ibid.*, pp. 14, 22, and 25.

85. Michael Weber, *Using Common Sense to Protect the Coasts: The Need to Expand the Coastal Barrier Resources System* (Coast Alliance, Washington, D.C., 1990), p. 5.

86. *Ibid.*, p. 11.

87. *Ibid.*, pp. 14–15.

88. Christopher P. White, *Chesapeake Bay, Nature of the Estuary: A Field Guide* (Tidewater, Centreville, Maryland, 1989), p. 5.

89. Tom Horton and William M. Eichbaum, *Turning the Tide: Saving the Chesapeake Bay* (Island Press, Washington, D.C., 1991), pp. 3–5.

90. *Ibid.*, pp. 5 and 11–17.

91. *Op. cit.* 88, pp. 13–18.

92. Robert E. Magnien, Robert M. Summers, and Kevin G. Sellner, "External Nutrient Sources, Internal Nutrient Pools, and Phytoplankton Production in Chesapeake Bay," *Estuaries*, Vol. 15, No. 4 (1992), pp. 502–503.

93. *Op. cit.* 89, pp. 21 and 23.

94. M. Gordon Wolman and Asher P. Schick, "Effects of Construction on Fluvial Sediment, Urban and Suburban Areas of Maryland," *Water Resources Research*, Vol. 3, No. 2 (1967), pp. 453–455.

95. *Op. cit.* 89, pp. 58–59.

96. *Op. cit.* 89, p. 61.

97. *Op. cit.* 89, p. 62.

98. *Op. cit.* 89, p. 73.

99. *Op. cit.* 89, pp. 71–72.

100. *Op. cit.* 89, pp. 97–99.

101. *Op. cit.* 89, pp. 92 and 190.

102. *Op. cit.* 89, pp. 60–61 and 74–75.

103. *Op. cit.* 89, p. 191.

104. Chesapeake Bay Program, *Progress at the Chesapeake Bay Program, '92 and '93* (U.S. Environmental Protection Agency, Annapolis, Maryland, 1993), pp. 7–9.

105. Gerald Winegrad, "The Critical Areas Legislation: A Necessary Step to Restore the Chesapeake Bay," University of Baltimore School of Law, *Law Forum*, Vol. 17, No. 1 (1986), pp. 3–5.

106. Francisco J. Pichon and Richard E. Bilsborrow, "Land-Use Systems, Deforestation and Associated Demographic Factors in the Humid Tropics: Farm-Level Evidence from Ecuador," paper prepared for the International Union for the Scientific Study of Population Seminar on Population and Deforestation in the Humid Tropics, Campinas, Brazil, November–December, 1992.

107. *Op. cit.* 89, p. 218.

108. *Op. cit.* 106.

109. International Labor Organization (ILO), unpublished data (ILO, Geneva, August 1993).

110. Stephen D. Mink, "Poverty, Population, and the Environment," World Bank Discussion Paper No. 189, The World Bank, Washington, D.C., 1993, pp. 8–10.

111. *Ibid.*, pp. 10–13.

112. *Op. cit.* 50, p. 12.

3. Women and Sustainable Development

As the 20th Century draws to a close, the role of women is under increasing scrutiny. Half the world's population is made up of women, yet for the most part they still do not have equal access to land, credit, technology, education, employment, and political power. The implications of this situation are more than that of simple inequity. In every society, women play critical roles; in rural areas, for example, they perform the bulk of household subsistence work and carry major household responsiblities for farming, food provision, health care, and the acquisition and stewardship of natural resources. Evidence indicates that in many societies, women have greater influence than men on rates of population growth and infant and child mortality, on health and nutrition, on children's education, and on natural resource management.

In short, women have a profound and pervasive effect on the well-being of their families, communities, and local ecosystems. Therefore, inequities that are detrimental to them—be it to their physical and mental health, income-earning ability, education, and/or decision-making power, to name just a few—are detrimental as well to society at large and to the environment.

Although definitions vary, in general the concept of sustainable development is based on the recognition that a nation cannot reach its economic goals without also achieving social and environmental goals—that is, universal education and employment opportunity, universal health and reproductive care, equitable access to and distribution of resources, stable populations, and a sustained natural resource base. While often difficult to quantify because of the lack of or local nature of data, there is also increasing recognition that, if women do indeed have a significant—and in some cases disproportionate—influence on many cross-cutting components of sustainable development, then the achievement of sustainable development is inextricably bound up with the establishment of women's equality; one cannot be accomplished without the other.

This chapter begins with a review of the international women's movement in the context of development. It then focuses primarily on rural women in Southern countries, discussing the valuable work they perform, the barriers they face, and why, for reasons of both equity and sustainable development, they must be given the opportunity to become full and equal par-

Box 3.1 New Perspectives on Women and Development

In recent years, theorists and practitioners have moved from the view of women in development (WID) that prevailed in the 1970s and 1980s to the more current concept of gender and development (GAD). The WID approach sees women essentially in isolation and seeks to integrate them into development efforts through such measures as increasing their access to credit, land, and employment. WID, as adopted by the international agencies, is based on an acceptance of existing social structures and traditional development objectives. WID believes that these objectives, especially those geared toward growth and productivity, would be better met if women were brought fully into the process (1) (2).

GAD believes that affirmative action strategies aimed at integrating women into ongoing development projects are not enough. Rather than focusing on women in isolation, GAD argues, it is important to understand the culturally variable social relationships between men and women (3). GAD is less concerned with women per se than with the assignment of specific roles, responsibilities, and expectations to women and men (4). GAD emphasizes that gender roles within households are diverse and complex, each with different obligations, use of resources, and returns to labor. Thus gender disaggregated data is needed to identify and compare male and female inputs, constraints, and outputs relevant to different projects, programs, and policies (5). Such gender information must become an integral part of development planning, if projects are to succeed. GAD also believes that the key problem in gender relationships is women's subordinate status to men. GAD calls for a fundamental reexamination of current social and political institutions, with the goal of giving women equality with men (6).

A grassroots group of global stature founded by developing-country women—DAWN, or Development Alternatives with Women for a New Era—also presents an alternative vision of women and development. In its groundbreaking book, *Development, Crises, and Alternative Visions: Third World Women's Perspectives* (1987), DAWN joins GAD proponents in questioning traditional efforts to integrate women into existing development programs. The integrationist approach, DAWN says, has had limited success partly because of the difficulty of overcoming cultural attitudes and prejudices. Of equal importance, however, is the fact that the model of development into which women are to be integrated is itself flawed. DAWN believes that development strategies striving for overall economic growth and increased agricultural and industrial productivity are inimical to women and their chances of achieving equality with men. What is needed is economic and social development tailored to human needs, which, among other things, gives women wider control over and access to economic and political power (7).

References and Notes

1. Eva M. Rathberger, "WID, WAD, GAD: Trends in Research and Practice" (International Development Research Centre, Ottawa, Canada, 1989), p. 6.
2. Caroline O.N. Moser, *Gender Planning and Development: Theory, Practice and Training* (Routledge, London, 1993), pp. 3–4.
3. Susan V. Poats and Hilary Sims Feldstein, "Introduction," in *Working Together: Gender Analysis in Agriculture*, H.S. Feldstein and S.V. Poats, eds. (Kumarian Press, West Hartford, Connecticut, 1989), pp. 2–3.
4. *Op. cit.* 1, p. 12.
5. Rae Lesser Blumberg, *Making the Case for the Gender Variable* (U.S. Agency for International Development, Washington, D.C., 1989), p. 96.
6. *Op. cit.* 2, p. 96.
7. Gita Sen and Caren Grown, *Development, Crises, and Alternative Visions*, (Monthly Review Press, New York, 1987), pp. 15–16 and 20.

ticipants in their societies and economies and in all development efforts.

HISTORY AND CONTEXT

The publication in 1970 of Ester Boserup's *A Role in Economic Development* was a milestone in the already growing international women's movement, one of the first books to document the contribution women make in the sphere of productive work (1). Boserup's work and that of others fostered the approach known as women in development, which gave birth to a body of research in the 1970s aimed at understanding women as an undervalued resource. Women, according to this view, could make more of an economic contribution to development if they were not neglected in development planning (2). (See Box 3.1.)

The 1970s also saw important strides toward fully integrating women in development efforts. The International Year of the Woman (1974) and the United Nations Decade for Women (1976–85) drew attention to the previously unrecognized contributions of, as well as the constraints on, women worldwide. Various groups systematically gathered information on women's roles from sectors such as agriculture, industry, commerce, education, and health, and from the formal and informal labor force. Agencies and organizations scrutinized their policies and assessed their agendas to determine how they could reduce women's workload and lift the veil of invisibility. In 1973, the U.S. Congress enacted the Percy Amendment to the Foreign Assistance Act, requiring bilateral programs "to give particular attention to those . . . activities that tend to integrate women into the national economies of foreign countries, thus improving their status and assisting the total development effort" (3). The United Nations Convention on the Elimination of All Forms of Discrimination against Women was adopted by the United Nations General Assembly in 1979. The United Nations Fund for Women and the International Research and Training Institute for the Advancement of Women were also started during this era.

Three global meetings took place as part of the U.N. Decade for Women—in Mexico City (1975), Copenhagen (1980), and Nairobi (1985). The convocation in Nairobi was perhaps the most significant, with more than 14,000 women and men from around the world in attendance. The conference report, *Forward Looking Strategies to the Year 2000*, along with the *Plan of Action* and the *Programme of Action*, charted among other things the growth in women's awareness of the policies needed to improve their status (4) (5) (6) (7). Critical to this growth was the commitment of numerous grassroots groups to equity, development, and peace.

Also critical was the growing harmony between environmentalists, women's advocates, development experts, and population specialists. This was invoked in

November 1991 when two meetings of importance with respect to women and sustainable development took place as part of the preliminaries to the United Nations Conference on Environment and Development (UNCED). The first was the Global Assembly of Women and the Environment: Partners in Life, organized by the Senior Women's Advisory Group of the United Nations Environment Programme (UNEP) and WorldWIDE, a Washington, D.C.-based international organization of women working on environmental issues. The purpose of this meeting was to demonstrate to UNCED and the world community that women, because of their experience, roles, and skills, "have specific and valuable contributions to make on environment and development issues . . . now being addressed by governments and the U.N." (8). The meeting was the culmination of a series of UNEP-sponsored regional assemblies, held between 1989 and 1991, whose themes focused on women and environmental management, and women and leadership.

The second meeting in November 1991 was the World Women's Congress for a Healthy Planet, convened by the New York–based Women's Environment and Development Organization. It drew 1,500 participants from around the world. By the end of the four-day conference, they had drawn up the Women's Action Agenda 21, calling for specific acts to address diversity, debt and trade, ethics, land rights and food security, biotechnology and biodiversity, information and education, and more.

These meetings, and women's subsequent powerful presence at UNCED, emphasized the role that women play in achieving sustainable development and the urgency of ensuring their inclusion in programs and policies everywhere.

THE MULTIPLE ROLES OF WOMEN

Throughout the world, women play key roles in productive and reproductive capacities, and as managers and users of local natural resources. Their productive roles, often undocumented, extend among other things to food output, service, farm, and export manufacturing labor, and the informal sector. In general, they also perform the bulk of household subsistence work.

Women as Income Earners

Time-use statistics considering all work, paid and unpaid, indicate that in almost all industrialized and developing regions of the world, women spend more time than men working. (See Figure 3.1.) Since 1970, women's share in the wage labor force has risen in all regions of the world, and almost everywhere more women are working outside the household than ever before. Although statistics often omit or obscure women's work, improved U.N. statistical methods show that, for example, 59 percent of women in eastern Asia, 60 percent in the former Soviet Union, and between 45 and 50 percent of women in Southeast Asia and sub-Saharan Africa are economically active (9).

The growth of the female labor force has to do not only with economic expansion but also with the increase in commercial agriculture and consequent land-

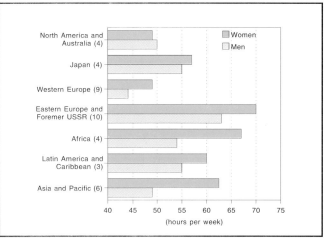

Figure 3.1 Women and Men's Working Time, Including Household Labor, 1976–88

Source: United Nations (U.N.), *World's Women, 1970–90, Trends and Statistics* (U.N., New York, 1991), p. 82.
Notes:
a. Numbers in parentheses refer to the number of studies in each region.
b. Estimates are based on studies conducted over various years from 1976–88.

lessness among the rural poor, prompting migration to cities. Although the migrant flow has consisted largely of men in most parts of the world, the proportion of migrating women is growing. In Latin America, in fact, women constitute the majority of urban migrants (10). In Africa and parts of Asia, by contrast, more limited urban growth and development over the last 20 years have meant that there were fewer wage labor opportunities for women (11).

Women's participation in the service sector, which offers a variety of low-paying (as well as some high-paying) jobs, has expanded in many parts of the world. In industrialized countries, nearly half of all service jobs are now performed by women. In Latin America and the Caribbean, between 60 and 70 percent of economically active women (on record) are employed in the service sector. Such increases are less prevalent in most other regions (12).

Women frequently work in the informal sector. Self-employment in unregulated industries and small-scale, service-related fields is common. In 1986, for example, women contributed 53.3 percent of Zambia's informal sector production (excluding agriculture and mining) and 43.2 percent of Malaysia's (13). Women usually comprise over half the borrowers in nongovernmental organization (NGO) projects targeting the smallest businesses: 85 percent of the borrowers in El Salvador's FEDECREDITO program, 60 percent in Indonesia's Badan Kredit Kecamatan program, and 97 percent in Zimbabwe's Federation of Rural Savings club (14). Many informal sector activities and related microenterprises result from agriculture, for instance, food vending and trading in household goods; other common ones include tailoring, domestic service, and artisanship. Changes are less dramatic in the formal industrial sector. Here, between 1970 and 1980, the proportion of women remained almost consistently low in every region (15).

Figure 3.2 Gender Labor Division in Africa, Early 1980s

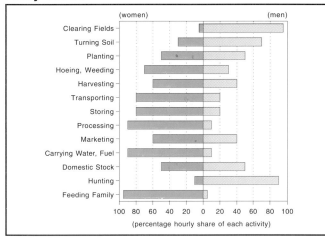

(women)　(men)

Clearing Fields
Turning Soil
Planting
Hoeing, Weeding
Harvesting
Transporting
Storing
Processing
Marketing
Carrying Water, Fuel
Domestic Stock
Hunting
Feeding Family

100 80 60 40 20 0 20 40 60 80 100
(percentage hourly share of each activity)

Source: Food and Agriculture Organization of the United Nations and Swedish International Development Authority (FAO/SIDA), *Restoring the Balance: Women and Forest Resource* (FAO/SIDA, Rome, 1988), p. 21.

Increasingly, women are employed in cash crop production—on their own farms, as laborers on plantations, and in the food industry. In Colombia, for example, women constitute 70 percent of paid workers in the flower export industry (16). And over the past two decades in India, their share of the agricultural wage labor force has gone up dramatically, exceeding the increase in men's share in most states (17).

Women's Unpaid Labor

Much of women's work in the developing world is performed in the noncash economy. Such labor includes subsistence agriculture; care for children, the elderly, and the disabled; provision of clothing and primary health care; cooking; cleaning; and sewing. Universally, women remain responsible for the bulk of household work even when employed outside the home. If women's unpaid domestic work were given economic value, gross domestic product (GDP) figures would almost certainly increase in all regions. Estimates of the value of such work vary. For example, studies from the early 1980s noted that in Norway, women's unpaid labor equaled 28 percent of GDP (based on equivalent market wages); in the United States, 23 percent; in the Philippines, 11 percent; and in Chile's and Venezuela's major cities, 15 and 22 percent, respectively (18). One study suggested that overall, unpaid female labor might add an estimated U.S. $4 trillion if included in statistics on the world economy (19).

Agriculture

In most of the developing world, women contribute significantly to agricultural production, as they did in the United States until farming was mechanized (20) (21) (22) (23). African farm women do 95 percent of the work related to feeding and caring for the family, including food production, while Asian women provide most of the labor for rice production. In Nepal's rice fields, women do 66 percent of the planting, 75 percent of the weeding, and 100 percent of the rice cleaning

and storage (24). Women's participation in agriculture varies between 19 and 35 percent in Latin America, and is as high as 54 percent in the Caribbean (25). Approximately one half of the world's food is grown by women, and an estimated two thirds of women workers in developing countries are in the agriculture sector (26). A great deal of their work consists of unpaid subsistence labor.

Specific farming tasks tend to be divided by gender, though women's responsibilities vary from region to region. In Africa, for example, they have traditionally hoed, planted, weeded, harvested, stored, and processed crops and food, while men have cleared the land and plowed the soil (27). (See Figure 3.2.) The introduction of modern cash cropping has shifted the balance of traditional tasks in many places, with men taking over crops explicitly for the market and women growing those for home consumption.

In many places, too, women are largely responsible for animal husbandry, tasks that include caring for livestock and poultry and collecting fodder (28). Studies in Egypt, Chile, Pakistan, and Swaziland, for example, show that between 80 and 100 percent of rural women take care of poultry (29).

Their agricultural work often instills in women valuable knowledge about local ecosystems, including soil features, multiple uses of crops, and health care for small livestock. Their experience is vital in maintaining crop diversity, as illustrated in areas of sub-Saharan Africa where women cultivate or collect more than 160 different species of plants on land fragments between men's crops and surrounding their communities (30). In the Andean regions of Bolivia, Colombia, and Peru, women develop and maintain the seed banks on which food production depends (31).

Forest Resources

For centuries, women have managed forests and used forest products (32) (33). In many developing countries, they are the ones who collect fuel, fodder, and food from trees and other plants. As in the case of agriculture, women see forest resources as multifunctional and use them in various ways to meet basic family needs. Men tend to use the same resources for commercial purposes as well as for their families (34).

Most household energy in the developing world is still generated by burning wood and other biomass, most of it gathered by women and children (35) (36) (37). (See Tables 3.1 and 21.2.) In Nepal, studies show, women and girls collect 84 percent of the fuel (38). Such work often takes women over formidable distances. For example, in rural Bangladesh, they spend an average of three to five hours a day searching for fuelwood. Girls begin this sort of work at an early age in many countries. In Africa, India, and other parts of south Asia, they commonly spend all day collecting fuel and water, doing domestic work, and farming, obviously at the expense of education (39).

Besides fuel, women collect and process many nonwood forest products, such as fodder, fiber, nuts, vegetables, and wild fruit. These items are important sources of protein and medicine for the family as well

Table 3.1 Time Spent Gathering Fuel, Early 1980s

Country	Average Hours per Day	Explanation of Work
Southern India (6 villages)	1.7	Women contribute 0.7 hours; children contribute 0.5
Gujarat, India	3.0	In family of 5, 1 member often spends all her/his time on it
Nepal	1–5	Often 1 adult and 1–2 children do fuelwood collection
Tanzania	8.0	Traditional women's work
Senegal	4–5	Often is carried about 45 km
Niger	4–6	Women sometimes walk 25 km
Kenya	3.5	Women do 75 percent of fuel gathering
Ghana	3.5-4	1 full day's search provides wood for 3 days
Peru	2.5	Women gather and cut wood

Source: Sheila Lewenhak, *The Revaluation of Women's Work* (Earthscan, London, 1989), p. 147.

Table 3.2 Hours Women Spend Drawing and Carrying Water, 1975–82

Region	Hours per Week
Africa	
Botswana, (rural areas)	5.5
Burkina Faso, Zimtenga region	4.4
Côte d'Ivoire, (rural farmers)	4.4
Ghana, (northern farms)	4.5
Mozambique, (villages)	
Dry season	15.3
Wet season	2.9
Senegal, (farming village)	17.5
Asia	
India, Baroda region	7.0
Nepal, (villages)	
Ages 5–9 years	1.5
Ages 10–14 years	4.9
Ages 15+ years	4.7
Pakistan, (village survey)	3.5

Source: United Nations (U.N.), *World's Women, 1970–90, Trends and Statistics* (U.N., New York, 1991), p. 75.

as a means of generating cash income (40). Women use forest products to make household items such as bowls, mats, and baskets, which may also be sold to generate income (41) (42). A 1988–89 study in Laos found that all village women in the area in question did some form of forest gathering; some relied entirely on forest products (using 141 different types) to support their families during seasons of variable rain (43).

Many rural women have developed considerable expertise in the practical application of resources from various tree species (44) (45). A survey in Sierra Leone revealed that women could name 31 products that they gathered or made from nearby flora, while men were able to name only 8 (46). Rural women are generally careful to conserve forests, and studies show they have a strong interest in safeguarding the supply of wood products (47) (48). They obtain fuel by collecting branches and dead logs rather than cutting living trees, and are often active in tree-planting efforts (49) (50).

Water Management

Throughout much of the South, in both rural and urban areas, women bear primary responsibility for collecting, supplying, and managing water. They take care of water sanitation, purification, storage, and use in cooking and cleaning, and they spend hours each day collecting and transporting water (51) (52) (53). (See Table 3.2.)

Although often hindered by lack of access to appropriate technology and information, women have developed various ways to conserve water (54). Often they are knowledgeable about the location, flow, and quality of local water sources vital to the livelihood of the community. In Yemen, women use the best water for drinking, cooking, and cleaning dishes and food, while "gray," or used, water is saved for washing clothes and watering plants (55). In rural areas of southern Nigeria, women do their house building and farm clearing in the rainy season so that they will have more time to collect water in the dry season, when that chore becomes more burdensome (56).

Health Care

In addition to being natural resource managers, women deliver basic health care in many parts of the

world, as nurses, healers, herbalists, nutritionists, hygiene specialists, and prenatal-, birth-, and childcare providers. The World Health Organization (WHO) recognizes women as the foremost practitioners of primary health care across the globe (57). An estimated 75 percent of health care is known to take place in the home, where women have the greatest responsibility (58). In many societies, they have developed a body of specialized health care knowledge, much of it relating to medicinal plants and passed down from generation to generation (59). Among the Huastec Indians in Mexico, for instance, the unique knowledge of *curanderas*, or female healers, has been documented as a vital part of health care (60).

Women generally make decisions regarding remedies for the ill, the type of care that should be received, and when outside help should be consulted. Mothers go to health centers when their children are ill and purchase medicine when it is available (61). And women everywhere are active in midwifery, with 60 to 80 percent of all births in developing countries being midwife assisted (62).

BARRIERS TO WOMEN'S FULL PARTICIPATION

In most societies worldwide, cultural and religious attitudes have resulted in discriminatory laws and/or practices that, beginning at birth, prevent women from becoming full and equal partners in their nations' societies and economies. Throughout most of their life and in most settings, women have less opportunity than men to pursue education and to develop economic self-sufficiency. The result is that women, particularly in the developing countries, represent the majority of the poor, and their numbers are growing (63) (64). In addition, although women make up approximately half of the world's population, they are two thirds of the world's illiterate (65). Statistics on poverty and illiteracy reflect discrimination in inheritance and landownership laws, employment and development policies, resource allocation, and the traditional division of labor.

Obviously, discrimination varies depending on country, culture, class, and locale, but in general, women are considered inferior and treated as such from birth (66). Perceived as having less economic value than sons, girls often receive less than boys when a family's resources are limited. Studies in India, Pakistan, Nepal, the Middle East, north Africa, and parts of sub-Saharan Africa show that girls are given less and poorer quality food, stay home from school at an earlier age, engage in hard labor earlier, and receive less medical care than boys (67) (68). In some places, this discrimination may be a cause of higher death rates for females than for males between infancy and age five. In the 1980s, mortality rates in early childhood were higher for females in Bangladesh, Pakistan, India, Jordan, Colombia, Nepal, Mexico, Turkey, and a number of other countries (69). A study in 1990 later showed that death rates were still higher for females in India (70).

In its most insidious form, gender discrimination manifests itself as violence against women, the practice of female infanticide, and the activities of the international sex trade (71). An estimated 80 million women in Africa, and millions more in the Middle East, have suffered female circumcision, a practice that poses serious health risks (72) (73). Far-reaching discrimination underlies many additional practices and this ultimately hinders the ability of societies to achieve sustainable forms of development.

Economic Constraints

Poverty, a major obstacle to the achievement of sustainable development, is the condition in which many women throughout the developing world live (74). The number of poor women continues to grow both in absolute terms and in relation to poor men. According to one estimate, poverty has increased by 47 percent among rural women over the past 20 years, compared with 30 percent among rural men (75). This trend reflects the fact that rural women often lack access to resources and is a reminder that much of their work is unpaid labor directed toward the support and survival of families (76) (77). Working as much as 16 hours a day, rural women can ill afford the time and energy to pursue cash-earning jobs or to develop new skills.

The growth in women's poverty is also a consequence of the economic crisis of the 1980s, which was particularly harmful to the poorest socioeconomic groups. The curtailment of social services, such as health care, child care, and family planning, brought about by the multilateral banks' stabilization and structural adjustment policies—macroeconomic reforms designed to alleviate developing country debt and economic stagnation—has in many cases forced women to make up the shortfall in these areas, increasing their unpaid work burden (78). (See Chapter 13, "International Institutions," Failures of Multilateral Aid.)

Women throughout the South are further disadvantaged by the fact that most of what they do outside the household, working as subsistence laborers or in the informal sector, is assigned little or no economic value by governments and therefore is uncounted in labor statistics and economic assessments. In Pakistan alone, an estimated 12 million women agricultural workers have been omitted from official labor statistics (79).

Moreover, methodologies for surveying and data analysis tend to be gender biased. For example, development planners generally assume that household heads are male, regardless of who is supporting the family (80). The result is that governments and development agencies, which are administered primarily by men, have failed both to integrate the concerns of women into mainstream economic policies and to make investments that would increase female productivity.

In recent decades, development policies have focused on export-oriented growth—cash crops, primary commodities, and industrial goods—largely the province of men (81). Relatively little direct support has gone to projects for traditional food crops grown by women (82). For example, a study of certain U.N. agencies found that in 1982, only 0.05 percent of the total allocation for agriculture went to programs for rural women (83). Historically, various development projects were formulated with the view that rural households are monolithic units—in other words, that projects designed to raise household income as a whole would benefit equally all members of the household, and that information, inputs, and technology passed on to the designated representative of the household (in most cases, the male) would likewise be shared equally with its other members. Many such projects failed to recognize the division by gender of labor and resources within households, as well as the division of returns to labor. The implications of this failure for some development projects has been significant. For example, women, particularly in Africa, often farm their own crops on separate plots in addition to working their husbands' plots. The sale of surplus food from their own crops gives them separate income to fulfill household obligations. If a development project causes women to lose control of their separate crops and/or income, then the project may not succeed. Studies have indicated that women try to direct labor toward activities under their control, even when activities beyond their control are more profitable (84).

The case of SEMRY I, an irrigated rice project in Cameroon, is an example. Planners found that farmers, through lack of interest, were leaving many fields uncultivated, with the result that the project was unable to grow enough rice to pay for itself. Although cultivation was done jointly by husband and wife, the husband received all the income, compensating his wife at his discretion. In addition, work in the rice fields competed directly with women's sorghum production and with other independent income-generating activities. Given the competition with sorghum, produced to meet subsistence needs and over which women had direct control, few had sufficent incentive to take on the cultivation of an additional rice field, the benefits from which depended on the uncertain inclinations of their husbands at harvest time (85).

An irrigated rice project in Gambia shows how production may even decrease when women lose control of their crops and income. In this case, even though women were the traditional cultivators and income beneficiaries of swamp rice, the development project was targeted to men. To keep women as labor on their

Table 3.3 Gender of Agricultural Extension Staff by Region, 1989

Region	Respondent Countries Number of	Administrators/ supervisors Male	Female	Subject-matter Specialists Male	Female	Fieldwork in Agriculture Male	Female	Fieldwork in Home Economics Male	Female	Total Extension Staff Total	Female (%)
Africa	27	1,971	92	4,178	467	23,658	2,069	221	1,034	42,117	10.46
Asia	22	17,105	3,218	30,801	5,882	77,099	3,002	44	3,059	280,415	14.75
Latin America	22	862	64	1,738	216	5,565	201	68	820	16,885	16.53
Near East	15	1,287	47	397	64	5,153	26	4	72	9,226	10.70
Europe	8	1,398	132	623	199	6,109	586	0	874	11,045	16.71
North America	3	613	322	3,579	1,127	3,406	368	44	2,724	15,350	39.62
Worldwide	**97**	**23,236**	**3,875**	**41,316**	**7,955**	**120,990**	**6,252**	**381**	**8,583**	**375,038**	**15.32**

Source: Food and Agriculture Organization of the United Nations (FAO), *Agricultural Extension and Farm Women in the 1980s* (FAO, Rome, 1993), Table 14, p. 42.

irrigated fields, the men prevented them from farming the irrigated rice land independently. In response, women held back their labor, and the result was decreased rice production (86).

Projects may also suffer when information and training are given only to the male head of household. In Thailand, the Northeast Rainfed Agricultural Development Project trained men who were only part-time farmers to carry out crop trials. The wives, also farmers, received no training. The result was that "crops were planted incorrectly and did not grow, the power tillers provided by the project could not be used, and a nitrogen-fixing crop intended to fertilize rice did not get planted. Even when the husband was present, advice on crop production was incorrectly transmitted from husband to wife" (87).

A final example comes from an integrated pest management (IPM) project in the Philippines. In this case, despite the fact that the male farmers who had received training seemed to understand the IPM concept, few were adopting it. Researchers discovered that although men did the physical labor associated with managing pests, it was women who made the crucial decisions about the kind and amount of pesticide to use. Even if the male farmers saw the value of IPM, their wives, who had received no information on it, did not, and continued to purchase pesticides. Once the women were allowed to participate in project discussions and training, there was an increase in the adoption of IPM because the women understood the alternatives to pesticide use (88).

Traditionally, agricultural extension services, based on Western models, have been staffed almost exclusively by men, and offered to men. In a 1989 global survey, the Food and Agriculture Organization of the United Nations (FAO) found that only 15 percent of the world's extension workers were women, ranging from approximately 40 percent in North America to less than 11 percent in Africa and the Middle East (89). (See Table 3.3.)

Technical innovations in agriculture, energy, and forestry have also often failed to reach women (90). In many cases, women lack access to technology simply because it is controlled by men or because they cannot afford to buy it. In other cases, government and development agencies have not invested in the development of technology tailored to the specific needs of women, including equipment that would reduce the amount of time and labor they spend on household tasks.

Most new agricultural technology—tractors, new seed varieties, fertilizer, and so forth—is geared to the promotion of industrial/export crop production, mainly the province of men. For example, in parts of Africa, while the introduction of animal-drawn plows allowed men to expand the amount of land under cultivation for cash crops, the plows were not always available to women for use in the cultivation of subsistence crops. Indeed, by expanding the amount of market cropland under cultivation, the plows may increase their work in cases where women are responsible for planting, weeding, and harvesting market crops (91). And, as studies in southern and southeastern Asia indicate, women's income may actually decrease after the introduction of technology. For instance, if women lack access to weeders used for cash crops, and have been displaced by weeders from paid work on those crops, the net effect is income loss (92).

Women, moreover, are less able than men to afford technology, a reflection not only of lower income but also of more limited access to credit. In Nigeria, the labor-intensive task of hand-grating cassava was traditionally performed by women. In the 1960s, mechanized graters were introduced from Benin, but most women lacked the capital to buy them. The industry consequently moved into the hands of men, 75 percent of whom owned their machines and controlled the profits. Women used the machines only as hired labor, which did not pay well enough to allow them to buy the machines themselves (93).

Too often technology aimed at women is inappropriate because women themselves have not been consulted during design and planning. A simple design flaw such as a well pump handle that is too high to reach, or a stove that is not adapted to the local cooking pot, can discourage use (94).

Efforts to develop income-generating projects for women tend to be similarly flawed. Typically, these projects are small in scale, initiated by NGOs, and funded by grants rather than loans from development agencies (95). Often they benefit only a small group and focus on traditional female activities such as sewing and cooking rather than introducing women to, and training them for, new areas of work. Many require women to volunteer their time and labor, making it difficult for those already burdened with nonpaid work to participate (96).

Poor women in both urban and rural areas have been neglected in other kinds of projects as well. For

Table 3.4 Women's Average Earnings as a Percentage of Men's, Selected Countries, 1980 and 1990

Country	In Agriculture		In Nonagricultural Activities	
	1980	1990	1980	1990
Costa Rica	78	90	70	66
Cyprus	57	61	54	61
Egypt			64[a]	114[b]
Hong Kong		76[c,d]		70[d]
Jordan		83		
Kenya	68	84	80	91
Korea, Republic of	74	71	44	54
Paraguay	72[e]	98	81[e]	76
Portugal	64			
Singapore		91	63[f]	71
Sri Lanka	85	92	88[g]	90[g]
Swaziland	49[h,i]	55[i]	66[h]	73[b]
Turkey	92[c,j]			
United Rep. Tanzania		85[j]		92[b]

Source: United Nations (U.N.) Women's Indicators and Statistics Database (Wisstat), Version 3 (U.N. Statistical Division, New York, forthcoming).

Figure 3.3 Female and Male Adult Literacy Rates, 1990

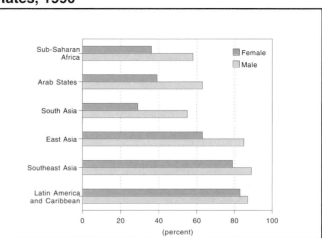

Source: United Nations Development Programme (UNDP), *Human Development Report, 1993* (UNDP, New York, 1993), p. 213.

example, governments and donors tend to invest in large-scale water schemes that favor large landholders rather than the small farms on which many women work. Social forestry projects have also largely excluded women. Out of 22 projects appraised by the World Bank between 1984 and 1987, only 1 explicitly included women as project beneficiaries (97).

In all countries, women wage laborers are almost always paid less than their male counterparts, even for the same work (98) (99). (See Table 3.4.) Although wage labor in rural and urban areas has brought some improvement to women, time-use statistics have shown that women workers throughout the world usually bear "double day" workloads—that is, they perform household tasks following a full schedule of paid work (100) (101). Household demands detract from women's ability to compete in the workplace.

Educational Constraints

A pervasive barrier to women's participation in sustainable development has been lack of education. In almost all areas of the world, women's literacy rates and levels of education and training are far below men's (102) (103). (See Figure 3.3.) Worldwide, in 1990, an estimated 601.6 million women (33.6 percent of women) compared with 346.5 million men (19.4 percent of men) were illiterate (104). Although the literacy gap has been narrowing in some regions, it remains wide, particularly in parts of Africa and Asia where the ratio approaches 2 to 1 (105).

Except in rich countries, girls receive much less schooling than boys (106). In many developing countries, girls are withdrawn from school earlier because parents, foreseeing the day when their daughters will marry and leave home, do not expect them to make an economic contribution to the family. Regarded as being more important to family sustenance than are boys, girls are kept at home to perform household work. This practice has trapped generation after generation of women in a cycle of illiteracy and poverty.

At secondary schools, vocational schools, and universities, the gap in male-female enrollment remains wide in all of the South except in most Latin American and Caribbean countries (107). Educational and training institutions are dominated by male administrators, and teachers in scientific and technical fields are primarily male. This means that development programs in agriculture and forestry, where women play an essential role, are planned, directed, staffed, and evaluated by men. And cultural traditions dictating that male experts focus on male farmers further exclude women from development projects (108).

Health Constraints

Women's health is a critical component of sustainable development. While most of the world's indigent suffer from poor health and nutrition, higher rates of malnutrition generally exist among females than among males of the same age groups (109). Half of all women in Africa and southern and western Asia, and two thirds of all pregnant women in these regions, are anemic (110). In many developing countries, food is distributed within households according to a member's status rather than nutritional needs. In India and Bangladesh, for instance, females from birth generally receive less and poorer quality food than males. Female babies are breast-fed for a shorter time and receive less cereal, fat, milk, sugar, and total calories than boys until the age of four and beyond (111). Similar discrimination in the allocation of household resources has been reported in the Middle East, North Africa, sub-Saharan Africa, and south Asia (112).

Malnutrition impairs the physical development of women, their health, and their capacity to bear healthy children. It also increases their susceptibility to illness, complicates pregnancy, and is correlated to maternal death during childbirth. In some countries in Africa and Asia, the maternal mortality rate per 100,000 live births reaches into the thousands (113).

Despite the fact that women are the primary providers of household health care, they often lack access to outside health care for themselves. Data show, for example, that in India fewer women than men survive common diseases, are treated in hospitals, are prescribed medication, or receive qualified, timely treatment. Restricted access to health services leaves women not only less capable of taking care of their own health but also that of their children, perpetuating a trend of high child mortality (114).

Lack of Reproductive Freedom

Reproductive practices are influenced by cultural and religious norms, economic and educational status, and access to relevant health services. These factors vary greatly depending on the region. Still, evidence from many countries shows that poor families tend to reproduce early and have many children, with little space between births (115) (116).

Women's poverty and limited education, self-determination, and access to economic opportunity and resources all contribute to high fertility rates (117). A primary reason for having many children is economic: offspring provide labor for basic survival and household income, as well as insurance against old age. For many poor families, too, children are a source of pleasure (118). In numerous cultures, an individual's social status depends on the number of children he or she has, especially sons (119).

High fertility rates are known to lead to various problems, including strained resources and endangered health for women and children (120). In some cases, development itself intensifies these problems. In Kenya, for example, post-independence policies on agriculture and the organization and delivery of health and education services, in addition to changes in family law, particularly with regard to marriage, divorce, inheritance, and property ownership, have encouraged high fertility (121).

Although fertility rates have gone down worldwide, many women still lack access to information and services, or cannot make use of them because of economic limitations or cultural norms. (See Figure 3.4.) Reproductive health services are available to approximately 95 percent of east Asian people, but only to 57 percent in Southeast Asia and Latin America, 54 percent in south Asia, 13–25 percent in the Arab states, and in sub-Saharan Africa, 9 percent (122).

Many women want greater control over their fertility. According to the United Nations Population Fund, there would be 27 to 35 percent fewer births in developing countries if women were able to have the number of children they wanted (123).

Lack of Access to Land and Natural Resources/Legal Rights

Throughout most of the developing world, women lack either ownership or effective control of land, water, and other resources. Some developing countries still function under the legacy of colonial rule and post-independence reforms that imposed title-deed systems and inheritance laws detrimental to women. In some areas, traditional communal rights that once gave women access to land, water, trees, and a variety of

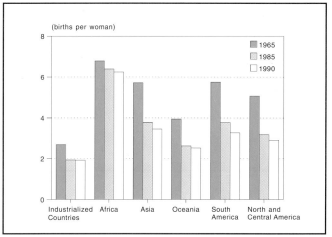

Figure 3.4 Total Fertility Rates, 1965–90

Source: United Nations (U.N.), *Demographic Indicators 1950–2025 (The 1992 Revision)*, on diskette (U.N., New York, 1993).

other resources were replaced by land-tenure systems based on exclusive use and ownership. In parts of Africa, women neither own land nor have rights to resources such as trees and crops on the land they cultivate (124). Though sometimes women own trees on land to which men hold title, many such systems of multiple use are being overridden by land-tenure reform based on freehold title, usually allocated to men. In Latin America, agrarian reform laws have largely failed to benefit women, primarily because, erroneously, females are not considered full-time producers or heads of household (125). Moreover, even where women have clear rights of land use, as among the Luo in Kenya, they may not be free to make decisions about the land independent of men (126).

Because of their lack of collateral based on land ownership, women in many developing countries have no credit or banking services. The FAO has estimated that women's share in agricultural credit is 10 percent or less (127). Even as the sole breadwinners, women are often denied credit because of biased loan policies. Without credit, they are unable to invest in timesaving equipment and fertilizer to improve their agricultural productivity and income.

In many developing countries, women also lack social security and rights pertaining to marital relations. For example, they often have no property rights in cases of abandonment or divorce (128). Labor laws seldom give them adequate protection against wage discrimination. And although women are gaining more responsibility as heads of household, they rarely hold rights appropriate to this social change. (See Figure 3.5.)

Environmental Degradation

Environmental destruction and degradation in the South almost inevitably increases the labor of rural women. For example, because of deforestation (as well as increasingly less open-access land), it has become more difficult and time-consuming for women to collect fuelwood and other forest products (129). Carrying loads up to 35 kilograms, they are forced to travel longer and longer distances, often as far as 10 kilome-

Figure 3.5 Households Headed by Women

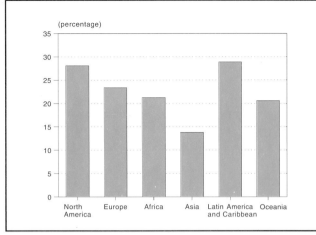

Source: United Nations (U.N.), U.N. Women's Indicators and Statistics Data Base (Wistat), Version 2 (U.N., New York, 1990).

ters from home (130). In the foothills of the Himalayas, for example, the gathering of firewood and fodder took no more than two hours a generation ago; now it takes a full day of walking through mountainous terrain (131). Over a 10-year period in the Sudan, the time it takes to collect fuelwood increased more than fourfold (132). When fuelwood is not available at all, women in some countries such as Bangladesh shift to alternative and sometimes inferior fuel, for instance, animal dung and crop residue. Not only do these take longer to burn but they also produce hazardous fumes. The use of dung as fuel also deprives the soil of nutrients needed for agricultural production. Lack of fuel sometimes forces women to reduce the number of hot meals their families receive (133) (134).

Like fuel gathering, water collection is becoming more difficult as desertification spreads and water sources are depleted. Women may spend up to four hours a day retrieving water for the home and the farm, often carrying 20 kilograms or more in containers on their backs, shoulders, or heads (135) (136).

Political Powerlessness

Women are virtually absent from decisionmaking positions in all realms of development and environmental management. Only 3.5 percent of the world's cabinet ministers are women, and in 93 countries women hold no ministerial positions. Only 6 of the 159 U.N. member countries were headed by women at the end of 1990. Women fill a mere 10 percent of the world's parliamentary positions, and rarely do they hold top-level positions in public administration (137). It should be noted as well that, on average, women represent less than 5 percent of management-level staff at bilateral and multilateral development agencies (138).

WOMEN AND SUSTAINABLE DEVELOPMENT

Education

Women's education and training programs—when integrated with basic health services, expanded economic opportunity, and enforced rights—are crucial to

the success of sustainable development. They raise female literacy and improve women's skills in agriculture, environmental management, and health care (139) (140). As female literacy goes up, fertility goes down, child and maternal mortality rates decrease, and the population as a whole becomes better nourished and healthier. (See Figures 3.6 and 3.7.)

Increasing women's education levels has proved to be one of the most effective ways to improve reproductive health and reduce fertility rates and unwanted births. According to World Bank studies, for every year of schooling a woman receives, her fertility rate is reduced by 10 percent (141).

Education broadens opportunity to earn income outside of the home and thus to pursue options other than childbearing and childcare. Educated women tend to have more decisionmaking authority within the household, communicate more with their husbands, and be more knowledgeable and assertive about family planning. They are more likely to marry later, to desire smaller families, to practice contraception (where it is available), and to have fewer, healthier children (142) (143). Fewer pregnancies reduce the risk of death from maternity-related causes and long-term physical stress.

Maternal education appears to have a greater effect on child health and survival than does paternal education. (See Figure 3.8.) Surveys in 25 developing countries show that, all other factors being equal, one to three years of maternal schooling can reduce child mortality rates by 15 percent, as opposed to only 6 percent through an equivalent level of paternal schooling (144). In general, educated women practice better hygiene, are more knowledgeable about nutrition and health problems, and are more inclined to seek professional help for such problems (145). The positive effect of maternal education continues after birth; children of educated mothers have lower risk of infection because of better domestic hygiene and are less susceptible to infection because of immunization and better food (146). Maternal education also appears to be the strongest determinant of children's education levels, particularly for daughters (147).

Training in nontraditional fields can increase women's economic welfare, skills, and confidence. One women's construction collective in Jamaica initiated a three-month training program in masonry and carpentry. Participants served in construction apprenticeships to learn electrical installation, painting, and plumbing (148). In other cases, programs in improved farming practices and agroforestry, such as those supported by the Pan American Development Fund in the Caribbean, have taught women new skills in resource management. Training women can have a multiplier effect, because women often act as local informal educators for other women, specifically with regard to resources, farming, and health (149).

Economic Opportunity

Improving economic opportunity for women is equally important to the goals of sustainable and equitable development. In general, health improves as income rises (although this can be affected by the

Figure 3.6 Mortality Rate for Children under 5 by Female Literacy, 1990–91

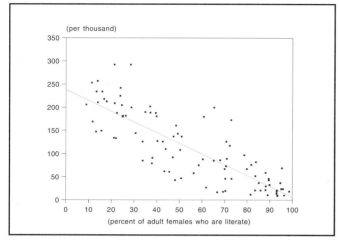

Sources:

1. United Nations Children's Fund (UNICEF), *The State of the World's Children, 1993* (UNICEF, New York, 1993).
2. United Nations Educational, Scientific and Cultural Organization (UNESCO), *Compendium of Statistics on Illiteracy, 1990* (UNESCO, Paris, 1990).

Note: Based on data reported from 93 countries. Each dot represents data from one country.

Figure 3.7 Fertility Rate by Female Literacy, 1990

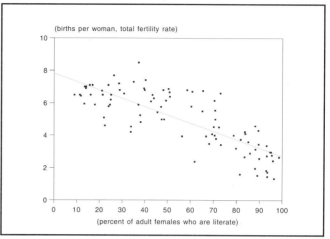

Sources:

1. United Nations Population Division, *Demographic Indicators 1950–2025 (The 1992 Revision)*, on diskette (U.N., New York, 1992).
2. United Nations Educational, Scientific and Cultural Organization (UNESCO), *Compendium of Statistics on Illiteracy, 1990* (UNESCO, Paris, 1990).

Note: Based on data reported from 93 countries. Each dot represents data from one country.

distribution of income within a household). The opportunity to both earn and retain control of income has a particularly significant effect on health and fertility rates. According to evidence in countries such as Jamaica, Guatemala, Sri Lanka, India, Cameroon, and Ghana, women in charge of expenditures usually spend their earnings on family nutrition and other subsistence needs, while men tend to spend a greater proportion of their earnings on consumer goods and entertainment (150) (151). One study showed that in Côte d'Ivoire, when household income under the control of women doubled, the proportion of the household budget spent for alcohol was reduced by 26 percent and for cigarettes by 14 percent. According to another study, to improve child nutrition by a specific measure in Guatemala, it takes 15 times more spending when income is earned by the father than by the mother (152). Like educated women, women who maintain control of their income also tend to have a greater input in fertility decisions. They are also more likely to give female offspring a greater share of household resources than are women in families that have no female wage earners (153) (154) (155).

Investments in credit for women bring in a high rate of return, often close to 100 percent. Perhaps the best known is the Grameen Bank in Bangladesh. Founded in 1976, this bank issues loans to its more than 500,000 members, 82 percent of whom are women. The average repayment rate is 97 percent. The Self-Employed Women's Association (SEWA) is a trade union in India sponsoring a cooperative credit and development program. Members are poor and many illiterate. After an initial struggle, the union's co-op bank has become a viable institution that is able to help its members (156). Women's World Banking, a New York-based institution established to advance and promote women's economic participation in all regions of the world, boasts

a better-than 95 percent repayment rate on its more than 70,000 loans (157).

Health

Reliable and high-quality services for reproductive health and family planning also promote sustainable development. When such services are affordable and accessible, women and men can make informed reproductive choices, plan births, and improve the health and chances for survival of their families. The greatest reduction in fertility rates results from the combination of women's improved economic and social status, education, and access to reproductive health services.

Land Tenure

Evidence from Africa and Asia has shown that securing women's access and tenure to land and resources is crucial to improving their productivity and economic well-being. For example, women in West Bengal have lobbied for legal reform so that land is allocated in the name of both spouses, as wives and families carry on farming when men migrate to urban areas. Sri Lankan estate workers have been lobbying to obtain joint (husband-wife) title to plots and dwellings allocated by estate owners. In Kenya, women have gained rights to land by organizing in local groups to buy plots for raising produce and small animals. Some of Kenya's numerous women's farming cooperatives have become relatively large businesses (158).

Although data is scarce, there is evidence that if given the same land, input, education, and technology, females can equal or surpass males in agricultural output. A study in Kenya showed that by holding constant most of the factors of which women usually have less, female farmers would outproduce men by 6.6 percent in maize yields per hectare (159). A study in southern Cameroon, where women produce most

Figure 3.8 **Parent's Schooling and Percentage Reduction in Child Mortality in Selected Countries, Late 1980s**

A. 4–6 Years of Education

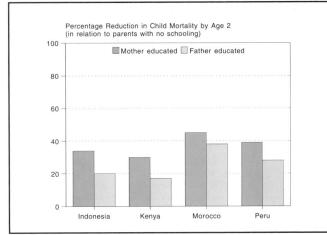

B. 7 Years or More of Education

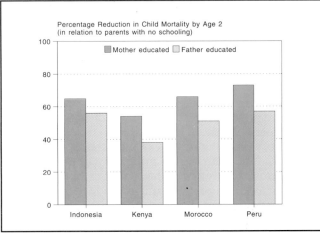

Source: The World Bank, *World Development Report, 1993* (Oxford University Press, New York, 1993), p. 43.

subsistence and locally marketed food (as they do in large regions of western, central, eastern, and southern Africa), found that "policies targeted at women are more likely to result in a significant production response at lower cost than policies [designed to attract] . . . more male labor into the food sector" (160).

Technology

Technology development aimed at giving women more time could have a powerful effect on their productivity as well as their well-being. Although most research on the impact of technology on productivity, income, and employment has concentrated on inputs such as tractors and fertilizers (largely used by men), there is evidence that labor-saving devices targeted to women's use—for example, hand-operated cornmills in Cameroon, fish-smoking ovens in Ghana, and rice-pounding machines in Guinea-Bissau—can result in women spending more time on income-generating activities, the care and feeding of their families, or even leisure activities (161). For example, the Kenya Water

for Health Organization (KWAHO), with support from UNIFEM, addressed urgent local water needs by mobilizing and training local people, mostly women, to install and repair pumps and improve sanitation techniques. After being trained, 24 women leaders organized 70 community-level committees to dig 85 boreholes and wells fitted with pumps, which serve a population of 27,000. No longer compelled to collect water, women found time for activities such as roof thatching, selling crafts, and buying a community grain mill (162). Beyond service to others, technology designed specifically for the purpose of alleviating women's workload and improving their health and status is valuable in its own right.

WOMEN'S INITIATIVES IN NATURAL RESOURCE MANAGEMENT

Faced with the problem of increasingly severe environmental stress in their communities, a growing number of women in the South are initiating projects—or playing leadership roles in programs introduced by outside agencies—aimed at improving environmental conditions and thus the quality of life.

Their initiatives span an array of issues, including forestry, agroforestry, agriculture, energy and water management, food processing, and urban pollution control. Many of the efforts seek to address problems of inadequate fuel, food, or water caused by soil erosion, deforestation, and pollution; and many have resulted in better resource management and community health conditions, two important goals of sustainable development. Some of the projects are self-sustaining and independent, while others receive assistance from development agencies, local or national governments, or NGOs (163) (164).

For example, in Andhra Pradesh, India, where much rainfed cropland is exhausted, village-level women's organizations developed the idea of collectively leasing and reviving the land with traditional farming techniques. Banks declined to assist the women, but the Deccan Development Society provided an initial loan. The project involved 400 women in 20 villages. Within three years, over 280 hectares of cropland was returned to production, and more land was added every year thereafter. Both international agencies and the Indian government have endorsed the program as a good example of sustainable development (165).

Soil erosion is a serious problem in Kenya as well. In many areas, hilly or arid land not suited for agriculture without terracing is cultivated because of population pressure. In the Katheka community, village leaders promoted the development of traditional, voluntary self-help groups known as *mwethya*. The mostly female *mwethya* consist of 25 to 35 members from the same farm neighborhood or household cluster. By 1987, there were 12 established groups with almost 400 members total. Through activities such as the construction of extensive terraces, check dams, and cutoff drains, they have made valuable contributions to Katheka's resource management efforts (166).

In Mexico, the combination of erosion and declining soil productivity has forced the nation into dependence on imported food and accelerated migration to cities. In one town, a group of housewives organized to fight the problem. They encouraged other women in the village schools and markets to collect and recycle their organic waste. The group collects and uses the material to fertilize and enrich agricultural soil. The effort eventually captured the attention and support of the Mexican government and served as a catalyst for similar efforts in other communities (167).

Many initiatives involving women seek to reduce food insecurity in drought-prone areas. In rural Botswana, for example, communities typically depend on livestock and arable agriculture to help meet their needs, yet frequent periods of drought threaten local economies and food supplies. Leaders of Thusano Lefatsheng, a small NGO set up in 1984, realized that indigenous food and medicinal plants, well adapted to the harsh climate, could provide an important alternative source of income, especially for rural women. The group has a small research farm. It purchases, processes, and markets indigenous veld products, promotes other indigenous products as new cash crops, and has developed a profitable, sustainable farming system that includes traditional crops, new crops, medicinal plants, trees, and livestock. By 1989, 1,500 harvesters and 10 processors were involved in these activities, mostly women from poverty-stricken areas. Demand for the new crops is growing, both in domestic and European markets (168).

Other initiatives aim to reduce the time women spend gathering fuelwood, to replace traditional cooking methods, or to find more sustainable energy sources for cooking.

In the Sudan-Sahelian region of Ghana, population growth rates in the 3 to 3.5 percent range increased demand for farm land and fuelwood, which resulted in widespread tree cutting, severe fuelwood shortages, declining land productivity, and accelerated siltation in dams. In 1988, a company managing two dams in the region, with support from the United Nations Development Programme (UNDP) and the government of Ghana, began a major agroforestry project. It worked with 19 groups of women farmers, providing free tree seedlings and encouraging them to plant the trees in woodlots, in alley-cropping orchards on farms, and along streams and boundaries. To date, thousands of trees have been planted by the 3,400 women participants. The project has improved soil fertility and should reduce the need for expensive fertilizer. When they mature, the woodlots will allow women to spend less time and money obtaining fuelwood (169).

In 1982, in response to fuelwood scarcity in the Ruiru area of Kenya, Sophia Kiarie started the Bellerive Foundation's first tree nursery program, which among other things distributes and plants seedlings with the help of various organizations including schools. Tree seedlings are nurtured to maturity, which has resulted in a survival rate of 50 to 95 percent. The program also encourages the creation of "green islands," of which about 60 have been established, each with 500 to 5,000 trees, and of tree belts on farms. The program's overall results are impressive:

about 100,000 people have planted some 2 million trees since the program began (170).

Water is another focus of women's initiatives. In Tripoli, Honduras, the government installed a water system. Hillside agriculture, mountainside grazing, and severe deforestation had all contributed to the buildup of sediment in the system's plumbing, making the water dangerous to drink and causing many diseases. In 1990, some women in the community formed a group to address this and other environmental problems. With the help of Carmen Bustillo, a promoter of women's groups for the Honduran Office of Natural Resources, they started a project to educate the women and, later on, the men of the community about the effects of deforestation and soil erosion. They built wood-conserving stoves, which reduced fuelwood consumption and protected women and their families from smoke inhalation. They planted trees in deforested areas near the water system and built outdoor lined sinks to improve health conditions. As a result of all these efforts, mountainside erosion was cut almost by half and water quality was markedly improved (171). In fact the project was so successful that FAO, its funder, plans to start others around the world.

In the 1980s, the village of Ban Bok in rural Thailand experienced severe water shortages during the dry season. Only 3 of the village's 41 households had latrines; diseases such as diarrhea and conjunctivitis were common. In response, the Girl Guide Association of Thailand included Ban Bok in a program to promote women's participation, education, and leadership in village-level water supply and sanitation projects. Fieldworkers, many of them women, held informal discussions in homes to identify needs and find solutions. The program included a latrine-building campaign, training in fish farming and mushroom cultivation, a health campaign, a community credit fund, and a project to build a well. All the households in the village now have latrines, water supplies have been expanded and upgraded, diets and incomes have improved, and the prevailing attitude about women's participation in development activity is more positive (172).

Women are also active in addressing environmental pollution that endangers health. In the Comas District in Lima, Peru, most residents are extremely poor and lack access to health care, education, and employment. In January 1991, a cholera epidemic broke out that could have been devastating. Garbage had accumulated in many areas, attracting large rodents and insects; latrines were poorly maintained; and water was often stored under unsanitary conditions. More than half the residents did not have potable water or adequate sewage.

In response, a Peruvian NGO obtained commitments from 200 women coordinators and approximately 1,500 mothers on its grassroots committees to start a public clean-up campaign. They removed the garbage, fumigated 5,000 centers where milk was prepared and distributed, and cleaned 3,000 latrines. Notices about the epidemic were placed in public places, and 10,000 pamphlets were distributed describing how to prevent the disease from spreading. Another NGO supported

Box 3.2 Global Goals for the 1990s

Many multilateral organizations, including most United Nations agencies and other influential independent groups, have tried to synthesize the many issues dealing with women and development into lists of recommended national and international actions. Excerpts from two such lists are presented here. The first was developed by the United Nations Population Fund and published as part of *Investing in Women: The Focus of the '90s* (1). The recommendations are directed primarily at governments but also at international and nongovernmental organizations. They specify the need to:

1. Document and publicize women's vital contribution to development.

■ Ensure that national statistics—on employment, mortality, morbidity, etc.—are disaggregated by sex;
■ Investigate and quantify the unpaid work of women as well as their work in the informal sector;
■ Assign an economic value to women's unpaid work;
■ Ensure timely and regular availability of socioeconomic indicators on women; and
■ Provide the widest possible audience with accurate and full information on women's productive and reproductive responsibilities.

2. Increase women's productivity and remove barriers to productive resources.

■ Repeal all laws and practices preventing or restricting women from owning and administering productive resources;
■ Recognize that women's access to technology and training has to be guaranteed in all aspects of the economy, not only in those occupations and tasks traditionally perceived as women's domain;
■ Ensure that women have access to credit without collateral and improved access to markets in the agricultural and informal sectors;
■ Establish and enforce laws of equal pay for work of equal value; and
■ Emphasize measures to relieve women's workload—including improved domestic technology and family planning services.

3. Provide family planning.

■ Provide high-quality services and a wide variety of family-planning methods;
■ Provide appropriate and special family-planning information and services for those who are often excluded, including men, teenagers, unmarried, and newly married women;

■ Ensure that women are consulted and involved at every level in the organization of family-planning services;
■ Ensure that prevention and treatment of infertility, and counseling on AIDS, is an effective part of family-planning services; and
■ Improve the quality of contraceptive care and ensure that services are user friendly and client oriented.

4. Improve the health of women.

■ Train traditional birth attendants in hygiene, in promoting the benefits of birth spacing, and in ensuring that "at risk" births take place in a clinic setting;
■ Concentrate interventions . . . on women who have lost two babies;
■ Provide supplementary food for malnourished mothers—especially teenage mothers—to reduce the incidence of low-birth-weight babies to fewer than 10 percent of live births by the year 2000;
■ Monitor nutrition of preschool children—with separate norms for boys and girls—and ensure that at least 90 percent of children have a weight for age corresponding to international . . . norms;
■ Educate parents about the need to care for their daughters equally with their sons; and
■ Train women to assume supervisory and decisionmaking roles in the health sector.

5. Expand education.

■ Expand girls' enrollment in school and their retention in the school system by active recruitment, counseling of dropouts, and reducing school fees if necessary;
■ Halt the practice of expelling pregnant teenagers from school and encourage them to continue their education before and after the birth;
■ Include sex education, family planning, and family responsibility in school curricula for children before they reach the age of first sexual experience; and
■ Encourage both girls and boys to study the whole range of subjects.

6. Establish equality of opportunity.

■ Ratify and implement the International Convention on the Elimination of all Forms of Discrimination against Women;
■ Review the legal system to remove barriers to women's full participation in society and the family on an equal basis with men, and eliminate the legal basis for discrimination;
■ Educate both men and women at all levels, starting in the school system, to accept the principle that women and men are equal in value and have equal rights in society and the family; and

■ Promote women's access to decision-making and leadership positions in government and the private sector, and ensure women's involvement in the design and implementation of policies and programs affecting women.

One of the important products of the 1992 United Nations Conference on Environment and Development was Agenda 21, an ambitious outline of actions necessary to sustainable development. Article 24 is devoted to the role and advancement of women in this process. Most of the recommendations are directed at national governments. For example, the signers agree that governments should:

■ Increase the proportion of women decisionmakers, planners, technical advisers, managers, and extension workers in environment and development fields;
■ Increase educational and training opportunities for women in science, technology and management of the environment;
■ Promote the provision of environmentally sound technologies that have been designed, developed, and improved in consultation with women;
■ Take urgent measures to avert the ongoing rapid environmental and economic degradation in developing countries that generally affects the lives of women and children; and
■ Develop gender-sensitive databases and encourage research on issues such as the impact on women of structural adjustment programs and environmental degradation, and the links between gender relations, environment, and development.

A few of the recommendations are directed at international organizations. For example, Article 24 urges the United Nations secretary general to review the entire United Nations system to see how environment and development programs and women's participation could be strengthened. It also urges the United Nations Fund for Women to establish regular consultations with donors in collaboration with the United Nations Children's Fund, and the United Nations Development Programme to establish a women's "focal point" on development and environment in each of its offices (2).

References and Notes

1. Nafis Sadik, *Investing in Women: The Focus of the '90s* (United Nations Population Fund, New York, 1990), pp. 30–31.
2. United Nations (U.N.) Environment Programme, *Agenda 21: The United Nations Programme of Action from Rio* (U.N., New York, 1993), Art. 24.

the effort by giving weekly training on hygiene and environmental sanitation to 100 women coordinators. Several Northern NGOs provided a total of about $20,000 to support the project. As a result of all these efforts, the epidemic was contained. Today an intense campaign is being waged to educate residents about environmental sanitation and waste management (173).

Many useful initiatives are inexpensive. In many parts of rural Indonesia, for example, sewage pollutes water and spreads disease. To help combat the problem, a group of women launched a community awareness program that included a radio broadcast about sanitation and health. This attracted a large listening audience among farm women in south Sumatra. Many used the information to install latrines or to improve the quality of drinking water, which led to a reduction in waterborne disease. A total of $270 had been spent by November 1991 on this project (174).

CONCLUSION

Traditional market-oriented development policies that have failed to consider equity, the environment, human development, and women's roles in society are believed by a growing number of experts to have contributed to poverty, an increase in economic and gender inequities, and environmental degradation. Such policies, by often overlooking or even undermining women's well-being and participation in their communities, have not only hurt women but also hindered the achievement of broad sustainable development goals.

Sustainable development makes paramount human interest and values and recognizes the complex links between the well-being of individuals, families, communities, and ecosystems on the one hand, and the health and prosperity of nations on the other. Sustainable development is a dynamic, interactive process grounded in participation, local strength, and equity. Achieving sustainable development means opening up to fresh views about women and about nature. It also means setting goals. (See Box 3.2.)

In an era of growing consciousness about the fragility of the Earth and all its inhabitants, internationalists must ask: Who is development for, and who should be designing new development strategies? What are reasonable objectives, and what processes will ensure that those objectives are sensibly met? If women in subsistence economies are the major suppliers of food, fuel, and water for their families, why is their access to resources declining? If those same women are valuable food producers, if they are versed in biological diversity, and if in many cases they have a greater impact than men on health, nutrition, and fertility rates—why are they still denied full partnership in development? Such issues of equity and justice must be addressed so that universal sustainable development goals—poverty alleviation, protected ecosystems, a balance between human activity and environmental resources—can be achieved (175).

This chapter was written by Ann Thrupp of WRI's Center for International Development and Environment; Elayne Clift, a freelance writer based in Washington, D.C.; and Deborah Estes of the World Resources *staff. Contributions were also made by Robert Livernash of the* World Resources *staff.*

References and Notes

1. Ester Boserup, *Woman's Role in Economic Development* (Earthscan, London, 1989), p. 1.
2. Caroline O.N. Moser, *Gender Planning and Development: Theory, Practice and Training* (Routledge, London, 1993), p. 2.
3. Elayne Clift and Farah Ebrahimi, "Overview," *A.I.D. Evaluation News: Focus on Women in Development*, Vol. 3, No. 3 (1991), pp. l–2.
4. United Nations (U.N.), *Forward Looking Strategies for the Advancement of Women*, Report of the World Conference to Review and Appraise the Achievements of the U.N. Decade for Women: Equality, Development and Peace (U.N., New York, 1986).
5. United Nations (U.N.), *World Plan of Action for the Implementation of the Objectives of the [International Women's Year] IWY*, Report of the World Conference of the IWY (U.N., New York, 1976).
6. United Nations (U.N.), *World Program of Action for the Implementation of the Objectives of the U.N. Decade for Women*, Report of the U.N. World Conference of the U.N. Decade for Women (U.N., New York, 1980).
7. Irene Tinker and Jane Jaquette, "U.N. Decade for Women: Its Impact and Legacy," *World Development*, Vol. 15, No. 3 (1987), pp. 419 and 422.
8. "Women's Perspectives on the Environment: Recommendations of the Global Assembly," in *Proceedings of the Global Assembly of Women and the Environment: "Partners in Life,"* Vol. 1, Joan Martin-Brown and Waafas Ofosu-Amaah, eds. (United Nations Environment Programme and WorldWIDE Network, Washington, D.C., 1992), p. 123.
9. The United Nations (U.N.) Statistical Office defines economic activity as that which contributes to the economy and includes paid work and some unpaid work, such as subsistence agricultural labor. It highlights the difficulty of fully counting this work, particularly rural women's contributions, because of interviewer biases and local variations in work-time definition. See U.N., *The World's Women, 1970–90: Trends and Statistics*, Social Statistics and Indicators Series K, No. 8 (U.N., New York, 1991), pp. 84–85.
10. Women and Development Unit, United Nations Economic Commission for Latin America and the Caribbean (ECLAC), *Major Changes and Crisis: The Impact on Women in Latin America and the Caribbean* (ECLAC, Santiago, Chile, 1992), pp. 159–160.
11. *Op. cit.* 9.
12. *Op. cit.* 9, p. 92.
13. *Op. cit.* 9, Table 6.16B.
14. Marguerite Berger, "Giving Women Credit: The Strengths and Limitations of Credit as a Tool for Alleviating Poverty," *World Development*, Vol. 17, No. 7 (1989), p. 1025.
15. *Op. cit.* 9, p. 91.
16. *Op. cit.* 10, p. 102.
17. Lynn Bennett, "Women, Poverty and Productivity in India," World Bank Economic Development Institute Seminar Paper No. 43, The World Bank, Washington, D.C., 1992, pp. 22–23.
18. *Op. cit.* 9, Table 6.17.
19. Ruth Leger Sivard, *Women: A World Survey* (World Priorities, Washington, D.C., 1985), p. 5.
20. *Op. cit.* 9, pp. 90–91.
21. Sheila Lewenhak, *The Revaluation of Women's Work* (Earthscan, London, 1992), pp. 83–89.
22. Ruth Dixon-Mueller, *Women's Work in Third World Agriculture: Concepts and Indicators*, Women, Work and Development Series No. 9 (International Labor Office, Geneva, 1985), p. v.
23. Jean Davison, "Land and Women's Agricultural Production: The Context," in *Agriculture, Women and Land: The African Experience*, Jean Davison, ed. (Westview, Boulder, Colorado, 1988), pp. 1–2.
24. Food and Agriculture Organization of the United Nations (FAO), "The Need for Improved Agricultural Extension Services for Women Engaged in Agriculture," Expert Consultation on Women in Food Production (FAO, Rome, 1983), p. 2.
25. Food and Agriculture Organization of the United Nations (FAO), "The Role of

Women in Agricultural Production," Expert Consultation on Women in Food Production (FAO, Rome, 1983), n.p.

26. Mayra Buvinic and Sally W. Yudelman, *Women, Poverty and Progress in the Third World*, Headline Series No. 289 (Foreign Policy Association, New York, 1989), p. 22.

27. *Op. cit.* 1, pp. 16–17.

28. Annabel Rhodda, *Women and the Environment* (Zed, London, 1991), p. 59.

29. *Op. cit.* 24, p. 3.

30. Dianne E. Rocheleau, "Whose Common Future? A Land-User Approach to Gendered Rights and Responsibilities in Rural Landscapes," paper prepared for the Workshop on Gender and Environment, Swedish International Development Authority/World Conservation Union, Stockholm, October 1991.

31. Jodi Jacobson, "Closing the Gender Gap in Development," in *State of the World, 1993: A Worldwatch Institute Report on Progress toward a Sustainable Society*, Linda Starke, ed. (W.W. Norton, New York, 1993), p. 68.

32. Bina Agarwal, *Cold Hearths and Barren Slopes: The Woodfuel Crisis in the Third World* (The Riverdale Company/Institute of Economic Growth, Riverdale, Maryland, 1986), n.p.

33. Theresa Aloo, "Forestry and the Untrained Kenyan Woman," in *Women and the Environmental Crisis: A Report of the Proceedings of the Workshops on Women, Environment and Development*, Dorothy K. Munyakho, ed. (Environment Liaison Centre, Nairobi, Kenya, 1985), p. 26.

34. Irene Dankelman and Joan Davidson, *Women and Environment in the Third World: Alliance for the Future* (Earthscan/International Union for Conservation of Nature and Natural Resources, London, 1989), p. 43.

35. Food and Agriculture Organization of the United Nations and Swedish International Development Authority (FAO/SIDA), *Restoring the Balance: Women and Forest Resources* (FAO/SIDA, Rome, 1991), p. 6.

36. *Op. cit.* 21, p. 147.

37. *Op. cit.* 32, Table 1.

38. *Op. cit.* 35.

39. Barbara Herz, K. Subbarao, Masooma Habib, *et al.*, "Letting Girls Learn: Promising Approaches in Primary and Secondary Education," World Bank Discussion Paper No. 133, The World Bank, Washington, D.C., 1991, p. 32.

40. *Op. cit.* 35, pp. 3–5 and 8–13.

41. Paula J. Williams, "Women, Children, and Forest Resources in Africa: Case Studies and Issues," paper presented at the Symposium on the Impact of Environmental Degradation and Poverty on Women and Children, United Nations Conference on Environment and Development, Geneva, May 1991.

42. *Op. cit.* 28, p. 51.

43. Carol Ireson, "Women's Forest Work in Laos," *Society and Natural Resources*, Vol. 4, No. 1 (1991), p. 30.

44. *Op. cit.* 30.

45. *Op. cit.* 41.

46. *Op. cit.* 35, p. 5.

47. Dianne E. Rocheleau, "Gender, Ecology and the Science of Survival: Stories and Lessons from Kenya," *Agriculture and Human Values* (Winter–Spring 1991), p. 160.

48. *Op. cit.* 35, n.p.

49. *Op. cit.* 41.

50. *Op. cit.* 34, pp. 46 and 57–65.

51. Women and the International Drinking Water Supply and Sanitation Decade (IDWSSD), (The Inter-Agency Task Force on Women and the IDWSSD/United Nations International Research and Training Insti-

tute for the Advancement of Women/United Nations Children's Fund, Santo Domingo, Dominican Republic, 1990), pp. 6–7.

52. *Op. cit.* 21, pp. 52 and 55–58.

53. Vandana Shiva, "Where Has All the Water Gone? The Case of Water and Feminism in India," in *Women and the Environmental Crisis: A Report of the Proceedings of the Workshops on Women, Environment and Development* (Environment Liaison Centre, Nairobi, Kenya, 1985), p. 61.

54. *Op. cit.* 51, pp. 8–9.

55. Christine Ansell, quoted in Van Wijk-Sybesma, *Participation of Women in Water Supply and Sanitation: Roles and Realities* (International Reference Centre for Community Water Supply and Sanitation, The Hague, 1985, n.p.), cited in Annabel Rhodda, *Women and the Environment* (Zed, London, 1991), p. 54.

56. *Op. cit.* 21, p. 53.

57. United Nations (U.N.), *Women: Challenge for the Year 2000* (U.N., New York, 1991), p. 16.

58. Lowell S. Levin, Alfred H. Katz, and Eric Holst, *Self-Care: Lay Initiatives in Health* (Prodist, New York, 1979), cited in Francine Coeytaux, *The Role of the Family in Health: Appropriate Research Methods* (World Health Organization, Geneva, 1984), p. 2.

59. Lucie S. Kelly, "Women's Special Heritage: Creating an Enlarged Vision of Society," in *Women in Health and Development: Report of the International Seminar at the Aga Khan University*, Khaula Y. Qureshi and Asma F. Qureshi, eds. (United Nations Children's Fund/Norwegian Agency for Development Cooperation, Karachi, Pakistan, 1990), p. 16.

60. Janis Alcorn, *Huastec Mayan Ethnobotany* (University of Texas Press, Austin, 1984), n.p.

61. *Op. cit.* 59.

62. Joanne Leslie and Geeta Rao Gupta, *Utilization of Services for Maternal Nutrition and Health Care* (International Center for Research on Women, Washington, D.C., 1989), cited in Judith Timyan, Susan J. Griffey Brechin, Diana M. Measham, *et al.*, "Access to Care: More Than a Problem of Distance," in *The Health of Women: A Global Perspective*, Marge Koblinsky, Judith Timyan, and Jill Gay, eds. (Westview Press, Boulder, Colorado, 1993), p. 221.

63. Idriss Jazairy, Mohiuddin Alamgir, and Theresa Panuccio, *The State of World Rural Poverty: An Inquiry into Its Causes and Consequences* (International Fund for Agricultural Development/New York University Press, New York, 1992), p. 273.

64. *Op. cit.* 26, p. 9.

65. Jonathan Power, *The Report on Rural Women Living in Poverty* (International Fund for Agricultural Development, Geneva, 1992), p. 13.

66. John Ward Anderson and Molly Moore, "Born Oppressed: Women in the Developing World Face Cradle-to-Grave Discrimination, Poverty," *Washington Post* (February 14, 1993), p. 48, sec. A.

67. Meera Chatterjee, "Indian Women: Their Health and Economic Productivity," World Bank Discussion Paper No. 109, The World Bank, Washington, D.C., 1990, pp. vii–x.

68. Jodi L. Jacobson, "Women's Health: The Price of Poverty," in *The Health of Women: A Global Perspective*, Marge Koblinsky, Judith Timyan, and Jill Gay, eds. (Westview Press, Boulder, Colorado, 1993), p. 19.

69. Nafis Sadik, *Investing in Women: The Focus of the 90s*, (United Nations Fund for Population Activities, New York, 1990), p. 6.

70. *Op. cit.* 67, pp. 68–69.

71. Judy Ell-Bushra and Eugenia Piza Lopez, "Gender-Related Violence: Its Scope and

Relevance," *Focus on Gender*, Vol. l, No. 2 (1993), pp. 3–4.

72. *Op. cit.* 57, p. 22.

73. *Op. cit.* 66.

74. *Op. cit.* 26, p. 9.

75. *Op. cit.* 63, p. 273.

76. *Op. cit.* 9, pp. 4–5.

77. *Op. cit.* 26, p. 20.

78. *Op. cit.* 9, p. 95.

79. United Nations Children's Fund (UNICEF), Government of Pakistan, *Situation Analysis of Children and Women in Pakistan* (UNICEF, Islamabad, Pakistan, 1992), p. 95.

80. Irene Tinker, "Feminizing Development for Growth with Equity," paper presented at Global Objectives Conference at University of California, Davis, March–April l990.

81. *Op. cit.* 9, p. 2.

82. Comba Marenah, "Producing Food: The Gambian Woman's Burden," in *Women and the Environmental Crisis: A Report of the Proceedings of the Workshops on Women, Environment and Development* (Environment Liaison Centre, Nairobi, Kenya, 1985), p. 56.

83. Gita Sen and Caren Grown, *Development, Crises, and Alternative Visions: Third World Women's Perspectives* (Monthly Review Press, New York, 1987), p. 44.

84. Rae Lesser Blumberg, *Making the Case for the Gender Variable: Women and the Wealth and Well-Being of Nations*, Women in Development Technical Reports in Gender and Development No. 1 (U.S. Agency for International Development, Washington, D.C., 1989), pp. 15–18.

85. Christine Jones, "The Impact of the SEMRY I Irrigated Rice Production Project on the Organization of Production and Consumption at the Intrahousehold Level" (U.S. Agency for International Development, Washington, D.C., 1983), cited in Rae Lesser Blumberg, *Making the Case for the Gender Variable: Women and the Wealth and Well-Being of Nations*, Women in Development Technical Reports in Gender and Development No. 1 (U.S. Agency for International Development, Washington, D.C., 1989), pp. 16–17.

86. Jennie Dey, "Development Planning in the Gambia: The Gap between Planners' and Farmers' Perceptions, Expectations, and Objectives," *World Development*, Vol. 10, No. 5 (1982), pp. 377–396, cited in Rae Lesser Blumberg, *Making the Case for the Gender Variable: Women and the Wealth and Well-Being of Nations*, Women in Development Technical Reports in Gender and Development No. 1 (U.S. Agency for International Development, Washington, D.C., 1989), pp. 16–17.

87. Alice Stewart Carloni, *Women in Development: AID's Experience, 1973–85*, Vol. 1 Synthesis Paper, Program Evaluation Report No. 18 (U.S. Agency for International Development, Washington, D.C., 1987), cited in Rae Lesser Blumberg, *Making the Case for the Gender Variable: Women and the Wealth and Well-Being of Nations*, Women in Development Technical Reports in Gender and Development No. 1 (U.S. Agency for International Development, Washington, D.C., 1989), pp. 16–17.

88. *Op. cit.* 84, p. 96.

89. Food and Agriculture Organization of the United Nations (FAO), *Agricultural Extension and Farm Women in the 1980s* (FAO, Rome, 1993), p. 41.

90. Kevin Cleaver and Götz Schreiber, *The Population, Agriculture and Environment Nexus in Sub-Saharan Africa*, Agriculture and Rural Development Series No. 1 (The World Bank, Washington, D.C., 1992), p. 56.

91. *Ibid.*

92. G. Scott and M. Carr, "The Impact of Technology Choices on Rural Women in Bangladesh," staff working paper, The World

Bank, Washington, D.C., 1985, cited in Marilyn Carr and Ruby Sandhu, *Women, Technology, and Rural Productivity*, United Nations (U.N.) Fund for Women Occasional Paper No. 6 (U.N., New York, 1987), p. 41.

93. Selina Adjebeng-Asem, "Grating without Drudgery," *Appropriate Technology*, Vol. 16, No. 3 (1989), pp. 18–20.

94. *Op. cit.* 55, p. 102.

95. Caroline O.N. Moser, "Gender Planning in the Third World: Meeting Practical and Strategic Gender Needs," *World Development*, Vol. 17, No. 11 (1989), p. 1812.

96. Mayra Buvinic, "Projects for Women in the Third World: Explaining Their Misbehavior," *World Development*, Vol. 14, No. 5 (1986), p. 655.

97. Augusta Molnar and Götz Schreiber, "Women and Forestry: Operational Issues," Women in Development Working Paper No. 184, The World Bank, Washington, D.C., 1989, Box 2.

98. *Op. cit.* 9, p. 88.

99. *Op. cit.* 9, pp. 22–23.

100. *Op. cit.* 1, pp. 78–79.

101. *Op. cit.* 9, p. 81.

102. M. Anne Hill and Elizabeth M. King, "Women's Education in the Third World: An Overview," in "Women's Education in Developing Countries: Barriers, Benefits and Policy," Elizabeth M. King and M. Anne Hill, eds., Population and Human Resources, Education and Employment Background Paper No. 40, The World Bank, Washington, D.C., 1991, p. 1.

103. *Op. cit.* 9, pp. 45–48.

104. *Op. cit.* 57, p. 28.

105. United Nations Educational, Scientific and Cultural Organization (UNESCO), *Compendium of Statistics on Illiteracy, 1990*, No. 31 (UNESCO, Paris, 1990), Table 2.

106. *Op. cit.* 39, Figure 1.2.

107. *Op. cit.* 9, pp. 45–48.

108. *Op. cit.* 80.

109. Kathleen M. Merchant and Kathleen M. Kurz, "Women's Nutrition through the Life Cycle: Social and Biological Vulnerabilities," in *The Health of Women: A Global Perspective*, Marge Koblinsky, Judith Timyan, and Jill Gay, eds. (Westview Press, Boulder, Colorado, 1993), p. 64.

110. World Health Organization (WHO), *World Health Statistics Quarterly*, No. 38 (WHO, Geneva, 1985), cited in United Nations (U.N.), *The World's Women 1970–90: Trends and Statistics*, Social Statistics and Indicators Series K, No. 8 (U.N., New York, 1991), Table 4.6.

111. *Op. cit.* 67, p. 18.

112. *Op. cit.* 69, p. 19.

113. F.T. Sai and J. Nassim, "The Need for a Reproductive Health Approach," *International Journal of Gynecology and Obstetrics*, Supplement 3: *Women's Health in the Third World: The Impact of Unwanted Pregnancy* (1989), pp. 103–113, cited in Andrea Eschen and Maxine Whittaker, "Family Planning: A Base to Build on for Women's Reproductive Health Services," in *The Health of Women: A Global Perspective*, Marge Koblinsky, Judith Timyan, and Jill Gay, eds. (Westview Press, Boulder, Colorado, 1993), p. 105.

114. *Op. cit.* 67, p. 53.

115. Nafis Sadik, *The State of World Population, 1990* (United Nations Fund for Population Activities, New York, 1990), pp. 14–17.

116. *Op. cit.* 69, p. 4.

117. *Op. cit.* 69, p. 4.

118. *Op. cit.* 69, pp. 5–6.

119. *Op. cit.* 28, p. 68.

120. Andrea Eschen and Maxine Whittaker, "Family Planning: A Base to Build on for Women's Reproductive Health Services," in *The Health of Women: A Global Perspective*, Marge Koblinsky, Judith Timyan, and Jill Gay, eds. (Westview Press, Boulder, Colorado, 1993), pp. 105–106.

121. Frank Odile and Geoffry McNicoll, "An Interpretation of Fertility and Population Policy in Kenya," *Population and Development Review*, Vol. 13, No. 2 (1987), pp. 221–226.

122. United Nations Population Fund (UNFPA), *The State of World Population 1993* (UNFPA, New York, 1993), p. 39.

123. *Op. cit.* 69, p. 19.

124. Dianne E. Rocheleau, "Women, Trees and Tenure: Implications for Agroforestry," in *Whose Trees? Proprietary Dimensions of Forestry*, Louise Fortmann and John W. Bruce, eds. (Westview Press, Boulder, Colorado, 1988), pp. 255–256 and 258–259.

125. *Op. cit.* 65, p. 35.

126. *Op. cit.* 124, pp. 263.

127. United Nations (U.N.) Center for Social Development and Humanitarian Affairs, *1989 World Survey on the Role of Women in Development* (U.N., New York, 1989), p. 104, cited in Margaret Snyder, *The Key to Ending Hunger*, The Hunger Project Paper No. 8 (The Hunger Project, New York, 1990), p. 14.

128. *Op. cit.* 35, p. 21.

129. *Op. cit.* 32, pp. 15–16.

130. *Op. cit.* 34, p. 69.

131. Erik P. Eckholm, "The Other Energy Crisis," WorldWatch Institute Paper No. 1, WorldWatch Institute, Washington, D.C., 1975, p. 7, cited in Bina Agarwal, *Cold Hearths and Barren Slopes: The Woodfuel Crisis in the Third World* (The Riverdale Company, Riverdale, Maryland, 1986), p. 21.

132. Turi Hammer Digerness, "Wood for Fuel: The Energy Situation in Bara, The Sudan," University of Bergen Department of Geography paper, Bergen, Norway, 1977, cited in Bina Agarwal, *Cold Hearths and Barren Slopes: The Woodfuel Crisis in the Third World* (The Riverdale Company, Riverdale, Maryland, 1986), p. 21.

133. Eric Eckholm, Gerald Foley, Geoffrey Barnard, *et al.*, *Fuelwood: The Energy Crisis That Won't Go Away* (Earthscan/International Institute for Environment and Development, London, 1984), p. 15.

134. *Op. cit.* 32, pp. 21–26.

135. *Op. cit.* 34, p. 32.

136. *Op. cit.* 28, pp. 51–52.

137. *Op. cit.* 9, pp. 31–32.

138. Madelyn Blair, President, Pelerei Inc., Jefferson, Maryland, 1993 (personal communication).

139. *Op. cit.* 102, pp. 17–19.

140. *Op. cit.* 39, pp. 17–19.

141. Lawrence Summers, "The Most Influential Investment," *People and the Planet*, Vol. 2, No. 1 (1993), p. 10.

142. *Op. cit.* 69, p. 5.

143. *Op. cit.* 39, pp. 19–21.

144. The World Bank, *World Development Report, 1993: Investing in Health* (Oxford University Press, New York, 1993), pp. 42–43.

145. *Op. cit.* 67, p. 53.

146. *Op. cit.* 144, p. 42.

147. *Op. cit.* 39, pp. 20–21.

148. Margaret Snyder, *Women: The Key to Ending Hunger*, Hunger Project Paper No. 8 (The Hunger Project, New York, 1990), p. 15.

149. *Op. cit.* 28, p. 104.

150. *Op. cit.* 84, pp. 8–9.

151. Mayra Buvinic and Margaret Lycette, "Women, Poverty and Development in the Third World," in *Strengthening the Poor: What Have We Learned?*, John P. Lewis, ed. (Overseas Development Council and Transaction Books, Washington, D.C., 1988), pp. 153–154.

152. *Op. cit.* 144, p. 41.

153. *Op. cit.* 84, pp. 8–10.

154. *Op. cit.* 151.

155. *Op. cit.* 67, p. 57.

156. Ela Bhatt, "Toward Empowerment," *World Development*, Vol. 17, No. 7 (1989), pp. 1059–1065.

157. Daniel F. Cuff, "Helping Women Abroad Get Started in Business," *New York Times* (November 13, 1990), p. 5, sec. D.

158. *Op. cit.* 21, pp. 106–107.

159. Peter Moock, "The Efficiency of Women as Farm Managers: Kenya," *American Journal of Agricultural Economics*, Vol. 58 (December 1976), p. 833, cited in Rae Lesser Blumberg, *Making the Case for the Gender Variable: Women and the Wealth and Well-Being of Nations*, Women in Development Technical Reports in Gender and Development No. 1 (U.S. Agency for International Development, Washington, D.C., 1989), pp. 25–26.

160. Jeanne K. Henn, "Intra-Household Dynamics and State Policies as Constraints on Food Production: Results of a 1985 Agroeconomic Survey in Cameroon," in *Gender Issues in Farming Systems Research and Extension*, Susan V. Poats, Marianne Schmink, and Anita Spring, eds. (Westview Press, Boulder, Colorado, 1988), pp. 315 and 328.

161. Marilyn Carr and Ruby Sandhu, *Women, Technology, and Rural Productivity*, United Nations (U.N.) Fund for Women Occasional Paper No. 6, (U.N., New York, 1987), p. 48.

162. *Op. cit.* 148, pp. 7–8.

163. *Op. cit.* 83, pp. 89–96.

164. Joan Martin-Brown and Waafas Ofosu-Amaah, eds., *Proceedings of the Global Assembly of Women and the Environment: "Partners in Life,"* Vol. 1 (United Nations Environment Programme and WorldWIDE Network, Washington, D.C., 1992), n.p.

165. Vasantha Kannabiran, "Deccan Development Society of India," in *Proceedings of the Global Assembly of Women and the Environment: "Partners in Life,"* Vol. 2, Waafas Ofosu-Amaah and Wendy Philleo, eds. (United Nations Environment Programme and WorldWIDE Network, Washington, D.C., 1992), p. 116.

166. Charity Kabutha, "Erosion Control in Katheka, Kenya," in *Proceedings of the Global Assembly of Women and the Environment: "Partners in Life,"* Vol. 2, Waafas Ofosu-Amaah and Wendy Philleo, eds. (United Nations Environment Programme and WorldWIDE Network, Washington, D.C., 1992), p. 43.

167. Gema Zendejas Huerta, "Women Fight against the Erosion of the Land in Mexico," in *Proceedings of the Global Assembly of Women and the Environment: "Partners in Life,"* Vol. 2, Waafas Ofosu-Amaah and Wendy Philleo, eds. (United Nations Environment Programme and WorldWIDE Network, Washington, D.C., 1992), p. 204.

168. Bonnake Tsimako, "Thusano Lefatsheng Promotes Sustainable Harvest of Veld Products, Botswana," in *Proceedings of the Global Assembly of Women and the Environment: "Partners in Life,"* Vol. 2, Waafas Ofosu-Amaah and Wendy Philleo, eds. (United Nations Environment Programme and WorldWIDE Network, Washington, D.C., 1992), p. 53.

169. Benedicta Kamboe, "Tono-Vea Agroforestry Project in Ghana Checks Desertification," in *Proceedings of the Global Assembly of Women and the Environment: "Partners in Life,"* Vol. 2, Waafas Ofosu-Amaah and Wendy Philleo, eds. (United Nations Environment Programme and WorldWIDE Network, Washington, D.C., 1992), p. 61.

170. Sophia W. Kiarie, "Green Islands Program in Ruiru, Kenya," in *Proceedings of the Global Assembly of Women and the Environment: "Partners in Life,"* Vol. 2, Waafas Ofosu-

Amaah and Wendy Philleo, eds. (United Nations Environment Programme and World-WIDE Network, Washington, D.C., 1992), p. 62.

171. Carmen Bustillo Turcios, "Women's Group in Tripoli, Honduras, Addresses Watershed Degradation Related to Deforestation," in *Proceedings of the Global Assembly of Women and the Environment: "Partners in Life,"* Vol. 2, Waafas Ofosu-Amaah and Wendy Philleo, eds. (United Nations Environment Programme and WorldWIDE Network, Washington, D.C., 1992), p. 226.

172. Daranee Wenuchan, "Girl Guide Association of Thailand's Water and Sanitation Program in Ban Bok Village," in *Proceedings of the Global Assembly on Women and the Environment: "Partners in Life,"* Vol. 2, Waafas Ofosu-Amaah and Wendy Philleo, eds. (United Nations Environment Programme and WorldWIDE Network, Washington, D.C., 1992), p. 152.

173. Rosa Arteaga Sato, "Peruvian Women Plan Sanitary Education against Cholera Epidemic in Comas District," in *Proceedings of the Global Assembly of Women and the Environment: "Partners in Life,"* Vol. 2, Waafas Ofosu-Amaah and Wendy Philleo, eds. (United Nations Environment Programme and WorldWIDE Network, Washington, D.C., 1992), p. 213.

174. Fitri Aini, "Radio Show Spreads the Word about Water, Health, and Sanitation to Thousands in Indonesia," in *Proceedings of the Global Assembly on Women and the Environment: "Partners in Life,"* Vol. 2, Waafas Ofosu-Amaah and Wendy Philleo, eds. (United Nations Environment Programme and WorldWIDE Network, Washington, D.C., 1992), p. 138.

175. *Op. cit.* 31, p. 76.

4. China

In a nation so vast and populous as China, environmental successes and failures have international repercussions. For example, the nation's reliance on coal to meet future domestic electricity demand has implications for any international effort to cut fossil fuel emissions in the hope of reducing the risk of global warming. And efforts to phase out ozone-depleting chlorofluorocarbons (CFCs) in industrialized countries could be partially offset by the growing Chinese refrigerator industry.

Along with a large and expanding population, China's remarkable record of economic growth explains its potential to affect the global environment as well as ecosystems within its own borders.

The economic numbers—growth averaging 9.7 percent annually between the onset of economic reform in 1978 to 1988, almost 13 percent in 1992, and about 14 percent in the first five months of 1993—seem to understate the boom that is under way, especially in southeastern China (1) (2) (3) (4). Goods are abundant, and life for the average person is clearly better than it was two decades ago. By some measures, China now has one of the largest economies in the world.

The typical standard of living, however, is meager compared with that in many industrialized countries. And the pace of growth may not be maintained. By

mid-1993, some serious cracks were developing in China's economy, notably an increase in inflation to about 20 percent annually in big cities (5). Meanwhile, poverty remains a severe problem, especially in the more remote interior regions of the country.

More so than the economic numbers, the population numbers reflect Chinese reality. The population, 1.15 billion now, is heading for 1.3 billion by the year 2000 and 1.5 billion by 2020. If these figures are abstract, one need only witness the daily traffic jams in Beijing or the throngs in the old market of Shanghai to understand that population growth is a pressing concern for China's leaders. (See Box 4.1.)

The combination of these two factors—booming economic growth and a teeming population—is threatening China's environment and resources. Water supplies in the north are dwindling, while most of the nation's rivers, especially in urban areas, are seriously polluted. Particulates and sulfur dioxide foul the air of many cities and cause widespread health problems.

The Chinese government intends to increase spending on environmental protection from 45 billion *renminbi* (RMB) (0.67 percent of gross national product) in 1986–90 to a projected RMB 83 billion (0.85 percent of projected GNP) in 1991–95. (In mid-1993, U.S.$1 roughly equaled RMB 5.7. See Chapter 15, "Basic Eco-

Box 4.1 China's Population Future

The fate of China's environment may ultimately depend on the pace of population growth and China's ability to stabilize it.

The 1990 census put China's total population at 1.13 billion. With about 17 million people added every year, the population will increase to about 1.3 billion by the year 2000. If the total fertility rate remains at the 1990 level, the population will reach 2 billion by the year 2050 and continue to grow thereafter [1]. If the fertility rate falls slightly, the population could level off at about 1.5 billion by 2050 and then decline to 1.4 billion by 2100 [2]. (See Figure 1.)

China is making remarkable strides in reducing the growth rate. In the period from 1990 to 1995, the population is expected to increase at an average annual rate of 1.4 percent, substantially below the 2 percent average rate for developing countries as a whole. Whereas China now has 37 percent of Asia's population, by the year 2025 it is projected to have 31 percent of the total [3].

China's demographic face is changing in several significant ways. For example, the population is aging. The number of people 65 or older is expected to be 90 million in the year 2000 and 167 million by 2020, compared with the elderly population of 66 million in 1990 [4]. This change has many important economic implications, particularly as most rural elderly have no old-age pensions and must rely on adult children for support [5].

The population is also becoming more urban. Using a relatively conservative definition of urban population, the 1990 census estimated China's at 297 million, an increase of nearly 90 million since 1982. Beijing's population increased by 17 percent and Shanghai's by 13 percent during this period. The rate of natural increase was estimated at 8 percent in Beijing and 5 percent in Shanghai; the rest of the growth was due to in-migration, reflecting, in part, mounting population shifts following the economic reforms of the 1980s and the decollectivization of agriculture [6].

During the mid-1960s, agricultural collectives provided the funds for a new rural health system that included a network of more than 1 million trained paramedics, popularly known as barefoot doctors, plus town and county health clinics that placed a high priority on family planning and provided free contraceptive services. These new services, coupled with heightened political pressure to limit family size, led to a dramatic halving of the fertility rate in the 1970s [7].

During the 1980s, the family planning program changed substantially. When agricultural collectives were dismantled, the government had to establish a new system of family planning clinics at the town and county levels to replace the communal health system. It was then that the government began to promote the one-child family, providing financial rewards to couples who limited themselves to one child. The program was unpopular in rural areas, where the preference for sons was still strong and the shift to private farming motivated people to have more than one child. Minority populations have always been exempted from the program. The one-child campaign is still strictly implemented in urban areas, but the government, trying a different tack in its attempt to curb growth, is now putting more emphasis on elevating the status of women, providing old-age security, and improving family planning and maternal-child health services [8].

Figure 1 China's Population, 1950–2025

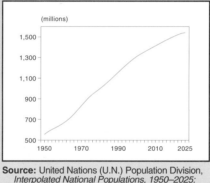

Source: United Nations (U.N.) Population Division, *Interpolated National Populations, 1950–2025: The 1992 Revision* (U.N., New York, 1993).

References and Notes

1. H. Yuan Tien, *et al.*, "China's Demographic Dilemmas," *Population Bulletin*, Vol. 47, No. 1 (1992), pp. 5 and 38–39.
2. United Nations, *Long-Range World Population Projections: Two Centuries of Population Growth, 1950–2150* (U.N., New York, 1992), p. 22.
3. United Nations (U.N.) Population Fund (UNFPA), *The State of World Population, 1993* (UNFPA, New York, 1993), pp. 2 and 48.
4. United Nations (U.N.) Population Division, *World Population Prospects, 1950–2025 (The 1992 Revision)*, on diskette (U.N., New York, 1993).
5. *Op. cit.* 1, p. 21.
6. *Op. cit.* 1, pp. 25–26.
7. Judith Banister, *China's Changing Population* (Stanford University Press, Stanford, California, 1987), pp. 61–62, 70–71, 169–170 and 353.
8. Shanti R. Conly and Sharon L. Camp, *China's Family Planning Program: Challenging the Myths* (The Population Crisis Committee, Washington, D.C., 1992), pp. 8–10 and 22–23.

nomic Indicators.") This amount may not be sufficient for, as the government itself estimates, spending needs to be at least 1.5 percent of GNP just to control current environmental degradation [6].

Despite talk of balancing environmental protection and development, Chinese policy is heavily tilted toward the latter; as the Chinese put it, one should not "give up eating for fear of choking" [7].

Efforts to tackle environmental problems have yielded some results, though scarce financial resources tend to make any solution only partial. Another constraint is the inefficient use of basic resources such as coal and water, which are heavily subsidized.

Much of China's environmental policy rests on the principle that the polluter pays. Rapid economic growth should enable the government to build on this, as should further efforts to remove resource subsidies and to decentralize decisionmaking authority by placing it in the hands of individual enterprises. No doubt enterprises faced with budget constraints and compelled to pay market prices for resources will find ways to avoid squandering them.

Will China's future policy be enough to absorb the impact of continued population growth and rapid economic expansion? A strengthened environmental partnership with industrialized nations and international institutions could make the difference between China's falling behind or moving ahead in this area.

THE POLITICAL AND ECONOMIC CONTEXT

It is difficult for most outside observers to comprehend the turbulence and pain of China's modern experience. In the first half of the 20th Century, the nation was devastated by a stream of civil war, famine, flooding, and foreign invasion that helps explain why China's elderly leaders are so steadfast in their efforts to maintain order and stability today [8].

Between 1959 and 1961, mismanagement, the turbulent aftermath of forced economic development under the Great Leap Forward, and natural catastrophes produced a famine that killed an estimated 30 million people—outside of World War II, no event in history has taken a greater toll on human life (9) (10). Today, flooding continues to plague the country to the tune of RMB 72.5 billion ($12.7 billion) in 1991 alone (11).

The Great Leap Forward was soon followed by the chaos of the Cultural Revolution, which lasted from 1966 to 1976 and wreaked havoc on the environment. In the 1960s, millions of hectares of forestland were converted to cropland to achieve Mao Zedong's goal of raising grain production (12). Widespread tree cutting exacerbated soil erosion and desertification, which devoured at least 4 million hectares of arable land between the 1950s and 1970s (13) (14).

China's approach to environmental issues began to change in the 1970s. In June 1972, a Chinese delegation attended the United Nations Conference on the Human Environment at Stockholm, where the severity of environmental problems in China became clear. In August 1973, the first National Environmental Protection Conference, held in Beijing, provided a forum for the development of China's policy in this area and led to the creation of environmental protection agencies at both the central and the local levels (15) (16). Mao's death in 1976 accelerated policy reassessment. For example, the state undertook a massive new tree planting campaign to help protect soil and cropland (17). In addition, awareness grew of the adverse health and environmental impacts of highly polluting industry.

In 1978, Deng Xiaoping further opened China to the outside world and began introducing market-oriented reforms into the nation's economy. Agricultural reforms were first undertaken in the populous provinces of Anhui and Sichuan. Between 1979 and 1984, communes were gradually disbanded and farmers leased land for periods of 15 to 25 years after agreeing to turn over a percentage of their output to the state. A 25 percent (average) real increase was set in relative agricultural prices. The combined effect of these and other reforms, such as rapid growth of inputs and the creation of local markets, was a quick boost in production and large cash savings. In 1984, with pressure mounting to channel the savings into new industry, local authorities were granted permission to create township and village enterprises. Backed by a strong commitment from local government, the enterprises flourished, producing light industrial and consumer goods previously overlooked by state-run manufacturers (18).

Though uneven, China's economic performance since the post-1978 reform period has been impressive. Productivity gains average 3 to 4 percent a year, the share of trade in GNP rose from 10 percent in 1978 to over 30 percent in 1990, consumption has more than doubled, and about 160 million people have been lifted out of poverty since 1979 (19).

Today, China's economic system is an unusual hybrid still undergoing rapid transition. (See Figure 4.1.) The nonstate sector, that is, the private and collective sectors combined, grew at an annual rate of about 26

Figure 4.1 China's Industrial Output by Sector, 1985–91

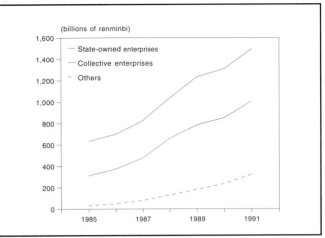

Source: State Statistical Bureau of the People's Republic of China, *China Statistical Yearbook, 1991* (China Statistical Information and Consultancy Service Center, Beijing, 1991), p. 353. Data for 1991 is from the Chinese-language edition of the 1992 yearbook.

percent between 1985 and 1990 and has increased its share of total industrial output from 22 percent in 1978 to 45 percent in 1990 (20)(21). The true private sector is small. Including joint ventures, it currently accounts for about 10 percent of industrial output, but that share is likely to grow to 25 percent by the end of the decade. The collective sector, a catch-all category that includes some private business as well as factories run by township governments, now produces about 35 percent of industrial output, a figure that should rise to nearly 50 percent by the end of the decade.

The trend toward decentralization, with the success it has generated, will no doubt extend into the future. The share of state-owned enterprises, currently 53 percent, is expected to shrink to about 27 percent by the end of the 1990s. Even with these changes, the government will continue to play a substantial role in managing the economy (22).

How does China currently make decisions about energy and environmental matters? As in many other industrialized nations, its decisionmaking structure is a behemoth embracing many different government institutions. (See Box 4.2.)

CHINA'S NATURAL ENDOWMENTS

While blessed with relatively abundant natural resources, China is cursed by their uneven distribution. Its territory is vast, like the United States, covering about 932 million hectares, or about 7 percent of the world's total land area. (See Chapter 17, "Land Cover and Settlements," Table 17.1.) About half of this area, especially in the northwest and the west, is either arid or semiarid (23). About 270 million hectares—29 percent of the country—consists of desert and rocky mountains (24). (See Figure 4.2.)

Cropland makes up about 96 million hectares, or 10 percent of China's total land area. The share of cropland per person is small, roughly 0.08 hectares, comparable to the per capita share in densely populated

Box 4.2 Decisionmaking in China

Decisionmaking in China is a convoluted process that traditionally works from the top down. The bureaucracy has many layers, beginning with 25 to 35 top leaders, various liaison leadership groups and staff, State Council commissions, ministries that implement national policy, and provincial governments and ministries. The Communist Party, of course, still exerts great influence (1).

Current economic reforms appear to be incorporating more autonomy into the decisionmaking process at the provincial level. This is especially the case in the fast-growing coastal and southern provinces.

The reforms of the past few decades now make consensus building a central feature of policymaking, which tends to be protracted, relatively loosely coordinated among agencies, and incremental (policies change only gradually). China is held together by the formal structure of authority, by the networks of hundreds of thousands of individuals bound by mutual obligation, loyalty, and by the total web of bargains among them (2).

External influences also affect Chinese decisionmaking. As part of China's effort to acquire modern technology and capital, Deng Xiaoping and his reformers expanded China's links with industrialized countries in the 1980s. Their modernization drive kindled concern about the industrialized world about environmental impacts. Donor agencies such as the World Bank insisted on environmental assessments in project evaluations, advanced industrial plants imported from abroad often included advanced pollution controls, and the government's efforts to bring product quality up to international standards included in many cases the adoption, in principle, of international standards for environmental protection as well (3).

Environmental Decisionmaking

As early as 1972, China prepared a statement on environmental policy for the United Nations Conference on the Human Environment held in Stockholm. That, in turn, led to the creation of an office that was a voice for environmental considerations in debates with production-oriented ministries. A decade later, that office became the National Environmental Protec-

tion Agency (NEPA), China's principal environmental organ (4).

Environmental issues affect many ministries, all of which need to be consulted and supportive if policies are to gather momentum. At the national level, the top consultative body is now the State Environmental Protection Commission (SEPC), which includes the heads of all relevant ministries and agencies. SEPC meets only quarterly and relies for administrative support on NEPA, which serves as its secretariat (5). Other commissions, notably the State Planning Commission (SPC) and the State Science and Technology Commission, have large full-time staffs and actively participate in the formulation of environmental policy. For example, the SPC played a lead role in preparing the report on environment and development for the United Nations Conference on Environment and Development in Rio de Janeiro in 1992 (6).

NEPA, which became an independent agency in 1988 but does not rank as a ministry, is responsible for all aspects of environmental policy and management. It shares authority with many other agencies, however. Marine environmental affairs are managed primarily by the State Oceanographic Administration and the Ministry of Agriculture and Fisheries. Conservation issues are handled in the main by resource agencies such as the Ministry of Forestry, the Ministry of Agriculture, and the Ministry of Water Resources. Energy issues are the province of the Ministry of Energy. The Ministry of Light Industry and the Ministry of Chemical Industry shoulder key responsibilities in the regulation of industrial pollution.

At the national level, staff and budgets are modest. NEPA's staff consists of about 300 people. This number is misleading, however, because many other institutions report to NEPA, among them the Chinese Research Academy of Environmental Sciences in Beijing, which conducts research on air and water pollution; the Nanjing Institute of Environmental Sciences, which concentrates on rural environmental issues; the South China Institute of Environmental Sciences in Guangzhou; the *China Environment News*, the official newspaper of NEPA; and the China Environmental Science Press, which edits and publishes

books on environmental protection (7). Other institutions not affiliated with NEPA, such as the Chinese Academy of Sciences, are also in the forefront of research on environmental and related health issues.

Below the national level, the environmental protection network includes 30 provincial, 366 municipal, and 2,084 county agencies. Provincial offices, responsible for the implementation of national policy, had about 8,000 staff by the end of 1990, in municipal offices nearly 24,000, and in county ones over 28,000. Nationwide, another 60,000 people were involved in environmental protection in industry and communications (8).

The basic law governing environmental issues is the Environmental Protection Law, first implemented in 1979 and amended in 1989. The 1989 version strengthened the enforcement authority of environmental protection bureaus by providing clear authority for on-site inspections and by requiring enterprises subject to them to cooperate. Many other laws cover more limited areas such as air or water pollution; a few areas such as solid and hazardous waste management are not yet regulated (9).

References and Notes

1. Kenneth Lieberthal and Michel Oksenberg, *Policy Making in China: Leaders, Structures, and Processes* (Princeton University Press, Princeton, New Jersey, 1988), pp. 21–24.
2. *Ibid.*, pp. 23–24 and 32.
3. Lester Ross, *Environmental Policy in China* (Indiana University Press, Bloomington and Indianapolis, 1988), pp. 204–206.
4. *Ibid.*, p. 204.
5. The World Bank, *China Environmental Strategy Paper* (The World Bank, Washington, D.C., 1992), p. 5.
6. *National Report of the People's Republic of China on Environment and Development* (China Environmental Science Press, Beijing, 1992), pp. 1–2 and 115–116.
7. National Environmental Protection Agency (NEPA), *Introduction to the Environmental Protection Organizations in China* (NEPA, Beijing, 1992), n.p.
8. *Ibid.*
9. *Op. cit.* 5, pp. 1–2.

Bangladesh and arid Saudi Arabia. (See Chapter 18, "Food and Agriculture," Table 18.2.)

Weather patterns in China are affected by cold, dry air from Siberia and monsoons from the south, resulting in irregular precipitation patterns. Densely populated eastern regions, especially the Hai, Huang (Yellow), and Huai River basins, experience recurring cycles of flooding and drought (25). (See Figure 4.3.) Precipitation is unevenly distributed. The south and

southeast usually receive 1,000 to 1,600 millimeters a year, while, in the north, Beijing averages about 600 millimeters, with wide variations from year to year (26).

Per capita water use falls below 500 metric tons annually in China, about 20 percent less than in India. (See Chapter 22, "Water," Table 22.1.) The region north of the Chang Jiang (Yangtze) River, which makes up about 60 percent of the land mass, claims only 20 percent of the country's water resources,

Figure 4.2 Map of China

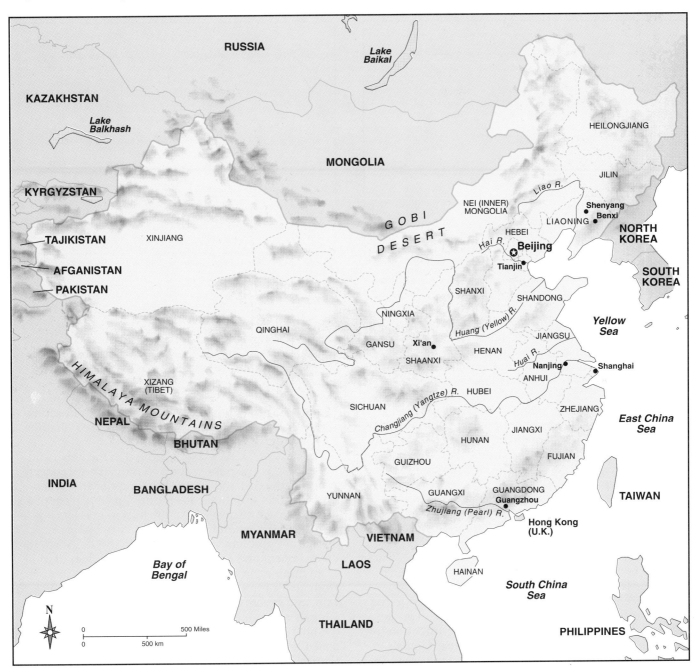

while in the Chang Jiang and Zhujiang (Pearl) River basins, water is abundant (27).

According to the latest government figures, about 13.6 percent of China—131 million hectares—is tree covered, with forests concentrated in the northeast and southwest (28) (29). Grassland ecosystems occupy about one third of the land, primarily in Inner Mongolia, Xinjiang, Tibet, and adjacent provinces. These grasslands have been grazed for thousands of years and today support millions of sheep, goats, cattle, horses, and camels (30).

China's coastline consists of 18,000 kilometers on the continent and 14,000 kilometers on thousands of islands. Marine waters, stretching across temperate, subtropical, and tropical zones, contain some 1,500 species of fish, of which 300 have economic value (31).

ENERGY: A CRITICAL ISSUE

China is already the third largest energy consumer in the world after the United States and the former Soviet Union and ranks fourth in electricity use (32). In 1990, China's commercial sector consumed the equivalent of more than 1 billion tons of coal, roughly 10 percent of global commercial energy consumption. (See Chapter 21, "Energy and Materials," Table 21.2.) The country's total energy consumption (commercial and noncommercial) in 1990 accounted for nearly 11 percent of global carbon dioxide (CO_2) emissions.

Figure 4.3 Area of China Affected by Floods and Drought, 1970–90

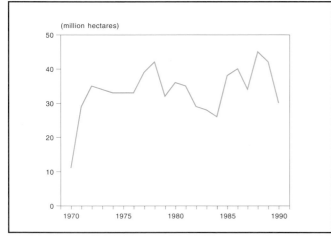

Source: Jikun Huang and Scott Rozelle, "Environmental Stress and Grain Yields in China," Chinese Rice Economy Project, China National Rice Research Institute, Beijing, and the Food Research Institute at Stanford University, Stanford, California, July 1993.

Figure 4.4 Total and Per Capita Commercial Energy Use in China, 1970–91

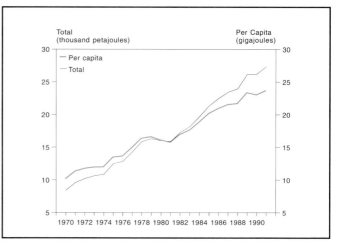

Source: United Nations Statistical Office (UNSO), *U.N. Energy Tape* (UNSO, New York, 1993).

China became one of the world's top energy users almost overnight: between 1970 and 1990, energy use shot up 208 percent, compared with an average increase of just 28 percent in the industrialized world. Commercial energy production alone increased 20-fold between 1952 and 1990, with electricity use more than doubling between 1980 and 1990 (33) (34). The rapid climb in energy consumption is projected to continue, driven by the goal of quadrupling economic output between 1980 and 2000. Estimates show a two- or threefold increase in consumption by 2025, accompanied by a steep rise in CO_2 emissions unless extraordinary measures are taken to wean China from coal (35) (36).

Despite these trends, per capita energy use is still low. (See Figure 4.4.) In 1990, for example, a typical Chinese household used less than 0.03 percent of the energy consumed in the average American home. This figure is now changing as modern appliances begin to find their way into many Chinese homes (37) (38).

China's energy growth has come at a high cost to the environment and public health. Fortunately, over the last decade, the government has turned its attention to reducing the adverse impacts of energy use. China's leaders acknowledge the need to replace inefficient equipment and curb harmful emissions. With capital to realize these goals being scarce, however, the priority is maintaining economic expansion to promote social development (39).

Current Patterns Of Energy Use

Coal, of which China has 11 percent of world reserves, forms the backbone of its energy system, supplying over 75 percent of all commercial energy. Most of this is used by the industrial sector. (See Figure 4.5.) By contrast, in the United States and the former Soviet Union, which also hold enormous reserves of coal, it accounts for about 25 percent of commercial energy (40) (41).

For many years, Chinese government officials have indicated that they would rely on coal for energy de-

velopment. That policy, however, was based on estimates of coal reserves that have been dramatically reduced. Whereas in 1987 China's proved recoverable reserves of coal were assessed at 730 million metric tons, a new survey estimates reserves of 114 million metric tons. This revised figure, just 15 percent of the previous estimate, may have significant implications for China's future energy policy (42) (43). (See Chapter 21, "Energy and Materials," Coal.)

The bulk of China's coal is located in the north and northwest, while population and industry are concentrated in the east and south. The long-distance transport that this situation calls for ties up 40 percent of an already taxed rail system and results in massive bottlenecks and coal shortages (44) (45).

Another problem with coal is the harm it does to the environment and to human health. Land degradation from mining, ground- and surface water pollution from acidic mine tailings and coal-washing refuse, acid rain, and severe air pollution are all byproducts of China's reliance on coal (46).

China commands many energy resources besides coal. Only 10 percent of the nation's hydroelectric potential, the largest such potential in the world, is currently exploited. Even so, hydropower is responsible for about 20 percent of China's electricity. One controversial project just getting under way, Three Gorges, would increase hydro capacity by nearly 50 percent (47). (See Box 4.3.) Many potential dam sites are not particularly feasible, being too remote or requiring long transmission lines, too affected by the seasons to supply primary energy, or too expensive to develop (48).

In addition to large hydro installations, China has extensively developed microhydro projects. More than 60,000 units have been installed with a capacity of less than 25 megawatts. Though these installations are often low powered, together accounting for only 6 percent of the nation's electricity in 1989, they nonetheless provide the only source of rural electricity in some areas and have proved crucial in promoting rural industry (49) (50) (51).

In the 1980s, China's oil reserves, while moderate by world standards, were important not only as a source of transport fuel and chemical feedstock but also as an export commodity. Oil exports declined from a high in 1985, however, and oil production grew at little more than 1 percent per year in the late 1980s (52) (53). If additional production is not brought on line, China may again become a net importer of oil (54). The Chinese have converted almost all of their oil-fired power plants to coal. The policy now is to divert oil to areas where it is more difficult to substitute other fuel sources (55). Oil currently makes up just 19 percent of China's energy mix (56).

China estimates its proven natural gas reserves at about 1.1 trillion cubic meters, but unproven reserves may be substantially higher (57). Natural gas supplies only about 25 percent of the nation's gas; most gas needs are met with liquified petroleum gas (LPG) and gasified coal (58). Although natural gas supplies are thought to be large, investment in exploration and infrastructure has been minimal (59), and natural gas currently plays a minor role, only about 2 percent of primary energy (60).

Shortages, Inefficiency, and Subsidies

Despite its resource endowment and the rapid expansion of its energy sector, persistent and severe shortages plague China. According to a 1990 *China Daily* report, in 1989 the nation produced 575 billion kilowatt-hours, 70 billion less than needed. As a result, about one third of China's industrial enterprises were unable to operate at full capacity (61). Residential customers, too, are subject to regular blackouts and brownouts. In addition, petroleum products are in short supply owing to an outdated refinery and distribution system (62).

The energy shortage affecting rural areas, where two thirds of the population reside, is perhaps more severe. Traditional biomass fuels such as firewood and straw, which account for about 80 percent of the energy used in rural households, are often unavailable (63). China consumes more of these fuels than any other nation, about 500 million tons annually, a rate not sustainable in the long run. Nearly half of all crop residue is burned, gradually draining humus from the soil, and firewood consumption is more than twice the sustainable harvest (64).

Although there has been a significant shift toward the use of commercial energy sources in the countryside, these sources are scarce. For example, 70 percent of rural households have access to electricity, but restricted supplies make rural electricity consumption just a fraction of urban consumption, which is itself small by Western standards (65). Chinese energy planners say that about 200 million rural Chinese have no electricity whatsoever (66).

Inefficiency plays a part in China's energy shortages. Though international comparisons are difficult to make (China does not have a fully convertible currency, nor does it use the U.N. System of National Ac-

Figure 4.5 China's Energy Use by Sector, 1989

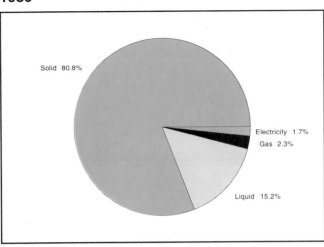

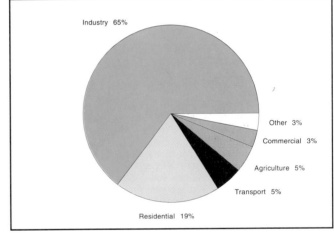

Sources:
1. United Nations (U.N.) Statistical Division, *U.N. Energy Tape* (U.N., New York, 1991).
2. International Energy Agency (IEA), *World Energy Statistics and Balances*, diskette (Organisation for Economic Co-operation and Development/IEA, Paris, 1991).

counts), one scholar believes that the country's energy efficiency is comparable to Poland's or the former Soviet Union's (67).

On average, China's major industries consume some 30 to 90 percent more energy than similar industries in developed countries (68). For example, steel production is 60 percent more energy intensive than in the industrialized world, and paper production requires about 40 percent more energy than elsewhere (69).

Among the biggest wasters of energy are China's half million small and medium-sized industrial boilers and kilns, most of which are coal fired (70). While modern boilers typically operate at 75 to 80 percent efficiency, Chinese boilers average about 55 to 60 percent; Chinese ovens and kilns operate in the 20 to 30 percent range, compared with the 50 to 60 percent range common in the industrialized world (71) (72). Upgrading or replacing this equipment alone could save some 100 million tons of raw coal per year, almost one tenth the amount of coal currently consumed (73). Other substan-

Box 4.3 The Three Gorges Controversy

In April 1992, the National People's Congress approved construction of the Three Gorges hydroelectric project on the Chang Jiang (Yangtze) River as part of China's 10-year development program (1). Approval brought the nation one step closer to realizing a project that has been debated for decades and remains deeply controversial both inside and outside China.

As planned, Three Gorges will be the world's largest and most complex hydroelectric dam. Its capacity, 17 million kilowatts, would top that of the largest dam currently operating by 40 percent (2). Its projected annual power generation of 84 billion kilowatt-hours is equivalent to a coal mine capacity of 40 to 50 million tons per year. The project will supply power mainly to the central China grid of Hubei, Hunan, Henan, and Jiangxi, and to the eastern China grid of Shanghai, Zhejiang, Jiangsu, and Anhui. It will take 15 to 18 years to build and cost (in 1990 prices) an estimated RMB 57 billion ($10.57 billion). Once completed, the dam would be 185 meters high and store 39.3 billion cubic meters of water (3).

The principal advantage of the project is that added power generation is desperately needed to keep pace with China's economic growth. It is estimated that China's power output must rise by 8 percent annually to keep pace with a 6 percent annual increase in gross national product. In practical terms, that means the nation's total 1990 power capacity of 130 million kilowatts must grow to 580 million by the year 2015 (4).

Chinese environmental officials note that the dam would relieve the danger of flooding in the chronically flood-prone middle and lower reaches of the Chang Jiang River valley. In addition, because generating electricity equal to the dam's projected annual output requires burning about 40 million tons of coal, the dam would substantially reduce emissions of sulfur dioxide and carbon dioxide (5).

Shipping coal by rail from the main production bases in Shanxi, Shaanxi, west Inner Mongolia, and Ningxia to Hebei and Henan is obstructed by natural features such as mountain passes. The option of building power plants in coal-producing areas is limited by scarce water resources near the main coal-production areas. Thus by lowering demand for coal, the dam would ease pressure on an overburdened rail transport network (6).

Outside China, the chief focus of opposition to the dam is the International Three Gorges Coalition headed by Green China, a group of Chinese students based in the United States. Other members include the Overseas Chinese Ecological Society, Friends of the Earth, and the Canadian group Probe International. There is considerable opposition within China as well, as evidenced by the fact that about one third of the 1992 National People's Congress either voted against authorizing Three Gorges or abstained (7).

Much of the criticism targets the project's social impact. Chinese officials estimate that the reservoir will partially or completely inundate 2 cities, 11 counties, 140 towns, 326 townships, and 1,351 villages. About 23,800 hectares of cultivated land will be submerged. According to estimates, more than 1.1 million people would have to be resettled, an expensive proposition accounting for about one third of the project's $10 billion cost. Many critics believe resettlement would fail, in light of its scale and the poor record of most other resettlement efforts. The government would construct new towns and urban areas, reclaim wasteland for cash crops, and house the resettlers on nearby hillsides (8) (9).

Concern has also been expressed about the project's ecological impact. The Yangtze dolphin, with a population of about 200 and one of the world's most endangered species, would be further threatened, along with the Chinese sturgeon

and many other fish species. The dam and reservoir would destroy some of China's finest scenery and an important source of tourism revenue (10).

Critics have other complaints. The quality of Shanghai's municipal and industrial water could deteriorate as the dam reduced river flow, disrupting the water supply to numerous downstream lakes and destroying the wetland habitat of numerous endangered species such as the Siberian crane. Furthermore, opponents maintain, silt trapped behind the dam would deprive downstream regions and the river's estuary of vital nutrients. Silt buildup behind the dam might also impede power generation (11).

References and Notes

1. Sun Haidong and Wang Guoning, "NPC Passes Three Gorges Project," *China Environment News*, No. 33 (April 1992), p. 1.
2. Lena H. Sun, "Dam Could Alter Face of China," *The Washington Post* (December 31, 1991), p. 1, sec. A.
3. Shen Gengcal, "Three Gorges Needs to Power Ahead," *China Environment News*, No. 32 (March 1992), pp. 4–5.
4. *Ibid.*, p. 4.
5. "NEPA Administrator Answers Focal Questions," *China Environment News*, No. 30 (January 1992), p. 6.
6. *Op. cit.* 3, pp. 4–5.
7. James McGregor, "Dam Vote, Rebuke of Li Reveal Defiant Legislature," *Asian Wall Street Journal Weekly* (April 13, 1992), p. 12.
8. James L. Tyson, "Critics Urge China to Consult on Dam Plan," *Christian Science Monitor* (July 22, 1991), p. 6.
9. Li Boning, "Building a New Life in Wake of Three Gorges," *China Environment News*, No. 33 (April 1992), pp. 4–5.
10. *Op. cit.* 8, p. 4.
11. Gráinne Ryder, "Exposing the Secrets of Three Gorges Dam," *World Rivers Review* (January/February 1989), pp. ii–iii.

tial energy savings could be realized throughout the industrial, residential, and transportation sectors.

In China, as in most developing nations, energy pricing has exacerbated shortage and waste. For many years, China's economic planners have fixed energy prices well below the cost of production, while establishing quotas for industrial and residential use. With a high value placed on gross production and with energy a negligible part of total operating costs, there has been little incentive to consume less than the full energy quota (74) (75). Significantly, in late 1993, China announced plans to decontrol coal prices in 1994.

When it became apparent in the late 1970s that energy shortages were holding back economic expansion, Chinese authorities formulated policies requiring industry, which accounts for nearly two thirds of total

commercial energy use, to start eliminating wasteful practices. Funds were made available for efficiency investment, and the importance of energy conservation was publicly stressed. China is in the process of refining its conservation policies (76). Though in this area it still lags behind many other countries, the nation has made remarkable progress in energy intensity, which, according to one estimate, went from 1.44 kg oe/$ (kilograms oil-equivalent per dollar) of gross domestic product in 1980 to 1.03 in 1988 (77).

FUTURE ENERGY PLANS

China expects to double its gross national product during the 1990s, well knowing that this goal hinges on rigorous energy planning (78). Official plans put equal

Figure 4.6 Industrial Carbon Dioxide Emissions in China, 1950–89

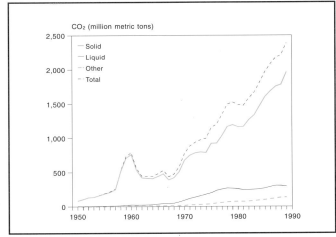
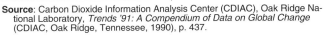

Source: Carbon Dioxide Information Analysis Center (CDIAC), Oak Ridge National Laboratory, *Trends '91: A Compendium of Data on Global Change* (CDIAC, Oak Ridge, Tennessee, 1990), p. 437.

weight on improving energy efficiency and expanding supply. The idea is to increase primary energy use 50 percent by 2000 and decrease energy intensity 50 percent during the same period (79). Government policy explicitly links energy development with national environmental goals. China plans to further develop hydropower, nuclear power, natural gas, and alternative energy, while making more efficient use of the coal it already burns (80).

China plans to double its hydropower capacity between 1989 and 2000. Some of this effort entails active promotion of microhydro facilities built by local governments for rural power (81). Natural gas and oil exploration will be accelerated, with gas promoted especially for residential heating and cooking (82). China has also begun to develop nuclear power, though it will remain a small part of the nation's total energy supply for the time being (83).

Emphasizing Coal for Electricity Generation
China hopes to reduce emissions as well as transportation problems associated with its dispersed coal network by converting more coal to clean electricity and distributing this by electrical grid. A program is already well under way to construct coal-fired generating plants that are larger and more efficient than older, smaller units. Many of these units will be built adjacent to coal mines, with power sent by high-voltage lines to circumvent coal transportation bottlenecks (84) (85). The potential for such plants is limited by a poor water supply in the coal-rich areas of Shanxi, Shaanxi, and Inner Mongolia, which contain 60 percent of China's coal reserves and almost all of its higher-quality coal (86).

Reforming Urban Energy Use
To continue along the path toward efficiency and cleaner city air, China plans to modernize urban coal technology. Replacing and refitting small and outdated industrial boilers is a high priority, though that

effort has been stymied by the surge in urban demand for electricity (87) (88).

Another priority is to reform residential coal use by encouraging cogeneration and the construction of gas lines and large central heating systems (district heating). City dwellers have traditionally used inefficient coal stoves for cooking, and many residential buildings depend on small, wasteful boilers for heat, resulting in serious indoor and outdoor air pollution (89) (90). The switch to gas appears likely in many cities.

Measures such as coal washing and molding coal into briquettes will also be stepped up. Coal briquettes burn up to 30 percent more efficiently than raw coal and, in residential use, produce 70 percent less carbon monoxide, 60 percent less dust, and 50 percent less sulfur dioxide (SO_2) (91).

Addressing the Rural Fuelwood Shortage
China intends to continue its effort to upgrade rural stoves and undertake a massive reforestation program to increase fuelwood supplies. To date, 150 million families—two thirds of the nation's rural households—are using stoves that are 30 percent more efficient than older stoves (92) (93). Of the 38 million hectares that have been reforested in China over the past four decades (94), almost 6 million hectares were planted specifically as fuelwood plantations (95).

In addition, for two decades, China has promoted a rural biogas program employing concrete digesters that convert animal and human waste into sludge for fertilizer and a methane-rich gas for cooking. Some 5 million digesters were in operation by 1989. Feedstock shortages have slowed biogas generation, however, and, in many cases, digesters are used to produce high-quality fertilizer rather than biogas (96). In the northern provinces, moreover, cold temperatures make digesters impractical for household heating (97).

Promoting Development of Renewables
China's interest in renewables, especially to meet rural energy needs, is growing. Though investment in this field is a tiny fraction of total energy investment, substantial progress has already been made in applying solar, wind, and even tidal technology to electricity production. For example, 12 Chinese factories now produce photovoltaic (PV) modules, and small 20- to 50-watt PV kits have become popular at remote sites. Larger installations are few but growing; a 20-kilowatt system was scheduled to be completed in 1992 (98).

Wind energy shows great potential. About 100,000 microwind units designed to power household lighting and television have been installed in remote northern and western provinces. About 10,000 wind pumps are in operation to extract groundwater in northern China and surface water in the south and east. In addition, six wind farms with a capacity of over 4 megawatts have been connected to electric grids in various parts of the country (99).

Rationalizing Energy Prices
China has promised to stop subsidizing energy within five years, which could help raise the capital needed

Figure 4.7 Cropland Area in China, 1961–90

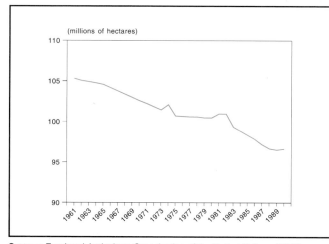

(millions of hectares)

Source: Food and Agriculture Organization of the United Nations (FAO), *Agrostat PC* (FAO, Rome, 1992).

Figure 4.8 Per Capita Arable and Permanent Cropland in China, 1961–90

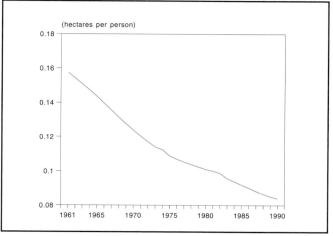

(hectares per person)

Sources:

1. Food and Agriculture Organization of the United Nations (FAO), *Agrostat PC* (FAO, Rome, 1992).
2. United Nations Population Division, *World Population Prospects, 1950–2025, The 1992 Revision*, diskette (U.N., New York, 1993).

for energy investment in the years ahead (100). Like most developing nations, China suffers a capital shortage. Given the capital-intensive nature of its expansion plans, capital constraints could slow the pace of development, especially in the face of the current global economic downturn.

BEYOND COAL: REDUCING CARBON EMISSIONS

China is the third largest emitter of CO_2 in the world, accounting for about 11 percent of global emissions. (See Chapter 23, "Atmosphere and Climate," Table 23.1.) Growth in CO_2 emissions has been dramatic; total emissions in 1989 were 18 times the 1952 level. (See Figure 4.6.) Coal accounts for about 80 percent of the total (101). Nonetheless, China's per capita CO_2 emissions from industrial sources are estimated at 2.16 metric tons in 1989, roughly half the world average and only about one tenth those of the United States. (See Chapter 23, "Atmosphere and Climate," Table 23.1.)

Some analysts think that China's plan to gradually deemphasize the predominance of coal should put much greater emphasis on natural gas (102) (103). Meanwhile, with coal still dominant, "clean coal" technologies have an important role to play. Coal gasification and conversion to hydrogen for use in fuel cells could well suit China's situation after the turn of the century. In urban applications, the 200°C heat produced by a hydrogen-fed fuel cell would be ideal for district heating applications such as those China is now encouraging (104). According to one scenario similar to that being planned for electricity, hydrogen produced from coal at the mine could be distributed by pipeline to points of use elsewhere (105).

Large-scale biomass gasification of plantation-raised timber could become a sustainable source of rural electricity with no net carbon release (106). A biomass-to-electricity project using forest plantations on currently deforested land is now moving forward in Yunnan Province in southern China. Tree planting started in 1992, and electricity generation is likely to begin by

1996 (107). This and further progress in wind, solar, and tidal technology could lay a sustainable energy foundation for China's future (108).

While existing technologies, for example, the infrastructure for handling gas, could go far toward satisfying China's growing appetite for energy while keeping the environmental impact under control, they are not likely to be adopted without considerable technical and financial support from other nations. Its expressed willingness to work with the global community in reducing carbon emissions notwithstanding, China remains adamant that economic development at home should not suffer to solve a problem it regards as largely created by the industrialized world (109) (110).

MAJOR RESOURCE AND ENVIRONMENTAL PROBLEMS

China's environment faces degradation on two fronts. First is the natural resource base. Several issues are pressing, particularly the declining quantity of water in the north but also the loss of forests, coastal wetlands, and wildlife habitat, the conversion of arable land to other uses, and the degradation of cropland.

Second, and perhaps the more urgent, is environmental pollution. Chinese officials believe that the most serious problems in this area are urban air and water quality, rural industrial pollution, and noise. Other significant problems include contaminated rural drinking water, indoor air pollution, acid rain, industrial and domestic solid-waste disposal, hazardous waste, vehicular emissions, and the emission of greenhouse gases (111).

THE RESOURCE BASE

Farmland Conversion

Changing patterns of land use, particularly the conversion of farmland to other purposes, is a source of some debate in China. Those alarmed about the loss of farmland note the present dearth of arable land per capita and maintain that further shrinkage could threaten China's ability to feed its growing population. Crop production on remaining lands, they point out, will become more intense and inevitably more environmentally damaging.

Others note that land can be used for activities more lucrative than agriculture, and that, thus far, productivity increases have more than offset production losses due to changing patterns of land use. For example, between 1983 and 1992 in the rural areas of Beijing, the total area (counting double-cropped hectares as 2 hectares) under cultivation declined from 638,000 hectares to 590,000, but both grain and vegetable output went up (grain from 2 million metric tons to 2.8, vegetables from 2 million metric tons to 3.7) (112). Furthermore, declining self-sufficiency in food production might be offset by continued economic growth, which generates foreign exchange to buy food from abroad.

Both skeptics and alarmists would probably agree on some points. First, effective land-use planning could discourage conversion of the most productive farmland. Second, declining self-sufficiency would force China to use scarce hard currency to buy food from abroad, slowing investment in the new equipment that is supporting the nation's swift economic growth. There seem to be good reasons for pursuing farmland preservation.

How serious is the problem? The Food and Agriculture Organization of the United Nations estimates that China's cropland declined from 105.2 million hectares in 1961 to 96.6 million in 1990. (See Figures 4.7 and 4.8.) These numbers could be underestimated by as much as 20 to 30 percent (113) (114). Local officials and farmers often underreport their area to reduce tax or quota obligations. In addition, perhaps 40 percent of the land taken out of cultivation in recent years has been converted to productive forest and grassland (115).

The Chinese Academy of Sciences estimates that net cropland area (including newly reclaimed land) is shrinking 333,000 hectares per year (116). In the 1990s, losses to housing, industrial construction, mining, hydropower, transportation, shelterbelts, and environmental degradation will probably range from 3 to 6 million hectares (117).

The loss of cropland has largely been offset by an increase in double cropping. China's total sown area, counting a hectare that is cropped twice as two hectares, rose slightly during the 1980s to reach a total of 148.3 million hectares (118). (See Figure 4.9.)

In addition, the loss of cultivated land has to some extent been offset by the reclamation of other areas usually described as wasteland. China uses this term to cover environmentally valuable wetlands. The government estimates that more than 10 million hectares of seashore can be turned into farmland (119), but this could have serious environmental repercussions. The reclamation of other wasteland such as abandoned mining sites could bring environmental benefits along with new farmland.

The total amount of potentially reclaimable land has been estimated at 30 to 35 million hectares, but only about 10 million hectares could be turned into cropland, of which roughly one third might be high-yield. In all likelihood, this reclaimed land would be less productive than farmland converted to other uses (120).

Increased food demand will have to be met primarily through higher yields on remaining land and more intensive cropping (121). Chinese officials say their primary strategy in the 1990s will be to raise yields on less productive land by expanding inputs such as fertilizer and high-yield seeds (122). This strategy could result in fertilizer and pesticide runoff, a principal source of rural water pollution.

Chinese officials are taking some steps to slow the conversion of prime farmland to residential and industrial use. Some provinces impose heavy taxes on converted farmland and use the revenue to develop new farmland (123). In Sichuan's Chengdu Plain, officials have designated 1.6 million hectares as an arable land reserve that cannot be converted for nonagricultural purposes (124).

In fact, China is developing comprehensive zoning for the entire country. At least five provinces have completed plans. Local governments must develop plans compatible with provincial plans. One central goal here is to prevent the net loss of farmland so that land lost to industrial or residential development will be offset by the conversion of other land for agriculture elsewhere in the province. In theory, land use rights will not be given to any conversion proposal that fails to conform to a zoning plan, but it is probable that in practice, intense development pressure will often override these planning goals (125).

Land Degradation

Land conversion is not the only threat to Chinese agriculture; land degradation is another. China now has about 153 million hectares of desert, nearly 16 percent of its total land area (126). About 5 percent of this area has undergone a natural process of desertification (127). The rate of desertification appears to be increasing and is currently estimated at 210,000 hectares per year, up from about 156,000 annually two decades ago (128). Nearly 4 million hectares of farmland and almost 5 million hectares of pastureland are threatened by desertification (129). Direct economic losses from sandstorms are considerable, averaging about RMB 4.5 billion ($800 million) per year (130).

To combat desertification, sand-break forests were built on 870,000 hectares in 1992, bringing the cumulative total of sand-break forests to about 10 million hectares. This has benefited about 8.9 million hectares of desertified land, and about 1.3 million hectares of new farmland within forested greenbelts. It has also protected about 11 million hectares of low-yield farmland from sandstorms (131).

About 7 million hectares of irrigated farmland are affected by salinization, largely because of inadequate drainage or improper irrigation. (See Figure 4.10.) The government has started a program to install drainage networks in salinized areas. Though in the North China Plain about 2.7 million hectares are affected (132), salinization may have receded over the past 20

Figure 4.9 Index of Multiple Cropping in China, 1970–90

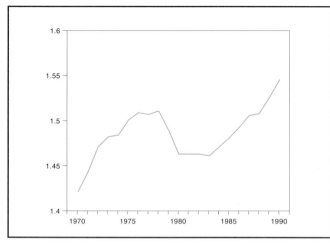

Source: Jikun Huang and Scott Rozelle, "Environmental Stress and Grain Yields in China," Chinese Rice Economy Project, China National Rice Research Institute, Beijing, and the Food Research Institute at Stanford University, Stanford, California, July 1993.

Figure 4.10 Area Affected by Salinity and Alkalinity in China, 1975–90

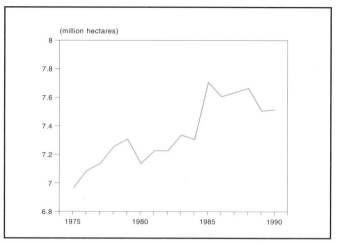

Source: Jikun Huang and Scott Rozelle, "Environmental Stress and Grain Yields in China," Chinese Rice Economy Project, China National Rice Research Institute, Beijing, and the Food Research Institute at Stanford University, Stanford, California, July 1993.

years as a result of better drainage, shifts in cropping, and natural phenomena such as drought (133).

Yields on about 4.3 million hectares of rice paddies are compromised by waterlogging and low oxygen (134).

The use of untreated urban sewage and industrial effluent for irrigation impairs soil chemistry and has destroyed about 2.6 million hectares of farmland. This practice, continuing on about 1.4 million hectares, has resulted in unsafe levels of toxic residue in a small but significant proportion of crops (135).

Soil Erosion

Soil erosion in China is serious and apparently getting worse. According to one government estimate, the total amount of eroded land went from 129 million hectares in 1985 to 162 million in 1991. Erosion control is practiced on 55 million hectares or about 34 percent of the total (136). (See Table 4.1.)

Soil erosion appears to be taking a serious toll on China's agricultural production. From 1983 to 1989, for example, natural phenomena restrained growth in grain yields by roughly 60 percent. About half of this figure can be attributed to an increased incidence of flooding and drought, but soil erosion and environmental problems associated with more intensive farming practices also played their part, the latter perhaps costing China as much as 5.7 million metric tons of grain annually in the late 1980s (137).

Grain yields are also affected when eroding soil clogs irrigation systems. In Guangxi Province, officials claim more than 20 percent of the irrigation network has been silted up (138).

About 65 percent of China's land lies on slopes or other fragile terrain, and in many regions it has been cultivated without protective measures such as ground cover. Water runoff and soil erosion are widespread, and most severe in the middle reaches of the Huang River, the red soil region south of the Chang Jiang River, the northeast plains and northwest grasslands (139).

Heavy soil erosion raises the risk of flooding in China's rivers. For example, soil runoff in the Huang River has elevated the riverbed in some areas from 3 to 10 meters above the fields. The river is contained only by embankments (140).

Extensive efforts—including reforestation, better management of native vegetation, and construction of bench terraces and gully controls—are under way to reduce soil erosion in the Huang River basin. The problem could be significantly mitigated by leaving crop residue in place after harvesting, planting cover crops and vegetative barriers on slopes, or combining agricultural crops with tree production (agroforestry) (141).

In the red soils region south of the Chang Jiang river, once-forested upland areas are seriously degraded. Prevailing practice is to stabilize this land through terracing, but a recent World Bank mission concluded that stabilization with plants such as vetiver grass may be less costly and more effective than terracing. The mission also recommended more farm animals to produce additional organic matter and techniques such as contour planting (142).

A number of efforts are under way to improve degraded land in southern China. One, called "stereoagriculture," applies ecological principles in hilly areas with varied topographical features. Typically, hilltops are restored as forests to reduce soil erosion and runoff, while hillsides are managed as forests to be exploited for local fuel and timber. Foothills are mixed agroforestry systems supporting orchards, livestock, and crops and using leguminous crops as a source of nitrogen. Lowlands, devoted to grain production, livestock, and aquaculture, are tended under the traditional dike-pond system (143).

Water Resources in the North

The paucity of water in northern China and in parts of southern China is degrading the environment and limiting prospects for economic growth in the region.

China consumes about 460 billion cubic meters of water annually (144). About 87 percent of that is used in agriculture, 6 percent for domestic purposes, and 7 percent in industry. (See Chapter 22, "Water," Table 22.1.) Demand for water is expected to soar by the beginning of the century, especially in the residential and industrial sectors (145) (146).

Finding new water sources to meet the demand will be difficult. Some 300 cities in northern China experience water shortages, 50 of them severely. Elsewhere, supplies are almost fully utilized. In some areas of northern China, as much as 68 percent of surface water and 84 percent of groundwater are already used (147), and the water table is falling in many places. In fact, the exploitation of underground sources is so aggressive that in some cities such as Tianjin, the ground level is actually dropping and sea water is entering underground reserves (148).

Traditionally, the Chinese government has responded to extra demand for water with increased supplies (149). For many years it has been considering a massive transfer of water from the Yangtze River in the south via canals to the country's northern region. The construction of three major south-north canals would be hugely expensive and has been opposed in the south because of the likely impact on ports and harbors there and the possibility of salt water entering city freshwater supplies (150) (151) (152). Construction of the most eastern of these routes, which includes modernizing the old Grand Canal, is already proceeding.

The government also favors the south as a location for industries that consume heavy amounts of water, though State Planning Commission officials say northern industries are often reluctant to go along with this policy (153). Rather than moving industries, which would raise other costs such as coal transportation, it may be more cost-effective to build on recent successes in recycling industrial water (154).

Chinese officials are also considering policies to encourage water conservation. Water prices are usually far below the cost of operating delivery facilities. Users, typically charged a flat rate, have no incentive to reduce consumption (155).

In 1990, the State Council announced that the price of water should go up (156). In some places, the price already has, and gradual hikes appear likely in the coming years. But prices will have to climb much further to incite agricultural and industrial users to conserve water or invest in conservation technologies. In a growing number of cities, residential water use is monitored by meter, but water is still too cheap to spur residential consumers to conserve (157).

Forests

China's current program of extensive reforestation comes after several centuries of massive forest loss. Most of China's virgin forest has been destroyed, with remnants only in the Greater and Lesser Hinggan Mountains and the Changbai Mountains in the northeast, in remote parts of Guangdong, Yunnan, and Sichuan provinces, and in the river valleys of the Qinghai-Tibetan plateau (158).

Table 4.1 Eroded Land and Erosion Control in China, 1985–91

Land Category	Year					
	1985	1987	1988	1989	1990	1991
Total eroded area (millions of km²)	1.29	1.32	1.33	1.34	1.36	1.62
Land area in erosion control programs	0.46	0.49	0.51	0.52	0.53	0.55
Eroded land in control programs (%)	35	37	38	38	39	34

Source: Scott Rozelle and Jikun Huang, "Poverty, Population and Environmental Degradation in China," paper prepared for the International Symposium on Sustainable Agriculture and Rural Development, China Academy of Agricultural Sciences, Beijing, May 1993, Table 1.

Pressure on forestland has been severe for decades. In the Xishuang Banna Autonomous Region, forest cover dropped from 60 percent in the early 1950s to 30 percent recently, and in neighboring Guizhou Province from about the same level to 14.5 percent. Similar declines have occurred in the western forests of Sichuan Province and elsewhere (159).

Demand for wood persistently exceeds supply. In 1986, for example, Sichuan felled 30 million cubic meters of timber but grew only 15 million; Yunnan's annual harvest was more than three times that prescribed under the state plan; Jilin's harvest exceeded growth by 2 million cubic meters; and in Liaoning, demand for wood exceeded official supply by over 1.5 million cubic meters. These figures do not include trees lost to illegal felling, which appears to be widespread, and fire (160).

Coastal Wetlands

Wetland ecosystems comprise about 7 percent of China's land area. China has about 3.1 million hectares of coastal marshes and mudflats, mostly around Hangzhou Bay, the estuary of the Huang River in Bohai Gulf, and the estuaries of the Shuangtaizi, Liao, and Hun rivers in Liaoning Province. There are about 11 million hectares of inland marsh, primarily in the Three Rivers Plain of Heilongjiang, the Greater and Lesser Hinggan Mountains, the Changbai Mountains, and the Qinghai-Tibetan plateau (161).

In China, officials still tend to view wetlands as wasteland to be converted to agricultural or industrial uses, overlooking ecological and attendant economic benefits such as natural flood protection and improved water quality. The prevailing attitude could have grave consequences. Coastal wetlands, under heavy pressure, may disappear in eastern China within the next two decades. Some 40,000 hectares of mudflats in Jiangsu, Zhejiang, Fujian, Guangdong, and Liaoning have been converted to grain, cotton, and sugarcane fields since 1949 (162).

Efforts to conserve coastal wetlands have been ineffective. China's Oceanographic Administration's Department of Islands and Coastal Zones has drafted a plan to balance coastal development and environmental protection, but such plans, considered obstructionist, are often ignored by local authorities (163).

It is likely that the loss of coastal wetlands has contributed, along with overfishing and marine pollution, to the depletion of China's offshore fish resources since the 1970s (164).

ENVIRONMENTAL POLLUTION

Urban Air Pollution

China's use of coal as its principal source of energy exacts a heavy price in air pollution, and thus human health. In some major cities in the north, for example, Beijing and Shenyang, air pollution is compounded by poor air dispersal and low-level temperature inversions. Urban centers in that region record some of the highest readings in the world for total suspended particulates (TSP) and SO_2. (See Figures 4.11 and 4.12.)

Coal is not the only source of particulate matter. Much of it is wind-blown dust from the desert, the Loess Plateau, or unpaved roads in urban centers. In Beijing, 40 to 60 percent of ambient TSP has been estimated to be natural dust particles, larger than human-generated particles, and thus probably less of a health risk (165).

In the center of Xi'an, for example, suspended particulates in the late 1980s averaged 565 micrograms per cubic meter (mcg/m³) annually, several times higher than the World Health Organization average annual guideline of 60 to 90 mcg/m³. TSP readings in the center of Xi'an rose 35 percent between 1981–84 and 1985–89 (166). In 1992, the daily average of suspended particulates for northern cities as a whole was 403 mcg/m³, down 6 percent from the previous year, and for southern cities 243 mcg/m³, up 8 percent (167).

In the north, the acidity of precipitation has remained at normal levels because SO_2 is neutralized by alkaline particulate matter that originates in China's interior deserts. In southern China, acid precipitation is a growing problem, especially in large areas of Sichuan, Guangxi, Hunan, Jiangxi, and Guangdong. Several cities in the region register annual average pH levels between 4 and 4.5, comparable to areas of North America and Europe most afflicted by acid precipitation (168).

Air quality readings during the 1980s do not show a uniform trend for all cities, though there were some distinct trends in individual cities for which data are available, such as a 36 percent increase in SO_2 levels in central Shanghai (169). Emissions currently appear to be increasing. Nationwide emissions of SO_2 were estimated at 16.85 million metric tons in 1992, up 4 percent from 1991 and 13 percent from 1990. Soot emissions (14.1 million tons) rose 7.6 percent from 1991 to 1992, while industrial fly ash (5.8 million tons) dropped by 0.5 percent (170) (171).

Coal burning is a major source of particulates and SO_2. Other factors such as diesel exhaust from trucks and background dust in arid areas add to the particulate problem (172).

Economic development over the past 15 years has created the common image of Chinese urbanites transporting themselves by bicycle. However, rapid growth has also added cars and motor scooters to the road, raising the possibility of a large-scale shift from bicycles to fueled vehicles (173). This development, if not accompanied by any pollution control technology, would substantially increase some pollutants such as hydrocarbons, carbon monoxide, nitrous oxide, and black smoke.

Air pollution takes a heavy toll on human health in China. Chronic obstructive pulmonary disease (COPD), linked to exposure to fine particulates, SO_2, and cigarette smoke among other factors, accounted for 26 percent of all deaths in China in 1988. The standardized (COPD) death rate, 162.6 per 100,000 people, is five times higher in China than in the United States (174). Indoor exposure to emissions from poor-quality coal used for cooking and heating is also a major health risk, increasing the incidence of both pulmonary disease and stroke (175) (176).

The price of pollution is high. For China's urban areas as a whole, the annual cost of air pollution-related morbidity might be around RMB 5 billion ($880 million). This estimate does not include indirect costs such as pollution-induced damage to food crops. Total annual air pollution damages are roughly RMB 15 billion ($2.6 billion) (177).

Numerous opportunities exist to reduce the environmental impact of coal burning. Increased coal washing can reduce ash and sulfur content, transportation and disposal costs, and emissions (178) (179). Saving higher-grade coal for specific uses might also help, for example, by changing distribution so that better quality coal went to consumers in dense urban areas and for use in household stoves and industrial boilers (180).

Basic economic reforms could dramatically curb coal consumption in China. The environmental impact of its centralized economy is profound: inefficiency may cause 30 percent or more of all pollution. The economic reforms of the 1980s gave enterprises more rein and incentive to operate more efficiently, though state enterprises are still not entirely responsible for their balance sheets. Granting enterprises full responsibility would encourage conservation of raw materials and recycling of waste products. An arm's-length relationship between ministries and business management would also make it easier for environmental protection bureaus to enforce their regulations (181).

Economic reforms will be more effective if they include price reform. In recent years, at least half of China's domestic coal has been sold below the cost of mining it. Similarly, low gas prices have discouraged investment in natural gas infrastructure. Coal and gas prices are now rising; further increases will give enterprises a much stronger incentive to use energy efficiently and to invest in energy-saving technologies (182). (See Figure 4.13.) Higher coal and gas prices will also make alternative energy sources such as solar more attractive.

Many cities are already switching to natural gas; Benxi, once one of the most polluted cities in China, launched a comprehensive attack on pollution that includes a goal to increase gas use from 43.8 percent to 70 percent by 1995 (183).

Initiatives based on the principle that polluters pay are promising. For example, Benxi's comprehensive cleanup effort is financed in part by fees on factories that create pollution in the course of manufacturing

Figure 4.11 Average Atmospheric Concentration of Suspended Particulate Matter (SPM) in Selected Chinese Cities

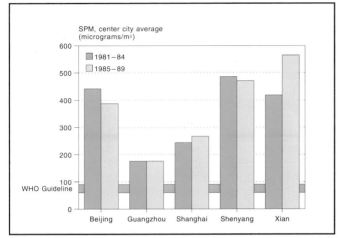

Source: Rudolf Orthofer, Program Officer, Global Environment Monitoring System (GEMS), Nairobi, Kenya, 1993 (personal communication), based on data compiled by WHO/UNEP-GEMS Urban Air Quality Monitoring Project (GEMS/Air).

Figure 4.12 Average Atmospheric Concentration of Sulfur Dioxide in Selected Chinese Cities

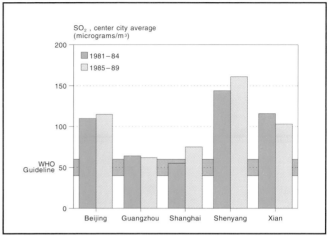

Source: Rudolf Orthofer, Program Officer, Global Environment Monitoring System (GEMS), Nairobi, Kenya, 1993 (personal communication), based on data compiled by WHO/UNEP-GEMS Urban Air Quality Monitoring Project (GEMS/Air).

products from raw materials (184). Sichuan province intends to impose a tax on polluting inputs such as coal. This will encourage conservation and the use of coal with less sulfur and ash, if not the installation of pollution control equipment (185).

The possibilities of cutting air pollution through conservation are manifold. They include the installation of central heating systems, improvement of the heat controls on small coal stoves, the use of available industrial energy (waste heat and gas), the insulation of housing stock in northern cities, the use of meters nationwide, and support for energy-efficient technologies for lighting and refrigeration (186).

Finally, China's assortment of environmental policy mechanisms includes many instruments to control air pollution, especially in the case of new facilities. All new projects are expected to adhere to the so-called three simultaneous steps, incorporating environmental protection into the design, construction, and operation of facilities. New facilities are expected to set aside 7 percent of their capital budget for environmental protection and can be fined for infractions or shut down for noncompliance (187) (188).

Local environmental protection bureaus have the authority to call for environmental impact assessments (EIAs) on all large and medium-sized construction projects. In the past, projects were often approved by the government before completion of an EIA. The 1989 Environmental Protection Law now requires that EIAs be approved before development plans (189).

In practice, local environmental bureaus are fairly selective in calling for EIAs. In Guangdong's Nanhai County, one of the fastest-growing counties in China, 3,000 new enterprises opened in 1991, of which only 130 were required to provide formal EIAs. Of the 130 companies assessed—they were in areas such as electroplating, dyeing and printing, and chemical manufacturing—the bureau rejected four, including one new

power station. Rejection does not necessarily mean plants will not be built; they may be modified or moved to another location. The power station was moved to another site so that its air emissions would not affect Guangzhou.

Nanhai is initiating a regulation requiring all new potentially polluting industries to pay 30 percent of total construction costs to the local environmental bureau. The money will be returned after pollution control equipment is properly installed (190).

Another broad mechanism to control urban pollutants is the environmental responsibility system. This involves various types of contracts designed to enact environmental protection. A contract for the city of Tianjin proposed increasing the percentage of industrial wastewater treated and the per capita green area (191).

Though such contracts are voluntary and there usually is little or no penalty for failure, they do offer incentives to meet targets. For example, the central government might grant cooperative businesses greater control over their foreign exchange and more discretion in the handling of profits. Local governments can earn money and awards for meeting their targets. The system seems to have focused the attention of municipal leaders on environmental issues and raising public awareness (192).

Urban Water Pollution

Many of China's rivers are polluted, most severely in urban areas. About 80 percent of urban river water is polluted to some degree, commonly with ammonium nitrate, volatile phenol, and oxygen-consuming organic matter (193).

In 1992, the volume of wastewater for the nation as a whole (not including discharge from village enterprises) was 36.7 billion tons, 9 percent higher than in the previous year. This increase was attributed to nonindustrial sources, for the total volume of industrial

Figure 4.13 Overall Retail Fuel Prices in China, 1950–91

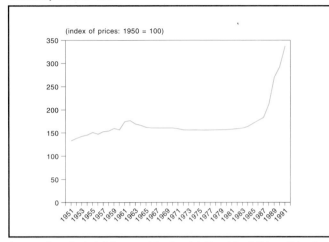

(index of prices: 1950 = 100)

Source: State Statistical Bureau of the People's Republic of China, *China Statistical Yearbook, 1991* (China Statistical Information and Consultancy Service Center, Beijing, 1991), p. 204.

Note: Data for 1991 is from the Chinese-language edition of the 1992 yearbook.

wastewater (23.4 billion tons or 64 percent of all wastewater) actually declined about 1 percent from 1991 to 1992 (194).

From year to year, the official government figures show sharp fluctuations in the levels of some industrial water pollutants. (The numbers, based on a rudimentary monitoring system, should be considered with caution.) Figures for 1992 reveal several significant declines, including reductions of 17 percent in heavy metals, 22 percent in arsenic, 23 percent in cyanide, 18 percent in volatile phenols, and 5 percent in petrol pollutants (195).

In 1992, 68.6 percent of industrial wastewater and 18.5 percent of municipal wastewater received some treatment. The rest, however, entered rivers, lakes, and seas without treatment, exacerbating the pollution that has devastated marine resources in China and the health of its citizens. For the four major fish species in the Chang Jiang River, production of fry has declined from 20 billion in the 1970s to 1 billion (196). And in 1989, seafood contaminated by sewage caused an outbreak of hepatitis A in Shanghai that affected over 300,000 people (197) (198).

Urban drinking water is generally poor, though the incidence of illness from contaminated drinking water is reduced by the widespread practice of boiling water. Boiling does not eliminate all problems, though. In outlying areas of Beijing, for example, it is estimated that the uncontrolled irrigation of market crops with raw sewage may cause intestinal worm disease among children. Nor does boiling eliminate toxins. Industrial waste is probably contributing dangerous amounts of chemicals, including carcinogenic compounds, to urban drinking water (199). There have been some reports of arsenic poisoning caused by drinking city water (200).

China has an array of policy mechanisms to control and reduce water pollution. For example, a wastewater discharge permit system is being implemented in 230 urban centers (about 60 percent of the country's

medium to large cities) and should cover most major polluters in each one. Under this system, polluting facilities each receive a permit that sets a limit on the total volume of discharged pollutants allowed. Local environmental protection bureaus monitor each facility for compliance (201).

China has also developed national standards for the discharge of water pollutants. These standards are generally not so strict as to be unattainable, but strict enough to reduce pollution and adverse effects on public health, according to the World Bank (202).

An important complement to the development of effluent standards is the pollution levy system, which imposes a fee on facilities that violate standards. If there are repeated violations, fines may be imposed as well. Official figures indicate that the government is making steady progress in implementing the system. In recent years, fees have risen about 15 to 18 percent annually (203) (204) (205) (206); in 1992 the total for both air and water violations rose to RMB 2.4 billion ($420 million) (207). Most of the fees are reabsorbed by business in the form of grants or low-interest loans for plant-level waste treatment facilities, or for operation and maintenance activities that reduce pollution (208).

In theory, the pollution levy system is promising because, following the polluter-pays principle, it encourages polluters to reduce emissions and provides a source of funds to finance controls. In practice, the system needs to be honed.

For example, fines against polluting facilities are low, a mere 0.1 percent or so of production costs in the machine-building and paper industries, and considerably less than that in the chemical, metallurgy, leather, and brewing industries (209). Because fees are so small, most firms choose to pay them rather than invest in pollution control equipment. Hiking fees above the marginal cost of investing in treatment equipment should improve the system. Furthermore, levies are assessed on the basis of the most highly concentrated of the measured pollutants rather than on the total volume of all pollutants emitted. China's National Environmental Protection Agency is considering revising the system, while cities such as Shanghai are now charging companies for the quantity of every pollutant discharged rather than only the principal pollutant (210).

New pollution control equipment aside, Chinese officials estimate that better operation and maintenance encouraged by higher fees could lower pollutants by 20 to 40 percent and for relatively little cost (211). Requiring that the fee be paid out of profits rather than passed along to consumers would prod enterprises to look for low-cost solutions (212). Another promising reform would be channeling loans competitively through investment companies. An experiment with this in Shenyang proved more effective than the old grant system (213).

RURAL POLLUTION

The agricultural reforms of the late 1970s and early 1980s boosted production and cash savings in rural areas. Eager to use funds to build their economies, local leaders aggressively developed township and village in-

Figure 4.14 Fertilizer Consumption in China, 1961–91

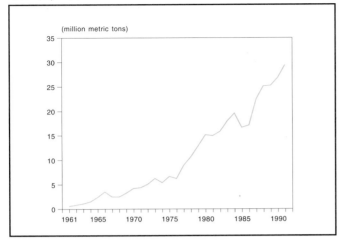

Source: Food and Agriculture Organization of the United Nations (FAO), *Agrostat PC* (FAO, Rome, 1993).

Figure 4.15 Cereal Production and Cereal Area in China, 1961–92

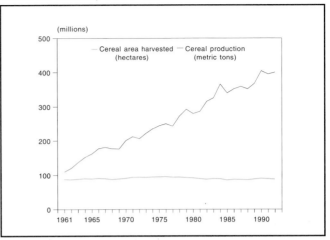

Source: Food and Agriculture Organization of the United Nations (FAO), *Agrostat PC* (FAO, Rome, 1993).
Note: Cereal area harvested includes double and triple cropping.

dustries and enterprises (TVIEs). Most of these small firms were in light industry, a highly profitable and relatively neglected area (214).

TVIEs grew at a phenomenal annual rate of 30 percent in the 1980s (215). From 1984 to 1988, the number of TVIEs increased from 4.8 million to 7.7 million, the value of their output nearly quadrupled, and their share of total industrial output reached 28 percent. In high-growth areas such as Jiangsu Province, TVIEs now account for nearly half of industrial output (216).

While certainly a positive development for China's economy, TVIEs nevertheless pose dilemmas for environmental managers. Installations tend to use outdated technology and are not well designed or built. Operation and maintenance are below standard, while pollution control equipment is lacking or ineffective. It is difficult to regulate TVIEs because they are dispersed and small, and supervision is divided between the Ministry of Agriculture and the National Environmental Protection Agency (217). A survey found that in 1989, only 14.8 percent of TVIEs complied with wastewater discharge regulations (218).

Being primarily in light industry, TVIEs contribute less pollution to the environment than their 28 percent share of output. For example, in 1991, the first national survey of the environmental impact of TVIEs estimated their combined effluent at 1.83 billion metric tons, roughly 7 percent of total industrial effluent, and the SO_2 emissions at 2.22 million metric tons, about 12 percent of the total for this pollutant (219).

A few industries account for the lion's share of TVIE pollution. The brick and tile industry discharges about two thirds of all TVIE soot, the porcelain and pottery industry emits more than half of all SO_2, the cement industry is responsible for more than three fourths of all fly ash emissions, and the pulp and paper industry accounts for nearly 44 percent of wastewater discharge (220).

Chinese officials are placing high priority on improved environmental controls for TVIEs. For example, in 1991, almost 1,700 such businesses either closed

down, temporarily stopped production, merged with other plants, or changed their product or location because of pollution. That year, nearly half of TVIEs were participating in the EIA system, and about RMB 170 million ($30 million) was collected in pollution discharge fees (221). In many areas, however, TVIEs contribute only about 30 percent of what is actually owed for pollution, largely because of local pressure to treat them less stringently (222).

Authorizing and equipping local governments to create industrial development zones or industrial estates for TVIEs, where it would be possible to treat industrial waste collectively, might improve the level of waste treatment for TVIEs and lower their pollution control costs (223).

Agriculture

Traditional Chinese agriculture is labor-intensive, relies heavily on draft animals and organic recycling, and employs rotation of crops such as soil-enriching legumes. This pattern has changed dramatically over the past few decades. Consumption of chemical fertilizer tripled between 1978 and 1988; organic manure, once the dominant source of agricultural nutrients, now accounts for less than 40 percent of fertilizer (224). (See Figure 4.14.) Largely owing to small tractors and trucks, the number of farm workers dropped almost 50 million during the 1980s, a decline expected to continue in the 1990s (225). Crop rotation is also waning: in parts of Jilin Province, for example, continuous corn planting accounts for 40 to 70 percent of the total planted area (226).

Such changes fueled explosive growth in China's agricultural production, as illustrated by cereal output, while at the same time accelerating environmental degradation. (See Figure 4.15.) Chemical fertilizers run off farm fields and contribute to water pollution. Continuous corn cropping depletes organic matter and nutrients in soil and aggravates pest and disease outbreaks. Studies in northeast China indicate that continuous corn cropping may reduce yields by 4.5 percent annually (227). Furthermore, enhanced production in livestock and poultry facilities can add to water pollution (228).

Scattered evidence points to a substantial decline in the organic content of crop soil. Some regional surveys indicate that the percentage of organic matter in the soil has fallen from about 9 percent several decades ago to about 3 percent today (229). The area fertilized with green manure shrank from 9.9 million hectares in 1975 to 4.2 million hectares in 1990 (230).

The Ministry of Agriculture has sponsored an impressive "ecological agriculture" program at about 400 trial sites (on about 1.7 percent of total cropland). The pilot promotes heavy use of organic fertilizer, production of biogas fuel, and sustainable crop, livestock, and fish production. Though yields and revenues apparently surpass those for conventional agricultural systems, the program is not catching on yet, in part because the trial sites benefit from subsidies and intensive political support that are not easily replicated (231).

China is a world leader in research on integrated pest management and biological pest controls. A national pest surveillance and monitoring system helps determine threshold treatment levels. Most of the techniques are not yet widely applied, one reason being the weak link between research institutes and extension services (232).

Some aspects of China's national farm policies push farmers in other directions. Subsidies for chemical fertilizer may encourage overuse, for example. National grain quotas discourage alternative, specialized cropping patterns. The quotas are weakening, however, as farmers convert more farmland to cash crops and emphasis shifts toward improved yields through improved and more efficient techniques (233).

Methane contributes significantly to the greenhouse effect, and Chinese officials are beginning to consider ways to reduce its release from two sources: rice paddies and ruminant animals. Chinese scientists are now learning about methane emission monitoring and cultivation techniques to minimize methane release from flooded rice paddies. Improved nutrition would reduce methane emissions from ruminants (234).

GLOBAL ISSUES: CFCs AND CO₂

China's soaring economic growth holds important implications for global climate change and ozone depletion. For example, booming sales of refrigerators, which jumped from 0.2 per hundred Chinese households in 1981 to 42.3 in 1990, and other products that use CFCs are stepping up CFC production (235) (236). The government estimates that production of all ozone-depleting substances, estimated at 48,000 metric tons in 1991, would rise to nearly 117,000 metric tons by the end of the decade if demand continues unrestrained (237).

China signed the Montreal Protocol on Substances that Deplete the Ozone Layer and is working to introduce CFC substitutes. China has proposed a complete phaseout of ozone-depleting substances in aerosols by the year 1997 and in the foam industry by the year 2000. The phaseout program, however, is contingent on financial assistance and technology transfers (238).

Figure 4.16 Use of China's Forests in 11 Sample Counties, 1980 and 1990

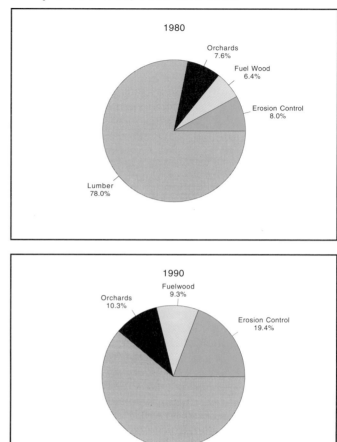

Source: Scott Rozelle, Susan Lund, Zuo Ting, *et al.*, "Rural Policy and Forest Degradation in China," Food Research Institute at Stanford University, Stanford, California, 1993.

China is seeking approximately $2.1 billion from the Montreal Protocol's Multilateral Fund, $1.4 billion for the phaseout and $660 million to cover the higher cost of substitute refrigerants (239).

China faces a more daunting task in responding to international calls to reduce the risk of global warming by cutting emissions of CO2. Even with efforts to restructure the economy and promote energy efficiency, growing energy demand is likely to triple coal consumption and CO2 emissions over the next 35 years (240).

China was among the first 10 countries to ratify the U.N. Framework Convention on Climate Change. The nation appears willing to help prevent global warming, provided that financial and technical assistance is made available.

RESTORATION PROGRAMS: REFORESTATION AND PROTECTED AREAS

China is investing considerable time, energy and money in restoring and protecting its environment. Two programs are particularly notable: one to increase total forest cover, the other to develop an extensive, linked system of protected habitat.

Forest Programs

Four decades of afforestation have yielded impressive results in China. New forests have been planted over vast areas of the nation, protecting crops, reducing soil erosion in agricultural areas, providing a source of local timber and fuelwood, and reducing pressure on China's mature forests. But the program has not been an unalloyed success. Until the late 1970s, emphasis was put on the quantity of trees planted rather than their survival; as a result of this, and widespread pest infestations and forest fire damage, only about 30 percent lived (241). Since the 1980s, when the program was adjusted, the survival rate has apparently improved.

Estimates of China's total forest cover, depending on how that is defined, vary from 11 to 14 percent (242). Ministry of Forestry officials put forest cover at 13.6 percent (131 million hectares) in 1992, up from 8.6 percent in 1949 (243) (244). Massive reforestation projects are under way in the north, the upstream and mid-stream regions of the Chang Jiang River, the plains, and the Taihang Mountains, as well as along the coast (245). The largest single such effort, being undertaken in southeast China, also involves a conversion of degraded natural forests to exotic tree species such as slash and loblolly pine from the United States (246).

During the 1990s, the government hopes to plant an additional 57.2 million hectares of forest. Of this total, 39.6 million hectares will be planted by hand and cultivated. Assuming a 70 percent survival rate, the program would bring total forest cover to about 168 million hectares, or roughly 17 percent of China's total area (247) (248).

These aggregate figures disguise some disturbing trends. Increases in forest cover are primarily due to new tree plantations, while natural forests continue to decline. Natural tropical forestland in Hainan, for example, declined from 25 percent of the island's total area in 1956 to 8.5 percent in 1981. For the country as a whole, it is estimated that virgin forest shrank from about 98 million hectares in 1973–76 to about 86 million hectares in 1984–88 (249). Forests were selectively logged for commercially valuable species, then cleared and planted with monoculture species such as larch in the northeast and rubber in Hainan (250). (Chinese officials say that now only degraded lands are used for rubber plantations (251).) Thus, while total forest cover may be expanding, the native populations and the genetic diversity of China's natural forestland continue to decline.

During the 1980s, in a sample of 11 counties, the proportion of forests in high-quality timber declined from 78 percent to 61 percent. (See Figure 4.16.) These woods were replanted in orchards and protection forests. Compared with natural forest, they have less biomass, less absorptive soil, less diversity of flora and fauna, and poorer ground cover (252).

With demand for wood still outpacing supply by about 28 to 30 million cubic meters, the pressure on natural forestland should continue (253). One opinion is that the annual timber harvest far exceeds incremental growth, and that the shortfall will probably not be made up by new plantation production in this century (254). Total forest area has likely expanded somewhat over the past decade, but timber volume has declined. Of the country's 140 forest bureaus, 25 have almost run out of forest reserves and 61 report that trees are being felled at unsustainable rates (255).

Protected Areas

The giant panda, the most visible symbol of China's endangered wildlife, is only one species in a nation that ranks among the top 10 in the world for the diversity of their mammal, bird, amphibian, and flowering plant species (256). Many other species in China are also endangered, including the tiger, snow leopard, white-lip deer, golden monkey, and green turtle, plus plants such as the Korean pine and dragon spruce (257).

Loss of habitat from human population pressure is a major threat to China's plants and wildlife. Animal populations continue to be depleted by overhunting and collecting for taxidermy and medicine. China, aware of these problems, is moving rapidly to create a system of nature reserves. Beginning with 59 reserves in 1979, the system had 606 totaling 40 million hectares by 1990. The government plans to add another 10 million hectares by the end of the century (258).

In a 1992 World Wide Fund for Nature/Ministry of Forestry workshop on conservation priorities, it was estimated that there were 820 existing or proposed protected areas in China. Forty were deemed exceptionally significant for reasons such as biodiversity, endemic species, ecosystem intactness, uniqueness and sustainability, and size. These 40 areas actually include 118 existing or proposed sites that could be linked by habitat corridors to form larger conservation units. Five of the proposed areas could be joined with conservation units across China's borders. Workshop participants concluded that there are several important gaps in the current system, particularly in the Tian Shan region in the northwest, the southeastern stretch of the Himalayas, and the central part of northern China (259).

With so many protected areas sprouting up, management has been understandably strained. Typically, managers have limited funds and little decisionmaking authority. For example, the Ministry of Forestry controls pandas in the wild, while the Ministry of Construction manages their captive counterparts, a situation that invites conflict and breeds reluctance to share information and resources (260). Six different national agencies have administrative responsibility for some sites, and not all agencies have expertise in nature conservation.

This chapter was written by Robert Livernash, World Resources staff member. The energy section was written by Gregory Mock, contributing editor of World Resources.

References and Notes

1. The World Bank, *World Tables, 1993*, STARS, on diskette (The World Bank, Washington, D.C., 1993).

2. Nicholas D. Kristof, "Chinese Communism's Secret Aim: Capitalism," *New York Times* (October 19, 1992), p. 6, sec. A.

3. Richard L. Holman, "China Boosts Growth Forecast," *The Wall Street Journal* (October 12, 1992), p. 6, sec. A.

4. "China at Boiling-Point," *The Economist*, Vol. 328, No. 7819 (1993), p. 15.

5. *Ibid.*

6. The World Bank, unpublished data (The World Bank, Washington, D.C., 1992).

7. *National Report of the People's Republic of China on Environment and Development* (China Environmental Science Press, Beijing, 1992), p. 108.

8. *Op. cit.* 2, p. 6, sec. A.

9. Basil Ashton, Kenneth Hill, Alan Piazza, *et al.*, "Famine in China, 1958–61," *Population and Development Review*, Vol. 10, No. 4 (1984), pp. 614 and 624–630.

10. Gil Elliot, *Twentieth Century Book of the Dead* (Charles Scribner's Sons, New York, 1972), pp. 83–88.

11. Vaclav Smil, "Environmental Change as a Source of Conflict and Economic Losses in China," Project on Environmental Change and Acute Conflicts, Occasional Paper No. 2, University of Toronto, Canada, and American Academy of Arts and Sciences, Cambridge, Massachusetts, 1992, pp. 25–30.

12. Vaclav Smil, *The Bad Earth: Environmental Degradation in China* (M.E. Sharpe, Armonk, New York, and ZED, London, 1984), pp. 15–16.

13. George Tseo, "The Greening of China," *Earthwatch* (May/June 1992), p. 23.

14. "1992 Report on the Environment in China," *China Environment News*, No. 47 (June 1993), p. 5.

15. Zhang Kunmin, "The Past, Present, and Future of Environmental Protection in the PRC," *The American Asian Review*, Vol. 8, No. 2 (1990), pp. 6–7.

16. Lester Ross, *Environmental Policy in China* (Indiana University Press, Bloomington and Indianapolis, 1989), pp. 137–138.

17. *Op. cit.* 13, p. 23.

18. The World Bank, *China Country Economic Memorandum: Reform and the Role of the Plan in the 1990s* (The World Bank, Washington, D.C., 1992), pp. 43–44 and 50.

19. *Ibid.*, pp. viii–ix.

20. State Statistical Bureau of the People's Republic of China, *China Statistical Yearbook, 1991* (China Statistical Information and Consultancy Service Center, Beijing, 1991), p. 353.

21. William U. Chandler, "Hearing on the Energy Needs of the People's Republic of China: An Energy Profile of China," testimony before the U.S. Senate Committee on Energy and Natural Resources, Washington, D.C. (March 11, 1992), p. 6.

22. *Op. cit.* 2, p. 6, sec. A.

23. *Op. cit.* 20, p. 2.

24. *Op. cit.* 7, p. 17.

25. *Op. cit.* 12, pp. 5–6.

26. Manfred Domrös and Peng Gongbing, *The Climate of China* (Springer-Verlag, Berlin, 1988), pp. 140 and 174.

27. Vaclav Smil, *China's Environmental Crisis* (M.E. Sharpe, Armonk, New York, 1993), p. 41.

28. *Op. cit.* 7, p. 19.

29. "Forest Coverage Hits 13.63% in 1992," *China Environment News*, No. 43 (February 1993), p. 1.

30. *Op. cit.* 6.

31. *Op. cit.* 7, pp. 19–20.

32. United Nations Statistical Office (UNSO), *U.N. Energy Tape* (UNSO, New York, 1993).

33. *Op. cit.* 20, p. 407.

34. *Op. cit.* 32.

35. Wu Zongxin and Wei Zhihong, "Policies to Promote Energy Conservation in China," *Energy Policy*, Vol. 19, No. 10 (1991), pp. 934–939.

36. Robert Perlack, Milton Russell, and Zhongmin Shen, "Reducing Greenhouse Gas Emissions in China: Institutional, Legal, and Cultural Constraints and Opportunities," *Global Environmental Change*, Vol. 3, No. 1 (1993), pp. 81–82.

37. William Chandler, Alexei Makarov, and Zhou Dadi, "Energy for the Soviet Union, Eastern Europe, and China," *Scientific American* (September 1990), p. 121.

38. Mark Levine, Feng Liu, and Jonathan Sinton, "China's Energy System: Historical Evolution, Current Issues, and Prospects," *Annual Review of Energy and the Environment*, Vol. 17 (1992), p. 419.

39. Robert Perlack and Milton Russell, "Energy and Environmental Policy in China," *Annual Review of Energy and the Environment*, Vol. 16 (1991), pp. 207 and 222–232.

40. *Ibid.*, pp. 207–209.

41. *Op. cit.* 36, p. 81.

42. World Energy Conference, *1989 Survey of Energy Resources* (World Energy Conference, London, 1989), p. 17.

43. World Energy Council, *1992 Survey of Energy Resources* (World Energy Council, London, 1992), p. 20.

44. F. Liu, W.B. Davis, and M.D. Levine, *An Overview of Energy Supply and Demand in China*, (Lawrence Berkeley Laboratory, University of California, Berkeley, 1992), p. 4.

45. *Op. cit.* 38, p. 411.

46. *Op. cit.* 39, pp. 210–211.

47. Huang Yicheng, "Strategic Alternatives for Coordinated Development of Energy and Environment in China," recommendations to the China Council for International Cooperation on Environment and Development, Paper No. 5, Agenda Item 4C, Beijing, 1992, p. 2.

48. J. Stapleton Roy, U.S. Ambassador to China, Beijing, 1993 (personal communication).

49. Chen Yingrong, "Renewables in China," *Energy Policy*, Vol. 19, No. 9 (1991), p. 893.

50. International Energy Agency (IEA), *Energy Statistics and Balances of Non-OECD Countries, 1989–90* (IEA, Paris, 1992), p. 175.

51. *Op. cit.* 38, p. 413.

52. *Op. cit.* 20, p. 411.

53. Larry Chuen-ho Chow, "The Rise and Fall of Chinese Oil Production in the 1980s," *Energy Policy*, Vol. 19, No. 9 (1991), pp. 870 and 877.

54. Lester Ross, Attorney, Jones, Day, Reavis, and Pogue, New York, 1993 (personal communication).

55. *Op. cit.* 48.

56. *Op. cit.* 20, p. 407.

57. *Op. cit.* 43, p. 75.

58. *Op. cit.* 48.

59. *Op. cit.* 38, p. 410.

60. Qu Geping, "China's Dual-Thrust Energy Strategy," *Energy Policy*, Vol. 20, No. 6 (1992), pp. 501–504.

61. Chen Xiao, "Efficient Energy Use Still the Key," *China Daily* (April 21, 1990), p. 4.

62. *Op. cit.* 39, p. 217.

63. *Op. cit.* 39, pp. 212 and 218.

64. *Op. cit.* 44, pp. 38, 39 and 67.

65. *Op. cit.* 39, pp. 212, 213 and 218.

66. *Op. cit.* 48.

67. *Op. cit.* 27, p. 74.

68. *Op. cit.* 47, p. 3.

69. *Op. cit.* 38, pp. 421–422.

70. *Op. cit.* 35, p. 936.

71. *Op. cit.* 38, p. 421.

72. Vaclav Smil, *Energy in China's Modernization: Advances and Limitations* (M.E. Sharpe, Armonk, New York, 1988), p. 123.

73. *Op. cit.* 47, p. 3.

74. *Op. cit.* 38, p. 422.

75. Jonathan Sinton, Research Assistant, Energy Analysis Program, Lawrence Berkeley Laboratory, Berkeley, California, 1992 (personal communication).

76. *Op. cit.* 38, pp. 414 and 423–433.

77. *Op. cit.* 6.

78. *Op. cit.* 49, p. 892.

79. *Op. cit.* 60, pp. 501–504.

80. *Op. cit.* 60, pp. 501–504.

81. *Op. cit.* 60, pp. 503–504.

82. *Op. cit.* 39, p. 221.

83. *Op. cit.* 60, pp. 503–504.

84. *Op. cit.* 39, pp. 219–220.

85. *Op. cit.* 60, pp. 504–505.

86. *Op. cit.* 48.

87. *Op. cit.* 60, p. 505.

88. *Op. cit.* 48.

89. *Op. cit.* 39, pp. 220–221.

90. *Op. cit.* 60, p. 505.

91. *Op. cit.* 60, p. 505.

92. *Op. cit.* 14, p. 6.

93. *Op. cit.* 72, pp. 190–191.

94. *Op. cit.* 7, p. 35.

95. *Op. cit.* 44, p. 33.

96. *Op. cit.* 39, p. 221.

97. *Op. cit.* 27, pp. 104–105.

98. Hu Chengchun and Lu Weide, "Solar Energy Utilization in China," *Ecodecision* (March 1992), p. 61.

99. *Op. cit.* 49, p. 894.

100. "China to Free Some Prices," *Wall Street Journal* (June 18, 1992), p. 13, sec. A.

101. Carbon Dioxide Information Analysis Center (CDIAC), Oak Ridge National Laboratory, *Trends '91: A Compendium of Data on Global Change* (CDIAC, Oak Ridge, Tennessee, 1991), pp. 389 and 407.

102. *Op. cit.* 39, p. 208.

103. Robert Williams, "The Potential for Reducing CO_2 Emissions with Modern Energy Technology: An Illustrative Scenario for the Power Sector in China," *Science and Global Security*, Vol. 2, No. 1/2 (1991), pp. 6–9.

104. *Ibid.*, pp. 9–15.

105. *Ibid.*, pp. 9–15.

106. *Ibid.*, pp. 15–19.

107. Milton Russell, Director, Energy, Environment and Resources Center, University of Tennessee, Knoxville, Tennessee, 1993 (personal communication).

108. *Op. cit.* 49, pp. 892–896.

109. *Op. cit.* 7, pp. 106–111.

110. *Op. cit.* 60, pp. 505–506.

111. *Op. cit.* 6.

112. James E. Nickum, Senior Fellow, Program on Environment, The East-West Center, Honolulu, 1993 (personal communication).

113. *Op. cit.* 20, p. 283.
114. *Op. cit.* 27, p. 55.
115. *Op. cit.* 6.
116. K.K. Chadha, "China's Grim Challenge," *Far Eastern Agriculture* (July/August 1992), p. 32.
117. *Op. cit.* 27, p. 145.
118. *Op. cit.* 20, p. 308.
119. Leo A. Orleans, "Loss and Misuse of China's Cultivated Land," in U.S. Congress, Joint Economic Committee, *China's Economic Dilemmas in the 1990s: The Problems of Reforms, Modernization, and Interdependence*, Committee Print, April 1991, p. 411.
120. *Op. cit.* 27, pp. 149–150.
121. *Op. cit.* 7, p. 47.
122. Jiang Tian Zhong, Deputy Chief of Division, Bureau of Environmental Protection and Energy, Ministry of Agriculture, Beijing, 1992 (personal communication).
123. *Op. cit.* 6.
124. *Op. cit.* 27, p. 147.
125. Christopher Muller, Chief, International Affairs, Bureau of Land Management, U.S. Department of the Interior, Washington, D.C., 1992 (personal communication).
126. *Op. cit.* 14, p. 5.
127. *Op. cit.* 6.
128. *Op. cit.* 14, p. 5.
129. *Op. cit.* 7, p. 47.
130. *Op. cit.* 14, p. 5.
131. *Op. cit.* 14, p. 6.
132. *Op. cit.* 6.
133. *Op. cit.* 112.
134. Deng Nan, "Sound Utilization of Land Resources and Improvement of the Eco-Environment for Promotion of Social Development," *Improving Degraded Lands: Promising Experiences from South China*, Walter Parham, Patricia Darana, and Alison Hess, eds. (Bishop Museum Press, Honolulu, 1993), p. 15.
135. *Op. cit.* 6.
136. Scott Rozelle and Jikun Huang, "Poverty, Population and Environmental Degradation in China," paper prepared for the International Symposium on Sustainable Agriculture and Rural Development, Chinese Academy of Rural Sciences, Beijing, May 1993.
137. Jikun Huang and Scott Rozelle, "Environmental Stress and Grain Yields in China," Chinese Rice Economy Project, China National Rice Research Institute, Beijing, and the Food Research Institute at Stanford University, Stanford, California, July 1993.
138. *Ibid.*
139. *Op. cit.* 6.
140. He Bochuan, *China on the Edge: The Crisis of Ecology and Development* (China Books and Periodicals, San Francisco, 1991), p. 30.
141. M.G. Cook, W. Cheng, and S.M. Chu, "Erosion in the Loess Plateau Region of China," *Agricultural Reform and Development in China*, T. Tso, ed. (IDEALS, Beltsville, Maryland, 1990), pp. 319–320.
142. *Op. cit.* 6.
143. Walter E. Parham, Patricia J. Durana, and Alison L. Hess, "Degraded Tropical Lands of China: Problems and Opportunities," in *Improving Degraded Lands: Promising Experiences from South China*, Walter E. Parham, Patricia J. Durana, and Alison L. Hess, eds. (Bishop Museum Press, Honolulu, 1993), p. 8.
144. *Op. cit.* 7, p. 56.
145. *Op. cit.* 7, p. 56.
146. *Op. cit.* 16, p. 94.
147. *Op. cit.* 7, pp. 55–56.
148. He Jun, "Water Crisis Menacing the Nation," *China Daily* (January 27, 1992), p. 5.
149. *Op. cit.* 16, p. 96.

150. Bruce Stone, "The Chang Jiang Diversion Project: An Overview of Economic and Environmental Issues," in *Long Distance Water Transfer: A Chinese Case Study and International Experiences*, Asit K. Biswas, Zuo Dakang, James E. Nickum, *et al.*, eds. (Tycooly, Dublin, 1983), pp. 194–197.
151. Shen Huanting, Mao Zhichang, Gu Guochuan, *et al.*, "The Effect of South-to-North Water Transfer on Saltwater Intrusion in the Chang Jiang Estuary," in *Long Distance Water Transfer: A Chinese Case Study and International Experiences*, Asit K. Biswas, Zuo Dakang, James E. Nickum, *et al.*, eds. (Tycooly, Dublin, 1983), pp. 352–359.
152. Dong Shi, "Water Crisis in North China and Counter-Measures," *Beijing Review* (April 2–8, 1990), p. 33.
153. Li Fuxian, Deputy Director, Department of Spatial Planning and Regional Economy, State Planning Commission, Beijing, 1992 (personal communication).
154. *Op. cit.* 112.
155. *Op. cit.* 16, pp. 96–98.
156. Martin Lees, "China and the World in the Nineties," summary report of the International Conference on the Integration of Economic Development and Environment in China, Beijing, April 1991.
157. *Op. cit.* 6, pp. 36–37.
158. S.D. Richardson, *Forests and Forestry in China* (Island Press, Washington, D.C., 1990), p. 10.
159. *Op. cit.* 140, p. 26.
160. *Op. cit.* 158, pp. 111–112.
161. *Op. cit.* 6.
162. *Op. cit.* 6.
163. *Op. cit.* 6.
164. *Op. cit.* 7, p. 57.
165. Rudolf Orthofer, Program Officer, Global Environment Monitoring System, Nairobi, Kenya, 1993 (personal communication).
166. *Ibid.*
167. *Op. cit.* 14, p. 4.
168. *Op. cit.* 27, p. 118.
169. *Op. cit.* 165.
170. *Op. cit.* 14, p. 4.
171. "1991 Communiqué on the State of the Environment in China," *China Environment News*, No. 35 (June 1992), p. 6.
172. *Op. cit.* 6.
173. "Auto Industry Sets New Record in First Half," *Beijing Xinhua* (August 3, 1993), reprinted in *Foreign Broadcast Information Service Daily Report: China* (August 5, 1993), pp. 43–44.
174. *Op. cit.* 6.
175. Xiping Xu, Douglas W. Dockery, and Lihua Wang, "Effects of Air Pollution on Adult Pulmonary Function," *Archives of Environmental Health*, Vol. 46, No. 4 (1991), p. 198.
176. Zuo-Feng Zhang, Shun-Zhang Yu, and Guo-Dong Zhou, "Indoor Air Pollution of Coal Fumes as a Risk Factor of Stroke, Shanghai," *American Journal of Public Health*, Vol. 78, No. 8 (1988), pp. 975–976.
177. *Op. cit.* 11, pp. 25–30.
178. Zhyong Wang, "Reducing Air Pollution from Electric Power Generation in China," *Environmental Conservation*, Vol. 18, No. 3 (1991), p. 244.
179. Richard A. Carpenter, "Final Report of the International Workshop on the Control of Environmental Pollution in China," paper prepared for the United Nations Development Programme (UNDP) and the State Science and Technology Commission, Beijing, February 1990.
180. *Op. cit.* 6.
181. *Op. cit.* 6.
182. *Op. cit.* 6.
183. Ren Wei, "Benxi Gets a Clean Sweep," *Beijing Review* (December 2–8, 1991), p. 25.

184. *Ibid.*, p. 23.
185. *Op. cit.* 6.
186. *Op. cit.* 6.
187. *Op. cit.* 6.
188. Lester Ross, Chenge Weixue, Mitchell A. Silk, *et al.*, "Cracking Down on Polluters," *The China Business Review* (July-August 1990), p. 39.
189. Lester Ross, "Environmental Protection in China: Policies, Problems, and Foreign Relations," paper prepared for the Conference on the Foreign Relations of China's Environmental Policy, Racine, Wisconsin, August 1991.
190. Liang Run Qiu, Deputy Director, Nanhai County Environmental Protection Bureau, Guangdong Province, 1992 (personal communication).
191. *Op. cit.* 6.
192. *Op. cit.* 6.
193. *Op. cit.* 14, p. 4.
194. *Op. cit.* 14, p. 4.
195. *Op. cit.* 14, p. 4.
196. Qu Geping, Administrator, China National Environmental Protection Agency, Beijing, 1993 (personal communication).
197. *Op. cit.* 14, pp. 5, 7.
198. *Op. cit.* 6, p. 10.
199. Daniel Okun and Zhang Chonghua, "Excerpts from the Report of the Water Group," in Richard A. Carpenter, "Final Report of the International Workshop on the Control of Environmental Pollution in China," paper prepared for UNDP and the State Science and Technology Commission, Beijing, February 1990.
200. *Op. cit.* 6.
201. *Op. cit.* 7, p. 83.
202. *Op. cit.* 6.
203. *Op. cit.* 6.
204. "1990s Communiqué on the State of the Environment," *China Environment News*, No. 23 (June 1991), p. 8.
205. *Op. cit.* 171, p. 3.
206. *Op. cit.* 14, p. 7.
207. *Op. cit.* 14, p. 5.
208. *Op. cit.* 6.
209. Xiong Zhihong, "Heavier Fines are Imposed on Pollution," *China Environment News*, No. 25 (August 1991), p. 1.
210. *Op. cit.* 188, p. 41.
211. *Op. cit.* 6.
212. *Op. cit.* 6.
213. "Better Use of Fees Will Help the Pollution Battle," *China Environment News*, No. 27 (October 1991), p. 4.
214. *Op. cit.* 18, p. 43.
215. *Op. cit.* 18, p. 50.
216. *Op. cit.* 6.
217. *Op. cit.* 6.
218. *Op. cit.* 171, p. 7.
219. *Op. cit.* 171, pp. 6–7.
220. *Op. cit.* 171, p. 7.
221. *Op. cit.* 171, p. 3.
222. *Op. cit.* 6.
223. *Op. cit.* 6.
224. *Op. cit.* 6.
225. Vaclav Smil, "Energy Cost of Chinese Crop Farming," in *Agricultural Reform and Development in China*, T. Tso, ed. (IDEALS, Beltsville, Maryland, 1990), p. 260.
226. Wen Dazhong and David Pimentel, "Ecological Resource Management for a Productive, Sustainable Agriculture in Northeast China," in *Agricultural Reform and Development in China*, T. Tso, ed. (IDEALS, Beltsville, Maryland, 1990), p. 302.
227. *Ibid.*, p. 302.
228. *Op. cit.* 48.
229. *Op. cit.* 27, p. 58.

230. *Op. cit.* 137.
231. *Op. cit.* 6.
232. *Op. cit.* 6.
233. *Op. cit.* 48.
234. *Op. cit.* 48.
235. *Op. cit.* 18, p. 51.
236. "China Takes a Firm Stance to Cut CFCs," *China Environment News* (July 1991), p. 4.
237. National Environmental Protection Agency (NEPA), "China Country Program for the Phaseout of Ozone-Depleting Substances under the Montreal Protocol," report submitted to the Ninth Meeting of the Executive Committee of the Multilateral Fund of the Montreal Protocol, Montreal, March 1993.
238. *Ibid.*
239. *Ibid.*
240. *Op. cit.* 37, p. 125.
241. *Op. cit.* 27, pp. 59–62.
242. Stanley Krugman, Director, Forest Management Research, U.S. Department of Agriculture (USDA), Washington, D.C., 1992 (personal communication).
243. *Op. cit.* 14, p. 5.
244. *Op. cit.* 7, p. 35.
245. *Op. cit.* 7, pp. 33–35.
246. *Op. cit.* 242.
247. Zhang Zhida, Director, Afforestation, Ministry of Forestry, Beijing, 1992 (personal communication).
248. Wang Dongtai, "Afforesting Project for 2000 Boosts Timber," *China Daily* (October 6, 1990), p. 1.
249. *Op. cit.* 6.
250. *Op. cit.* 6.
251. Walter E. Parham, Research Associate, Bishop Museum, Honolulu, 1993 (personal communication).
252. Scott Rozelle, Susan Lund, Zuo Ting, *et al.*, "Rural Policy and Forest Degradation in China," Food Research Institute at Stanford University, Stanford, California, 1993.
253. *Op. cit.* 6.
254. *Op. cit.* 158, p. 110.
255. Qu Geping and Li Jinchang, "An Outline of Study on China's Population-Environment Issues," draft report for NEPA, Beijing, 1990, p. 19.
256. Jeffrey A. McNeely, Kenton R. Miller, Walter V. Reid, *et al.*, *Conserving the World's Biological Diversity* (International Union for Conservation of Nature, Gland, Switzerland, 1990), p. 89.
257. Zhao Yuqing, "China's Nature Preserves Rapidly Expand," *Beijing Review* (April 29–May 5, 1991), p. 28.
258. *Op. cit.* 7, pp. 41, 59 and 92.
259. Catherine Cheung Pui Shan, "MOF/WWF Workshop on Conservation Priorities in China," Report of Proceedings, Ministry of Forestry, Beijing, and World Wildlife Fund, Vienna, Virginia, 1992, pp. 3–4 and 39.
260. Sheryl WuDunn, "Pessimism Is Growing on Saving Pandas from Extinction," *New York Times* (June 11, 1991), p. 4, sec. C.

5. India

One of the great challenges India faces over the next several decades is how to speed economic growth without exhausting the resources on which that growth relies. Environmental health is of utmost importance to India's future. Good soil is critical, for example, to provide the ever increasing population with food and livestock fodder, as well as income from exportable cash crops. Forests support water retention in river catchments, provide fuel for heating and cooking, and supply fodder for about 100 million livestock.

One obstacle to conserving and improving India's environment is the momentum of population growth. At a busy intersection near the All India Institute of Medical Sciences in New Delhi, a population clock adds about 3,000 babies every hour to the national census count. At this rate, the clock could read about 905 million in January 1994 (1), over 1 billion by the year 2000, and 1.4 billion by the year 2025 (2). It is India's daunting task to support this vast population, currently 16 percent of the world total, with just 2.3 percent of the world's land resources and 1.7 percent of the world's forest stock (3).

Rapid population growth creates many pressures. In rural areas, it calls for intensified agricultural production, which raises the risk of environmental degradation. In urban areas, it requires municipal governments to install more basic services, or it simply swells the ranks of those not receiving such services.

Climatic uncertainties are a continuing problem. Harvests in 600,000 villages—and national prosperity —have traditionally depended on a successful southwest monsoon, the source of about three fourths of India's annual rainfall (4). In recent years, the growth of irrigation and diversification into manufacturing have helped mitigate the problem, but rainfed agriculture continues to be central to the economy (5).

Ethnic diversity is another challenge. Many differences in culture, language, religion, and economic condition separate India's states and regions. (See Figure 5.1.) For example, five poor states—Bihar, Madhya Pradesh, Orissa, Rajasthan, and Uttar Pradesh—lag far behind the rest of the country in nearly all measures of human and economic development, while several states in the south and the northwest have done better in some respects than the nation as a whole. (See Figure 5.2.) Female literacy and infant mortality statistics vary widely from state to state, and some individual states also have ethnic and socioeconomic disparities (6) (7). (See Table 5.1.)

Kerala, in particular, has made remarkable strides in areas such as health care and education. Over several decades, the state government carried out land reform, mandated education through the tenth grade, insti-

Figure 5.1 Map of India

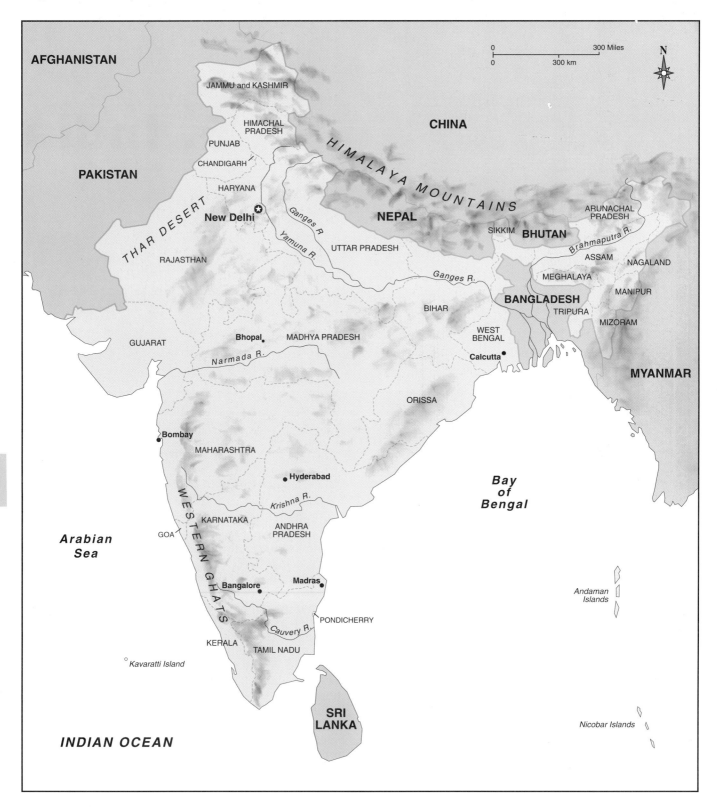

tuted a minimum wage and the right of labor to organize, and built the most extensive medical facilities in India. The results are impressive: despite a per capita income of about $300, many indicators such as literacy, infant mortality, and life expectancy are close to industrialized countries with far higher per capita incomes (8).

India's diversity is also a source of creativity and strength. For instance, an estimated 10,000 nongovernmental organizations (NGOs) are active throughout the country in environment and development work. These range from national agencies such as the Centre for Science and Environment to regional organizations

Figure 5.2 Average Fertility Rate in India, Major States

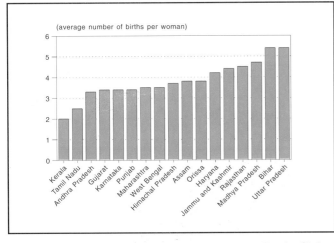

(average number of births per woman)

Source: Shanti R. Conly and Sharon L. Camp, *India's Family Planning Challenge: From Rhetoric to Action* (Population Action International, Washington, D.C., 1992), p. 11.

Table 5.1 Per Capita Spending on Health and Education by State
(1980–91, in rupees)

Health Spending (per capita) 1986–87	Infant Mortality (per 1,000) 1989	States	Education Spending (per capita) 1980–87	Literacy Rate (percent) 1991
30.4	81	Andhra Pradesh	67.7	45.1
15.0	91	Bihar	37.0	38.5
39.6	86	Gujarat	81.4	60.9
37.5	82	Haryana	66.6	55.3
23.2	80	Karnataka	65.4	56.0
29.3	22	Kerala	103.0	90.6
18.3	117	Madhya Pradesh	46.5	43.5
44.7	59	Maharashtra	79.6	63.1
32.2	122	Orissa	49.8	48.6
32.8	67	Punjab	81.7	57.1
32.8	96	Rajasthan	60.3	38.8
33.3	68	Tamil Nadu	59.1	63.7
19.1	118	Uttar Pradesh	42.1	41.7
25.4	77	West Bengal	68.0	57.7

Sources:
1. Martin Ravallion and K. Subbarao, "Adjustment and Human Development in India," in *Journal of Indian School of Political Economy*, Vol. 4, No. 1 (January–March 1992), p. 69.
2. Ashish Bose, *Demographic Diversity in India: 1991 Census* (B.R. Publishing, Delhi, 1991), pp. 62, 89.

Table 5.2 Population in India below Poverty Line

Region	1987–88	1983–84	1977–78	1972–73
Number of poor (millions)				
Rural	196.0	221.5	253.1	244.2
Urban	41.7	49.5	53.7	47.3
Total	**237.7**	**271.0**	**306.8**	**291.5**
Poverty rate (percent)				
Rural	33.4	40.4	51.2	54.1
Urban	20.1	28.1	38.2	41.2
Total	**29.9**	**37.4**	**48.3**	**51.5**

Source: Tata Services, *Statistical Outline of India, 1992–93* (Tata Services, Bombay, 1992), p. 27.
Note: Poverty is defined in relation to the expenditure required for a daily calorie intake of 2,400 per person in rural areas and 2,100 in urban areas. This expenditure is officially estimated at (rupees) Rs. 181.50 per capita per month in rural areas and Rs. 209.50 in urban areas at 1991–92 prices.

such as the Bombay Environmental Action Group, which addresses urban land use and industrial zoning in the Bombay area (9). A local example is the Institute of Rural Reconstruction, which has developed the idea of "nutrition gardens" in five villages in the drought-prone Thane district of Maharashtra. Men and women are trained to produce drought-resistant fruits and vegetables whose deep roots ensure survival during the dry months (10).

Economic growth is essential for the Indian government to improve the quality of life of the poor. In 1987–88 the poor officially totaled 238 million people, or 30 percent of the population (11).

To liberalize the economy and accelerate growth, the Narasimha Rao government adopted economic reforms. As a result the gross domestic product grew from 2 percent annually in 1991 to a projected 4 percent in 1993, and the annual inflation rate declined from 17 percent in mid-1991 to less than 7 percent in early 1993 (12). The new strategy could also create badly needed capital to invest in resource projects and environmental protection.

The economic reforms could also result in higher cereal prices, which in the short run might adversely affect low-income groups (13). The hope is that India will avoid carrying out its economic reforms at the expense of the poor.

THE DEMOGRAPHIC AND SOCIAL LANDSCAPE

The number of people living below the poverty line decreased from 52 percent of the population in 1972–73 to 30 percent of the population in 1987–88 (14). (See Table 5.2.) However, poverty remains a serious problem.

Roughly four out of five of India's poor live in rural areas. The poorest households tend to have many children or other dependents. If the rural poor own land, it is usually unproductive and they lack the income or credit to improve it. Opportunities for self-employment are limited. While poor men can take temporary agricultural jobs, most poor women do not have this option (15) (16).

Historically, poverty has been more prevalent in the countryside than in the city. Since the late 1980s, this pattern seems to have changed: the prevalence of extreme poverty is now about equal or perhaps slightly higher in urban areas. The urban poor have greater access to social services than do their rural counterparts. Public health spending per capita is over six times higher in urban areas (17). Nevertheless, many urban poor are unable to afford medical care and housing.

The strong link between poverty and health is manifested most clearly in the inability of the poor to obtain an adequate diet. Although India is self-sufficient in food-grain production, malnutrition remains a serious problem. From 1975 to 1989, in fact, the total percentage of Indian households with adequate nutrition stayed about the same, even though food production rose (18). Many other factors contribute to malnutrition, including local dietary habits, weaning and child-feeding practices, the status of women in the family, and decisionmaking within the family (19).

Roughly 40 percent of India's population is affected by malnutrition (20). Particularly vulnerable are landless

Box 5.1 India's Population: A Critical Issue

India's 1991 census estimated the country's total population at 844 million, 160 million more people than in 1981 (1). The population is projected to be 914 million by January 1994 (2); by the year 2000, it will exceed 1 billion. (See Figure 1.) Early in the next century, India should surpass China as the most populous country in the world (3). In part, such rapid growth is an indirect result of India's mortality rate, which fell from roughly 16 per 1,000 in the early 1970s to about 10 per 1,000 by 1989 (4).

Demographic pressures on the environment are likely with increases in population density. From 1901 to 1951, India's population density went from 77 people to 117 people per square kilometer. From 1981 to 1991, density increased from 216 to 267 people per square kilometer. In other words, there was a bigger rise in density in just one decade, the 1980s, than in the first five decades of the century (5). In several states, population density now exceeds 400 people per square kilometer. (See Figure 2.)

These aggregate figures disguise vast demographic differences among India's various states. The transition from high to low fertility is nearly complete in some states, notably Kerala and Tamil Nadu in the south. The average fertility rate in Kerala, for example, is two children. The average number of births per woman is just above three children in a second group of states, including Punjab, Maharashtra, Gujarat, and Karnataka (6).

India's demographic vulnerability is concentrated in a half dozen other states, primarily in the north. The most notable are Bihar and Uttar Pradesh, where the average number of births per woman is still nearly six. On a wide variety of other indicators—the infant mortality rate, the female literacy rate, the average age at marriage, per capita income, percentage of population below the poverty line—these six states also rank at the bottom (7). The average national fertility rate is about four children per woman of childbearing age, still about double the replacement level of slightly over two children (8).

Many factors help to explain the difference. The traditional preference for sons is stronger in the north than in the south, for example. In the northern states, daughters are considered something of a liability because of the tradition that requires parents to provide a dowry at the time of a daughter's marriage, and because a daughter, absorbed by her husband's family, is unable to assist her own parents in old age. Women tend to marry outside their own village, thus losing property rights and control over economic resources. In the southern state of Kerala, by contrast, the social status of women is much higher, as is reflected in the inheritance laws of some communities. Among the Nairs, for instance, property is traditionally inherited by daughters (9).

India was one of the first nations to recognize the implications of rapid popula-

Figure 1 Estimated and Projected Population for India, 1950–2150

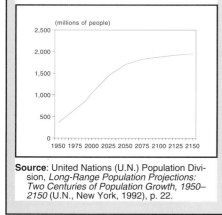

(millions of people)

Source: United Nations (U.N.) Population Division, *Long-Range Population Projections: Two Centuries of Population Growth, 1950–2150* (U.N., New York, 1992), p. 22.

Figure 2 Population Density Among Major States, 1991

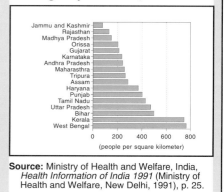

(people per square kilometer)

Source: Ministry of Health and Welfare, India, *Health Information of India 1991* (Ministry of Health and Welfare, New Delhi, 1991), p. 25.

agricultural laborers, urban slum dwellers, and remote tribal communities. Nearly 50 percent of the agricultural workers have an inadequate diet (21). The most common nutritional disorders are protein energy malnutrition, which affects about 1 percent of children under 5, and deficiencies of iron, iodine, and vitamins A and B.

India does have a relatively well-developed social welfare program. For example, the Public Distribution System (PDS) now circulates about 15 to 19 million metric tons of food grain annually. The PDS has averted famine over the last four decades, but critics suggest it could redirect subsidies to poorer areas and target the neediest people within those areas (22) (23). The system could be expanded in rural and remote areas, and distribute coarse food grains, millet, maize, and pulses in appropriate regions (24).

Like the PDS, India's Primary Health Centres (PHCs) target the poor. But most PHCs have small staffs, inadequate budgets, medicine shortages, and high staff absenteeism (25).

To face a possible resurgence of communicable diseases such as malaria and Japanese encephalitis and the spread of acquired immune deficiency syndrome (AIDS), India needs to develop a strong health system (26). Many efforts are under way to improve services. Staff at the King Edward Memorial Hospital, in Maharashtra, is attempting to develop a system of comprehensive primary health care with community participation (27). In Bombay, Streehitakarini, a grassroots women's organization, relies on locally recruited women as part of this effort to deliver maternal, pediatric, and family planning services to 100,000 slum dwellers (28). The Parivar Seva Sanstha (Family Services Organization) is using modern management and marketing techniques to develop a network of clinics, primarily in northern India, which focus on women's reproductive health care (29).

Problems of poverty in India are closely linked to the status of women. To take just one example, the literacy rate for the country as a whole was provisionally estimated at 52 percent in 1991, but the rate for women was just 39 percent. (See Table 5.3.)

Investment in women's education is a critical component of the transition to lower fertility rates. Yet poverty and environmental degradation can undermine this effort as young girls skip school to collect fuel, fodder, and water for the household (30). (See Chapter 3, "Women and Sustainable Development.")

Box 5.1

tion growth for future development when in 1951 it announced an official policy to lower the birthrate. After four decades, an extensive network of clinics is in place around the country, providing contraceptive and maternal and child health care services. As birth control has become more socially acceptable, birthrates have fallen. (See Figure 3.) More than 90 million unintended births have been prevented since the program began. Fertility decline is largely the result of family planning efforts rather than social and economic changes (10).

The pattern of choice among contraceptive options varies from state to state. In Kerala and Maharashtra, sterilization is relatively acceptable, whereas conventional contraceptives are not widely used. In Bihar and Uttar Pradesh, there has been resistance to both sterilization and conventional contraception (11).

Despite some success, India's population control program has fallen far short of its potential. Political support has been inconsistent. Certain program abuses, especially overzealous sterilization efforts during the mid-1970s, eroded support. Family planning options in India remain limited, even though the country has a highly developed drug industry capable of manufacturing contraceptives. There appears to be enormous scope for the expanded use of contraceptives (12).

Indian and international family planning experts agree that the government's top priority should be to broaden the options and expand the availability of reversible contraception. There is also consensus about the need for a large-scale training effort to upgrade the technical and counseling skills of family welfare personnel, outreach programs, a replacement for the present system of sterilization targets, a pluralistic program that draws more on the private sector, and intensified public education (13) (14). The Rao government has shown some support for these goals, at least on paper, issuing an action plan that vows to improve the quality of services, reduce the emphasis on sterilization targets, and expand the availability of reversible methods (15).

Figure 3 Trends in Fertility in India, 1950–90

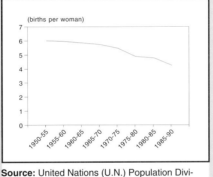

Source: United Nations (U.N.) Population Division, *Demographic Indicators 1950–2025 (the 1992 Revision)*, on diskette (U.N., New York, 1993), p. 498.

References and Notes

1. Ashish Bose, *Demographic Diversity of India: 1991 Census* (B.R. Publishing, Delhi, 1991), p. 47.
2. United Nations (U.N.) Population Division, *Interpolated National Populations 1950-2025 (The 1992 Revision)*, on diskette, (U.N., New York, 1993).
3. United Nations (U.N.), *Long-range World Population Projections* (U.N., New York, 1992), p. 22.
4. *Op. cit.* 1, p. 68.
5. Ministry of Health and Welfare, India, *Health Information of India* (Ministry of Health and Welfare, New Delhi, 1992), p. 24.
6. Shanti R. Conly and Sharon L. Camp, *India's Family Planning Challenge: From Rhetoric to Action* (The Population Crisis Committee, Washington, D.C., 1992), pp. 10–11.
7. *Op. cit.* 1, p. 4.
8. *Op. cit.* 6, p. 1.
9. *Op. cit.* 6, pp. 15–19.
10. *Op. cit.* 6, pp. 1, 10.
11. Central Statistical Organization (CSO), *Statistical Abstract 1990* (CSO, New Delhi, 1992), p. 515.
12. *Op. cit.* 6, pp. 7–8, 13, 21, 29, 36–37, 50–51.
13. *Op. cit.* 6, pp. 44–53.
14. Robert S. McNamara, "A Global Population Policy to Advance Human Development in the 21st Century, with Particular Reference to India," Rajiv Gandhi Memorial Lecture, New Delhi, May 23, 1992, pp. 37–38.
15. *Op. cit.* 6, p. 9.

Population Growth And Urbanization

City dwellers make up 26 percent of the country's total population. India's urban population, at a total of 217 million, is the second largest in the world and is projected to grow to 290–350 million by 2000. (See Figure 5.3.)

These people are increasingly concentrated in comparatively larger cities; the share of the urban population living in cities over 100,000 rose from 51 percent in 1961 to 65 percent in 1991. The number of cities over 1 million has also grown rapidly, nearly doubling since 1981 from 12 to 23, while their share of the urban population has jumped from 26.8 percent to over 35 percent (31). Reproduction now accounts for about 60 percent of urban population growth; growth as a result of migration from the countryside dropped from about 40 percent in the 1970s to about 33 percent in the 1980s (32).

The contribution of India's urban sector to net domestic product rose from 29 percent in 1950–51 to 41 percent by 1980–81; and it is likely to be over 60 percent by 2001. Roughly two thirds of the employment in manufacturing, trade, commerce, and the transport sector is concentrated in urban areas.

The benefits of this economic growth are not shared by all. In addition to poverty, inadequate shelter is a major problem in urban areas, especially large cities

such as Calcutta, Bombay, Delhi, Madras, and Kanpur, where one third to one half of the population lives in slums and squatter settlements. About 15 percent of the male work force and 25 percent of the female work force have no regular employment (33).

THE POLITICAL AND INSTITUTIONAL CONTEXT

India's eighth five-year plan suggests that environmental objectives are almost synonymous with human development. The plan's objectives are to generate adequate employment, contain population growth, universalize elementary education, eliminate illiteracy among 15- to 35-year-olds, deliver safe drinking water and primary health care to the entire population, expand and diversify agriculture for self-sufficiency and exportable surpluses, and strengthen infrastructure (energy, transport, communication, irrigation) to sustain growth. The plan recognizes that "environment, ecology, and development must be balanced to meet the needs of the society" (34).

Controlling Industrial Pollution

Since the 1970s, and especially in the wake of the accident at the Union Carbide plant in Bhopal in the mid-

Table 5.3 Literacy Rates in India, 1951–91
(percent of population)

Year	Total Population	Males	Females
1951	18.33	27.16	8.86
1961	28.31	40.40	15.34
1971	34.45	45.95	21.97
1981	43.56	56.37	29.75
	(41.42)	(53.45)	(28.46)
1991	52.11	63.86	39.42

Source: Ashish Bose, *Demographic Diversity of India: 1991 Census* (B.R. Publishing, New Delhi, 1991), p. 50.
Note: a. Literacy rates for 1951, 1961 and 1971 relate to population aged 5 years and older. Rates for the years 1981 and 1991 relate to the population aged 7 years and older. Rates for the population aged 5 years and older in 1981 in parentheses.

1980s, the Indian government has enacted legislation to govern industrial pollutants and has created agencies to enforce the laws. (See Box 5.2)

India's Central and State Pollution Control Boards are an outgrowth of the 1974 Water Prevention and Control of Pollution Act. The boards set water quality and effluent standards, inspect industrial plants, and order them to observe certain environmental conditions to continue operating, and issue permits for waste discharge into water bodies. They monitor compliance with the 1974 act and prosecute violations (35).

The 1981 Air Prevention and Control of Pollution Act gave the boards an additional responsibility: protecting air quality. They were authorized to establish standards for air quality and the emission of airborne pollutants as well as procedures for monitoring and enforcement. As under the water act, industrial facilities must obtain permission from the state pollution control board or some other designated authority to emit airborne pollutants (36).

The 1986 Environment Protection Act and Rules authorized the central government to protect and improve environmental quality, control and reduce pollution from all sources, and prohibit or restrict the location or operation of an industrial facility on environmental grounds. It established comprehensive national discharge standards to regulate wastewater products from some industries (37).

New companies must go through an elaborate clearance process, in some cases including an environmental impact assessment, before they begin operations. How thorough the process is partly depends on the proposed plant location and whether it will be polluting. After a plant opens, consent to operate is routinely required from the state pollution control board that certifies compliance with environmental regulations. Established industrial facilities must renew their consent to operate every few years (38).

Progress in controlling industrial pollution is often offset by the pace of industrial expansion. Many noncomplying industries are tolerated because of the immense workload at the boards and the lack of staff, budget, equipment, and facilities. Boards are sometimes reluctant to close facilities because of social and employment considerations. Fines and penalties for noncompliance are generally not steep enough to induce industries to invest in pollution control equipment (39). Occasionally, companies are unable to

Figure 5.3 Trends and Projections in India's Urban and Rural Population Growth, 1950–2025

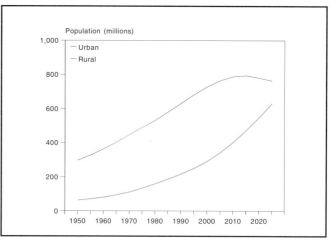

Source: United Nations (U.N.) Population Division, *Urban and Rural Areas 1992*, on diskette (U.N., New York, 1993).

comply with pollution laws because of technical constraints, lack of land to install pollution control systems, or inability to obtain credit (40).

Underfunding and understaffing make it difficult for control boards to deal with small industries. And most small companies are ill-equipped to comply with the law. Owners may be unaware of pollution control requirements or may lack the analytical expertise or the financial resources to meet them. A protracted legal battle is frequently considered cheaper in the long run than installing pollution control equipment (41).

Forestry Management

The government's high profile in forestry management dates back to the late 19th Century and decisions made by the British colonial administration. To provide timber for an expanding railway network and for shipping and defense, the administration enacted laws in 1865 and 1878 that effectively granted the government control of India's forests. The 1878 law divided forests into three categories: unclassified, protected, and reserved, with the latter being the most regulated and restricted (42) (43). Today, 97 percent of India's forestland is publicly owned and 85 percent is managed by state forestry departments (44).

These colonial laws had several unfortunate consequences. Foresters tended to try to limit people's access to forests and to treat agriculture and forestry separately. Tribal forest communities had no ownership rights and only limited use of the forest (45). Conflict often arose between government forest managers and shifting cultivators or local inhabitants who wanted to have access to the forest for firewood and other forest resources (46).

Official foresters mainly concentrated on timber extraction. The government frequently sold wood at low prices, prompting paper mills and plywood companies to maximize short-term profits by harvesting until a resource was exhausted, then moving to another area. In regions such as the Uttara Kannada district of Karnataka, companies exhausted the more accessible deciduous forests and then went after even more remote evergreen forests (47).

In the race to extract timber, forest products that could be used as fuel, food, raw building materials, and medicine were largely overlooked. One such resource is the *tendu* plant, whose leaves are used in cigarette making (48). This approach also reduced the incentive for local residents to harvest fuelwood, fodder, and other products on a sustainable basis (49).

Recently the government has begun involving village communities and non-governmental organizations in forest management. (See Participatory Forest Management below.)

ENVIRONMENTAL CONDITIONS

Perhaps the most significant environmental problem and threat to public health in both urban and rural India is inadequate access to clean water and sanitation. In rural India, other environmental problems include land degradation, loss of soil nutrients, forest and groundwater depletion, and diminishing biodiversity. In urban India, air pollution from industrial sources and vehicles is a serious problem, as are living conditions in squatter settlements.

National Problems: Water Supply and Sanitation

The World Health Organization (WHO) has estimated that in developing countries, 75 percent of all illnesses and 80 percent of child mortality cases are associated with unsafe disposal of excrement, poor hygiene, and water supplies that are inadequate in quantity or quality (50).

WHO clean-water standards require that 98 percent of water samples from any one area be completely free of coliform bacteria. By this measure, most of India's surface water resources are polluted. The Yamuna receives an estimated 200 million liters of untreated sewage every day as it passes by New Delhi, raising the coliform count from 7,500 per 100 milliliters above the city to 24 million below the city (51). About 70 percent of India's water is seriously polluted (52). A 1990 government survey showed coliform levels to be a serious problem at many urban locations on the Ganges and on sections of other rivers (53).

The Indian government reports that by early 1992, 78 percent of rural Indians and 85 percent of urban Indians had access to potable water. Sanitation services were available to almost 48 percent of the urban population but less than 3 percent of the rural population (54). Some cities such as Madras must limit the number of hours when water is available (55).

The irony is that, in the midst of water scarcity, about one fourth (40 million hectares) of India's cropland is flood-prone; in an average year, flash floods occur on about 9 million hectares of cropland (56). Aside from its devastating impacts on housing, crops, and food supplies, flooding raises health risks. The lack of potable drinking water, for example, leads to gastroenteritis and higher mortality among children (57).

Figure 5.4 Percentage of India's Land Cover, 1991

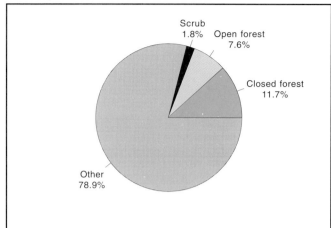

Source: Ministry of Environment and Forest, India, *The State of Forest Report, 1991* (Ministry of Forests, New Delhi, 1991), p. 7.
Note: Does not include mangrove forests (4,244 square kilometers or 0.13 percent of total area) or uninterpreted area under clouds and in shadows (19,093 square kilometers, or 0.58 percent of total area).

Key Problems In Rural India

Forests

A 1991 government assessment of forest cover estimated India's forest cover at 63.9 million hectares, about 19 percent of the country's total geographical area (58).

Forestland with a crown density of 40 percent or more covers 38.5 million hectares, or about 11.7 percent of India's total area. (See Figure 5.4.) Open forestland with a crown density of 10 to 40 percent covers 25 million hectares or about 7.6 percent of the country (59).

The 1991 survey reflected a modest annual increase of about 28,000 hectares of forest cover since an earlier survey in 1989. This small increase could have been caused by technical changes in assessment techniques, for instance, better satellite imagery, more accurate interpretation, and corrections in geographical area. Nonetheless, the findings reversed the trend of previous surveys, which had shown annual deforestation of about 47,000 hectares in the early 1980s (60). India has suffered massive losses: forests covered over 40 percent of its land mass barely a century ago (61).

Although forest area is not currently shrinking, forest degradation continues. Wood is the primary fuel for the rural population and forest cover near cities is diminishing as a result of urban demand. India's forests can sustainably provide an estimated 41 million cubic meters of fuelwood per year, yet current annual demand is thought to be 240 million cubic meters (62) (63). (See Box 5.3.)

Many Indians establish temporary farm plots by burning off the natural vegetation. There are an estimated 30 million itinerant cultivators in the northeastern area of the country alone (64).

In addition to fuelwood, forests in many areas are used for livestock fodder, which leaves trees severely pruned or defoliated, and for livestock grazing, which depletes soil nutrients. About 25 percent of India's 400 million livestock graze on tracts of forestland that have

Box 5.2 Environmental Regulations in India

The December 1984 accident at the Union Carbide plant in Bhopal, which released deadly methyl isocyanate gas into the air and killed more than 2,000 people, was a strong impetus for new environmental regulations in India [1] [2] [3].

The Ministry of Environment and Forests reviewed existing regulations while the Ministry of Labour reviewed the Factories Act of 1948. Their initial response was to make environmental regulations more stringent and enact statutes for the storage and handling of hazardous materials. After a detailed review of the 1974 Water Prevention and Control of Pollution Act and the 1981 Air Prevention and Control of Pollution Act, the government enacted a comprehensive Environmental Protection Act in 1986 [4].

The act subjected the use of hazardous substances to the law, made all the officers of a firm liable for violations under the act, authorized the Ministry of Environment and Forests to initiate action to close down any firm that violated the act's restrictions regarding effluent discharge, and permitted individuals to initiate legal action against anyone violating the act. Industries not meeting environmental standards would have to devise a remedial program within a specific time or close down. Since passage of the 1986 act, the ministry has issued numerous closure notices. However, firms routinely obtain stays against closure, shifting decisions to the judiciary and stalling action for years.

In 1989, using the powers conferred by the 1986 act, the government issued rules for the management and handling of hazardous waste [5]. For the first time, they specifically identified hazardous and toxic chemicals, flammable chemicals, and explosives. Any organization handling hazardous waste must take all practical steps to ensure that it is properly collected, stored, and disposed of directly or through the operator of a facility. Though the rules were published in 1989, state governments have not yet identified disposal sites. In November of the same year, more rules were issued covering the manufacture, storage, and importation of hazardous chemicals. Organizations handling such materials must provide safety data sheets on request, as well as information to persons likely to be affected by a major accident.

Another act, issued in January 1991, requires public liability insurance to cover people affected by an accident that occurs

Table 1 Environmental Assessment of Projects
May 1992–January 1993

Sector	Projects Pending at Beginning of the Year	Projects Received	Projects Appraised	Projects Cleared	Projects Rejected	Projects Seeking Additional Information
Mining	18	37	63	20	2	33
Industries	27	25	44	31	13	8
Atomic power	3	—	2	2	—	1
Thermal power	8	12	39	13	—	7
River valley projects	6	20	26	5	12	9
Other sectors (transport, tourism, ports, harbors, highways, air ports, communications, etc.)	17	34	73	30	2	19
Total	**79**	**128**	**247**	**101**	**29**	**77**

Source: Ministry of Environment and Forests, India, *Annual Report 1992–93* (Ministry of Environment and Forests, New Delhi, 1993), p. 47.

an estimated capacity of only 31 million livestock [65]. In spite of this, the number of livestock grazing in forests is rising.

Another major pressure on forest resources is the increasing demand for timber and paper. From 1980–81 to 1991–92, for example, paper production rose 105 percent and wood production rose significantly [66].

If the burden on India's forests is not eased, the result will be continued forest fragmentation and declining forest health and productivity.

Salinized and Waterlogged Cropland

Soil degradation affects about 85 million hectares of farm land in India [67]. Water and wind erosion, salinity, waterlogging, and loss of soil nutrients seriously affect agricultural production [68] [69].

Of particular importance to Indian agriculture are the two problems typically associated with canal irrigation—waterlogging and salinity. Salinity occurs when the water table rises as water drains from irrigated land over a period of years. When the table is a meter or so below the soil, water flows to the surface, evaporates, and leaves salt deposits.

A related problem is secondary salinization, which occurs when poor-quality groundwater is pumped up and applied to crops by farmers anxious to augment scarce surface supplies. Groundwater, often containing more salt than canal water, tends to leave a higher concentration of salt in the soil as it evaporates [70].

A December 1991 study by the director of the Central Soil Salinity Research Institute estimated that salinity affected 8.5 million hectares [71]. Other estimates are lower [72]. Of India's 47.5 million hectares of irrigated land, about 3 million hectares are believed to be affected by salinity. It is a particularly serious problem in Uttar Pradesh and Gujarat [73].

Another effect of canal irrigation, waterlogging, occurs when the water table rises to within 3 meters of a crop's roots, impeding their ability to absorb oxygen and ultimately compromising crop yields. Estimates of the amount of waterlogged crop land in India vary from 1.6 to 8.5 million hectares. This wide range reflects differences in the definition of waterlogging [74] [75].

Many factors contribute to waterlogging. These include inadequate drainage, improper balance in the use of groundwater and surface water, seepage and percolation from unlined channels, overwatering, planting crops not suited to specific soils, and inadequate preparation of land before irrigation.

Waterlogging is most serious in Haryana, Punjab, West Bengal, Andhra Pradesh, and Maharashtra. In these areas, it is reducing yields and wasting large amounts of water that could be used in places with no irrigation, thus extending the total area of land suited

while handling hazardous substances (6). Every owner of hazardous substances must take out an insurance policy for people likely to be affected in the event of an accident. Compensation (reimbursement of medical expenses up to $400 or $800 for fatal accidents) has to be paid within 30 days of an accident. For new facilities, the provisions of this act are compulsory. In the case of older units, they still have to be implemented, although some large firms have already done so.

Another regulatory change mandated that after 1992–93, firms within the jurisdiction of the Environmental Protection Act must conduct environmental audits annually and submit them to their state pollution control board. The first audit reports were to be submitted by May 1993. One obstacle promises to be the pollution control boards, which are already understaffed and have not been adequately trained in audit reviews.

Another major institutional change introduced after the Bhopal accident affected environmental impact assessments (EIAs) (7). The change required an EIA for specified industries, including small or private companies. Earlier EIAs were carried out only for big government projects. Reviews will be made by either the state or the central government. (See Table 1.)

Another institutional response to the problems highlighted at Bhopal has been

from the judiciary (8). Indian courts never used to entertain cases such as public interest litigation where appellants had no standing. Recently, however, the courts have been invoking a provision of the constitution, stating that it is the fundamental duty of every Indian citizen to protect and improve the natural environment and to have compassion for living creatures. The Supreme Court has taken up three types of public interest litigation—cases filed by voluntary organizations, public-minded individuals, and judges. In one landmark judgment on pollution from small-scale tanneries, the verdict stated that like an industry that cannot pay minimum wages to its workers, a tannery unable to set up a primary pollution control facility should be closed, regardless of its size or budgetary constraints. This carries major implications for small industries.

Even as India's environmental awareness, regulatory and procedural changes, as well as more stringent action by the courts have increased, compliance with the new controls has been sluggish. There are several reasons, among them financial constraints faced by firms, understaffed pollution control boards, the lack of a comprehensive industrial zoning policy, poor commitment at the corporate level, and the dearth of relevant, cost-effective technology. In the long run, the "polluter pays principle" and the "anticipate and pre-

vent" strategies have to be dovetailed. If the technical capability of state pollution control boards and environmental departments was bolstered, staffs could assess the effectiveness of various strategies proposed by manufacturing firms as well as propose safeguards for the environment (9).

References and Notes

1. B. Bowonder and S.S. Arvind, "Environmental Regulations and Litigation in India," *Project Appraisal*, Vol. 4, No. 4 (1989), pp. 182–195.
2. Centre for Science and Environment, *The State of India's Environment, 1984-85* (Centre for Science and Environment, New Delhi, 1985), pp. 206, 210, 227–232.
3. Michael R. Reich and B. Bowonder, "Environmental Policy in India: Strategies for Better Implementation," *Policy Studies Journal*, Vol. 20, No. 4 (1992), pp. 643–659.
4. Central Pollution Control Board, India, *Pollution Control Law Series: PCL/2/1992, Pollution Control Acts, Rules, and Notifications Issues Thereunder* (Central Pollution Control Board, New Delhi, 1992), pp. 207– 222.
5. *Ibid.*, pp. 351–367.
6. *Ibid.*, pp. 443–472.
7. K. Khanna, "Conceptual Framework and Role of EIA," paper prepared for the Indo-Dutch Seminar on Environmental Impact Assessment, Ministry of Environment and Forests, New Delhi, 1989, pp. 47–80.
8. *Op. cit.* 1, pp. 187–192.
9. *Op. cit.* 3, pp. 650–658.

for agriculture (76). The problem is acute at the Sriramsagar irrigation project in Andhra Pradesh, the Tawa project in Madhya Pradesh, and the Tungabhadra project in Karnataka. A detailed survey of the change in agricultural output before and after waterlogging shows a 30 percent reduction in production and increased salinity (77).

Various avenues exist for alleviating the severity of waterlogging. These include educating farmers about efficient water use, improving groundwater monitoring, setting market-based pricing for water and distribution, providing drainage in all new irrigation projects, establishing disincentives for water overuse, promoting supplementary use of groundwater, and better coordinating of watershed management (78).

Investment in irrigation drainage is often minimal. Existing drains may be poorly maintained or badly silted and overgrown with weeds. According to statistics from the World Bank, state funding for the maintenance of drains is typically only 10 to 20 percent of the total amount required (79).

In most irrigation systems, farmers at the "head" receive more water than farmers at the "tail," resulting in waterlogging and salinization near the head. Better water management would redress this imbalance. In some areas, supplementary (or conjunctive) use of groundwater for irrigation helps combat a rising water table (80).

Loss of Soil Nutrients

In some areas, soil nutrients are being rapidly lost. The problem seems most severe in parts of the black-soil region of central and southern India, where more than half of the estimated national losses of nitrogen and phosphorus are occurring (81).

Many small farms and heavily planted soils are also lacking in micronutrients such as zinc, copper, iron, manganese, and boron. Such shortages, a major impediment to agricultural production, are difficult to detect without soil analysis. Zinc deficiency has been reported in various states, among them Madhya Pradesh, Tamil Nadu, Andhra Pradesh, and Uttar Pradesh. About 67 percent of soil samples taken in a 1988–89 national survey were low in zinc. Copper deficiency is acute in Uttar Pradesh, iron deficiency in Haryana, manganese deficiency in Uttar Pradesh, and boron deficiency in Bihar (82).

Groundwater Depletion and Pollution

Over the past decade, the number of agricultural pumps used in India more than doubled, rising from 4.33 million in 1980–81 to 9.1 million in 1991–92 (83). A study of the Ludhiana district in Punjab, a semiarid area that relies heavily on irrigation water from wells, found that the water table fell by roughly 0.8 meters annually in the mid- to late 1980s. Electricity subsidies,

Figure 5.5 Cities in India with Wastewater Disposal Facilities, 1988

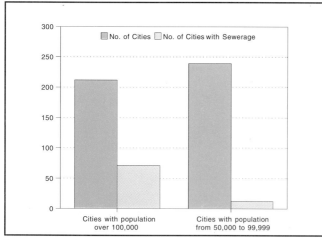

Sources:
1. Central Pollution Control Board (CPCB), "Status of Water Supply and Wastewater Collection, Treatment and Disposal in Class I Cities, 1988," Control of Urban Pollution Series, CUPS/30/1989-90 (CPCB, New Delhi, 1990), p. 36.
2. CPCB, "Status of Water Supply and Wastewater Collection, Treatment and Disposal in Class II Towns, 1988," Control of Urban Pollution Series, CUPS/31/1989–90 (CPCB, New Delhi, 1990), p. 13.

Figure 5.6 Trends in Registered Motor Vehicles in India, 1971–89

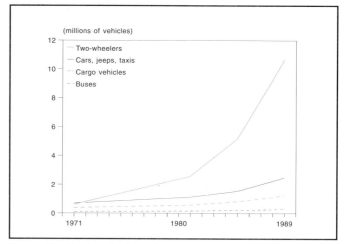

Source: Tata Services, *Statistical Outline of India, 1992–93* (Tata Services, Bombay, 1992), p. 87.

which encourage overirrigation by providing cheap energy to operate pumps, exacerbate the problem of groundwater depletion. The study concludes that rice production, because of its heavy water requirements, is inherently unsustainable in Ludhiana; only a maize-wheat rotation would completely eliminate the reduction in groundwater levels (84).

How extensively is India's groundwater used? Of the 3,841 administrative blocks in the country, it is estimated, 620 (16 percent) are either fully exploiting or overexploiting their groundwater. Development is most intense in Punjab, Haryana, Gujarat, and Tamil Nadu (85).

Pollution from agriculture is another threat. Pollution caused by the leaching of nitrogen fertilizers has been detected in the groundwater in many areas. In Haryana, for example, some well water is reported to have nitrate concentrations ranging from 114 milligrams (mg)/liter to 1,800 mg/liter, far above the 45 mg/liter national standard (86).

Indoor Air Pollution

Indoor air pollution is particularly serious in rural areas. Smoke from wood and other biomass fuels used for household cooking could be responsible for about 50 percent of total human exposure to particulates (87). Indoor pollution is especially severe in poorly ventilated homes in the winter when the air is dense with particulates, smoke, and hazardous organic compounds. Exposure to these pollutants and poor nutrition increases susceptibility to respiratory disease (88).

Key Urban Environmental Problems

India's urban areas are a difficult environmental management problem. The worst conditions prevail in most squatter settlements, which usually lack adequate water supply and sanitation facilities. In 1991, an estimated 20 million people living in 23 major metro-

politan areas—more than 28 percent of the population—were residing in squatter settlements (89).

One reason local governments are unable to provide water and sanitation facilities in these areas is that many residents live in makeshift huts to which they have no ownership rights. Some major urban centers cannot meet the existing demand for water or the increase in demand caused by a growing population (90).

Cities often increase the water supply without any concomitant increase in wastewater treatment. According to a survey conducted by the Central Pollution Control Board in 1988, of 212 class I cities (populations of more than 100,000), only 71 had sewer systems. (See Figure 5.5.) Of the 6.5 billion liters of sewage generated daily in the 12 major metropolitan areas, only 1.5 billion liters was collected. The state capitals of Lucknow and Jaipur had no sewage treatment facilities and cities with sewer systems only provided coverage to about 60 percent of their population (91).

Air pollution is also a serious concern in urban areas. Emissions of suspended particulates have increased in Bombay, Calcutta, and Delhi, according to the Global Environmental Monitoring System. Levels of suspended particulates considerably exceed standards prescribed by WHO. Nitrogen oxide levels in three cities still fall below WHO guidelines, but are rapidly rising, a matter or concern because of trends in the number of motor vehicles (92). (See Figure 5.6.)

In Bombay, where there are higher levels of sulfur dioxide, there has been an increased prevalence of breathing difficulties, coughs, and colds. Mortality data between 1971 and 1979 establish a link between dense air pollution in Bombay and a higher rate of death from respiratory and cardiac conditions, as well as cancer (93).

Industrial Air Pollution

The data on industrial pollution in India are relatively scarce. Estimates of the magnitude of toxic emissions, however, suggest that the problem is serious and growing. (See Chapter 12, "Industry.")

Most industrial air pollution is in the form of suspended particulates. Emissions from utilities and major industries (including textiles, chemicals, iron and steel, cement, fertilizer, and paper) are already substantial in most regions of the country and may rise considerably over the next two decades (94). (See Figure 5.7.)

The Indian government identified 17 highly polluting industries and directed them to comply with pollution control requirements by the end of 1993. By mid-1993, of 1,541 highly polluting companies, 1,003 (65 percent) had installed pollution control facilities that complied with the government's effluent and emission standards (95).

Industrial Waste

Industrial wastewater, only about one fourth of India's total wastewater by volume, is over one half of the total water pollutant load. Most industrial wastewater comes from large and medium sized facilities, especially in the chemical industry and related sectors (96) (97). Although the water act was passed more than two decades ago, relatively little industrial wastewater is treated.

Indian industries also produce a large quantity of solid and hazardous waste. Major generators of solid waste include thermal power plants, which turn out about 30 million metric tons of coal ash annually; iron and steel mills, which create about 35 million metric

---

Box 5.3 India's Fuelwood Market Dynamics

During the last 15 years, a sharp increase in the price of commercial fuels (kerosene, coal, and charcoal) has forced the urban poor of India to use fuelwood for cooking food. Studies show heavy fuelwood consumption in Bangalore (460,000 metric tons in 1983) and Hyderabad (370,000 tons in 1985) (1). In Hyderabad, the principal users of fuelwood are hotels and restaurants (34 percent), squatters (21 percent), and alcohol distilleries (18 percent) (2) (3) (4). This city has more than 500,000 squatters, mostly day laborers who have no other fuel for cooking and buy their fuelwood at the end of the day (5).

Fuelwood is transported to cities by both truck and train from outlying fuelwood-producing areas, in the case of Hyderabad, 50 to 280 kilometers away and anywhere from 40 to 700 kilometers from Bangalore.

Rising demand for fuelwood in urban markets has elevated the price. (See Table 1.) This trend has had two major impacts. First, it has increased the flow of fuelwood into the more lucrative urban market, reducing supplies in rural areas where fuelwood was once mostly a noncommercial product. Shortages in rural markets induce illegal fuelwood collection and tempt unemployed men and women to earn a livelihood by selling it in cities.

Table 1 Fuelwood Prices in Selected Cities

Cities	Fuelwood Price, per ton		
	1960	1986	1992
Ahmedabad	90	740	1,191
Bangalore	47	657	1,135
Bombay	84	1,232	1,812
Calcutta	93	1,040	1,585
Hyderabad	66	667	917

Sources:
1. For 1960 and 1986 prices: B. Bowonder, S.S.R. Prasad, and N.V.M. Unni, "Dynamics of Fuelwood Prices in India," *World Development*, Vol. 16, No. 10 (1988), p. 1221.
2. For 1992 prices: B. Bowonder, Dean of Research, Administrative Staff College of India, Hyderabad, India, 1993 (personal communication).

Table 2 Closed Forest Cover around Urban Centers

Urban Center	1960 (square kilometers)	1986 (square kilometers)
Ajmer (Rajasthan)	259	124
Ammathi (Karnataka)	8,275	5,625
Amritsar (Punjab)	208	111
Bangalore (Karnataka)	3,853	2,762
Bhavnagar (Gujarat)	112	9
Bhopal (Madhya Pradesh)	3,031	1,417
Bombay (Maharashtra)	5,649	3,672
Chikmagalur (Karnataka)	7,912	6,175
Coimbatore (Tamil Nadu)	5,525	4,700
Delhi (Delhi)	254	101
Gwalior (Madhya Pradesh)	1,353	515
Hyderabad (Andhra Pradesh)	40	26
Indore (Madhya Pradesh)	3,770	1,070
Jaipur (Rajasthan)	1,534	786
Madras (Tamil Nadu)	918	568
Monghyr (Bihar)	1,069	875
Nagpur (Maharashtra)	3,116	2,051
Varanasi (Uttar Pradesh)	1,785	1,072

Source: B. Bowonder, S.S.R. Prasad, and N.V.M. Unni, "Dynamics of Fuelwood Prices in India, *World Development*," Vol. 16, No. 10 (1988), p. 1218.

Though the wood fetches a high return for the sellers who collect it, they do not replant. This accelerates forest depletion (6).

The other major impact of the rising demand for fuelwood in urban centers is the devastation of forest cover near cities. A study of changes in forest cover within a radius of 100 kilometers from the center of 33 major Indian cities, carried out with satellite imagery maps prepared by India's National Remote Sensing Agency, indicates a sharp reduction in closed forests around these cities (7). (See Table 2.)

The National Commission on Urbanization has called attention to the problem but jurisdictional roadblocks have hindered initiatives. Further forest depletion can only be curbed by widespread, innovative measures. These include providing fuelwood to the urban poor through extensive city forestry programs, promoting fuel-efficient cookstoves among urban groups, starting high-density plantations to augment the supply, preparing detailed supply and demand plans for critical districts, and weaning heavy users such as bakeries and hotels from the use of fuelwood (8).

References and Notes

1. A.K.N. Reddy and B.S. Reddy, "Energy in a Stratified Society: A Case Study of Fuelwood in Bangalore," *Economic and Political Weekly*, Vol. 18, No. 41 (1983), pp. 1757–1770.
2. B. Bowonder, S.S.R. Prasad, and K. Raghuram, "Fuelwood Use in Urban Centers: A Case Study of Hyderabad," *Natural Resources Forum*, Vol. 11, No. 2 (1987), pp. 189–194.
3. B. Bowonder, V.V.R. Prasad, and S. Prasad, "Fuelwood Consumption in the Hyderabad Metropolitan Area," *Landscape and Urban Planning*, Vol. 14 (1987), pp. 31-43.
4. B. Bowonder, K. Raghuram, A.V. Ramanamurthy, *et al.*, Energy Consumption Pattern in the Hyderabad Urban Area (Administrative Staff College of India, Hyderabad, 1986), p. 85.
5. *Op. cit.* 3, pp. 32, 41.
6. B. Bowonder, S.S.R. Prasad, and N.V.M. Unni, "Dynamics of Fuelwood Prices in India," *World Development*, Vol. 16, No. 10 (1988), pp. 1217–1219.
7. *Ibid.*, pp. 1218–1220.
8. *Ibid.*, pp. 1221–1228.

tons of slag; nonferrous metal industries such as aluminum, zinc, and copper; and the sugar and fertilizer industries. Most of the waste is dumped on land (98).

It is estimated that about one third of the large and medium water-polluting companies generate hazardous wastes, notably the petrochemical, pharmaceutical, pesticide, paint and dye, petroleum, fertilizer, asbestos, caustic soda, inorganic chemical, and general engineering industries. Rough estimates, based on overall economic activity, indicate that in 1984 about 300,000 metric tons of hazardous waste were generated in India. Disposal of these wastes is largely uncontrolled; dumping on public land or in municipal solid waste disposal sites is common (99).

Health officials are concerned about the effects of hazardous waste on humans, especially in places such as Patancheru, Andhra Pradesh, where over 60 chemical and other factories discharge their toxic waste directly into freshwater streams (100). Groundwater near one city in the north, where plants produce bicycle parts, hosiery items, and sporting goods, contains a toxic mix of cyanide, manganese, and chromium in concentrations up to seven times higher than WHO limits for potable water (101).

Vehicular Emissions

Heavy vehicles are a significant source of air pollution in large cities, as are motor scooters and other small vehicles (102). Between 1981 and 1989, the number of two-wheelers quadrupled, totaling 10.6 million in 1989, and growth is expected to continue (103). Most two-wheelers emit harmful unburnt hydrocarbons (104).

PROMISING INITIATIVES

Several promising initiatives are under way to address environmental problems. These include a program to clean up the Ganges and other major river systems, incentives for industrial pollution control, greater community participation in forest management, a 20-year effort to protect India's tiger population, and a new effort to protect elephants.

Controlling Pollution In The Ganges

To Indians, the Ganges—or, as they call it, Ganga—is more than just a river that provides water and supports agriculture: hundreds of millions consider it holy. Pilgrims throng to the Ganges to bathe in its waters or cast the ashes of a cremated body adrift, thereby freeing the soul from the eternal cycle of death and rebirth. These age-old practices help to pollute the Ganges.

Cleaning up the Ganges is a staggering task. The river is more than 2,500 kilometers and on its banks are 25 of India's largest towns with populations exceeding 100,000. They generate nearly 1,400 million liters of sewage every day (105). In 1985, the Central Ganga Authority (CGA) was created to implement a plan to clean up the most polluted sections of the river, in Uttar Pradesh, Bihar, and West Bengal. The project's first phase aimed to intercept, divert, and treat 870 million liters of sewage a day; 405 million liters per day had been diverted as of December 1991 (106).

The Ganga plan includes sewage treatment plants, low-cost sanitation facilities, electric crematoria and more efficient wood-based crematoria, and on the waterfront, regulation of traffic, separate sites for washing clothes, and the construction and renovation of bathing ponds. The government has gone so far as to introduce into the river specially bred snapping turtles that eat corpses but do not nip bathers (107) (108).

Controlling industrial pollution requires building effluent treatment plants, enforcing quality standards, and closing polluting units, if necessary. The CGA identified 68 industrial units as gross polluters. By 1992, 43 of these had installed effluent treatment plants and 7 were in the process of doing so, 10 units were closed, and action had been initiated against the remaining 8 (109). But in some industries, such as leather tanning in Jajmau, progress has been slow (110).

The cost of the first phase of the plan exceeds $120 million, raising questions about the best way to use the money. One critic questions the value of water-quality monitoring stations and arbitrary standards of quality without in-depth, location-specific studies of the river and its capacity to assimilate waste (111).

Another question concerns pollution control costs. Though the central government has paid for constructing some facilities, state governments are reluctant to bear recurring maintenance and operating costs (112).

Cost, however, has not dampened willingness to deal with riverine pollution. Plans to clean up more rivers are being developed on the lines of the Ganga plan. A $330 million national river action plan has been proposed for stretches of 13 waterways and a plan to clean up the Yamuna River, which flows through New Delhi, is already under way (113) (114).

Participatory Forest Management

In the 1970s and 1980s, the government's attempts to deal with the fuelwood and fodder crisis centered on India's social forestry program, which encouraged private farms and community wood lots. The program helped increase supplies of timber, construction poles, and pulp, but did little to stop forestland degradation. Attempts by roughly 100,000 government forest officers to regulate access to these resources proved impossible; some 300 million rural people, and a huge population of cattle and other grazing animals, were depleting forest resources (115).

In the late 1980s and early 1990s, the government's approach to forest management changed to include greater participation from village communities and nongovernmental organizations. The 1990 guidelines to the 1988 National Forest Policy Act support various measures toward this end: forming partnerships between communities and forest departments facilitated by nongovernmental organizations; granting forest access and benefits to communities involved in forest regeneration; giving communities rights to all nonwood forest products and a share of the tree harvest; encouraging joint development of 10-year forest management plans; and forbidding grazing, farming, and tree cutting except as outlined in the 10-year plans (116). As a result, between 1987 and 1993, 11 states passed orders

Figure 5.7 Trends and Projections in the Emission of Selected Pollutants from Major Industrial Sources and Thermal Power Plants in India, 1990–2010

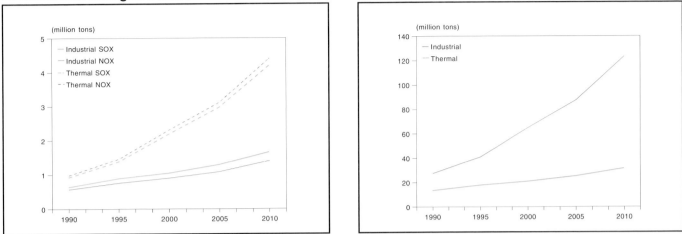

A. Sulfur and Nitrogen Oxides

B. Suspended Particulates

Source: Tata Energy Research Institute (TERI), *Environmental Considerations in Energy Development*, final report submitted to the Asian Development Bank, New Delhi, 1992, pp. 73, 83.

and resolutions to provide greater authority and rights to communities that protect public forestland (117).

The environmental and economic benefits of community participation can be dramatic. In the 1970s in Haryana, for example, government leaders became concerned about the heavy siltation of Sukhna Lake near Chandigarh. A survey of the watershed found that the problem was mainly caused by overgrazing, illicit tree removal, and poor agricultural practices in the surrounding ecosystem. Every effort by the forest department to stop grazing in woods was unsuccessful. The only way to stop the degradation, foresters realized, was to encourage the local communities to manage the forests prudently and in partnership with the government (118).

One early attempt to build community support was in the village of Sukhomajri, a major source of silt in Sukhna Lake. More than 70 percent of the 1,200 millimeters of annual rainfall disappeared as runoff, carrying with it some 700 tons of silt per hectare. Sukhomajri's 100 hectares of agricultural rainfed land could not support a human population of 455 and a cattle population of 411, which increased villagers' dependence on the hills for fuel and fodder. There were no irrigation facilities and groundwater development was prohibitively expensive. Fodder production from the hills averaged a meager 40 kilograms of grass per hectare per year, but in the absence of an alternative, no attempts were made to limit grazing (119).

Local leaders mobilized interest in rehabilitating the hills by focusing on water. A small earthen dam was constructed in 1976–77 above a gully head and grass was planted to stabilize the sides of the gully. Some of the water irrigated marginal agricultural fields, which tripled crop yields. The improved harvest increased byproducts of wheat straw and corn stalks, reducing dependence on fodder from forestland. Aware now of the economic benefits of rehabilitating the hills, villagers planted grass and prohibited grazing there, thus

supplying themselves with a harvestable fodder crop and reducing soil erosion (120).

The Haryana Forest Department tried to replicate this successful program, constructing 54 new dams in 39 villages from 1983 to 1988. But the department lacked the resources to help communities organize local watershed management societies, considered a key factor in early successes. By the late 1980s, the department realized that it needed to strengthen its capacity to motivate villagers: they should assume the responsibility for watershed management before dams are constructed or grass leases granted (121).

This participatory approach holds great potential. After construction of earthen dams boosts crop yields, villagers start protecting the watershed and forest cover and composition improve dramatically. In Nada, another village in Haryana, hills that produced 40 kilograms of grass per hectare in the 1970s produced more than 2,000 kilograms per hectare in 1986 and tree biomass increased (122).

The difficulty of participatory forest management is dealing with the political complexity of Indian villages, with their unique cultural traditions, various castes, and division of labor between genders and among subgroups. What the Haryana foresters discovered is that joint management agreements must be the result of a dialogue in which all village subgroups become convinced of the benefits of cooperation (123). In Sukhomajri, the Hill Resources Management Society consists of one member from each household. The society makes sure that no household grazes its animals in the watershed and that resources (wood, water, and grass) are distributed equitably among households. Another important element of success is creating a new institution rather than working with existing *Panchayats* (town councils), which are often the product of factionalism within a village or among several villages and thus tend to divide communities (124).

Involving women in watershed management groups is also crucial, because women are usually responsible for collecting and processing fuelwood, fodder, food, and water. Experience has shown that successful community management groups have a guaranteed minimum number of women participants. Nongovernmental organizations, acting as intermediaries between forest departments and communities, help to maximize participation by women and other marginalized community members (125).

Such flexible fine-tuning has produced results: successful community forestry programs are now under way in parts of West Bengal, Orissa, Uttar Pradesh, Haryana, Madhya Pradesh, and Gujarat (126) (127). In West Bengal, some 2,000 rural communities now look after about 250,000 hectares of natural *sal* forest, which supply a variety of medicinal, fiber, fodder, fuel, and food products for the participants (128). In Orissa, 3 to 10 percent of all reserve and protected forestland receives informal community protection. In the Uttar Pradesh hills, up to 30 percent of all forestland is managed by local communities. Throughout India, over 500,000 hectares of reserve and protected forestland is already under community protection through joint management agreements, and communities are beginning work with forest department staff in Jammu and Kashmir, Tamil Nadu, Karnataka, and Bihar (129).

In addition, nongovernmental organizations have begun training forest department staff in community organizing techniques. A national support group has been established to assist state-level joint forest management programs with research and training activities and donor agencies are expanding their projects to include natural regeneration and community forest protection and management (130).

According to an analysis of Landsat imagery, some 30 million hectares of degraded state forestland could be regenerated naturally with community involvement at only one twentieth the cost per hectare required to establish tree plantations (131).

Wastelands Development

India has also begun a major program to reforest the denuded lands that cover nearly 130 million hectares. The Wasteland Development Program started in 1985 with tree planting but soon found that additional measures were needed to stem erosion and reduce local exploitation of young growth. A new approach begun in 1990 entails a more comprehensive effort to address entire watersheds and involve local people. The pace of reforestation picked up considerably in the late 1980s, reaching over 2 million hectares annually by 1989 and totaling more than 15 million hectares since 1985 (132) (133). In the early 1990s, the program's targets and achievements were scaled back (134).

Project Tiger

At the turn of the century an estimated 40,000 tigers roamed India's forests. But human population growth, the clearing of wilderness for agriculture and cattle grazing, commercial forestry, and hunting took a devastating toll on the tiger population (135). By the late 1960s, Indian conservationists and the international community began to voice serious concerns about the fate of the tiger and several other rare species in India. A tiger census in 1972 indicated the urgency of the problem: the population had dwindled to 1,827 (136).

The turning point came in 1970 when the Indian government imposed a national ban on tiger hunting. In 1973, the Indian Board for Wildlife set up a special task force to maintain the tiger population and preserve its essential habitat (137).

Preserving the tiger's habitat was complex: most prospective tiger reserves were subject to ongoing human use, including commercial forestry, grazing, and interior settlement. The task force decided that reserves should include a core area free from all human interference and a buffer area for conservation-oriented land use. With support from the central and state governments and the World Wildlife Fund, nine tiger reserves were established in 1973–74. Management plans eliminated forestry operations and grazing in the core areas and provided for the relocation of villages (138). Project Tiger currently has 19 reserves with a gross area of nearly 30,000 square kilometers and a core area of over 12,000 square kilometers (139).

The tiger population, estimated at 268 in the original nine reserves, is now thought to exceed 1,300. Many other endangered species, including swamp deer, elephants, and rhinos, have benefited from the reserves, and there has been a significant improvement in overall floral and faunal diversity, particularly in the core areas (140) (141). Many problems remain, however. The medicinal use of tiger bones in some East Asian countries makes the animals a constant target for poachers, a threat that has intensified in India with the sharp decline in tiger numbers in Southeast Asia (142).

In addition to its efforts on behalf of tigers, the government recently launched Project Elephant to protect India's population of roughly 20,000 elephants. Unlike tiger reserves with their strictly protected core areas, these new reserves will accommodate human activities such as sustained-yield forestry and slow-rotation shifting cultivation that are consistent with elephant conservation. Eleven reserves have been identified, mostly in the eastern and southern sections of the country (143).

More initiatives are being discussed for other vulnerable and endangered animal species, including the snow leopard, wild ass, and musk deer (144). (See Box 5.4.)

Incentives For Pollution Control

The Indian government has taken a variety of measures to control industrial pollution. Several incentives are in place to encourage the purchase of pollution control equipment—such as reduced excise taxes, an accelerated depreciation allowance, a reduced maximum customs duty, and soft loans and grants for financing (145). The fiscal incentives to date have been relatively expensive to administer and have had a limited effect in stimulating entrepreneurs to invest in pollution control equipment. The common view is that such equipment will not show any return on investment (146).

The government is also implementing a grant program to construct common wastewater treatment facili-

Table 5.4 India's Cropped Area, Irrigated Area, and Fertilizer Use, 1960–91

Year	Cropped Area (million hectares)	Irrigated Area (million hectares)	Area under High-Yield Varieties (million hectares)	Fertilizer Use (000 metric tons of nutrients)
1960–61	133.2	24.7	—	293
1970–71	140.8	31.1	15.4	2,177
1980–81	140.0	38.7	43.1	5,516
1985–86	140.9	42.1	55.4	—
1989–90	143.0	46.5	61.2	11,568
1990–91[a]	143.0	47.5	63.9	12,567

Source: Tata Services, *Statistical Outline of India, 1992–93* (Tata Services, Bombay, 1992), pp. 56 and 60.
Note: a. Including area sown/irrigated more than once, cropped area was 182.5 million hectares in 1990–91 and irrigated area was 59 million hectares.

Figure 5.8 Index of Total and Per Capita Food Production in India, 1970–92

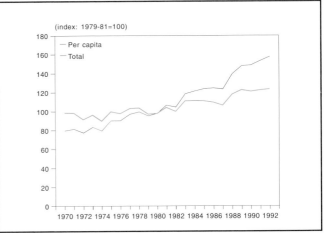

Source: Food and Agriculture Organization of the United Nations (FAO), *Agrostat PC,* on diskette (FAO, Rome, 1993).

ties to handle effluent from multiple industrial installations (147). This is one practical way to solve the dilemma of small-scale industries unable to afford pollution control equipment. Because many medium- and small-scale industries are clustered in state-sponsored industrial estates, common treatment facilities may be a practical and cost-effective solution (148). Variations in wastewater quality, however, pose problems for operational management at such facilities.

DEVELOPMENT CHALLENGES

Food and energy production are the most critical of India's many developmental challenges. Growth in production is essential and the challenge for Indian policymakers is to enhance production in food and energy with minimal environmental damage.

Food Production And Sustainability

Like so many other issues affecting India, agriculture is a complex subject because of the vast differences among regions.

Roughly one third of the country's crop land is irrigated; the rest depends on rainfall. About 62 percent of total cropped area is planted with high-yield varieties, ranging from 44 percent of land planted in maize to 85 percent of land planted in wheat (149). Most of India's farms are small. A survey in 1985–86 found that 58 percent of all farms were less than 1 hectare, 18 percent were 1 to 2 hectares, 14 percent were 2 to 4 hectares, 8 percent were 4 to 10 hectares, and 2 percent were larger than 10 hectares. Marginal and small farms up to 2 hectares make up only 29 percent of the total area; farms larger than 4 hectares make up 49 percent (150).

Over the last four decades, India more than tripled food production primarily because of the use of high-yield varieties of grain. In 1990–91 alone, production topped 176 million tons. Production gains outpaced population and expanded the daily amount of food grain available per capita from 395 to 510 grams by 1991 (most of the gains in per capita availability occurred in the 1950s) (151) (152). Considering that the population rose by 483 million during those four decades, this is an impressive achievement.

However, not all regions nor all crops share this success. While yields of wheat, rice, and sugar cane, to name a few, have gone up spectacularly, the production of pulses—the major source of food protein (in-

cluding lentils and peas) in a predominantly vegetarian population—has not kept pace (153).

One factor affecting food production is the government's pricing policy for inputs. Prices are often subsidized but artificially low prices offer little incentive for more efficient production. A second is availability of credit or soft loans to buy high-yield seed varieties, fertilizers, and pesticides (154). Production is also influenced by the vagaries of the monsoon rains. The subcontinents's main source of rain, the southwest monsoon, begins in June and recedes in September. However, rain can set in or end earlier or later, it can be copious or sparse in the same year over various parts of the country, and it can vary greatly in intensity. If it falls during the harvest, crops can be ruined. For instance, because of the erratic monsoon in 1991–92, food grain production was 5.3 percent below that in 1990–91, when rains were normal (155).

Raising productivity on existing lands is the only viable option in the race to keep up with demand for food as there is little room to develop new farmland. Roughly half of India's land mass is used for agriculture, a figure exceeded only in Bangladesh among the world's major developing countries and far higher than the world average of 11 percent (156).

The Production Challenge: Past and Future

The development and rapid spread of high-yield varieties of wheat and rice in the mid-1960s was the key ingredient in a dramatic increase in yield, especially in the states of Punjab, Haryana, and western Uttar Pradesh (157). In Punjab and Haryana other factors played a role as well: expanded irrigation, favorable topography featuring large stretches of relatively flat land, easy-to-work soil, and more fertilizer (158) (159). Irrigation in particular has reduced India's susceptibility to drought and helped take some pressure off rainfed land by allowing second crops (160). (See Table 5.4.) Aside from irrigation, Punjab had many advantages over other regions, including a relatively effective transportation and marketing infrastructure, more landownership and larger average farms, electric power in rural areas, and technical support from the Punjab Agricultural University (161).

With Punjab leading the way, India's nationwide statistics show impressive gains in many areas of food production, which is up in both absolute and per capita terms. (See Figure 5.8.) About 30 percent of growth came from expanding the area of farmland and about 70 percent from improved average yields; since the late 1970s, most of the increase is attributable to higher yields (162). Average cereal yields nevertheless remain below those of China, Sri Lanka, and Indonesia. (See Chapter 18, "Food and Agriculture," Table 18.1.)

Growth in milk and egg production was even more dramatic with dairy and poultry enterprises providing substantially higher returns per hectare than crop farming (163). A Punjab Agricultural University study found that returns from dairy farming can be anywhere from 1.5 to 4.5 times greater than those from cereal production per unit area (164). Such enterprises, being relatively labor-intensive, created new jobs and brought about health and nutritional improvements. In Tamil Nadu, for example, average per capita milk consumption went from about 40 grams per day in 1947 to about 170 grams per day in 1993 (165).

The production of pulses has not grown despite their value as a source of protein and their ability to enrich the soil by taking nitrogen from the air. The share of pulses in the production of food crops (here including cereals and pulses) declined from 10.9 percent in 1970–71 to 8 percent in 1990–91; per capita consumption in 1990 was slightly more than half that in 1961 (166). Typically, farmers who grow pulses earn a much lower share of the market price than those who grow rice or wheat. Less land is being devoted to pulses; they are often mixed with coarse cereals such as sorghum and maize, and when irrigation becomes available, these crops are replaced with wheat or rice (167).

Irrigation

Although irrigation boosts yields dramatically, India could enhance food production with more efficient farming. The average yield of rice in Punjab is 3.5 tons per hectare, but 4 to 6 tons is not an unrealistic target. Wheat production could be improved by roughly the same amount (168) (169).

Irrigation has not achieved its full potential for several reasons. Some lands still have to be leveled and field channels constructed to direct the flow of water. Moreover, it takes time for farmers accustomed to rainfed agriculture to switch to irrigated agriculture (170). Bringing more area under irrigation is increasingly expensive (171). Major new irrigation works also bring social and environmental costs—the resettlement of people displaced by large dams, the loss of biodiversity in submerged areas, and so on. A case in point is the controversial Sardar Sarovar dam on the Narmada River. Owing to stringent terms of resettlement stipulated by the World Bank, the government decided to build the dam without aid from that source (172) (173).

Private groundwater irrigation with shallow wells serving about 3 to 4 hectares appears to be the most

Table 5.5 Distribution of Sown Area and Rainwater Availability in India

Rainfall Zone (millimeters)	Geographical Area (million hectares)	Net Sown Area (million hectares)
100–500	52	29
500–750	40	22
750–1,000	66	34
1,000–2,500	137	44
2,500	33	14
Total	**328[a]**	**143[b]**

Source: J.C. Katyal, "Dryland Farming: Corporatisation Indispensable," *The Hindu: Survey of Indian Agriculture, 1992* (S. Rangarajan, Madras, 1993), p. 21.
Notes:
a. Includes bodies of water.
b. Includes 47.5 million hectares that are irrigated.

cost-effective investment, bringing a favorable return of 30 percent or more, partly because of government subsidies (174). Another option in the search for enhanced production is the conjunctive use of canal- and groundwater to prevent waterlogging and groundwater depletion. This practice, which requires better water management techniques by farmers, has not been easy to establish.

The average yield of 2 tons of cereals per irrigated hectare, though more than twice that of rainfed land, is low compared with the average yield of irrigated cropland in other countries. The solutions appear to depend primarily on improved water management and greater involvement of local farmers (175). Current management systems suffer from heavy reliance on top-down administrative structures that limit the role of farmers, poor coordination among support agencies, and sometimes inefficient and inequitable methods of water distribution (176).

Rainfed Agriculture

Rainfed agriculture, which accounts for roughly two thirds (68 percent) of the total cultivated area in India, is crucial to its food production. Managing the small, fragmented holdings where this type of farming is typically practiced calls for a cooperative approach if economies of scale are to be utilized (177) (178).

The areas that depend on rainfed agriculture are diverse. Some, such as the coastal lands of Kerala, Karnataka, Goa, and Maharashtra, receive more than 2,500 millimeters of rain a year, while others rely on a scarce 100 to 500 millimeters. (See Table 5.5.) Soil may be fertile, black, and rich in organic matter, or stony with low water retention and few nutrients. In some rainfed areas, agricultural extension services are operating, in others they are largely neglected.

Rain brings about 400 million hectare-meters of water to India each year. About 40 percent of the available surface flow can be diverted to large reservoirs, leaving 60 percent potentially available for collection. It is estimated that in areas receiving up to 1,000 millimeters of precipitation annually, 6.3 million hectare-meters could be collected (179).

Improved farming practices in rainfed areas could enhance production otherwise curbed by poor soils, in particular the black and red types found in central and south India. Black soil is characterized by low infiltra-

Box 5.4 India's Biodiversity

India, considered one of the world's leading "megadiversity" states, is home to about 16,000 species of flowering plants, 372 species of mammals, 1,230 species of birds, and 399 species of reptiles (1) (2) (3). In addition, it is an important center of genetic diversity in crops—especially rice, sugar cane, mangoes, cucumbers, black peppers, and eggplants—and in medicinal and aromatic plants (4) (5). Areas rich in biodiversity include northeastern India, the Western Ghats region in southern India, the Bastar region in central India, the Andaman and Nicobar islands, and the Sunderbans mangrove forests (6). Two of the regions, Northeast India and the Western Ghats, are recognized internationally as biodiversity "hot spots" (7).

The traditional environmental emphasis has been to protect large mammals such as tigers, rhinos, and elephants. By June 1993, India had 331 protected areas totaling 13.2 million hectares (8). Some of these protected areas are under considerable pressure. Kanha National Park, one of the best tiger preserves in central India, has suffered from the setting of fires and poaching by tribal people displaced from the reserve. Dandeli, the largest wildlife sanctuary in the Western Ghats, has been badly degraded by a paper mill and dams constructed in its midst (9).

With the aim of better protecting India's wildlife, a review of possible new sites recommends a total of 148 national parks and 503 sanctuaries. These would encompass 151,342 square kilometers or 4.6 percent of the country's total area (10).

Protecting large mammals is a particularly difficult challenge, especially given India's population pressures and food requirements. For example, elephants eat fresh plants and grasses equivalent to 6 percent of their body weight each day. An elephant herd requires a range of 100 to 500 square kilometers, yet, in some areas, elephant habitat is narrow—only 2 to 3 kilometers wide. Many habitats have been fragmented by tea and coffee plantations in the Western Ghats, cultivation in the Eastern Ghats, and agriculture and dams elsewhere (11).

Plant biodiversity also needs to be recognized and preserved. Some 43 distinct groupings of vegetation types have been identified in India as well as localities of great significance for the conservation of these types (12). One method of preservation is to support traditional conservation areas such as sacred groves. The system of sacred groves is still largely intact in the tribal hill state of Mizoram. There is also an old Indian tradition of preserving trees of the genus *Ficus*, often the only large trees in town and city centers. This genus is now considered a keystone resource in tropical forests (13). If ecosystems are to function, however, reserves large enough to protect a full complement of species must be set aside.

The indigenous people and local communities must have a stake in India's biodiversity if it is to be preserved. Local residents are more likely to be invested in preservation if their land tenure is stable and property rights are clearly defined. On an institutional level, a national biodiversity coordinating body could promote preservation policies and help oversee a long-term biodiversity conservation and utilization strategy for India (14).

References and Notes

1. World Conservation Monitoring Centre unpublished data, Cambridge, U.K., 1993.

2. T.N. Khoshoo, "Conservation of Biodiversity in Biosphere," in *Indian Geosphere Biosphere Programme: Some Aspects*, T.N. Khoshoo and M. Sharma, eds. (Har-Anand, New Delhi, 1991), p. 208.

3. These figures from Indian sources differ somewhat from those given by international sources. (See World Conservation Monitoring Centre, *Global Biodiversity* [Chapman and Hall, London, 1992], pp. 80 and 139.) (See also Chapter 20, "Biodiversity," Tables 20.4 and 20.5 in this volume for international estimates.)

4. *Op. cit.* 2.

5. World Conservation Monitoring Centre, *Global Biodiversity* (Chapman and Hall, London, 1992), p. 338.

6. P.S. Ramakrishnan, "International Sustainable Biosphere Initiative: A Participatory Research Agenda for India," *Current Science*, Vol. 63, No. 3 (1992), p. 129.

7. Norman Myers, "Threatened Biotas: Hot Spots in Tropical Forests," *The Environmentalist*, Vol. 8 (1988), pp. 187–208.

8. See Chapter 20, "Wildlife and Habitat," Table 20.1.

9. Madhav Gadgil, "Conserving India's Biodiversity: The Societal Context," *Evolutionary Trends in Plants*, Vol. 5, No. 1 (1991), p. 7.

10. *Op. cit.* 2, pp. 201–202.

11. R. Sukumar, "The Elephant Populations of India: Strategies for Conservation," *Proceedings of the Indian Academy of Sciences*, Animal Sciences/Plant Sciences supplement (Bangalore, November 1986), pp. 64, 66.

12. Madhav Gadgil and V.M. Meher-Homji, "Localities of Great Significance to Conservation of India's Biological Diversity," *Proceedings of the Indian Academy of Sciences*, Animal Sciences/Plant Sciences supplement (Bangalore, November 1986), pp. 165–180.

13. *Op. cit.* 10, p. 5.

14. T. N. Khoshoo, Tata Energy Research Institute, New Delhi, 1993 (personal communication).

---

tion and sheet erosion. Red soil has poor water retention and a tendency to crust (180). In black-soil areas, improved practices include cultivation immediately after harvesting the post-rainy season crop; construction of field and community drains; land leveling; dry sowing or early sowing of rainy season crops; sowing with improved seed, a moderate amount of fertilizer, and better placement techniques; and timely plant protection. Demonstrations of this novel system generated a 250 percent rate of return on the additional investment. Grain yields averaged 4,000 kilograms per hectare compared with about 600 to 800 kilograms using traditional practices (181). Demonstrations always yield results that exceed those in practice, but the test does suggest that rainfed agriculture has the potential to boost production substantially.

Fertilizer

By the early 1990s, Indian farmers were using about 72 kilograms of fertilizer per hectare. This is a striking increase from the 0.55 kilogram average in 1950–51, but the current applications are nevertheless lower than in many other developing countries (182). (See Chapter 18, "Food and Agriculture," Table 18.2.)

Fertilizer is used on about 62 percent of India's farmland; about 43 percent of rainfed land is fertilized. Fertilizer use was hindered by deficient research and extension services, inadequate efforts to convince farmers about returns on fertilizer in rainfed areas, the slow expansion of fertilizer distribution networks, a shortfall in domestic fertilizer production, and bias toward irrigation and high-yield seed varieties in government-extended production credit to farmers. Ample opportunity exists in India to improve the use and effectiveness of fertilizer, especially on rainfed land (183).

Farmers in many cases may be applying too much of one type of nutrient, typically nitrogen, and not enough of others. It is estimated, for example, that the soil in 46 percent of India's districts is low in phosphorus (184). In part, this can be attributed to the fact that

Figure 5.9 Total and Per Capita Commercial Energy Use in India, 1970–91

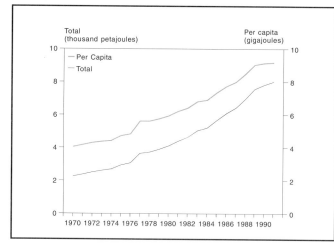

Source: United Nations Statistical Division (UNSD), *U.N. Energy Tape* (UNSD, New York, 1993).

soil-testing facilities are not widely used to advise farmers on fertilizer needs. Such testing could boost yields and efficiency by eliminating nutrient deficiencies and unnecessary fertilizer applications (185).

A production goal of 219 million metric tons of food grain by the year 2000 would require a 6 percent annual increase in fertilizer application. To maintain growth at this pace there will have to be a rapid improvement in the provision of credit and services to farmers and in the dissemination of knowledge about fertilizer in different locations and on different crops (186).

Energy

Because of its size, India is one of the largest consumers of energy in the developing world and is among the top 20 consumers of commercial energy in the world (187). (See Figure 5.9.) On a per capita basis, however, its use of commercial energy is only one eighth the world average (188).

In the 1980s, India's commercial energy sector grew about 6 percent a year, with electricity use growing faster at 9 percent annually (189). Meanwhile, the economy grew at an annual rate of 5 percent, with industrial output rising 6.3 percent a year (190). (See Chapter 15, "Basic Economic Indicators," Table 15.1.) In the early 1990s, however, economic growth turned sluggish.

Despite this economic setback, the energy sector's expansion from a small base in the 1950s continues, pushed by a spreading industrial base, population growth, and the rise in residential energy use that accompanies higher incomes and greater access to consumer products among middle- and upper-income groups. However, the shortage of capital resources for energy sector expansion has repeatedly forced the government to postpone ambitious development plans.

India's importance as a global energy consumer will continue to rise. Indeed, if current demographic and energy trends hold, within the next 40 years the country will surpass China in total population and rival it in energy use (as well as in total greenhouse gas emissions). Projections show that India's energy demand

could increase fourfold by 2025, while its carbon emissions could increase sixfold as traditional biomass fuels are displaced by higher fossil fuel use (191).

Today, on a per capita basis, India uses much less energy than industrialized nations. In 1991, the average American consumed 35 times more commercial energy than the average Indian (192). However, India's energy situation is also very different from that of most other developing nations. Utilities recently began to privatize, and a solid indigenous technology base and research capability could encourage the country to adopt progressive energy technologies (193).

In 1991–92, 27 percent of India's import payments went to buy petroleum (194). With demand for petroleum rising and domestic production stagnant, India can only become more dependent on imported oil. Meanwhile, the market for kerosene and diesel fuel is expanding, a trend that in the absence of short-term substitutes for these fuels promises to continue (195).

The government has established energy conservation targets for each major industry and the transport sector. Several conservation programs have been launched, including loan programs to encourage investment in more energy-efficient equipment and research programs to help develop equipment and appliances suited to the Indian market (196).

Energy Resources

To power its economic engine, India can draw from a mix of energy resources. (See Figure 5.10.) Foremost among these is coal, India's largest energy resource other than biomass (197). Today, coal provides almost 40 percent of the nation's total energy requirements and is the source of about 60 percent of its commercial energy. With the surge in demand for commercial energy over the last two decades and the need to minimize oil imports, coal has become a critical energy source. From 1980 to 1991–92, coal production more than doubled to 229 million tons, and it is expected to reach 400 million tons by the turn of the century (198) (199).

Indian coal is low in sulfur but contains 25 to 40 percent ash (200). Ash causes problems for utilities, such as clogged boiler grates and questions about disposal. Another obstacle is coal distribution: severe bottlenecks develop on national rail lines between the eastern coal regions and delivery points to the west and south (201) (202). Unfortunately, Indian coal destined for the power sector does not receive the washing that decreases ash and contaminants, improves quality, and reduces volume for easier transport (203) (204).

Coal dominates India's energy mix, but oil accounts for about one third of all commercial energy. India rapidly developed its domestic oil resources in the 1970s and early 1980s, more than quadrupling production to keep up with rising demand and reduce foreign oil dependence. Since 1985, however, production has been relatively stagnant; the estimated 30 million tons produced in 1991–92 was actually about 10 percent below levels achieved in the previous two years. Still a net oil importer, India must spend about one quarter of its foreign exchange earnings, down from about three quarters in the early 1980s, on oil (205) (206) (207).

Table 5.6 Energy Consumed in Steel Manufacturing in Selected Countries, 1985

Countries		Gigacalories per Ton of Steel Produced
Germany	(average for all plants)	5.20
India	Bhilai Steel Plant	8.90
	Durgaphur Steel Plant	11.45
	Rourkela Steel Plant	11.12
	Bokaro Steel Plant	10.81
	Tata Steel Plant	9.68
Italy	(average for all integrated plants)	4.01
Japan	(average for all integrated plants)	4.09
Korea	(Pohang Steel Plant)	5.21
France	(average for all plants)	5.70
USA	(average for all plants)	6.00

Source: B. Bowonder and T. Miyake, "Measurement of Technology at Industry Level: A Case Study of the Steel Industry in India and Japan," *Science and Public Policy*, Vol. 15, No. 4 (1988), p. 255.

Natural gas today supplies about 8 percent of India's commercial energy needs, but its share is growing. India's natural gas is usually a by-product of oil activities and the amount available cannot be scaled back without cutting oil production, even though present gas production greatly exceeds the country's ability to ship and use it. Consequently, some 30 percent is burned off. Now new gas facilities are rapidly coming on line and official plans cite gas as a major part of India's future energy makeup (208) (209).

The potential for augmenting hydro capacity, an important source of electricity in India, is great. But high capital costs, remote sites, and swelling resistance to large hydro facilities on environmental and social grounds has slowed development (210). Microhydro projects, currently few in number, are now being actively promoted by the government for local power (211). (See Chapter 9, "Energy," Aggressive Development of Renewable Energy Sources.)

Traditional biomass fuels—about 250 million tons a year—provide from one third to one half of India's total energy needs and over three quarters of all household energy (212) (213). Many urban residents still rely on firewood from the surrounding countryside, while traditional fuels are nearly indispensable to rural families, which make up nearly three quarters of the population. Commercial fuels are scarcer and more expensive outside urban distribution areas. Only about one third of Indian homes currently have electricity (214).

Energy Shortages and Inefficiency

Like many quickly developing nations, India suffers energy shortages that have severe economic side effects. Over the last decade, shortages of coal and electricity have progressively worsened, largely because of low energy prices that do not provide sufficient return to producers (215). Electric power generation falls some 10 percent short of demand on a nationwide basis, with even greater shortages in some regions (216). As a result, utilities resort to scheduled power outages and many industries shut down during peak load times. Even with planning, unscheduled brownouts and blackouts are common (217). Economic losses associated with these power shortages are estimated at 1 to 2 percent of the national income (218).

Figure 5.10 India's Energy Use by Sector, 1990–91, and Mix of Energy Sources, 1988

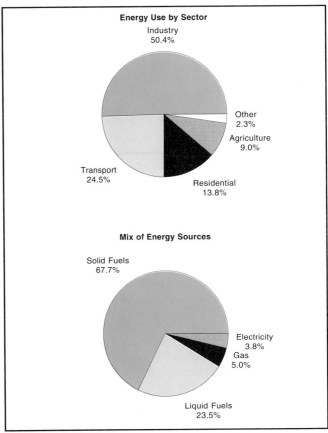

Energy Use by Sector

Industry 50.4%
Other 2.3%
Agriculture 9.0%
Residential 13.8%
Transport 24.5%

Mix of Energy Sources

Solid Fuels 67.7%
Electricity 3.8%
Gas 5.0%
Liquid Fuels 23.5%

Sources:
1. United Nations Statistical Division (UNSD), *U.N. Energy Tape* (UNSD, New York, 1993).
2. Tata Services, *Statistical Outline of India, 1992–93* (Tata Services, Bombay, 1992), p. 68.

Losses would undoubtedly be larger but for the fact that many industries have invested in backup generators. Unfortunately, these divert capital that might be put to some better use and drive up diesel fuel consumption, further inflating oil imports (219).

Widespread inefficiency intensifies energy shortfalls. More than 20 percent of the electricity generated by the nation's power plants, for example, is lost during transmission and distribution, even though present technology applications have the potential to reduce transmission and distribution losses in developing countries to as low as 7 to 10 percent (220) (221). Outdated equipment and processes make Indian industries considerably less efficient than their counterparts in the industrialized world. For example, steel requires at least twice as much energy to manufacture in India than in industrialized countries (222) (223). (See Table 5.6.)

The steel industry, India's largest energy user, recently realized a 10 percent energy savings by improving monitoring and operating procedures. There is potential for greater efficiency, with appropriate investments, as high as 45 percent or more (224). Boilers, for example, burn over 60 percent of the subcontinent's industrial fuel but fall far below modern efficiency standards. According to one study, a successful boiler re-building and replacement program could cut national energy consumption in boilers by as much as 12 percent by the year 2000 (225).

Another recent study estimated that by 2005, the electricity consumption could be slashed by 20 percent through a combination of measures including refitting inefficient irrigation pumps, using compact fluorescent instead of incandescent bulbs in newly constructed buildings, improving industrial operations and maintenance, and promoting high-efficiency motors. Such innovations could be frustrated, however, by the electricity shutdowns and extreme fluctuations in voltage experienced in most regions of the country (226) (227).

Various barriers impede progress toward energy efficiency. Subsidies that keep energy prices artificially low are the most notable. Until quite recently, in fact, the price of coal was lower than the cost of production. (See Figure 5.10.) As for electricity, the cost of producing one kilowatt-hour (kWh) in 1991 was about 3.5 cents, whereas actual returns were estimated at 2.75 cents per kWh. Low tariffs for agricultural pumping, in particular, have resulted in huge losses for state electricity boards, hindering their ability to fund future power generation (228). By the end of 1991, the accumulated losses of all state electricity operations due to subsidies was approximately $1.65 billion (229). The situation is only deteriorating. For 1992–93 alone, the annual loss is estimated at $750 million (230).

Planning the Future

While the government does seek to promote conservation, it is relying mainly on continued expansion of the energy sector. Production of coal, oil, and gas is slated to jump, while electricity-generating capacity will be added at a record pace (231) (232). India may lack the capital to meet these goals. Until recently, the government planned to increase power generation by 50 percent between 1990 and 1995, but the price tag of $50 billion for new power plants and $23 billion for the fuels to run them could well prove too high (233).

To help solve its financing problems, the government recently decided to solicit private investment in new power projects, a radical step in a country where most utilities are state-run monopolies (234) (235). Ensuring a good return on private investment without adding expensive subsidies will pressure the government to raise energy prices, a politically unpopular move that has nonetheless been urged by experts for years (236).

The government also hopes to save money and speed plant expansion by encouraging the use of natural gas, both to replace petroleum products in industrial applications and to generate electricity. Natural gas-fired power stations, which are cheaper and faster to build than coal-fired plants, may make up 20 percent of the planned addition to generating capacity during the early 1990s (237) (238). There are additional benefits to promoting this resource. India's natural gas supplies exceed its oil reserves, and natural gas is more environmentally friendly than coal (239) (240).

Rural Energy and Renewables

India has adopted several strategies to solve rural energy problems. To promote energy efficiency and reduce fuelwood demand, an extensive program to upgrade rural stoves was begun in 1983 (241). Other steps include actively encouraging the replacement of traditional biomass fuels and charcoal with commercial fuels such as liquified petroleum gas, kerosene, and coal and pursuing an aggressive, expensive rural electrification program. A sizable reforestation effort was undertaken in the last decade to increase fuelwood supplies and combat deforestation. (See Participatory Forest Management and Wastelands Development sections above). Considerable research has been done to select appropriate tree species for fuelwood plantations, particularly on degraded sites that may be arid, saline, or eroded (242).

The government has actively pushed the development of a number of renewable energy technologies. Lately, the conversion of biomass to energy has received a good deal of attention in India because of the tremendous potential within the nation for producing biomass through agriculture or agroforestry. For example, using conventional boilers in industrial cogeneration facilities to burn agricultural waste such as rice hulls or sugar cane residue, could immediately increase rural electricity supplies (243) (244). Indian researchers have developed biomass gasifiers that can replace fuel in diesel engines or generators or be used for process heat (245). In addition, the government has made a concerted effort to promote biogas in rural homes, with the result that more than 1.6 million family-size biogas systems are now in place (246). (See Chapter 9, "Energy," Case 2: Biogas Electricity in India.)

Other renewable energy technologies that are developing are solar and wind. India has the largest solar cooking program in the world; over 238,000 solar cookers had been sold by December 1992. Solar collectors to heat industrial and domestic water are more common; by the end of 1992 the total area given over to their installation was 228,000 square meters (247). India has also commercialized the manufacture of photovoltaic cells (248). Today, over 8,300 villages have lighting systems derived from this source (249).

Wind turbines show particular promise, especially in producing commercial-scale quantities of electricity. As of December 1992, wind farm capacity was estimated at 45 megawatts (MW) of electricity, about half of it connected to the commercial grid and about 7.5 MW available to the private sector. Wind surveys show that India has the potential to generate 16,800 to 50,000 MW from wind power. The state utilities in both Gujarat and Tamil Nadu have expressed interest in further wind farm development (250) (251). (See Chapter 9, "Energy," Case 4: Wind Power in India.)

India's small-scale hydropower program (capacity less than 3 MW) is progressing as well. Over 86 MW of capacity are installed, over 100 MW are scheduled to be added over the next four years, and the total estimated potential is 5,000 MW (252).

As in many other countries, both industrialized and developing, renewable energy technologies could do much to solve India's energy problems. In 1989, an official in charge of developing these technologies remarked that renewables, owing to their short gestation period, could supply up to 20 percent of India's total energy needs by 2000 (253). But to reach this point will require both a change of thinking and an intensified commitment of resources over the next few years, not only on the part of the Indian Energy Ministry but also of international lenders and aid agencies (254).

One promising example of such commitment is the India Renewable Resources Development Project. Under the project, the government will receive $234 million from international and bilateral sources. The funds will establish 100 MW of small hydro, 85 MW of wind farm, and 2.5 MW of solar photovoltaic capacity (255). Commercial energy needs, however, will not be fully met by renewable resources because their potential capacity still falls far short of demand.

To secure an energy future for its growing population, India must continue developing a jigsaw puzzle of resources and implementing a variety of measures to make pricing more rational, manage demand, conserve energy, and boost supply.

The India chapter was written by Robert Livernash of the World Resources *staff. Dr. B. Bowonder, dean of research at the Administrative Staff College of India at Hyderabad, wrote the boxes on environmental regulations and fuelwood and made numerous other contributions to the draft. Yateen Joshi of the Tata Energy Research Institute in New Delhi assisted in the research and also contributed to the chapter. Gregory Mock,* World Resources *contributing editor, wrote the first draft of the energy section.*

References and Notes

1. United Nations (U.N.) Population Division, *World Population Prospects: The 1992 Revision* (U.N., New York, forthcoming).
2. United Nations (U.N.), *Long-Range World Population Projections* (U.N., New York, 1992), p. 22.
3. B. Bowonder, S.S.R. Prasad, and N.V.M. Unni, "Afforestation in India," *Land Use Policy*, Vol. 4, No. 2 (1987), pp. 133–146.
4. J.C. Katyal, "Dryland Farming: Corporatisation Indispensable," *The Hindu: Survey of Indian Agriculture, 1992* (S. Rangarajan, Madras, 1993), p. 17.
5. The Economist Intelligence Unit, *India: Nepal Country Report: No. 2* (Business International, London, 1992), p. 6.
6. Tata Services, *Statistical Outline of India, 1992–93* (Tata Services, Bombay, 1992), p. 28.
7. Ashish Bose, *Demographic Diversity of India: 1991 Census* (B.R. Publishing, Delhi, 1991), pp. 53, 61, and 89.
8. Ann Austin, "State of Grace," *Earthwatch* (March/April 1993), pp. 23–27.
9. Daryl Ditz, Associate, Program in Technology and the Environment, World Resources Institute, Washington, D.C., 1993 (personal communication).
10. Neelam Singh, "Nutrition Gardens," *Health for the Millions*, Vol. 18, Nos. 1 and 2 (Voluntary Health Association of India, New Delhi, February/April 1992), p. 5.
11. *Op. cit.* 6, p. 27.
12. "Harvesting India's Reforms," *The Economist* (March 6, 1993), p. 33.
13. R. Radhakrishna, "Market Intervention and Food," Centre for Economic and Social Studies paper, Hyderabad, n.d., p. 27.
14. *Op. cit.* 6, pp. 27 and 222.
15. The World Bank, *World Development Report, 1990* (Oxford University Press, Oxford and New York, 1990), pp. 30–31.
16. O.P. Dasgupta, "Population, Resources and Poverty," *AMBIO*, Vol. 21, No. 1 (1992), pp. 95–101.
17. Martin Ravallion and K. Subbarao, "Adjustment and Human Development in India," *Journal of Indian School of Political Economy*, Vol. 4, No. 1 (January–March 1992), p. 57.

18. United Nations (U.N.) Children's Fund, *Children and Women in India: A Situation Analysis, 1990* (U.N. Children's Fund, New Delhi, 1990), pp. 35–36.
19. Almas Ali, "Nutrition," *Health for the Millions* (February/April 1992), p. 2.
20. *Ibid.*, pp. 3–4.
21. *Ibid.*, pp. 3–4.
22. *Op. cit.* 6, p. 55.
23. *Op. cit.* 17, pp. 72 and 75.
24. *Op. cit.* 19, p. 5.
25. Alok Mukhopadhyay, "Health Systems and Services," Health for the Millions (February/April 1992), pp. 8 and 12.
26. *Ibid*, p. 11.
27. Veena Soni Raleigh, "King Edward Memorial Hospital Rural Health Project," *Anubhav* (Ford Foundation, New Delhi, 1987), p. 1.
28. Veena Raleigh, "Streehitakarini," *Anubhav* (Ford Foundation, New Delhi, n.d.), p. 1.
29. Neera Kuckreja Sohoni, "Parivar Seva Sanstha," *Anubhav* (Ford Foundation, New Delhi, 1988), pp. 1 and 32.
30. Bina Agarwal, "The Gender and Environment Debate: Lessons from India," *Feminist Studies*, No. 1 (Spring 1992), p. 134.
31. Om Prakash Mathur, "Responding to India's Urban Challenge: A Research Agenda for the 1990s," National Institute of Public Finance and Policy draft paper, New Delhi, 1993, pp. 6–7.
32. *Ibid.*, p. 8.
33. *Ibid.*, pp. 9–12.
34. Planning Commission, Government of India, *Eighth Five-Year Plan, 1992–97*, Vol. 1 (Controller of Publications, Delhi, 1992), pp. 9 and 15.
35. The World Bank, *Staff Appraisal Report: India Industrial Pollution Control Project* (The World Bank, Asia Technical Department, Industry and Finance Division, 1991), p. 4.
36. *Ibid.*, pp. 4–5.
37. *Ibid.*, p. 5.
38. *Ibid.*, pp. 5–6.
39. *Ibid.*, pp. 5–6.

40. B. Bowonder, *Implementing Environmental Policy in India* (Friedrich Ebert Stiftung, New Delhi, 1988), p. 4.
41. K.P. Nyati, *Problems of Pollution and Its Control in Small-Scale Industries* (Friedrich Ebert Stiftung, New Delhi, 1988), pp. 12–18.
42. Ramachandra Guha, "Forestry in British and Post-British India: A Historical Analysis," *Economic and Political Weekly* (October 29, 1983), p. 1883.
43. Simon Commander, "Managing Indian Forests: A Case for the Reform of Property Rights," *Development Policy Review*, Vol. 4 (1986), pp. 328–329.
44. The World Conservation Union (formerly the International Union for Conservation of Nature and Natural Resources), *The Conservation Atlas of Tropical Forests: Asia and the Pacific*, N. Mark Collins, Jeffrey A. Sayer, and Timothy C. Whitmore, eds. (Macmillan Press, London and Basingstoke, U.K., 1991), p. 128.
45. *Op. cit.* 43, p. 329.
46. U. Bannerjee, "Participatory Forest Management in West Bengal," *Forest Regeneration Through Community Protection: The West Bengal Experience*, proceedings of the Working Group on Forest Protection Committees, Calcutta, June 21–22, 1989, K.C. Malhotra and Mark Poffenberger, eds. (Ford Foundation, New Delhi, n.d.), pp. 1–2.
47. Madhav Gadgil, "Restoring India's Forest Wealth," *Nature and Resources*, Vol. 27, No. 2 (1991), pp. 15–16.
48. K.C. Malhotra and Mark Poffenberger, eds., *Forest Regeneration Through Community Protection: The West Bengal Experience*, proceedings of the Working Group on Forest Protection Committees, Calcutta, June 21–22, 1989 (Ford Foundation, New Delhi, n.d.), Introduction p. 1.
49. *Op. cit.* 47, p. 17.
50. Center for International Environment and Development, World Resources Institute, *Toward an Environmental and Natural Resource Management Strategy for ANE Countries in the 1990s*, report for the U.S. Agency for International Development (U.S. AID) (U.S. AID, Washington, D.C., 1990), p. 40.

51. *Ibid.*, p. 39.
52. Ministry of Environment and Forests, India, *Environment and Development: Traditions, Concerns and Efforts in India*, report submitted to the United Nations Conference on Environment and Development (Centre for Environment Education, Ahmedabad, 1992), p. 41.
53. Central Pollution Control Board (CPCB), *Annual Report, 1991–92* (CPCB, New Delhi, 1992), p. 19.
54. Planning Commission, Government of India, *Eighth Five-Year Plan: 1992–97*, Vol. II (Controller of Publications, Delhi, 1992), pp. 378–379.
55. "An Acute Problem," *The Hindu* (May 13, 1993), reprinted in *Green File*, No. 65 (May 1–31, 1993), p. 64.
56. Centre for Science and Environment, *Floods, Flood Plains and Environmental Myths* (Centre for Science and Environment, New Delhi, 1991), pp. 4–6.
57. Jill Carr-Harris, "Environment and Health," *Health for the Millions* (February/April 1992), p. 17.
58. Ministry of Environment and Forests, India, *The State of Forest Report 1991* (Ministry of Environment and Forests, Dehra Dun, n.d.), p. 7.
59. *Ibid.*
60. *Ibid.*, pp. 7–9.
61. *Op. cit.* 43, p. 325.
62. *Op. cit.* 44, p. 133.
63. United Nations Food and Agriculture Organization (FAO), *Forest Products Yearbook, 1991* (FAO, Rome, 1993), pp. 22 and 24.
64. P.S. Ramakrishnan, *Shifting Agriculture and Sustainable Development*, Man and the Biosphere series, Vol. 10 (UNESCO, Paris, 1992), pp. 7–10 and 42–44.
65. *Op. cit.* 44, p. 133.
66. *Op. cit.* 6, p. 70.
67. *Op. cit.* 52, pp. 11–12.
68. *Op. cit.* 52, pp. 11–12.
69. Gautam Sethi, "Degradation of the Soil Resource," Tata Energy Research Institute draft paper, New Delhi, n.d., p. 3.
70. Mark Svendsen, Research Fellow, International Food Policy Research Institute, Washington, D.C., 1993 (personal communication).
71. *Ibid.*
72. *Op. cit.* 69, pp. 3–4.
73. Ministry of Water Resources, India, *Waterlogging, Soil Salinity and Alkalinity: Report of the Working Group on Problem Identification in Irrigated Areas with Suggested Remedial Measures* (Ministry of Water Resources, New Delhi, 1991), pp. 59 and 63.
74. *Ibid.*, p. 43.
75. O.P. Singh and I.P. Abrol, *Historical Investigations of Waterlogging and Salinity Problem in Irrigated Agriculture in India* (Central Soil Salinity Research Institute, Karnal, 1992), p. 53.
76. B. Bowonder, K.V. Ramana, C. Ravi, *et al.*, "Land Use, Waterlogging, and Irrigation Management," *Land Use Policy*, Vol. 3, No. 3 (1987), p. 332.
77. *Ibid.*, pp. 333–336.
78. *Ibid.*, p. 339.
79. The World Bank, *India Irrigation Sector Review*, Vol. 2 (Supplementary Analysis), (The World Bank, Washington, D.C., 1991), p. 72.
80. *Ibid.*, p. 73.
81. *Op. cit.* 69, pp. 22–23 and 26.
82. Indian Institute of Soil Science, *All India Coordinated Scheme of Micro and Secondary Nutrients and Pollutant Elements in Soils and Plants*, annual report, 1988–89 (Indian Institute of Soil Science, Bhopal, 1990), pp. 16–18.

83. Economic Intelligence Service, *Current Energy Scene in India* (Centre for Monitoring Indian Economy, Bombay, 1992), pp. 2–13.
84. R.P.S. Malik and Paul Faeth, "Rice-Wheat Production in Northwest India," in *Agricultural Policy and Sustainability: Case Studies from India, Chile, the Philippines and the United States*, Paul Faeth, ed. (World Resources Institute, Washington, D.C., 1993), pp. 17–31.
85. S.V.S. Jeneja, Asian Development Bank, Noida, Uttar Pradesh, 1992 (personal communication).
86. Central Ground Water Board, Ministry of Water Resources, India, *Status of Ground Water Pollution in India* (Ground Water Pollution Directorate, Lucknow, Uttar Pradesh, 1991), pp. 19 and 32.
87. Kirk R. Smith and Susan A. Thorneloe, "Household Fuels in Developing Countries: Global Warming, Health, and Energy Implications," paper prepared for the 1992 Greenhouse Gas Emissions and Mitigation Research Symposium, Washington, D.C., August 1992, pp. 10–11.
88. Kirk R. Smith, *Biofuels, Air Pollution, and Health: A Global Review* (Plenum Press, New York, 1987), pp. 25, 41–57, and 207–209.
89. V. Agarwala, Ministry of Urban Development, New Delhi, 1993 (personal communication).
90. B. Bowonder, "Environmental Management Problems in India," *Environmental Management*, Vol. 10, No. 5 (1986), pp. 599–609.
91. Central Pollution Control Board (CPCB), *Control of Urban Pollution Series: CUPS/30/1989-90, Status of Water Supply and Wastewater Collection: Treatment and Disposal in Class I Cities, 1988*, Control of Urban Pollution series 30, 1989–90 (CPCB, New Delhi, 1991), pp. 32 and 36.
92. The World Health Organization and the United Nations Environment Programme, *Urban Air Pollution in Megacities of the World* (Blackwell, Oxford, U.K., 1992), pp. 12, 70–73, 95–98, and 103–105.
93. *Ibid.*, pp. 74–75.
94. Tata Energy Research Institute (TERI), *Environmental Considerations in Energy Development*, final report submitted to the Asian Development Bank (TERI, New Delhi, July 1992), pp. 72–73 and 82–83.
95. Dilip Biswas, Chairman, Central Pollution Control Board, New Delhi, 1993 (personal communication to Dr. T.N. Khoshoo, Jawaharlal Nehru Fellow, Tata Energy Research Institute).
96. Ministry of Environment and Forests, India, *Policy Statement for Abatement of Pollution, 1992* (Ministry of Environment and Forests, New Delhi, 1992), p. 2.
97. *Op. cit.* 35, p. 1.
98. Ministry of Environment and Forests, India, "Industrial Waste Management," report of sub-group 2 of the National Waste Management Council, August 1990, pp. i, 3, and 17.
99. P.V.R. Subrahmanyan and Kanchana Swaminathan, "Hazardous Waste Management in India," paper presented at the First International Technology Fair and Hi-Tech Seminar on Electronics, Communication and Environment Protection, Bangalore, August 21, 1991, pp. 8–9 and 13.
100. *Op. cit.* 52.
101. *Op. cit.* 41, pp. 9–10.
102. *Op. cit.* 52, p. 40.
103. *Op. cit.* 6, p. 87.
104. *Op. cit.* 90, p. 602.
105. Ministry of Environment and Forests, India, *Annual Report, 1991–92* (Ministry of Environment and Forests, New Delhi, n.d.), p. 54.

106. *Ibid.*
107. *Ibid.*, pp. 50–52.
108. John Ward Anderson, "The Great Cleanup of the Holy Ganges," *The Washington Post* (September 25, 1992), p. A1.
109. Ministry of Information and Broadcasting, India, *India 1992* (Ministry of Information and Broadcasting, New Delhi, 1993), p. 180.
110. *Op. cit.* 8.
111. D.S. Bhargava, "Why the Ganga Could Not Be Cleaned," *Environmental Conservation*, Vol. 19, No. 2 (Summer 1992), pp. 170–172.
112. Dinesh C. Sharma, "650-CR Plan Cleared to Clean Yamuna," *Business and Political Observer* (November 26, 1992), reprinted in *Green File*, No. 59 (November 1–30, 1992), p. 49.
113. N. Suresh, "Rs. 1,000-Crore Plan to Clean 13 Rivers," *Times of India* (November 18, 1992), reprinted in *Green File*, No. 59 (November 1–30, 1992), p. 48.
114. T.N. Khoshoo, Jawaharlal Nehru Fellow, Tata Energy Research Institute, New Delhi, 1993 (personal communication).
115. Mark Poffenberger, ed., *Forest Management Partnerships: Regenerating India's Forests*, Executive Summary of the Workshop on Sustainable Forestry, New Delhi, September 10–12, 1990 (The Ford Foundation and Indian Environmental Society, New Delhi, n.d.) pp. 1–2.
116. *Ibid.*, p. 6.
117. Mark Poffenberger, Consultant, Center for Southeast Asia Studies, University of California at Berkeley, 1993 (personal communication).
118. S.K. Dhar, "Early Experiences with Hill Resource Societies as Joint Forest Managers," in S.K. Dhar, J.R. Gupta, and Madhu Sarin, *Participatory Forest Management in the Shivalik Hills: Experiences of the Haryana Forest Department*, Sustainable Forest Management Working Paper No. 5, Ford Foundation, New Delhi, n.d., p. 2.
119. *Ibid.*, p. 3.
120. *Ibid.*, pp. 3–5.
121. *Ibid.*, pp. 6–7.
122. *Ibid.*, pp. 5–6.
123. *Ibid.*, p. 19.
124. Anil Agarwal and Sunita Narain, *Towards Green Villages* (Centre for Science and Environment, New Delhi, 1989), pp. 19 and 21.
125. *Op. cit.* 115, pp. 6 and 20.
126. *Op. cit.* 115, pp. 16–17.
127. Samar Singh, Secretary General, World Wide Fund for Nature: India, New Delhi, 1993 (personal communication).
128. Mark Poffenberger and Samar Singh, "Forest Management Partnerships: Regenerating India's Forests," *Unasylva*, Vol. 43, No. 170 (1992), p. 46.
129. *Op. cit.* 115, p. 2.
130. *Op. cit.* 117.
131. *Op. cit.* 115, p. 3.
132. Ministry of Environment and Forests, India, *Developing India's Wastelands* (Ministry of Environment and Forests, New Delhi, n.d.), p. 8.
133. Tata Energy Research Institute, *Environmental Considerations in Energy Development: India Country Study*, final report submitted to the Asian Development Bank (TERI, New Delhi, 1991), p. 5.
134. *Op. cit.* 105, p. 58.
135. Ministry of Environment and Forests, India, *Project Tiger, 1990* (Ministry of Environment and Forests, New Delhi, n.d.), pp. 1–2.
136. *Ibid.*
137. *Ibid.*, p. 2.
138. *Ibid.*, pp. 3–5.

139. Ministry of Environment and Forests, India, *A Review of Project Tiger, 1993* (Ministry of Environment and Forests, New Delhi, 1993), p. 2.

140. *Op. cit.* 135, pp. 5–6.

141. *Op. cit.* 139.

142. *Op. cit.* 139, p. 30.

143. Ministry of Environment and Forests, India, *Project Elephant* (Ministry of Environment and Forests, New Delhi, 1993), pp. 34, 38, and 40–45.

144. *Op. cit.* 114.

145. *Op. cit.* 35, pp. 12–13.

146. *Op. cit.* 35, pp. 10–13.

147. *Op. cit.* 96, p. 6.

148. *Op. cit.* 35, pp. 7–9.

149. *Op. cit.* 6, pp. 56 and 60.

150. Fertilizer Association of India, *Fertilizer Statistics, 1991–92* (Fertilizer Association of India, New Delhi, 1992), p. III-72.

151. *Op. cit.* 54, p. 1.

152. *Op. cit.* 6, pp. 40 and 54.

153. *Op. cit.* 6, pp. 53–54.

154. Ministry of Finance, India, *Economic Survey, 1992-93,* (Ministry of Finance, New Delhi, 1993), pp. 164 and 169.

155. *Ibid.*, p. 153.

156. United Nations Environment Programme, *Environmental Data Report* (Blackwell, Oxford, U.K., 1991), pp. 152–158.

157. James A. Hanson, *India: Recent Developments and Medium-Term Issues* (The World Bank, Washington, D.C., 1989), pp. xx–xxi and 27–28.

158. G.S. Bhalla, G.K. Chadha, S.P. Kashyap, *et al.*, *Agricultural Growth and Structural Changes in the Punjab Economy: An Input-Output Analysis*, Research Report No. 82 (International Food Policy Research Institute, Washington, D.C., 1990), p. 9.

159. Anya McGuirk and Yair Mundlak, *Incentives and Constraints in the Transformation of Punjab Agriculture*, Research Report No. 87 (International Food Policy Research Institute, Washington, D.C., 1990), p. 17.

160. *Op. cit.* 79, p. 70.

161. M.S. Swaminathan, Director, Center for Research on Sustainable Agricultural and Rural Development, Madras, 1992 (personal communication).

162. J.S. Sarma and Vasant Gandhi, *Production and Consumption of Foodgrains in India: Implications of Accelerated Economic Growth and Poverty Alleviation*, Research Report No. 81 (International Food Policy Research Institute, Washington, D.C., 1990), pp. 17 and 18.

163. *Op. cit.* 154, p. S-28.

164. R.M. Acharya, "Sustainable Animal Husbandry," in *Sustainable Management of Natural Resources*, T.N. Khoshoo and Manju Sharma, eds. (Malhotra, New Delhi, 1992), p. 262.

165. V.D. Padmanaban, Professor and Head, Department of Animal Biotechnology, Madras Veterinary College, Madras, 1992 (personal communication).

166. Total food grain production is calculated using the weight of milled rice. The cereal production figures in Part IV of *World Resources* are calculated using the weight of paddy rice, which is about 50 percent more than the weight of milled rice because it includes the weight of the rice husks.

167. S.E. Aranha, "Pulses: Relegated to Rainfed Lands," in *The Hindu: Survey of Indian Agriculture, 1992* (S. Rangarjan, Madras, 1993), pp. 43–45.

168. B. Venkateswarlu, "Rice: East Merits More Attention," *The Hindu: Survey of Indian Agriculture, 1992*, p. 24.

169. M.V. Rao, "Wheat: Rise in Productivity Crucial," in *The Hindu: Survey of Indian Agriculture, 1992* (S. Rangarjan, Madras 1993), p. 31.

170. *Op. cit.* 154, p. 161.

171. Mark Svendsen, "Sources of Future Growth in Indian Irrigated Agriculture," in *Future Directions for Indian Irrigation*, Ruth Meinzen-Dick and Mark Svendsen, eds. (International Food Policy Research Institute, Washington, D.C., 1991), pp. 59–60.

172. "India Snubs World Bank Aid," *Wall Street Journal* (March 31, 1993), p. A10.

173. Paul Kurian, "Narmada Project and Opting Out of WB Loan," *Deccan Herald* (Bangalore), May 17, 1993, reprinted in *Green File*, No. 65 (May 1–31, 1993), pp. 30–31.

174. *Op. cit.* 79, p. 10.

175. *Op. cit.* 79, pp. 4 and 33–43.

176. Anthony Bottrall, "Overview," in *Future Directions for Indian Irrigation*, Ruth Meinzen-Dick and Mark Svendsen, eds. (International Food Policy Research Institute, Washington, D.C., 1991), p. 150.

177. *Op. cit.* 4, p. 20.

178. Inderjit Singh, *Land and Labor in South Asia* (The World Bank, Washington, D.C., 1988), pp. 13-14.

179. *Op. cit.* 4, pp. 20–21.

180. R.P. Singh, "Problems and Prospects of Dryland Agriculture in India," in *Land and Soils*, T.N. Khoshoo and B.L. Deekshatulu, eds. (Har-Anand, New Delhi, 1992), p. 267.

181. S.M. Virmani, "Agricultural Climatic Environment of Semi-Arid India: Some Issues, Problems, and Solutions," in *Land and Soils*, T.N. Khoshoo and B.L. Deekshatulu, eds. (Har-Anand, New Delhi, 1992), pp. 261–263.

182. *Op. cit.* 109, p. 528.

183. Gunvant M. Desai, "Issues and Themes in Growth of Fertilizer Use in India: An Agenda for Further Research and Future Policies," *Journal of the Indian Society of Agricultural Statistics*, Vol. 43, No. 1 (April 1991), pp. 89 and 93–94.

184. Gunvant M. Desai and Vasant Gandhi, "Phosphorus for Sustainable Growth in Asia: An Assessment of Alternative Sources and Management," paper prepared for the Symposium on Phosphorus Requirements for Sustainable Agriculture in Asia and Pacific Region, International Rice Research Institute, Los Banos, Philippines, March, 1989.

185. *Op. cit.* 183, p. 94.

186. *Op. cit.* 162, p. 85.

187. U.S. Congress, Office of Technology Assessment (OTA), *Fueling Development: Energy Technologies for Developing Countries* (OTA, Washington, D.C., 1992), pp. 26–27.

188. *Op. cit.* 109, p. 472.

189. Malaine Manzo, Energy Specialist, The World Bank, Washington, D.C., 1992 (personal communication).

190. The World Bank, *World Development Report 1993* (The International Bank for Reconstruction and Development/The World Bank, Washington, D.C., 1993), p. 240.

191. Jayant Sathaye and Nina Goldman, eds., *CO₂ Emissions from Developing Countries: Better Understanding the Role of Energy in the Long Term, Vol. 3: China, India, and South Korea*, (Lawrence Berkeley Laboratory, Berkeley, California, 1991), pp. 1 and 17.

192. United Nations Statistical Division (UNSD), *1991 Energy Statistics Yearbook* (UNSD, New York, 1993), Table 3, pp. 62–111.

193. R. Govinda Rao, Gautam Dutt, and Michael Philips, *The Least Cost Energy Path for India: Energy Efficient Investments for the Multilateral Development Banks* (International Institute for Energy Conservation, Washington, D.C., 1991), p. ix.

194. *Op. cit.* 6, p. 99.

195. *Op. cit.* 6, p. 63.

196. *Op. cit.* 193, pp. 15–19.

197. Tata Energy Research Institute (TERI), *Energy Data, Directory, and Yearbook, 1990–91* (TERI, New Delhi, 1992), p. 37.

198. Asian Development Bank (ADB), *Environmental Considerations in Energy Development* (ADB, Manila, 1991), p. 24.

199. *Op. cit.* 197, pp. 38–39.

200. *Op. cit.* 198, p. 263.

201. *Op. cit.* 198, pp. 265–267.

202. *Op. cit.* 197, p. 39.

203. *Op. cit.* 187, pp. 246–247.

204. *Op. cit.* 197, p. 47.

205. *Op. cit.* 197, p. 8.

206. *Op. cit.* 198.

207. *Op. cit.* 83, pp. 1-1, 1-2.

208. *Op. cit.* 83, pp. 1-1, 1-2.

209. *Op. cit.* 197, pp. 8 and 58.

210. *Op. cit.* 198, pp. 24 and 274.

211. *Op. cit.* 54, pp. 200–202.

212. *Op. cit.* 198, pp. 263 and 268.

213. *Op. cit.* 197, pp. 5 and 151.

214. Ashok Gadgil and Gilberto De Martini Jannuzzi, "Conservation Potential of Compact Fluorescent Lamps in India and Brazil," *Energy Policy*, Vol. 19, No. 5 (June 1991), p. 451.

215. *Op. cit.* 54, p. 166.

216. Arun Sanghvi, "Power Shortages in Developing Countries," *Energy Policy*, Vol. 19, No. 5 (June 1991), p. 427.

217. *Op. cit.* 214, pp. 450–451.

218. *Op. cit.* 216, p. 428.

219. *Op. cit.* 216, p. 430.

220. *Op. cit.* 191, p. 15.

221. Gunter Schramm, "Issues and Problems in the Power Sectors of Developing Countries," *Energy Policy*. Vol. 21, No. 7 (July 1993), p. 740.

222. *Op. cit.* 191, pp. 75 and 76.

223. B. Bowonder and T. Miyake, "Measurement of Technology at Industry Level: A Case Study of the Steel Industry in India and Japan," *Science and Public Policy*, Vol. 15, No. 4 (1988), pp. 253–257.

224. *Op. cit.* 193, pp. 8 and 15.

225. *Op. cit.* 193, pp. 4, 9, and 46–47.

226. Steven Nadel, Virendra Kothari, and S. Gopinath, *Opportunities for Improving End-Use Electricity Efficiency in India* (American Council for an Energy-Efficient Economy, Washington, D.C., 1991), pp. S-4, S-7, S-14, and S-15.

227. *Op. cit.* 83, pp. 2–11.

228. *Op. cit.* 83, pp. 2–15.

229. *Op. cit.* 83, pp. 2–14 and 2–43.

230. *Op. cit.* 154, p. 178.

231. S. Meyers, J. Sathaye, O. Masera, and A. Ketoff, *Plans for the Power Sector in 13 Major Developing Countries* (Lawrence Berkeley Laboratory, Berkeley, California, 1989), pp. 3-5 to 3-8.

232. *Op. cit.* 193, pp. 6–7.

233. *Op. cit.* 193, pp. 6–7.

234. Bhaskar Natarajan, Fellow, Tata Energy Research Institute, New Delhi, 1992 (personal communication).

235. James Sullivan, "Private Power in Developing Countries: Early Experience and a Framework for Development," *Annual Review of Energy*, Vol. 15 (1990), pp. 348–349.

236. *Op. cit.* 234.

237. *Op. cit.* 198, p. 268.

238. *Op. cit.* 231, pp. 3-5 and 3-7.

239. N. Mongia, R. Bhatia, J. Sathaye, *et al.*, "Cost of Reducing CO2 Emissions from India: Imperatives for International Transfer of Resources and Technologies," *Energy Policy*, Vol. 19, No. 10 (December 1991), pp. 984–986.

240. Robert Williams, Senior Research Scientist, Center for Energy and Environmental Studies, Princeton University, Princeton, New Jersey, 1992 (personal communication).

241. Maheshwar Dayal, *Renewable Energy: Environment and Development* (Konark, Delhi, India, 1989), pp. 62–63.

242. *Ibid.*, pp. 20–30.

243. *Ibid.*, pp. 31–34.

244. Matthew S. Mendis, President, Alternative Energy Development, Silver Spring, Maryland, 1992 (personal communication).

245. *Op. cit.* 241, pp. 32–34 and 41–47.

246. Tata Energy Research Institute (TERI), "Rays of Hope: Renewable Energy for Sustainable Development" (TERI, New Delhi, 1993), p. 2.

247. C.S. Sinha, Tata Energy Research Institute, New Delhi, 1993 (personal communication).

248. Planning Commission, India, *Eighth Five-Year Plan, Vol. ii* (Government of India Planning Commission, New Delhi, n.d.), p. 199.

249. *Op. cit.* 246.

250. *Op. cit.* 234.

251. *Op. cit.* 247.

252. *Op. cit.* 247.

253. M. Dayal, "Role of Renewable Energy Sources in Reducing Global Warming and Climatic Change," in *Global Warming and Climate Change: Perspectives from Developing Countries*, S. Gupta and R.K. Pachauri, eds. (Tata Energy Research Institute, New Delhi, 1989), p. 181.

254. *Op. cit.* 244.

255. *Op. cit.* 247.

6. Food and Agriculture

Agricultural production in much of the developing world has been an extraordinary success over the past several decades, but the pressure to grow more food will continue as populations rise. With land growing scarcer, most future production gains will have to come from greater average yields per hectare. Yet in Asia, yield gains are generally slowing, while in sub-Saharan Africa the gap between supply and demand is expected to widen.

Such circumstances would seem to call for an even greater investment in agricultural research and development. In fact, public research spending slowed considerably in the 1980s, both at the national and international levels.

Two of the many important issues facing agriculture over the next few decades are discussed here. First is the use of pesticides in developing countries. Pesticides, one foundation of the remarkable production hikes over the past few decades, continue to underpin many national development strategies in developing countries. Yet considerable research suggests that the benefits of pesticides have been exaggerated and that,

as currently used, they pose substantial dangers both to the environment and to human health.

The second issue, agricultural biotechnology, is an important source of hope for the future. Biotechnology offers numerous possibilities for agriculture. But these potential advances are decades away from realization, carry some risk, and will not displace current agricultural practices altogether. Moreover, while the developing world is most in need of biotechnology's innovations, current research is concentrated on high-value crops grown in the industrialized world.

CONDITIONS AND TRENDS

Global agriculture's steady gains in production over the past several decades have not fully overcome the problem of rising demand caused by soaring population growth and uneven production progress among regions. The challenge is immense: by the year 2050, global demand for food may be three times greater than today (1). Moreover, during the past two decades the production growth rate has declined, dropping

Figure 6.1 Index of Food Production by Region, 1970–92

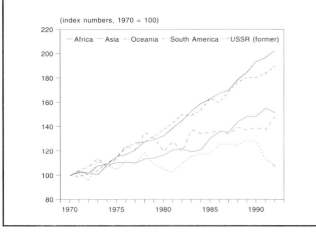

(index numbers, 1970 = 100)

Africa — Asia — Oceania — South America ··· USSR (former)

Source: Food and Agriculture Organization of the United Nations (FAO), *Agrostat PC*, on diskette (FAO, Rome, 1993).

Figure 6.2 Index of Per Capita Food Production by Region, 1970–92

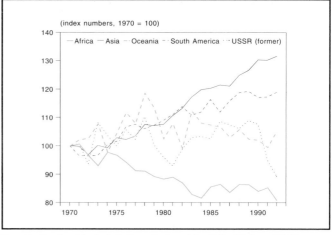

(index numbers, 1970 = 100)

Africa — Asia — Oceania — South America ··· USSR (former)

Source: Food and Agriculture Organization of the United Nations (FAO), *Agrostat PC*, on diskette (FAO, Rome, 1993).

from 3 percent annually during the l960s to 2.4 percent in the 1970s and finally to 2.2 percent in the l980s (2).

In 1991, global agricultural production actually fell, the first decline since 1983 and one that can be attributed to reduced harvests in North America, Australia, Eastern Europe, and the former U.S.S.R. (3). In the developing world, gross agricultural production continued to increase—by 2.3 percent in 1991—most notably in Asia and South America. (See Figures 6.1. and 6.2.) But per capita production figures for Africa, where population growth has steadily outpaced food production, have fallen. The African countries of Sierra Leone, Somalia, and Zimbabwe were among eight developing nations that experienced serious declines in 1990–91 (4) (5). As for Oceania and the former U.S.S.R., production has fluctuated dramatically over the last 22 years .

The absolute number of undernourished people in the world has decreased since 1969–71, as a result of better global per capita dietary energy supplies and an improving food distribution system (6). (See Table 6.1.) This was not the trend in all regions. The number of chronically undernourished in Africa went from about 101 million in 1969–71 to 168 million in 1988–90, while the proportion of undernourished persons to the general population only dropped 2 percent. At the same time, Asia experienced the largest decline in the proportion of undernourished, from 40 to 19 percent, but it supports the largest absolute population of undernourished. The United Nations Food and Agriculture

Organization (FAO) estimates that in 1988–90, 528 million people were chronically malnourished in Asia—67 percent of all such people in developing regions (7).

CRITICAL ISSUES: YIELD TRENDS AND SUB-SAHARAN AFRICA

On a global basis, average yields per hectare of wheat, rice, and maize have climbed fairly steadily since 1961. (See Figure 6.3.) The aggregate figures nonetheless mask some disturbing regional trends. In Asia, for example, rice yields rose dramatically in the 1960s with the introduction of new varieties and management practices. Yields continued to increase in the 1970s, but in the 1980s began to level off or decline.

In the Philippines, average wet-season rice yields increased from about 2.5 tons per hectare in 1966 to about 4.2 tons per hectare in Central Luzon province and 4.7 tons per hectare in Laguna Province by the early 1980s. By 1990, however, yields in both areas were 0.5 tons per hectare lower than in the early 1980s. In Ludhiana District in India's Punjab, average rice yields went from 1.8 to 4.0 tons per hectare in the 1970s, but have stayed about the same since 1980 (8).

Declining yields have also occurred in experimental plots at the International Rice Research Institute (IRRI) in the Philippines. The pattern was exhibited in fields with optimal inputs as well as those without nutrient inputs. Despite continual replacement of older varieties with improved ones, none of the IRRI's long-term

Table 6.1 Prevalence of Chronic Undernutrition in Developing Regions

Region	1969–71 Millions of Undernourished	1969–71 Proportion of Total Population %	1979–81 Millions of Undernourished	1979–81 Proportion of Total Population %	1988–90 Millions of Undernourished	1988–90 Proportion of Total Population %
Africa	101	35	128	33	168	33
Asia	751	40	645	28	528	19
Latin America	54	19	47	13	59	13
Middle East	35	22	24	12	31	12
Total Developing Regions	**941**	**36**	**844**	**26**	**786**	**20**

Source: Food and Agriculture Organization of the United Nations (FAO), *The State of Food and Agriculture, 1992* (FAO, Rome, 1992), p. 22.
Note: Seventy-two countries with a population of less than 1 million, representing 0.6 percent of the developing world's population, were excluded from the table totals.

Figure 6.3 World Average of Per-Hectare Yields of Major Food Crops, 1961–92

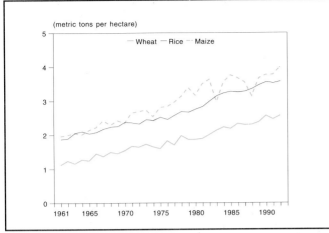

Source: Food and Agriculture Organization of the United Nations (FAO), *Agrostat PC*, on diskette (FAO, Rome, 1993).

Figure 6.4 World Production of Selected Food Crops, 1970–92

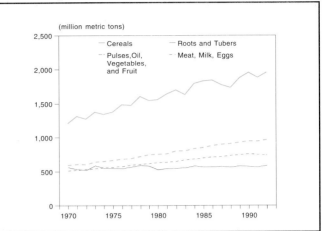

Source: Food and Agriculture Organization of the United Nations (FAO), *Agrostat PC*, on diskette (FAO, Rome, 1993).

experiments currently show yield gains. The causes are not clear; current research is testing the hypothesis that in continuously submerged soil, organic matter undergoes changes that over time reduce the nitrogen available to rice crops. Additional research is planned to see if similar processes may contribute to waning productivity in farmers' fields (9).

Trends in yields are not the only factors affecting rice in Asia. Other phenomena that may be discouraging production of the crop include changing dietary habits, depressed world prices, and shrinking investment in new irrigation by major development banks and national governments (10).

Sub-Saharan Africa

Most global and regional projections suggest that the amount of cereal imported by developing countries will rise by one half during the next two decades (11).

In some rapidly developing countries, this trend may not impose an intolerable economic burden. In sub-Saharan Africa, however, the food import gap could be as high as 50 million metric tons—one third of projected consumption—by the year 2000. The region may not be able to pay the costs. Sub-Saharan Africa's external debt (as a percentage of exports of goods and services) more than tripled during the 1980s. Furthermore, buying food requires a growth in household purchasing power, yet strategies to promote rural employment and raise the incomes of small farmers have proven elusive. Finally, even if world cereal prices remain relatively stable, in most inland rural areas of Africa, prices for imported commodities typically run 100 to 200 percent higher than on the coast because of transfer costs (12). In light of these circumstances, programs to boost agricultural production and economic growth in sub-Saharan Africa appear urgent.

Production of Major Food Crops

The production of major food crops has climbed steadily over the last 20 years, growing 1.45 percent annually between 1981 and 1991. Between 1990 and 1991,

however, production fell from a record 1,971 million metric tons to 1,890 million metric tons (13).

Cereal production has nearly doubled since 1970, while the production of roots and tubers has remained relatively stable. (See Figure 6.4.) Global production of root crops for 1991 remained at the 1990 level of 574 million tons. Over the 1981–91 period, pulse production has increased at an annual rate of 3.34 percent, most of which went to human food consumption as opposed to feed consumption for livestock (14).

Global stocks increased from 365 million metric tons in 1984 to 464 million metric tons in 1986 and then fell back to the 300–343 million metric ton range (15). U.S. production of cereal has had a significant impact on global stocks, which, since 1960, have shown a generally upward trend. (See Figure 6.5.) Africa (7.8 million metric tons) and Latin America (10.7 million metric tons) together accounted for approximately 5 percent of global cereal stocks for 1992 (16).

Food Aid Flows

The 13.2 million tons of cereal delivered globally as aid in 1991 represented 0.7 percent of world cereal production (17) (18) and approximately 7 percent of stocks in industrialized countries (19).

Regional estimates of food aid flows fluctuated between 1987 and 1991. Africa and Asia received the largest amounts of food aid overall. (See Figure 6.6.) Sub-Saharan Africa received the largest volume of food aid in 1991, major recipients being Ethiopia, Sudan, Mozambique, Malawi, Liberia, and Angola (20). In 1992, the Horn of Africa (Ethiopia, Somalia, and the Sudan) suffered severe food shortages, the latter two because of civil strife as well as low rainfall.

Food aid declined in Latin America, the Caribbean, Eastern Europe, and the former Soviet Union. The Asia/Pacific and North Africa/Middle East regions saw slight increases from 1990 aid levels.

Agricultural Prices

Many less developed countries that depend heavily on earnings from agricultural exports see their economies

Figure 6.5 Ending Stocks of Total Grains, 1960–92

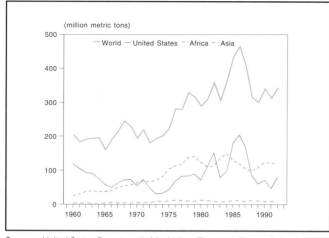

Source: United States Department of Agriculture/Economic Research Service (USDA/ERS), *PS&D View '92*, on diskette (USDA/ERS, Washington, D.C., 1992).

hurt by low prices. Other countries that produce little and import a lot benefit by low prices. With a few exceptions, prices of agricultural commodities have fallen globally over the last 15 years (21) (22). (See Table 15.4.) In 1990–91, the overall level of prices for agricultural exports fell by 6 percent in the developing world, while the overall decline for industrialized countries was 4 percent. The prices of coffee, cocoa, tea, sugar, cotton, and jute saw substantial drops (23).

Real prices (constant dollar prices) of agricultural exports declined slightly less than current dollar prices during 1991 (24). These prices represent 64 percent of the 1979–81 average level for developing countries and 81 percent for industrialized countries (25). Higher prices for agricultural commodities in industrialized countries usually reflect subsidies, tariffs, and price guarantees, which keep the local price above the global market price (26). In addition, in industrialized countries farmers earn a greater share of their income

Figure 6.6 Total Food Aid Deliveries by Region, 1987–91

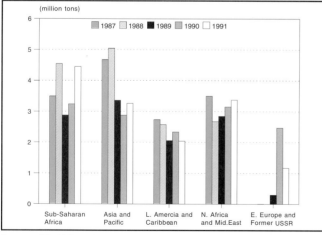

Source: World Food Programme (WFP), *1992 Food Aid Review* (WFP, Rome, 1992), p. 12.

Figure 6.7 Index of Food Exports from Developing Countries by Volume and Value, 1970–91

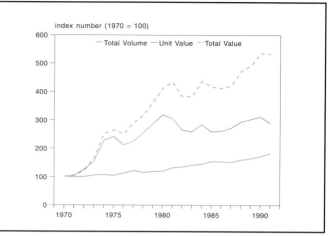

Source: Food and Agriculture Organization of the United Nations (FAO), *Agrostat PC*, on diskette (FAO, Rome, 1993).

from relatively expensive livestock and horticultural products, whereas in developing countries they earn proportionately more from cereals, roots, and tubers (27).

The total volume of exports from developing countries has risen steadily since 1970, while unit value rose and then plateaued during the early 1980s. (See Figure 6.7.) The total value of imports for developing countries rose to roughly seven times the 1970 level by the early 1980s with total volume increasing approximately two and one-half times. (See Figure 6.8.)

Agricultural Research and Development

Productivity gains to meet future demands for food and fiber depend to a large extent on current agricultural research.

Global investment in public research climbed substantially between 1961 and 1985. (See Tables 6.2 and 18.5.) During this period, the total number of agricultural researchers rose at an average annual rate of 4.2 percent—in developing countries 7.2 percent, in industrialized countries 1.7 percent. While the developing world enjoyed 6.3 percent annual growth in research expenditure, the average for 1961–65 and 1981–85, the growth rate slowed considerably in the early 1980s. In fact, the 1976–80 to 1981–85 annual rate of growth in real research expenditures was only 0.7 percent for sub-Saharan Africa and 0.9 percent for Latin America and the Caribbean (28).

Based on a study of 83 countries, 68 percent of agricultural researchers are engaged in crop research, 19 percent in livestock research, 7 percent in forestry research, and 6 percent in fisheries research (29).

In 1971, 20 donor countries established the Consultative Group on International Agricultural Research (CGIAR) as an umbrella body that by 1980 included 13 international research centers. By 1990, there were 18 centers and 40 donors. The CGIAR budget rose from $20 million in 1971 to $280 million in 1990. In inflation-adjusted terms, CGIAR spending grew rapidly during the 1970s, slowed in the 1980s, and has stagnated or declined over the past few years (30). (See Figure 6.9.)

Figure 6.8 Index of Food Imports into Developing Countries by Volume and Value, 1970–91

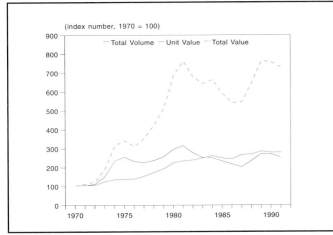
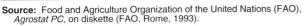

Source: Food and Agriculture Organization of the United Nations (FAO), *Agrostat PC*, on diskette (FAO, Rome, 1993).

CGIAR research initially focused on Asia, but in the early 1980s the emphasis shifted to sub-Saharan Africa. Between 1986 and 1988, that region received 39 percent of CGIAR's core funding, Asia received 26 percent, Latin America and the Caribbean 21 percent, and West Asia and North Africa 14 percent (31).

The system's commodity orientation, like its regional focus, has been redirected. Since CGIAR's establishment, expenditure on cereals steadily declined and by 1986–88 was about 40 percent of total spending. Potatoes, roots and tubers, and legumes accounted for 24 percent, and livestock research accounted for 20 percent of the total (32). Currently, 30 percent of CGIAR funds target production technologies for marginal lands, roughly in proportion to the percentage of the population living in these areas (33).

FOCUS ON PESTICIDE USE IN DEVELOPING COUNTRIES

Pesticides have played a significant role in increasing agricultural production in the developing world over the last several decades. Along with chemical fertilizers, high-yield crop varieties, and intensive agricultural practices, pesticides have formed one of the foundations of the so-called Green Revolution. Heavily promoted by manufacturers, international aid agencies, and the governments of developing nations, pesticides until recently were viewed as the quickest path to food self-sufficiency and as a means to expand agricultural exports needed to fund cash-poor economies. Developing world policymakers frequently consider pesticide use essential to national development.

Although pesticide use in the South is apparently still on the rise, this trend has recently come under scrutiny by the combined efforts of grassroots watchdog groups, farmers' organizations, and labor unions, as well as the FAO, the World Health Organization (WHO), the United Nations Environment Programme, and other national and international nongovernmental

Figure 6.9 Consultative Group on International Agricultural Research (CGIAR) Expenditures, 1971–89

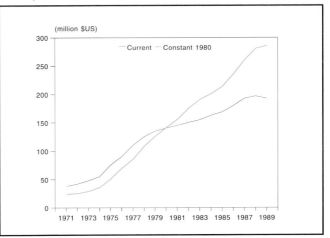

Source: International Service for National Agricultural Research (ISNAR), *Summary of Agricultural Research Policy: International Quantitative Perspectives* (ISNAR, The Hague, 1992), p. 13.

organizations. Consequently, many developing nations are now experimenting with alternatives. Several notable successes showcase the benefits of pesticide reform and highlight steps for achieving further success.

THE DEVELOPING WORLD PESTICIDE MARKET

On a global scale, a relatively small number of crops—among them corn, rice, cotton, soybeans, and wheat (many critical to developing economies)—receives the

Table 6.2 Annual Agricultural Research Personnel and Expenditures, Regional Totals, 1961–65 to 1981–85

Region	Agricultural Research Personnel (full-time equivalents)			Growth Rate[a] (%)
	1961–65	1971–75	1981–85	
Sub-Saharan Africa (43)[b]	1,323	2,416	4,941	6.8
China	7,469	11,781	36,335	8.2
Asia and Pacific, excluding China (28)	6,641	12,439	22,576	6.3
Latin America and Caribbean (38)	2,666	5,840	9,000	6.3
West Asia and North America (20)	2,157	4,746	8,995	7.4
Less-developed countries (130)	20,256	37,221	81,848	7.2
More-developed countries (22)	40,395	48,123	56,376	1.7
Total (152)	**60,651**	**85,344**	**138,224**	**4.2**

	Agricultural Research Expenditures[c] (million 1980 PPP dollars)			
Sub-Saharan Africa (43)[a]	149.5	276.9	372.3	4.7
China	486.7	874.8	1,712.7	6.5
Asia and Pacific, excluding China (28)	316.7	651.5	1,159.6	6.7
Latin America and Caribbean (38)	229.1	486.6	708.8	5.8
West Asia and North America (20)	126.9	300.7	455.4	6.6
Less-developed countries (130)	1,308.9	2,590.5	4,408.7	6.3
More-developed countries (22)	2,190.7	3,726.3	4,812.9	4.0
Total (152)	**3,499.6**	**6,316.8**	**9,221.6**	**5.0**

Source: Jock R. Anderson, Philip G. Pardey, and Johannes Roseboom, "Sustaining Growth in Agriculture: A Quantitative Review of Agricultural Research Investments" (*Agricultural Economics*, forthcoming).
Notes: Because of rounding, totals may not add up exactly.
a. Compound annual average growth rate between 1961–65 and 1981–85.
b. Figures in parentheses indicate the number of countries in the regional totals.
c. For more information, see Chapter 15, "Basic Economic Indicators," Technical Note 15.1 and Chapter 18, "Food and Agriculture," Technical Note 18.5.

Figure 6.10 World Agrochemical Market, 1991

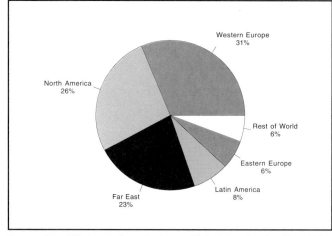

Source: Wood Mackenzie Consultants, unpublished data, London, May 1993.

bulk of pesticides. Currently, rice and cotton make up the largest part of the world pesticide market (34) (35).

Ever since 1941, when DDT ushered in the synthetic-pesticide era, the developing world has been a lucrative market for pesticides. Poor nations bought chemicals both for public health purposes, such as mosquito abatement in malaria control, and for agriculture, especially on large plantations producing export crops such as bananas, coffee, cotton, cocoa, coconuts, pineapples, palm oil, and sugar cane. Even so, developing countries accounted for only a small fraction of global pesticide use in the 1940s and 1950s (36) (37) (38) (39).

With the high-input, chemical-intensive agriculture that marked the Green Revolution in the 1960s and 1970s, pesticide use in the developing countries soared. In India alone, treated acreage expanded from just 6 million hectares in 1960 to over 80 million hectares in the mid-1980s (40). According to World Bank estimates, the Asia-Pacific pesticide market grew to $2.5 billion annually in the mid-1980s (41) (42). Indonesia, Pakistan, the Philippines, and Sri Lanka all saw increases in their pesticide consumption of more than 10 percent per year between 1980 and 1985 (43).

While industrialized countries still consume most of the world's pesticides (See Figure 6.10.), use in the United States has leveled off in recent years, while use grew slightly in Western Europe (44). Thus the developing world constitutes an increasingly important segment of the pesticide market which tops $21 billion annually. Developing nations currently purchase about 31 percent of world pesticide exports (45) (46) (47) (48). Indeed, with growth in the Northern pesticide market flattening over the last decade or so, manufacturers have turned more attention to Southern markets that retain ample potential for expansion (49) (50) (51).

Many of the pesticides exported to developing nations have been banned or restricted for health and environmental reasons in the countries where they are manufactured. Products such as DDT, chlordane, and heptachlor, prohibited for farm use in most industrialized countries, are still commonly used in developing nations. Some evidence indicates that the practice of pesticide dumping may be intensifying. For example,

U.S. customs records show that the manufacturer of chlordane, one of the most toxic and persistent pesticides ever formulated, increased its exports tenfold between 1987 and 1990 to over 3.6 tons per day (52) (53).

Indigenous production of pesticides has expanded to take advantage of what many governments of developing countries see as a lucrative industrial venture: supplying their own domestic needs and creating an export industry to fill the regional demands. While overall pesticide use in India is among the lowest in the world, its pesticide production increased 13-fold from 1970 to 1980 and now supplies roughly 90 percent of the indigenous demand (54) (55).

WHY MORE PESTICIDES?

The galloping spread of Western-style intensive agriculture, coupled with the movement toward commodity agriculture and away from traditional subsistence farming, has fueled pesticide use in the developing world (56) (57) (58).

While chemical fertilizers, irrigation, and high-yield crop varieties have increased productivity, they have also encouraged agricultural practices that make crops more vulnerable to pest attack. Large monocultures and year-round plantings of a single crop create ideal conditions for massive pest outbreaks, as demonstrated repeatedly on Southern plantation crops. In Asia, techniques such as direct rice sowing encouraged weeds, and nitrogen fertilizers heightened rice's susceptibility to certain diseases such as sheath blight (59) (60).

At a macroeconomic level, export agriculture, which comprises a large percentage of Southern pesticide use, has grown along with pressure to repay mounting foreign debt. Intensifying international competition in the agricultural export market has forced ever greater reliance on pesticides as tools to maximize yields (61).

Farmers' misconceptions also contribute to the use of pesticides, which are often viewed as progressive and modern—a legacy of years of preaching from agrochemical salespeople and agricultural extension agents who paid little heed to the practical limits and substantial risks of the chemicals they were peddling. Many farmers regard pesticides as cheap insurance against the risk of crop loss, one of the few concrete steps they can take to reduce the natural uncertainties of their trade (62).

SUBSIDIZING PESTICIDES

Until recently, the rise in consumption was encouraged in many developing nations through costly subsidies, tax incentives, and agricultural extension programs. Total subsidies have ranged from 15 to 90 percent of the retail cost of pesticides, with the annual value running into the hundreds of millions of dollars in some cases (63). In recent years, however, some developing countries have reduced their subsidies, sometimes in response to structural adjustment programs (64).

By depressing pesticide costs, such policies can lead to overuse, such as the practice of frequent spraying as "insurance," although the benefits in terms of increased crop yields may be marginal or nonexistent. By skewing the economics of pesticide use, subsidies also discourage more traditional and alternative pest-control strategies that are less chemical-intensive. Pesticide-free approaches may take more time and labor, but they reduce pollution and the incidence of agriculture-related health problems (65) (66).

Furthermore, serious questions of social equity arise when governments push pesticides. Wealthier landowners and large corporations benefit more from subsidies than smaller farmers. At the same time, the social costs of treating crops with pesticides—for instance, direct worker contamination, tainted water supplies, and food residues—tend to fall disproportionately on those who benefit least from the incentives (67).

THE PESTICIDE TREADMILL

Despite their prominence in world agriculture, pesticides have by no means ended the problems they were meant to solve. In fact, in the 50 years since pesticide use became widespread, the percentage of crop loss from pest damage has not measurably declined. Insects, weeds, and plant diseases still claim 30 to 35 percent of total crop production today—about the same percentage estimated for the prechemical era (68) (69) (70). While the intensified agricultural practices of this period raised global crop production, they also compromised the immunity of many crops to pest attack. Just keeping the percentage of crop losses constant as total production has risen is an accomplishment, though it falls far short of the panacea pesticides were once envisioned to be (71) (72). (See Figure 6.11.)

The ability of some pests to develop resistance curbs the effectiveness of many commercial chemicals. Most individuals in a pest population die when exposed to a pesticide, but a few, whose genetic makeup allows them to detoxify the poison, survive to breed. Those who inherit this resistance dominate in succeeding generations, and efforts to eradicate the population with the original chemical are increasingly futile (73) (74).

Resistance has accelerated since it was first observed on a large scale with DDT in the late 1940s. Today more than 500 insect and mite species are immune to one or more insecticides. Similarly, before 1970, few weeds were resistant, but since that time, 113 have developed the ability to detoxify one or more herbicides. About 150 plant pathogens such as fungus and bacteria are now shielded against fungicides (75) (76) (77).

Exacerbating this problem, pesticides can wipe out pest predators and thereby upset nature's own method of control. In fact, insecticides are often more deadly to beneficial predators than to the pests themselves. Once freed from natural biological controls, pest populations may experience quick resurgence. The elimination of pest predators has also been known to cause secondary pest outbreaks, that is, initially small populations swell to attain pest status (78).

A typical response to such complications is to increase pesticide dosages or the frequency of spraying. This may offer temporary relief but only hastens the trend toward resistance or secondary outbreaks. Farmers become trapped on the pesticide treadmill, a cycle of reliance on chemicals that offers diminishing returns while demanding greater cash outlays (79) (80) (81).

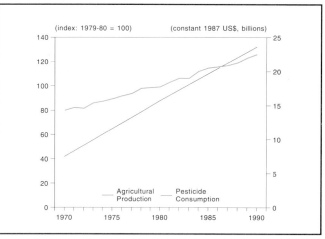

Figure 6.11 Agricultural Production Index and Pesticide Consumption, 1970–90

Source: The Food and Agriculture Organization of the United Nations (FAO), *Agrostat PC* on diskette (FAO, Rome, 1993), and Wood Mackenzie Consultants Limited, unpublished data, May 1993.

The tropical environment of many developing countries makes the tendency toward pest resistance and resurgence particularly worrisome. Heavy use of insecticides and quick reproduction are ideal conditions under which insects build resistance. Not surprisingly, resistance and secondary outbreaks have been observed in a number of Southern crops.

The best-documented case is cotton. It is one of the world's most important agricultural commodities, particularly for developing nations, which are responsible for about two thirds of global production (82) (83). It is also one of the most chemical-intensive crops in the world, consuming more than 10 percent of pesticides worldwide (84). For example, between the 1950s and the 1970s, cotton growers in Central America had to increase the average number of insecticide applications per season fourfold, from 10 to 40. Even so, declining yields and falling profits forced many into bankruptcy. In northeastern Mexico alone, the resistance of tobacco budworms—a secondary pest that emerged from efforts to eradicate the boll weevil—devastated the cotton industry, reducing crop acreage from 300,000 hectares in the 1960s to less than 500 hectares in 1970 and forcing an exodus of cotton workers (85) (86).

In Egypt, to cite another example, the use of DDT to control the American bollworm caused a species of white fly, which had been a secondary pest, to explode in the late 1970s, supplanting the bollworm as that country's worst cotton pest. Studies subsequently showed that DDT treatment actually stimulated white flies to produce a higher number of eggs than unsprayed flies (87).

ENVIRONMENTAL COSTS OF PESTICIDE USE

Pesticides are a nearly ubiquitous pollutant. By design, they are biocides, compounds intended to be lethal to their targets. Unfortunately, only a handful restrict their toxic effects to the target pest. Most make their presence felt across a broad spectrum, doing widespread incidental damage to diverse wildlife, plant life, and soil and water organisms (88) (89) (90).

Table 6.3 Major Pesticides

Insecticides		
Type	Examples	Persistence
Chlorinated hydrocarbons	DDT, aldrin, dieldrin, endrin, heptachlor, toxaphene, lindane, chlordane, kepone, mirex	High (2–15 years)
Organophosphates	Malathion, parathion, monocrotophos, methamidophos, methyl parathion, DDVP	Low to moderate (normally 1–12 weeks, but some can last several years)
Carbamates	Carbaryl, maneb, priopoxor, mexicabate, aldicarb, aminocarb	Usually low (days to weeks)
Pyrethroids	Pemethrin, decamethrin	Usually low (days to weeks)

Herbicides		
Type	Examples	Effects
Contact	Triazines such as atrazine and paraquat	Kills foliage by interfering with photosynthesis
Systemic	Phenoxy compounds such as 2,4-D, 2,4,5-T, and silvex; substitutes ureas such as diuron, norea, fenuron, and other nitrogen-containing compounds such as daminozide (Alar), glyphsate	Absorption creates excess growth hormones; plants die because they cannot obtain enough nutrients to sustain their greatly accelerated growth
Soil Sterilants	Trifluralin, diphenamid, dalapon, butylate	Kills soil microorganisms essential to plant growth; most also act as systemic herbicides

Source: G. Tyler Miller Jr., *Living in the Environment* (Wadsworth, Belmont, California, 1990), p. 551.

The heart of the problem is that an extremely small percentage of the pesticide applied on a given field—less than 0.1 percent for many insecticides—actually reaches the target organism; the rest, by definition, becomes an environmental contaminant (91).

Even carefully applied pesticides can dissipate in the air as vapor, in water runoff, or in the soil by leaching to the groundwater below. Pesticide contamination of groundwater sources has become increasingly common in recent years, endangering local water supplies and polluting aquatic systems in many nations. The herbicide atrazine, one of the most commonly used pesticides, is now also one of the most common water contaminants (92). (See Table 6.3.)

Pesticide contaminants affect wildlife both directly and indirectly. The poisoning of bees and other pollinators; of birds feeding on contaminated seed; and of raptors and mammals feeding on contaminated rodents has been copiously documented over the years. Wholesale elimination of helpful soil-dwelling insects and microorganisms that build soil and plant nutrition sometimes occurs, essentially sterilizing the soil (93) (94) (95).

Many modern pesticides are particularly toxic to water-dwelling insects, plankton, crustaceans, and fish. Low levels of atrazine in streams, ponds, and estuaries can harm whole ecosystems, inhibiting algae and plankton growth and affecting the diet and reproduction of fish and other organisms (96) (97).

A less obvious but potentially devastating effect involves the ability of pesticides to interfere with the endocrine and immune systems of animals, including humans. The endocrine system regulates the production and function of hormones that control everything from reproduction to the development of young (98) (99). The amount of pesticide needed to trigger damage can be small, leading scientists to fear that present contamination levels pose an imminent risk of population-wide effects on some wildlife species (100).

Toxic effects may be exacerbated by persistence of a pesticide. Compounds such as DDT and dieldrin can linger in the environment for decades, and, even where DDT has been banned for years, residues have yet to disappear. Many developing countries still make liberal use of this and other tenacious chemicals. While newer classes of pesticides such as organophosphates and carbamates generally break down faster than DDT and its relatives, they tend to be more acutely toxic to nontarget organisms (101) (102) (103).

Some pesticides accumulate in the tissue of exposed organisms, extending their destructive potential far beyond the farm. Those animals highest on the food chain, including humans, are often at the greatest risk. This became evident in the 1960s and 1970s when populations of predatory birds, such as eagles and peregrine falcons, declined because of the widespread use of organochlorines (104) (105).

HUMAN HEALTH: THE GROWING COSTS

The threat pesticides pose to human health is particularly potent in the developing world, where most serious exposure occurs. Indeed, pesticide poisoning is disconcertingly common in developing nations, representing a major occupational hazard for farmers and their families (106) (107) (108). According to one study of Malaysia, in the 1980s more than 7 percent of all users suffered some form of pesticide poisoning, and nearly 15 percent reported they had experienced such poisoning at least once in their lives (109).

The problem is not unique to Malaysia. According to the latest (1990) estimate published by WHO, occupational pesticide poisoning may affect as many as 25 million—or 3 percent—of the agricultural workforce each year in the South (110). In Africa alone, where some 80 percent of the populace is involved in agriculture, as many as 11 million cases of acute pesticide exposures occur each year, according to a recent study by the Helsinki Institute of Occupational Health (111). Most of these victims do not seek medical treatment, so their cases are not reflected in official reports (112). (See Table 6.4.)

Plantation workers and farmers growing cash crops are most likely to suffer from pesticide exposure. For example, extremely high exposure has been documented among Central American cotton and banana plantation workers (113) (114). In one particularly tragic incident in Costa Rica, some 1,500 males working on banana plantations became sterile in the 1970s after repeated contact with the pesticide dibromochloropropane, a potent nematode killer (115).

The high incidence of pesticide-related health problems in many developing countries stems largely from improper handling, application, and storage practices. Three quarters of all pesticides are applied by hand or tractor, with the operator close by. Though many pesticides are readily absorbed through the skin or lungs, the use of protective equipment is rare, especially in the hot and humid conditions of the tropics (116) (117) (118).

Formal training is uncommon, labels may not contain appropriate instructions, or they may not be printed in the local language. In the case of illiterate farmers, of course, printed warnings go unread (119) (120) (121). In a recent survey of Malaysian farm workers responsible for spraying pesticides, 93 percent did not know how to differentiate the color bands on labels indicating toxicity levels (122).

With little access to running water, many pesticide workers are unable to clean up. Pesticide-coated clothes enter the home and spread contamination to other family members. To make matters worse, homemakers frequently recycle pesticide containers to store drinking water and food (123) (124) (125).

Children are particularly susceptible to pesticides, some of which are believed to impair brain functions much in the manner of lead (126). Where pesticide use has been heavy, contamination, especially from organochlorines such as DDT, is found in breast milk at alarmingly high levels (127). And it is common in developing countries for children to work or play in fields treated with pesticides (128).

While attention is largely focused on the high incidence of acute exposure, there is substantial evidence that pesticides can cause chronic health conditions such as cancer and other systemic dysfunctions (129). Many pesticides may suppress the human immune system, making exposed persons—particularly undernourished children and seniors—vulnerable to infectious agents (130). In addition, some compounds, even at low doses, disrupt human endocrine functions (131).

These effects are not confined to farm workers. Residues in food and water extend the sphere of pesticides' possible influence to a much larger population. A number of studies throughout the developing world have reported dangerously steep levels of contamination on locally grown produce and in fish (132).

Another severe hazard involves large stocks of pesticides such as DDT and dieldrin that have accumulated over the years in many developing countries. The FAO has identified more than 7 million kilograms of outdated and unusable pesticides in 35 countries that require safe disposal (133). Often containers are leaking, corroded, or unlabeled. Cleanup is sure to be expensive, and most countries are ill-equipped to foot the

Table 6.4 Estimated Annual Impact of Pesticides in Developing Countries

Population Groups at Risk	Character of Exposure	Estimated Overall Annual Impact
Pesticide formulators, mixers, applicators, pickers, and suicides and mass poisoning	Single and short-term, very high level exposure	3,000,000 exposed, 220,000 deaths
Pesticide manufacturers, formulators, mixers, applicators, and pickers	Long-term, high-level exposure	735,000 suffer from specific chronic effects of long-term exposure
All population groups	Long-term, low-level exposure	37,000 suffer from chronic effects of long-term exposure (cancer)

Source: World Health Organization (WHO), *Our Planet, Our Health* (WHO, Geneva, 1992), p. 81.

bill. Cleanup costs in Africa alone are estimated at $100 million (134).

PESTICIDE ALTERNATIVES

Alternatives to exclusive reliance on chemical pesticides do exist, some of which are currently being applied in the developing world as well as the industrialized world. The most common alternative approach is known as integrated pest management (IPM), in which both crop and pest are seen as part of a dynamic agroecosystem. IPM attempts to capitalize on natural biological factors that limit pest outbreaks, only using chemicals as a last resort (135) (136) (137).

Central to IPM is the idea that effective crop protection does not require the ecological disruption of completely wiping out pests. The goal is to reduce crop damage to a level where it is economically tolerable, using control measures whose cost, both economic and ecological, is not excessive (138) (139).

A number of nonchemical cultural practices form the core of IPM. These include crop rotation, planting more than one crop, early or delayed planting to protect a crop during the most vulnerable stages of growth, manipulation of water and fertilizer, field sanitation (such as plowing under harvest stubble to remove pest hideaways), and the use of "trap crops" to lure pests away from the main crop. One classic example of IPM comes from the Nicaraguan cotton fields. Several rows of cotton are planted a few months ahead of the regular crop to attract boll weevils, which can be destroyed by hand or with pesticides without affecting the main field (140) (141).

Biological control, one of the most powerful IPM methods, employs natural predators, parasites, and diseases to keep pest populations below harmful levels. For example, India, China, and a number of other countries raise the parasitic wasp *Trichogramma* in commercial facilities and release it to control corn, cotton, rice, and sugar cane pests (142) (143) (144).

A crucial step in IPM is to determine economic damage thresholds. These help farmers decide when to take action if preventive measures are insufficient. The farmer develops a monitoring system to count pests, track their life cycle, and ascertain whether it is time for remedial intervention (145). When pest numbers surge beyond the economic damage threshold and re-

Box 6.1   Pest Control Without Pesticides: Indonesia's IPM Success

Among the most successful integrated pest management (IPM) programs in the world is that under way to protect Indonesia's rice harvest, the nation's most important crop. Established in 1986 after conventional pesticides failed to control rice pests, the program has yielded substantial economic, environmental, and health benefits, eliciting broad support from farmers and policymakers. It is regarded as proof that reorienting a nation's agriculture away from heavy pesticide use is both possible and prudent and does not mean compromising the gains of the Green Revolution.

Indonesia began applying pesticides to its rice paddies only in the late 1960s, when it set the goal of meeting its own rice needs domestically. Over the next 15 years, Indonesia used the Green Revolution package of inputs—new rice varieties, irrigation systems, fertilizers, and pesticides—to transform itself from the world's largest rice importer to being self-sufficient in rice in 1984. That year, Indonesia accounted for 20 percent of the global use of rice pesticides. The government promoted heavy use by subsidizing 85 percent of the cost of pesticides, believing that pesticides were necessary to maintain high yields (1) (2).

Just the opposite proved true: pesticides made rice production unstable. From the beginning, chemicals caused the classic problems of pest resistance and resurgence, with consequent crop losses. The most serious pest was the brown plant hopper, which sucks juices from the rice stem and weakens the plant. Before pesticides, the plant hopper was not a problem; by 1977, losses from this insect had reduced the rice harvest by over 1 million tons—enough to feed 2.5 million people (3) (4) (5).

Widespread planting of plant hopper–resistant rice varieties temporarily halted damage in the early 1980s. By 1985, however, plant hoppers were feeding voraciously on the new varieties. In 1986, the population exploded to the catastrophic levels of 1977, threatening over 50 percent of the rice harvest in Java, the nation's most important rice-growing region. Indonesia's rice self-sufficiency, so recently attained, seemed doomed (6) (7).

Studies of the plant hopper's life cycle indicated that further pesticide use would only make matters worse. In fields sprayed with pesticide, roughly eight times as many plant hopper eggs survived as in unsprayed fields, whereas in the latter, natural predators such as spiders and wasps kept the pest under complete biological control (8) (9) (10).

Armed with this knowledge, as well as results from pilot studies of IPM techniques in fields, cabinet ministers convinced Indonesian president Suharto to take decisive action. In November 1986, the president issued a decree banning 57 of the 66 pesticides used on rice, phasing out pesticide subsidies over a two-year period, and diverting some of this money to fund Indonesia's IPM program, including a major farmer education program (11) (12).

Results since 1986 have exceeded all expectations. Indonesia's rice harvest climbed 15 percent, while national pesticide use declined 60 percent, and more than 250,000 farmers have been trained in IPM techniques, most since 1989 (13) (14) (15). The economic benefits have been profound as well. Indonesia's treasury has saved $120 million per year by terminating pesticide subsidies, and individual farmers have saved out-of-pocket costs for pesticides and spray equipment (16). By 1990, the economic impact of IPM was already calculated at well over $1 billion, and total savings have continued to accrue yearly since then (17).

As for the environment, the use of thousands of tons of toxic contaminants have been eliminated, with health benefits to farmers, villagers, rice consumers, and wildlife. Rice paddy fish, a traditional food source eliminated by pesticides, have returned to many fields (18).

The resounding success of Indonesia's IPM program can be attributed to training. "Farmer field schools," created with the guidance of the U.N. Food and Agriculture Organization (FAO), help farmers control their operations by teaching them about the rice agroecosystem. This helps them make more informed crop decisions

---

medial measures are deemed necessary, IPM tries to minimize their environmental impact. If pesticides are used, dosages and application times are carefully adjusted to avoid killing pest predators (146).

Often, "microbial pesticides," that is, suspensions of bacteria, viruses, or fungi, are better able to target a given insect than synthetic pesticides. *Bacillus thuringiensis* (BT) is the best known natural pesticide and has been used in many nations to control mosquito larvae (147).

IPM IN THE DEVELOPING WORLD

Using IPM concepts, developing countries have chalked up some successes that prove the yield gains of the Green Revolution do not have to come from pesticides alone. The power of national IPM programs to preserve agricultural gains while protecting public health and decreasing costs is perhaps most notable in Indonesia and Cuba. (See Box 6.1.)

In both countries, nationwide IPM programs have received substantial and continued support from the national government. Cuba's program is notable for its extensive effort to develop and field-test biological controls, which have been applied on a variety of crops from sugar cane to citrus fruits and vegetables. These technical accomplishments are accompanied by government curbs on pesticide use and a system of worker safety and medical monitoring for pesticide applications. In part because of this program, Cuba cut its pesticide imports during the 1980s by 70 percent (148) (149).

Despite such inspiring examples, the prognosis for IPM in the developing world is still uncertain. Asia, which shares many of the problems in rice culture that drove Indonesia to adopt its innovative program, holds promise for widescale adoption of IPM techniques (150) (151) (152) (153) (154). Currently, the FAO is sponsoring IPM programs for rice in eight Asian countries in addition to Indonesia: China, Bangladesh, India, Thailand, Vietnam, the Philippines, Sri Lanka, and Malaysia. IPM projects targeting vegetables have started in six Asian countries. Together, these programs have trained hundreds of thousands of farmers in IPM methods and saved millions of dollars in pesticides, not to mention the associated health and environmental benefits (155) (156) (157) (158).

These trends have been encouraged by the activism of grassroots consumer groups, farmers, and nongovernmental organizations dedicated to stopping the health abuses caused by indiscriminate pesticide use. Recently, groups from many countries started coordinating regionally. The Pesticide Action Network, a coalition of over 300 organizations in 50 countries with regional centers on every continent, is one example of regional coordination (159) (160).

Box 6.1

and frees them from dependence on the agricultural extension agent (19) (20).

Farmers convene at the school once a week for an entire crop cycle, 10 to 12 weeks, to identify pests and predators and study plant health, water management, and the effects of weather on pest cycles. Using this knowledge and their experience, each group manages a test plot to apply and evaluate IPM methods (21).

Farmers have responded with enthusiasm to the field schools. Indeed, IPM has become something of a social movement among rice farmers, with its techniques spreading from person to person in a manner unprecedented in other extension programs. Many village leaders and local officials have publicly endorsed the program, and some have used local money to help pay for IPM training so that implementation would proceed faster (22).

Can the IPM program continue to live up to its billing? So far, indications are that it can. The brown planthopper declined sharply after the program began and has not been a pest since. And in 1990, IPM headed off an even greater challenge. An outbreak of white rice stemborer, a traditional, sporadic pest, alarmed farmers in west Java. Despite desperate calls to relax the pesticide ban, local and national government officials continued to support IPM, funding instead a massive effort to teach 75,000 affected farmers how to recognize and destroy stemborer eggs. Later, over 300,000 people mobilized to

search the paddies for egg masses, a campaign so effective that only a handful of paddies were infested in 1991 (23) (24).

IPM proponents believe Indonesia's success can be duplicated in other rice-producing nations of the region. The planthopper has made inroads in many neighboring nations. In 1989–90, Thailand suffered the largest planthopper outbreak in its history, and infestations plagued Vietnam in 1990–91. Significantly, a pilot program in Bangladesh has shown positive results: farmers who received IPM training spent 75 percent less on pesticides than their untrained counterparts while producing 13.5 percent more rice (25) (26).

References and Notes

1. Peter Kenmore, "Getting Policies Right, Keeping Policies Right: Indonesia's Integrated Pest Management Policy, Production and Environment," paper presented at the Asia Region and Private Enterprise Environment and Agriculture Officers' Conference, Sri Lanka, September 1991.
2. L. Ross Brownhall, Kees G. Ercleens, Ward Heneveld, *et al.*, *Mid-Term Review of FAO Intercountry Program for the Development and Application of Integrated Pest Control in Rice in South and Southeast Asia: Phase II, Mission Report, November 1990* (Food and Agriculture Organization of the United Nations, Rome, 1990), pp. 19–20, 58.
3. *Op. cit.* 1.
4. *Op. cit.* 2.
5. Michael Hansen, *Escape from the Pesticide Treadmill: Alternative to Pesticides in Developing Countries* (Institute for Consumer Policy Research, Mount Vernon, New York, 1987), p. 134.
6. *Op. cit.* 1.
7. *Op. cit.* 2, p. 25.
8. *Op. cit.* 1.
9. Richard Stone, "Researchers Score Victory over Pesticides—and Pests—in Asia," *Science*, Vol. 256, No. 5057 (1992), p. 1272.
10. *Op. cit.* 5, p. 139.
11. *Op. cit.* 1.
12. *Op. cit.* 9.
13. Peter Kenmore, Entomologist and Consultant to the Indonesian Integrated Pest Management Programme, Food and Agriculture Organization of the United Nations, Manila, Philippines, 1993 (personal communication).
14. *Ibid.*
15. *Op. cit.* 9.
16. The Indonesian Integrated Pest Management (IPM) Programme, *Farmers as Experts* (The Indonesian IPM Programme, Jakarta, 1990), p. 4.
17. *Op. cit.* 1.
18. James Tarrant, "An Environmental Study of the Proposed Indonesian National IPM Programme Support Project," a report to the FAO Cooperative Program in support of a proposed World Bank loan project, Washington, D.C., 1992, pp.44–45.
19. *Op. cit.* 9.
20. *Op. cit.* 18, p. 45.
21. *Op. cit.* 16, pp. 7–8.
22. *Op. cit.* 1.
23. *Op. cit.* 1.
24. *Op. cit.* 9, p. 1273.
25. *Op. cit.* 1.
26. *Op. cit.* 9, p. 1273.

Such groups are beginning to exert some influence on national pesticide policies. In 1991, the Dominican Republic responded to nine years of antipesticide campaigning by banning 20 hazardous pesticides, while in 1992, the Philippines took action to ban four of the country's most widely used toxic chemicals. In both cases, the action affects a substantial share of the national pesticide market (161) (162).

Still, IPM is more the exception than the rule in most developing nations, its full incorporation into national agricultural policies faces barriers. Even though it has been widespread for only a few decades, pesticide use is the accepted agricultural mode. Corporate pesticide interests, moreover, wield enormous financial power; having battled to maintain their market dominance, they will not give up easily (163) (164) (165).

ENCOURAGING THE SWITCH

For most developing nations, stepping off the pesticide treadmill requires government commitment at several different levels, from farmer outreach at the bottom to national pesticide policy at the top.

Experience in Indonesia and elsewhere demonstrates that a key ingredient of successful IPM programs is outreach and training. Programs must not only school farmers in the particulars of IPM techniques but also al-

low them to verify for themselves the economic and health advantages these techniques confer. IPM skills such as pest scouting and determining damage thresholds are not difficult to learn, and, once absorbed, they can easily be spread abroad through local networks (166).

Such outreach must be supported by an infrastructure of research and technical services. Ideally, the infrastructure would develop pest controls that respond to local needs and would help farmers analyze and adapt to changing conditions. And, because the benefits of IPM are magnified if many producers in a given area embrace its techniques, authorities ought to encourage a coordinated, regionwide approach (167) (168).

At the highest level, national pesticide policies must discourage bias toward pesticides and encourage alternatives. This means eliminating pesticide subsidies, formulating and enforcing regulations on pesticide packaging, labeling, and advertising, banning or restricting particularly hazardous chemicals, and establishing political and economic support for IPM development (169) (170) (171).

Weaning governments from excessive reliance on pesticides is only one aspect of a more general reorientation of agriculture worldwide toward more sustainable practices. To be most effective, pesticide reforms should go hand in hand with tillage and cropping practices that better utilize water and nutrients, minimize soil erosion and water pollution, and strenthen agro-ecosystems against disruption by pests (172).

FOCUS ON BIOTECHNOLOGY

The tools of modern biotechnology, which include genetic engineering, cell and plant tissue culture, and enhanced fermentation for mass-producing microorganisms, offer hope of further expanding the global food supply while lightening the environmental burden of modern agricultural practices. In the near term, biotechnology may enhance yields, bolster the pest and disease resistance of some critical crops, improve the nutritional value of some foods, and make others easier to process or less prone to loss during harvesting or shipping. (See Box 6.2.) In the longer term, biotechnology could improve the tolerance of staple crops to environmental stresses such as drought and enable some plants to fix nitrogen in the manner of legumes. (See Table 6.5.) In effect, if carefully applied, biotechnology could ease some of the biological and environmental factors that now limit production, while reducing the need for inputs such as pesticides that carry a high price for both the farmer and the environment.

Yet biotechnology is certainly no panacea. It will not displace traditional breeding programs or pest management and cultivation practices that strive to minimize ecological damage and soil loss. Nor will it end world hunger. Biotechnology's contribution to agricultural productivity, moreover, will take decades to realize. After more than 20 years of costly research, the first products from the agricultural biotechnology pipeline have just begun to appear in global markets. By most accounts, biotechnological advances will not begin to make a noticeable difference in world agriculture until the turn of the century. In contrast to the rapid production increases associated with the Green Revolution, biotechnology's "gene revolution" promises to proceed slowly, though ultimately to have a much larger impact.

The advent of biotechnology is not without risk or controversy. Fears that the release of genetically altered plants or microorganisms could upset natural ecosystems have prompted a cautious regulatory approach in several countries, and many biotechnology companies still question whether consumers will accept food from genetically engineered crops.

In addition, some observers feel biotechnology's potential to improve world agriculture has been exaggerated. As with the Green Revolution, hidden costs to both the environment and to farm culture and economy will ultimately appear, they argue. Others believe that commercial interests could drive exploitation of biotechnology to favor the most lucrative applications rather than those addressing the most pressing needs.

For the developing world, realizing the promise of agricultural biotechnology is a particular challenge. Underdeveloped nations are most in need of the agricultural gains that biotechnology promises, yet these are the nations least able to profit from current work overwhelmingly directed toward high-value crops grown in industrialized countries. Moreover, genetic manipulations could actually do short-term harm to some developing economies by cutting into key export crops. This is the case with recent alterations of certain oil seed crops and plants such as cocoa.

While efforts are under way to bridge the biotechnology gap between rich and poor nations through technology sharing, the real work of building an indigenous biotechnology capacity focused on agricultural problems in the developing world has just begun. Issues that will need to be addressed include technical assistance, product licensing, and cooperative arrangements between the public and private sectors, as well as the much thornier issues of protecting intellectual property through patents and compensating developing nations for the use of their genetic resources.

THE BIOTECH TOOLBOX

Several key technologies define biotechnology and give it broad potential for agriculture. The most important and controversial of these is genetic engineering, by which useful DNA material is identified in one organism and transferred into the genetic makeup of another unrelated one.

Recombinant DNA techniques allow researchers, using special enzymes, to splice in selected genes that control important traits such as insect resistance or the timing of fruit ripening. Implanted genes can come from other species, and they can cross from the animal to the plant kingdom and vice versa. In many instances, genes contain fragments from several different donors (173) (174).

Before insertion, genes may be tailored to modify and enhance their expression in the host plant. Or they may be tagged with DNA segments, enabling identification in the new plant and in subsequent plant crosses and genetic manipulations. Advances in the science of reading and marking genes have led to rapid progress in constructing "gene maps" of important crop species. Both genetic engineers and conventional plant breeders have begun to use maps to locate desirable genes and to choose plants to cross (175) (176) (177) (178).

Over the last five years, tremendous progress has been made in the technology of inserting genetic material into a target plant so that it is stable and functions normally, most notably with broad-leafed plants such as tomatoes, potatoes, soybeans, cotton, and canola (rapeseed). These are easier than cereal crops to alter genetically, although recent advances have been made with grains as well. One technique is the "gene gun" that projects DNA-coated particles into a plant cell without destroying its structure (179) (180) (181).

Cell and tissue culture, which enables a complete plant to regenerate from a single cell, a mass of unorganized cells called a callus, or even a piece of root or shoot, is a second critical area of progress in biotechnology. A plant cell or tissue is exposed to a succession of nutrients and hormones in a laboratory culture, stimulating plant development in vitro. The breadth of culture applications makes this a central aspect of biotechnology, one that has already brought advances to both developing and industrialized nations (182) (183).

Table 6.5 Prospective Biotechnology Food Products

Genetic Modification	Crop Type	Benefit
Controlled ripening	Tomato, pea, pepper, tropical fruits	Will permit the shipping of vine ripened tomatoes; improved quality and shelf life; improved food processing quality
High solids content	Tomato, potato	Improved food processing quality
Insect resistance	Cotton, corn, potatoes, tomatoes	Will reduce amount of insecticides needed for pest management
Fungal resistance	Pepper, tomato	Will reduce the amount of fungicides needed for pest management
Viral resistance	Potatoes, tomatoes, cantaloupe, squash, cucumbers, alfalfa, corn, oilseed rape (canola), soybeans, grapes	Many plant viruses are transmitted by insects; by increasing viral resistance, the need for insecticide can be reduced
Herbicide tolerance	Corn, cotton, soybeans, tomatoes, oilseed rape (canola)	Will shift the use of herbicides to lower amounts of environmentally "soft" herbicides for weed control; reduced groundwater contamination
Improved nutrition	Corn, sunflowers, soybeans	Storage proteins from other plant varieties will increase the amount of essential amino acids in the host crop
Improved nutrition	Oilseed rape (canola)	Oil producing pathway altered to increase the amount of unsaturated oils in the plant (i.e. healthier oils)
Freezing tolerance	Tomato, fruits, vegetables	Improved textural properties
Heat stability	Oilseed rape (canola), peanut	Improved processing quality; permits new food uses of healthier oils
Low caffeine content	Coffee	Naturally decaffeinated coffee
Controlled starch build-up	Corn, peas	Will retain sweetness during entire shelf-life
Various	Vegetables	Enhanced properties believed to reduce the risks of human disease

Source: Biotechnology Industry Organization (BIO), *Developments in Agricultural Biotechnology: An Industrial Perspective* (BIO, Washington, D.C., November 1992), p. 3.

The most common commercial use of tissue culture is clonal propagation, the mass production of genetic duplicates or clones of desirable plant varieties that can then be planted in the field like conventional seedlings. Clonal propagation has proven particularly valuable for plants normally produced from tubers or cuttings, or that are difficult or time-consuming to culture from seed. Potatoes, bananas, orchids, and oil palms are all regularly cloned (184) (185).

Regeneration from tissue culture can be used to produce disease-free plants, eliminating both viruses and microorganisms from the original plant material. This technology, essential to breeding programs, restores diseased plant lines and facilitates the international transfer of pathogen-free germ plasm. More important, it enhances crop yields. Virus-free seed varieties are already crucial to commercial potato culture, and, according to one estimate, virus-free cassava, sweet potatoes, and yams—Southern subsistence crops that suffer extensive virus-related losses—could double in production in some areas (186) (187) (188).

Beyond clonal propagation, tissue culture is an essential element of genetic engineering work, because it allows a cell whose genetic material has been altered to regenerate into a viable plant. This step, often more difficult than the genetic transfer itself, stands as a substantial barrier to the development of transgenic crops, especially cereal grains such as corn and wheat (189) (190).

Tissue culture techniques have the potential to bring about a radical departure from traditional agriculture. Some current work seeks to induce cells to produce only the desired food product instead of developing into a full-grown plant—for example, the strawberry fruit without the stem, leaves, or roots. Such "laboratory farming" could be one means of overcoming drought, insect damage, and other variables that plague traditional farms (191).

This strategy has already been commercially applied to some high-value plants grown only for the chemicals they produce, such as food flavorings and certain drugs. One California company can now produce extract from large-scale vanilla-orchid cell cultures at one fifth the cost of natural vanilla. Several firms are exploring the use of tissue culture to produce the cancer drug taxol, which comes from the bark of a rare yew tree (192) (193) (194).

Some researchers have suggested that with the appropriate digestive enzymes, which are now under development, cellulose from vast crops of drought-resistant woody perennials could be converted directly to sugar syrups, which would in turn become the basis for foods made by laboratory tissue culture (195).

Advocates say such modifications of the natural food chain could result in better use of marginal lands and minimize the effect of ecological disturbances associated with annual crop agriculture (196). Others believe these radical alternatives ignore the nutritional and cultural dimensions of agriculture and offer far less benefit than reorientation of current farming practices toward sustainable methods (197).

The use of monoclonal antibodies is a third significant area of agricultural biotechnology. In 1975, scientists learned how to clone individual antibodies—proteins produced by the animal and plant immune system in response to invasion by foreign substances (antigens)—in quantity. The ability to mass-produce pure clones of virtually any antibody has given rise to a burgeoning agricultural diagnostics industry (198) (199). Tests using specific antibodies can now help detect and differentiate among a host of plant and animal pathogens, viral, bacterial, and fungal. Many test kits could be made simple enough for use in the field. For example, the farmer might simply crush plant tissue or take a blood sample from a stock animal, apply a reagent, and look for a color change to discover whether a given disease agent is present. Quick and accurate diagnosis could speed treatment and reduce losses. Currently, however, the expense and dearth of test kits limit their use in the developing world (200).

Monoclonal antibodies also play an important role in the development of new animal vaccines by helping

Box 6.2   The Potential of Transgenic Crops

No other aspect of modern biotechnology holds more promise than the application of recombinant DNA techniques to modify crops. In the United States alone, the private sector has invested more than $1 billion in the development of so-called transgenic varieties that could well undergird agricultural commerce in the future (1). Today, nearly 50 species of crop plants can be genetically transformed, many of which should see commercial release within this decade (2) (3).

Insect and Disease Resistance

Insects and plant pathogens constitute one of the greatest sources of crop loss. Implanting genes that make crops resistant to disease, pests, and environmental stress has been a cornerstone of transgenic crop development, and researchers have achieved some impressive results (4).

Initial work focused on implanting genes from *Bacillus thuringiensis* (BT), a common bacterium that produces a toxin active against certain damaging caterpillars. BT, used as a "biopesticide" on crops for over 30 years, has proven nontoxic to mammals, birds, and most nontarget insects. Implanting other toxin-producing genes—some of them from venomous arachnids—may also prove fruitful (5) (6) (7) (8) (9). Several crops—most notably cotton, corn, and potatoes—have already been engineered to produce the BT toxin in their tissues and will be released in the United States once they win government approval, possibly by 1995 (10) (11) (12) (13).

Though the genetic protection currently being engineered into crops is only active against a narrow range of pests, some researchers claim it will still substantially reduce the use of insecticides, as just a few pest species are usually responsible for most damage on any given crop. Some in industry believe that in the next 10 to 20 years, genetically programmed resistance will account for a large percentage of insect control for annual crops (14).

The movement to create crops with BT-based resistance calls for industry acceptance of some aspects of integrated pest management to keep insects from becoming immune to the BT toxin. Already, several cases of insect populations grown tolerant of the most common BT toxins have been reported (15) (16).

To counter the tendency toward resistance, researchers have begun to advise farmers not to plant uniform stands of BT-containing crops. One recommended alternative is to grow unprotected crops among the gene-altered varieties, creating small "refuges" of plants to sustain a population of insects susceptible to the BT toxin (17) (18).

Work on genetically engineered resistance to viruses and disease agents is also proceeding apace. Scientists have discovered that implanting crops with genes responsible for making the protein coat of a virus often confers resistance to that virus. Potatoes, tomatoes, melons, tobacco, squash, alfalfa, soybeans, corn, and rice have all been modified with this strategy. Efforts to impart resistance to fungal and bacterial diseases, using genes from an assortment of bacteria and plants, have also met with some success (19) (20) (21).

Modified Fruit Ripening

To prevent bruising, tomatoes and many other soft fruits are harvested prematurely and ripened artificially after shipping, a practice that kills flavor. Despite this, up to 30 percent of the world's fresh tomato crop is lost to rotting and damage from handling (22).

Geneticists have isolated several genes that control aspects of the ripening process and inserted them into tomato plants. The first transgenic "whole-food product," scheduled to receive U.S. government approval in fall 1993, is Calgene's "Flavr-Savr" tomato. Modified to block synthesis of an enzyme responsible for softening, the fruit can remain on the vine longer and develop a more succulent flavor before being shipped to stores (23) (24) (25).

About 40 other fruits and vegetables, including berries, peaches, pears, apples, melons, mangoes, and papayas, undergo a ripening process not unlike that of tomatoes and should be responsive to similar transformation (26).

Additional work has concentrated on altering the sugar or starch content of crops such as potatoes, corn, peas, and tomatoes to sweeten them or improve processing. For example, researchers have raised the starch content in some potatoes by as much as 40 percent, which makes them easier to process into potato chips. Controlled conversion of sugar to starch in corn and peas helps them retain their sweetness longer after picking (27) (28).

Stress Tolerance

To date, the efforts of genetic engineers to increase plant tolerance to phenomena such as drought, heat, cold, and high aluminum or salt content in soil have not been productive (29) (30) (31).

Nonetheless, gene maps and markers are helping untangle the complex mechanisms of tolerance. Genes that control responses to major plant stresses have been identified in various crops such as rice and cotton, and their functions are being evaluated (32) (33) (34).

Stress-tolerant crops could be of particular benefit to the developing world, allowing better use of marginal lands where drought, heat, and poor soil constrain production. For example, developing rice more resistant to drought could enhance production where irrigation is not available (35) (36) (37).

Improved Nutritional Content

Genetic manipulation has the potential to alter the nutrient content of many foods. In hopes of correcting the vitamin A deficiency common among rice eaters in the developing world, researchers are attempting to induce production of vitamin A in rice kernels (38).

Corn and soybeans are the subject of work to enhance protein quality by inserting genes that elevate the level of methionine, an essential amino acid. Most current work on protein enhancement is directed toward improving the nutritional balance

identify the strain of a disease organism and by characterizing its surface proteins (201).

With fermentation and enzyme technology, another biotechnology whose application has rapidly expanded, microorganisms and their byproducts are produced for use on an industrial scale. The genetic material of microorganisms is often altered to supply specialized proteins in bulk. While so far this technique has been employed mostly to mass-produce high-value pharmaceuticals, it is useful in the manufacture of certain agricultural products. One is the animal growth hormone bovine somatotropin (BST, also called bovine growth hormone). Feeding BST to dairy herds is known to increase milk production from 5 to 20 percent, though it may also make the cow more susceptible to health problems such as mastitis, an inflammation of the udder. Another product of this technology is porcine somatotropin, which causes hogs to grow more quickly and produce leaner meat (202) (203) (204).

Various new reproductive techniques for livestock come under the rubric of biotechnology. Embryo transfer involves stimulation of the female to produce multiple eggs for artificial insemination. The embryos are subsequently transplanted to surrogate mothers. In a more recent refinement of this technique, the eggs are removed, fertilized in vitro, and subsequently cloned

Box 6.2

of commercial animal feed so that supplements could be eliminated (39) (40).

Modified Oil Crops

Several companies have active programs to modify the chemical content of certain oil crops. For example, the California company Calgene is developing a number of different rapeseed lines, each engineered to produce a specialty oil. These include oil with enhanced levels of laurate and myristate for use in soap and shampoo, oil that solidifies at room temperature without hydrogenation for healthier margarine, cooking oil with reduced saturated fat, cocoa butter substitute for making chocolate, and liquid wax for high-temperature lubricants and cosmetics. Because many of these oils are currently derived from tropical sources, success with these crops could gravely affect the export markets of the South (41) (42) (43) (44).

Biosynthesis of Plastics and Other Chemical Commodities

Researchers in the United States recently induced a small plant from the mustard family to produce a biodegradable plastic called polyhydroxybutyrate (PHB), similar to the petroleum-based plastic polypropylene. The plastic is scattered throughout the plant in discrete granules (45) (46).

Researchers expect to be able to splice the PHB-making gene, which was originally found in a species of soil bacteria, into plants such as potatoes, where the plastic could be stored in the tuber for convenient harvesting and processing. Preliminary studies indicate that biosynthesis of other polymers besides PHB can also be genetically induced (47) (48).

If plant-based production of biodegradable plastic becomes feasible and competitive in the marketplace, it could reduce the disposal nuisance associated with present plastics, and it might benefit many countries in the developing world without petrochemical refining facilities or the abundant oil reserves necessary for making petroleum-based plastics.

References and Notes

1. Joan Hamilton and James Ellis, "A Storm Is Breaking Down on the Farm," *Business Week* (December 14, 1992), p. 98.
2. Robert Fraley, "Sustaining the Food Supply," *Bio/Technology*, Vol. 10 (January 1992), p. 42.
3. *Op. cit.*
4. *Op. cit.* 2, pp. 40–41.
5. *Op. cit.* 2, p. 40.
6. Jerald Feitelson, Jewel Payne, and Leo Kim, "Bacillus Thuringiensis: Insects and Beyond," *Bio/Technology*, Vol. 10 (March 1992), pp. 271– 275.
7. William Stevens, "Tests Speed Effectiveness of Biological Pesticide," *New York Times* (July 5, 1991), p. 10, sec. A.
8. Maliyakal E. John and James McD. Stewart, "Genes for Jeans: Biotechnological Advances in Cotton," *Trends in Biotechnology*, Vol. 10 (May 1992), pp. 166–167.
9. Charles Gasser and Robert Fraley, "Transgenic Crops," *Scientific American* (June 1992), pp. 65–66.
10. Dan Layman, Administrator, Plant Biotechnology, Ciba- Geigy, Greensboro, North Carolina, 1992 (personal communication).
11. *Op. cit.* 2, p. 40.
12. Gordon Conway and Jules Pretty, *Unwelcome Harvest: Agriculture and Pollution* (Earthscan, London, 1991), p. 21, Table 2.2.
13. Robert Horsch, Biologist, Monsanto, St. Louis, Missouri, 1992 (personal communication).
14. *Op. cit.* 2, p. 40.
15. Shericca Williams, Leslie Friedrich, Sandra Dincher, *et al.*, "Chemical Regulation of Bacillus Thuringiensis Delta-Endotoxin Expression in Transgenic Plants," *Bio/Technology*, Vol. 10 (May 1992), pp. 540–541.
16. William Stevens, "Power of Natural Pest-Killer Wanes From Overuse," *New York Times* (December 29, 1992), p. 1, sec. C.
17. *Op. cit.* 15.
18. *Op. cit.* 16.
19. *Op. cit.* 2, p. 41.
20. Eduardo Bejarano and Conrad Lichtenstein, "Prospects for Engineering Virus Resistance in Plants with Antisense RNA," *Trends in Biotechnology*, Vol. 10 4 (November 1992), p. 383.
21. Industrial Biotechnology Association (IBA), *Developments in Agricultural Biotech-*

nology: An Industrial Perspective (IBA, Washington, D.C., 1992), p. 3.
22. Calgene, Prospectus for Calgene common stock (Calgene, Davis, California, January 1993), pp. 20–21.
23. *Ibid.*
24. *Op. cit.* 2, p. 41.
25. Simon Best, Managing Director of Zeneca A.Z.P., Zeneca Seeds, Wilmington, Delaware, 1992 (personal communication).
26. *Ibid.*
27. *Op. cit.* 2, p. 41.
28. *Op. cit.* 21.
29. Gary Toenniessen, Associate Director, Rockefeller Foundation, New York, 1993 (personal communication).
30. *Op. cit.* 8, pp. 167–168.
31. *Op. cit.* 2, p. 41.
32. *Op. cit.* 29.
33. Gary Toenniessen, "Rice Biotechnology: Progress and Prospects," paper presented at the Society of Chemical Industries Conference on Pest Management in Rice, London, June 1990.
34. *Op. cit.* 2, p. 41.
35. *Op. cit.* 29.
36. Teresa Albor, "Scientists Develop Rice for Low-Quality Farmland," *Christian Science Monitor* (November 28, 1992), p. 10.
37. John Komen, "WARDA: Rice Research in West Africa," *Biotechnology and Development Monitor*, Vol. 10 (March 1992), pp. 10–11.
38. *Op. cit.* 29.
39. Larry Beach, Molecular Biologist, Pioneer Hi-Bred International, Des Moines, Iowa, 1992 (personal communication).
40. *Op. cit.* 2.
41. *Op. cit.* 22, pp. 22–24.
42. Sally Lehrman, "Splicing Genes, Slicing Exports," *Washington Post* (September 27, 1992), p. 6, sec. H.
43. *Op. cit.* 2, pp. 41–42.
44. *Op. cit.* 2, pp. 40–41.
45. Jim Detjen, "Scientists' Genetically Engineered Weed Can Grow Plastic," *Journal of Commerce* (April 27, 1992), p. 10, sec. A.
46. Amal Kumar Naj, "Plant's Genes Are Engineered to Yield Plastic," *Wall Street Journal* (April 24, 1992), p. 1, sec. B.
47. *Op. cit.* 45.
48. *Op. cit.* 46.

to increase the number of offspring (205). Both techniques enable breeders to boost the reproduction rate of desirable cattle, speeding introduction of genetically outstanding stocks into a herd. In international trade of breeding stock, embryo transfer ensures disease-free exchanges and improves the survival rate of transported animals, which receive immunities to local pathogens in their indigenous mother's first milk (206) (207).

BIOTECH BARRIERS: BIOSAFETY AND REGULATION

While the potential benefits of biotechnology are great, most policymakers acknowledge the need for some

type of oversight to shield natural ecosystems and human consumers from any risks in genetic manipulation. Biosafety—minimizing risk when a genetically altered organism is commercialized—has been the subject of lengthy debate from which no uniform international guidelines have emerged. Though efforts are under way to help standardize international regulatory requirements, given the economic interests at stake and the lack of evidence about potential risks, it may be difficult to achieve agreement (208).

The worry is that genetic tinkering could give some plants, animals, or microorganisms a competitive edge, allowing them to outcompete unaltered organisms and thus potentially alter ecosystem dynamics (209) (210). History offers numerous examples of the unintended release of foreign insects or other pests into environments where they proliferated and wreaked havoc. In the 1860s, the European gypsy moth was accidentally released in the United States, where it now defoliates an extensive tract of hardwood forest each year (211).

Outcrossing, that is, when an altered organism reproduces with native species and spreads its new genes abroad, is another concern, especially with respect to microorganisms, crop plants, and insects that might breed with weed species (212) (213).

In light of such risks, many industrialized countries have regulated field tests and been cautious about permitting transgenic crops in the food supply. However, more than 1,000 field tests of engineered plants have been conducted under fairly stringent regulations in various countries with no record of untoward effects, and concern has ebbed in many quarters. In May 1993, the U.S. Department of Agriculture eased regulations governing tests for six crops that had been reviewed and field-tested earlier (214).

In another significant decision, the U.S. Food and Drug Administration ruled that genetically engineered food crops would not be given special regulation simply because of their laboratory origins. Instead, they would receive special testing for safety only if genetic changes introduced exotic substances into food or increased levels of toxins or potential allergens. In addition, there would be no special labeling of genetically altered foods unless the new food was noticeably different from consumer expectations (215) (216).

The ruling was widely viewed as a victory by the international biotechnology industry, which tends to regard government regulation as even more daunting than the technical challenge of genetically altering crops. Despite the U.S. action, there is no assurance that the European Community, also in the midst of formulating its biotech regulations, will be as liberal in its approach (217) (218).

Consumer acceptance is another formidable obstacle to the widespread adoption of genetically altered crops. Substantial opposition to some biotech products has already surfaced in a few nations. For example, the growth hormone BST has been blocked in the United States by the combined actions of consumer groups concerned about its safety—despite the assurances of scientists—and of dairy farmers worried about the effect of increased milk production on prices (219) (220).

BIOTECHNOLOGY AND THE DEVELOPING WORLD

Over the next 25 years, the World Bank estimates that food production in the developing world will have to double just to keep pace with population growth. While there is still room to elevate food production through traditional breeding programs and expanded use of fertilizers and irrigation, experts caution that these means alone cannot double the food supply (221).

Thus, if developing nations are to have enough food in the years to come, harnessing the potential of biotechnology is not just an option, it is a critical necessity. Conditioning crops to absorb environmental stresses such as drought could allow marginal lands to be pressed into service as well as reduce the wide fluctuations in food supply that plague developing nations (222) (223). Likewise, improving the pest and disease resistance of staple crops might gradually increase yields and help protect the health of wildlife and farmers by reducing pesticide use. Enhancing the nutritional value of staples would mean squeezing more from every bushel produced (224) (225).

However, significant barriers stand in the way of biotechnology's application in the developing world. Perhaps most daunting, control of the tools and products of biotechnology is currently concentrated in the industrialized world, especially the United States and Western Europe, home to the bulk of the research and investment in genetic engineering (226).

Unlike the Green Revolution's plant science, which was carried out primarily at public research institutions and made available to developing nations without charge, modern biotechnology is not available to those who cannot pay for it. Commercial interests dominated by a small list of large transnational chemical, seed, pesticide, and food-processing companies largely control biotechnology development, enforcing their command through patents and proprietary research (227). Until an indigenous biotechnology capacity emerges in the developing world, it will have to buy the benefits of biotechnology, and it will grow more and more dependent on the industrialized world for inputs (228).

Perhaps a more serious and basic problem is that the research priorities of biotechnology companies, set by the lucrative markets of the industrialized world, largely ignore the special needs of the South. For example, much initial work has been directed toward developing herbicide-resistant crops and improving the ripening qualities of tomatoes and other soft produce; these efforts have little immediate relevance to small farmers in poor countries (229) (230). Indeed, important subsistence crops such as rice, millet, and cassava have received scant attention from the private sector, and overall spending on biotechnology research for the South is at least an order of magnitude lower than for the North (231).

Even in those developing nations that have initiated programs in biotechnology, the emphasis is often on improving export crops at the expense of subsistence crops because exports underpin many national economies. For example, in India, where the private sector has recently begun to invest in biotechnology, most commercial tissue culture research targets exports such as spices, sugar cane, and tropical fruits (232) (233) (234).

This research orientation toward the industrialized world also stands to hurt many developing nations, at least in the short term, by displacing some of their traditional exports with biotechnology substitutes. For example, cell culture manufacture of vanilla flavoring at highly competitive prices could drastically reduce vanilla exports from countries such as Madagascar, one of the world's poorest nations and also one of the largest exporters of vanilla beans (235) (236) (237).

Much more damaging could be work on replacements for coconut and palm kernel oil, important exports for a variety of tropical nations such as Indonesia, the Philippines, Brazil, Nigeria, and Malaysia. The global market for coconut oil alone is nearly $2 billion per year (238). These oils are important ingredients in soaps, detergents, personal care products, marine oils, and lubricants. Genetic engineers at Calgene, Inc., a biotechnology firm in California, are developing new forms of rapeseed oil chemically similar to coconut and palm oil. They are also working on substitutes for cocoa butter, the second most important tropical commodity after coffee (239) (240).

PROTECTING INTELLECTUAL PROPERTY

One consequence of heavy commercial involvement in modern biotechnology has been an increasingly bitter struggle between the South and the North over patent protection of "intellectual property"—the skills, processes, and germ plasm that go into biotechnology products. In fact, this is one of the primary obstacles impeding the flow of biotechnology products to the developing world (241) (242) (243) (244) (245).

Biotechnology could develop into a phenomenally lucrative field: industry projections set global sales at $70 billion by 2000, mostly from bioengineered agricultural and pharmaceutical products. Banking on this promise, many biotechnology companies have invested heavily for over a decade, relying on the patent system to protect their investment (246) (247).

The biotechnology industry argues that patent protection spurs innovation and investment. Indeed, most of the progress in agricultural biotechnology has come since the 1980s when landmark rulings in the United States allowed the patenting of all life forms except humans. Without such protection, the industry believes, the private sector would pull out, investment capital would dry up, and technical progress would slow to a crawl (248) (249) (250) (251).

Most developing nations refuse to grant or respect patents on plants and animals. They see patent protection of the kind promoted by the United States as a form of monopoly control: it will increase the flow of money and resources—in the form of royalties and licensing agreements—from South to North, and restrict the development of an indigenous biotechnology sector in the South by discouraging the free exchange of germ plasm among plant breeders. Strict patent protection, it is argued, tends to preserve the position of current technology leaders, thus working against the interests of the South (252) (253) (254) (255).

Concern over intellectual property has already effectively restricted the availability of biotechnology products in some countries, because many companies flatly refuse to operate in arenas where they feel their products may be appropriated without licensing agreements. Pioneer Hi-Bred, the world's largest seed company, has declined to work in countries that cannot ensure protection of its germ plasm (256).

International debate has been fierce. The United States, which is leading the race to commercialize biotechnology products, views patent protection as crucial to its economic competitiveness. In the current round of trade talks on the General Agreement on Tariffs and Trade, it has actively pushed for such protection to be made internationally binding (257) (258) (259). At the same time, the United States has vigorously lobbied other countries to bring their patent systems in line with its own, using what many developing nations regard as strong-arm tactics. Brazil, India, Thailand, China, and others have been threatened with trade sanctions to produce patent compliance, and in a few cases sanctions have been applied. As a result, several developing nations recently enacted changes in their patent laws. Mexico's system, modified in 1991 to permit patenting of plant varieties and microorganisms, is frequently put forward by the United States as a model for the South (260) (261) (262) (263) (264).

The dispute over intellectual property has important implications for the conduct of biotechnology research at the International Agricultural Research Centers, a collection of specialized institutions whose mission is to improve agriculture in poor countries. The centers, which include the International Rice Research Institute and the International Institute of Tropical Agriculture, were the driving force behind the high-yield grain varieties introduced during the Green Revolution (265) (266). Commercial biotechnology's practice of routinely patenting every new advance may compromise the ability of these centers to conduct cutting-edge research by restricting access to the most advanced germ plasm and research techniques. Just as importantly, it raises the question of whether the centers will begin to patent their own innovations; traditionally, their work has been free to all. In a recent policy statement, the centers reaffirmed their commitment to the open-door policy, saying they will seek patents only for defensive reasons, that is, to ensure access to new products and processes for developing nations (267).

COMPENSATION FOR GENETIC RESOURCE USE

Part of the debate over intellectual property is the issue of compensating developing nations for use of genetic material found within their borders. Plant breeders and pharmaceutical companies routinely come to tropical nations, the world's storehouse of biological diversity, to look for plant breeding materials and new drugs. Typically, materials are taken without compensating—or even informing—the host nation.

Developing nations, increasingly aware that their biological diversity represents a valuable national resource, view the lack of compensation as not only unjust but inconsistent. After all, no one is free to plunder natural resources such as oil, timber, and minerals (268) (269) (270). The growing value attached to useful genes because of biotechnology, and the fact that many of these genes end up patented, only makes the current practice more intolerable to host nations. Their genetic capital leaves the country free of charge, only to return in the form of expensive new seeds, drugs, and other patented items (271) (272) (273).

The Convention on Biodiversity, signed by 157 nations at the June 1992 Earth Summit in Rio de Janeiro, recognizes the validity of these complaints and stipulates that developing nations should receive some compensation for the export of their germ plasm. Explicit valuation of genetic resources in international commerce is expected to sweeten the incentive for nations to preserve their biodiversity, as this can now be justified on economic and ecological grounds (274) (275).

In addition, the Convention contains language promoting the transfer of biotechnologies to developing countries that provide a genetic resource, thus encouraging them to participate in research and make better use of their own biodiversity. Other statements in the Convention give developing nations access to technologies that result from in situ germ plasm discoveries—even if these discoveries are patented—though the mechanism to achieve this is not specified. Most nations found the Convention's language on biotechnology and patents sufficiently qualified to protect their interests. The United States, which initially refused to sign, later relented and added its signature (276) (277).

Even before the signing of the Convention, some companies saw the wisdom of joining in partnership with a developing nation to explore commercial uses of its germ plasm. In September 1991, Merck, the world's largest pharmaceutical company, entered into a two-year, $1.1 million deal with Costa Rica's National Biodiversity Institute (INBio) to prospect for promising drugs (278) (279) (280). Under the agreement, a model of the kind of cooperation envisioned in the Convention, INBio will provide extracts from hundreds of wild plants, animals, and insects to be screened for their drug potential. Merck will retain the patent rights on any product resulting from the venture but will pay INBio royalties to be used in part for biodiversity conservation activities. Merck will also provide training and technical assistance to Costa Rica as it builds up an indigenous drug research capacity, hoping to profit from its own resources (281) (282) (283).

BUILDING THIRD WORLD BIOTECHNOLOGY

Despite limited finances and governmental haggling over intellectual property rights, considerable effort has been made to share the benefits of biotechnology with the South and equip it with an indigenous biotechnology capacity.

Several larger developing nations such as India, China, and Brazil are already pursuing vigorous biotechnology programs of their own, focusing on more accessible technologies such as tissue culture and fermentation biology. India has a sophisticated scientific infrastructure including several national agricultural laboratories as well as a budding biotechnology industry. Among other areas of research, well-established programs are under way in the tissue culture of tuber crops, spices, and aromatic and medicinal plants. The Indian program also covers genetic engineering work on crops such as cotton and corn (284) (285).

In most of the developing world, however, scientific infrastructure and capital are more limited. In response to this situation, different programs have been set up to transfer key technologies and develop the scientific base to apply them. Some programs are primarily public sector and financed by aid agencies.

Perhaps the premier example is the Rockefeller Rice Biotechnology Network, begun in 1985 and now supporting 120 rice research projects in a host of countries (286) (287). A prominent feature of the Rockefeller program is its goal of raising the number of rice researchers in the developing world. To that end, about two thirds of the scientists and all of the trainees involved are from developing countries. Research coming out of the Rockefeller program has produced major progress in the areas of rice disease, pest resistance, nutrition enhancement, and genetic mapping of the rice genome. India, China, Thailand, and other countries have already begun to test new strains of rice emanating from the program (288) (289).

The network strategy, that is, linking scattered researchers through a single funding and communication mechanism, has been tried successfully with other crops. For example, Centro Internacional de Agricultura Tropical, an international research institute based in Colombia, hosts the cassava biotechnology network and a recently formed bean biotechnology network (290).

Parts of the private sector have stepped forward to do their part, resulting in several creative public-private collaborations over the last several years. In a project funded by the U.S. Agency for International Development (U.S. AID), Monsanto, a biotechnology leader in the United States, is collaborating with a Kenyan researcher to use the company's genetic engineering technology for incorporating virus resistance into African sweet potatoes (291) (292) (293).

In another U.S. AID-supported venture, Zeneca, a large British seed and bioscience conglomerate, will work with Indonesia to develop an insect-resistant corn variety suited to the tropics, and a team of Indonesian scientists will be trained in genetic engineering. The International Service for the Acquisition of Agri-Biotechnological Applications, an international non-profit agency, exists solely to foster direct exchange of proprietary biotechnology to developing nations (294) (295).

In some cases, private corporations are willing to share some or all of their technology in selected markets where they do not expect to compete. Zeneca plans to make its technology for screening corn that can tolerate high-acid tropical soil available to the international laboratory system for free distribution anywhere Zeneca is not active. Likewise, Monsanto has donated its virus-resistance technology for use in areas where the company has no commercial interest (296) (297).

Though these and similar programs inspire hope, they are still limited in scope and means. If the capacity building they foster is to succeed, observers point out, continued attention and expanded funding will be required from the industrialized world. Technology transfer alone cannot redress the present unequal distribution of biotechnology's benefits; only by developing its own robust biotechnology capability can the South protect its export markets and fully address its unique crop and livestock needs (298).

BIOTECH TRADEOFFS: KEEPING PERSPECTIVE

Without denying the tremendous potential for agricultural gain that biotechnology offers in both developing and industrialized nations, many experts caution that biotechnology's benefits should not be oversold, nor its potential for negative impacts overlooked when evaluating its role in global agriculture (299) (300) (301) (302).

Some fear that widespread acceptance of a limited selection of bioengineered seeds or laboratory-produced clones may lead to a loss of genetic diversity among farm crops as local strains are replaced, much in the way that modern hybrid seed has displaced many traditional local varieties. The movement toward genetic uniformity could mean greater susceptibility to large-scale pest or disease attack or other environmental disruptions, a problem that has long plagued monoculture farming. Furthermore, dependence on outside sources for clones and specialized seed could erode the self-reliance of farmers and raise costs, as high-tech planting materials tend to be more expensive than cuttings or seeds supplied locally (303) (304) (305).

In some cases, the very possibilities of biotechnology may be a source of conflict. For instance, current work to develop crop varieties with drought resistance, greater salt tolerance, or the ability to fix their own nitrogen could make food production possible on more marginal lands. Yet widespread exploitation of these lands, many of which are fragile, could easily destroy their habitat or increase soil erosion (306).

Similarly, success in implanting the so-called BT gene in a variety of crops has made genetically based insect protection a reality, yet it has also prompted concern about human health. The long-term effect on humans of ingesting the exotic plant protein responsible for protecting against insects is not yet fully known; it may not be entirely benign (307) (308) (309).

Concern has also been raised that government funding of biotechnology research, particularly in developing nations, diverts resources from essential research in conventional plant breeding, plant pathology, and agronomy—work that cannot be ignored if global food production is to be maximized in the years ahead (310).

Critics hope that acknowledging the possible disadvantages of current trends will help correct the vision of biotechnology as modern agriculture's silver bullet come to solve all ills. A more useful view, they contend, is of agricultural biotechnology as one of several avenues leading toward sustainable agriculture, which, if it is to succeed, must also address tillage and irrigation practices, cropping patterns, pesticide use, government agricultural policies, and the complex workings of global economic markets (311) (312).

The Conditions and Trends section was written by Steven McCann of the World Resources *staff. The Focus On section was written by contributing editor Gregory Mock.*

References and Notes

1. Pierre R. Crosson, "Sustainable Agriculture," *Resources*, No. 106 (Winter 1992), p. 14.
2. Nikos Alexandratos, Chief of the Global Perspective Studies Unit, Economic and Social Policy Department, Food and Agriculture Organization of the United Nations, 1993 (personal communication).
3. Food and Agriculture Organization of the United Nations (FAO), *The State of Food and Agriculture, 1992* (FAO, Rome, 1992), p. 16.
4. The other countries were Mongolia, Vanuatu, Iraq, Jordan, and Yemen.
5. *Op. cit.* 3, p. 19.
6. *Op. cit.* 3, p. 22.
7. *Op. cit.* 3, p. 22.
8. K.G. Cassman and P.L. Pingali, "Extrapolating Trends from Long-Term Experiments to Farmer's Fields: The Case of Irrigated Rice Systems in Asia," paper presented at the Working Conference on Measuring Sustainability Using Long-Term Experiments, Rothamsted Experimental Station, U.K., April, 1993.
9. *Ibid.*
10. Christopher L. Delgado and Per Pinstrup-Andersen, "Agricultural Productivity in the Third World: Patterns and Strategic Issues," keynote address to the 1993 American Agricultural Economics Association (AAEA)/International Food Policy Research Institute (IFPRI) Conference Workshop Post-Green Revolution Agricultural Development Strategies in the Third World: What Next?, Orlando, Florida, July, 1993.
11. *Ibid.*
12. *Ibid.*
13. *Op. cit.* 3.

14. *Op. cit.* 3.
15. U.S. Department of Agriculture, Economic Research Service (USDA-ERS), *PS&D View '92*, on diskette (USDA-ERS, Washington, D.C., 1992).
16. *Ibid.*
17. The World Food Programme (WFP), *1992 Food Aid Review* (WFP, Rome, 1992), p. 10.
18. Food and Agriculture Organization of the United Nations (FAO), *FAO Quarterly Bulletin of Statistics*, Vol. 5, No. 4 (1992), p. 26.
19. *Ibid.*, p. 16.
20. *Op. cit.* 17, p. 11.
21. Martin Brown and Ian Goldin, *The Future of Agriculture: Developing Country Implications* (Development Centre of the Organisation for Economic Co-operation and Development, Paris, 1992), p. 91.
22. *Op. cit.* 3, p. 27.
23. *Op. cit.* 3, p. 27.
24. *Op. cit.* 3, p. 27.
25. *Op. cit.* 3, p. 27.
26. David Grigg, "World Agriculture: Production and Productivity in the Late 1980s," *Geography*, Vol. 77, No. 335, Part 2 (1992), p. 100.
27. *Ibid.*
28. Jock R. Anderson, Philip G. Pardey, and Johannes Roseboom, "Sustaining Growth in Agriculture: A Quantitative Review of Agricultural Research Investments," International Service for National Agricultural Research, The Hague, The Netherlands, 1993, p. 4.
29. *Ibid.*, p. 9.
30. *Ibid.*, pp. 16–17.

31. *Ibid.*, p. 18.
32. *Ibid.*
33. *Ibid.*, p. 19.
34. Gordon Conway and Jules Pretty, *Unwelcome Harvest: Agriculture and Pollution* (Earthscan, London, 1991), p. 21.
35. James J. Tarrant, *An Environmental Study of the Proposed Indonesian National IPM Programme Support Project*, Food and Agriculture Organization of the United Nations Cooperative Programme, Jakarta, 1992, p. 12.
36. Michael Hansen, *Escape from the Pesticide Treadmill: Alternative to Pesticides in Developing Countries* (Institute for Consumer Policy Research, Mount Vernon, New York, 1987), pp. 12–13.
37. Lori Ann Thrupp, "Pesticides and Policies: Approaches to Pest-Control Dilemmas in Nicaragua and Costa Rica," *Latin American Perspectives*, Vol. 15, No. 4 (1988), pp. 41–42.
38. Foundation for Advancements in Science and Education (FASE), "Exporting Banned and Hazardous Pesticides: A Preliminary Report," *FASE Reports*, Vol. 9, No. 1 (FASE, Los Angeles, 1991), p. S-6.
39. *Op. cit.* 34, p. 19.
40. Sandra Postel, "Defusing the Toxics Threat: Controlling Pesticides and Industrial Waste," Worldwatch Paper No. 79, Worldwatch Institute, Washington, D.C., 1987, p. 10.
41. United Nations Industrial Development Organization (UNIDO), "Global Overview of the Pesticide Industry Subsector," Sectoral Working Paper No. V.88-31250, UNIDO, New York, 1988, pp. 11 and 14, Table 11.

42. The World Bank, *World Development Report* (The World Bank, Washington, D.C., 1992), p. 140.

43. *Ibid.*

44. World Health Organization (WHO), *Our Planet, Our Health: Report of the WHO Commission on Health and Environment* (WHO, Geneva, 1992).

45. *Op. cit.* 41, p. 15.

46. *Op. cit.* 34, pp. 19–20.

47. Food and Agriculture Organization of the United Nations (FAO), *Agrostat-PC 1993*, on diskette (FAO, Rome, 1993).

48. Pan American Health Organization, WHO, *Pesticides and Health in the Americas* (WHO, Washington, D.C., 1993), p. 10.

49. Ernst and Young, *National Agricultural Chemicals Association 1990 Pesticide Export Survey* (Ernst and Young, Washington, D.C., 1990), p. 3.

50. *Op. cit.* 41, p. 52.

51. Lori Ann Thrupp, Director of Sustainable Agriculture, Center for International Development and Environment, Washington, D.C., 1993 (personal communication).

52. *Op. cit.* 38, pp. S-1 to S-8.

53. Foundation for Advancements in Science and Education (FASE), "FASE Report Stirs Export Debate," *FASE Reports*, Vol. 10, No. 1 (FASE, Los Angeles, 1992), p. 3.

54. Jumanah Farah, "Pesticide Policies in Developing Countries: Do They Encourage Excessive Pesticide Use?" Working paper, Agriculture and Natural Resources Department, Agricultural Policies (The World Bank, Washington, D.C., 1993), pp. 44–45.

55. *Op. cit.* 41, pp. 54–55.

56. *Op. cit.* 37.

57. *Op. cit.* 34, p. 27.

58. Lori Ann Thrupp, "Inappropriate Incentives for Pesticide Use: Agricultural Credit Requirements in Developing Countries," *Agriculture and Human Values* (Summer/Fall 1990), p. 63.

59. *Op. cit.* 34, p. 27.

60. *Op. cit.* 37, pp. 41–43.

61. *Op. cit.* 58, p. 63.

62. *Op. cit.* 34, pp. 28–29.

63. *Op. cit.* 54, pp. 26, 43, 47, 50–51, and 56.

64. Robert Repetto, *Paying the Price: Pesticide Subsidies in Developing Nations* (World Resources Institute, Washington, D.C., 1985), pp. 1–6.

65. *Ibid.*, pp. 1–4, 12.

66. *Op. cit.* 34, p. 26.

67. *Op. cit.* 64, pp. 1 and 4.

68. *Op. cit.* 34, pp. 22–23.

69. David Pimentel, "Diversification of Biological Control Strategies in Agriculture," *Crop Protection*, Vol. 10 (1991), p. 243.

70. *Op. cit.* 40, p. 19.

71. *Op. cit.* 34, pp. 22–23.

72. David Pimentel, Lori McLaughlin, Andrew Zepp, *et al.*, "Environmental and Economic Impacts of Reducing U.S. Agricultural Pesticide Use," in *CRC Handbook of Pest Management in Agriculture*, D. Pimentel, ed., Vol. 1, 2nd ed. (CRC Press, Boca Raton, Florida, 1991), p. 682.

73. Michael Dover and Brian Croft, *Getting Tough: Public Policy and the Management of Pesticide Resistance* (World Resources Institute, Washington, D.C., 1984), pp. 1–8.

74. *Op. cit.* 36, pp. 21–22.

75. *Op. cit.* 36, pp. 21–22.

76. Peter Weber, "A Place for Pesticides?" *World Watch*, Vol. 15, No. 3 (1992), pp. 22–23.

77. *Op. cit.* 73, p. 6.

78. *Op. cit.* 36, p. 22.

79. Lori Ann Thrupp, "Entrapment and Escape from Fruitless Insecticide Use: Lessons for the Banana Sector of Costa Rica," *International Journal of Environmental Studies*, Vol. 36 (1990), pp. 174–175.

80. *Op. cit.* 36, pp. 21–22.

81. *Op. cit.* 36, p. 22.

82. *Op. cit.* 47.

83. *Op. cit.* 3, p. 17, Table 5, and pp. 27–28.

84. *Op. cit.* 34, p. 21, Table 2.2.

85. *Op. cit.* 37, p. 43.

86. Terry Gips, *Breaking the Pesiticide Habit: Alternatives to 12 Hazardous Pesticides*, International Alliance for Sustainable Agriculture (IASA) Publication No. 1987-1 (IASA, Minneapolis, Minnesota, 1987), pp. 44–45.

87. V. Dittrich, S.O. Hassan and G.H. Ernst, "Sudanese Cotton and the Whitefly: A Case Study of the Emergence of a New Primary Pest," in *Crop Protection* (1985) 4 (2), pp. 161–176.

88. *Op. cit.* 42.

89. *Op. cit.* 34, pp. 17 and 32–81.

90. *Op. cit.* 86, p. 2.

91. David Pimentel and Lois Levitan, "Pesticides: Where Do They Go?," *The Journal of Pesticide Reform*, Vol. 7, No. 4 (1988), pp. 2–5.

92. Bob Uhlir, "Atrazine," *Journal of Pesticide Reform*, Vol. 11, No. 4 (1991), p. 35.

93. *Op. cit.* 34, pp. 35–44 and 56–57.

94. *Op. cit.* 36, p. 18.

95. *Op. cit.* 86, pp. 19–26.

96. *Op. cit.* 92, pp. 34–35.

97. *Op. cit.* 34, pp. 47 and 56–57.

98. Howard A. Barn, Phyllis Blair, Sophie Brasseur, *et al.*, "Statement from the Work Session on Chemically Induced Alterations in Sexual Development: The Wildlife/Human Connection," Wingspread Retreat, Racine, Wisconsin, July 1991, pp. 1–4.

99. Theo Colburn, "Listening to the Lakes," *Pesticides and You*, Vol. 12, No. 2. (Natinal Coalition Against the Misuse of Pesticides, Washington, D.C., June 1992), pp. 4–8.

100. Howard A. Bern, Phyllis Blair, Sophie Brasseur, *et al.*, "Statement from the Work Session on Chemically Induced Alterations in Sexual Development: The Wildlife/Human Connection," Wingspread Retreat, Racine, Wisconsin, July 1991, pp. 1–4.

101. *Op. cit.* 34, pp. 40–41.

102. *Op. cit.* 36, pp. 17–19.

103. Organochlorine pesticides are insecticides such as DDT, BHC, lindane, dieldrin, aldrin, toxaphene, and heptachlor. For further information see *op. cit.* 36, p.14 and *op. cit.* 48, p. 3.

104. *Op. cit.* 91, p. 4.

105. *Op. cit.* 34, pp. 57–68.

106. *Op. cit.* 38, pp. S-1 to S-8.

107. World Health Organization (WHO), *Public Health Impact of Pesticides Used in Agriculture* (WHO, Geneva, 1990), pp. 79–86.

108. J. Jeyaratnam, "Acute Pesticide Poisoning: A Major Global Health Problem," *World Health Statistics Quarterly*, Vol. 43 (1990), pp. 139–143.

109. *Ibid.*, p. 142, Table 3.

110. *Ibid.*, p. 141.

111. *Op. cit.* 38, p. S-8.

112. *Op. cit.* 108, p. 141.

113. *Op. cit.* 107.

114. *Op. cit.* 37, pp. 43–44.

115. Lori Ann Thrupp, "Sterilization of Workers from Pesticide Exposure: Causes and Consequences of DBCP-Induced Damage in Costa Rica and Beyond," *International Journal of Health Services*, Vol. 21, No. 4 (1991), pp. 731–739.

116. Carl Smith and Shelley Beckmann, Foundation for Advancements in Science and Education, "Unregistered and Restricted-Use Pesticide Exports in 1990," statement before the House Subcommittee on International Economic Policy and Trade, Hearings, February 20, 1992 (unpublished, Washington, D.C.), pp. 5–6.

117. *Op. cit.* 38, p. S-3.

118. *Op. cit.* 107, pp. 77–78.

119. *Op. cit.* 116.

120. *Op. cit.* 38, p. S-3.

121. *Op. cit.* 107, pp. 77–78.

122. Pesticide Action Network (PAN), "Victims without Voice," *Pesticide Monitor*, Vol. 1, No. 3 (PAN, San Francisco, 1992), p. 1.

123. *Op. cit.* 116.

124. Arif Jamal, "Pesticide Tragedies in Sudan," *Global Pesticide Campaigner*, Vol. 2, No. 1 (Pesticide Action Network, San Francisco, 1992), pp. 4–5.

125. *Op. cit.* 122, p. 3.

126. Foundataion for Advancement in Science and Education (FASE), "Lead, Pesticides, and Children," *FASE Reports*, Vol. 10, No. 1 (1992), pp. 4–5.

127. *Op. cit.* 42.

128. Commission on Life Sciences, *Pesticides in the Diets of Infants and Children* (Commission on Life Sciences, National Association of Sciences, Washington, D.C., 1993), pp. 1–12.

129. *Op. cit.* 107, pp. 87–88.

130. Robert Repetto, "Policy Implications of Possible Effects of Pesticides on the Immune System," paper presented at the Conference on Pesticides and Health, Bellagio, Italy, April 1992.

131. *Op. cit.* 100.

132. *Op. cit.* 34, p. 137.

133. Bill Barclay and John Steggall, "Obsolete Pesticides Crisis," *Global Pesticide Campaigner*, Vol. 2, No. 1 (1992), p. 1.

134. *Ibid.*, pp. 1 and 11–12.

135. Food and Agricultural Organization of the United Nations (FAO), *Report of the First Session of the FAO Panel of Experts on Integrated Pest Control* (FAO, Rome, 1967), pp. 2–3, as cited in Michael Hansen, *Escape from the Pesticide Treadmill: Alternative to Pesticides in Developing Countries* (Institute for Consumer Policy Research, Mount Vernon, New York, 1987), pp. 33–34.

136. *Op. cit.* 36, pp. 33–41.

137. *Op. cit.* 40, pp. 25–26.

138. *Op. cit.* 36, pp. 35–36.

139. *Op. cit.* 40, pp. 25–26.

140. *Op. cit.* 36, pp. 35–41, and 113.

141. *Op. cit.* 86, pp. 28–29.

142. *Op. cit.* 36, pp. 36–39.

143. *Op. cit.* 86, pp. 29–30.

144. *Op. cit.* 40, pp. 33–34.

145. *Op. cit.* 36, pp. 35–41.

146. *Op. cit.* 36, p. 38.

147. *Op. cit.* 36, pp. 38–39.

148. Peter Rosset, Latin American Studies Program, Stanford University, Stanford, California, 1993 (personal communication).

149. Lori Ann Thrupp, "Breaking Chemical Dependency in Agriculture: The Remarkable Case of Cuba," unpublished manuscript, University of California, Berkeley, 1989.

150. Peter Kenmore, Entomologist and Consultant to Indonesian Integrated Pest Management Programme, Food and Agricultural Organization of the United Nations, Manila, Philippines, 1993 (personal communication).

151. Roger Bloom, Deputy Agricultural Development Officer, Asia Bureau, U.S. Agency for International Development (U.S. AID), Washington, D.C., 1993 (personal communication).

152. Tim O'Hare, Economist, Latin American Bureau, U.S. Agency for International Development, Washington, D.C., 1993 (personal communication).

153. James Tarrant, Consultant to Indonesian National Integrated Pest Management Pro-

gramme, U.S. Agency for International Development, Washington, D.C., 1993 (personal communication).

154. *Op. cit.* 148.

155. Peter Kenmore, "Getting Policies Right, Keeping Policies Right: Indonesia's Integrated Pest Management Policy, Production and Environment," paper presented at the Asia Region and Private Enterprise (ARPE) Environment and Agriculture Officers' Conference, Sri Lanka, September 1991.

156. *Op. cit.* 150.

157. *Op. cit.* 153.

158. L. Ross Brownhall, Kees G. Eveleens, Ward Heneveld, *et al.*, *Mid-Term Review of FAO Intercountry Program for the Development and Application of Integrated Pest Control in Rice in South and Southeast Asia: Phase II, Mission Report, November 1990* (Food and Agricultural Organization of the United Nations, Rome, 1990), pp. 39–70.

159. Kai Siedenburg, "Philippine Pesticide Bans Show NGO Strength," *Global Pesticide Campaigner*, Vol. 2, No. 3 (1992), pp. 1 and 6–7.

160. Ron Nigh, "Grassroots Leadership Provokes New Approach to Malaria Control," *Global Pesticide Campaigner*, Vol. 2, No. 1 (1992), pp. 1, 10–11, and 20.

161. *Op. cit.* 159, pp. 1 and 6.

162. Antonio Thomen, "Dominican Republic Bans Dirty Dozen—Industry Fights Back," *Global Pesticide Campaigner*, Vol. 2, No. 1 (1992), p. 3.

163. *Op. cit.* 35.

164. *Op. cit.* 153.

165. *Op. cit.* 148.

166. *Op. cit.* 158, pp. 39–68.

167. *Op. cit.* 158, pp. 39–68.

168. *Op. cit.* 51.

169. *Op. cit.* 35.

170. *Op. cit.* 64.

171. *Op. cit.* 51.

172. *Op. cit.* 51.

173. Charles Gasser and Robert Fraley, "Transgenic Crops," *Scientific American* (June 1992), pp. 62–65.

174. Henk Hobbelink, *Biotechnology and the Future of World Agriculture* (Zed Books, London, 1991), pp. 21–22.

175. *Op. cit.* 173.

176. Robert Cowen, "Farmers to Benefit from World Biotech Revolution," *Christian Science Monitor* (February 18, 1992), p. 9.

177. Gary Toenniessen, Associate Director, Rockefeller Foundation, New York, 1993 (personal communication).

178. Gary Toenniessen, "Rice Biotechnology: Prospects and Prospects," paper presented at the Society of Chemical Industries Conference on Pest Management in Rice, London, June 1990.

179. *Op. cit.* 173, pp. 62–65.

180. Robert Fraley, "Sustaining the Food Supply," *Bio/Technology*, Vol. 10 (January 1992), pp. 40–43.

181. Alice Cantwell, "Grace, DuPont to Share Licensing of Gene Technology," *Journal of Commerce* (April 23, 1992), p. 9, sec. A.

182. National Research Council, Board on Science and Technology for International Development, *Priorities in Biotechnology Research for International Development* (National Academy Press, Washington, D.C., 1982), pp. 131–139, 152–154, and 230–233.

183. *Op. cit.* 174, pp. 26–27.

184. *Op. cit.* 182, pp. 133–134, 152–154, and 236–237.

185. M.S. Swaminathan, ed., *Biotechnology in Agriculture: A Dialogue* (Macmillan, Madras, India, 1991), pp. 90–94.

186. *Op. cit.* 182, pp. 134, 152–154, and 237–238.

187. *Op. cit.* 185, p. 92.

188. "Kenya Receives Plant Improvement Technology to Fight World Hunger," Monsanto press release, February 14, 1993.

189. *Op. cit.* 173, pp. 63–64.

190. H.S. Gupta and A. Pattanayak, "Plant Regeneration from Mesophyll Protoplasts of Rice," *Bio/Technology*, Vol. 11 (January 1993), p. 90.

191. Malcolm Gladwell, "Biotechnologists Forging New Links in Food Chain," *Washington Post* (September 29, 1989), p. 3, sec. A.

192. Sally Lehrman, "Splicing Genes, Slicing Exports," *Washington Post* (September 27, 1992), p. 1, sec. H.

193. J. Komen, "Screening Plants for New Drugs," *Biotechnology and Development Monitor*, No. 9 (December 1991), p. 6.

194. Jane Brody, "Gardens of Plant Tissue in Labs Seen as Factories for Vital Drugs," *New York Times* (November 20, 1990), p. 1, sec. C.

195. Martin Rogoff and Stephen Rawlins, "Food Security: A Technological Alternative," *BioScience*, Vol. 37, No. 11 (1987), p. 801.

196. *Ibid.*, pp. 800–807.

197. Rebecca Goldburp, *Biotechnology's Bitter Harvest: Herbicide-Tolerant Crops and the Threat to Sustainable Agriculture*, Biotechnology Working Group, 1990.

198. *Op. cit.* 182, pp. 96–106 and 150–151.

199. Petra Smits, "Modern Agricultural Diagnostics: Relevance and Applicability for Developing Countries," *Biotechnology and Development Monitor*, No. 10 (March 1992), pp. 20–21.

200. *Op. cit.* 177.

201. *Op. cit.* 182, pp. 183–185.

202. Laurent Belsie, "Biotechnology Promises Fresh Gains," *Christian Science Monitor* (October 28, 1992), pp. 9 and 12.

203. Industrial Biotechnology Association (IBA), *Agriculture and the New Biology* (IBA, Washington, D.C., 1987), p. 6.

204. Neill Schaller, Associate Director, Henry A. Wallace Institute for Alternative Agriculture, Greenbelt, Maryland, 1993 (personal communication).

205. Jos Bijman, "Can Biotechnology Help to Increase Livestock Productivity?" *Biotechnology and Development Monitor*, No. 11 (June 1992), pp. 3–5.

206. *Ibid.*

207. *Op. cit.* 182, pp. 151–152.

208. Anders Nilsson, "International Efforts to Prevent Bio-Hazards," *Biotechnology and Development Monitor*, No. 10 (March 1992), pp. 16–18.

209. D. Pimentel, M. Hunter, J. La Gro, *et al.*, "Benefits and Risks of Genetic Engineering in Agriculture," *BioScience*, Vol. 39, No. 9 (1989), pp. 606–610.

210. Christopher Andreae, "Engineered Plants Are Put to Field Test," *Christian Science Monitor* (September 4, 1991), p. 12.

211. "A Pox on the Gypsy Moth," *Technology Review*, Vol. 96, No. 2 (February/March 1993), p. 72.

212. *Op. cit.* 209.

213. *Op. cit.* 210.

214. John H. Payne, Acting Director, Biotechnology Biologics and Environmental Protection, Animal and Plant Health Inspection Service, United States Department of Agriculture, Washington, D.C., 1993 (personal communication).

215. Warren Leary, "Gene-Altered Food Held by the FDA to Pose Little Risk," *New York Times* (May 26, 1992), p. 1, sec. A.

216. Malcolm Gladwell, "Biotech Food Products Won't Require Special Rules, FDA Decides," *Washington Post* (May 26, 1992), p. 4, sec. A.

217. *Op. cit.* 180, p. 43.

218. Paula Green, "U.S. Biotechnology Industry Faces Fight over Regulation," *Journal of Commerce*, Vol. 392, No. 27 (1992), p. 1-A.

219. Joan Hamilton and James Ellis, "A Storm is Breaking Down on the Farm," *Business Week* (December 14, 1992), pp. 98–101.

220. Henry Miller, "Putting the BST Human-Health Controversy to Rest," *Bio/Technology*, Vol. 10 (February 1992), p. 147.

221. The World Bank, "Agricultural Biotechnology: The Next Green Revolution," Technical Paper No. 133 (The World Bank, Washington, D.C., 1991), p. 5.

222. *Ibid.*, pp. 5 and 6.

223. *Op. cit.* 180, p. 40.

224. *Op. cit.* 221, pp. vii and 5–6.

225. *Op. cit.* 180, p. 42.

226. *Op. cit.* 174, pp. 30–48.

227. *Op. cit.* 174, pp. 30–48 and 120–121.

228. *Op. cit.* 174, pp. 30–48 and 119–120.

229. John Hodgson, "Feeding the World," *Bio/Technology*, Vol. 10 (January 1992), pp. 47–50.

230. James Ellis, "Can Biotech Put Bread on Third World Tables?" *Business Week* (December 14, 1992), p. 100.

231. *Op. cit.* 229.

232. R. Ravi Srinavas, "Private Investment in Biotechnology Promoted in India," *Biotechnology and Development Monitor*, No. 11 (June 1992), p. 17.

233. *Op. cit.* 174, pp. 123–133.

234. *Op. cit.* 229, p. 50.

235. *Op. cit.* 221, p. 6.

236. *Op. cit.* 192.

237. Food and Agricultural Organization of the United Nations (FAO), *FAO Trade Statistics 1991*, (FAO, Rome, 1991), p. 213.

238. *Op. cit.* 192.

239. Calgene, prospectus for Calgene common stock (Calgene, Davis, California, January 1993).

240. *Op. cit.* 192.

241. *Op. cit.* 174, pp. 99–116.

242. *Op. cit.* 180, p. 43.

243. J. van Wijk, "GATT and the Legal Protection of Plants in the Third World," *Biotechnology and Development Monitor*, No. 10 (March 1992), pp. 14–15.

244. Kevin Watkins, "Battle for the Rights to Life," *The Guardian* (February 7, 1992, London), p. 27.

245. Paula Green, "Battle Rages over Right to Patent Living Things," *Journal of Commerce* (December 16, 1991), p. 1-A.

246. *Op. cit.* 218.

247. *Op. cit.* 174, pp. 104–108.

248. *Op. cit.* 174, pp. 99–116.

249. *Op. cit.* 244.

250. *Op. cit.* 245.

251. Charles F. Warren, Deputy Director, Patent Examining Group 1800: Biotechnology, U.S. Department of Commerce, 1993 (personal communication).

252. *Op. cit.* 174, pp. 99–116.

253. *Op. cit.* 243, p. 14.

254. *Op. cit.* 244.

255. *Op. cit.* 245, p. 1-A.

256. Larry Beach, Molecular Biologist, Pioneer Hi-Bred, Des Moines, Iowa, 1993 (personal communication).

257. *Op. cit.* 243, p. 14.

258. *Op. cit.* 244.

259. *Op. cit.* 245.

260. R. Pistorius, "Retaliation against Thailand for its Patent Law," *Biotechnology and Development Monitor*, No. 7 (June 1991), p. 22.

261. J. van Wijk, "Plant Varieties Patentable in Mexico," *Biotechnology and Development Monitor*, No. 9 (December 1991), p. 20.

262. Paula Green, "Andean Nations Stiffen Patent Laws," *Journal of Commerce* (August 4, 1992), p. 1-A.

263. J. van Wijk, "India's Patent Law Under Debate," *Biotechnology and Development Monitor*, No. 5 (December 1990), p. 15.

264. *Op. cit.* 174, pp. 102–103.

265. John Komen, "CGIAR Statement on Genetic Resources and Intellectual Property," *Biotechnology and Development Monitor*, No. 11 (June 1992), p. 20.

266. *Op. cit.* 174, pp. 120–123.

267. *Op. cit.* 265.

268. *Op. cit.* 244.

269. *Op. cit.* 245.

270. Jessica Mathews, "The Race to Claim the Gene," *Washington Post* (November 17, 1991), p. 7, sec. C.

271. *Op. cit.* 244.

272. *Op. cit.* 245.

273. *Op. cit.* 270.

274. See also: Earth Summit: final Texts, *Convention on Biological Diversity*, (UNCED, Rio de Janeiro, 1992), p. 9.

275. Graeme Browning, "Biodiversity Battle," *National Journal* (August 8, 1992), p. 1828.

276. *Op. cit.* 274, p. 9.

277. *Op. cit.* 275, p. 1827.

278. Walter Reid, Sarah Laird, Carrie Meyer, *et al.*, Biodiversity Prospecting: Using Guidelines for Genetic Resources for Sustainable Development, (World Resources Institute, Instituto Nacional de Biodiversidad, Rainforest Alliance, USA, and African Centre for Technology Studies, Washington, D.C., 1993), p. 1.

279. *Op. cit.* 275.

280. William Stevens, "Costa Rica in Pact to Search for Forest Drugs," *New York Times* (September 24, 1991), p. 8, sec. B.

281. *Op. cit.* 278.

282. *Op. cit.* 275.

283. *Op. cit.* 280.

284. *Op. cit.* 221, p. 11.

285. R. Pistorius, "Biotechnology in India," *Biotechnology and Development Monitor*, No. 5 (December 1990), pp. 10–12.

286. *Op. cit.* 177.

287. *Op. cit.* 230.

288. *Op. cit.* 177.

289. *Op. cit.* 230.

290. J. Komen, "CIAT's Advanced Biotechnology Networks," *Biotechnology and Development Monitor*, No. 6 (March 1991), pp. 19–20.

291. "Biotechnology Services for Third World Agriculture," *Biotechnology and Development Monitor*, No. 9 (December 1991), p. 16.

292. *Op. cit.* 188.

293. *Op. cit.* 230.

294. Agricultural Biotechnology for Sustainable Productivity, "The ICI Relationship," *Biolink*, Vol. 1, No. 1 (1992), p. 7.

295. *Op. cit.* 291, p. 17.

296. Simon Best, Managing Director, Zeneca A.Z.Q., Zeneca Seeds, Wilmington, Delaware, February 1992 (personal communication).

297. *Op. cit.* 229, p. 47.

298. Gabrielle Persley, Biotechnology Analyst, The World Bank, Washington, D.C., 1993 (personal communication).

299. *Op. cit.* 209.

300. *Op. cit.* 51.

301. *Op. cit.* 204.

302. Walter V. Reid, Vice-President for Program, World Resources Institute, Washington, D.C., 1993 (personal communication).

303. The Keystone Center, *Keystone International Dialogue Series on Plant Resources, Oslo Plenary Session, Final Consensus Report: Global Initiative for the Security and Sustainable Use of Plant Genetic Resources* (Genetic Resources Communications Systems, Washington, D.C., 1991), pp. 13–14.

304. *Op. cit.* 174, pp. 26–27.

305. *Op. cit.* 209, p. 609.

306. *Op. cit.* 302.

307. Rebecca Goldburg and Gabrielle Tjaden, "Are B.T.K. Plants Really Safe To Eat?," *Bio/Technology*, Vol. 8 (Nov. 1990), pp. 1011–1015.

308. Douglas McCormick, "Still a Few Bugs in the System," *Bio/Technology*, Vol. 8 (Nov. 1990), p. 981.

309. *Op. cit.* 173, pp. 65–66.

310. D. Pimentel, Professor, Department of Entomology, Cornell University, Ithaca, New York, April 1993 (personal communication).

311. *Op. cit.* 204.

312. *Op. cit.* 302.

7. Forests and Rangelands

A 1990 United Nations (U.N.) assessment of tropical forests for the first time separates tropical forests into various ecological types—rain, moist, dry—and identifies those countries where deforestation is most significant within each type. This and other studies also suggest that the area of degraded and fragmented tropical forest may be significantly larger than the actual deforested area.

Meanwhile, there is considerable uncertainty about the future development of international agreements and institutions geared toward establishing policies to protect the world's forests.

This volume of *World Resources* continues a region-by-region examination of the world's rangelands, this time focusing on rangelands in North America. Like nearly all other regions, North American rangelands have been significantly degraded by livestock grazing and other factors. But prospects for reversing negative trends in North American rangelands are more favorable, since these rangelands do not face the population pressures or uncontrolled access problems that are typical in many developing countries.

Regions covered in previous volumes include Africa in *World Resources 1986*, Western Asia in *World Resources 1987*, selected Asian countries in *World Resources 1988–89*, and Latin America (including Mexico) in *World Resources 1990–91*. The discussion in this volume covers lands in Canada and the United States.

CONDITIONS AND TRENDS

NEW GLOBAL FOREST RESOURCE ASSESSMENTS

The U.N. assessment of tropical forests for the first time sheds light on deforestation (defined as the permanent depletion of the crown cover of trees to less than 10 percent) trends in different types of forests and identifies those countries where deforestation is most significant for each individual forest type. For example, the new study shows that Brazil and Indonesia apparently account for about 45 percent of global rainforest loss.

This assessment and a separate study of Brazilian Amazonian forests also suggest that the area of de-

Figure 7.1 Estimated Annual Forest Change Rates, 1981–90

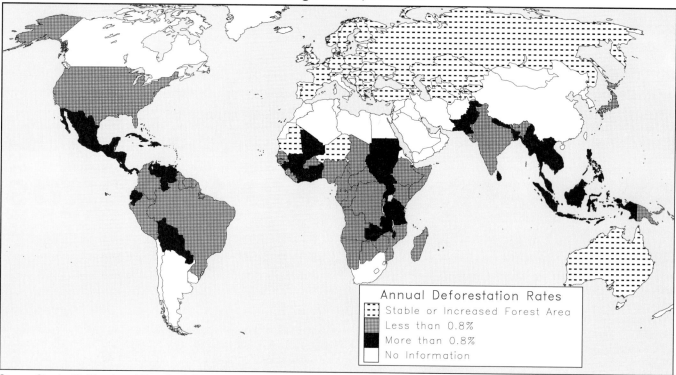

Annual Deforestation Rates
Stable or Increased Forest Area
Less than 0.8%
More than 0.8%
No Information

Source: Chapter 19, "Forests and Rangelands," Table 19.1.
Note: The global deforestation average for the tropics is 0.8 percent per year.

graded and fragmented tropical forest may be significantly larger than the actual deforested area, indicating that habitat loss—and therefore biodiversity loss—is proceeding much faster than deforestation figures would imply.

The new assessment, published in three parts, was prepared by the Food and Agriculture Organization of the United Nations (FAO). The first study, released in February 1992, describes conditions in temperate forests in industrialized countries; the second study, completed in August 1993, does the same for tropical forests in developing countries; the third study, expected in early 1994, will cover nontropical developing countries such as China and Argentina. A number of other assessments, many of which use satellite imagery, are also under way (1).

These studies represent the most recent and comprehensive quantitative assessment of the world's forests. For the first time, the FAO has examined conditions in specific forest ecosystems, looked at problems such as degradation and changes in biomass, and identified those countries with the highest rates of deforestation by ecosystem type. This last assessment could enable government policymakers and international aid donors to develop conservation priorities based on type.

Though the FAO's findings are comprehensive, they must be treated with caution. Most of the data came from national forest inventory reports, which were reviewed, adjusted to a common set of classifications, and combined in a database. The database was then adjusted to a common base year and changes in forest cover between 1980 and 1990 were calculated with the

help of a model. The reliability of these modeled estimates largely depends on the accuracy of the model and the accuracy of the primary data source. Good forestry information is scarce in Africa, less so in Latin America, and compared to these regions, widely available in Asia.

The tropical forest report also included a sample survey of forest cover changes based on high-resolution satellite data. For each of 117 sample sites, one image taken around 1980 and a second around 1990 were visually interpreted by an expert familiar with the location's vegetation and land use. The temperate forest report was based on data collected in questionnaires and supplemented with information from national reports and expert judgments. Surprisingly, this assessment did not provide conclusive estimates for changes in temperate forest area, even though data-generating sources are more common in temperate than in tropical regions. (For a detailed discussion of the methodology used by the FAO, see Chapter 19, "Forests and Rangelands.")

Some nations dispute the FAO's findings. For example, the government of Indonesia believes the FAO's deforestation estimate is much too high (2).

KEY FINDINGS

The FAO reports include the following:
■ Between 1980 and 1990, tropical forest areas have been shrinking on average 15.4 million hectares (0.8 percent) per year. The 76 countries studied in the 1990 assessment include about 98 percent of tropical land area.

Figure 7.2 Tropical Forest Area by Region

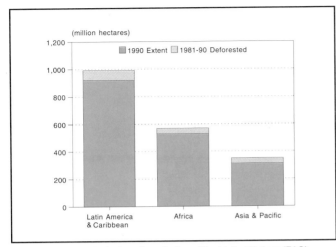

Source: Food and Agriculture Organization of the United Nations (FAO), *Forest Resources Assessment, 1990: Tropical Countries*, FAO Forestry Paper 112 (FAO, Rome, 1993), p. 25.

Figure 7.3 Tropical Rainforest Lost, 1981–90: Percentage Share of Top Five Countries

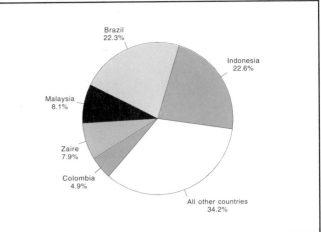

Source: Food and Agriculture Organization of the United Nations (FAO), *Forest Resources Assessment, 1990: Tropical Countries*, FAO Forestry Paper 112 (FAO, Rome, 1993), Tables 8a, 8b, and 8c.

Over the past decade, 154 million hectares of tropical forests, equivalent to almost three times the land area of France, have been converted to other land use (3).

■ Whether rates of deforestation have worsened significantly is difficult to determine. Preliminary research by the FAO indicates that rates of deforestation in the 1970s were substantially higher than previously thought. As a result, current indications show that deforestation rates in the 1980s were worse than in the 1970s, but comparisons between the two periods are difficult because of differences in methodology.

■ Forest area in industrialized countries has increased slightly over the past decade (4). (See Chapter 19, "Forests and Rangelands," Table 19.1.)

■ Global loss of above-ground biomass from deforestation in tropical countries is estimated at 2.5 gigatons annually during the past 10 years (5). This is equivalent to 4.1 gigatons of carbon dioxide, roughly 80 percent of the United States' total carbon dioxide emissions from energy use and cement production in 1990. (See Chapter 23, "Atmosphere and Climate," Table 24.1.)

■ Degradation and fragmentation of remaining forestland continue to threaten the diversity of plant and animal life, both in tropical and temperate regions. Evidence from Africa and Brazil suggest that the area of degraded and fragmented forestland may be much larger than the deforested area.

■ The area of plantations spread rapidly in the 1980s, rising from 18 million hectares in 1980 to more than 40 million hectares by 1990. About three fourths of all plantations are in Asia.

■ No significant increase took place in the sustainably managed forest area. But, log production rose steadily, with most of the cutting occurring in primary forests.

At the end of 1990, tropical forests were estimated to cover 1,756 million hectares, with 52 percent (918 million hectares) in South America and the Caribbean, 30 percent (528 million hectares) in Africa, and 18 percent (311 million hectares) in the Asia and Pacific region.

Half of the world's tropical forests were located in four countries: Brazil, Zaire, Indonesia, and Peru (6) (7).

All but a few tropical countries showed a decline in forest area. Six countries—Brazil, Indonesia, Zaire, Mexico, Bolivia, and Venezuela—accounted for about half of the deforestation in the tropical region, according to the FAO (8). (See Figure 7.1.)

Changes from closed to open forest (a decline in the density of the forest canopy as a result of grazing, fires, logging, or fuelwood gathering) and declines in biomass were classified as forest degradation and are not included in deforestation statistics (9).

The Asia and Pacific region, which has less remaining forest than other tropical regions, has the highest average annual deforestation rate (1.2 percent), followed by South America and the Caribbean (0.8 percent) and Africa (0.7 percent). In terms of total tropical forest area lost per year, South America and the Caribbean (7.4 million hectares) lead the way, followed by Africa (4.1 million hectares) and the Asia and Pacific region (3.9 million hectares) (10). (See Figure 7.2.)

Two subregions, continental Southeast Asia and Central America and Mexico, have the world's highest annual deforestation rate, both about twice the global average for the tropics. These rates can be primarily attributed to the clearing of the small area of remaining intact forest (11). While the annual deforestation rate between the 1980 and the 1990 assessment did not change significantly for Central America and the Caribbean—increasing in Honduras and Mexico and declining in Costa Rica—the FAO did report a significant acceleration for continental Southeast Asia. With the exception of Laos, all other countries of that region—Cambodia, Myanmar, Thailand, and Viet Nam—experienced a sharp rise in their respective annual deforestation rates. Several factors have contributed to this situation: the thriving economies in Thailand and Viet Nam, a growing demand for agricultural land and timber, an increased investment in the region from Japan and its

Figure 7.4 Tropical Moist Deciduous Forest Lost, 1981–90: Percentage Share of Top Five Countries

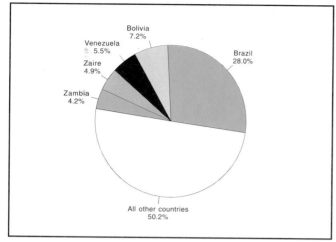

Source: Food and Agriculture Organization of the United Nations (FAO), *Forest Resources Assessment, 1990: Tropical Countries*, FAO Forestry Paper 112 (FAO, Rome, 1993), Tables 8a, 8b, and 8c.

Figure 7.5 Tropical Dry Forest Lost, 1981–90: Percentage Share of Top Five Countries

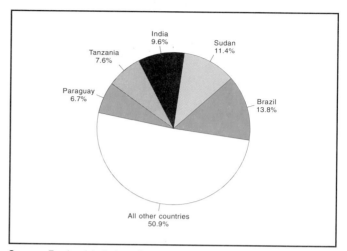

Source: Food and Agriculture Organization of the United Nations (FAO), *Forest Resources Assessment, 1990: Tropical Countries*, FAO Forestry Paper 112 (FAO, Rome, 1993), Tables 8a, 8b, and 8c.
Note: This includes dry deciduous, very dry, and desert forest.

Asian neighbors, and timber sales by governments or rebel groups.

TROPICAL FORESTS

Forest Changes by Ecological Zone

The FAO divides lowland forests into five categories based on precipitation and type: rainforest, moist deciduous, dry deciduous, very dry deciduous, and desert. A sixth category, hill and mountain forest above 800 meters in altitude, can include forests with wet, moist, or dry characteristics. (See Chapter 19, "Forests and Rangelands," Table 19.2.)

Over the past decade, the greatest loss of forest area in the tropics has occurred in easily accessible lowland forests, with 6.1 million hectares (1 percent) of moist deciduous forest and 4.6 million hectares (0.6 percent) of rainforest disappearing annually.

Deforestation in rainforest and moist deciduous forest areas is of global significance because it affects regions rich in biodiversity. The removal of forests in dry areas depletes already scarce resources such as fuelwood and fodder. Evidence from the Sahel region of the Sahara suggests that the availability of forest resources is critical in determining the carrying capacity of its agricultural and pastoral communities (12).

Rainforest. Roughly 0.6 percent of the world's rainforest—4.6 million hectares—is lost annually. Asia leads losses with 2.2 million hectares per year. Latin America and the Caribbean convert 1.9 million hectares and Africa 470,000 hectares of rainforest per year (13).

Two countries, Indonesia and Brazil, each losing perhaps 1 million hectares annually over the last decade, account for about 45 percent of the world's total loss of rainforest (14). (See Figure 7.3.)

Moist deciduous forest. About 6.1 million hectares (1 percent) of moist deciduous forest disappeared annually between 1980 and 1990. The largest regional share

of this loss was seen in Latin America and the Caribbean (3.2 million hectares per year). Africa followed, experiencing an annual loss of 2.2 million hectares, while the Asia and Pacific region lost 660,000 hectares.

Brazil (1.7 million hectares per year) and Bolivia (440,000 hectares per year) accounted for 35 percent of annual average global loss of moist deciduous forest. The addition of Venezuela and Zaire brings this percentage up to 45 percent (15). (See Figure 7.4.)

Dry deciduous forest. Brazil (310,000 hectares) and India (210,000 hectares) are reported to have lost the most forestland in this class over the last decade. Together with Sudan and Paraguay, they account for more than 40 percent of the global average of 1.8 million hectares in this ecozone (16). (See Figure 7.5.)

Very dry forest. Annual global deforestation for the very dry forest zone is 341,000 hectares. Sudan loses the most in this category (81,000 hectares per year), followed by Botswana (58,000 hectares). Along with a third African country, Tanzania (41,000 hectares), their contribution to the global deforestation of this type of forest is 53 percent (17).

Desert forest. Global annual deforestation for this category is currently estimated at 82,000 hectares. Two countries, Mexico with 35,000 hectares and Pakistan with 16,000 hectares per year, are responsible for about 60 percent of that total (18).

Hill and montane forest. Hills and mountains lose about 2.5 million hectares of forestland a year, with Brazil (640,000 hectares per year), Mexico (370,000 hectares), and Indonesia (150,000 hectares) accounting for 46 percent of the total global loss. (See Figure 7.6.) Of all zones, the hill and montane zone is experiencing the fastest rate of loss (1.1 percent). At the end of 1990, 29 percent of the world's hill and montane zone was covered by forest (19). If slopes are left without protective ground cover, runoff and soil erosion can increase.

Figure 7.6 Tropical Montane Forest Lost, 1981–90: Percentage Share of Top Five Countries

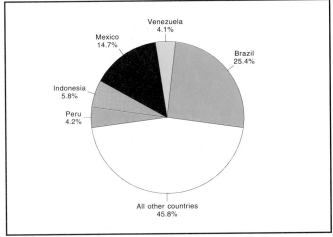

Source: Food and Agriculture Organization of the United Nations (FAO), *Forest Resources Assessment, 1990: Tropical Countries,* FAO Forestry Paper 112 (FAO, Rome, 1993), Tables 8a, 8b, and 8c.

Degradation and Fragmentation

Evidence from Brazil and West Africa suggests that forest degradation and fragmentation may play a more important role than outright conversion of forestland to other uses in the loss of wooded habitat.

Degradation and fragmentation of remaining forests can magnify the impact of deforestation on biodiversity. Degradation can result in the removal of plants and trees important in the life cycle of other species, erosion, changes in the local environment, and other processes adversely affecting local wildlife. Fragmentation can result in patches of habitat that are too small to support remaining populations of resident plants and animals (20).

In Africa, forest conversion from 1980 to 1990 accounted for only about one fourth of the changes in forest cover. During that time, a higher percentage of forest was deforested, fragmented, and degraded in Africa's moist lowland zone than in the dry lowland and moist mountain zones. This was the result of agricultural activity and higher population densities in the moist lowland zone (21).

A U.S. National Aeronautics and Space Administration study of deforestation and fragmentation in the Brazilian Amazon Basin from 1978 to 1988 found that only 39 percent of the altered forest habitat came from outright conversion to other uses. Some 58 percent of the altered habitat occurred through exposure to newly cleared areas. Forest edges are vulnerable to degradation and species loss resulting from microclimate changes, disturbance by humans, and invading edge species. The remaining 3 percent of forest habitat alteration resulted from fragmentation (22).

Brazil and West Africa show distinctive fragmentation patterns. In most of West Africa, once closed forests are now small forest islands surrounded by cropland. In the Brazilian Amazon, deforestation is moving from the edges to the center; fragmentation patterns are determined by the creation of roads and the conversion of land for grazing and other uses (23).

Figure 7.7 Tropical Forest Biomass by Ecoregion, Continental Asia, 1990

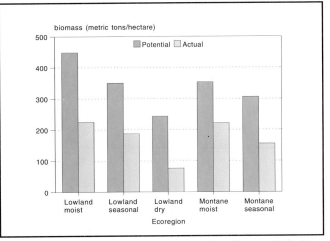

Source: Food and Agriculture Organization of the United Nations (FAO), *Forest Resources Assessment, 1990: Tropical Countries,* FAO Forestry Paper 112 (FAO, Rome, 1993), p. 33.

Preliminary results of the FAO's remote sensing sample sites for Brazil and Asia indicate that changes in continuous forest cover are occurring there at much higher rates than in Africa, as a result of high population densities, planned resettlements, and resource exploitation, among other factors. In Brazil, almost all of the changes in forest area have resulted from direct conversion to nonwooded area, while data suggest that in Africa and Asia, a more gradual process of fragmentation and degradation is taking place (24).

The FAO's specific study on the process of deforestation and forest degradation on the African continent is based on 31 samples of satellite data. These samples, each covering one image taken around 1980 and another around 1990, are a broad representation of the ecological forest conditions on that continent. An analysis of the samples found that about 8.4 percent of the closed forest cover was altered over that 10-year period. Of that, 34.1 percent went into short-fallow agriculture, primarily a result of increased resource pressure from rural populations; 24.8 percent degraded to open forest; 16.1 percent was converted for other land uses such as permanent agriculture; and 19 percent became fragmented forest, a result of clearing many small tracts of land dispersed in the original closed-forest area (25).

The FAO attempted to get a broader picture of changes in forest resources by examining continuous forest, which includes closed forest, open forest, and areas that lie fallow for long periods. The analysis found that about 8.7 percent of all continuous forest had changed over the 10-year period, but that roughly half of this area had changed in ways—from closed to fragmented forest, for example—that might not be counted in deforestation estimates (26).

Biomass Changes

Though lacking forest inventory data that would provide reliable estimates of woody biomass volume and change, the FAO nevertheless provided estimates for

Figure 7.8 Tropical Forest Management by Region

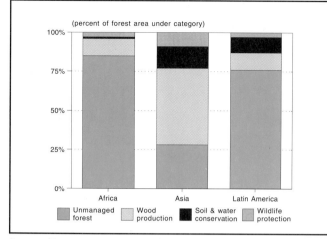

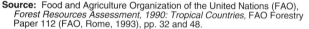

Source: Food and Agriculture Organization of the United Nations (FAO), *Forest Resources Assessment, 1990: Tropical Countries,* FAO Forestry Paper 112 (FAO, Rome, 1993), pp. 32 and 48.

Figure 7.9 Production of Nonconiferous Industrial Roundwood in the Tropics, 1961–90

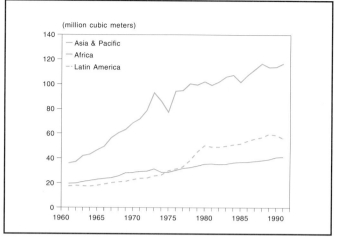

Source: Food and Agriculture Organization of the United Nations (FAO), *Agrostat PC,* on diskette (FAO, Rome, 1993).

above-ground biomass by converting available forestry information (on a volume-per-unit area) to biomass density and total biomass. These figures have to be interpreted with caution, because the underlying data are usually rough estimates and because the reliability of factors and weights used to convert volumes to biomass is unknown.

Global loss of above-ground biomass from deforestation is estimated at 2.5 gigatons per year. About 50 percent of the loss occurs in Latin America, 30 percent in Asia, and 20 percent in Africa. A comparison of potential and actual biomass of tropical forestland in Asia shows a 50 percent reduction for most ecological zones. The greatest reduction, almost 70 percent, occurred in lowland dry forests in continental Asia. A reduction in potential biomass can be interpreted as a surrogate measure of degradation (27). (See Figure 7.7.)

Forest Management and Wood Production

About 30 percent (522 million hectares) of tropical forest cover is under some sort of management. Asia has demarcated 49 percent of its forestland for wood production, while Latin America and Africa have each set aside 11 percent. About 14 percent of Asian forestland is managed to protect soil and hydrological functions. In Latin America, this share is 10 percent, while in Africa, it is around 1 percent.

Asia has the largest percentage of forest area set aside for wildlife protection (9 percent); Africa and Latin America each have about 3 percent of their forest designated for the same purpose (28). (See Figure 7.8.)

Logging has increased in all three tropical regions—Africa, Asia, and Latin America—with a consistent rise in both total area logged and total volume of wood removed (29). The removal of trees, depending on the intensity of harvesting and the terrain, causes immediate damage to surrounding forest and soil and can have long-term effects on the ecosystem, for example, increasing remaining forestland's vulnerability to storms and fires (30) (31).

The volume of industrial roundwood production has grown steadily in Asia and Latin America, while Africa seems to have reached a plateau at 40 million cubic meters per year. (See Figure 7.9.) Globally, 5.9 million hectares are logged annually in the tropics, with the greatest loss occurring in primary forests (4.9 million hectares). Over the past 30 years, the area of primary forests logged yearly has more than doubled, while logging in secondary forests has increased by a factor of 4.5. (See Figures 7.10A, B, and C.) Commercial timber harvest volume, on the average, is highest in Asia (33 cubic meters per hectare), followed by Africa (14 cubic meters per hectare) and Latin America (8 cubic meters per hectare) (32).

Plantations

The FAO estimates that there are 43.8 million hectares of industrial and nonindustrial forest plantations in the tropical zone. Five countries—India, Indonesia, Brazil, Viet Nam, and Thailand—are home to 85 percent of these plantations.

To calculate a global average survival rate for plantation seedlings of 70 percent, the FAO used survival rates from 56 plantation inventories. This reduces the figure for total global net plantation area at the end of 1990 to 30.7 million hectares. The FAO estimates that 2.6 million hectares of new plantations appear yearly, of which about 1.8 million survive. Plantations are planted primarily with eucalyptus, pine, teak, and acacia trees (33).

On average, 6 hectares are deforested per year for every hectare put into forest plantations. The ratio of deforestation to established plantation is 32:1 for Africa, 2:1 for Asia, and 6:1 for Latin America. The exceptions are India, which plants four times the area that it deforests annually, and Cuba and Haiti, where the area of annual deforestation is about the same as the area of new plantations (34).

The creation of forest plantations to produce tropical timber can bring economic benefits and provide some ecosystem services, such as watershed and soil protection, especially if suitable tree species are planted on previously degraded land. However, when tree monocultures replace native forests, much of an area's biodiversity is lost. The FAO could not decide if plantations were established on forested or nonforested land (35).

TEMPERATE FORESTS

Estimates of Area and Change

At the end of 1990, just about half of the world's forests were located in the industrialized countries of the temperate zone. Another 7 percent were in other temperate countries, including China, Mongolia, Argentina, and Chile. The remainder, 43 percent, could be found in the tropics (36).

Almost 40 percent of the land in the FAO's temperate forest study was classified as forest and other wooded land. Of the 2,063 million hectares of forest covering industrialized countries, over two thirds were in three countries: the republics of the former Soviet Union (941 million hectares), Canada (453 million hectares), and the United States (296 million hectares).

The forest resources of the 34 countries covered in the FAO study differ greatly. In some countries—including Iceland, Ireland, the Netherlands, and the United Kingdom—less than 10 percent of the land is forested; in others, such as Japan, Sweden, and Finland, more than 60 percent is forested. Canada has the most forest area per person (17 hectares), while the Netherlands has the least (0.02 hectares per person) (37).

The FAO could not provide conclusive estimates of the changes in total forest area for the temperate zone. However, it was able to calculate changes in forest cover for Europe, where it is estimated that total wooded area expanded by 2 million hectares between 1980 and 1990. Additional data imply that forest area increased in the former Soviet Union, and declined slightly in the United States, Japan, and Canada. This suggests a net increase in forest area in the temperate zone over the past decade (38).

Paralleling this expansion in area has been a long-term increase in forest volume and biomass. Thus, in global terms, temperate forests in industrialized countries have been a net carbon sink over the past decade.

Degradation

The total increase in forest biomass and area in the temperate zone over the past decade masks forest degradation occurring in some areas and the disappearance of old-growth forests.

The degree of degradation for European forests is assessed annually by the Economic Commission for Europe (ECE) and the European Community (EC). A 1991 ECE/EC survey estimated that 22.2 percent of European trees showed moderate to severe defoliation, up from 20.8 percent in 1990. Scientists believe that forest decline is caused by factors such as air pollutants, pests, drought, and nutrient loss. The relative contribution of different factors varies from country to country, depending on conditions such as soil type (39).

Figure 7.10 Tropical Forest Area Logged, 1961–90

A. Asia and the Pacific Region

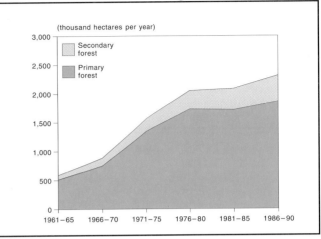

B. Africa

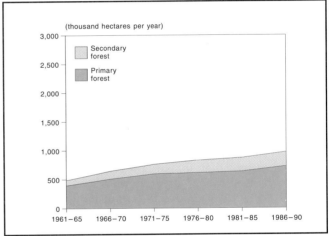

C. South America

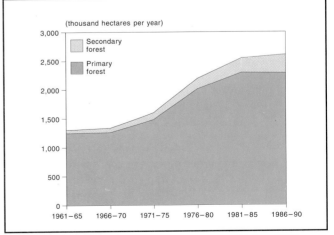

Source: Food and Agriculture Organization of the United Nations (FAO), *Forest Resources Assessment, 1990: Tropical Countries,* FAO Forestry Paper 112 (FAO, Rome, 1993), pp. 53–54.

Quantitative information on the extent of global old-growth forest is scarce and not part of any global or regional monitoring effort, though rough estimates exist for some countries. No generally accepted definition of old-growth forest exists. Usually, forests that have a natural variation of tree species and include trees over 200 years old are defined as old-growth. Old-growth forests are important for biodiversity conservation, as they are an important habitat for many species (40).

Most experts believe that about 1 percent of Western Europe's forests can be classified as old-growth, most of it now in small isolated remnants. Central and Eastern Europe and the Baltic states retain slightly more old-growth forest. Other temperate regions still have comparatively large tracts. Thirteen percent of the forests in the northwest United States are old growth, 40 percent in Canada's British Columbia, 25 percent in New Zealand, 5–20 percent in Australia, and significant tracts in northern Russia and Siberia. Little of the old-growth in temperate regions is fully protected (41).

INSTITUTIONAL DEVELOPMENTS

The development of international institutions to protect the world's forests is a source of considerable debate and uncertainty. Existing institutions have been heavily criticized and weakened to a point where there is no clear institutional leadership on forest issues at the global level; at the same time, there is little agreement on the shape or structure of new institutions.

Within the United Nations, the acknowledged leader on forestry issues has been the FAO, which took the lead role in the management of the Tropical Forestry Action Plan (TFAP). TFAP was launched in June 1985. The plan established a forum for development agencies to coordinate their forestry programs and a process whereby tropical countries could formulate their own programs. It was hoped programs would be funded by the development agencies. But many national plans were criticized for ignoring the policy-related and root causes of deforestation; donor funding did not materialize as expected, and TFAP was criticized for having—at best—a modest impact on reducing deforestation. As an effort to reduce tropical deforestation globally, TFAP seems to have lost most of its momentum, but it remains important as a mechanism to coordinate donor actions at the national level in countries where programs are under way (42).

The International Tropical Timber Agreement (ITTA) and its coordinating body, the International Tropical Timber Organization, were established to protect the future of the tropical timber trade, encourage nontimber products and services, and conserve forest ecosystems. In 1993, ITTA was being renegotiated, and there was heated debate over whether in the future it should include all timbers. Brazil, Malaysia, and some Northern nongovernmental organizations (NGOs) supported this proposal; consumer countries were generally opposed (43).

The 1992 United Nations Conference on Environment and Development (UNCED) provided a focal point of sorts for institutional developments on forests. UNCED's statement of forest principles, various chapters of Agenda 21, and the conventions on climate change and biodiversity all reinforce the critical role of forests in the overall fabric of sustainable development. The United Nations Commission on Sustainable Development, created to monitor progress on environmental and development issues, is expected to review progress on forestry issues in 1997.

In the meantime, a coalition that includes prominent citizens from both tropical and temperate countries and leading scientists in climate change and forestry has proposed the creation of an independent world commission on forests and sustainable development. The U.N. secretary general would appoint the chairman and vice chairman of the commission, who would in turn appoint the other 20 to 25 members (44).

Helped by a small secretariat and using U.N. information resources, the commission would have a broad mandate. It would look at the economic, social, ecological, and political issues associated with forests; propose ways to strengthen sources of data on forests; explore means of improving international economic relations, so as to reduce pressure on forests; and examine existing forms of international cooperation. Its findings would be submitted to the United Nations in time for the 1997 review of forest principles. The commission could also serve as a negotiating forum for international forestry agreements (45).

Meanwhile, commercial and economic pressures related to forestry are intensifying. For example, many countries are considering bans on imports from tropical forests that do not carry an environmental label. Such nontariff barriers could violate the UNCED statement of forest principles, according to which "trade in forest products should be based on nondiscriminatory and multilaterally agreed rules and procedures consistent with international trade law and practices" (46). To deal with this problem, the recently inaugurated Forest Stewardship Council (FSC)—a diverse body that includes forest industry representatives, environmentalists, and indigenous peoples—is generating a set of principles and criteria that would define forest stewardship. The FSC would accredit local certification programs regarding forest products.

The FSC program could help consumers determine the validity of certification claims. Though it faces a series of difficult political and technical hurdles, the FSC could become a major independent force leading the way to timber certification worldwide (47).

A great deal of activity is also taking place at the national and local level. Many international NGOs are trying to encourage partnerships with groups in developing countries to replace the traditional donor-recipient approach to managing forestry. Many countries also are attempting to decentralize their efforts, for example, by encouraging local initiatives in sustainable forestry management.

FOCUS ON NORTH AMERICAN RANGELANDS

North American range conditions are reported to be on a par with or slightly better than those elsewhere.

Nearly all the world's rangelands except those in the Arctic have been substantially degraded by livestock grazing, the introduction of exotic species, fuelwood harvesting, suppression of the natural fire cycle, wildlife depredation, and conversion to cropland or housing. (See Figure 7.11.) Rangelands in North America, however, are not subject to the same uncontrolled access and population pressures as in many developing countries. Thus the outlook is more favorable for reversing negative trends and restoring degraded sites. Even so, because of past management practices, it is likely that many of the continent's rangelands will never regain their former ecological complexity (48).

The term *rangeland* refers to land on which native vegetation is predominantly grasses, forbs, and shrubs, plants well suited as forage for wildlife and livestock (49) (50). North American rangelands are typically located in arid or semiarid climates, most notably in the West where annual rainfall averages 50 centimeters or less. Western rangelands occur in shortgrass prairies and other natural grasslands, shrublands, savannahs, deserts, alpine meadows, coastal marshes, and wet meadows. Rangelands occur in the eastern half of the continent as wet meadows, tallgrass prairies, mountain balds, and marshes. Extensive rangelands also cover the northern tier of the continent in the form of tundra (51).

In addition to these natural rangelands, many forest habitats have been converted to permanent pasture or grassland, which provides substantial forage and can be considered rangeland. In fact, the well-watered pastures of the eastern continent, largely converted forestlands, are many times more productive on a biomass-per-hectare basis than the arid western range. Most forestlands also support a rich understory of grasses, shrubs, and forbs, contributing to the total range forage available (52).

EXTENT AND USE

Land managed as rangeland makes up one third of the land base of the United States—some 312 million hectares (770 million acres) (53). About two thirds of this rangeland is privately owned or under state or local government control. The remaining one third, about 112 million hectares (276 million acres), is federally owned public range and usually includes the more arid or less productive sites (54).

In the 48 contiguous states, many tracts of public rangeland are leased by private grazing interests under a permit system; private rangeland is also largely used for commercial grazing. In fact, for the last 130 years North American rangeland, except in the Arctic, has been used primarily for livestock grazing (55). Such grazing has been and continues to be one of the most ubiquitous agents of ecological change on North American rangeland, particularly in the arid West (56). In the southwestern United States, for example, 85 percent of all land is considered rangeland, and livestock graze 90 percent of it (57). Not surprisingly, the condition of southwestern rangeland has reflected the evolution in range management practices over the years.

Figure 7.11 Range Degradation Since 1945

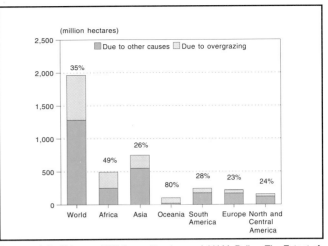

Source: L.R. Oldeman, V.W.P. van Engelen, and J.H.M. Pulles, The Extent of Human-Induced Soil Degradation," Annex 5 of L.R. Oldeman, R.T.A. Hakkeling, and W.G. Sombroek, *World Map of the Status of Human-Induced Soil Degradation: An Explanatory Note*, rev. 2nd edition (International Soil Reference and Information Centre, Wageningen, the Netherlands, 1990), as presented in *World Resources 1992–93*, Table 19.4, p. 290.
Note: Percentages indicate contribution of overgrazing to total degraded area.

Alaskan rangeland covers about 80 million hectares (200 million acres). A small portion of that is grazed by domesticated reindeer, but most is used exclusively by wildlife (58).

In Canada, rangeland suitable for livestock is far less extensive than in the United States—about 28.1 million hectares (69.4 million acres) (59)—but significant areas of tundra provide forage for deer, caribou, elk, and other wildlife species. Most managed ranges, some two thirds, are on public land in southern Canada under lease to private ranchers. This land is generally administered at the provincial level, with limited input from the federal government (60) (61) (62).

Though North American livestock include sheep, goats, horses, and reindeer, cattle are by far the most numerous. U.S. cattle, numbering more than 100 million (including dairy cows), account for over 95 percent of all annual forage consumption by U.S. livestock (63). Canadian range supports 13 million cattle (64).

Rangeland also provides essential habitat for a wide variety of wildlife and plant species. Native range ecosystems, even many disturbed sites, typically exhibit surprising biodiversity. For example, plant surveys have identified more than 400 plant species on some remnant tallgrass prairie sites (65). (See Figure 7.12.) Though modern ranges are hardly pristine, their importance to wildlife is nonetheless paramount. An estimated 84 percent of mammal species and 74 percent of the bird species found in the United States are associated with rangeland ecosystems (66) (67).

In addition, rangelands act as critical watersheds throughout North America, providing both surface and groundwater resources as they absorb and slowly release rainfall. The current impetus to improve the continent's range conditions largely stems from a desire to restore the functions of watersheds. Overgrazing has compromised the soil's ability to absorb rain and resulted in excessive runoff, erosion, siltation, and flooding (68) (69) (70).

Figure 7.12 U.S. Nationally Threatened Plants by Ecosystem Type, 1990

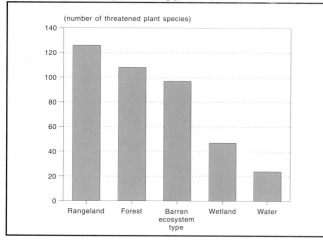

(number of threatened plant species)

Source: Curtis A. Flather, Linda A. Joyce, and Carol A. Bloomgarden, "Species Endangerment Patterns in the United States," U.S. Department of Agriculture (USDA), Forest Service Technical Report 241, USDA, Fort Collins, Colorado, 1994, Table 3.

Finally, rangeland is a valuable resource for recreation. While the use of rangeland to produce livestock forage has declined somewhat over the last two decades, its use for activities such as hunting, hiking, and camping has risen dramatically. In fact, management plans for public rangeland now often sanction recreational use and sometimes recognize it as a significant source of income for local economies (71) (72).

EARLY ABUSE OF RANGELAND

In general, North American range conditions reflect a pattern of early abuse by cattlemen and sheep herders, followed by slow recovery as ranching and public land management practices improved. According to some reports, rangelands are in better shape today than at any time this century, but many are still degraded (73) (74) (75). Several studies indicate that western rangelands now produce less than half of the livestock forage they produced before the advent of commercial grazing (76).

The results of abusive grazing practices, particularly on arid western rangeland, are well chronicled. Drawn by lush grasslands and mountain meadows, ranchers increased their herds in the late 1800s to well above the land's long-term carrying capacity. Unrestricted, year-round grazing on overstocked ranges, exacerbated by drought, denuded uplands and subjected them to severe erosion (77) (78) (79). With livestock trampling along waterways and sediment washed from bare slopes, riparian areas were also left decimated (80).

On many rangelands, soil compaction and reduced plant cover from overgrazing decreased the soil's ability to absorb infrequent rain and started a general drying trend. Lower water tables and a decreased flow are common symptoms of this phenomenon in many western waterways (81) (82).

In many areas, changes in plant cover, documented by photos and historic accounts, have been dramatic. Grazing virtually wiped out native perennial grasses in some rangelands, allowing shrubby vegetation such as sagebrush, mesquite, and juniper, plants whose deep roots can lower water tables and alter the local hydrological balance, to move in. The disruption of the natural fire cycle, which acted as a check on shrub invasion, exacerbated this trend (83) (84).

Laws restricting grazing were eventually enacted in the United States and Canada. More influential was the soil conservation movement of the 1930s, spurred by the disastrous Dust Bowl era and the bitter lessons it taught about farming and ranching arid lands. Conservationists began to refine range science and livestock management to prevent further damage and allow the land to heal.

However, the arid lands of the West often recover slowly, as harsh temperatures and scant rainfall make the growing season short (85) (86). While improvement is expected, experts agree that many North American ranges, having suffered the loss of soil and native species and the invasion of exotic species, will never fully return to their former condition (87) (88).

In general, the potential for recovery of Canadian rangelands may be somewhat higher. Settlement of the Canadian frontier occurred somewhat later, and abusive grazing was short-lived (from the early 1900s to the 1940s), less widespread, and less damaging than in the United States (89).

MONITORING RANGE CONDITIONS

Interpreting current range conditions and trends is controversial. Rangeland monitoring data are often incomplete or questionable. Local rangeland data in the United States have been collected sporadically because of tight budgets and limited personnel; evaluations of some sites are more than 20 years old (90).

In Canada, formal assessments are carried out on most provincial rangeland, but the methods, intensity, and frequency of monitoring vary. No monitoring system is in place for private land, and there is no federal or even provincial database of range conditions to give an overview of data collected locally or regionally (91).

Also, there has been disagreement over just how to evaluate range status. Early on, it was judged only by the land's ability to produce livestock forage. Now, managers use a system based on the ecological status of a site (92) (93).

Ecological status is determined by comparing a site's present vegetation—species composition, diversity, distribution, and quantity—to its "potential natural community" or "climax community," that is, the vegetation that would dominate the site over time in the absence of human interference. A rating of excellent, good, fair, or poor is assigned, based on how closely the range vegetation resembles the climax condition. Excellent equals 76–100 percent climax vegetation; good, 51–75 percent; fair, 26–50 percent; and poor, 0–25 percent (94) (95).

This method of quantifying ecological status is based on the theory, adopted some 40 years ago, that rangeland not covered in climax vegetation follows a fairly predictable path of plant succession that ultimately reestablishes the climax community. The expectation, then, is that rangeland in poor or fair condition will naturally progress toward the original climax community if managed correctly.

Within the last several years, this approach, while still the basis of most range data, has come under increasing attack. Some range managers complain that it is based on a faulty ecological model, does not accurately reflect range conditions, and compares against a standard—the original mix of plants—no longer attainable in many cases.

Critics contend that soil loss, the local extinction of some plant species, and the widespread invasion of exotic plant and animal species have effectively established a new climax state for some ranges. These areas may never reach their former climax state, no matter how well managed. However, if managed properly, they may produce sufficient plant cover to protect soil, provide forage and habitat for some animal species, and preserve watershed functions (96) (97).

Plant succession theory, the underpinning of the current ecological status method of range evaluation, is now challenged by the "stable state and transition" model. This holds that various stable states, or stable vegetation communities, can exist on a site depending on the combined effect of natural forces such as fire, grazing, rainfall, and other factors. According to this theory, if an environmental disruption occurs—drought or overgrazing, for instance—it may push a rangeland over the threshold to a new stable state, and natural processes will not necessarily return it to its former state. In other words, a single climax community does not define natural succession. It may proceed along several alternate paths, depending on the circumstances. This model is particularly applicable to many arid or mountain rangelands, where crucial climatic variables like rainfall and fire oscillate widely from year to year (98) (99).

In response to these concerns, the U.S. Forest Service and the U.S. Bureau of Land Management are shifting to an assessment system based on the "desired plant community" for each range. The desired plant community is determined by considering the original climax vegetation, the site's potential, and possible "resource outputs" from a given range—for example, livestock and wildlife forage, wildlife habitat, and watershed preservation. Range conditions are, then, judged as either satisfactory or unsatisfactory relative to the desired plant community (100) (101) (102).

Some environmentalists and many range managers fear that a monitoring system based on desired plant communities could discount the degraded condition of some ranges unless ecological criteria—rather than commodity factors such as maximizing livestock forage—are the primary basis for defining the desired plant community (103).

CURRENT RANGE STATUS

Disputes over evaluation methods aside, the most reliable and comprehensive data currently available on rangeland still follow the ecological status model. These data reveal that only a small portion, about 4 percent, of nonarctic rangeland in the United States is in excellent condition (i.e., covered in climax vegeta-

tion). Most rangeland in the United States is in good or fair condition, but a significant portion, about 15 percent, is categorized as poor.

Conditions in Canada reportedly follow this general pattern as well. Few Canadian rangelands are in excellent condition, while roughly two thirds are in good or fair condition (104) (105) (106).

Data on range trends—if a site is moving toward or away from climax conditions—measure how well rangelands are being managed. Plant vigor, species composition, vegetational litter cover, abundance of seedlings, invasion of weed species, and the condition of the soil surface are all important in assessing whether a range is deteriorating or recuperating (107).

About 86 percent of U.S. rangelands either are moving toward climax condition, are stable, or exhibit no discernible trend, while 14 percent are declining in status. The highest percentage of deteriorating ranges exist in the most arid regions, the Southwest and the Great Basin. Though no data are available on Canadian range trends, again the pattern is expected to reflect what exists in the United States, with the majority of ranges stable or improving but a significant percentage still declining (108).

Arctic rangelands are generally in excellent ecological condition because of remoteness and limited commercial grazing. In Alaska, where commercial reindeer herds once numbered 600,000 head, some overgrazing has occurred on lichen rangelands but only in small pockets. The current reindeer population is about 35,000 on the Seward Peninsula and nearby islands, and most rangelands in fair and poor condition are said to be improving (109).

How figures are used to evaluate overall range health often depends on who is doing the analysis. Livestock trade organizations and federal agencies responsible for public range management usually interpret trends as positive, to show that progress is being made, if slowly, in rehabilitating degraded ranges. For example, the Bureau of Land Management, which administers many of the public ranges in the western United States, reports that the condition of its ranges has improved over the last 50 years: the range area in excellent or good condition has doubled since 1936, while the area in poor condition has shrunk by half (110). Veteran ecologists and government range specialists often report overall improvement in conditions in many areas (111) (112).

Many environmentalists and other critics of range management policies feel the numbers deliver a more sober message: that more than 50 percent of U.S. range is still producing at less than half its former potential after more than 50 years of management ostensibly directed toward recovery and sustainable use. Progress on the range, critics contend, has fallen far short of the stated goals, with wildlife and watersheds still suffering and substantial acreage declining because of the continued overgrazing (113).

REASONS FOR CONTINUED RANGE DECLINE

The continued decline in some rangeland conditions can be attributed in large part to improper livestock management. Detrimental policies include overstocking (too many animals for the available feed), uneven grazing so that some areas are more adversely affected than others, and heavy year-round grazing that leaves range plants no time for regrowth and reproduction.

In a 1988 analysis, the U.S. General Accounting Office (GAO) reported that approximately 20 percent of the grazing parcels on federal land were overstocked, and that these areas were much more likely to be deteriorating (114). Likewise, the U.S. Soil Conservation Service reported in 1987 that conditions on one third of private U.S. rangeland—some 54 million hectares (134 million acres)—could be improved by controlling livestock numbers and adjusting when and how long the animals graze (115).

Drought, which has plagued western states for much of the last decade, can greatly accelerate range decline by diminishing forage supplies. Another threat is crossbreeding, which has made the average cow 15–30 percent larger over the past few decades and raised the risk of overstocking. To meet higher feed requirements, ranchers must either reduce the number of livestock or increase the production of forage (116) (117).

Experts also attribute some loss of range productivity to continued brush invasion, which is especially severe on western rangeland now that the incidence of wildfire has been reduced (118).

Most artificial brush removal efforts, employing herbicides or tractors, were curtailed in the 1970s because of environmental and financial costs. Even prescribed burning, the least expensive and most environmentally acceptable control technique, faces new restrictions owing to the effects of smoke on air quality (119). Researchers estimate that approximately 40.5 million hectares (100 million acres) of western range are threatened by sagebrush or juniper encroachment (120).

LIVESTOCK GRAZING AND WILDLIFE

While livestock grazing—with proper monitoring—may be compatible with maintaining good wildlife habitat, over the years its influence on wildlife has generally been negative (121) (122) (123).

Steep declines in wildlife numbers, particularly of large game animals such as bison, elk, and antelope, accompanied the settlement of the Great Plains and other western ranges. The initial cause was overhunting and conversion of native habitat to cropland. The subsequent establishment of the livestock industry, requiring direct competition for forage resources and habitat, helped keep these numbers low (124).

Although livestock numbers are down today, competition with wildlife still exists. Cattle and sheep, fairly adaptable, wide-spectrum foragers, outcompete many wild species whose food needs are more restrictive. Nonetheless, because of less hunting, fewer cattle, and a general improvement in habitat and increased forage, populations of some game animals have gained over the past few decades (125) (126).

In some respects, however, this limited success has only highlighted the inherent conflicts between wildlife and grazing interests when resources are limited. For instance, in recent years elk numbers have risen

sharply in several areas, causing problems even on ranges where livestock are managed well (127) (128).

Large game animals are not the only species to suffer. Overgrazing has profoundly upset the dynamics of many range ecosystems, reducing biodiversity and altering the feeding and breeding patterns of birds, small mammals, reptiles, and insects (129) (130) (131).

Perhaps the single greatest conflict between wildlife and livestock is the widespread disruption of riparian areas by poorly managed cattle (132). Livestock can degrade riparian zones by overgrazing and trampling streamside vegetation, destroying banks and thereby increasing sediment levels and bacterial counts in the water, and raising water temperatures. Thus forage and cover are reduced, along with the ability of fish and other aquatic organisms to spawn (133). Such damage has helped make fish species the fastest-disappearing wildlife group in the United States (134).

Fortunately, riparian zones can be restored. Fencing to restrict stream access and developing off-stream watering sites to accommodate livestock are two common measures for initiating recovery. In many cases, partial livestock use can eventually be resumed. However, permanent closure of the stream zone may be required if livestock cannot be tightly controlled (135).

Sometimes recovery is rapid and remarkable. Once grazing is controlled, stream banks may stabilize within a few years and then exhibit a gradual rise in forage production, as fish populations in the stream revive. This happened in Bear Creek, Oregon, after grazing duration and timing were adjusted to fit the mountain pasture site; within a decade, forage increased fivefold and rainbow trout returned. Sometimes a stream that has been intermittent or just a trickle for decades resumes a continuous flow as the natural sponge of the riparian zone is rejuvenated (136).

In many instances, recovery is a long-term process that may never result in complete restoration, especially if adjacent upland ranges remain in poor condition, pouring runoff and sediment into the vulnerable riparian zone (137). For lasting riparian recovery, there must be a larger recovery effort aimed at improving range conditions in the entire watershed (138).

Livestock grazing can also drastically affect the distribution of some species. In the United States, for example, the conversion of grassland to shrubland has eliminated the pronghorn antelope from much of its range in the Southwest and helped reduce bighorn sheep to remnant herds throughout the West (139).

The irrigation of pasture to support livestock in arid areas is another indirect influence on wildlife prospects. When water is diverted for irrigation, the levels of western streams are lowered and the supply available to wildlife is reduced (140) (141).

Other activities associated with livestock grazing are particularly hard on some wildlife species. Among the worst are longstanding government-sponsored programs of predator control that have decimated numerous populations such as wolves and mountain lions (142). In the name of protecting livestock, thousands of animals are killed annually without regard to their larger ecological roles and effect on other wildlife spe-

Box 7.1 Short-Duration Grazing: Reclaiming or Ruining the Range?

Short-duration grazing is rotational grazing in which a range is divided into many pastures that are each grazed intensively for just a few days, then rested for a period of many weeks. The most common form of short-duration grazing—and easily the most controversial grazing system today—is known as the Savory grazing method or, more recently, as holistic resource management (HRM) (1) (2).

Originated by wildlife biologist Allan Savory on the veld of Zimbabwe, HRM postulates that periods of intense grazing are actually necessary to restore most degraded rangelands. Rest alone does not bring recovery; instead, it is unnatural and will harm the range (3). Savory believes that the close cropping, extensive trampling, and concentrated dropping of urine and dung associated with intense but brief grazing replicate the natural-use pattern of large mammals such as bison and elk that once roamed the range in herds. According to HRM advocates, this "herd effect" stimulates range plants by fertilizing them and brushing off dead leaf matter that might otherwise give too much shade. Moreover, the argument goes, concentrated trampling increases water infiltration by breaking up crusts on the surface (4) (5) (6) (7).

The most controversial aspect of the HRM method is that, in most cases, it calls for more livestock to produce the herd effects. Disagreeing that many rangelands are overstocked, Savory believes that understocking has actually helped degrade rangelands: small numbers of continuously grazing cattle, widely dispersed, promote overgrazing without providing the benefits of the herd effect. Higher stock rates would be supported by the fuller use of all available forage—forage that ordinarily would not be consumed by more wide-ranging livestock (8) (9).

Advocates are careful to point out that the intensive grazing practices of HRM are just part of a larger system of land management whose goal is to adopt a whole-ecosystem approach to ranching. Continuous monitoring of range conditions and adjustment to changing conditions such as drought are prominent features of the HRM approach (10) (11).

Advocates of HRM claim impressive results, including increased forage production, improved wildlife habitat, and rejuvenation of shrub-infested areas without the use of herbicides. For example, after four years of holistic management, owners of one ranch in Nevada reported 87 percent less bare ground in areas they monitored, more wildlife diversity, better

water retention, significantly more riparian vegetation, and restoration of perennial grasses—all during a drought (12) (13).

Most evidence for the success of HRM grazing methods remains anecdotal. Meanwhile, published reports critical of these methods have accumulated. For example, research on the effect of frequent livestock trampling shows increased erosion and declining water infiltration. Other research suggests that there is no apparent difference between short-duration grazing and other grazing systems in terms of their effect on the quantity of vegetation growth and cover. This is not surprising, detractors of HRM say, because the major factor limiting forage growth on arid ranges is precipitation, not shading or other phenomena that HRM grazing seeks to influence (14) (15) (16).

Many environmentalists are harsher in their criticism of HRM. Despite its high-minded goals, they complain, it is being used by some as an unscientific excuse to run larger numbers of cattle on already overstocked rangelands (17). The extensive fencing required for HRM grazing is also a cause for concern, especially on public rangeland, both because it may restrict the movement of wildlife and because it blocks recreational access. Also, with additional animals on the range, damage can occur more quickly, and be more severe if stock is not moved on schedule (18).

Public range managers and many range scientists are more neutral in their appraisal of HRM grazing, and comment that the system has merit but is not universally applicable (19) (20) (21). Some believe HRM may work better on plains, where moisture is higher, plants grow faster, and heavy-grazing bison once lived. It may be less appropriate west of the Rockies, where there is no historic evidence of high-impact grazing (22) (23).

Others speculate that if there is benefit in Savory's system, it may come not from intensive grazing, but from the ecosystem approach that HRM fosters and the increased attention such management pays to the land through frequent monitoring and reevaluation (24).

References and Notes

1. Sam Bingham, "Allan Savory: Creator of a Socratic Approach to Land Management," *High Country News* (April 27, 1987, Paonia, Colorado), pp. 11 and 13.
2. Steve Johnson, "Allan Savory: Guru of False Hopes and an Overstocked Range," *High Country News* (April 27, 1987, Paonia, Colorado), pp. 12 and 16.
3. *Op. cit.* 1.
4. Sam Bingham, "Where Animals Save the Land," *World Monitor* (September 1990), pp. 34–40.
5. *Op. cit.* 1.
6. Allan Savory, "Time and Overgrazing," *Holistic Resource Management Newsletter*, No. 37 (Center for Holistic Resource Management, Albuquerque, New Mexico, Fall 1992), pp. 5–6.
7. Allan Savory, "The Critical Role of Predators," *Holistic Resource Management Newsletter*, No. 35 (Center for Holistic Resource Management, Albuquerque, New Mexico, Spring 1992), p. 3.
8. *Op. cit.* 4.
9. *Op. cit.* 1.
10. Jody Butterfield, Editor, *Holistic Resource Management Newsletter*, Albuquerque, New Mexico, 1993 (personal communication).
11. Dayle Flanigan, Ranger, U.S. Forest Service, Austin, Nevada, 1993 (personal communication).
12. Tommie Martin, "Finding Common Ground," *Holistic Resource Management Newsletter*, No. 37 (Center for Holistic Resource Management, Albuquerque, New Mexico, Fall 1992), pp. 7–10.
13. *Op. cit.* 11.
14. R.D. Pieper and R.K. Heitschmidt, "Is Short-Duration Grazing the Answer?" *Journal of Soil and Water Conservation*, Vol. 43, No. 2 (1988), pp. 134–135.
15. R. Hart, M. Samuel, P. Test, *et al.*, "Cattle, Vegetation, and Economic Responses to Grazing Systems and Grazing Pressure," *Journal of Range Management*, Vol. 41, No. 4 (1988), p. 263.
16. Jon Skovlin, "Southern Africa's Experience with Intensive Short-Duration Grazing," *Rangelands*, Vol. 9, No. 4 (1987), pp. 162–167.
17. *Op. cit.* 2.
18. Steve Johnson, Wildlife Advocate, Native Ecosystems, Tucson, Arizona, 1993 (personal communication).
19. Robert Williamson, Director of Range Management, U.S. Forest Service, Washington, D.C., 1993 (personal communication).
20. Mel George, Range Scientist, University of California Agricultural Extension, Davis, California, 1992 (personal communication).
21. Dan Merkel, Range Scientist, U.S. Environmental Protection Agency, Denver, Colorado, 1993 (personal communication).
22. Jerry L. Holechek, Professor of Animal and Range Sciences, New Mexico State University, Las Cruces, New Mexico, 1992 (personal communication).
23. Barry Adams, Range Specialist, Alberta Public Lands, Lethbridge, Alberta, 1993 (personal communication).
24. *Op. cit.* 14, p. 136.

cies. This elimination is achieved with techniques such as trapping or poison—methods that wildlife advocates consider inhumane (143).

At least some of the negative effects of livestock grazing on wildlife stem not from ecological factors, but

from an institutional bias against wildlife. Federally owned ranges in the United States are home to more than 3,000 wildlife species, including about one third of the nation's threatened or endangered species. Yet, according to the GAO, management of these ranges heavily favors grazing interests even when they directly threaten wildlife (144). Less than 5 percent of the budget and staffing of the Bureau of Land Management and the Forest Service, the GAO reports, is devoted to wildlife management, though these federal agencies are required by law to manage their ranges under multiple-use guidelines that specifically recognize the importance of wildlife (145).

In drawing up land-use plans and issuing grazing permits, the bulk of available forage is routinely allocated to livestock (146) (147). On 35 percent of U.S. national wildlife refuges, livestock grazing is permitted as a secondary use, despite the fact that in more than half of these locations, refuge managers say, grazing is harmful to wildlife (148).

MANAGING LIVESTOCK FOR REDUCED IMPACT

With livestock grazing the most powerful human influence on rangeland other than housing development and conversion to cropland, considerable attention has been directed to minimizing its impact. Controlling the timing, duration, and intensity of grazing appears to be the key.

Many perennial range grasses, particularly prairie grasses, are adapted to periodic, sometimes intense grazing. Periods of rest allow grazed perennials to replenish leaf area, set seed, and store food reserves in their roots (149) (150). Continuous or too frequent access by large numbers of cattle to the same range impedes the ability of new growth to store food. When perennial grasses are repeatedly cropped back, leaf growth takes precedence over root growth. With continued severe grazing, roots die and plants become less vigorous. The result is reduced forage and greater plant susceptibility to drought and disease. Watershed protection also suffers as plant cover and leaf litter diminish, leaving erodible, exposed soil (151) (152).

Livestock do not graze on all plant species equally; they concentrate on the most palatable and nutritious first. Thus grazing can lead to the disappearance of beneficial species, the dominance of less palatable species, and the invasion of aggressive weeds, brush, and poisonous plants (153) (154).

Livestock managers generally control such undesirable impacts by adjusting three critical variables: the number of livestock per hectare of range, called the stocking rate; the grazing system, in other words, the location and timing of grazing; and the placement of watering sites and salt blocks, which can spread grazing more evenly over the range.

The single most important factor is the stocking rate, because it directly influences the total amount of forage removed from the range (155) (156). The number of cattle or sheep a range can sustain depends on vegetation as well as precipitation. Prairies, which receive more rainfall, can stand somewhat heavier grazing than can the desert or mountain rangelands of the U.S. West. Plants in dry areas regenerate much more slowly than those in humid areas (157) (158) (159).

Research shows that, over the long term, many desert and mountain rangelands can tolerate light to moderate stock levels that result in the consumption of about 30 to 35 percent of the forage. With this practice, conditions on many degraded ranges could gradually improve and forage production increase (160) (161).

However, traditional stocking practice on arid western range is to allow the consumption of 50 percent or more of available forage, a level more appropriate to productive prairie grassland (162). Therefore, in some areas, ranges have continued to decline. Studies show that reducing consumption from heavy (60–80 percent) to moderate (40–60 percent) or from moderate to light (20–40 percent) can raise overall forage production by about one third (163).

In addition to determining an appropriate stocking rate, range managers must choose a system that will best regulate how and when livestock graze. Even with livestock numbers low, poor distribution or timing of grazing can quickly degrade a rangeland. Over the years, a number of systems have been developed, the most appropriate for a given range depending on the local climate, the steepness of the terrain, and the competing needs of various range users (164).

Continuous grazing, where livestock are set out on a single tract for prolonged periods, is more popular than other systems because it requires less direct management and fewer fences and roads. Continuous grazing need not be abusive, if the stocking rate is moderate or light, the terrain mostly flat so that grazing is more or less even, and access to streamside or other vulnerable vegetation regulated. Impact is further reduced if watering sites and salt blocks are moved or periodically "rested" to allow an area to recover from heavy traffic (165) (166) (167).

Other grazing systems involve various strategies for rotating livestock from one area to another, with the goal of periodically resting vegetation (168). Despite the cost of fencing and moving cattle and the years it takes to master the new system, rotational grazing has steadily gained popularity over the last two decades because it offers better control over livestock distribution and feeding patterns (169). Rotational grazing is particularly beneficial in areas with steep terrain to ensure that grazing pressure is not confined to lowland areas, which cattle generally prefer (170).

Other benefits include an average 13 percent increase in forage production compared with continuously grazed ranges when stocking levels are moderate (171). Wildlife benefit from increased cover on the rest pasture: feeding and nesting are easier for birds and small mammals, and large game animals can roam an area free of disturbance from livestock (172).

The simplest rotational system divides the range up and then grazes the separate pastures in a regular sequence. (See Box 7.1.) Deferred rotation, an important variation of the model, delays the start of grazing in the spring to protect plants during a particularly vulnerable growth period. Deferred grazing allows plants to set seed and complete much of their growth cycle before defoliation begins (173) (174).

Another option is complete rest from grazing for one or more years. This system, often used on severely degraded rangelands, is frequently preferred by environmentalists and wildlife advocates. Rest not only allows range plants to grow more abundantly but also allows plant litter to accumulate, conserving scarce moisture. In one survey of a variety of test plots throughout the U.S. West, researchers found that rangelands that had rested from 4 to 60 years produced an average of 68 percent more plant growth than those subject to moderate grazing (175).

Most observers caution that the ability of a degraded rangeland to recover if allowed to rest indefinitely varies. Some interventions, such as brush control, prescribed burns, species reintroduction, or occasional grazing may be required for full restoration (176) (177).

PUBLIC RANGE: HOW MUCH GRAZING?

An unprecedented demand for recreational access and an environmental awakening have combined to focus public attention on range conditions and management as never before (178).

Though "multiple use" of rangelands—for forage, recreation, wildlife, and other purposes—has been public policy for decades, in practice, an acceptable balance of uses has been difficult to achieve. Inevitably, the debate focuses on livestock grazing on public lands. What are its benefits and costs, and to whom? How much should be permitted?

Environmentalists maintain that the benefits are actually much less than is generally perceived. Public rangelands produce only a small percent—less than 3 percent, by one estimate—of total livestock feed in the United States. Moreover, the number of ranchers using public lands is fairly small, about 23,000 or 1 percent of U.S. livestock producers. This meager production on such extensive public acreage—about one third of the land area in the West is federal range—can be attributed to the fact that public rangelands are generally the driest and least productive sites (179) (180) (181).

But while livestock production is marginal on these lands, they are increasingly valuable for other possible uses, which most environmentalists believe directly conflict with grazing as currently practiced. They contend that safeguarding public rangelands requires lowering the number of livestock there, more carefully regulating grazing, and elevating the interests of wildlife to a more prominent place in management. Other environmentalists go farther: they maintain that only complete removal of livestock from the public range will allow full recovery of its ecosystems (182) (183) (184).

Livestock ranchers counter that cattle and sheep, when properly managed, can be a tool for maintaining rangeland health. Judiciously regulated grazing pressure, they argue, stimulates seed dispersal and the growth of range grasses. They also stress that their profession, which continues to be an important feature of western culture and economy, will suffer if ranching is limited on public land (185) (186) (187) (188).

The conflict between these groups is particularly apparent in the debate about public land grazing fees. Current fees are low compared with prices to graze livestock on private land. In 1992, ranchers paid $1.93 per animal unit month (AUM)—the amount of forage one 1,000-pound cow or five sheep eat in one month—to use public land, while the fee on comparable private land ranged from $5.50 per AUM in Nevada to $12 per AUM in Nebraska and the Dakotas (189) (190).

Moreover, government grazing programs are heavily subsidized. For example, in 1990 the Bureau of Land Management spent nearly $50 million to administer its grazing leases but collected only $19 million in grazing fees. Additional subsidies include predator-control and range-improvement programs that fund such projects as livestock water development and brush control. Environmentalists and other critics claim such public funding cannot be justified on environmental or economic grounds. Grazing fees of two to four times the current rate, they argue, would both discourage abuse of range resources and bring the subsidies down to a more modest level (191) (192). Efforts are under way in the Clinton Administration to raise grazing fees on public lands.

Livestock interests maintain that private rangeland offers fencing and other services that public rangeland often lacks. Paying a higher price for public range would place a burden on the rancher and devalue the land for grazing purposes. More important, ranchers regard their use of the land as a public service: they keep the land in production, provide a valuable commodity to the American market, and protect rangeland from damage by uncontrolled public access (193) (194) (195).

CHANGING RANGE PERSPECTIVES

No matter what the grazing fee, livestock are not likely to disappear from public rangeland in either the United States or Canada. However, in response to public concern, managers have adopted a more ecological approach to their ranges (196) (197). For instance, in its recent initiative "Change on the Range," the U.S. Forest Service states that livestock numbers on its lands are likely to decline, at least in the short term, as it curtails the use of marginally productive sites and seeks to rehabilitate deteriorating rangeland (198).

Government officials have also acknowledged that some of the least productive and most fragile rangeland may indeed be more valuable as wildlife habitat and watershed. Even on the most productive sites, range managers maintain, their new ecosystem approach will result in grazing being used as a land management tool, that is, as a means of maintaining the plant community appropriate for that site (199) (200).

RANCH ECONOMY IN TRANSITION

The management of private rangeland has also begun to change, partially in response to the harsh economics of modern livestock ranching. Expensive techniques such as fertilization, seeding, and brush removal that were used in the 1960s and 1970s have all been severely curtailed (201) (202).

Many range advisers are now recommending a low-input approach that favors better breeding programs, more efficient placement of watering stations, more careful attention to stocking rates that minimize supplemental feeding, and other inexpensive approaches to increase ranch efficiency (203). In addition, many ranchers are seeking other sources of income on their private ranges to augment livestock income. Some are taking advantage of the rising demand for recreation by charging for such activities as hunting, fishing, and wilderness pack trips. In northern New Mexico, for example, several private ranches receive from $2,000 to $30,000 annually from hunting fees (204). Some ranchers in Texas have even introduced African game species to their ranges to capitalize on the lucrative game-hunting market (205).

To the extent that these new uses encourage better stewardship and more attention to wildlife needs, they may promote range recovery. They have the added

benefit of providing a financial bridge to a diversified ranch economy that moves away from exclusive focus on livestock.

The Conditions and Trends section was written by Norbert Henninger, an associate in WRI's Center for International Development and Environment and Dirk Bryant of the World Resources staff. The Focus On section was written by contributing editor Gregory Mock.

References and Notes

1. A number of countries, among them Brazil and Thailand, have begun to develop their own forest monitoring programs. Other assessments that map forest area with the help of satellite imagery include the Tropical Ecosystem Environment Observations by Satellite (TREES) project, the International Geosphere-Biosphere Programme Data and Information System (IGBP-DIS), and the Landsat Pathfinder project. Both TREES, a tropical forest monitoring project undertaken by the Commission of the European Community and the European Space Agency, and IGBP-DIS, a global land-cover assessment conducted by the International Council of Scientific Unions, are using coarse spatial resolution Advanced Very-High Resolution Radiometer data, while the Landsat Pathfinder project, sponsored by a number of U.S. agencies, is employing high spatial resolution Landsat images to map tropical rainforests. Results from these inventories are expected to be made available to the public over the next two years.

2. Nelson P. Hutabarat, Agricultural Attache, Embassy of the Republic of Indonesia, Washington, D.C., 1993 (personal communication).

3. Food and Agriculture Organization of the United Nations (FAO), *Forest Resources Assessment, 1990: Tropical Countries*, FAO Forestry Paper 112 (FAO, Rome, 1993), p. 25.

4. Nigel Dudley, *Forests in Trouble: A Review of the Status of Temperate Forests Worldwide* (World Wildlife Fund, Gland, Switzerland, 1992), p. 22.

5. *Op. cit.* 3, p. 31.

6. The Food and Agriculture Organization of the United Nations defines forests as ecosystems with a crown cover of more than 10 percent of trees or bamboo, characterized by distinctive wild flora and fauna, natural soil conditions, and no agriculture.

7. *Op. cit.* 3, Tables 3a, 3b, and 3c.

8. *Op. cit.* 3, Tables 4a, 4b, and 4c.

9. *Op. cit.* 3, p. 10.

10. *Op. cit.* 3, pp. 24–25.

11. *Op. cit.* 3.

12. Jean Eugene Gorse and David R. Steeds, *Desertification in the Sahelian and Sudanian Zones of West Africa*, World Bank Technical Paper Number 61 (The World Bank, Washington, D.C., 1987), pp. 45–48.

13. *Op. cit.* 3, pp. 28 and 31.

14. *Op. cit.* 3, Tables 8a, 8b, and 8c.

15. *Op. cit.* 3, pp. 28 and 31, and Tables 8a, 8b, and 8c.

16. *Op. cit.* 3, Tables 8a, 8b, and 8c.

17. *Op. cit.* 3, Tables 8a, 8b, and 8c.

18. *Op. cit.* 3, Tables 8a, 8b, and 8c.

19. *Op. cit.* 3, pp. 28–29 and Tables 8a, 8b, and 8c.

20. Christopher Uhl and J. Boone Kauffman, "Deforestation, Fire, Susceptibility, and Potential Tree Responses to Fire in the Eastern Amazon," *Ecology*, Vol. 71, No. 2 (1990), pp. 437–449.

21. *Op. cit.* 3, p. 38.

22. David Skole and Compton Tucker, "Tropical Deforestation and Habitat Fragmentation in the Amazon: Satellite Data from 1978 to 1988," *Science*, Vol. 260, No. 5116 (June 25, 1993), pp. 1905–1909.

23. *Op. cit.* 3, pp. 42–46.

24. *Op. cit.* 3, pp. 42–46.

25. *Op. cit.* 3, pp. 33–36.

26. *Op. cit.* 3, pp. 34–38.

27. *Op. cit.* 3, pp. 31–33.

28. *Op. cit.* 3, p. 48 and Tables 3a, 3b, and 3c.

29. *Op. cit.* 3, pp. 51–53.

30. A.D. Johns, "Species Conservation in Managed Tropical Forests," in *Tropical Deforestation and Species Extinctions*, T.C. Whitmore and J.A. Sayers, eds. (Chapman and Hall, London, 1992), pp. 23–25.

31. *Op. cit.* 20.

32. *Op. cit.* 3, p. 52.

33. *Op. cit.* 3, pp. 55–59.

34. *Op. cit.* 3, Tables 4a, 4b, and 4c.

35. *Op. cit.* 3, p. 55.

36. United Nations Economic Commission for Europe (UN-ECE)/Food and Agriculture Organization of the United Nations (FAO), *The Forest Resources of the Temperate Zones: Main Findings of the UN-ECE/FAO 1990 Forest Resource Assessment* (U.N., New York, 1992), p. 1.

37. *Ibid.*, pp. 16–17.

38. *Ibid.*, pp. 46–47 and 295.

39. Derek Denniston, "Air Pollution Damaging Forests," in *Vital Signs, 1993*, Lester R. Brown, Hal Kane, and Ed Ayres, eds. (W.W. Norton, New York, 1993), p. 108.

40. *Op. cit.* 4, pp. 33–36 and 40–42.

41. *Op. cit.* 4, pp. 9, 31, 67–68, 72–73, 89–90, and 115.

42. Thomas H. Fox, Director, Center for International Development and Environment, World Resources Institute, Washington, D.C., 1993 (personal communication).

43. Nigel Sizer, Associate, Program in Biological Resources and Institutions, World Resources Institute, Washington, D.C., 1993 (personal communication).

44. Organizing committee for the establishment of an independent World Commission on Forests and Sustainable Development, "World Commission on Forests and Sustainable Development: Possible Mandate, Key Issues, Strategy, and Work Plan," Organiz-

ing committee for the establishment of an independent World Commission on Forests and Sustainable Development, Woods Hole, Massachusetts, 1993, pp. 2–5.

45. *Ibid.*, pp. 4–6.

46. "Statement of Forest Principles," in *Agenda 21: Programme of Action for Sustainable Development* (U.N., New York, 1993), p. 294.

47. Bruce Cabarle, Associate, Latin America and the Caribbean Program, Center for International Development and Environment, World Resources Institute, Washington, D.C., 1993 (personal communication).

48. Dennis Child, National Program Leader for Range, Agricultural Research Service, U.S. Department of Agriculture, Beltsville, Maryland, 1991 (personal communication).

49. Linda Joyce, *An Analysis of the Range Forage Situation in the United States, 1989–2040*, (United States Department of Agriculture, Forest Service, Washington, D.C., 1989), p. 9.

50. Lynn Huntsinger, Assistant Professor, Department of Forestry and Resource Management, University of California, Berkeley, California, 1992 (personal communication).

51. *Op. cit.* 49.

52. *Op. cit.* 49.

53. *Op. cit.* 49.

54. *Op. cit.* 49, p. 10.

55. *Op. cit.* 49, pp. 1–55.

56. Frederic H. Wagoner, "Livestock Grazing and the Livestock Industry," in *Wildlife and America*, Howard Brokaw, ed. (Council on Environmental Quality, Washington, D.C., 1978), p. 138.

57. *Op. cit.* 49, p. 41.

58. J. David Swanson, State Range Conservationist, United States Department of Agriculture, Soil Conservation Service, Anchorage, Alaska, 1993 (personal communication).

59. This figure includes both rangeland and cultivated pasture used for forage. Food and Agriculture Organization of the United Nations (FAO), *1991 Production Yearbook*, Vol. 45 (FAO, Rome, 1991), p. 6, Table 1.

60. Richard Burroughs, User Services, Agriculture Division, Statistics Canada, Ottawa, Ontario, 1993 (personal communication).

61. Barry Adams, Range Specialist, Alberta Public Lands, Lethbridge, Alberta, 1991 (personal communication).

62. Donald Gayton, Range Manager, British Columbia Ministry of Forests, Nelson, British Columbia, 1993 (personal communication).

63. *Op. cit.* 49, p. 18.

64. *Op. cit.* 60.

65. Harvey Payne, Director, Tallgrass Prairie Preserve, Pawhuska, Oklahoma, 1993 (personal communication).

66. Curtis H. Flather and Thomas W. Hoekstra, *An Analysis of the Wildlife and Fish Situation in the United States, 1989–2040*, General Technical Report RM-178 (United States Department of Agriculture, Forest Service, Washington, D.C., 1989), p. 9.

67. Curtis H. Flather, Research Wildlife Biologist, Rocky Mountain Forest Range Experiment, Fort Collins, Colorado, 1993 (personal communication).

68. Ed Chaney, Wayne Elmore, and William Platts, *Livestock Grazing on Western Riparian Areas* (U.S. Environmental Protection Agency, Washington, D.C., 1990), pp. 2–6.

69. *Op. cit.* 49, p. 8.

70. Dan Merkel, Range Specialist, U.S. Environmental Protection Agency, Denver, Colorado, 1993 (personal communication).

71. *Op. cit.* 49, p. 8.

72. Jerry L. Holechek, Professor, Animal and Range Science, New Mexico State University, Las Cruces, New Mexico, 1992 (personal communication).

73. U.S. Bureau of Land Management, *State of the Public Rangelands, 1990* (Department of the Interior, Washington, D.C., 1990), p. 2.

74. U.S. General Accounting Office (GAO), *Rangeland Management: More Emphasis Needed on Declining and Overstocked Grazing Allotments*, (GAO, Washington, D.C., 1988), pp. 10 and 25.

75. David Sheridan, *Desertification of the United States* (U.S. Government Printing Office, Washington, D.C., 1981), p. 9.

76. Thadis Box, Professor of Range Science, New Mexico State University, Las Cruces, New Mexico, 1993 (personal communication).

77. *Op. cit.* 73.

78. World Resources Institute and International Institute for Environment and Development, *World Resources 1987* (Basic Books, New York, 1987), p. 67.

79. C.H. Herbal, "Vegetation Changes on Arid Rangelands of the Southwestern United States," in *Rangelands: A Resource under Siege*, P.J. Joss, P.W. Lynch, and O.B. Williams, eds. (Cambridge University Press, Cambridge, U.K., 1986), p. 8.

80. Ed Chaney, Wayne Elmore, and William Platts, *Livestock Grazing on Western Riparian Areas* (U.S. Environmental Protection Agency, Washington, D.C., 1990), pp. 2–6.

81. *Ibid.*, pp. 2–7.

82. *Op. cit.* 78.

83. *Op. cit.* 79.

84. William Kruger, Chairman, Range Science Department, Oregon State University, Corvallis, Oregon, 1993 (personal communication).

85. *Op. cit.* 73.

86. *Op. cit.* 48.

87. *Op. cit.* 48.

88. *Op. cit.* 84.

89. *Op. cit.* 61.

90. *Op. cit.* 74, pp. 20–24 and 30.

91. *Op. cit.* 61.

92. Society for Range Management (SRM), *Assessment of Rangeland Condition and Trend of the United States, 1989* (SRM, Denver, Colorado, 1989), pp. 2–12.

93. *Op. cit.* 49, pp. 13–14.

94. *Op. cit.* 92, p. 8.

95. *Op. cit.* 49, pp. 14–17.

96. Robert Williamson, Director, Forest Service Range Management, U.S. Department of Agriculture, Washington, D.C., 1991 and 1993 (personal communication).

97. *Op. cit.* 48.

98. W. Laycock, "Stable States and Thresholds of Range Condition on North American

99. Rangelands: A Viewpoint," *Journal of Range Management*, Vol. 44, No. 5 (1991), p. 427.

99. M. Friedel, "Range Condition Assessment and the Concept of Thresholds: A Viewpoint," *Journal of Range Management*, Vol. 44, No. 5 (1991), p. 422.

100. *Op. cit.* 96.

101. Kurt Kotter, Range Conservationist, Bureau of Land Management, Washington, D.C., 1993 (personal communication).

102. T. Quigley, "New Criteria for Measuring Range Management Activities," U.S. Forest Service General Technical Report (draft), U.S. Forest Service, Washington, D.C., 1989, pp. 1–37.

103. *Op. cit.* 61.

104. *Op. cit.* 61.

105. *Op. cit.* 62.

106. James Romo, Department of Crop Sciences and Plant Ecology, University of Saskatchewan, Saskatoon, Saskatchewan, 1993 (personal communication).

107. *Op. cit.* 49, p. 15.

108. Dee Quinton, Research Scientist, Rangelands Research Station, Kamloops, British Columbia, May 1993 (personal communication).

109. *Op. cit.* 58.

110. *Op. cit.* 73, p. 6.

111. *Op. cit.* 70.

112. Harold Heady, Range Scientist Emeritus, University of California, Berkeley, California, 1993 (personal communication).

113. George Weurthner, "Some Ecological Costs of Livestock," *Wild Earth*, Vol. 2, No. 1 (1992), p. 10.

114. *Op. cit.* 74, p. 27.

115. *Op. cit.* 49, p. 89.

116. *Op. cit.* 61.

117. John Winder, Assistant Professor, Department of Animal and Range Sciences, New Mexico State University, Las Cruces, New Mexico, 1993 (personal communication).

118. *Op. cit.* 84.

119. *Op. cit.* 96.

120. *Op. cit.* 84.

121. *Op. cit.* 56, pp. 121–145.

122. *Op. cit.* 72.

123. *Op. cit.* 113, pp. 10–14.

124. *Op. cit.* 56, p. 124.

125. *Op. cit.* 56, pp. 121–125.

126. *Op. cit.* 73, p. 7.

127. U.S. Forest Service, *Livestock/Big Game Interaction: Activity Review, Intermountain and Southwest Regions* (U.S. Forest Service, Washington, D.C., 1990), pp. 1–6.

128. *Op. cit.* 96.

129. *Op. cit.* 56, pp. 123–126.

130. *Op. cit.* 113, pp. 10–14.

131. George Wuerthner, "Public Lands Grazing: What Benefits at What Cost?" *Western Wildlands* (Fall 1989), p. 27.

132. *Op. cit.* 49, p. 85.

133. Bradley Shepard, "Grazing Allotment Administration along Streams Supporting Cutthroat Trout in Montana," *Rangelands*, Vol. 14, No. 4 (1992), p. 243.

134. *Op. cit.* 131.

135. *Op. cit.* 68, p. 38.

136. *Op. cit.* 68, p. 14.

137. *Op. cit.* 68, pp. 20 and 38–39.

138. *Op. cit.* 70.

139. *Op. cit.* 56, p. 125.

140. *Op. cit.* 113, pp. 11–12.

141. Montana Department of Fish, Wildlife, and Parks, Dewatered Streams List, Helena, Montana, 1991.

142. *Op. cit.* 131.

143. Lynn Jacobs, *Waste of the West* (Lynn Jacobs, Tucson, Arizona, 1991), pp. 252–291.

144. U.S. General Accounting Office (GAO), *Public Land Management: Attention to Wildlife Is Limited*, (GAO, Washington, D.C., 1991), pp. 2–5 and 8.

145. *Ibid.*, pp. 2–5 and 18.

146. *Ibid.*, pp. 34 and 38–39.

147. George Wuerthner, Wildlife Ecologist, Livingston, Montana, 1992 (personal communication).

148. U.S. General Accounting Office (GAO), *National Wildlife Refuges: Continuing Problems with Incompatible Uses Call for Bold Action* (GAO, Washington, D.C., 1989), pp. 2–5, 17, and 20–21.

149. John Merrill, "The XXX Ranch: Managing Range for Ecology and Economy," Publication No. YS-83-1, chapter offprint from *1983 Yearbook of Agriculture* (U.S. Department of Agriculture, Washington, D.C., 1983), pp. 87–94.

150. B.W. Adams, G. Ehlert, and A. Robertson, "Grazing Systems for Public Grazing Lands," *Range Notes* No. 10 (Alberta Forestry Lands and Wildlife, Public Lands Division, Lethbridge, Alberta, January 1991), pp. 1–8.

151. *Op. cit.* 68, p. 36.

152. Allan Savory, "Time and Overgrazing," *Holistic Resource Management Newsletter*, No. 37 (Center for Holistic Resource Management, Albuquerque, New Mexico, Fall 1992), p. 5.

153. *Op. cit.* 68, p. 36.

154. *Op. cit.* 56, p. 124.

155. Jerry L. Holechek and Rex Pieper, "Estimation of Stocking Rate on New Mexico Rangelands," *Journal of Soil and Water Conservation*, Vol. 47, No. 1 (1992), p. 116.

156. H. Walt Van Poollen and John R. Lacey, "Herbage Response to Grazing Systems and Stocking Intensities," *Journal of Range Management*, Vol. 32, No. 4 (1979), p. 250.

157. Jerry L. Holechek, "Considerations Concerning Grazing Systems," *Rangelands*, Vol. 5, No. 5 (1983), p. 208.

158. Jerry L. Holechek, "Chihuahuan Desert Rangeland, Livestock Grazing, and Sustainability," *Rangelands*, Vol. 13, No. 3 (1991), p. 115.

159. Jerry L. Holechek, "An Approach for Setting the Stocking Rate," *Rangelands*, Vol. 10, No. 1 (1988), p. 11.

160. *Op. cit.* 158.

161. *Op. cit.* 159.

162. *Op. cit.* 158.

163. *Op. cit.* 156.

164. *Op. cit.* 157, pp. 208–211.

165. *Op. cit.* 72.

166. *Op. cit.* 157.

167. *Op. cit.* 150, pp. 2–3.

168. *Op. cit.* 150.

169. Mel George, Range Scientist, University of California Agricultural Extension, Davis, California, 1993 (personal communication).

170. *Op. cit.* 157, pp. 208–209.

171. *Op. cit.* 156.

172. *Op. cit.* 157, pp. 208–209.

173. *Op. cit.* 157, pp. 208–210.

174. *Op. cit.* 150, pp. 3–7.

175. John R. Lacey and H. Walt Van Poollen, "Comparison of Herbage Production on Moderately Grazed and Ungrazed Western Ranges," *Journal of Range Management*, Vol. 34, No. 3 (1981), pp. 210–212.

176. Larry Ford, Plant Ecologist, U.S. Agency for International Development, Washington, D.C., 1993 (personal communication).

177. *Op. cit.* 50.

178. U.S. Forest Service, *The Forest Service Program for Forest and Rangeland Resources* (U.S. Department of Agriculture, Washington, D.C., 1990), pp. 5.16–5.18.

179. *Op. cit.* 143, pp. 25–27.

180. U.S. House of Representatives, Committee on Government Operations, *Federal Grazing Program: All Is Not Well on the Range*, Committee Print, May, 1986.

181. U.S. General Accounting Office (GAO), *Rangeland Management: BLM's Hot Desert Grazing Program Merits Reconsideration* (GAO, Washington, D.C., 1991), p. 43.

182. Lynn Jacobs, "Amazing Graze: How the Livestock Industry is Ruining the American West," *Desertification Control Bulletin*, No. 17 (1988), pp. 13–17.

183. *Op. cit.* 131, pp. 24–29.

184. George Wuerthner, "The Price Is Wrong," *Sierra* (October 1990), pp. 38–45.

185. *Op. cit.*, 149, p. 87.

186. John Merrill, Director, Ranch Management Program, Texas Christian University, Fort Worth, Texas, 1993 (personal communication).

187. *Op. cit.* 96.

188. *Op. cit.* 181, pp. 49–50.

189. "Selected Grazing Lease Activities: Bureau of Land Management," (U.S. Department of the Interior, Washington, D.C., 1992), pp. 28–31.

190. Steve Richardson, Legislative Assistant, House Subcommittee on Environment, Energy, and Natural Resources, Washington, D.C., 1993 (personal communication).

191. *Op. cit.* 189.

192. *Op. cit.* 190.

193. Darwin Nielsen, "Total Cost of Grazing Public Lands," *Western Livestock Journal* (January 14, 1991), p. 10.

194. *Op. cit.* 186.

195. Tom Bartlett, Range Economist, Colorado State University, Fort Collins, Colorado, 1992 (personal communication).

196. *Op. cit.* 96.

197. *Op. cit.* 61.

198. U.S. Forest Service, *The Forest Service Program for Forest and Rangeland Resources* (U.S. Department of Agriculture, Washington, D.C., 1990), pp. 5.16–5.18.

199. *Op. cit.* 96.

200. *Op. cit.* 48.

201. *Op. cit.* 96.

202. Jerry Holechek and Jerry Hawkes, "Desert and Prairie Ranching Profitability under Changing Economic Conditions," *Rangelands*, Vol. 15, No. 3 (1993), pp. 104–109.

203. *Ibid.*

204. *Ibid.*

205. Harlan Degarmo, Range Division, Soil Conservation Service, U.S. Department of Agriculture, Washington, D.C., 1993 (personal communication).

8. Biodiversity

By some accounts, the world is on the verge of an episode of major species extinction, rivaling five other documented periods over the past half billion years during which a significant portion of global fauna and flora were wiped out (1) (2) (3). The most recent event occurred 65 million years ago when the dinosaurs disappeared. Unlike previous die-offs, for which climatic, geologic, and other natural phenomena were to blame, experts say the current episode is driven by anthropogenic factors: the rapid conversion and degradation of habitat for human use; the accidental and deliberate introduction of exotic species; overharvesting of animals, fish, and plants; pollution; human-caused global climate change; industrial agriculture and forestry; and other activities that destroy or impair natural ecosystems and the species within them (4).

Experts suggest that following each previous extinction episode, it took 10 million years or more for the number of species to return to the level of diversity existing prior to the event in question. If their warnings prove true, the effect of human activities on biodiversity—the variation of genes within a species and the overall diversity of species, communities, and ecosystems—will be irreparable if continued unchecked, within the time frame of subsequent generations, and perhaps within the lifetime of the human race itself (5).

Skeptics note that only a small fraction of the world's plants and animals have become extinct over the past few centuries, and that fear of a massive species die-off is overblown (6).

This chapter examines recent trends in species and habitat loss, efforts under way to protect biodiversity, and the Convention on Biological Diversity, a global agreement to protect and promote the sustainable use of the Earth's living resources. Most of the material that follows deals with terrestrial diversity. (For a discussion of freshwater and marine diversity, see Chapter 10, "Water.")

CONDITIONS AND TRENDS

Key Issues

BIODIVERSITY: WHAT IT IS, WHY IT IS IMPORTANT

Scientists define biodiversity at several levels: genetic diversity, the variation between individuals and between populations within a species; species diversity, the different types of plants, animals, and other life forms within a region; and community or ecosystem diversity, the variety of habitats found within an area (grassland, marsh, and woodland, for instance). Some add a fourth level: functional diversity, the different roles organisms play within an ecosystem, which would distinguish, for example, between the energy-capturing role of a plant and the role of an herbivore in keeping plant growth in check.

Practical value can be attached to biodiversity at each of these levels. Genetic diversity is important in corn crops, for instance, because the unique characteristics of some corn populations leave them resistant to certain pests. Farmers can select for these traits when faced with infestations, rather than resigning themselves to heavy pesticide use or high crop loss.

Species diversity provides us with a host of wild and domestic plant, fish, and animal products used for medicines, cosmetics, industrial products, fuel and building materials, and food, among other things (7). Products extracted from wild species are the basis of traditional and modern medicines. Currently, one quarter of pharmaceuticals dispensed in the United States contain active ingredients derived from plant products (8). New medicinal plants, as well as new food sources adapted to difficult climate and soil conditions, may improve the health and living standards of growing human populations around the world.

Diversity is important in ecosystems partly because of the human services they provide—cycling water, gas, nutrients, and other materials. Wetlands, for example, ameliorate water flow resulting from rainfall, filtering sediments in the process. Another example is the role mycorrhizal fungi and soil fauna play in making nutrients available to plants, vital for maintaining the production of food, forage, and timber crops. Along with these practical functions, biodiversity is valued by many for the recreational and nontangible benefits that wildlife and wild areas offer.

Levels and Patterns of Diversity

Although humans have been systematically counting and classifying other living things for at least two centuries, estimates of how many species there are vary significantly. Best guesses put the total number of species at between 3 and 30 million, of which at most 1.8 million have been identified to date (9). While most birds, mammals, and plants are already in the scientific record, little is known about other orders such as the insects, which make up an overwhelming majority of species described to date, or microorganisms (viruses, protozoa, and bacteria), which recent work reveals to be much more diverse than scientists had previously believed (10) (11).

Knowing how many and what kinds of species exist is important both for discovering new crops, medicines, and other natural products of value and for preventing future extinction. By locating and protecting areas rich in species diversity, we can reduce the level of extinction more than if we merely preserved areas on an ad hoc basis (12). For this reason, scientists attempt to classify "hotspots," areas particularly rich in species or where many endemic species (those with limited ranges) are found. This approach is useful for protecting global biodiversity, but it gives short shrift to diversity at the local level. To preserve only biologically rich areas is to ignore the importance of less diverse areas, such as those found in some arid zones or those that provide sources of wild products essential to the survival of local people.

Most of the world's biodiversity is located in the tropics—some 40 to 90 percent of the world's species live in tropical forests (13) (14) (15). Norman Myers, a noted environmentalist, has defined 18 global hotspots, based both on high plant endemism and how threatened they are by human activity; 14 of these areas are located in tropical forests (16). Birdlife International recently gathered information on all bird species with breeding ranges of under 50,000 square kilometers. They found that three quarters of the zones where these species breed are in tropical areas, and that 20 percent of all bird species were restricted to 2 percent of the Earth's land area (17). Areas with Mediterranean-like climates, coral reefs, islands, and some lakes are other habitats particularly rich in diversity.

Species Loss

The fossil record indicates that, on average, a species persists between 1 and 10 million years before succumbing to factors such as climate change, or random events such as persistent drought, natural catastrophe, the emergence of a new predator, or genetic mutation (18). A conservative estimate places background extinction rates over geologic time at 1 mammal species every 400 years and 1 bird species every 200 years (19). But recorded extinctions over the past 400 years indicate that 58 mammal species and 115 bird species have disappeared, most of these on islands (20).

There are at least three reasons why recorded recent extinctions underestimate actual rates of species loss. First, these figures represent only known extinctions. Given incomplete knowledge of even the bird and mammal taxa, it is almost certain that some species disappeared without ever being described. Second, these numbers do not include extinctions that have happened within the past few decades. According to internationally recognized criteria, a species is not classified as extinct until 50 years after its last sighting. Third, much of the widespread destruction of habitat and populations in tropical areas, where most species are found, has taken place only recently. Affected populations may persist for a few generations but are doomed when their numbers drop below the point where they can rebound from hardship brought about by drought, disease, predation, and other phenomena. By many estimates, a given species must have a population of at least several thousand individuals to survive such events over the long term, although this number, known as the minimum viable population size, differs from species to species (21).

About 12 percent of mammal species and 11 percent of bird species were classified as threatened in 1990 (22). The percentage of threatened species in other groups—such as reptiles, amphibians, fish, and insects—was lower, most likely reflecting the far less complete information available for these taxonomic groups. (See Figure 8.1.)

Figure 8.1 Percentage of Animal Species Known to be Globally Threatened, 1990

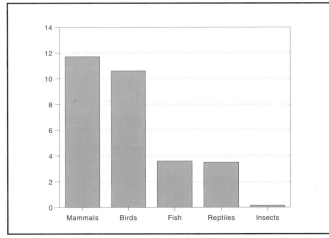

Source: World Conservation Monitoring Centre, *Global Biodiversity: Status of the Earth's Living Resources* (Chapman and Hall, London, 1992), p. 236.

Figure 8.2 Known Causes of Animal Extinctions since 1600

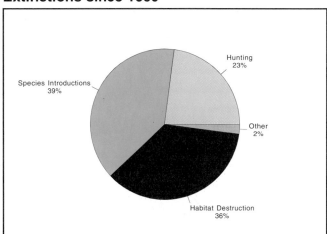

Source: World Conservation Monioring Centre, *Global Biodiversity: Status of the Earth's Living Resources* (Chapman and Hall, London, 1992), p. 199.
Notes:
a. Percentage of extinctions by cause is weighted where more than one factor is involved in a given extinction.
b. Animals include mammals, birds, molluscs, and other nonplant species.

At the national level, at least, current methods for classifying the status of species may not reflect how threatened they really are. An analysis of endangered taxa (species and subspecies) in the United States found that populations of vertebrate animals averaged 1,075 individuals and plants averaged less than 120 individuals by the time they were listed as endangered, suggesting that for some populations, a taxa may be doomed to local extinction by the time it is classified as threatened (23).

The World Conservation Union, formerly known as the International Union for Conservation of Nature and Natural Resources, classifies the global status of species. It is currently evaluating a new classification method, known as the Mace-Landy criteria, that would take into account viable size, range, and numbers of population, where known, when determining whether or not a species is endangered (24). To what extent this method, as currently proposed, will affect the number of species listed is unknown. Reviews of an earlier draft of the method suggested that indeed there would be a substantial increase in the number listed as threatened, primarily through the evaluation of species whose status is currently unknown (25).

Various projections, based largely on current trends of habitat destruction in the tropics, suggest that between 1 and 11 percent of the world's species per decade will be committed to extinction between 1975 and 2015 (some estimates refer to shorter periods) (26). One intermediate estimate projects that 4–8 percent of closed tropical forest species will be doomed to extinction over the next 25 years, if current rates of deforestation persist. This figure might be higher if deforestation accelerates, or if habitat modification favors areas rich in diversity (27).

THREATS TO BIODIVERSITY

A World Conservation Union analysis of animal extinctions since 1600 found that where the cause was known, 39 percent had resulted from species introduc-

tions, 36 percent from habitat destruction, and 23 percent from hunting and deliberate extermination. (See Figure 8.2.) While the analysis focuses on island species, it is generally agreed that these factors, particularly species introduction and habitat loss, are major threats to biodiversity everywhere.

When new species are deliberately or accidentally introduced to an area, they can wipe out local flora and fauna either by preying on them or by outcompeting them for food and space. Island species have been especially vulnerable to domestic livestock, pets, and other introduced species because, having evolved in isolation, many never developed defenses against predators and herbivores.

Habitat loss is considered the biggest current threat to biodiversity (28). There are estimates of how much natural vegetation has been converted to human use since Europeans first arrived in South America (1492 A.D.), but comparably detailed estimates of habitat loss do not exist for all regions of the globe. (See Figure 8.3.) While South America has lost more closed forest (moderately to densely wooded areas) than any other habitat type, it is savannah-grassland, almost one quarter of it lost, that has undergone the largest percentage decrease since preagricultural times (29). The effects of this loss on mammal species diversity is of particular concern, as one recent study found grassland, scrubland, desert, and other dryland areas in South America to have the highest endemic mammalian diversity of any habitat type in the region, including tropical forestland (30).

Habitat loss takes several forms: outright loss of areas used by wild species; degradation, for example, from vegetation removal and erosion, which deprive native species of food, shelter, and breeding areas; and fragmentation, when native species are squeezed onto small patches of undisturbed land surrounded by areas cleared for agriculture and other purposes. In the

Figure 8.3 Natural Vegetation Loss in Select South American Countries as of 1988

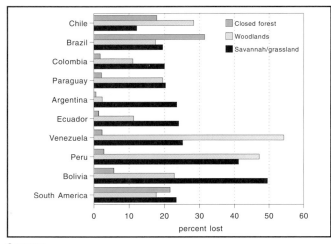

Sources:

1. Thomas Stone, "South America's Vanishing Natural Vegetation," *Cultural Survival Quarterly*, Vol. 16, No. 3 (1992), pp. 67–70.
2. T. Stone, P. Schlesinger, G. Woodwell, *et al.*, "A Map of the Vegetation of South America Based on Satellite Imagery," *Photogrammetric Engineering and Remote Sensing* (in press, 1994).

Notes:

a. Loss covers period after European arrival on continent.
b. Data are not comparable with forest extent data provided in Chapter 19, "Forests and Rangelands," Table 19.1 because of differences in methodology between the two studies.

Table 8.1 Gray Wolf Population and Range, Selected Countries, 1990

Country	Number of Wolves Remaining	% Range Occupied	Population Trend
Canada			
Northwest Territories	5,000–15,000	100	V
Ontario and Quebec	<10,000	80	V
United States			
Alaska	6,000	100	V
Minnesota	1,200	30	V
Mexico	<10	<10	E
Sweden and Norway	<10	<10	E
Finland	<100	<10	E/L
Syria	200–500	10	L
Iran	1,000	80	V
Afghanistan	1,000?	90	V/D?
India	1,000–2,000	20	E/L
European USSR (former)	20,000	60	V
Asian USSR (former)	50,000	75	V
Poland	900	90	V
Romania	2,000?	20	D
Greece	500	60	V/D
Yugoslavia (former)	2,000	55	D
Italy	250	10	L
Spain	500–1,000	10	L
Portugal	150	20	L

Source: J.R. Ginsberg and D.W. MacDonald, *Foxes, Wolves, Jackals, and Dogs: An Action Plan for the Conservation of Canids* (World Conservation Union, Gland, Switzerland, 1990), pp. 37–39.

Note: V = viable, at least in the short term, D = decreasing, L = lingering, and E = highly endangered.

latter case, ecosystem functions such as the hydrological cycle may be interrupted, native species may be crowded out because fragments are too small, and fragment edges may prove uninhabitable to plants and animals associated with the habitat type because of exposure to wind, sunlight, new predators, and other factors (referred to by ecologists as edge effect).

While much attention has been paid to deforestation and other examples of habitat destruction, few attempts have been made to measure the loss of habitat through fragmentation and edge effect. A 1993 study of deforestation and fragmentation in the Brazilian Amazon basin between 1978 and 1988 found that of total habitat affected, only 39 percent could be attributed to outright forest conversion; the rest occurred through fragmentation and edge effect (31). (See Chapter 7, "Forests and Rangelands.")

Habitat loss, not only through outright conversion to human use but also through degradation and fragmentation, is difficult to measure. Human disturbance, only a surrogate measure of habitat loss, is based on the assumption that human activity is associated with habitat conversion, fragmentation, and degradation. In 1993, Conservation International mapped areas of the globe over 40,000 hectares in size that have undergone low, moderate, and high levels of human disturbance. Their study used deforestation, forest degradation, human population density, and other data from various sources (32). Less than half of the world's vegetated land remains in relatively undisturbed areas. (See Figures 8.4 and 8.5.) On a regional basis, South America has the highest percentage of vegetated land in such areas (63 percent); Europe has the lowest (12 percent)—almost all of its relatively undisturbed area located in northern countries such as Norway and Iceland (33).

In measuring how much habitat is left, some experts look to areas where large carnivores and grazing animals still exist. The rationale is that if the biggest animals (often referred to as the umbrella species) still survive within a region, then there is still enough wilderness left to support most of the other inhabitants within that ecosystem, as smaller species generally require less range (34). The presence of wolves, for example, provides an indicator of remaining habitat in various countries of the world. (See Table 8.1.) Often umbrella species play a key role in the functioning of an ecosystem, and their removal signifies that the system has been impaired. Elephants, another umbrella species, may be critical to maintaining African grasslands. In some areas where savannah elephants have been removed, grasslands have reverted to bush, changing the complement of native species (35).

The absence of an umbrella species may not always indicate too little habitat. Large mammals such as elephants—particularly prior to a global ban on ivory trading in 1989, which reduced elephant poaching—are often targeted by hunters (36). Overharvesting species is still a major threat to biodiversity despite international agreements such as the Convention on International Trade in Endangered Species of Flora and Fauna (CITES), which was the mechanism used for halting the ivory trade. This treaty regulates international trade in wild plant and animal products, banning trade in products from endangered species, known as Appendix I species, and requiring export nations to harvest Appendix II species, those that could become endangered through uncontrolled trade, at sustainable yields.

The wild bird trade is one example of how trade threatens species despite CITES protection. Continued

Figure 8.4 Degree of Human Disturbance, Total Land Area

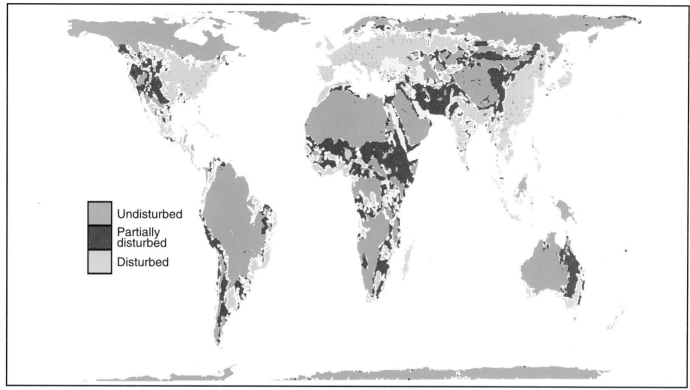

Undisturbed

Partially disturbed

Disturbed

Source: Lee Hannah, unpublished map (Conservation International, Washington, D.C., 1993).
Note: For details on definitions and methodology, refer to Chapter 20, "Biodiversity," Sources and Technical Notes to Table 20.2.

trade for the pet market has been specifically implicated in the decline of over 40 parrot species (37). Instead of assigning sustainable harvest quotas based on population surveys, export nations often set quotas at previous years' export numbers. In other cases, birds are shipped with incomplete or inaccurate documentation to comply with CITES provisions. Most import nations, lax about inspecting paperwork and shipments, are also to blame. The United States, the world's largest importer of pet birds during the 1980s, established a moratorium on CITES-listed commercial wild bird imports to take effect in November 1993 (38) (39).

Pollution threatens biodiversity, particularly in aquatic areas. There is evidence that a mysterious worldwide decline in amphibian species may be caused in part by various types of pollution, including acid rain from industrial emissions and forest burning (40). (See Chapter 10, "Water.")

When a species goes extinct or is extirpated from an area, there is generally more than one cause. Habitat destruction leaves populations isolated in fragments, where they become vulnerable to outside predators—either introduced or associated with cleared areas—and to human hunters living on adjacent lands.

PROTECTING BIODIVERSITY

There are two management-level approaches to biodiversity conservation: protecting individual species and populations, and protecting the habitats they live in. Efforts directed at species and populations, while important, are time and resource intensive and thus can

only support a small percentage of threatened species. Measures include offering legal protection to individual species, developing management plans targeted at protecting them, and ex situ conservation, that is, protecting animal and plant populations in zoos and seed banks. (See Table 8.2.) Ex situ conservation serves both as insurance against the loss of genetic and species diversity in the wild and as a source for occasional re-

Figure 8.5 Degree of Human Disturbance, Vegetated Land Area

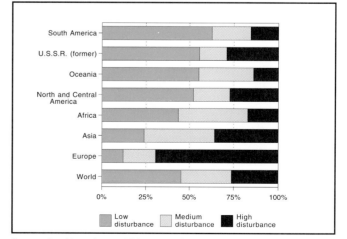

Source: Lee Hannah, unpublished data (Conservation International, Washington, D.C., 1993).
Note: For details on definitions and methodology, refer to Chapter 20, "Biodiversity," Sources and Technical Notes to Table 20.2.

Box 8.1 How Effective are Protected Areas in Conserving Biodiversity?

Historically, protected areas have been the main tool used by governments to conserve biodiversity. Modern parks and reserves were first established in the late 1800s, although forest reserves existed in India and other countries as far back as the fourth century B.C. (1). Currently, 6 percent of the world's land area is either strictly or partially protected. North and Central America have set aside the highest percentage of land in parks and reserves (almost 12 percent), while the countries of the former Soviet Union have set aside the least, just over 1 percent. (See Table 1.) While protected areas are invaluable in conserving habitat and species, the current network of parks and reserves raises specific concerns about ecosystem representation, size, community participation, and management effectiveness (2) (3) (4).

Often governments set aside less useful land for protection (5). For example, a large percentage of parks and reserves are established in mountainous areas covered by rock and ice (6). To encourage preservation of a broad range of ecosystems, the World Conservation Union, the independent global body that oversees efforts to conserve biodiversity, established a goal of having 10 percent of each of the world's major biomes (a broad regional ecological community) protected by the year 2000.

This and other goals, including ". . . an agreement to establish a global network of . . ." well-managed marine protected areas, formed the basis of the Caracas Action Plan, developed during the Fourth World Congress on National Parks and Protected Areas in Caracas, Venezuela, in 1992 (7).

Roughly 5 percent of the world's biomes were protected by 1990. (See Table 2.) Temperate grasslands and lake systems, the most poorly represented biomes, had about 1 percent of their total area protected. Only subtropical and temperate rainforests and woodlands, 9.3 percent of which are protected, are close to the 10 percent goal set out in the Caracas Action Plan.

How realistic is the 10 percent goal? For some biomes, it may be difficult to find enough remaining undeveloped land to protect. Only 7.5 percent of the world's evergreen sclerophyllous forest, typical of the Mediterranean region, remains in areas of relatively little human disturbance. Less than 10 percent of temperate broadleaf forest, once predominant in Europe, the eastern United States, and parts of Asia, is located in low-disturbance areas. Some of the most threatened biomes are located in the temperate, industrialized world. If biodiversity is to be protected at the ecosys-

tem level, habitat preservation in industrialized countries may be of most immediate concern.

Another problem has to do with the size of protected areas. Managed as separate entities, without consideration of the surrounding landscape, they risk becoming islands of undisturbed land hemmed in by cropland and human-dominated areas. The result would be parks and reserves too small to hold viable populations of some of their largest carnivores and herbivores (8). Some large species require millions of hectares of land to support several thousand individuals, the population size generally considered necessary for long-term survival. Less than 2 percent of the world's protected areas are at least 1 million hectares in size, one conservative estimate of the minimum habitat requirement for maintaining viable populations of the largest mammals (9). (See Table 1.) Moreover, parks and reserves rarely encompass the full range of habitats exploited by species during seasonal movements, for example, the spawning migration of some fish or the biannual movement of migratory birds (10).

Some experts advocate a network of numerous small protected areas rather than a few large reserves. Thus, if disease or natural disaster should decimate popula-

Table 1 Protected Area Coverage by Region, 1993

Regions	Protected Areas[a]		Percent of Land Area Protected	Percent of Protected Areas in Parks/Reserves At Least 1 Million Hectares in Size[a]	
	Total Number	Total Area (000 ha)		Area	Number
World	**8,619**	**792,265.6**	**5.9**	**55.7**	**1.5**
Africa	704	138,892.7	4.6	58.5	4.8
Asia	2,181	121,160.9	4.4	40.1	0.8
North and Central America	1,752	263,249.8	11.7	73.1	2.1
South America	667	114,595.9	6.4	48.6	3.7
Europe	2,177	45,533.0	9.3	4.2	0.0
USSR (former)	218	24,329.8	1.1	23.7	1.8
Oceania	920	84,503.5	9.9	65.8	1.2

Source: World Conservation Monitoring Centre (WCMC), unpublished data (WCMC, Cambridge, U.K., June 1993).
Note: a. Areas in International Union for Nature and the Conservation of Natural Resources I-V categories. World total excludes Antarctica.

leases to reintroduce or bolster wild populations. In addition, seed banks are a source of genetic diversity for agricultural research.

Parks and reserves, where human activity is strictly curtailed, at least in theory, form the bulwark of conventional habitat conservation. There are deficiencies in the current protected-area network. (See Box 8.1.) These include incomplete representation of habitat types, limited size, and failure to provide for human residents in surrounding areas. Protected areas also fail to conserve biodiversity on human-settled lands.

Policymakers and managers are expanding the network of parks and reserves and redefining the protected-area concept to better accommodate humans and safeguard biodiversity. They are also expanding

the management scale to consider biodiversity at the landscape level, that is, the matrix of habitats located on settled and undeveloped lands. Facing scarce financial resources, policymakers and managers are increasingly turning to private and community groups for support of expansion and management.

Integrated conservation-development projects (ICDPs) represent a new management approach that seeks to reduce human impact on protected areas by providing local populations with sustainable, income-generating opportunities. Many ICDPs are far-reaching, managing protected areas within the context of the surrounding landscape. The broad variety of ICDPs range from community development initiatives in areas bordering parks to regional land use planning tar-

Box 8.1

tions in one park, representative populations will still remain in other, unaffected parks. This approach would also protect a greater range of habitat types than would large reserves alone (11) (12). Another advantage is that protected areas as small as 10 hectares can preserve viable populations of plants, which make up a large percentage of the Earth's biodiversity (13).

In reality, few countries are able to protect areas as large as 1 million hectares. Some experts think that population viability can be maintained within smaller reserves by linking them with wildlife corridors, which would permit individuals to disperse and interbreed (14).

Protected areas in many parts of the world exist in name only. Though legally protected, parks are threatened by farmers, poachers, and herders and their livestock, and mining and other illegal activities occur within their borders (15).

Despite problems, protected areas play a critical role in preserving the Earth's biodiversity. Recent studies in Africa and Asia have found that a large percentage of local fauna is afforded protection within existing parks and reserves (16) (17).

References and Notes

1. World Conservation Monitoring Centre, *Global Biodiversity: Status of the Earth's Living Resources* (Chapman and Hall, London, 1992), p. 447.
2. *Ibid.*, pp. 451 and 459.
3. Craig L. Shafer, *Nature Reserves: Island Theory and Conservation Practice* (Smithsonian Institution Press, Washington, D.C., 1990), pp. 1–2.
4. Michael Wells, Katrina Brandon, and Lee Hannah, *People and Parks Linking Protected Area Management with Local Communities* (The World Bank/World Wildlife Fund/U.S. Agency for International Development, Washington, D.C., 1992), p. 1.
5. *Op. cit.* 1, p. 459.
6. *Op. cit.* 1, p. 452.

7. World Conservation Union (IUCN), "Parks for Life: a New Beginning," *IUCN Bulletin*, Vol. 23, No. 2 (1992), p. 10.
8. *Op. cit.* 3, p. 1.
9. Christine M. Schonewald-Cox, "Conclusions: Guidelines to Management: A Beginning Attempt," in *Genetics and Conservation: A Reference for Managing Wild Animal and Plant Populations*, Christine M. Schonewald-Cox, Steven M. Chambers, Bruce MacBryde, *et al.*, eds. (Benjamin/Cummings, Menlo Park, California, 1983), p. 416.
10. Kenton R. Miller and Andrew Lawton, *Balancing the Scales: Policies for Increasing Biodiversity's Chances through Bioregional Management* (World Resources Institute, Washington, D.C., 1993), p. 4.
11. *Op. cit.* 3, p. 81.
12. D.S. Simberloff and N. Gotelli, "Effects of Insularization on Plant Species Richness in the Prairie-Forest Ecotone," *Biological Conservation*, Vol. 29 (1984), pp. 27–46, cited in Craig L. Shafer, *Nature Reserves: Island The-*

ory and Conservation Practice (Smithsonian Institution Press, Washington, D.C., 1990), p. 81.
13. Jeffrey A. McNeely, Kenton R. Miller, Walter V. Reid, *et al.*, *Conserving the World's Biological Diversity* (World Conservation Union/World Resources Institute/Conservation International/World Wildlife Fund/The World Bank, Gland, Switzerland, 1990), p. 61.
14. *Op. cit.* 3, pp. 81–84.
15. *Op. cit.* 4, pp. 11–13.
16. Jeffrey A. Sayer and Simon Stuart, "Biological Diversity and Tropical Forests," *Environmental Conservation*, Vol. 15, No. 3 (1988), pp. 193–194.
17. P. Round, *The Status and Conservation of Resident Forest Birds in Thailand* (Association for the Conservation of Wildlife, Bangkok, 1985), cited in World Conservation Monitoring Centre, *Global Biodiversity: Status of the Earth's Living Resources* (Chapman and Hall, London, 1992), p. 561.

Table 2 Percentage of Biome Types Protected and Subject to Low Human Disturbance, 1990

Biome Type	Percent of Biome Area Protected	Percent of Biome Area Subject to Low Human Disturbance
Subtropical/temperate rainforests/woodlands	9.3	33.0
Mixed mountain systems	7.7	29.3
Mixed island systems	7.6	46.6
Tundra communities	7.5	97.0
Tropical humid forests	5.0	63.2
Tropical dry forests/woodlands	4.7	29.0
Evergreen sclerophyllous forests	4.7	7.5
Tropical grasslands/savannahs	4.7	74.0
Warm deserts/semideserts	3.9	58.9
Cold-winter deserts	3.9	47.4
Temperate broadleaf forests	3.2	9.7
Temperate needle-leaf forests/woodlands	2.9	81.7
Lake systems	1.3	X
Temperate grasslands	0.8	27.6
Average	**4.8**	**43.2**

Sources:
1. Adapted from World Conservation Monitoring Centre, *Global Biodiversity Status of the Earth's Living Resources* (Chapman and Hall, London, 1992).
2. Lee Hannah, unpublished data (Conservation International, Washington, D.C., June 1993).
Notes: Biome type definitions follow Udvardy classification scheme. The percentage of mixed island systems protected is likely an overestimate, as a result of including marine protected areas. X indicates no data available.

geted at protected areas and surrounding lands (41). Biosphere reserves are well-known examples, although only some are managed with both conservation and development in mind (42). These reserves consist of protected core areas, often existing parks, surrounded by buffer zones and transition areas where some human activity is permitted. The biosphere model offers local people economic opportunity through the sustainable management of resources in noncore areas of the reserve, while extending the total area managed for biodiversity beyond core boundaries.

In many cases, governments lack the staff or financial resources to manage an existing network of protected areas, much less to invest in the creation of new reserves. One solution is to work with private and non-

governmental organizations (NGOs). Private groups can raise money to purchase land for protection and to support conservation in existing parks. They are often in a better position than government agencies to negotiate land use disputes and to incorporate local interests in management decisions. In some Latin American countries, including Belize, El Salvador, and Ecuador, NGO and community groups currently manage protected areas (43).

Bioregional management, conducted at the landscape level as part of other land management efforts, allows for biodiversity conservation at all levels, from maintaining ecosystem function to preserving genetic diversity within individual populations. Only by managing entire watersheds can hydrological cycles be

Table 8.2 Ex Situ Conservation of the World's Mammals, 1991

Threatened Taxa[a]	Number	Total Threatened Mammal (%) Taxa[b]
In captivity	213	32
With captive population of at least 50 individuals[c]	104	16
With captive population of at least 500 individuals	14	2
Threatened taxa found only in captivity	2	0[d]

Source: C.D. Magin, T.J. Johnson, B. Groombridge, et al., "Species Extinctions, Endangerment and Captive Breeding," in *Creative Conservation: Interactive Management of Wild and Captive Animals*, P.J. Olney, G.M. Mace, and A.T.C. Feistner, eds. (Chapman and Hall, London, in press).

Notes:
a. Threatened taxa include both species and subspecies. The total number of threatened taxa in captivity is likely an underestimate, as not all zoos report their data.
b. Total threatened mammal taxa as of 1990.
c. Many experts estimate that a breeding population size of at least 50 is essential for the short-term preservation of most mammalian species. Note that the captive population figure is for the total number of breeding and nonbreeding individuals.

maintained or the habitat needs of broad-ranging species be accounted for. The approach entails coordinating government agencies, community leaders, businesses, and private groups within a region so that biodiversity concerns are included in the planning process. Examples of bioregional management can be found in Greater Yellowstone Park and the Adirondack Mountains of the United States, the Greater Serengeti region of Tanzania, Wadden Zee in the Netherlands, and the Great Barrier Reef in Australia (44).

Conservation—at the population and species level through ex situ collections and species management plans, at the community and ecosystem level through protected areas, and at the ecosystem and landscape levels through bioregional management—is key to preventing the major extinction that some experts foretell. The Biodiversity Convention is an important global step in integrating these and other approaches to conserve biodiversity for future generations.

FOCUS ON THE CONVENTION ON BIOLOGICAL DIVERSITY

Key Issues

TRENDS IN BIODIVERSITY PROTECTION

The Convention on Biological Diversity, signed by 158 governments at the 1992 United Nations Conference on Environment and Development (UNCED), (commonly called the Earth Summit) reflects growing international concern about biodiversity loss. The challenge that lies ahead is to translate international political commitment into effective action at the national, scientific, and popular levels.

Along with scientific consensus, popular concern over biodiversity loss has swelled, although it is expressed differently in various parts of the world. In the industrialized countries of the North, the threat to well-known and -liked species—whales, tigers, elephants, and pandas, for example—has awakened the public to the specter of biodiversity loss (45). Tropical deforestation has also been a focus of concern in the North partly because of fear that the loss of such a vast genetic storehouse would foreclose options for the development of new medicines, crops, and other goods and services of value to humanity. In addition, the well-publicized threat to the traditional indigenous communities that inhabit tropical forests has stirred the conscience of some circles in the North.

Similar concerns are expressed by many in the developing South. Governments there, however, focus more on the critical role biological resources play in their economies and development plans. For many of the billions of rural people who depend on wild and cultivated biological resources for their livelihood, the key issue is the erosion of access to these resources at the local level. Access is increasingly restricted by both national development and conservation initiatives, threatening some local communities' very cultural and physical survival. Southern governments and the rural people they govern may have a stake in biodiversity, but their interests sometimes conflict.

THE CONTEXT FOR THE CONVENTION

Governments have long acknowledged the importance of conserving wild nature by establishing parks and protected areas. In the past three decades, the number of protected areas worldwide has increased from 1,433 to 8,619 (from 130 million to 792 million hectares) (46).

At the international level, numerous treaties, conventions, and multilateral and bilateral agreements address aspects of biodiversity conservation, including protection of certain species and ecosystems, and regulation of international trade in endangered species. (See Chapter 24, "Policies and Institutions," Table 24.1.) In the mid-1980s, however, a growing number of experts, advocates, and governments began to articulate the need for a more comprehensive framework for international cooperation in stemming biodiversity loss. One major catalyst for this view was the World Commission on Environment and Development (WCED), or the Brundtland Commission (47).

Between 1984 and 1989, well before governmental negotiations on a treaty began, the World Conservation Union prepared successive drafts of articles for inclusion in such a treaty (48). The drafts highlighted a number of issues that would become key points for negotiation of the actual Convention, including proposals for a global list of critical sites for biodiversity conservation, an international fund based on the "polluter pays" principle, and a new regime for returning the benefits of genetic resource development to those countries that possess and conserve them (49) (50).

In 1987, the United States provided further impetus with a proposal for development of an international agreement on species and habitat protection (51). In the same year, the Governing Council of the United Nations Environment Programme (UNEP) established the ad hoc Working Group of Experts on Biological Diversity to investigate the feasibility of an umbrella agreement (52). This group concluded that a new global treaty on biodiversity was indeed needed. UNEP's Governing Council then established the ad hoc Working Group of Legal and Technical Experts, which met twice before being transformed into the Intergovernmental Negotiating Committee for the Convention on Biological Diversity (INC). The INC met in five sessions between June 1991 and May 1992. The Convention was negotiated in these seven sessions.

Concurrently with this process, the United Nations Development Programme (UNDP) and other sponsors in 1988 commissioned the International Conservation Financing Project, which recommended creation of an "international environmental facility" (53). In March 1990, a version of this recommendation was taken up by 17 donor countries at a meeting convened by the World Bank. By the fall of the following year, the Global Environment Facility (GEF) had been established as a joint venture of the World Bank, UNDP, and UNEP, to run in a pilot phase from July 1991 through June 1994. Resources of some $1.2 billion were pledged by donor governments, and four program areas were delineated, one being biodiversity conservation (54). (See Figures 8.6 and 8.7.)

While all of these initiatives largely focused on biodiversity loss in natural ecosystems, a debate on agricultural genetic resources intensified in the early 1980s. Southern countries began to question what they maintained was the practice of companies based in gene-poor Northern countries: obtaining diverse agricultural genetic material free of charge from a gene-rich developing country, then patenting seed varieties produced from that material and selling them back to the country of origin. The debate quickly escalated into a "seed war" between the North and the South, and efforts to resolve the issue at the international level have been largely ineffective (55).

NEGOTIATION AND CURRENT STATUS OF THE CONVENTION

The convention negotiating process began with the conviction, particularly among developed countries, that the result would be a comprehensive agreement on the conservation of species. From the outset, however, some countries sought to enlarge the focus to encompass issues bearing on the interaction between environment and development with the result that a number of contentious issues were brought into the debate:

■ The cost of taking measures to conserve biodiversity versus the cost of not taking them;
■ Different ways of regulating access to genetic resources;
■ Access to and transfer of technology, including biotechnology, in a manner that conserves biodiversity;
■ Sources of and mechanisms for funding the measures agreed upon; and
■ Consequences for trade and development of different ways of implementing biodiversity conservation (56).

The developing countries argued that because most biodiversity was located within their borders, the cost of conserving it could fall disproportionately on them. They wanted the Convention to explicitly tie conserva-

tion commitments to measures promoting sustainable use of biological resources, to increase funding from industrialized countries, and to ensure that the benefits of exploiting genetic resources, particularly through biotechnology, would be equitably shared between the North and the South. Thus the negotiations became, in part, a proxy for the much wider debate over the nature of North-South aid and trade, and the fairness of the global economic system.

The impending June 1992 Earth Summit (UNCED) complicated matters. Although in 1991–92 UNCED preparations ran on a legally and institutionally distinct track, they influenced the Convention negotiations in three important ways. First, UNCED became a de facto deadline for completion of a Convention text, without which it is unlikely that the Convention could have been completed in the time it was. Some governments—notably the United States and France—felt that the rush prevented resolution of a number of contentious issues.

Second, the concurrent negotiation of the biodiversity chapter of UNCED's official set of recommendations, Agenda 21, provided a parallel forum for countries either to reopen issues that had been settled in the INC or to create precedents for points not yet agreed upon in the Convention process.

Third, UNCED had a strong impact on the Convention through the pressure it exerted for rapid development of the GEF. Although the GEF was newly established, its major donors—who viewed some variant of the GEF as the only acceptable model for an international environmental funding mechanism—were anxious that it establish a track record by the time of the Earth Summit. In May 1992, the GEF's record on biodiversity was largely on paper. Although funding had been committed, almost all projects were still in preparation. Nonetheless, developing countries accepted the GEF as the interim funding mechanism for the Convention, as long as it was restructured to meet their concerns about the strength of their role in its governance.

With the Earth Summit less than two weeks away, the final session of the INC was held in May 1992 in Nairobi. There was still no agreement on several key provisions. The INC chairman and secretary general (UNEP's executive director) introduced a new draft, with compromise language based on informal consultations with a number of delegations, as a take-it-or-leave-it package. The final full text of the agreement did not emerge until May 22, 30 minutes before the Conference for the Adoption of the Agreed Text of the Convention on Biological Diversity. As a result of the either-or approach, delegates agreed on and initialed the Convention text, although some did so with strong misgivings (57). The Conference's formal report, together with a number of resolutions, constitutes the Nairobi Final Act, a document of some importance for the Convention's implementation (58).

While adoption of the agreed text at Nairobi allowed the Convention to be opened for signature at the Earth Summit a few weeks later, statements by a number of governments at the Conference on the Agreed Text referred to the fact that on certain key issues, the dele-

Figure 8.6 Number of Biodiversity Projects Funded through 1993 by Region

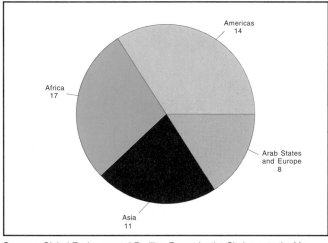

Source: Global Environmental Facility, *Report by the Chairman to the May 1993 Participants' Meeting, Part One: Main Report* (The World Bank/United Nations Development Programme/United Nations Environment Programme, Beijing, May 1993), p. 11.

Figure 8.7 Spending on Global Environmental Facility Biodiversity Projects Funded through 1993 by Region (US$ Million)

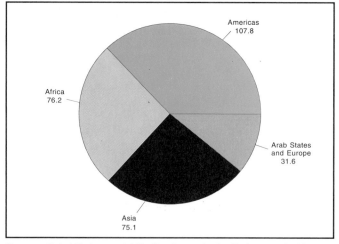

Source: Global Environmental Facility, *Report by the Chairman to the May 1993 Participants' Meeting, Part One: Main Report* (The World Bank/United Nations Development Programme/United Nations Environment Programme, Beijing, May 1993), p. 11.

gates had "agreed to disagree," expecting to deal with unresolved issues at a later stage. Nineteen donor countries joined in a statement expressing their concern that the provisions on financial resources not be interpreted as requiring mandatory assessments and contributions from them (59).

Possibly the most negative statements made at the conclusion of the Nairobi negotiations came from France and the United States. Their statements were directed at the negotiating process itself. France "expected practical and sound provisions to strengthen the conservation of biodiversity. Such provisions are few and too vague . . . France regrets that the manner in which the text of the Convention was adopted did not allow it to make a compromise proposal on the question of the global approach to biological diversity" (60). France, which did not initial the final text, did go on to sign the Convention at Rio. The head of the delegation to Rio, as well as three French ambassadors, noted publicly at a luncheon in honor of the INC chairman that the French delegation in Nairobi had been extreme in its criticism of the negotiations (61).

The United States initialed the text but expressed its regret that a number of issues related to intellectual property rights, finances and the GEF, technology transfer, and biotechnology, among others, had not been adequately addressed. The United States commented, "Procedurally, we believe that the hasty and disjointed approach to the preparation of this Convention has deprived delegations of the ability to consider the text as a whole before adoption. Further, it has not resulted in a text that reflects well on the international treaty-making process in the environmental field" (62).

Just before the Earth Summit, the U.S. government issued a statement that it would not sign the Biodiversity Convention at Rio, citing its provisions on intellectual property rights, funding, and biotechnology (63). The refusal created criticism and controversy at the Earth Summit and briefly put biodiversity at the top of the news around the world. While some branded the United States an "environmental outlaw," the U.S. biotechnology industry strongly supported the decision, arguing that "what is happening in Rio is nothing short of a diplomatic mugging" (64). A year later, under a new president, the United States reversed its position and signed the Convention (65). The three concerns the United States raised at Rio, however, remain contentious, and their resolution is one of the major tasks facing governments as they move to ratify and implement the Convention.

Since the Earth Summit, action to implement the Convention's objectives has moved forward quickly. Drawing on Resolution 2 of the Nairobi Final Act, UNEP's Governing Council established the Intergovernmental Committee on the Convention on Biological Diversity (ICCBD), which met for the first time in October 1993 in Geneva. UNEP's executive director also established four expert panels to study solutions for problems not solved in the negotiations (66). In addition, a fifth review panel prepared revised guidelines for biodiversity country studies (67). Concurrent and intensive negotiations were also held throughout 1993 to restructure and replenish the GEF so that it can operate the interim funding mechanism for the Convention.

On September 30, 1993, Mongolia became the thirtieth country to ratify the Convention, which took effect 90 days later (68). (See Chapter 24, "Policies and Institutions," Table 24.1 Technical Notes.)

The Convention: An Overview

The Convention on Biological Diversity is a document of 25 pages consisting of a preamble, 42 articles, and 2 annexes. The paramount institution presiding over the Convention's implementation is the Conference of the Parties, which became a legal entity when the Convention took effect and which will meet periodically. A secretariat and a scientific and technological advisory committee are also envisioned as part of the Convention's administrative structure (69).

Conceptually, the Convention has four parts. The preamble and Articles 1 through 5 lay out general objectives, definitions, principles, and jurisdiction. Articles 6 through 14 elaborate the commitments of each individual party to conserve biodiversity and promote its sustainable use. Articles 15 through 22 deal with the relationships between parties relevant to implementing the Convention, including financial relationships, and between the Convention and other international legal instruments. Articles 23 through 42 detail the administrative and procedural mechanisms by which the Convention regime will operate.

The Convention's preamble is nonbinding, but it expands on the reasons for the binding parts and on the concerns and expectations of signatories. Among other things, it recognizes the intrinsic value of biodiversity, its importance to human welfare, the sovereign right of states over their own biodiversity, and their responsibility for conserving it. The preamble also notes that:

■ Certain human activities are reducing biodiversity;
■ The scientific, technological, and institutional capacity to conserve biodiversity needs to be strengthened, and lack of scientific certainty about the issue should not be used as a reason for postponing action;
■ "Economic and social development and poverty eradication are the first and overriding priorities of developing countries;"
■ Substantial new investment will be required to conserve biodiversity, thus developing countries will need to be provided "new and additional financial resources and appropriate access to relevant technologies;" and
■ Intergovernmental cooperation is necessary for effective biodiversity conservation.

The preamble also notes the importance of the role of women, "indigenous and local communities embodying traditional lifestyles," and NGOs, as well as the "special conditions of the least-developed countries and small island states."

The Convention provides a broad framework of national and international obligations. Many articles provide clear direction for actions that parties must take, although these are generally laced with qualifiers that allow countries a good deal of latitude in interpretation. There are a number of issues on which countries do not yet agree, a state of affairs reflected in the ambiguous language of some articles.

CONTENTIOUS ISSUES

Financial Resources and Mechanisms

Article 20 states that developing countries will "require new and additional resources" to meet their obligations under the Convention. Indeed, "the extent to which developing country Parties will effectively implement their commitments under this Convention will depend on the effective implementation by developed country Parties" of their financial commitments (70). Two controversial issues remain: the amount of money that industrialized nations will provide and the

mechanism that will be used to control and account for those funds (71).

Article 20 attempts to strike a balance between developing countries' concern that they not take on obligations to step up biodiversity conservation without a commitment to help pay for it, and Northern countries' concern that their contributions be in amounts and on terms that they voluntarily accept. The financial mechanism set up under Article 21 to collect and administer funds has thus become a key point of contention between North and South.

The industrialized nations want their financial contributions to be managed by an institution over which they exercise effective control in policy and program decisions, and which is accountable both to them and to recipient countries for fund use. Developing countries, on the other hand, favor a U.N.-style majority-rule institution (one country, one vote), or at least one in which they have an equal voice with donors in setting policies and priorities and in allocating funds. Developing countries thus face a tradeoff between a financial mechanism with few resources over which they exercise significant control, and a more generously funded institution controlled by the donors.

In the early 1980s, for example, the Food and Agriculture Organization of the United Nations (FAO), which is subject to majority rule and therefore to control by developing countries, set up the Fund for Conservation of Plant Genetic Resources. This has never attracted significant contributions. The donor-controlled GEF, however, attracted some $1.3 billion just a few years later (72).

Given the clear preference of donor governments for the GEF model, developing countries reluctantly accepted the GEF as the interim Convention funding mechanism, but on the conditions of Articles 21 and 39 that it be "fully restructured" under the "authority and guidance of" the Conference of the Parties (73). In hopes that the GEF would be adopted as the financial mechanism supporting the Convention, the GEF Participants' Meeting in April 1992 acknowledged that universal membership is important; it called for a mixed decisionmaking system, using consensus first, then a voting system, if necessary, to ensure balanced "representation of the interests of developing countries while giving due weight to the funding efforts of donor countries" (74).

It is likely that the GEF will in some form become the permanent funding mechanism for the Convention. Negotiations over the GEF's restructuring will thus be a key forum—perhaps *the* key forum—for determining the Convention's future effectiveness. But hard bargaining lies ahead.

Some observers have noted that much of the debate over international environmental institutions, especially on financial obligations and equitable decisionmaking, has not been fruitful because it uncritically accepts the conventional international law perspective that (a) the only entities with the power to negotiate or decide at the international level are nation-states; (b) that a state is the sole international representative of everyone within its borders; and (c) that it is the legitimate international representative of its citizens, regardless of the means by which it acquired or keeps power. Thus, discussions of democracy and participation in relation to the Convention and GEF have only considered relations among governments. What is needed, some critics argue, is a radical change in international law that breaks the monopoly of the nation-states' hold over legitimacy in international forums, and that recognizes the right of citizens' groups and individuals to participate (75) (76). On the other hand, others might fairly question the legitimacy of nongovernmental entities that claim to more truly represent particular populations or interests. Who, after all, elected them?

Access to Genetic Resources

Before the Convention, unmodified genetic resources were held to be the common heritage of humankind, subject to free access. While free access was never meant to imply an abdication of national sovereignty, Article 15 clearly establishes that the authority to determine access to genetic resources rests with national governments and is subject to national legislation. Any collection of genetic resources can only be made with prior informed consent from the country of origin. It goes on to say, however, that countries must not unduly hinder access. These access provisions do not apply to genetic resources removed from a country before the Convention took effect. Simply put, those genetic resources stored in gene banks and collections outside of the country of origin—most of which are in developed countries—are outside of the Convention's provisions, no matter how they were acquired.

Applying the Convention's access provisions retroactively to genetic material existing outside of its country of origin would be legally and logistically improbable, so the exception in Article 15 makes practical sense. On the other hand, many people, particularly in developing countries, consider this unfair: genes collected in the past under the banner of free access, and frequently without any sort of prior informed consent, might end up as the intellectual property of either international gene banks or private firms.

The Consultative Group on International Agricultural Research (CGIAR), a consortium of donors supporting the work of 18 international centers that have gene repositories, does not apply intellectual property protection to any of the materials held in trust. Currently it is exploring ways by which the same conditions can be applied to recipients (such as national research institutions and private firms) of the materials from their gene banks (77).

A CGIAR working document, however, notes that in the changing research environment occasioned by modern biotechnology, the centers need to collaborate with a wide range of agencies in both the public and private sectors that increasingly protect their inventions through holding intellectual property rights (IPRs). While the centers do not generally seek intellectual property protection, they may do so on a case-by-case basis. Any such IPRs, however, will be "exercised without compromising in any manner whatsoever the fundamental position of the CGIAR regarding the free access by developing countries to knowledge, technology, materials and plant genetic resources" (78). The status of third parties, such as multinational corporations that use CGIAR genetic resources in modified commercial products for which they obtain intellectual property rights, is still unclear. And the centers in the CGIAR system are by no means the only existing international ex situ collections.

The Convention's failure to address this significant loophole led the final Nairobi Conference to adopt a resolution recognizing the need to resolve the issue with the FAO Global System for the Conservation and Sustainable Use of Plant Genetic Resources (79). It is likely to remain a significant and contentious issue.

Transfer of Technology

Article 16 is perhaps the most convoluted provision in the Convention, and was one of the hardest fought in the negotiations. It establishes the obligation of all parties to facilitate the transfer of, or provide access to, technologies relevant to the Convention's objectives, and elaborates the terms for transfers, including the treatment of patents and other IPRs. Because transfers are subject to "mutually agreed terms," it seems clear that this provision does not envision compulsory transfers of proprietary technology.

Despite the fact that Article 15 places access to genetic resources under national sovereignty and control, developing countries were not willing to rely on this to guarantee transfer of technologies that utilize their genetic resources, fearing an imbalance of negotiating power between developing country governments and large multinational corporations. This fear is not unjustified—the research budget of the Monsanto corporation, for example, is nearly the same as that of all national agricultural research programs in South America and that of all CGIAR centers combined (80) (81).

Developing countries sought through Article 16 to commit industrialized countries to ensuring that companies taking advantage of Southern genetic resources would give source countries access to technologies developed with those resources, including technologies protected by various IPRs (82). In turn, industrialized countries sought to ensure that Article 16 would not obligate them to force their industries to turn over patented technologies to Southern governments or firms. The result is an article whose language is confusing and subject to divergent interpretations.

The controversy over Article 16 must be seen in the context of the larger debate over IPRs. As the Biodiversity Convention was taking shape, negotiators for the General Agreement on Tariffs and Trade (GATT) were grappling with IPR issues as well. Since the beginning of the Uruguay Round of GATT negotiations in 1987, the United States has pushed for an agreement on trade-related intellectual property rights (TRIPS) that would impose legal obligations on signatories to provide minimum standards of IPR protection. Many developing countries, viewing IPRs as a way not only of denying them access to technologies but also of raising their price, resisted the imposition of new IPR standards in the GATT talks.

Table 8.3 Select International Companies Active in Plant and Other Natural Product Collection and Screening, 1950 to the Present

Company	Products Collected	Cancer	AIDS	Inflammation	Cardio-vascular Problems	Gastro-intestinal Problems	Other
Abbott Laboratories	Microbes, plants				•		•
Boehringer Ingelheim	Microbes, plants				•		
Bristol-Myers Sqibb	Fungi, microbes, marine plants	•					•
CIBA-GEIGY	Microbes, marine plants	•		•	•		•
Eli Lilly	Plants, algae	•			•		
Glaxo Group Research	Fungi, microbes, marine plants	•		•	•	•	•
Inverni della Beffa	Plants			•			•
Merck and Company	Fungi, microbes, marine plants	•		•	•	•	•
Miles	Microbes, plants, marine fungi				•		•
Monsanto	Plants, microbes			•	•		
National Cancer Institute	Plants, microbes, insects, marine fungi, algae, invertebrates	•				•	
Pfizer	Plants, spider venom	•		•	•	•	•
Pharmagenesis	Natural products used in traditional Asian medicine			•			•
Phytopharmaceuticals	Plants	•					
Rhone-Poulenc Rorer	Plants, marine microbes	•	•		•		•
Shaman Pharmaceuticals	Plants						
SmithKline Beecham	Microbes, marine plants			•		•	
Sphinx Pharmaceuticals	Plants, marine fungi, algae	•				•	
Sterling Winthrop	Microbes, marine plants	•		•			
Syntex Laboratories	Plants, microbes	•		•	•		•
Upjohn Company	Plants, microbes		•		•		•

Source: Walter Reid, Sarah Laird, Carrie Meyer, *et al.*, *Biodiversity Prospecting: Using Genetic Resources for Sustainable Development* (World Resources Institute, Washington, D.C., 1993), pp. 8–13.

The United States and other industrialized countries argued that extending strong IPR protection to developing countries would be an incentive for both technology transfer and domestic research and technology development in those countries. Industrialized countries therefore feared the impact of the Convention's technology transfer provisions on TRIPS and on the GATT negotiations in general. Some developing countries were aware of this potential link, and attempted to get language into the Convention that might weaken the TRIPS agreement (83). However, other Southern countries such as Brazil may have viewed the "IPR card" as a negotiating tactic to be given up in exchange for Northern concessions on financing. In Brazil, for example, NGOs observed that the government's "demand for access to cutting-edge technologies simply is not to be taken seriously." Given moves by the government in 1991 to introduce an industrial property bill abdicating free access to proprietary technologies, overwhelming government cutbacks in support for science and technology, and the lack of government interest in more accessible technologies for sustainable development programs, "[t]his demand for access to technologies can therefore be interpreted as a bargaining chip to be played (and given up) at the right moment of negotiations on access to financing" (84).

Despite its convoluted language, Article 16 sets out some basic principles and provides room for further elaboration as the Convention regime is developed among its parties. It recognizes that access to and transfer of technology, including biotechnology, between parties are essential to the goals of the Convention, and binds parties to try to "provide and/or facilitate access for and transfer to other Contracting Parties of technologies that are relevant to the conservation and sustainable use of biological diversity or make use of

genetic resources and do not cause significant damage to the environment."

Following this provision in Article 16 are four subsections that strike a balance between the demand of developing countries that they be given access to and transfer of technology on terms more favorable than those provided by market exchanges, and the demand of industrialized countries that any such transfers be on mutually agreed terms and not infringe on existing IPR protection. The Bush administration largely based its refusal to sign the Convention at Rio on this provision, believing it could be interpreted to require the compulsory transfer of patented biotechnologies to developing countries. Several detailed legal analyses of the provision, however, concluded that a fair interpretation of the provision in fact strongly protects IPRs (85). Indeed, a number of countries with strong biotechnology and pharmaceutical industries have signed the Convention and intend to ratify it, and even in the United States, biotechnology representatives seem to have become less concerned with the Convention's IPR ramifications as they have become more familiar with the text (86). (See Table 8.3.)

The Convention also raises issues concerning rights relating to indigenous peoples and genetic resources. India's neem tree (*Azarichdita indica*) illustrates the problems involved. Throughout the country, communities have invested centuries of care and knowledge in propagating and using neem as a biopesticide, soap, toothpaste, and medicine. Since the early 1980s, however, U.S. patents have been granted to several multinational corporations for neem resources effective against certain cancers and as an insecticide (87). Azadirachtin, the significant active component of neem, is a "product of nature" and therefore unpatentable, but

---

Box 8.2 **Implementing the Biodiversity Convention: Ten Immediate Actions that Countries Can Take**

Resolution of these contentious issues is likely to take time—time that the Earth's diminishing biodiversity does not have. While a great deal of attention is being devoted to ambiguous and disputed parts of the Convention, there are 10 areas where action can begin now. These are as follows:

1. Develop national plans, strategies, and/or policies to conserve biodiversity and ensure that use of the elements of biodiversity is sustainable (Article 6).
2. Conduct biodiversity inventories and surveys, identify activities that adversely affect biodiversity, and develop a system for organizing and maintaining this information (Article 7).
3. Establish or strengthen networks of national protected areas in order to protect

species, habitats, representative ecosystems, and genetic variability within species (Article 8).
4. Control, eradicate, or prevent the introduction of alien species that threaten ecosystems, habitats, or indigenous species (Article 8).
5. Manage biological resources, outside of protected areas, including degraded ecosystems, with a view to ensuring that their use is sustainable (Articles 8 and 10), and adopt economic and social incentives to that end (Article 11).
6. Develop or maintain necessary legislation and/or other regulatory provisions for the protection of threatened species and populations (Article 8).
7. Establish and/or strengthen facilities for the ex situ conservation of biodiversity

that support and complement in situ conservation efforts (Article 9).
8. Establish environmental impact assessment legislation and processes that take into account the impact on biodiversity of planned or existing projects, programs, or policies, and encourage public participation (Article 14).
9. Consider options for development of national and/or state/provincial regulations governing access to and exploitation of genetic resources (Article 15).
10. In industrialized countries, increase the amount of funding for effective biodiversity conservation in developing countries that undertake the actions noted above (Article 20).

---

when the compound is altered in a laboratory it is patentable under U.S. law (88). An Indian research report argues that the neem patents are for products and processes derived from neem and from indigenous knowledge and technologies, and that only minor modifications in traditional compounds and uses have been made (89). Allowing U.S. patent protection for neem products, the report goes on, is to condone "theft of knowledge and resources" (90).

Indigenous knowledge does not, in any case, receive much protection under the Biodiversity Convention. Article 8 mandates that parties "respect, preserve and maintain knowledge, innovations and practices of indigenous and local communities embodying traditional lifestyles . . . and promote their wider application with the approval and involvement of the holders of such knowledge, innovations and practices and encourage the equitable sharing of benefits arising [from them]." Several other articles include similar references. There is, however, no language that unequivocally guarantees indigenous peoples rights in traditional knowledge (91). It appears, therefore, that as corporate IPRs for genetic resources and the inventions derived from them expand, those of indigenous communities may contract. Correcting this growing imbalance is not only a matter of fairness. Indigenous people, like everyone else, require concrete incentives to preserve biodiversity.

Managing the Risks of Biotechnology

Along with the debate on how to share the benefits of gene-based biotechnology, controversy over managing its risks arose, but was not resolved, in negotiation of the Convention. Specifically, Article 19 calls on parties to consider a protocol (a legally binding agreement under the authority of the Convention) "setting out appropriate procedures . . . in the field of safe transfer, handling and use of any living modified organism resulting from biotechnology that may have adverse ef-

fect on the conservation and sustainable use of biodiversity." While most governments favored a protocol, a few questioned the scientific rationale for assuming that the release of genetically modified organisms poses significant risks (92).

Whether or not such a protocol emerges, Article 19 requires parties to make available any information on organisms they are transferring and on relevant regulations in their own jurisdictions, to the receiving party or parties.

OUTLOOK

The completion of the Biodiversity Convention is an important step toward slowing the loss of global biodiversity and instituting more sustainable and equitable ways of using the Earth's living resources. It is, however, only one step on a long journey that will extend through this decade and beyond. (See Box 8.2.) The Convention is a useful framework for action, but it is not a substitute for action. If its promise is to be realized, work will have to proceed on a number of complementary tracks that draw in a wide range of actors and interests.

First, more and more governments must move quickly to ratify the Convention, and they must work together to establish a strong institutional structure to guide and encourage its implementation. While the Convention took effect in December 1993 with 30 signatories, it will not gain much stature until considerably more countries, in particular the major powers of the North and South, sign on. In the meantime, governments can lay the groundwork for the Conference of the Parties through support for the interim secretariat and completion of the work mandated to the ICCBD in the Nairobi Final Act. Governments should also make sure that nongovernmental participation in the Convention process is firmly established and carries into the permanent Convention regime.

Box 8.3 Guidelines for Planning Biodiversity Conservation

All sectors that influence biodiversity should help plan its conservation.

If biodiversity conservation is to expand beyond the traditional agenda—protected areas, programs to protect individual species, and ex situ conservation—then the broader mandate must be reflected in national planning. All affected sectors and groups should be allowed to present their views and priorities and held accountable for how their activities and investments affect the country's biodiversity.

Biodiversity planning must involve bottom-up and participatory negotiations, and priorities must be set at a bioregional level.

Although coordination between national government agencies is essential for effective planning, many other interests depend on biodiversity, influence it, are knowledgeable about it, and have perspectives different from those of government agencies. Because hard choices must be made in planning, negotiation and compromise are essential. Effective negotiation takes time and costs money, and the process of coming to terms is likely to be initially contentious. But there is no other way to develop a plan that represents a broad range of interests and that has a hope of being implemented. Moreover, the interests of particular bioregions within a country need to be directly represented in planning. As a practical matter, once broad national goals are set, state or provincial planning meetings should flesh out actions to achieve these goals.

The ultimate planning authority for biodiversity conservation should rest with agencies that have real power.

When the locus of planning is a relatively weak agency, plans rarely work. Effective planning requires leadership by one or more agencies with real power to allocate resources and set national priorities. For this reason, agencies charged with managing protected areas, forestry, or wildlife may not be the most suitable political center of biodiversity planning, even though they will certainly be important participants. Rather, ministries or departments of planning or finance—or those

with equivalent power—should catalyze biodiversity planning, capitalizing on their proven ability to elicit cross-sector cooperation.

Biodiversity planners must set clear objectives and priorities.

Part of effective planning is deciding what *not* to do. Financial, human, and institutional resources for conservation are limited, and a lengthy wish list of everything that might be done with unlimited resources is no plan at all. Effective planning begins with the elaboration of national objectives derived from broad-based participation. Once a consensus forms, practical priorities can be set for policy reform, legal change, institutional fortification, human resources development, and investments in the field.

Policy reform and institutional change must be central elements of biodiversity planning.

Most national environmental planning focuses on developing investment projects and getting them into the national plan. However, no conservation investment or project should be approved until the policies and institutions that influence it are scrutinized. Indeed, concrete plans for eliminating or reducing policy weaknesses and institutional problems must be part of the plan. Since planning is too often equated with haggling over how to spend money, policy and institutional reform must be explicitly written into the legal terms of reference for planning and championed by those in charge of planning.

The full range of conservation options must be considered in developing biodiversity plans.

No single tool—be it national parks, zoos, agroforestry, or seed banks—can meet all the objectives of biodiversity conservation. Quite the contrary, the full range of options must be systematically considered in developing national action plans. Traditionally, however, in situ and ex situ conservation techniques have been developed and managed piecemeal by separate agencies and private institutions. As a result, broad understanding of the ad-

vantages and limitations of each approach is lacking.

Biodiversity planning must include systematic attention to implementation.

Environmental planning, indeed national plans of any sort, have earned a bad name among those eager for swift, effective action. All too frequently, elaborate plans languish forgotten on the shelf. Lack of attention to implementation may be partly to blame. Implementation is often overlooked because institutions' formal mandates are often confused with their true operating capacity. For example, ministries of forestry in many countries are legally responsible for managing vast portions of public forest estate but do not actually plant or harvest many trees. Similarly, many nongovernmental organizations have a deeply held commitment to habitat preservation but lack the wherewithal needed to bring it about. Institutions involved in planning must honestly evaluate their strengths and weaknesses. They must be prepared to shoulder more or less authority and responsibility where circumstances dictate, and they must decide how to strengthen their ability to implement a conservation plan.

Mechanisms for monitoring implementation must be built into planning.

A program for monitoring implementation must be clearly defined, and it should include milestones and criteria for measuring success. Ongoing evaluation not only ensures implementation, it also provides the feedback needed to improve a plan in response to changing circumstances. Implementation depends not only on the commitment of real programs and funds by governments but also on citizen participation. Just as keen public interest is critical at the front end of planning, citizens are needed as watchdogs as a plan is implemented.

Source: Adapted from World Resources Institute (WRI), World Conservation Union, and United Nations Environment Programme, *Global Biodiversity Strategy* (WRI, Washington, D.C., 1992), pp. 35–36.

Once the Convention takes effect, parties should move rapidly to resolve those issues on which there is not yet a clear consensus. The most pressing, in addition to the controversies already discussed, are (a) property rights with GATT and other international legal regimes, (b) the intent, language, and mechanisms for technology cooperation and transfer, (c) the Convention's treatment of biotechnology risk and safety issues, (d) the intent and language of the Convention regarding agreed full incremental costs and the structuring and funding of a permanent financial mechanism. While some work can begin on these issues now—restructuring the GEF to serve as the interim fi-

nancial mechanism, for example—many governments are understandably resistant to collateral negotiations that might upset the delicate balance the Convention's official structure and procedures represent. Progress will probably be best facilitated through negotiation of protocols and annexes to the Convention, both of which it provides for. The need for clarification and consensus on these issues is urgent, for in the absence of common understanding some governments may issue unilateral interpretations that conflict with each other and slow implementation.

Meanwhile, governments should move without delay to implement the many articles that are in accord with their own national policies, laws, and regulations. Many governments are already doing so. With assistance from UNEP, some 20 countries of the North and South have found it useful to conduct biodiversity country studies as a preliminary step toward developing the national biodiversity strategy, action plan, or policy framework the Convention requires of each party. (See Box 8.3.) Some countries have completed action plans and are working to implement them. Examples from among these countries include Chile, China, Indonesia, and Viet Nam.

Other countries, such as Costa Rica and, more recently, the United States, are working to develop comprehensive surveys and inventories of their biotic wealth, the foundation for virtually all actions under the Convention (93) (94). Canada, during the ratification process, conducted a systematic review of its laws and policies to determine where it complies with the Convention and where policy change and investment still need to be made (95).

Countries can also review their policies in sectors such as protected areas, forestry, agriculture, and fisheries, and change those policies that do not yet take biodiversity into account.

Perhaps most important on the legal front, countries need to develop or review legislation regulating international access to genetic resources within their borders. This is particularly important for gene-rich developing countries. The Convention grants broad discretion to national governments in setting up such legislation. Developing workable legislation and building the capacity of institutions to enforce and monitor it will take time, and the sooner a country develops its system of access control, the better positioned it will be within the Convention regime.

At the international level, governments and other entities are already cooperating in the preparation of the Global Biodiversity Assessment (GBA), funded by the GEF and carried out under the auspices of UNEP with the participation of a wide range of scientific experts (96). The GBA is meant to be an authoritative assessment of the current state of knowledge on biodiversity, its conservation, and its utilization. Done well, the GBA would provide a badly needed global information base, one useful to the Convention process. The key to GBA's success, however, will be political acceptability, which in turn will be based on scrupulous scientific objectivity, broad participation from all regions and sectors, and dissemination in a form that is comprehensible and useful to policymakers and those who advise and influence them.

Governments must recognize that while they are the main actors in realizing the objectives of the Convention, they are not the only ones. The model of governance that is assumed to prevail in the chambers of international diplomacy—governments decide, and the rest of society obeys—is largely fiction when it comes to biodiversity. Governments will only be able to carry out their biodiversity policies by gaining the support of the diverse sectors of civil society. After all, it is the daily decisions and actions of billions of individual citizens that actually determine biodiversity's fate.

Governments should open the process of implementing the Convention's objectives to all parties whose interests are affected, and whose views, resources, and skills can be brought to bear on the task. Specific methods for doing so should include:

■ Establishing national and local forums to debate, inform, and shape policies and initiatives that relate to the Convention's objectives;

■ Fully informing the public about policy decisions under consideration to further the Convention's implementation; and

■ Establishing procedures for environmental impact assessments that fully consider impacts on biodiversity and that guarantee effective public participation.

At the international level, governments can mobilize participation in the Convention process by granting broad observer status for NGOs in the Conference of the Parties and providing financial support to encourage participation. Governments may also want to consider putting NGOs and other civil representatives on their official delegations.

International dialogue on biodiversity, such as that being held under the auspices of the Global Biodiversity Forum, has been supported by a wide variety of public and private entities around the world. The forum's premise is simple: biodiversity conservation generally, and the Convention in particular, cannot be carried out without broad-based discussion of key issues. Therefore the forum brings together representatives from government, intergovernmental agencies, NGOs, grassroots organizations, and the private business sector to discuss important and contentious issues as well as to advance knowledge of biodiversity. Consensus is sought but not forced. The Forum is not a formal institution, nor does it claim to be the sole venue for such dialogue.

While governments can give support and legitimacy to all these efforts to broaden the constituency for conserving biodiversity and implementing the Convention, NGOs and other private entities should also be involved in this effort. The Earth's living creatures and ecological systems do not belong exclusively to governments. All of humanity has a stake in achieving the Convention's objectives, and all of humanity's diverse energies and skills will be needed toward that end.

The Conditions and Trends section was written by Dirk Bryant of the World Resources *staff. Focus On was written by Charles Barber, Senior Associate with the World Resources Institute Program in Biological Resources.*

References and Notes

1. Edward O. Wilson, "Is Humanity Suicidal? We're Flirting with the Extinction of Our Species," *The New York Times Magazine* (May 30, 1993), p. 28.

2. Norman Myers, "A Major Extinction Spasm: Predictable and Inevitable?" in *Conservation for the Twenty-First Century*, David Western and Mary Pearl, eds. (Oxford University Press, New York, 1989), pp. 42 and 47–48.

3. World Conservation Monitoring Centre, *Global Biodiversity: Status of the Earth's Living Resources* (Chapman and Hall, London, 1992), pp. 196–197.

4. World Resources Institute (WRI), World Conservation Union, and United Nations Environment Programme, *Global Biodiversity Strategy* (WRI, Washington, D.C., 1992), pp. 7 and 11–12.

5. *Op. cit.* 1.

6. Julian Simon and Aaron Wildavsky, "Facts, Not Species, Are Periled," *The New York Times* (May 13, 1993), p. 15, sec. A.

7. *Op. cit.* 4, pp. 2–3.

8. *Op. cit.* 4, p. 4.

9. Robert M. May, "How Many Species Inhabit the Earth?" *Scientific American*, Vol. 267, No. 4 (1992), pp. 42–44.

10. *Ibid.*, pp. 43 and 47.

11. Walter V. Reid, Jeffrey McNeely, Daniel Tunstall, *et al.*, *Biodiversity Indicators for Policy-makers* (World Resources Institute, Washington, D.C., 1993), p. 23.

12. *Op. cit.* 3, pp. 154–155.

13. P.H. Raven, "Biological Resources and Global Stability," in *Evolution and Coadaptation in Biotic Communities*, S. Kawano, J.H. Connell, and T. Hidaka, eds. (University of Tokyo, 1988), pp. 16 and 23.

14. Norman Myers, *Conversion of Tropical Moist Forests* (National Academy of Sciences, Washington, D.C., 1980), p. 14.

15. W. Reid and K. Miller, *Keeping Options Alive: The Scientific Basis for Conserving Biodiversity* (World Resources Institute, Washington, D.C., 1989), p. 15.

16. Norman Myers, "The Biodiversity Challenge: Expanded Hotspots Analysis," *The Environmentalist*, Vol. 10, No. 4 (1990), pp. 243–256.

17. C.J. Bibby, N.J. Collar, M.J. Crosby, *et al.*, *Putting Biodiversity on the Map: Priority Areas for Global Conservation* (International Council for Bird Preservation, Cambridge, U.K., 1992), p. 1.

18. Walter V. Reid and D.M. Raup, "Cohort Analysis of Generic Survivorship," *Paleobiology*, Vol. 4 (1978), pp. 1–15, cited in "How Many Species Will There Be?" in *Tropical Deforestation and Species Extinction*, J. Sayer and T. Whitmore, eds. (Chapman and Hall, New York, 1992), p. 56.

19. *Op. cit.* 3, p. 197.

20. *Op. cit.* 3, Table 16.1.

21. David S. Wilcove, Margaret McMillan, and Keith C. Winston, "What Exactly Is an Endangered Species? An Analysis of the U.S. Endangered Species List, 1985–91," *Conservation Biology*, Vol. 7, No. 1 (1993), p. 92.

22. *Op. cit.* 3, p. 236.

23. *Op. cit.* 21, pp. 87 and 92.

24. Rosemarie S. Gnam, "Comments Invited on Species Risk," *BioScience*, Vol. 43, No. 7 (1993), p. 430.

25. Georgina Mace, Research Fellow, Zoological Society of London, 1993 (personal communication).

26. Walter V. Reid, "How Many Species Will There Be?" in *Tropical Deforestation and Species Extinction*, T.C. Whitmore and J.A. Sayer, eds. (Chapman and Hall, London, 1992), Table 3.2.

27. *Ibid.*, p. 68.

28. *Op. cit.* 3, p. 202.

29. Thomas A. Stone and Peter Schlesinger, "Using 1 Km Resolution Satellite Data to Classify the Vegetation of South America," Woods Hole Research Center draft, Woods Hole, Massachusetts, 1992, p. 90.

30. Michael A. Mares, "Neotropical Mammals and the Myth of Amazonian Biodiversity," *Science*, Vol. 255 (February 21, 1992), pp. 976–977.

31. David Skole and Compton Tucker, "Tropical Deforestation and Habitat Fragmentation in the Amazon: Satellite Data from 1978 to 1988," *Science*, Vol. 260, No. 5116 (1993), p. 1906.

32. Lee Hannah, unpublished data (Conservation International, Washington, D.C., September 1993).

33. *Ibid.*

34. *Op. cit.* 11, p. 14.

35. William K. Stevens, "Huge Conservation Effort Aims to Save Vanishing Architect of the Savannah," *New York Times* (February 28, 1989), pp. 1 and 15, sec. c.

36. The African Elephant Conservation Coordinating Group (AECCG), *The African Elephant Conservation Review* (AECCG, Oxford, U.K., 1991), p. 1.

37. Wildlife Conservation International (WCI), *The Wild Bird Trade: When a Bird in the Hand Means None in the Bush*, WCI Policy Report No. 2 (New York Zoological Society, Bronx, New York, 1992), p. 5.

38. *Ibid.*, pp. 10–16.

39. Dorene Bolze, Policy Analyst, Wildlife Conservation Society, The Bronx, New York, 1993 (personal communication).

40. David Sarokin and Jay Schulkin, "The Role of Pollution in Large-Scale Population Disturbances, Part 2: Terrestrial Populations," *Environmental Science and Technology*, Vol. 26, No. 9 (1992), p. 1695.

41. Michael Wells, Katrina Brandon, and Lee Hannah, *People and Parks: Linking Protected Area Management with Local Communities* (The World Bank/World Wildlife Fund/ U.S. Agency for International Development, Washington, D.C., 1992), p. 3.

42. Valerie Barzetti, ed., *Parks and Progress: Protected Areas and Economic Development in Latin America and the Caribbean* (World Conservation Union, Cambridge, U.K., 1993), pp. 53–54.

43. *Ibid.*, p. 55.

44. Kenton R. Miller and Andrew Lawton, *Balancing the Scales: Policies for Increasing Biodiversity's Chances through Bioregional Management* (World Resources Institute, Washington, D.C., 1993), p. 2.

45. The industrialized countries of the North, with relatively high per capita income and relatively less biological diversity per unit of area, are expected to provide additional financial resources for biodiversity conservation in developing countries. While not all Southern countries are rich in biodiversity, they have tended to speak as a block in Convention negotiations.

46. *Op. cit.* 3, Table 29.2.

47. The World Commission on Environment and Development, *Our Common Future* (Oxford University Press, Oxford, U.K., 1987), p. 162.

48. The World Conservation Union Environmental Law Centre, *The Convention on Biological Diversity: An Explanatory Guide*, draft (Bonn, Germany, October 1993), p. 2.

49. David Bell, "The 1992 Convention on Biological Diversity: The Significance of the United States' Objections at the Earth Summit," *George Washington University Journal of International Law and Economics*, Vol. 26, No. 3 (1993), in press.

50. World Conservation Union (IUCN), "Draft Articles Prepared by IUCN for Inclusion in a Proposed Convention in the Conservation of Biological Diversity and for the Establishment of a Fund for the Purpose," IUCN Draft No. 6 (final), Gland, Switzerland, June 1989, Arts. 5, 15–16, and 26.2.

51. *Op. cit.* 49.

52. United Nations Environment Programme Governing Council Decision 14/26, June 17, 1987, cited in World Conservation Union (IUCN), "Draft Articles Prepared by IUCN for Inclusion in a Proposed Convention on the Conservation of Biological Diversity and for the Establishment of a Fund for the Purpose," IUCN Draft No. 6 (final), Gland, Switzerland, June 1989, Explanatory Notes, p. 2.

53. International Conservation Financing Project, *Natural Endowments: Financing Resource Conservation for Development* (World Resources Institute, Washington, D.C., 1989), p. 11.

54. David Reed, ed., *The Global Environment Facility: Sharing Responsibility for the Biosphere*, Vol. 2 (World Wide Fund for Nature, Washington, D.C., 1993), pp. 4–5.

55. Walter V. Reid, Sara A. Laird, Carrie A. Meyer, *et al.*, *Biodiversity Prospecting: Using Genetic Resources for Sustainable Development* (World Resources Institute, Washington, D.C., 1993), p. 23.

56. Vicente Sanchez, "The Convention on Biological Diversity," paper presented at the Second Asia-Pacific Regional Consultation on Biodiversity, Bangkok, Thailand, January–February 1993.

57. France did not initial the text but did sign the Convention at Rio. The United States, on the other hand, initialed the text but did not sign at Rio.

58. United Nations Environment Programme (UNEP), "Conference for the Adoption of the Agreed Text of the Convention on Biological Diversity: Nairobi Final Act," Intergovernmental Negotiating Committee, UNEP, Nairobi, Kenya, 1992, pp. 1 and 5.

59. "Declaration of Australia, Austria, Belgium, *et al.*" in United Nations Environment Programme (UNEP), "Conference for the Adoption of the Agreed Text of the Convention on Biological Diversity: Nairobi Final Act," Intergovernmental Negotiating Committee, UNEP, Nairobi, Kenya, 1992, p. 15.

60. "Declaration of France," in United Nations Environment Programme (UNEP), "Conference for the Adoption of the Agreed Text of the Convention on Biological Diversity: Nairobi Final Act," Intergovernmental Negotiating Committee, UNEP, Nairobi, Kenya, 1992, p. 19.

61. Ambassador Vicente Sanchez, Chairman, Intergovernmental Negotiating Committee, Nairobi, Kenya, 1993 (personal communication).

62. "Declaration of the United States," in United Nations Environment Programme

(UNEP), "Conference for the Adoption of the Agreed Text of the Convention on Biological Diversity: Nairobi Final Act," Intergovernmental Negotiating Committee, UNEP, Nairobi, Kenya, 1992), p. 25.

63. U.S. Department of State, "Convention on Biological Diversity," May 29, 1992 (press release).

64. Association of Biotechnology Companies, "President Bush Is Right Not to Sign Biodiversity Treaty," June 11, 1992 (press release).

65. "U.S. Signs Treaty: Global Patent Protection for Biotechnology Urged," *Bureau of National Affairs International Environment Reporter*, Vol. 16, No. 2 (1993), p. 432.

66. The panel topics were as follows: "Priorities for action and agenda for scientific and technological research" (Panel 1); "Evaluation of potential economic implications for conservation of biological diversity and its sustainable use, and evaluation of biological and genetic resources" (Panel 2); "Technology transfer and financial issues" (Panel 3); and "[Needs for, elements for inclusion in and modalities of] a protocol for transfer and handling of any living modified organism resulting from biotechnology" (Panel 4).

67. A number of such country studies have been prepared during and after the negotiating process, under the aegis of the United Nations Environment Programme and funded, in the case of many developing country studies, by Global Environment Facility. The review panel's mandate was to revise the guidelines based on the experience of the first group of studies, completed in January 1992.

68. Interim Secretariat, Convention on Biological Diversity, "The Biodiversity Treaty: In 90 Days It Will Enter into Force," September 30, 1993 (press release).

69. This section is based largely on the document itself, "Convention on Biological Diversity," treaty opened for signature at the United Nations Conference on Environment and Development, Rio de Janeiro, June 1992.

70. "Convention on Biological Diversity," treaty opened for signature at the United Nations Conference on Environment and Development, Rio de Janeiro, June 1992, Article 20.

71. John H Barton, "Biodiversity at Rio," *Bioscience*, Vol. 42, No. 10 (1992), p. 774.

72. *Ibid.*

73. *Op. cit.* 70, Arts. 21 and 39.

74. Global Environmental Facility (GEF), "The Pilot Phase and Beyond," GEF Working Paper No. 1, The World Bank, Washington, D.C., 1992, pp. 5–7.

75. Hilary French, "Strengthening Global Environmental Governance," in *State of the World 1992*, Lester Brown, Holly Brough, Alan Durning, *et al.*, eds. (W.W. Norton, New York, 1992), pp. 172–173.

76. David Downes, "Don't Blame It on Rio," *The Environmental Forum*, Vol. 9, No. 3 (1992), pp. 20–23.

77. Consultative Group on International Agricultural Research, "The Convention on Biological Diversity and the CGIAR," paper presented at the Global Biodiversity Forum, World Conservation Union/World Resources Institute/African Center for Technology Studies, Gland, Switzerland, October 1993.

78. "CGIAR Working Document on Genetic Resources and Intellectual Property," in *Summary of Proceedings and Decisions of the CGIAR Mid-term Meeting in Istanbul* (Consultative Group on International Agricultural Research, Washington, D.C., 1992), Annex 3, p. 22.

79. "Resolution 3: The Interrelationship between the Convention on Biological Diversity and the Promotion of Sustainable Agriculture," United Nations Environment Programme (UNEP), *Conference for the Adoption of the Agreed Text of the Convention on Biological Diversity: Nairobi Final Act* (UNEP Intergovernmental Negotiating Committee, Nairobi, Kenya, May 1992), pp. 10–11.

80. Philip Pardey and Johannes Roseboom, *ISNAR Agricultural Research Indicators Series: A Global Data Base on National Agricultural Research Systems* (Cambridge University Press, New York, 1989), n.p.

81. M. Collinson and K. Wright, "Biotechnology and the International Agricultural Research Centers of the CGIAR," paper presented at the 21st Conference of the International Agricultural Economists, Tokyo, August 1991, cited in World Resources Institute (WRI)/World Conservation Union/United Nations Environment Programme, *Global Biodiversity Strategy* (WRI, Washington, D.C., 1992), p. 110.

82. Gareth Porter, "The United States and the Biodiversity Convention: The Case for Participation," Environmental and Energy Study Institute, Paper on Environment and Development No. 1, Washington, D.C., 1992, p. 5.

83. *Ibid.*, p. 7.

84. David Hathaway, "Some Biodiversity Issues in Brazil," notes prepared for discussion at L'accès aux Ressources Génétiques: Un Enjeu de Développement, *Journée d' Etudes*, Paris, 1993.

85. *Op. cit.* 82, p. 19.

86. In January 1993, several environmental, policy research, and industry groups (Merck, Genentech, Shaman Pharmaceuticals, the World Wildlife Fund, the World Resources Institute, and the Environmental and Energy Study Institute) met to discuss the concerns of U.S. industry and to reach a common interpretation of the Convention.

Agreement was not difficult for this working group, whose main objective was to educate other corporations still fearful of the Convention and its strong language protecting international property rights, and to demonstrate to the U.S. government that both industry and environmental groups could support U.S. signature of the Convention. **Source:** United States Biodiversity Network (BioNet), "A Matter of Interpretation: The Strategy of U.S. NGOs toward the Convention on Biological Diversity," BioNet, Washington, D.C., 1993, pp. 3–4.

87. The Neem Campaign, *Intellectual Piracy and the Neem Patents* (The Research Foundation for Science, Technology and Natural Resource Policy, Dehradun, India, 1993), pp. 7–10.

88. Josephine R. Axt, M. Lynne Corn, Margaret Lee, *et al.*, *Biotechnology, Indigenous Peoples, and Intellectual Property Rights* (Congressional Research Service, Washington, D.C., 1993), pp. 54–55.

89. *Op. cit.* 87, p. 11.

90. Vandana Shiva, "Cultivating Biodiversity: From Reports to Action," paper presented at Norway/United Nations Environment Programme Experts Conference on Biodiversity, Trondheim, Norway, May 1993.

91. *Op. cit.* 88, p. 43.

92. United Nations Environment Programme (UNEP), Expert Panels Established to Follow Up on the Convention on Biological Diversity, *Report of Panel IV: Consideration of the Need for and Modalities of a Protocol Setting Out Appropriate Procedures* (UNEP, Nairobi, Kenya, 1993), pp. 12–13 and 24–30.

93. Rodrigo Gámez, Alfio Piva, Ana Sittenfeld, *et al.*, "Costa Rica's Conservation Program and National Biodiversity Institute (INBio)," in Walter Reid, Sarah Laird, Carrie Meyer, *et al.*, *Biodiversity Prospecting: Using Genetic Resources for Sustainable Development* (World Resources Institute, Washington, D.C., 1993), p. 57.

94. U.S. Department of the Interior (USDI), *A Proposal to Establish a National Biological Survey within the Department of the Interior* (USDI, Washington, D.C., 1993), pp. 1–2.

95. Ambassador Arthur Campeau, "The Process of Ratification," in *Proceedings of the Norway/UNEP Expert Conference on Biodiversity* (Norwegian Ministry of Environment/United Nations Environment Programme, Trondheim, Norway, 1993), p. 173.

96. Minutes of the Meeting of the Steering Group for the Global Biodiversity Assessment, United Nations Environment Programme, Trondheim, Norway, May–June 1993.

9. Energy

Energy is central to industrial development and to providing many vital services that improve the human condition—refrigeration for foods, fuels that are clean cooking, light for reading, motive power for transport, and electricity for modern communications such as telephone and television.

Although there is no evidence that the world has begun a transition away from dependence on fossil fuels, there is growing recognition that the environmental consequences—local, regional, and especially global—of these energy sources may prove serious enough to constrain their use.

In the South, shortages of energy are a serious constraint on development. Per capita use of energy in the developing world is less than one sixth that of the industrialized world, and energy services are scarce. In meeting their growing energy needs, developing countries face the challenges of overcoming widespread technical inefficiencies, capital constraints, and a pattern of subsidies that undercut incentives for conservation.

This chapter surveys the world's energy balance sheet—production, consumption, and resources. It reviews energy prospects in developing nations, including the potential for renewable energy sources and the critical role that the industrialized world must play. Finally, the chapter considers five case studies which

have had successes in field testing new energy approaches in the developing world.

CONDITIONS AND TRENDS

Recent years have seen significant changes in the world's energy balance sheet. A number of factors contributed to these changes: energy production and consumption are waning in the former Soviet Union, the 1991 Persian Gulf War curbed oil production in the Middle East, and the estimate of China's coal resources classified as "proven recoverable reserves" has been lowered dramatically.

Fossil fuels remain essential to the economies of modern industrial nations. Indeed, fossil fuel production and consumption continue to rise almost everywhere. The same can be said of electricity from large-scale hydroelectric and nuclear sources, which together supply the bulk of commercial energy from non-fossil fuel sources. Commercial energy from alternative renewable sources—nontraditional biomass, solar, wind, wave, geothermal, small-scale hydro, and ocean thermal—continues to reflect more future promise than current practice, although wind power may soon be more widely harnessed on a commercial scale. In many less developed countries, traditional, often

Table 9.1 Commercial Energy Production and Consumption by Region and by Fuel, 1991
(petajoules)[a]

Region	Liquid[b] Production	Liquid[b] Consumption	Gas[c] Production	Gas[c] Consumption	Solid[d] Production	Solid[d] Consumption	Primary Electricity Production Nuclear[e]	Primary Electricity Production Hydro[f,g]	Primary Electricity Consumption	Total Production	Total Consumption
World	132,992	119,178	76,275	76,315	93,689	93,947	22,669	9,311	31,990	334,890	321,430
Developing countries	78,715	31,471	15,147	11,872	37,736	36,870	857	3,231	4,007	135,686	84,290
Oil-exporting developing	65,156	12,603	11,125	7,927	1,140	564	33	566	589	78,020	21,683
OPEC[h]	50,862	7,568	8,934	6,088	525	304	0	198	196	60,519	14,156
Non-OPEC oil-exporting[i]	14,293	5,035	2,191	1,839	615	260	33	368	394	17,501	7,528
Oil-importing developing[j]	13,559	18,868	4,022	3,945	36,596	36,306	824	2,665	3,488	57,666	62,607
Africa oil-importing	625	988	14	62	4,115	2,917	46	151	199	4,951	4,167
Asia and Oceania oil-importing	9,170	13,002	2,730	2,530	31,671	32,638	678	1,290	1,965	45,539	50,135
Latin America oil-importing	3,764	4,878	1,277	1,353	810	751	101	1,224	1,323	7,176	8,305
Industrialized countries	54,195	86,072	61,093	64,328	56,334	56,558	21,427	6,058	27,527	199,107	234,485
OECD industrialized	31,969	67,978	31,482	37,894	37,331	38,789	18,513	5,048	23,610	125,343	168,271
North America[k]	21,875	34,562	23,883	23,987	23,704	20,730	7,609	2,716	10,339	79,787	89,618
Western Europe[l]	8,829	22,928	7,490	10,911	9,002	12,868	8,575	1,698	10,308	32,594	57,015
Pacific[m]	1,265	10,488	1,108	2,996	4,625	5,191	2,329	635	2,963	9,962	21,638
Non-OECD industrialized	22,226	18,094	28,611	26,434	19,003	17,769	2,915	1,009	3,917	73,764	66,214
Central Europe	514	2,367	1,199	2,595	6,284	5,695	602	162	827	8,761	11,484
Former Soviet Union	21,712	15,727	27,412	23,839	12,719	12,074	2,313	847	3,090	65,003	54,730

Source: United Nations (U.N.) Statistical Division, *U.N. Energy Tape* (U.N., New York, 1991).
Notes: Totals may not add because of rounding. a. One petajoule (PJ) = 10^15 joules = 947.8 x 10^9 BTUs. b. Includes crude petroleum gas liquids. c. Includes natural gas and other petroleum gases. d. Includes bituminous coal, lignite, peat, and oil shale burned directly. e. Production and consumption of electricity from nuclear generating facilities are calculated as the energy used to generate the electricity (30% efficient); electricity from geothermal sources is similarly calculated (10% efficiency). f. Production and consumption of electricity from hydro-powered sources are assessed at the heat value of electricity (1 kWh = 3.6 million joules), the equivalent of assuming a 100% efficiency. g. Includes electricity generated from geothermal and wind. h. Algeria, Gabon, Indonesia, Iran, Iraq, Kuwait, Libya, Nigeria, Qatar, Saudi Arabia, the United Arab Emirates, and Venezuela. i. Developing countries whose exports of petroleum and gas including reexports account for at least 30% of merchandise exports: Afghanistan, Angola, Bahrain, Bolivia, Brunei, the Congo, Ecuador, Egypt, Mexico, the Netherlands Antilles, Oman, Syria, Trinidad and Tobago, and Yemen. j. Also includes countries self-sufficient in oil whose oil exports are less than 30% of merchandise exports. k. Canada and the United States. l. Does not include Turkey, which is included in total for Asia and Oceania oil-importing. m. Australia, Japan, and New Zealand.

noncommercial, fuels such as wood remain primary sources of energy.

ENERGY PRODUCTION AND CONSUMPTION

Worldwide commercial energy production was 35 percent higher in 1991 than in 1971. From 1990 to 1991, however, production fell 0.025 percent to 334.9 exajoules (1 exajoule equals 10^18 joules). This is only the third interruption since 1950 of a steady climb in global production, the others occurring in 1973–74 and 1979–81. Total commercial energy consumption, on the other hand, rose 1 percent between 1990 and 1991. Over the last 20 years, in fact, energy consumption declined only in 1980, 1981, and 1990 (1). (See Table 9.1 and Figures 9.1, 9.2, and 9.3.)

Global per capita consumption of commercial energy in 1991 stood at 59 gigajoules (1 gigajoule equals 10^9 joules), down just slightly from the previous two years. This recent trend was driven primarily by only moderate growth in total consumption in the United States and Canada, and the steep decline (2.7 percent between 1990 and 1991) in total consumption in the former Soviet Union. Together those regions were responsible for almost 45 percent of the total global energy consumption. Energy consumption in Central Europe also fell.

Estimates of average global per capita consumption mask sharp differences in consumption around the world. Per capita consumption in Africa is only 12 gigajoules, or 20 percent of the global average, while in Europe it is 136 gigajoules (2.3 times the global average), and in the United States, which is the largest consumer of energy, it is 320 gigajoules (5.4 times the

global average). (See Chapter 21, "Energy and Materials," Table 21.2.)

Liquid fuels, primarily derived from petroleum, continue to dominate the world's energy mix. Global consumption increased by 0.8 percent from 1990 to 1991, to make up 37.1 percent of all commercial energy consumption; in this same period, global production fell 0.55 percent to make up 39.7 percent of all commercial energy production. National dependence on liquid fuels varies widely from 100 percent in Mauritania to 15.2 percent in China. Many countries such as Kenya that produce no petroleum, or only a fraction of what they need, depend on oil-exporting countries and the international market to supply this essential commodity of modern economies.

Solid fuels (primarily hard coals, soft coals or lignite, and peat) constitute 28 percent of global energy production and 29.2 percent of consumption. Trade in coal is extremely limited, compared with the trade in liquid fuels, with many countries neither producing nor consuming solid fossil fuels. Nevertheless, for some countries, solid fuels are the dominant energy source. In China, for example, they account for 80.8 percent of all commercial energy consumption, in India 67.7 percent, and in the Democratic People's Republic of Korea 88.7 percent.

The production and consumption of gaseous fuels (primarily natural gas) is the fastest growing part of the world energy mix. Global production increased 9 percent between 1988 and 1991 and now represents 22.8 percent of global production and 23.7 percent of global consumption of energy. Highly efficient combined-cycle turbines and natural gas's relatively benign environmental impact are what make this fuel so

Table 9.2 Proven Commercial Energy Reserves, 1990

(fossil fuel proven [petajoules])[a]

Region	Coal			Oil		Natural Gas		Total Reserves
	Hard Coal Reserves	Soft Coal Reserves	R/P[b] Years	Reserves	R/P Years	Reserves	R/P Years	
World	**19,841,141**	**4,582,845**	**209**	**5,639,794**	**45**	**5,004,802**	**52**	**34,578,702**
Developing countries	**6,711,060**	**734,799**	**163**	**5,030,292**	**68**	**2,358,035**	**96**	**14,344,306**
Oil-exporting developing	**296,158**	**336,743**	**911**	**4,780,005**	**78**	**2,058,015**	**106**	**6,982,042**
OPEC[c]	247,255	335, 696	1,511	4,397,271	91	1,904,014	116	6,394,357
Non-OPEC oil-exporting developing[d]	49,903	1,047	164	382,734	30	154,001	50	587,684
Oil-importing developing[e]	**6,413,902**	**398,055**	**152**	**250,287**	**19**	**300,020**	**58**	**7,362,264**
Africa oil-importing	1,724,503	56	341	14,864	24	27,017	827	1,766,440
Asia and Oceania oil-importing	261,766	1,494	333	43,017	12	44,153	28	350,432
Latin America oil-importing	4,427,631	396,506	123	192,405	22	228,849	65	5,245,391
Industrialized countries	**13,130,081**	**3,848,046**	**239**	**609,502**	**12**	**2,646,768**	**37**	**20,234,397**
OECD industrialized	**8,205,121**	**1,907,746**	**231**	**264,443**	**10**	**507,729**	**14**	**10,885,039**
North America[f]	5,983,709	485,668	242	179,204	10	304,933	11	6,953,513
Western Europe[g]	826,610	836,790	144	77,531	10	178,443	21	1,919,375
Pacific[h]	1,394,802	585,287	358	7,708	7	24,353	21	2,012,150
Non-OECD industrialized	**4,924,960**	**1,940,300**	**252**	**345,059**	**14**	**2,139,039**	**62**	**9,349,358**
Central Europe	989,650	544,300	161	10,099	15	21,094	13	1,565,143
Former Soviet Union	3,935,310	1,396,000	300	334,960	14	2,117,945	65	7,784,215

Sources:
1. World Energy Council (WEC), *1992 Survey of Energy Resources* (WEC, London, 1992), pp. 20–21, 42–43, and 71.
2. United Nations (U.N.) Statistical Office, *U.N. Energy Tape* (U.N., New York, 1993).
Notes: Totals may not add up because of rounding. a. One petajoule (PJ) = 10^{15} joules = 947.8 x 10^{9} BTUs. Conversion factors: 1 million metric tons of oil equivalent = 41.87 PJ, 1 billion cubic meters natural gas = 38.84 PJ, 1 million metric tons of coal equivalent (hard coal) = 27.91 PJ, 1 million metric tons of coal equivalent (soft coal) = 13.96 PJ. b. R/P is the ratio of proven reserves to 1990 production rate. c. Algeria, Gabon, Indonesia, Iran, Iraq, Kuwait, Libya, Nigeria, Qatar, Saudi Arabia, the United Arab Emirates, and Venezuela. d. Developing countries whose exports of petroleum and gas including reexports account for at least 30% of merchandise exports: Afghanistan, Angola, Bahrain, Bolivia, Brunei, the Congo, Ecuador, Egypt, Mexico, the Netherlands Antilles, Oman, Syria, Trinidad and Tobago, and Yemen. e. Also incudes countries self-sufficient in oil whose oil exports are less than 30% of merchandise exports. f. Canada and the United States. g. Does not include Turkey, which belongs in total for Asia and Oceania oil-importing countries. h. Australia, Japan, and New Zealand.

attractive (2). Some countries supply a significant fraction of their fuel needs by importing natural gas. In Japan, natural gas makes up 12.5 percent of total energy consumption even though domestic production meets only 4.1 percent of demand for that fuel. In Finland, which produces no natural gas, 11.1 percent of energy is consumed in the form of natural gas.

The most important sources of primary electricity, that is, electricity produced from any source other than fossil fuel-fired thermal plants, are large-scale hydroelectric plants and nuclear-fueled thermal plants (3). Primary electrical production accounts for 9.5 percent of the world's energy supplies and almost 10 percent of its energy consumption. Nuclear power provides about two thirds of primary electricity, hydroelectric power almost all the rest. Both nuclear and hydroelectric require massive investment and technical expertise. Many countries have only limited potential to develop hydroelectric power. (See Chapter 21, "Energy and Materials," Table 21.3.)

Wind, geothermal, solar power, and small-scale hydro continue to show promise. Important producers of wind power are the United States (2,500 gigawatt-hours (GWh) in 1989), Denmark (744 GWh in 1990), and Australia (125 GWh in 1990) (4). In 1990, world energy production from geothermal sources exceeded 30,000 GWh, the largest producers being the United States (16,900 GWh), the Philippines (5,470 GWh), and Mexico (5,124 GWh) (5). Electric power from solar energy is still small from photovoltaic sources and amounts to just over 700 GWh from thermal solar sources, most of which is produced in the United States, specifically the deserts of California. Small-scale hydroelectric power mostly fulfills specialized needs

such as applications in remote areas. The installed capacity of hydroelectric plants less than 2 megawatts in size is only 1.9 percent of the capacity of larger plants (6).

INDUSTRIALIZED COUNTRIES

The Organisation for Economic Co-operation and Development

In 1991, the Organisation for Economic Co-operation and Development (OECD), an organization of industrialized nations, accounted for 52.4 percent of total world energy consumption but only 37.4 percent of

Figure 9.1 Commercial Energy Consumption, 1971–91

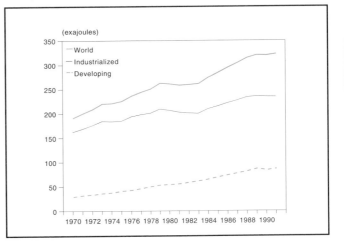

Source: United Nations (U.N.) Statistical Division, *U.N. Energy Tape* (U.N., New York, 1993).

Figure 9.2 Commercial Energy Consumption in Industrialized Countries, 1971–91

A. All Industrialized Countries

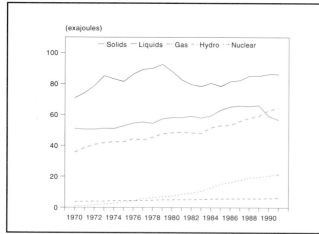

B. OECD Industrialized Countries

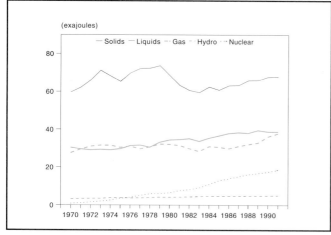

C. Central Europe and the Soviet Union

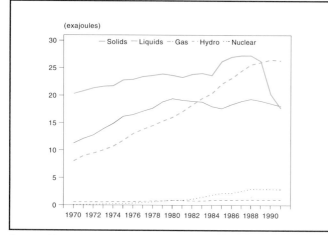

Source: United Nations Statistical Division, *U.N. Energy Tape* (U.N., New York, 1993).

global production. OECD countries produced 74.5 percent of what they consumed.

Since the oil shocks of the 1970s, coal use has grown in OECD countries, especially the United States and Australia, and it remains the major energy production source in OECD countries. (See Figure 9.2B.)For their oil-hungry economies, OECD countries depend on imports, primarily from Persian Gulf states.

Central Europe and the Former Soviet Union

The global plateau in energy production clearly results from the dramatic production decline in the former Soviet Union. The nations of Central Europe and those that once formed the Soviet Union together produce 22 percent of the world's supply of energy and account for 20.6 percent of world consumption. Between 1988 (the peak year so far) and 1991, however, total energy production in the former Soviet Union fell 11.3 percent. Energy from solid fuels fell 27.9 percent and energy from liquid fuels 17.3 percent (gas edged up and primary electricity production dropped slightly). (See Figure 9.2C.) Consumption also fell—an overall 8.5 percent between 1988 and 1991—helping explain the sluggish global growth of consumption in the last few years. The declines mirror social and economic upheaval in the region, including unprecedented strikes by coal miners. Potential for gains in efficiency are evident in both Central Europe and the former Soviet Union: the region's energy intensity (energy use per dollar of gross national product) was more than twice that in North America. (See Chapter 21, "Energy and Materials," Table 21.2.)

DEVELOPING COUNTRIES

Developing countries produce the remainder of global energy (50.5 percent) but consume only 26.2 percent of the global total. (See Chapter 1, "Natural Resource Consumption," Figure 1.2, and Chapter 21, "Energy and Materials.")

Oil-Exporting Nations

Twenty-six countries, together accounting for about 23 percent of global oil production, depend on oil for 30 percent or more of their total exports. During 1991, this supply was threatened by the outbreak of war involving or affecting the nations in the Persian Gulf. Oil production dropped in Iraq (-86.9 percent, or 3,718 petajoules) and Kuwait (-84.1 percent, or 2,212 petajoules), about 4.5 percent of global oil production. At the same time, 85 percent of the decline was made up by production increases in Saudi Arabia (+26.2 percent, or 3,722 petajoules), the United Arab Emirates (+12.0 percent, or 541 petajoules), Iran (+7.8 percent, or 527 petajoules), Syria (+20.6 percent, or 198 petajoules), Oman (+3.2 percent, or 46 petajoules), and Turkey (+18.1 percent, or 28 petajoules) (7). (See Figure 9.3B.)

Oil-Importing and Self-Sufficient Nations

Other developing nations are not so well endowed with oil. These range from countries that are nearly self-sufficient in energy to those that rely on imports for all their supplies.

India, a modest importer of energy (18 percent), is self-sufficient in coal and able to supply much of its rising demand for petroleum. China, despite its huge and accelerating demand, exports energy equal to 6 percent of domestic consumption, primarily because of rapid increases in coal production. Afghanistan exports 12 percent, being self-sufficient because of modest internal demand, and Argentina, blessed with a near balance between domestic demand and supply, imports 3 percent.

Some other countries find that dependence on foreign energy upsets their balance of payments and piles up external debt. Many of the poorest countries import all of their energy. For example, The Gambia, Mauritania, Equatorial Guinea, and Somalia, all of which rely on imported energy, are also all heavily in debt. (See Chapter 15, "Basic Economic Indicators," Table 15.2.)

ENERGY RESOURCES

The World Energy Council, in its 16th *Survey of Energy Resources*, found that "the fears of imminent [resource] exhaustion that were widely held 20 years ago are now considered to have been unfounded. The concepts of exhaustion, or even scarcity, fail to appear anywhere in this survey" (8). Estimates of proven recoverable reserves of petroleum rose 11.4 percent between the end of 1987 and the end of 1990, while those of natural gas liquid rose 5.3 percent and those of natural gas rose 17.9 percent. These increases can be attributed to both the reevaluation of existing reserves and the discovery of new reserves. Given current economic conditions and technologies, proven reserves alone could supply petroleum needs for 40 years, natural gas for 50 years, and coal for well over 200 years; there is also the expectation that new fossil fuel reserves will be discovered in the coming years (9) (10). (See Table 9.2 and Chapter 21, "Energy and Materials," Table 21.3.)

Coal

In 1987, China was believed to have 45.7 percent of all the world's proven recoverable reserves of coal, totaling 1.6×10^{12} metric tons. Drastically revised estimates for 1990, however, show that country with 11 percent of a diminished global reserve of 1×10^{12} metric tons, a 35 percent decline for the world and an 84.3 percent decline for China. Estimates of proved recoverable coal reserves outside of China actually grew 6.6 percent from 1987 to 1990 (11) (12). The World Energy Council, in a laconic footnote to this dramatic change, explained, "The Reserves data presented in this Survey differ considerably from those in the *1989 Survey of Energy Resources*. The figures in this Survey are based on a new study" (13). More recent Chinese sources, however, continue to emphasize China's huge coal resources (14). What appears uncertain is the fraction of Chinese resources that can be accurately classified as proven recoverable reserves, that is, those extractable under local economic and technical conditions. Even with the lower estimate of proven recoverable reserves, China's coal would last for many decades if current consumption rates held. For the long term, the

Figure 9.3 Commercial Energy Consumption in Developing Countries, 1971–91

A. All Developing Countries

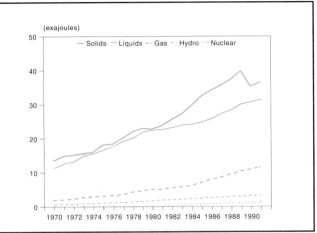

B. Oil-Exporting Developing Countries

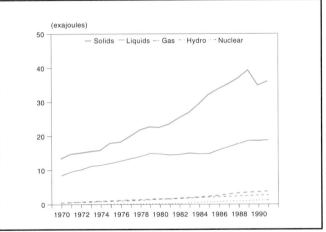

C. Oil-Importing Developing Countries

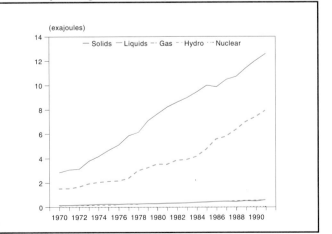

Source: United Nations (U.N.) Statistical Division, *U.N. Energy Tape* (U.N., New York, 1993).

new estimates, if confirmed, should be taken into account by energy and development planners.

Petroleum

Estimates of global petroleum reserves increased 10 percent between 1987 and 1990, primarily owing to the reevaluation of reserves in the Persian Gulf states. The estimates refer to the period prior to the Gulf War, but total reserves in the region are not expected to have been significantly affected by that event. Outside of the Gulf states, reserve estimates fell between 1987 and 1990—in the United States 3.3 percent, and in Europe 23.3 percent. The Russian Federation's high-yield oil fields are 60 to 90 percent depleted (which also explains recent declines in production) (15). Estimates of the Federation's resources may rise after Western technology and investment begin to have an effect.

Natural Gas

Proven recoverable reserves of natural gas remain on the rise, going up 17.9 percent between the end of 1987 and the end of 1990. During that time, proven recoverable reserves in the former Soviet Union jumped a full 32.7 percent to compose 42.3 percent of the world's total resource. Demand for gas is growing, and supplies have dwindled in some countries where demand is already relatively high. Between 1987 and 1990, reserves declined 21.3 percent in Western Europe and 15 percent in the United States. The imbalance in consumption and reserves, coupled with the environmental advantages of natural gas over other fossil fuels, should stimulate international trade and extend new economic opportunities to those countries well endowed in this resource.

Nuclear Power

Global proven reserves of uranium (outside of China, Central Europe, and the former Soviet Union), recoverable at the rate of U.S. $130/kilogram, dropped 10 percent between 1987 and 1990 (16). This reduction can be attributed primarily to mines closing after an excess supply caused uranium prices to collapse.

Hydroelectric Power

Only 15.3 percent of the world's exploitable hydroelectric potential was used in 1990. The former Soviet Union had the largest exploitable potential (3,831,000 GWh/year), followed by China, Brazil, Indonesia, Canada, and Zaire. Global installed capacity grew 6.9 percent between 1987 and 1990. China and Brazil together were responsible for 38.6 percent of the increase. Growing awareness of environmental and social costs of large-scale hydroelectric projects does not appear to have slowed their development. Ongoing construction should increase installed capacity at the rate of 2.5 to 3.0 percent annually, continuing a 20-year trend (17) (18).

FOCUS ON ENERGY PROSPECTS FOR DEVELOPING NATIONS

An adequate and reliable energy supply is central to meeting the goals of development and economic growth in the developing world. Without heating, re-

frigeration, lighting, and mechanical power, development would be inconceivable; these and other energy services literally fuel the engine of economic growth and pave the way for improved living standards.

Building a sector capable of delivering energy services is itself one of the most complex and expensive aspects of national development. The tremendous capital costs associated with constructing power plants and transmission lines, for example, or acquiring, transporting, and refining primary fuels such as coal and oil consume a significant portion of the financial resources available to developing nations for economic and social development. Indeed, as much as 40 percent of total public investment goes to capitalizing the energy sector in many nations of the South, which accounts for a high percentage of their current foreign debt (19).

In addition to the economic cost of meeting the developing world's rising energy needs, the environmental price is steep. Over the last two decades, rapid expansion of the energy sector in the South has been accompanied by a decline in urban air quality as well as serious land and water degradation from mineral exploitation and fuelwood harvesting. And as energy use rises, so does the emission of greenhouse gases, though the developing world still only accounts for a modest percentage of global emissions. Growth along conventional lines will only intensify these trends.

Herein lie the challenges that developing nations face in meeting their current and future energy needs. Significant opportunities now exist—in the form of new energy technologies and potential policy reforms—for these nations to align development and environmental goals. Industrialized nations have an important role to play in providing commercially viable alternative technologies, implementing model sustainable energy policies, and generating innovative financial mechanisms to help developing countries adopt these technologies.

ENERGY USE IN THE DEVELOPING WORLD

Energy consumers in the developing world fall into two distinct groups with different energy sources and needs. Those with access to modern commercial fuels—coal, petroleum products, natural gas, and electricity—live primarily in urban areas where there are sizable industries, utility grids, and fuel distribution systems. Those who live in rural areas continue to rely heavily on traditional biomass fuels—wood, crop waste, and animal dung. (Biomass fuels supply roughly one third of the South's energy needs.) The typical rural economy is subsistence-based and has little access to commercial fuels and services. Animal and human muscle contribute much of the energy for agriculture and transportation; fuelwood is burned for cooking, heating, and some industrial uses (20). (See Chapter 21, "Energy and Materials," Table 21.2.)

Energy consumption, much lower in developing than in industrialized nations, reflects disparities in economic activity and living standards. Developing countries account for 75 percent of world population, but consume only about 30 percent of the global energy budget (about 26 percent of all the commercial energy sources and 85 percent of all the traditional biomass fuels) (21).

The difference in per capita energy consumption is even more pronounced. Per capita consumption (including both commercial and traditional fuels) in the developing world is less than one sixth that in the industrialized world, and less than one tenth that in the United States (22). The disparity is smaller than 20 years ago: over the past two decades, energy consumption in the South has risen more than seven times faster than in the North, driven by rapidly expanding economies, rising populations, and increasing urbanization (23). In spite of this growth in consumption, energy services in developing nations are scarce for all but a wealthy minority (24).

Both industrial and residential demand have outstripped growth in power-generating capacity and in production and use of coal and oil, leading to electricity and primary-fuel shortages. Commercial energy shortages, aside from their inconvenience, often measurably decrease national productivity. Factories suffer regular black- or brownouts, industrial boilers lack fuel, backup diesel generators must be purchased—these are common pitfalls of shortages (25) (26) (27). And the price is high. In India, for example, economic losses associated with such power shortages are estimated at 1 to 2 percent of the national income (28).

In the noncommercial sector, the expanded population has created chronic shortages of traditional fuel along with a legacy of environmental degradation and declining soil fertility. Fuelwood is disappearing and people are burning more crop residue and animal manure instead of returning them to the soil (29) (30).

The developing world faces several structural problems that exacerbate already inadequate energy supplies. Foremost among these is widespread inefficiency: energy is lost at every stage of production, distribution, and use, and losses generally exceed those in industrialized countries. Power plants in the developing world consume, on average, 15–30 percent more fuel per unit of electricity produced than efficiently operated plants elsewhere. Lack of proper maintenance and poor-quality fuel further erode the capacity and reliability of power plants (31).

Distribution networks compound energy waste. Because of outdated, inefficient, ill-maintained equipment, low-voltage lines serving widely dispersed rural customers, and pilferage, losses between power station and customer average about 17 percent in the South, as opposed to 6–8 percent in the North (32) (33) (34). Old industrial boilers and low-efficiency motors are still commonly used, partly because of the lack of capital to replace them. In the home, people often burn raw coal, wood, and other biofuels in open fireplaces and low-efficiency stoves and heaters, wasting energy and releasing dangerous pollutants. The traditional "three-stone stove," in use throughout much of the developing world, has a typical efficiency of only 10 percent, compared with an average efficiency of about 60 percent for a modern gas stove (35) (36).

Government policies regulating energy prices and subsidies exacerbate the problem of waste in poor countries by effectively discouraging conservation. To keep energy affordable, prices charged to consumers—particularly for electricity—are generally kept far below the costs of producing energy. On average, consumers in the developing world cover only 60 percent of the real cost of the energy they receive, requiring massive subsidies by central governments to keep their energy sectors afloat (37) (38) (39) (40).

Low energy prices have another drawback: they leave little incentive for conservation because the financial reward, savings on utility bills, is small compared to the effort and expense of conservation measures. A lack of market penalties can have undesired effects, particularly where energy supply is already limited (41). For example, in India, where farmers pay low electricity prices, the proliferation and overuse of inefficient electric irrigation pumps have driven up agricultural demand for electricity by 15 percent annually and contributed to system overloads (42) (43) (44).

ENERGY DEMAND: A COSTLY FUTURE

Energy demand in the future, it seems, will only grow. According to the U.S. Office of Technology Assessment, commercial energy use in developing nations could triple over the next 30 years, with their share of total global commercial energy consumption rising from 26 percent in 1991 to 40 percent in 2020 (45). Electricity demand in the South is projected to rise an average of nearly 7 percent a year through the 1990s; in some nations, demand is growing by 10 percent or more annually (46) (47).

If this anticipated demand were met using conventional means, the environmental consequences could be dire at both local and global levels. In addition to worsening urban smog and regional acid rain, growing consumption of fossil fuels would have a profound effect on efforts aimed at reducing the threat of global warming. The developing world's share of energy-related carbon dioxide emissions would increase from 26 percent in 1985 to 44 percent by 2025. Other impacts might be equally severe, including additional land disturbance from mining, defoliation and soil degradation associated with fuelwood collection, and habitat loss and displacement of indigenous peoples resulting from large hydroelectric developments (48) (49).

However, while energy use in the developing world will undoubtedly continue to climb, there is widespread skepticism about whether the conventional energy supply can expand fast enough to meet projected demand, because of the expense involved and the limited financial resources of developing nations (50) (51) (52). A study in 1988 concluded that, depending on the rate of economic growth, $1.7 to 4 trillion would be required to finance the South's energy needs over the following 20 years at existing levels of energy efficiency—a rate of investment 1.5 to 4 times greater than at present (53). (See Figure 9.4.)

Yet investment in debt-strapped developing nations is falling, not rising, and there is little prospect that adequate funds will be available from either domestic or international sources for the kind of expansion energy planners in these nations envision. Shortage of

Figure 9.4 Projected Growth in Electricity Consumption, 1980-2010

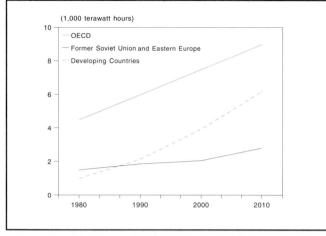

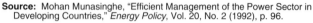

Source: Mohan Munasinghe, "Efficient Management of the Power Sector in Developing Countries," *Energy Policy*, Vol. 20, No. 2 (1992), p. 96.

capital promises to become the single greatest barrier to expanding the conventional energy infrastructure in the near future (54) (55).

IMPROVING ENERGY EFFICIENCY

Given the limitations on expanding the energy sector, aggressive investment in energy efficiency, which extracts more services such as light or mechanical power from the same energy input, is a potent tool for developing countries. Indeed, energy efficiency is now widely regarded as a correlate of any workable scheme for sustainable development, because it reduces environmental and economic costs of expanding the energy services on which development depends (56).

Current technology makes possible immediate, substantial energy savings that can reduce present shortages as well as future demand. Acquiring such technology is economically attractive: lower energy costs usually pay for the investment, and often within a short time. One study estimates that as much as 25 percent of the energy used in the developing world could be saved with investments that paid for themselves in two years or less, with even greater savings realized over the longer term (57).

Adopting new technologies is not the sole means of improving energy efficiency. Good operational and management practices, many of them straightforward and inexpensive, can minimize energy waste. It has been shown in Kenya that housekeeping measures such as shutting down machinery not in use can deliver energy savings of up to 10 percent (58) (59).

At a macroeconomic level the argument for efficiency is even more persuasive, offering at least a partial solution to the capital scarcity that plagues energy sectors (60). According to two independent studies, over the next several decades the adoption of energy-efficient technology, by reducing growth in demand, could reduce the South's capital requirements for energy-sector expansion by half. This would free up investment funds while still fueling growth (61) (62).

Opportunities for increasing energy efficiency abound, and the potential for savings is particularly large in connection with electricity, on which many of the services associated with a rising living standard—lighting, refrigeration, air conditioning—depend (63).

In the developing world, the use of more efficient appliances and processes could result in energy savings of as much as 50 percent, with consumers reaping savings of some 25 percent over the life of the equipment, according to the U.S. Office of Technology Assessment (64). On the supply side, 15 percent increases in power plant efficiency and a decrease in transmission losses of about 6 percent are possible. Together with a 25 percent increase in end-use efficiency, these efforts could cut electricity generation needs by some 40 percent, leading to tremendous capital investment savings (65).

In the noncommercial sector, improving the efficiency of traditional appliances such as wood or kerosene stoves could bring substantial energy savings and ease the present energy crisis in rural areas. Several fuel-efficient stoves are already in production, and many developing nations—Kenya, India, and China, for example—have active programs to distribute them to rural residents (66) (67) (68) (69) (70). (See Table 9.3.) In addition, the transportation sector offers developing countries tremendous opportunities for saving energy through efficiency measures, including proper road and vehicle maintenance and development of fuel-efficient vehicles and mass-transit systems (71) (72) (73).

Despite the obvious economic advantages, developing nations have been slow to embrace the concept of energy efficiency. For one, energy planning has traditionally focused on increasing supply as fast as possible, not managing supply to maximize services. Until recently, investment in energy efficiency was not a priority (74) (75) (76). This began to change with the recent surge of interest in "integrated resource planning," a more far-reaching approach toward planning that looks for the least-cost option to meet demand for services. Integrated resource planning, which explicitly recognizes the economic advantage of investment in energy efficiency, emphasizes the need for national utilities to encourage conservation among customers, not simply to facilitate electricity use (77).

Another barrier to adopting efficiency measures is economic instability. Hyperinflation causes interest rates to rise, dries up investment capital, and makes it difficult to calculate the payback period for efficiency investments, reducing their attractiveness (78).

Obstacles to embracing energy conservation also exist at the consumer level. For example, energy-efficient equipment and appliances are frequently not available. Many of those that are come from foreign countries and may be subject to high import tariffs. In any case, consumers tend to be put off by the higher initial cost of energy-efficient appliances (79) (80) (81) (82).

To address these type of problems, governments in developing countries will need to adopt a combination of policy changes. These include raising energy prices (while targeting subsidies for the poor), establishing efficiency standards for appliances and manufacturing equipment, exempting efficient equipment from burdensome duties and taxes, and creating rebate programs to offset the higher purchase cost of efficient appliances (83) (84) (85) (86) (87).

IMPROVING SUPPLY TECHNOLOGIES

Even if considerable progress is made in efficiency in the developing world, new energy sources will ultimately be required to meet continuing development demands (88). Advances in technology now offer developing nations a number of options to expand their energy supply, enabling them to avoid the more pollution- and energy-intensive development paths that industrialized nations have pursued (89).

In the foreseeable future, fossil fuels will remain a primary source of commercial energy. New technologies are allowing nations to continue to upgrade both efficiency and environmental performance (90). Among the most promising of the new technologies for electricity generation are the latest natural gas-fired turbines, whose advantages relative to conventional coal-fired power plants include low capital cost, low emissions, and high efficiency (91) (92).

The most advanced gas turbine, when combined with a steam turbine to utilize waste heat, can currently reach an efficiency of nearly 50 percent, with a 60 percent efficiency projected beyond the turn of the century; this compares with an efficiency of about 35 percent for a modern coal-fired power plant with environmental controls (93) (94). Moreover, capital costs for a gas turbine installation are only about one third those for a coal-fired plant installation, and the unit price of gas turbines is dropping, making them extremely cost-competitive (95) (96) (97).

Gas turbines derived from aircraft engine technology are modular in design, so they can be installed quickly, usually within a year or less. By varying the number of individual turbine units, such installations can be sized to match energy needs. Any country with a commercial airline industry has the required maintenance infrastructure, and replacement units can be flown quickly even to remote sites (98) (99). Gas turbines also offer environmental advantages: minimal sulfur emissions, virtually no airborne particulates, and carbon dioxide emissions up to 60 percent less per kilowatt-hour than those from coal-fired plants (100) (101).

Gas turbines would require substantially more gas production and a much greater gas-handling infrastructure than most developing nations now have. Natural gas is more widely distributed among developing nations than oil, and supplies are large enough to last nearly three times longer than the developing world's scarce oil reserves (102). Thus gas has the potential to be a good bridge between fossil fuels and future renewable energy sources, not least because of its impressive environmental advantages (103) (104).

Nonetheless, gas is currently underutilized in the developing world. Much of it is burned off owing to lack of markets, processing facilities, and distribution networks. New exploration technologies and a wider appreciation of the benefits of gas may help ease this situation. The use of gas to generate electricity would not necessarily require extensive pipeline develop-

Table 9.3 Cost and Efficiency of Alternative Cooking Technologies, 1991

Stoves	Efficiency		Stove Capital Cost (US$)
	Stove (percent)	System (percent)	
Traditional			
Dung	11–15	10–14	0.00
Agricultural residues	13–17	12–16	0.00
Wood	15–19	14–18	0.00
Wood (commercial)	15–19	14–18	0.00
Charcoal	19–23	8–12	3.00
Improved biomass			
Wood	27–32	26–31	6.00
Charcoal	29–34	13–17	8.00
Wood II	40–44	38–42	10.00
Liquid			
Kerosene wick	40–45	36–41	20.00
Kerosene pressure	45–50	41–45	40.00
Alcohol wick	40–45	33–37	20.00
Alcohol pressure	45–50	37–42	40.00
Gas			
Central gasifier	55–60	39–42	20.00
Site gasifier	40–45	39–44	50.00
Biogas	55–60	54–59	20.00[a]
LPG	55–60	48–53	50.00
Natural gas	55–60	53–58	20.00
Electric			
Resistance	60–65	17–21	75.00
Microwave	55–60	16–20	250.00
Solar			
Solar box oven	25–30	25–30	25.00

Source: U.S. Congress, Office of Technology Assessment (OTA), *Fueling Development: Energy Technology for Developing Countries* (OTA, Washington, D.C., 1992), p. 296.
Note: a. Substantial capital costs are required for the fuel system and extensive labor is involved in collecting the biomass and dung to be put in the digester.

ment; generation plants could be located close to gas reservoirs, and electricity distributed by grid. Still, additional use of gas in industrial and residential sectors would entail considerable capital outlays for infrastructure development (105) (106).

Despite its adverse impact on the environment, coal use in the developing world is projected to double in the next 30 years. It is rising particularly rapidly in China and India, where coal is the primary source of commercial energy (107). Clean-coal technologies to decrease emissions (other than carbon dioxide) and increase efficiency will thus become much more important in developing nations, especially for electricity generation. Fluidized bed combustion (FBC), which is the most common clean-coal technology, is increasingly being applied in both India and China. It works especially well there because FBC systems tolerate the poor-quality coal in these countries better than conventional coal boilers (108).

Perhaps the clean-coal technology that holds the greatest promise for the developing world is coal gasification. Coal is converted to gas at high temperatures and burned in a high-efficiency turbine similar to the type used in the natural gas applications described above. The most advanced applications of this technology will likely achieve overall efficiencies of 42 percent by the turn of the century, at lower capital costs than conventional coal plants (109) (110).

Moreover, coal gasification may lead to other, cleaner applications in the years ahead. With existing technology, gasified coal could be used to produce high-quality hydrogen gas, which in turn could be used in fuel cells to generate electricity or to power electric vehicles when fuel cell technologies mature. A coal plant with fuel cells could reach an efficiency of nearly 60 percent, as fuel cells convert fuel directly into electricity without first burning it. The capital costs of this new technology are still high but should fall considerably as development proceeds (111) (112) (113).

AGGRESSIVE DEVELOPMENT OF RENEWABLE ENERGY SOURCES

Long-term sustainable development in all countries requires a gradual move toward renewable sources of energy, such as wind, solar, hydro, and biomass, that are both more equitably distributed and less environmentally destructive than current fossil fuel sources (114).

Developing countries (other than in the Middle East) possess less than 20 percent of the world's crude oil reserves, and only about half of all developing countries have known recoverable reserves. Nonetheless, with the notable exception of China and India, which have extensive coal resources, most developing nations rely on oil, and often siphon off a high percentage of foreign exchange earnings to finance its purchase (115).

Aggressive development of renewable energy sources offers developing nations the prospect of increasing energy self-reliance, both nationally and locally, and reaping the attendant economic and security benefits. And, because of their ability to function independently of utility grids, renewables such as solar photovoltaic (PV) arrays and wind turbines could be particularly important in providing power to remote areas (116). The prospect of such decentralized installations is particularly attractive in light of the limited success of current rural electrification programs in addressing energy needs in the South. Among other problems, these programs are costly, and transmission lines experience significant energy loss (117) (118) (119).

With the exception of hydroelectric power, renewable energy technologies have had a hard time penetrating the energy sectors of developing nations, despite numerous and varied demonstration projects over the last 20 years. There are several reasons, including lack of commitment on the part of energy planners, technical failures attributable to poor capacity for local maintenance, and the cost of many new technologies, especially relative to oil prices (120).

Two decades of technical development and substantial field experience, nonetheless, have reduced the price of these technologies and widened their applicability in developing countries. Wind turbines and PV arrays are already cost-effective at many remote sites (121). For example, the price of wind energy has dropped by two thirds over the last decade, and some 20,000 electricity-generating wind turbines (and a large number of wind-powered water pumps) have been installed worldwide. (See Figure 9.5.) The technology is beginning to mature (122). Improved designs soon to be commercially available may make wind

power (at favorable sites) cheaper than electricity from new coal- or oil-fired plants. In the future that wind energy may be used more widely to feed utility grids in both developing and industrialized nations (123) (124).

Photovoltaics have shown similar cost declines. The demand for PV assemblies, which have proven highly reliable in the developing world, is growing steadily. With prices projected to fall even further in the next decade, the worldwide market for photovoltaics is likely to expand rapidly (125) (126) (127). "Low-tech" solar applications, for example, cookers, water heaters, kilns, and crop dryers, have had some success in nations such as India and China. According to reports from China, that country has installed some 1.5 million square meters of solar heat collectors, and it manufactures about 200,000 square meters each year. Most likely, as they are further refined and their advantages recognized, solar applications will continue to increase in popularity (128) (129) (130) (131).

Hydroelectric development could continue to expand energy supplies in the developing world. The only large-scale commercial renewable energy source in the developing world, hydropower contributes a significant portion of the total electricity generated there. Yet only a small fraction of its potential—less than 10 percent, according to one estimate—has been exploited so far (132) (133).

Nevertheless, the large hydro projects of the past have considerable drawbacks that will probably limit hydro development significantly. These include high capital costs, long lead times of 7 to 10 years, and the environmental and social consequences of flooding large areas and displacing local residents (134) (135).

Hydropower's greatest potential appears to be micro-hydro installations, much smaller units of up to 100 kilowatts that can often function without a reservoir for water storage. In many cases, they are a convenient source of local power, relatively easy to construct and environmentally more benign, though still expensive. Both China and India have active microhydro programs, and considerable potential for this energy application exists in other developing nations (136) (137) (138).

Another area with great potential is that of finding new ways to convert biomass to energy, either in the form of electricity, process heat for industry, or a gas suitable for cooking or fueling a diesel engine. The current use of fuelwood, dung, and crop residue for cooking and heating is extremely inefficient. Helping rural residents adopt more efficient methods of handling biomass would both increase living standards and ease pressure on fuelwood supplies (139).

One promising route is to gasify biomass rather than immediately burning it, a process that is easier than gasifying coal. The basic technology for biomass gasification has been available since well before World War II, but technical refinements have only recently begun to make it more attractive. The gas can be used either directly as a cooking or engine fuel or, in the highest-technology applications, to fuel a high-efficiency gas turbine generating electricity, a process similar to that of coal gasification. Biomass gasifier/gas-turbine systems are in the process of being commercialized and should be available by the mid-1990s with efficiencies of 40 percent or more (140) (141).

Some analysts envision large-scale gasification integrated with biomass plantations on degraded lands. This might bring several benefits to rural communities: efficient electrification, employment, and the restoration of degraded acreage (142) (143). In fact, a project to create electricity by growing forest biomass on deforested lands is moving forward in China's Yunnan Province. Tree planting started in 1992, and electricity will probably be generated by 1996 (144) (145).

Some experts fear that large biomass plantations are environmentally risky and may not be sustainable in the long run. Some of the potential problems include soil erosion, loss of soil nutrients, groundwater contamination from fertilizers and pesticides, and increased demand for irrigation (146) (147).

Direct conversion of biomass to liquid fuel such as ethanol and methanol shows promise for developing nations. Most notably, biomass-generated fuel could be used as a substitute for petroleum-based fuel in the transportation sector, which accounts for a high percentage of oil consumption in the South. Currently, converting sugar cane to ethanol by fermentation offers the easiest route to liquid-fuel production (148) (149).

Brazil's well-known sugar cane-to-ethanol fuel program, which provided drivers with more than half of their transportation fuel in 1988, has shown that biomass-to-fuel conversion can be applied successfully on a massive scale. However, a recent drop in oil prices and a rise in the cost of sugar have made the program less attractive (150). New conversion technologies could make conversion of wood chips or other plant materials cost-competitive by the turn of the century, even if today's depressed oil prices persist (151) (152).

THE ROLE OF THE INDUSTRIALIZED WORLD

With such diverse new energy and energy-saving technologies available to developing countries, a future that accommodates development at minimum economic and environmental cost—sustainable development—begins to look feasible. Yet it is not likely to evolve without sustained international cooperation (153) (154). (See *World Resources 1992–93*, pp. 155–156.)

In the effort to enable sustainable development in the South, the North has a three-part role to play: as a continuing source of commercially viable, progressive energy technologies; as a source of technical assistance and innovative financing to encourage and assist the South in learning to utilize these technologies; and as an exemplar, adopting these technologies at home in the attempt to build and demonstrate model sustainable energy programs (155) (156) (157) (158).

Without leadership in developing and actively promoting advanced energy technologies for fossil fuels and renewables, it is unlikely that these technologies will be speedily adopted in the South. Developing nations do not command sufficient technical and financial resources to drive research and development, and they harbor institutional biases favoring conventional fossil fuel and hydroelectric approaches (159) (160). In order to lead, the North must commit itself to a more effi-

Figure 9.5 Cost of Electricity from Wind Energy at Two Interest Rates, 1985–94

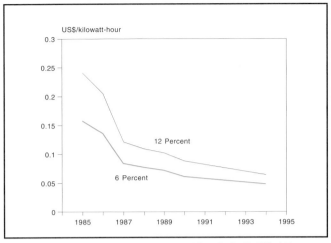

Source: Alfred J. Cavallo, Susan M. Hock, and Don R. Smith, "Wind Energy: Technology and Economics," in *Renewable Energy: Sources for Fuels and Electricity*, Thomas B. Johansson, Henry Kelly, Amulya K.N. Reddy, *et al.*, eds. (Island Press, Washington, D.C., 1993), pp. 121–156.

cient and sustainable energy future and support this commitment with additional resources and policy reforms of its own (161) (162) (163) (164) (165).

Financing will be a barrier to investment in the best energy technologies, even if developing nations are diligent in pursuing energy efficiency and thus reduce their capital needs (166). Revising aid programs and the loan policies of multilateral development banks to target renewables, efficiency programs, and advanced fossil fuel technologies is an essential first step in bridging the funding gap (167) (168). In 1993, the World Bank took such a step by announcing new principles aimed at the development and adoption of cleaner and more energy-efficient technologies (169).

Yet it is not sufficient simply to redeploy funding sources. Substantial increases in financial assistance from the North are required if the South is to make rapid progress in embracing efficient and sustainable energy sources. The return on this investment could be substantial on a global level in terms of reduced carbon dioxide emissions and on a local level in terms of advancing development (170) (171).

One international funding mechanism already pursuing such mutually beneficial investment is the Global Environmental Facility (GEF). Jointly administered by the World Bank, the United Nations Development Programme, and the United Nations Environment Programme, the GEF finances projects in the South that will provide benefits for both national development and the global environment (172) (173). (See Chapter 13, "International Institutions.")

As of mid-1993, the GEF had awarded grants of $290 million for energy-related activities, providing partial funding for projects that could not otherwise compete with conventional energy projects for World Bank financing. Activities are split between those designed to increase the efficiency of fossil fuel use, for example, reducing leakage on a gas pipeline in China's Sichuan Province, and those that promote development of alternative energy sources, for instance, generating biogas from municipal waste in Tanzania (174).

Other creative financing mechanisms may also be in sight. One involves utilities in the North that wish to expand; to offset the increase in carbon emissions, they could finance energy efficiency projects or alternative energy development in the South. This sort of tradeoff may become more attractive as international pressure to limit carbon emissions mounts (175).

Joint ventures and other arrangements between business partners in developing and industrialized countries will also be an important source of investment capital and energy-efficient technologies for the South. The possibilities for fruitful collaboration would rapidly expand if industrialized nations genuinely pursued sustainable energy policies of their own, creating a robust market for energy-efficient or alternative energy technologies at home and prompting investment to expand the market abroad (176) (177) (178).

SUSTAINABLE OPTIONS FOR THE DEVELOPING WORLD: SELECTED CASE STUDIES

Of the many new energy technologies and management approaches field-tested in the developing world over the last two decades, several have met with considerable success. A few are profiled here to indicate the opportunities available.

Most of the technologies described below are past the experimental stage and now provide reliable energy at a cost generally comparable to that of energy from conventional sources. Indeed, what these cases suggest is that the technologies themselves are not the stumbling block so much as factors such as shortages of capital, skilled labor, or community institutions.

Case 1: Solar Photovoltaics in the Dominican Republic

About 2 billion people in rural areas of the South still lack electricity from a central grid system (power plants that distribute electricity over a wide area via power lines) (179). Most of these people make do with kerosene lamps for domestic lighting and disposable zinc-carbon batteries, costing $30 to $60 per kilowatt-hour, to power transistor radios or televisions (180).

In most countries, the prospects for extending grids to rural areas are not good. Priority usually goes to urban areas with dense populations and relatively low transmission and distribution costs (181). Extension of rural grids is costly (about $10,000 per kilometer, according to the World Bank) and highly subsidized. Rural grids, moreover, are typically inefficient (182) (183).

One promising alternative is the installation of small solar PV systems in rural households. The complete system usually consists of one or two solar modules, a control box, a storage battery, wiring, and lighting fixtures. A typical 48-watt system provides 6 kilowatt-hours of electricity per month and costs about $600. It provides enough electricity for five lights, a radio/cassette player, a television, and a blender (184).

Several countries are launching programs to bring PV systems to rural areas. One of the most successful is in the Dominican Republic. The program, started by

Enersol Associates, a U.S.-based nonprofit international development organization, draws primarily on the strength of local private institutions (185). Enersol's approach involves three ongoing institutions: a rural-development nongovernmental organization (NGO) charged with establishing a revolving credit fund, a community association that uses the money provided by the NGO to extend loans to rural households, and a service enterprise that provides the PV hardware and performs system maintenance (186).

To start a project, a development professional from a local NGO usually encourages participation at the local level. Technical assistance and specialized training extend for a three- to five-year period. Enersol has conducted many one-week workshops to give development workers and community leaders an overview of solar-based rural electrification. The workshop includes hands-on installation of PV systems and lectures about electricity, revolving credit fund management, and project development. Enersol also conducts a program of technician workshops to teach local people how to install and maintain simple PV systems (187).

The approach seems to be taking hold. About 1,500 systems have been installed in the Dominican Republic since 1985. The biggest obstacle to further growth appears to be lack of credit for two- to three-year financing of systems (188). Estimates suggest that about 20 percent of the Dominican Republic's 380,000 rural families who lack electricity could afford a 35–40 watt PV system to satisfy their basic needs (189).

Similar programs using PV systems are under way in a number of other developing countries, including Sri Lanka and Indonesia (190) (191).

Case 2: Biogas Electricity in India

Another alternative to the electric grid is the community-sized biogas digester, which converts organic material into energy by way of fermentation. For example, manure from village cattle can be used to feed the biogas digester and produce a 60:40 mixture of methane and carbon dioxide. This is used to cook, produce electricity for lighting, or pump drinking water. The residue from the digester is available as fertilizer (192) (193).

Family-sized biogas digesters are now relatively common in countries such as China and India. In China, an estimated 4.6 million biogas digesters currently in use (mostly in the south) produce 1 to 1.5 cubic meters of biogas a day for six to eight months out of the year (194). Family-sized biogas digesters are also common in India. An estimated 87,000 digesters were installed from April to December 1991 (195).

Although community-sized digesters are more economical than family-sized ones, they are relatively uncommon, in part because of the difficulty of organization and equitable distribution of costs and benefits among the villagers (196). One example of a community digester is located in the town of Pura in southern India. The Pura project is supported by the Karnataka State Council for Science and Technology and by the Centre for Application of Science and Technology to Rural Areas situated at the Indian Institute of Science in Bangalore (197) (198).

In 1991, Pura had 87 households and a cattle population of 248. About half the households received grid electricity from an unreliable system. The biogas plant began to provide gas to the village in 1982, but the project stopped in 1984 because the digester did not supply enough energy for every family to cook both daily meals. However, the community strongly supported use of the biogas digester to produce electricity for drinking water, and in 1987 the project was revived, this time with the addition of a dual-fuel engine to generate electricity (199) (200).

Biogas from the digester passes through a condensation trap and is mixed with diesel fuel to operate the generator. The electricity runs a pump that brings water 50 meters up to an overhead tank; the water then flows by gravity to 9 street taps and 29 household taps. The generator also provides fluorescent lighting to households (201).

The biogas system has numerous advantages. It is clean, self-reliant, renewable, and inexpensive, and it employs local people. It also provides better and more accessible drinking water, and better and more reliable illumination than a grid system. The sludge fertilizer that is its byproduct has twice the nitrogen content of farmyard manure (202).

The biogas system generates income from the fees villagers pay for private water taps and for the electricity used in lighting. In the early stages, the plant was only operating enough (4.2 hours per day) to cover about half of its recurring expenses, not to start paying off the capital investment. As demand for electricity rises along with the dung supply to meet that demand, income from the plant should increase. Once it is operating six hours a day, a surplus will be generated. When demand increases to the level where it operates the same number of hours as a central station plant (15.1 hours a day), the biogas plant will produce electricity at a lower unit cost than the grid system (203).

The Indian government is offering to help finance the capital costs of community biogas plants and the early stages of operation and maintenance. The government set a target of 120 new community and institutional biogas plants for 1991–92 (204).

Case 3: National Energy Conservation Programs

Many developing countries are finding electricity conservation programs to be a cost-effective alternative to the construction of new hydroelectric or fossil fuel plants. In Brazil, it is estimated that the cost of electricity conservation is only about half the long-run marginal cost of supplying electricity to high-voltage industrial customers and about one fourth the cost of supplying low-voltage commercial and residential customers (205). In developing countries, improving the efficiency of electric lights, motors, and appliances typically costs $300 to $1,000 per kilowatt saved, compared with $1,500 to $3,000 per kilowatt supplied from new hydroelectric or fossil fuel plants (206).

Conservation also reduces the risk of electricity shortages, lowers investment requirements for the utility sector, and helps make industries and products more competitive in world markets. Compared with supplying additional electricity, conservation has significant environmental and social advantages. New hydro plants inundate large areas of land and require extensive resettlement, while fossil fuel plants cause serious air pollution and generate substantial waste; conservation can avoid drawbacks such as these (207).

A wide variety of beneficial initiatives is possible in a national electricity conservation program. These include performance testing, labeling, and setting minimum efficiency standards for electric equipment; performing energy audits; setting up training courses, as well as technology development and commercialization programs; establishing building codes, energy management requirements, and electric rate incentives; giving rebates to purchasers of high-efficiency equipment; arranging favorable financing and tax structures; and starting least-cost or integrated-resource utility planning (208).

One of the most successful national programs to date has been Brazil's National Electricity Conservation Program (PROCEL). Started in 1985, it concentrates on technology research and development, demonstrations, education and promotion, direct installation of conservation equipment, development of standards and regulatory legislation, incentives, and joint projects with utilities and other organizations (209).

PROCEL is based at Eletrobras, the federally owned utility holding and coordinating company, which has almost entirely financed the program. Projects are carried out by state and local utilities, research organizations, and private companies. In five years, PROCEL invested a total of $20 million in 150 projects, with organizations conducting the projects providing matching funds (210).

PROCEL's most effective policies include support for the development of a number of energy-efficient technologies, such as reflectors for fluorescent fixtures; standardized testing of refrigerators and freezers, which has stimulated Brazilian manufacturers to improve the efficiency of their products; and the direct replacement of incandescent street lamps with mercury vapor and high-pressure sodium lamps (211).

Since its inception, PROCEL has had a noticeable impact on Brazil's electricity consumption, with direct savings as of 1989 estimated at 1,070 gigawatt-hours per year. That is equal to the power supplied by about 280 megawatts of hydroelectric capacity, which would have cost $600 million in power plants, transmission lines, and distribution facilities (212). Although a budgetary crisis forced Eletrobras to scale back PROCEL's activities in the early 1990s, strong interest in efficiency measures continues. For example, the market for energy-efficient lighting products has been doubling every two years since 1988, and in 1991 a special task force helped reduce electricity use in ministry buildings in Brasilia by 17 percent (213) (214).

Case 4: Wind Power in India

Wind power has emerged as a significant dependable renewable energy technology. Over 12 countries have substantial wind energy programs, and worldwide there are more than 20,000 wind turbines with a capacity that exceeds 2,200 megawatts (215). On the best sites, wind energy is nearly competitive with fossil fuels (216).

In the early 1980s, wind turbines experienced numerous technical problems such as blade cracks that undermined their case as reliable harnesses of power. Since 1984, however, turbine efficiency has dramatically improved, costs per unit have fallen, and there have been advances in other areas such as site selection and wind farm design (217).

The leading developers of this technology are Denmark, which now supplies about 3 percent of its electricity from some 3,400 turbines, and California, which generates roughly 1 percent of its electricity from about 15,000 turbines (218) (219) (220).

Among developing countries, India is moving forward with an ambitious program that now includes over 250 installed turbines at 12 locations with a capacity of more than 45 megawatts. The government has set a target of 3,000 megawatts of capacity by the year 2000. So far, India's wind machines have been reliable and operate at high performance levels (221) (222) (223).

Under the sponsorship of the Ministry of Energy's Department of Non-Conventional Energy Sources, India has undertaken a comprehensive survey of its wind energy resources. The potential for wind power generation based solely on land availability, wind speeds, and economic viability may be as much as 150,000 megawatts, but the technically realizable potential (calculated by taking into consideration such limiting factors as availability of the grid) is estimated to be about 20,000 to 40,000 megawatts (224) (225).

Capital costs for a wind power plant in India are comparable to those for a new coal-fired power plant located some distance from mines. Wind power is already cheaper than diesel power. This advantage should widen because the cost of thermal/diesel power operation will continue to increase, while the cost of wind power generation should decline as the technology continues to improve (226).

Wind power has several other advantages: it is environmentally friendly; operation and maintenance costs are low; planning and construction of new projects generally take only one to two years; and wind farms can be located in small, decentralized areas, preventing the transmission and distribution losses experienced with distant conventional power plants (227).

The major impediments to wind power development in India are shortage of investment capital, lack of experienced manpower for specific projects, and limited world supplies of hardware coupled with increas-

ing demand for that hardware from the United States, Europe, and elsewhere (228). One Indian company has developed a wind generator, however, so India may soon have its own production capacity (229).

Case 5: Fuel Ethanol Production in Zimbabwe

Landlocked Zimbabwe must import petroleum fuel either by pipeline from Mozambique or by road and rail through South Africa. Given Zimbabwe's geographical position and the high cost of oil imports, the government has turned part of its efficient sugar industry to the production of fuel alcohol.

In the late 1970s, Triangle Limited, a company that grows sugar cane on 13,000 hectares of irrigated land, approached the government about building a fuel alcohol plant and marketing the fuel solely through the federally owned oil procurement company. Government officials reacted enthusiastically, but they put a strict limit on the amount of foreign currency that could be used in the construction of the plant. Though it was designed by a German team, 60 percent of the plant was fabricated and constructed in Zimbabwe. The cost came to $6.4 million (in 1980), the lowest capital cost per liter for any ethanol plant in the world. The plant has been operating since 1980, and there have been few maintenance problems so far.

The blend of alcohol in petrol was originally set at 15 percent but dropped to about 12 percent as a result of rising fuel consumption and a variable alcohol supply. On occasion, the plant has exceeded its expected production of about 40 million liters of alcohol per year. However, when there is severe drought or a poor cane harvest, reducing feedstock, production can be severely limited.

Waste from the plant is diluted with water and applied as fertilizer to about half of the sugar plantation. The fertilizer, which provides the soil with all necessary phosphates and an excess of potassium, has increased crop yields by 7 percent.

The plant has enabled Zimbabwe to diversify its agroindustry and freed it somewhat from the vagaries of external oil and commodities markets (230) (231).

The Conditions and Trends section was written by Eric Rodenburg, World Resources *staff member. The Focus On section was written by Gregory Mock, contributing editor to* World Resources, *and Robert Livernash of the* World Resources *staff.*

References and Notes

1. United Nations (U.N.) Statistical Division, *U.N. Energy Tape* (U.N., New York, 1993).
2. World Energy Council (WEC), *1992 Survey of Energy Resources* (WEC, London, 1992), p. 14.
3. The U.N. Statistical Office has changed its method of calculating primary electrical production. Except for electricity from nuclear power and geothermal energy, sources continue to be calculated on the energy content of the electricity generated. Nuclear

power is calculated as the amount of fossil fuel energy required to generate the same amount of electricity based on an efficiency of 33 percent, and geothermal energy is calculated based on an efficiency of 10 percent. These changes have been applied retroactively to the entire energy database.

4. *Op. cit.* 2, p. 198.
5. *Op. cit.* 2, p. 184.
6. *Op. cit.* 2, pp. 114–119 and 174.

7. United Nations (U.N.) Statistical Division, *1991 Energy Statistics Yearbook* (U.N., New York, forthcoming).
8. *Op. cit.* 2, p. 13.
9. World Energy Conference, *1989 Survey of Energy Resources* (World Energy Conference, London, 1989), pp. 39–40 and 64–65.
10. *Op. cit.* 2, pp. 13, 42–43, and 71.
11. *Op. cit.* 9, pp. 16–17.
12. *Op. cit.* 2, pp. 20–21.

13. *Op. cit.* 2, p. 34.
14. Tse Pui-Kwan, Country Specialist, U.S. Bureau of Mines, Washington, D.C., 1993 (personal communication).
15. A. Konoplyanik, "Russia Struggling to Revive Production, Rebuild Oil Industry," *Oil and Gas Journal* (August 2, 1993), pp. 43–44.
16. *Op. cit.* 2, p. 87.
17. *Op. cit.* 2, pp. 109–116.
18. *Op. cit.* 9, pp. 102–104.
19. Mohan Munasinghe, *Electric Power Economics* (Butterworths, London, 1990), pp. 4–5.
20. U.S. Congress, Office of Technology Assessment (OTA), *Fueling Development: Energy Technologies for Developing Countries* (OTA, Washington, D.C., 1992), pp. 23–27 and 33–34.
21. Gregory Kats, "The Earth Summit: Opportunity for Energy Reform," *Energy Policy*, Vol. 20, No. 6 (1992), p. 547.
22. José Goldemberg, Thomas B. Johansson, Amulya K.N. Reddy, *et al.*, *Energy for a Sustainable World* (Wiley Eastern, New Delhi, 1988), p. 191.
23. Mark Levine, Ashok Gadgil, Steven Meyers, *et al.*, *Energy Efficiency, Developing Nations, and Eastern Europe: A Report to the U.S. Working Group on Global Energy Efficiency* (International Institute for Energy Conservation, Washington, D.C., 1991), pp. 2 and 9.
24. Amulya Reddy and José Goldemberg, "Energy for the Developing World," *Scientific American* (September 1990), p. 111.
25. U.S. Agency for International Development (U.S. AID), "Power Shortages in Developing Countries: Magnitude, Impacts, Solutions, and the Role of the Private Sector," a report to the U.S. Congress (U.S. AID, Washington, D.C., March 1988), pp. 17–22.
26. Jayant Sathaye and Ashok Gadgil, "Aggressive Cost-Effective Electricity Conservation," *Energy Policy*, Vol. 20, No. 2 (1992), p. 163.
27. *Op. cit.* 20, p. 180.
28. Arun Sanghvi, "Power Shortages in Developing Countries: Impacts and Policies Implications," *Energy Policy*, Vol. 19, No. 5 (1991), p. 428.
29. Hussein Rady, "Renewable Energy in Rural Areas of Developing Countries," *Energy Policy*, Vol. 20, No. 6 (1992), pp. 582–583.
30. F. Liu, W.B. Davis, and M.D. Levine, *An Overview of Energy Supply and Demand in China*, (Lawrence Berkeley Laboratory, University of California, Berkeley, California, 1992), p. 67.
31. *Op. cit.* 25, pp. 35–37.
32. José R. Escay, *Summary 1988 Power Data Sheets for 100 Developing Countries* (The World Bank, Washington, D.C., 1991), pp. 1–2.
33. Mohan Munasinghe, "Efficient Management of the Power Sector in Developing Countries," *Energy Policy*, Vol. 20, No. 2 (1992), p. 99.
34. *Op. cit.* 20, p. 292.
35. *Op. cit.* 29, p. 584.
36. *Op. cit.* 20, pp. 24, 53, 56–62, 96, and 133–134.
37. *Op. cit.* 33, pp. 99–100.
38. *Op. cit.* 20, p. 8.
39. Gerald Foley, "Rural Electrification in the Developing World," *Energy Policy*, Vol. 20, No. 2 (1992), pp. 146–147.
40. Howard Geller, *Efficient Electricity Use: A Development Strategy for Brazil* (American Council for an Energy-Efficient Economy, Washington, D.C., 1991), pp. 62–63.
41. *Op. cit.* 20, pp. 52–53.
42. *Op. cit.* 39, pp. 148–149.
43. *Op. cit.* 21, p. 555.
44. Ministry of Information and Broadcasting, India, *India 1992* (Ministry of Information and Broadcasting, New Delhi, 1993), p. 472.
45. *Op. cit.* 20, pp. 3 and 27.

46. *Op. cit.* 20, p. 5.
47. Edwin A. Moore and George Smith, *Capital Expenditures for Electric Power in the Developing Countries in the 1990s* (The World Bank, Washington, D.C., 1990), p. 4.
48. *Op. cit.* 24, p. 111.
49. *Op. cit.* 20, pp. 37–40.
50. Andrew Barnett, "The Financing of Electric Power Projects in Developing Countries," *Energy Policy*, Vol. 20, No. 4 (1992), p. 332.
51. *Op. cit.* 20, pp. 29–30.
52. *Op. cit.* 33, p. 95.
53. *Op. cit.* 25, p. 10.
54. *Op. cit.* 50, p. 332.
55. *Op. cit.* 26, p. 163.
56. *Op. cit.* 24, pp. 111–113.
57. *Op. cit.* 23, p. 22.
58. O. Davidson and S. Karekezi, *A New Environmentally Sound Energy Strategy for the Development of Sub-Saharan Africa* (African Energy Policy Research Network, Nairobi, Kenya, 1992), p. 15.
59. Stephen Karekezi, Energy Analyst, African Energy Policy Research Network, Nairobi, Kenya, 1993 (personal communication).
60. *Op. cit.* 26, p. 163.
61. *Op. cit.* 23, pp. 3 and 32–35.
62. *Op. cit.* 25, pp. 9–13.
63. *Op. cit.* 20, pp. 5–6 and 23.
64. *Op. cit.* 20, pp. 5–6.
65. *Op. cit.* 23, p. 22.
66. Maheshwar Dayal, *Renewable Energy: Environment and Development* (Konark, Delhi, India, 1989), pp. 62–63.
67. R. Govinda Rao, Gautam Dutt, and Michael Philips, *The Least Cost Energy Path for India: Energy Efficient Investments for the Multilateral Development Banks* (International Institute for Energy Conservation, Washington, D.C., 1991), pp. 13 and 17.
68. Robert Perlack and Milton Russell, "Energy and Environmental Policy in China," *Annual Review of Energy and the Environment*, Vol. 16 (1991), p. 221.
69. *Op. cit.* 29, p. 585.
70. *Op. cit.* 59.
71. *Op. cit.* 20, pp. 145–150.
72. *Op. cit.* 58, p. 16.
73. *Op. cit.* 59.
74. Amulya Reddy, "Barriers to Improvements in Energy Efficiency," *Energy Policy*, Vol. 19, No. 10 (1991), pp. 953–961.
75. *Op. cit.* 20, pp. 5–9.
76. *Op. cit.* 26, pp. 167–172.
77. *Op. cit.* 20, pp. 7–9 and 87.
78. *Op. cit.* 40, p. 63.
79. *Op. cit.* 74, pp. 953–961.
80. *Op. cit.* 20, pp. 8–9 and 83–84.
81. *Op. cit.* 26, pp. 167–172.
82. B.N. Lohani and A.M. Azimi, "Barriers to Energy End-Use Efficiency," *Energy Policy*, Vol. 20, No. 6 (1992), pp. 533–545.
83. *Op. cit.* 74, pp. 953–961.
84. *Op. cit.* 20, pp. 5–9.
85. *Op. cit.* 26, pp. 167–172.
86. *Op. cit.* 82, pp. 533–545.
87. José Goldemberg, Thomas B. Johansson, Amulya K.N. Reddy, *et al.*, *Energy for Development* (World Resources Institute, Washington, D.C., 1987), p. 64.
88. *Op. cit.* 20, p. 179.
89. *Op. cit.* 20, p. 32.
90. In this and the following section, emphasis is placed on new, efficient fossil fuel technologies and alternative energy technologies, while little mention is made of the nuclear energy option. Despite the current involvement of a few of the larger developing nations, most notably India and China, in nuclear energy development, the chances

that, in the foreseeable future, nuclear energy will significantly contribute to the energy picture in the South are considered minimal by most experts, owing to high capital costs, slow construction, poor economic performance records to date, and the environmental risks involved in fueling, operating, and decommissioning of nuclear facilities as well as in nuclear waste disposal.
91. *Op. cit.* 44, p. 498.
92. Robert Williams, "The Potential for Reducing CO_2 Emissions with Modern Energy Technology: An Illustrative Scenario for the Power Sector in China," *Science and Global Security*, Vol. 2 (1991), p. 7.
93. *Ibid.*
94. *Op. cit.* 20, pp. 196–197.
95. *Op. cit.* 21, p. 554.
96. R. Williams and E. Larson, "Advanced Gasification-Based Biomass Power Generation," in *Renewable Energy: Sources for Fuels and Electricity*, Thomas B. Johansson, Henry Kelly, Amulya K.N. Reddy, *et al.*, eds. (Island Press, Washington, D.C., 1993), p. 741.
97. *Op. cit.* 20, pp. 305–307, Table B-1.
98. *Op. cit.* 96, p. 736.
99. *Op. cit.* 20, pp. 196–197.
100. *Op. cit.* 20, pp. 196–197.
101. J. Alan Brewster, Senior Vice President, World Resources Institute, Washington, D.C., 1993 (personal communication).
102. *Op. cit.* 20, p. 235.
103. *Op. cit.* 21, p. 554.
104. *Op. cit.* 20, p. 197.
105. *Op. cit.* 20, pp. 234–236, 240, and 243.
106. The World Bank, *World Development Report 1992* (Oxford University Press, New York, 1992), p. 120.
107. *Op. cit.* 20, pp. 244–245.
108. *Op. cit.* 20, pp. 190–192.
109. Thomas B. Johansson, Henry Kelly, Amulya K.N. Reddy, *et al.*, "Renewable Fuels and Electricity for a Growing World," in *Renewable Energy: Sources for Fuels and Electricity*, Thomas B. Johansson, Henry Kelly, Amulya K.N. Reddy, *et al.*, eds. (Island Press, Washington, D.C., 1993), p. 23.
110. *Op. cit.* 20, pp. 192–193.
111. *Op. cit.* 109, pp. 23 and 34–35.
112. *Op. cit.* 20, pp. 200 and 306.
113. *Op. cit.* 92, pp. 9–11.
114. *Op. cit.* 22, p. 376.
115. *Op. cit.* 20, pp. 233–235.
116. *Op. cit.* 20, p. 202.
117. C.S. Sinha and T.C. Kandpal, "Decentralized v. Grid Electricity for Rural India: The Economic Factors," *Energy Policy*, Vol. 19, No. 5 (1991), pp. 441–448.
118. *Op. cit.* 20, pp. 211–213.
119. Deborah Bleviss, Executive Director, International Institute for Energy Conservation, Washington, D.C., 1993 (personal communication).
120. Gerald Foley, "Renewable Energy in Third World Energy Assistance," *Energy Policy*, Vol. 20, No. 4 (1992), pp. 355–361.
121. *Op. cit.* 20, p. 10.
122. *Op. cit.* 21, p. 555.
123. *Op. cit.* 109, pp. 18–19.
124. Alfred J. Cavallo, Susan M. Hock, and Don R. Smith, "Wind Energy: Technology and Economics," in *Renewable Energy: Sources for Fuels and Electricity*, Thomas B. Johansson, Henry Kelly, Amulya K.N. Reddy, *et al.*, eds. (Island Press, Washington, D.C., 1993), pp. 121–122.
125. *Op. cit.* 109, p. 21.
126. *Op. cit.* 20, p. 205.
127. Henry Kelly, "Introduction to Photovoltaic Technology," in *Renewable Energy: Sources for Fuels and Electricity*, Thomas B. Johans-

son, Henry Kelly, Amulya K.N. Reddy, *et al*., eds. (Island Press, Washington, D.C., 1993), pp. 297–298.

128. M. Dayal, "Role of Renewable Energy Sources in Reducing Global Warming and Climatic Change," in *Global Warming and Climate Change: Perspectives From Developing Countries*, S. Gupta and R.K. Pachauri, eds. (Tata Energy Research Institute, New Delhi, India, 1989), p. 180.

129. Chen Yingrong, "Renewables in China," *Energy Policy*, Vol. 19, No. 9 (1991), pp. 895–896.

130. Wang Qingyi, "China's Energy: Challenge and Strategy," *International Journal of Global Energy Issues*, Vol. 1, Nos. 1 and 2 (1989), p. 43.

131. *Op. cit.* 59.

132. *Op. cit.* 20, pp. 193–194.

133. José Moreira and Alan Poole, "Hydropower and Its Constraints," in *Renewable Energy: Sources for Fuels and Electricity*, Thomas B. Johansson, Henry Kelly, Amulya K.N. Reddy, *et al*., eds. (Island Press, Washington, D.C., 1993), p. 77.

134. *Op. cit.* 20, pp. 193–194 and 305–308, Table B-1.

135. *Op. cit.* 133, p. 92.

136. *Op. cit.* 20, pp. 206–208.

137. *Op. cit.* 133, pp. 85–87.

138. *Op. cit.* 44, p. 498.

139. *Op. cit.* 20, pp. 214–222.

140. *Op. cit.* 20, pp. 214–222.

141. *Op. cit.* 109, p. 18.

142. David Hall, Frank Rosillo-Calle, Robert H. Williams, *et al*., "Biomass for Energy: Supply Prospects," in *Renewable Energy: Sources for Fuels and Electricity*, Thomas B. Johansson, Henry Kelly, Amulya K.N. Reddy, *et al*., eds. (Island Press, Washington, D.C., 1993), p. 593.

143. *Ibid.*

144. Milton Russell, *Electricity from Biomass: Two Potential Chinese Projects* (Energy, Environment and Resources Center, University of Tennessee, Knoxville, 1991), pp. 1–50.

145. Milton Russell, Director, Joint Institute for Energy and Environment, University of Tennessee, Knoxville, 1993 (personal communication).

146. James MacKenzie, Senior Associate, World Resources Institute, Washington, D.C., 1993 (personal communication).

147. *Op. cit.* 109, p. 13.

148. *Op. cit.* 109, pp. 35–40.

149. *Op. cit.* 20, pp. 145, 172–175, 222–227, and 247–258.

150. *Op. cit.* 20, pp. 172–175.

151. *Op. cit.* 109, pp. 35–40.

152. Charles E. Wyman, Richard L. Bain, Norman D. Hinman, *et al*., "Ethanol and Methanol from Cellulosic Biomass," in *Renewable Energy: Sources for Fuels and Electricity*, Thomas B. Johansson, Henry Kelly, Amulya K.N. Reddy, *et al*., eds. (Island Press, Washington, D.C., 1993), p. 865.

153. Maurice Strong, "Energy, Environment and Development," *Energy Policy*, Vol. 20, No. 6 (1992), p. 494.

154. *Op. cit.* 109, p. 43.

155. *Op. cit.* 153, p. 494.

156. *Op. cit.* 33, p. 99.

157. *Op. cit.* 59.

158. *Op. cit.* 40, pp. 127–133.

159. *Op. cit.* 109, p. 43.

160. *Op. cit.* 33, p. 99.

161. *Op. cit.* 109, p. 43.

162. *Op. cit.* 33, p. 99.

163. *Op. cit.* 59.

164. *Op. cit.* 146.

165. *Op. cit.* 40, pp. 127–129.

166. *Op. cit.* 20, p. 14.

167. Michael Philips, *The Least Cost Energy Path for Developing Countries: Energy-Efficient Investments for the Multilateral Development Banks* (International Institute for Energy Conservation, Washington, D.C., 1991), p. xix.

168. *Op. cit.* 40, pp. 129–130.

169. The World Bank, *Energy Efficiency and Conservation in the Developing World: The World Bank's Role* (The World Bank, Washington, D.C., 1993), pp. 10–12.

170. *Op. cit.* 153, p. 494.

171. *Op. cit.* 20, p. 14.

172. *Op. cit.* 33, p. 102.

173. Charles Feinstein, GEF Operations Officer for Global Warming Projects, The World Bank, Washington, D.C., 1993 (personal communication).

174. *Ibid.*

175. Walter Reid, Vice President, World Resources Institute, Washington, D.C., 1993 (personal communication).

176. *Op. cit.* 24, p. 118.

177. *Op. cit.* 59.

178. *Op. cit.* 20, p. 86.

179. Derek Lovejoy, "Electrification of Rural Areas by Solar PV," *Natural Resources Forum*, Vol. 16, No. 2 (1992), p. 102.

180. Richard D. Hansen, "Solar-Based Rural Electrification in the Dominican Republic," paper presented at the Finesse Workshop, Kuala Lumpur, Malaysia, October 1991.

181. *Op. cit.* 179, pp. 102–103.

182. The World Bank, "Finesse: You Can Bank on It," pamphlet prepared by the Asia Technical Department, The World Bank, Washington, D.C., n.d.

183. *Op. cit.* 179, p. 103.

184. *Op. cit.* 180.

185. *Op. cit.* 180.

186. *Op. cit.* 180.

187. *Op. cit.* 180.

188. *Op. cit.* 180.

189. *Op. cit.* 179, p. 107.

190. *Op. cit.* 182.

191. *Op. cit.* 179, pp. 107–108.

192. *Op. cit.* 20, pp. 219–222.

193. P. Rajabapaiah, S. Jayakumar, and Amulya K.N. Reddy, "Biogas Electricity: The Pura Village Case Study," in *Renewable Energy: Sources for Fuels and Electricity*, Thomas B. Johansson, Henry Kelly, Amulya K.N. Reddy, *et al*., eds. (Island Press, Washington, D.C., 1993), p. 788.

194. *Op. cit.* 129, p. 895.

195. Ministry of Power and Non-Conventional Energy Sources, Department of Non-Conventional Energy Sources (DNES), India, *Annual Report, 1991–92* (DNES, New Delhi, n.d.), pp. 4 and 9.

196. *Op. cit.* 193.

197. D.O. Hall, F. Rosillo-Calle, and P. de Groot, "Biomass Energy: Lessons from Case Studies in Developing Countries," *Energy Policy*, Vol. 20, No. 1 (1992), p. 70.

198. *Op. cit.* 193, p. 814.

199. *Op. cit.* 193, pp. 790 and 796–797.

200. *Op. cit.* 197, pp. 70–71.

201. *Op. cit.* 193, pp. 796–798.

202. *Op. cit.* 193, pp. 789 and 813.

203. *Op. cit.* 193, pp. 808 and 811–812.

204. *Op. cit.* 195, pp. 6–7.

205. *Op. cit.* 40, p. 7.

206. Steven Nadel, Howard Geller, and Marc Ledbetter, "A Review of Electricity Conservation Programs for Developing Countries," paper prepared for the American Council for an Energy-Efficient Economy, n.d.

207. *Op. cit.* 40, pp. 7–9.

208. *Op. cit.* 206.

209. *Op. cit.* 40, p. 67.

210. *Op. cit.* 40, p. 67.

211. Howard S. Geller and José E. Moreira, "Brazil Encourages Electricity Savings," *Forum for Applied Research and Public Policy* (forthcoming).

212. *Op. cit.* 40, p. 67.

213. *Op. cit.* 211.

214. Howard S. Geller, Executive Director, American Council for an Energy-Efficient Economy, Washington, D.C., 1993 (personal communication).

215. Kevin Rackstraw, Director of International Programs, American Wind Energy Association, Washington, D.C., 1993 (personal communication).

216. *Op. cit.* 124, p. 121.

217. Alexi Clarke, "Wind Energy: Progress and Potential," *Energy Policy*, Vol. 19, No. 8 (1991), pp. 744–745.

218. Gordon Mackenzie, Senior Energy Planner, United Nations Environment Programme Collaborating Centre on Energy and Environment, Roskilde, Denmark, 1993 (personal communication).

219. *Op. cit.* 217, p. 742.

220. *Op. cit.* 124, pp. 121–122.

221. Ajit K. Gupta and J. Gururaja, *Perspectives on Wind Power Development in India* (Department of Non-conventional Energy Sources, Ministry of Energy, New Delhi, n.d.), pp. 21 and 25.

222. *Op. cit.* 217, p. 742.

223. C.S. Sinha, Tata Energy Research Institute, New Delhi, 1993 (personal communication).

224. Tata Energy Research Institute, "Environmental Considerations in Energy Development," final report submitted to the Asian Development Bank, New Delhi, 1992, p. 23.

225. *Op. cit.* 221, pp. 18–19.

226. *Op. cit.* 221, p. 24.

227. *Op. cit.* 221, p. 24.

228. *Op. cit.* 224, p. 110.

229. *Op. cit.* 195, p. 26.

230. *Op. cit.* 197, pp. 68–70.

231. C. Wenman, "The Production and Use of Fuel Ethanol in Zimbabwe," in *Energy from Biomass*, W. Palz, J. Combs, and D.O. Hall, eds. (Elsevier, London, 1985), pp. 172–177.

10. Water

While the oceans of the world contain a seemingly unlimited supply of water, freshwater for human use is a fragile, finite resource. And yet the demand for freshwater continues to grow with the human population. The diversion of freshwater to supply agricultural, industrial, domestic, and municipal needs stretches hydrological systems, both natural and man-made, to the limit. Within a nation, these needs compete for a supply of freshwater that may already be scarce and may vary drastically both seasonally and geographically. Among nations, competition for water of high quality is a cause of conflict that only promises to intensify. Mutually exclusive demands on a scarce but life-giving resource are not easily resolved. (See Box 10.1.)

The world's marine ecosystems support vast numbers of fish that are a vital part of the global food supply. An estimated 1 billion people, mostly in developing countries, depend on fish as their sole source of protein. Yet there are signs that many of the world's marine fisheries are in serious trouble.

This chapter examines declines in two large-scale marine fisheries, the anchovy fishery off the coast of Peru and Chile and the groundfish fishery off the coast of the northeastern United States. In the case of the anchovy fishery, complex changes in the ocean ecosystem and unrestricted fishing were important factors in the declining catch. In the groundfish case, overfishing seems to be the primary factor. Management reforms could rebuild stocks, but such reforms are difficult to implement.

CONDITIONS AND TRENDS

Ninety-seven percent of the world's water is contained in saline oceans; of what remains, 69 percent is in the form of snow and ice (1). Freshwater for human use, found in lakes, swamps, and rivers, makes up only 0.008 percent of the Earth's water. (See Figure 10.1.) Because the water cycle renews the flow of rivers, groundwater, and glaciers, actual runoff from these sources might exceed 47,000 cubic kilometers per year, although estimates range as low as 31,000 cubic kilometers (2) (3). (See Figure 10.2.)

Freshwater is distributed unevenly over the Earth's surface. The world's natural store of freshwater is concentrated in the high latitudes—the glaciers of Greenland and Antarctica and the lakes of North America and Russia. Water supplies also vary widely by latitude, being concentrated in tropical humid zones. Brazil, for example, accounts for over 13 percent of the world's total renewable supply of freshwater (excluding that of Antarctica), most of it in rivers. (See Chapter 22, "Water," Table 22.1.) Not only is freshwater

Figure 10.1 Global Total Water and Freshwater Reserves

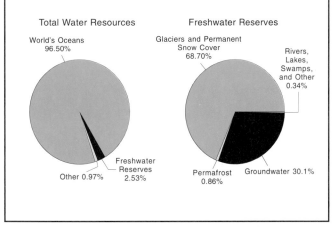

Source: Igor A. Shiklomanov, "World Fresh Water Resources," in *Water in Crisis*, Peter H. Gleick, ed. (Oxford University Press, New York, 1993), p. 13.

Figure 10.3 Global Water Withdrawal by Sector, 1900–2000

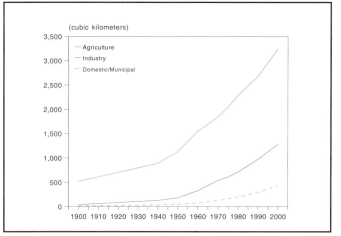

Source: Igor A. Shiklomanov, "World Fresh Water Resources," in *Water in Crisis*, Peter H. Gleick, ed. (Oxford University Press, New York, 1993), p. 20.

unevenly distributed, but in many areas quantities of it also peak seasonally. For instance, more than 65 percent of Australia's runoff occurs in January, February, and March (4).

To modify such seasonal and geographical variations, humans have built thousands of large dams (36,000 or more over 15 meters in height) (5). By the late 1980s, these impounded more than 5,000 cubic kilometers of freshwater, and the total is expected to rise to as much as 7,500 cubic kilometers by the year 2000 if current plans for dam building are carried out (6). Whether they will be built is open to question, for, in recent years, controversy has been growing about the potential impact of large dams on human populations and natural ecosystems.

Irrigation, the largest consumer of freshwater, not least because of evaporation and evapotranspiration, will likely be expanded to meet the demand for food as the human population grows. Between 1900 and the

year 2000, agricultural water consumption will have grown sixfold to 3,250 cubic kilometers. (See Figure 10.3.)

Global Trends

LEGAL MEASURES AND POTENTIAL CONFLICT

Many of the important water basins of the world are shared by more than one country. Common basins make up 60 percent of the total area of Africa and South America (7). The importance that nations attach to their water resources is reflected in the existence of over 2,000 treaties relating to common basins, for example, the United States and Canada's Great Lakes Compact (8). But, in many areas, treaties are either nonexistent or inadequate. The Nile Waters Agreement of 1959, a Sudanese and Egyptian attempt to distribute the flow of that river, ignores the requirements and demands of upstream users such as Ethiopia.

Besides direct bilateral agreements to manage resources, a body of international law has grown up based on the principle that no state can harm other states in its use and management of the common resource. But there is still no mechanism for solving competing claims. The most common conflict occurs between upstream users who claim sovereign rights to water that originates or flows through their territory (including the right to use, store, divert, or pollute) and downstream users who demand that the watercourse be maintained in its natural state (9).

The potential for conflict over shared water resources is most obvious in the Nile Basin, southwest Asia, and the Middle East. Dispute over control of the headwaters of the Jordan River (a basin shared by Syria, Jordan, Lebanon, and Israel) and the possibility that the rivers might be diverted into the Israeli National Water Carrier helped spark the 1967 Arab-Israeli war (10). Today, despite new regional peace initiatives, the danger of conflict continues, especially with Israel's unrestricted use of groundwater from the Jordan River basin in occupied territories.

Figure 10.2 Annual River Runoff

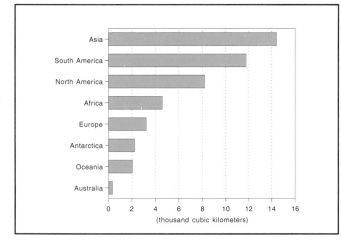

Source: Igor A. Shiklomanov, "World Fresh Water Resources," in *Water in Crisis*, Peter H. Gleick, ed. (Oxford University Press, New York, 1993), p. 15.

Figure 10.4 Global Marine Fish Catch and Estimated Potential Sustainable Yield, 1970–91

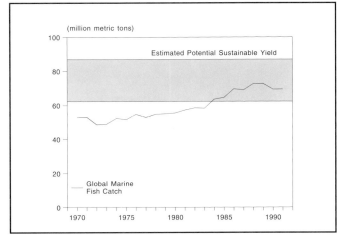

Sources:
1. Food and Agriculture Organization of the United Nations (FAO), *FAO Fishstat 1992*, on diskette (FAO, Rome, 1992).
2. M.A. Robinson, "Trends and Prospects in World Fisheries," Fisheries Circular No. 772, Food and Agricultural Organization of the United Nations, FAO, Rome, 1984.

Table 10.1 Operating Costs and Revenues for the Global Fishing Fleet, 1989

Annual Operating Costs	Amount (millions of US$)
Routine maintenance	30,207
Insurance	7,193
Supplies and gear	18,506
Fuel	13,685
Labor	22,587
Total annual operating costs	92,178
Gross revenue from 1989 catch	69,704
1989 deficit (excluding debt servicing)	22,474

Source: Food and Agriculture Organization of the United Nations (FAO), *Marine Fisheries and the Law of the Sea: A Decade of Change* (FAO, Rome, 1992), pp. 20 and 58.

Iraq depends on the Tigris and Euphrates rivers for its water, most of which originates in Turkey and Syria. Recent years have seen the construction of a system of dams on the Euphrates by Turkey (the Greater Anatolia Project), an effort that is expected to reduce Iraq's receipt of Euphrates water to as little as 10 percent of normal flow (Syria's receipt may fall to 60 percent of normal levels) (11).

The Nile River is the longest in the world—its basin embraces parts of nine countries. Egypt is totally dependent on the Nile's flow. Its agreement with Sudan, the only agreement governing water rights, totally allocates the river's downstream flow (as it was in 1959, the year of signing) without reference to the demands of upstream users. The bulk of water reaching Egypt originates in Ethiopia and flows through the Sudan, via the Blue Nile, where it joins the remnants of the White Nile at Khartoum. A project to enhance the flow of the White Nile by building a canal to bypass the Sudd (a large swamp in the southern Sudan where much of the White Nile's flow is lost to evaporation) was one factor that began the continuing civil war in the Sudan. Development of Ethiopia's hydroelectric and irrigation infrastructure could reduce the flow of the Blue Nile by almost 9 percent. If managed successfully, this would not necessarily cut supplies to Egypt (evaporation losses at Aswan and elsewhere exceed this reduction), but Egypt is unwilling to accept any diminished supply (12).

There are precedents for a peaceful and even equitable resolution of potential conflicts over water resources. India and Pakistan have managed to share development of the Indus River. India and Bangladesh have agreed to maintain minimal flows on the Ganges. The United States and Mexico have drawn up terms for the Colorado and Rio Grande rivers. Argentina and Brazil have agreed on the management of the Paraná River to maintain Argentina's development potential (13).

TOXIC TIDES

Dramatic fluctuations in marine life over the past two decades have been attributed variously to anthropogenic global warming, pollution, disease, and long-term climate cycles affecting water temperature and currents. One notable phenomenon is the incidence of phytoplankton blooms, known alternatively as red, green, and brown tides (14) (15).

Algal blooms appear to be occurring more frequently and are showing up in waters where they have never been observed before (16). Many of the algae produce toxins that, once ingested by mollusks and fish, either kill or accumulate in them, endangering their predators in turn. Indirect poisoning by algal toxins has been well documented in humans, sea birds, and whales and other marine mammals. One bloom off the coast of Guatemala in 1987 poisoned nearly 200 people, killing 26 (17). Along the east coast of the United States in 1987–88, 740 dead dolphins washed up on beaches in the most extensive such kill ever recorded; estimates of total dolphin deaths in that incident range from 1,500 to 2,500 (18).

One newly discovered algae family (dinoflagellate) that actually seems to prey on fish may be the culprit behind unexplained fish deaths that have occurred in various regions of the world over the past 20 years. Resting on an estuary floor, they swim up the water column when a school of fish passes overhead and release toxins that disable their prey, sometimes causing numerous deaths. The algae feed on fish tissue before drifting back to the estuary floor and encysting themselves. Although this behavior has only been described in North Carolina estuaries, the algae are suspected to be widespread because they tolerate broad temperature and salinity ranges (19).

The increased incidence of toxic blooms could be the result of pollution and exotic species introduced by humans (20). Sewage and agricultural runoff stimulate algal growth in coastal waters, and algae species may be transported to new areas in the ballast water of ships (21). Whatever their cause, more frequent blooms, along with fluctuating populations of other marine organisms, may be a symptom of declining health in marine ecosystems around the globe (22). In the absence of

Box 10.1 Freshwater Biodiversity

The biodiversity of freshwater lakes, streams, rivers, and wetlands may be the most threatened ecosystems on Earth. Fully one fifth of the world's freshwater fish are either endangered or extinct. (See Figure 1.) This number is much higher in some industrialized countries; it reaches 72 percent in former West Germany, for instance (1). The status of freshwater species other than fish is not fully known, but many appear endangered too. Amphibian populations around the world are in decline; in North America, 43 percent of freshwater mussel species and subspecies either have disappeared or are in trouble (2).

The extent of this threat is difficult to gauge because so little is known about freshwater biodiversity. Freshwater species that have never been described disappear without anyone's knowledge. Land vertebrates are fairly well known: on average, perhaps two new birds are discovered annually. In contrast, about 200 new freshwater fish species are identified each year, leading experts to believe that at least half of the world's vertebrates are fish (3). In the Amazon basin, where freshwater diversity is richest, as many as 3,000 fish species may exist, although only 1,800 have been catalogued to date. The Amazon and its tributaries host seed-eating fish that forage in seasonally flooded forests, the world's largest freshwater turtle, and the half-blind boto dolphin (which hunts its prey by echolocation) (4).

Freshwater systems tend to be the first habitats to experience degradation because humans congregate along waterways. These areas provide drinking and irrigation water, protein (fish and crustaceans, for example), disposal for sewage,

and a transportation medium, while fertile floodplain soils attract farming. Aquatic species are especially vulnerable to changes that result from development, since many are confined to individual watersheds and cannot readily disperse to undisturbed areas.

Other characteristics make freshwater ecosystems more vulnerable than terrestrial or ocean ecosystems. Watercourses are uniquely open, that is, there is a constant flow of materials through the ecosystem. This exposes river species to events outside of their immediate habitat, such as

Figure 1 Total Freshwater Fish Species with Threatened / Special Concern Status

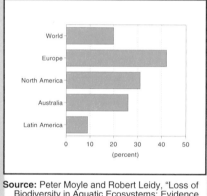

Source: Peter Moyle and Robert Leidy, "Loss of Biodiversity in Aquatic Ecosystems: Evidence from Fish Faunas," in *Conservation Biology: The Theory and Practice of Nature Conservation, Preservation and Management*, Peggy L. Fiedler and Subodh K. Jain, eds. (Chapman and Hall, New York, 1992), pp. 135 and 140.

an oil spill or deforestation upstream. Lakes and ponds are vulnerable for the opposite reason: essentially closed systems, their natural cycles take a long time to flush out contaminants.

In much of Africa and South America, the overharvesting of species and the introduction of exotic species are among the gravest threats to freshwater biodiversity (5). Nile perch, brought to East Africa's Lake Victoria around 1960 to "improve" local fishing for sport and food, are destroying one of the world's most diverse collections of freshwater fauna. Lake Victoria, like other lakes in the region, has an extremely high level of endemism, with over 200 species of freshwater fish of the family *Cichlidae* unique to it alone. Predation by the Nile perch appears to be driving many of these species to extinction, although additional factors may be involved in the cichlid's decline (6).

Elsewhere, exotic species outcompete or interbreed with native fauna. Brown trout, carp, and other fish have been introduced to streams and rivers around the world for food and sport. Where native fauna are not wiped out, they may be poisoned to improve conditions for the exotic fishery. Exotics are also introduced through accidental or deliberate release of bait fish and aquarium species. When watersheds are linked for hydropower or navigational canals, whole assemblages of fauna may intermix (7).

Introductions have contributed to the demise of 68 percent of North American fish species, according to one study (8). The same study found habitat loss, a contributing factor in 73 percent of extinctions, to be the primary threat to the region's fish.

---

long-term monitoring of affected populations or the ecosystems with which they are associated, the evidence of decline is inconclusive at this point (23).

FOCUS ON MARINE FISHERIES

With the inexorable rise in the world's human population, the demand for food is exerting ever more pressure on marine fisheries at a time when most traditional fish stocks, according to the Food and Agricultural Organization of the United Nations (FAO), are already being fished at maximum rates. More fishing probably will not boost yields (24). The global marine catch did increase during the past decade, but this can be largely attributed to greater exploitation of less valuable species, masking declines in the catch of more profitable species such as Atlantic cod and haddock (25).

The best current global estimate of the potential sustainable yield of marine fish is between 62 and 87 million metric tons, a level attained in the mid-1980s (26). (See Figure 10.4.) Clearly, unless nations take decisive, timely action to control fish exploitation, the popula-

tion of many fish species will drop below levels necessary to assure maximum yields. This development could seriously disrupt ecosystems, put thousands of fishers out of work, and prove disastrous to the estimated 1 billion people, most of whom live in developing countries, who depend on fish as their sole source of protein (27).

Current fishing practices deplete some stocks and are inefficient. An FAO review of fishing revenues and costs found that the global fleet was operating at a loss of $22 million in 1989; when capital costs were included, the loss was $54 million. (See Table 10.1.) Direct and indirect government subsidies are credited with offsetting much of this loss (28). For example, governments effectively subsidize the fishing industry by paying access fees for fishing in the exclusive economic zones of foreign countries, while at the same time providing domestic fishers free access to their own zones (29).

The problem of overcapitalization—overinvestment in new vessels and processing equipment—is often the indirect result of the natural fluctuation of many fish

Box 10.1

(See Figure 2.) Water projects and the degradation and conversion of adjacent terrestrial vegetation are primary causes of biodiversity loss, particularly in industrialized regions. Dams interrupt spawning migrations of salmon and other fish, and by changing the temperature, flow, and chemistry of water, render it unfit for many species.

Riverine and adjacent terrestrial ecosystems are interdependent. Floodplains benefit from silt deposited as a result of periodic flooding, while freshwater species use seasonally flooded areas for foraging and spawning. These processes are interrupted by dams, dikes, and channels, which drive many species to extinction and greatly reduce productivity. Logging along streams exposes waterways to sunlight, fluctuating water levels, and siltation, all of which contribute to the demise of native species.

Pollution, as well as the deliberate poisoning of waterways, has contributed to over one third of North American fish extinctions. (See Figure 2.) Acid rain, sewage, and agricultural chemicals and waste all threaten freshwater biodiversity in many parts of the world. Toxic chemicals and oxygen deprivation resulting from the conversion of organic matter have virtually sterilized many of Europe's major rivers, although a number of them are in the process of recovery.

When biodiversity has been lost primarily through pollution to rivers, prospects for recovery are good once the pollutant is removed because rivers flush themselves out quickly. Still, toxic chemicals may remain in a riverbed for years, and extirpated species will not reappear unless

reintroduced. More difficult than reintroducing species is recreating freshwater habitat after it has been destroyed. To boost an ecosystem's productivity, native vegetation can be planted along waterways and stream channels reconstructed to resemble their former state (9).

Habitat restoration is expensive. Protecting remaining aquatic habitats is the best and most economical way to conserve freshwater biodiversity. Current efforts focus on preserving individual species by listing them as endangered and enacting subsequent recovery programs. Waterways are rarely protected in their own right; those covered under the U.S. Wild and Scenic Rivers Act are a notable excep-

tion. When lakes and rivers are protected, it is because they lie in or flow through parks and reserves. These are usually designed to protect terrestrial habitat and, because waterways often cut across administrative boundaries, watersheds are generally protected or managed in piecemeal fashion. Thus, even protected segments are vulnerable to unregulated upstream activity. If freshwater biodiversity is to be preserved, protected areas and management plans should cover entire watersheds (10).

Figure 2 Factors Contributing to North American Freshwater Fish Extinction, 1900–84

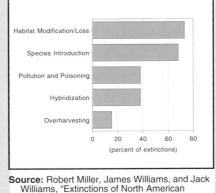

(percent of extinctions)

Source: Robert Miller, James Williams, and Jack Williams, "Extinctions of North American Fishes during the Past Century," *Fisheries*, Vol. 4, No. 6 (1989), pp. 34 and 36.

References and Notes

1. Robert M. Hughes and Reed F. Noss, "Biological Diversity and Biological Integrity: Current Concerns for Lakes and Streams," *Fisheries*, Vol. 17, No. 3 (1992), p. 13.
2. J. David Allan and Alexander S. Flecker, "Biodiversity Conservation in Running Waters," *BioScience*, Vol. 43, No. 1 (1993), p. 35.
3. *Ibid.*, p. 32.
4. Michael Goulding, "Flooded Forests of the Amazon," *Scientific American*, Vol. 268, No. 3 (1993), pp. 117–118.
5. World Resources Institute (WRI), The World Conservation Union, and the United Nations Environment Programme, *Global Biodiversity Strategy* (WRI, Washington, D.C., 1992), p. 11.
6. Daniel Miller, "Introductions and Extinction of Fish in the African Great Lakes," *Tree*, Vol. 4, No. 2 (1989), p. 56.
7. *Op. cit.* 2, pp. 38–39.
8. Robert Miller, James Williams, and Jack Williams, "Extinctions of North American Fishes During the Past Century," *Fisheries*, Vol. 14, No. 6 (1989), p. 34.
9. *Ibid.*, p. 41.
10. *Op. cit.* 2, p. 42.

stocks. When stocks are high, the fishing industry buys new boats and equipment, often with government support. When fish populations decline, either as part of a natural cycle or from too much fishing, the industry puts pressure on government for subsidies to protect jobs and investment. Both uncontrolled growth of fleets when stocks are high and subsidized fishing during periods of population decline contribute to excessive exploitation of fisheries (30).

What follows are two case studies of large-scale marine fisheries that have been exhausted by these trends and a discussion of possible solutions. The fisheries, Peruvian anchovies and northeastern U.S. groundfish, were selected to provide a reasonably balanced perspective—one is in a developing country in the southern hemisphere and the other in a developed nation in the northern hemisphere.

PERUVIAN ANCHOVY FISHERY

Upwelling systems are where cold, nutrient-rich waters from the ocean's depths rise and mix with surface

water. Only 0.1 percent of the Earth's oceans consist of upwelling systems yet they contribute roughly 50 percent of the world's fish catch (31). The major upwelling systems of the world are located off the west coasts of North and South America and Africa and off the coasts of Arabia and Somalia in the Arabian Sea. (See Figure 10.5.)

The Humboldt current upwelling system, off the coast of Peru and Chile, is one of the richest marine ecosystems on the planet. During the 1960s and 1970s, the Humboldt system provided nearly 20 percent of the world's fish landings (32). It is characterized by cool surface water (an August mean of 16.5° C), high densities of phytoplankton (flora) and zooplankton (fauna), and relatively few links in the food chain between primary-producing phytoplankton and harvestable fish (33) (34). Yet because of an unusual combination of climatic and human-induced factors, the biomass of the six major species in the system plummeted 50 percent between 1959 and 1989, and the balance of species changed significantly (35).

Figure 10.5 Major Ocean Upwellings of the World

Source: Woods Hole Oceanographic Institute, unpublished data (Woods Hole, Massachusetts, 1993).

Evolution of the Anchovy Fishery

Before 1950, fish in Peru were harvested mainly for human consumption, and the fishery was small. In 1950, the total catch in Peru was 86,723 metric tons (36). In 1953, the first fish meal processing plants were built in Peru, a speculative venture designed to make use of a large and relatively untapped resource, anchovies, to produce oil and fish meal for export. Over the next several years, anchovy fishing rose in response to the growing demand of the plants. Within just nine years, Peru became the number one fishing nation in the world by volume (37), with anchovies making up roughly 94 percent of its total catch (38) (39).

These were boom years in Peru. Anchovy fishing intensified during the 1960s as more and more fish meal plants were constructed. During the seven-month fishing season in 1969–70, Peru's fleet of 1,700 purse seiners—up from 100 in 1953—brought in 11 million metric tons of anchovies. (In 1969, the U.S. catch for all fish and shellfish was about 2.5 million metric tons (40) (41).)

How much longer could the Peruvian anchovy fishery sustain such exploitation? A group representing FAO and the Peruvian government's Ocean Institute (Instituto del Mar del Peru) began investigating in the 1960s. The number of fish meal plants and vessels fishing for anchovy seemed to be straining a resource whose historic population levels and dynamics were poorly understood (42). The group's biologists estimated the maximum sustainable yield of anchovies at 9.5 million metric tons per year—including nearly 2 million metric tons thought to be consumed by seabirds. In 1970, the group issued a warning: if the anchovy catch remained above 9.5 million metric tons, the fishery would be in imminent danger of collapse (43).

The Peruvian government turned a deaf ear. Fish meal prices were high in 1969 because overfishing had recently led to a collapse of herring fisheries in Nor-

way and Iceland (44). Peruvian officials, hoping to earn more hard currency through the export of fish meal, were also unwilling to risk declining employment in the industry. In 1970, a harvest of 12.4 million metric tons was allowed; in 1971, 10.5 million metric tons was allowed (45).

Causes of the Collapse

In March 1972, fishermen were delighted at the apparent superabundance of anchovies, which they scooped up near the shore at the record-setting pace of over 170,000 tons per day. Later, biologists learned that the fish had been corralled near the shore by warmer-than-normal water. Soon the dense schools of fish disappeared; by the end of the season, only 2.5 million metric tons had been netted (46).

El Niño had arrived—a phenomenon characterized by the appearance of warm surface water off Peru and Ecuador that persists for 6 to 18 months. During El Niño, which occurs at irregular intervals every three to seven years, fewer nutrients rise to the ocean surface, with a consequent reduction in phytoplankton growth. Because phytoplankton is the first link of the food chain, this reduction causes the decline of all the other elements: zooplankton, fish, birds, and mammals (47).

Over the next four years, the Peruvian anchovy fleet landed only a fraction of its previous catch: in 1973, 1.8 million metric tons; 1974, 3.6 million metric tons; 1975, 3.1 million metric tons; and 1976, 3.9 million metric tons. Additional warming episodes in 1976–77 and 1986–87 were accompanied by further declines in the anchovy biomass (48). (See Figure 10.6.) From 1977 to 1987, the catch averaged about 1.2 million metric tons per year (49) (50).

An Ecosystem Approach to Management

The significant changes to Peruvian waters brought about by El Niño—average ocean temperatures are now 2°C warmer than 30 years ago—has attracted attention from scientists worldwide (51). Over the past two decades, they have been piecing together the complex dynamics of the Humboldt current ecosystem, devising strategies that may help rebuild the anchovy stocks while allowing fishery managers to anticipate and respond to future occurrences of El Niño.

Today, the misconception persists that El Niño was responsible for the demise of Peru's anchovy fishery (52). Most research, however, supports the idea that although El Niño contributed to the collapse, it was unrestricted fishing that placed the resource in jeopardy. According to one hypothesis, in addition to reducing plankton production, El Niño's warmer sea surface temperatures caused anchovies to collect in isolated pockets of cold, upwelling water, making them easy prey to fishermen (53). These pockets normally protect cold-water species until warm water retreats. But when fishermen targeted anchovies in their sanctuaries, the population fell below the level required for rapid regrowth (54). Warmer water also created a habitat favorable to anchovy predators such as mackerel and horse mackerel.

The combination of a higher predation rate and lower anchovy biomass (one quarter of its 1960s level) does not bode well for the stock, although there are signs that it may be slowly gaining (55) (56). Meanwhile, sardines have increased in population to become the most important fishery in Peru, though their catch volume and value are far below levels attained for anchovies at their peak.

The collapse of the Peruvian anchovy industry revealed that traditional fishery management models were inadequate for the Humboldt current ecosystem. Most, based on the analysis of single species, did not consider the effects of environmental change (57) (58). A more comprehensive, ecosystemwide plan was needed that took into account interspecies dynamics and variations in climate.

The events that caused the collapse of the Peruvian anchovy fishery form a scenario that has been repeated often around the world (59). Rapid anthropogenic declines have occurred in many other related fisheries, for example, California sardines, North Sea herring, and Atlanto-Scandic herring. In each case, economic and political considerations dominated decisions regarding targeted fish stocks. Either biological and related environmental data about the relevant resource was scarce, or, if data was available, fishery managers decided to disregard it.

This general scenario has also emerged in the groundfish fishery off the northeastern coast of the United States.

NEW ENGLAND GROUNDFISH

The continental shelf off the New England coast of the United States encompasses the Gulf of Maine, Georges Bank, and the Mid-Atlantic Bight. Home to one of the most productive and studied ecosystems in the world, it has been overfished for the past three decades (60). Stocks of primary targeted species, including groundfish that live near the ocean floor—Atlantic cod, had-

Figure 10.6 Estimated Anchovy Biomass in the Peruvian Upwelling Ecosystem, 1953–88

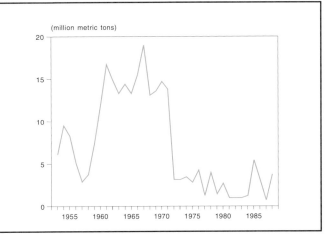

Source: Peter Muck, "Major Trends in the Pelagic Ecosystem off Peru and Their Implications for Management," in *The Peruvian Upwelling Ecosystem: Dynamics and Interactions* (Instituto del Mar del Peru, Callao, 1989), p. 388.

dock, redfish, hake, pollock, and flounder—are now at or near record low levels (61). Though everything from polluted water to climate change has been offered as reasons for the decline of New England's groundfish industry, most observers agree that overfishing is primarily to blame (62). One problem is that regulations are designed not to conserve fish resources but to avoid burdening the fishing industry. The regulations that exist, moreover, have not proven enforceable.

New England has experienced cycles of overfishing since the middle of the 19th Century. The introduction in 1905 of the otter trawl, a cylindrical net dragged across the ocean floor, raised concerns about loss of immature groundfish on Georges Bank. By the mid-1930s, haddock, which had become the primary New England fishery, showed signs of severe depletion (63) (64) (65). Over the past three decades or so, stocks have twice experienced significant decline. In the 1960s, long-distance fishing fleets, mainly from the Soviet Union, Poland, Spain, and Germany, began harvesting in the international waters off New England (more than 12 miles from the coast). Before the fleets arrived, annual yields from Georges Bank had averaged about 95,000 metric tons, most of it taken by U.S. vessels. From 1961 to 1974, this rose sharply to about 427,000 metric tons, most of this caught by ships from countries other than the United States (66).

As early as 1964, the International Commission for the Northwest Atlantic Fisheries (ICNAF) warned that fishing probably exceeded the sustainable level for fish stocks (67). But fishery managers, in what has been called a delaying tactic, questioned the accuracy of scientific assessments and called for further studies (68).

Not until 10 years later were measures taken to reduce the catch through the establishment of a total allowable catch for each species and a quota system for member nations. Although these efforts proved ineffective in reducing fishing pressure, they achieved some success in rebuilding stocks. Nations were suspected

Box 10.2 West Atlantic Bluefin Tuna

Among the largest, fastest, and most sought-after fish in the ocean is the bluefin tuna, *Thunnus thynnus*. It can weigh up to 700 kilograms and swim as fast as 90 kilometers an hour (1). Though not an endangered species, it has become so valuable that overfishing has caused stocks in some regions, notably the west Atlantic, to fall precipitously over the past decade.

Despite the efforts of the International Commission for the Conservation of Atlantic Tuna (ICCAT), which has monitored and regulated the fishery since 1969, the stock of west Atlantic bluefin (WAB) shrank more than 80 percent between 1970 and 1993 (2). Particularly worrisome is the decline of the breeding stock, fish 8 years and older, whose population has dropped 90 percent since 1970 (3). (See Figures 1 and 2.)

Figure 1 Total West Atlantic Bluefin Tuna Catch, 1970–92

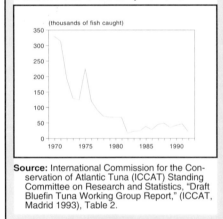

(thousands of fish caught)

Source: International Commission for the Conservation of Atlantic Tuna (ICCAT) Standing Committee on Research and Statistics, "Draft Bluefin Tuna Working Group Report," (ICCAT, Madrid 1993), Table 2.

Why such a sudden collapse? Recently in Japan, bluefins became fashionable fare as sushi and sashimi, driving up demand. And as bluefin landings dwindled, the price skyrocketed, luring even more people into the fishery. In 1992, a record $67,500 was paid for a single 225-kilogram bluefin on the wholesale market, though the average price for the sushi and sashimi market was closer to $10,000 to $15,000 per fish (4) (5).

While a variant of gold rush fever threatens the fishery, political differences among nations do not help. Conflict has attended much of the history of ICCAT, made up of about 20 nations whose citizens harvest tuna in the Atlantic, mostly in international waters (6). ICCAT was formed because Atlantic tuna stocks were spiraling downward in the 1960s, and there was no agency regulating the fleets that fished for them (7).

The obstacles confronting ICCAT, daunting in 1969, remain in place. The combination of slow stock recovery, high prices that spur the industry to press for elevated catch limits, and varying commitments to conservation by fishing nations, is, according to one biologist familiar with the WAB fishery, "about the worst possible combination of factors to hand to a fisheries manager" (8).

The WAB stock is managed by a combination of catch restrictions, minimum size limits, and closed areas (9). Though ICCAT's mandate is to manage the fishery with the goal of maintaining maximum sustainable yields, critics charge that catch limits have long exceeded that level (10).

ICCAT's lack of effectiveness has many causes. One is the inherent difficulty of

getting numerous countries to agree on fishing and conservation objectives. Regulations are viewed by some nations as too restrictive, too lax by others (11). For example, in 1981, a two-year reduced catch of WAB (totaling 565 metric tons for the two years) was recommended by the U.S. National Marine Fisheries Service (NMFS). ICCAT considered the proposal, but Canada complained that its domestic fishery would suffer as a result. The United States and Canada then agreed to a catch of 800 metric tons to be split among themselves and Japan. ICCAT allowed these nations to decide how to allocate the 800 metric tons; at a separate meeting, the three agreed to raise the catch to 1,160 metric

Figure 2 Estimated Population of West Atlantic Bluefin Tuna Age 8 and Over, 1970–93

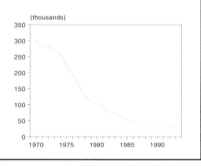

(thousands)

Source: International Commission for the Conservation of Atlantic Tuna (ICCAT) Standing Committee on Research and Statistics, "Draft Bluefin Tuna Working Group Report," (ICCAT, Madrid, 1993), Table 4.

of exceeding their quotas and falsifying catch statistics (69). (See Box 10.2.)

Disturbed by the trend, U.S. fishing interests applied pressure on the U.S. Government to limit foreign fleets (70). In 1976, mainly as a response to the situation in New England, the U.S. Congress passed the Magnuson Fishery Conservation and Management Act. This Act gave the federal government control over fish resources in waters up to 200 miles from the U.S. coastline, including the primary New England fishing zones.

At the time, many New England fishers saw the Magnuson Act as a bonanza that would allow them free access to resources that had previously been taken by other nations. Simply removing non-U.S. vessels from the fishery, they felt, would be sufficient to conserve stocks. Fishery biologists, on the other hand, viewed the act as a mandate to rebuild exhausted stocks through careful regulation (71) (72). Conflict seemed inevitable.

Under the Magnuson Act, fishery management is regulated by eight regional councils made up of indus-

try representatives and government officials. (Ultimate responsibility for management lies with the National Marine Fisheries Service of the U.S. Department of Commerce (73) (74).) In 1977, the New England Fishery Management Council, using the ICNAF format, applied a quota system designed to control fishing of depleted stocks. Fishers, who quickly attained their quotas, complained that stock assessments were too conservative. The council accommodated them by inflating quotas (75).

The quota system did appear to be effective in reducing the catch of cod, haddock, and yellowtail flounder (76). From historic lows in 1974, their populations peaked in 1978 (77). Then new vessels began entering the fishery, lured by low-cost government loans and the specter of easy wealth. Between 1977 and 1984, the number of otter trawlers rose from 650 to 1,021, and improved technology allowed the fleet to catch more fish in less time (78). With so much more fishing, quotas were reached more quickly, shutting down fisheries for extended periods and disrupting the market (79).

Box 10.2

tons (12). Two years later, the quota was raised to 2,660 metric tons (13).

Another problem with ICCAT is that, like all international commissions formed by treaty, it has no enforcement power; that function is left to the signatory nations themselves. When an NMFS study found that, during the 1982 season, Japanese WAB fishers significantly underreported their catch rates, ICCAT was unable to take punitive action (14).

For the most part, however, it appears that ICCAT regulations have been enforced by member nations through their own national regulatory agencies (15). The problem now appears to be that the ICCAT catch limit for WAB (2,660 metric tons annually) is simply too high. Compounding this is the fact that non-ICCAT countries are taking a significant percentage of WAB—as much as 80 percent of the total catch landed by ICCAT nations (16).

To address the problem of overfishing, the U.S. National Audubon Society lobbied in 1992 to have WAB declared an endangered species under the Convention on International Trade in Endangered Species (CITES). This would have banned exports of the fish by CITES members. A Swedish proposal to this effect, made at the 1992 CITES meeting, was withdrawn when four ICCAT members committed to reduce catch levels if WAB was not listed. Those reductions were never made (17).

Japan, and at times the United States, has called for a 50 percent reduction in the ICCAT catch level for WAB. But other nations, notably Canada, have resisted. At the 1991 ICCAT meeting, delegates agreed on a 10 percent total cut for 1992–93 (18) (19). Japan has also called for measures to

be taken against WAB fishers from non-ICCAT nations, a suggestion resisted by the European Community, some of whose members do not belong to ICCAT. Meanwhile, ICCAT has proposed a certification program to track the origin of WAB imports and discourage non-ICCAT nations from fishing (20) (21).

Critics claim that ICCAT still has not established a plan for rebuilding WAB stocks, although it was slated to do this in 1993 (22) (23). In its defense, ICCAT maintains that current catch rates and size limits are sufficient to allow the stock to recover within 30 years, though in the short term the status of WAB is uncertain. Supporters point to an encouraging rise in the number of younger fish (24) (25).

The next few years will be critical for WAB. If the population continues to decline, pressure may be brought to bear on ICCAT by member-nation governments and environmental groups to take more effective action.

References and Notes

1. Carl Safina, "Bluefin Tuna in the West Atlantic: Negligent Management and the Making of an Endangered Species," *Conservation Biology*, Vol. 7, No. 2 (1993), p. 229.
2. International Commission for the Conservation of Atlantic Tuna (ICCAT) Standing Committee on Research and Statistics, *Bluefin Tuna Working Group Report*, (ICCAT, Madrid, 1993), Table 4.
3. *Ibid.*
4. "Record Price Paid for Bluefin Tuna," International Commission for the Conservation of Atlantic Tuna (ICCAT) *Watch Newsletter*, Vol. 1, No. 1 (World Wildlife Fund, Washington, D.C., August 1992), p. 4.
5. William K. Stevens, "Appetite for Sushi Threatens Giant Tuna," *New York Times* (September 17, 1991), p. 1, sec. C.
6. *Op. cit.* 1.
7. Michael J.A. Butler, "Plight of the Bluefin Tuna," *National Geographic* (August 1982), p. 231.
8. Pamela Mace, Fisheries Consultant, Silver Spring, Maryland, 1993 (personal communication).
9. Richard B. Deriso and William H. Bayliff, eds., *World Meeting on Stock Assessment of Bluefin Tunas: Strengths and Weaknesses* (Inter-American Tropical Tuna Commission, La Jolla, California, 1991), p. 91.
10. *Op. cit.* 1.
11. National Oceanic and Atmospheric Administration (NOAA), *Our Living Oceans: The First Annual Report on the Status of U.S. Living Marine Resources* (NOAA, Washington, D.C., 1991), p. 37.
12. David C. Hoover, "A Case against International Management of Highly Migratory Marine Fishery Resources: The Atlantic Bluefin Tuna," *Environmental Affairs Law Review*, Vol. 11, No. 1 (1983), pp. 29–32.
13. *Op. cit.* 1, p. 230.
14. *Op. cit.* 12, pp. 20 and 43.
15. *Op. cit.* 9.
16. *Op. cit.* 1, p. 230.
17. *Op. cit.* 1, pp. 230–232.
18. *Op. cit.* 1, p. 232.
19. Russell Drumm, "An International Fuss over Bluefin Tuna," *National Fisherman* (February 1992), pp. 13–15 and 76.
20. *Op. cit.* 1, pp. 231–233.
21. "ICCAT Makes Steady Progress on Bluefin and Swordfish," *National Fisherman* (February 1993), pp. 16–17.
22. *Op. cit.* 1, pp. 232–233.
23. *Op. cit.* 21, p. 16.
24. *Op. cit.* 9, p. 92.
25. *Op. cit.* 19.

From Direct to Indirect Controls

In 1982, after strong lobbying by the fishing industry, quota-based management, a form of direct fishery control, was replaced by a system of indirect controls over such things as mesh and minimum fish size. Spawning areas remained off limits as in the previous plan. Since 1982, species have been added to the management plan and minor modifications made, but the overall approach remains the same.

After a decade under the new system, critics charge that it has failed to curb overfishing. Between 1982 and 1991, the level of fishing effort rose 13 percent while the total catch declined by 43 percent. (See Figure 10.7.) The total groundfish population decreased by 65 percent between 1977 and 1987 (80). Some stocks reached record low levels by the early 1990s. Overharvesting also altered the balance of fish populations: skates and dogfish replaced cod and codlike fish as the dominant finfish species on Georges Bank. (See Figure 10.8.) Even if fishing were to stop completely, one study reported in 1990, harvestable stocks would take

5 to 20 years to return to sustainable levels (81). The groundfish catch in 1992 was less than half of its long-term potential sustainable level, causing estimated annual economic losses of more than $100 million (82) (83).

Evidence suggests that the New England Fishery Management Council has paid more attention to the short-term economic needs of commercial fishers than to the conservation of fish stocks, which is one of the primary objectives of the Magnuson Act (84). Fishing industry representatives have dominated the Council, leading to charges of conflict of interest (85) (86). The Council refuses to establish direct control over the fishery by setting limits on the size of the fleet and the total catch.

One form of indirect control is the net used in otter trawling, the primary method of catching New England groundfish. Trawl nets capture by size, not species, a problem in areas where groundfish species share habitat. The size of the mesh at the rear of a net, known as the cod end, is regulated to allow undersized fish to escape, but once the cod end fills up, no

Box 10.3 New Zealand: A Management Model?

New Zealand's marine fishery has been hailed as the most progressively managed in the world (1). The quota-based management system now in place, introduced on a national scale in 1986, was designed to reduce overfishing, downsize an overcapitalized industry, and avoid burdensome regulations (2). While many experts point to New Zealand as the model for future global fishery management, others believe its performance record is still unclear.

New Zealand, though small, has the fourth largest exclusive economic zone in the world (4.5 million square kilometers) (3). In 1989, the value of its fishery was N.Z. $950 million (U.S. $570 million) (4).

Before 1986, New Zealand had an open-access inshore fishery. There were closed areas and seasons, minimum fish sizes, and designated ports for fishing vessels, but no controls on the number of people fishing. Offshore, however, the fishery had been regulated by quota since 1978, when New Zealand's jurisdiction was extended to 200 miles off the coast. The system was enacted not to stem overfishing or overcapitalization but to prevent them altogether. The government's positive experience with offshore fishery management seems to have encouraged the transfer of the quota system to the troubled inshore fishery (5) (6).

The core of New Zealand's system is the individual transferable quota (ITQ). A limited number of ITQ "owners" have the right to harvest a given amount of fish, which are considered private property. Annual fish stock assessments determine the total allowable catch (TAC) for each harvested species. Fishers who own an ITQ have the right to their harvests or to sell or trade their quota (7).

In theory, ITQs result in a number of advantages. First, they provide economic security to fishers who know in advance how much fish they can harvest each year. With the element of competition removed, fishers are no longer compelled to catch as many fish as possible in the shortest time. They can concentrate on operating in the most economic manner, fishing at times when their catch will bring the highest price (8). And because the ITQ is transferable, it should naturally flow from the least to the most efficient harvesters (9) (10).

Second, because fishers have an exclusive right to their resource, they have more at stake in conserving it and tend to comply with regulations, reducing the need for enforcement.

And third, if biological assessments are accurate, fish stocks can be maintained at sustainable yield levels, giving fishery managers greater control over resources.

Although New Zealand's experience has roughly followed this scenario, there have been some problems implementing the system. Stock assessments have been inadequate because of a lack of data. The fishing industry is continually pushing for the highest possible quotas, and some fishers misreport their catch in an attempt to take more fish than they are allotted. Quota enforcement, moreover, is severely limited (11).

Unlike many of their counterparts in other parts of the world, New Zealand's fishers, for the most part, have embraced the ITQ system. Nearly 60 percent, according to one study conducted six months after it was instituted, thought the ITQ system was better than the previous management system (12) (13). But they do complain about the cost of quotas and about the wisdom of some catch levels (14).

At the outset, levels were set for most of the major harvestable species. The law required that levels ensure a maximum sustainable yield. Fixed quotas were then distributed to fishers based on their recent catch record. For some species, there were too many fishers for the size of the TAC. So the government bought back quotas from fishers, spending NZ $42.4 million (US $22 million) in 1986 and reducing the number of fishers in certain fisheries (15).

Most government and industry officials believe the ITQ system was necessary to conserve stocks (16). But measuring performance is not a simple task, and some authorities disagree with the general opinion that fish stocks have improved. One reason it is difficult to measure performance is that stock assessments are by nature imprecise. Stocks can vary from year to year, depending on environmental and other factors. And in New Zealand's case, historic scientific data may have been too sketchy to allow for knowledgeable estimates today. A stock of orange roughy, for example, was initially given a catch level three times higher than the most optimistic sustained-yield estimates, and it will probably be some time before the assessment process is refined enough to ensure sustainable yields for that fish (17).

Because quotas were at first allotted by weight rather than percentage of the total catch, the government could not change the amount each fisher caught unless it

---

fish of any size can escape (87) (88). Bycatch—the unintended capture of marine animals, most of which are discarded and die—is especially a problem when it consists of depleted species. For instance, haddock, a severely overfished species, is often netted by trawlers that target pollock (89) (90). Bycatch often goes unreported because fishermen do not want to risk penalties for netting protected species.

Another problem unheeded by the New England Fishery Council is that small-mesh nets are allowed on board in large-mesh areas. This makes regulations difficult to enforce. Violators who use small-mesh nets in these areas cannot be caught except by surprise. According to a 1989 report, violations are common (91). As early as 1979, the U.S. Coast Guard suggested that only one mesh size be allowed in a given area (92). This advice has been ignored by the Council, mainly because carrying a single mesh size would inconvenience some fishers (93).

Another failure of the Council is that it has not limited the number of fishers or the size (and hence the catch capacity) of vessels. Owing to unrestricted access,

the level of fishing effort doubled between 1977 and 1985 (94) (95). With such a large number of boats fishing, the Council was pressured into giving fishers more of the resource than was biologically justified (96). Such open access, coupled with an unlimited total catch, has been a formula for disaster in New England.

Solutions to Overfishing in New England

To rebuild the groundfish stocks of New England, a number of solutions are being considered. One is to change the Magnuson Act itself, eliminating, or at least limiting, the power of the fishing industry to set catch levels and allocate resources. To prevent overfishing, the final decision on harvest levels should rest not with a regional management council but rather with an agency such as the National Marine Fisheries Service, which has access to the best scientific analyses. The regional council would then be allowed to allocate quotas. To dilute the power of the fishing industry in management decisions, councils could include more public-interest representatives on the grounds that a publicly owned resource is at stake (97).

Box 10.3

bought back some of the quota. The prospect of spending millions of dollars to do this prompted New Zealand to change its quota system from fixed to variable tonnage in 1990. When fishers lost quota after the switch, the government negotiated an out-of-court settlement to compensate them. To reduce landings now, the government scales back the catch level (18).

Bycatch remains a critical conservation issue in New Zealand. Unavoidably, fishers catch species for which they do not own quota. By law, a fisher must either trade sufficient ITQ to cover the bycatch or turn bycatch over to the government. Yet without compensation, there is no incentive to bring bycatch ashore. Officials are trying to work out a way to discourage at-sea dumping by establishing a penalty high enough to discourage targeting a bycatch species, yet low enough to make it worthwhile to land (19) (20).

Another obstacle to conservation is the illegal practice of highgrading—discarding a less valuable size or species of fish in order to keep a more valuable one. If fishers are entitled to a certain amount of fish, it is to their advantage to land only the most profitable ones. Nobody knows how common highgrading is in New Zealand, nor does there appear to be any practical way to prevent it (21).

On the economic front, evidence suggests that New Zealand's ITQ system is reducing fleet size somewhat. At the outset, in 1986, larger companies that presumably could harvest fish at less cost than smaller ones owned much of the quota. But since then, some larger firms have leased quotas to small companies, which now make

up the same percentage of the fleet as before 1986. The number of middle-sized firms has declined (22).

A big winner under the ITQ system was supposed to have been New Zealand's government. It charges an annual "resource royalty" to fishers who own quota, which averaged N.Z. $20 million (U.S. $12 million) between 1986 and 1989. That money—plus the revenue generated from selling quota in 1986—has paid for research and enforcement as well as added to the national treasury (23). But expensive litigation in cases involving the fishing industry and native Maori people has drained much of the profit. And some observers assert that the revenue hasn't found its way back to fishery budgets, leaving research and enforcement programs underfunded (24).

Several limited ITQ systems are in place in Iceland, Canada, Australia, and the United States. Acceptance in these countries has been slow, not least because fishers are reluctant to change their competitive, winner-take-all tradition (25). Before plunging into such a radically different management system, fishers and fishery managers around the world are waiting for more quantifiable results from New Zealand and elsewhere.

References and Notes

1. Todd Campbell, "World Fisheries Management Earns Poor Marks," *National Fisherman* (Yearbook 1991), p. 45.
2. Michael P. Sissenwine and Pamela M. Mace, "ITQs in New Zealand: The Era of Fixed Quota in Perpetuity," *Fishery Bulletin*, Vol. 90, No. 1 (1992), p. 148.
3. *Ibid.*
4. Arch Davis, "New Zealand System Puts the Squeeze on Fishermen," *National Fisherman* (February 1992), p. 24.
5. Ian N. Clark, Philip J. Major, and Nina Mollet, "Development and Implementation of New Zealand's ITQ Management System," *Marine Resource Economics*, Vol. 5, No. 4 (1988), p. 331.
6. *Op. cit.* 2, pp. 148–149.
7. *Op. cit.* 2, p. 149.
8. Donald R. Leal, "Using Property Rights to Regulate Fish Harvest," *The Christian Science Monitor* (July 30, 1992), p. 18.
9. *Op. cit.* 2, p. 147.
10. *Op. cit.* 5.
11. Pamela Mace, Fisheries Consultant, Silver Spring, Maryland, 1993 (personal communication).
12. *Op. cit.* 2, p. 147.
13. Christopher M. Dewees, "Assessment of the Implementation of Individual Transferable Quotas in New Zealand's Inshore Fishery," *North American Journal of Fishery Management*, Vol. 9 (1988), p. 137.
14. *Op. cit.* 2, p. 154.
15. *Op. cit.* 2, pp. 149–150.
16. *Op. cit.* 4, p. 23.
17. *Op. cit.* 2, pp. 152–159.
18. Rick O. Boyd and Chrisopher M. Dewees, "Putting Theory into Practice: Individual Transferable Quotas in New Zealand's Fisheries," *Society and Natural Resources*, Vol. 5, No. 2 (1992), pp. 192–193.
19. *Op. cit.* 5, pp. 343 and 346.
20. *Op. cit.* 2, pp. 155–156.
21. *Op. cit.* 2, p. 156.
22. *Op. cit.* 4, p. 25.
23. *Op. cit.* 2, pp. 151 and 153–154.
24. *Op. cit.* 11.
25. *Op. cit.* 8.

Some observers believe that the most effective way to address the problems inherent in crowded open-access fisheries such as New England's is to place limits on access and on catches. One possible model, favored by managers but resisted by fishers, would be a variation of the individual transferable quota (ITQ) system now being used in New Zealand and select U.S. fisheries (98). (See Box 10.3.) Under ITQ management, biologists assess fish stocks and determine optimum catch levels to maintain sustainable fisheries. The catch is then divided among fishers, whose shares, based on individual catches from recent years, can be sold or traded.

An example relevant to New England is Canadian groundfishing off the coast of Nova Scotia, now controlled by an experimental ITQ system (99). The effects on fish stocks are still unknown, though research vessels of the National Oceanic and Atmospheric Administration report that there are more groundfish on the Canadian side of the border running across Georges Bank, suggesting that tighter controls are having a positive effect (100). And Pacific halibut fishers in Canada, also operating under an ITQ program, fetch

higher prices for their catch than their U.S. counterparts, who operate under an open-access system (101).

In 1989, the U.S. Department of Commerce issued guidelines requiring regional councils to establish measurable definitions of overfishing and to take steps that would reduce fishing to sustainable levels. The New England Fishery Management Council's September 1993 draft proposal called for a 50 percent reduction in fishing mortality over a seven-year period, a moratorium on new permits, and an increase in mesh size from 5.5 to 6 inches (102) (103) (104). If such measures are not enough to restore the New England fishery, the United States may be forced to go the more draconian—but in the long term assuredly more successful—route used by Canada. In 1992 that country imposed a two-year moratorium on cod fishing in Newfoundland (105).

ONE SOLUTION FOR PERU AND NEW ENGLAND

The fishery problems in Peru and New England, though different, have some similarities. In both places, controls on the industry's size or rate of growth

Figure 10.7 Total Catch versus Level of Effort, Georges Bank, 1976–91

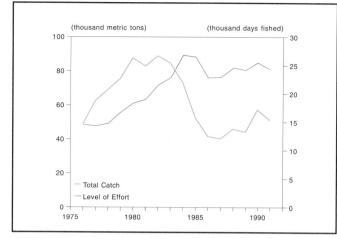

Source: National Marine Fisheries Service, unpublished data, Northeast Fisheries Science Center, 1993.

were minimal; in fact, government encouraged growth. Large sectors of both economies became dependent on a few species of fish, creating tremendous pressure on fishery managers to provide steady access to those fish. As fishing vessels proliferated, fish-catching technology improved, the processing infrastruc-ture expanded, and fishing intensified beyond the point of maximum sustainable yield (106) (107) (108).

Also, in both Peru and New England the sustainable-yield estimates of biologists went unheeded. Instead, fishery managers chose to maximize exploitation rates for the short term, a decision that ultimately devastated the economies it was meant to bolster.

Finally, in both Peru and New England the balance of species was altered. Skates and dogfish took over from groundfish as the dominant species in New England (109) (110). (See Figure 10.8.) In the Peruvian upwelling ecosystem, anchovies, which accounted for nearly 90 percent of fish biomass throughout the 1960s, now share dominance with sardines (111). Because some of the new dominant species prey on members of the former dominant species, New England ground-fish and Peruvian anchovies will probably have a difficult time recovering.

Management That Works

The simplest and most reliable way to rebuild depleted fish stocks is to reduce catch levels. In just about every instance where this has happened—for instance, with Pacific halibut, northwest Atlantic mackerel, North Sea herring, and Atlantic salmon—stocks have been restored to earlier levels (112). While the logic of reducing harvests is inescapable, the social implications are enormous. For example, Canada's difficult de-

Box 10.4 Marine Biodiversity

Over 90 percent of the world's living biomass is contained in the oceans, which cover 71 percent of the Earth's surface. Despite the predominance of marine ecosystems, only a small percentage of the oceans has been sampled. New marine phenomena, communities, and species are constantly being identified (1). In 1977, hydrothermal vents, or undersea hot springs, were discovered on the ocean floor. They support diverse communities, not through the photosynthetic activity of primary producers such as plants or algae but through the chemical breakdown of hydrogen sulfide and other compounds to create energy. Marine biodiversity is so poorly known that we continue to discover even large vertebrates. In 1938, the coelacanth fish, long thought extinct, was found living in the Indian Ocean. In recent years, specimens of the megamouth shark, a 5-meter-long filterfeeder, were caught.

How diverse are marine ecosystems? Recent discoveries have upped estimates of total marine species from 160,000 in 1971 to at least 10 million species, possibly more, today (2) (3). Although the marine environment may not rival its terrestrial counterpart in total number of species, it is more diverse in measures of uniqueness—of a total of 33 animal phyla, 32 are found in the ocean and 15 are exclusively marine—and of function—that is, for the variety of lifestyles its species has evolved to survive (4). For example, marine organ-

isms ranging from zooplankton to baleen whales have adapted filter-feeding strategies to capture their food, a rare if nonexistent phenomenon on land. Marine ecosystems also exhibit more complex food webs.

Marine biodiversity provides a wealth of services. Photosynthetic phytoplankton lock up atmospheric carbon, a primary contributor to global warming. Fish and shellfish provide a plentiful supply of protein to human populations worldwide. Seaweed derivatives are used in the production of food, cosmetics, shampoo, detergent, and industrial lubricants. And because many marine organisms rely on chemical defenses, the oceans are a promising source of new medicine. The same chemicals that protect species against predators may serve humanity in combating hypertension, cardiovascular problems, and viral and bacterial infections.

Threats to marine biodiversity include water and air pollution, silt and chemical runoff from land, the introduction of exotic species, changes related to ozone depletion, and global climate change. Marine organisms are particularly vulnerable to pollutants for two reasons: their aquatic environment easily spreads harmful substances, and many of these organisms are free-floating, at least in the juvenile stage, so they are specially vulnerable to toxins as they are dispersed.

Of direct concern to biologists studying marine biodiversity is the depletion of spe-cies and the destruction of habitats they depend on. The North Atlantic and central and southern Pacific fisheries are generally overexploited, as are select stocks in many of the remaining major global fisheries (5). Habitats are affected both directly, for instance by oil spills, and indirectly, through such activities as waste disposal and abusive land practices that send sediments and pollutants into rivers where they eventually empty into the ocean (6).

Of all marine habitats, those in coastal waters are under the greatest pressure. Ninety percent of the world's marine fish catch (measured by weight) depend on coastal habitats for at least part of their life cycles (7). Coral reefs, which rival rainforests in diversity, are being destroyed through siltation, coral mining, and pollution. Mangroves, which line one quarter of tropical coastlines, are being cut down for lumber, fuelwood and to build aquaculture ponds. More than half of Indomalaysia and Africa's original mangroves have been destroyed (8). Estuaries and wetlands, important sites for migratory species, are threatened in many areas by coastal development. Deeper waters, whose floors were more recently found to be rich in diversity, are threatened by the disposal of toxic chemicals (9).

Because the ocean beyond territorial waters is an open-access resource, it is difficult to prevent the excessive fishing, mining, and dumping that threaten ma-

cision to cut back fish harvests has meant thousands of lost jobs.

In most depleted fisheries this step can not be avoided. But in some parts of the world, two concepts are gaining attention that, if supported by fishery managers and combined with greater controls, could provide a more effective paradigm for managing fisheries and preventing overfishing: placing greater value on the preservation of whole ocean ecosystems and viewing these ecosystems as integrated units.

When a species is overfished, genetic diversity within that species is reduced. So, frequently, is the population and diversity of other organisms connected to that species, the "predators, symbionts, competitors and prey" (113). The consequences of overfishing, then, may go far beyond what is readily apparent. In the case of Peru, for example, the elimination of vast numbers of anchovies depleted bird species that depend on them for food (114). Yet most fishery management programs do not address the issue of nontarget species (115).

The biological consequences of altering the balance of species in an ecosystem are not known. But if biodiversity is indeed worth preserving, there is compelling reason to investigate this issue. (See Box 10.4.)

To preserve biodiversity, it is vital to maintain the integrity of entire living systems (116). All pertinent elements of an ecosystem need to be studied in relation to each other, not as isolated units of knowledge. This, in

Figure 10.8 Georges Bank Catch Composition, 1963 and 1990

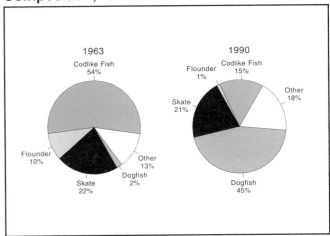

Sources:
1. Northeast Fisheries Science Center (NEFSC), unpublished data (NEFSC, Woods Hole, Massachusetts, May 1993).
2. Mark Alan Lovewell, "Georges Bank: An American Tragedy," *Vineyard Gazette* (January 8, 1993, Martha's Vineyard, Massachusetts), p. 1 and 8, sec. B.

a general sense, is what the Large Marine Ecosystem (LME) concept is all about.

The idea, which originated in the mid-1970s, can be thought of as bioregionalism for the sea. LMEs are defined as ecologically coherent areas of the ocean that

Box 10.4

rine biodiversity. A handful of international agreements such as the United Nations Convention on the Law of the Sea (ratified as of November 16, 1993 by 60 nations; it will take effect on November 16, 1994) and regional sea conventions attempt to regulate these activities (10). Even within territorial waters, few countries have the ability to oversee their marine resources adequately, and few attempt an integrated approach to managing coastal regions. Countries have been slow to establish marine parks and reserves: less than 1 percent of marine areas is currently protected (11). The Caracas Action Plan, drawn up in Venezuela at the 1992 World Congress on National Parks and Protected Areas, calls for a representative global network of marine protected areas to spur further protection. The plan's target is to have at least 20 percent of the world's coastal zones operating under management plans by the year 2000 (12).

The Center for Marine Conservation's Global Marine Biological Diversity Strategy, published in 1993 and sponsored by the United Nations Environment Programme, World Bank, World Conservation Union, and World Wildlife Fund, recommends a series of actions at the international, national, and local levels to protect marine diversity. These include reducing the consumption and waste of marine resources, slowing and later stopping the growth of coastal human popula-

tions, strengthening intergovernmental laws and institutions concerned with marine issues, fostering environmentally friendly trade and technology, promoting integrated coastal resource management, developing management plans for species located in the territories of more than one country or in international waters, and expanding marine biodiversity research and monitoring (13). This strategy is the first comprehensive, worldwide approach to protecting marine biodiversity. Its effectiveness will depend on whether government policymakers, intergovernmental institutions, and nongovernmental organizations implement these measures.

References and Notes

1. Sylvia Earle, "Foreword," in *The Living Ocean: Understanding and Protecting Marine Biodiversity* (Island Press, Washington, D.C., 1991), p. xiv.
2. Albert Manville, "Maintaining Marine Biodiversity: The Missing Link in Global Ecosystem Management" in *Transactions of the 57th North American Wildlife and Natural Resources Conference* (Wildlife Management Institute, Washington, D.C., 1992), pp. 403–404.
3. J.F. Grassle and N.J. Maceolek, "Deep-Sea Species Richness: Regional and Local Diversity Estimates from Quantitative Bottom Samples," *American Naturalist*, Vol. 139 (1992), pp. 333–336.
4. Elliott A. Norse, ed., *Global Marine Biological Diversity: A Strategy for Building Conser-*

vation into Decision Making (Island Press, Washington, D.C., 1993), pp. 14–15.
5. Food and Agriculture Organization of the United Nations (FAO), "Agriculture Towards 2010," (FAO, Rome, 1993, unpublished).
6. G. Carleton Ray, "Ecological Diversity in Coastal Zones and Oceans," in *Biodiversity*, E.O. Wilson, ed. (National Academy Press, Washington, D.C., 1988), p. 37.
7. Food and Agriculture Organization of the United Nations (FAO), Committee on Fisheries, *Environment and Sustainability in Fisheries* (FAO, Rome, February 1991), p.7.
8. World Resources Institute in collaboration with the United Nations Environment Programme and the United Nations Development Programme, *World Resources 1990-91* (Oxford University Press, New York, 1990), p. 124.
9. Boyce Thorne-Miller and John Catena, *The Living Ocean: Understanding and Protecting Marine Biodiversity* (Island Press, Washington, D.C., 1991), p. 63.
10. Charles Higginson, Executive Director, Council on Ocean Law, Washington, D.C., 1993 (personal communication).
11. Graeme Kelleher and Chris Bleakley, *Conservation of Global Marine Biodiversity: The Role of Marine Protected Areas* (The World Bank, Washington, D.C., 1992), p. 1.
12. "Fourth World Congress on Parks and Protected Areas: Caracas," *Biodiversity Conservation Strategy Update*, Vol. 3, No. 1 (1992), p. 2.
13. *Op. cit.* 4, pp. 283–287.

are 200,000 square kilometers or more in size. So far, 49 have been defined on the margins of the world's oceans, encompassing the most commercially productive fisheries and accounting for 95 percent of the world's annual harvest (117).

An LME approach to fishery management evaluates an individual fish stock, as traditional single-species management does, but also looks at the stock's competitors and predators. It is critical to monitor fish stocks accurately and understand inter- and intraspecies dynamics (118), for if fishers have little faith in the accuracy of stock assessments, they may disregard catch limits or lobby to have them raised. Imprecise biological data also makes it difficult to set a total catch limit that will sustain a species.

For the past several decades, the fisheries of the LME that comprise the northeast U.S. continental shelf have been monitored and analyzed by research vessels that regularly conduct trawl surveys (119). Consequently, the biological database for New England is extensive and, for the most part, accurate. One conclusion from this long-term monitoring is that overfishing was indeed primarily responsible for the decline of groundfish and other commercially valuable species in New England. Data show that the carrying capacity of the ocean for finfish has not changed, and the biomass of finfish is approximately the same. Overfishing simply altered the makeup of populations, allowing sand eels, dogfish, and skates to replace groundfish (120).

As part of an LME approach to the management of New England groundfish, a strategy known as "adaptive management," one that deliberately manipulates population balances, might be attempted (121). One researcher estimates that reducing predation by targeting fish-eating species on Georges Bank might double the fish yield (122). Others caution against meddling with population dynamics over a large geographic expanse because of the unknown consequences to the ecosystem as a whole (123).

A strategy similar to adaptive management could be used in the Humboldt current LME off Peru. During El Niño, when warmer water causes predators of the anchovy such as mackerel to thrive, an effort would be made to fish for these species. One drawback is the low demand for these predatory fish, however, the fishery could be subsidized with profits from the anchovy-based fish meal industry (124).

Another important part of an LME approach to the Humboldt current ecosystem would be to forecast El Niño more accurately. With better information, managers could shut down the anchovy fishery before a warming episode occurred, protecting the fish from undue environmental stress. Yet some observers question the value of El Niño forecasts if long-term sustainable fish harvests are not a priority for managers (125).

Regardless of how New England groundfish or Humboldt current anchovy are managed, it is unlikely that these species will ever be completely destroyed by humans. In fact, there has never been a documented case of human exploitation driving a marine fish species to extinction, though individual stocks such as New England haddock have been virtually eliminated (126). Nonetheless, people must realize that traditional attitudes about fishery resources and management no longer work. Gone are the days of record landings, little competition, and high profits. Only through more enlightened and integrated approaches, which keep politics and biology clearly separated and bring exploitation rates under tighter control, will depleted fish populations begin to recover to sustainable levels.

The Conditions and Trends section was written by Eric Rodenburg and Dirk Bryant of the World Resources *staff. The Focus On section was written by Scott McCredie, a freelance writer based in Seattle, Washington.*

References and Notes

1. Igor A. Shiklomanov, "World Fresh Water Resources," in *Water in Crisis*, Peter H. Gleick, ed. (Oxford University Press, New York, 1993), pp. 13–14.

2. *Ibid.*, p. 15.

3. World Resources Institute in collaboration with the United Nations Environment Programme and the United Nations Development Programme, *World Resources 1990–91* (Oxford University Press, New York, 1990), p. 168.

4. *Op. cit.* 1, pp. 16–17.

5. The International Commission on Large Dams (ICOLD), *World Register of Dams, 1988 Updating* (ICOLD, Paris, 1989), pp. 25–27.

6. *Op. cit.* 1, p. 14.

7. Stephen C. McCaffrey, "Water, Politics, and International Law," in *Water in Crisis*, Peter H. Gleick, ed. (Oxford University Press, New York, 1993), p. 92.

8. *Ibid.*, p. 97.

9. Miguel Solanes, "Legal and Institutional Aspects of River Basin Development," *Water International*, Vol. 17, No. 3 (1992), p. 116.

10. *Op. cit.* 7, pp. 92–93.

11. *Op. cit.* 7, p. 93.

12. Dale Whittington and Elizabeth McClelland, "Opportunities for Regional and International Cooperation in the Nile Basin," *Water International*, Vol. 17, No. 3 (1992), pp. 144–154.

13. *Op. cit.* 7, pp. 94–97.

14. David Sarokin and Jay Schulkin, "The Role of Pollution in Large-Scale Population Disturbances, Part 1: Aquatic Populations," *Environmental Science and Technology*, Vol. 26, No. 8 (1992), pp. 1476–1478 and 1482–1483.

15. Patrick Hughes, "Killer Algae," *Discover*, Vol. 14, No. 4 (April 1993), p. 72.

16. *Op. cit.* 14, p. 1482.

17. *Op. cit.* 15

18. *Op. cit.* 14, pp. 1478–1479.

19. JoAnn Burkholder, Edward Noga, Cecil Hobbs, *et al.*, "New 'Phantom' Dinoflagellate Is the Causative Agent of Major Estuarine Fish Kills," *Nature*, Vol. 358, No. 6385 (1992), pp. 407–410.

20. Elizabeth Culotta, "Red Menace in the World's Oceans," *Science*, Vol. 257, No. 5076 (1992), p. 1476.

21. *Ibid.*

22. Theodore Smayda, Professor of Oceanography, University of Rhode Island, Kingston, Rhode Island, 1993 (personal communication).

23. *Op. cit.* 20, pp. 1476–1477.

24. Food and Agriculture Organization of the United Nations (FAO), *Recent Developments in World Fisheries* (FAO, Rome, 1991), p. 1.

25. Food and Agriculture Organization of the United Nations (FAO), "Marine Fisheries and the Law of the Sea: A Decade of Change," FAO Fisheries Circular No. 853 (FAO Fisheries Department, Rome, 1992), pp. 4–7.

26. Although the term "sustainable yield" has been widely used for years, a growing number of scientists are abandoning it. The term

assumes that there is a "magic number" that can be calculated and used to set harvest limits, but in reality this number fluctuates according to climate, region, the degree of fishing pressure, and inter-species dynamics. One possible term that better reflects the uncertainty of a given harvest level is "likely production potential." Source: S. Garcia, Director, Fishery Resources and Environment Division, Fisheries Department, Food and Agriculture Organization of the United Nations, Rome, 1993 (personal communication); James R. McGoodwin, *Crisis in the World's Fisheries: People, Problems, and Policies* (Stanford University Press, Stanford, California, 1990), pp. 155–160; and Elliot A. Norse, ed., *Global Marine Biological Diversity: A Strategy for Building Conservation into Decision Making* (Island Press, Washington, D.C., 1993), p. 91.

27. James R. McGoodwin, *Crisis in the World's Fisheries: People, Problems, and Policies* (Stanford University Press, Stanford, California, 1990), p. 3.

28. *Op. cit.* 25, pp. 19 and 34.

29. *Op. cit.* 25, pp. 19, 21, 26, and 34.

30. Donald Ludwig, Ray Hilborn, and Carl Walters, "Uncertainty, Resource Exploitation, and Conservation: Lessons from History," *Science*, Vol. 260, No. 5104 (April 2, 1993), p. 17.

31. John H. Ryther, "Photosynthesis and Fish Production in the Sea," *Science*, Vol. 166, No. 3901 (October 3, 1969), p. 75.

32. Cesar N. Caviedes and Timothy J. Fik, "The Peru-Chile Eastern Pacific Fisheries and Climatic Oscillation," in *Climate Variability, Climate Change and Fisheries*, Michael H. Glantz, ed. (Cambridge University Press, Cambridge, U.K., 1992), p. 355.

33. *Op. cit.* 31.

34. Richard T. Barber and Francisco P. Chavez, "Biological Consequences of El Niño," *Science*, Vol. 222, No. 4629 (December 16, 1983), p. 1203.

35. Peter Muck, "Major Trends in the Pelagic Ecosystem off Peru and Their Implications for Management," in *The Peruvian Upwelling Ecosystem: Dynamics and Interactions*, D. Pauly, P. Muck, J. Mendo, *et al.*, eds. (Instituto del Mar del Peru, Callao, 1989), pp. 392–393 and 398–400.

36. *Op. cit.* 32, pp. 357–358.

37. *Op. cit.* 32, p. 357.

38. *Op. cit.* 32, pp. 357–358.

39. *Op. cit.* 35, p. 391.

40. *Op. cit.* 35, p. 391.

41. J. Dana Thompson, "Climate, Upwelling, and Biological Productivity," in *Resource Management and Environmental Uncertainty: Lessons from Coastal Upwelling Fisheries*, Michael H. Glantz and J. Dana Thompson, eds. (John Wiley, New York, 1981), pp. 20–21.

42. Instituto del Mar del Peru, "Panel of Experts' Report (1970) on the Economic Effects of Alternative Regulatory Measures in the Peruvian Anchoveta Fishery," in *Resource Management and Environmental Uncertainty: Lessons from Coastal Upwelling Fisheries*, Michael H. Glantz and J. Dana Thompson, eds. (John Wiley, New York, 1981), pp. 375–388.

43. *Ibid.*, pp. 369–375.

44. Gerald J. Paulik, "Anchovies, Birds, and Fishermen in the Peru Current," in *Resource Management and Environmental Uncertainty: Lessons from Coastal Upwelling Fisheries*, Michael H. Glantz and J. Dana Thompson, eds. (John Wiley, New York, 1981), p. 73.

45. *Op. cit.* 32, p. 359.

46. *Op. cit.* 41, p. 28.

47. *Op. cit.* 34, 1203–1204.

48. *Op. cit.* 32, p. 363.

49. *Op. cit.* 41, p. 29.

50. *Op. cit.* 35, p. 389.

51. *Op. cit.* 35, p. 391.

52. William E. Evans, "Management of Large Marine Ecosystems," in *Biomass Yields and Geography of Large Marine Ecosystems*, Kenneth Sherman and Lewis M. Alexander, eds. (Westview Press, Boulder, Colorado, 1989), pp. 463–464.

53. *Op. cit.* 35, p. 399–400.

54. *Op. cit.* 32, p. 369.

55. *Op. cit.* 35, pp. 397 and 399.

56. *Op. cit.* 32, pp. 362–364.

57. John A. Gulland, "Managing Fisheries in an Imperfect World: The Nature of the Imperfection," in *Global Fisheries: Perspectives for the 80's*, Brian J. Rothschild, ed. (Springer-Verlag, New York, 1983), p. 183.

58. *Op. cit.* 35, pp. 399–400.

59. Michael H. Glantz, "Considerations of the Societal Value of an El Niño Forecast and the 1972–1973 El Niño," in *Resource Management and Environmental Uncertainty: Lessons from Coastal Upwelling Fisheries*, Michael H. Glantz and J. Dana Thompson, eds. (John Wiley, New York, 1981), p. 469.

60. Kenneth Sherman, "The Large Marine Ecosystem Concept: Research and Management Strategy for Living Marine Resources," *Ecological Applications*, Vol. 1, No. 4 (1991), p. 354.

61. National Oceanic and Atmospheric Administration (NOAA), *Status of Fishery Resources off the Northeastern United States for 1992* (NOAA, Woods Hole, Massachusetts, 1992), pp. 13–16.

62. *Ibid.*, p. 16.

63. Daniel Merriman, "The History of Georges Bank," in *Georges Bank: Past, Present, and Future of a Marine Environment*, Guy C. McLeod and John H. Prescott, eds. (Westview Press, Boulder, Colorado, 1982), pp. 23–26.

64. Richard C. Hennemuth and Susan Rockwell, "History of Fisheries Conservation and Management," in *Georges Bank*, Richard Backus, ed. (MIT Press, Boston, 1987), p. 434.

65. Fredric M. Serchuk and Susan E. Wigley, "Assessment and Management of the Georges Bank Cod Fishery: An Historical Review and Evaluation," *Journal of Northwest Atlantic Fisheries Science*, Vol. 13 (1992), p. 28.

66. *Op. cit.* 64, p. 437.

67. *Op. cit.* 64, p. 437.

68. Vaughn Anthony, Chief Scientific Adviser, Northeast Fisheries Science Center, National Marine Fisheries Service, Woods Hole, Massachusetts, 1993 (personal communication).

69. *Op. cit.* 64, pp. 438–443.

70. Henry Lyman, "The Role of the New England Regional Fishery Management Council on Georges Bank," in *Georges Bank: Past, Present and Future of a Marine Environment*, Guy C. McLeod and John H. Prescott, eds. (Westview Press, Boulder, Colorado, 1982), p. 142.

71. *Op. cit.* 64, p. 443.

72. Vaughn Anthony, "The New England Groundfish Fishery after 10 Years under the Magnuson Fishery Conservation and Management Act," *North American Journal of Fisheries Management*, Vol. 10, No. 2 (1990), pp. 178–181.

73. National Fish and Wildlife Foundation (NFWF), "Needs Assessment of the National Marine Fisheries Service" NFWF, Washington, D.C., 1990, p. 41.

74. *Op. cit.* 64, p. 443.

75. J.L. McHugh, "Jeffersonian Democracy and the Fisheries Revisited," in *Global Fisheries: Perspectives for the 80's*, Brian J. Rothschild, ed. (Springer-Verlag, New York, 1983), pp. 87–88.

76. New England Fishery Management Council (NEFMC), "Draft of Amendment No. 5 to

Fishery Management Plan," NEFMC, Saugus, Massachusetts, 1992, p. 4.

77. *Op. cit.* 61, p. 12.

78. Massachusetts Offshore Groundfish Task Force (MOGT), *New England Groundfish in Crisis—Again* (MOGT, Boston, 1990), p. 6.

79. *Op. cit.* 76.

80. *Op. cit.* 72, p. 175.

81. *Op. cit.* 73, p. 74.

82. Vaughn Anthony, "The State of Groundfish Resources off the Northeastern United States," *Fisheries*, Vol. 18, No. 3 (1993), pp. 16–17.

83. Steven F. Edwards and Steven A. Murawski, "Potential Economic Benefits from Efficient Harvest of New England Groundfish," *North American Journal of Fisheries Management* (in press).

84. *Op. cit.* 73, p. 47.

85. Comptroller General of the United States (CGUS), *Progress and Problems of Fisheries Management under the Fishery Conservation and Management Act* (CGUS, Washington, D.C., 1979), p. 77.

86. *Op. cit.* 73, pp. 42–43.

87. Kris Freeman, "Mesh-Size Study Confirms Fisherman's Observations," *National Fisherman* (June 1992), p. 23.

88. *Op. cit.* 73, p. 107.

89. National Oceanic and Atmospheric Administration (NOAA), *Our Living Oceans: The First Annual Report on The Status of U.S. Living Marine Resources* (NOAA, Washington, D.C., 1991), p. 26.

90. *Op. cit.* 73, p. 107.

91. *Op. cit.* 78, p. 27.

92. *Op. cit.* 85, p. 79.

93. Susan Pollack, "New England Regulatory Knot Tightens around Groundfishermen," *National Fisherman*, (April 1991), p. 13.

94. *Op. cit.* 72, p. 184.

95. *Op. cit.* 78, p. 7.

96. *Op. cit.* 73, pp. 87–88.

97. *Op. cit.* 73, pp. 43 and 87–88.

98. Michael Weber, Marine Resources Management Specialist, National Marine Fisheries Service, Silver Spring, Maryland, 1993 (personal communication).

99. Nancy Griffin, "Inshore Draggermen Hit Rough Water under New System," *National Fisherman* (June 1992), p. 29.

100. Mark Alan Lovewell, "Hague Line Parts Waters of Two Great Nations," *Vineyard Gazette* (January 8, 1993), Martha's Vineyard, Massachusetts, p. 7, sec. B.

101. *Op. cit.* 98.

102. *Op. cit.* 76, pp. 7, 8, 17, and 30.

103. Pat Fiorelli, Public Information Officer, New England Fisheries Management Council, Saugus, Massachusetts, 1993 (personal communication).

104. "Northeast Fishermen Present Their Own Proposals," *National Fisherman* (July 1993), pp. 12–13.

105. Alan Harman, "Newfoundland Cod Fishery Closed for Two Years," *National Fisherman* (September 1992), p. 19.

106. S. Garcia, Director, Fishery Resources and Environment Division, Fisheries Department, Food and Agriculture Organization of the United Nations, Rome, 1993 (personal communication).

107. *Op. cit.* 27, pp. 155–160.

108. Elliott A. Norse, ed., *Global Marine Biological Diversity: A Strategy for Building Conservation into Decision Making* (Island Press, Washington, D.C., 1993), p. 91.

109. Steven A. Murawski, "Can We Manage Our Multispecies Fisheries?" *Fisheries*, Vol. 16, No. 5 (1991), p. 9.

110. R.K. Mayo, M.J. Fogarty, and F.M. Serchuk, "Aggregate Fish Biomass and Yield on

Georges Bank, 1960–1987, " *Journal of North-west Atlantic Fisheries Science*, Vol. 14 (1992), pp. 70–72.

111. *Op. cit.* 35, p. 388.
112. *Op. cit.* 68.
113. *Op. cit.* 108, pp. 89–90.
114. *Op. cit.* 35, pp. 390–391.
115. Boyce Thorne-Miller and John Catena, *The Living Ocean: Understanding and Protecting Marine Biodiversity* (Island Press, Washington, D.C., 1991), p. 83.
116. *Op. cit.* 108, pp. 186–187.
117. Kenneth Sherman, "Sustainability of Resources in Large Marine Ecosystems," in *Food Chains, Yields, Models, and Management of Large Marine Ecosystems*, Kenneth Sherman, Lewis M. Alexander, and Barry D.

Gold, eds. (Westview Press, Colorado, 1991), pp. 2–5.

118. *Ibid.*, pp. 3–5 and 10.
119. Kenneth Sherman, "Large Marine Ecosystems and Fisheries," paper presented at the United Nations University International Conference on the Definitions and Measurement of Sustainability: The Biophysical Foundations, The World Bank, Washington, D.C., June 1992.
120. *Ibid.*
121. Jeremy S. Collie, "Adaptive Strategies for Management of Fisheries Resources in Large Marine Ecosystems," in *Food Chains, Yields, Models, and Management of Large Marine Ecosystems*, Kenneth Sherman, Lewis M. Alexander, and Barry D. Gold, eds.

(Westview Press, Boulder, Colorado, 1991), pp. 225–227.

122. John Byrne, "Large Marine Ecosystems and the Future of Ocean Studies: A Perspective," in *Variability and Management of Large Marine Ecosystems*, Kenneth Sherman and Lewis Alexander, eds. (Westview Press, Boulder, Colorado, 1986), pp. 304–305.
123. John Pearce, Deputy Director, Northeast Fisheries, Science Center, National Marine Fisheries Serivce, Woods Hole, Massachusetts, 1993 (personal communication).
124. *Op. cit.* 35, p. 400.
125. *Op. cit.* 59, p. 468.
126. *Op. cit.* 108, p. 90.

11. Atmosphere and Climate

The thin skin of air that surrounds the planet is being affected by human activities as never before. Despite decades of warnings about air pollution and legislated efforts to control it, urban people are still being exposed to unacceptable levels of toxic pollutants, forests are still being degraded by acid deposition generated by faraway industry, and greenhouse gases continue to accumulate in the atmosphere.

The impact of human activities on Earth's climate is under intense scientific study. There is new evidence of how anthropogenic air pollutants and volcanic eruptions can temporarily cool the climate, and new concern that temperature-induced changes in ocean circulation could give rise to rapid shifts in climate. Nonetheless, many gaps in scientific understanding of the climate system remain, including how fast the climate will respond to greenhouse gases, forcing uncertainties in the global carbon budget.

This chapter reports on air pollution in urban megacities, on transboundary air pollution in Europe, on greenhouse gas emissions, and on the status of the Climate Convention. It also surveys the state of climate science and reports on new developments and continuing puzzles in this field.

CONDITIONS AND TRENDS

Now at 45 percent, the proportion of the global population living in urban areas could climb to 50 percent by the turn of the century (1). The megacities of the world lie under heavy clouds of industrial and vehicular pollution. Usually generated by the combustion of fossil fuels, the degree of air pollution depends on pollution reduction efforts, choice of fuels, technologies available, climate, weather, and topography.

Air pollution does not respect boundaries. It affects agriculture and ecosystems far from its source. European forests show the impact of transboundary pollution. More recently, world attention has been drawn to the potential danger of greenhouse gases. If they continue to be pumped into the air at the present rate, they could bring global climate change. The United Nations (U.N.) Framework Convention on Climate Change is an attempt to control them.

URBAN AIR POLLUTION: THE MEGACITIES

While some megacities represent extreme cases, there is no escaping air pollution or its health consequences in most of the world's cities. According to a 1988 assessment, more than 600 million people live in urban areas where sulfur dioxide (SO_2) levels exceed World Health Organization (WHO) guidelines, and over 1.25 billion live in cities with unacceptable levels of suspended particulate matter (SPM) (2). (See Table 11.1.)

The Megacities Study of 1992

WHO and the U.N. Environment Programme (UNEP) joined forces in 1992 to publish *Urban Air Pollution in the Megacities of the World*, a study covering 20 of the world's 24 megacities (3). The study has its weaknesses. Real differences in methods, concepts, standards, and calibration mark the reporting on various cities and countries. There are gaps in the coverage of important pollutants. Nonetheless, the megacities study is significant because it used all available data to provide the first global look at the state of the atmosphere in numerous urban environments.

Megacities are defined in the study as those urban areas that have more than 10 million people or will have more than 10 million by the year 2000, as estimated by the United Nations in *Prospects for World Urbanization, 1988* (4) (5). Every city studied had at least one major pollutant that exceeded WHO health guidelines, 14 cities had at least two, and 7 cities had at least three. (See Table 11.2.)

SO_2 remains a serious problem in Beijing, Mexico City, and Seoul, but it has become less of a problem elsewhere and in 12 cities does not even appear to be a threat. Suspended particulate matter, which can have especially toxic effects if it carries heavy metals or hydrocarbons, does not affect New York, London, or Los Angeles, but it is a serious problem in 12 megacities. Lead concentrations afflict Cairo and Karachi but not most megacities. Carbon monoxide, heavily concentrated in Mexico City's air, is not a problem at all in six of the megacities. Nitrogen dioxide (NO_2) is serious nowhere, even negligible in 10 cities. Information on ozone is poor but, of the cities measured, Los Angeles, Mexico City, São Paulo, and Tokyo fare the worst.

Of the cities for which there is sufficient data to compare, Mexico City has the worst overall air pollution—serious levels of SO_2, SPM, carbon monoxide, and ozone, and heavy levels of lead and NO_2. For megacities in general, SPM is the single most threatening air pollutant. Particularly hazardous blends of SO_2 and SPM occur in five centers: Beijing, Mexico City, Rio de Janeiro, Seoul, and Shanghai. Only 6 of the 20 megacities have adequate air quality monitoring (6), and efforts to gather and interpret data on related health risks and effects are lacking. (See Table 11.3.)

TRANSBOUNDARY AIR POLLUTION IN EUROPE

Air pollutants that give rise to acid precipitation and ozone are still pumped into the atmosphere in large quantities. According to *Acid News*, a Swedish Government newsletter, "Acid is being deposited in amounts that are damaging to the environment over three-quar-

Table 11.1 World Health Organization Air Pollutant Guidelines

Pollutant ($\mu g\ m^{-3}$)	Time Weighted Averages (μg = micrograms, 0.000001 grams)			
	One Hour	One Day	One Year	Other Period
Sulfur dioxide	350	100-150	40-60	500 (10 min.)
Suspended Particulate Matter				
Black Smoke	100-150	40-60		
Total Suspended	150-30	60-90		230 (<2% of days)
Lead			0.5-0.1	
Carbon Monoxide	30	10[a]		60 (30 min.) 100 (15 min.)
Nitrogen Oxide	400	150		190-320 (<once per month)
Ozone	150-200	100-120[a]		

Source: World Health Organization and United Nations Environment Programme, *Urban Air Pollution in the Megacities of the World* (Blackwell Reference, Oxford, U.K., 1992), p. 12.

Note: a. Eight hours. The World Health Organization (WHO) sets guidelines for exposure to many air pollutants. Air pollution monitors measure the amount of a pollutant either continuously or by periodic observation. Measurements are usually averaged (the sum of observations is divided by the number of observations) over a certain time period. Measurements are for both acute and chronic exposure. For example, a 10-minute average sulfur dioxide concentration of 500 micrograms per cubic meter ($\mu g\ m^{-3}$) of air exceeds the WHO health standard for short-term exposure while an annual average concentration of 35 $\mu g\ m^{-3}$ does not exceed WHO guidelines for long-term exposure. Health effects of pollutants measured are: sulfur dioxide (increased mortality, morbidity, impaired pulmonary function), suspended particulate matter (increased mortality, morbidity, impaired pulmonary function), lead (impaired liver and kidney functions and neurological damage), carbon monoxide (cardiovascular and neurological damage), nitrogen oxide (respiratory system inflammatory and permeability responses, lung function decrements, increases in airway reactivity), and ozone (respiratory system inflammatory and permeability responses, lung function decrements, increases in airway reactivity; eye, nose, and throat irritation, headaches).

ters of Europe. In some central and northwestern parts of the continent the depositions are twenty times higher, if not more, than the ecosystems can withstand without becoming damaged—twenty times more, that is, than the so-called critical loads" (7). In 1979 the U.N. Economic Commission for Europe (UNECE) called for a Convention on Long-Range Transboundary Air Pollution to supply a forum for the formation of a viable abatement strategy in Europe.

Sulfur Dioxide

SO_2 not only affects human health in urban areas but also acts as a precursor to sulfuric acid in dry deposition and precipitation, which can erode buildings, kill aquatic organisms, and damage habitat. In 1985, the Convention on Long-Range Transboundary Air Pollution supplied the framework for the Sulfur Protocol that called on signatories to reduce national emissions 30 percent from 1980 levels by 1993. A new agreement is not expected for some time, although the commitment to reductions still exists. The next stage of reduction, for which it will be far more difficult to achieve consensus, will entail targets set by estimates of critical thresholds for deposition and air pollution (8).

In the meantime, signatory countries have in large part met the goal of reducing their SO_2 emissions by 30 percent. Between 1980 and 1990, all signatories reduced emissions. Total German emissions, while a full 23 percent below 1980 levels, were still high as a result of the reunification of East and West Germany. Many

Table 11.2 Status of Pollutants in the Megacities, 1992

City	SO$_2$	SPM	Pb^a	CO	NO$_2$	O$_3$
Bangkok	□	●	■	□	□	□
Beijing	●	●	□	○	□	■
Bombay	□	●	□	□	□	○
Buenos Aires	○	■	□	□	○	○
Cairo	○	●	●	■	○	○
Calcutta	□	●	□	○	□	○
Delhi	□	●	□	□	□	○
Jakarta	□	●	■	■	□	■
Karachi	□	●	●	○	○	○
London	□	□	□	■	□	□
Los Angeles	□	■	□	■	■	●
Manila	□	●	■	○	○	○
Mexico City	●	●	■	●	■	●
Moscow	○	■	□	■	■	○
New York	□	□	□	■	□	■
Rio de Janeiro	■	■	□	□	○	○
São Paulo	□	■	□	■	■	●
Seoul	●	●	□	□	□	□
Shanghai	■	●	○	○	○	○
Tokyo	□	□	○	□	□	●

Source: World Health Organization and United Nations Environment Programme, *Urban Air Pollution in Megacities of the World* (Blackwell Reference, Oxford, U.K., 1992), p. 39.
Notes:
● Serious problem, WHO guidelines exceeded by more than a factor of two.
■ Moderate to heavy pollution, WHO guidelines exceeded by up to a factor of two (short-term guidelines exceeded on a regular basis at certain times).
□ Low pollution, Who guidelines normally met (short-term guidelines are exceeded occasionally).
○ No data available or insufficeint data for assessment.

Table 11.3 Air Pollution Monitoring in the Megacities, 1992

City	SO$_2$	SPM	Pb^a	CO	NO$_2$	O$_3$	Emissions Inventory
Bangkok	□	□	○	○	○	■	■
Beijing	□	□	○	○	○	○	○
Bombay	○	○	■	●	○	●	●
Buenos Aires	●	○	●	●	●	●	■
Cairo	■	□	●	●	●	●	●
Calcutta	○	○	○	●	●	●	○
Delhi	○	○	■	●	○	●	○
Jakarta	○	○	■	●	●	●	■
Karachi	●	●	●	●	●	●	○
London	□	○	○	○	○	○	○
Los Angeles	□	□	□	□	□	□	○
Manila	○	○	■	●	●	●	●
Mexico City	□	□	□	□	□	□	□
Moscow	●	■	■	■	■	●	■
New York	□	□	□	□	□	□	○
Rio de Janeiro	□	□	□	○	●	●	■
São Paulo	□	□	■	□	□	□	□
Seoul	□	□	○	□	□	□	○
Shanghai	□	□	○	●	●	●	○
Tokyo	□	□	□	□	□	□	○

Source: World Health Organization and United Nations Environment Programme, *Urban Air Pollution in Megacities of the World* (Blackwell Reference, Oxford, U.K., 1992), p. 36.
Notes:
a. Pb = lead.
● None or not known
■ Rudimentary
○ Adequate
□ Good

nonsignatory nations also dramatically reduced their sulfur dioxide outputs. (See Table 11.4.) Total emissions in Europe dropped from about 55 million metric tons in 1980 to just over 40 million in 1991 (9).

Nitrogen Oxides

Nitrogen emissions contribute to the formation of ozone, which damages human health, cropland, and biota. In the presence of sunlight, nitrogen oxides react with volatile organic compounds (VOCs) to form tropospheric ozone, a form of oxygen that is toxic to living things, including human beings. Nitrogen oxides are also a precursor of nitric acid in rainwater, and they reinforce the deleterious effects of SO$_2$ on artifacts, aquatic organisms, agriculture, and habitat. Total emissions of nitrogen oxides in Europe actually increased 5 percent between 1980 and 1991 (10). Signatories to the Nitrogen Protocol of the Convention on Long-Range Transboundary Air Pollution have committed to reduce their emissions (11).

Volatile Organic Compounds and Ozone

A protocol on VOCs, signed in November 1991, added another layer to the basic framework of the Convention on Long-Range Transboundary Air Pollution. The Protocol promises to reduce VOC emissions 30 percent from 1989 levels by the year 1999. Good baseline data on emissions are not yet available, so that measuring any changes will be difficult. The degree to which ozone forms depends on the ratio of VOCs to nitrogen oxides. A recent attempt to model the results of reducing VOCs to agreed levels, however, suggests that long-term average levels of ozone would not change much (only 4 to 8 percent in northwestern Europe), although the model projects that peak episodes would be significantly reduced (acute ozone exposure of 40 parts per billion could drop as much as 15 to 20 percent in northwestern Europe) (12).

Forest Damage

Europe's most recent forest damage assessment attempted to document the degree of defoliation, some of which can be attributed to acid deposition, for broadleaf trees and conifers. (See Table 11.5.) In 1991, fully 18.5 percent of Europe's broadleaf trees and 24.4 percent of its conifers were moderately or severely defoliated. (Moderate defoliation is defined as loss of leaves from 25 to 60 percent; severe is over 60 percent. Trees 100 percent defoliated, considered dead, are still included in this category.) Certain countries far exceeded the European average. In the United Kingdom, 56.7 percent of trees were at least moderately defoliated, in Poland 45 percent, and in Czechoslovakia 41.3 percent. Of course, within a given country there are regional variations. Defoliation, for instance, tends to be worse in mountain regions. And in any particular year, defoliation varies depending on factors other than acid deposition such as wind and frost damage (13).

GREENHOUSE GASES AND CLIMATE

Greenhouse Gas Emissions

The "greenhouse effect" refers to the phenomenon by which the Earth's atmosphere traps infrared radiation, or heat. Gases that cause the greenhouse effect are for the most part natural compounds—water vapor, CO$_2$,

Table 11.4 Changes in Sulfur Dioxide Emissions, 1980–90

Country	1980-90 Percent Reduction
Parties to the Protocol to the 1979 Convention on Long-Range Transboundary Air Pollution on the Reduction of Sulfur Emissions	
Austria	77.33
Belorussia	19.46
Belgium	46.50
Bulgaria	1.46
Canada	19.81
Czechoslovakia	21.19
Denmark	60.09
Finland	55.48
France	62.25
Germany[a]	23.41
Hungary	38.11
Italy	42.63
Liechtenstein	75.00
Luxembourg	33.33
Netherlands	55.58
Norway	61.43
Russian Federation[b]	37.72
Sweden	67.44
Switzerland	50.79
Ukraine	27.74
ECE region total	**33.03**
Parties to the Convention, nonparties to the "Sulfur Protocol"	
Greece	-25.00[c]
Iceland	0.00
Ireland	24.32
Poland	21.71
Portugal	23.31
Romania	0.00
Spain	30.22
Turkey	-28.26
United Kingdom	22.95
United States	9.40
Yugoslavia (former)	-13.85[c]
ECE region total	**12.44**
Other European countries (nonparties to the Convention)	
Albania	0.00
Europe total	28.71
USA and Canada total	**11.12**
ECE region total	**22.30**

Source: Strategies and Policies for Air Pollution Abatement, 1992 revision, UNECE 1992.

Notes:
a. Data for Germany include both the former Federal Republic of Germany and the former German Democratic Republic.
b. Within the European area only.
c. Negative number implies an increase.

Table 11.5 Forest Damage in Europe

(Percentage of trees with greater than 25 percent defoliation)

Country	1991
Austria	7.5
Belgium	17.9
Czechoslovakia	41.3
Denmark	29.9
Estonia	28.0[a]
Finland	16.0
France	7.1
Germany	25.2
Greece	16.9
Hungary	19.6
Ireland	15.0[a]
Italy	16.4
Lithuania	23.9
Liechtenstein	19.0
Luxembourg	20.8
Netherlands	17.2
Norway	19.7
Poland	45.0
Portugal	29.6
Romania	9.7
Russia	26.0[a]
Slovenia	15.9
Spain	7.3
Sweden	12.0
Switzerland	19.0
United Kingdom	56.7
Yugoslavia	9.8

Source: Swedish NGO Secretariat on Acid Rain, "Forest Damage in Europe," *Environmental Factsheet,* No. 1 (Swedish NGO Secretariat on Acid Rain, Göteborg, Sweden, December 1992), p. iv.
Note: a. Conifers only

methane, and nitrous oxide—that keep the Earth habitable. But human activity is increasing the concentration of these and other gases, for example, the industrial compounds known as chlorofluorocarbons (CFCs). The trend, if continued, is expected by atmospheric scientists to lead to global climate change with uncertain but potentially grave long-term effects. (See Focus on Climate Change: State of the Science, below.)

In an important turning point, global emissions of the major greenhouse gases resulting from human activity have begun to decline. In 1991, 22.7 metric tons of CO_2 were emitted from industrial sources (up 2 percent from 1989) and 3.4 billion metric tons from land

clearing (down 47 percent from 1989), representing an overall decrease of 11 percent. (See Tables 23.1 and 23.2.) This reduction occurred despite the oil well fires ignited in Kuwait by Iraqi military forces during the Persian Gulf War, which generated 2.1 percent of global industrial CO_2 emissions in 1991. Methane emissions in 1991 totaled 250 million metric tons (down 7.4 percent from 1989), while emissions of CFC-11 and -12 amounted to 400,000 metric tons (a decrease of 16.7 percent from 1989). (See Table 23.3.)

This pattern may be short-lived, as it reflects current sharp declines in fossil fuel use in the former Soviet Union, slow growth in the industrial world's energy consumption, and lower estimates of the rate of tropical deforestation. Energy use and emissions could mount when global economic growth resumes. In the case of CFC emissions, however, lower releases result from policy action, namely the accelerated phaseout of the manufacture and use of CFCs pursuant to international agreements. Thus the new trend offers encouragement in so far as it demonstrates that the international community is able to alter human activity to protect the global environment.

Even with the current decline in emissions, greenhouse gases continue to accumulate. The Intergovernmental Panel on Climate Change (IPCC) has estimated that an immediate 60 percent reduction in emissions of long-lived gases (smaller reductions for short-lived gases) would be required to stabilize atmospheric concentrations (14). As long as concentrations continue to rise, so does the warming potential of the atmosphere and hence the risk of global climate change.

National Rankings

A new international Convention on Climate Change that came into force in March, 1994, would require national inventories of greenhouse gas emissions. (See Status of the Climate Convention, below.) Inventories would help develop a comprehensive picture of greenhouse gases and their sources, part of an extended effort to control and limit the effects of emissions. In the absence of inventories, an estimate of each country's greenhouse gas emissions for 1991 has been used to calculate national contributions to (or relative shares of) the increase in the warming potential of the atmosphere for that year. Table 11.6 gives the national rank and percent share of the increase in the atmosphere's warming potential attributable to countries that in 1991 emitted the largest amounts of CO_2, methane, and CFCs. The countries are ranked by their Greenhouse Index. (See Box 11.1.) The United States and the former Soviet Union together contribute 32.8 percent of the total atmospheric impact of current global emissions, 19.1 and 13.6 percent respectively. If taken as a single unit, the European Community would rank third at 12.4 percent. As it is, the top six emitters, two of which are developing countries, contribute 55.8 percent of global emissions.

Compared to their Greenhouse Index rankings for 1989, Brazil moved up one place to fifth and India fell two places to seventh. (See *World Resources 1992–93*, Table 13.4.) The 1991 index uses new estimates by the U.N. Food and Agriculture Organization of annual average deforestation between 1980 and 1990 in calculations of CO_2 emissions. The new (higher) deforestation estimate for Brazil, disputed by that country, is the primary cause of its change in rank. (See Chapter 19, "Forests and Rangelands," Table 19.1.) India fell in the ranking because of the new deforestation estimates and the lower weight now given to methane emissions. Mexico's rank also declined significantly from 9th to 14th. Because of the oil well fires in Kuwait, which were assigned to Iraq, Iraq moved from 50th to 11th in rank.

Table 11.6 Greenhouse Index Ranking and Percent Share of Global Emissions, 1991

Rank	Country	Percent	Rank	Country	Percent
1.	United States	19.14	26.	Czechoslovakia	0.70
2.	Former Soviet Union	13.63	27.	Malaysia	0.61
3.	China	9.92	28.	Colombia	0.61
4.	Japan	5.05	29.	Netherlands	0.59
5.	Brazil	4.33	30.	Philippines	0.59
6.	Germany[a]	3.75	31.	Myanmar	0.55
7.	India	3.68	32.	Argentina	0.54
8.	United Kingdom	2.37	33.	Turkey	0.53
9.	Indonesia	1.89	34.	Romania	0.52
10.	Italy	1.72	35.	Bulgaria	0.51
11.	Iraq	1.71	36.	Bolivia	0.48
12.	France	1.63	37.	Pakistan	0.46
13.	Canada	1.62	38.	Belgium	0.40
14.	Mexico	1.43	39.	Peru	0.39
15.	Poland	1.16	40.	Yugoslavia	0.36
16.	Australia	1.13	41.	Nigeria	0.35
17.	South Africa	1.12	42.	Egypt	0.34
18.	Spain	1.01	43.	Viet Nam	0.32
19.	Venezuela	1.01	44.	Greece	0.31
20.	Republic of Korea	0.98	45.	Ecuador	0.30
21.	Zaire	0.93	46.	Bangladesh	0.29
22.	Thailand	0.88	47.	Hungary	0.26
23.	Korea, Democratic		48.	Austria	0.25
	People's Republic	0.84	49.	Demark	0.24
24.	Islamic Rep of Iran	0.82	50.	Algeria	0.23
25.	Saudi Arabia	0.78			

Sources:
1. World Resources Institute calculations.
2. Chapter 23, "Atmosphere and Climate," Tables 23.1 and 23.2.
Note: a. Data for Germany include both the former Federal Republic of Germany and the former German Democratic Republic.

Per Capita Rankings

Table 11.7 provides per capita rank and a measure of per capita emissions of CO_2, methane, and CFCs for 1991. The measure used is the ratio of a country's per capita emissions to the world median per capita figure, which for 1991 was 2.59 metric tons of CO_2 equivalent per person (the same as the per capita estimate for China). Some countries high on the list of total emitters disappear from the list of the highest per capita emitters (China, India, and Brazil, for example). The four highest per capita emitters either are large producers of oil (Qatar, the United Arab Emirates, and Brunei) or experienced severe deforestation during the 1980s (Gabon). Iraq moved temporarily into sixth place. Among

Box 11.1 Calculating a Greenhouse Index

Estimates here of national greenhouse gas emissions are based on anthropogenic sources of carbon dioxide (CO_2) (as calculated from data on fossil fuel combustion, cement manufacture, and deforestation), methane (from data on landfills, coal extraction, oil and gas production, wet rice agriculture, and livestock production), and the two main chlorofluorocarbons (CFCs) (from data on the use of CFC-11 and -12). (See Tables 23.1 and 23.2.)

Using the method proposed by the Intergovernmental Panel on Climate Change (IPCC), emission estimates for each gas are combined with another factor, the global warming potential, to give an overall index of each country's contribution to the increase in the warming potential of the atmosphere in a given year [1]. Global warming potentials account for the atmospheric lifetime of each gas and its relative efficiency in absorbing infrared radiation. (See *World Resources 1992–93*, p. 207.)

Differences from estimates for earlier years can be attributed to changes in the activities giving rise to emissions, a continuing reduction in global CFC emissions, and scientific advances in determining the global warming potential of greenhouse gases, especially methane [2].

References and Notes

1. IPCC, *Climate Change 1992: The Supplementary Report to the IPCC Scientific Assessment*, J.T. Houghton, B.A. Callander, and S.K. Varney, eds. (Cambridge University Press, Cambridge, U.K., 1992), p. 15, Table 3. Direct global warming potential for a 100-year period is given as 1 for CO_2, 11 for CH_4 (methane), 3,400 for CFC-11, and 7,100 for CFC-12.
2. J.W. Elkins, T.M. Thompson, T.H. Swanson, *et al.*, "Decrease in the Growth Rates of Atmospheric Chlorofluorocarbons 11 and 12," *Nature*, Vol. 364, No. 6440 (1993), pp. 780–783.

Table 11.7 Relative Per Capita Greenhouse Emissions, 1991

Rank	Country	Per Capita Measure[a]	Rank	Country	Per Capita Measure[a]
1.	Qatar	18.63	27.	Netherlands	4.66
2.	Gabon	17.03	28.	Finland	4.60
3.	United Arab Emirates	16.15	29.	Korea, Democratic People's Republic	4.48
4.	Brunei	11.51	30.	New Zealand	4.42
5.	Luxembourg	11.41	31.	Panama	4.13
6.	Iraq	10.84	32.	Bahamas	4.00
7.	United States	8.95	33.	Malaysia	3.93
8.	Bahrain	8.43	34.	Israel	3.90
9.	Australia	7.70	35.	Austria	3.88
10.	Bolivia	7.68	36.	Libya	3.68
11.	Canada	7.10	37.	Guyana	3.67
12.	Bulgaria	6.74	38.	Nicaragua	3.64
13.	Suriname	6.63	39.	Greece	3.61
14.	Trinidad and Tobago	6.53	40.	Poland	3.56
15.	Singapore	6.33	41.	Italy	3.53
16.	Venezuela	6.01	42.	South Africa	3.39
17.	Saudi Arabia	5.95	43.	France	3.39
18.	Former Soviet Union	5.68	44.	Brazil	3.37
19.	Norway	5.68	45.	Iceland	3.32
20.	Denmark	5.61	46.	Ecuador	3.23
21.	Germany[b]	5.54	47.	Cyprus	3.15
22.	Czechoslovakia	5.30	48.	Switzerland	3.09
23.	United Kingdom	4.87	49.	Spain	3.05
24.	Japan	4.81	50.	Paraguay	3.04
25.	Ireland	4.80			
26.	Belgium	4.76			

Sources:
1. World Resources Institute calculations.
2. Chapter 23, "Atmosphere and Climate," Tables 23.1 and 23.2.
Note:
a. World median = 1.
b. Data for Germany include both the former Federal Republic of Germany and the former German Democratic Republic.

Table 11.8 Fifty Countries with the Highest Industrial Emissions of Carbon Dioxide (CO_2), 1991

Rank	Country	Total CO_2 Emissions (million metric tons)	Rank	Country	Total CO_2 Emissions (million metric tons)
1.	United States	4,931,630	26.	Romania	138,027
2.	Former Soviet Union	3,581,179	27.	Venezuela	121,604
3.	China	2,543,380	28.	Argentina	115,848
4.	Japan	1,091,147	29.	Belgium	102,079
5.	Germany[a]	969,630	30.	Thailand	100,896
6.	India	703,550	31.	Nigeria	91,930
7.	United Kingdom	577,157	32.	Yugoslavia	87,225
8.	Iraq	520,281	33.	Egypt	81,667
9.	Canada	410,628	34.	Greece	72,866
10.	Italy	402,516	35.	Pakistan	68,487
11.	France	374,113	36.	Hungary	63,574
12.	Mexico	339,873	37.	Denmark	63,054
13.	Poland	308,164	38.	Malaysia	61,196
14.	South Africa	278,695	39.	Austria	60,331
15.	Republic of Korea	264,647	40.	United Arab Emirates	59,459
16.	Australia	261,818			
17.	Korea, Democratic People's Republic	243,235	41.	Norway	58,672
			42.	Colombia	57,503
18.	Islamic Republic of Iran	222,361	43.	Bulgaria	56,675
19.	Spain	219,877	44.	Algeria	55,194
20.	Brazil	215,601	45.	Sweden	53,498
21.	Saudi Arabia	214,919	46.	Finland	52,047
22.	Czechoslovakia	191,356	47.	Philippines	44,587
23.	Indonesia	170,468	48.	Libya	43,008
24.	Turkey	142,555	49.	Switzerland	41,843
25.	Netherlands	138,990	50.	Portugal	41,792

Source: Chapter 23, "Atmosphere and Climate," Table 23.1.
Note: a. Data for Germany include the former Federal Republic of Germany and the former German Democratic Republic.

industrialized countries, Luxembourg, the United States, and Australia rank highest. Per capita emissions in the United States are almost 9 times those of China and almost 18 times those of India, reflecting the great disparities in per capita emissions between industrialized and developing countries. (See Figure 11.1.)

Industrial CO_2 Emissions

Industrial processes that generate CO_2—the burning of fossil fuel and the production of cement—constitute the dominant anthropogenic source of greenhouse gases. Thus these activities represent the greatest opportunity for reductions of greenhouse gases emitted to the atmosphere. Major industrial and large developing countries such as China and India rank high on the international list of those with the largest emissions of industrial CO_2. (See Table 11.8.) On a per capita basis, however, China and India rank relatively low.

Status of the Climate Convention

In June 1992, more than 150 countries signed the U.N. Framework Convention on Climate Change, a centerpiece of the Earth Summit in Rio de Janeiro (15). To garner such support on an issue as complex as climate change was a major achievement, but the real challenge is yet to come: backing up those words with meaningful action.

The first step in the process is for the signatories to ratify the treaty. So far, this has typically been done through legislative action requiring broad support at home. More than the required 50 signatories had ratified the treaty by the end of 1993 (16) and it became legally binding on March 21, 1994.

Within six months following ratification, certain nations, mainly industrialized, must produce a national action plan (NAP) detailing mitigation policies and projecting the level of greenhouse gas emissions that they propose to allow in the future. NAPs are submitted to the Conference of Parties, which is the organization of signatories created to be the supreme body of the Framework Convention.

One year after NAPs are submitted, the Conference of Parties plans to hold a session to review the actions proposed by each signatory. Thereafter, the treaty will move from general principles to specific requirements that signatories must obey to avoid penalty. The Framework Convention on Climate Change may become to the future agreement what the 1985 Vienna Convention was to the 1987 Montreal Protocol, the widely respected law on ozone-depleting substances.

The Conference of Parties will be guided by the Intergovernmental Negotiating Committee (INC), an international body created by the U.N. General Assembly. The INC, with working groups on greenhouse gases and financing, will develop an agenda to monitor the issues. The Conference of Parties will also closely watch the latest climate research reported by the IPCC.

The Framework Convention's path will require countries to balance international pressure for bold commitment with internal pressure to minimize economic and political costs. Significant progress needs to be made in a few major areas that now threaten the agreement, including financing and institution building.

National emissions limitations may be harder to achieve than originally expected. Gains from energy efficiency, generally viewed as the least-cost avenue to-

Figure 11.1 Per Capita Greenhouse Gas Emissions of the 15 Countries with the Highest Total Emissions, 1991

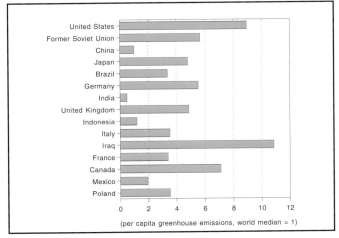

Sources:
1. World Resources Institute calculations.
2. Chapter 23, "Atmosphere and Climate," Tables 23.1 and 23.2.
Note: Data for Germany include both the former Federal Republic of Germany and the former German Democratic Republic.

Figure 11.2 Per Capita Carbon Dioxide (CO_2) Releases for the 15 Countries with the Highest Total Emissions by Industry Sources, 1991

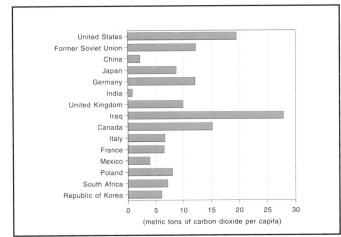

Source: Carbon Dioxide Information Analysis Center (CDIAC), Oak Ridge National Laboratory, unpublished data (CDIAC, Oak Ridge, Tennessee, August 1993).
Note: Data for Germany include both the former Federal Republic of Germany and the former German Democratic Republic.

ward reduction, may not be the only solution. Economic incentives, such as a tax on fossil fuels, can be effective but politically sensitive. An option is joint implementation, whereby two or more countries work together to meet the goals of the Convention. In the typical joint implementation, an industrialized country invests in emissions reductions in a lower-income country. Developing countries, from the start of climate negotiations, have expressed their need for significant assistance in this area. Participation on the part of China and India, essential if global emissions are to be curbed, depends on some level of assistance. Joint implementation and technology transfer could enable both developing and industrialized countries to make strong commitments to the climate treaty.

Another challenge to the climate treaty is developing the institutions to make emissions reductions possible. Joint implementation and other forms of financial assistance integral to any strategy to prevent climate change will only work as effectively as the institutions that handle them. The Framework Convention chose the Global Environment Facility (GEF), a three-year-old pilot project of UNEP, the U.N. Development Programme, and the World Bank as the financial mechanism for the treaty. GEF has been developing its capacity to handle this new type of aid. It will be equally important for developing countries, governments, and nongovernmental organizations to learn to carry out emissions reductions.

Finally, leadership will be essential to global cooperation on preventing climate change. Countries, particularly poorer ones, are not likely to make strong unilateral commitments. At the Earth Summit, the United States refused to join Japan and the European Community in committing to reducing greenhouse gas emissions to 1990 levels by the year 2000. The United States reversed its position a year later and on Earth

Day 1993, President Bill Clinton announced that the United States would commit to the goals of the Framework Convention (17).

FOCUS ON CLIMATE CHANGE: STATE OF THE SCIENCE

Over the last decade, policymakers around the world have struggled to gauge the risks of global warming and frame an appropriate response. During this period, climate change science has developed rapidly. Progress has not produced simple answers. If anything, recent research confirms the complexity of the climate system. For example, new findings on the role of local air pollution and ozone depletion in moderating the greenhouse effect have lowered computer projections of the rate of global warming. And new evidence about past climate changes casts doubt on the prevailing view of climate stability.

Nonetheless, advances in the science reaffirm the generally held belief that progressive warming is caused by increasing greenhouse gas concentrations in the atmosphere. Considerable uncertainty about the scale, timing, and regional distribution of global warming remains and will continue to plague forecasts, perhaps for two more decades. But the outlines of a global assessment of climate change have clearly emerged, and the international scientific community is now moving toward consensus.

Consensus first emerged in the 1990 report of the IPCC, sponsored jointly by UNEP and the World Meteorological Organization (WMO). The IPCC report, with contributions from nearly 400 of the world's leading climate experts, distilled the best available knowledge and remains the most comprehensive summary of climate change science.

Among the IPCC's conclusions was that global mean temperatures will likely rise at a rate of 0.3° C per decade if current emission trends continue—a global warming rate faster than any in the last 10,000 years. At this rate, temperatures would rise about 1° C by 2025 and 3° C before the end of the next century. At the same time, sea levels would probably rise some 65 centimeters by 2100 (18).

In 1992, the IPCC updated its initial report to include the results of the latest research. Computer models incorporating these findings have lowered estimates of the rate of global temperature and sea level rise by about 20 to 30 percent, but have left intact the IPCC's broad view of climate change (19). (See Box 11.2.)

RECENT EVIDENCE FOR GLOBAL WARMING

The most direct evidence of global warming comes from analysis of temperature records covering the last 130 years. Recent reexamination of the records confirms the IPCC's original view that global mean temperatures have risen 0.3 to 0.6° C during this time (20). This estimate appears reliable, for the rise is documented in three independent sets of data: air temperatures over land, air temperatures over the ocean, and sea surface temperatures (21).

A separate analysis of sea surface records along the California coast recently found temperature rise of the water column's top 100 meters of 0.8° C over the last 42 years. This increase was accompanied by an annual rise in sea level of 1 to 3 millimeters (22). Because it occurred over a short time span, the temperature rise, though small, is considered significant; global temperatures have fluctuated by only about 2.0°C since the end of the last ice age some 10,000 years ago (23) (24).

Moreover, a string of warm years beginning in 1980 has continued into the 1990s. Eight of the hottest years in the temperature record have occurred over a 12-year period (25) (26). To some scientists this is hard to explain except by greenhouse warming (27).

Though scrutiny of global temperature logs indicates that warming has occurred, the pattern of warming is unexpected, at least in the northern hemisphere. Data from three continents there show that over the last four decades warmer temperatures have occurred mainly at nighttime, with daytime temperatures registering only minor increases (28) (29). Scientists strongly suspect that part of the blame lies with airborne sulfur pollution, which acts as a kind of greenhouse shade and reduces the daytime heating (30) (31). (See Sulfate and Smoke Aerosols, below.)

Other evidence also points to a rise in surface temperatures over the last century. Temperature profiles of the Earth taken from boreholes drilled for geothermal or mineral exploration are a convenient tool for scientists studying this subject. Heat diffuses down from the Earth's surface at a rate of about 1 meter per year. By plotting a profile of temperatures at increasing depths, scientists can produce a historical record of broad temperature trends at the surface. Borehole records from areas as diverse as Alaska and Africa reflect a distinct warming curve (32) (33) (34).

It is still hotly debated whether all or part of this century-old trend can be explained by human contributions to the greenhouse effect. The warming detected in temperature and borehole records to date has not exceeded the limits of natural climate variability. Indeed, meteorological evidence that the air was cooler in many regions of the world around the end of the 19th Century suggests that some of the warming noted in borehole records since then—particularly in the early 20th Century—is a natural thermal rebound. Borehole profiles recently compiled for areas in Canada and the southwestern United States confirm that thermal recovery contributed to warming in these areas (35) (36).

Nonetheless, the view that warming has accelerated during the last few decades is supported by strong evidence: the rapid melting of glaciers outside the polar zone over the last 30 years and a decrease in snow cover in some areas (37) (38). Data from UNEP's World Glacier Inventory clearly indicate that most glaciers around the world have retreated since the turn of the century (39). Glaciologists believe that tropical glaciers and icecaps, being particularly sensitive to climate change, may serve as a barometer for global warming (40) (41). They are alarmed by the rapid recession of ice masses in parts of Asia, Africa, and South America.

In some cases, melting has been dramatic. For example, the glacier on Africa's Mount Kenya shrank by 40 percent from 1963 to 1987, and the average ice thickness decreased 14.5 meters—a melting rate much higher than that recorded for the period between 1899 and 1963 (42). Ice cores recovered at the Quelccaya icecap in Peru indicate that recent melting there is faster than at any time in 500 years. One glacier descending from Quelccaya has receded at a rate of 14 meters per year since 1984—almost three times the rate observed between 1963 and 1978. Cores from icecaps in China and the former Soviet republic of Kirghizia show warming over the last 50 years (43).

Some scientists have suggested that a rise in humidity is increasing heat transfer from the atmosphere to the ice and thus hastening melting (44). The IPCC reports some evidence for higher humidity levels in the tropics since the mid-1960s. This observation is consistent with the greenhouse theory, which predicts that humidity will rise as sea surface temperatures grow warmer and evaporation increases (45) (46) (47).

The northern hemisphere has also experienced warmer conditions in the last few decades (48). Decreases in snow cover have averaged about 8 percent since 1973. Melting has been most pronounced in Eurasia, totaling about 9 percent in the spring and 13 percent in the fall (49).

The warming trend on Earth may be accompanied by a cooling trend in the mesosphere, the atmospheric layer above the stratosphere extending between the altitudes of 55 and 80 kilometers. Greenhouse theory suggests that warming in the lower atmosphere will cool the mesosphere by increasing infrared radiation emitted from this layer to space (50).

Recent analyses of atmospheric temperature trends signal a decrease of about 2°C in the lower mesosphere. This decrease, distinct from stratospheric cooling caused by ozone depletion, is broadly consistent with the cooling scientists expect from the buildup of greenhouse gases over the last 15 to 20 years. (See

CFCs and Stratospheric Cooling, below.) Cooling in the lower mesosphere may be one of the more direct reflections of humankind's contribution to the greenhouse effect (51) (52) (53).

Additional evidence of mesospheric cooling comes from observation of a narrow band of sodium atoms in the upper atmosphere. The height of this band can be measured quite accurately. It has dropped about 1 kilometer since 1972, suggesting that the mesosphere cooled and subsequently contracted (54) (55).

AIR POLLUTION AND ATMOSPHERIC DYNAMICS: COOLING THE GREENHOUSE

One of the most significant recent developments in climate change science is the growing understanding of the effect of ozone depletion and airborne particulates. Both phenomena have had a cooling influence over some regions of the globe, and as a result greenhouse warming has been less pronounced than expected. Unfortunately, these cooling agents may alter other aspects of the climate system and greatly complicate predictions of global warming effects at both local and regional levels.

CFCs and Stratospheric Cooling

CFCs are potent greenhouse gases once thought responsible for as much as 20 percent of the greenhouse warming attributable to human activity (56). Since the 1970s, these long-lived industrial chemicals have contributed to the progressive depletion of the stratospheric ozone layer (57). Recent work suggests that the heat-trapping properties of CFCs may be offset by stratospheric cooling resulting from their role in ozone loss (58).

Ozone, better known for its ability to absorb dangerous ultraviolet radiation before it reaches Earth, also functions as a natural greenhouse gas. Over the last 20 years, a slight cooling of 0.3 to $0.5°$ C per decade has been measured in the lower stratosphere, where ozone loss is greatest. In other words, the ozone layer is reflecting less heat back to Earth (59). The global average of lower-stratospheric cooling appears nearly to balance the warming properties of CFCs (60).

This cancellation of competing greenhouse effects is not necessarily reassuring. Ozone depletion, greatest over the poles and high latitudes, decreases toward the equator; its greenhouse cooling effect is not evenly distributed over the globe. By contrast, CO_2 and other greenhouse gases warm the globe rather uniformly. Potentially uneven warming could influence atmospheric circulation and the distribution of global warming effects. This in turn could change weather patterns or other climatic phenomena. Looked at in this light, CFCs do not appear so greenhouse-benign (61).

Sulfate and Smoke Aerosols

Perhaps more significant to the greenhouse balance sheet are the cooling effects of atmospheric aerosols. These tiny droplets or solid particles have physical and chemical properties that allow a broad array of atmospheric interactions. The effect of the natural aerosol sources, including volcanoes and forest fires, is substantially less than that of human activities—the combustion of fossil fuel and the burning of grassland and tropical rainforest (62) (63).

The most ubiquitous aerosols originate in SO_2 emissions from energy and industrial sectors, the same sources that emit much of the world's CO_2. As scientists have known for some time, sulfate aerosols block out sunlight. They scatter light both directly—an effect that is responsible for much of the urban haze—and indirectly by serving as nuclei around which water droplets condense. These droplets make clouds brighter and more reflective (64).

Only recently have researchers found that the reflective properties of sulfate aerosols have a substantial

Box 11.2 Global Climate Change: The Scientific Consensus

The scientific consensus on global climate change is represented by the findings of the Intergovernmental Panel on Climate Change (IPCC), which brings together several hundred of the world's leading atmospheric scientists under the auspices of the World Meteorological Organization and the United Nations Environment Programme. What is that consensus in practical terms? Jerry Mahlman, director of the Geophysical Fluid Dynamics Laboratory of the U.S. National Oceanic and Atmospheric Administration, has attempted to answer that question by restating IPCC consensus in the following terms: *virtually certain* (nearly unanimous agreement among scientists and no credible alternative view), *very probable* (roughly a 9 out of 10 chance of occurring), *probable* (roughly a 2 out of 3 chance of occurring), and *uncertain* (hypothesized effect for which evidence is lacking).

Table 1. Degree of Consensus on Various Climate Change Issues

Issue	Statement	Consensus
Basic characteristics	Fundamental physics of the greenhouse effect	*Vitually certain*
	Added greenhouse gases add heat	*Virtually certain*
	Greenhouse gases increasing because of human activity	*Virtually certain*
	Significant reduction of uncertainty will require a decade or more	*Virtually certain*
	Full recovery will require many centuries	*Virtually certain*
Projected effects by mid-21st Century	Large stratospheric cooling	*Virtually certain*
	Global-mean surface precipitation increase	*Very probable*
	Reduction of sea ice	*Very probable*
	Arctic winter surface warming	*Very probable*
	Rise in global sea level	*Very probable*
	Local details of climate change	*Uncertain*
	Tropical storm increases	*Uncertain*
	Details of next 25 years	*Uncertain*

shading effect. This effect could rival the greenhouse warming exerted by CO_2 and other trace gases, at least over industrialized regions of the northern hemisphere where 90 percent of sulfur emissions originate (65). Initial calculations, though uncertain, show that direct aerosol shading and indirect shading may each be responsible for blocking about 0.5 watt of energy per square meter of the planet ($0.5 W/m^2$) (66) (67). This is roughly one quarter of the 2 to 2.5 W/m^2 of heat energy added to the Earth's surface by the accumulation of greenhouse gases since the Industrial Revolution. The figure may help explain why the global warming observed to date is only about one half of what climate models predict (68) (69).

While sulfate aerosols exert most of their cooling effect in the northern hemisphere, smoke may serve a similar role in the tropics, where the burning of rainforest, agricultural waste, and wood for fuel in homes is prevalent (70). Human activity is responsible for about half of the approximately 5 billion tons of plant material burned every year worldwide (71).

When the shading effect of sulfate aerosols became apparent, researchers analyzed smoke aerosols and found that their global effect could be as large as 2 W/m_2—in the range of sulfate aerosols (72). Some scientists caution that their estimates are still uncertain. For example, if smoke contains large amounts of black soot, which absorbs heat rather than reflecting it, then smoke's cooling effect may be considerably less than has been calculated (73).

Climatologists warn that aerosol cooling does not offer any lasting protection from greenhouse warming. One reason is the uneven distribution of cooling effects. In heavily industrialized areas of the northern hemisphere and where biomass burning is heavy, aerosols undoubtedly counter some greenhouse warming. But over the continental regions of the southern hemisphere and over the oceans of both hemispheres, where aerosol influence is limited, greenhouse warming will likely proceed unabated (74) (75).

Furthermore, aerosol cooling, the result of scattered light, does not take place at night, whereas greenhouse warming occurs at all hours. Scientists suspect that this may explain why much recent warming in the northern hemisphere has occurred at night (76). Studies show that in the northern hemisphere, temperature records correlate with sulfur emission trends from coal burning over the last century. Cooler summer temperatures reflect concentrated sulfur emissions in heavily industrialized areas (77).

The influence of aerosols is also limited by their short residence in the atmosphere, about a week. They do not build up over time as greenhouse gases do. Pollution control programs targeting sulfur emissions might quickly unmask a significant latent warming trend now hidden by aerosol cooling (78) (79).

It is clear that aerosol shading and greenhouse warming do not cancel each other out. In fact, recent evidence shows that sulfate aerosols promote ozone-destroying chemical reactions. Other evidence suggests that these aerosols may inhibit precipitation from clouds (80). In addition, in the Arctic, aerosols tend to

trap heat by capturing some of the sunlight reflected off of the ice (81) (82). And it has long been known that sulfate aerosols can lead to acid rain and snow as well as dry-acid deposition.

The cooling influence of aerosols may not be entirely beneficial, either. Like ozone-depletion cooling, aerosol cooling is uneven and may be causing large-scale changes in weather patterns and climate cycles (83). Vertical temperature profiles in the atmosphere could be affected, for aerosols can warm local pockets at those altitudes where they are most concentrated (84). Moreover, by interfering with cloud dynamics, aerosols might be altering the global water cycle, for instance, precipitation patterns and the amount of atmospheric humidity (85).

Volcanoes and Climate

Although human activity accounts for most aerosol cooling, natural aerosol sources can affect the climate, especially over short periods of one to three years (86). Volcanic eruptions are among the most significant of these natural sources. The latitude and timing of an eruption, as well as the amount of sulfur released, determine the severity of its effect (87).

In little more than a decade, two climate-cooling eruptions have taken place. The explosion of Mexico's El Chichon in 1982 injected some 12 megatons of sulfate aerosol into the stratosphere, apparently lowering global temperatures by 0.2° C for a few years (88).

Meanwhile, climatologists have observed a more extreme effect from the 1991 eruption of Mount Pinatubo in the Philippines, which released more than twice as much sulfur into the stratosphere as El Chichon. So far, surface temperatures have dropped about 0.5° C, and the lower stratosphere has cooled as much as 1.0° C over the northern midlatitudes where Pinatubo's aerosols are most concentrated. Some additional minor cooling is expected before global temperatures rebound in 1994 (89) (90) (91).

OCEAN CIRCULATION AND RAPID CLIMATE SHIFTS

The ocean is one of the most important factors shaping climate. It plays several roles in global warming. First and foremost, the ocean is a climate stabilizer. Because its enormous volume heats and cools slowly, the ocean tends to moderate the seasonal fluctuations to which the atmosphere is subject. The ocean also absorbs some of the heat trapped by greenhouse gases (92).

By contrast, the ocean may occasionally instigate dramatic climate shifts. Recent evidence indicates that alterations in ocean circulation patterns around the world may have triggered temperature changes of more than 5° C within periods as short as 40 years (93).

Data collected from the Greenland icecap in the 1980s suggested that at the end of the last ice age air temperatures there had warmed about 7° C within 50 years. More recent data from Greenland's ice cores indicate that such a sharp temperature swing could occur in as little as two years. At first, scientists did not know if this swing was a purely local phenomenon (94) (95) (96). Information since gleaned from ocean sediment cores reveals that large, rapid fluctuations in ocean temperature caused atmospheric warming over the whole North Atlantic region (97).

The rapidity of such temperature changes—significantly larger than greenhouse-related changes projected by climate models—unnerved climatologists. The climate system may be much more volatile than assumed, and the assumption that greenhouse-driven warming will be gradual over the next century or so may be misleading (98). Instead, warming could take place in sudden leaps as the climate—driven by the ocean—oscillates between stable states (99).

The source of this instability can be traced to the ocean's role in transporting heat from the tropics to the poles. The sea's deep currents function as a huge conveyor belt, carrying cold, salty water from the North Atlantic along the ocean bottom in a circuitous path around Africa and Australia and then into the Pacific. There the frigid water upwells. A shallower return circuit brings warm, less briny Pacific water to the Atlantic, and warms the European land mass (100).

For several years, scientists have theorized that this system could stall out under certain conditions, quickly altering climate patterns (101). The stalling and renewal of current flow and heat transport would explain the discontinuous warming that characterized the world's emergence from the last ice age. In fact, on-again off-again current flow has recently been linked to the interrupted melting of the massive arctic ice sheets 12,000 to 15,000 years ago (102).

The cause of ocean current oscillation lies in a region of the North Atlantic off the coast of Iceland. Here, warm Gulf Stream water from the south, enriched with salt from rapid evaporation at warmer latitudes, meets frigid arctic winds blowing from Canada. With this rapid cooling, the salty water grows dense and sinks into the abyss, forming what oceanographers call North Atlantic "deep water," the driving force of the ocean conveyor belt (103) (104).

Apparently, the conveyor stops rather easily. In the past, it is thought, massive influxes of freshwater from melting continental ice sheets kept North Atlantic waters too buoyant to sink, halting the formation of deep water. The European continent cooled as the heat transport along its coast ceased (105).

The fear today is that greenhouse warming could similarly prevent the formation of North Atlantic deep water. It would do so in one of several ways: by increasing arctic runoff from melting snow and ice; by altering the balance between evaporation and precipitation in the North Atlantic; or, eventually, by warming the ocean so much that surface water, no matter how much salt it contained, would not become dense enough to sink (106) (107).

Rapid climate fluctuations in the wake of a stalled conveyor would severely affect the functioning of the biosphere. Few ecosystems would have time to adapt to the temperature shifts. There might be other serious repercussions. For example, deep water is one of the important mixing mechanisms in the ocean, and the rate of mixing is the limiting factor in determining how much CO_2 the ocean can absorb from the atmos-

phere (108) (109). A stalled current could substantially reduce the ocean's role as a carbon sink.

Smaller changes in ocean dynamics can apparently affect world climate within periods as short as a decade or so. Recent evidence shows that from 1976 to 1988, El Niño—the name for ocean currents that periodically warm the western Pacific, affecting weather across North America and as far off as sub-Saharan Africa—was thrown off. This disrupted regional climate patterns, causing unusually severe storms in southern California and a series of uncommon freezes in Florida. Climatologists are unsure how such sudden shifts begin and end. Despite the uncertainty, such shifts lend credence to the view that, even in the short run, climate change may take place more in fits and starts than in smooth transitions (110).

BALANCING THE CARBON BUDGET

CO_2, the predominant greenhouse gas, is responsible for approximately 60 percent of the greenhouse warming that has occurred since preindustrial times. According to projections, CO_2 will play a similar role in the years ahead (111). Thus, determining the fate of carbon dioxide after it is released into the atmosphere—how much will be taken up by plants and the oceans, and how much will remain in the atmosphere—is crucial to predicting when and how greenhouse warming will affect the climate (112). (See Box 11.3.)

But a clear picture of the global carbon budget—the balance sheet of sources and sinks of CO_2 and other forms of carbon, such as plant and animal tissues—continues to elude climate researchers (113). As yet, the carbon output of given sources cannot be accurately determined. The IPCC estimates that the combustion of fossil fuels accounts for about 6 billion tons of carbon released yearly, while biomass burning—from tropical forest and grassland burning—contributes another 1.6 billion tons or so (114).

Pinning down the amount of carbon in sinks is even more difficult. The atmosphere, the ocean, and the land with its plants and animals comprise the world's three major carbon sinks. The only sink whose carbon content is known with any certainty is the atmosphere. Because scientists can precisely monitor rising atmospheric CO_2 levels, they know that approximately 46 percent of all carbon emissions remain in the atmosphere—about 3.56 billion tons of carbon a year (115). How the remaining 4.1 billion tons divides between the land and ocean sinks is one of the great riddles of climate science (116) (117). New field observations and improved computer models of ocean-atmosphere dynamics reinforce what some earlier research indicated: the oceans take up about 2 billion tons of carbon per year, with more absorbed in the northern hemisphere than in the southern (118) (119) (120) (121).

That leaves more than 2 billion tons of carbon per year unaccounted for. For want of a better explanation, some scientists assume that this is the amount of carbon in the terrestrial sink, stored by the world's plants as increased growth. But how and exactly where this storage occurs is uncertain, for increases in biomass of this order are very difficult to confirm (122).

Box 11.3 Plant Growth in a Greenhouse World: Responding to Enhanced CO_2

Plants are the most basic elements of every terrestrial ecosystem, so their response to enhanced carbon dioxide (CO_2) levels, as well as to warmer temperatures and altered moisture patterns, will play a predominant role in determining the overall effect of climate change on the terrestrial biosphere [1].

While climatologists rarely speak with certainty when making projections, they are confident that CO_2 levels will be markedly higher within a half century or so, regardless of whether or how much global temperatures have risen. Even if emission rates were to remain at current levels, CO_2 concentrations in the atmosphere would increase from their present level of 350 parts per million to about 450 parts per million by 2050—nearly a 30 percent rise [2]. From there, CO_2 levels would probably keep on rising in the absence of radical emission reductions.

How will plants respond? More than a decade of research reveals that the response to elevated CO_2 levels is not uniform among plants: some species grow more with extra CO_2, while others gain no advantage [3]. This disparity could mean a competitive edge for some, which could in turn dramatically affect the composition and functioning of ecosystems [4]. Moreover, additional carbon storage due to increased plant growth may be minimized by a host of factors, and thus cannot be taken for granted [5].

Initial studies showing enhanced plant growth in the presence of elevated CO_2 levels, known as CO_2 fertilization, led some to suggest that higher levels would spur a global rise in biomass and thus increase the terrestrial carbon sink. Subsequent ecosystem-level studies revealed a much more complex situation [6].

No one doubts that CO_2 fertilization is a phenomenon, one that works, at least in part, by enhancing photosynthesis. With sufficient nutrients and optimum temperatures, CO_2 fertilization can promote tissue growth and agricultural yields. For example, grain yields increase by about one third when plants are grown with elevated levels of CO_2 [7].

Not all species respond so robustly to enriched CO_2. Those that stand to gain the most belong to the C3 group of plants, so named because they use a three-carbon molecule during photosynthesis. Perhaps 95 percent of all plant species belong to this group, including many important agricultural crops and virtually all forest trees [8] [9].

A second group of plants, called C4 plants, responds less well to CO_2 enrichment. Corn, millet, and sugarcane are C4 species, as are many other grass species from hot, dry tropical regions [10].

Even among C3 species, there is wide variation in the response to CO_2. Some respond only slightly, while many react with an initial burst of enhanced photosynthesis that tapers off over time for reasons not yet understood [11].

In any case, plant response is always highly dependent on environmental conditions. Biologists are quick to point out that the favorable conditions that typify most agricultural settings—an unlimited nutrient and water supply, optimum plant spacing, and the absence of herbivores—are unlikely to be present in natural ecosystems [12] [13]. In natural settings, competition for scarce resources may considerably limit the CO_2 fertilization effect [14]. Some studies indicate that, in natural settings, elevated CO_2 levels have less of an effect on plant growth than such factors as light and nutrient availability [15]. For instance, tundra grassland responds only slightly to increased CO_2, presumably because permafrost severely restricts nutrient availability. On the other hand, marshland plants in the Chesapeake Bay area, where water and nutrients are abundant, show pronounced growth with additional CO_2 [16] [17].

Though little research has been done on whole-forest responses to elevated CO_2 levels, there is no reason to believe that net growth occurs in forest ecosystems [18] [19]. In one recent experiment, yellow poplar trees, common in eastern U.S. forests, showed no net increase in carbon storage after three years in high-CO_2 forest conditions, despite a consistently elevated photosynthesis rate. Higher growth was revealed not in more wood production or leaf mass, but in greater root production [20].

On the positive side, increased CO_2 apparently enhances plant utilization of water and other nutrients. Leaves lose less water, and soil organisms that fix nitrogen, such as mycorrhizal fungi, thrive. Thus plants are better able to withstand

Many biologists are uneasy about trends that would shrink the terrestrial sink: the large-scale destruction of tropical forests, and pollution-related declines in the health of some temperate forests in Europe and elsewhere. Many assume from the scant biological evidence available that temperate forests, which have the potential to absorb carbon in the billions of tons, are already in equilibrium with the atmosphere, absorbing and releasing equal amounts of CO_2 rather than storing additional carbon [123].

However, recent findings in Europe suggest that, over the last 20 years, growth in temperate forests of the northern hemisphere could account for the uptake of a sizable fraction of the "missing" carbon. Despite some severe forest loss and the widespread acidification of soil from acid rain, European forests apparently gained biomass during the 1970s and 1980s [124].

Projections based on forest surveys conducted by the U.N. Economic Commission for Europe show a 25 percent increase in growing stock—the volume of living trees—in European forests from 1971 to 1990 [125]. Researchers theorize that the fertilizing effects of added nitrogen from acid rain and increasing CO_2 offset the negative effects of pollution in most locations. This resulted in greater carbon storage than expected, about 85 to 120 million tons per year during the 1970s and 1980s [126]. If a similar phenomenon occurred in temperate forests on other continents, it would identify at least part of the elusive terrestrial sink.

If this is how the terrestrial sink operates, will it continue to function as in the past, or will natural biological limits or climate changes brought on by global warming diminish its storage capacity? Scientists caution that unless pollution subsides, its negative effects, which are cumulative, will likely retard European forest growth [127]. Moreover, natural recovery of forestland heavily cut in the last century will taper off at some point, and the fertilization benefits of additional nitrogen and CO_2 may reach a saturation point. So the continued ability of temperate forests to absorb new carbon is anything but assured [128] [129].

REFINING GREENHOUSE PROJECTIONS: CLIMATE MODEL UPDATE

Climatologists have wasted little time incorporating the latest findings on stratospheric cooling and sulfate aerosols into their computer models. Some modelers have balanced the carbon budget in their models by as-

Box 11.3

environmental stresses and to absorb nutrients, an advantage in less fertile soil [21]. Because a forest ecosystem's potential to store carbon over the long term depends in good measure on its ability to survive environmental stresses, CO_2 enrichment could ultimately be an important contributor to the terrestrial carbon sink [22].

What about the apparent increase in biomass in some temperate forests over the last several decades? Some biologists believe this growth stems from a combination of factors, including natural recovery from earlier overcutting, higher temperatures, and CO_2 and nitrogen fertilization. The growth may well taper off as other factors, such as nutrient availability and competition for space come into play [23].

Regardless of how it influences total carbon storage, CO_2 enrichment is bound to have an impact on ecosystems. For example, the composition of plant communities will likely change as different responses to heightened CO_2 result in some plants competing more successfully. C4 plants may have a disadvantage and decline or disappear from some settings [24].

CO_2 enrichment would have other ecosystemwide effects. For reasons unknown, CO_2-enriched foliage contains less nitrogen, making it less palatable to herbivores. This could diminish herbivore populations, setting in motion a cascade of ecosystem changes that eventually could alter the balance of species [25] [26].

Of course, plant response to higher CO_2 levels must be weighed against competing responses to other climate variables, for instance, higher temperatures and altered precipitation patterns. One widely acknowledged effect of higher temperatures is to shift the optimum growing range of plants toward higher latitudes. This can cause a rapid and large-scale reorganization of plant communities, as happened some 9,000 to 12,000 years ago, at the end of the last ice age [27].

If, because of higher temperatures, some forested areas shrank and gave way to herbaceous or shrubby vegetation, it could result in a net carbon release to the atmosphere, easily overwhelming positive CO_2 fertilization effects. Indeed, one recent computer model of plant response to warming showed a net CO_2 release. Higher soil respiration rates could be expected to add to this carbon burden as decomposition of buried plant materials sped up in warmer soil. Some researchers have already found evidence for higher CO_2 releases from tundra soils in northern Alaska over the last decade [28] [29] [30].

References and Notes

1. Fakhri Bazzaz and Eric Fajer, "Plant Life in a CO_2-Rich World," *Scientific American* (January 1992), p. 69.
2. Intergovernmental Panel on Climate Change (IPCC), *Climate Change: The IPCC Scientific Assessment*, J.T. Houghton, G.J. Jenkins, and J.J. Ephraums, eds. (Cambridge University Press, Cambridge, U.K., 1990), p. 289.
3. *Op. cit.* 1.
4. *Op. cit.* 1, p. 71.
5. *Op. cit.* 1, pp. 70–74.
6. *Op. cit.* 1, p. 68.
7. *Op. cit.* 1, p. 71.
8. *Op. cit.* 1, pp. 69–70.
9. *Op. cit.* 2.
10. *Op. cit.* 1, p. 71.
11. *Op. cit.* 1, p. 70.
12. *Op. cit.* 2, p. 290.
13. Fakhri Bazzaz, H.H. Timpken Professor of Science, Harvard University, Boston, 1992 (personal communication).
14. *Ibid.*
15. *Op. cit.* 1, p. 70.
16. *Op. cit.* 2, p. 292.
17. *Op. cit.* 1, p. 70.
18. *Op. cit.* 2, p. 292.
19. *Op. cit.* 1, p. 71.
20. Richard Norby *et al.*, "Productivity and Compensatory Responses of Yellow-Poplar Trees in Elevated CO_2," *Nature*, Vol. 357 (May 28, 1992), pp. 322–324.
21. *Op. cit.* 1, pp. 68 and 73.
22. *Op. cit.* 20, p. 324.
23. *Op. cit.* 13.
24. *Op. cit.* 1, pp. 68 and 71–72.
25. *Op. cit.* 13.
26. *Op. cit.* 1, p. 72.
27. Bette Hileman, "Web of Interactions Makes It Difficult to Untangle Global Warming Data," *Chemical and Engineering News*, Vol. 70, No. 17 (April 27, 1992), p. 13.
28. *Op. cit.* 1, pp. 73–74.
29. *Op. cit.* 2, pp. 294–300.
30. Richard Monastersky, "Plants and Soils May Worsen Global Warming," *Science News*, Vol. 143, No. 7 (February 13, 1993), p. 100.

suming a CO_2 fertilization effect that would enhance plant growth. As expected, these refinements have significantly adjusted projections for global warming over the next century or so.

In general, the projected rate of warming and consequent sea level rise is 20 to 30 percent less than in previous models. According to one update, the expected rise in global mean temperature from 1990 to 2100 is 2.5° C, compared with 3.3° C calculated by the older models—a 24 percent decline. Likewise, the expected sea level rise from 1990 to 2100 was rolled back 27 percent, from 66 to 48 centimeters. Though these are sig-

Box 11.4 Long-term Effects of Increased Atmospheric Carbon Dioxide

A recent scientific report suggested that, if current patterns of carbon dioxide (CO_2) emission continue over the next century, the world's climate may heat up for 500 years [1]. Based on a study with an ocean-atmosphere circulation model, Syukuro Manabe and Ronald J. Stouffer of the U.S. National Oceanic and Atmospheric Administration found that profound changes could occur in deep-ocean circulation, with the result that the Earth's carbon cycle would be altered. Theirs is one of the first attempts to study the consequences of CO_2 emissions over a period of centu-

ries, and its findings should be regarded as preliminary.

The study nonetheless suggests that if the present trends of greenhouse gas emissions prevail over the next century, atmospheric concentrations of CO_2 or equivalent gases would quadruple. Atmospheric temperatures would continue to increase, rising as much as 7° C in 500 years. Sea levels would rise by about 2 meters from the thermal expansion of oceans alone (this does not even consider melting ice sheets, which could also increase sea levels). Most alarming, the ocean would set-

tle into a stable pattern, its surface and deep waters no longer mixing. This could conceivably compromise marine biological activity, and by greatly reducing the ocean's ability to absorb CO_2, alter the Earth's carbon cycle.

References and Notes

1. Syukuro Manabe and Ronald Stouffer, "Century-Scale Effects of Increased Atmospheric CO_2 on the Ocean-Atmosphere System," *Nature*, Vol. 364, No. 6434 (1993), pp. 215–218.

Figure 11.3 Global Land-Sea Temperatures, 1861-1989

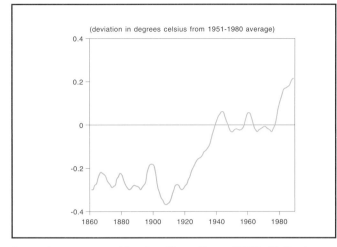

(deviation in degrees celsius from 1951-1980 average)

Source: Intergovernmental Panel on Climate Change (IPCC), J.T. Houghton, G.J. Jenkins, and J.J. Ephraums, eds., *Climate Change: The IPCC Scientific Assessment* (Cambridge University Press, Cambridge, U.K., 1991), p. 213.

nificant reductions, modelers are hardly sanguine: the projected rate of warming is still about five times higher than that observed over the last century (130). (See Figure 11.3.)

Ironically, these models suggest that earlier models may have underestimated the sensitivity of the climate to CO_2 increases, since they did not account for the cooling effects of aerosols and ozone depletion. Instead of a 2.5° C rise in global mean temperature when the atmospheric CO_2 level doubles, updated models calculate a rise of more like 3.4°C if there were no masking effect from aerosols and ozone depletion (131). Thus, the climate may be even more vulnerable to greenhouse warming than anticipated.

Significantly, the refined models do not indicate a decrease in the magnitude of eventual warming; they only show a moderation of the rate at which warming occurs. Scientists warn that the cooling effect of aerosols and ozone depletion will pale over the long term next to the relentless rise in CO_2, a long-lived gas whose concentrations are expected to increase (132).

Lending credence to the latest models is a recent analysis of how Earth's past climate responded to changes in CO_2 levels and other influences. According to this study, which examined the relation between CO_2 levels and global temperatures in much colder and in much warmer eras of the past, the Earth tends to warm by about 2.3° C when the CO_2 level doubles. This is close to the 2.5° C rise that the latest models predict for a doubling in the CO_2 level. (See Box 11.4.)

CONTINUED MODEL UNCERTAINTIES

Climate models remain flawed in several key areas. The greatest source of uncertainty concerns clouds, which play a crucial role in regulating Earth's radiation (133). Clouds exercise competing influences on cli-

mate: they reflect sunlight into space and thus cool the planet, and at the same time they reflect heat radiated from the planet's surface back to Earth (134).

Research reveals that the cooling effect of clouds currently predominates, but modelers do not know how clouds will respond in a warmer world. Global warming could affect the number of clouds as well as their location, altitude, and reflective properties (135) (136) (137). A decade or more of observation may be required to produce accurate models of cloud dynamics (138).

Ocean dynamics are a second major area of concern for modelers. Current circulation models are fairly crude; they do not quantify the movement of deep currents, or the diffusion of heat down from the ocean surface. Both phenomena are critical parameters in determining how much greenhouse heat the ocean will absorb, suppressing temperature rises over land. To achieve meaningful circulation models will require decades of dedicated work (139).

A third area of uncertainty involves atmospheric chemistry. Such important greenhouse gases as methane and ground-level ozone—distinct from stratospheric ozone—are part of a complicated web of chemical reactions and counterreactions that cannot yet be modeled (140). For example, nitrogen oxide and unburned hydrocarbon from auto exhaust combine to form ozone, which in turn generates chemical reactions that destroy methane. Such complications make it a daunting task to calculate the sources and sinks of many trace greenhouse gases (141) (142) (143).

A final source of uncertainty for modelers is the biosphere's reaction to greenhouse conditions. If the effect of higher CO_2 levels and warmer temperatures is to promote plant growth, then a net sequestering of carbon might occur and help to slow warming, at least for a time. But the opposite might occur if rapidly changing climate conditions upset delicately balanced ecosystems. The result could be a major reorganization of plant communities and a net loss of biomass (144) (145). (See Box 11.3.) Indeed, some recent studies indicate that a transition period during which ecosystems adjusted to warmer conditions would result in far more CO_2 release than storage, exacerbating the warming trend (146). In fact, current warming in the Alaskan tundra may have already prompted CO_2 release there (147).

While these flaws obscure the picture of how global warming will play out in the short term, they do not hide the long-term dimensions of the greenhouse problem. Climatologists still emphasize the simplest truth about the greenhouse effect: regardless of climate feedback mechanisms or pollutants that may temporarily slow the rate of warming, a continued increase in greenhouse gases will heat up the Earth over time (148).

The Focus On section was written by World Resources *contributing editor Gregory Mock. Allen Hammond, Eric Rodenburg, and Rob Gramlich of the* World Resources *staff contributed to Conditions and Trends.*

References and Notes

1. United Nations (U.N.) Population Division, *Urban and Rural Areas, 1950–2025 (The 1992 Revision)*, on diskette (U.N., New York, 1993).

2. Global Environment Monitoring System/AIR Monitoring Project, Monitoring and Assessment Research Centre (MARC), *Assessment of Urban Air Quality (MARC, London, 1988)*, pp. 20, 34.

3. World Health Organization and United Nations Environment Programme, *Urban Air Pollution in Megacities of the World* (Blackwell Reference, Oxford, U.K., 1992).

4. The United Nations (U.N.), *Prospects of World Urbanization, 1988*, Population Studies, No. 112 (U.N., New York, 1993).

5. Definitions used for megacity population estimates in this study of urban air quality are not the most recent available and can differ from those used for other purposes. A megacity is not defined by administrative boundaries *per se* but by the United Nations assessment of the built-up area surrounding the core.

6. *Op. cit.* 3, p. 45.

7. Christer Agren, "Critical Loads: Often Far Exceeded," *Acid News*, No. 1 (Swedish Nongovernmental Organization Secretariat on Acid Rain, Göteborg, Sweden, March 1992), pp. 12–13.

8. Christer Agren, "New Sulphur Protocol: Drawn-out Negotiations," *Acid News*, No. 5 (Swedish Nongovernmental Organization Secretariat on Acid Rain, Göteborg, Sweden, December 1992), p. 5.

9. European Monitoring and Evaluation Programme (EMEP), *Calculated Budgets for Airborne Acidifying Components in Europe, 1985, 1987, 1988, 1989, 1990 and 1991* (Norwegian Meteorological Institute, Oslo, 1992), p. 11.

10. *Ibid.*, p. 14.

11. C. Ian Jackson, "A Tenth Anniversary Review of the ECE Convention on Long-Range Transboundary Air Pollution," *International Environmental Affairs*, Vol. 2, No. 3 (1990), p. 224.

12. D. Simpson and H. Styve, *The Effects of the VOC Protocol on Ozone Concentrations in Europe* (Norwegian Meteorological Institute, Oslo, 1992), pp. 12–15.

13. Swedish NGO Secretariat on Acid Rain, "Forest Damage in Europe," *Environmental Factsheet*, No. 1 (Swedish NGO Secretariat on Acid Rain, Göteborg, Sweden, December 1992), p. ii.

14. Intergovernmental Panel on Climate Change (IPCC), *Climate Change: The IPCC Scientific Assessment*, J.T. Houghton, G.J. Jenkins, and J.J. Ephraums, eds. (Cambridge University Press, Cambridge, U.K., 1990), pp. xvii–xviii.

15. United Nations (U.N.), Conference on Environment and Development, *Framework Convention of Climate Change*, final text (U.N., New York, May 9, 1992).

16. "United Nations (U.N.), Framework Convention on Climate Change," in *Multilateral Treaties Deposited with the Secretary General* (U.N., New York, 1993), pp. 837–838 and Supplement.

17. Bill Clinton, "Remarks by the President in Earth Day Speech," speech presented at the U.S. Botanic Gardens, Washington, D.C., April 21, 1993.

18. *Op. cit.* 14, p. xi.

19. T.M.L. Wigley and S.C.B. Raper, "Implications for Climate and Sea Level of Revised IPCC Emissions Scenarios," *Nature*, Vol. 357, No. 6376 (1992), pp. 299–300.

20. Intergovernmental Panel on Climate Change (IPCC), *Climate Change 1992: The Supplementary Report to the IPCC Scientific Assessment*, J.T. Houghton, B.A. Callander, and S.K. Varney, eds. (Cambridge University Press, Cambridge, U.K., 1992), p. 17.

21. *Op. cit.* 14, p. 199.

22. Dean Roemmich, "Ocean Warming and Sea Level Rise along the Southwest U.S. Coast," *Science*, Vol. 257, No. 5068 (1992), pp. 373–375.

23. *Op. cit.* 14, p. 199.

24. Bette Hileman, "Web of Interactions Makes It Difficult to Untangle Global Warming Data," *Chemical and Engineering News*, Vol. 70, No. 17 (American Chemical Society, Washington, D.C., April 27, 1992), p. 8.

25. *Op. cit.* 20, p. 17.

26. *Op. cit.* 24, p. 8.

27. *Op. cit.* 24, p. 8.

28. *Op. cit.* 20, p. 17.

29. Richard Monastersky, "Industrial Countries Warmed Most at Night," *Science News*, Vol. 141, No. 1 (1992), p. 4.

30. Richard Monastersky, "Haze Clouds the Greenhouse," *Science News*, Vol. 141, No. 15 (1992), pp. 232–233.

31. James Hansen, Atmospheric Modeler, Goddard Space Institute, New York, 1993 (personal communication).

32. Tim Appenzeller, "Ground Truth," *The Sciences* (March/April 1991), pp. 8–9.

33. *Op. cit.* 24, p. 19.

34. Kelin Wang and Trevor Lewis, "Geothermal Evidence from Canada for a Cold Period before Recent Climatic Warming," *Science*, Vol. 256, No. 5059 (1992), pp. 1003–1005.

35. *Op. cit.* 32, p. 9.

36. *Op. cit.* 34.

37. Richard Monastersky, "Signs of Global Warming Found in Ice," *Science News*, Vol. 141, No. 10 (1992), p. 148.

38. *Op. cit.* 20, p. 19.

39. International Association of Hydrological Sciences (IAHS) (International Commission on Snow and Ice)/UNEP/UNESCO, *World Glacier Inventory: Status 1988*, W. Haeberli, H. Bosch, K. Sherler, *et al.*, eds. (IAHS, Wallingford, U.K., 1989).

40. Stefan Hastenrath, "Greenhouse Indicators in Kenya," *Nature*, Vol. 355, No. 6360 (1992), pp. 503–504.

41. *Op. cit.* 37.

42. *Op. cit.* 40.

43. *Op. cit.* 37.

44. *Op. cit.* 40.

45. *Op. cit.* 40.

46. *Op. cit.* 14, p. 222.

47. *Op. cit.* 20, p. 19.

48. *Op. cit.* 20, p. 19.

49. *Op. cit.* 14, pp. 223–224.

50. Rolando Garcia, "Middle Atmosphere Cooling," *Nature*, Vol. 357, No. 6373 (1992), p. 18.

51. *Ibid.*

52. Rolando Garcia, Upper-Atmosphere Chemist, National Center for Atmospheric Research, Boulder, Colorado, 1992 (personal communication).

53. World Meteorological Organization (WMO)/United Nations Environment Programme (UNEP), *Scientific Assessment of Ozone Depletion, 1991* (WMO/UNEP, Nairobi, 1991), pp. 2–12.

54. *Op. cit.* 50.

55. *Op. cit.* 52.

56. World Resources Institute in collaboration with the United Nations Environment Programme and the United Nations Development Programme, *World Resources 1990–91* (Oxford University Press, New York, 1990), p. 24, Table 2.4.

57. F. Sherwood Roland, "Stratospheric Ozone Depletion by Chlorofluorocarbons," *Ambio*, Vol. 19, No. 6–7 (1990), pp. 281–292.

58. V. Ramaswamy *et al.*, "Radiative Forcing of Climate From Halocarbon-Induced Global Stratospheric Ozone Loss," *Nature*, Vol. 355, No. 6363 (1992), pp. 810–812.

59. *Op. cit.* 53.

60. Jeffrey Kiehl, "Cold Comfort in the Greenhouse," *Nature*, Vol. 355, No. 6363 (1992), p. 773.

61. *Ibid.*

62. R.J. Charlson *et al.*, "Climate Forcing by Anthropogenic Aerosols," *Science*, Vol. 255, No. 5043 (1992), p. 424.

63. *Op. cit.* 20, p. 9.

64. *Op. cit.* 30.

65. *Op. cit.* 62, p. 423–425.

66. *Op. cit.* 31.

67. James Hansen, Andrew Lacis, Reto Ruedy, *et al.*, "How Sensitive Is the World's Climate?" *Research and Exploration*, Vol. 9, No. 2 (1993), p. 152.

68. *Op. cit.* 62, p. 426.

69. Richard Kerr, "Pollutant Haze Cools the Greenhouse," *Science*, Vol. 255, No. 5045 (1992), p. 683.

70. Joyce Penner, Robert Dickinson, and Christine O'Neill, "Effects of Aerosol from Biomass Burning on the Global Radiation Budget," *Science*, Vol. 256, No. 5062 (1992), p. 1432.

71. Associated Press, "Fires Said to Delay Greenhouse Effect," *Washington Post* (June 5, 1992), p. 42, sec. A.

72. *Op. cit.* 70, p. 1433.

73. Richard Monastersky, "A Smoke Screen for Greenhouse Warming?" *Science News*, Vol. 141, No. 21 (1992), p. 343.

74. *Ibid.*

75. *Op. cit.* 69.

76. *Op. cit.* 30.

77. "Seasonal Signs of Pollutant Cooling," *Science News*, Vol. 141, No. 22 (1992), p. 365.

78. *Op. cit.* 73.

79. *Op. cit.* 69.

80. *Op. cit.* 30.

81. J. Harte and J. Williams, "Arctic Aerosol and Arctic Climate: Results from an Energy Budget Model," *Climatic Change*, Vol. 13, No. 2 (1988), pp. 161–189.

82. John Harte, Professor of Energy and Resources, University of California, Berkeley, 1992 (personal communication).

83. Jeremy Hales, Principal Atmospheric Scientist, Envair, Kennewick, Washington, 1992 (personal communication).

84. *Op. cit.* 70, p. 1433.

85. *Op. cit.* 62.

86. American Geophysical Union (AGU), *Volcanism and Climate Change* (AGU, Washington, D.C., 1992), p. 3.

87. *Ibid.*, pp. 2–3.

88. *Ibid.*, pp. 3, 15.

89. *Ibid.*, pp. 3, 9.

90. K. Hoppe, "Mount Pinatubo's Cloud Shades Global Climate," *Science News*, Vol. 142, No. 3 (1992), p. 37.

91. "The Volcanic Mirror over Earth," *Science News*, Vol. 143, No. 11 (1993), p. 175.

92. *Op. cit.* 14, pp. 179, 320–321.

93. Scott Lehman and Lloyd Keigwin, "Sudden Changes in North Atlantic Circulation during the Last Deglaciation," *Nature*, Vol. 356, No. 6372 (1992), p. 757.

94. Woods Hole Oceanographic Institution, "New Evidence Indicates Global Climate Change May Occur Suddenly," April 30, 1992, p. 3 (press release).

95. Richard Monastersky, "Tales from Ice Time," *Science News*, Vol. 140, No. 11 (September 14, 1991), pp. 171–172.

96. Richard Monastersky, "Ice Core Shows Speedy Climate Change," *Science News*, Vol. 142, No. 24 (December 12, 1992), p. 404.

97. *Op. cit.* 93.

98. Lloyd Keigwin, Associate Scientist, Woods Hole Oceanographic Institution, Woods Hole, Massachusetts, 1992 (personal communication).

99. *Op. cit.* 93, p. 761.

100. Wallace Broecker, "The Biggest Chill," *Natural History* (October 1987), pp. 78–79.

101. *Ibid.*

102. Christopher Charles and Richard Fairbanks, "Evidence from Southern Ocean Sediments for the Effect of North Atlantic Deep-Water Flux on Climate," *Nature*, Vol. 355, No. 6359 (January 30, 1992), p. 416.

103. *Op. cit.* 100, p. 77.

104. *Op. cit.* 94.

105. *Op. cit.* 94.

106. *Op. cit.* 98.

107. *Op. cit.* 94.

108. *Op. cit.* 14, p. 9.

109. *Op. cit.* 56, p. 22.

110. Richard Kerr, "Unmasking a Shifty Climate System," *Science*, Vol. 255, No. 5051 (March 20, 1992), pp. 1508–1510.

111. *Op. cit.* 14, pp. 55–56.

112. Richard Kerr, "Fugitive Carbon Dioxide: It's Not Hiding in the Ocean," *Science*, Vol. 256, No. 5053 (1992), p. 35.

113. *Ibid.*

114. *Op. cit.* 20, p. 8.

115. *Op. cit.* 20, p. 13.

116. Paul Quay, B. Tilbrook, and C.S. Wong, "Oceanic Uptake of Fossil Fuel CO_2: Carbon-13 Evidence," *Science*, Vol. 256, No. 5053 (1991), p. 74.

117. *Op. cit.* 112.

118. Jorge Sarmiento and Eric Sundquist, "Revised Budget for the Oceanic Uptake of Anthropogenic Carbon Dioxide," *Nature*, Vol. 356, No. 6370 (1992), pp. 589–593.

119. *Op. cit.* 116.

120. *Op. cit.* 112.

121. *Op. cit.* 20, pp. 8–9.

122. *Op. cit.* 14, p. 17.

123. P.E. Kauppi, K. Mieliainen, and K. Kuusela, "Biomass and Carbon Budget of European Forests, 1971–90," *Science*, Vol. 256, No. 5053 (1992), p. 73.

124. *Ibid.*, pp. 70–74.

125. *Ibid.*, p. 71.

126. *Ibid.*

127. *Ibid.*

128. *Op. cit.* 14, p. 17.

129. Fakhri Bazzaz, H.H. Timken Professor of Science, Harvard University, Boston, 1992 (personal communication).

130. *Op. cit.* 19, p. 299.

131. *Op. cit.* 19, p. 300.

132. Jerry Mahlman, director, National Oceanic and Atmospheric Administration Geophysical Fluid Dynamics Laboratory, Princeton, New Jersey, 1992 (personal communication).

133. *Ibid.*

134. V. Ramanathan, B. Barkstrom, and E. Harrison, "Climate and the Earth's Radiation Budget," *Physics Today* (May 1989), p. 30.

135. *Op. cit.* 82.

136. *Op. cit.* 24, p. 13.

137. *Op. cit.* 56, p. 22.

138. *Op. cit.* 14, p. 319.

139. *Op. cit.* 14, pp. 320–321.

140. *Op. cit.* 24, p. 9.

141. *Op. cit.* 24, p. 14.

142. *Op. cit.* 53, pp. 5–1 to 5–21.

143. Jos Lelieveld and Paul Crutzen, "Indirect Chemical Effects of Methane on Climate Warming," *Nature*, Vol. 355, No. 6358 (1992), p. 340.

144. *Op. cit.* 24, p. 13.

145. Fakhri Bazzaz and Eric Fajer, "Plant Life in a CO_2-Rich World," *Scientific American*, Vol. 266, No. 1 (1992), p. 74.

146. Richard Monastersky, "Plants and Soils May Worsen Global Warming," *Science News*, Vol. 143, No. 7 (February 13, 1993), p. 100.

147. *Ibid.*

148. *Op. cit.* 132.

12. Industry

A requirement for development in any country is a viable industrial base—a prime source of the goods and services, employment, and national wealth that sustain economies. However, industrial activities, including mining, are directly responsible for much of the pollution that degrades the environment. They also affect the environment by shaping consumption into a resource-intensive pattern.

Industrial processes, characteristically, alter the natural flow of materials. Today's industrial flows are immense and often disruptive to local environments. Environmental degradation can occur when natural resources are extracted or processed, and when end products are used or discarded. (See Chapter 1, "Natural Resource Consumption.") For some toxic substances such as heavy metals, the global industrial flow already exceeds the natural flow. In areas polluted as a result of industrial activity, concentrations of toxic substances often exceed the levels normally found in soil, waterways, and sediment. When toxic substances accumulate in the environment and in food chains, they can profoundly disrupt biological processes.

Industrial processes also alter the physical and chemical composition of materials, introducing novel substances into the environment. More than 50,000 different chemical substances are produced annually.

Some, such as many halogenated chemicals, can be toxic or carcinogenic. And some, such as polychlorinated biphenyls, are long-lived and can be stored in living tissue, especially fat. They tend to concentrate as they pass through the food chain from "grazers" to predator species.

In addition to their direct toxic effects, materials from industrial processes can have dangerous indirect effects when they react with the environment. Inorganic mercury, for example, is converted by certain anaerobic bacteria to organic (methylated) forms that can accumulate in freshwater and marine food chains. It was methyl mercury that caused Minimata disease, a sometimes fatal neurological disorder first observed among birds, cats, and fishermen living on the shores of Japan's Minimata Bay. To cite another example, chlorofluorocarbons (CFCs), which are extremely inert and unreactive until broken up by ultraviolet radiation in the stratosphere, release atomic chlorine that degrades the Earth's protective ozone layer.

In short, the current pattern of industrial activity—altering the natural flow of materials and introducing novel chemicals into the environment on a vast scale—is "toxifying" the environment, a term that, as used here, encompasses a wide range of direct and indirect effects. Some analysts fear that the toxic burden is nearing a threshold beyond which it will destabilize ecosystems and alter planetwide nutrient cycles (1) (2). What is certain is that long-lived toxic materials will continue to accumulate and the risk of widespread environmental damage will continue to grow until industrial patterns change.

Any serious effort to pursue sustainable global development thus must confront the formidable task of transforming industrial practices. Clearly, if industry is to provide for today's and tomorrow's needs without undue environmental degradation—the goal of sustainable development—new processes will be needed that use less virgin material, produce markedly less pollution or waste per unit of product, and minimize indirect environmental effects. Another consideration critical to sustainable development is the overall "metabolism" of industrial activity; this includes the products industry creates and their ultimate use and disposal.

Fortunately, there has been a distinct heightening of environmental awareness among leading companies in many industries since the mid-1980s. Worldwide, more than 1,100 firms have endorsed the Business Charter for Sustainable Development, setting forth broad environmental principles for corporate conduct (3) (4). The chemical industry's "Responsible Care" program, which started in Canada, has now spread throughout the world. In the United States alone, more than 1,100 companies have publicly committed themselves to the Environmental Protection Agency's (U.S. EPA's) 33/50 program, which has set voluntary targets for reducing discharges of potentially toxic pollutants by 1995 (5). Meanwhile, a host of so-called green products catering to newfound consumer sensitivity to the environment has appeared.

In some cases, this new regard for the environment does not extend much beyond looking green, capitalizing on the latest consumer fad, or anticipating the next regulatory hurdle. But for an increasing—if still small—number of companies of all sizes, reducing the environmental impact of their extraction and production processes and of the products themselves as they are used and discarded, has become a matter of strategic importance. In fact, for some of these companies, environmental stewardship has become a business opportunity rather than simply an expensive burden—a chance to improve both company image and production efficiency at the same time, with increased competitiveness as the result.

In a few well-publicized cases, this convergence of environmental and business goals has already brought tangible benefits, with companies saving tens of millions of dollars in material, energy, and waste disposal costs. More important, these cases have paved the way for the first serious consideration by business of the idea of sustainable industrial practice.

Forward-looking companies have begun to realize that minimizing overall waste and emissions is a key to maximizing productivity and thus to surviving in the marketplace of the future. This realization implies a profound change in business culture and practice—what some have boldly called a second industrial revolution—one that views industrial products and processes as part of a larger industrial ecosystem, eventually forming a nearly closed system of material flows.

TOXIFICATION OF THE ENVIRONMENT BY INDUSTRIAL ACTIVITY

Few would argue that current industrial practice is sustainable. The mass of industrial materials used, and the waste generated, is staggering. In the United States alone, industry devours nearly 2.7 billion metric tons of raw material a year, not counting stone, sand, and gravel. (See Chapter 1, "Natural Resource Consumption.") In the extraction process, U.S. industry creates 6.9 billion metric tons of solid waste annually (6), in addition to about 7.7 billion metric tons of solid waste from metal and mineral processing (7). Each year it also emits a huge quantity of gas and liquid pollutants, including more than 120 million metric tons of conventional air pollutants and more than 4.9 billion metric tons of carbon dioxide. (See Chapter 23, "Atmosphere and Climate," Tables 23.1, 23.5, and 23.6.)

Toxicity and the Environment

Exposure to toxic materials can cause acute illness or death, as the 1984 Bhopal tragedy in India painfully illustrated. Low levels of exposure may impair development in the young. Neurological problems, for example, have been associated with low-level lead poisoning. Chemicals in the food chain that accumulate in the body can lead to reproductive failures such as those caused by DDT in hawks and eagles. Toxic compounds can induce mutagenesis (gene alteration) whose effects are felt in future generations. Toxic materials may also lead or contribute to chronic disease or altered metabolic activity resulting in reduced capability or productivity, such as human lung damage caused by high levels of sulfur dioxide or curtailed crop growth caused by exposure to ozone.

Environmental toxification can also result from chemical imbalances within an organism, an ecosystem, or a geophysical system. Excessive nutrients, for example, are credited with the increasing occurrence of algae blooms in estuaries and enclosed seas in many parts of the world. Blooms, by exhausting dissolved oxygen in the water or releasing toxins, have in turn led to widespread fish kills (8). (See Chapter 10, "Water," Toxic Tides.)

Sometimes environmental toxification arises from industrial emissions of substances not normally regarded as toxic. As already mentioned, when CFCs break up in the stratosphere and degrade the Earth's protective ozone layer, it intensifies the ultraviolet flux to which zooplankton and fish in shallow surface waters near Antarctica are exposed during part of the year. Another well-known example is urban smog. Unburned hydrocarbons from gasoline and nitrogen oxides from high-temperature combustion combine in the presence of sunlight to form ozone, a reactive form of oxygen that is damaging to plants and, if breathed directly, to animals (including people).

A more controversial example of indirect environmental damage is acid precipitation stemming from

Table 12.1 U.S. Heavy Metal Emissions from Consumptive Uses, 1980

(metric tons)

Source	Silver	Arsenic	Cadmium[a]	Chromium	Copper	Mercury[b]	Lead	Zinc
Metallic (except coating and electrical)	12.0[c]	0.0	0.0	2.0	11.1		1.2	0.5
Protective coverings								
Plating and coating			140.0	0.2				8.8
Paints and pigments			120.0	6.5			49.0	78.0
Electrical								
Batteries and equipment	2.0	2.0	7.8			200.0	8.5	0.1
Other	9.3					18.0		
Chemical								
Industrial catalyst, reagents, etc.	110.0	490.0		1.3	4.2	410.0		2.6
Consumer uses, additives, etc.	670.0		29.0	0.4			120,000.0	19.0
Biocidal poison								
Agricultural pesticide, herbicide, fungicides		3,000.0			0.2	16.0		0.2
Nonagricultural pesticides (except medical)		5,900.0		1.0		240.0		0.3
Medical, dental, pharmaceutical	21.0	20.0				8.4		1.0
Miscellaneous not elsewhere categorized	6.3		1.0	2.1		7.0	1.3	
Total	**830.0**	**9,400.0**	**290.0**	**12.0**	**16.0**	**890.0**	**120,000.0**	**110.0**

Sources:
1. Robert U. Ayres, Leslie W. Ayres, Joel A. Tarr, *et al., An Historical Reconstruction of Major Pollutant Levels in the Hudson-Raritan Basin: 1880–1980* (U.S. National Oceanic and Atmospheric Administration, Rockville, Maryland, 1988), pp. 40–58.
2. Robert U. Ayres, Sandoz Professor of Management and the Environment, The European Institute of Business Administration, Fontainebleau, France, 1993 (personal communication).

Notes:
a. In 1979.
b. In 1977.
c. Includes plating and coating.

sulfur and nitrogen oxide emissions during fuel combustion. These gaseous oxides react with water in the air or on the surface of small particles to produce sulfuric and nitric acids. Acid precipitation acidifies soil unless it is heavily buffered. The soil, in turn, can release otherwise immobilized metals—both naturally occurring aluminum, whose ions are toxic to plants, and heavy metals, often spread from smelters and in fly ash from coal burning. This sequence appears to have contributed to the degradation (*Waldsterben*) of Germany's Black Forest and many of the wooded slopes of the Alps. As trees die, topsoil erodes and can deposit heavy metals into stream and estuary sediment. Some metals such as mercury, arsenic, and cadmium are mobilized from sediment and converted to soluble form by bacteria, increasing the risk that they will enter the food chain. Metals can also become rapidly oxidized and converted to soluble form when sediment is dredged and exposed to oxygen (9) (10).

Large accumulations of heavy metals reside in the soils and sediments in some areas, the legacy of many forms of past industrial activity. Lead arsenate was heavily used as an insecticide, especially in apple orchards; arsenic is still widely used as a herbicide and in wood preservatives along with copper and chromium compounds. Mercury compounds were used for pigments, antimildew and antibarnacle paints, to control fungal diseases in plants, and to protect seeds from rot. Historically, mercury has been used in very large quantities (especially in South America) to refine gold and silver ores, a practice that continues among wildcat miners in the region today.

Tetraethyl and tetramethyl lead have been used as octane enhancers in gasoline for half a century (leaded gasoline is still common in much of the world). "White lead" paint was widely used to protect wood for more than a century, and "red lead" is still used to protect steel from rust. Zinc-based compounds were also widely used for pigments, as were chromium (chrome yellow) and cadmium (red and orange). The yellow paint used on streets and roads in the United States and the paint used on some construction equipment are chrome based. Zinc oxide (with cadmium traces) is used extensively in tires. Chromium compounds continue to be used for tanning leather and as an algicide for commercial air conditioners. Copper sulfate was, and still is, widely used to protect grape vines from fungus infections (11). Table 12.1 gives information on the consumptive uses of heavy metals in the United States in 1980.

Soft coal, whose ash contains trace quantities of many toxic metals, continues to be burned widely in many urban areas. Phosphate fertilizers containing cadmium also continue to be widely used.

Global anthropogenic emissions of many materials, including sulfur and nitrogen, now rival or exceed the flow of these materials from natural sources (12). (See Chapter 23, "Atmosphere and Climate," Table 23.5.) The emissions of toxic heavy metals such as lead, mercury, copper, cadmium, arsenic, chromium, and zinc exceed natural sources by a factor of 10 or more. (See Table 12.2.) Some analysts see such comparisons as evidence that industrial activity could overwhelm many natural ecosystems (13) (14).

Assessing Industrial Releases

According to the U.S. EPA, emissions of more than 300 toxic materials in the United States amounted to about

Table 12.2 Estimated Annual Global Emissions of Toxic Metals, 1980

Metals	Human Activity (thousand metric tons)	Natural Activity (thousand metric tons)	Ratio of Human to Natural Activity
Lead	2,000	6	333
Zinc	840	36	23
Copper	260	19	14
Vanadium	210	65	3
Nickel	98	28	4
Chromium	94	58	2
Arsenic	78	21	4
Antimony	38	1	38
Selenium	14	3	5
Cadmium	6	0	20

Source: James N. Galloway, J. David Thornton, Stephen A. Norton, *et al.*, "Trace Metals in Atmospheric Deposition: A Review and Assessment," *Atmospheric Environment*, Vol. 16, No. 7 (1982), p. 1678.

2.2 million metric tons in 1991 (15). Each year, data are reported factory by factory and made public in the Toxics Release Inventory (TRI). The TRI totals do not include hazardous materials that are incorporated in products (many of which end up in the environment), reports from nearly one third of U.S. factories, or emissions of all materials likely to be toxic. The TRI figures also do not distinguish among materials of widely varying toxicity.

When TRI data are scrutinized, additional questions about the inventory arise. Independent estimates for a number of toxic materials, based on calculations of materials balances for the primary industrial processes involved, suggest that TRI figures may understate U.S. emissions or releases for some important toxins by as much as a factor of 10. (See Table 12.3.) The apparent discrepancy may result from reporting rules that do not account for hazardous material in "nonhazardous" waste streams or in certain commercial products used

by small businesses and households. Thus the TRI, though the world's most detailed database of industrial emissions, must be approached cautiously; at best, its data represent lower-bound estimates.

The United States, as the world's largest producer and consumer of industrial materials, is also probably the world's top producer of toxic wastes. Although the Soviet Union was once a strong contender for that distinction, precise comparison between countries is not possible, because few release information on toxic emissions and the industrial processes that produce them, and many do not collect information on toxic (or other) emissions at all. Process-specific data, where it does exist, is often not published for fear of revealing proprietary information. As a result, in most countries, citizens and even government officials have little reliable information about the toxic substances emitted by industrial activity within their borders. Likewise, neither governments nor international development organizations have a way to gauge the environmental effects of industrial development plans.

Some information of global interest can be gleaned from the TRI, however. A study by the World Bank compared emissions as recorded in the TRI and other U.S. EPA databases with U.S. census data on manufacturing activity for a huge sample of industrial facilities—approximately 13,000 factories in all regions of the United States. The result is an index of pollution intensity (the environmental risk from industrial emissions per unit of manufacturing activity) for each of 1,500 industrial sectors or product categories.

The study created four separate indexes: direct risk to humans; direct risk to aquatic organisms (aquatic organisms are generally more sensitive to toxins than mammals); heavy metals (which, by accumulating in living tissue and food chains, can pose a long-term

Table 12.3 U.S. Toxic Emissions Estimates Assessed, 1989

(thousand metric tons)

Chemical	Apparent Consumption	Materials Balance Total Emission Losses	Emission Reported in TRI	Losses Unaccounted for by TRI
Benzene	7,360.0	390.6	14.6	376.0
Toluene	3,071.7	1,345.4	158.5	1,186.9
Xylenes, mixed	3,419.2	839.4	86.5	752.9
m-Xylene	34.6	7.1	1.6	5.5
o-Xylene	509.6	104.2	1.3	102.9
p-Xylene	2,510.9	190.6	3.2	187.4
Carbon tetrachloride	400.2	11.2	2.3	8.9
Chloroform	224.8	46.4	12.2	34.2
Methylene chloride	183.1	162.9	70.3	92.6
Perchloroethylene	252.9	183.0	17.1	165.9
Trichloroethylene	68.9	65.5	26.2	39.3
1,1,1-Trichloroethane	303.4	283.1	88.1	195.1
Methyl ethyl ketone	239.2	242.0	73.1	168.9
Methyl isobutyl ketone	91.2	82.1	20.2	61.9
Cadmium	3.6	4.6	0.9	3.7
Chromium	536.9	443.0	31.2	411.8
Mercury	1.6	1.6	0.1	1.5
Nickel	159.2	141.8	8.7	133.1
Cyanides	629.7	182.5	5.3	177.2
Hydrogen cyanide	543.0	95.7	1.4	94.2
Other	86.8	86.9	3.9	82.9
Total	**20,000.8**	**4,727.2**	**621.6**	**4,105.6**

Source: Robert U. Ayres and Leslie W. Ayres, "Use of Materials Balances to Estimate Aggregate Waste Generation in the U.S. (Excluding Chemicals)," INSEAD Working Paper Series, European Institute of Business Administration, Fontainebleau, France, 1993.
Note: Toxics Release Inventory as compiled and published by the United States Environmental Protection Agency (U.S. EPA), Office of Pollution Prevention and Toxics (U.S. EPA, Washington, D.C., 1991).

risk); and conventional pollutants. Manufacturing activity was measured in units of a product's dollar value and data were combined in standard economic sectors for ease of comparison with economic data (16). By applying U.S.-based intensities to sectoral economic data for other countries, the World Bank study makes it possible to estimate an approximate lower bound for toxic emissions in these countries. (See Table 12.4.)

Estimating releases from other countries remains problematic because manufacturing practices can vary significantly. For instance, because there are no phosphate ores in western Europe, the German chemical industry does not include a phosphate rock-processing sector, a major source of toxic emissions in the United States. Preliminary results from additional work by the World Bank suggest that emissions estimates may be too low as TRI data reflect "post-treatment" emissions, and developing countries tend to have less efficient equipment and practices (17). But in the absence of reliable data, the estimates provide some information on the environmental burden accumulating in each country. It is noteworthy that estimated emissions of heavy metals in Japan are higher than those in the United States, reflecting a metal-intensive manufacturing sector, and that two developing countries, China and India, also have larger estimated emissions than a number of Organisation for Economic Co-operation and Development countries, pointing to significant industrial activity.

Looking to the Future

Considering the already heavy environmental risks posed by current industrial practices, any significant expansion could become ecologically untenable. Yet such an expansion is what global development may imply, as the global industrial economy expands and as developing countries supply unmet needs and rising expectations (and incomes). Within the next 60 years, the global economy is projected to grow fivefold (18). In such a world, just holding the present—possibly unsustainable—environmental burden constant would require cutting the current environmental impact per unit of gross national product by 80 percent (19).

TOWARD SUSTAINABLE PRACTICES

The case for clean industry is easy to make on ecological or humanitarian grounds. But there are also compelling economic reasons for industry to embrace sustainable practices. For one, the cost of cleaning up pollution—from disposing of toxic waste to installing and maintaining control devices that treat harmful emissions—is already high and climbing in most industrial countries (20). In the United States, in fact, pollution abatement costs are rising faster than the growth rate of industrial production. (See Figure 12.1.) Disposal costs for some toxic wastes have risen as high as $10,000 per ton. U.S. manufacturers spend more than $40 billion annually on pollution control (21) (22).

Adopting cleaner processes can not only save on pollution control costs but also make manufacturing more efficient, thus increasing profits. And by converting a higher percentage of raw materials into useful prod-

Table 12.4 Lower-Bound Estimates of Annual Toxic Releases

(million metric tons)

Country	Human Risk Exposure	Aquatic Organism Risk Exposure	Heavy Metal Exposure	Year of Data
United States	18,004.1	21,212.1	911.4	1986
Japan	13,715.1	15,877.1	1,033.7	1988
Germany	9,451.7	12,086.4	412.6	1988
France	5,507.4	6,989.5	265.2	1988
Italy	4,077.3	5,185.7	195.7	1987
United Kingdom	3,983.0	4,683.4	204.6	1987
China	3,226.0	4,097.7	155.1	1987
Canada	1,900.3	2,224.0	115.1	1987
Spain	1,327.3	1,549.9	82.5	1987
India	1,193.0	1,450.1	73.8	1986
Netherlands	1,136.1	1,442.3	47.2	1987
Korea, Republic of	1,126.0	1,283.3	84.9	1987
Australia	783.9	924.5	70.8	1988
Sweden	705.9	808.6	49.6	1988
South Africa	636.4	796.5	41.9	1981
Austria	620.1	754.3	39.0	1987
Finland	516.6	609.4	29.1	1988
Turkey	453.2	539.4	30.4	1987
Norway	383.6	454.4	35.4	1988
Hungary	303.9	389.1	15.5	1988
Denmark	296.6	355.0	9.9	1988
Singapore	277.1	358.6	7.6	1988
Hong Kong	231.3	277.1	8.0	1987
Portugal	227.7	268.2	7.5	1987
Greece	217.6	263.6	12.5	1985
Ireland	206.2	269.7	3.2	1986
Venezuela	198.1	232.5	15.1	1986
Indonesia	195.3	246.7	6.8	1986
New Zealand	183.4	221.1	8.5	1986
Malaysia	181.3	216.5	8.6	1987
Poland	167.5	198.6	13.5	1988
Colombia	145.5	177.7	4.8	1986
Thailand	136.8	166.7	5.9	1986
Syrian Arab Republic	131.5	169.0	2.5	1987
Philippines	118.2	143.0	6.8	1987
Morocco	110.9	143.4	2.7	1987
Pakistan	96.5	120.2	2.7	1984
Kuwait	65.5	79.6	0.8	1986
Tunisia	63.7	83.8	1.2	1981
Luxembourg	61.5	73.8	8.8	1988
Uruguay	34.7	42.3	0.9	1987
Bangladesh	33.9	42.4	0.9	1986
Zimbabwe	28.6	34.9	1.7	1986
Côte d'Ivoire	28.5	36.4	0.5	1982
Ecuador	25.5	30.5	1.0	1987
Costa Rica	24.6	31.5	0.3	1988
Nigeria	22.5	26.6	0.7	1983
Guatemala	21.0	26.7	0.5	1988
Libya	13.4	17.1	0.1	1980
Dominican Republic	13.2	16.2	0.4	1984
Cyprus	12.9	16.2	0.2	1988
Senegal	11.3	14.6	0.3	1984
Yemen	11.2	14.9	0.1	1988
Panama	11.2	13.7	0.3	1985
Ethiopia	9.3	11.0	0.3	1987
Sri Lanka	8.6	10.6	0.3	1987
El Salvador	7.7	9.4	0.2	1985
Mauritius	7.1	9.2	0.2	1988
Cameroon	6.8	7.8	1.1	1979
Malta	4.5	5.7	0.1	1985
Papua New Guinea	3.5	4.3	0.1	1985
Madagascar	2.7	3.6	0.0	1985
Fiji	1.7	2.0	0.1	1985
Rwanda	1.6	2.1	0.1	1986
Malawi	1.6	1.9	0.0	1986
Ghana	1.3	1.5	0.2	1983
Kenya	1.3	1.6	0.0	1982
Central African Republic	1.2	1.6	0.0	1986
Congo	1.2	1.5	0.0	1985
Botswana	1.1	1.4	0.0	1986

Source: The World Bank, unpublished data (The World Bank, Washington, D.C., May 1993).

Note: A complete description of the Industrial Pollution Projection System used for these estimates will be published as a working paper by the Environment and Infrastructure Division of the World Bank Policy Research Department.

Figure 12.1 U.S. Pollution Abatement
Expenditure, 1980–91

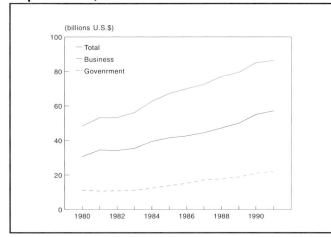

Sources:
1. Gary L. Rutledge and Mary L. Leonard, "Pollution Abatement and Control Expenditures, 1987–1991," *Survey of Current Business*, Vol. 73, No. 5 (1993), pp. 60–61.
2. Gary L. Rutledge and Mary L. Leonard, "Pollution Abatement and Control Expenditures, 1972–1990," *Survey of Current Business*, Vol. 72, No. 6 (1992), pp. 35–37.

ucts, clean processes can bring savings on material as well as waste disposal. For example, with computer modeling, Dow Chemical Corporation was able to refine the synthesis of agricultural chemicals at its Pittsburg, California, plant, cutting the need for a key reactant by some 80 percent, eliminating 1,000 metric tons of waste per year, and saving $8 million annually (23). Greater efficiency, combined with less waste disposal and lower liability costs, forms a powerful economic argument for cleaner processes.

The Green Factor

The rise in consumer consciousness about the environment is another factor influencing businesses to adopt sustainable practices. Indeed, evidence of environmentally responsible behavior has become an essential element of modern business success. The emergence of the so-called green factor has prompted businesses to realize the significant market potential for environmentally friendly products—everything from mercury-free batteries to recycled paper (24).

Along with this heightened sensitivity to environmental concerns has come increasing pressure from local community groups, environmental organizations, and government regulators for industries to reduce their pollutant emissions. Industries are being asked to make full public disclosures of toxic emissions for each facility they operate (25).

In 1986, the United States enacted a right-to-know law that required industries to quantify their emissions of the 313 toxic substances covered by the TRI. The specter of public accounting prompted business managers, many of whom had no overall picture of company emissions, to rethink their operations (26) (27). Despite limitations in the TRI, it has become an important bench mark for measuring companies' commitment to cleaning up and thus a powerful public relations tool for use against reluctant industries. Similar toxics report-

ing laws are now on the books or under active consideration in other countries, including Canada, Australia, and India. The European Community is formulating a multinational toxics inventory (28) (29) (30).

The demand for full disclosure along with growing public concern has coaxed many companies to expand their view of who has a legitimate stake in their operations. Today, for some leading companies, "stakeholders" include not just stockholders, lenders, and regulators but also employees, customers, suppliers, trade associations, community and environmental groups, the public at large, and in the widest sense, future generations and the biosphere as a whole (31) (32). In response to these numerous stakeholders, a growing number of companies have set public goals for pollution reduction and are adopting some type of pollution prevention program. Several major transnational corporations have developed ambitious cleanup targets (33).

For instance, 3M Company, which operates in more than 20 countries, has pledged to reduce all hazardous and nonhazardous emissions to air, water, and land by 90 percent by the year 2000 (using 1987 emissions as a base), and to cut all waste generation in half by 2000 (34). To achieve these goals, 3M has begun developing closed-loop and zero-waste processes (35). Monsanto Company recently achieved its goal of reducing toxic air emissions by 90 percent and has now committed to cutting all toxic releases by 70 percent (from a 1990 base) by 1995 (36) (37).

The willingness of some industrial firms to extend their cleanup efforts beyond mere compliance with minimum legal standards is an important beginning. Widespread adoption of this attitude, partly as a result of educational efforts, will be an important part of any substantive movement toward sustainable practices. Without the active participation of business, overall progress will be difficult, despite increasingly strict environmental regulations.

One advantage to business of a proactive approach is that it can begin to set the agenda of industrial transformation rather than have the pace and direction of change dictated by regulatory agencies or other outside influences. In this way, it can manage change in a manner that makes better economic sense, using the green factor itself to maintain or achieve a competitive edge in present and future markets (38).

Initial Steps toward Clean Industry

Industries striving for sustainable practices invariably begin by accepting the central tenet of modern pollution prevention: reducing waste or pollution at the source is inherently good business because it is more efficient and less costly than attempting to clean up pollution once it is produced (39) (40) (41). This philosophy differs markedly from traditional approaches to waste management and pollution control, which center on end-of-pipe technologies such as stack scrubbers, incinerators, and water treatment facilities that merely remove or detoxify wastes without fundamentally affecting the industrial processes that produce them. Pollution prevention adopts a front-end approach, attacking the source of waste by adjusting process technologies and controls, cleaning and handling practices, product design and packaging, and even transportation practices. Zero-emission or zero-waste processes are the goal of this approach. Complete pollution prevention is probably an impossible goal because of the inevitability of technical limitations and human error (42) (43).

The pollution prevention approach follows a natural hierarchy of waste management options: reduce waste at the source; reuse or recycle waste that is produced, preferably on site and directly back into the production process; or treat waste that cannot be prevented or recycled with the latest technology to detoxify, remove, or destroy it. Waste should be disposed of or released into the environment only as a last resort (44) (45).

Progress in pollution prevention comes through a variety of different routes. Simple measures that conserve materials and avoid spoilage or needless contamination often help reduce waste at little cost in time and energy. For instance, many industries have found that a simple step like redesigning cleaning processes can both save water and reduce the volume of wastewater generated (46) (47) (48) (49).

Second-order measures involve substituting more benign substances for toxic materials or redesigning manufacturing processes to recycle or eliminate a given waste. This approach has been widely employed to cut emissions of volatile organic solvents used extensively in manufacturing. Many businesses have begun capturing and recycling these solvents back into manufacturing processes. Others have phased out solvents altogether by substituting water-based processes. Microelectronics manufacturers on several continents, for example, have managed to replace CFCs and other ozone-depleting solvents with water-based cleaning operations, and car manufacturers are phasing in water-based paints in their shops (50) (51).

New technologies such as sophisticated chemical sensors and computerized process controls also have an important role to play in cleaning up industrial processes. By monitoring process conditions and precisely regulating the flow of reactants or energy, these technologies can increase efficiency and minimize waste (52). By modifying manufacturing processes and improving process controls, Intel, a major U.S. computer chip maker, decreased the amount of hazardous waste requiring treatment and disposal by about 95 percent between 1985 and 1993, even as annual sales increased by 500 percent (53).

To support these changes on the factory floor, companies must change the method they use to measure waste and account for waste cleanup in their budgets. Most companies do not have a comprehensive view of their waste streams—where the constituent waste components originate and exactly how much each waste costs to manage (54) (55). Simply assembling this information often reveals opportunities to develop a more efficient operation.

For the sake of convenience, expenses for a variety of waste treatment, disposal, and administrative functions have too often been lumped together under the general category of environmental management, so

that there is little accountability on the production line for the cost of pollutants produced there. In effect, this practice hides the true cost of products and processes from production managers and undervalues the advantages of many pollution prevention strategies. Cost-accounting procedures that charge specific waste producers within a company for the pollutants they create provide internal incentive for waste reduction and enable managers to evaluate more accurately the economic benefits and costs of process adjustments (56) (57).

Green Design

Introducing environmental consciousness into the design phase of products and processes is one of the most effective methods of pollution prevention. Decisions made during the design stage set parameters for the manufacturing process and ultimately determine the kind of waste produced. Green design marks the point where the difficult transition away from current practice begins in earnest (58) (59) (60).

Traditionally, industrial design has focused on maximum product performance and ease of production at minimum cost, ignoring the overall environmental impact of raw material acquisition, production processes, and the product itself. The goal of green design, by contrast, is to minimize the environmental impact of a product throughout its life cycle without compromising its performance. As with other aspects of pollution prevention, green design sees environmental friendliness as an opportunity, not a constraint (61).

Green design can be aided by an exercise called life cycle assessment (LCA). LCA seeks to quantify or at least assess the total environmental burden (including energy expenditure) of procuring raw materials for a product and manufacturing, distributing, using, and disposing of it (62). From this vantage point, designers can identify opportunities for reducing a product's impact, for example, where resource use and waste production might be minimized during manufacture or where the product might be reused or recycled at the end of its lifespan. Such opportunities might include reducing the use of toxic materials during production, including recycled material in the product, using less of a given material to perform the same function, increasing the energy efficiency of the final product, or extending the product lifespan by substituting more durable materials or design (63) (64).

While tradeoffs with nonenvironmental considerations are inevitable, the results of green design can be significant. Polaroid Corporation used it in creating a new high-definition film in 1991. Designers were able to substitute less toxic materials in the manufacturing process, cutting toxic waste by about one third without sacrificing quality standards (65).

Green design also gives special consideration to the fate of a product at the end of its life. Some products can be designed for disassembly or breakdown and subsequent use in other manufacturing processes, thereby keeping the materials within the industrial loop. Other products can be designed for composting or some other means of disposal that is safe and may itself provide environmental benefits (66).

In some cases, manufacturers of durable goods such as cars, major appliances, and business machines have already begun to design their products for ease of disassembly or for direct remanufacture. Often they use fewer parts or materials and label components such as plastics for easy separation prior to recycling (67).

Industrial Ecology

Industrial sustainability may not be achieved by individual companies acting in isolation. One alternative approach is to practice pollution prevention, green design, and closed-loop materials cycling on a systemwide basis. Obviously, this would require close connection among suppliers, producers, distributors, users, and waste recovery or disposal entities. The approach, which is known as industrial ecology, seeks to structure the world's industrial base along the lines of natural ecosystems, whose cyclical flows of material and energy are both efficient and sustainable (68) (69) (70) (71) (72).

Industrial ecology eschews the traditional linear model of industrial production in which waste is considered inevitable. In a natural ecosystem, there is no real waste. Resources are conserved, for example, when one organism uses another's byproducts or decay as food. Similarly, an industrial ecosystem would consist of complex "food webs" that allow spent products, waste, and byproducts to flow between industries (and consumers) in a multidimensional system of recycling and reuse. Incorporating waste streams into the manufacture of new products would become an integral part of the industrial process (73) (74) (75).

Industrial ecology redefines waste as a starting material for another industrial process. The idea is that processes can be designed as much for the useful byproducts they produce as for the primary products (76). The results could even be counterintuitive—for example, a process producing a large quantity of easily used waste might be preferable to a more efficient process producing a small amount of waste for which there is little use (77).

All this is theory. In practice, constructing the recycling infrastructure and consumer culture to support industrial ecosystems will prove challenging. One place where this challenge has been met, albeit on a limited scale, is the town of Kalundborg, Denmark. Here, industrial waste and waste process heat are exchanged in a cooperative arrangement among a power plant, an oil refinery, a pharmaceutical manufacturer, a plasterboard factory, a cement producer, farmers, and the utility that provides residential heat for local residents. The arrangement, which has been financially beneficial to all parties, is a working model of a small industrial ecosystem (78) (79).

One of the difficulties industries could face in striving for a closed-loop cycle is that many materials are dissipated. Products such as brake shoes, lubricant, pesticides, and paint are all essentially impossible to collect and reclaim as they are currently used (80).

Even where materials are reused, the cycle may not be truly closed. Certain types of paper and plastic are difficult to reprocess for their original purpose. Reclaimed material tends to cascade down the industrial food web to progressively more limited uses until it can only be burned for energy or discarded (81).

Greening the Marketplace

Success in transforming industry through new technology, innovative design, and better systems management will depend in large part on realigning global economic markets—the major determinant of most business behavior—to support the green revolution. This means that the prices placed on products must be changed to reflect the full environmental cost of their production (82) (83) (84).

Current markets often offer little incentive for environmentally responsible behavior. Companies and consumers are frequently insulated from the direct costs of the environmental degradation their activities incur. Typically, these costs—in the form of smog, groundwater contamination, pesticide residue, acid rain, loss of biological diversity—are borne by individuals not directly responsible for them or by the global community at large. When companies are made to internalize the costs—called full-cost pricing—then market forces will begin to penalize environmentally harmful practices and reward benign ones (85) (86).

While the logic of full-cost pricing is simple, bringing it about on a global scale is not. Industry might help realign markets by adopting environmental accounting procedures that highlight the cost of pollution and by practicing pollution prevention to increase efficiency. But industry's efforts will be fruitless unless there is also government involvement in adjusting tax and regulatory policies to intervene in markets on behalf of the environment (87) (88) (89).

Many policy mechanisms are available to government to prompt industry to internalize environmental costs. Taxes can be imposed on pollution emissions, energy consumption, and the use of virgin material or toxic substances. A complementary strategy is eliminating government subsidies that impede environmental goals. Subsidies, which range from tax incentives for extractive activities such as oil and gas production, mining, and logging to artificially low charges for energy or water, can lead to overuse of resources and serious environmental contamination (90) (91).

Another, more indirect scheme is emissions trading, where a limited pool of credits are exchanged on the open market to reward those who emit less. This sort of scheme is favored by companies because it allows them to decide on their own how to achieve environmental objectives at minimum cost (92) (93).

In addition to economic instruments, governments can influence markets through environmental regulation. Current regulations often take the form of "command and control," that is, they specify emission standards or disposal practices for toxic materials and prohibit certain polluting activities. Such regulations, while effective within their sphere, focus attention on specific pollutants in isolation, prompting investment in end-of-the-pipe pollution control rather than changes in industrial practice to realize the overall goal of pollution prevention (94) (95) (96). A few governments are now expanding their efforts to embrace the pollution prevention ethic without abandoning the command- and control-approach altogether.

In some cases, this has meant greater emphasis on cooperative arrangements with industry to coax it into reducing pollution beyond levels required by statute. The success of the U.S. EPA's 33/50 program, which has resulted in voluntary pledges from companies to reduce emissions of 17 priority pollutants by a total of nearly 354 million pounds by 1995, is seen as a signal that a less adversarial relationship with industry can sometimes be practical and cost-effective (97) (98) (99) (100). It should be noted, however, that the pledged reductions will probably be obtained by a variety of methods, not just pollution prevention.

Environmental product policy has also become an area of great interest to the international community over the last several years, particularly in Europe, where a variety of statutes and voluntary covenants have been put in place to encourage recycling of containers and packaging materials and to promote green design. Perhaps the most visible and controversial example is Germany's packaging law, which holds product manufacturers directly responsible for collecting and recycling the packaging they use. The law aims for a recycling rate of 80 percent of all packaging materials by 1995, a target which is admittedly ambitious and of uncertain feasibility. Japan has initiated an ambitious recycling program as well, targeting a 60 percent recovery rate for paper, aluminum, glass, steel cans, and batteries by 1995 (101).

Yet another way governments have sought to influence market behavior is by setting and enforcing standards for "ecolabeling." The goal is to employ labels to inform consumers about the environmental impact of the products they purchase. Environmental labeling programs are under way in Canada, Japan, India, several European nations, and (in the private sector) in the United States (102) (103).

Managing Change

The goal of industrial sustainability entails more than just a transformation of technology and its applications, experts warn. It involves, more fundamentally, a revolution in corporate culture—that is, in the philosophy business uses to make decisions. Indeed, the limiting factor in most pollution prevention efforts to date and the key constraint in accomplishing the transition to sustainable practices is not technology but management practices (104) (105) (106).

In other words, the transformation to sustainability must begin in the boardroom, where the management attitudes, organizational structures, and performance incentives are all shaped. Without a change in corporate culture to embrace the prevention ethic and the strategic value of sustainable practices, any change in technology will be largely reactive and based on short-term compliance (107) (108) (109).

The corporate changes required by the goal of sustainability will probably come about slowly. The proactive approach of pollution prevention, in which environmental criteria are part of each business decision and environmental performance is rewarded on a par with production performance, is likely to develop much more slowly than the technological transformation itself (110) (111). In fact, real progress could take a decade or more. Once the fundamental change in business thinking is made, however, progress is expected to be more rapid and profound (112) (113).

Will such gradual change be enough to prevent rapid environmental decline and accommodate world development in the interim? Few experts hazard a guess, but most agree that the momentum toward transforming industrial practice is building steadily. The strategic value of operating with the future in mind is beginning—at least in a few companies—to reshape the conception of what comprises sound business practice (114) (115).

The section on toxification was written by Dr. Robert Ayres, Sandoz Professor of Environmental Management at the European Institute of Business Administration in Fontainebleau, France, and by Allen Hammond of the World Resources staff. The section on sustainable industrial practice was written by contributing editor Gregory Mock.

References and Notes

1. Robert U. Ayres, "Toxic Heavy Metals, Material Cycle Optimization," *Proceedings of the National Academy of Sciences*, Vol. 89 (1992), p. 816.

2. Jerome O. Nriagu, "Global Metal Pollution," *Environment*, Vol. 32, No. 7 (1990), pp. 29–32.

3. Stephen Schmidheiny, *Changing Course: A Global Perspective on Development and the Environment* (MIT Press, Cambridge, Massachusetts, 1992), p. 6.

4. International Chamber of Commerce (ICC), *Supporting Companies and Business Organizations* (ICC, Paris, 1993), n.p.

5. U.S. Environmental Protection Agency (EPA), "EPA's 33/50 Program: Third Progress Update," EPA Report No. 745-R-93-0001 (EPA, Washington, D.C., 1993), p. 1.

6. U.S. Environmental Protection Agency (EPA), *Screening Survey of Industrial Subtitle D Establishments* (EPA, Washington, D.C., 1987), pp. 2-2 and C-8.

7. Robert U. Ayres, Sandoz Professor of Management and the Environment, The European Institute of Business Administration, Fontainebleau, France, 1993 (personal communication).

8. Elliott A. Norse, ed., *Global Marine Biological Diversity: A Strategy for Building Conservation into Decision Making* (Island Press, Washington, D.C., 1993), pp. 123–127.

9. William M. Stigliani, "Change in Valued 'Capacities' of Soil and Sediments as Indicators of Nonlinear and Time-Delayed Environmental Effects," *Environmental Monitoring and Assessment*, Vol. 10, No. 3 (1988), pp. 245–307.

10. William M. Stigliani, Peter R. Jaffe, and Stefan Anderberg, "Heavy Metal Pollution in the Rhine Basin," *Environmental Science and Technology*, Vol. 27, No. 5 (1993), pp. 790–792.

11. *Op. cit.* 1, pp. 815–820.

12. Intergovernmental Panel on Climate Change (IPCC), *Climate Change: The IPCC Scientific Assessment*, J.T. Houghton, G.J. Jenkins, and J.J. Ephraums, eds. (Cambridge University Press, Cambridge, U.K., 1990), pp. 30–33.

13. Hardin Tibbs, "Industrial Ecology: An Agenda for Environmental Management," *Pollution Prevention Review*, Vol. 2, No. 2 (1992), p. 168.

14. *Op. cit.* 1, pp. 815–816.

15. U.S. Environmental Protection Agency (EPA), *1991 Toxics Release Inventory* (EPA,

Office of Pollution Prevention and Toxics, Washington, D.C., 1993), p. 15.

16. David Wheeler, Mala Hettige, Paul Martin, *et al.*, "The Industrial Pollution Projection System," unpublished paper, The World Bank, Washington, D.C., 1993.

17. Mala Hettige, Economist, The World Bank, Washington, D.C., 1993 (personal communication).

18. James Gustave Speth, "The Transition to a Sustainable Society," *Proceedings of the National Academy of Sciences*, Vol. 89 (1992), p. 870.

19. Bruce Smart, *Beyond Compliance: A New Industry View of the Environment* (World Resources Institute, Washington, D.C., 1992), p. 5.

20. C. Kumar N. Patel, "Industrial Ecology," *Proceedings of the National Academy of Sciences*, Vol. 89 (1992), p. 798.

21. *Ibid.*

22. *Op. cit.* 3, p. 100.

23. *Op. cit.* 3, p. 268.

24. *Op. cit.* 19, pp. 83–96.

25. International Institute for Sustainable Development (IISD), *Coming Clean* (IISD, Winnipeg, Manitoba, Canada, 1993), pp. 6–9.

26. David Sarokin, *Toxic Releases from Multinational Corporations* (The Public Data Project, Washington, D.C., 1992), p. 2.

27. "Emissions Zero: Profits One," in *Saving the Planet: Environmentally Advantaged Technologies for Economic Growth*, a special supplement of *Business Week* (December 30, 1991), p. 10.

28. *Op. cit.* 26.

29. World Wildlife Fund (WWF), "The Right to Know: The Promise of Low-Cost Public Inventories of Toxic Chemicals," draft report, WWF, Washington, D.C., 1993, pp. 3 and 30.

30. *Op. cit.* 27, p. 9.

31. *Op. cit.* 25, p. 13.

32. *Op. cit.* 3, pp. 10–11.

33. *Op. cit.* 3, pp. 99–100.

34. *Op. cit.* 19, p. 15.

35. Richard Renner, Public Relations Counselor, 3M Company, St. Paul, Minnesota, 1993 (personal communication).

36. Monsanto Company, *Environmental Annual Review 1992* (Monsanto, St. Louis, Missouri, 1992), p. 18.

37. Monsanto Company, *Environmental Annual Review 1993* (Monsanto, St. Louis, Missouri, 1993), pp. 16–18.

38. *Op. cit.* 3, pp. 100–101.

39. Joel Hirschhorn, "The Technological Potential: Pollution Prevention," paper presented at *Toward 2000: Environment, Technology, and the New Century*, World Resources Institute, Annapolis, Maryland, June 1990.

40. *Op. cit.* 3, pp. 101–106.

41. U.S. Environmental Protection Agency (EPA), *The Design for the Environment Program: Cleaner Technologies for a Safer Future* (EPA, Washington, D.C., n.d.), p. 1.

42. *Op. cit.* 39.

43. *Op. cit.* 27, pp. 11–18.

44. *Op. cit.* 19, pp. 12–14.

45. *Op. cit.* 27, p. 11.

46. Joel Hirschhorn, "Technological Potential in Pollution Prevention," *Pollution Prevention*, Vol. 1, No. 2 (1991), pp. 21–24.

47. Ann Thayer, "Pollution Reduction," *Chemical and Engineering News* (November 16, 1992), pp. 35–36.

48. *Op. cit.* 3, pp. 101–102.

49. *Op. cit.* 27, pp. 11–15.

50. *Op. cit.* 3, pp. 102–103.

51. *Op. cit.* 27, pp. 11–15.

52. George Heaton, Robert Repetto, and Rodney Sobin, *Transforming Technology: An Agenda for Environmentally Sustainable Growth* (World Resources Institute, Washington, D.C., 1991), pp. 17–18.

53. Terry McManus, Manager, Corporate Environmental Affairs, Intel Corporation, Chandler, Arizona, 1993 (personal communication).

54. U.S. Environmental Protection Agency (EPA), *Design for the Environment Fact Sheet: Accounting and Insurance Projects; Applications for Pollution Prevention in Financial Professions* (EPA, Washington, D.C., 1993), pp. 2–3.

55. *Op. cit.* 46, p. 27.

56. *Op. cit.* 54.

57. *Op. cit.* 46, p. 27.

58. U.S. Office of Technology Assessment (OTA), *Green Products by Design: Choices for a Cleaner Environment* (OTA, Washington, D.C., 1992), p. 3.

59. *Op. cit.* 41.

60. Elizabeth Corcoran, "Thinking Green: Can Environmentalism Be a Strategic Advantage?" *Scientific American*, Vol. 267, No. 6 (December 1992), pp. 44–45.

61. *Op. cit.* 58, pp. 35–43.

62. *Op. cit.* 58, pp. 60–62.

63. James Fava, Frank Consoli, and Richard Denison, "Analysis of Product Life Cycle Assessment (LCA) Applications," paper presented at the Society for Environmental Toxicology, Europe, Workshop on LCA, Leiden, The Netherlands, December 1991.

64. *Op. cit.* 58, pp. 37–38.

65. Polaroid Corporation, *Polaroid Report on the Environment, 1991* (Polaroid Corporation, Boston, 1992), p. 18.

66. *Op. cit.* 58, pp. 39–43.

67. *Op. cit.* 58, pp. 39–42 and 59.

68. *Op. cit.* 13, pp. 168–170.

69. Robert Frosch, "Industrial Ecology: A Philosophical Introduction," *Proceedings of the National Academy of Sciences*, Vol. 89 (1992), pp. 800–803.

70. *Op. cit.* 20, pp. 798–799.

71. *Op. cit.* 58, pp. 54–56.

72. Robert Frosch, "Strategies for Manufacturing," *Scientific American*, Vol. 261, No. 3 (1989), pp. 144–146.

73. *Op. cit.* 13, pp. 168–170.

74. *Op. cit.* 69, pp. 800–801.

75. U.S. Environmental Protection Agency (EPA), *An Introduction to EPA's Design for the Environment Program*, pamphlet (EPA, Washington, D.C., 1993), p. 1.

76. *Op. cit.* 69, pp. 800–801.

77. *Op. cit.* 72, p. 149.

78. *Op. cit.* 13, pp. 171–172.

79. *Op. cit.* 58, p. 57.

80. *Op. cit.* 1, pp. 815–820.

81. *Op. cit.* 69, p. 801.

82. *Op. cit.* 3, pp. 15–33.

83. *Op. cit.* 72, pp. 151–152.

84. *Op. cit.* 18, p. 871.

85. *Op. cit.* 3, pp. 15–18.

86. *Op. cit.* 18, p. 871.

87. *Op. cit.* 3, pp. 15–19.

88. *Op. cit.* 18, p. 871.

89. *Op. cit.* 69, pp. 802–803.

90. *Op. cit.* 3, pp. 21–28.

91. *Op. cit.* 18, p. 871.

92. *Op. cit.* 3, pp. 21–28.

93. *Op. cit.* 18, p. 871.

94. Carol Browner, *U.S. Environmental Protection Agency Administrator's Earth Day 1993 Message*, pamphlet (EPA, Washington, D.C., 1993), pp. 1–4.

95. *Op. cit.* 3, pp. 19–21.

96. *Op. cit.* 18, p. 872.

97. *Op. cit.* 94.

98. *Op. cit.* 5.

99. *Op. cit.* 3, pp. 21–28.

100. *Op. cit.* 18, p. 872.

101. *Op. cit.* 58, pp. 67–75.

102. *Op. cit.* 58, pp. 67–75.

103. Norman Dean, "Life-Cycle Review as a Tool in Standard Setting," in *Rethinking the Materials We Use: A New Focus for Pollution Policy*, Ken Geiser and Frances H. Irwin, eds., (World Wildlife Fund, Washington, D.C., 1993), pp. 49–54.

104. Bruce Piasecki, "Industrial Ecology: An Emerging Management Science," *Proceedings of the National Academy of Sciences*, Vol. 89 (1992), p. 874.

105. John Ehrenfeld, Director, Technology, Business, and Environment Program, Massachusetts Institute of Technology, Cambridge, Massachusetts, 1993 (personal communication).

106. *Op. cit.* 39.

107. *Op. cit.* 104.

108. *Op. cit.* 39.

109. *Op. cit.* 105.

110. *Op. cit.* 105.

111. Hardin Tibbs, Strategic Consultant, Global Business Network, Emeryville, California, 1993 (personal communication).

112. *Op. cit.* 105.

113. *Op. cit.* 111.

114. *Op. cit.* 105.

115. *Op. cit.* 111.

13. International Institutions

The opportunity for international and regional institutions to encourage actions by national governments that promote sustainable development has never been greater. Public awareness of the urgent need for concerted action has been growing in many countries. In June 1992, the United Nations Conference on Environment and Development (UNCED) called for the creation of new, and the strengthening of existing, international institutions to enhance support for environment and development. The agreements signed at that meeting laid the groundwork for increased cooperation on sustainable development issues. The Global Environment Facility (GEF), a pilot program established in 1991 and managed by the World Bank, the United Nations Development Programme (UNDP), and the United Nations Environmental Programme (UNEP), is being evaluated as a possible financial mechanism for addressing key global environmental issues. And the upcoming 50th anniversary of the United Nations will be a useful occasion to reevaluate the role and function of the United Nations system in the post–cold war world of the 21st Century.

THE GROWING ROLE OF INTERNATIONAL ENVIRONMENTAL GOVERNANCE

In the last 10 years, environmental issues have gradually become more important in the conduct of international relations. Once considered scientific and technical issues outside mainstream diplomatic channels, environmental problems today are intricately linked with other crucial global issues, including the future of North-South relations and the liberalization of world trade (1).

A number of factors are responsible for this shift. Evidence of the extent of anthropogenic environmental deterioration has been mounting rapidly. Since the 1972 United Nations Conference on the Human Environment in Stockholm, it has been increasingly recognized that environmental deterioration and the depletion of natural resources create cycles of poverty and further environmental degradation in many areas of the world (2). Although analyses of the problems and proposed solutions frequently differ, growing awareness in both industrialized and developing countries that local and national actions affect life-sustaining global systems and cycles gives new urgency to the call for international solutions. The accumulated technical and institutional experience of the last decades makes effective international action possible if existing treaties are fully activated and institutions functional (3).

Increasingly, solutions to environmental problems such as transboundary airborne and waterborne pollution, ozone depletion, and climate change require action by all responsible countries. As deforestation and species loss suggest, there is little incentive for a nation unilaterally to address problems caused by the cumulative actions of many.

Of more than 170 environmental treaties that have been adopted, more than two thirds have been adopted since the United Nations Conference on the Human Environment in 1972 (4). Rhetorical commitment, however, can be stronger than willingness to undertake national policies and cooperate in international efforts to support global environmental goals. Moreover, most multilateral environmental agreements are not yet subject to international adjudication; instead, complex, reciprocal procedures are used to impose sanctions for noncompliance (5). Pressure from other treaty parties, the public, and interested nongovernmental organizations (NGOs) are important mechanisms for ensuring compliance (6).

UNCED: RHETORIC OR ACTION?

UNCED, held in Rio de Janeiro in June 1992 and popularly known as the Earth Summit, is the most recent and most dramatic international attempt to promote sustainable development. The largest international conference ever held and the first environmental meeting with heads of state, it was attended by 8,000 delegates, 9,000 members of the press, and 3,000 NGO representatives (7). More than 20,000 individuals from 171 countries attended the Global Forum held concurrently (8).

Delegates to UNCED approved three documents that had been previously drafted:

■ The Rio Declaration on Environment and Development, a set of 27 principles outlining the rights and responsibilities of countries toward the environment. This nonbinding declaration reflects concern about the ability of the deteriorating environment to sustain life as well as awareness that long-term economic progress and the need for environmental protection must be seen as interdependent (9).
■ A statement of 15 principles for the sustainable management of forests as the basis for further negotiations on an international forestry agreement. A nonbinding declaration, this document consists of general principles rather than a specific program of action, reflecting wide differences between industrialized and developing countries (10).
■ Agenda 21, a comprehensive plan to guide national and international action toward sustainable development. The 40-chapter plan covers many environmental and development program areas, defining problems and objectives, outlining specific steps for implementation, and giving estimates for funding (11).

In addition, two international treaties that were not part of the formal groundwork for UNCED were signed—the United Nations Framework Convention on Climate Change and the United Nations Convention on Biological Diversity. The Climate Convention addresses the build-up of greenhouse gas emissions in the Earth's atmosphere; at the insistence of the United States, it does not include binding targets, but it does require signatories to conduct national inventories of greenhouse gas emissions and submit action plans for controlling emissions (12). The Biodiversity Convention addresses issues related to conservation of biological diversity, the sustainable use of its components, and the equitable sharing of the commercial benefits derived from genetic resources. This controversial convention gives national governments the authority to exploit genetic resources within their own borders and, among other things, to negotiate access to the technologies that use those resources, consistent with the protection of intellectual property rights (13). These conventions go into effect 90 days after the appropriate number of states (50 for the climate treaty, 30 for the biological diversity treaty) deposit their instruments of "ratification, acceptance, approval, or accession" (14).

Of course, signing documents does not ensure implementation; the real test of UNCED's success will be the extent to which governments follow up on the commitments they made in Rio. There, in discussions on international institutional issues, debate was divided not along North-South or regional lines, as in talks on more specific issues, but rather on the definition of sustainable development and the prospects for reform of the U.N. system. Reaching an agreement to institutionalize a process to monitor progress was widely regarded as one of the quiet successes of the Earth Summit (15).

AFTER RIO: INSTITUTIONAL REFORMS

The monitoring agent agreed upon at UNCED, perhaps its most significant achievement, is the high-level United Nations Commission on Sustainable Development (CSD). CSD's task is to encourage and oversee progress in implementing Agenda 21 at national, regional, and global levels and to promote integrated, rationalized decisionmaking on environmental and development issues (16). On February 12, 1993, the United Nations Economic and Social Council (ECOSOC) formally established CSD, which held its first meeting in June of that year (17). CSD reports to ECOSOC and through it makes recommendations to the General Assembly, which, as the principal intergovernmental policymaking organ, plans to hold a special session no later than 1997 to review and appraise implementation of Agenda 21.

CSD's 53 seats are apportioned as follows: 13 to Western Europe and North America, 13 to Africa, 11 to Asia, 10 to Latin America and the Caribbean, and 6 to Eastern Europe (18). CSD has no legal or budgetary authority over the national or international programs it reviews. Rather, it serves as a forum for reviewing sustainable development issues across sectors, building political consensus about problem areas, exchanging information and ideas about solutions, and forging partnerships to address areas of mutual concern. NGOs may use CSD as a forum to mobilize and maintain pressure on governments and international institutions so that they keep their commitments and to provide independent assessments of programs and policies (19).

A real challenge for CSD will be to examine various international economic, social, and environmental efforts throughout the U.N. system and help coordinate them. CSD is specifically charged with monitoring commitments to provide financial resources and transfer technology (20). Critics hope that CSD will make it possible to identify and respond in timely fashion to emerging issues and problems (21).

Another major international mechanism for coordinating implementation of Agenda 21 is the United Nations Administrative Committee on Coordination. Headed by the U.N. secretary general, this interagency committee links the heads of major U.N. agencies and organs, including multilateral financial institutions. In October 1992, the Inter-Agency Committee on Sustainable Development, composed of senior agency officials, was established to prepare recommendations for the ACC on how to improve coordination among various U.N. agencies (22). In July 1993, the U.N. secretary general appointed a 21-member board in response to an Agenda 21 recommendation for a high-level advisory group consisting of prominent people in the environmental and development fields, with solid representation from the international scientific and technological community. The board's task is to advise intergovernmental bodies, the secretary general, and the United Nations as a whole (23) (24).

In general, Agenda 21 gives high priority to NGOs, which played an unprecedented role in preparations for UNCED and at the conference itself, in some cases by participating in official delegations and in others by putting effective pressure on governments and raising public awareness (25). Recognizing the extent to which environmental protection and sustainable development depend on NGOs, Agenda 21 calls on the U.N. system to include them in the review process, take account of their findings in reports to the secretary general, and establish procedures to expand their participation and accreditation in the UNCED followup process (26). At the first official meeting of CSD, NGOs continued to have the same kind of access to formal meetings and informal working groups as at UNCED and its preparatory meetings. They made oral and written statements, suggested text changes, and consulted with governments and the commission secretariat; NGO representatives were also, in some cases, included in governmental delegations (27). The arrangements for this level of NGO participation were designed to maintain the momentum of the UNCED process; at the same time, ECOSOC has undertaken a review of NGO participation in U.N. activities that is expected to result in procedural changes for making increased NGO participation routine (28).

Agenda 21 also recommends that international institutions dealing with environmental and development issues be strengthened, particularly UNEP, which will play a more prominent role in guiding and coordinating environmental policy in the context of development (29); UNDP, which will lead the effort to build capacity at the national, regional, and global levels; the

United Nations Conference on Trade and Development, which will concern itself with relationships among development, international trade, and environmental interests; and the United Nations Sudano-Sahelian Office, because of its work on drought, desertification, and land resource management (30). Agenda 21 calls on these institutions to improve their performance and their collaboration with one another; it does not address the question of how their mandates could be strengthened or additional resources provided. As part of its followup to UNCED, UNDP has created a new unit charged with promoting Agenda 21. Called "Capacity 21," this facility's objective is to help developing countries incorporate principles of sustainable development into national programs and processes. It is also intended to strengthen the sustainable development aspects of UNDP generally. Capacity 21 is considered a temporary facility whose activities and additional funding should eventually be incorporated into the regular UNDP program (31) (32).

The potential of regional and subregional organizations to advance sustainable development is also recognized in Agenda 21, which stresses their role in capacity building, integrating environmental concerns in development policies, and promoting cooperation on transboundary issues (33). Such organizations could also facilitate consultation processes, exchanges of information in the implementation of Agenda 21, progress reviews, and the delivery of development assistance within their particular regions (34). The United Nations' regional economic commissions are required to report to ECOSOC through CSD on their specific plans to implement Agenda 21 no later than 1994 (35).

The number of regional institutions has grown dramatically since the founding of the United Nations (36). Today, there are five U.N. regional economic commissions; six regional development banks; regional divisions and offices of such U.N. agencies as UNEP and the World Health Organization; and over a dozen other regional economic, political, and technical organizations. Although, in principle, they expand the opportunities for shared governance affecting sustainable development, no real mechanisms exist for coordinating activities or policies among or even within regions.

OTHER INSTITUTIONAL DEVELOPMENTS

To keep up pressure on governments to pursue sustainable development agendas, Maurice Strong, secretary general of the Earth Summit, and other independent leaders, scientists, and experts formed the Earth Council in late 1992. The Earth Council is committed to maintaining the momentum generated at UNCED by evaluating and reporting on public and private activities related to sustainable development. From Costa Rican headquarters, the council will work with other NGOs to promote independent evaluations of progress in meeting Agenda 21 objectives (37).

Despite the participation of NGOs and other private interests, UNCED was primarily a meeting of governments that now bears major responsibility for following up on the commitments made at Rio. Agenda 21 stresses the importance of integrating national efforts on behalf of the environment and development and calls on aid agencies to facilitate this process. Governments, too, are the ones that must ratify and implement the treaties signed at UNCED. A detailed report of national actions released by the National Resources Defense Council (U.S.) one year after UNCED paints a mixed picture of movement and inertia, highlights the difficulty of obtaining progress reports, and calls on CSD to make national reporting mandatory (38).

THE FUTURE OF INTERNATIONAL ENVIRONMENTAL GOVERNANCE

In recent years there has been no systematic review of the programs and agencies involved in development issues, even though the United Nations and international development agencies have the capacity to do so. Attempts to enhance U.N. influence on development policy by administering funds centrally through UNDP have, in the opinion of some, failed. Today, only 14 percent of official development assistance flows through the United Nations, and only 30 percent of that through UNDP (39). The United Nations' systemwide environmental program, coordinated by UNEP, could become a mechanism for evaluating accomplishments but has not been used for this purpose yet.

In 1980, the Committee on International Development Institutions on the Environment (CIDIE) was established to conduct regular reviews of agencies' procedures and projects supporting sustainable development. Thus far, CIDIE has not fulfilled its potential to help governments develop the capability to deal with sustainable development or coordinate development and financing agencies. Nevertheless, with a mixed membership of U.N. and non-U.N. institutions and of global and regional agencies, it holds promise in this area (40) (41) (42).

In recent decades, the Development Assistance Committee (DAC) of the Organisation for Economic Co-operation and Development (OECD) has sought to coordinate policy on issues affecting development (including trade, foreign investment, and debt) as well as to improve the quality of development assistance. As part of this effort, DAC has devised methods for doing environmental impact assessments and has conducted a survey of its members' procedures for reporting on environmental aid (43).

Even with threats to the environment mounting, the U.N. system's shortcomings in terms of managing, coordinating, and evaluating international environmental and development issues have become more serious. Its components compete for financial resources; financial and policy commitments made by various agencies remain uncoordinated; and despite the U.N.'s original mandate to deal with international economic issues, the most important economic and financial decisions are made by international financial institutions and at economic summits convened by major industrialized countries (44) (45).

In 1985, the United Nations marked its 40th anniversary, an occasion that prompted rethinking in many quarters about its role and the mechanisms for carrying that out. Agenda 21 could be critical to any process of change initiated by the U.N. anniversary. Its targets might provide the framework for a new system of measuring actions in the area of sustainable development and of holding countries and agencies, the United Nations and others, accountable. CSD and the new mandate of ACC represent steps in this direction. Other steps include Agenda 21's recommendation to strengthen the U.N. information base through improved data collection and analysis. Indicators such as gross national product (GNP) do not provide sufficient information on sustainability; social, development, demographic, and environmental factors need to be assessed as part of the decisionmaking process on environmental and development issues. (See also Chapter 1, "Natural Resource Consumption," and Chapter 3, "Women and Sustainable Development.") Specifically, Agenda 21 recommends greater support for Earthwatch, the systemwide environmental monitoring program, and calls for a similar program that would collect economic and social statistics (46).

Reform must extend beyond the United Nations to draw on the capacities and commitments of governments, NGOs, and intergovernmental bodies. In 1990, a group convened by former West German Chancellor Willy Brandt reviewed the work and proposals of commissions that had met over the previous decade on North-South relations, disarmament and security, environment and development, and South-South cooperation. Also taking into consideration changes in East-West relations, Brandt's group concluded that the challenges of the 1990s could be met only by coordinated multilateral action. Their work led to the Stockholm Initiative on Global Security and Governance and later to the Commission on Global Governance, cochaired by former Prime Minister Ingvar Carlsson of Sweden and former British Commonwealth Secretary Sir Shridath S. Ramphal of Guyana. The commission is assessing existing international structures in a post- cold war context, the need to expand participation in global decisionmaking and proposals to reform the United Nations and international financial institutions, in addition to such specific topics as environment and development and conflict intervention (47) (48) (49).

FOCUS ON MULTILATERAL FUNDING FOR SUSTAINABLE DEVELOPMENT

According to the UNCED secretariat, the average annual cost of implementing the conference's proposed activities in developing countries exceeds $600 billion, including approximately $125 billion in grants or concessions from the international community (50). The World Bank had previously identified the need for an investment of $75 billion annually for a priority list of environmental and related social programs (51).

The amount of external assistance required by Agenda 21 is far higher than the nearly $57 billion in official development assistance (ODA) that the North provided the South in 1991. (See Figure 13.1A.) Developing countries and the UNCED secretariat stressed at Rio, however, that the target could almost be met if in-

Figure 13.1 Net Official Development Assistance from Development Assistance Countries (DACs), 1991

A. In Billion U.S. Dollars

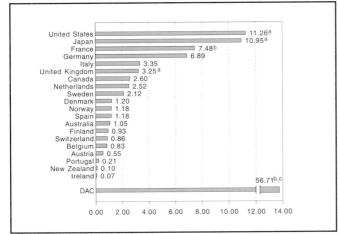

B. As Percentage of GNP

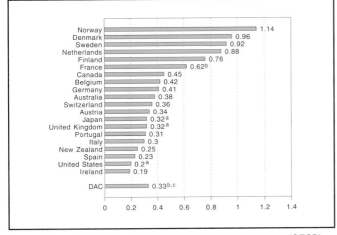

Source: Organisation for Economic Co-operation and Development (OECD), *Development Co-Operation: 1992 Report* (OECD, Paris, 1992), Chart 2, p. 24.
Notes:
a. Includes forgiveness of nonofficial development assistance debt.
b. Includes overseas territories but excludes overseas departments.
c. Excludes forgiveness of nonofficial development assistance debt.

dustrialized countries raised their assistance from the current average of 0.33 percent of GNP to the long-stated goal of 0.7 percent of GNP (52).

Of the 21 industrialized countries belonging to DAC, only six have reached or are approaching this level. (See Figure 13.1B.) While some countries reaffirmed their commitment to reach the U.N. target of 0.7 percent of GNP for ODA in Agenda 21 and to reach it as soon as possible, others (the United States and Switzerland) promised only to put forth their best effort to increase their ODA (53) (54).

Net resource flows to developing countries in 1991 reached almost $131 billion. This amount included about $4 billion in aid from non-DAC sources (Arab countries and drastically declining amounts from the former Soviet Union), $55.4 billion from private sources (including $28 billion in foreign direct invest-

ment and $5 billion in grants from NGOs), and $3.1 billion in export credits (55).

In 1991, 28 percent of the $57 billion in ODA from DAC was in the form of multilateral aid and the rest was made in direct bilateral transfers. (See Box 13.1.) The proportion of aid provided from OECD-DAC members through multilateral channels, which increased from 18 percent in the early 1970s to 30 percent of total ODA in the mid-1970s, has fallen in recent years. Declines in contributions from some of the largest donors, including the United States, Japan, and Italy, have been especially pronounced (56).

Still, multilateral organizations provide far more funds to developing countries than ODA figures ($16 billion in 1989–91) imply. In fact, in 1990, net multilateral disbursements to developing countries amounted to $24 billion, of which $13.8 billion was concessional assistance and $10.2 billion nonconcessional (57). (See Chapter 15, "Basic Economic Indicators," Technical Notes to Table 15.2.)

Ensuring that existing development funds incorporate sustainable development considerations in policies and projects is one of the most efficient and quickest ways to move toward more environmentally benign development. Many donors, both bilateral and multilateral, have strengthened their capacity to promote sustainable development through foreign assistance programs. Measures include more stringent environmental impact assessment requirements, increased funds for natural resource management and protection, and a commitment to alleviating poverty. Nevertheless, critics contend that development assistance agencies too often undermine rather than promote sustainable development, and that reform is needed in the quality of aid provided and in the concept of development promoted.

FAILURES OF MULTILATERAL AID

Development assistance, and multilateral assistance in particular, has come under widespread criticism in recent years from a variety of sources—NGOs, research institutions, scholars, multilateral development bank (MDB) officials themselves, and women's advocates. Only by promoting the principles of poverty alleviation, human development, environmental protection, and widespread participation, critics maintain, will the concept of sustainable development ever be viable. They charge that MDBs, especially the World Bank, support projects undermining these basic principles of sustainability, fail to consult those most affected by a project, and promote policies that adversely affect the environment and the poorest sectors of society.

Lack of emphasis on sustainable development. MDBs, the argument goes, have too often supported projects and sectors that fail to contribute to, or impede, sustainable development. Most notable are large projects such as irrigation systems and hydroelectric dams that result in widespread salinization and waterlogging, loss of cultivable land and forests, forced migration, disease, soil erosion, loss of biological diversity, and so forth. Not only do MDBs fund the wrong projects, they frequently fail to support those sectors that can contribute most to sustainable development in poor countries (58). For example, a 1991 study of MDB energy investments, which average more than $5 billion per year, shows that over the past decade less than 1 percent went to improvements in energy efficiency, even though this sort of investment often produces more energy per dollar than investments to increase energy supply (59).

Critics fault MDBs for failing to include social and environmental costs in their calculations of a project's expected rate of return. Some estimates suggest that if the costs of resource degradation and depletion as well as negative effects on human health, living standards, and social conditions are taken into account, the return of many supposedly successful projects would be nil or even negative (60).

An internal review of World Bank lending concluded that even based on the bank's own criteria of economic return, more than 37 percent of projects reviewed in 1991 should have been considered unsatisfactory. In the water supply and sanitation sector, 43 percent of projects in their fourth or fifth year of implementation were experiencing major problems; in the agriculture sector, 42 percent (61). Critics argue, moreover, that of the 58 percent of presumably successful agriculture projects, not all benefit the poor or are structured so as to protect the environment (62).

Lack of consultation with those most affected. A frequent criticism of large development projects is that they benefit one group at the expense of another, with the rural poor receiving the least benefit. A related complaint is that MDBs and developing nations often deny affected communities, NGOs, and the public access to information about potentially adverse environmental consequences of development proposals.

Critics want MDBs considering a loan to consult with all those who would be affected by proposed projects and to ensure that any disadvantaged groups be compensated and harm minimized (63). A recent increase in NGO involvement in project implementation is considered a welcome but still inadequate development.

Negative effects of structural adjustment lending. The most severe condemnation of the MDBs is related to the growing trend since 1980 for these institutions to shift lending and grants away from projects toward support of stabilization and structural adjustment policies. These two sets of macroeconomic policies are designed to correct debtor countries' problems of external debt and economic stagnation. Stabilization programs of the International Monetary Fund aim to correct a debtor country's short-run balance of payment problems; the structural adjustment policies of the World Bank are intended to promote long-term economic growth (64). Both stabilization and structural adjustment usually include policies to reduce aggregate demand (for example, by cutting public spending, increasing taxes, and reducing the money supply), and policies to restructure the economy (for example, trade and exchange rate reform, changes in the structure of public spending, and measures to improve factor markets and mobility) (65).

After a decade of experience with such programs, the development community remains divided about their value and impact. Proponents, though acknowledging that the programs have introduced severe setbacks to some sectors of the economy and society, argue that "among countries requiring adjustment, those that have carried out major adjustments have performed better on average in terms of their aggregate economic activity than those that have not . . ." (66). Specifically, in reviewing its policy-based loans, the World Bank contends that in middle- and low-income countries that received intensive adjustment lending in the 1970s and 1980s, the poor were visibly better off than they would have been without any systematic adjustment effort. Whether this path or an alternative would have served them better, however, is as yet undetermined. The Bank also points to lower fiscal deficits, lower foreign exchange rates, and lower inflation in 1986–90 as proof that adjustment lending benefited those countries that respected the conditions of the loans (67).

Opponents of stabilization and structural adjustment maintain that these programs have not only failed to achieve their macroeconomic objectives but also were extremely harmful to the poorest sectors of society and to the environment. In its analysis of the impact of World Bank adjustment programs, the United Nations Economic Commission for Africa (ECA), for example, charged that the Bank's report of "better overall economic performance in countries that pursue strong reform programs than in those that do not" (68) is neither realistic nor credible because it ignores factors such as weather, commodities markets, and debt. In addition, based on criteria used by stabilization and structural adjustment promoters themselves, Africa's basic development objectives, including food self-sufficiency, sustainable growth, and the alleviation of poverty, have not been supported by these policies (69).

The ECA charges that the social consequences of adjustment include declining per capita income and wages, rising unemployment and underemployment, deteriorating social services, falling educational and training standards, growing malnutrition and other health problems, and more poverty and income inequality. The ECA proposed an alternative: a framework that emphasizes human development and strengthened institutions while simultaneously promoting sustainable development.

A 1992 study of stabilization and structural adjustment in the Philippines concluded that its impact on natural resources and the environment has been severe, but for different reasons than have usually been cited. Critics had charged that the program forced the Philippines to export natural resources more rapidly to service its debt, but the worldwide economic slump and limited domestic supplies made this impossible; rather, it forced millions of unemployed and impoverished people into marginal upland forests and coastal areas for a subsistence livelihood (70).

Critics are moving the debate away from whether MDB assistance should entail structural adjustment and toward the question of how macroeconomic policies can restructure economies so as to eliminate the burden on the poor, ensure sustainable management

Box 13.1 Trends in Official Development Assistance by Major Donors

In 1991, the 21 countries of the Development Assistance Committee (DAC) of the Organisation for Economic Co-operation and Development (OECD) gave $57 billion in official development assistance (ODA) to developing countries and multilateral institutions, with approximately four fifths provided on a bilateral basis. That same year, non-OECD sources— Central and Eastern European countries, the former Soviet Union, Arab countries, and a small number of developing countries—gave another $4 billion, down from $8.6 billion in 1990 (1).

Over the last decade, the total volume of DAC aid rose at an average annual rate of 2.4 percent, resulting in an increase of more than $11 billion between 1980–81 and 1990–91, largely attributable to actual and relative increases in donations from Japan, France, and Italy, as well as Finland, Portugal, Norway, and Switzerland. Only the United Kingdom, Belgium, and New Zealand decreased their aid in absolute terms during this period. Meanwhile, ODA as a percentage of gross national product (GNP) declined in the Netherlands, Australia, Germany, and the United States. The largest donors in absolute terms in 1990–91 were the United States and Japan, followed by France and Germany (2).

For more than two decades, the DAC average of ODA as a percentage of GNP has hovered just below 0.35 percent, exactly half the internationally agreed target of 0.7 percent. Considerable shifts have taken place in aid from individual donors. The ODA/GNP ratios of the United States and the United Kingdom are now 0.20 and 0.32 percent, respectively, while Scandinavian countries and the Netherlands have reached or exceed the 0.7 ODA/GNP target, with France not far behind at 0.61 percent (3).

Over half of DAC aid goes to low-income countries. The European Community, Scandinavia, and Canada focus heavily on sub-Saharan Africa. U.S. aid

goes primarily to the Middle East (Israel and Egypt), sub-Saharan Africa, and Central America. Japan, which provides aid to Asian countries, has recently increased its aid to sub-Saharan Africa (4).

Many countries are reevaluating both the level and the focus of their aid, in light of the end of the cold war, domestic and global economic restrictions, and the pressing development needs of the poorest countries. Despite the consensus expressed at the United Nations Conference on Environment and Development that bilateral assistance programs need to be strengthened in order to promote sustainable development, it is not clear whether sufficient additional resources will be available. Nevertheless, some countries, notably France and Japan, appear likely to increase their levels of ODA in real terms (5). In the United States, the Agency for International Development has begun a reorganization process that is intended to

Figure 1 Net Disbursements of Official Development Assistance (ODA) from Development Assistance Countries, 1987–91

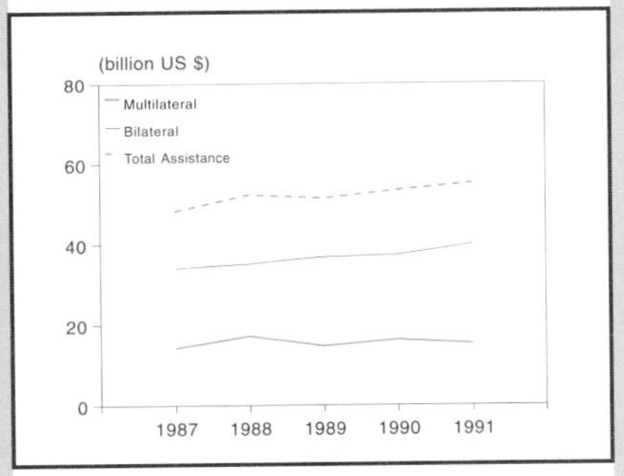

Source: Organisation for Economic Co-operation and Development (OECD), *Development Co-Operation: 1992 Report* (OECD, Paris 1992), Table V-2, p. 87.

strengthen the agency's "effectiveness and efficiency" in achieving its goals of "promoting sustainable development abroad, responding to natural and man-made disasters, and addressing key global problems" (6). Total U.S. foreign assistance appropriations (including security assistance) declined by $1.3 billion between FY 1993 and FY 1994. Subsequently, another $200 million was cut from FY 1994 and, as of November 1993, additional cuts were being proposed (7) (8). The Administration is developing new foreign assistance legislation that will enable AID to focus on a limited number of objectives under the broad sustainable development goal (9) (10).

References and Notes

1. Organisation for Economic Co-operation and Development (OECD), *Development Cooperation: 1992 Report* (OECD, Paris, 1992), pp. ii, 83, 92, and 111–112.

2. *Ibid.*, pp. 88–89.

3. *Ibid.*, pp. 87 and 89.

4. *Ibid.*, pp. 26 and 27.

5. *Ibid.*, p. 95.

6. U.S. Agency for International Development (U.S. AID), "Reorganization Plan for the Agency for International Development," U.S. AID, Washington, D.C., October 1993, p. 1.

7. U.S. Agency for International Development, Congressional Presentation, Summary Tables, June 2, 1993.

8. Budget Office staff member, U.S. Agency for International Development, Washington, D.C., November 1993 (personal communication).

9. U.S. Agency for International Development (U.S. AID), "What Are the Major A.I.D.-Related Improvements in the New Bill?" Fact Sheet (U.S. AID, Office of External Affairs, Washington, D.C., Fall 1993).

10. J. Brian Atwood, Administrator, U.S. Agency for International Development, "Agency Reorganization Plan," memorandum, General Notice ES 10-1-93.

of natural resources, and protect the environment. Policies must be designed, they say, to reduce environmental damage and simultaneously promote such economic objectives as fiscal balance, the alleviation of poverty, and economic efficiency (71).

Now that the end of the cold war has reduced competition among donors trying to win friends through politically motivated bilateral aid, interest in multilateral development assistance is growing. How can it be made more effective? One recent study of the United Nations' economic, social, and development activities recommended a stronger operational role for the United Nations and its specialized agencies, as well as a clearer delineation of roles based on comparative advantage between the United Nations as a whole and the World Bank group. Specialization and coordina-

tion could make the entire system of international institutions more effective (72).

THE GLOBAL ENVIRONMENT FACILITY

GEF is a three-year pilot program running from 1991 to 1994 to help developing countries deal with global environmental concerns. Praised by some as an important tool for future multilateral cooperation on environmental issues, it is roundly criticized by others for not addressing the key environmental concerns of developing countries. In fact, debate over the extent and nature of GEF reforms has become for some an opportunity to address the reform of development assistance in general. GEF, managed jointly by the World Bank, UNDP, and UNEP, provides resources to fund that

Table 13.1 Approved Expenditures for the Global Environment Facility's Pilot Phase, 1991–94
(million US$)

Expense Category	Africa	Asia	Arab States and Europe	Latin America and Caribbean	Global	Total	Percentage of Total
Biodiversity	76.2	75.1	31.6	107.8	12.8	303.5	42
Global warming	55.0	128.5	55.2	29.9	27.4	296.0	40
International waters	16.0	38.0	45.9	19.5	2.6	121.9	17
Ozone	0.0	0.0	3.8	1.9	0.0	5.7	1
Total[a]	147.2	241.6	136.4	159.1	42.8	727.1[b]	100
Percentage of total	20.0	33.0	19.0	22.0	6.0	100.0	

Source: Global Environment Facility, "Report by the Chairman to the May 1993 Participants' Meeting, Part 1: Main Report," The World Bank, Washington, D.C., 1993, Table 4, p.11.
Notes:
a. Totals may not add because of rounding.
b. Total core fund available is $862 million.

portion of proposed development activities that generates global environmental benefits but would not otherwise be funded as part of national development. It provides resources in four specific categories: climate change, biological diversity, international waters, and ozone depletion. In 1992, land degradation issues related to these focal areas, particularly desertification and deforestation, became eligible for funding as well (73).

The World Bank houses the GEF secretariat, acts as trustee and administrator for the GEF program, and manages GEF investment projects. UNDP is responsible for GEF technical assistance, capacity building, and project preparation. UNEP ensures that GEF's policy framework reflects existing and emerging conventions and protocols, supports a secretariat for the Scientific and Technical Advisory Panel, and plays a role in strategic planning (74).

GEF's core fund during the pilot phase amounts to approximately $862 million. (See Table 13.1.) According to the initiators of the original international environmental facility concept, this should all be from new contributions; that is, in addition to existing ODA contributions. Because of the difficulty in tracking these contributions, however, it is suspected that some—particularly cofinancing and parallel financing arrangements from bilateral development agencies—are just a relabeling of existing commitments (75) (76). The Montreal Protocol Multilateral Fund, established in late 1990 to help developing countries defray the costs of phasing out ozone-depleting substances, is one example of the confusion surrounding GEF financing arrangements. When Protocol projects are approved, UNEP, which acts as secretariat for the Multilateral Fund, transfers the approved funds to the GEF's Ozone Projects Trust Fund. The World Bank then uses those funds for implementation of the project (77).

With this and other structural problems in mind, critics began to push for reform of the GEF as early as December 1991, when member governments asked the implementing agencies to review operational ideas for a post-pilot phase of the GEF (78). The pilot phase is under scrutiny from developed and developing countries, as well as from NGOs. Participants in GEF and outside critics are pressuring for policy, institutional, and managerial reforms and expressing concern about participation and access of affected groups both in in-

ternational GEF structures and in the project cycle in their respective countries. The kind and extent of reforms needed are the major topic of the semi-annual meetings of GEF participants.

A second source of pressure for reform developed out of the preparatory process for UNCED. Donor governments had indicated their wish to adapt the GEF to serve as a financial mechanism for implementing the Biodiversity and Climate Change conventions, after they were accepted at UNCED. The signers of the conventions agreed to use a mechanism such as the GEF on an interim basis for the incremental costs of implementation. Both conventions specified, however, that the mechanism would have to incorporate an equitable and balanced system of representation, a democratic and transparent system of governance, and universal membership. The conventions also stipulated that the financing mechanism shall function "under the authority and guidance of, and be accountable to" the parties to the conventions (79). It was clear after UNCED that such a relationship would depend on significant reforms in the GEF. The future role of the GEF therefore depends, in considerable part, on the willingness of the parties to these conventions—as well as future international environmental agreements—to use the facility as their funding mechanism (80).

In fact, prior to UNCED, donor governments had indicated their preference to adapt the GEF as the umbrella financing mechanism for the climate change and biological diversity conventions. A forward-looking document approved by the participants in April 1992 recognized the need for universal membership, equitable participation, increased accountability in decision-making, and a significant role for the private sector and NGOs. Such principles, it was thought, would provide the basis for more specific substantive reforms (81). Critics, however, contend that these principles for reform fall short of addressing underlying problems in development assistance generally.

Specifically, critics are concerned that GEF's scientific and technical criteria result in projects that put a bandaid on environmental failures and ignore the underlying causes of environmental deterioration. The proper role for GEF, they say, is to help countries make the transition to a model of sustainable development that incorporates global environmental costs (82).

Some NGOs in developing nations argue that the very premise of GEF is faulty—that the environmental areas on which it focuses do not represent the key environmental concerns of the South. GEF's priorities reflect Northern demands that developing countries forego development in the name of saving the planet (83). A joint statement by NGOs from Africa, Latin America, and southern Asia suggests that an ideal global environmental fund would address issues in the context of regionally defined needs, for example, the need to alleviate poverty and achieve sustainable development in Asia (84).

Critics further charge that because of its relationship to UNDP, UNEP, and the World Bank, GEF will find it difficult if not impossible to construct a new model of development. As a captive of these agencies—in particular, the World Bank, with its restrictive information policies, propensity for large projects, and poor environmental record—GEF will not be able to develop programs premised on promoting sustainability, for that would undermine "the development strategy embedded in the logic of the institutions themselves" (85).

Such are the issues to be resolved before GEF or some alternate structure can become a financial mechanism for addressing pressing global environmental problems and promoting the kind of sustainable development agreed upon at UNCED (86) (87) (88) (89) (90) (91). A number of solutions have been put forward:

■ Decisionmaking authority over both policies and specific projects should reside with recipient countries as well as with donors. Some analysts believe there should be a voting system that gives some measure of control to donors.

■ Participation by NGOs and community-based organizations in defining GEF policies and in developing individual-country programs should be expanded. Similarly, increased, continuous access by affected groups to detailed documentation about GEF projects and associated loans is seen as essential.

■ GEF should not limit itself to four program areas focused on global issues but rather address beneficiaries' regional and local priorities, including poverty, underdevelopment, and Northern consumption. Others caution against overburdening a new and still developing mechanism.

■ Additional proposals include changing the criteria used in reviewing projects to embrace social and economic factors rather than just scientific and technical ones; increasing the proportion of resources available for small- and medium-sized projects and community-based initiatives; expanding participation so that other international organizations are project principals, not just cofinancing or implementing agencies; and shifting support from the incremental costs of standard development projects toward programs that encourage sustainable strategies.

GEF pilot resources are miniscule in relation to the total financial needs outlined in Agenda 21 and elsewhere. Even if its budget is expanded from $1 billion to $3 or even $4 billion, the main impact of GEF is still likely to come from its ability to reshape traditional development lending and to serve as a catalyst for a wider range of international capital transfers, including private investment.

THE FUTURE OF MULTILATERAL AID

There is growing recognition of the relationship between the development issues of concern to the South and the global environmental issues of concern to the North, as well as growing appreciation of the need for assistance in meeting the challenges of sustainable development. At the same time, donor countries confronted with tight budgets and competing priorities face increasing domestic resistance to the concept of providing foreign aid. Thus at the very time when many leaders are acknowledging the need for international assistance, they have the difficult task of persuading their domestic constituencies to support it.

Moreover, the number of countries with claims on foreign assistance has increased and changes are being made in the traditional classification of developing countries. In 1993, the DAC of the OECD added five central Asian republics of the former Soviet Union (Kazakhstan, Tajikistan, Turkmenistan, Uzbekistan, and Kyrgzstan) to its list of developing-country aid recipients, since these countries' economic situation resembled that of developing countries. DAC has also determined that as of 1996, six traditional aid recipients that now have average annual incomes above $10,000 per capita will no longer be eligible to receive official development assistance; these are Singapore, Brunei, the Bahamas, Qatar, United Arab Emirates, and Kuwait. While the loss of aid from the former Soviet Union and some Eastern European countries has been partially made up by new donors such as Taiwan and the Republic of Korea, the overall aid picture is hard to assess (92).

At the same time, emergencies including famine, drought, and regional conflict are diverting resources that might otherwise be devoted to the pursuit of sustainable development. Emergency assistance is often carried out with development funds, as in the 1991 Persian Gulf War and in 1992 for use in war-torn and drought-stricken African countries. Countries recovering from war, such as Angola, Cambodia, and Nicaragua, can also be expected to make new claims on development funding (93).

A critical question for the remainder of the 1990s is how much aid will be available to meet these multiplying needs. The question, avoided at UNCED, will be an important part of the follow-up process.

At Rio, it was agreed that the tenth replenishment of funds for the International Development Association (IDA) would be a good time to examine ways to help "the poorest countries meet their sustainable development objectives as contained in Agenda 21" (94). IDA is the window of the World Bank through which "soft," or interest-free, loans are provided to the poorest countries. The IDA 10 negotiations, completed in December 1992, resulted in an $18 billion replenishment for the three-year period beginning July 1, 1993. Another $4 billion in payment of IDA credits will bring total available resources for the three-year period to $22 billion.

In real terms, this is comparable to the amount available in IDA 9, covering the period from 1990 to 1993, during which nine new countries became IDA borrowers. Donors agreed that IDA credits should support poverty reduction, economic reform, and environmental sustainability, but they did not commit to specific increases in funding (95).

Many NGOs in both developed and developing countries are highly critical of the social and environmental impacts of IDA's past lending practices. Some, in fact, have called for cuts in IDA funding, with the withheld portion reprogrammed to help poor countries, until substantial reforms are made. African NGOs, on the other hand, have argued that such a move would hurt their countries even more. Thus, among the reforms being advocated are an independent appeals mechanism for people affected by projects, a new policy broadening access to information, the adoption of an index reflecting possible impacts on natural resource bases, and greater ownership of projects on the part of borrowers (96).

Agenda 21 did not press the issue of where sustainable development funding would come from. This consensus document went a long way toward outlining a new vision of the world, but it could be passed only by avoiding some of the most difficult issues. Others have been less reluctant to spell out measures that could secure the needed funds.

A number of proposals for international environmental taxation have been made in recent years. These include taxes on global income, fossil fuel consumption, pollutants, the use of global commons such as the oceans, international trade in certain natural resources, defense expenditures or arms trading, and energy-wasting consumer items (97). Another idea is to issue permits to emit certain quantities of greenhouse gases, which could be sold by countries not using their allowed quota to countries exceeding theirs.

Another potential source of development funding is the "peace dividend" resulting from reduced military spending in the post-cold war era. It is estimated to be around $100 billion per year for developed countries (perhaps rising to between $200 and $300 billion annually by the end of the century). The North's peace dividend over the course of the 1990s could be roughly $1,500 to $2,000 billion (98). Potential savings from reduced military expenditure by developing countries have been estimated at $30 to $40 billion per year. Urgent domestic problems will make legitimate demands

on these savings, but the commitment of even a portion for international cooperation (members of the Stockholm Initiative suggest one third) could provide significant resources for development (99).

BEYOND AID

Equally important to ensuring long-term sustainability is reform of the international trade and financial systems that still favor industrialized nations. The debt of many Southern countries makes investment in human development and environmental protection difficult, if not impossible. Exacerbating this situation is the tendency of Southern countries to draw on their natural resource base in an effort to expand exports and thereby finance external debt. Some countries, in fact, are paying more to service their debt than they receive in new resources (100).

Trade protections for industrialized nations, particularly nontariff barriers, have increased substantially in recent years, costing Southern countries between $10 and $15 billion per year in textile and clothing exports alone (101). The combination of high debt and inability to expand exports in environmentally sound ways is a major impediment to sustainable development in the South (102) (103).

Both the process leading to, and the documents resulting from, UNCED represent major steps in the international community's willingness to acknowledge the importance of environmentally sustainable development, and to commit to at least some actions toward that goal. The challenge now is for all countries, industrialized and developing, to undertake the national and international actions to pursue that goal. These include not only providing funds and technical assistance but also making significant policy reforms.

The challenge for Southern countries is to devise coherent national (and perhaps regional) development strategies incorporating economic and environmental objectives. For Northern countries, it is to recognize more explicitly their responsibility for current levels of environmental deterioration and their role in promoting more sustainable development.

This chapter was written by Rosemarie Philips, a writer and editor in Alexandria, Virginia, who specializes in environment and development issues.

References and Notes

1. Gareth Porter and Janet Welsh Brown, *Global Environmental Politics*, Dilemmas in World Politics Series (Westview Press, Boulder, Colorado, 1991), pp. 1–2.

2. World Resources Institute in collaboration with the United Nations Environment Programme and the United Nations Development Programme, *World Resources 1992–93* (Oxford University Press, New York, 1992), p. 2.

3. Peter H. Sand, *Lessons Learned in Global Environmental Governance* (World Resources Institute, Washington, D.C., 1990), pp. 1 and 34–35.

4. Hillary E. French, "After the Environmental Summit: The Future of Environmental Governance," Worldwatch Paper No. 107, Worldwatch Institute, Washington, D.C., 1992, p. 6.

5. *Op. cit.* 3, pp. 21 and 22.

6. U.S. General Accounting Office (GAO), *International Environment: International Agreements Are Not Well Monitored*, GAO/RCED-92-43 (GAO, Washington, D.C., 1992), pp. 10 and 12.

7. Richard N. Gardner, *Negotiating Survival: Four Priorities After Rio* (Council on Foreign Relations Press, New York, 1992), p. 1.

8. "14 Incredible Days in June: An Overview of the '92 Global Forum," *Network '92*, No. 18 (Centre for Our Common Future, Geneva, June-July 1992), pp. 8–9.

9. United Nations Environment Programme (UNEP), "Rio Declaration and Forest Princi-

ples" (UNEP, Rio de Janeiro, June 3–14, 1992), introduction.

10. *Ibid.*

11. United Nations Environment Programme (UNEP), "Agenda 21: The United Nations Programme of Action from Rio" (UNEP, Rio de Janeiro, 1992).

12. United Nations Environment Programme (UNEP), Convention on Climate Change (UNEP, Rio de Janeiro, 1992).

13. United Nations Environment Programme (UNEP), Convention on Biological Diversity (UNEP, Rio de Janeiro, 1992), Art. 1, p. 2; Art. 3, p. 4; and Art. 16, p. 9.

14. *Op. cit.* 12, Art. 23, p. 19 and *op. cit.* 13, Art. 36, p. 18.

15. Kathryn G. Sessions, *Institutionalizing the Earth Summit: The United Nations Commission on Sustainable Development*, United Nations Management and Decision-Making Project of the United Nations Association of the United States of America (UNA-USA) Occasional Paper No. 7 (UNA-USA, New York, October 1992), pp. 1–3.

16. *Op. cit.* 11, Ch. 38, Art. 11, p. 275.

17. David E. Pitt, "Finally, the Next Steps: New U.N. Commissioners Pledge Rio Accords Will Be Carefully Monitored," *Earth Times*, Vol. 5, No. 2 (1993), pp. 1 and 16.

18. David E. Pitt, "Who's Who in the Commission," *Earth Times*, Vol. 5, No. 2 (1993), p. 16.

19. Kathryn G. Sessions, Policy Analyst, United Nations Association of the United States of America, Washington, D.C., 1993 (personal communication).

20. Lee A. Kimball, "Institutional Developments," *Yearbook of International Environmental Law*, Vol. 3, Part 2 (Graham & Trotman, Norwell, Massachusetts, 1993), p. 183.

21. Lee A. Kimball, "International Institutions: What Happens after the Rio Conference?" *International Journal of Sustainable Development*, Vol. 1, No. 3 (1992), p. 6.

22. *Op. cit.* 20, pp. 183–184.

23. *Op. cit.* 11, Ch. 38, Art. 18, p. 277.

24. United Nations, "Secretary General Appoints 21-Person Advisory Board on Sustainable Development," July 1, 1993 (press release).

25. *Op. cit.* 15, p. 11.

26. Op. cit. 11, Ch. 38, Art. 11, p. 276 and Art. 42–44, p. 280.

27. United Nations Non-Governmental Liaison Service, "E & D File: Briefings on UNCED Follow-up," Vol. 2, No. 10 (1993), pp. 1–2.

28. Marina Lent, Program Officer, United Nations Non-Governmental Liaison Service, New York, November 1993 (personal communication).

29. *Op. cit.* 11, Ch. 38, Art. 21, p. 277.

30. *Op. cit.* 11, Ch. 38, Art. 24–27, p. 278.

31. United Nations Development Programme (UNDP), Environment and Natural Resources Group, "Capacity 21: Most Often Asked Questions," UNDP, New York, 1993, p. 1.

32. United Nations Development Program (UNDP), "The Current Status of Capacity 21: Notice to Field Offices," UNDP, New York, September 1993, p. 6.

33. *Op. cit.* 11, Ch. 38, Art. 29, p. 279.

34. *Op. cit.* 11, Ch. 37, Art. 11, p. 273.

35. *Op. cit.* 21, p. 182.

36. Lee A. Kimball and William C. Boyd, *Forging International Agreement: Strengthening Inter-Governmental Institutions for Environment and Development* (World Resources Institute, Washington, D.C., 1992), p. 68.

37. The Earth Council, "Maurice Strong Announces Plans for the Earth Council," October 8, 1992 (press release).

38. Natural Resources Defense Council (NRDC), *One Year after Rio, Keeping the Promises of the Earth Summit: A Country-by-Country Progress Report*, Earth Summit Watch (NRDC, New York, 1993), pp. 14–15.

39. *Op. cit.* 36, p. 50.

40. The Committee on International Development Institutions on the Environment has 15 members: the African Development Bank, Arab Bank for Economic Development of Africa, Asian Development Bank, Caribbean Development Bank, Central American Bank for Economic Integration, European Development Fund, European Investment Bank, Food and Agriculture Organization of the United Nations, Inter-American Development Bank, International Fund for Agricultural Development, Nordic Investment Bank, Organization of American States, United Nations Development Programme, International Bank for Reconstruction and Development, and World Food Program.

41. Lee A. Kimball and William C. Boyd, "International Institutional Arrangements for Environment and Development: A Post-Rio Assessment," *Review of the European Community and International Environmental Law*, Vol. 1, No. 33 (1992), pp. 295–306.

42. H. Abaza, Chief, Environment and Economics Unit, United Nations Environment Programme, Nairobi, 1993 (personal communication).

43. Organisation for Economic Co-operation and Development (OECD), *Development Co-operation: 1992 Report* (OECD, Paris, 1992), pp. 3–5, 9–10, and 22.

44. *Op. cit.* 36, pp. 32–33.

45. Dick Thornburgh, Undersecretary General for Administration and Management of the United Nations, "Report to the Secretary-General of the United Nations," United Nations, New York, 1993, n.p.

46. *Op. cit.* 11, Ch. 40, Art. 4, p. 284; Art. 8, p. 285; and Art. 12, p. 286.

47. *Common Responsibility in the 1990s: The Stockholm Initiative on Global Security and Governance*, Stockholm, April 22, 1991, p. 5.

48. David G. Pitt, "Global Commission Sharpens Mission," *The Earth Times: Geneva Report*, Vol. 5., No. 2 (1993), p. 5.

49. David E. Pitt, "Global Governance: Statement of Purpose," *The Earth Times: Geneva Report*, Vol. 5, No. 2 (1993), p. 7.

50. *Op. cit.* 11, Ch. 33, Art. 18, p. 251.

51. The World Bank, *World Development Report, 1992: Development and the Environment* (Oxford University Press, New York, 1992), p. 173.

52. Patti L. Petesch, "After the Earth Summit: The Action Agenda," Overseas Development Council (ODC) Policy Focus No. 4, ODC, Washington, D.C., 1992, p. 4.

53. *Op. cit.* 11, Ch. 33, Art. 13, p. 250.

54. *Op. cit.* 52.

55. *Op. cit.* 43, pp. 25, 77–78, and 111.

56. *Op. cit.* 43, Table V-5, pp. 92–93 and 111.

57. *Op. cit.* 43, Table 28, p. A-28 and Table V-5, p. 92.

58. Raymond F. Mikesell and Larry Williams, *International Banks and the Environment: From Growth to Sustainability, An Unfinished Agenda* (Sierra Club Books, San Francisco, 1992), p. 282.

59. Michael Philips, *The Least Cost Energy Path for Developing Countries: Energy Efficient Investments for the Multilateral Development Banks* (International Institute for Energy Conservation, Washington, D.C., 1991), pp. xv and 1–2.

60. *Op. cit.* 58, p. 281.

61. Portfolio Management Task Force, "Effective Implementation: Key to Development Impact," Report No. 92-195 (The World Bank, Washington, D.C., 1992), p. ii.

62. "Foreign Aid: What Counts toward Sustainable Development and Humanitarian Relief?" Bread for the World Institute discussion paper, Silver Spring, Maryland, 1993, pp. 85–86.

63. *Op. cit.* 58, p. 283.

64. Fahrettin Yagci, Steven Kamin, and Vicki Rosenbaum, "Structural Adjustment Lending: An Evaluation of Program Design," Staff Working Paper No. 735, The World Bank, Washington, D.C., 1985, p. 8.

65. Wilfrido Cruz and Robert Repetto, *The Environmental Effects of Stabilization and Structural Adjustment Programs: The Philippines Case* (World Resources Institute, Washington, D.C., 1992), p. 51.

66. The World Bank, *Restructuring Economies in Distress*, p. 544, quoted in David Reed, "Diverging Views on the Adjustment Debate," in David Reed, ed., *Structural Adjustment and the Environment* (Westview Press, Boulder, Colorado, 1992), p. 22.

67. The World Bank Country Economics Department, *Adjustment Lending and Mobilization of Private and Public Resources for Growth* (The World Bank, Washington, D.C., 1992), pp. 1, 4, and 23.

68. The World Bank and United Nations (U.N.) Development Programme, *Africa's Adjustment and Growth in the 1980s*, p. iii, quoted in United Nations Economic Commission for Africa, *African Alternative Framework to Structural Adjustment Programs for Socioeconomic Recovery and Transformation*, (U.N., New York, 1989), p. 22.

69. United Nations (U.N.) Economic Commission for Africa, *African Alternative Framework to Structural Adjustment Programs for Socio-Economic Recovery and Transformation* (U.N., New York, 1989), pp. 23–26.

70. *Op. cit.* 65, pp. 6–9.

71. *Op. cit.* 65, pp. 67–68.

72. The Nordic United Nations Project, *The United Nations in Development: Reform Issues in the Economic and Social Fields: A Nordic Perspective* (Almquist and Wiksell International, Stockholm, 1991), p. 7.

73. Global Environment Facility, "The Pilot Phase and Beyond," Working Paper Series No. 1, The World Bank, Washington, D.C., 1992, pp. 1–2.

74. *Ibid.*, pp. 8–9, 13, 15, and 18.

75. Global Environment Facility, "Report by the Chairman to the May 1993 Participants' Meeting, Part 1: Main Report," The World Bank, Washington, D.C., 1993, p. 20.

76. David Reed, "The GEF Experience in Perspective," in *The Global Environment Facility: Sharing Responsibility for the Biosphere*, Vol. 2, David Reed, ed. (World Wide Fund for Nature, Washington, D.C., 1993), pp. 18–19.

77. Alexander Wood, "Study 3: The Interim Multilateral Fund for the Implementation of the Montreal Protocol," in *The Global Environment Facility: Sharing Responsibility for the Biosphere*, Vol. 2, David Reed, ed. (World Wide Fund for Nature, Washington, D.C., 1993), pp. 82–85.

78. *Op. cit.* 76, pp. 8–9.

79. *Op. cit.* 13, Art. 11, p. 13.

80. David Reed, ed., *The Global Environment Facility: Sharing Responsibility for the Biosphere*, Vol. 2 (World Wide Fund for Nature, Washington, D.C., 1993), p. 9.

81. *Op. cit.* 73, pp. 12 and 13.

82. *Op. cit.* 76, p. 29.

83. Vandana Shiva, *Global Environment Facility*, Part 3, *Perpetuating Non-Democratic Decision-Making*, United Nations Commission on Economic Development Briefing Paper No.

15 (Third World Network, Penang, Malaysia, 1992), pp. 1–3.

84. World Wide Fund for Nature, *The Southern Green Fund: Views from the South on the Global Environment Facility* (World Wide Fund for Nature, Gland, Switzerland, 1993), pp. 7 and 53.

85. *Op. cit.* 76, p. 30.

86. *Op. cit.* 84, pp. 5–9.

87. David Reed, "Recommendations for Reform," in *The Global Environment Facility: Sharing Responsibility for the Biosphere*, Vol. 2, David Reed, ed. (World Wide Fund for Nature, Washington, D.C., 1993), pp. 35–38.

88. Russell A. Mittermeier and Ian A. Bowles, "The GEF and Biodiversity Convention: Lessons to Date and Recommendations for Future Action," discussion paper, Conservation International, Washington, D.C., 1993, pp. 15–18.

89. Martin Holdgate, Director General, World Conservation Union, Gland, Switzerland, November 11, 1992 (open letter to Union members).

90. Environmental Defense Fund, "Open Letter to the GEF Participants' Meeting on Governance and Replenishment," Rome, March, 1993.

91. *Op. cit.* 83, pp. 1–3.

92. *Op. cit.* 43, pp. 94–95.

93. *Op. cit.* 43, p. 94.

94. *Op. cit.* 11, Ch. 33, Art. 14, p. 250.

95. "IDA and the Tenth Replenishment," World Bank Information Brief No. B.02.4-93, The World Bank, Washington, D.C., 1993, pp. 1–2.

96. Barbara J. Bramble, Director, International Programs, National Wildlife Federation (NWF), statement before the U.S. House of Representatives Subcommittee on International Development, Finance, Trade, and Monetary Policy, *Concerning the Tenth Replenishment of the International Development Association and the Global Environment Facility*, Hearings, May 5, 1993 (NWF, Washington, D.C., 1993), pp. 1–14, and Lori Udall, Staff Attorney, International Program, Environmental Defense Fund (EDF), statement before the U.S. House of Representatives Subcommittee on International Development, Finance, Trade, and Monetary Policy, Concerning the Environmental and Social Impacts of the International Development Association, Hearings, May 5, 1993 (EDF, Washington, D.C., 1993), pp. 2–3.

97. United Nations Development Programme, *Human Development Report, 1992* (Oxford University Press, New York, 1992), p. 84, Box 5.3.

98. *Op. cit.* 47, pp. 12–13.

99. *Op. cit.* 47, p. 12.

100. *Op. cit.* 2, p. 12.

101. Stuart K. Tucker and Lori L. Lylton, "Global Textile and Apparel Trade, A Policy Unraveled," Overseas Development Council (ODC) Policy Focus No. 4 (ODC, Washington, D.C., 1991), n.p., cited in Patti L. Petesch, *North-South Environmental Strategies, Costs, and Bargains* (ODC, Washington, D.C., 1992), pp. 88–89.

102. *Ibid.*, n.p.

103. *Op. cit.* 47, pp. 18–20.

14. National and Local Policies and Institutions

Major international conferences and agreements are trying to point the world toward an environmentally sustainable future. But the effort to reduce environmental pollution and manage resources on a more sustainable basis still remains largely the responsibility of people at the national and local levels.

The situations facing national officials in the 1990s vary greatly. Most industrialized nations have considerable data on environmental pollution and its health effects, whereas many developing nations have little. Some nations have large and vocal public constituencies pressing for environmental improvements; many others have none. Some have a large corps of trained environmental officials, a comprehensive body of environmental law, and the authority to enforce that law; many have laws on paper, but few staff and little enforcement capacity.

Most national leaders are looking for ways to get their economies growing. The urgency of economic growth usually overrides concern about its environmental implications, but in more and more cases, national leaders are aware of the need to reduce pollution and use resources more efficiently while spurring the economy.

In virtually all countries, the question of how best to reduce environmental pollution and nurture resources is controversial. For example, most industrialized countries have relied on the traditional "command and control" approach, wherein national regulations limit pollution primarily through end-of-pipe technologies. This approach has been relatively successful in improving water quality and lowering emissions of conventional air pollutants. It has been less successful in decreasing the volume of solid waste and in managing toxic and hazardous waste.

Leaders of industrialized nations are under considerable pressure to modify this approach, however. International economic competition compels nations to manage pollution in the most cost-effective way, while strained budgets force government managers to reexamine pollution control costs.

But there are strong counterpressures. Many governments, though recognizing that subsidies for natural resources encourage inefficient use, find it difficult to remove subsidies because of political pressure exerted by beneficiaries. And while there is a general consensus among industrialized countries to implement the "polluter pays" principle, the private sector often resists, arguing that imposed higher costs will reduce its ability to compete.

A few industrial countries are beginning to rethink environmental issues in the broader context of sustainable development, for example, encouraging more efficient industrial processes and less resource-intensive consumption. The Netherlands, discussed in more detail later, is the first industrial country to systematically attempt to devise policies that will alter production and consumption patterns and bring that country toward sustainability. Its National Environmental Policy Plan (NEPP) and National Environmental Policy Plan Plus have a goal of sharply reducing the growth of energy and resource use by the year 2000. The Dutch hope to meet this goal partly by persuading industry to change its manufacturing processes.

The situation in developing countries is similar in some respects to that in industrialized countries, but fundamentally different in others. For example, governments in both industrialized and developing countries face competing demands for limited financial resources. In developing countries, however, financial resources are more limited and the pressure to use those resources for economic growth greater. In both industrialized and developing countries responsibility for environmental management may be spread among several institutions with overlapping authority.

Many developing countries have a more limited institutional capacity. They may have shortages of staff, critical skills, and equipment to monitor environmental pollution, and a limited capacity to enforce environmental regulations and establish clear priorities.

To set priorities requires an understanding of the extent and consequences of environmental degradation. Yet most developing countries have little data on the amount of water pollution in their rivers, lakes, and aquifers, and of air pollution in their urban centers. Information on the use of forest and land resources is often outdated, and there may not be much known about the condition of critical ecosystems such as coastal zones or watersheds.

Many developing countries are also undergoing a fundamental economic shift from central planning or protection of domestic producers toward market-oriented reform. Decentralization is reinforced by growing evidence that widespread local participation is critical to the success of any environment/development project. Such change can have important benefits, such as improving energy efficiency, but it poses difficult challenges for environmental managers. Managers at the state or local level may be given greater responsibility, for example, but without additional resources to cope with that responsibility.

This chapter discusses in more detail the experience of the Netherlands, Chile, and Madagascar. Chile is a developing country that in recent years has rapidly shifted to a market economy. It is making a serious effort to identify and cope with environmental problems and, while most of its environmental policies and institutions are relatively new, they demonstrate what can be accomplished by a determined, democratically elected government and its citizenry. Madagascar may well have the most advanced national environmental action plan (NEAP) in Africa. The need for sustainable development seems acute on the island because its problems of population growth and poverty are so severe. Although economic and political obstacles threaten to block the NEAP's progress, this small country's experiences thus far offer several lessons for environmental planners in other countries.

PLANNING FOR THE FUTURE

International donors have increasingly urged developing countries to gather basic information about environmental conditions and trends within their borders and to formulate strategies to deal with problems. By the early 1990s, virtually every country in the world had prepared a national report on its environment; most of the reports were published between 1987 and 1992 (1). (See Table 14.1.) Although they have much in common, these reports do contain some important differences. Many reports are primarily informational in scope: they give the available data and assess the environmental conditions.

In the early 1980s, donors such as the U.S. Agency for International Development (U.S. AID) supported the preparation of country environmental profiles. In effect, these compiled and analyzed information on environmental conditions and trends, described relevant legal and institutional settings, assessed government environmental policies, provided a framework to resolve environment/development conflicts, and proposed policy changes to promote sustainable development. Profiles were produced for about 70 developing countries, mostly in the early 1980s.

Several industrialized countries, notably Canada, Denmark, and the Netherlands, have supported environmental profiles to help the donor country identify ways to incorporate environmental concerns into development assistance to the South.

Many developing countries have begun preparing state-of-the-environment reports to learn more about the environment and help formulate policy. The United Nations Environment Programme supports the preparation of state-of-the-environment reports in several countries, as does the Organization of American States (OAS) and the Japanese Overseas Economic Cooperation Fund (OECF).

Prior to the 1992 United Nations Conference on Environment and Development (UNCED), most developing nations prepared national reports on environmental and development issues.

International nongovernmental organizations (NGOs) have been active in preparing studies that consider a particular issue. For example, the World Conservation Union (formerly the International Union for Conservation of Nature and Natural Resources) (IUCN), has prepared a number of country studies on the conservation of tropical forests, while the World Conservation Monitoring Centre has prepared biodiversity profiles for more than two dozen developing countries.

Other reports put more emphasis on identifying the most urgent environmental issues and preparing plans of action to handle them. Reports include national conservation strategies, which were conceived by IUCN and others in 1980, and NEAPs, which have been promoted by the World Bank since 1987.

National conservation strategies attempt to identify a country's basic resources and the condition of those resources, determine the most urgent environmental needs and assign priorities, and build the financial and institutional capacity to tackle problems. National conservation strategies and related studies are under way

Table 14.1 Environmental Action Plans and Strategies, 1993

Types of Action Plans and Strategies	Africa		Central America and the Caribbean		South America		Asia		Oceania		Total	
	pub[a]	in prep[b]	pub	in prep	pub	in prep	pub	in prep	pub	in prep	pub	in prep
Canada (CIDA) Environmental Strategies	1	3	1	1			3				5	4
Denmark (DANIDA) Environmental Profiles	3						2				5	
Netherlands Environmental Profiles	5	2					3				8	2
United Kingdom/EC/Australia Environmental Synopses	3	28	4			3	2	2		5	5	42
United States (U.S. AID) Country Environmental Profiles	4		11		5		6				26	
United States (U.S. AID) Tropical Forests/ Biodiversity Assessments	10	3	5		3		5	1	6		29	4
CILSS Antidesertification Plans	6										6	
World Bank National Environmental Action Plans	7	11		9		3	2	14			9	37
IUCN National Conservation Strategies	14	3	2	7		3	9	8		2	25	23
IUCN Conservation of Forest Ecosystem Studies	8										8	
WCMC Biological Diversity Profiles	13		1		4		5		1		24	
Tropical Forestry Action Programme	6	21	7	5	6	3	8	5	2	1	29	35
State-of-the-Environment Reports	8	2	2	2	3	2	13	4	1		27	10
UNCED National Report	37	6	8	3	7		22	5	8		82	14
Other Policy, Management, and Environmental Studies	13		3		7		12		1		36	
Total	**138**	**79**	**39**	**31**	**36**	**14**	**92**	**39**	**19**	**8**	**324**	**171**

Source: World Resources Institute (WRI), International Institute for Environment and Development, and the World Conservation Union, *1993 Directory of Country Environmental Studies* (WRI, Washington, D.C., 1992), pp.10–16.
Notes: Country updates or republished revisions are not counted.
a. Pub = published.
b. In prep = in preparation.

in more than 65 countries. Although IUCN originated the concept, many countries, including China and India, have undertaken conservation strategies without IUCN involvement.

National environmental action plans are usually prepared by host country organizations with technical and/or financial assistance from the World Bank. These plans provide a framework to integrate environmental considerations into a nation's overall economic and social development strategy. They usually include proposals for a variety of environmentally related investment projects. By November 1992, NEAPs had been completed in seven countries and about 40 more were in progress.

Canada and the Netherlands have also produced green plans—comprehensive national programs for environmental and resource management. And the Asian Development Bank and others are supporting the preparation of national environmental management plans for many island countries in the South Pacific.

Many other plans are proposed. UNCED's Agenda 21, for example, calls for national sustainable development strategies. National plans are expected as part of two UNCED agreements, the United Nations Framework Convention on Climate Change and the United Nations Convention on Biological Diversity. (See Chapter 8, "Biodiversity," Focus on Convention on Biological Diversity.)

CASE 1: THE NETHERLANDS' PLAN— A GLOBAL FIRST

The Netherlands is one of the first nations to convert the principles of sustainable development into a series of concrete steps. The dramatic decision to embrace these principles came after decades of industrial growth and a gradual buildup of pollution in the na-

tion's air, soil, and water. For nearly a century, the Nuisance Act of 1875 served as the single environmental law in the Netherlands (2). After World War II, the country was racked by the same environmental problems that developed in other industrialized nations. In the early 1970s, the Netherlands took steps to control pollution through specific laws, but nearly two decades later it concluded that these were not sufficiently integrated (3). Some signs of improvement could be seen, for example, there were notable improvements in air quality in Rotterdam. On balance, however, the nation's booming industrial base, which included chemical manufacturing and oil refining, had overwhelmed the regulatory process, and by the mid-1980s the Netherlands ranked among the dirtiest of the industrialized countries (4) (5). (See Box 14.1.)

One symbol of environmental decline was a drop in the population of the country's beloved seals—from roughly 10,000 in 1900 to fewer than 600 in 1991 (6) (7). Between 1950 and 1991, 500 of some 1,400 species of higher plants declined in numbers, and more than 70 were extirpated in the Netherlands; the number of breeding birds fell by one third (8). Other signs of deterioration ranged from acidification and the presence of toxic industrial and agricultural wastes in the soil, air, and groundwater to growing noise and congestion.

The Political and Scientific Context

The Netherlands found inspiration in the 1987 report of the World Commission on Environment and Development, popularly known as the Brundtland Report, which called on nations to rethink environmental and economic goals in terms of sustainable development (9). The Brundtland Report prompted the Dutch to devise a vision of sustainable development that would reduce energy and material consumption, integrate

Box 14.1 The Netherlands: The Role of Size and Location

Located on the North Sea in the deltas formed by three major rivers—the Rhine, Meuse, and Scheldt—the Netherlands is a country largely made by human ingenuity. It maintains a complex system of water management that dates back to the Middle Ages; lakes and marshes have been drained, water rerouted through canals, and land reclaimed from the sea and surrounded by protective dikes. About 30 percent of the Netherlands' entire land mass actually lies below sea level. The country is also highly developed. While vestiges of ecosystems remain, including some 400 nature reserves, many of them are polluted (1) (2).

Roughly 60 percent of the population lives on reclaimed land, whose vulnerability was made very clear during a flood in 1953 (3). This is one reason the Dutch have paid so much attention to the potential impact of global warming, which some scientists believe could speed icecap melting and raise sea levels (4). The Dutch have taken a lead in urging restrictions on the burning of fossil fuel and deforestation, a second cause of warming. While the technology theoretically exists to deal with higher sea levels, the cost would be intolerable, according to a government spokesperson, who says that under the worst global warming scenario, half the country could become uninhabitable (5).

While the Netherlands is responsible for many of its environmental problems, much of its pollution comes from outside its borders (6). For example, one third of the nation's drinking water comes from the Rhine and the Meuse rivers, which carry vast quantities of industrial waste

The Netherlands

from Germany and other countries. The Rhine River basin alone covers some 185,000 square kilometers in more than five countries. One of them is Switzerland, which created environmental havoc in 1986 by flushing "a wave of poison" into the river while fighting a fire that had broken out in a pesticide warehouse. (The following year, the Netherlands and other countries along the Rhine sponsored an action program aimed at restoring the river's ecosystem.) Similarly, the North Sea has been a receptacle for industrial and agricultural wastes such as polychlorinated biphenyls, cadmium, benzene, and lead, which enter it by way of rivers and the air (7).

In 1990, countries bordering the North Sea agreed to cut the toxins going into the air and water by 50 percent or more between 1985 and 1995; dioxins, mercury, cadmium, and lead are slated to be cut 70 percent or more. The agreement also calls for a 50 percent reduction in emissions of

nitrogen and phosphorous. These nutrients cause the excessive growth and heavy use of oxygen by aquatic plants, to the detriment of fish and other species in the shallow waters of the North Sea (8).

Noting its own impact on the environment in the South, the Netherlands' 1992 report to the United Nations Conference on Environment and Development blamed Dutch farmers for importing much of their feed from developing countries. "The Netherlands," it commented, "produces its current agricultural output by exploiting approximately more than twice as much agricultural land outside the country than within the country" (9).

References and Notes

1. H.W. Kroes, ed., *Essential Environmental Information: The Netherlands, 1991* (Ministry of Housing, Physical Planning and Environment, The Hague, 1991), pp. 24 and 26.
2. Ministry of Housing, Physical Planning and Environment (VROM), *Netherlands National Report to UNCED 1992* (VROM, The Hague, 1992), p. 5.
3. *Ibid.*
4. F. Langeweg, *Concern for Tomorrow: A National Environmental Survey, 1985–2010* (National Institute of Public Health and Environmental Protection, Bilthoven, The Netherlands, 1989), p. 44.
5. Hans van Zijst, Counselor for Health and Environment, Royal Netherlands Embassy, Washington, D.C., 1992 (personal communication).
6. *Op. cit.* 2, p. 64.
7. *Op. cit.* 1, pp. 29–38, 45–47, and 244.
8. *Op. cit.* 1; pp. 45–48.
9. *Op. cit.* 2, p. 64.

various aspects of environmental protection, and wed environmental goals to economic policy.

In 1988, the Dutch National Institute of Public Health and Environmental Protection issued its seminal environmental survey, *Concern for Tomorrow*. This not only identified the nation's key environmental problems but also categorized them as local (short-term and generally reversible problems such as noise and some air pollution); regional (such as groundwater pollution); fluvial (systematic and incidental damage to rivers, which carry toxics downstream); continental (border-crossing pollution, resulting in such things as soil acidification and air pollution in other countries), and global (ozone depletion and climate change caused by greenhouse gases) (10).

The report became a best seller in the Netherlands and was responsible for a new era of environmental awareness. The commitment that the nation's leadership had made to this new approach was underscored by Queen Beatrix during her 1988 Christmas message, when she observed, "The Earth is slowly dying, and the inconceivable—the end of life itself—is actually becoming conceivable" (11).

A third report, prepared by the Central Economic Council, found that the national economic impact of new environmental policies would be manageable (12).

These three reports enhanced the bargaining power of the Dutch directorate-general of environment and laid the groundwork for a policy debate (13). The ultimate result of the debate was a strategy for achieving sustainable development, NEPP (14). A subsequent document, NEPP Plus, was adopted by the Dutch cabinet in 1990 to speed up policy implementation (15).

The policy debate began in the summer of 1986 and went through three phases. The first phase, which lasted a year and a half, concentrated on initiating administrative activity essential to the process of developing a plan. The principal participants were midlevel government officials, largely from three ministries: housing, physical planning, and environment; agriculture, nature management, and fisheries; and transport and public works. A large number of working, project, and study groups were set up; only a few officials understood the structures and links that would guide comprehensive data collection. These efforts were relatively free of political pressure, in part because during this period there were frequent personnel changes at the ministries' upper levels (16).

During the next phase, from the spring of 1988 to the beginning of 1989, plan development was simplified and dominated by a relatively small group of senior officials. Their emphasis was on determining the key issues of sustainable development, analyzing various alternatives from an economic perspective, negotiating the contents of the NEPP, and writing the report (17).

In the spring of 1989, while in its final phase, the project became part of political debate, increasingly involving the prime minister and ministries such as finance that had not participated before. By the end of this debate, environmental considerations ranked with full employment and reduction in the budget deficit as cornerstones of Dutch policy development (18).

Diverse interest groups, including four different ministries and various provincial and municipal governments, were involved in policy formation through workshops and hearings at the early stages. Allowing their voices to be heard from the beginning, rather than confronting them with an end product, was a key factor in building consensus for the plan (19).

The NEPP that emerged is an ambitious, action-oriented (some 220 steps are prescribed), and tough document (20) (21). At the outset, it declares that environmental problems are connected and that society must end its practice of making others pay the cost of environmental deterioration—for example, when one generation borrows resources from future generations or one nation prospers at the expense of environmental protection in a less-developed one (22).

One of the NEPP's governing principles is that polluters pay. Where possible, the cost of cleaning up should be assigned to an identifiable individual or group that bears responsibility. As the NEPP Plus explained, this principle boils down to establishing direct regulations that exact the cost of cleanup through specific levies imposed on known polluters (23).

The Dutch government also uses other laws and regulations, including licensing requirements, to achieve its goals. Economic incentives appear in the form of energy and environmental taxes and subsidies for industry to test new ways of doing business.

The general hope is to shift the Netherlands from the command-and-control approach of traditional environmental laws and toward a structure promoting sustainable development through economic incentive, social institutions, and self-regulation. For example, the government has been seeking to negotiate covenants with target groups such as oil refineries that will spell out specific goals and deadlines; by late 1992, 18 covenants were on paper and 12 were in the works (24). Some covenants are expected to specify procedures should the target group fail to meet environmental goals or deadlines. The flexibility of this approach ensures cost-effectiveness. Later on, when covenants are supported by legislation, noncooperative firms will be forced to change. "It's a semivoluntary approach with the understanding that there's a stick behind our backs," explains one government spokesperson (25) (26) (27). Every year, the Dutch environmental ministry issues a new four-year plan. The business community is invited to participate in its development, in the hope that such participation will prod individual companies toward more enlightened practices. As Dutch Environmental Minister Hans Alders has observed, however, "The problem is that the government expects concrete results, and that it would rather see them today than tomorrow. . . . It would be an illusion to think this will be easy" (28).

The NEPP's Overall Goals

The NEPP broadly defines sustainable development as meeting these difficult, long-range objectives: the consumption of no more energy than can be recovered from the sun, the treatment of all waste as raw material, and the promotion of "high-quality" products—products that last, can be repaired, and are suitable for recycling. Because these goals cannot be met in one generation, the NEPP's immediate emphasis is on incremental improvements (29).

Some of the improvements themselves are ambitious. Agricultural chemicals, for example, are not simply to be regulated; the use of certain toxic compounds is to be slashed 50 to 70 percent (30). Consumption of energy and raw materials is expected to be reduced drastically, and most emissions are targeted for an 80 to 90 percent cut before the year 2010 (31). Specific goals include stabilizing carbon dioxide (CO_2) emissions at the 1989–90 level (estimated at 182 megatons CO_2/year) by 1994–95, and reducing emissions to below that level by the year 2000; a phaseout of chlorofluorocarbons by 1998; lowered emission ceilings on sulfur dioxide and other causes of acidification; stepped-up manure treatment to reduce eutrophication (the harmful loading of soil and water with dissolved nutrients such as phosphates); more recycling and less consumption of raw material; noise control; and reduced use of water (32) (33). (See Figures 14.1, 14.2, and 14.3.)

Previously, industry was free to pass along the cost of pollution and resources to future generations and society at large. One new goal is "integrated life-cycle management," a novel concept aimed at reducing overall resource consumption by closing loops in the use of energy and materials (34). (See Chapter 12, "Industry," Toward Sustainable Practices.)

The NEPP projects a government expenditure equivalent to U.S. $6 billion between 1990 and 1994 (this expenditure is above and beyond the cost of implementing previous environmental programs). To help cover the cost, the average Dutch household is now paying the equivalent of $20 a month in new taxes (35). Industry ultimately will pay many additional costs. For example, Royal Dutch Shell has committed an investment of more than $1.6 billion between 1993 and 1997 to help renovate a refinery in Rotterdam. The goal of this renovation is to reduce pollution and create cleaner products (36). In 1988, the private sector spent $1.9 billion on environmental programs, while the public sector invested $2.9 billion; by 1996, the cost to the private sector will top that of the public sector (37).

Figure 14.1 Greenhouse Gas Emission Index, the Netherlands, 1980–91

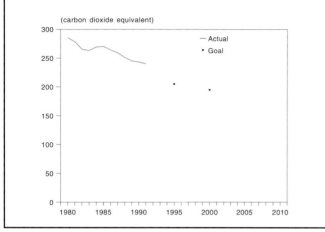

Source: Albert Adriaanse, *Environmental Policy Performance Indicators* (Sdu Uitgeverij Koninginnegracht, The Hague, 1993), pp. 20 and 24.
Note: The Greenhouse Gas Emissions Index was calculated by estimating the emissions of carbon dioxide from fossil fuels, methane—mostly from agricultural activities—nitrogen oxides from combustion processes, and chlorofluorocarbons and halons. These were each weighted by their warming potential compared to carbon dioxide to estimate their carbon dioxide equivalent warming.

Figure 14.2 Eutrophication Index, the Netherlands, 1980–91

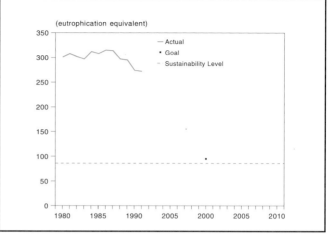

Source: Albert Adriaanse, *Environmental Policy Performance Indicators* (Sdu Uitgeverij Koninginnegracht, The Hague, 1993), pp. 39 and 44.
Note: The Eutrophication Index uses emissions of phosphorus (in the form of phosphate) and nitrogen (calculated from fertilizer and manure use as well as waste dumping), weighted by their natural proportion in the Dutch environment.

Target Groups

The Dutch environmental bureaucracy has identified primary target groups that will be largely responsible for achieving the nation's strategic plan (38).

Agriculture

While agriculture contributes less than 5 percent to the Netherlands' gross domestic product, it generates about a quarter of Dutch exports (39). (See Chapter 15, "Basic Economic Indicators," Table 15.1.) The Netherlands cultivates potatoes, tomatoes, and flowering bulbs, among other things, for export, and it also raises chickens, cows, and pigs, sustaining more farm animals (120 million) than people (15 million) (40). Livestock management is highly efficient (the Netherlands boasts one of the world's highest milk yields per cow) if environmentally hazardous (41). Agriculture's contribution to the nation's pollution rose from 20 percent to 35 percent between 1982 and 1992. Heavy use of pesticides, herbicides, and fertilizer are to blame, along with production of manure that outpaces the country's ability to process it (42). Some 85 percent of the nitrogen and phosphorus applied annually in the Netherlands comes from animal manure and fertilizer (43) (44).

One result is eutrophication, which can harm plant life, drinking water, and ironically, cattle and crops (45). Furthermore, applications of ammonia fertilizer have contributed to soil acidification. A new soil protection law and subsequent regulations, including manure quotas, went into effect in 1987. With adoption of the NEPP in 1989, the agricultural sector was asked to cut ammonia emissions to 30 percent of the 1980 level by the year 2000 (46). Farmers were called on to install manure processing plants, a solution described by one 1991 government report as "proceeding very slowly" and "relatively expensive"; manure surpluses have

been projected at 5.5 million tons in 1995 and 7 million tons in 2000 (47).

The government estimates that farm land receives 21 million kilograms of active ingredients in pesticide every year, with 4 to 5 million kilograms ending up in the air, soil, and groundwater. The goal for the year 2000 is to cut pesticide use to half of 1985 levels (48).

Industry

Dutch industry has made some strides in controlling air and water emissions since the mid-1970s. Emissions of heavy metals and organic micropollutants to surface water fell 50 to 90 percent, for example, between 1975 and 1985 (49). But the NEPP envisions much tougher environmental protection, which it hopes to achieve by collaborating with industry and giving it some flexibility in achieving specific goals.

The chemical industry is the focus of special concern, not only because it is responsible for much of the country's visible air and water pollution, but because it has already made enormous progress in pollution control, leaving the hardest, most expensive improvements for implementation before 2015. Among the NEPP's goals are reducing the risk of chemical accidents; cutting emissions of certain substances by 50 percent, with greater reductions for benzene, chloromethane, dichloroethane, copper, and cadmium; and finding alternatives for the chlorofluorocarbons used by industry and for certain pesticides. (See Figure 14.4.) Chemical manufacturers have been asked to work with government to develop integrated production cycles, which would reduce waste and pollution (50).

Transportation

To discourage commuting by car, the government has cut the travel tax deduction and raised excise taxes on

Figure 14.3 Acidification Index, the Netherlands, 1980–91

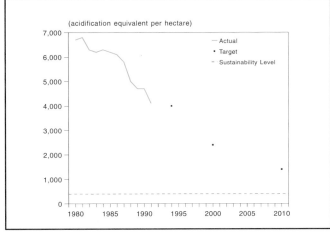

(acidification equivalent per hectare)

— Actual
• Target
– Sustainability Level

Source: Albert Adriaanse, *Environmental Policy Performance Indicators* (Sdu Uitgeverij Koninginnegracht, The Hague, 1993), pp. 33 and 36.
Note: The Acidification Index was calculated using the three main substances responsible for acid deposition in The Netherlands, sulfur dioxide, nitrogen oxides, and ammonia. The index is the number of acid equivalents deposited per hectare per year (from both domestic and foreign sources) and converts these substances to an acidification equivalent corresponding to 32 grams (g.) of sulfur dioxide, 46 g. of nitrogen dioxide, and 17 g. of ammonia.

Figure 14.4 Toxic and Hazardous Pollution Index, the Netherlands, 1980–91

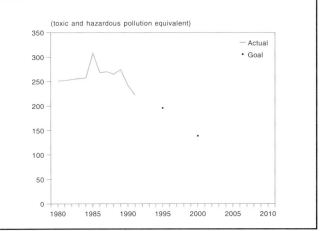

(toxic and hazardous pollution equivalent)

— Actual
• Goal

Source: Albert Adriaanse, *Environmental Policy Performance Indicators* (Sdu Uitgeverij Koninginnegracht, The Hague, 1993), pp. 47 and 53.
Note: The Toxic and Hazardous Waste Index was calculated by using the emissions of the most hazardous substances in three main categories (pesticides, other wastes of high priority, and radioactive substances) weighted according to their toxicity and residence time in the environment.

gasoline and diesel oil. Gasoline already costs more than U.S. $1 per liter, yet sales are as high as ever (51).

To control traffic in Amsterdam, portions of downtown have been made off limits to cars, and commuters have been encouraged to use bikes and streetcars. The government has pledged new funds to improve the public transit system, and land use planning is expected to further curb automobile use (52) (53) (54).

The Energy Sector

The NEPP asks power plants to make improvements that would help prevent acidification. This could require a covenant aimed at cutting emissions as well as strengthened licensing standards at the provincial level. Utilities have been encouraged to explore the possibility of burning waste for energy (55).

The NEPP envisions increased commitment to energy conservation, renewable energy, and waste recycling—goals the government is exploring not only with domestic energy producers but with other European Community countries as well.

Construction

The construction industry is expected to pay "explicit attention" to the environmental impact of building methods and products with an eye toward reducing the use of nonrenewable material and tropical forest products. Builders have been asked to recycle twice as much construction and demolition waste, and to raise awareness of environmental issues among architects and homeowners (56).

Consumers and Retail Trade

While environmental awareness is acute in the Netherlands as a whole, the NEPP points out that individual citizens want "bigger houses and greater mobility." In-

creasingly, consumers are being asked to adopt more environmentally conscious ways. Among the NEPP's goals by the year 2000 are to have consumers improve waste handling. There will be separate collection of organic waste, used batteries, certain chemical wastes, tin, glass, textiles, and paper, and 50 percent of the organic household waste will be composted. Among other improvements in household energy efficiency, electricity consumption will be kept at 1985 levels. The growth of passenger kilometers (using 1985 as a baseline) will be cut by 15 percent, and the use of solvents will be cut by 50 percent (57).

The retail trade industry is expected to step up efforts to inform consumers about the relative environmental merits of various products, to stock more environmentally friendly products, to assist with recycling programs, and to discourage suppliers from using wasteful packaging or manufacturing environmentally unfriendly products (58).

The Waste Sector

The NEPP calls for improved, industrywide planning and coordination of incineration, dumping, composting, and reuse. Waste will be separated more aggressively, and waste incineration and dumping will meet new pollution control standards (59).

Water supply boards are expected to improve production methods, help devise ways to store chemically suspect sludge, pay more attention to drinking water quality, and encourage consumers to conserve. Sewage treatment plants are to reduce levels of phosphorus and nitrogen in the water and to stop the flow of polluted water into certain areas. And finally, firms that specialize in pollution control have been asked to focus less on filtration and emission controls and more on sustainable development—that is, structural changes in industry and society that will provide a reduction in the areas of pollution production and resource consumption (60).

Finally, the NEPP appeals to research institutions, educational establishments, unions, and nongovernmental organizations to raise the public's environmental awareness (61).

Building Support

In addition to measures to educate the public about the need for sustainable development and lifestyle changes, the Netherlands has tried to avoid showdowns between government regulators and industry by bringing together different factions and attempting to achieve consensus. The leadership of Prime Minister Ruud Lubbers, not to mention the fact that the largest share of the initial cost of implementing the NEPP's goals will be paid by the government, has been a big help in this effort (62) (63) (64) (65).

Because the deadline for many of the NEPP's objectives is generous—25 years or one generation—general support has not been hard to gather (66). But meeting the staggered deadlines between 1990 and 2010 will be difficult, and few underestimate the daunting economic and technological challenges that lie ahead. Politically, the NEPP faces challenges as well. Because the Netherlands does a great deal of business overseas—three fifths of the gross domestic product is earned through exports—there is the issue of international trade and competition (67). Some Dutch industrial and agricultural enterprises may be put at a disadvantage if asked to meet environmental requirements that are not imposed on their foreign competition. An example is a proposed tax on fuel, based on its carbon dioxide content, which would hurt Dutch industry if it were not imposed throughout the European Community.

Many of the ordained steps could be painful for industry and consumers alike, raising serious questions about how quickly and effectively the nation's environmental goals will be attained. In early 1992, some corporations reportedly threatened to withdraw from the Netherlands rather than accept proposed energy and environmental levies on the use of such things as fossil fuel, groundwater, and pesticides (68). The citizenry, although it is largely supportive of the country's strong environmental stance, nonetheless maintains more cars per square kilometer than any other country and has resisted calls to give them up—despite the nation's superb system of mass transit and such punishing disincentives as a 45 percent sales tax on automobiles (69) (70) (71). And among all European nations, the Dutch rank first in the amount of commercial energy consumed per person. (See Chapter 21, "Energy and Materials," Table 21.2.)

Dutch farmers have been slow to change from artificial fertilizer and pesticides to integrated pest management and low-input farming techniques (72). Because the Netherlands is a major exporter of agricultural goods, they are understandably concerned about being able to maintain their competitive position in the international market.

The Netherlands' environmental NGOs, which generally favor even tougher positions than some of those that have been adopted by the NEPP, do not believe industry will shut down operations overnight rather than comply with enlightened environmental management. As one environmental activist explained, the Netherlands has "industrial peace" as well as a highly educated work force that would be difficult to replace (73). Yet some business leaders say that over the long term, the rising cost of doing business may force them to invest overseas even while maintaining operations in the Netherlands (74).

Despite these reservations, there remains widespread support for the NEPP among the general public and the business community.

CASE 2: ENVIRONMENTAL PLANNING IN CHILE

With annual economic growth averaging more than 6 percent between 1987 and 1991 and reaching 10 percent in 1992, Chile has become by far the most vibrant economy of Latin America (75) (76). Success, however, has not come without significant cost to the country's natural resource base and environment.

Unlike the Netherlands, Chile entered the 1990s lacking both a coherent body of environmental law and a central environmental authority (77). The cavalier approach to pollution control and conservation that had characterized the dictatorship of General Augusto Pinochet began to change under the democratic government of President Patricio Aylwin, who took office in 1990. Along with a concerted effort to document and control environmental problems, there has been an emphasis on the need to decentralize responsibility for the enforcement of the country's environmental laws and regulations. Meanwhile, not only is the economy growing but so is the influence of Chile's NGOs, which have played a key role in raising environmental awareness in the country. (See Box 14.2.)

At the very beginning of his administration, President Aylwin created an interministerial advisory commission to formulate and coordinate environmental policy (78). This commission and its technical secretariat, together known as CONAMA (Comisión Nacional del Medio Ambiente), have become a focal point for a nation that is now attempting to broaden its understanding of the ways that human activity affects the environment and identify ways to mitigate the damage without sacrificing goals for economic development. The concept of sustainable development is receiving support from the highest levels of government. This was expressed by President Aylwin himself in a speech to the Chilean National Congress: "We believe that true development entails the conservation of nature and [enhances] the quality of human life, and therefore growth ought to occur in such a way that it does not harm the environment" (79).

Impacts of Rapid Economic Growth

Chile is long and narrow (4,300 kilometers north to south and about 160 kilometers wide on average), with the Andes Mountains forming the eastern border and the Pacific Ocean the western. The country's climate and terrain shift dramatically from the northern part, primarily desert, down through temperate regions and

Box 14.2   Chile: Raising Public Awareness

The roots of Chile's most current resolve to curtail environmental pollution can be traced back to the days of the Pinochet regime when a group of academics formed a nongovernmental organization, the Center for Environmental Research and Planning (CIPMA). At a time when citizens were shut out of most decisionmaking, CIPMA became a tool for raising public awareness and delicately tapping Chile's democratic potential. Being an environmental group, CIPMA attracted supporters from the entire political spectrum, according to its president, Guillermo Geisse. And because it emphasized the scientific aspects of environmentalism, CIPMA was less vulnerable to censorship by the military regime, which gave no priority to environmental matters.

In 1983, the group began holding national meetings every three years; the most recent, convened in 1992, reportedly attracted 800 participants. While CIPMA has remained nonpartisan, it links conser-

Chile

vation to economic development and social equity. According to Geisse, "To conserve we have to grow, and to grow we have to conserve."

Although in the 1980s the government was reluctant to crack down on industrial pollution, some producers were persuaded to upgrade their environmental

standards, a process to which CIPMA contributed significantly. And when democracy returned to Chile, public support for the environment was strong enough to speed the adoption of new policies. Meanwhile, other nongovernmental organizations, notably the National Committee for the Defense of Flora and Fauna, a large entity whose main focus is preservation, lent their support to the environmental cause.

The linking of economic, social, and environmental goals has enabled Chile to build sustainable development policy. For its effort Chile has attracted widespread support: in 1993, for example, CIPMA received about half of its funding from organizations and businesses in Chile and about half from sources in the United States, the Netherlands, and Sweden.

Source: Guillermo Geisse, President, Center for Environmental Research and Planning, Santiago, Chile, 1993 (personal communication).

then on to a southern third that is so cold and wet as to discourage habitation.

Like many Latin American countries Chile is a former Spanish colony, but unlike some, it has a strong democratic tradition (Pinochet's military rule was an anomaly). The development of a manufacturing sector has helped urbanize the population and has contributed to economic growth that is the envy of Latin America. (See Chapter 17, "Land Cover and Settlements," Table 17.2.) Roughly half of Chile's families still live in poverty, but literacy rates are high (80) (81). (See Chapter 16, "Population and Human Development," Table 16.5.).

Chile's economy relies heavily on exploitation of natural resources—mining, farming, forestry, and fishing. More recently, economic growth has been spurred by the development of a solid industrial base geared toward adding value to natural resources and making them export products. Both exploitation and exportation, as well as the evolution of the Chilean economy over the last two decades, are key to understanding the pressing need to address environmental matters.

Mineral Industry

Mining is still Chile's dominant economic activity. Coal, saltpeter, and finally copper have fueled growth for many years. Diversification through the extraction of gold, silver, and molybdenum is a more recent development. Valued at $4.4 billion in 1991, exports of mineral products account for roughly half of the country's total exports and are expected to increase (82) (83).

Over the last two decades, the mining sector has grown significantly. Chile is the world's largest producer and exporter of copper (84). The government mining sector alone doubled copper production from 600,000 metric tons in 1980 to 1,200,000 in 1990 (85). (See Figure 14.5.)

CODELCO, the state-owned copper company, owns about one quarter of Chile's mines, produces about three quarters of its copper, and is one of the nation's most egregious polluters (86).

Flora and fauna have been seriously damaged in the coastal area near Chañaral because of the discharge of tailings into the Rio Salado by CODELCO's Salvador mining installations. This problem resulted in the first citizen-sponsored environmental litigation in Chile. The courts finally ordered CODELCO to cease the discharge of tailings and invest $21 million in cleanup (87).

As a whole, the mining sector is Chile's most significant source of industrial contamination, polluting both urban and rural environments. Sulfur dioxide and arsenic contamination at smelter sites is a serious issue for workers and nearby residents (88).

Agricultural Sector

Over the last 15 years, most agricultural development has been driven by agroindustry, specifically the production of fresh fruit for export. This subsector increased its share of total agricultural exports from 36 percent in 1970 to over 70 percent after 1988 (89). In 1991, Chile was responsible for more than 14 percent of world exports of fresh fruit grown in temperate climates (grapes, apples, and pears topped the list) (90). It exported $1 billion worth of fruit in 1992. In addition, Chile is now the third largest supplier of wine to the United States (91) (92).

Along with intensified production has come more extensive use of agricultural chemicals. Between 1980 and 1991, Chile's pesticide imports increased 150 percent, from $20 million to $50 million, and fertilizer consumption showed a similar rate of increase (93). Agricultural chemicals in soil runoff have contaminated water supplies. Various agricultural and industrial

Figure 14.5 Chile's Copper Mining, 1970–91

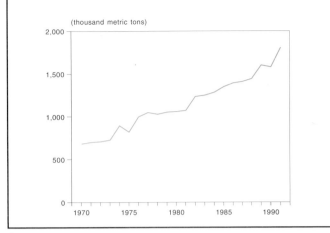

Sources:
1. Metallgesellschaft Aktiengesellschaft, *Metallstatistik, 1970–80* (Metallgesellschaft Aktiengesellschaft, Frankfurt, Germany, 1981), p. 30.
2. World Bureau of Metal Statistics, *World Metal Statistics* (World Bureau of Metal Statistics, London, 1992), pp. 23 and 26.

techniques have had other adverse effects, among them soil erosion, desertification, flooding, water salinization, and the contamination of irrigation water (94). Poor disposal of liquid and solid waste from the use of agricultural chemicals is causing health problems that are compounded by mine wastes (95).

Forestry Sector

Between 1974 and 1990, forestry activity grew as a percentage of gross national product from 4.8 percent to 7.5 percent. Two processes account for this rapid expansion: the planting of exotic species such as eucalyptus in areas where poor agricultural practices had rendered the soil useless for other purposes, and more recently, converting native forests into plantations for exotic species (96) (97).

In 1991, exports by the forestry sector and related industries were valued at $750 million, accounting for 8 percent of total exports (98). While most forestry revenues are generated by pine trees, native forest species are being harvested for export at a rapid rate; the most common product is chipped wood (99). Exports grew from 0.2 million cubic meters in 1986 to 4.5 million cubic meters in 1991 (100). Overall, between 1980 and 1990, the number of forestry exporters increased from 253 to 589, the number of products from 54 to 350, and the number of markets from 49 to 72 countries in the five continents (101).

Of Chile's 34 million hectares of territory suitable for forestry only, 11 million are classified as sustainable-yield production forest and 23 million as protection forest. All but 25 percent of the production forest (2.7 million hectares) has been destroyed, and more than half of the protection forest (13 million hectares) has been cleared. Most of the cleared areas suffer some degree of erosion (102). The government subsidizes reforestation by paying 75 to 95 percent of plantation costs in treeless areas. In some cases, however, clear-cut land is turned into pine tree plantations and the native spe-

cies are lost (103). Plantations are more susceptible to fire and typically require heavy pesticide use (104).

Chile is also a major exporter of industrial wood and paper (105). These industries discharge a large quantity of effluent, which contributes to both soil and water contamination; air is contaminated by gases and other harmful substances emitted from the plants (106).

Fishing Industry

For decades, Chile has benefited from one of the longest, richest stretches of coastline in the world. The coastal ecosystem supports a seemingly inexhaustible supply of fish, crustaceans, and molluscs. (See Chapter 10, "Water," The Humboldt Current Upwelling System.) In 1991, exports of fish and fish products earned the equivalent of more than $1 billion (107). Between 1978 and 1989, as fishing techniques grew more technologically sophisticated and the government maintained a laissez-faire approach to the conservation of natural resources, the fishing industry enjoyed an annual growth rate of 9 percent (108). The average annual catch in 1989–91 was 5.9 million metric tons, double the average annual catch between 1979 and 1981. (See Figure 14.6 and Chapter 22, "Water," Table 22.5.) More than 90 percent of this catch was harvested by large vessels for sale overseas (109).

This growth in yield meant immediate economic gains for some but had negative long-term ecological and economic implications. According to one calculation, a sustainable maximum harvest would have been 3.5 million metric tons, and the average size and age of the catch seemed to indicate overfishing (110). Having invested in large, technologically superior vessels, however, the fishing industry was reluctant to reduce its take, despite the long-term prognosis.

Meanwhile, parallel advances were made in aquaculture, with some 38,000 metric tons of salmon produced in 1990, also mostly for export (111). Chile produced some 46,000 tons of salmon in 1992, making it the world's second largest producer (112). Against a backdrop of concern over future supplies of fish in the wild, aquaculture presented its own problems, including the displacement of native species and the contamination of some water supplies (113).

Chile's coastal bounty is likely to be decreased by several factors. There are virtually no controls on the dumping of industrial waste and sewage into rivers that empty into the ocean. The pollution flows from cities, mines, farms, and factories, threatening valuable coastal resources and marring beaches used by tourists and others (114). According to a 1988 report, two of the most polluted coastal areas, near the cities of Valparaiso and Concepción, annually receive some 244.4 million cubic meters of industrial discharge, chiefly from copper mines, cellulose and paper factories, fish meal and fish oil facilities, and oil refineries. Nationwide, Chile dumps 709 million cubic meters of domestic waste into coastal waters each year (115).

Industrialization and Human Settlements

Among the costs of shifting from a socialist regime to a free-market, export-oriented economy has been mounting industrial pollution, which affects air and water quality and public health (116).

The lack of effective sewage treatment in Chile's urban areas alone poses significant environmental and public health risks. About 86 percent of Chile's population lives in urban areas, with the overwhelming concentration—4.4 million people, out of a total population of 13.2 million—in metropolitan Santiago, the nation's capital and largest city (117). Rivers and an open canal running through Santiago carry untreated sewage, and the contaminated water is used for irrigation during summer months. When the affected crops include vegetables and fruits that are eaten raw, it can lead to outbreaks of typhoid and cholera (118).

Santiago's air pollution is a serious problem. (See Figure 14.7.) The sprawling city, located at the foot of the Andes, is boxed in by mountains on three sides. It often sits under a thick blanket of smog created by vehicle exhaust, dust from unpaved roads and eroded hillsides, and industrial facilities (119). As often as one day out of six during the winter, air quality reaches critical levels. Fine particulate matter is a prominent public health problem, with fumes from diesel buses and traffic congestion in general contributing their part. The Pinochet regime's hands-off philosophy led, among other things, to the deregulation of public transportation. When the public sector bus monopoly ended, bus operators moved toward cheaper buses that pollute more (120) (121).

Enacting Environmental Policies

Because Santiago is such a visible symbol of environmental degradation, it has become a focus of public and political concern. A special autonomous commission was created to tackle air pollution there, and in early 1991 Chile took 2,600 aging, polluting buses off the streets. Other reforms include tougher emissions standards for new buses, limits on the kinds of buses that operate downtown, and pavement on once dusty streets (122). Furthermore, to reduce industrial emissions, companies in the Santiago area are now allowed to trade pollution permits. This experiment in the use of economic incentives, too new to evaluate, gives each company a pollution ceiling; any company that reduces its emissions can sell its unused "pollution rights" to a company that sees this option as more economical than investing in controls (123).

The Aylwin administration has also addressed exploitation of marine resources by enacting a new fishing law aimed at curbing overfishing of certain species. The result of sensitive negotiations with the industry, the law went into effect in 1990. As in the case of pollution control, the new fishing law is an important component of Chile's evolving approach to environmental problems, namely the use of economic incentives to change behavior (124).

The government has also resorted to issuing presidential decrees aimed at controlling such specific problems as sulfur dioxide emissions (125). It is credited with halting at least one major wood chip project in a native forest (126). Located in southern Chile and known as Terra Nova, the project is on hold while its

Figure 14.6 Chile's Total Marine Fish Catch, 1970–91

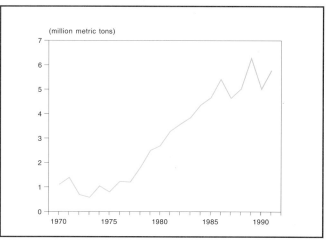

Source: Food and Agriculture Organization of the United Nations (FAO), *Fishstat-PC*, on diskette (FAO, Rome, 1992).

merits are debated (127). Though environmental assessments have yet to become institutionalized, it is becoming standard practice for public agencies to demand them, especially in the mining industry and public works (128). One assessment, for example, led to efforts aimed at protecting the rare Chilean Conure parrot when a dam project threatened its habitat (129).

Institutionalizing Change

When President Aylwin took office, Chile had environmental rules and regulations, but they were fragmented, issues were addressed exclusively from a sectoral perspective, and existing policy and legislation focused on just a few areas such as forestry and fishing. Several laws assigned specific responsibility to a series of sectoral agencies that lacked both a comprehensive perspective of the environment and common guiding principles. Lack of coordination, ambiguity, and duplication of effort were the main features of a weak environmental management structure (130).

Along with the restoration of democracy in Chile came the view that there is no contradiction between economic development and environmental conservation. Indeed, as some government officials have pointed out, "If development is not sustainable, it cannot be called development" (131).

Experience in Latin America has shown that concentrating all environmental policymaking and implementation in one agency or ministry with scarce resources is likely to render the institution powerless in the face of the formidable challenges that it will inevitably confront (132). Thus, rather than setting up an environmental ministry, the Aylwin administration settled on the idea of a coordinating body, CONAMA, which is expected to strengthen public sector capabilities, carry out needed policy research, frame legislation, and create the system under which the environmental impact of proposed projects can be assessed (133).

The philosophy behind the coordinating body is that the environment is not a sector per se but a phenome-

Figure 14.7 Trends in Number of Days of Unhealthy Air, Santiago, 1989–92

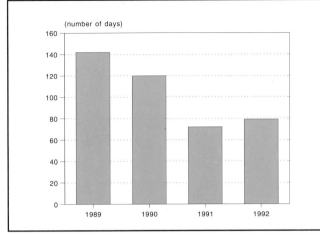

Source: Comisión Nacional del Medio Ambiente (CONAMA), unpublished data (CONAMA, Santiago, Chile, July 1993).
Note: Unhealthy air includes air quality classified as bad, critical, or dangerous.

non that permeates all human activities. Therefore, environmental issues must be approached comprehensively at the highest level. The current government has also recognized the danger of depriving agencies of their specific environmental mandates and concentrating them into a single body: agencies would abandon the responsibility of curbing the adverse environmental effects of their respective sector's activities (134).

In response to this concern, CONAMA's political direction has been given to a committee integrated by various ministries, among them economy, education, public works, agriculture, mining, housing, and transport. Each ministry has a unit responsible for addressing environmental issues in its purview, according to the policies set forth by CONAMA. In accordance with Chile's commitment to decentralization, regional environmental commissions known as COREMAs have been established. COREMAs are responsible for developing environmental plans and programs that reflect particular regional needs and are in accordance with CONAMA's overall environmental policy (135).

The Role of Environmental Legislation

CONAMA, which spent its early days defining its mission and struggling for a degree of independence, assumed the task of reviewing more than 2,000 Chilean laws that relate to the environment. It created a regulatory framework for dealing with problems through a comprehensive law that is expected to be enacted in February 1994 (136) (137) (138).

CONAMA and other institutions involved in the process of creating a legal environmental framework were confronted with a major challenge: reconciling the need to continue profiting from the exploitation of natural resources while maintaining sustainable yields (in fishing, forestry, and farming) and controlling pollution. The environmental law they drafted has four main objectives:

1. To guarantee the constitutional right of all Chileans to live in a clean environment;

2. To create the institutions that enable government to address existing problems and prevent new ones;

3. To establish the means for implementing a policy geared toward protection of natural resources and preservation of biodiversity; and

4. To provide a general framework for legislation relevant to individual sectors (139).

Underlying these four objectives is a series of principles of which the most important are as follows:

■ *Prevention.* Rules and regulations should aim at avoiding environmental problems—through environmental education and scientific research; environmental assessments for projects expected to have a significant environmental impact; management plans for renewable natural resources; preventive plans for areas where contamination threatens to surpass established limits; and a rule concerning individual responsibility, mandating that economic sanctions will apply to anyone damaging the environment.

■ *Polluters must pay.* Businesses must incorporate in their production budgets all pollution-prevention investments. The cost of implementing decontamination plans will be paid by polluters; only in critical cases will the government subsidize the process.

■ *Participation.* Because all Chileans have a stake in environmental protection, CONAMA and the COREMAs have provisions for citizen participation. CONAMA's consultative council will include two representatives from the academic community, two from business, two from labor, and two from NGOs.

■ *Gradualism.* Not all problems are to be addressed at once. Priorities must be established through consensus, and laws and regulations must be created—or adapted—to respond to the most pressing issues facing each sector or natural resource (140).

Ultimately, it appears, Chile's environmental policy and regulatory framework will combine a traditional command-and-control approach—involving, for example, American-style laws and regulations to control specific pollutants and processes—and a market-based approach that uses economic incentives to encourage sound environmental decisions. Suggesting that both approaches have merit, a 1992 World Bank report pointed out that regulations are needed when access to air, water, forests, and fisheries is open and uncontrolled, and when critical aspects of public health are at stake, while at the same time, economic incentives such as tradable pollution permits can be effective in a growth economy (141).

Gathering Support

Commitment to sustainable development, as reflected in Chile's 1992 report to UNCED, has helped attract international support for the nation's environmental policies and institutions. The international aid community, including the World Bank, U.S. AID, and the Inter-American Development Bank, has supported various projects designed to help Chile incorporate environmental and social costs in its market economy.

Projects funded by the Inter-American Development Bank have advanced air and water pollution control in Santiago (142). In 1989, in the context of fostering democratic institutions in Chile, U.S. AID launched a program aimed at supporting public and private institutions working on environmental issues (143). Since then, U.S. AID has focused on helping CONAMA fulfill its catalytic role in environmental policymaking, planning, and management. U.S. AID has sponsored several of CONAMA's initiatives, including development of a system for tracking environmental indicators; a series of workshops that led to the publication of a two-volume environmental atlas identifying major environmental problems in the country's 13 regions; and a second series of workshops that helped raise CONAMA's profile and establish environmental policy (144). Created with the help of a team of specialists from Universidad Católica de Chile in Santiago, the atlas's success encouraged CONAMA to begin work on a state of the environment report which should be published by 1994.

As the country moves toward more sophisticated environmental protection, it has strong public support but faces a number of social and institutional barriers. These include a dearth of environmental professionals, lack of information about industrial pollution, and the absence of clear institutional authority for pollution monitoring and control (145). To help address these problems, the World Bank provided CONAMA with an $11.5 million loan in 1992. Among other things, the loan will boost CONAMA's technical secretariat, support the development of an information base, provide environmental assessment training at the national level, and fund environmental projects in the mining, forestry, and industrial sectors (146) (147).

Public spending on the environment was five to six times higher in 1992 than in the 1980s, according to the business organization Amcham Chile (148). In total, the Chilean government expects to spend the equivalent of $32.8 million to establish an institutional framework for managing environmental protection and natural resource conservation and controlling specific problems (149). The private sector has dramatically increased spending as well. To cope with toxic waste alone, major industrial companies are investing an estimated $100 million per year (150).

Free Trade and the Environment

At this time the potential impact of a free trade agreement expected to be negotiated with the United States is unclear. While some have argued that increased trade and investment would set back Chile's environmental goals, others believe an agreement would elevate environmental standards and controls (151). Referring to an ongoing debate among Latin American countries, Chile's ambassador to the OAS, Heraldo Muñoz, remarked, "Some say the more free trade and privatization, the worse it will be for the environment because the desire for profits will predominate." He observed, however, that some of the most industrialized, free-market nations also have the most advanced environmental regulations (152).

Chile's concern with the environmental variable increased when Mexico was required by the United States to sign side agreements involving labor rights and environmental standards in the North American Free Trade Agreement. Chilean officials have complained that there is a danger in making the environment another kind of nontariff barrier to free trade (153), while pointing to the progress they have made in terms of rewriting their environmental laws to require that new mines and industrial plants live up to stiffer standards than the old ones (154).

CASE 3: MADAGASCAR—PIONEERING THE PLANNING PROCESS IN AFRICA

In 1987, Madagascar initiated an NEAP, one of the world's first developing countries to do so. By 1993, recognizing the need to reverse environmental degradation, 30 other countries in Africa had initiated a similar environmental planning process (155). But despite progress and support both internally and from numerous international donors, Madagascar's NEAP faces an uphill battle. Challenges include crushing poverty (per capita income in Madagascar is about U.S. $210 a year), poor prospects for economic change, and logistical problems such as inadequate roads (156). (See Chapter 15, "Basic Economic Indicators," Table 15.1)

Madagascar's economic and environmental problems are entwined. Thus it is important to look at the NEAP in the context of efforts not only to raise environmental awareness but also to expand economic opportunity for the Malagasy people.

Poverty and Population

Madagascar is located 400 kilometers from the east coast of Africa. (See Figure 14.9.) Poverty is pervasive and has been exacerbated in recent years by a population growing at an annual rate of 3.3 percent, a diminishing natural resource base, political and economic mismanagement, and decreasing terms of trade for its major export crops. (See Figure 14.8 and Chapter 16, "Population and Human Development," Table 16.1.) Population density, relatively low overall, is high in certain areas. In these areas, land has been subdivided into farms too small to feed families, forcing some farmers to plant on slopes. This has led to erosion and silting in downstream rice fields (157). Contributing to erosion are huge circular ravines, which send thousands of tons of soil and sediment into downstream rivers and fields when rainstorms occur (158).

Only a small portion of the cultivated land is owned by those who farm it, so few farmers have a stake in preserving the soil (159). With the population growing, farmers have made further incursions into the island's tropical forests, slashing and burning to create new farms in an age-old tradition called *tavy*. The resulting soil erosion only intensifies pressure to cut more forests and create more farmland—a devastating, self-destructive cycle (160). At current rates of population growth, according to one calculation, the last bit of forest could vanish in only 15 to 20 years (161).

A Unique Island

The fourth largest island in the world, Madagascar split away from the African mainland about 165 mil-

Figure 14.8 Madagascar Population and Per Capita Gross National Product, 1970–91

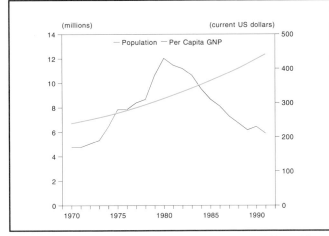

Source: United Nations (U.N.) Population Division, *Interpolated National Populations 1950–2025 (The 1992 Revision)*, on diskette (U.N., New York, 1993), and The World Bank, unpublished data (The World Bank, Washington, D.C., 1993).

lion years ago. Some scientists believe that its ancestral primates floated from Africa on "rafts" of matted vegetation about 100 million years later. "Arriving thus," writes paleontologist Ian Tattersall of the American Museum of Natural History, they "would have found an incredible wealth of ecological opportunities on an island that is only slightly smaller than Texas and topographically, climatically, and ecologically much more diverse" (162). That diversity, reflected in the evolution of at least 45 lemur species by the time human beings arrived there, has turned it into a focus of concern for proponents of biodiversity preservation.

For example, the island is unique in its population of lower primates that are active during the day (163). Twenty-eight of its 31 species of primates, many of which face some degree of endangerment, exist in Madagascar alone. (See Table 14.2.) Numerous other mammal species, as well as reptile, amphibian, bird, and plant species, are endemic or unique to the island. Madagascar is one of the world's 12 "megadiversity countries," which together account for approximately 70 percent of the world's biological diversity (164).

The first human settlers arrived about 2,000 years ago. They encountered a heavily forested island about 1,600 kilometers long and 580 kilometers at its widest, large enough to encompass five major hydrological regions, with a climate dominated by wide variations in rainfall and tropical hurricanes and soil composed of unusually erodible clay (165) (166). Hunting and habitat destruction almost immediately threatened the island's large birds and mammals. Extinct today as a result of human activity are the exotic elephant bird, which may have weighed half a ton, six genera of lemurs, two giant turtle species, an aardvark species, and countless plant species (167) (168).

The Changing Human Habitat

Scientists dispute the extent of Madagascar's original rainforest and thus the degree of its destruction. But clearly much of the damage has been recent. According to one estimate, by 1985, humans had cleared two thirds of the forest that had been standing at the turn of the century (169); according to another, 90 percent of the island's original rainforest was gone by 1990 (170).

Typically, farmers cut down large trees and underbrush to sow rice. Within two or three years, erosion and soil exhaustion put an end to productivity, and farmers use the land as long as possible for cattle grazing, burning it periodically to encourage a fresh crop of grass. Meanwhile, the forest cannot reseed (171). The Malagasy burn about 1 million hectares of land a year (172). What remains of the forest runs along the eastern coast and in isolated pockets of the west (173) (174) (175).

The island depends on wood for more than 80 percent of its energy needs. (See Chapter 21, "Energy and Materials," Table 21.2.) It lacks funds to develop other resources. The leading agricultural product is rice; in 1991, more than 40 percent of 2.6 million hectares of cultivated land was devoted to paddies. Though Madagascar exported rice until the early 1970s, it now must import the crop, and increased demand is forcing farmers to rely on *tavy* (176) (177). Madagascar grows other products for export, a legacy of French colonial rule that began in the late 19th Century. Among the exports are coffee, vanilla, and pepper (178).

The country boasts nearly 40 parks and natural reserves, but it lacks the personnel and financial means to manage these areas and to discourage itinerant farmers, charcoal makers, and other poachers (179) (180).

Traditionally, choice land has been held by the elite, and those lower in the social hierarchy have depended on sharecropping and a shared property system. This pattern, in conjunction with the pressures of poverty, is probably responsible for the degree of exploitation seen in Madagascar. During the colonial era the pattern intensified, with French settlers receiving large land grants. A 1911 law further restricted the land rights of the Malagasy by rejecting their centuries-old system of shifting cultivation (181) (182).

Figure 14.9 Map of Madagascar

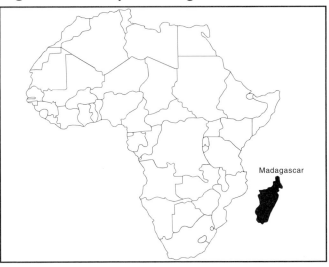

Table 14.2 Number of Primate Species and Degree of Threat, Madagascar and Africa, 1992

Region	Taxa			Critical Subspecies	Endangered Subspecies	Vulnerable Subspecies	Safe Subspecies	Total Threatened		
	Genera	Species	Subspecies[a]					Genera	Species	Subspecies
Africa	18	67	156	7	12	46	91	16	45	65
Madagascar	14	31	49	7	10	8	24	7	16	25

Source: Miranda Stevenson, Anne Baker, and Thomas J. Foose, "Conservation Assessment and Management Plan for Primates," in *Conservation Assessment and Management Plans (GCAP) Review Summary Reports,* Captive Breeding Specialist Group, 1992 Annual Meeting, Vancouver, B.C., p. 39.
Notes: a. Subspecies data represent the total number of species and subspecies (or total taxa). Criteria for estimating the risk of extinction of taxa are based on information about size, distribution, and trend of their population as well as conditions of their habitat. Critical indicates a 50 percent probability of extinction within five years or two generations, whichever is longer. Endangered indicates a 20 percent probability of extinction within 20 years or 10 generations, whichever is longer. Vulnerable indicates a 10 percent probability of extinction within 100 years.

Today one challenge is to give citizens a stake in soil conservation, in the words of one recent report, to "increase incentives for local stewardship of public lands and waters" (183). Some believe that owning land is the vital first step in creating better stewardship, but not everyone agrees; the concepts of private property and entrepreneurship, they argue, will not easily take root in a country that has no such traditions (184). To this day, observes Frederic L. Pryor, author of an exhaustive World Bank study of Madagascar, Malagasy farming practices involve an intricate inheritance system that, for example, may give a family access to certain land only in certain months. Communal rights come into play because cattle may graze in common pasture and because the irrigation of rice typically requires shared effort. In Pryor's view, one of the most important factors contributing to what he calls "tenure insecurity" has been a deterioration of the social order in rural areas, spawning crop theft in the 1980s in addition to the centuries-old problem of cattle rustling (185).

Social disorder has occurred against a backdrop of political crisis. Corruption reportedly has plagued the government and tainted some environmental programs (186). However, following a general strike throughout much of 1991, a new constitution was adopted, and in February 1993 long-time President Didier Ratsiraka lost an election to reformist leader Albert Zafy (187). Although Madagascar is making the transition to a more democratic, free-enterprise system, few expect immediate change.

Introducing Madagascar's NEAP

In recent years the government, more aware of serious environmental degradation in both urban and rural areas, has recognized the need for effective planning to reverse this devastating trend.

On a practical level, Madagascar's nascent planning process is grappling with the need for sustainable practices and economic alternatives that will simultaneously increase production and reduce habitat destruction. Politically, the process faces challenges, among them the need for national leadership, support for emerging environmental programs and those who staff them, and local and regional input as the Malagasy people gain control over their future and an understanding of their stake in bringing about change.

In 1990 the NEAP, its groundwork laid in the mid-1980s, was created with the assistance of a consortium of donors and ratified. It sets up a framework for environmental planning and programs to proceed in tandem with specific objectives, such as establishing natural resource management practices and combating poverty. One overriding objective is to put in place an effective institutional and legal structure for environmental management of the country as a whole (188). With its 15-to-20-year time frame, the NEAP is expected to yield tangible results only if development needs are addressed simultaneously (189).

The first of three five-year program phases began soon after the passage of the Environmental Charter in 1990 (190). It has seven components:
■ Protection and management of biodiversity, and establishment of a network of parks and reserves;
■ Soil conservation and reforestation, carried out with local community participation;
■ Mapping and gathering geographic information;
■ Establishment of clear boundaries for protected areas, and improving land security through titling;
■ Environmental training, education, and awareness;
■ Research on land, coastal, and marine ecosystems; and
■ The strengthening of environmental institutions, protection procedures, and a database (191).

By 1993, eight institutional bodies were involved in implementing the NEAP, including the Office National de l'Environnement (ONE). This semiautonomous unit, attached to the Ministry of State for Agriculture and Rural Development, is responsible for formulating and monitoring policy and coordinating the entire environmental action plan. ONE is a small, influential agency expected to develop into a national institution capable of managing Madagascar's complex environmental problems. Other implementing bodies include the National Association for Environmental Action (ANAE), an NGO that sponsors small projects to test protection and rural development ideas; the National Association for the Management of Protected Areas (ANGAP), charged with coordinating activities in and around some 50 protected areas; the national forestry department; the agency which is charged with land titling; and institutes that are devoted to mapping and studying Madagascar's environmental and maritime resources (192) (193).

Implementation of the NEAP's first five-year phase is expected to cost $86 million, $17 million of it provided by the Malagasy government. The rest is being provided by private environmental groups, including the U.S. division of the World Wildlife Fund, which has been involved in Madagascar for a quarter of a century; the United Nations Development Programme; the World Bank; the African Development Bank;

French, Swiss, and Norwegian donors; and U.S. AID, active in Madagascar since 1984 (194) (195).

In a joint project, the World Wildlife Fund and U.S. AID arranged a 1989 "debt-for-nature" agreement in Madagascar, which provides that commercial or official creditors cancel debt on the condition that those financial resources be invested in programs to promote environmental sustainability. This frees local currency for the government's Ministry of Water and Forests. The money has been set aside to recruit and train conservation agents (196).

Institutional Obstacles

Madagascar, like many other countries, has had a hard time establishing an effective institutional structure for saving the environment. With few qualified staff and organizational difficulties, ONE has not yet been able to fulfill its responsibilities as mandated by Madagascar's environmental code. Lines of authority are unclear, mandates overlap, there is little coordination between agencies with environmental responsibilities, and enforcement of environmental law is lax (197).

At the same time, the NEAP's main projects, particularly those managed by ANGAP and ANAE, have progressed (198). ANAE, for example, was actively involved in three small projects designed to reseed areas that had lost most of their forest cover. It also continued to work with local communities on a project to reduce slash-and-burn farming by turning marshy areas into rice fields. And it helped one group repair a small irrigation dam so the town could cultivate rice (199).

A World Bank draft report, based on a 1990 field trip to several Malagasy villages, concluded that residents' top priorities were road and other infrastructure improvement, better farming and antierosion techniques, access to clean water and health services, and better education. The report emphasized the need for greater grassroots participation in environmental planning, believed critical to the development of strong local institutions, and recommended that village councils be given a clearer role in determining land titles (200).

While international interest in Madagascar's environmental plight has helped raise the country's profile, it has also created problems—coordinating technical assistance from abroad, for example, and supporting the island's own institutions. Though it now has a professional staff, ONE suffered from government restructuring and a lack of political clout in the early 1990s (201).

The Future

While Madagascar's environmental planning has experienced political and structural setbacks, it has garnered much international support. Donors such as the World Bank are expected to pour more than $300 million into the country over the next one or two decades (202). A U.S. AID-sponsored multidonor secretariat, located in World Bank offices in Madagascar, is coordinating the various donor activities. In the meantime, Madagascar continues to search for management structures that are in accordance with its cultural, social, and political system.

Madagascar's preliminary efforts to achieve sustainable development offer several lessons for other countries, among them the need for high-level government support and advocacy. Because sustainable development is a relatively new concept, and because public awareness is key to success, the endorsement of a nation's political leaders is critical.

The Madagascar case also makes clear that when conflicts arise among competing factions—as they inevitably will—a country's environmental agency must have the authority to step in and make a final decision. That authority will not be effective unless the agency is positioned at the highest levels of government.

Finally, Madagascar demonstrates that an environmental agency's authority and effectiveness depend on qualified, motivated staff professionals. They can add credibility and visibility to the drive for sustainable development, especially when their decisions are based on established technical expertise.

This chapter was written primarily by Deborah Baldwin, a freelance writer based in Washington, D.C. Additional contributions were made by Robert Livernash of the World Resources *staff and Patricia Ardila, a consultant on Latin American issues.*

References and Notes

1. The information presented here is available in much more detail in the *1993 Directory of Country Environmental Studies*, prepared jointly by the International Institute for Environment and Development, the World Conservation Union, and the World Resources Institute. This report provides a detailed list, including abstracts and biblio- graphic information, of all the major natural resource and environmental studies that have been published on developing countries in recent years.

2. F. Langeweg, ed., *Concern for Tomorrow: A National Environmental Survey, 1985–2010* (National Institute of Public Health and Environmental Protection, Bilthoven, The Netherlands, 1989), p. xi.

3. H.W. Kroes, ed., *Essential Environmental Information: The Netherlands, 1991* (Ministry of Housing, Physical Planning and Environment, The Hague, 1991), pp. 2 and 257–274.

4. Ministry of Housing, Physical Planning and Environment, *Netherlands National Report to UNCED, 1992* (Ministry of Housing, Physical Planning and Environment, The Hague, 1992), pp. 6–7.

5. David Lawday, "Cleaning up the West's Dirtiest Nation," *U.S. News and World Report* (September 11, 1989), p. 68.

6. Anthony Bailey, "Letter from the Netherlands," *The New Yorker* (August 12, 1991), p. 56.

7. *Op. cit.* 2, p. 119.

8. *Op. cit.* 4, p. 14.

9. Ministry of Housing, Physical Planning, and Environment (VROM), *To Choose or to Lose: National Environmental Policy Plan* (VROM, The Hague, The Netherlands, 1989), p. 5.

10. *Op. cit.* 2, pp. vii and 3–5.

11. *Op. cit.* 6, pp. 52 and 63.

12. Jan A. de Koning, "Evaluation of the Development Process of the Dutch National Environmental Policy Plan-90," report prepared for the Netherlands Ministry of Housing, Physical Planning and Environment, The Hague, 1990, p. 10.

13. *Ibid.*

14. *Op. cit.* 9.

15. Ministry of Housing, Physical Planning and Environment (VROM), *National Environ-*

mental Policy Plan Plus (VROM, The Hague, 1990), p. 16.

16. *Op. cit.* 12, pp. 6–9.

17. *Op. cit.* 12, p. 7.

18. *Op. cit.* 12, pp. 7–8.

19. *Op. cit.* 12, pp. 10–11.

20. *Op. cit.* 9, pp. 129–130.

21. Robert Cahn, "Where Green Is the Color," *The Amicus Journal* (Fall 1992), pp. 8 and 10.

22. *Op. cit.* 9, pp. 9–10.

23. *Op. cit.* 15, pp. 87–89.

24. Hans van Zijst, Counselor for Health and Environment, Royal Netherlands Embassy, Washington, D.C., 1992 (personal communication).

25. *Op. cit.* 9, pp. 179–181.

26. "Alders on Government/Industry Cooperation," *Environmental News from the Netherlands*, No. 4 (Ministry of Housing, Physical Planning and Environment, The Hague, December 1991), p. 6.

27. *Op. cit.* 24.

28. *Op. cit.* 26, p. 7.

29. *Op. cit.* 9, pp. 82–84.

30. *Op. cit.* 9, p. 140.

31. R.J.M. Maas, "Summary," in *National Environmental Outlook, 1990–2010* (National Institute of Public Health and Environmental Protection, Bilthoven, The Netherlands, 1992), p. 11.

32. Albert Adriaanse, *Environmental Policy Performance Indicators* (Sdu Uitgeverij Koninginnegracht, The Hague, 1993), pp. 24–25.

33. *Op. cit.* 9, pp. 23–27, 132–139, and 145–154.

34. *Op. cit.* 9, p. 82.

35. *Op. cit.* 24.

36. Shell Netherlands, "Press Information," January 19, 1993 (press release).

37. *Op. cit.* 24.

38. *Op. cit.* 9, pp. 188–229.

39. Food and Agriculture Organization of the United Nations (FAO), *Agrostat PC*, on diskette (FAO, Rome, 1993).

40. *Op. cit.* 4, p. 44.

41. Food and Agriculture Organization of the United Nations (FAO), *FAO Yearbook: Trade 1991* (FAO, Rome, 1992), pp. 218–219.

42. *Op. cit.* 4, pp. 21 and 43–44.

43. W.J. Willems and N.J.P. Hoogervorst, "Over-Fertilization of the Soil and Groundwater Eutrophication," in *National Environmental Outlook, 1990–2010* (National Institute of Public Health and Environmental Protection, Bilthoven, The Netherlands, 1992), p. 275.

44. *Op. cit.* 2, p. 153.

45. *Op. cit.* 43.

46. *Op. cit.* 9, p. 33.

47. *Op. cit.* 43, pp. 289–290.

48. R. van den Berg, "Pesticides in Soil and Groundwater," in *National Environmental Outlook, 1990–2010* (National Institute of Public Health and Environmental Protection, Bilthoven, The Netherlands, 1992), p. 299.

49. *Op. cit.* 4, p. 25.

50. *Op. cit.* 9, pp. 211–212.

51. *Op. cit.* 24.

52. *Op. cit.* 9, pp. 194–196.

53. *Op. cit.* 15, pp. 6 and 9–10.

54. Margaret Kriz, "Europe's Cooldown," *National Journal* (November 28, 1992), p. 2728.

55. *Op. cit.* 9, pp. 213–214.

56. *Op. cit.* 9, p. 216.

57. *Op. cit.* 9, p. 219.

58. *Op. cit.* 9, p. 222.

59. *Op. cit.* 9, pp. 223–224.

60. *Op. cit.* 9, pp. 223–226.

61. *Op. cit.* 9, pp. 227–229.

62. Sheila Rule, "Politics as Usual over the Dutch Environment," *New York Times* (June 11, 1989), p. 10.

63. *Op. cit.* 9, pp. 30 and 171–175.

64. Ministry of Housing, Physical Planning and Environment (VROM), *Environmental Programme, 1992–95* (VROM, The Hague, 1992), p. 24.

65. *Op. cit.* 24.

66. *Op. cit.* 64, p. 7.

67. *Op. cit.* 4, p. 28.

68. Peter Spinks, "Industrial Giants Poised to Quit the Netherlands," *New Scientist* (February 15, 1992), p. 17.

69. United Nations Development Programme (UNDP), *Human Development Report, 1993* (UNDP, New York, 1993), pp. 199 and 207–208.

70. *Op. cit.* 24.

71. Policy Implications of Greenhouse Warming: Mitigation, Adaptation, and the Science Base (National Academy Press, Washington, D.C., 1992), p. 316.

72. Marijke Brunt, Press Officer, Foundation for Nature and the Environment, Utrecht, The Netherlands, 1992 (personal communication).

73. *Ibid.*

74. Leen Koster, Manager, Environmental Affairs, Shell Netherlands, Rotterdam, The Netherlands, 1992 (personal communication).

75. The World Bank, unpublished data (The World Bank, Washington, D.C., March 1993).

76. Thomas Kamm, "Chile's Economy Roars as Exports Take Off in Post–Pinochet Era," *Wall Street Journal* (January 25, 1993), p. 1, sec. A.

77. Luis Alvarado, "Environment and Development: A View from Chile," in *Environment and Diplomacy in the Americas*, Heraldo Muñoz, ed. (Lynne Rienner, Boulder, Colorado, 1992), p. 19.

78. Walter Arensberg, Deputy Director, Center for International Development and Environment, World Resources Institute, Washington, D.C., 1992 (personal communication).

79. Patricio Aylwin Azocar, President of Chile, Speech to the National Congress, translated by Carlos Linares from the Spanish, Valparaíso, May 21, 1993.

80. U.S. General Accounting Office (GAO), *Chilean Trade: Factors Affecting U.S. Trade and Investment* (GAO, Washington, D.C., 1992), p. 2.

81. *Op. cit.* 76.

82. The Economist Intelligence Unit, *Chile Country Report No. 4, 1992* (Business International, London, 1992), p. 3.

83. Comisión Nacional del Medio Ambiente (CONAMA), *Informe Nacional a la Conferencia de las Naciones Unidas sobre Medio Ambiente y Desarrollo* (CONAMA, Santiago, 1992), pp. 28–31.

84. United Nations (U.N.), *1990 International Trade Statistics Yearbook* (U.N., New York, 1992), pp. 560–561.

85. *Op. cit.* 83, p. 28.

86. *Op. cit.* 80, p. 15.

87. The World Bank, "Staff Appraisal Report: Chile, Environmental Institutions Development Project," The World Bank, Washington, D.C., 1992, p. 6.

88. *Ibid.*

89. *Op. cit.* 83, p. 13.

90. *Op. cit.* 39.

91. *Op. cit.* 76, p. 8, sec. A.

92. *Op. cit.* 80, p. 19.

93. *Op. cit.* 39.

94. Walter Arensberg, Mary Louise Higgins, Rafael Asenjo, *et al.*, "Environment and Natural Resources Strategy in Chile," paper prepared for the U.S. Agency for International Development/Chile, Washington, D.C., 1989, pp. 15–18.

95. *Op. cit.* 83, p. 66.

96. *Op. cit.* 83, p. 22.

97. *Op. cit.* 87, p. 4.

98. *Op. cit.* 41, p. 350.

99. *Op. cit.* 87, p. 63.

100. *Op. cit.* 39.

101. *Op. cit.* 83, p. 27.

102. *Op. cit.* 94, p. 21.

103. Kari Keipi, Senior Forester, Inter-American Development Bank, Washington, D.C., 1993 (personal communication).

104. *Op. cit.* 94, p. 22.

105. The World Bank, *Environment and Development in Latin America and the Caribbean: The Role of the World Bank* (The World Bank, Washington, D.C., 1992), p. 26.

106. *Op. cit.* 83, p. 58.

107. Food and Agriculture Organization of the United Nations (FAO), *FAO Yearbook: Fishery Statistics, 1991* (FAO, Rome, 1993), p. 23.

108. Food and Agriculture Organization of the United Nations (FAO), *Fishstat-PC*, on diskette (FAO, Rome, 1993).

109. *Op. cit.* 94, p. 27.

110. *Op. cit.* 94, p. 27.

111. *Op. cit.* 87, p. 5.

112. *Op. cit.* 82, p. 18.

113. *Op. cit.* 94, p. 28.

114. *Op. cit.* 87, pp. 6 and 66.

115. United Nations Environment Programme (UNEP), *Regional Cooperation on Environmental Protection of the Marine and Coastal Areas of the Pacific Basin* (UNEP, Nairobi, Kenya, 1991), p. 6.

116. *Op. cit.* 78.

117. *Op. cit.* 87, p. 2.

118. *Op. cit.* 87, pp. 6 and 66.

119. *Op. cit.* 94, p. 33.

120. *Op. cit.* 87, pp. 66–67.

121. *Op. cit.* 105, pp. 22–23.

122. *Op. cit.* 87, p. 67.

123. *Op. cit.* 105, p. 22.

124. The World Bank, *World Development Report, 1992: Development and the Environment* (Oxford University Press, New York, 1992), p. 84.

125. *Op. cit.* 80, p. 25.

126. *Op. cit.* 105, p. 27.

127. John A. Dixon, Senior Environmental Economist, The World Bank, Washington, D.C., 1993 (personal communication).

128. Guillermo Geisse, President, Center for Environmental Research and Planning, Santiago, 1993 (personal communication).

129. *Op. cit.* 105, p. 29.

130. Rafael Asenjo, "La Institucionalidad Ambiental en el Proyecto de Ley de Bases del Medio Ambiente," in *Discusiones y Aportes al Proyecto de Ley de Bases del Medio Ambiente* (Centro de Estudios Públicos Working Document No. 191, Santiago, 1993), pp. 4 and 13.

131. *Ibid.*, p. 7.

132. Raúl Brañes, *Aspectos Institucionales y Jurídicos del Medio Ambiente, Incluida la Participación de la Organizaciones No Gubernamentales en la Gestión Ambiental* (Inter-American Development Bank, Washington, D.C., 1991), pp. 78–81.

133. Carlos Linares, Executive Director, Salva Natura, San Salvador, El Salvador, 1992 (personal communication).

134. *Op. cit.* 130, pp. 10 and 16.

135. Comisión Nacional del Medio Ambiente (CONAMA), *Se Plantea un Gran Desafío*

para Chile (CONAMA, Santiago, 1993), pp. 3–5.

136. Op. cit. 78.

137. Op. cit. 80, p. 24.

138. Rafael Asenjo, Director, Comisión Nacional del Medio Ambiente, Santiago, Chile, 1993 (personal communication).

139. "La Política Ambiental en Chile y la Responsabilidad del Sector Público y Privado Frente a los Problemas de Contaminación," Comisión Nacional del Medio Ambiente, Working Document, Santiago, 1993, pp. 1–2.

140. Op. cit. 135, pp. 20–21.

141. Op. cit. 105, pp. 20–22.

142. Marc Dourojeanni, Environment Protection Division Chief, Inter-American Development Bank, Washington, D.C., 1992 (personal communication).

143. Op. cit. 133.

144. Op. cit. 78.

145. Op. cit. 87, pp. 52, 56, and 68.

146. Op. cit. 105, p. 37.

147. Op. cit. 75.

148. Mauricio Roldán, Environment Committee, AmCham Chile, Santiago, 1993 (personal communication).

149. Op. cit. 87, pp. 12 and 18.

150. Op. cit. 148, p. 2.

151. Andrea Butelmann and Alicia Frohmann, "U.S.-Chile Free Trade," in The Premise and the Promise: Free Trade in the Americas, Sylvia Saborio, ed. (Transaction, New Brunswick, New Jersey, 1992), p. 190.

152. Don Podesta, "The Environment Running Second," Washington Post (February 4, 1993), p. 14, sec. A.

153. Rafael Asenjo, presentation at the Seminario International "Ambiente/Empresa," Comisión Nacional del Medio Ambiente, Riverside, California, September 8, 1993.

154. Jerry Hagstrom, "Making Chile's Case," National Journal (July 3, 1993), p. 1704.

155. Kirk Talbott, "Elusive Success: Institutional Priorities and the Role of Coordination: A Case Study of the Madagascar National Environmental Action Plan," Issues in Development (World Resources Institute, Washington, D.C., May 1993), pp. 1–3.

156. Albert Michael Greve, Coordinator, Multi-Donor Secretariat, The World Bank, Washington, D.C. 1993 (personal communication).

157. The World Bank, U.S. Agency for International Development, Coopération Suisse, et al., Madagascar Environmental Action Plan, Vol. 1 (The World Bank, Washington, D.C., 1988), pp. 34 and 54.

158. Philemon Randrianarijaona, "The Erosion of Madagascar," Ambio, Vol. 12, No. 6 (1983), p. 308.

159. "Staff Appraisal Report: Democratic Republic of Madagascar, Environment Program" (The World Bank, Washington, D.C., 1990), p. 5.

160. Frederick L. Pryor, Malawi and Madagascar: The Political Economy of Poverty, Equity, and Growth (Oxford University Press, New York, 1990), pp. 198–199.

161. Sylvia da Silva, "Saving Madagascar," Swiss Review of World Affairs (June 1991), p. 22.

162. Ian Tattersall, "Madagascar's Lemurs," Scientific American, Vol. 268, No. 1 (1993), p. 110.

163. Ibid., pp. 110 and 112.

164. Jeffrey A. McNeely, Kenton R. Miller, Walter V. Reid, et al., Conserving the World's Biological Diversity (The World Conservation Union, Gland, Switzerland, 1990), pp. 89–90 and 95.

165. Knut Opsal and Kirk Talbott, "The Implementation of the Madagascar Environmental Action Plan: Possibilities and Constraints for Local Participation," Aften Technical Note No. 9, The World Bank, Washington, D.C., 1990, p. 15.

166. Op. cit. 160, p. 198.

167. Op. cit. 162, p. 115.

168. Op. cit. 164, p. 95.

169. Glen M. Green and Robert W. Sussman, "Deforestation History of the Eastern Rain Forests of Madagascar from Satellite Images," Science, Vol. 248, No. 4952 (1990), pp. 212–215.

170. Op. cit. 165, p. 16.

171. Op. cit. 161, p. 23.

172. Op. cit. 160, p. 198.

173. Op. cit. 169.

174. Op. cit. 162, pp. 116–117.

175. Op. cit. 158, p. 309.

176. Op. cit. 39.

177. Op. cit. 157, pp. 31–32.

178. Op. cit. 39.

179. Op. cit. 157, p. 27.

180. World Wildlife Fund (WWF), WWF Madagascar Country Plan, FY 92/93–FY 96/97, draft (WWF, Washington, D.C., September 1992), pp. 8–9, and 21–22.

181. Op. cit. 165, p. 17.

182. Op. cit. 160, pp. 208 and 410.

183. World Resources Institute (WRI), The World Conservation Union, formerly the International Union for Conservation of Nature and Natural Resources (IUCN), and United Nations Environment Programme (UNEP), Global Biodiversity Strategy: Guidelines for Action to Save, Study, and Use Earth's Biotic Wealth Sustainably and Equitably (WRI, IUCN, and UNEP, Washington, D.C., 1992), p. 82.

184. Leonard P. Hirsch, International Liaison, Smithsonian Institution Office of International Relations, Washington, D.C., 1993 (personal communication).

185. Op. cit. 160, p. 410.

186. Op. cit. 184.

187. "Start Again," The Economist (February 20, 1993), pp. 42 and 44.

188. Op. cit. 155, pp. 2–3.

189. Anthony Pryor, Natural Resources Policy Adviser, U.S. Agency for International Development, Washington, D.C., 1993 (personal communication).

190. Op. cit. 155, p. 4.

191. Op. cit. 159, pp. 12–13.

192. Op. cit. 155, pp. 3–5.

193. Luciano Mosele, Agricultural Economist, The World Bank, Washington, D.C., 1993 (personal communication).

194. "Environment Program 1, Financial Plan Summary," Madagascar Environment Program Newsletter, Vol. 2, No. 2 (The World Bank, Washington, D.C., March 1992), p. 8.

195. Op. cit. 189.

196. Op. cit. 180, p. 48.

197. Op. cit. 155, pp. 4–6.

198. Op. cit. 155, p. 4.

199. "The National Association for Environmental Actions Forges Ahead," Madagascar Environment Program Newsletter, Vol. 2, No. 2 (The World Bank, Washington, D.C., March 1992), p. 2.

200. Op. cit. 165, pp. 7, 9–12, and 17.

201. Op. cit. 155, pp. 4–10.

202. Op. cit. 161, p. 24.

Part IV. Data Tables

The data and notes in Part IV of this report (Chapters 15–24) provide background information essential to any informed discussion of the interlocked themes of environment and development. Along with other data sets presented in previous editions of this report, *World Resources 1994–95* has found and published data for a variety of relevant variables, selecting those sets with the best quality and broadest country coverage. Where possible, data are given that inform arguments presented in Parts I, II, and III of this report, but data are also provided that document conditions and trends in the resource base, provide surrogate measures of the environment's health, and illuminate its economic and human dimensions. These data, with associated detailed sources and explanatory notes (often including comments on data quality), will enable the reader to undertake informed analysis, double check the assertions of authors or authorities, both here and elsewhere, and understand the global context of national detail.

None of this work would have been possible without the invaluable cooperation of many international organizations, academics, and national governments who provide, review, and comment on these data and explanatory notes. Certain organizations have been especially helpful: the United Nations Food and Agriculture Organization (FAO), by providing agricultural, fisheries, land use, and forestry data; the World Bank, by supplying and explaining economic data; the United Nations Statistical Division (UNSTAT), by providing population and energy data; and the World Conservation Monitoring Centre, by supplying data relevant to biodiversity. Data sources, including institutions, are formally acknowledged in the Sources and Technical Notes of each of these data chapters; individuals are formally acknowledged following the Preface of this report.

High-quality, environmentally relevant, and internationally comparable data sets are difficult to amass. The collection and aggregation of such information is given short shrift by many of the national governments that could be expected to fund, collect, and use such information, as well as make it available for international dissemination. In the absence of adequate and timely data, data providers sometimes extrapolate, interpolate, or model—instead of surveying, measuring, and collecting. High-quality data collection activities are expensive, and even technical solutions that have the potential of reducing costs, such as remote aerial or satellite sensing, still require expensive "ground

truthing"—that is, calibrating the technology against the hard truth of the real world.

What is adequate data quality for one purpose might be totally inadequate for another. The estimates of carbon dioxide emissions from industrial sources presented in Table 23.1 are believed to be within 10 percent of the global total but less accurate for individual countries. These data are of sufficient quality to rank countries and to understand the magnitude of global and national emissions and are good enough to show the change in magnitude of a country's emissions over time. These data would, however, be inadequate for a country to use to manage its emissions to achieve some national purpose.

Some data sets have a historical role as important indicators, a role that depends more on custom than on the quality of measurement. Three such data sets are infant and child (0 to 5 years) mortality rates and life expectancy. The statistical infrastructure necessary to measure these parameters is simply lacking in much of the developing world outside of the Americas. Age-specific mortality rates are poorly correlated and such rates are poor predictors of life expectancy. Calculations of mortality require age-specific mortality rates, from all ages, derived from detailed birth and death records. In the absence of such data, indirect methods are used and estimates based on model life tables are reported. Child mortality rates using these indirect methods are considered robust and the mortality measure least influenced by the choice of a particular model life table. There is not enough information for 18 countries to use even these indirect techniques to estimate child mortality. Nonetheless, measures of mortality are used as an input into innumerable comparisons and aggregated indicators and to judge governments and compare countries.

Among sectors, the data sets with the best global quality are those related to economics and the production (and, to a lesser extent, consumption) of commercial fuels. Even with these data, however, the user must keep in mind each data set's limitations when using it in calculations and comparisons. As illustrated in Table 15.1, measures of nations' incomes will differ whether using gross national product (GNP) or gross domestic product; GNP accounts for gross factor income from abroad. In addition, comparisons will differ depending on whether 3-year average currency exchange rates, single-year exchange rates, or conversion rates derived from studies of purchasing power are used. The conversion of energy production from different sources into common units (petajoules in Table 21.1) requires an understanding of the source-specific energy of specific fuels. Where known, average national energy content factors were used here. While energy production figures are based on government and private-sector reports of actual production, energy consumption is estimated from known production, imports, exports, and stock changes, and so is removed from any observation of actual consumption.

There is a common expectation that data such as cereal production or fuel consumption will vary from year to year and that other data, such as total land area, are inherently stable. Some data sets are surprisingly variable. The areas of large natural lakes seem to vary significantly, both because of local weather events and according to who reports their area; Table 22.2 gives a best judgment based on various sources. Still other data sets, such as estimates of energy and mineral reserves, are surprisingly mutable—dependent as they are on current exploration effort and economic conditions.

There is always a delay in assembling, analyzing, and reporting data. Many of the internationally comparable data sets reported have additional delays due to the gathering, harmonizing, and verifying of diverse national data sets. *World Resources 1994–95*, prepared during 1993, attempts to provide the most recent data available, which are generally, but not always, through 1991. Data for the most recent years—in many data sets—can be thought of as works-in-progress, subject to modification as the responsible international organizations obtain final assessments or more complete information. UNSTAT recently froze its compilation of energy statistics for 1950 through 1970 in its current form. Its time series for 1971 through the present are still subject to change as better or more complete data become available.

Other data sets become available only occasionally. The FAO performs an assessment of the world's forests every 10 years (reported in Chapter 19, "Forests and Rangelands," for the decade 1981–90). Such time gaps, and associated changes in methods, motives, and raw information, mean that sequential data sets are not strictly comparable and that their analysis requires considerable effort and subjective judgments. The World Energy Council assembles estimates of world energy reserves (see Table 21.3) every 3 years (most recently in 1992 assembling data for 1990), and thus major changes (e.g., the extent of China's estimated proven recoverable coal reserves compared to those es-

timated in 1989 for 1987) do not enter the global discussion on energy-related matters in a timely fashion.

Ultimately, the availability of data depends on the existence of a political will and statistical infrastructure sufficient to ensure its collection, at the national level, for the purposes of *World Resources 1994–95*. Often, for many important environmentally relevant data series, this national will and infrastructure either do not exist or exist only in the most developed countries. Simple health and mortality data are only readily available from developed countries and from the developing countries of the Americas. The Organisation for Economic Co-operation and Development (OECD) collects data on industrial waste generation (see Table 21.6) from its members (although differences in definition make their comparison difficult); no comparable data set exists for non-OECD countries, many of which do not collect or estimate these data. Likewise, there is no global map of land use—at a reasonable scale (see Table 17.1 for gross estimates at a national scale); no complete, harmonized assessment of habitat loss (see Table 22.2 for recent estimates); no reliable data that would allow national comparisons of soil loss; and no comparable data on the extent and conditions of natural rangelands.

At the same time, some progress is being made. Global monitoring systems are being developed for the climate, the oceans, and terrestrial systems. The use of standard definitions and classifications for many parameters is reasonably well advanced for the European region and initiatives to extend their applicability on a wider scale are under way.

The long-term, seemingly mundane collection, analysis, and dissemination of data is frequently not given high priority against competing demands for scarce financial and human resources. Yet decisionmakers need to set priorities, rationally allocate and manage resources, plan for the future, and even build political consensus. Data is needed for early warning of future emergencies; to provide a basis for optimally allocating scarce personnel and financial resources in the face of competing demands; to monitor compliance with national laws or international conventions; or to help generate political interest in the sustainability of local, national, regional, and global systems.

Decisionmakers are often ill-served by the current paucity of information about important environmental variables. Yet, even in the absence of adequate information, necessary decisions will continue to be made or—just as important—not made.

15. Basic Economic Indicators

Aggregate measures of economic activities give policymakers some of the most important information they need to make decisions. This chapter provides a basic set of economic indicators that policymakers and the public can use to give an economic context to discussions of the environment and development.

Many traditional economic indicators fail to account for the depletion or deterioration of natural resources, the long-term consequences of such depletion, the equitable distribution of income within a country, or the sustainability of current economic practices. Still, the indicators provided here are useful for showing the differences between the wealthiest and poorest countries. For example, the 1991 U.S. gross national product (GNP) estimate of $5.6 trillion is substantially larger than that of any other country; Japan has the second largest estimated GNP—$3.3 trillion.

The comparison of GNP and gross domestic product (GDP) estimates among countries based on market exchange rates must be carefully made as sometimes rapid variations occur in those exchange rates. GDP estimates based on Purchasing Power Parities (PPPs), which reflect relative price levels in different countries, are designed to provide a more stable and realistic comparison. For example, Japan's 1991 per capita exchange rate-based GDP was $26,984 compared to $19,390 based on 1991 PPPs. For many of the poorer countries, PPP estimates of per capita GDP improve relative position. India, for example, jumps from $288 to $1,150, Chile from $2,538 to $7,060 and Kenya from $399 to $1,350.

Table 15.2 shows that the United States and Japan gave the most official development assistance (ODA) between 1989 and 1991, averaging $10.1 and $9.6 billion a year, respectively. For the same period, Egypt ($3.9 billion) and China ($2.1 billion) were the largest recipients of ODA, followed by Bangladesh ($2.0 billion), Indonesia ($1.8 billion), and India ($1.7 billion). On a per capita basis, Israel ($225 per person) received the most ODA, while the United Arab Emirates gave the most ($347 per person). ODA receipts represent over 70 percent of the GNP of Mozambique and Guinea-Bissau, while Denmark, Norway, and Sweden each gave approximately 1 percent of their GNP to ODA.

The total external debt of developing countries was approximately $1.5 trillion in 1991. The three-year averages of total external debt in Table 15.2 identify Brazil, Mexico, and India as having the greatest debts. For many developing countries, external debt is a large proportion of GNP and debt service takes a significant portion of the total foreign exchange earned from the export of goods and services, thereby limiting the potential for investment or consumption. For example, Hungary's external long-term public debt was 63 percent of its GNP for the period 1989–91, and its debt service represented 38 percent of its total export earnings.

Table 15.3 presents statistics concerning monetary and human resources invested in military establishments throughout the world. The United States ($227 billion) spent roughly 2.5 times as much as the former U.S.S.R. ($92 billion) during 1991. The third largest defense expenditure is attributed to Saudi Arabia (approximately $35 billion). Note that the Gulf War occurred in 1991.

In 1991, China had the largest standing army, with over 3 million soldiers, and the Republic of Korea had the largest number of reservists, estimated at 4.5 million. The three largest arms exporters during 1988 were China, the United States, and the former U.S.S.R., and in terms of arms trade as a percentage of total imports for the same period, Ethiopia, Nicaragua, and the Syrian Arab Republic imported the largest percentages of arms (81, 66, and 59 percent, respectively).

Many developing countries, such as Mozambique and Tanzania, which produce more than 60 percent of their GDP in the agricultural sector (see Table 15.1), are sharply affected by commodity price declines. Table 15.4 shows that commodity price indexes for all categories of commodities (except timber) have declined since 1975.

Table 15.5 presents data on the flow of international trade among the major international economic groups. Since 1965, fully 60 to 75 percent of international trade has been among developed nations in the Organisation for Economic Co-operation and Development.

Table 15.1 Gross National and Domestic Product

	Gross National Product (GNP) 1991 {a}		Gross Domestic Product (GDP) Exchange Rate Based (GDP) 1991 {b}		Purchasing Power Parity (PPP) 1991 {c}		Average Annual Growth Rate (percent)		Distribution of GDP, 1991 (percent)		
	Total (million $US)	Per Capita ($US)	Total (million $US)	Per Capita ($US)	Total (million $I)	Per Capita ($I)	GNP {d} 1980-91	GDP {e} 1980-91	Agriculture	Industry	Services
WORLD											
AFRICA											
Algeria	51,060	1,991	42,933	1,674	144,627	5,640	2.1	3.0	14.0 f	50.0 f	36.0 f
Angola	X	X	8,375	879	X	X	X	X	X	X	X
Benin	1,854	389	1,898	398	7,151	1,500 g	2.1	2.4	36.1	13.2	50.7
Botswana	3,399	2,666	3,688	2,893	5,980	4,690 g	9.3	9.8	5.5	58.5	36.0
Burkina Faso	2,683	290	2,753	298	6,936	750	4.0	4.0	44.0 f	20.0 f	37.0 f
Burundi	1,230	218	1,170	207	4,072	720	4.3	4.0	55.0 f	16.0 f	29.0 f
Cameroon	10,174	858	11,674	985	28,457	2,400 g	2.1	1.4	23.0	29.4	47.6
Central African Rep	1,258	407	1,278	413	3,368	1,090	1.2	1.4	41.0 f	16.0 f	42.0 f
Chad	1,206	212	1,297	228	4,155	730	6.3	5.5	43.0 f	18.0 f	39.0 f
Congo	2,436	1,060	2,722	1,185	6,434	2,800 g	3.1	3.3	13.2	38.2	48.7
Cote d'Ivoire	8,416	677	9,503	764	18,778	1,510 g	0.3	(0.5)	38.0 f	22.0 f	40.0 f
Djibouti	X	X	445	982	X	X	X	X	X	X	X
Egypt	32,783	611	32,790	611	193,072	3,600 g	4.5	4.8	18.0 f	30.0 f	52.0 f
Equatorial Guinea	124	345	131	363	X	X	5.8	X	X	X	X
Ethiopia	6,313	123	6,602	129	19,010	370 g	1.5	1.6	47.0 f	13.0 f	40.0 f
Gabon	4,643	3,879	5,435	4,540	X	X	(0.9)	0.2	9.0	49.1	41.9
Gambia, The	324	367	341	386	X	X	3.2	X	28.5 h	13.8 h	57.6 h
Ghana	6,496	420	7,000	452	30,968	2,000	3.1	3.2	51.1	16.9	32.0
Guinea	2,952	498	3,180	536	X	X	X	X	32.0	32.6	35.4
Guinea-Bissau	184	187	211	214	679	690	3.3	3.7	46.3	15.8	37.9
Kenya	8,529	350	8,261	339	32,933	1,350 g	4.1	4.2	27.0 f	22.0 f	51.0 f
Lesotho	1,042	582	601	336	3,385	1,890	2.7	5.5	14.0 f	38.0 f	48.0 f
Liberia	X	X	X	X	X	X	X	X	X	X	X
Libya	X	X	X	X	X	X	X	X	X	X	X
Madagascar	2,574	207	2,673	215	8,812	710 g	0.5	1.1	33.0 f	14.0 f	53.0 f
Malawi	1,997	200	2,192	220	7,989	800 g	3.5	3.1	35.0 f	20.0 f	45.0 f
Mali	2,387	251	2,451	258	4,565	480 g	2.5	2.5	42.1	14.2	43.7
Mauritania	1,042	500	1,130	543	2,895	1,390	0.6	1.4	22.0 f	31.0 f	47.0 f
Mauritius	2,585	2,380	2,730	2,514	12,141	11,180 g	7.2	6.7	11.0 f	33.0 f	56.0 f
Morocco	26,530	1,033	27,653	1,077	85,795	3,340 g	4.3	4.2	16.8	32.8	50.4
Mozambique	1,221	84	1,328	92	8,697	600	(1.1)	(0.1)	64.0 f	15.0 f	21.0 f
Namibia	2,354	1,584	2,278	1,533	X	X	1.6	1.0	10.0 f	28.0 f	62.0 f
Niger	2,419	303	2,328	291	6,309	790	(0.9)	(1.0)	34.8	15.9	49.3
Nigeria	34,226	305	34,124	304	152,418	1,360 g	1.4	1.9	37.0 f	38.0 f	26.0 f
Rwanda	2,052	282	1,630	224	4,944	680 g	0.5	0.6	40.2	18.7	41.2
Senegal	5,544	736	5,639	749	12,649	1,680 g	2.9	3.1	20.3	18.6	61.1
Sierra Leone	860	202	755	177	3,409	800 g	1.1	1.1	X	X	X
Somalia	X	X	X	X	X	X	X	X	X	X	X
South Africa	98,854	2,543	107,437	2,763	X	X	3.3	1.3	5.0 f	44.0 f	51.0 f
Sudan	X	X	7,310	282	X	X	0.3	X	X	X	X
Swaziland	933	1,210	942	1,222	X	X	6.8	X	X	X	X
Tanzania	2,561	95	3,183	118	15,332	570 g	2.0	2.9	61.0 f	5.0 f	34.0 f
Togo	1,558	427	1,637	449	4,775	1,310	1.8	1.8	33.0	22.2	44.8
Tunisia	12,377	1,504	13,183	1,602	38,585	4,690 g	3.5	3.7	18.0	32.0	50.0
Uganda	2,949	163	2,566	142	20,285	1,120	5.9	X	51.0 f	12.0 f	37.0 f
Zaire	X	X	X	X	X	X	1.6	X	X	X	X
Zambia	3,508	418	3,628	432	8,473	1,010 g	0.7	0.8	18.2	45.3	36.5
Zimbabwe	6,586	641	6,324	616	22,175	2,160 g	3.6	3.1	20.0 f	32.0 f	49.0 f
ASIA											
Afghanistan	X	X	X	X	X	X	X	X	X	X	X
Bangladesh	23,883	205	23,394	201	135,075	1,160 g	4.2	4.3	36.8	15.8	47.4
Bhutan	275	174	253	160	977	620	9.0	7.6	43.0 f	27.0 f	29.0 f
Cambodia	1,730	202	1,965	230	X	X	X	X	48.9	12.4	38.6
China	425,623	364	371,455	317	1,966,771	1,680 i	9.4	9.4	28.4	38.8	32.8
India	284,658	330	248,583	288	992,157	1,150 g	5.5	5.4	31.0 f	27.0 f	41.0 f
Indonesia	111,165	592	115,878	617	512,487	2,730 j	5.8	5.6	21.4	39.3	39.2
Iran, Islamic Rep	136,348	2,274	117,190	1,955	279,957	4,670 g	2.5	2.2	21.0 f	21.0 f	58.0 f
Iraq	X	X	X	X	X	X	X	X	X	X	X
Israel	59,879	12,293	63,032	12,940	65,564	13,460 j	3.7	3.7	X	X	X
Japan	3,326,646	26,824	3,346,486	26,984	2,404,709	19,390 k	4.3	4.2	2.5	42.0	55.5
Jordan	3,880	935	4,082	984	20,196	4,870	0.6	(1.5)	7.0 f	26.0 f	67.0 f
Korea, Dem People's Rep	X	X	X	X	X	X	X	X	X	X	X
Korea, Rep	274,875	6,277	282,970	6,462	364,341	8,320 g	10.0	9.6	9.0	44.7	46.3
Kuwait	X	X	11,199	5,369	X	X	X	X	0.6	51.0	48.4
Lao People's Dem Rep	943	218	1,033	238	8,367	1,930	4.2	X	X	X	X
Lebanon	X	X	4,304	1,546	X	X	X	X	X	X	X
Malaysia	45,798	2,497	47,104	2,568	135,731	7,400 l	5.6	5.7	X	X	X
Mongolia	X	X	756	336	X	X	X	X	16.6	33.5	49.9
Myanmar	X	X	28,278	662	X	X	X	X	X	X	X
Nepal	3,420	170	3,333	166	22,681	1,130	4.7	X	59.0 f	14.0 f	27.0 f
Oman	9,714	6,148	10,236	6,479	14,204	8,990	9.3	7.9	3.3	57.7	39.0
Pakistan	46,566	383	45,294	373	239,325	1,970 g	6.5	6.1	26.0 f	26.0 f	49.0 f
Philippines	46,466	728	45,162	708	155,718	2,440 g	1.2	1.1	22.1	34.9	43.0
Saudi Arabia	121,452	7,893	108,640	7,060	166,949	10,850	0.4	(0.2)	6.7	52.4	40.9
Singapore	39,067	14,263	40,201	14,677	43,167	15,760	7.1	6.6	0.3	37.4	62.3
Sri Lanka	8,638	495	9,054	519	46,216	2,650 g	4.0	4.0	27.0 f	25.0 f	48.0 f
Syrian Arab Rep	14,607	1,141	17,236	1,346	X	X	1.4	2.6	29.8	23.4	46.8
Thailand	94,022	1,697	98,261	1,774	291,921	5,270 g	7.8	7.9	12.7	39.7	47.6
Turkey	102,495	1,793	107,842	1,886	276,683	4,840 k	5.4	5.0	18.0 f	34.0 f	49.0 f
United Arab Emirates	36,137	22,170	34,323	21,057	X	X	(1.8)	X	X	X	X
Viet Nam	X	X	6,970	102	X	X	X	X	38.6	23.7	37.7
Yemen	6,746	557	8,341	689	X	X	X	X	X	X	X

Estimates, 1980–91

Table 15.1

	Gross National Product (GNP) 1991 {a}		Gross Domestic Product (GDP) Exchange Rate Based (GDP) 1991 {b}		Purchasing Power Parity (PPP) 1991 {c}		Average Annual Growth Rate (percent)		Distribution of GDP, 1991 (percent)		
	Total (million $US)	Per Capita ($US)	Total (million $US)	Per Capita ($US)	Total (million $I)	Per Capita ($I)	GNP {d} 1980-91	GDP {e} 1980-91	Agriculture	Industry	Services
NORTH & CENTRAL AMERICA											
Belize	422	2,176	420	2,165	X	X	5.3	X	21.9 h	24.8 h	53.3 h
Canada	559,825	20,740	582,000	21,561	521,505	19,320 k	3.1	3.1	3.0 m	33.8 m	63.2 m
Costa Rica	5,733	1,841	5,635	1,810	15,876	5,100 j	3.4	3.1	15.8	25.7	58.5
Cuba	X	X	X	X	X	X	X	X	X	X	X
Dominican Rep	6,751	922	7,148	976	22,549	3,080 j	1.9	1.7	17.5	26.2	56.3
El Salvador	5,740	1,087	5,915	1,120	11,143	2,110 j	1.1	1.0	11.2	23.3	65.5
Guatemala	8,939	944	9,353	988	30,105	3,180 j	1.0	1.1	25.7	19.7	54.6
Haiti	2,479	375	2,641	399	8,075	1,220	(0.6)	(0.7)	X	X	X
Honduras	3,112	587	3,004	567	9,642	1,820 j	2.6	2.7	20.0	23.5	45.6
Jamaica	3,532	1,446	3,497	1,431	8,966	3,670 j	1.0	1.6	5.0	43.9	51.1
Mexico	256,422	2,971	286,628	3,321	618,864	7,170 l	1.5	1.2	8.0	30.7	61.3
Nicaragua	1,079	283	1,736	456	9,708	2,550	(1.4)	(1.9)	31.1	20.0	48.9
Panama	5,259	2,133	5,544	2,248	12,108	4,910 j	0.3	0.5	9.9	10.0	80.1
Trinidad and Tobago	4,745	3,793	4,939	3,948	10,483	8,380 k,j	(3.9)	(4.4)	2.5	38.6	58.9
United States	5,645,415	22,356	5,610,802	22,219 n	5,588,356	22,130 k,n	3.1	2.6	2.0 o	29.3 o	68.6 o
SOUTH AMERICA											
Argentina	129,723	3,966	189,720	5,800	167,485	5,120 j	(0.2)	(0.4)	8.1	36.0	55.9
Bolivia	4,808	654	5,020	683	15,941	2,170 j	0.5	0.3	X	X	X
Brazil	442,698	2,920	405,771	2,677	794,394	5,240 j	2.5	2.5	10.0 f	39.0 f	51.0 f
Chile	31,582	2,359	33,977	2,538	94,512	7,060 j	3.4	3.6	X	X	X
Colombia	41,207	1,254	41,700	1,269	179,421	5,460 j	3.2	3.7	16.1	36.5	47.4
Ecuador	10,907	1,010	11,663	1,080	44,712	4,140 j	2.0	2.1	13.4	37.9	48.7
Guyana	242	302	349	435	X	X	(3.8)	X	X	X	X
Paraguay	5,568	1,266	6,249	1,421	15,038	3,420 j	2.3	2.7	27.8	23.1	49.1
Peru	23,434	1,065	21,899	996	68,408	3,110 j	(0.4)	(0.4)	0.0	0.0	0.0
Suriname	1,666	3,874	1,941	4,513	X	X	(2.2)	X	11.1 h	26.8 h	62.1 h
Uruguay	8,971	2,883	9,804	3,150	20,757	6,670 j	0.2	0.6	11.3	32.1	56.6
Venezuela	53,880	2,728	53,441	2,705	160,394	8,120 j	1.1	1.5	5.4	50.2	44.4
EUROPE											
Albania	X	X	1,154	351	X	X	X	X	X	X	X
Austria	158,054	20,410	163,992	21,177	136,991	17,690 k	2.3	2.3	3.2	36.1	60.7
Belgium	190,140	19,043	196,873	19,717	174,837	17,510 k	2.2	2.1	1.8	30.1	68.1
Bulgaria	16,316	1,818	12,687	1,414	44,696	4,980	1.7	1.9	17.7	51.3	31.0
Czechoslovakia (former)	38,810	2,473	33,172	2,114	98,565	6,280	0.7	0.6	8.0 f	56.0 f	36.0 f
Denmark	122,484	23,793	130,277	25,306	92,046	17,880 k	2.2	2.3	5.0 f	28.0 f	67.0 f
Finland	120,326	24,089	124,542	24,933	80,569	16,130 k	2.9	3.0	6.0 f	34.0 f	60.0 f
France	1,166,992	20,486	1,199,287	21,053	1,049,865	18,430 k	2.3	2.3	3.4	29.0	67.6
Germany	1,533,932	19,204	1,574,317	19,709	1,579,168	19,770 k	2.3	2.3	1.5	38.7	59.8
Greece	66,300	6,530	70,572	6,951	77,975	7,680 k	1.6	1.8	17.0 f	27.0 f	56.0 f
Hungary	28,436	2,700	31,593	3,000	64,035	6,080 g	0.5	0.6	12.6	32.4	55.0
Iceland	5,994	23,324	6,490	25,252	X	X	2.4	X	12.0 p	29.0 p	59.0 p
Ireland	39,270	11,245	43,432	12,434	39,925	11,430 k	2.4	3.5	11.0 f	9.0 f	80.0 f
Italy	1,073,075	18,588	1,150,517	19,930	983,702	17,040 k	2.4	2.4	3.2	33.3	63.5
Netherlands	283,798	18,858	290,725	19,319	253,124	16,820 k	2.1	2.1	4.0	29.3	66.7
Norway	102,684	24,065	105,922	24,824	73,264	17,170 k	2.5	2.7	3.1	35.6	61.3
Poland	68,439	1,787	78,031	2,037	172,382	4,500 g	1.2	1.1	8.4	54.2	37.4
Portugal	58,636	5,944	65,103	6,599	93,224	9,450 k	3.2	2.9	8.7 o	37.1 o	54.2 o
Romania	32,120	1,380	27,619	1,187	160,584	6,900 l	0.3	0.1	18.0	53.9	28.1
Spain	487,150	12,482	527,284	13,510	494,485	12,670 k	3.2	3.2	5.3 m	35.0 m	59.7 m
Sweden	217,438	25,254	236,947	27,520	150,589	17,490 k	2.0	2.0	3.0 f	34.0 f	63.0 f
Switzerland	228,923	33,850	232,000	34,304	147,298	21,780 k	2.2	2.2	3.6 q	35.5 q	60.9 q
United Kingdom	955,828	16,606	1,009,499	17,538	940,530	16,340 k	2.8	2.9	1.7 o	36.3 o	62.0 o
Yugoslavia (former)	X	X	X	X	X	X	(0.7)	0.8	12.0 f	48.0 f	40.0 f
U.S.S.R. (former)											
Armenia	6,583	1,928	701	205	15,739	4,610 i	2.9	X	X	X	X
Azerbaijan	8,866	1,232	X	X	26,417	3,670 i	1.9	X	33.0	35.0	31.0
Belarus	33,795	3,288	X	X	70,411	6,850 i	4.0	X	X	X	X
Estonia	6,200	3,914	X	X	12,815	8,090 i	2.8	X	15.6	46.8	37.6
Georgia	9,778	1,788	X	X	20,071	3,670 i	2.9	X	X	X	X
Kazakhstan	34,227	2,026	X	X	75,850	4,490 i	2.1	X	X	X	X
Kyrgyzstan	5,183	1,163	6,727	1,509	14,619	3,280 i	4.1	X	33.7	38.3	28.0
Latvia	10,342	3,850	X	X	20,252	7,540 i	3.4	X	18.1	47.4	34.5
Lithuania	9,046	2,415	X	X	20,266	5,410 i	3.4	X	27.7	43.3	29.0
Moldova	7,422	1,700	14,171	3,246	20,258	4,640 i	2.7	X	30.7	39.4	29.8
Russian Federation	515,989	3,469	X	X	1,030,531	6,930 i	2.0	X	17.0	49.0	34.0
Tajikistan	3,793	697	X	X	11,861	2,180 i	2.9	X	X	X	X
Turkmenistan	5,419	1,439	X	X	13,328	3,540 i	3.2	X	X	X	X
Ukraine	114,052	2,191	168,800	3,243	269,598	5,180 i	2.7	X	33.3	31.1	34.4
Uzbekistan	20,510	978	X	X	58,523	2,790 i	3.4	X	X	X	X
OCEANIA											
Australia	296,051	17,068	300,900	17,348	289,315	16,680 k	2.8	3.1	3.3	30.9	65.8
Fiji	1,423	1,945	1,475	2,015	X	X	1.5	X	X	X	X
New Zealand	42,106	12,301	42,233	12,338	47,819	13,970 k	1.0	1.5	8.4 m	26.9 m	64.8 m
Papua New Guinea	3,693	932	3,787	955	7,254	1,830	1.7	2.0	29.0	30.4	40.6
Solomon Islands	226	684	217	656	X	X	6.7	X	X	X	X

Sources: The World Bank and United Nations Population Division.
Notes: a. Current U.S. dollars (Atlas methodology). b. Current 1991 U.S. dollars. c. Current 1991 international dollars ($I). d. Constant GNP. e. Constant GDP. f. From the "World Development Report 1993." g. Extrapolated from 1985 International Comparison Programme (ICP) estimates and scaled up by the corresponding U.S. deflator. h. Data are for 1990. i. These values are subject to more than the usual margin of error (see Technical Notes). j. Extrapolated from 1980 ICP estimates. k. 1991 ICP estimates. l. Extrapolated from 1975 ICP estimates. m. Data are for 1988. n. GDP figures are from different sources and differ slightly. o. Data are for 1987. p. Data are for 1989. q. Data are for 1985.
0 = zero or less than half of the unit of measure; X = not available; negative numbers are shown in parentheses.
For additional information, see Sources and Technical Notes.

Table 15.2 Official Development Assistance and External

	Average Annual Official Development Assistance (ODA) (million $US) {a}		ODA as a Percentage of GNP {a}	1991 ODA Per Capita ($US) {a}	Total External Debt (million $US)		Disbursed Long-Term Public Debt (million $US)	% of GNP	Debt Service as a Percentage of: Exports of Goods and Services	Current Borrowing	Current Borrowing Per Capita ($US)
	1982-84	1989-91	1989-91	1989-91	1979-81	1989-91	1989-91	1989-91	1989-91	1989-91	1989-91
WORLD											
AFRICA											
Algeria	49	261	0.5	14	18,742	29,001	26,804	47.1	70.6	134.9	358.5
Angola	84	219	2.9 b	26	X	7,679	X	X	X	X	X
Benin	82	265	15.7	57	435	1,220	1,162	68.6	8.2	26.9	6.8
Botswana	103	147	5.3	103	140	522	518	18.7	15.5	157.1	66.4
Burkina Faso	195	327	13.2	41	318	820	756	30.6	12.7	36.8	4.4
Burundi	136	204	17.4	26	160	918	860	73.4	40.1	43.5	7.6
Cameroon	176	488	4.5	43	2,388	5,547	4,511	41.8	21.0	65.7	38.7
Central African Rep	99	217	18.3	73	187	772	713	60.4	12.1	24.0	8.1
Chad	92	278	25.9	47	225	489	439	41.0	5.2	12.2	2.1
Congo	103	147	6.3	58	1,353	4,338	3,851	164.0	29.5	288.9	166.3
Cote d'Ivoire	140	563	6.3	48	5,751	16,522	9,679	108.1	41.4	98.9	119.4
Djibouti	76	124	X	225	29	196	156	X	8.4	67.8	33.0
Egypt	1,577	3,890	11.9	86	20,105	42,384	37,614	115.6	35.6	144.2	58.2
Equatorial Guinea	13	60	44.1	167	69	219	206	151.7	11.4	40.3	13.2
Ethiopia	454	890	14.6	19	890	3,221	3,106	51.0	32.8	76.3	4.3
Gabon	67	138	3.5	119	1,456	3,488	2,781	69.4	8.7	173.3	169.9
Gambia, The	48	93	31.3	107	131	346	301	101.1	16.4	134.8	37.2
Ghana	157	552	9.5	39	1,406	3,720	2,652	45.6	37.2	88.2	24.5
Guinea	97	324	13.0	56	1,176	2,366	2,201	88.3	18.7	60.5	24.1
Guinea-Bissau	64	125	70.4	125	114	562	527	296.0	27.1	25.7	9.2
Kenya	432	978	11.3	36	3,179	6,566	4,525	52.2	34.6	111.0	31.0
Lesotho	101	131	13.4	70	69	380	363	37.2	28.3	46.2	13.6
Liberia	120	106	X	54	696	1,476	1,106	X	X	X	X
Libya	(63)	19	0.1 b	4	X	X	X	X	X	X	X
Madagascar	204	358	13.8	29	1,189	3,426	3,214	124.0	40.5	87.6	15.7
Malawi	132	462	27.2	49	764	1,554	1,401	82.7	26.6	78.9	11.7
Mali	255	445	19.2	43	711	2,358	2,247	96.8	13.4	42.2	5.7
Mauritania	180	222	22.4	100	836	2,108	1,870	188.0	20.6	108.2	52.7
Mauritius	41	81	3.3	87	462	921	725	29.4	9.5	112.4	142.6
Morocco	514	901	3.7	47	9,634	21,998	20,916	86.1	35.6	165.6	82.7
Mozambique	257	944	75.2	71	X	4,227	4,001	319.0	21.6	30.4	3.7
Namibia	X	98	4.9	120	X	X	X	X	X	X	X
Niger	198	359	15.6	52	837	1,656	1,246	54.1	35.0	105.2	17.0
Nigeria	39	291	1.0	3	9,109	33,017	32,275	106.7	24.7	263.0	27.6
Rwanda	155	284	13.4	45	181	739	689	32.5	13.2	33.5	3.6
Senegal	325	737	14.2	102	1,422	3,510	2,818	54.2	24.4	139.0	46.4
Sierra Leone	70	93	9.9	25	449	1,030	589	62.9	8.0	38.3	2.8
Somalia	385	450 c	0.5 c	32	755	2,069	1,838 c	187.2 c	24.7	37.6	1.6
South Africa	X	X	X	X	X	X	X	X	X	X	X
Sudan	780	805	6.9 b	32	5,068	10,828	8,949	0.8 b	9.3	30.5	2.2
Swaziland	30	44	5.5	62	190	261	251	31.6	9.8	187.8	51.3
Tanzania	616	1,040	39.3	39	2,397	5,661	5,412	204.8	27.4	48.5	5.1
Togo	100	197	13.3	55	1,002	1,270	1,059	71.4	11.8	110.8	21.7
Tunisia	203	333	2.9	38	3,511	7,646	6,636	58.4	26.3	125.8	161.2
Uganda	144	522	16.9	31	656	2,481	2,145	69.3	87.1	54.9	8.3
Zaire	325	706 c	8.5 c	13	4,957	9,677	7,938 c	95.7 c	26.7	116.8	10.1
Zambia	262	491	16.3 c	70	3,294	6,354	4,507 c	149.9 c	28.1	137.8	39.9
Zimbabwe	242	330	5.0	37	868	3,155	2,448	37.3	24.6	116.1	49.5
ASIA											
Afghanistan	258	277	X	29	X	X	X	X	X	X	X
Bangladesh	1,221	2,013	9.1	18	3,898	11,990	11,153	50.3	33.2	60.5	5.5
Bhutan	14	48	17.8	35	X	82	80	29.9	7.6	61.1	3.9
Cambodia	123	45	7.8	7	X	X	X	X	X	X	X
China	450	2,099	0.5	2	4,161	52,704	44,254	10.6	10.8	75.3	6.1
India	1,671	1,678	0.6	2	20,381	68,208	59,731	20.3	30.9	113.1	8.3
Indonesia	775	1,773	1.8	9	20,779	64,844	44,699	44.5	34.6	106.1	52.7
Iran, Islamic Rep	31	93	0.1	1	2,767	8,563	2,132	1.6	3.8	154.0	10.8
Iraq	12	29 c	0.1 c	22	X	X	X	X	X	X	X
Israel	1,145	1,310	2.5	280	X	X	X	X	X	X	X
Japan	(3,701)	(9,662)	(0.3)	(88)	X	X	X	X	X	X	X
Jordan	758	609	13.5	161	1,923	7,983	7,026	155.9	25.0	85.7	150.3
Korea, Dem People's Rep	43	8	0.0 b	X	X	X	X	X	X	X	X
Korea, Rep	2	37	0.0	3	28,451	36,098	19,354	8.3	10.0	132.8	177.5
Kuwait	(1,054)	(354)	(0.5) b	(187)	X	X	X	X	X	X	X
Lao People's Dem Rep	109	150	17.3	37	290	1,047	1,032	118.4	9.8	9.5	2.2
Lebanon	130	169	X	50	472	1,631	546	X	X	183.6	56.3
Malaysia	213	356	0.9	25	6,915	19,149	15,135	36.5	11.9	178.6	218.3
Mongolia	611	12	0.2 b	8	X	X	X	X	X	X	X
Myanmar	310	173	1.1 b	4	1,498	4,379	4,349	24.8 b	38.1	85.3	2.7
Nepal	201	442	13.1	20	210	1,587	1,523	45.3	16.2	35.5	3.4
Oman	90	33	0.4	9	671	2,735	2,365	27.4	X	177.7	434.0
Pakistan	839	1,153	2.6	10	9,798	20,628	16,191	36.6	28.5	105.3	15.9
Philippines	387	1,119	2.5	19	17,161	30,121	23,428	53.1	27.0	177.8	54.7
Saudi Arabia	(3,390)	(2,134)	(2.0)	(108)	X	X	X	X	X	X	X
Singapore	25	25	0.1	7	X	X	X	X	X	X	X
Sri Lanka	452	620	7.8	37	1,877	5,857	4,957	62.1	18.0	74.0	24.0
Syrian Arab Rep	874	341	2.8	17	3,561	16,415	15,198	122.7	49.0	139.6	87.9
Thailand	433	759	1.0	13	8,598	29,156	12,758	16.2	16.3	103.4	89.3
Turkey	420	1,003	1.1	29	18,083	46,936	37,541	41.8	37.7	148.2	132.8
United Arab Emirates	(277)	(109) d	(0.4)	(346)	X	X	X	X	X	X	X
Viet Nam	1,279	179	1.9 b	3	X	X	X	X	X	X	X
Yemen	563 e	340	3.7 f	20	X	X	4,991	79.8 f	X	62.0	16.8

Debt Indicators, 1979–91

Table 15.2

	Average Annual Official Development Assistance (ODA) (million $US) {a}		ODA as a Percentage of GNP {a}	1991 ODA Per Capita ($US) {a}	Total External Debt (million $US)		Disbursed Long-Term Public Debt		Debt Service as a Percentage of:		Current Borrowing Per Capita ($US)
							(million $US)	% of GNP	Exports of Goods and Services	Current Borrowing	
	1982-84	1989-91	1989-91	1989-91	1979-81	1989-91	1989-91	1989-91	1989-91	1989-91	1989-91
NORTH & CENTRAL AMERICA											
Belize	14	29	7.9	144	65	153	136	37.6	14.9	89.6	102.8
Canada	(1,417)	(2,465)	(0.5)	(96)	X	X	X	X	0.0	X	X
Costa Rica	183	217	4.1	62	2,693	3,963	3,317	62.9	21.3	188.9	138.9
Cuba	697	50	X	4	X	X	X	X	X	X	X
Dominican Rep	141	111	1.8	13	1,961	3,865	3,414	56.9	13.9	180.6	38.7
El Salvador	257	362	6.9	55	976	2,113	1,921	36.5	26.1	100.7	40.3
Guatemala	68	217	2.6	20	1,157	2,519	2,120	25.0	17.2	203.2	28.9
Haiti	132	193	8.1	30	327	793	680	28.5	17.7	111.7	5.7
Honduras	211	347	10.0	63	1,451	3,229	2,969	86.0	28.3	110.4	53.8
Jamaica	177	246	8.1	81	1,970	4,410	3,784	124.5	30.3	206.5	280.5
Mexico	118	147	0.1	2	59,456	98,180	77,099	36.1	34.4	189.8	159.6
Nicaragua	198	421	25.0	179	2,032	8,771	8,093	480.4	19.0	36.4	38.1
Panama	53	76	3.9	45	2,981	5,623	3,954	203.5	9.8	1,238.3	67.3
Trinidad and Tobago	5	8	0.2	7	853	2,275	1,842	42.1	15.9	348.7	269.9
United States	(8,331)	(10,111)	(0.2)	(45)	X	X	X	X	X	X	X
SOUTH AMERICA											
Argentina	50	217	0.3	8	27,921	56,261	48,010	60.8	42.6	468.4	179.7
Bolivia	165	499	10.8	74	2,819	4,136	3,545	77.0	36.5	104.4	47.0
Brazil	159	189	0.0	1	70,898	108,988	85,202	21.3	45.2	173.1	72.1
Chile	(2)	95	0.4	9	12,369	18,355	10,415	40.3	30.2	173.1	236.7
Colombia	91	102	0.3	4	7,175	17,146	14,391	35.6	45.6	177.6	113.7
Ecuador	84	177	1.7	19	6,062	10,470	9,749	95.2	32.6	160.9	101.7
Guyana	36	93	28.1	156	766	1,838	1,567	476.0	61.9	163.7	188.6
Paraguay	62	87	1.8	25	970	2,120	1,870	38.1	12.7	162.3	52.7
Peru	272	349	1.3	15	9,080	16,153	13,408	50.6	17.3	205.1	31.9
Suriname	37	50	3.3	93	X	X	X	X	X	X	X
Uruguay	4	50	0.6	19	1,719	4,243	2,943	36.0	40.0	170.3	279.0
Venezuela	12	39	0.1	4	28,499	33,372	25,023	49.2	24.4	236.3	211.4
EUROPE											
Albania	X	108	X	92	X	X	X	X	X	X	X
Austria	(192)	(408)	(0.3)	(71)	X	X	X	X	X	X	X
Belgium	(473)	(808)	(0.5)	(83)	X	X	X	X	X	X	X
Bulgaria	X	X	X	X	X	10,681	9,982	48.5	25.7	133.5	205.4
Czechoslovakia (former)	X	X	X	X	X	8,710	5,225	11.0	10.5	106.4	102.9
Denmark	(420)	(1,103)	(1.0)	(233)	X	X	X	X	X	X	X
Finland	(158)	(827)	(0.7)	(186)	X	X	X	X	X	X	X
France	(3,879)	(6,838)	(0.6)	(131)	X	X	X	X	X	X	X
Germany	X	(6,053)	(0.4) f	(86)	X	X	X	X	X	X	X
Greece	12	34	0.1	4	X	X	X	X	X	X	X
Hungary	X	X	X	X	9,472	21,439	17,949	63.1	37.6	138.8	374.8
Iceland	X	X	X	X	X	X	X	X	X	X	X
Ireland	(38)	(59)	(0.2)	(21)	X	X	X	X	X	X	X
Italy	(926)	(3,453)	(0.4)	(58)	X	X	X	X	X	X	X
Netherlands	(1,312)	(2,383)	(0.9)	(167)	X	X	X	X	X	X	X
Norway	(561)	(1,100)	(1.1)	(276)	X	X	X	X	X	X	X
Poland	X	X	X	X	X	41,042	39,296	57.7	7.2	208.7	30.5
Portugal	64	(108)	(0.2)	(22)	9,736	24,400	16,982	33.1	40.6	106.4	496.3
Romania	X	X	X	X	7,931	939	129	0.3	10.4	542.6	29.8
Spain	(149)	(891)	(0.2)	(30)	X	X	X	X	X	X	X
Sweden	(827)	(1,974)	(1.0)	(246)	X	X	X	X	X	X	X
Switzerland	(286)	(724)	(0.3)	(128)	X	X	X	X	X	X	X
United Kingdom	(1,613)	(2,824)	(0.3)	(56)	X	X	X	X	X	X	X
Yugoslavia (former)	(1)	74	0.1 c	5	18,367	17,793	13,716 c	19.7 c	30.6	349.6	174.0
U.S.S.R. (former)	(2,674)	(1,287)	X	(4)	X	X	45,924	X	X	X	41.7
Armenia	X	X	X	X	X	X	X	X	X	X	X
Azerbaijan	X	X	X	X	X	X	X	X	X	X	X
Belarus	X	X	X	X	X	X	X	X	X	X	X
Estonia	X	X	X	X	X	X	X	X	X	X	X
Georgia	X	X	X	X	X	X	X	X	X	X	X
Kazakhstan	X	X	X	X	X	X	X	X	X	X	X
Kyrgyzstan	X	X	X	X	X	X	X	X	X	X	X
Latvia	X	X	X	X	X	X	X	X	X	X	X
Lithuania	X	X	X	X	X	X	X	X	X	X	X
Moldova	X	X	X	X	X	X	X	X	X	X	X
Russian Federation	X	X	X	X	X	X	X	X	X	X	X
Tajikistan	X	X	X	X	X	X	X	X	X	X	X
Turkmenistan	X	X	X	X	X	X	X	X	X	X	X
Ukraine	X	X	X	X	X	X	X	X	X	X	X
Uzbekistan	X	X	X	X	X	X	X	X	X	X	X
OCEANIA											
Australia	(801)	(1,008)	(0.4)	(61)	X	X	X	X	X	X	X
Fiji	33	46	3.6	63	265	393	290	21.4	12.1	314.7	137.9
New Zealand	(60)	(94)	(0.2)	(29)	X	X	X	X	X	X	X
Papua New Guinea	322	365	11.0	96	837	2,545	1,477	44.1	38.3	97.8	135.6
Solomon Islands	25	44	21.0	121	19	118	101	44.9	10.8	220.3	36.2

Sources: Organisation for Economic Co-operation and Development, the World Bank, and United Nations Population Division.
Notes: a. For ODA, flows to recipients are shown as positive numbers; flows from donors are shown as negative numbers (in parentheses). b. Data are for 1989 only.
c. Data are for 1988 through 1990. d. 1989 data are incomplete. e. Includes data from both the former Arab Republic of Yemen and the former People's
Democratic Republic of Yemen. f. Data are for 1991.
0 = zero or less than half of the unit of measure; X = not available.
For additional information, see Sources and Technical Notes.

Table 15.3 Defense Expenditures, Military Personnel,

	Defense Expenditures ($US million)		Numbers in Armed Forces (1,000) {a}		Estimated Reservists (1,000) {b}	Victims of Conflict {c}		Location of Refugees and Asylum Seekers	Arms Trade			
						Military Deaths	Civilian Deaths	Seekers	Exports (million $US)	Percent of Total Exports	Imports (million $US)	Percent of Total Imports
	1985	1991	1985	1991	1991			1992	1988	1988	1988	1988
WORLD	X	X	26,423.1	24,908.1	5,602.0	X	X	17,556,900	48,640	1.7	48,610	1.7
AFRICA	X	X	1,826.3	2,098.3	X	X	X	5,698,450	110	0.2	4,870	7.1
Algeria	953	971	170.0	139.0	150	X	X	210,000	0	0.0	825	10.6
Angola	1,147	X	49.5	100.0	50	21,000	320,000	9,000	0	X	1,600	X
Benin	21	13	4.5	4.4	X	X	X	4,300	0	X	10	X
Botswana	22	79	3.0	4.5	X	X	X	500	0	0.0	30	X
Burkina Faso	34	62	4.0	8.7	X	X	X	6,300	0	X	10	X
Burundi	35	X	5.2	7.2	X	X	X	107,350	0	0.0	10	4.9
Cameroon	159	94	7.3	11.7	X	X	X	1,500	0	0.0	5	0.4
Central African Rep	X	X	2.3	6.5	X	X	X	18,000	0	X	0	0.0
Chad	37	X	12.2	17.0	X	X	X	X	0	0.0	40	9.5
Congo	56	X	8.7	8.8	X	X	X	9,400	0	X	20	3.5
Cote d'Ivoire	76	X	13.2	7.1	12	X	X	195,500	0	X	0	0.0
Djibouti	32	X	3.0	3.8	X	X	X	96,000	X	X	X	X
Egypt	4,143	3,582	445.0	410.0	604	X	X	10,650	170	2.9	725	3.1
Equatorial Guinea	X	X	2.2	1.3	X	X	X	X	0	0.0	0	0.0
Ethiopia	447	1,217	217.0	320.0	X	X	X	416,000	0	0.0	725	80.6
Gabon	79	X	2.4	4.8	X	X	X	200	0	0.0	5	0.5
Gambia, The	2	X	0.5	0.9	X	X	X	3,300	0	0.0	10	X
Ghana	63	69	15.1	12.2	0	X	X	12,100	0	0.0	10	1.1
Guinea	X	X	9.9	9.7	X	X	X	485,000	0	0.0	20	X
Guinea-Bissau	11	X	8.6	9.2	X	X	X	12,000	0	0.0	30	X
Kenya	256	X	13.7	23.6	X	X	X	422,900	0	0.0	160	8.0
Lesotho	X	X	X	2.0	X	X	X	200	0	0.0	0	0.0
Liberia	28	X	6.8	7.8	50	1,000	9,000	100,000	0	0.0	10	X
Libya	1,350	X	73.0	85.0	40	X	X	X	50	0.8	575	11.5
Madagascar	54	39	21.1	21.0	X	X	X	X	0	0.0	10	X
Malawi	21	X	5.3	7.3	1	X	X	1,070,000	0	0.0	0	0.0
Mali	30	X	4.9	7.3	X	X	X	10,000	0	0.0	70	13.6
Mauritania	X	27	8.5	9.6	X	X	X	40,000	0	0.0	10	X
Mauritius	X	X	X	X	X	X	X	X	0	0.0	0	0.0
Morocco	641	730	149.0	195.5	100	X	X	800	0	0.0	90	1.9
Mozambique	239	230	15.8	50.2	X	50,000	1,000,000	250	0	0.0	160	X
Namibia	X	33	X	9.0	X	X	X	150	X	X	X	X
Niger	12	X	2.2	3.3	X	X	X	3,600	0	0.0	0	0.0
Nigeria	1,251	814	94.0	76.0	X	X	X	2,900	0	0.0	150	X
Rwanda	X	X	5.2	5.2	X	X	X	24,500	0	0.0	0	0.0
Senegal	63	68	10.1	9.7	X	X	X	55,100	0	0.0	10	X
Sierra Leone	5	X	3.1	6.2	X	X	X	7,600	0	0.0	0	0.0
Somalia	46	X	62.7	64.5	X	5,000	50,000	10,000	0	0.0	30	X
South Africa	1,951	2,063	106.4	72.4	650	0	10,000	250,000	60	0.3	0	0.0
Sudan	207	X	56.6	82.5	X	6,000	500,000	750,500	0	0.0	60	5.7
Swaziland	X	X	X	X	X	X	X	52,000	0	0.0	0	0.0
Tanzania	280	X	40.4	46.8	10	X	X	257,800	0	0.0	70	8.6
Togo	19	X	3.6	5.9	X	X	X	350	0	0.0	0	0.0
Tunisia	417	323	35.1	35.0	X	X	X	X	0	0.0	20	0.5
Uganda	53	70	20.0	70.0	X	X	X	179,600	0	0.0	80	14.7
Zaire	81	X	48.0	51.0	X	X	X	442,400	0	0.0	10	1.3
Zambia	295	61	16.2	16.2	X	X	X	155,700	0	0.0	0	0.0
Zimbabwe	284	312	41.0	48.5	X	X	X	265,000	0	0.0	0	0.0
ASIA	X	X	11,905.9	12,019.0	X	X	X	X	4,055	X	28,040	X
Afghanistan	287	X	47.0	45.0	X	X	X	52,000	0	0.0	X	0.0
Bangladesh	169	234	91.3	107.0	X	X	X	245,300	0	0.0	80	2.6
Bhutan	X	X	X	X	X	X	X	X	X	X	X	X
Cambodia	X	X	35.0	111.8	X	X	X	X	0	0.0	240	X
China	10,615	12,025	3,900.0	3,030.0	1,200	0	2,000	12,500	3,100	6.5	270	0.5
India	6,263	7,990	1,260.0	1,265.0	655	4,000	12,000	378,000	0	0.0	3,200	16.7
Indonesia	2,341	1,739	278.1	283.0	400	X	X	15,600	0	0.0	130	1.0
Iran, Islamic Rep	14,223	4,270	305.0	528.0	350	X	X	2,781,800	0	0.0	2,000	18.2
Iraq	12,868	X	520.0	382.5	650	X	X	64,600	80	0.6	4,600	37.1
Israel	5,052	3,239	142.0	175.0	430	X	X	X	140	1.5	1,900	12.6
Japan	13,151	16,464	243.0	246.0	48	X	·X	700	70	0.0	1,100	0.6
Jordan	523	594	70.3	98.3	35	X	X	1,010,850	40	3.9	320	11.6
Korea, Dem People's Rep	4,156	5,328	838.0	1,132.0	540	X	X	150	470	19.6	1,000	32.3
Korea, Rep	4,399	6,359	598.0	633.0	4,500	X	X	150	50	0.1	600	1.2
Kuwait	1,796	7,959	12.0	11.7	19	0	1,000	X	0	0.0	190	3.6
Lao People's Dem Rep	X	X	53.7	55.1	X	X	X	X	0	0.0	150	X
Lebanon	X	20	17.4	36.8	X	22,000	41,000	322,900	0	0.0	10	0.4
Malaysia	1,764	1,670	110.0	127.5	44	X	X	16,700	0	0.0	30	0.2
Mongolia	233	268	33.0	15.5	200	X	X	X	0	0.0	0	0.0
Myanmar	228	298	186.0	286.0	X	X	X	X	0	0.0	30	12.3
Nepal	36	35	25.0	35.0	X	X	X	89,400	0	0.0	0	0.0
Oman	2,157	1,182	2.5	35.7	X	X	X	X	0	0.0	30	1.4
Pakistan	2,076	3,014	482.8	580.0	513	X	X	1,577,000	10	0.2	340	5.2
Philippines	474	843	114.8	106.5	131	X	X	5,600	0	0.0	60	0.7
Saudi Arabia	17,693	35,438	62.5	102.0	75	X	X	27,400	5	0.0	3,000	14.9
Singapore	1,188	1,518	55.0	55.5	292	X	X	100	10	0.0	310	0.7
Sri Lanka	228	340	21.6	105.9	12	12,000	18,000	X	0	0.0	20	0.9
Syrian Arab Rep	3,483	3,095	402.5	408.0	400	X	X	307,500	0	0.0	1,300	58.5
Thailand	1,517	1,761	235.3	283.0	500	X	X	255,000	0	0.0	525	2.7
Turkey	1,649	2,014	630.0	579.2	1,107	X	X	31,700	0	0.0	775	5.4
United Arab Emirates	2,043	4,249	43.0	54.5	X	X	X	X	0	0.0	60	0.7
Viet Nam	X	X	1,027.0	1,041.0	1,000	X	X	19,000	70	X	1,500	X
Yemen	792	910	64.1	63.5	40	X	X	52,500	X	X	X	X

and Refugees, 1985–92

Table 15.3

	Defense Expenditures ($US million)		Numbers in Armed Forces (1,000) {a}		Estimated Reservists (1,000) {b}	Victims of Conflict {c}		Location of Refugees and Asylum Seekers	Arms Trade			
						Military	Civilian		Exports (million $US)	Percent of Total Exports	Imports (million $US)	Percent of Total Imports
	1985	1991	1985	1991	1991	Deaths	Deaths	1992	1988	1988	1988	1988
NORTH & CENTRAL AMERICA	X	X	2,724.0	2,516.5	X	X	X	X	14,710	X	3,340	X
Belize	4	9	0.6	0.8	1	X	X	8,700	X	X	X	X
Canada	7,566	7,358	83.0	84.0	30	X	X	37,700	180	0.2	210	0.2
Costa Rica	29	48	X	X	X	X	X	34,350	0	0.0	0	0.0
Cuba	1,597	1,272	161.5	175.0	1,435	X	X	1,100	230	4.2	1,700	22.4
Dominican Rep	51	22	22.2	22.2	X	X	X	X	0	0.0	5	0.3
El Salvador	252	201	41.7	43.7	X	25,000	50,000	250	0	0.0	60	X
Guatemala	197	158	31.7	44.6	5	40,000	100,000	4,900	0	0.0	5	0.3
Haiti	31	21	6.9	7.4	X	X	X	X	0	0.0	0	0.0
Honduras	72	82	16.6	17.5	60	X	X	150	0	0.0	40	4.5
Jamaica	18	23	2.1	3.4	1	X	X	X	0	0.0	0	0.0
Mexico	1,241	917	129.1	175.0	300	X	X	47,300	0	0.0	60	0.3
Nicaragua	637	225	62.9	14.7	X	X	X	5,850	0	0.0	525	65.6
Panama	97	73	12.0	11.7	X	X	X	850	0	0.0	10	1.3
Trinidad and Tobago	73	X	2.1	2.7	X	X	X	X	0	0.0	0	0.0
United States	258,165	227,055	2,151.6	1,913.8	1,784	X	X	103,700	14,300	4.4	725	0.2
SOUTH AMERICA	X	X	853.2	914.2	X	X	X	X	690	X	545	X
Argentina	1,889	1,161	108.0	65.0	377	X	X	X	30	0.3	20	0.4
Bolivia	127	122	27.6	31.5	X	X	X	X	0	0.0	10	1.7
Brazil	1,737	1,081	276.0	296.7	1,515	X	X	200	380	1.1	260	1.6
Chile	1,242	735	101.0	91.8	45	X	X	X	280	4.0	30	0.6
Colombia	274	1,403	66.2	139.0	117	8,000	14,000	400	0	0.0	60	1.2
Ecuador	284	401	42.5	57.5	100	X	X	200	0	0.0	40	2.3
Guyana	45	X	6.6	2.0	2	X	X	X	0	0.0	0	0.0
Paraguay	60	X	14.4	16.0	45	X	X	X	0	0.0	30	5.2
Peru	641	605	128.0	112.0	188	8,000	9,000	400	0	0.0	30	1.0
Suriname	23	16	2.0	3.0	X	X	X	X	0	0.0	0	0.0
Uruguay	128	143	31.9	24.7	X	X	X	100	0	0.0	5	0.4
Venezuela	824	1,525	49.0	75.0	X	X	X	1,350	0	0.0	60	0.5
EUROPE	X	X	3,725.0	3,284.8	X	X	X	X	28,820	1.9	9,755	0.6
Albania	189	103	40.4	40.0	155	X	X	X	0	0.0	0	0.0
Austria	892	813	54.7	52.0	200	X	X	82,100	60	0.2	1,300	3.6
Belgium	2,428	1,505	91.6	80.7	229	X	X	19,100	20	0.0	575	0.7
Bulgaria	1,656	1,790	148.5	107.0	473	X	X	X	380	1.9	400	1.9
Czechoslovakia (former)	4,849	2,800	203.3	145.8	495	X	X	2,200	850	3.2	210	0.8
Denmark	1,259	1,272	29.6	29.2	72	X	X	13,900	0	0.0	200	0.8
Finland	807	1,084	36.5	32.8	700	X	X	3,500	10	0.0	70	0.3
France	20,780	18,044	464.3	453.1	419	X	X	29,400	1,890	1.1	140	0.1
Germany	19,922 d	16,450 d	478.0 d	447.0 d	905 d	X	X	536,000	X	X	X	X
Greece	2,331	1,977	201.5	158.5	406	X	X	1,900	30	0.6	575	4.7
Hungary	2,402	1,230	106.0	80.8	192	X	X	40,000	160	0.8	60	0.3
Iceland	X	X	X	X	X	X	X	X	0	0.0	0	0.0
Ireland	320	278	13.7	13.0	16	X	X	X	0	0.0	10	0.1
Italy	9,733	9,146	385.1	361.4	584	X	X	19,100	390	0.3	270	0.2
Netherlands	3,884	3,947	105.5	93.0	144	X	X	24,600	525	0.5	410	0.4
Norway	1,797	1,864	37.0	32.7	285	X	X	5,700	10	0.0	230	1.0
Poland	5,760	2,200	319.0	296.5	435	X	X	1,500	675	2.2	1,000	3.8
Portugal	654	638	73.0	55.3	190	X	X	X	110	1.0	50	0.3
Romania	1,395	1,150	189.5	200.0	593	X	X	X	150	X	20	X
Spain	3,969	3,484	320.0	217.0	498	X	X	12,700	150	0.4	900	1.5
Sweden	3,192	2,788	65.7	60.5	709	X	X	88,400	210	0.4	150	0.3
Switzerland	1,930	1,853	35.0	35.0	625	X	X	81,700	110	0.2	90	0.2
United Kingdom	23,791	22,420	327.1	293.5	353	X	X	24,600	725	0.5	625	0.3
Yugoslavia (former)	1,692	3,490	X	X	X	X	X	621,600	200	1.6	40	0.3
U.S.S.R. (former)	241,500	91,631	5,300.0	3,988.0	5,602	X	X	X	21,400	19.3	1,100	1.0
Armenia	X	X	X	X	X	X	X	300,000	X	X	X	X
Azerbaijan	X	X	X	X	X	X	X	246,000	X	X	X	X
Belarus	X	X	X	X	X	X	X	3,700	X	X	X	X
Estonia	X	X	X	X	X	X	X	X	X	X	X	X
Georgia	X	X	X	X	X	X	X	X	X	X	X	X
Kazakhstan	X	X	X	X	X	X	X	X	X	X	X	X
Kyrgyzstan	X	X	X	X	X	X	X	X	X	X	X	X
Latvia	X	X	X	X	X	X	X	X	X	X	X	X
Lithuania	X	X	X	X	X	X	X	X	X	X	X	X
Moldova	X	X	X	X	X	X	X	X	X	X	X	X
Russian Federation	X	X	X	X	X	X	X	460,000	X	X	X	X
Tajikistan	X	X	X	X	X	X	X	X	X	X	X	X
Turkmenistan	X	X	X	X	X	X	X	40,000	X	X	X	X
Ukraine	X	X	X	X	X	X	X	X	X	X	X	X
Uzbekistan	X	X	X	X	X	X	X	X	X	X	X	X
OCEANIA	X	X	88.7	87.3	X	X	X	X	65	0.1	1,410	3.1
Australia	4,668	4,210	70.4	67.9	29	X	X	24,000	40	0.1	70	0.2
Fiji	14	23	2.7	5.0	5	X	X	X	0	0.0	0	0.0
New Zealand	454	423	12.4	10.9	9	X	X	X	5	0.1	80	1.1
Papua New Guinea	34	37	3.2	3.5	X	X	X	3,800	0	0.0	30	2.2
Solomon Islands	X	X	X	X	X	X	X	X	X	X	X	X

Sources: The International Institute for Strategic Studies, World Priorities, U.S. Committee for Refugees, and the World Bank.
Notes: a. Global and regional totals of numbers in armed forces only include countries listed here. b. Global and regional totals of estimated reservists only include countries listed here. c. Data refer to the total number of war or war-related deaths occurring from the beginning of the conflict until 1990. d. Data are for the former Federal Republic of Germany. 0 = zero or less than half of the unit of measure; X = not available.
For additional information, see Sources and Technical Notes.

Table 15.4 World Commodity Indexes and Prices, 1975–92

Commodity Indexes (based on constant prices with 1990 = 100)

	1975	1980	1981	1982	1983	1984	1985	1986	1987	1988	1989	1990	1991	1992
Petroleum	113	199	223	205	190	190	183	78	91	67	81	100	80	76
33 NONFUEL COMMODITIES	159	168	147	134	144	149	132	112	102	114	113	100	94	86
Total Agriculture	185	193	168	151	166	175	151	132	110	117	112	100	96	85
Total Food	196	198	172	155	168	182	159	143	110	121	115	100	95	85
-Beverages	168	234	194	201	208	246	224	233	139	145	120	100	92	74
-Cereals	259	183	194	144	159	155	135	100	86	108	116	100	100	94
-Fats and Oils	222	205	197	163	196	236	164	107	114	139	126	100	102	105
-Other Foods	177	165	126	108	117	106	102	91	91	95	102	100	93	84
Nonfood Agricultural Products	150	179	155	138	159	151	126	97	110	104	105	100	97	82
Timber	62	129	102	104	99	117	94	89	119	116	113	100	103	112
Metals and Minerals	135	134	119	112	117	111	105	82	85	109	114	100	89	83

Commodity Prices (in constant 1990 $US)

	$US/Unit	1975	1980	1981	1982	1983	1984	1985	1986	1987	1988	1989	1990	1991	1992
Cocoa (New York & London)	kg	2.76	3.62	2.88	2.44	3.05	3.52	3.29	2.56	2.24	1.66	1.31	1.27	1.17	1.03
Coffee (Other Mild Arabicas)	kg	3.19	4.82	3.97	4.34	4.19	4.69	4.71	5.31	2.82	3.18	2.52	1.97	1.83	1.32
Tea (World)	kg	3.06	3.10	2.79	2.72	3.35	5.08	2.89	2.38	1.92	1.88	2.13	2.03	1.81	1.88
Rice (Thailand)	mt	803.1	603.0	668.1	411.7	398.2	370.5	314.7	260.2	259.2	316.2	338.3	287.2	308.0	269.7
Grain Sorghum (U.S.)	mt	247.5	179.1	174.9	152.5	185.2	174.9	150.1	102.0	81.9	103.3	111.9	103.9	103.0	96.4
Maize (U.S.)	mt	264.5	174.1	181.0	153.6	195.6	199.7	163.6	108.3	85.2	112.2	117.8	109.3	105.2	97.8
Wheat (Canada)	mt	401.0	265.1	271.8	234.0	243.8	243.1	252.6	198.5	150.3	188.3	212.6	156.2	140.0	166.1
Sugar (World)	kg	1.00	0.88	0.51	0.26	0.27	0.17	0.13	0.16	0.17	0.24	0.30	0.28	0.19	0.19
Beef (U.S.)	kg	2.94	3.83	3.42	3.36	3.51	3.34	3.14	2.59	2.69	2.64	2.71	2.56	2.61	2.30
Lamb (New Zealand)	kg	3.15	4.01	3.79	3.34	2.78	2.82	2.69	2.66	2.43	2.53	2.45	2.66	2.28	2.49
Bananas (Any Origin)	mt	545.7	526.6	555.4	526.1	616.7	543.0	554.4	471.9	411.3	501.6	577.7	540.9	548.1	443.9
Oranges (Mediterranean)	mt	504.3	542.7	560.5	540.5	536.7	517.9	580.8	486.7	513.3	475.7	470.6	531.1	510.4	459.0
Copra (Philippines)	mt	566.9	629.0	524.4	441.6	713.4	1,043.5	562.7	243.5	347.8	417.6	367.6	230.7	280.6	356.9
Coconut Oil (Phil. & Indonesia)	mt	870.4	936.2	788.7	652.7	1,049.8	1,696.7	860.1	367.2	497.5	592.6	546.0	336.5	424.2	541.9
Groundnut Meal (Any Origin)	mt	309.7	333.9	329.4	292.3	329.4	274.9	214.3	204.0	182.4	219.8	210.5	184.8	147.0	146.1
Groundnut Oil (Nigeria)	mt	1,897.8	1,193.6	1,443.1	822.1	1,022.4	1,494.0	1,319.2	703.4	562.8	619.3	818.6	963.7	876.6	572.3
Linseed (Canada)	mt	747.6	487.6	490.3	418.8	398.8	437.9	399.4	257.1	190.2	308.5	364.5	314.0	204.7	198.0
Linseed Oil (Any Origin)	mt	1,550.5	968.6	913.4	729.6	697.0	840.6	915.5	518.0	353.4	547.7	799.8	709.0	430.1	372.7
Palm Kernels (Nigeria)	mt	457.4	479.5	439.1	372.5	525.4	775.9	424.2	175.5	203.7	280.1	265.2	188.0	215.5	215.8
Palm Oil (Malaysia)	mt	960.4	810.8	789.8	625.6	721.1	1,071.0	730.3	317.7	386.1	458.7	370.2	289.8	332.1	369.2
Soybeans (U.S.)	mt	486.4	411.6	399.1	343.8	405.0	414.5	326.5	257.1	243.1	318.4	290.5	246.8	234.7	221.0
Soybean Oil (Any Origin)	mt	1,369.2	828.8	701.5	628.7	757.9	1,063.9	833.8	422.8	376.0	485.8	456.4	447.0	444.6	402.4
Soybean Meal (U.S.)	mt	342.8	364.0	349.6	307.1	342.0	289.8	228.9	228.7	228.5	280.7	259.8	200.2	193.1	191.8
Fish Meal (Peru)	mt	541.9	700.3	647.7	496.1	651.5	548.1	408.2	396.8	431.1	570.8	431.5	412.2	468.1	451.8
Cotton ("A" Index)	kg	2.57	2.84	2.55	2.24	2.67	2.62	1.92	1.31	1.86	1.47	1.77	1.82	1.64	1.20
Burlap (U.S.)	meter	0.49	0.50	0.39	0.38	0.42	0.54	0.50	0.31	0.30	0.32	0.33	0.31	0.30	0.27
Jute (Bangladesh)	mt	820.6	428.0	381.8	401.7	434.6	780.0	849.7	333.9	363.3	388.2	394.4	408.3	372.6	299.9
Sisal (East Africa)	mt	1,282.9	1,062.7	892.6	833.5	809.7	858.2	766.8	635.4	576.3	578.1	689.9	715.0	655.4	474.4
Wool (New Zealand)	kg	6.06	6.39	5.92	5.52	5.23	5.40	5.19	4.09	5.08	6.08	5.65	4.07	3.46	3.69
Rubber (New York)	kg	1.46	2.26	1.73	1.41	1.78	1.61	1.35	1.17	1.26	1.35	1.18	1.02	0.99	0.96
Logs (Malaysia)	cm	131.2	271.6	215.3	219.1	208.8	245.7	198.5	187.0	249.2	245.0	237.3	210.4	217.2	234.9
Plywood (Philippines)	sheet	2.69	3.80	3.39	3.27	3.31	3.34	3.07	3.38	4.49	3.76	3.70	3.55	3.65	3.57
Sawnwood (Malaysia)	cm	368.1	507.3	434.7	424.5	437.7	450.8	402.8	329.1	310.8	321.7	445.7	524.2	462.3	481.4
Tobacco (India)	mt	3,605.4	3,195.8	3,252.1	3,387.2	3,228.8	2,924.3	2,842.6	2,348.9	2,082.4	2,036.5	1,997.9	1,964.0	2,161.1	1,848.4
Coal (U.S.)	mt	X	59.89	78.19	73.37	64.00	71.42	67.93	54.27	40.75	38.93	42.79	41.80	40.65	38.09
Crude Petroleum (OPEC, Spot)	bbl	24.11	42.38	47.47	43.57	40.41	40.41	38.92	16.81	19.36	14.27	17.22	21.30	16.95	16.23
Gasoline (Europe)	mt	266.1	497.4	490.0	454.8	369.6	378.3	372.0	180.5	192.8	165.8	202.9	252.3	218.9	X
Fuel Oil (Europe)	mt	137.4	235.9	253.9	231.3	235.3	262.2	220.7	90.9	112.0	71.2	91.2	98.6	75.1	X
Aluminum (LME)	mt	1,762.9	2,023.1	1,747.9	1,394.2	2,069.6	1,838.4	1,517.5	1,421.7	1,761.6	2,676.5	2,061.3	1,639.0	1,275.7	1,176.9
Bauxite (Jamaica)	mt	55.96	57.25	55.36	50.60	49.91	48.49	48.49	43.73	34.61	29.27	31.79	36.34	34.40	30.02
Copper (LME)	mt	2,736.1	3,031.8	2,410.6	2,080.7	2,289.5	2,024.0	2,066.2	1,698.4	2,006.4	2,729.7	3,009.4	2,661.5	2,291.1	2,140.3
Lead (LME)	kg	0.92	1.26	1.01	0.77	0.61	0.65	0.57	0.50	0.67	0.69	0.71	0.81	0.55	0.51
Tin (Malaysia)	kg	14.80	22.84	19.46	18.20	18.75	18.30	16.82	7.62	7.53	7.40	9.02	6.09	5.37	5.62'
Zinc (LME)	kg	1.64	1.06	1.17	1.05	1.10	1.35	1.14	0.93	0.90	1.30	1.75	1.51	1.09	1.16
Iron Ore (Brazil)	mt fe	38.27	39.03	38.87	45.68	41.71	38.43	38.72	32.46	27.58	24.66	28.00	30.80	32.57	29.65
Manganese Ore (India)	10 kg	3.05	2.18	2.32	2.31	2.18	2.10	2.06	X	X	X	X	X	X	X
Nickel (LME)	mt	10,108.8	9,057.5	8,238.4	6,799.0	6,720.6	6,983.5	7,141.5	4,798.1	5,484.2	14,456.3	14,060.4	8,864.1	7,989.4	6,569.0
Phosphate Rock (Morocco)	mt	148.2	64.9	68.5	59.6	53.1	56.3	49.4	42.3	34.9	37.8	43.1	40.5	41.6	39.2
Diammonium Phosphate (U.S.)	mt	537.5	308.7	269.9	256.9	263.9	277.9	246.4	190.6	195.5	206.2	182.6	171.4	169.4	136.2
Potassium Chloride (Canada)	mt	179.8	161.0	156.4	114.7	108.3	123.0	122.4	85.1	77.7	91.8	104.5	98.1	106.7	105.2
Triple Superphosphate (U.S.)	mt	446.8	250.1	222.8	194.0	194.2	192.5	176.4	149.6	155.3	165.8	152.1	131.8	130.4	113.2
Urea (Any Origin)	mt	438.0	308.6	298.9	223.2	194.7	251.7	198.7	132.3	131.2	162.6	139.7	157.0	168.5	131.6

Source: The World Bank.
Notes: LME = London Metal Exchange; mt = metric ton; kg = kilogram; bbl = barrel; fe = iron; X = not available.
For additional information, see Sources and Technical Notes.

Table 15.5 International Trade Flows, 1965–90

Agriculture, Food, and Beverages (SITC categories 0 and 1)

		Imports ($US million) OECD Countries	Developing Countries	Transitional Countries	Total
	1990	OECD	157,672	39,084	8,317	205,074
		Developing	54,810	18,722	9,011	82,544
		Transitional	4,852	1,217	3,062	9,132
		Total	217,334	59,025	20,391	296,750
	1985	OECD	80,617	26,453	7,102	114,172
		Developing	32,698	13,053	8,429	54,180
		Transitional	2,359	1,538	4,004	7,901
		Total	115,674	41,045	19,535	176,253
Exports ($US million)	1980	OECD	87,425	30,905	12,565	130,984
		Developing	36,886	13,840	6,813	57,539
		Transitional	2,183	697	5,438	8,318
		Total	126,493	45,442	24,815	196,750
	1970	OECD	18,966	4,534	1,171	24,671
		Developing	10,089	2,172	1,899	14,160
		Transitional	920	331	2,136	3,387
		Total	29,975	7,038	5,206	42,219
	1965	OECD	13,279	3,369	1,267	17,915
		Developing	6,987	1,894	1,702	10,583
		Transitional	575	150	1,618	2,343
		Total	20,841	5,413	4,587	30,841

Industrial Raw Materials and Edible Oils (SITC categories 2 and 4)

		OECD Countries	Developing Countries	Transitional Countries	Total
	1990	OECD	98,837	22,808	2,193	123,838
		Developing	34,267	17,369	1,525	53,161
		Transitional	5,561	1,257	1,741	8,559
		Total	138,665	41,434	5,459	185,558
	1985	OECD	57,240	13,992	2,261	73,493
		Developing	20,864	10,999	3,324	35,188
		Transitional	3,002	1,088	3,462	7,551
		Total	81,106	26,079	9,047	116,232
Exports ($US million)	1980	OECD	66,720	13,890	2,622	83,232
		Developing	27,603	10,405	2,285	40,293
		Transitional	6,382	1,054	4,552	11,988
		Total	100,705	25,349	9,459	135,513
	1970	OECD	17,589	1,869	659	20,117
		Developing	7,401	1,646	927	9,974
		Transitional	1,557	323	1,691	3,571
		Total	26,547	3,838	3,277	33,662
	1965	OECD	12,074	1,269	613	13,956
		Developing	5,974	1,166	899	8,039
		Transitional	907	141	1,248	2,296
		Total	18,955	2,576	2,760	24,291

Mineral Fuels (SITC category 3)

		OECD Countries	Developing Countries	Transitional Countries	Total
	1990	OECD	91,392	11,233	1,106	103,731
		Developing	159,721	39,850	2,320	201,891
		Transitional	20,833	2,499	6,301	29,633
		Total	271,946	53,582	9,727	335,255
	1985	OECD	90,752	7,331	1,269	99,352
		Developing	144,443	64,794	3,234	212,471
		Transitional	23,217	4,614	23,542	51,374
		Total	258,412	76,739	28,045	363,197
Exports ($US million)	1980	OECD	80,587	6,017	608	87,212
		Developing	269,454	66,403	4,165	340,022
		Transitional	28,389	5,310	13,093	46,792
		Total	378,430	77,730	17,866	474,026
	1970	OECD	7,027	606	182	7,815
		Developing	14,887	3,429	181	18,497
		Transitional	979	296	1,616	2,891
		Total	22,893	4,331	1,979	29,203
	1965	OECD	3,948	456	9	4,413
		Developing	8,983	2,002	37	11,022
		Transitional	1,029	456	1,423	2,908
		Total	13,960	2,914	1,469	18,343

Manufactures (SITC categories 5 through 9)

		Imports ($US million) OECD Countries	Developing Countries	Transitional Countries	Total
	1990	OECD	1,578,007	377,995	41,688	1,997,690
		Developing	278,812	143,390	5,969	428,171
		Transitional	26,936	12,600	33,709	73,245
		Total	1,883,755	533,985	81,366	2,499,106
	1985	OECD	750,102	223,046	31,206	1,004,354
		Developing	105,601	56,819	3,491	165,911
		Transitional	17,284	17,886	60,622	95,792
		Total	872,987	297,751	95,319	1,266,057
	1980	OECD	716,789	240,508	37,361	994,658
		Developing	94,455	50,836	9,841	155,132
		Transitional	17,493	10,028	65,816	93,337
		Total	828,737	301,372	113,018	1,243,127
	1970	OECD	137,144	33,409	5,929	176,482
		Developing	11,477	4,640	917	17,034
		Transitional	3,435	3,458	15,887	22,780
		Total	152,056	41,507	22,733	216,296
	1965	OECD	71,143	21,166	2,852	95,161
		Developing	5,759	2,628	802	9,189
		Transitional	2,033	2,540	9,794	14,367
		Total	78,935	26,334	13,448	118,717

Total Trade

		OECD Countries	Developing Countries	Transitional Countries	Total
	1990	OECD	1,925,909	451,122	53,304	2,430,335
		Developing	527,610	219,333	18,825	765,768
		Transitional	58,182	17,574	44,813	120,569
		Total	2,511,701	688,029	116,942	3,316,672
	1985	OECD	978,711	270,821	41,838	1,291,370
		Developing	303,607	145,665	18,478	467,750
		Transitional	45,861	25,127	91,630	162,618
		Total	1,328,179	441,613	151,946	1,921,738
	1980	OECD	951,521	291,319	53,156	1,295,996
		Developing	428,398	141,483	23,103	592,984
		Transitional	54,446	17,090	88,899	160,435
		Total	1,434,365	449,892	165,158	2,049,415
	1970	OECD	181,224	40,185	7,960	229,369
		Developing	43,218	11,887	3,925	59,030
		Transitional	6,920	4,408	21,330	32,658
		Total	231,362	56,480	33,215	321,057
	1965	OECD	100,719	26,222	4,750	131,691
		Developing	27,393	7,690	3,439	38,522
		Transitional	4,565	3,285	14,083	21,933
		Total	132,677	37,197	22,272	192,146

Source: United Nations Macroeconomic and Social Policy Analysis Division.
Notes: The rows of the world trade matrices show export values and the columns show import values.
For a description of country division breakdowns, see Technical Note for Table 15.5.
Data are reported in free-on-board (FOB) valuations and expressed in current U.S. dollars.
SITC = Standard International Trade Classification.
For additional information, see Sources and Technical Notes.

Sources and Technical Notes

Table 15.1 Gross National and Domestic Product Estimates, 1980–91

Sources: 1991 Gross national product (GNP) and gross domestic product (GDP): The World Bank, unpublished data (The World Bank, Washington, D.C., November 1993). Population figures for calculations: United Nations (U.N.) Population Division *Interpolated National Populations, 1950–2025 (The 1992 Revision)*, on diskette (U.N., New York, 1993). Per capita purchasing power parity (PPP) and average annual growth rates of GDP: The World Bank, *World Development Report 1993* (The World Bank, Washington, D.C., 1993). Average annual growth rates of GNP: The World Bank, *The World Bank Atlas* (The World Bank, Washington, D.C. 1992). Distribution of GDP: The World Bank, *World Tables 1993*, on diskette (The World Bank, Washington, D.C., 1993).

Gross national product is the sum of two components: the GDP and net factor income from abroad. GDP is the final output of goods and services produced by the domestic economy, including net exports of goods and nonfactor services. Net factor income from abroad is income in the form of overseas workers' remittances, interest on loans, profits, and other factor payments that residents receive from abroad, less payments made for factor services (i.e., labor and capital). Most countries estimate GDP by the production method. This method sums the final outputs of the various sectors of the economy (e.g., agriculture, manufacturing, and government services), from which the value of the inputs to production have been subtracted.

GNP estimates at current purchaser values (market prices) in U.S. dollars are calculated according to the *World Bank Atlas* methodology. GNP estimates in local currencies were converted to U.S. dollars using a three-year average exchange rate, adjusted for domestic and U.S. inflation. The *Atlas* method of averaging three years of exchange rates smoothes fluctuations due to the currency market and provides a more reliable measure, over time, of gross output than do estimates based on a single year's exchange rate.

The *gross domestic product* estimates at purchaser values (market prices) are in 1991 U.S. dollars (based on 1991 exchange rates), and are the sum of GDP at factor cost (value added in the agriculture, industry, and services sectors) and indirect taxes, less subsidies. World Bank GDP estimates accord with the United Nations System of National Accounts.

Per capita estimates of GNP and GDP for 1991 are calculated using United Nations Population Division data.

Total and per capita purchasing power parity are GDP estimates based on the purchasing power of currencies rather than on current exchange rates. The estimates are a blend of extrapolated and regression-based num-

bers, using the results of the International Comparison Progamme (ICP).

The ICP benchmark studies are (essentially) multilateral pricing exercises. The intercountry price comparisons have been reported in six phases: 1970, 1973, 1975, 1980, 1985, and 1990. Another benchmark study is under way with 1993 as the reference year. For countries that have ever participated in the ICP, as well as for China and the economies of the former U.S.S.R., the latest available PPP-based values are extrapolated to 1991 using World Bank estimates of growth rates and are converted to current "international dollars" ($I) by scaling all results up by the U.S. inflation rate. Footnotes indicate for which year PPP-based data were extrapolated, and those figures that are not footnoted were obtained by regression. Estimates for the former U.S.S.R. countries are based on partial and preliminary ICP data from 1990; the estimate for China was calculated by the World Bank. See *World Development Report 1993*, Technical Note for Table 30, for more information.

ICP recasts traditional national accounts through special price collections and the disaggregation of GDP by expenditure components. ICP details are reported by national statistical offices, and the results are coordinated by the United Nations Statistical Division, with support from other international agencies, particularly the Statistical Office of the European Communities and the Organisation for Economic Co-operation and Development. Sixty-four countries participated in ICP Phase V. The next round of ICP surveys for 1993 is expected to cover more than 80 countries, including China and several states of the former U.S.S.R.

The international dollar has the same purchasing power over total GDP as the U.S. dollar in a given year, but purchasing power over subaggregates is determined by average international prices at that level rather than by U.S. relative prices. The international dollar values, which are different from the U.S. dollar values of GNP or GDP, are obtained using special conversion factors designed to equalize the purchasing powers of different currencies. This conversion factor, the PPP, is defined as the number of units of a country's currency required to buy the same amounts of goods and services in the domestic market as $1 would buy in the United States. The computation involves deriving implicit quantities from national accounts expenditure data and specially collected price data and then revaluing the implicit quantities in each country at a single set of average prices. The average price index thus equalizes dollar prices in every country so that cross-country comparisons of GDP based on them reflect differences in quantities of goods and services free of price-level differentials. This procedure is designed to bring cross-country comparisons in line with cross-time real value comparisons that are based on con-

stant price series. PPP estimates tend to lower per capita GDPs in industrialized countries and raise per capita GDPs in developing countries.

The *average annual growth rates* of GNP and GDP are least-squares calculations of productivity growth based on constant price GNP and GDP data. That is, the GNP and GDP estimates have been adjusted to exclude inflation.

The *distribution of GDP* is calculated using current local currency units provided in the *World Tables 1993*. *Agriculture* includes agricultural and livestock production and services, logging, forestry, fishing, and hunting. *Industry* comprises mining and quarrying; manufacturing; construction; and electricity, gas, and water. *Services* include wholesale and retail trade; transport, storage, and communications; banking, insurance, and real estate; public administration and defense; ownership of dwellings; and others. The *distribution of GDP* does not always add up to 100 percent due to rounding.

Although considerable effort has been made to standardize economic data according to the United Nations System of National Accounts, care should be taken when interpreting the indicators presented in Table 15.1. Intercountry and intertemporal comparisons using economic data involve complicated technical problems that are not easily resolved; therefore, readers are urged to read these data as characterizing major differences between economies rather than as precise, quantitative measurements.

Table 15.2 Official Development Assistance and External Debt Indicators, 1979–91

Sources: Official development assistance (ODA): Organisation for Economic Co-operation and Development (OECD), *Development Co-operation* (OECD, Paris, 1984, 1986, 1987, 1988, 1989, 1990, 1991, and 1992), and *Geographical Distribution of Financial Flows to Developing Countries 1981/84, 1983/86, 1984/87, 1986/89, and 1988/91* (OECD, Paris, 1986, 1988, 1989, 1991, and 1993). ODA as a percentage of Gross National Product (GNP) was calculated using The World Bank, The World Bank Atlas (The World Bank, Washington, D.C., 1992). Population figures for per capita estimates of ODA and current borrowing: United Nations (U.N.) Population Division, *Interpolated National Populations, 1950–2025 (The 1992 Revision)*, on diskette (U.N., New York, 1993). External debt, disbursed long-term public debt, debt service, and current borrowing: The World Bank, *World Debt Tables 1992–93*, on diskette (The World Bank, Washington, D.C., May 1993). Exports of goods and services: The World Bank, unpublished data (The World Bank, Washington, D.C., March 1993).

Net *average annual official development assistance* (in current U.S. dollars) is the net amount of disbursed grants and concessional loans given or received by a country.

Grants include gifts of money, goods, or services for which no repayment is required. A concessional loan has a grant element of 25 percent or more. The grant element is the amount by which the face value of the loan exceeds its present market value because of below-market interest rates, favorable maturity schedules, or repayment grace periods. Nonconcessional loans are not a component of ODA.

ODA contributions are shown as negative numbers (in parentheses); receipts are shown as positive numbers. Data for donor countries include contributions made directly to developing countries and through multilateral institutions.

ODA sources include the development assistance agencies of OECD and Organization of Petroleum Exporting Countries members as well as other countries. Grants and concessional loans to and from multilateral development agencies are also included in contributions and receipts. OECD gathers ODA data through questionnaires and reports from countries and multilateral agencies. Only limited data are available on ODA flows among developing countries.

The GNP data used to calculate *ODA as a percentage of GNP* were *Atlas* GNP estimates (calculated using exchange rates averaged over three-year periods). For full comparability of these ratios, the GNP figures should be at current prices and calculated using single-year exchange rates, like the ODA figures.

The *1991 ODA per capita* estimates are calculated using 1991 ODA estimates in current dollars and United Nations Population Division population data.

The World Bank operates the Debtor Reporting System (DRS), which compiles reports supplied by 116 of the Bank's member countries. Countries submit detailed reports on the annual status, transactions, and terms of the long-term external debt of public agencies and of publicly guaranteed private debt. Additional data are drawn from the World Bank, the International Monetary Fund (IMF), regional development banks, government lending agencies, and the Creditor Reporting System (CRS). The CRS is operated by OECD to compile reports from the members of its Development Assistance Committee.

Total external debt (current U.S. dollars) includes long-term debt outstanding, private nonguaranteed debt outstanding, use of IMF credit, and short-term debt. A long-term debt is an obligation with a maturity of at least one year that is owed to nonresidents and is repayable in foreign currency, goods, or services. Long-term debt is divided into long-term public debt and long-term publicly guaranteed private debt. A short-term debt is a public or publicly guaranteed private debt that has a maturity of one year or less. This class of debt is especially difficult for countries to monitor. Only a few countries supply these data through the DRS; the World Bank supplements these data with creditor-country reports, information from international clearinghouse banks, and other sources to derive rough estimates of short-term debt.

Use of IMF credit refers to all drawings on the Fund's General Resources Account. Use of IMF credit is converted to dollars by applying the average special drawing right exchange rate in effect for the year being calculated.

A private debt is an external obligation of a private debtor that is not guaranteed by a public entity. Data for this class of debt are less extensive than those for public debt; many countries do not report these data through the DRS. These data are included in the total when available.

A *disbursed long-term public debt* is an outstanding public or publicly guaranteed long-term debt. A public debt is an obligation of a national or subnational government or its agencies and autonomous bodies. A publicly guaranteed debt is an external obligation of a private debtor guaranteed for repayment by a public entity.

Long-term public debt as a percentage of GNP is calculated using the disbursed long-term public debt described previously and the *Atlas* GNP estimates defined in the Technical Note for Table 15.1. Again, for full comparability, the GNP estimates should be at current prices and using single-year exchange data, like the long-term public debt data.

Total *debt service* (in foreign currencies, goods, and services) comprises interest payments and principal repayments made on the disbursed long-term public debt and private, nonguaranteed debt, IMF debt repurchases, IMF charges, and interest payments on short-term debt.

Exports of goods and services are the total value (current prices in U.S. dollars) of goods and nonfactor services sold to the rest of the world. *Current borrowing* is the total long-term debt disbursed during the specified years. *Current borrowing per capita* was calculated using the United Nations Population Division data noted previously. This source is described more fully in the Technical Note for Table 16.1.

Debt data are reported to the World Bank in the units of currency in which they are payable. The World Bank converts these data to U.S. dollars, using the IMF par values, central rates, or the current market rates, where appropriate. Debt service data are converted to U.S. dollars at the average exchange rate for the given year. Comparability of data among countries and years is limited by variations in methods, definitions, and comprehensiveness of data collection and reporting. Refer to the World Bank's *World Debt Tables 1992–93*, Vols. 1 and 2, for details.

ODA figures are derived from the annual questionnaire completed by each Development Assistance Committee member country; for nonmembers, values are based on information published by governments or provided directly to the OECD by them.

External debt data pertain to only those countries within the DRS, which focuses on low- and middle-income economies. Many economies are not represented within the system, and the estimates that are presented may not be comprehensive due to different reporting frameworks. These data

do not account for the term structure and the concessionality mix of debt, which can lead to a misrepresentation of a country's underlying solvency.

Table 15.3 Defense Expenditures, Military Personnel, and Refugees, 1985–92

Sources: Defense expenditures, numbers in armed forces, and estimated reservists: The International Institute for Strategic Studies (IISS), *The Military Balance, 1992–93* (IISS, London, 1992). Victims of conflict: Ruth Leger Sivard, *World Military and Social Expenditures 1991* (World Priorities, Washington, D.C., 1991). Refugees: U.S. Committee for Refugees (USCR), *World Refugee Survey 1993* (USCR, Washington, D.C., 1993). The arms trade: The World Bank, unpublished data (The World Bank, Washington, D.C., March 1993).

Defense expenditures were compiled using national definitions and, when possible, were converted to constant 1987 dollars using International Monetary Fund (IMF) exchange rates. When IMF rates were not available, published annual exchange rates were averaged and used to estimate constant 1987 dollars. The IMF reporting system for military expenditures, which is used by most countries, includes all spending on regular military forces and military aid (including equipment and training) to other nations. Some estimates include internal security expenditures. The North Atlantic Treaty Organization (NATO) reporting system also includes military pensions, host government expenses for NATO tenant forces, and NATO infrastructure and civilian staff costs.

Numbers in armed forces refers to all active servicemen and women on full-time duty (including conscripts and long-term assignments from the reserves). Reservists and paramilitary forces are not included in these estimates.

Reserves are formations and units that are not fully staffed or operational in peacetime, but that can be mobilized in an emergency. *Estimated reservists* are those persons committed to rejoining the armed forces in an emergency and usually include all men and women within five years of their active service period.

Both *military deaths* and *civilian deaths* data are taken from *World Military and Social Expenditures 1991* and refer to the total number of war or war-related deaths occurring from the beginning of a conflict to 1990. These are not annual data but, instead, accumulated totals for the conflict period. The information on deaths associated with wars is incomplete, and all estimates must be used with caution.

The definition of a refugee is limited and specifically includes persons in need of protection or assistance. The 1951 United Nations Convention Relating to the Status of Refugees classifies a person in flight from a country as a "refugee" if his or her flight is based on a "well-founded fear of being persecuted for reasons of race, religion, nationality, membership in a particular social group, or political opinion." The USCR reports that this definition has been somewhat broadened, at least in Africa, to include flight due to "external aggression, occupation, foreign domination, or events seriously disturbing to the public order." *Location of refugees and asylum seekers* refers to refugees who require assistance or international protection and are unable or unwilling to repatriate because of fears of violence and persecution. The estimates include all the refugees registered with the United Nations High Commissioner on Refugees. The USCR has also included in these data those who clearly would be registered as refugees if the country or refuge to which they had gone had asked the High Commission to assist them. Several outcomes are possible for refugees, including repatriation, continuing status as a refugee in the country of asylum, and permanent resettlement in a third country.

The *arms trade* data are from the World Bank. Trade estimates include transfers to governments of conventional military equipment and of commodities considered (primarily) military in nature. Estimates are in constant 1987 U.S. dollars. For further information, see *World Military Expenditures and Arms Transfers 1989*, published by the U.S. Arms Control and Disarmament Agency.

Table 15.4 World Commodity Indexes and Prices, 1975–92

Source: The World Bank, unpublished data (The World Bank, Washington, D.C., August 1993).

Price data are compiled from major international marketplaces for standard grades of each commodity. For example, maize refers to No. 2, yellow, FOB (free on board) U.S. gulf ports. The 1990 U.S. constant dollar figures were derived by converting current average monthly prices in local currencies to U.S. dollars using average monthly exchange rates. These average monthly dollar figures were then averaged to produce an average annual dollar figure, which was adjusted to 1990 constant dollars using the manufacturing unit value index. This index is a composite price index of all manufactured goods exported by the G-5 countries (the United States, the United Kingdom, France, Germany, and Japan) to developing countries.

The aggregate price indexes have the following components:

1. *33 Nonfuel commodities*: individual commodities listed under items 4–10, below.
2. *Total agriculture*: total food and nonfood agricultural products.
3. *Total food*: beverages, cereals, fats and oils, and other foods.
4. *Beverages*: coffee, cocoa, and tea.
5. *Cereals*: maize, rice, wheat, and grain sorghum.
6. *Fats and oils*: palm, coconut, and groundnut oils; soybeans; copra; groundnut meal; and soybean meal.
7. *Other foods*: sugar, beef, bananas, and oranges.
8. *Nonfood agricultural products*: cotton, jute, rubber, and tobacco.
9. *Timber*: logs.
10. *Metals and minerals*: copper, tin, nickel, bauxite, aluminum, iron ore, lead, zinc, and phosphate rock.

The commodity prices reported here are specific to the markets named. The commodities themselves are often defined more specifically than is suggested in the table (e.g., wheat (Canada), No. 1, Western Red Spring (CWRS), in store, St. Lawrence, export price; lamb (New Zealand), frozen whole carcasses, wholesale price, Smithfield market, London; coffee (ICO), indicator price, other mild arabicas, average New York and Bremen/Hamburg markets, exdock).

Table 15.5 International Trade Flows, 1965–90

Source: United Nations (U.N.) Macroeconomic and Social Policy Analysis Division, unpublished data (U.N. New York, 1993).

Original estimates of commodity composition and direction of trade for 78 countries and regions (i.e., groupings of small countries) are in four broad commodity classifications: (1) *agriculture* (including tobacco and live animals), *food and beverages* (Standard International Trade Classification (SITC) categories 0 and 1); (2) *industrial raw materials and edible oils* (SITC categories 2 and 4); (3) *mineral fuels* (SITC category 3); and (4) *manufactures* (SITC categories 5 through 9). Estimates for total merchandise trade have also been prepared.

The data used were those reported to the United Nations Statistical Office, supplemented, when necessary, with other information. Annual trade matrices showing exports along rows and imports along columns were prepared from these tabulations. Data were reported in FREE ON BOARD (FOB) valuations and expressed in current U.S. dollars.

Trade flows are measured between three country groupings: (1) Organisation for Economic Co-operation and Development (OECD) countries, (2) developing countries, and (3) transitional countries. The OECD countries are Australia, Austria, Belgium, Canada, Denmark, Finland, France, Germany, Greece, Iceland, Ireland, Italy, Japan, Luxembourg, the Netherlands, New Zealand, Norway, Portugal, Spain, Sweden, Switzerland, the United Kingdom, and the United States. The transitional countries are all those in eastern Europe and the former U.S.S.R., namely Albania, Armenia, Azerbaijan, Belarus, Bulgaria, Czechoslovakia (former), Estonia, Georgia, Hungary, Kazakhstan, Kyrgyzstan, Latvia, Lithuania, Moldova, Poland, Romania, the Russian Federation, Tajikistan, Turkmenistan, Ukraine, and Uzbekistan. The developing countries category includes all other countries.

16. Population and Human Development

Public perceptions of global population growth and policy responses to that growth range from pessimistic (population growth is the most pressing problem facing humanity) to optimistic (population growth is not a major problem but part of the larger equation of economic development). Meanwhile, the world's population increased from 2.52 billion in 1950 to 5.57 billion in 1993 and is projected to reach approximately 10 billion by the year 2050.

This chapter presents demographic, health, and education data necessary to understand both global population and the quality of human life throughout the world. Table 16.1 presents population and labor force size and growth rate statistics for countries, regions, and the world. Africa's total population is increasing the fastest of any continent (by approximately 20 million people per year between 1990 and 1995) and is projected to total 1.58 billion people by the year 2025, up from 702 million in 1993. In terms of a sheer increase in numbers, Africa does not compare to Asia, which will gain 58 million people annually between 1990 and 1995. By 2025, the United Nations Population Division projects the population of Asia to number close to 5 billion, with China and India alone accounting for 60 percent of the Asian population and 35 percent of the global population.

Although populations in other world regions are not increasing as rapidly as in Africa, nor as dramatically as in Asia, individual countries will see drastic changes. For example, many of the poorer countries of Central and South America are expected to experience dramatic increases in population over a 30-year period. Between 1995 and 2025, Nicaragua's population is projected to increase by 105 percent, Bolivia's by 75 percent, and Paraguay's by 88 percent.

Tables 16.2, 16.3, 16.4, and 16.5 present other demographic, health, and education indicators that illustrate important trends and challenges facing nations and the global community.

Birth rates, death rates, and total fertility rates fell between 1970–75 and 1990–95, indicating that people are living longer and producing fewer offspring than before. Comparisons between developed and developing countries continue to show large differences in these rates. For example, the U.S. estimated birth rate of 15.9 per 1,000, death rate of 9 per 1,000, total fertility rate of 2.1, and life expectancy of 75.9 years for the period 1990–95 differ dramatically from those estimated for Malawi, which has a crude birth rate of 54.5, a crude death rate of 22, a total fertility rate of 7.6, and a life expectancy of 44.2 years.

Countries with large percentages of the population aged 15 years or younger will see the greatest future population growth as these people reach childbearing age. Africa, with approximately 45 percent of the population in this category, faces the difficult challenge of providing basic access to education, health services, and job opportunities for the growing population. Industrialized countries, especially Northern European countries, confront different challenges. With relatively few young people and a long life expectancy, these countries are increasingly faced with supporting a growing proportion of retirees.

Table 16.5 shows that the World Health Organization and the United Nations Children's Fund almost reached their 1990 goal of immunizing 80 percent of all children worldwide against infectious diseases such as tetanus, measles, polio, diphtheria, pertussis (whooping cough), and tuberculosis, thereby saving an estimated 3 million children's lives each year and protecting many more from paralysis, malnutrition, blindness, and deafness.

Education not only affects people's health and reproductive behavior, it is also an important factor in economic development. Tables 16.5 and 16.6 indicate considerable improvement over the 20-year period between 1970 and 1990, although female literacy rates continued to lag behind those of males in many developing countries. In some cases, the ratio of literate females to males actually declined (e.g., in Botswana, Sierra Leone, and Uganda).

Table 16.6 addresses differences between the sexes, the status of women, and family life. Almost universally, life expectancy rates for females are higher than those for males. Labor force data reveal that the formal working sector includes more males than females, and contraception statistics reflect different levels of education and health services available to women.

Table 16.1 Size and Growth of Population and Labor Force,

	Population (millions)				Average Annual Population Change (percent)			Average Annual Increment to the Population (thousands)			Average Annual Growth of the Labor Force (percent)	
	1950	1990	1995	2025	1980-85	1990-95	2000-2005	1980-85	1990-95	2000-2005	1981-90	1991-2000
WORLD	2,516.19	5,295.30	5,759.28	8,472.45	1.75	1.68	1.43	81,538	92,795	91,981		
AFRICA	222.46	642.58	744.01	1,582.54	2.91	2.93	2.70	15,028	20,286	24,734		
Algeria	8.75	24.96	28.58	51.83	3.01	2.71	2.50	610	724	872	3.7	3.7
Angola	4.13	9.19	11.07	26.62	2.63	3.72	3.05	197	376	431	1.8	2.1
Benin	2.05	4.62	5.40	12.35	2.82	3.11	2.91	105	155	196	2.1	2.6
Botswana	0.39	1.24	1.43	2.85	3.40	2.92	2.69	33	39	47	3.3	3.4
Burkina Faso	3.65	8.99	10.35	22.63	2.50	2.81	2.69	185	272	341	2.0	2.2
Burundi	2.46	5.49	6.34	13.39	2.80	2.88	2.53	124	170	195	2.1	2.5
Cameroon	4.47	11.52	13.28	29.26	2.83	2.83	2.84	263	350	467	1.9	2.3
Central African Rep	1.31	3.01	3.43	7.05	2.58	2.62	2.31	64	84	95	1.4	1.9
Chad	2.66	5.55	6.36	12.91	2.28	2.72	2.47	108	162	192	1.9	2.1
Congo	0.81	2.23	2.59	5.76	2.82	3.00	2.67	51	72	85	1.9	2.4
Cote d'Ivoire	2.78	11.98	14.40	37.94	3.86	3.68	3.28	348	484	608	2.6	2.6
Djibouti	0.06	0.44	0.51	1.16	4.46	3.01	2.88	15	14	18	X	X
Egypt	20.33	52.43	58.52	93.54	2.58	2.20	1.90	1,127	1,219	1,295	2.6	2.7
Equatorial Guinea	0.23	0.35	0.40	0.80	7.22	2.55	2.41	19	10	12	X	X
Ethiopia	19.57	49.83	58.04	130.67	2.12	3.05	2.84	867	1,642	2,054	1.9	2.2
Gabon	0.47	1.16	1.37	2.87	4.01	3.31	2.64	36	42	45	0.6	1.1
Gambia, The	0.29	0.86	0.98	1.88	3.01	2.60	2.34	21	24	27	X	X
Ghana	4.90	15.02	17.45	37.99	3.58	3.00	2.81	421	487	609	2.7	3.0
Guinea	2.55	5.76	6.70	15.09	2.23	3.04	2.86	105	189	239	1.7	1.9
Guinea-Bissau	0.51	0.96	1.07	1.98	1.87	2.14	2.12	16	22	27	X	X
Kenya	6.27	23.59	27.89	63.83	3.56	3.35	3.12	648	860	1,107	3.5	3.7
Lesotho	0.73	1.75	1.98	3.78	2.78	2.47	2.39	40	46	57	2.0	2.2
Liberia	0.82	2.58	3.04	7.23	3.17	3.32	3.08	65	93	119	2.3	2.8
Libya	1.03	4.55	5.41	12.87	4.37	3.47	3.20	149	172	221	3.6	3.5
Madagascar	4.23	12.01	14.16	33.75	3.06	3.29	3.06	290	429	549	2.0	2.3
Malawi	2.88	9.58	11.30	24.92	3.42	3.31	2.42	230	344	324	2.6	2.7
Mali	3.52	9.21	10.80	24.58	2.85	3.17	2.91	210	317	394	2.6	2.8
Mauritania	0.83	2.02	2.34	4.99	2.60	2.86	2.68	43	62	77	2.8	3.2
Mauritius	0.49	1.08	1.13	1.40	1.09	1.00	0.85	11	11	10	2.9	1.9
Morocco	8.95	25.06	28.26	47.48	2.56	2.40	2.12	529	640	709	3.2	3.0
Mozambique	6.20	14.20	16.36	36.29	2.27	2.83	2.87	290	432	600	2.0	2.0
Namibia	0.51	1.44	1.69	3.75	2.94	3.18	2.91	34	50	61	2.4	2.8
Niger	2.40	7.73	9.10	21.29	3.36	3.26	3.02	204	274	347	2.4	2.7
Nigeria	32.94	108.54	126.93	285.82	3.20	3.13	2.95	2,717	3,677	4,695	2.7	2.9
Rwanda	2.12	7.03	8.33	20.60	2.87	3.40	3.09	159	261	327	2.8	3.0
Senegal	2.50	7.33	8.39	17.08	2.81	2.70	2.59	167	212	265	1.9	2.1
Sierra Leone	1.94	4.15	4.74	9.80	2.32	2.66	2.54	80	118	146	1.2	1.5
Somalia	3.07	8.68	10.17	23.40	3.20	3.18	2.99	232	299	383	1.7	1.9
South Africa	13.68	37.96	42.74	73.21	2.58	2.37	2.07	814	956	1,047	2.8	2.8
Sudan	9.19	25.20	28.96	60.60	3.11	2.78	2.65	628	751	940	2.9	3.2
Swaziland	0.26	0.75	0.86	1.74	3.07	2.68	2.64	19	22	28	X	X
Tanzania	7.89	25.99	30.74	74.17	3.28	3.36	2.99	663	950	1,156	2.9	3.1
Togo	1.33	3.53	4.14	9.38	2.93	3.18	2.93	83	121	152	2.3	2.5
Tunisia	3.53	8.06	8.93	13.43	2.57	2.06	1.51	175	175	154	3.1	2.7
Uganda	4.76	17.56	20.41	45.93	2.72	3.00	2.68	383	569	670	2.8	3.0
Zaire	12.18	37.39	43.81	104.53	3.18	3.17	2.98	932	1,285	1,636	2.3	2.6
Zambia	2.44	8.14	9.38	20.98	3.58	2.84	2.56	225	249	292	3.3	3.6
Zimbabwe	2.73	9.95	11.54	22.89	3.22	2.97	2.48	249	318	348	2.8	3.1
ASIA	1,377.26	3,117.84	3,407.59	4,900.26	1.91	1.78	1.39	51,710	57,950	53,070		
Afghanistan	8.96	16.56	23.20	45.83	(2.02)	6.74	2.36	(309)	1,328	672	2.6	2.2
Bangladesh	41.78	113.68	128.25	223.25	2.68	2.41	2.18	2,528	2,913	3,329	2.9	3.0
Bhutan	0.73	1.54	1.73	3.40	2.10	2.33	2.43	27	38	50	1.9	1.9
Cambodia	4.35	8.34	9.45	16.72	2.40	2.50	2.07	166	222	231	1.9	1.7
China	554.76	1,153.47	1,238.32	1,539.76	1.44	1.42	0.78	14,888	16,970	10,417	2.2	1.1
India	357.56	846.19	931.04	1,393.87	2.14	1.91	1.65	15,559	16,971	17,463	2.0	1.8
Indonesia	79.54	184.28	201.48	283.32	2.06	1.78	1.28	3,275	3,439	2,874	2.4	2.1
Iran, Islamic Rep	16.91	58.27	66.72	144.63	4.40	2.71	2.98	1,932	1,691	2,507	3.3	3.2
Iraq	5.16	18.08	21.22	46.26	3.27	3.21	2.92	462	629	779	3.7	4.1
Israel	1.26	4.66	5.88	8.15	1.75	4.67	1.33	71	245	87	2.2	2.0
Japan	83.63	123.54	125.88	127.03	0.68	0.38	0.27	806	468	350	0.9	0.3
Jordan	1.24	4.01	4.76	10.81	3.07	3.42	3.11	97	149	190	4.4	4.1
Korea, Dem People's Rep	9.73	21.77	23.92	33.34	1.71	1.88	1.21	326	430	325	2.9	2.8
Korea, Rep	20.36	43.38	45.18	50.29	1.36	0.82	0.59	536	361	281	2.4	1.8
Kuwait	0.15	2.14	1.60	2.79	4.48	(5.80)	2.58	69	(108)	47	5.2	3.2
Lao People's Dem Rep	1.76	4.20	4.88	9.41	2.29	3.00	2.50	78	136	149	2.0	2.2
Lebanon	1.44	2.74	3.03	4.48	(0.01)	2.00	1.46	(0)	58	50	2.1	2.6
Malaysia	6.11	17.89	20.13	31.27	2.60	2.35	1.73	383	447	401	2.9	2.6
Mongolia	0.76	2.19	2.50	4.58	2.76	2.63	2.34	49	62	70	2.9	2.8
Myanmar	17.83	41.83	46.55	75.60	2.09	2.14	1.87	745	945	1,012	X	X
Nepal	8.18	19.57	22.12	40.06	2.85	2.45	2.27	456	511	598	2.3	2.3
Oman	0.41	1.52	1.82	4.71	4.91	3.57	3.41	55	60	81	3.8	2.9
Pakistan	39.51	118.12	134.97	259.56	3.31	2.67	2.54	3,075	3,370	4,193	2.9	3.0
Philippines	20.99	62.44	69.26	105.15	2.58	2.07	1.70	1,342	1,364	1,347	2.5	2.4
Saudi Arabia	3.20	14.87	17.61	40.43	5.57	3.38	3.04	601	548	680	4.0	3.4
Singapore	1.02	2.71	2.85	3.31	1.16	1.03	0.67	29	29	20	1.5	0.6
Sri Lanka	7.68	17.22	18.35	24.74	1.67	1.27	1.04	258	226	209	1.6	1.6
Syrian Arab Rep	3.50	12.36	14.78	35.25	3.46	3.58	3.30	329	484	630	3.6	4.1
Thailand	20.01	54.68	58.27	72.26	1.83	1.27	0.92	894	718	577	2.3	1.6
Turkey	20.81	55.99	62.03	92.88	2.50	2.05	1.61	1,181	1,208	1,145	2.2	2.0
United Arab Emirates	0.07	1.59	1.79	2.79	5.69	2.33	1.86	67	39	38	4.0	1.8
Viet Nam	29.95	66.69	73.81	116.96	2.18	2.03	1.85	1,237	1,425	1,581	2.8	2.6
Yemen	4.32	11.68	13.90	34.24	3.43	3.47	3.24	308	443	577	X	X

Table 16.1

	Population (millions)				Average Annual Population Change (percent)			Average Annual Increment to the Population (thousands)			Average Annual Growth of the Labor Force (percent)	
	1950	1990	1995	2025	1980-85	1990-95	2000-2005	1980-85	1990-95	2000-2005	1981-90	1991-2000
NORTH & CENTRAL AMERICA	202.61	390.05	418.55	559.75	1.68	1.65	1.29	4,677	5,701	5,088		
Belize	0.07	0.19	0.21	0.29	2.63	2.03	1.46	4	4	3	X	X
Canada	13.74	26.64	28.54	38.36	0.90	1.38	1.19	222	380	374	1.2	0.8
Costa Rica	0.86	3.04	3.42	5.61	2.91	2.41	1.84	72	78	73	2.8	2.4
Cuba	5.85	10.61	11.09	12.99	0.81	0.89	0.59	80	97	69	2.3	1.3
Dominican Rep	2.35	7.17	7.92	11.45	2.38	1.98	1.48	144	149	132	3.4	2.8
El Salvador	1.94	5.17	5.77	9.74	0.92	2.18	2.00	43	119	135	3.1	3.2
Guatemala	2.97	9.20	10.62	21.67	2.82	2.88	2.68	209	285	350	2.9	3.4
Haiti	3.26	6.49	7.18	13.13	1.83	2.03	2.06	102	139	173	2.0	2.3
Honduras	1.40	5.14	5.97	11.51	3.59	3.00	2.48	144	166	180	3.9	3.9
Jamaica	1.40	2.42	2.55	3.51	1.60	1.02	1.14	36	25	31	2.8	2.2
Mexico	27.30	84.49	93.67	137.48	2.40	2.06	1.55	1,710	1,837	1,651	3.2	2.9
Nicaragua	1.11	3.68	4.43	9.08	2.83	3.74	2.78	85	151	154	3.8	4.0
Panama	0.89	2.42	2.66	3.86	2.17	1.90	1.48	45	48	45	2.9	2.4
Trinidad and Tobago	0.64	1.24	1.31	1.78	1.40	1.08	0.76	16	14	10	2.4	2.0
United States	152.27	249.98	263.14	322.01	0.92	1.03	0.76	2,142	2,633	2,121	1.1	0.8
SOUTH AMERICA	111.59	294.12	319.71	451.95	2.15	1.67	1.35	5,446	5,119	4,808		
Argentina	17.15	32.32	34.26	45.51	1.43	1.17	1.07	419	388	399	1.1	1.6
Bolivia	2.77	7.17	8.07	14.10	2.55	2.37	2.13	152	181	203	2.8	2.6
Brazil	53.44	149.04	161.38	219.67	2.23	1.59	1.22	2,856	2,468	2,172	2.2	2.1
Chile	6.08	13.17	14.24	19.77	1.68	1.55	1.24	195	213	195	2.4	1.5
Colombia	11.95	32.30	35.10	49.36	2.11	1.66	1.34	591	560	526	2.7	2.3
Ecuador	3.31	10.55	11.82	18.64	2.72	2.28	1.80	237	255	247	3.0	2.8
Guyana	0.42	0.80	0.83	1.14	0.80	0.94	1.05	6	8	10	X	X
Paraguay	1.35	4.28	4.89	9.18	3.20	2.69	2.31	109	123	135	3.0	2.8
Peru	7.63	21.55	23.85	37.35	2.31	2.03	1.77	424	461	485	2.9	2.8
Suriname	0.22	0.42	0.46	0.67	1.66	1.86	1.23	6	8	6	X	X
Uruguay	2.24	3.09	3.19	3.69	0.64	0.58	0.55	19	18	18	0.7	1.0
Venezuela	5.01	19.32	21.48	32.67	2.66	2.12	1.66	428	432	407	3.3	2.9
EUROPE	398.14	509.04	516.04	541.78	0.31	0.27	0.27	1,546	1,400	1,411		
Albania	1.23	3.25	3.39	4.46	2.07	0.84	1.08	58	28	40	2.8	2.2
Austria	6.94	7.71	7.86	8.26	0.02	0.38	0.24	2	30	19	0.6	(0.0)
Belgium	8.64	9.97	10.03	9.91	0.01	0.13	0.03	1	13	4	0.5	0.0
Bulgaria	7.25	8.99	8.89	8.80	0.22	(0.23)	(0.02)	20	(21)	(2)	(0.0)	0.3
Czechoslovakia (former)	12.39	15.66	15.88	17.92	0.24	0.27	0.57	38	43	94	0.4	0.8
Denmark	4.27	5.14	5.19	5.14	0.00	0.20	0.11	(0)	10	6	0.5	0.1
Finland	4.01	4.98	5.05	5.17	0.51	0.26	0.20	24	13	10	0.7	0.2
France	41.83	56.72	57.77	60.79	0.47	0.37	0.25	258	210	149	0.8	0.4
Germany	68.38	79.48	81.26	83.88	(0.16)	0.44	0.22	(127)	357	184	0.4	(0.5)
Greece	7.57	10.12	10.25	10.10	0.60	0.26	0.07	58	26	7	0.5	0.2
Hungary	9.34	10.55	10.47	10.40	(0.12)	(0.15)	0.10	(12)	(16)	10	0.1	0.4
Iceland	0.14	0.26	0.27	0.34	1.13	1.04	0.96	3	3	3	X	X
Ireland	2.97	3.50	3.47	3.58	0.87	(0.19)	0.01	30	(7)	0	1.6	1.5
Italy	47.10	57.66	57.91	56.24	0.25	0.09	0.07	141	49	43	0.6	(0.0)
Netherlands	10.11	14.94	15.50	17.67	0.48	0.73	0.67	68	111	109	1.2	0.3
Norway	3.27	4.25	4.36	4.92	0.32	0.51	0.51	13	22	23	0.8	0.6
Poland	24.82	38.18	38.74	43.79	0.90	0.29	0.49	326	111	195	0.6	0.8
Portugal	8.41	9.87	9.88	10.13	0.28	0.03	0.13	28	3	12	0.9	0.8
Romania	16.31	23.21	23.51	26.27	0.47	0.26	0.47	105	60	115	0.7	0.7
Spain	28.01	38.96	39.28	40.61	0.49	0.16	0.22	186	63	86	1.1	0.7
Sweden	7.01	8.57	8.77	9.53	0.10	0.48	0.35	8	41	32	0.4	0.2
Switzerland	4.69	6.71	6.96	7.70	0.47	0.71	0.49	30	49	35	0.5	(0.2)
United Kingdom	50.62	57.41	58.09	60.25	0.10	0.24	0.19	58	136	111	0.4	0.1
Yugoslavia (former)	16.35	23.81	24.11	26.08	0.72	0.25	0.38	164	61	93	0.9	0.7
U.S.S.R. (former)	174.46	281.34	288.56	344.46	0.89	0.51	0.65	2,341	1,444	1,962	0.7	0.6
Armenia	X	3.33	3.73	X	X	2.30	X	X	79	X	X	X
Azerbaijan	X	7.13	7.45	X	X	0.80	X	X	63	X	X	X
Belarus	X	10.26	10.31	X	X	0.10	X	X	10	X	X	X
Estonia	1.10	1.58	1.57	1.67	0.75	(0.15)	0.32	56	(2)	5	X	X
Georgia	X	5.46	5.47	X	X	0.10	X	X	3	X	X	X
Kazakhstan	X	16.74	17.44	X	X	0.80	X	X	139	X	X	X
Kyrgyzstan	X	4.39	4.69	X	X	1.30	X	X	60	X	X	X
Latvia	1.95	2.69	2.65	2.75	0.61	(0.28)	0.22	16	(7)	6	X	X
Lithuania	2.57	3.73	3.77	4.14	0.88	0.21	0.42	31	8	16	X	X
Moldova	X	4.36	4.35	X	X	0.00	X	X	(3)	X	X	X
Russian Federation	X	148.28	149.74	X	X	0.20	X	X	291	X	X	X
Tajikistan	X	5.30	6.01	X	X	2.50	X	X	140	X	X	X
Turkmenistan	X	3.67	4.16	X	X	2.50	X	X	98	X	X	X
Ukraine	X	51.89	52.39	X	X	0.20	X	X	101	X	X	X
Uzbekistan	X	20.51	22.83	X	X	2.10	X	X	463	X	X	X
OCEANIA	12.62	26.69	28.79	41.34	1.51	1.51	1.37	358	420	439		
Australia	8.22	17.09	18.34	25.21	1.40	1.41	1.21	213	250	245	1.7	1.2
Fiji	0.29	0.73	0.76	0.97	1.97	0.96	1.02	13	7	8	X	X
New Zealand	1.91	3.39	3.55	4.28	0.84	0.92	0.77	27	32	29	1.6	1.0
Papua New Guinea	1.61	3.88	4.34	7.77	2.29	2.29	2.20	75	94	113	2.1	2.0
Solomon Islands	0.09	0.32	0.38	0.84	3.50	3.32	3.05	9	12	15	X	X

Source: United Nations Population Division and International Labour Office.
Notes: World and regional totals include countries not listed here.
0 = zero or less than half the unit of measure; X = not available; negative numbers are shown in parentheses.
For additional information, see Sources and Technical Notes.

Table 16.2 Trends in Births, Life Expectancy, Fertility, and

	Crude Birth Rate (births per 1,000 population)		Life Expectancy at Birth (years)		Total Fertility Rate		Percentage of Population in Specific Age Groups					
							1975			1995		
	1970-75	1990-95	1970-75	1990-95	1970-75	1990-95	<15	15-65	>65	<15	15-65	>65
WORLD	31.5	26.0	57.9	64.7	4.5	3.3	36.9	57.4	5.7	31.9	61.6	6.5
AFRICA	46.8	43.0	46.1	53.0	6.6	6.0	44.9	52.0	3.0	44.8	52.1	3.1
Algeria	48.0	34.0	54.5	66.2	7.4	4.9	47.6	48.2	4.2	41.4	55.2	3.4
Angola	49.0	51.3	38.0	46.5	6.6	7.2	44.2	52.9	3.0	47.1	50.0	2.9
Benin	49.4	48.9	40.0	46.3	7.1	7.1	44.8	51.6	3.6	47.3	49.8	2.9
Botswana	52.1	38.4	51.0	61.0	6.9	5.1	50.2	47.7	2.1	44.9	51.8	3.3
Burkina Faso	47.8	46.7	41.2	48.3	6.4	6.5	44.0	53.3	2.8	44.9	52.0	3.1
Burundi	44.0	46.0	44.0	48.1	6.8	6.8	45.5	51.1	3.5	46.3	50.7	2.9
Cameroon	45.3	40.7	45.8	56.0	6.3	5.7	43.4	53.1	3.6	44.0	52.4	3.6
Central African Rep	43.1	44.5	43.0	47.0	5.7	6.2	40.6	55.5	3.9	45.2	51.0	3.8
Chad	44.6	43.7	39.0	47.5	6.0	5.9	41.7	54.7	3.6	43.4	53.0	3.6
Congo	46.1	44.7	46.7	51.5	6.3	6.3	44.4	52.2	3.5	45.7	51.0	3.3
Cote d'Ivoire	51.1	49.9	45.4	51.5	7.4	7.4	45.8	51.8	2.4	49.0	48.4	2.6
Djibouti	50.4	46.5	41.0	48.9	6.6	6.6	42.8	54.7	2.5	45.8	51.7	2.5
Egypt	38.4	31.3	52.1	61.6	5.5	4.1	40.0	55.8	4.2	37.9	57.9	4.2
Equatorial Guinea	42.4	43.5	40.5	48.0	5.7	5.9	40.4	55.1	4.4	43.3	52.8	4.0
Ethiopia	48.0	49.1	41.0	47.0	6.8	7.0	44.4	53.0	2.6	46.5	50.7	2.8
Gabon	30.9	42.6	45.0	53.5	4.3	5.3	32.3	61.9	5.8	35.9	58.3	5.8
Gambia, The	49.2	44.1	37.0	45.0	6.5	6.1	42.2	54.9	2.9	43.9	53.1	3.1
Ghana	45.8	41.7	50.0	56.0	6.6	6.0	45.4	51.9	2.7	45.3	51.8	2.9
Guinea	51.6	50.6	37.3	44.5	7.0	7.0	45.3	52.1	2.6	47.1	50.3	2.6
Guinea-Bissau	41.4	42.7	36.5	43.5	5.4	5.8	38.1	58.1	3.8	41.7	54.2	4.1
Kenya	52.9	43.7	51.0	58.9	8.1	6.3	49.1	47.2	3.7	47.4	49.7	2.9
Lesotho	42.4	34.4	50.4	60.5	5.7	4.7	41.7	54.7	3.6	40.7	55.3	3.9
Liberia	48.1	47.3	47.5	55.4	6.8	6.8	44.1	52.2	3.7	46.0	50.4	3.7
Libya	49.0	41.9	52.9	63.1	7.6	6.4	46.0	51.7	2.2	45.4	52.0	2.6
Madagascar	46.0	45.5	46.5	55.5	6.6	6.6	44.0	53.0	2.9	45.7	51.4	2.9
Malawi	56.6	54.5	41.0	44.2	7.4	7.6	47.2	50.6	2.2	49.2	48.2	2.6
Mali	51.0	50.7	38.5	46.0	7.1	7.1	46.0	51.5	2.5	47.4	50.0	2.5
Mauritania	47.0	46.0	40.0	48.0	6.5	6.5	43.3	53.8	3.0	45.0	51.9	3.1
Mauritius	26.1	18.1	62.9	70.0	3.3	2.0	39.7	57.5	2.8	26.7	67.5	5.8
Morocco	45.6	32.3	52.9	63.3	6.9	4.4	47.2	49.2	3.7	38.7	57.4	3.9
Mozambique	45.7	45.1	42.5	46.8	6.5	6.5	43.8	53.1	3.1	44.9	51.9	3.3
Namibia	43.6	42.5	48.7	58.7	6.0	6.0	43.7	52.9	3.3	45.0	51.7	3.4
Niger	52.3	51.3	39.0	46.5	7.1	7.1	46.4	51.2	2.4	48.1	49.4	2.5
Nigeria	49.3	45.2	44.5	52.5	6.9	6.4	46.5	51.1	2.4	47.0	50.4	2.6
Rwanda	52.9	52.1	44.6	46.2	8.3	8.5	48.3	49.3	2.4	49.8	47.8	2.3
Senegal	49.2	43.0	40.3	49.3	7.0	6.1	44.8	52.4	2.8	44.6	52.5	2.9
Sierra Leone	48.9	48.2	35.0	43.0	6.5	6.5	42.5	54.4	3.1	44.9	51.9	3.1
Somalia	50.1	50.2	41.0	47.0	7.0	7.0	45.4	51.6	3.0	47.5	49.8	2.7
South Africa	39.7	31.3	53.9	62.9	5.5	4.1	40.8	55.4	3.8	37.5	58.5	4.0
Sudan	47.0	42.0	42.6	51.8	6.7	6.1	44.4	52.8	2.7	44.5	52.6	2.9
Swaziland	47.5	37.2	47.3	58.0	6.5	4.9	45.6	51.5	2.9	42.5	54.4	3.1
Tanzania	49.6	48.1	46.5	50.9	6.8	6.8	47.9	49.8	2.3	48.0	49.6	2.5
Togo	45.6	44.5	45.5	55.0	6.6	6.6	44.2	52.7	3.1	45.7	51.1	3.2
Tunisia	37.1	27.0	55.6	67.8	6.2	3.4	43.8	52.7	3.5	35.2	60.4	4.4
Uganda	50.3	51.0	46.5	41.8	6.9	7.3	47.4	50.1	2.5	48.7	48.9	2.4
Zaire	47.7	47.5	46.1	51.6	6.3	6.7	45.3	52.0	2.8	48.1	49.0	2.8
Zambia	49.1	46.4	47.3	44.1	6.9	6.3	46.5	50.9	2.6	48.5	49.3	2.2
Zimbabwe	48.6	40.6	51.5	55.8	7.2	5.3	49.0	48.4	2.6	44.6	52.6	2.8
ASIA	34.9	26.3	56.1	64.8	5.1	3.2	39.9	56.0	4.1	32.3	62.3	5.4
Afghanistan	51.6	52.8	38.0	43.5	7.1	6.9	43.8	53.9	2.4	40.0	57.4	2.6
Bangladesh	48.5	38.5	44.9	52.8	7.0	4.7	45.9	50.5	3.6	40.3	56.7	3.0
Bhutan	41.8	40.0	40.7	48.5	6.0	5.9	40.1	56.7	3.2	40.8	55.8	3.4
Cambodia	39.9	39.2	40.3	51.1	5.5	4.5	41.6	55.6	2.8	41.9	55.4	2.8
China	30.6	20.8	63.2	70.9	4.8	2.2	39.5	56.1	4.4	27.3	66.4	6.3
India	38.2	29.2	50.3	60.4	5.4	3.9	39.8	56.4	3.8	34.9	60.3	4.9
Indonesia	38.2	26.6	49.3	62.7	5.1	3.1	42.0	54.8	3.2	33.4	62.2	4.4
Iran, Islamic Rep	44.1	39.9	55.9	67.2	6.5	6.0	45.4	51.3	3.3	45.9	50.3	3.8
Iraq	47.4	38.8	57.0	66.0	7.1	5.7	46.6	50.9	2.5	43.8	53.3	3.0
Israel	27.4	21.1	71.6	76.5	3.8	2.9	32.9	59.4	7.8	28.8	61.5	9.7
Japan	19.2	11.2	73.3	78.7	2.1	1.7	24.3	67.8	7.9	16.8	69.2	13.9
Jordan	50.0	39.5	56.6	67.9	7.8	5.7	47.2	50.0	2.8	43.6	53.7	2.7
Korea, Dem People's Rep	35.8	24.2	61.5	71.1	5.7	2.4	45.1	51.7	3.1	29.1	66.3	4.6
Korea, Rep	28.8	16.3	61.5	70.8	4.1	1.8	37.7	58.6	3.6	23.3	71.3	5.4
Kuwait	44.4	28.2	67.3	74.7	6.9	3.7	44.4	54.0	1.6	41.1	57.2	1.7
Lao People's Dem Rep	44.4	45.2	40.4	51.0	6.2	6.7	42.1	55.2	2.7	44.8	52.2	3.0
Lebanon	32.1	27.1	65.0	68.5	4.9	3.1	41.2	53.8	5.0	34.2	60.3	5.5
Malaysia	34.7	28.6	63.0	70.8	5.2	3.6	42.1	54.2	3.7	37.9	58.2	3.9
Mongolia	41.5	34.0	53.8	63.7	5.8	4.6	43.8	53.3	2.9	40.2	56.5	3.3
Myanmar	39.9	32.5	49.8	57.6	5.8	4.2	40.7	55.4	3.8	37.4	58.5	4.1
Nepal	47.1	37.5	43.3	53.5	6.5	5.5	42.9	53.8	3.3	43.1	53.8	3.2
Oman	49.6	40.5	49.0	69.6	7.2	6.7	44.6	52.6	2.7	46.5	50.7	2.7
Pakistan	47.5	40.6	49.0	59.0	7.0	6.2	45.5	51.6	3.0	43.6	53.4	2.9
Philippines	38.4	30.3	57.8	65.0	5.5	3.9	43.6	53.8	2.7	38.4	58.3	3.3
Saudi Arabia	47.6	35.8	53.9	69.2	7.3	6.4	44.3	52.7	3.0	42.0	55.3	2.7
Singapore	21.2	15.9	69.5	74.5	2.6	1.8	32.9	63.0	4.1	22.6	70.9	6.4
Sri Lanka	28.9	20.8	65.0	71.6	4.0	2.5	39.4	56.6	4.1	30.3	63.8	5.9
Syrian Arab Rep	46.6	42.4	57.0	67.1	7.7	6.2	48.5	47.8	3.7	47.6	49.6	2.8
Thailand	35.1	20.5	59.6	69.3	5.0	2.2	44.9	52.1	3.0	29.2	66.3	4.5
Turkey	34.5	28.1	57.9	67.3	5.0	3.5	40.1	55.4	4.5	33.7	61.5	4.8
United Arab Emirates	33.0	21.2	62.5	71.2	6.4	4.5	28.3	69.7	2.0	28.9	68.9	2.2
Viet Nam	37.6	29.2	50.3	63.8	5.9	3.9	43.7	52.3	4.0	37.0	58.1	4.9
Yemen	53.2	48.3	42.6	52.7	7.8	7.2	50.9	46.5	2.6	49.3	48.3	2.4

Age Structure, 1970–95

Table 16.2

	Crude Birth Rate (births per 1,000 population)		Life Expectancy at Birth (years)		Total Fertility Rate		Percentage of Population in Specific Age Groups					
							1975			1995		
	1970-75	1990-95	1970-75	1990-95	1970-75	1990-95	<15	15-65	>65	<15	15-65	>65
NORTH & CENTRAL AMERICA	29.3	22.8	66.5	72.8	4.2	2.8	30.5	60.9	8.6	26.6	63.5	10.0
Belize	X	X	X	X	X	X	X	X	X	X	X	X
Canada	16.0	14.2	73.1	77.4	2.0	1.8	26.4	65.0	8.5	20.7	67.3	12.0
Costa Rica	31.5	26.3	68.1	76.3	4.3	3.1	42.2	54.4	3.4	35.0	60.3	4.7
Cuba	26.7	17.4	70.9	75.7	3.6	1.9	37.3	55.9	6.7	23.2	67.8	9.0
Dominican Rep	38.8	28.3	59.9	67.5	5.6	3.3	45.3	51.6	3.0	36.3	59.9	3.9
El Salvador	42.8	33.5	58.7	66.4	6.1	4.0	45.9	51.2	2.9	40.7	55.2	4.1
Guatemala	44.6	38.7	54.0	64.8	6.5	5.4	45.7	51.5	2.8	44.3	52.2	3.5
Haiti	38.6	35.3	48.5	56.6	5.8	4.8	41.1	54.3	4.6	40.2	55.8	3.9
Honduras	48.7	37.1	54.0	65.8	7.4	4.9	48.2	49.1	2.7	43.2	53.4	3.3
Jamaica	32.5	22.0	68.6	73.6	5.0	2.4	45.2	49.0	5.8	30.9	62.6	6.4
Mexico	42.7	27.9	62.9	70.3	6.4	3.2	46.6	49.8	3.6	36.0	60.0	4.0
Nicaragua	47.2	40.5	55.3	66.7	6.8	5.0	48.0	49.5	2.5	45.9	51.0	3.1
Panama	35.7	24.9	66.3	72.7	4.9	2.9	43.1	53.0	3.9	33.2	61.8	5.1
Trinidad and Tobago	27.0	23.3	65.7	71.3	3.5	2.7	38.0	57.0	4.9	33.8	60.5	5.7
United States	15.7	15.9	71.3	75.9	2.0	2.1	25.2	64.3	10.5	21.9	65.5	12.6
SOUTH AMERICA	33.0	24.2	60.7	67.4	4.6	2.9	39.5	56.2	4.3	32.6	62.0	5.4
Argentina	23.4	20.3	67.2	71.3	3.2	2.8	29.2	63.2	7.6	28.3	62.1	9.6
Bolivia	45.4	34.4	46.7	61.2	6.5	4.6	43.2	53.5	3.3	39.7	56.4	3.9
Brazil	33.6	23.3	59.8	66.2	4.7	2.8	40.1	56.2	3.7	32.2	62.7	5.2
Chile	27.6	22.5	63.6	72.0	3.6	2.7	36.8	57.8	5.4	30.5	63.2	6.4
Colombia	32.6	24.0	61.7	69.3	4.7	2.7	43.1	53.4	3.5	32.9	62.6	4.5
Ecuador	41.2	29.7	58.9	66.6	6.1	3.6	44.7	51.7	3.6	37.1	58.9	4.0
Guyana	35.0	25.1	60.0	65.2	4.9	2.6	44.1	52.2	3.7	32.3	63.8	4.0
Paraguay	36.6	33.0	65.6	67.3	5.7	4.3	44.3	52.2	3.5	39.6	56.8	3.6
Peru	40.5	29.0	55.5	64.6	6.0	3.6	43.2	53.2	3.5	35.5	60.4	4.1
Suriname	34.6	25.6	64.0	70.3	5.3	2.7	47.5	48.6	3.8	34.1	61.3	4.5
Uruguay	21.1	17.1	68.8	72.5	3.0	2.3	27.7	62.7	9.6	24.4	63.3	12.3
Venezuela	36.1	26.1	66.2	70.3	5.0	3.1	43.5	53.4	3.1	34.7	61.1	4.1
EUROPE	15.7	12.7	71.5	75.2	2.2	1.7	23.9	63.8	12.3	19.0	66.9	14.1
Albania	31.9	22.7	67.7	73.4	4.7	2.7	39.9	55.6	4.5	31.2	63.2	5.7
Austria	13.7	11.6	70.6	76.0	2.0	1.5	23.2	61.9	14.9	17.5	67.0	15.4
Belgium	13.6	12.1	71.4	76.0	1.9	1.7	22.2	63.9	13.9	18.0	66.4	15.7
Bulgaria	16.2	12.5	71.2	72.0	2.2	1.8	22.0	67.1	10.9	19.2	66.3	14.4
Czechoslovakia (former)	18.0	14.0	70.0	72.5	2.3	2.0	23.4	64.5	12.1	20.9	67.0	12.1
Denmark	14.6	12.5	73.6	75.6	2.0	1.7	22.6	64.0	13.4	17.1	67.5	15.4
Finland	13.2	12.8	70.7	75.7	1.6	1.8	22.0	67.4	10.6	18.9	67.0	14.1
France	16.3	13.5	72.4	76.9	2.3	1.8	23.9	62.6	13.5	19.8	65.3	14.9
Germany	11.4	11.3	71.0	76.0	1.6	1.5	21.5	63.6	14.8	17.1	68.1	14.8
Greece	15.9	10.4	72.3	77.6	2.3	1.5	23.9	63.9	12.2	17.3	67.2	15.4
Hungary	15.7	12.3	69.9	70.3	2.1	1.8	20.3	67.0	12.6	18.5	67.7	13.9
Iceland	21.0	17.4	74.3	78.2	2.8	2.2	29.8	61.0	9.2	24.3	64.6	11.2
Ireland	22.1	14.4	71.3	75.3	3.8	2.1	31.2	57.8	11.0	24.7	63.7	11.6
Italy	16.1	10.0	72.1	77.2	2.3	1.3	24.2	63.7	12.0	15.4	69.0	15.6
Netherlands	15.4	13.7	74.0	77.4	2.0	1.7	25.3	63.9	10.8	18.6	68.3	13.0
Norway	16.8	14.7	74.4	77.1	2.3	2.0	23.8	62.5	13.7	19.6	64.4	15.9
Poland	17.8	14.3	70.4	71.7	2.3	2.1	24.0	66.4	9.5	23.5	65.6	10.9
Portugal	19.5	11.6	68.0	74.6	2.8	1.5	27.9	62.2	9.9	18.5	67.3	14.2
Romania	19.3	15.7	69.0	70.1	2.6	2.1	25.2	65.2	9.6	22.2	66.4	11.3
Spain	19.5	10.8	72.9	77.6	2.9	1.4	27.6	62.4	10.0	17.0	68.3	14.7
Sweden	13.6	14.0	74.7	77.9	1.9	2.1	20.7	64.2	15.1	18.8	63.8	17.4
Switzerland	14.2	12.7	73.8	78.0	1.8	1.7	22.4	65.0	12.6	17.2	67.7	15.1
United Kingdom	14.5	13.9	72.0	76.2	2.0	1.9	23.3	62.7	14.0	19.7	64.7	15.6
Yugoslavia (former)	18.2	14.1	68.4	72.1	2.3	1.9	25.7	65.7	8.6	21.6	67.8	10.6
U.S.S.R. (former)	18.1	16.5	68.6	70.4	2.4	2.3	26.1	64.4	9.5	25.1	64.0	10.9
Armenia	X	23.0 a	X	71.0 a	X	2.6 a	X	X	X	30.0 b	64.0 b	6.0 b
Azerbaijan	X	27.0 a	X	70.0 a	X	2.8 a	X	X	X	33.0 b	62.0 b	5.0 b
Belarus	X	16.0 a	X	72.0 a	X	2.0 a	X	X	X	23.0 b	66.0 b	11.0 b
Estonia	15.4	14.0	70.5	71.5	2.2	2.1	24.1	67.7	8.2	23.6	67.8	8.6
Georgia	X	18.0 a	X	72.0 a	X	2.3 a	X	X	X	25.0 b	66.0 b	9.0 b
Kazakhstan	X	24.0 a	X	69.0 a	X	3.0 a	X	X	X	32.0 b	62.0 b	6.0 b
Kyrgyzstan	X	31.0 a	X	68.0 a	X	4.0 a	X	X	X	38.0 b	57.0 b	5.0 b
Latvia	14.4	13.9	70.1	71.3	2.0	2.0	23.5	67.3	9.2	23.6	67.6	8.8
Lithuania	16.6	14.8	71.3	73.0	2.3	2.0	27.5	63.3	9.2	24.0	67.1	8.9
Moldova	X	21.0 a	X	68.0 a	X	2.6 a	X	X	X	28.0 b	64.0 b	8.0 b
Russian Federation	X	16.0 a	X	70.0 a	X	2.1 a	X	X	X	23.0 b	67.0 b	10.0 b
Tajikistan	X	40.0 a	X	70.0 a	X	5.4 a	X	X	X	43.0 b	53.0 b	4.0 b
Turkmenistan	X	36.0 a	X	65.0 a	X	4.6 a	X	X	X	41.0 b	55.0 b	4.0 b
Ukraine	X	14.0 a	X	71.0 a	X	2.0 a	X	X	X	21.0 b	67.0 b	12.0 b
Uzbekistan	X	36.0 a	X	69.0 a	X	4.4 a	X	X	X	41.0 b	55.0 b	4.0 b
OCEANIA	23.9	19.3	66.8	72.6	3.2	2.5	31.0	61.5	7.5	26.0	64.5	9.5
Australia	19.6	15.1	71.7	76.9	2.5	1.9	27.6	63.7	8.7	21.7	66.8	11.6
Fiji	32.5	23.5	65.1	71.5	4.2	3.0	39.9	57.5	2.6	35.0	61.0	3.9
New Zealand	20.8	17.4	71.7	75.7	2.8	2.1	30.0	61.3	8.7	23.0	65.8	11.2
Papua New Guinea	41.0	33.5	47.7	55.9	6.1	4.9	42.0	54.9	3.1	39.8	57.5	2.6
Solomon Islands	47.2	37.5	62.0	70.4	7.2	5.4	46.5	49.5	4.0	44.3	53.1	2.6

Source: United Nations Population Division.
Notes: a. Data are for 1985-90. b. Data are for 1990.
World and regional totals include countries not listed here.
X = not available.
For additional information, see Sources and Technical Notes.

Table 16.3 Mortality and Nutrition, 1970–95

	Crude Death Rate (per 1,000 population)		Infant Mortality Rate (per 1,000 live births)		Under-five Mortality Rate (per 1,000 live births)			Maternal Mortality Rate (per 100,000 live births)	Wasting (percentage of children aged 12-23 months)	Stunting (percentage of children aged 24-59 months)	Per Capita Average Calories Available (as percentage of need)	Percentage Share of Household Consumption Expenditure for Food
	1970-75	1990-95	1970-75	1990-95	1960	1980	1991	1980-90	1980-91	1980-91	1988-90	1980/85
WORLD	12	9	92	62								
AFRICA	19	14	135	95								
Algeria	15	7	132	61	243	145	67	140	4	13	123	X
Angola	26	19	173	124	345	261	297	X	X	X	80	X
Benin	26	18	136	87	310	176	150	160	X	X	104	37
Botswana	17	9	94	60	170	94	62	200	X	X	97	35
Burkina Faso	25	18	173	118	318	218	159	810	X	X	94	X
Burundi	20	17	137	106	255	193	180	X	10	60	84	X
Cameroon	20	12	119	63	264	173	125	430	2	43	95	24
Central African Rep	22	18	132	105	294	202	182	600	X	X	82	X
Chad	25	18	166	122	325	254	216	960	X	X	73	X
Congo	19	15	90	82	220	125	110	900	13	33	103	42
Cote d'Ivoire	19	15	129	91	300	180	130	X	17	20	111	40
Djibouti	23	17	154	112	289	199	164	X	X	X	X	X
Egypt	16	9	150	57	258	180	76	320	4	32	132	50
Equatorial Guinea	24	18	157	117	316	243	206	X	X	X	X	X
Ethiopia	23	19	155	122	294	260	216	X	19	43	73	50
Gabon	20	16	132	94	287	194	164	190	X	X	104	X
Gambia, The	27	19	179	132	375	278	238	X	X	X	X	X
Ghana	16	12	107	81	215	157	170	1,000	15	39	93	50 a
Guinea	27	20	177	134	337	276	238	800	X	X	97	X
Guinea-Bissau	27	21	183	140	336	290	246	700	X	X	97	X
Kenya	17	10	98	66	202	112	78	170	5	32	89	39
Lesotho	19	10	130	79	204	173	158	X	7	23	93	X
Liberia	20	14	182	126	288	235	219	X	X	X	98	X
Libya	15	8	117	68	269	150	112	80	X	X	140	X
Madagascar	19	13	172	110	364	216	176	570	17	56	95	59
Malawi	24	22	191	142	365	290	230	170	8	61	88	55
Mali	25	19	203	159	400	310	230	2,000	16	34	96	57
Mauritania	24	18	160	117	321	249	213	X	18	65	106	X
Mauritius	7	7	55	21	84	42	26	99	16	22	128	24
Morocco	16	8	122	68	215	145	72	X	X	X	X	40
Mozambique	22	18	168	147	331	269	297	300	X	X	77	X
Namibia	17	11	113	70	206	114	84	370	9	30	X	X
Niger	25	19	167	124	320	320	320	700	23	38	95	X
Nigeria	20	14	135	96	204	196	191	800	16	54	93	52
Rwanda	21	18	142	110	191	222	222	210	1	34	82	30
Senegal	24	16	122	80	303	221	155	600	8	28	98	50
Sierra Leone	29	22	193	143	385	301	257	450	14	X	83	56
Somalia	24	19	155	122	294	246	215	1,100	X	X	81	X
South Africa	14	9	76	53	126	91	73	83	X	X	128	34
Sudan	21	14	145	99	292	210	172	550	13	32	87	60 a
Swaziland	18	10	133	73	233	151	116	X	X	X	X	X
Tanzania	19	15	130	102	249	202	180	340	X	X	95	64
Togo	19	13	129	85	264	175	143	420	10	37	99	X
Tunisia	12	6	120	43	244	102	46	50	4	23	131	37
Uganda	19	21	116	104	218	181	185	300	4	25	93	X
Zaire	19	15	117	93	286	204	190	800	X	X	96	55
Zambia	18	18	100	84	220	160	197	150	10	59	87	37
Zimbabwe	15	11	93	59	181	125	90	X	2	31	94	40
ASIA	12	8	98	62								
Afghanistan	26	22	194	162	360	280	260	640	X	X	72	X
Bangladesh	21	14	140	108	247	211	140	600	16	65	88	59
Bhutan	23	17	178	129	324	249	210	1,310	4	56	128	X
Cambodia	23	14	181	116	217	330	193	500	X	X	96	X
China	9	7	61	27	209	65	43	95	8	41	112	61 b
India	16	10	132	88	236	177	131	460	27	65	101	52
Indonesia	17	9	114	65	216	128	111	450	X	X	121	48
Iran, Islamic Rep	15	7	122	40	233	126	67	120	23	55	125	37
Iraq	15	7	96	58	171	83	X	120	X	X	128	X
Israel	7	7	23	9	39	19	12	3	X	X	125	21
Japan	7	8	12	5	40	11	6	11	X	X	125	16
Jordan	14	6	82	36	149	66	X	48	3	21	110	35
Korea, Dem People's Rep	8	5	47	24	120	43	35	41	X	X	121	X
Korea, Rep	9	6	47	21	124	18	10	26	X	X	120	35
Kuwait	5	2	43	14	128	35	16	6	2	14	X	X
Lao People's Dem Rep	23	15	145	97	233	190	152	X	20	44	111	X
Lebanon	9	7	48	34	91	62	48	X	X	X	127	X
Malaysia	9	5	42	14	105	42	21	59	6	X	120	23 a
Mongolia	13	8	98	60	185	112	85	140	X	X	97	X
Myanmar	16	11	122	81	237	146	120	460	X	X	114	X
Nepal	21	13	153	99	279	177	135	830	X	X	100	57
Oman	20	5	145	30	300	95	35	X	X	X	X	X
Pakistan	18	11	140	98	221	151	139	500	11	60	99	54
Philippines	10	7	71	40	102	70	62	100	14	45	104	51
Saudi Arabia	17	5	105	31	292	90	45	90	X	X	121	X
Singapore	5	6	19	7	40	13	8	10	X	X	136	19
Sri Lanka	8	6	56	24	130	52	X	80	21	39	101	43
Syrian Arab Rep	12	6	88	39	201	73	44	140	X	X	126	X
Thailand	9	6	65	26	146	61	36	71	10	28	103	30
Turkey	12	7	138	56	217	141	95	150	X	X	127	40
United Arab Emirates	10	4	57	22	240	64	24	X	X	X	X	X
Viet Nam	14	9	106	36	219	105	55	120	12	49	103	X
Yemen	22	14	168	106	378	236	187	X	15	X	X	X

Table 16.3

	Estimated and Projected								Wasting (percentage of children aged 12-23 months)	Stunting (percentage of children aged 24-59 months)	Per Capita Average Calories Available (as percentage of need)	Percentage Share of Household Consumption Expenditure for Food
	Crude Death Rate (per 1,000 population)		Infant Mortality Rate (per 1,000 live births)		Under-five Mortality Rate (per 1,000 live births)			Maternal Mortality Rate (per 100,000 live births)				
	1970-75	1990-95	1970-75	1990-95	1960	1980	1991	1980-90	1980-91	1980-91	1988-90	1980/85
NORTH & CENTRAL AMERICA												
Belize	X	X	X	X	X	X	X	X	X	X	X	X
Canada	7	8	16	7	33	13	9	5	X	X	122	11
Costa Rica	6	4	53	14	112	29	16	36	3	8	121	33
Cuba	7	7	38	14	50	26	X	39	1	X	135	X
Dominican Rep	10	6	94	57	152	94	X	X	3	26	102	46
El Salvador	11	7	99	46	210	120	70	X	3	36	102	33
Guatemala	13	8	95	48	205	136	85	200	3	68	103	36
Haiti	18	12	135	86	270	195	140	340	17	51	89	X
Honduras	14	7	101	60	203	100	62	220	2	34	98	39
Jamaica	8	6	42	14	76	39	16	120	6	7	114	39
Mexico	9	6	68	35	141	81	39	110	6	22	131	35 b
Nicaragua	13	7	100	52	209	143	86	X	X	22	99	X
Panama	7	5	43	21	104	31	21	60	7	24	98	38
Trinidad and Tobago	8	6	42	18	73	40	24	110	5	4	114	X
United States	9	9	18	8	30	15	11	8	X	X	138	13
SOUTH AMERICA	10	7	84	51								
Argentina	9	9	49	29	68	41	26	140	X	X	131	35
Bolivia	19	9	151	85	252	170	125	600	2	51	84	33 a
Brazil	10	7	91	57	181	93	69	200	2	15	114	35
Chile	9	6	70	17	138	35	20	67	1	10	102	29
Colombia	9	6	73	37	132	59	X	200	5	18	106	29
Ecuador	11	7	95	57	180	101	63	170	4	39	105	30
Guyana	10	7	79	48	126	88	71	X	X	X	X	X
Paraguay	7	6	55	47	90	61	X	300	X	17	116	30
Peru	13	8	110	76	236	130	X	300	3	43	87	35
Suriname	8	6	49	28	96	52	38	X	X	X	X	X
Uruguay	10	10	46	20	47	42	23	36	X	16	101	31
Venezuela	7	5	49	33	70	42	X	X	4	7	99	23
EUROPE	10	11	24	10								
Albania	7	5	58	23	151	57	33	X	X	X	107	X
Austria	13	11	24	8	43	17	9	8	X	X	133	16
Belgium	12	11	19	8	35	15	9	3	X	X	149	15
Bulgaria	9	12	26	14	70	25	18	X	X	X	X	X
Czechoslovakia (former)	11	11	21	10	33	20	13	10	X	X	145	X
Denmark	10	12	12	7	25	10	9	3	X	X	135	13
Finland	10	10	12	6	28	9	7	11	X	X	113	16
France	11	10	16	7	34	13	9	9	X	X	143	16
Germany	12	11	21	7	40	16	9	5	X	X	X	X
Greece	9	10	34	8	64	23	11	5	X	X	151	30
Hungary	12	14	34	14	57	26	16	15	X	X	137	25
Iceland	7	7	12	5	22	9	5	X	X	X	X	X
Ireland	11	9	18	7	36	14	9	2	X	X	157	22
Italy	10	10	26	8	50	17	10	4	X	X	139	19
Netherlands	8	9	12	7	22	11	9	10	X	X	114	13
Norway	10	11	12	8	23	11	10	3	X	X	120	15
Poland	8	10	27	15	70	24	18	11	X	X	131	29
Portugal	11	10	45	12	112	31	16	10	X	X	136	34
Romania	9	11	40	23	82	36	34	150	X	X	116	X
Spain	8	9	21	6	57	16	10	5	X	X	141	24
Sweden	10	12	10	6	20	9	7	5	X	X	111	13
Switzerland	9	10	13	7	27	11	9	5	X	X	130	17 a
United Kingdom	12	12	17	7	27	14	9	8	X	X	130	12
Yugoslavia (former)	9	10	45	22	113	37	23	8	X	X	140	27
U.S.S.R. (former)	9	10	26	20	53	37	31	21	X	X	132	X
Armenia	X	6 c	X	23 c	X	X	X	35	X	X	X	X
Azerbaijan	X	7 c	X	28 c	X	X	X	29	X	X	X	X
Belarus	X	10 c	X	13 c	X	X	X	25	X	X	X	X
Estonia	11	12	17	13	X	X	X	41 a	X	X	X	X
Georgia	X	9 c	X	22 c	X	X	X	55	X	X	X	X
Kazakhstan	X	8 c	X	28 c	X	X	X	53	X	X	X	X
Kyrgyzstan	X	7 c	X	36 c	X	X	X	43	X	X	X	X
Latvia	11	12	17	10	X	X	X	57 a	X	X	X	X
Lithuania	9	10	18	10	X	X	X	29 a	X	X	X	X
Moldova	X	10 c	X	24 c	X	X	X	34	X	X	X	X
Russian Federation	X	11 c	X	19 c	X	X	X	49	X	X	X	X
Tajikistan	X	7 c	X	46 c	X	X	X	39	X	X	X	X
Turkmenistan	X	8 c	X	54 c	X	X	X	55	X	X	X	X
Ukraine	X	12 c	X	14 c	X	X	X	33	X	X	X	X
Uzbekistan	X	7 c	X	43 c	X	X	X	43	X	X	X	X
OCEANIA	10	8	40	22								
Australia	9	8	17	7	24	13	10	3	X	X	124	13
Fiji	6	5	45	23	97	42	31	X	X	X	X	X
New Zealand	8	8	16	8	26	16	12	13	X	X	131	12
Papua New Guinea	17	11	100	54	248	95	80	900	X	X	114	X
Solomon Islands	9	4	61	27	X	X	X	X	X	X	X	X

Sources: United Nations Population Division, United Nations Children's Fund, and the World Bank.
Notes: a. World Bank estimate. b. World Bank estimate, includes beverages and tobacco. c. Data are for 1985-90.
World and regional totals include countries not listed here.
X = not available.
For additional information, see Sources and Technical Notes.

Table 16.4 Access to Safe Drinking Water, Sanitation, and

	Percentage of Population with Access to:								Health Services 1985-88			Percentage of Total Central Government Expenditure for Health	
	Safe Drinking Water				Sanitation Services								
	Urban		Rural		Urban		Rural						
	1980	1990	1980	1990	1980	1990	1980	1990	All	Urban	Rural	1972	1990
WORLD													
AFRICA													
Algeria	X	X	X	X	X	X	X	X	88	100	80	X	X
Angola	85	73	10	20	40	25	15	20	30 a	X	X	X	X
Benin	26	73	15	43	48	60	4	35	18	X	X	X	X
Botswana	X	100	X	88	X	100	X	85	89 a	100 a	85 a	6 b	4.8 b
Burkina Faso	27	44 c	31	70	38	35 c	5	5 c	49 a	51 a	48 a	8.2	X
Burundi	90	92	20	43	40	64	35	16	61	X	X	6	X
Cameroon	X	42	X	45	X	X	X	X	41	44	39	X	3.4
Central African Rep	X	19	X	26	X	45	X	46	45	X	X	X	X
Chad	X	X	X	X	X	X	X	X	30	X	X	4.4	X
Congo	36	92 c	3	2 c	17	X	0	2	83	97	70	X	X
Cote d'Ivoire	X	57	X	80	X	81	X	100	30 a	61 a	11 a	X	X
Djibouti	50	50 c	20	21 c	43	94 c	20	50 c	X	X	X	X	X
Egypt	88	95	64	86	45	80	10	26	X	X	X	X	2.8
Equatorial Guinea	47 d	65	X	18	99 d	54	X	24	X	X	X	X	X
Ethiopia	X	70 c	X	11 c	X	97 c	X	7 c	46	X	X	5.7	X
Gabon	X	90 c	X	50 c	X	X	X	X	90 a	X	X	X	X
Gambia, The	85	100	X	48	X	100	X	27	X	X	X	X	X
Ghana	72	63	33	39	47	63	17	60	60	92	45	6.3 b	9 b
Guinea	69	100	2	37	54	65	1	0	47	100	40	X	X
Guinea-Bissau	18	18 c	8	27 c	21	30 c	13	18 c	X	X	X	X	X
Kenya	85	X	15	X	89	X	19	X	X	X	X	7.9 b	5.4 b
Lesotho	37	59 c	11	45 c	13	14 c	14	23 c	80	X	X	8	7.4
Liberia	X	93 c	16	22 c	18	4 c,e	5	8 c	39	50	30	9.8	5.4
Libya	100	100 c	90	80 c	100	100 c	72	85 c	X	X	X	X	X
Madagascar	80	62	7	10	9	X	X	X	56	X	X	4.2	X
Malawi	77	66 c	37	49 c	100	X	81	X	80	X	X	5.5 b	7.4 b
Mali	37	41	0	4	79	81	0	10	15	X	X	X	2.1
Mauritania	80	67 c	85	65 c	5	34 c	X	X	40	X	X	X	X
Mauritius	100	100	98	100	100	100	90	100	100	100	100	10.3	8.6
Morocco	100	100	X	18	X	100	X	19 c	70	100	50	4.8	X
Mozambique	X	44 c	X	17 c	X	61 c	X	11 c	39	100	30	X	X
Namibia	X	90	X	37	X	24	X	11	X	X	X	X	11.1
Niger	41	98	32	45	36	71	3	4	41	99	30	X	X
Nigeria	60	100	30	22	X	80	X	11	66	85	62	3.6 b	X
Rwanda	48	84	55	67	60	88	50	17	27 a	60 a	25 a	5.7	X
Senegal	33	65	25	26	5	57	2	38	40	X	X	X	X
Sierra Leone	50	80 c	2	20	31	55	6	31	X	X	X	5.3 b	3.6 b
Somalia	60	50 c	20	29 c	45	41 c	5	5 c	27 a	50 a	15 a	7.2 b	X
South Africa	X	X	X	X	X	X	X	X	X	X	X	X	X
Sudan	X	90 f	31	20 f	63	40 f	0	5 f	51	90	40	5.4 b	X
Swaziland	X	100 g	X	7 g	X	100 g	X	25 g	X	X	X	X	X
Tanzania	X	75 c	X	46 c	X	76 c	X	77 c	76 a	99 a	72 a	7.2	X
Togo	70	100 c	31	61 c	24	42 c	10	16 c	61	X	X	X	X
Tunisia	100	100 c	17	31 c	100	71 c	X	15 c	90 a	100 a	80 a	7.4	6.1
Uganda	45	60	8	30	40	32	10	60	61	90	57	5.3	X
Zaire	X	68	X	24	X	46	X	11	26	40	17	2.4	0.1
Zambia	65	76 c	32	43 c	100	77 c	48	34 c	75 a	100 a	50 a	7.4 b	7.4 b
Zimbabwe	X	95 c	X	80 c	X	95 c	X	22 c	71	100	62	X	7.6
ASIA													
Afghanistan	28	40	8	19	X	13	X	X	29	80	17	X	X
Bangladesh	26	39	40	89	21	40	1	4	45	X	X	5 b	4.8 b
Bhutan	50	60	5	30	X	80	X	3	65	X	X	X	5.3
Cambodia	X	X	X	X	X	X	X	X	53	80	50	X	X
China	X	87	X	68	X	100	X	81	90	100	88	X	X
India	77	86	31	69	27	44	1	3	X	X	X	1.5	1.6
Indonesia	35	35	19	33	29	79	21	30	80	X	X	1.4	2
Iran, Islamic Rep	X	100 c	X	75 c	X	100 c	X	35 c	80	95	65	3.6	8.5
Iraq	X	93	X	41	X	96	X	18	93	97	78	X	X
Israel	X	100 h	X	97 h	X	99 h	X	95 h	X	X	X	X	4.1
Japan	X	100	X	85	X	X	X	X	X	X	X	X	X
Jordan	100	100 c	65	97 c	94	100 c	34	100 c	97	98	95	3.8	5.8
Korea, Dem People's Rep	X	100 h	X	100 h	X	100 h	X	100 h	X	X	X	X	X
Korea, Rep	86	100	61	76	100	67	100	12	93	97	86	1.2	2.2
Kuwait	X	100 h	X	X	X	100 h	X	X	100	X	X	5.5	7.4
Lao People's Dem Rep	21	47	12	25	11	30	3	8	67	X	X	X	X
Lebanon	100	X	100	X	94	X	18	X	X	X	X	X	X
Malaysia	90	96	49	66	100	94	55	94	X	X	X	X	X
Mongolia	X	100	X	58	X	100	X	47	X	X	X	X	X
Myanmar	38	79	15	72	38	50	15	13	33	100	11	6.1	4.6
Nepal	83	66	7	34	16	34	1	3	X	X	X	4.7	4.8
Oman	X	87	X	42	X	100	X	34	91	100	90	5.9	4.6
Pakistan	72	82	20	42	42	53	2	12	55	99	35	1.1	0.7
Philippines	65	93	43	72	81	79	67	63	X	X	X	3.2 b	4.1 b
Saudi Arabia	92	100 c	87	74 c	81	100 c	50	30 c	97	100	88	X	X
Singapore	100	100	NA	NA	80	99	NA	2	100	100	NA	7.8	4.7
Sri Lanka	65	80	18	55	80	68	63	45	93 a	X	X	6.4	5.4
Syrian Arab Rep	98	91 h	54	68 h	74	72 h	28	55 h	75 a	92 a	60 a	1.4	1.3
Thailand	65	67 c	63	85	64	84 c	41	86	90	90	90	3.7	6.8
Turkey	95	100 g	62	70 g	56	95 g	X	90 g	X	X	X	3.2	3.6
United Arab Emirates	95	100 h	81	100 h	93	100 h	22	77 f	99	X	X	4.3 b	6.9 b
Viet Nam	X	47	32	33	X	23	55	10	80	100	75	X	X
Yemen	X	X	X	X	X	X	X	X	38	X	X	X	X

Health Services, 1972–90

Table 16.4

	Percentage of Population with Access to:								Health Services 1985-88			Percentage of Total Central Government Expenditure for Health	
	Safe Drinking Water				Sanitation Services								
	Urban		Rural		Urban		Rural						
	1980	1990	1980	1990	1980	1990	1980	1990	All	Urban	Rural	1972	1990
NORTH & CENTRAL AMERICA													
Belize	X	94 c	36	53	62	76	75	22	X	X	X	X	X
Canada	X	100 g	X	100 g	X	X	X	X	X	X	X	7.6	5.5
Costa Rica	100	100 c	68	84 c	93	100 c	82	93 c	80 a	100 a	63 a	4	26.3
Cuba	X	100	X	91	X	100	X	68	X	X	X	X	X
Dominican Rep	85	82	33	45	25	95	4	75	80	X	X	11.7	11.3
El Salvador	67	87	40	15	80	85	26	38	56	80	40	10.9 b	7.8 b
Guatemala	89	92	18	43	45	72	20	52	34	47	25	9.5	9.9
Haiti	48	56	8	35	39	44	10	17	50	X	X	X	X
Honduras	50	85	40	48	40	89	26	42	66	80	56	10.2	X
Jamaica	X	95 c	X .	46 c	X	14 e	X	X	90	X	X	X	X
Mexico	64	94	43	49	51	85	12	12	78	80	60	4.5	1.9
Nicaragua	91	76	10	21	35	32 e	X	X	83	100	60	4	X
Panama	100	100 c	65	66 c	62	100 c	28	68 c	80 a	95 a	64 a	15.1	17.9
Trinidad and Tobago	100	100	93	88	95	100	88	92	99	X	X	X	X
United States	X	X	X	X	X	X	X	X	X	X	X	8.6	13.5
SOUTH AMERICA													
Argentina	65	73 c	17	17 c	89	100 c	32	29 c	71	80	21	X	2
Bolivia	69	76	10	30	37	38	4	14	63	90	36	X	2.3
Brazil	80	95	51	61	32	84	X	32	X	X	X	6.7	7.2
Chile	100	100 c	17	21 c	99	100 c	X	6 c	97	X	X	10	5.9
Colombia	X	87	79	82	100	84	4	18	60	X	X	X	X
Ecuador	82	63	16	44	39	56	14	38	75	92	40	4.5 b	11 b
Guyana	X	100	60	71	100	97	80	81	89	X	X	X	X
Paraguay	39	61	10	9	95	31	89	60	61	X	X	3.5	4.3
Peru	68	68	21	24	57	76	0	20	75	X	X	5.5 b	5.1 b
Suriname	X	82 c	79	56 c	100	64 c	79	36 c	X	X	X	X	X
Uruguay	96	100	2	5 c	59	60 c	60	65 c	82	X	X	1.6	4.5
Venezuela	91	89 c	50	36	90	97 c	70	72	X	X	X	11.7	X
EUROPE													
Albania	X	100 g	X	95 g	X	100 g	X	100 g	X	X	X	X	X
Austria	X	100 g	X	100 g	X	100 g	X	100 g	X	X	X	10.1	12.9
Belgium	X	100 h	X	100 h	X	100 h	X	100 h	X	X	X	1.5	X
Bulgaria	X	100 h	X	96 h	X	100 h	X	100 h	X	X	X	X	4.1
Czechoslovakia (former)	X	100 g	X	100 g	X	100 g	X	100 g	X	X	X	X	X.4
Denmark	X	100 h	X	100 h	X	100 h	X	100 h	X	X	X	10	1.1
Finland	X	99 g	X	90 g	X	100 g	X	100 g	X	X	X	10.6	10.8
France	X	100 g	X	100 g	X	100 g	X	100 g	X	X	X	X	15.2
Germany	X	100 f	X	100 f	X	X	X	X	X	X	X	X	X
Greece	X	100 g	X	95 g	X	100 g	X	95 g	X	X	X	7.4	X
Hungary	X	100 g	X	95 g	X	100 g	X	100 g	X	X	X	X	7.9
Iceland	X	100 g	X	100 g	X	100 g	X	100 g	X	X	X	X	X
Ireland	X	100 g	X	100 g	X	100 g	X	100 g	X	X	X	X	12.1
Italy	X	100 g	X	100 g	X	100 g	X	100 g	X	X	X	13.5	11.3
Netherlands	X	100 g	X	100 g	X	100 g	X	100 g	X	X	X	12.1	11.7
Norway	X	100 h	X	100 h	X	100 g	X	100 g	X	X	X	12.3	10.4
Poland	X	94 g	X	82 g	X	100 g	X	100 g	X	X	X	X	X
Portugal	X	97 g	X	90 g	X	100 g	X	95 g	X	X	X	X.5	8.7
Romania	X	100 g	X	90 g	X	100 g	X	95 g	X	X	X	X.9	12.8
Spain	X	100 g	X	100 g	X	100 g	X	100 g	X	X	X	X	X
Sweden	X	100 h	X	100 h	X	100 h	X	100 h	X	X	X	3.6	X.9
Switzerland	X	100 h	X	100 h	X	100 f	X	100 f	X	X	X	10	X
United Kingdom	X	100 g	X	100 g	X	100 g	X	100 g	X	X	X	12.2	14.6
Yugoslavia (former)	X	100 f	X	65 f	X	78 f	X	46 f	X	X	X	24.8	X
U.S.S.R. (former)	X	100 g	X	100 g	X	100 g	X	100 g	X	X	X	X	X
Armenia	X	X	X	X	X	X	X	X	X	X	X	X	X
Azerbaijan	X	X	X	X	X	X	X	X	X	X	X	X	X
Belarus	X	X	X	X	X	X	X	X	X	X	X	X	X
Estonia	X	X	X	X	X	X	X	X	X	X	X	X	X
Georgia	X	X	X	X	X	X	X	X	X	X	X	X	X
Kazakhstan	X	X	X	X	X	X	X	X	X	X	X	X	X
Kyrgyzstan	X	X	X	X	X	X	X	X	X	X	X	X	X
Latvia	X	X	X	X	X	X	X	X	X	X	X	X	X
Lithuania	X	X	X	X	X	X	X	X	X	X	X	X	X
Moldova	X	X	X	X	X	X	X	X	X	X	X	X	X
Russian Federation	X	X	X	X	X	X	X	X	X	X	X	X	X
Tajikistan	X	X	X	X	X	X	X	X	X	X	X	X	X
Turkmenistan	X	X	X	X	X	X	X	X	X	X	X	X	X
Ukraine	X	X	X	X	X	X	X	X	X	X	X	X	X
Uzbekistan	X	X	X	X	X	X	X	X	X	X	X	X	X
OCEANIA													
Australia	X	100	X	100	X	100	X	100	X	X	X	7	12.8
Fiji	94	96 i	66	69 i	85	91 c	60	65 c	X	X	X	X	X
New Zealand	X	100	X	82	X	100	X	88	X	X	X	14.8 b	12.7 b
Papua New Guinea	55	94	10	20	96	57	3	56	96	X	X	X	9.4 b
Solomon Islands	91	82 c	20	58	82	73	10	2	X	X	X	X	X

Sources: World Health Organization, United Nations Development Progamme, United Nations Children's Fund, and the World Bank.
Notes: a. Indicates data that refer to only part of a country, years other than 1985-1988, or differ from the standard definition. b. Data are for budgetary accounts only.
c. 1988 data. d. 1983 data. e. Population served by sewer connection only. f. 1986 data. g. 1985 data. h. 1987 data. i. Population served by house connection only.
0 = zero or less than 0.5 percent; X = not available; NA = not applicable.
For additional information, see Sources and Technical Notes.

Table 16.5 Education and Child Health, 1970–91

	Adult Female Literacy (percent)		Adult Male Literacy (percent)		Gross Primary School Enrollment (as a percentage of age group) Female		Male		Births Attended by Trained Personnel (percent)	ORT{a} Use (percent)	Low-Birth-weight Infants (percent)	Percentage of 1-Year-Olds Fully Immunized in 1991 Against:			
	1970	1990	1970	1990	1960	1990	1960	1990	1983-91	1987-91	1990	TB	DPT	Polio	Measles
WORLD												86	78	79	77
AFRICA												80	56	56	55
Algeria	11	46	39	70	37	89 b	55	105 b	15	26	9	99	89	89	83
Angola	7	29	16	56	14	85 b	30	102 b	15	48	19	53	26	26	39
Benin	8	16	23	32	15	44 c	38	87 c	45	45	X	X	X	X	X
Botswana	44	65	37	84	48	117 c	35	112 c	78	64	8	92	86	82	78
Burkina Faso	3	9	13	28	5	27 c	12	44 c	30	X	21	84	37	37	42
Burundi	10	40	29	61	10	66	33	86	19	49	X	88	83	89	75
Cameroon	19	43	47	66	37	104	77	121	45	84	13	76	56	54	56
Central African Rep	6	25	26	52	11	58	50	85	66	24	15	96	82	82	82
Chad	2	18	20	42	4	34	29	80	15	15	X	40	18	18	28
Congo	19	44	50	70	53	X	103	X	X	26	16	83	70	70	60
Cote d'Ivoire	10	40	26	67	22	66	62	88	20	16	14	63	48	48	42
Djibouti	X	X	X	X	X	X	X	X	X	X	X	81	81	81	79
Egypt	20	34	50	63	52	89 c	80	104 c	35	58	10	92	86	86	89
Equatorial Guinea	X	37	X	64	54	120	92	122	X	X	X	97	78	75	88
Ethiopia	X	X	8	X	3	33	9	50	14	38	16	57	44	44	37
Gabon	22	49	43	74	X	X	X	X	80	10	X	96	78	78	76
Gambia, The	X	16	X	39	10	52	21	79	X	X	X	97	85	89	87
Ghana	18	51	43	70	31	65	58	81	55	21	17	88	45	44	34
Guinea	7	13	21	35	9	19	27	39	25	65	21	57	41	41	39
Guinea-Bissau	6	24	13	50	X	42 c	X	76 c	27	5	20	94	63	63	52
Kenya	19	59	44	80	29	98	62	101	50	69	16	X	36	42	36
Lesotho	74	X	49	X	109	128	73	111	40	68	11	97	76	75	76
Liberia	8	29	27	50	13	28	40	45	58	9	X	X	X	X	X
Libya	13	50	60	75	24	X	92	X	76	60	X	91	62	62	59
Madagascar	43	73	56	88	57	94	74	102	62	11	10	67	46	46	33
Malawi	18	X	42	X	26	65	50	80	45	14	20	96	81	78	78
Mali	4	24	11	41	5	17	13	28	32	X	17	68	35	35	40
Mauritania	X	21	X	47	3	50	12	66	20	X	11	64	29	27	32
Mauritius	59	X	77	X	90	110	96	109	85	7	9	94	90	90	84
Morocco	10	38	34	61	28	61	69	88	X	X	X	89	79	79	76
Mozambique	14	21	29	45	43	76	71	97	25	30	20	30	19	19	23
Namibia	X	X	X	X	X	X	X	X	X	X	12	85	53	53	41
Niger	2	17	6	40	3	24	8	42	47	54	15	38	18	18	24
Nigeria	14	40	35	62	31	79	54	98	37	35	16	96	65	65	70
Rwanda	21	37	43	64	29	69	65	70	22	24	17	94	89	89	89
Senegal	5	25	18	52	18	51	37	72	41	27	11	92	60	66	59
Sierra Leone	8	11	18	31	15	56	30	73	25	60	17	94	65	65	63
Somalia	1	14	5	36	2	17	6	27	2	78	16	31	18	18	30
South Africa	X	X	X	X	85	X	94	X	X	X	X	85	67	69	63
Sudan	6	12	28	43	11	44	29	63	69	37	15	66	63	63	58
Swaziland	X	X	X	X	58	106	58	107	X	X	X	66	79	79	70
Tanzania	18	X	48	X	16	72	33	69	60	83	14	89	79	74	75
Togo	7	31	27	56	25	86	64	126	15	33	20	93	73	72	61
Tunisia	17	56	44	74	43	110	88	126	68	63	8	80	90	90	80
Uganda	30	35	52	62	18	71	39	77	38	30	X	73	50	50	56
Zaire	22	61	61	84	32	75	89	89	X	45	15	65	32	31	31
Zambia	37	65	66	81	40	99	61	108	38	89	13	97	79	78	76
Zimbabwe	47	60	63	74	65	132 d	82	139 d	60	77	14	87	89	88	87
ASIA															
Afghanistan	2	14	13	44	2	18	14	41	9	26	20	X	X	X	X
Bangladesh	12	22	36	47	31	55	80	72	5	26	50	89	63	63	59
Bhutan	X	25	X	51	0	26	5	38	7	65	X	98	95	95	89
Cambodia	23	22	X	48	X	X	X	X	47	6	X	55	38	39	38
China	X	62	X	84	90	122	131	136	94	54	9	99	97	98	98
India	20	34	47	62	44	85	83	113	33	14	33	85	83	83	77
Indonesia	42	68	66	84	58	115	78	119	32	45	14	89	89	84	80
Iran, Islamic Rep	17	43	40	65	28	104	59	118	70	71	9	92	88	88	84
Iraq	18	49	50	70	36	100	94	108	50	70	15	89	69	69	73
Israel	83	X	93	X	97	95 c	99	92 c	99	X	7	0	85	85	88
Japan	99	X	99	X	102	102 c	103	102 c	100	X	6	85	87	90	66 e
Jordan	29	70	64	89	59	99 c	94	98 c	87	77	7	X	92	92	85
Korea, Dem People's Rep	X	X	X	X	X	103 c	X	110 c	100	72	X	99	90	98	96 e
Korea, Rep	81	94	94	99	94	99	108	98	89	X	9	72	74	74	93 e
Kuwait	42	67	65	77	99	98	132	101	99	10	7	X	76	76	63
Lao People's Dem Rep	28	X	37	X	20	113	43	129	X	30	18	34	22	22	48
Lebanon	58	73	79	88	105	95	112	108	45	10	10	X	85	85	51
Malaysia	48	70	71	87	79	100	108	101	82	47	10	98	91	91	79 e
Mongolia	74	X	87	X	80	102	80	102	99	59	10	87	84	84	86
Myanmar	57	72	85	89	52	100 c	61	106 c	57	19	16	X	X	X	X
Nepal	3	13	23	38	3	70	19	116	6	14	X	83	74	74	64
Oman	X	X	X	X	X	97 c	X	106 c	60	19	10	92	94	94	96
Pakistan	11	21	30	47	11	36	39	60	40	34	25	91	81	81	77
Philippines	81	90	84	90	93	109	98	110	55	25	15	96	88	90	88
Saudi Arabia	2	48	15	73	3	73	32	84	90	45	7	99	94	94	90
Singapore	55	X	82	X	101	110	120	114	100	X	7	99	91	91	92 e
Sri Lanka	69	84	85	93	X	X	X	X	94	76	25	89	86	86	79
Syrian Arab Rep	20	51	60	78	39	106	89	116	61	89	11	95	89	89	84
Thailand	72	90	86	96	88	94	97	99	71	43	13	84	69	69	60
Turkey	34	71	69	90	58	118	90	123	77	X	8	X	X	X	X
United Arab Emirates	7	X	24	X	X	95	X	98	99	81	6	95	85	85	92
Viet Nam	X	84	X	92	X	99 c	X	105 c	95	53	17	91	88	88	88
Yemen	X	X	X	X	0	48	17	119	12	7	19	77	62	62	64

Table 16.5

| | Adult Female Literacy (percent) | | Adult Male Literacy (percent) | | Gross Primary School Enrollment (as a percentage of age group) | | | | Births Attended by Trained Personnel (percent) | ORT{a} Use (percent) | Low-Birth-weight Infants (percent) | Percentage of 1-Year-Olds Fully Immunized in 1991 Against: | | | |
| | | | | | Female | | Male | | | | | | | | |
	1970	1990	1970	1990	1960	1990	1960	1990	1983-91	1987-91	1990	TB	DPT	Polio	Measles
NORTH & CENTRAL AMERICA															
Belize	X	X	X	X	X	X	X	X	X	X	6	79	82	82	86
Canada	X	X	X	X	105	105 c	108	105 c	99	X	6	X	85	85	85 e
Costa Rica	87	93	88	93	95	99 c	94	101	93	78	8	81	90	89	96 e
Cuba	87	93	86	95	110	101	109	108	90	80	16	98	100	97	100
Dominican Rep	65	82	69	85	74	103 d	75	99 d	92	31	11	44	47	64	69
El Salvador	53	70	61	76	56	80	59	78	50	45	14	66	60	60	53
Guatemala	37	47	51	63	39	75	48	86	34	24	15	43	63	69	49
Haiti	17	47	26	59	39	98	50	104	20	20	9	72	41	40	31
Honduras	50	71	55	76	67	113	68	111	90	70	11	100	94	93	86
Jamaica	97	99	96	98	79	107	78	106	82	10	12	94	85	86	77
Mexico	69	85	78	90	75	118	80	121	77	66	15	87	63	95	78 e
Nicaragua	57	X	58	X	59	108	57	97	73	40	10	75	71	83	54
Panama	81	88	81	88	86	106	89	111	96	55	10	87	82	82	80
Trinidad and Tobago	X	X	X	X	108	106	111	103	98	70	7	X	82	81	93
United States	99	X	99	X	X	100 c	X	101 c	99	X	X	0	67	53	80 e
SOUTH AMERICA															
Argentina	92	95	94	96	99	107	99	108	87	70	12	100	84	88	100
Bolivia	46	71	68	85	43	87	70	97	54	63	11	67	58	67	73
Brazil	63	80	69	83	56	101	58	109	95	62	7	75	80	96	83
Chile	88	93	90	94	86	110	87	113	98	1	10	90	91	91	93
Colombia	76	86	79	88	74	124	74	121	94	40	11	93	87	94	82 e
Ecuador	68	84	75	88	75	118	82	119	56	70	X	83	59	62	54
Guyana	89	95	94	98	99	91	110	92	X	X	8	89	81	81	76
Paraguay	75	88	85	92	94	101	106	105	66	42	11	96	88	90	88
Peru	60	79	81	92	74	122	98	123	52	X	X	78	71	74	59
Suriname	X	95	X	95	106	132	113	139	X	X	8	X	75	72	84 e
Uruguay	93	96	93	97	117	109	117	111	96	96	9	99	88	88	82 e
Venezuela	71	90	79	87	99	109	98	110	69	80	X	79	60	71	61
EUROPE												75	85	82	82
Albania	X	X	X	X	86	98 c	102	99 c	99	X	6	94	94	96	96
Austria	X	X	X	X	104	103 c	106	104 c	X	X	6	97	90	90	60
Belgium	99	X	99	X	108	101 c	111	101 c	100	X	X	0	87	99	85
Bulgaria	89	X	94	X	92	96 c	94	98 c	100	X	6	100	99	99	97
Czechoslovakia (former)	X	X	X	X	93	93 c	93	92 c	100	X	6	98	99	99	98
Denmark	X	X	X	X	103	98 c	103	97 c	100	X	4	0	99 f	99	86
Finland	X	X	X	X	95	99 c	100	99 c	100	X	5	99	95	97	97
France	98	X	99	X	143	111 c	144	114 c	94	X	X	80	95	87	71
Germany	X	X	X	X	X	102 c	X	103 c	99	X	6	84	95	95	80
Greece	76	89	93	98	101	102 c	104	101 c	97	X	9	56	54	77	76
Hungary	98	X	98	X	100	97 c	103	96 c	99	X	X	99	100	98	100
Iceland	X	X	X	X	X	X	X	X	X	X	4	0	99	99	99
Ireland	X	X	X	X	112	101 c	107	100 c	X	X	5	0	65	63	78
Italy	93	96	95	98	109	96 c	112	96 c	X	X	6	6	95 f	85	50
Netherlands	X	X	X	X	104	117 c	105	114 c	100	X	4	X	97	97	94
Norway	X	X	X	X	100	98 c	100	98 c	X	X	X	95	91	86	90
Poland	97	X	98	X	107	99 c	110	99 c	100	X	5	94	98	98	94
Portugal	65	82	78	89	129	123 c	132	131 c	90	X	7	88	95	95	96
Romania	91	X	96	X	95	95 c	101	96 c	100	X	4	99	97	90	92
Spain	87	93	93	97	116	110 c	106	112 c	96	X	5	0	96	94	97
Sweden	X	X	X	X	96	104 c	95	104 c	100	X	5	14	99 f	99	95
Switzerland	X	X	X	X	118	X	118	X	99	X	7	0	89	95	83
United Kingdom	X	X	X	X	92	106 c	92	105 c	100	X	X	90	90	95	89
Yugoslavia (former)	76	88	92	97	108	94 c	113	95 c	86	X	X	84	87	84	84
U.S.S.R. (former)	97	X	98	X	100	105 c	100	104 c	X	X	X	90	79	74	85
Armenia	X	X	X	X	X	X	X	X	X	X	X	X	X	96	92
Azerbaijan	X	X	X	X	X	X	X	X	X	X	X	X	X	93	91
Belarus	X	X	X	X	X	X	X	X	X	X	X	X	X	90	95
Estonia	X	X	X	X	X	X	X	X	X	X	X	X	X	70	86
Georgia	X	X	X	X	X	X	X	X	X	X	X	X	X	80	74
Kazakhstan	X	X	X	X	X	X	X	X	X	X	X	X	X	86	94
Kyrgyzstan	X	X	X	X	X	X	X	X	X	X	X	X	X	72	91
Latvia	X	X	X	X	X	X	X	X	X	X	X	X	X	89	96
Lithuania	X	X	X	X	X	X	X	X	X	X	X	X	X	80	86
Moldova	X	X	X	X	X	X	X	X	X	X	X	X	X	92	95
Russian Federation	X	X	X	X	X	X	X	X	X	X	X	X	X	75	79
Tajikistan	X	X	X	X	X	X	X	X	X	X	X	X	X	90	89
Turkmenistan	X	X	X	X	X	X	X	X	X	X	X	X	X	84	68
Ukraine	X	X	X	X	X	X	X	X	X	X	X	X	X	81	88
Uzbekistan	X	X	X	X	X	X	X	X	X	X	X	X	X	61	81
OCEANIA															
Australia	X	X	X	X	103	105 c	103	106 c	99	X	X	0	95	72	86 e
Fiji	X	X	X	X	84	109	88	108	X	X	6	100	99	100	93 e
New Zealand	X	X	X	X	106	106 c	110	106 c	99	X	23	20	81	68	82 e
Papua New Guinea	24	38	39	65	15	68	24	80	20	46	X	98	74	75	73 e
Solomon Islands	X	X	X	X	X	X	X	X	X	X	X	X	74	74	76

Sources: United Nations Children's Fund; United Nations Educational, Scientific and Cultural Organization; and the World Health Organization.
Notes: a. Oral Rehydration Therapy. b. 1984 data. c. Data are for 1986-90. d. 1986 data. e. Measles immunization given at, or later than, 12 months and up to 2 years of age. f. DT only.
0 = zero or less than half the unit of measure; X = not available.
For additional information, see Sources and Technical Notes.

Table 16.6 World's Women, 1970–92

	Females as a Percentage of Males — Life Expectancy		Females as a Percentage of Males — Literacy		Females as a Percentage of Total Labor Force	Mean Years of School for Persons Age 25 and Above 1990		Couples Using Contraception (percent; latest yr)	Average Age of First Marriage (latest yr)		Year Women Received Vote{a}	Females per 100 Males (latest yr)		Households Headed by Women (percent; latest yr)
	1970	1990	1970	1990	1992	Female	Male	latest yr	Female	Male		Urban	Rural	
WORLD	105	106				4.3	5.8							
AFRICA	107	106												
Algeria	104	103	28	65	10	0.8	4.4	51 b	21	25	1962	102	100	X
Angola	109	108	44	51	38	1.0	2.0	X	X	X	1975	X	X	X
Benin	108	107	35	49	47	0.3	1.1	9 c	18	25	1956	98	111	X
Botswana	107	111	119	78	35	2.4	2.5	33	26	31	1965	95	115	45
Burkina Faso	109	108	23	32	46	0.1	0.1	X	17	27	X	X	X	5
Burundi	108	107	34	65	47	0.2	0.5	9	21	24	1961	79	108	X
Cameroon	107	106	40	64	33	0.8	2.5	16 b	19	26	1946	93	104	14 d
Central African Rep	113	112	23	48	45	0.5	1.6	X	18	23	1986	109	108	X
Chad	109	107	10	42	21	0.1	0.3	X	X	X	X	X	X	X
Congo	112	111	38	63	39	1.1	3.1	X	22	27	1963	92	110	21
Cote d'Ivoire	108	107	38	60	34	0.9	2.9	3	19	27	1952	X	X	X
Djibouti	108	107	X	X	X	0.2	0.5	X	X	X	1946	X	X	X
Egypt	105	104	40	54	10	1.6	3.9	48 b	21	27	1956	95	96	X
Equatorial Guinea	108	107	X	58	40	0.3	1.3	X	X	X	1963	X	X	X
Ethiopia	108	107	X	X	37	0.7	1.5	4 b	17	23	X	115	98	X
Gabon	108	107	51	66	37	1.3	3.9	X	X	X	1956	90	112	X
Gambia, The	109	108	X	41	40	0.2	0.9	X	X	X	1960	X	X	X
Ghana	107	107	42	73	40	2.2	4.8	13	19	X	X	X	X	27
Guinea	103	102	33	38	39	0.3	1.3	X	X	X	X	95	104	X
Guinea-Bissau	109	108	46	48	40	0.1	0.5	X	X	X	1977	X	X	X
Kenya	109	107	43	73	39	1.3	3.2	27	20	26	1963	82	105	30
Lesotho	111	109	151	X	43	4.0	2.7	5	21	26	X	118	100	X
Liberia	107	104	30	58	30	0.8	3.2	6	19	27	1946	X	X	15
Libya	106	106	22	67	10	1.3	5.5	X	19	25	1969	X	X	X
Madagascar	107	106	77	83	39	1.7	2.6	17 b	20	24	1959	103	99	15
Malawi	103	104	43	X	41	1.1	2.4	7	18	23	1964	86	110	29
Mali	109	108	36	59	16	0.1	0.5	5	16	X	1956	103	105	15
Mauritania	108	107	X	45	23	0.1	0.5	4	19	27	X	85	104	X
Mauritius	106	111	77	X	27	3.3	4.8	75	24	28	1956	100	99	19
Morocco	106	106	29	62	21	1.5	4.1	42 b	22	27	1963	99	100	17
Mozambique	108	107	48	47	47	1.2	2.1	X	18	23	1975	88	108	X
Namibia	106	105	X	X	24	1.7	1.7	26	X	X	1989	90	112	X
Niger	109	107	33	42	46	0.1	0.2	4 b	X	X	1948	X	X	X
Nigeria	108	107	40	63	34	0.5	1.8	6	19	X	X	93	105	X
Rwanda	108	107	49	58	47	0.5	1.6	10	21	X	1961	82	107	25
Senegal	105	104	28	48	39	0.4	1.3	11	18	28	1945	103	102	X
Sierra Leone	109	108	44	37	32	0.4	1.4	X	X	X	1951	X	X	X
Somalia	108	107	20	39	38	0.1	0.3	X	20	27	1956	X	X	X
South Africa	110	110	X	X	36	3.7	4.1	50	26	28	X	99	107	X
Sudan	106	105	21	27	22	0.5	1.1	9	21	X	1953	88	99	22 e
Swaziland	110	107	X	X	38	3.3	4.0	20	X	X	1968	X	X	X
Tanzania	108	107	38	X	47	1.3	2.8	10 b	19	25	1959	93	106	X
Togo	108	107	26	54	36	0.8	2.4	16 c	19	27	1956	101	103	X
Tunisia	102	102	39	76	25	1.2	3.0	50	24	28	1959	97	96	10
Uganda	107	107	58	56	41	0.6	1.6	5	18	24	1962	86	104	X
Zaire	108	107	36	73	35	0.8	2.4	X	20	25	1967	97	105	X
Zambia	107	104	56	81	30	1.7	3.7	15	19	25	1962	97	109	28
Zimbabwe	107	106	75	82	34	1.7	4.2	43	20	25	1957	88	110	X
ASIA	101	103												
Afghanistan	100	102	15	32	9	0.2	1.4	2	18	25	1965	94 f	95 f	X
Bangladesh	96	99	33	47	8	0.9	3.1	40 b	17	24	1947	84	96	17
Bhutan	104	102	X	48	32	0.1	0.3	X	X	X	1953	X	X	X
Cambodia	107	106	X	46	37	1.7	2.3	X	X	X	X	97	101	X
China	103	104	X	73	43	3.6	6.0	72	22	25	1949	96	96	X
India	97	100	43	55	25	1.2	3.5	43	19	23	1950	89	96	X
Indonesia	104	106	64	81	31	2.9	5.0	50 b	21	25	1945	101	101	14
Iran, Islamic Rep	99	101	43	67	19	3.1	4.6	49	20	24	1963	95	96	7
Iraq	103	105	36	71	22	3.9	5.7	14 b	21	25	1980	93	100	X
Israel	105	105	89	X	34	9.0	10.9	X	24	26	1948	101	94	18
Japan	108	108	100	X	38	10.6	10.8	64	26	30	1945/1947	103	105	15
Jordan	106	106	45	79	11	4.0	6.0	35	23	27	1974	93	94	X
Korea, Dem People's Rep	106	110	X	X	46	4.6	7.4	X	X	X	1946	X	X	X
Korea, Rep	106	110	86	94	34	6.7	11.0	79	25	28	1948	101	98	15
Kuwait	106	105	65	87	16	4.7	6.0	35	22	25	X	X	X	5
Lao People's Dem Rep	107	106	76	X	44	2.1	3.6	X	X	X	1948	X	X	X
Lebanon	106	106	73	83	28	3.5	5.3	53	X	X	1926	104	103	X
Malaysia	106	106	68	81	35	5.0	5.6	48	24	27	1957	99	100	X
Mongolia	105	104	85	X	46	7.2	7.6	X	X	X	1923-1924	101	98	X
Myanmar	107	106	67	81	37	2.1	3.0	X	22	25	X	101	102	16 g
Nepal	98	98	13	35	33	1.0	3.2	14	18	22	1951	87	96	X
Oman	105	105	X	X	9	0.3	1.4	9 b	X	X	X	X	X	X
Pakistan	95	100	37	45	13	0.7	3.0	12	20	25	1937	87	92	4
Philippines	106	106	96	99	31	7.0	7.8	36	22	25	1937	105	96	11
Saudi Arabia	106	104	13	66	8	1.5	5.9	X	X	X	X	X	X	X
Singapore	106	108	67	X	32	3.1	4.7	74	26	28	1948	98	91	18
Sri Lanka	102	108	81	89	27	6.1	7.7	62	24	28	1931	91	98	17
Syrian Arab Rep	106	106	33	65	18	3.1	5.2	20	22 h	26 h	1949	93 h	98 h	13
Thailand	108	108	84	94	44	3.3	4.3	66	23	25	1932	104	100	16 i
Turkey	106	108	49	79	34	2.3	4.7	63	21	24	1930/1934	91	102	10
United Arab Emirates	106	106	29	X	7	5.2	5.1	X	18	26	X	47	36	X
Viet Nam	110	107	X	91	47	3.4	5.8	53	X	X	1946	94	109	X
Yemen	101	101	X	X	14	0.2	1.3	7 b	18	22	1967/1970	90 j	111 j	X

Table 16.6

	Females as a Percentage of Males Life Expectancy		Females as a Percentage of Males Literacy		Females as a Percentage of Total Labor Force	Mean Years of School for Persons Age 25 and Above 1990		Couples Using Contraception (percent;	Average Age of First Marriage (latest yr)		Year Women Received	Females per 100 Males (latest yr)		Households Headed by Women (percent;
	1970	1990	1970	1990	1992	Female	Male	latest yr)	Female	Male	Vote{a}	Urban	Rural	latest yr)
NORTH & CENTRAL AMERICA														
Belize	X	X	X	X	X	4.4	4.8	47 b	X	X	1945	X	X	X
Canada	109	109	X	X	40	11.9	12.3	73	24	27	1917/1969	106	94	25
Costa Rica	106	106	99	101	22	5.6	5.8	70	22	25	1949	109	93	18 d
Cuba	105	105	101	98	32	7.7	7.5	70	20	24	1934	103	89	28
Dominican Rep	106	107	94	96	16	4.5	4.9	56 b	X	X	1942	X	X	X
El Salvador	107	115	87	92	25	4.1	4.1	47	19	25	1961	110	99	22
Guatemala	105	108	73	75	17	3.8	4.4	23	21	24	1945	105	93	X
Haiti	106	106	65	80	41	1.3	2.0	10	24	27	1950	125	101	X
Honduras	107	107	91	94	20	3.7	4.0	41	20	24	1957	107	95	22
Jamaica	106	106	101	100	46	5.2	5.3	55	30 k	31	1944	114	98	34
Mexico	106	110	88	95	27	4.6	4.8	53	21	24	1947	105	97	X
Nicaragua	106	112	98	X	26	4.5	4.1	27	20	25	1955	116	92	X
Panama	104	106	100	100	28	6.9	6.5	64 l	21	25	1941/1946	105	90	22 m
Trinidad and Tobago	107	107	X	X	30	8.1	8.0	53	22 n	28	1946	103	98	25
United States	111	110	100	X	41	12.4	12.2	74	23	25	1920	108	100	31
SOUTH AMERICA	108	109												
Argentina	110	110	98	100	28	8.9	8.5	X	23	25	1947	105	86	19
Bolivia	110	108	68	83	26	3.0	5.0	30	22	25	1938/1952	105	100	X
Brazil	107	109	91	97	28	3.8	4.0	66	23	26	1934	104 o	92 o	14
Chile	111	110	98	100	29	7.2	7.8	X	24	26	1931/1949	106	84	22 i
Colombia	106	109	96	98	22	7.3	6.9	66	23	26	1957	110	88	X
Ecuador	105	107	91	95	19	5.3	5.8	53	21	24	1946	103	94	X
Guyana	106	109	95	98	25	4.9	5.4	31	24	26	1953	108	98	24
Paraguay	106	107	88	96	21	4.6	5.2	48	22	26	1961	107	94	X
Peru	106	107	74	86	24	5.7	7.1	59	23	26	1950	100 o	96 o	23
Suriname	107	107	X	100	30	4.0	4.3	X	X	X	1953	X	X	X
Uruguay	110	109	100	99	31	8.2	7.4	X	22	25	1932	110	71	21
Venezuela	107	109	90	103	28	6.2	6.4	49	21	25	1947	100 o	87 o	22
EUROPE	109	110												
Albania	104	109	X	X	41	5.0	7.0	X	X	X	1945	97	93	X
Austria	110	109	X	X	40	10.5	11.5	71	24	27	1918	117	105	31
Belgium	110	109	100	X	34	10.7	10.7	79 b	22	25	1919/1948	105	99	21
Bulgaria	106	109	95	X	46	6.4	7.6	76	21	25	1944	103	102	X
Czechoslovakia (former)	110	111	X	X	X	8.4	9.5	X	22	25	1920	107	103	23
Denmark	107	108	X	X	45	10.3	10.5	78	26	28	1915	106	88	X
Finland	112	111	X	X	47	10.5	10.7	80	25	27	1906	111	100	X
France	111	112	99	X	40	11.7	11.5	80	24	26	1944	107	100	22
Germany	109	109	X	X	39	10.6	11.7	X	X	X	1918	110 p	106 p	X
Greece	105	107	82	91	27	6.5	7.3	X	23	28	1952	106	100	16
Hungary	108	112	100	X	45	9.7	9.5	73	21	25	1945	109	104	20 q
Iceland	108	107	X	X	43	9.0	8.8	X	X	X	1915	100	86	X
Ireland	107	108	X	X	29	8.8	8.6	X	23	24	1918	106	93	X
Italy	108	109	98	99	32	7.3	7.4	78 r	23	27	1945	X	X	20 i
Netherlands	108	109	X	X	31	10.8	10.4	76	23	26	1919	103	97	X
Norway	108	109	X	X	41	11.5	11.7	76	24	26	1907/1913	111	100	38
Poland	109	113	99	X	46	7.7	8.3	75 s	23	26	1918	108	100	27
Portugal	110	110	83	92	37	5.2	6.8	66	22	25	1931/1976	113	105	18 i
Romania	106	109	95	X	47	6.6	7.4	58 s	21	25	1929/1946	104	102	X
Spain	108	108	94	96	24	6.5	7.0	59	23	26	1931	104	98	16
Sweden	106	108	X	X	45	11.1	11.1	78	28	30	1918-1921	105	89	27
Switzerland	108	109	X	X	36	10.7	11.5	71	25	28	1971	109	100	25
United Kingdom	109	108	X	X	39	11.6	11.4	81	23	25	1918/1928	105	97	25 t
Yugoslavia (former)	107	108	83	90	X	X	X	55 s	22	26	1949	105	100	X
U.S.S.R. (former)	113	114	99	X	X	X	X	X	22	24	1918	113	114	X
Armenia	X	110 u	X	X	X	X	X	12 u	X	X	X	X	X	X
Azerbaijan	X	112 u	X	X	X	X	X	7 u	X	X	X	X	X	X
Belarus	X	114 u	X	X	X	X	X	13 u	X	X	X	X	X	X
Estonia	X	115 u	X	X	X	X	X	26 u	X	X	X	X	X	X
Georgia	X	111 u	X	X	X	X	X	8 u	X	X	X	X	X	X
Kazakhstan	X	114 u	X	X	X	X	X	22 u	X	X	X	X	X	X
Kyrgyzstan	X	113 u	X	X	X	X	X	25 u	X	X	X	X	X	X
Latvia	X	116 u	X	X	X	X	X	19 u	X	X	X	X	X	X
Lithuania	X	115 u	X	X	X	X	X	12 u	X	X	X	X	X	X
Moldova	X	110 u	X	X	X	X	X	15 u	X	X	X	X	X	X
Russian Federation	X	116 u	X	X	X	X	X	22 u	X	X	X	X	X	X
Tajikistan	X	108 u	X	X	X	X	X	15 u	X	X	X	X	X	X
Turkmenistan	X	111 u	X	X	X	X	X	12 u	X	X	X	X	X	X
Ukraine	X	114 u	X	X	X	X	X	15 u	X	X	X	X	X	X
Uzbekistan	X	110 u	X	X	X	X	X	19 u	X	X	X	X	X	X
OCEANIA	108	108												
Australia	110	109	X	X	38	X	X	76	24	26	1901/1967	103	89	25 i
Fiji	105	106	X	X	21	4.6	5.6	41	22	25	X	100	95	X
New Zealand	109	109	X	X	X	X	X	70	25	27	1893	104	89	24
Papua New Guinea	99	103	62	58	35	0.6	1.2	X	X	X	1975	73	94	X
Solomon Islands	X	X	X	X	X	0.8	1.2	X	X	X	1945	64	95	X

Sources: United Nations Population Division; United Nations Children's Fund; United Nations Educational, Scientific and Cultural Organization; United Nations Department of Economic and Social Information and Policy Analysis; United Nations Development Programme; the World Bank; and United Nations Department of International Economic and Social Affairs.

Notes: a. For additional information concerning the year women received the right to vote, see Sources and Technical Notes. b. Preliminary and provisional. c. Women who have not resumed sexual relations since last pregnancy are not counted as users of contraception. d. Including collective households. e. Refers to the settled population only. f. Excluding nomads. g. Excluding 1,183,005 persons from restricted areas. h. Including Palestinian refugees. i. Percentage of families. j. Data refer to former Democratic Yemen only. k. Data are for only those women who are not attending primary or secondary school on a full-time basis. l. Excluding douche, abstinence, and folk methods. m. Excluding indigenous areas and the former Canal Zone. n. Data include legal, consensual and visiting unions. o. Excluding Indian jungle population. p. Data refer to the former Democratic Republic of Germany. q. Excluding 124,917 where head of household is not determined. r. Use since last pregnancy (since marriage if no pregnancy). s. Excluding sterilization. t. England and Wales only. u. Data are from the "Human Development Report 1993."

Sources and Technical Notes

Table 16.1 Size and Growth of Population and Labor Force, 1950–2025

Sources: United Nations (U.N.) Population Division, *Interpolated National Populations (The 1992 Revision),* on diskette (U.N., New York, 1993); and International Labour Office (ILO), unpublished data (ILO, Geneva, 1993).

Population refers to the midyear population. Most data are estimates based on population censuses and surveys. All projections are for the medium-case scenario. (See the following discussion.) The *average annual population change* takes into account the effects of international migration.

Many of the values in Tables 16.1–16.3 are estimated using demographic models based on several kinds of demographic parameters: a country's population size, age and sex distribution, fertility and mortality rates by age and sex groups, growth rates of urban and rural populations, and the levels of internal and international migration.

Information collected through recent population censuses and surveys is used to calculate or estimate these parameters, but accuracy varies. The United Nations Population Division's Department of Economic and Social Information and Policy Analysis compiles and evaluates census and survey results from all countries. These data are adjusted for overenumeration and underenumeration of certain age and sex groups (i.e., infants, female children, and young males), misreporting of age and sex distributions, and changes in definitions, when necessary. These adjustments incorporate data from civil registrations, population surveys, earlier censuses, and, when necessary, population models based on information from socioeconomically similar countries. (Because the figures have been adjusted, they are not strictly comparable to the official statistics compiled by the United Nations Statistical Office and published in the *Demographic Yearbook*.)

After the figures for population size and age/sex composition have been adjusted, these data are scaled to 1990. Similar estimates are made for each five-year period between 1950 and 1990. Historical data are used when deemed accurate, also with adjustments and scaling. However, accurate historical data do not exist for many developing countries. In such cases, the Population Division uses available information and demographic models to estimate the main demographic parameters. Projections are based on estimates of the 1990 base-year population. Age- and sex-specific mortality rates are applied to the base-year population to determine the number of survivors at the end of each five-year period. Births are projected by applying age-specific fertility rates to the projected female population. Births are distributed by an assumed sex ratio, and the appropriate age- and sex-specific survival rates are applied.

Future migration rates are also estimated on an age- and sex-specific basis. Combining future fertility, mortality, and migration rates yields the projected *population size, average annual population change,* and *average annual increment to the population.*

Assumptions about future mortality, fertility, and migration rates are made on a country-by-country basis and, when possible, are based on historical trends. While projections are always of questionable quality, U.N. demographic models are based on surveys and censuses with well-understood qualities, which make these data fairly reliable.

The labor force includes all people who produce economic goods and services. It includes all employed people (employers, the self-employed, salaried employees, wage earners, unpaid family workers, members of producer cooperatives, and members of the armed forces), and the unemployed (experienced workers and those looking for work for the first time).

The ILO determines the *average annual growth of the labor force* by multiplying the activity rates of age/sex groups (the economically active fraction of an age/sex group) by the number of people in those groups. Activity rates are based on information from national censuses and labor force surveys. The ILO adjusts national labor force statistics when necessary to conform to international definitions. The growth of age/sex groups is provided to the ILO by the United Nations Population Division.

Table 16.2 Trends in Births, Life Expectancy, Fertility, and Age Structure, 1970–95

Sources: United Nations (U.N.) Population Division, *Demographic Indicators, 1950–2025 (The 1992 Revision),* on diskette (U.N., New York, 1993); and U.N. Population Division, *Sex and Age, 1950–2025 (The 1992 Revision),* on diskette (U.N., New York, 1993).

The *crude birth rate* is derived by dividing the number of live births in a given year by the midyear population. This ratio is then multiplied by 1,000.

Life expectancy at birth is the average number of years that a newborn baby is expected to live if the age-specific mortality rates effective at the year of birth apply throughout his or her lifetime.

The *total fertility rate* is an estimate of the number of children that an average woman would have if current age-specific fertility rates remained constant during her reproductive years.

The *percentage of population in specific age groups* shows a country's age structure: 0–14, 15–65, and over 65 years. It is useful for inferring dependency, needs for education and employment, potential fertility, and other age-related factors. For additional details on data collection, estimation, and projection methods, refer to the sources or to the Technical Notes for Table 16.1.

Table 16.3 Mortality and Nutrition, 1970–95

Sources: Crude death rate and infant mortality rate data: United Nations (U.N.) Population Division, *Demographic Indicators 1950–2025 (The 1992 Revision),* on diskette (U.N., New York, 1993); Under-five mortality rate: U.N. Children's Fund (UNICEF), unpublished data (UNICEF, New York, 1993); Maternal mortality rate, wasting, stunting, and per capita average calories available as a percentage of need: UNICEF, *State of the World's Children 1993* (UNICEF, New York, 1993); Percentage share of household consumption expenditure for food: The World Bank, *World Development Report 1992* (Oxford University Press, New York, 1992).

The *crude death rate* is derived by dividing the number of deaths in a year by the midyear population and multiplying by 1,000.

The *infant mortality rate* is the probability of dying by exact age 1, multiplied by 1,000. The U.N. Population Division provides this cohort measure.

Under-five mortality rate is the probability of dying by exact age 5, multiplied by 1,000. UNICEF provides this cohort measure, which is derived from *Child Mortality Since the 1960s—a Database for Developing Countries* (U.N., New York, 1992) and from infant mortality estimates provided by the U.N. Population Division. The mix is the result of a move from modeled estimates to estimates based on a periodically updated child mortality data base.

Maternal mortality rate is the number of deaths from pregnancy- or childbirth-related causes per 100,000 live births. A maternal death is defined by the World Health Organization (WHO) as the death of a woman while pregnant or within 42 days of termination of pregnancy from any cause related to or aggravated by the pregnancy, including abortion. Most official maternal mortality rates are underestimated because of underreporting, incorrect classification, and unavailable cause of death information. In some countries, over 60 percent of women's deaths are registered without a specified cause. Maternal deaths are highest among women of ages 10–15 years, over 40 years, and in women with five or more children. Data are provided to UNICEF by WHO and refer to a single year between 1980 and 1990. Data for a few countries are outside the range of years indicated.

Wasting indicates current acute malnutrition and refers to the percentage of children between the ages of 12 and 23 months whose weight-for-height is below minus 2 standard deviations from the median of the reference population as defined by the U.S. National Center for Health Statistics (NCHS).

Stunting, an indicator of chronic undernutrition, refers to the percentage of children between the ages of 24 and 59 months whose height-for-age is below minus 2 standard deviations from the median of the reference population. NCHS, among others, has found that healthy children in one country differ little, as a group, in terms of weight and height from healthy children in other countries. WHO has accepted the NCHS weight-for-age and weight-for-height standards; however, a number of countries still use local reference populations, and the estimates provided may utilize a number of sources, not solely or primarily the WHO database. Children with low weight-for-age are at a high risk of mortality. Data on wasting and stunting, provided to UNICEF by WHO, refer to a single year between 1980 and 1991. Data for some countries are outside the range of years or ages indicated. Data for wasting and stunting are generally good if derived from recent national household surveys, such as the Demographic and Health Surveys, but are not good if they are old or from local subnational studies.

The *per capita average calories available (as percentage of need)* are calories from all food sources: domestic production, international trade, stock draw-downs, and foreign aid. The quantity of food available for human consumption, as estimated by the Food and Agriculture Organization of the United Nations (FAO), is the amount that reaches the consumer. The calories actually consumed may be lower than the figures shown, depending on how much is lost during home storage, preparation, and cooking, and how much is fed to pets and domestic animals or discarded. Estimates of daily caloric requirements vary for individual countries according to the population's age distribution and estimated level of activity.

According to the World Bank, *percentage share of total household consumption expenditure for food* is calculated in national market prices using details of the gross domestic product collected as part of the International Comparison Program (ICP) Phases IV (1980) and V (1985). For countries not included in the ICP survey, these data are estimated using less detailed national accounts. Except where noted, these data refer to either 1980 or 1985. Consumption, as used here, refers to private (nongovernment) consumption as defined in the U.N.'s System of National Accounts. These data are collected through household censuses and surveys and therefore can suffer from sampling frame biases. In addition, the national accounting method used to estimate food expenditures may skew or distort these data.

Table 16.4 Access to Safe Drinking Water, Sanitation, and Health Services, 1972–90

Sources: Drinking water and sanitation: World Health Organization (WHO), The International Drinking Water Supply and Sanitation Decade: End of Decade Review (as at December 1990) (WHO, Geneva, August 1992); WHO, The International Drinking Water Supply and Sanitation Decade: Review of Mid-Decade Progress (as at December 1985) (WHO, Geneva, September 1987);

WHO, The International Drinking Water Supply and Sanitation Decade: Review of National Progress (as at December 1983); WHO, The International Drinking Water Supply and Sanitation Decade: Review of National Baseline Data: December 1980 (WHO, Geneva, 1984); WHO, Global Strategy for Health for All. Monitoring 1988–1989. Detailed Analysis of Global Indicators (WHO, Geneva, May 1989); and unpublished data (WHO, Geneva, July 1991). Access to health services: United Nations Children's Fund (UNICEF), State of the World's Children 1993 (UNICEF, New York, 1993). Percentage of total central government expenditure for health: The World Bank, World Development Report 1992 (Oxford University Press, New York, 1992).

WHO collected data on drinking water and sanitation from national governments in 1980, 1983, 1985, 1988, and 1990 using questionnaires completed by public health officials, WHO experts, and Resident Representatives of the United Nations Development Programme (UNDP). Data for a number of countries were gathered during 1986–87. For several African countries, dates were not indicated.

WHO defines reasonable access to *safe drinking water* in an urban area as access to piped water or a public standpipe within 200 meters of a dwelling or housing unit. In rural areas, reasonable access implies that a family member need not spend a disproportionate part of the day fetching water. "Safe" drinking water includes treated surface water and untreated water from protected springs, boreholes, and sanitary wells. Definitions of safe water and appropriate access to sanitation and health services vary depending upon location and condition of local resources.

Urban areas with access to *sanitation services* are defined as urban populations served by connections to public sewers or household systems such as pit privies, pour-flush latrines, septic tanks, communal toilets, and other such facilities. Rural populations with access were defined as those with adequate disposal such as pit privies and pour-flush latrines. Application of these definitions may vary, and comparisons can therefore be misleading.

The population with access to *health services* is defined by WHO as the proportion of the population having treatment for common diseases and injuries and a regular supply of at least 20 essential drugs available within one hour's walk or travel (expressed as a percentage).

The *percentage of total central government expenditure for health* includes expenditures on hospitals, maternity and dental centers, clinics, health insurance schemes, and family planning. These data are from the International Monetary Fund (IMF) *Government Finance Statistics 1990* and IMF data files. The percentage of total government expenditures is calculated from figures in national currencies and does not include expenditures by state, provincial, or local governments, or private expenditures. For these reasons, these statistics are not directly comparable across all economies and

may in fact misrepresent the allocation of resources for health. "Central government" can either refer to consolidated or budgetary accounting. The most common method, consolidated accounting, incorporates all central government finances into one overall account, whereas the budgetary accounting method may not include all of the expenditures by all central government units. Countries reporting budgetary data are footnoted.

Table 16.5 Education and Child Health, 1970–91

Sources: Adult literacy for 1970: United Nations Children's Fund (UNICEF), *State of the World's Children 1989, State of the World's Children 1991*, and *State of the World's Children 1993* (UNICEF, New York, 1989, 1991, and 1993); Adult literacy for 1990: United Nations Educational, Scientific and Cultural Organization (UNESCO), *Compendium of Statistics on Illiteracy–1990 Edition* (UNESCO, Paris, 1990); Gross primary school enrollment (as a percentage of age group): *Trends and Projections of Enrollment by Level of Education and by Age (1960–2025)* as assessed in 1989 (UNESCO, Paris, 1989); and UNICEF, *State of the World's Children 1993* (UNICEF, New York, 1993); Births attended by trained personnel, ORT use, and low-birth-weight infants: UNICEF *State of the World's Children 1993* (UNICEF, New York, 1993); percentage of 1-year-olds fully immunized in 1991: World Health Organization, unpublished data, May 1993.

Adult female and *adult male literacy rates* refer to the percentage of people over the age of 15 who can read and write. UNESCO recommends defining illiterate as a person who cannot both read with understanding and write a short, simple statement about his or her everyday life. This concept is widely accepted, but its interpretation and application vary. It does not include people who, though familiar with the basics of reading and writing, do not have the skills to function at a reasonable level in their own society. Actual definitions of adult literacy are not strictly comparable among countries. Literacy data for 1990 are projected from past census figures, using current estimates of age, group size, and country populations (where available). In many cases, these data are based on subnational censuses and surveys that are projected to the national level.

The *gross primary school enrollment ratio (as a percentage of age group)* data for females and males are provided by UNESCO. These data entail two periods, 1960 and 1990, except where footnoted. UNESCO defines the primary school enrollment ratio as the total enrollment, regardless of age, divided by the population of the age group that corresponds to a specific level of education. Primary education is level 1 of the International Standard Classification of Education and its principal function is to provide the basic elements of education, such as those provided by elementary and primary schools. Intercountry comparisons should be made cautiously as regulations for this level are extremely flexible.

The *percentage of births attended by trained personnel* includes all health personnel accepted by national authorities as part of the health system. The types of personnel included vary by country. Some countries include traditional birth attendants and midwives; others, only doctors. WHO provides these data to UNICEF.

ORT (oral rehydration therapy) *use* refers to administration of oral rehydration salts or appropriate household solutions to children to combat diarrheal diseases leading to dehydration or malnutrition.

The *percentage of low-birth-weight infants* refers to all babies weighing less than 2,500 grams at birth. WHO has adopted the standard that healthy babies, regardless of race, should weigh more than 2,500 grams at birth. These data are provided by UNICEF and WHO, and refer to a single year between 1980 and 1990.

Immunization data show the *percentage of 1-year-olds fully immunized in 1991 against*: TB (tuberculosis), DPT (diphtheria, pertussis [whooping cough], and tetanus), polio, and measles. Most data refer to the immunization situation in 1991.

Table 16.6 World's Women, 1970–92

Sources: Females as a percentage of males, life expectancy: United Nations (U.N.) Population Division, *Demographic Indicators, 1950–2025 (The 1992 Revision)*, on diskette (U.N., New York, 1993); Females as a percentage of males, literacy: U.N. Children's Fund (UNICEF), *State of the World's Children 1989, State of the World's Children 1991*, and *State of the World's Children 1993* (UNICEF, New York, 1989, 1991, and 1993); Adult literacy for 1990: U.N. Educational, Scientific and Cultural Organization (UNESCO), *Compendium of Statistics on Illiteracy—1990 Edition* (UNESCO, Paris, 1990); Females as a percentage of total labor force: The World Bank, *World Tables 1993*, on diskette (The World Bank, Washington, D.C., 1993); Mean years of school: United Nations Development Programme (UNDP), *Human Development Report 1992* (UNDP, New York, 1992); Percentage of couples using contraception: U.N. Population Division, *Contraceptive Use Database 1993*, unpublished data (U.N., New York, 1993); Average age of first marriage, year women received vote, females per 100 males for urban and rural areas, and percentage of households headed by women: U.N. Department of Economic and Social Information and Policy Analysis, Statistical Division, *Wistat, Women's Indicators and Statistics Spreadsheet Database for Microcomputers (Version 2)* (U.N., New York, 1991); and Wistat (version 3) (U.N., New York, forthcoming).

The *females as a percentage of males* data are derived by dividing the female figure by the male figure and multiplying by 100. The smaller the figure, the bigger the gap between genders. A figure above 100 indicates that the female average is higher than the male average.

Life expectancy at birth data are derived by dividing the number of years a newborn girl can expect to live (if the age-specific mortality rates effective at the year of birth apply throughout her lifetime) by the number of years a male can expect to live and multiplying by 100.

The adult female literacy rate is the ratio of the percentage of literate females (over age 15) to the percentage of literate males.

Females as a percentage of total labor force data refer to the proportion of the economically active population which are female.

The *mean years of school for females and males* is defined as the average number of years of schooling received for persons age 25 or over. UNESCO provides these data, which are compiled from national population censuses and surveys, to UNDP.

The percentage of *couples using contraception* is the level of current contraceptive use of any method among couples in which the woman is of childbearing age. These data were obtained from nationally representative sample surveys of women between the ages of 15 and 49 who are married or cohabiting. The ages of women interviewed for some surveys varied slightly from this range. Many of these surveys were conducted as part of the World Fertility Survey, contraceptive prevalence surveys, or Demographic Health Surveys.

The *average age of first marriage for females and males* is an indirect indicator of the number of children a woman is likely to bear. These data are derived on the basis of a single population census or demographic survey. The definition of marital status varies with the laws and customs of each country.

The *year women received vote* data are provided to the Inter-Parliamentary Union by national authorities. Only countries with a parliament as of 31 October 1991 participated in the survey. The dates identify the year all women, regardless of race, class, or education, received the right to vote for national offices.

In many countries, women were allowed restricted suffrage prior to the date identified. *Argentina:* In some provinces, women were given the right to vote at an earlier date. *Australia:* The Commonwealth Franchise Act of 1902 granted all 21-year-olds the right to vote (with the exception of aboriginals). Aboriginal women and men received full franchise in 1967. *Belgium:* In 1919, women political prisoners, and widows and mothers of servicemen and male civilians killed during World War I were given the right to vote. Universal suffrage was granted in 1948. *Bolivia:* Literate women were given the right to vote in 1938. Universal suffrage was granted in 1952. *Canada:* In 1917, women who had served in the military or who had a close male relative serving in the military (i.e., a father, son, or husband) were granted the right to vote at the federal level. The franchise at the federal level was opened to all women in 1918. Suffrage at the provincial level was not universal until 1969, when Quebec extended the right to vote to Indians. *Chile:* Women received the right to vote in municipal elections in 1931. Universal suffrage was extended in 1949. *Ecuador:* Women obtained the right to vote in 1946. Voting is mandatory for all literate citizens between ages 18 and 65; illiterate persons did not receive the vote until 1978. *Greece:* Women obtained the right to vote at the communal and municipal levels in 1949 and at the national level in 1952. *Japan:* Women received the right to vote in elections for the House of Representatives in 1945 and in elections for the House of Councillors in 1947. *Kenya:* European women were given the vote in 1919. Restricted suffrage was given to African men and women in 1956, but it was not until 1963 that all Kenyans received the right to vote. *Panama:* Limited suffrage was given to women in 1941. Universal suffrage was granted in 1946. *Portugal:* Women who had completed secondary or higher studies were granted the right to vote in 1931; men were required only to know how to read and write. Total equality between men and women was achieved in 1976. *Romania:* In 1929, women received a restricted right to vote, and in 1946, universal suffrage. *South Africa:* The electoral bill of December 26, 1993 provides for the first time, equal suffrage for both men and women of all races. The first election under this bill is scheduled for April 27, 1994. *Sweden:* Women were given the right to vote between 1918 and 1921. *Syrian Arab Republic:* Women were granted the right to vote over a period of time; at first, suffrage was limited to only those women who had reached an educational level equivalent to six classes of primary school. Later, women who were literate were granted the right to vote, but women only recently received universal suffrage. *Turkey:* Women received the right to vote in local elections in 1930. Women were given the right to vote in legislative elections in 1934. *United Arab Emirates:* According to the 1971 Constitution, "each Emirate shall be left to determine the method of selection of the citizens who shall represent it on the Federal National Council." *United Kingdom:* In 1918, women over the age of 30 years obtained the right to vote. Women received full voting equality in 1928. *Yemen:* Women of the People's Democratic Republic of Yemen and the Arab Republic of Yemen received the vote in 1967 and 1970, respectively. *Zimbabwe:* Limited suffrage was granted to black women in 1957.

The main source for *females per 100 males, urban and rural* data is the U.N. *Demographic Yearbook* which is based on official data submitted to the U.N. Statistical Division by national statistical services or other government offices.

The percentage of *households headed by women* is defined as either those households in which a woman is acknowledged as the head of household by the other members of the household or in which a woman is the person economically responsible for the household or the person with authority for managing household activities.

17. Land Cover and Settlements

The distribution of populations and agricultural areas across landscapes affects the quality of natural and urban environments. This chapter provides information on land use, urban and rural populations, and large cities. Data on transport, living conditions in megacities, unemployment, and the labor force provide surrogate measures of urban environmental quality.

Table 17.1 gives a breakdown of the types of land cover found within countries and how land use has changed over time. Domesticated land—land dedicated to raising crops and permanent pastureland for livestock—occupies over one third of the world's land surface (excluding Antarctica). Oceania has the highest percentage of domesticated land (57 percent), and the former U.S.S.R, the lowest (25 percent).

Oceania also has the lowest population density of any region, only 33 persons per 1,000 hectares, as compared to a global average of 427 persons per 1,000 hectares. As data in this table show, there is often no relation between the percentage of land given over to agriculture and permanent pasture and population density. Asia and Europe averaged over 1,000 people per 1,000 hectares. Of those countries with data, nine had population densities exceeding 3,000 per 1,000 hectares (one third of a hectare per person or less, if land were to be distributed equally among the population). These were: Singapore, Bangladesh, Mauritius, the Republic of Korea, the Netherlands, Japan, Belgium, Rwanda, and India.

Globally, the area under crops increased less than 2 percent between 1979–81 and 1989–91. Permanent pasture increased 2.4 percent, and forest and woodland (which includes woodlots and shelterbelts) decreased by almost 8 percent during this 10-year period. In Europe there was a decline both of crop land and permanent pasture over the decade, while North and Central America and the former U.S.S.R registered declines in crop land of 0.7 and 1 percent, respectively. In all other regions, the area used for crops and permanent pastures increased during the 1979–81 to 1989–91 period.

By 1995, over 45 percent of the world's population will be living in urban areas, as is shown in Table 17.2. This is a 10 percent increase in urban population as a percentage of total population over the past three decades. During this period, the world's urban popula-

tion grew almost 3 percent annually, as compared to a rural population growth of just over 1 percent annually. Rural populations actually declined in South America, Europe, and the former U.S.S.R from 1965 to 1995. This table also provides data on large cities of the world and their growth between 1965 and 1995 relative to the total population of the countries and regions where they are located. In 1990 376 cities had populations of at least 750,000. About 40 percent of these cities (149) are located in Asia.

On average there were nine people for every motor vehicle—commercial and private—in the world, as Table 17.2 shows. Regionally, Africa has fewer cars, buses, and trucks relative to its population (47 people per vehicle), while North and Central America and Oceania have the most (2 people per vehicle). These differences are even more dramatic at the country level. The United States, Canada, Australia, New Zealand, Iceland, and Italy all average fewer than 2 persons per vehicle. In contrast, Myanmar, Uganda, Ethiopia, and Bangladesh average more than 500 people per vehicle. Table 17.2 also provides information on labor force size; labor force distribution in the agricultural, industrial, and service sectors; and male and female unemployment during the late 1980s and early 1990s.

Table 17.3 profiles the world's 21 megacities, those urban agglomerations projected to have populations of at least 10 million people by the year 2000. Seventeen of these cities are located in developing countries: 11 in Asia, 2 in Africa (Cairo and Lagos), and 4 in the Americas. Of megacities in the developed countries, 2 are located in Japan (Osaka and Tokyo) and 2 in the United States (Los Angeles and New York). Of the 21 cities, Dacca, Bangladesh grew the fastest during the 1980–90 period (over 7 percent per year) while New York registered the slowest growth (0.3 percent per year). Table 17.3 provides five indicators of living conditions: percentage of household income spent on food, number of persons per room, percentage of households with electricity and with running water, and number of telephones per 100 people. Additional data are provided on the size of each megacity; its population in 1980 and 1990, and its projected population in the year 2000; and the number of registered motor vehicles.

Table 17.1 Land Area and Use, 1979–91

	Land Area (000 hectares)	Population Density, 1993 (per 1,000 hectares)	Domesticated Land as a Percentage of Land Area {a}	Cropland 1989-91	Cropland % Change Since 1979-81	Permanent Pasture 1989-91	Permanent Pasture % Change Since 1979-81	Forest and Woodland 1989-91	Forest and Woodland % Change Since 1979-81	Other Land 1989-91	Other Land % Change Since 1979-81	Built-up Area {b} 1986-89 (000 ha)
WORLD {c}	13,041,713	427	37	1,441,423	1.8	3,357,292	2.4	3,897,998	(7.8)	4,345,007	5.5	X
AFRICA	2,963,951	237	36	181,125	5.0	900,428	0.9	684,664	(3.8)	1,197,734	0.9	X
Algeria	238,174	114	16	7,646	1.9	31,043	(10.7)	4,065	(7.3)	195,420	2.0	X
Angola	124,670	82	26	3,417	0.5	29,000	0.0	52,300	(2.7)	39,953	3.7	X
Benin	11,062	459	21	1,863	3.9	442	0.0	3,470	(12.6)	5,287	8.9	X
Botswana	56,673	24	61	1,387	2.0	33,000	0.0	10,910	(0.9)	11,376	0.7	X
Burkina Faso	27,380	357	50	3,563	27.9	10,000	0.0	6,600	(8.3)	7,217	(2.4)	X
Burundi	2,565	2,337	88	1,341	3.0	914	0.8	66	7.6	243	(17.5)	X
Cameroon	46,540	270	33	7,012	1.2	8,300	0.0	24,540	(4.3)	6,688	17.9	X
Central African Rep	62,298	52	8	2,006	3.4	3,000	0.0	35,800	(0.3)	21,492	0.1	X
Chad	125,920	48	38	3,205	1.7	45,000	0.0	12,730	(5.9)	64,985	1.2	X
Congo	34,150	71	30	168	13.7	10,000	0.0	21,160	(0.9)	2,822	6.8	X
Cote d'Ivoire	31,800	421	52	3,680	19.0	13,000	0.0	7,330	(25.8)	7,790	33.6	X
Djibouti	2,318	208	9	0	0.0	200	0.0	6	0.0	2,112	0.0	X
Egypt	99,545	563	3	2,621	6.8	0	0.0	31	0.0	96,893	(0.2)	X
Equatorial Guinea	2,805	135	12	230	0.0	104	0.0	1,295	0.0	1,176	0.0	X
Ethiopia	110,100	496	53	13,930	0.4	44,900	(1.1)	27,100	(3.6)	24,170	6.4	X
Gabon	25,767	50	20	455	0.9	4,700	0.0	19,877	(0.7)	735	23.4	X
Gambia, The	1,000	932	27	179	14.5	90	0.0	156	(27.8)	575	6.9	X
Ghana	22,754	723	34	2,723	(2.6)	5,000	0.0	8,070	(8.0)	6,961	12.5	X
Guinea	24,586	256	28	729	3.4	6,150	0.0	14,580	(4.0)	3,127	22.6	X
Guinea-Bissau	2,812	366	50	337	17.9	1,080	0.0	1,070	0.0	325	(13.6)	X
Kenya	56,969	458	71	2,433	6.5	38,100	0.0	2,340	(7.9)	14,096	0.4	X
Lesotho	3,035	620	77	337	12.8	2,000	0.0	0	0.0	698	(5.2)	X
Liberia	9,675	294	63	373	0.5	5,700	0.0	1,740	(14.8)	1,862	19.2	X
Libya	175,954	29	9	2,155	3.6	13,300	2.6	690	15.0	159,809	(0.3)	X
Madagascar	58,154	228	64	3,099	3.3	34,000	0.0	15,530	(8.8)	5,525	34.0	X
Malawi	9,408	1,137	37	1,670	25.2	1,840	0.0	3,630	(22.8)	2,268	47.9	X
Mali	122,019	83	26	2,096	2.2	30,000	0.0	6,950	(4.2)	82,973	0.3	X
Mauritania	102,522	22	38	205	5.1	39,250	0.0	4,430	(2.2)	58,637	0.2	X
Mauritius	203	5,463	56	106	(0.9)	7	0.0	57	(1.7)	33	6.5	X
Morocco	44,630	604	68	9,278	15.4	20,900	1.5	9,006	15.6	5,446	(33.6)	X
Mozambique	78,409	195	60	3,120	1.3	44,000	0.0	14,260	(7.8)	17,029	7.3	X
Namibia	82,329	19	47	662	0.8	38,000	0.0	18,120	(1.6)	25,547	1.2	X
Niger	126,670	67	10	3,605	4.0	8,893	(6.6)	2,000	(23.1)	112,172	1.0	X
Nigeria	91,077	1,310	79	32,228	6.2	40,000	0.0	11,900	(20.1)	6,949	19.5	X
Rwanda	2,467	3,157	66	1,156	12.9	464	(16.0)	554	(5.1)	293	(4.5)	X
Senegal	19,253	413	28	2,350	0.0	3,100	0.0	10,550	(4.5)	3,253	18.3	X
Sierra Leone	7,162	627	40	635	8.6	2,204	0.0	2,060	(2.6)	2,263	0.2	X
Somalia	62,734	152	70	1,039	3.9	43,000	0.0	9,060	(1.1)	9,635	0.6	X
South Africa	122,104	334	77	13,174	(0.6)	81,378	(0.0)	4,515	7.1	23,037	(0.8)	X
Sudan	237,600	115	52	12,900	3.9	110,000	12.2	44,840	(6.3)	69,860	(11.9)	X
Swaziland	1,720	473	81	206	18.4	1,183	4.6	104	1.3	227	(27.3)	X
Tanzania	88,604	325	43	3,367	1.0	35,000	0.0	40,940	(2.8)	9,297	14.3	X
Togo	5,439	714	45	667	7.3	1,790	0.0	1,600	(5.9)	1,382	4.1	X
Tunisia	15,536	552	55	4,868	1.9	3,685	10.1	651	20.4	6,332	(7.9)	X
Uganda	19,955	964	43	6,722	18.3	1,800	0.0	5,560	(8.3)	5,873	(8.4)	X
Zaire	226,760	182	10	7,863	3.5	15,000	0.0	174,310	(1.9)	29,587	11.4	X
Zambia	74,339	120	47	5,268	3.1	30,000	0.0	28,850	(2.4)	10,221	5.6	X
Zimbabwe	38,667	282	20	2,812	8.8	4,856	0.0	19,130	(4.0)	11,869	5.1	X
ASIA	2,678,997	1,229	45	457,204	1.3	759,367	9.5	531,722	(4.9)	930,704	(4.6)	X
Afghanistan	65,209	315	58	8,054	0.0	30,000	0.0	1,900	0.0	25,255	(0.0)	X
Bangladesh	13,017	9,388	76	9,352	2.1	600	0.0	1,899	(13.4)	1,166	9.7	X
Bhutan	4,700	351	9	132	8.5	271	2.4	2,563	(0.6)	1,735	(0.1)	X
Cambodia	17,652	510	21	3,059	0.4	580	0.0	13,372	0.0	641	(2.0)	X
China	932,641	1,292	53	96,524	(4.0)	400,000	19.9	126,515	(6.5)	309,602	(14.7)	X
India	297,319	3,016	61	169,594	0.7	11,782	(2.6)	67,011	(0.7)	48,932	(1.0)	X
Indonesia	181,157	1,074	19	21,967	12.3	11,800	(1.5)	109,800	(6.6)	37,590	17.4	X
Iran, Islamic Rep	163,600	386	36	15,050	2.8	44,000	0.0	18,020	0.1	86,530	(0.5)	X
Iraq	43,737	455	22	5,450	0.2	4,000	0.0	1,887	(1.4)	32,400	0.0	X
Israel	2,033	2,662	29	436	5.1	147	22.2	119	2.3	1,332	(3.7)	X
Japan	37,652	3,319	14	4,595	(5.8)	647	11.8	25,105	(0.1)	7,305	3.5	X
Jordan	8,893	499	13	398	18.2	791	0.1	70	9.9	7,634	(0.9)	X
Korea, Dem People's Rep	12,041	1,915	17	2,003	5.4	50	0.0	8,970	0.0	1,018	(9.2)	X
Korea, Rep	9,873	4,508	22	2,109	(4.0)	80	56.9	6,480	(1.3)	1,204	13.8	X
Kuwait	1,782	1,024	8	5	275.0	136	1.5	2	0.0	1,639	(0.3)	X
Lao People's Dem Rep	23,080	200	7	908	3.6	800	0.0	12,700	(7.4)	8,672	12.7	X
Lebanon	1,023	2,836	30	301	(1.6)	10	0.0	80	(7.7)	632	1.9	X
Malaysia	32,855	586	15	4,880	1.5	27	0.0	19,361	(8.8)	8,587	26.4	X
Mongolia	156,650	15	80	1,386	17.0	124,386	0.8	13,915	(8.3)	16,964	0.6	X
Myanmar	65,754	678	16	10,053	0.2	359	(0.8)	32,405	1.0	22,937	(1.4)	X
Nepal	13,680	1,541	34	2,651	14.3	2,000	6.0	2,480	0.0	6,549	(6.4)	X
Oman	21,246	80	5	60	46.3	1,000	0.0	0	0.0	20,186	(0.1)	X
Pakistan	77,088	1,661	34	21,107	4.0	5,000	0.0	3,430	19.7	47,551	(2.8)	X
Philippines	29,817	2,232	31	7,973	2.5	1,257	24.0	10,350	(16.9)	10,237	19.5	X
Saudi Arabia	214,969	77	41	2,358	20.2	85,000	0.0	1,200	(2.2)	126,411	(0.3)	X
Singapore	61	45,869	2	1	(87.0)	0	0.0	3	0.0	57	13.2	X
Sri Lanka	6,463	2,769	36	1,901	1.5	439	0.0	2,075	17.9	2,048	(14.3)	X
Syrian Arab Rep	18,392	748	73	5,585	(2.2)	7,869	(5.6)	724	53.9	4,214	8.3	X
Thailand	51,089	1,113	47	23,042	25.5	830	29.7	14,113	(14.3)	13,104	(16.1)	X
Turkey	76,963	774	47	27,754	(2.9)	8,533	(12.0)	20,199	0.1	20,476	10.8	X
United Arab Emirates	8,360	204	3	39	69.6	200	0.0	3	12.5	8,118	(0.2)	X
Viet Nam	32,549	2,178	21	6,381	(2.9)	341	18.3	9,412	(21.2)	16,415	19.5	X
Yemen	52,797	246	33	1,603	9.5	16,065	0.0	4,060	0.0	31,069	(0.4)	X

Table 17.1

	Land Area (000 hectares)	Population Density, 1993 (per 1,000 hectares)	Domesticated Land as a Percentage of Land Area {a}	Cropland 1989-91	Cropland % Change Since 1979-81	Permanent Pasture 1989-91	Permanent Pasture % Change Since 1979-81	Forest and Woodland 1989-91	Forest and Woodland % Change Since 1979-81	Other Land 1989-91	Other Land % Change Since 1979-81	Built-up Area {b} 1986-89 (000 ha)
NORTH & CENTRAL AMERICA {d}	**2,137,681**	**190**	**30**	**271,780**	**(0.7)**	**362,084**	**1.0**	**709,830**	**0.3**	**793,987**	**(0.5)**	**X**
Belize	2,280	89	5	56	9.0	48	9.1	1,012	0.0	1,164	(0.7)	X
Canada	922,097	30	8	45,947	0.5	28,100	0.9	359,000	5.4	489,050	(3.7)	5,500
Costa Rica	5,106	640	56	529	4.5	2,327	15.6	1,640	(9.9)	611	(20.3)	X
Cuba	10,982	993	57	3,330	4.0	2,970	15.3	2,760	9.1	1,922	(28.1)	X
Dominican Rep	4,838	1,575	73	1,446	2.4	2,092	0.0	615	(3.1)	685	(2.0)	X
El Salvador	2,072	2,663	65	733	1.1	610	0.0	104	(25.7)	625	4.7	X
Guatemala	10,843	925	30	1,882	7.9	1,400	7.7	3,750	(17.6)	3,811	17.3	X
Haiti	2,756	2,501	51	905	1.7	497	(2.4)	38	(34.1)	1,316	1.3	X
Honduras	11,189	503	39	1,824	3.7	2,560	6.2	3,260	(18.8)	3,545	17.9	X
Jamaica	1,083	2,304	42	270	1.8	190	(8.1)	185	(5.1)	438	5.3	X
Mexico	190,869	472	52	24,713	0.7	74,499	0.0	42,460	(11.4)	49,197	12.1	X
Nicaragua	11,875	346	56	1,273	2.1	5,400	10.7	3,380	(24.7)	1,822	44.6	X
Panama	7,599	337	29	649	16.7	1,560	13.9	3,300	(20.4)	2,090	36.9	X
Trinidad and Tobago	513	2,493	26	120	3.4	11	0.0	220	(4.3)	162	3.8	X
United States	916,660	281	47	187,776	(1.5)	239,172	0.7	287,400	(2.5)	202,312	4.4	99,109
SOUTH AMERICA	**1,752,925**	**177**	**35**	**113,709**	**12.7**	**493,930**	**4.4**	**829,386**	**(5.1)**	**315,900**	**3.5**	**X**
Argentina	273,669	122	62	27,200	0.0	142,200	(0.7)	59,200	(1.4)	45,069	4.3	X
Bolivia	108,438	71	27	2,328	12.9	26,600	(1.7)	55,590	(1.1)	23,920	3.4	X
Brazil	845,651	185	29	59,933	23.1	184,200	7.5	493,030	(4.9)	108,488	1.2	X
Chile	74,880	184	24	4,400	3.9	13,500	3.8	8,800	1.3	48,180	(1.6)	X
Colombia	103,870	327	44	5,410	4.1	40,400	5.8	50,300	(5.6)	7,760	7.8	X
Ecuador	27,684	409	28	2,732	9.4	5,140	29.2	10,900	(21.9)	8,912	22.8	X
Guyana	19,685	41	9	495	0.1	1,230	0.8	16,369	0.0	1,591	(0.6)	X
Paraguay	39,730	117	59	2,199	26.7	21,100	33.5	13,800	(31.6)	2,631	30.3	X
Peru	128,000	179	24	3,730	6.1	27,120	0.0	68,400	(3.5)	28,750	8.6	X
Suriname	15,600	29	1	68	39.7	20	1.7	14,853	(0.2)	658	2.7	X
Uruguay	17,481	180	85	1,304	(9.5)	13,520	(0.8)	669	6.8	1,988	11.4	X
Venezuela	88,205	234	24	3,898	4.3	17,700	2.9	30,175	(8.8)	36,432	6.6	X
EUROPE	**472,740**	**1,086**	**47**	**138,480**	**(1.8)**	**83,130**	**(3.7)**	**157,327**	**0.9**	**93,810**	**4.6**	**X**
Albania	2,740	1,218	40	704	0.3	403	(3.0)	1,046	3.0	587	(3.3)	X
Austria	8,273	943	43	1,521	(7.0)	2,002	(1.9)	3,215	(2.0)	1,533	16.5	897
Belgium	3,023	3,311	46	764	(1.0)	613	(1.5)	612	X	1,036	X	X
Bulgaria	11,055	807	56	4,155	(1.1)	2,008	0.9	3,871	0.7	1,021	0.0	295
Czechoslovakia (former)	12,536	1,258	54	5,088	(1.9)	1,652	(2.2)	4,617	1.1	1,180	6.2	248
Denmark	4,239	1,219	66	2,561	(3.5)	216	(15.0)	493	0.0	969	15.6	314
Finland	30,461	165	9	2,471	(3.6)	123	(25.1)	23,222	(0.4)	4,645	5.3	898
France	55,010	1,043	56	19,187	1.5	11,381	(11.4)	14,817	1.6	9,625	11.0	2,910
Germany	34,931	2,308	50	12,002	(4.2)	5,329	(11.1)	10,403	1.2	7,197	15.8	X
Greece	12,890	792	71	3,909	(0.6)	5,255	0.0	2,620	0.1	1,106	2.2	489
Hungary	9,234	1,136	70	5,287	(0.9)	1,185	(8.2)	1,695	5.4	1,067	6.7	X
Iceland	10,025	26	23	8	0.0	2,274	0.0	120	0.0	7,623	0.0	10
Ireland	6,889	505	82	943	(15.0)	4,692	1.6	343	7.4	911	8.1	X
Italy	29,406	1,966	57	11,971	(3.7)	4,880	(5.0)	6,751	6.3	5,803	5.9	X
Netherlands	3,392	4,502	59	909	10.8	1,092	(9.2)	300	2.5	1,092	1.0	538
Norway	30,683	140	3	870	5.5	111	(4.8)	8,330	0.0	21,371	(0.2)	370
Poland	30,442	1,265	62	14,736	(1.3)	4,049	(0.1)	8,760	0.9	2,898	4.2	1,960
Portugal	9,195	1,073	44	3,171	1.0	838	0.0	2,968	0.0	2,218	(1.3)	X
Romania	23,034	1,015	64	10,038	(4.4)	4,737	6.1	6,684	1.8	1,575	4.5	901
Spain	49,944	784	61	20,195	(1.5)	10,270	(4.6)	15,786	1.4	3,693	18.7	1,968
Sweden	41,162	211	8	2,829	(4.9)	556	(23.0)	28,020	0.3	9,757	2.2	1,155
Switzerland	3,977	1,725	51	412	1.5	1,609	(0.3)	1,052	0.0	904	(0.1)	237
United Kingdom	24,160	2,393	74	6,665	(4.3)	11,186	(2.3)	2,391	13.8	3,918	7.2	X
Yugoslavia (former)	25,540	940	39	7,741	(1.8)	2,119	(0.6)	2,858	(1.4)	2,330	15.0	X
U.S.S.R. (former)	**2,190,070**	**131**	**25**	**229,257**	**(1.0)**	**326,933**	**1.7**	**827,800**	**(22.2)**	**806,080**	**40.7**	**X**
Armenia	2,840	1,256	X	500 e	1.6 e	750	7.1	X	X	X	X	X
Azerbaijan	8,610	852	X	1,600 e	15.7 e	2,200	0.0	X	X	X	X	X
Belarus	20,760	496	X	6,100 e	(1.6) e	3,100	(3.1)	X	X	X	X	X
Estonia	4,320	365	X	X	X	X	X	X	X	X	X	X
Georgia	6,970	785	X	800 e	1.7 e	2,050	2.5	X	X	X	X	X
Kazakhstan	266,980	64	X	35,600 e	0.5 e	161,800	2.7	X	X	X	X	X
Kyrgyzstan	19,130	239	X	1,400 e	6.5 e	8,650	(0.6)	X	X	X	X	X
Latvia	6,205	430	X	1,687 e	X	845	X	2,799	(61.7)	X	X	X
Lithuania	4,551	826	X	X	X	245	X	X	X	X	X	X
Moldova	3,370	1,293	X	1,700 e	(6.3) e	300	0.0	X	X	X	X	X
Russian Federation	1,699,580	88	X	132,100 e	(1.3) e	81,000	(3.2)	X	X	X	X	X
Tajikistan	14,270	401	X	800 e	0.5 e	3,315	3.6	X	X	X	X	X
Turkmenistan	48,810	81	X	1,200 e	39.6 e	33,460	14.2	X	X	X	X	X
Ukraine	60,355	865	69	34,807	X	6,900	3.0	X	X	X	X	X
Uzbekistan	42,540	515	X	4,500 e	11.1 e	21,600	(0.9)	X	X	X	X	X
OCEANIA	**845,349**	**33**	**57**	**49,868**	**9.9**	**431,420**	**(4.8)**	**157,268**	**(0.1)**	**206,792**	**9.1**	**X**
Australia	764,444	23	61	48,267	10.2	417,244	(4.8)	106,000	(0.2)	192,932	9.5	X
Fiji	1,827	409	16	241	2.3	60	0.0	1,185	0.0	341	(1.5)	X
New Zealand	26,799	130	52	416	(8.4)	13,627	(4.7)	7,347	4.2	5,409	8.2	X
Papua New Guinea	45,286	92	1	397	8.3	83	(20.1)	38,227	(0.4)	6,579	2.4	X
Solomon Islands	2,799	126	3	57	9.6	39	16.0	2,560	0.0	143	(3.4)	X

Sources: Food and Agriculture Organization of the United Nations, The United Nations Statistical Commission and Economic Commission for Europe, and other sources.

Notes: a. Domesticated land is the sum of cropland and permanent pasture. b. Data are for the latest year available during the 1986-89 period. c. Does not include Antarctica. d. Includes Greenland. e. Arable land only.
Regional totals include countries not listed.
0 = zero or less than half the unit of measure; X = not available; negative numbers are shown in parentheses.
For additional information, see Sources and Technical Notes.

Table 17.2 Urban and Rural Populations, Transport, and

| | Urban Population as a Percentage of Total | | Average Annual Population Change 1965-95 (percent) | | Cities With at Least 750,000 Inhabitants | | | Persons Per Vehicle | Total Labor Force 1989-91 {a} | Percentage of 1989-91 Labor Force in {a} | | | Percent Unemployment 1989-91 {a} | |
| | | | | | Percentage of Total Population | | Number of Cities | | | | | | | |
	1965	1995	Urban	Rural	1965	1995	1990	1991	(000)	Agri-culture	Industry	Services	Male	Female
WORLD	35.5	45.2	2.7	1.3	14.7	17.4	376	9	X	X	X	X	X	X
AFRICA	20.6	34.7	4.7	2.2	6.9	10.9	34	47	X	X	X	X	X	X
Algeria	37.6	55.8	4.3	1.8	9.0	13.0	1	20	4,418	X	X	X	17	16
Angola	12.5	32.2	5.9	1.7	6.1	19.9	1	60	X	X	X	X	X	X
Benin	13.0	41.8	6.8	1.3	4.4	20.0	1	125	52	X	X	X	X	X
Botswana	3.9	30.9	10.7	2.1	0.0	0.0	0	21	223	X	X	X	X	X
Burkina Faso	5.2	19.5	7.1	1.9	0.0	0.0	0	356	X	X	X	X	X	X
Burundi	2.2	6.1	5.8	2.2	0.0	0.0	0	290	47	X	X	X	X	X
Cameroon	16.4	44.9	6.3	1.3	6.2	18.4	2	67	X	X	X	X	X	X
Central African Rep	26.7	50.8	4.6	1.1	0.0	0.0	0	184	13	X	X	X	X	X
Chad	9.0	37.0	7.1	0.9	0.0	0.0	0	379	11	X	X	X	X	X
Congo	32.4	43.4	3.9	2.3	0.0	0.0	0	54	X	X	X	X	X	X
Cote d'Ivoire	23.1	43.6	6.2	2.9	7.0	19.1	1	47	385	X	X	X	X	X
Djibouti	55.1	82.8	6.6	1.8	0.0	0.0	0	29	X	X	X	X	X	X
Egypt	40.7	44.8	2.6	2.1	22.2	24.6	3	67	14,926	42	21	37	X	X
Equatorial Guinea	26.4	30.5	1.8	1.1	0.0	0.0	0	40	X	X	X	X	X	X
Ethiopia	7.6	13.4	4.5	2.3	2.2	3.8	1	875	X	X	X	X	X	X
Gabon	21.2	50.0	6.4	1.9	0.0	0.0	0	30	X	X	X	X	X	X
Gambia, The	13.6	25.5	5.2	2.5	0.0	0.0	0	104	31	X	X	X	X	X
Ghana	26.1	36.3	3.8	2.2	6.8	9.7	1	124	X	X	X	X	X	X
Guinea	11.7	29.6	5.4	1.4	4.8	22.5	1	220	X	X	X	X	X	X
Guinea-Bissau	14.4	22.2	3.9	2.1	0.0	0.0	0	173	X	X	X	X	X	X
Kenya	8.6	27.7	7.7	2.8	3.6	7.4	1	81	1,409	X	X	X	X	X
Lesotho	6.4	23.1	6.9	1.8	0.0	0.0	0	X	X	X	X	X	X	X
Liberia	22.1	50.6	6.1	1.6	0.0	0.0	0	222	X	X	X	X	X	X
Libya	27.4	86.0	8.1	(1.5)	23.6	80.1	2	6	X	X	X	X	X	X
Madagascar	12.4	27.1	5.6	2.3	0.0	0.0	0	156	X	X	X	X	X	X
Malawi	4.9	13.5	7.1	3.2	0.0	0.0	0	294	442	X	X	X	X	X
Mali	12.6	27.0	5.3	2.0	0.0	0.0	0	307	X	X	X	X	X	X
Mauritania	9.0	53.8	8.8	0.3	0.0	0.0	0	139	X	X	X	X	X	X
Mauritius	37.0	40.7	1.7	1.2	0.0	0.0	0	18	281	X	X	X	X	X
Morocco	31.9	48.4	4.0	1.6	9.0	11.6	1	26	X	X	X	X	14	20
Mozambique	4.6	34.3	9.4	1.0	3.1	13.7	1	129	X	X	X	X	X	X
Namibia	16.8	30.9	5.1	2.3	0.0	0.0	0	X	X	X	X	X	X	X
Niger	6.8	23.1	7.4	2.4	0.0	0.0	0	222	25	X	X	X	X	X
Nigeria	17.0	39.3	6.2	2.2	3.9	9.3	2	80	X	X	X	X	X	X
Rwanda	2.8	6.1	6.0	3.1	0.0	0.0	0	291	X	X	X	X	X	X
Senegal	32.7	42.3	3.7	2.3	12.9	23.8	1	55	X	X	X	X	X	X
Sierra Leone	15.4	36.2	5.2	1.3	0.0	0.0	0	89	X	X	X	X	X	X
Somalia	19.5	25.8	3.9	2.7	3.2	10.2	1	396	X	X	X	X	X	X
South Africa	47.3	50.8	2.8	2.4	23.3	20.7	6	7	X	X	X	X	9	9
Sudan	13.0	24.6	5.1	2.4	3.9	8.5	1	150	X	X	X	X	X	X
Swaziland	6.5	31.2	8.4	1.8	0.0	0.0	0	21	X	X	X	X	X	X
Tanzania	5.3	24.4	8.7	2.5	2.0	5.7	1	318	X	X	X	X	X	X
Togo	11.3	30.8	6.7	2.3	0.0	0.0	0	87	X	X	X	X	X	X
Tunisia	39.5	59.0	3.6	0.9	13.8	23.3	1	16	X	26	34	40	X	X
Uganda	6.5	12.5	5.4	2.9	2.8	4.7	1	702	X	X	X	X	X	X
Zaire	26.1	29.1	3.5	3.0	4.5	9.6	1	203	X	X	X	X	X	X
Zambia	23.3	43.1	5.4	2.2	4.4	14.1	1	49	360	X	X	X	X	X
Zimbabwe	14.4	32.1	6.0	2.4	6.1	9.1	1	39	X	X	X	X	X	X
ASIA	22.2	34.0	3.5	1.5	9.8	13.3	149	32	X	X	X	X	X	X
Afghanistan	9.4	20.0	4.8	1.8	3.1	8.8	1	242	X	X	X	X	X	X
Bangladesh	6.2	19.5	6.7	2.1	3.4	10.1	3	896	X	X	X	X	X	X
Bhutan	2.8	6.4	5.0	2.0	0.0	0.0	0	X	X	X	X	X	X	X
Cambodia	10.8	12.9	2.0	1.4	7.1	12.3	1	X	X	X	X	X	X	X
China	18.2	30.3	3.5	1.2	9.8	10.7	51	191	583,640	X	X	X	1	1
India	18.8	26.8	3.3	1.8	6.6	10.0	34	185	25,986	X	X	X	X	X
Indonesia	15.8	32.5	4.6	1.4	7.2	12.8	9	63	75,851	56	14	30	2	3
Iran, Islamic Rep	38.0	60.4	5.0	1.8	15.9	22.8	5	27	X	X	X	X	X	X
Iraq	50.7	74.6	4.7	1.1	20.2	21.3	1	19	X	X	X	X	X	X
Israel	80.9	92.7	3.3	(0.4)	34.4	38.4	1	5	1,583	4	29	68	9	13
Japan	67.3	77.9	1.3	(0.5)	26.2	38.0	7	2	63,690	7	35	59	2	2
Jordan	46.3	71.5	4.5	0.8	15.2	24.6	1	20	X	X	X	X	X	X
Korea, Dem People's Rep	45.1	61.3	3.3	1.0	6.2	10.3	1	X	X	X	X	X	X	X
Korea, Rep	32.4	77.6	4.6	(2.1)	24.0	57.9	7	10	18,576	17	36	48	2	2
Kuwait	77.7	97.0	4.9	(2.6)	78.3	68.0	1	3	X	X	X	X	X	X
Lao People's Dem Rep	8.3	21.7	5.7	1.8	0.0	0.0	0	255	X	X	X	X	X	X
Lebanon	49.5	87.2	3.1	(3.4)	38.0	58.7	1	X	X	X	X	X	X	X
Malaysia	26.1	47.2	4.6	1.4	4.1	10.4	1	8	6,685	26	28	46	X	X
Mongolia	42.1	60.9	4.1	1.5	0.0	0.0	0	X	X	X	X	X	X	X
Myanmar	21.0	26.2	3.0	2.0	4.8	8.3	1	611	15,221	70	9	21	X	X
Nepal	3.5	13.7	7.3	2.2	0.0	0.0	0	X	X	X	X	X	X	X
Oman	4.3	13.2	8.0	3.6	0.0	0.0	0	7	X	X	X	X	X	X
Pakistan	23.5	34.7	4.2	2.4	11.1	17.5	8	132	29,828	47	20	33	5	17
Philippines	31.6	45.7	3.9	1.8	9.8	16.9	2	104	22,979	45	16	39	9	13
Saudi Arabia	38.8	80.2	7.0	0.6	8.8	23.6	2	3	X	X	X	X	X	X
Singapore	100.0	100.0	1.4	NA	100.0	100.0	1	7	1,524	0	35	65	2	2
Sri Lanka	19.9	22.4	2.1	1.6	0.0	0.0	0	53	5,964	49	21	30	9	24
Syrian Arab Rep	40.0	52.4	4.4	2.7	24.7	26.5	2	50	X	23	29	48	X	X
Thailand	12.9	25.4	4.5	1.6	8.4	14.5	1	20	X	X	X	X	X	X
Turkey	34.1	68.8	4.7	(0.2)	15.1	23.8	5	22	19,492	49	20	31	8	6
United Arab Emirates	48.6	84.0	10.8	4.6	0.0	0.0	0	4	X	X	X	X	X	X
Viet Nam	16.4	20.8	3.0	2.0	1.8	1.7	1	X	X	X	X	X	X	X
Yemen	11.0	33.6	6.8	1.9	0.0	0.0	0	30	X	X	X	X	X	X

Labor Force, 1965–95

Table 17.2

	Urban Population as a Percentage of Total		Average Annual Population Change 1965-95 (percent)		Cities With at Least 750,000 Inhabitants Percentage of Total Population		Number of Cities	Persons Per Vehicle	Total Labor Force 1989-91 {a}	Percentage of 1989-91 Labor Force in {a}			Percent Unemployment 1989-91 {a}	
	1965	1995	Urban	Rural	1965	1995	1990	1991	(000)	Agri-culture	Industry	Services	Male	Female
NORTH & CENTRAL AMERICA	67.4	74.0	1.8	0.7	36.0	38.6	66	2	X	X	X	X	X	X
Belize	52.5	52.5	2.2	2.2	0.0	0.0	0	40	X	X	X	X	X	X
Canada	72.9	78.1	1.5	0.5	29.4	32.3	4	2	12,340	4	23	72	11	10
Costa Rica	38.1	49.7	3.7	2.1	23.8	25.7	1	12	1,007	25	27	48	5	7
Cuba	57.6	76.0	2.1	(0.7)	20.3	20.2	1	X	X	X	X	X	X	X
Dominican Rep	35.1	64.6	4.6	0.4	20.9	45.5	2	30	X	X	X	X	X	X
El Salvador	38.9	46.7	2.8	1.7	0.0	0.0	0	33	890	11	29	60	8	7
Guatemala	34.0	41.5	3.5	2.4	13.0	8.9	1	38	787	50	18	32	2	3
Haiti	17.6	31.6	3.9	1.2	8.3	17.6	1	120	2,339	X	X	X	X	X
Honduras	25.7	47.7	5.4	2.0	7.4	16.6	1	39	1,494	38	21	41	9	6
Jamaica	37.6	55.4	2.6	0.1	0.0	0.0	0	21	894	26	24	50	9	23
Mexico	54.9	75.3	3.7	0.6	25.1	31.0	9	8	8,899	23	29	48	3	3
Nicaragua	42.7	62.9	4.5	1.7	15.4	27.0	1	54	229	X	X	X	11	19
Panama	44.4	54.9	3.1	1.6	25.8	35.8	1	13	722	27	14	59	13	22
Trinidad and Tobago	63.7	66.6	1.4	1.0	0.0	0.0	0	6	401	10	33	57	16	23
United States	71.9	76.2	1.2	0.5	39.2	41.7	43	1	116,877	3	26	72	7	6
SOUTH AMERICA	55.9	78.0	3.3	(0.2)	26.0	36.8	35	12	X	X	X	X	X	X
Argentina	76.1	87.5	1.9	(0.7)	40.3	42.7	3	6	X	X	X	X	7	8
Bolivia	40.0	54.4	3.6	1.6	11.4	14.6	1	23	858	47	13	40	7	8
Brazil	50.4	78.7	3.7	(0.7)	24.7	40.8	17	11	X	X	X	X	X	X
Chile	71.7	85.9	2.3	(0.6)	28.1	37.6	1	13	4,540	19	26	55	5	6
Colombia	53.5	72.7	3.2	0.4	20.4	29.2	4	22	4,611	1	30	69	10	10
Ecuador	37.2	60.6	4.5	1.2	18.8	32.1	2	44	2,192	33	19	48	6	11
Guyana	29.2	35.3	1.5	0.6	0.0	0.0	0	24	X	X	X	X	X	X
Paraguay	36.2	50.7	4.1	2.1	18.4	23.9	1	40	495	1	26	73	5	5
Peru	51.9	72.2	3.6	0.6	19.4	31.3	1	35	2,377	1	25	75	5	7
Suriname	47.1	50.4	1.3	0.9	0.0	0.0	0	9	X	X	X	X	X	X
Uruguay	81.1	90.3	0.9	(1.6)	43.1	41.6	1	10	597	4	30	66	7	11
Venezuela	69.8	92.9	3.9	(1.9)	31.8	31.2	4	10	6,728	13	25	62	11	9
EUROPE	63.8	75.0	1.0	(0.8)	23.0	24.0	56	3	X	X	X	X	X	X
Albania	31.2	37.3	2.6	1.7	0.0	0.0	0	X	851	X	X	X	X	X
Austria	50.8	60.6	0.9	(0.5)	25.7	27.8	1	2	3,420	8	37	55	3	4
Belgium	93.4	96.7	0.3	(2.1)	11.0	13.4	1	2	3,637	3	28	69	5	12
Bulgaria	45.9	70.7	1.7	(1.8)	9.8	15.7	1	6	3,189	X	X	X	X	X
Czechoslovakia (former)	51.1	80.6	1.9	(2.7)	7.6	7.8	1	4	X	11	44	44	X	X
Denmark	77.1	85.5	0.6	(1.2)	28.9	25.7	1	3	2,670	6	27	67	X	X
Finland	43.9	60.3	1.4	(0.8)	11.7	20.7	1	2	2,366	8	29	63	9	6
France	67.1	72.8	0.8	(0.1)	22.2	22.4	4	2	22,068	6	29	65	7	12
Germany	78.0	86.5	0.6	(1.4)	42.1	44.1	16	2	36,626	4	40	56	4	5
Greece	47.5	65.0	1.7	(0.7)	33.2	44.3	2	4	3,719	24	28	48	4	12
Hungary	45.5	67.7	1.4	(1.6)	18.5	20.6	1	5	4,978	X	X	X	X	X
Iceland	82.7	91.6	1.5	(1.3)	0.0	0.0	0	2	125	X	X	X	X	X
Ireland	48.7	58.4	1.2	(0.1)	25.1	26.7	1	3	1,125	15	28	57	17	12
Italy	61.8	70.5	0.8	(0.5)	28.8	28.0	7	2	21,454	9	32	59	7	17
Netherlands	85.6	88.9	0.9	(0.1)	15.6	14.0	2	2	6,521	4	25	70	5	10
Norway	57.6	77.0	1.5	(1.5)	0.0	0.0	0	2	2,010	6	23	71	6	5
Poland	50.0	63.9	1.5	(0.4)	19.8	22.5	5	5	10,458	27	37	36	X	X
Portugal	23.9	36.4	1.7	(0.3)	10.6	17.1	1	4	4,718	18	34	48	3	6
Romania	37.7	56.2	2.1	(0.5)	7.9	9.7	1	14	8,102	29	43	28	X	X
Spain	61.3	80.7	1.6	(1.6)	15.6	22.9	2	3	12,609	11	34	55	12	24
Sweden	77.1	84.7	0.7	(0.9)	18.8	30.1	2	2	4,430	3	28	68	3	2
Switzerland	52.8	64.0	1.2	(0.3)	10.5	14.2	1	2	3,560	X	X	X	X	X
United Kingdom	87.1	89.5	0.3	(0.5)	28.3	23.0	4	2	26,049	2	29	68	7	6
Yugoslavia (former)	31.2	60.7	3.0	(1.1)	3.4	7.4	1	5	6,492	X	X	X	X	X
U.S.S.R. (former)	52.8	68.1	1.7	(0.5)	14.6	17.9	30	11 b	124,971	20	47	34	X	X
Armenia	X	X	X	X	X	34.5	1	X	X	X	X	X	X	X
Azerbaijan	X	X	X	X	X	24.6	1	X	X	X	X	X	X	X
Belarus	X	X	X	X	X	17.5	1	X	5,020	X	X	X	X	X
Estonia	61.5	73.1	1.2	(0.5)	0.0	0.0	0	X	790	X	X	X	X	X
Georgia	X	X	X	X	X	24.9	1	X	X	X	X	X	X	X
Kazakhstan	X	X	X	X	X	7.2	1	X	X	X	X	X	X	X
Kyrgyzstan	X	X	X	X	X	0.0	0	X	X	X	X	X	X	X
Latvia	59.6	72.9	1.2	(0.8)	29.1	35.4	1	X	X	X	X	X	X	X
Lithuania	44.9	72.1	2.4	(1.5)	0.0	0.0	0	X	X	X	X	X	X	X
Moldova	X	X	X	X	X	0.0	0	X	X	X	X	X	X	X
Russian Federation	X	X	X	X	X	20.8	16	X	X	X	X	X	X	X
Tajikistan	X	X	X	X	X	0.0	0	X	X	X	X	X	X	X
Turkmenistan	X	X	X	X	X	0.0	0	X	X	X	X	X	X	X
Ukraine	X	X	X	X	X	18.8	7	X	19,119	X	X	X	X	X
Uzbekistan	X	X	X	X	X	9.8	1	X	X	X	X	X	X	X
OCEANIA	68.6	71.0	1.8	1.4	39.2	41.3	6	2	X	X	X	X	X	X
Australia	83.0	85.2	1.7	1.1	55.7	59.9	5	2	7,713	5	24	70	10	9
Fiji	32.6	40.7	2.4	1.2	0.0	0.0	0	12	92	X	X	X	X	X
New Zealand	78.9	84.3	1.2	0.0	20.2	25.4	1	2	1,451	11	24	66	11	10
Papua New Guinea	5.2	17.8	6.7	1.9	0.0	0.0	0	X	X	X	X	X	X	X
Solomon Islands	8.8	17.1	5.8	3.1	0.0	0.0	0	X	27	X	X	X	X	X

Sources: United Nations Population Division, International Labour Office, and American Automobile Manufacturers Association.
Notes: a. Data are for the latest year available during the 1989-91 period. b. Excludes Estonia, Latvia, and Lithuania.
World and regional totals include countries not listed.
0 = zero or less than half the unit of measurement; X = not available; NA = not applicable; negative numbers are shown in parentheses.
For additional information, see Sources and Technical Notes.

Table 17.3 Twenty-one Megacities

Country and Megacity {a}	Size (000 ha)	Estimated and Projected Population Size (000) 1980	1990	2000	Annual Population Growth Rate 1980-90	Percentage of Household Income Spent on Food	Persons per Room	Percentage of Households With: Running Water	Electricity	Telephones Per 100 People	Motor Vehicle Registrations (000) 1989-90 {b}
Argentina											
Buenos Aires	700	9,918	11,448	12,822	1.4	40	1.3	80	91	14	1,000 c
Bangladesh											
Dacca	X	3,290	6,578	11,511	7.2	63	2.4	60	85	2	X
Brazil											
Rio de Janeiro	650	8,789	10,948	12,162	2.2	26	0.8	86	98	8	X
Sao Paulo	800	12,101	18,119	22,558	4.1	50	0.8	100	100	16	4,000
China											
Beijing	1,680	9,029	10,867	14,366	1.9	52	1.2	88	90	2	308 d
Shanghai	630	11,739	13,447	17,407	1.4	55	2.0	95	95	4	148
Tianjin	X	7,268	9,249	12,508	2.4	52	1.3	80	84	4	X
Egypt											
Cairo	21.4 e	6,852	8,633	10,761	2.3	47	1.5	91	98	4	939
India											
Bombay	60	8,067	12,223	18,142	4.2	57	4.2	92	78	5	588
Calcutta	130	9,030	10,741	12,675	1.8	60	3.0	51	63	2	500
Delhi	59.1 f	5,559	8,171	11,692	3.9	40	3.1	50	81	5	1,660
Indonesia											
Jakarta	59 g	5,985	9,206	13,380	4.4	45	3.4	75	94	3	1,380 h
Japan											
Osaka	X	9,990	10,482	10,601	0.5	18	0.6	96	100	42	X
Tokyo	216	21,854	25,013	27,956	1.4	18	0.9	100	100	44	4,400
Korea, Rep											
Seoul	165 i	8,283	10,979	12,949	2.9	34	2.0	100	100	22	2,660
Mexico											
Mexico City	250	13,888	15,085	16,190	0.8	41	1.9	92	97	6	2,500
Nigeria											
Lagos	X	4,385	7,742	13,480	5.8	58	5.8	47	53	1	X
Pakistan											
Karachi	353 j	5,023	7,943	11,895	4.7	43	3.3	66	84	2	650
Philippines											
Manila	64 g	5,966	8,882	12,582	4.1	38	3.0	89	93	9	510 k
United States											
Los Angeles	1,660	9,523	11,456	13,151	1.9	12	0.5	91	98	35	8,000
New York	359 g	15,601	16,056	16,645	0.3	16	0.5	99	100	56	1,780

Sources: Population Action International, United Nations Population Division, World Health Organization, and United Nations Environment Programme.

Notes: a. Megacities represented here are all cities projected to have a population of at least 10 million in the year 2000. b. Data are for the latest year available during the 1989-90 period. c. Estimate. d. 1991 data. e. Governate of Cairo only. f. 1981 data. g. Metropolitan area only. h. 1987 data. i. Greater Seoul only. j. 1982 data.
k. 1988 data.
X = not available.
For additional information, see Sources and Technical Notes.

Sources and Technical Notes

Table 17.1 Land Area and Use, 1979–91

Sources: Land area and use: Food and Agriculture Organization of the United Nations (FAO), *Agrostat-PC*, on diskette (FAO, Rome, July 1993); for countries of the former U.S.S.R. excluding Latvia, Lithuania, Ukraine, and former U.S.S.R. total: U.S. Central Intelligence Agency (CIA), *The World Factbook 1992* (CIA, Washington, D.C., 1992); population density: calculated from FAO land area data and population figures provided by the United Nations (U.N.) Population Division, *Interpolated National Populations (The 1992 Revision)*, on diskette (U.N., New York, 1993); built-up area: United Nations Statistical Commission and Economic Commission for Europe, *The Environment in Europe and North America: Annotated Statistics 1992* (U.N., New York, 1992).

Land area and *land use* data are provided to the FAO by national governments in response to annual questionnaires. The FAO also compiles data from national agricul-

tural censuses. When official information is lacking, the FAO prepares its own estimates or relies on unofficial data. Several countries use definitions of total area and land use that differ from those used in this chapter. Refer to the sources for details.

The FAO often adjusts the definitions of land use categories and sometimes substantially revises earlier data. For example, in 1985, the FAO began to exclude from the crop land category land used for shifting cultivation but currently lying fallow. Because land use changes can reflect changes in data-reporting procedures as well as actual land use changes, apparent trends should be interpreted with caution.

Land use data are periodically revised and may change significantly from year to year. For the most recent land use statistics, see the latest *FAO Production Yearbook*.

Land area data are for 1991. They exclude major inland water bodies, national claims to the continental shelf, and Exclusive Economic Zones. (See Chapter 22, "Water," Table 22.6.) Total land area for the former U.S.S.R. differs from the land area sum of

the individual countries, as different sources were used in compiling these data.

The world *population density* and *land use* figures refer to the six inhabited continents. Population density was derived by using the population figures for 1993 published by the United Nations Population Division and 1991 land area data from the FAO. Although the population figures were published in 1993, actual censuses and estimates were made in prior years. For additional information on population and methodology, see the Technical Notes to Table 16.1 in Chapter 16, "Population and Human Development."

Crop land includes land under temporary and permanent crops, temporary meadows, market and kitchen gardens, and land that is temporarily fallow. Permanent crops are those that do not need to be replanted after each harvest, such as cocoa, coffee, rubber, fruit, and vines. This category excludes land used to grow trees for wood or timber. *Permanent pasture* is land used for five or more years for forage, including natural crops and cultivated crops. This category is difficult for countries to assess because it includes wildland used for pasture. In addition, few countries regularly report data on permanent pasture. As a result, the absence of a change in permanent pasture area (e.g., 0 percent change for many African and Asian countries) may indicate differences in land classification and data reporting rather than actual conditions. Grassland not used for forage is included under *other land.*

Forest and woodland includes land under natural or planted stands of trees, as well as logged-over areas that will be reforested in the near future.

Other land includes uncultivated land, grassland not used for pasture, built-up areas, wetlands, wastelands, and roads.

Built-up area can refer to residential, recreational, and industrial lands, and areas covered by roads and other transport systems, as well as quarries and technical infrastructures. Differences in built-up area among countries are caused, in part, by definitional differences.

Table 17.2 Urban and Rural Populations, Transport, and Labor Force, 1965–95

Sources: Urban population as a percentage of total: United Nations (U.N.) Population Division, *Urban and Rural Areas, 1950–2025 (The 1992 Revision)*, on diskette, and *Interpolated National Populations (The 1992 Revision*, on diskette (U.N., New York, 1993); cities with at least 750,000 inhabitants: United Nations Population Division, *Urban Agglomerations, 1950–2010 (The 1992 Revision)*, on diskette (U.N., New York, 1993); number of vehicles: American Automobile Manufacturers Association (AAMA), *World Motor Vehicle Data* (AAMA, Detroit, Michigan, 1993); total labor force: International Labour Office (ILO), *STARS ILO Yearbook 1992*, on diskette (ILO, Geneva, 1992); labor force by sector and unemployment: ILO, *STARS World Labour Report Database 1992*, on diskette (ILO, Geneva, 1992).

Urban population as a percentage of total is the portion of the total population residing in urban areas. The rest of the population is defined as rural. Definitions of "urban" vary from country to country. For a list of individual country definitions, see the sources. For additional information on methods of data collection and estimation, refer to the Technical Note for Table 16.1 in Chapter 16, "Population and Human Development."

The *percentage of total population* in cities *with at least 750,000 inhabitants* was calculated using figures for populations of urban agglomerations of 750,000 or more residents reported in *Urban Agglomerations*

1950–2010, and total national population estimates and projections for 1960 and 1990 reported in *Interpolated National Populations (The 1992 Revision)*. In *Urban Agglomerations 1950–2010*, the United Nations provides estimates and projections of the populations of 348 urban agglomerations with 750,000 or more inhabitants in 1990, for each five-year period between 1950 and 2010.

The United Nations defines an "urban agglomeration" as "comprising the city or town proper and also the suburban fringe or thickly settled territory lying outside of, but adjacent to, the city boundaries. . . . For some countries or areas, the data relate to entire administrative divisions known, for example, as shi or municipos which are composed of a populated center and adjoining territory, some of which may contain other quite separate urban localities or be distinctly rural in character." For additional information, refer to the source.

Persons per vehicle was calculated by dividing the total population for 1991 as provided in *Interpolated National Populations (The 1992 Revision)* with the total number of private and commercial vehicles registered at the end of 1991 as reported by country sources to the AAMA.

All people who work or who are without work but are available for and are seeking work to produce economic goods and services make up the total labor force, which includes employed people and the unemployed (experienced workers who are without work as well as those looking for work for the first time). ILO provides labor force estimates and projections for men, women, and the total population. The data for *total labor force*, as well as *percentage of 1989–91 labor force in agriculture, industry*, and *services*, take into account information on the economically active population, which is obtained from national censuses of population, labor force sample surveys, and other surveys conducted through 1991. Estimates are based on midyear, medium- variant population figures. (See Chapter 16, "Population and Human Development," for further information on population projections.) Labor force data are for the latest year available during the 1989–91 period.

Percent unemployment includes all people who were unemployed, available for work, and seeking employment during the latest year of the 1989–91 period for which data were available. These data are based on labor force sample surveys and ILO estimates.

Table 17.3 Twenty-one Megacities

Sources: Size and motor vehicle registrations: United Nations Environment Pro-

gramme (UNEP) and World Health Organization (WHO), *Urban Air Pollution in Megacities of the World* (Blackwell, Oxford, U.K., 1992); population data: United Nations Population Division, *Urban Agglomerations, 1950–2010 (The 1992 Revision)*, on diskette (U.N., New York, 1993); living conditions: Population Action International (formerly Population Crisis Committee), *Cities: Life in the World's 100 Largest Metropolitan Areas Statistical Appendix*, on diskette (Population Action International, Washington, D.C., 1990).

Megacity size and *motor vehicle registrations* were culled by UNEP and WHO from various secondary sources, and therefore differences among cities in this table may be due, in part, to definitional differences. Except where otherwise indicated, size generally encompasses the greater metropolitan area and includes both the urban center and surrounding counties or municipalities. For example, the Delhi Metropolitan area includes the cities of Delhi and New Delhi. Motor vehicle registrations are the total number of private and commercial vehicles registered as of 1989 or 1990 (the latest year data were available), unless otherwise noted. Registrations for New York are only those vehicles registered in the city proper.

For information concerning the *population size* and *population growth rate*, please refer to the Technical Notes for Table 17.2 pertaining to data on cities with at least 750,000 inhabitants.

Data on *living conditions* were collected by Population Action International through a 1989 questionnaire survey of government, university, nongovernmental organization, and other experts in the world's 100 largest metropolitan areas. Recipients were asked to document the sources of their information or to provide estimates when published data were not available (these estimates are for varying years). Metropolitan area boundaries in this study encompassed the city center and suburbs, as well as more distant communities from which people either within the communities in question or within the metropolitan area commuted to work. Osaka, as defined in this study, includes Kobe and Kyoto. Tokyo includes Yokohama. *Persons per room* were calculated based on housing units defined as accommodating one family. Households equipped with *running water* include those serviced by water tanks. Households with *electricity* are those that receive this service 24 hours a day. *Telephones per 100 people* are based on number of working telephones only.

For additional information, refer to the source.

18. Food and Agriculture

Agriculture, broadly defined as the work of cultivating the soil, producing crops, and raising livestock, is the human activity that has had the greatest impact upon the Earth's environment. Globally, agriculture has been relatively successful in meeting the needs of the growing human population due to increases in agricultural labor, area under cultivation, irrigation, mechanization, crop breeding and research, and inputs of fertilizer and pesticides. With the global population projected to reach 10 billion by the year 2050, however, global agricultural production must expand 2.5 to 3 times to provide an adequate diet for the world's people.

Even though the world's food production has to date far outpaced its population growth, some regional and national data show reason for concern (see Table 18.1). The 22 percent increase in Africa's food production between 1980–82 and 1990–92 fell short of meeting demand; per capita food production dropped by 5 percent. Somali, Malawi, and Liberia experienced the most serious declines in food production over the 10-year period. In Asia, South America, Europe, and the former U.S.S.R., food production grew faster than the population.

Yield differences reflect the intensity of agricultural activity. On a global average, 1 hectare yielded about 2.76 metric tons of cereals and 12.20 metric tons of roots and tubers. However, 1 hectare in Africa yielded only 1.17 metric tons of cereals and 7.44 metric tons of roots and tubers, whereas, in Europe, the averages were 4.29 and 20.26 metric tons, respectively.

Differences in yields may be due to differences in agricultural systems, soil, climate, economic incentives, or amounts of agricultural inputs. Europe, for example, with roughly 10 percent of the world's agricultural crop land, applies approximately 19 percent of the world's fertilizer, whereas Africa, with 13 percent of the world's crop land, applies only 3 percent of the world's fertilizer (see Table 18.2). Notably, the fertilizer application rate has increased in Africa (by 11 percent), the former U.S.S.R. (by 19 percent), and Asia (by 84 percent) between 1979–81 and 1989–91 and has decreased in North and Central America, South America, Europe, and Oceania.

The geographic distribution of tractors and harvesters is similar to that of fertilizer use rates. Europe and North America, which together have less than one third of the world's crop land, possess 61 percent of the world's tractors and 42 percent of the world's harvesters. The United States alone has roughly 9 times as many tractors and 10 times as many harvesters as the whole of Africa. Canada and the United States together have roughly the same number of tractors as Asia.

Livestock continue to supply traction power for use in cultivation and harvesting in much of the world and is an important source of food, raw materials, fertilizer, and energy. Global populations of domestic animals are rising, with Africa, Asia, and South America registering increases in each of the six livestock categories (see Table 18.3). Notably, the world's chicken population has more than doubled since 1980–82. Asia's chicken population has risen by 359 percent, largely in China.

Food trade statistics show changing patterns of regional and national food self-sufficiency (see Table 18.4). Africa's imports of food have risen over the 10-year period from 1979–81 through 1989–91 in each of the three trade categories. The steady decline in world commodity prices (see Chapter 15, "Basic Economic Indicators," Table 15.4) means countries that export commodities face a decrease in earnings while countries that import commodities are finding them increasingly more affordable. The United States, Canada, and France are the largest net exporters of cereals, whereas the former U.S.S.R. and Japan are the greatest net importers.

Food aid often links agricultural areas producing subsidized surpluses with countries experiencing food deficits. The United States, Canada, Japan, and the European Community are the world's largest donors of cereals. Egypt and Bangladesh receive the largest amounts of cereal aid.

The agricultural productivity of 87 countries is considered in Table 18.5. The total agricultural gross domestic product (AGDP) is the value added after deducting agricultural and nonagricultural inputs used in production. AGDP per hectare of arable land estimates indicate that New Zealand and the Netherlands possess the most productive farmland, whereas AGDP per unit labor estimates characterize New Zealand and Australian farmers as the most productive, churning out $26,752 and $20,240 per labor unit input, respectively.

Agricultural research personnel and expenditure data describe resources devoted to national agricultural research systems. For the period 1981–1985, China, the United States, and Japan had the greatest investments in agricultural research, both in terms of personnel and expenditures (see Table 18.5).

Table 18.1 Food and Agricultural Production, 1980–92

| | Index of Agricultural Production (1979-81 = 100) | | | | Index of Food Production (1979-81 = 100) | | | | Average Production of Cereals | | Average Yields of Cereals | | Average Yields of Roots and Tubers | |
| | Total | | Per Capita | | Total | | Per Capita | | (000 metric tons) | Percent Change Since | Kilograms Per Hectare | Percent Change Since | Kilograms Per Hectare | Percent Change Since |
	1980-82	1990-92	1980-82	1990-92	1980-82	1990-92	1980-82	1990-92	1990-92	1980-82	1990-92	1980-82	1990-92	1980-82
WORLD	103	126	101	104	103	127	101	105	1,928,044	18	2,757	22	12,197	5
AFRICA	102	128	99	93	102	129	99	94	90,225	22	1,168	0	7,441	14
Algeria	103	168	100	123	103	167	100	122	2,818	46	926	38	8,153	24
Angola	100	102	97	75	100	106	97	78	372	2	410	(20)	3,897	11
Benin	98	171	96	124	98	163	95	118	558	58	862	28	9,383	28
Botswana	101	101	97	72	101	101	97	72	38	(1)	334	31	7,333	(0)
Burkina Faso	101	170	98	128	101	167	98	125	2,102	79	769	34	5,432	(42)
Burundi	101	132	99	96	103	135	100	99	300	35	1,382	30	7,657	9
Cameroon	104	113	101	82	104	114	101	83	915	2	1,140	31	5,132	30
Central African Rep	103	122	101	91	103	123	101	92	86	(24)	691	26	3,344	(2)
Chad	102	135	100	106	102	130	100	102	776	70	613	(2)	5,496	20
Congo	104	130	101	94	104	130	102	94	26	139	823	12	7,519	8
Cote d'Ivoire	101	135	97	89	101	141	97	93	1,239	41	891	(5)	5,472	(3)
Djibouti	X	X	X	X	X	X	X	X	X	X	X	X	X	X
Egypt	103	141	100	108	103	153	101	117	13,844	67	5,734	39	21,043	13
Equatorial Guinea	X	X	X	X	X	X	X	X	X	X	X	X	2,705	(9)
Ethiopia	101	112	99	85	101	113	99	85	6,587	11	1,282	4	3,616	(3)
Gabon	100	124	96	84	100	124	96	83	24	112	1,714	(4)	6,863	12
Gambia, The	117	122	114	88	117	118	114	86	108	17	1,098	(12)	3,000	0
Ghana	100	149	97	103	100	150	97	104	1,083	67	1,073	44	6,632	(5)
Guinea	103	133	101	100	103	130	101	98	922	27	807	(15)	7,543	6
Guinea-Bissau	107	136	104	110	107	137	104	110	172	34	1,534	112	6,786	20
Kenya	104	142	100	97	104	145	100	99	2,853	16	1,600	2	8,102	8
Lesotho	95	100	92	75	94	98	91	74	155	(5)	1,045	27	7,667	X
Liberia	103	74	100	52	104	92	100	65	106	(60)	778	(40)	6,712	(3)
Libya	109	142	104	92	109	142	104	92	290	15	674	23	8,055	18
Madagascar	102	122	99	86	103	123	100	87	2,561	19	1,976	21	6,386	12
Malawi	104	107	100	67	104	97	100	60	1,259	(7)	875	(25)	3,148	(29)
Mali	106	132	103	95	107	128	104	92	2,114	85	871	11	8,529	3
Mauritania	101	115	99	86	101	115	99	86	95	87	721	85	2,000	(29)
Mauritius	103	122	101	108	103	123	101	109	2	100	2,000	(33)	17,333	24
Morocco	105	162	102	122	105	162	102	122	5,966	55	1,110	26	17,112	28
Mozambique	101	98	98	82	101	100	99	84	506	(22)	337	(40)	3,874	(9)
Namibia	96	99	94	71	97	101	94	72	94	3	454	(4)	8,500	(5)
Niger	100	122	97	85	100	122	97	85	2,073	20	340	(20)	7,520	12
Nigeria	102	174	99	122	102	174	99	122	13,111	62	1,205	(14)	10,491	31
Rwanda	104	115	101	82	105	112	102	80	313	7	1,224	4	5,956	(30)
Senegal	110	130	107	96	109	130	106	96	926	4	803	12	3,400	(25)
Sierra Leone	103	120	101	92	104	115	102	88	503	(9)	1,115	(12)	4,481	41
Somalia	104	72	101	54	104	72	101	54	346	(2)	651	27	10,154	2
South Africa	101	97	98	74	101	97	98	74	8,868	(37)	1,584	(19)	15,026	29
Sudan	101	111	98	80	101	113	98	81	3,999	31	678	6	2,717	(19)
Swaziland	106	122	103	90	106	122	103	90	100	15	1,283	(3)	1,600	(17)
Tanzania	101	119	97	82	101	120	98	83	3,723	27	1,254	12	8,290	(13)
Togo	100	141	97	101	99	136	96	98	469	57	764	4	7,756	14
Tunisia	100	157	97	122	100	158	97	122	2,131	71	1,419	44	13,100	8
Uganda	105	146	102	105	105	146	102	105	1,580	42	1,438	(1)	6,304	(3)
Zaire	104	131	100	92	103	131	100	92	1,347	44	758	(7)	7,569	9
Zambia	100	127	97	87	101	125	97	86	1,012	7	1,253	(26)	3,828	9
Zimbabwe	103	113	100	79	106	101	103	71	1,715	(31)	1,195	(12)	4,714	19
ASIA	104	148	102	121	104	148	102	121	875,970	33	2,854	31	14,198	9
Afghanistan	98	76	100	69	99	77	100	69	2,616	(33)	1,156	(14)	17,205	14
Bangladesh	102	125	99	95	102	126	99	96	28,203	29	2,572	30	9,896	(2)
Bhutan	102	108	100	85	102	107	100	85	106	(35)	1,089	(25)	10,667	56
Cambodia	118	190	117	145	118	183	117	140	2,371	32	1,448	30	5,123	(21)
China	105	163	104	139	104	161	102	137	399,927	36	4,329	37	14,893	6
India	103	152	101	121	103	153	101	122	196,173	39	1,935	42	15,982	23
Indonesia	104	164	102	132	105	168	103	135	52,871	47	3,857	26	11,651	27
Iran, Islamic Rep	108	178	104	117	108	181	104	119	14,912	59	1,578	44	18,018	18
Iraq	107	121	104	85	107	122	104	85	2,482	24	861	(1)	15,472	(21)
Israel	102	122	100	96	101	139	99	109	256	1	2,397	22	32,474	(18)
Japan	98	96	98	90	99	99	98	93	13,985	2	5,704	11	25,284	9
Jordan	111	172	108	110	111	175	108	112	128	17	955	37	27,714	(1)
Korea, Dem People's Rep	102	127	101	104	102	126	101	103	10,086	7	6,497	6	13,094	5
Korea, Rep	97	115	96	100	97	117	96	102	8,058	2	5,808	19	20,595	19
Kuwait	X	X	X	X	X	X	X	X	2	400	5,000	X	X	X
Lao People's Dem Rep	108	143	106	106	108	143	106	106	1,470	30	2,333	58	8,632	(14)
Lebanon	108	187	108	179	108	193	109	185	80	129	1,983	38	19,050	18
Malaysia	107	185	104	139	110	227	107	171	1,928	(3)	2,815	0	8,890	(1)
Mongolia	101	104	98	77	101	105	98	77	537	36	904	24	10,821	41
Myanmar	108	122	106	96	108	124	106	98	14,137	(2)	2,726	(2)	8,840	(2)
Nepal	102	154	99	114	102	156	100	116	5,359	47	1,854	17	7,595	35
Oman	X	X	X	X	X	X	X	X	4	140	2,000	100	X	X
Pakistan	104	166	101	117	104	159	101	112	21,391	20	1,828	11	10,738	2
Philippines	103	118	101	90	103	118	100	90	14,086	26	2,031	20	6,629	5
Saudi Arabia	89	580	83	348	89	590	82	354	4,495	1,186	4,488	323	20,125	X
Singapore	96	82	95	73	96	83	95	73	0	X	X	X	X	X
Sri Lanka	101	97	99	83	102	99	100	84	2,432	10	2,880	11	8,702	(10)
Syrian Arab Rep	111	124	108	85	111	121	108	83	3,584	11	940	(21)	17,887	18
Thailand	104	134	102	113	104	129	102	109	22,438	8	2,052	6	14,055	(6)
Turkey	102	122	100	95	103	123	100	95	30,129	18	2,202	16	22,717	37
United Arab Emirates	X	X	X	X	X	X	X	X	8	100	4,000	(33)	X	X
Viet Nam	106	156	103	123	105	156	103	123	20,874	57	3,077	40	7,700	14
Yemen	X	X	X	X	X	X	X	X	X	X	X	X	X	X

Table 18.1

	Index of Agricultural Production (1979-81 = 100)				Index of Food Production (1979-81 = 100)				Average Production of Cereals		Average Yields of Cereals		Average Yields of Roots and Tubers	
	Total		Per Capita		Total		Per Capita		(000 metric tons)	Percent Change Since	Kilograms Per Hectare	Percent Change Since	Kilograms Per Hectare	Percent Change Since
	1980-82	1990-92	1980-82	1990-92	1980-82	1990-92	1980-82	1990-92	1990-92	1980-82	1990-92	1980-82	1990-92	1980-82
NORTH & CENTRAL AMERICA	102	111	100	96	102	112	101	96	398,318	3	4,040	13	20,718	11
Belize	106	119	104	90	106	119	104	90	24	(17)	1,490	(27)	X	X
Canada	108	123	107	110	108	125	107	111	52,855	9	2,531	9	25,409	6
Costa Rica	99	135	97	99	98	132	95	97	265	(15)	3,050	34	18,524	239
Cuba	102	105	101	95	102	104	101	94	491	(16)	2,346	(9)	5,029	(18)
Dominican Rep	101	108	99	84	102	111	99	86	522	12	3,744	15	7,183	22
El Salvador	95	94	94	81	93	123	92	105	849	28	1,876	13	16,125	17
Guatemala	102	118	100	86	105	133	102	97	1,385	18	1,891	22	4,974	45
Haiti	99	97	97	79	100	99	98	80	312	(23)	994	(4)	3,948	3
Honduras	102	138	99	96	104	133	100	92	690	38	1,377	9	7,714	33
Jamaica	96	117	94	103	95	117	94	103	3	(50)	1,000	(39)	13,172	13
Mexico	103	126	101	98	104	128	101	100	24,662	11	2,430	7	16,565	20
Nicaragua	92	74	89	54	87	86	84	63	446	5	1,498	(2)	11,750	10
Panama	103	111	101	88	103	110	101	87	306	19	1,796	17	5,750	(27)
Trinidad and Tobago	96	103	94	89	96	105	95	91	17	104	2,833	(9)	11,000	14
United States	102	108	101	97	102	108	101	97	315,486	1	4,881	18	33,070	13
SOUTH AMERICA	104	132	101	106	104	134	102	108	75,293	4	2,182	17	11,982	10
Argentina	102	113	100	98	102	113	100	97	21,874	(21)	2,610	15	18,931	29
Bolivia	105	151	102	115	106	154	103	117	853	22	1,423	16	6,878	24
Brazil	104	134	102	107	106	138	103	111	37,816	14	1,924	22	12,425	8
Chile	102	138	101	115	102	139	101	116	2,915	85	3,933	85	15,179	42
Colombia	101	137	99	111	101	140	99	113	3,979	16	2,489	2	11,743	5
Ecuador	103	145	100	109	104	146	101	110	1,462	95	1,783	1	6,397	(37)
Guyana	100	66	99	62	100	66	99	62	225	(22)	2,974	(3)	7,917	15
Paraguay	105	157	101	113	105	142	102	102	1,018	51	1,789	18	14,917	17
Peru	103	116	100	91	103	120	101	94	1,691	12	2,463	20	7,835	0
Suriname	102	101	101	83	102	101	101	83	208	(26)	3,692	(8)	X	X
Uruguay	108	123	107	115	108	122	107	114	1,224	16	2,451	35	7,121	26
Venezuela	102	131	99	100	102	132	99	100	2,003	33	2,452	28	8,730	6
EUROPE	102	107	101	104	102	107	101	104	281,421	10	4,295	17	20,264	10
Albania	102	92	100	74	103	94	101	76	700	(24)	2,598	3	6,833	5
Austria	105	109	105	105	105	109	105	105	4,882	3	5,404	21	24,122	(3)
Belgium {a}	100	122	100	120	100	122	100	120	2,213	6	6,256	23	34,776	(14)
Bulgaria	102	85	102	83	103	89	103	88	7,977	(8)	3,833	(8)	11,220	6
Czechoslovakia (former)	105	117	104	115	105	118	104	115	11,599	15	4,786	21	15,930	(6)
Denmark	104	133	104	132	104	133	104	132	8,645	16	5,460	31	35,000	18
Finland	101	110	100	105	101	110	100	105	3,566	17	3,394	30	19,875	28
France	101	106	101	100	101	106	101	100	58,595	23	6,372	31	32,868	8
Germany	X	X	X	X	X	X	X	X	24,672 b	X	5,670 b	X	29,994 b	X
Greece	105	111	105	106	106	107	105	101	5,396	(1)	3,700	10	21,985	31
Hungary	106	102	106	106	106	103	106	106	12,931	(7)	4,785	(2)	27,067	61
Iceland	102	90	101	80	102	90	101	80	X	X	X	X	11,000	(18)
Ireland	100	125	99	122	100	125	99	121	2,091	(0)	6,243	28	26,855	27
Italy	101	101	101	98	101	100	101	98	18,744	3	4,316	20	20,532	13
Netherlands	104	118	104	110	104	117	104	110	1,302	(1)	7,143	17	39,963	6
Norway	104	113	104	109	104	113	104	109	1,312	13	3,731	1	24,582	(8)
Poland	96	112	96	105	97	115	96	107	25,265	28	2,964	19	16,665	12
Portugal	96	130	96	128	96	130	96	129	1,473	17	1,854	57	10,879	25
Romania	100	79	100	75	100	79	100	75	16,253	(12)	2,800	(6)	9,883	(34)
Spain	103	120	102	115	102	120	102	115	17,526	21	2,313	19	19,669	24
Sweden	103	95	103	92	103	95	103	92	5,098	(10)	4,309	15	31,102	15
Switzerland	102	112	102	105	103	112	102	105	1,265	47	6,082	23	37,175	(4)
United Kingdom	102	115	102	112	102	115	102	112	22,466	10	6,332	24	38,596	13
Yugoslavia (former)	103	92	103	85	103	92	103	86	14,917	(7)	3,752	0	7,785	(15)
U.S.S.R. (former)	100	108	100	99	100	110	99	101	183,731	15	1,779	33	11,127	6
Armenia	X	X	X	X	X	X	X	X	274	8	1,918	10	11,871	(13)
Azerbaijan	X	X	X	X	X	X	X	X	1,328	18	2,187	(6)	8,106	5
Belarus	X	X	X	X	X	X	X	X	6,387	38	2,569	56	12,421	(9)
Estonia	X	X	X	X	X	X	X	X	830	(2)	1,971	(1)	13,085	(5)
Georgia	X	X	X	X	X	X	X	X	535	(5)	2,094	7	10,141	(14)
Kazakhstan	X	X	X	X	X	X	X	X	23,218	3	1,013	14	10,499	4
Kyrgyzstan	X	X	X	X	X	X	X	X	1,432	16	2,500	9	13,792	4
Latvia	X	X	X	X	X	X	X	X	1,340	42	1,965	43	12,033	(5)
Lithuania	X	X	X	X	X	X	X	X	2,807	47	2,666	50	12,530	0
Moldova	X	X	X	X	X	X	X	X	2,512	(2)	3,455	3	6,868	(20)
Russian Federation	X	X	X	X	X	X	X	X	100,220	13	1,701	35	10,627	9
Tajikistan	X	X	X	X	X	X	X	X	300	12	1,298	(5)	14,179	(16)
Turkmenistan	X	X	X	X	X	X	X	X	571	105	2,398	13	8,083	10
Ukraine	X	X	X	X	X	X	X	X	39,994	13	3,094	32	11,688	11
Uzbekistan	X	X	X	X	X	X	X	X	1,985	(25)	1,840	(18)	8,242	(20)
OCEANIA	98	113	97	95	97	112	96	95	23,085	22	1,733	50	11,480	9
Australia	95	117	94	99	93	113	92	96	22,214	23	1,691	52	27,728	14
Fiji	101	110	99	95	101	110	99	95	35	79	2,364	18	12,800	56
New Zealand	103	104	102	96	102	110	102	102	832	2	5,138	19	28,545	3
Papua New Guinea	103	130	100	101	103	133	101	104	3	(18)	1,500	(5)	7,226	2
Solomon Islands	104	137	100	94	104	137	100	94	0	(100)	X	X	18,167	22

Source: Food and Agriculture Organization of the United Nations.
Notes: a. Data for Belgium and Luxembourg are combined under Belgium. b. Data refer to the former Federal Republic of Germany only.
World and regional totals include some countries not listed here.
0 = zero or less than half of the unit of measure; X = not available; negative numbers are shown in parentheses.
For additional information, see Sources and Technical Notes.

Table 18.2 Agricultural Inputs, 1979–91

	Cropland		Irrigated Land as a Percentage of Crop Land		Average Annual Fertilizer Use (kilograms per hectare of crop land)		Pesticide Consumption (metric tons)	Tractors		Harvesters	
	Total Hectares (000)	Hectares Per Capita						Average Number	Percent Change Since	Average Number	Percent Change Since
	1991	1991	1979-81	1989-91	1979-81	1989-91	1989	1989-91	1979-81	1989-91	1979-81
WORLD	1,441,573	0.27	15	17	81	96	X	26,411,984	21	3,956,306	12
AFRICA	181,620	0.27	6	6	18	20	X	544,757	22	69,882	47
Algeria	7,653	0.30	3	5	25	15	X	90,833	93	9,267	108
Angola	3,450	0.36	X	X	4	4	X	10,283	0	X	X
Benin	1,870	0.39	0	0	1	4	85	127	22	X	X
Botswana	1,400	1.10	0	0	1	1	X	5,800	168	92	16
Burkina Faso	3,563	0.39	0	1	3	6	X	130	13	X	X
Burundi	1,350	0.24	4	5	1	2	251	134	49	X	X
Cameroon	7,020	0.59	0	0	5	3	3,096	1,077	94	X	X
Central African Rep	2,006	0.65	X	X	0	0	X	203	31	16	57
Chad	3,205	0.56	0	0	1	2	90	165	4	18	6
Congo	169	0.07	2	2	5	6	6	702	5	55	70
Cote d'Ivoire	3,690	0.30	1	2	16	10	X	3,550	16	62	66
Djibouti	X	X	X	X	X	X	3	8	33	X	X
Egypt	2,643	0.05	100	100	268	361	17,090	57,000	57	2,337	11
Equatorial Guinea	230	0.64	X	X	0	0	X	100	2	X	X
Ethiopia	13,930	0.27	1	1	3	7	X	3,900	(1)	150	(2)
Gabon	457	0.38	X	X	1	2	X	1,463	18	X	X
Gambia, The	180	0.20	7	7	13	7	X	43	(4)	5	25
Ghana	2,730	0.18	0	0	7	4	X	4,000	15	517	72
Guinea	730	0.12	1	3	1	2	X	270	80	X	X
Guinea-Bissau	340	0.35	X	X	2	3	X	19	21	X	X
Kenya	2,440	0.10	2	2	27	45	X	14,000	117	300	(19)
Lesotho	340	0.19	X	X	16	16	X	1,827	30	33	9
Liberia	373	0.14	1	1	12	3	X	330	11	X	X
Libya	2,160	0.46	11	11	30	37	X	32,323	38	3,410	31
Madagascar	3,102	0.25	22	30	3	3	X	2,887	9	147	19
Malawi	1,690	0.17	1	1	23	36	X	1,400	17	X	X
Mali	2,103	0.22	7	10	6	8	X	838	1	48	9
Mauritania	205	0.10	6	6	5	10	X	336	18	X	X
Mauritius	106	0.10	15	16	237	277	5	356	9	X	X
Morocco	9,420	0.37	15	14	25	35	X	38,952	49	4,622	31
Mozambique	3,130	0.22	2	4	10	1	X	5,750	0	X	X
Namibia	662	0.45	1	1	0	0	X	3,050	20	X	X
Niger	3,605	0.45	1	1	1	1	X	176	91	X	X
Nigeria	32,335	0.29	3	3	5	12	X	11,533	35	X	X
Rwanda	1,160	0.16	0	0	0	2	X	90	8	X	X
Senegal	2,350	0.31	7	8	10	6	X	490	8	153	10
Sierra Leone	636	0.15	3	5	5	2	X	530	106	6	350
Somalia	1,039	0.12	11	11	1	2	X	2,127	29	X	X
South Africa	13,174	0.34	8	9	82	59	X	167,000	(4)	43,500	48
Sudan	12,900	0.50	14	15	5	6	X	9,711	2	1,219	42
Swaziland	209	0.27	33	30	100	60	X	3,528	23	X	X
Tanzania	3,370	0.13	4	4	10	15	X	6,800	(32)	X	X
Togo	669	0.18	1	1	4	15	X	367	83	X	X
Tunisia	4,875	0.59	3	5	14	20	X	24,889	(4)	3,028	23
Uganda	6,750	0.37	0	0	0	0	X	4,500	74	15	47
Zaire	7,880	0.20	0	0	1	1	X	2,397	26	X	X
Zambia	5,268	0.63	0	1	14	13	X	5,883	27	285	4
Zimbabwe	2,814	0.27	6	8	59	56	4,268	20,400	1	593	6
ASIA	457,505	0.14	29	33	67	123	X	5,497,355	62	1,343,556	46
Afghanistan	8,054	0.46	31	34	6	6	X	847	9	X	X
Bangladesh	9,137	0.08	17	31	45	101	X	5,200	24	X	X
Bhutan	132	0.08	23	26	X	X	X	X	X	X	X
Cambodia	3,066	0.36	3	3	3	2	X	1,365	1	20	0
China	96,554	0.08	45	49	144	284	X	827,844	12	38,434	42
India	169,700	0.20	23	27	33	73	X	971,145	147	2,950	102
Indonesia	22,200	0.12	28	37	59	109	X	27,054	193	17,933	28
Iran, Islamic Rep	15,050	0.25	35	38	40	77	X	115,000	47	2,833	(7)
Iraq	5,450	0.29	32	47	17	34	X	36,062	55	2,264	(30)
Israel	436	0.09	49	46	186	240	X	27,600	5	270	(17)
Japan	4,552	0.04	63	62	412	402	X	2,052,443	55	1,213,990	43
Jordan	402	0.10	11	16	36	50	1,257	5,750	26	70	13
Korea, Dem People's Rep	2,010	0.09	59	71	397	409	X	73,000	65	X	X
Korea, Rep	2,091	0.05	60	64	368	440	X	41,835	1,366	43,518	3,295
Kuwait	5	0.00	75	40	250	133	X	120	362	X	X
Lao People's Dem Rep	912	0.21	12	13	3	2	X	870	65	X	X
Lebanon	306	0.11	28	29	117	93	X	3,000	0	95	6
Malaysia	4,880	0.27	7	7	89	188	X	12,133	56	X	X
Mongolia	1,396	0.62	3	6	8	12	48	11,526	18	2,515	7
Myanmar	10,057	0.24	10	10	11	7	75	12,000	37	46	77
Nepal	2,659	0.13	22	38	10	27	X	4,367	87	X	X
Oman	61	0.04	93	96	24	122	190	144	46	40	246
Pakistan	21,140	0.17	73	80	52	89	X	260,544	163	1,500	200
Philippines	7,980	0.13	16	20	43	65	X	10,317	(2)	660	50
Saudi Arabia	2,375	0.15	28	38	22	208	X	1,950	63	637	55
Singapore	1	0.00	X	X	X	X	X	62	41	X	X
Sri Lanka	1,903	0.11	28	27	81	98	X	31,470	33	6	89
Syrian Arab Rep	5,625	0.44	10	12	23	51	X	68,006	142	3,715	52
Thailand	23,160	0.42	16	19	16	39	36,694	157,000	108	X	X
Turkey	27,689	0.48	7	9	47	65	34,650	687,025	59	11,413	(13)
United Arab Emirates	39	0.02	22	13	159	359	X	180	13	5	88
Viet Nam	6,380	0.09	24	29	27	96	X	26,797	17	X	X
Yemen	X	X	X	X	X	X	X	X	X	X	X

Table 18.2

	Cropland		Irrigated Land as a Percentage of Crop Land		Average Annual Fertilizer Use (kilograms per hectare of crop land)		Pesticide Consumption (metric tons)	Tractors		Harvesters	
	Total Hectares (000) 1991	Hectares Per Capita 1991	1979-81	1989-91	1979-81	1989-91	1989	Average Number 1989-91	Percent Change Since 1979-81	Average Number 1989-91	Percent Change Since 1979-81
NORTH & CENTRAL AMERICA	271,798	0.69	10	10	91	87	X	5,813,808	3	851,331	(1)
Belize	57	0.29	3	4	32	89	X	1,090	36	44	46
Canada	45,930	1.70	1	2	41	46	X	775,133	18	155,533	(4)
Costa Rica	529	0.17	12	22	148	212	6,264	6,450	8	1,160	14
Cuba	3,330	0.31	24	27	167	158	X	77,694	14	7,321	28
Dominican Rep	1,446	0.20	12	16	43	60	X	2,330	8	X	X
El Salvador	733	0.14	15	16	103	105	X	3,417	4	395	27
Guatemala	1,885	0.20	4	4	53	71	X	4,200	5	3,020	16
Haiti	905	0.14	8	8	4	3	X	222	27	X	X
Honduras	1,842	0.35	5	5	15	14	X	3,470	7	X	X
Jamaica	271	0.11	12	13	63	94	X	3,060	9	X	X
Mexico	24,720	0.29	20	21	53	69	X	170,000	37	18,767	25
Nicaragua	1,273	0.33	6	7	37	29	X	2,600	19	X	X
Panama	654	0.27	5	5	55	50	X	5,086	(5)	1,085	(23)
Trinidad and Tobago	120	0.10	18	18	66	67	2,303	2,623	11	X	X
United States	187,776	0.74	11	10	108	99	X	4,749,000	(0)	664,000	(1)
SOUTH AMERICA	115,222	0.38	7	8	45	44	X	1,125,596	27	117,620	18
Argentina	27,200	0.83	6	6	4	6	X	203,000	11	48,433	10
Bolivia	2,358	0.32	7	7	2	3	X	5,200	30	117	3
Brazil	61,350	0.40	3	4	72	54	X	720,000	35	46,000	28
Chile	4,384	0.33	30	29	30	69	X	35,790	4	8,677	6
Colombia	5,430	0.17	8	10	58	104	20,019	35,600	25	2,700	29
Ecuador	2,750	0.25	21	20	30	28	X	8,700	38	760	28
Guyana	496	0.62	25	26	21	30	X	3,603	4	432	4
Paraguay	2,235	0.51	3	3	4	9	988	15,093	105	X	X
Peru	3,730	0.17	33	34	35	32	X	16,000	12	X	X
Suriname	68	0.16	86	87	68	20	636	1,287	17	265	36
Uruguay	1,304	0.42	5	9	55	57	X	32,901	0	4,660	0
Venezuela	3,905	0.20	4	5	54	116	X	48,000	26	5,567	72
EUROPE	138,024	0.27	10	12	225	192	X	10,384,879	23	831,233	2
Albania	700	0.21	53	60	130	114	X	12,300	21	1,780	28
Austria	1,524	0.20	0	0	246	199	X	351,444	10	27,048	(15)
Belgium {a}	818	0.08	0	0	523	470	9,664	116,704	1	8,133	(16)
Bulgaria	4,162	0.46	28	30	214	153	X	52,400	(15)	8,136	(17)
Czechoslovakia (former)	5,060	0.32	3	6	334	217	X	136,936	0	21,093	18
Denmark	2,558	0.50	14	17	244	243	X	162,950	(13)	33,039	(15)
Finland	2,524	0.51	2	3	187	174	2,252	237,333	12	48,333	7
France	19,234	0.34	5	6	301	301	X	1,465,000	0	153,000	5
Germany	12,002	0.15	X	4	X	520	36,937 b	1,564,421	X	156,053	X
Greece	3,912	0.39	24	31	143	172	8,151	210,000	48	6,499	5
Hungary	5,287	0.50	4	3	274	142	25,951	48,209	(14)	10,199	(26)
Iceland	8	0.03	X	X	X	X	X	11,122	(15)	18	17
Ireland	933	0.27	X	X	536	725	X	166,000	16	5,120	(3)
Italy	11,975	0.21	23	26	175	160	X	1,430,667	35	47,000	36
Netherlands	911	0.06	59	61	828	614	X	191,033	8	5,580	(7)
Norway	865	0.20	9	11	314	234	X	155,232	17	16,490	0
Poland	14,715	0.38	1	1	234	138	20,568	1,172,148	89	80,163	105
Portugal	3,173	0.32	20	20	86	84	X	136,516	61	7,558	68
Romania	10,020	0.43	22	32	136	98	X	137,200	(7)	38,366	(13)
Spain	20,089	0.51	15	17	77	98	X	739,745	42	48,692	14
Sweden	2,790	0.32	2	4	165	113	X	182,667	(1)	46,833	(7)
Switzerland	412	0.06	6	6	438	413	2,423	112,386	20	4,034	(23)
United Kingdom	6,600	0.11	2	2	316	350	X	504,927	(1)	49,000	(15)
Yugoslavia (former)	7,730	0.32	2	2	114	99	X	1,086,667	147	9,054	(2)
U.S.S.R. (former)	228,920	0.81	8	9	80	95	X	2,645,067	3	682,500	(6)
Armenia	1,200 c	0.36 c	23 d	25 c	X	39 c	X	13,300 e	3	1,400 e	(7)
Azerbaijan	3,800 c	0.53 c	34 d	37 c	X	38 c	X	38,850 e	10	4,400 e	2
Belarus	9,200 c	0.90 c	2 d	2 c	X	234 c	X	127,050 e	8	31,150 e	12
Estonia	X	X	X	X	X	X	X	21,197 e	X	1,908	X
Georgia	2,800 c	0.51 c	15 d	17 c	X	43 c	X	24,650 e	(2)	1,400 e	(13)
Kazakhstan	197,300 c	11.79 c	1 d	1 c	X	3 c	X	221,050 e	(7)	89,350 e	(18)
Kyrgyzstan	10,000 c	2.28 c	10 d	10 c	X	18 c	X	27,650 e	5	3,800 e	(14)
Latvia	2,531 c	0.94 c	X	X	X	151 c	X	40,749	X	4,341	X
Lithuania	X	X	X	X	X	X	X	49,000	X	7,233	X
Moldova	2,000 c	0.46 c	11 d	15 c	X	122 c	X	50,450 e	(1)	2,450 e	(37)
Russian Federation	212,800 c	1.44 c	2 d	3 c	X	52 c	X	1,368,450 e	3	409,540 e	(9)
Tajikistan	4,100 c	0.77 c	16 d	17 c	X	50 c	X	34,950 e	9	1,500 e	7
Turkmenistan	35,610 c	9.71 c	3 d	3 c	X	7 c	X	45,900 e	24	1,900 e	73
Ukraine	34,629 c	0.67 c	5 f	8 c	X	126 c	X	428,550 e	5	107,850 e	20
Uzbekistan	26,100 c	1.27 c	14 d	16 c	X	41 c	X	154,550 e	(2)	8,350 e	(4)
OCEANIA	48,484	1.79	4	4	37	34	X	400,532	(6)	60,184	(4)
Australia	46,877	2.70	4	4	27	26	X	317,000	(3)	56,700	(2)
Fiji	242	0.33	0	0	74	83	X	4,310	5	X	X
New Zealand	410	0.12	40	68	1,081	899	X	76,000	(17)	3,000	(30)
Papua New Guinea	407	0.10	X	X	21	33	1,367 g	1,143	(17)	471	26
Solomon Islands	57	0.17	X	X	0	0	X	X	X	X	X

Sources: Food and Agriculture Organization of the United Nations, and the United Nations Population Division.
Notes: a. Data for Belgium and Luxembourg are combined under Belgium. b. Data are for 1991. c. Data are for 1990. d. Data are for 1981. e. Data are for 1989 and 1990 only.
f. Data are for 1978. g. Data are for 1988.
0 = zero or less than half of the unit of measure; X = not available; negative numbers are shown in parentheses.
World and regional totals include some countries not listed here.
For additional information, see Sources and Technical Notes.

Table 18.3 Livestock Populations and Grain Consumed as

	Cattle		Sheep and Goats		Pigs		Equines		Buffaloes and Camels		Chickens		Grain Fed to Livestock as Percentage of Total Grain Consumption	
	Annual Average (000) 1990-92	Percent Change Since 1980-82	Annual Average (000) 1990-92	Percent Change Since 1980-82	Annual Average (000) 1990-92	Percent Change Since 1980-82	Annual Average (000) 1990-92	Percent Change Since 1980-82	Annual Average (000) 1990-92	Percent Change Since 1980-82	Annual Average (millions) 1990-92	Percent Change Since 1980-82	1972	1992
WORLD	1,284,680	4	1,785,436	13	861,263	10	119,509	7	164,648	16	17,224	132	41	37
AFRICA	188,461	8	374,048	15	17,769	69	18,934	14	15,710	2	905	54	5	16
Algeria	1,404	(1)	20,750	26	5	7	514	(40)	127	(16)	75	137	0	34
Angola	3,150	(2)	1,760	15	805	29	6	0	X	X	6	6	0	0
Benin	981	16	1,953	(1)	731	54	7	0	X	X	25	114	0	0
Botswana	2,565	(13)	2,411	211	16	220	190	23	X	X	2	100	0	0
Burkina Faso	4,016	43	11,925	64	521	116	441	41	12	9	17	53	0	2
Burundi	436	(10)	1,295	29	104	98	X	X	X	X	4	33	0	0
Cameroon	4,709	29	7,080	67	1,371	28	50	(2)	X	X	18	150	0	0
Central African Rep	2,657	51	1,406	32	435	57	X	X	X	X	3	50	X	X
Chad	4,401	(1)	4,908	(9)	14	54	455	3	561	26	4	33	0	0
Congo	68	7	380	55	52	118	X	X	X	X	2	100	0	0
Cote d'Ivoire	1,145	62	2,070	10	371	16	2	0	X	X	25	39	4	3
Djibouti	173	181	947	(2)	X	X	8	14	60	17	X	X	X	0
Egypt	2,869	54	8,902	122	109	308	1,497	(15)	3,181	29	35	25	0	34
Equatorial Guinea	5	25	44	7	5	7	X	X	X	X	X	X	X	X
Ethiopia	30,333	16	40,820	1	20	9	8,410	37	1,060	7	58	13	0	0
Gabon	28	425	246	33	162	37	X	X	X	X	2	0	0	0
Gambia, The	397	34	283	(7)	11	3	49	18	X	X	1	X	0	0
Ghana	1,282	50	4,814	23	491	29	11	(59)	X	X	11	10	0	5
Guinea	1,800	(0)	970	13	33	(18)	3	(25)	X	X	13	63	0	0
Guinea-Bissau	428	44	472	27	293	12	7	75	X	X	1	X	0	0
Kenya	12,598	23	14,172	8	105	29	2	0	813	34	25	47	2	1
Lesotho	537	(5)	2,520	19	75	8	251	21	X	X	1	0	0	0
Liberia	38	(5)	443	6	120	12	X	X	X	X	4	50	0	0
Libya	127	(14)	6,617	2	X	X	87	(5)	148	(2)	55	493	0	21
Madagascar	10,265	0	2,037	(15)	1,462	13	0	(100)	X	X	22	31	0	0
Malawi	901	6	1,033	28	235	17	2	100	X	X	9	13	0	0
Mali	5,189	(18)	12,735	1	66	36	670	(8)	247	(14)	22	65	0	3
Mauritania	1,383	1	8,740	11	X	X	171	10	977	32	4	33	0	0
Mauritius	34	20	102	28	12	54	X	X	X	X	2	0	0	0
Morocco	3,361	10	20,866	8	9	35	1,617	4	33	(72)	41	56	0	19
Mozambique	1,333	(4)	502	12	168	35	20	0	X	X	22	25	0	0
Namibia	2,106	(2)	5,120	3	51	33	127	7	X	X	X	X	X	X
Niger	1,767	(48)	8,445	(18)	38	19	525	(30)	362	(5)	19	78	0	0
Nigeria	15,160	24	36,594	75	4,334	333	1,172	27	18	4	130	56	0	1
Rwanda	597	(4)	1,480	18	139	8	X	X	X	X	1	0	0	0
Senegal	2,770	19	5,833	86	302	64	720	72	15	137	17	89	0	1
Sierra Leone	333	(8)	424	1	50	32	X	X	X	X	6	38	0	2
Somalia	2,267	(49)	20,000	(30)	6	(32)	46	(1)	5,000	(17)	2	(33)	53	4
South Africa	13,498	1	38,345	0	1,487	10	454	1	X	X	40	28	32	35
Sudan	21,070	8	37,429	19	X	X	702	(0)	2,766	2	33	20	0	0
Swaziland	736	13	370	7	28	77	13	(20)	X	X	1	0	0	0
Tanzania	13,134	2	12,411	28	327	139	175	6	X	X	23	19	0	3
Togo	300	28	3,388	195	739	230	5	200	X	X	7	233	0	17
Tunisia	630	8	7,516	29	6	58	363	11	230	34	41	56	15	26
Uganda	5,004	2	5,250	48	851	238	17	6	X	X	19	39	0	0
Zaire	1,600	36	3,980	16	830	21	X	X	X	X	21	32	0	0
Zambia	2,986	29	612	83	294	27	2	100	X	X	17	(2)	2	5
Zimbabwe	5,798	7	3,157	115	289	74	129	11	X	X	13	41	8	11
ASIA	392,882	11	735,135	22	442,958	20	44,338	11	146,405	17	11,036	359	9	16
Afghanistan	1,650	(56)	15,650	(28)	X	X	1,684	(3)	265	0	7	5	0	0
Bangladesh	23,481	7	21,168	111	X	X	X	X	801	68	67	22	0	0
Bhutan	414	34	88	206	73	31	54	32	4	(29)	X	X	X	0
Cambodia	2,175	134	X	X	1,641	408	18	116	768	90	8	118	X	X
China	79,455	50	209,397	12	370,436	19	26,863	16	22,172	15	8,380	790	12	19
India	192,576	2	158,690	18	10,450	7	2,588	27	80,092	16	380	121	1	3
Indonesia	10,892	55	17,167	43	7,150	112	750	18	3,349	35	582	213	2	8
Iran, Islamic Rep	7,043	26	69,086	36	0	(100)	2,279	(14)	494	34	165	60	11	18
Iraq	1,408	(5)	10,300	(22)	X	X	366	(30)	156	(37)	42	7	0	19
Israel	341	14	487	31	95	(7)	11	0	10	(9)	23	(7)	55	60
Japan	4,883	12	67	(15)	11,367	13	24	3	X	X	331	14	36	48
Jordan	31	10	2,299	54	X	X	26	5	18	26	47	62	18	40
Korea, Dem People's Rep	1,300	35	687	26	3,267	48	50	18	X	X	29	59	0	0
Korea, Rep	2,304	41	346	57	5,026	160	5	60	X	X	76	75	5	39
Kuwait	10	(51)	174	(53)	X	X	1	X	2	(59)	7	(31)	0	15
Lao People's Dem Rep	909	98	133	150	1,449	24	36	7	1,102	26	8	47	0	0
Lebanon	69	25	690	17	44	130	38	138	1	X	20	(10)	26	36
Malaysia	699	25	593	44	2,740	39	5	0	205	(24)	149	184	4	42
Mongolia	2,814	16	65,014	241	188	443	2,252	12	553	(7)	0	X	X	X
Myanmar	9,383	6	1,321	30	2,376	(8)	127	4	2,086	6	24	(6)	X	X
Nepal	6,261	(10)	6,269	15	588	54	X	X	3,038	24	7	17	0	0
Oman	138	0	868	11	X	X	26	8	90	76	3	350	0	0
Pakistan	17,711	14	63,338	32	X	X	3,972	31	18,878	48	155	149	3	4
Philippines	1,654	(14)	2,259	29	8,010	2	200	(9)	2,660	(7)	66	16	11	21
Saudi Arabia	207	(41)	9,351	50	X	X	112	(4)	416	42	80	219	0	71
Singapore	0	(100)	1	(78)	277	(69)	X	X	0	(100)	4	(74)	15	28
Sri Lanka	1,606	(5)	516	(3)	87	8	2	0	893	2	9	44	0	0
Syrian Arab Rep	773	(2)	16,147	41	1	50	232	(30)	6	(30)	15	7	0	29
Thailand	6,372	47	294	314	4,943	39	19	(18)	4,764	(21)	125	104	2	29
Turkey	11,841	(25)	52,772	(21)	10	(19)	1,734	(28)	381	(63)	100	76	26	33
United Arab Emirates	52	94	960	93	X	X	X	X	119	91	7	163	0	0
Viet Nam	3,151	87	419	121	12,207	23	143	19	2,864	23	80	53	0	0
Yemen	X	X	X	X	X	X	X	X	X	X	X	X	X	0

Feed, 1972–92

Table 18.3

	Cattle		Sheep and Goats		Pigs		Equines		Buffaloes and Camels		Chickens		Grain Fed to Livestock as Percentage of Total Grain Consumption	
	Annual Average (000) 1990-92	Percent Change Since 1980-82	Annual Average (000) 1990-92	Percent Change Since 1980-82	Annual Average (000) 1990-92	Percent Change Since 1980-82	Annual Average (000) 1990-92	Percent Change Since 1980-82	Annual Average (000) 1990-92	Percent Change Since 1980-82	Annual Average (millions) 1990-92	Percent Change Since 1980-82	1972	1992
NORTH & CENTRAL AMERICA	163,063	(7)	34,839	(2)	89,053	(8)	21,760	3	9	13	1,898	30		
Belize	52	4	5	25	26	59	9	0	X	X	1	X	X	X
Canada	12,698	(5)	845	5	10,390	5	421	12	X	X	114	21	77	75
Costa Rica	1,737	(23)	5	36	225	(5)	126	1	X	X	4	(25)	16	46
Cuba	4,847	(5)	487	6	1,867	30	664	(21)	X	X	28	15	0	0
Dominican Rep	2,320	21	674	28	650	459	594	40	X	X	28	121	24	42
El Salvador	1,246	14	20	11	312	(23)	121	7	X	X	4	(20)	27	20
Guatemala	2,069	(0)	751	7	1,107	48	161	10	X	X	10	(27)	7	27
Haiti	1,383	26	1,292	19	920	(14)	725	3	X	X	13	135	0	2
Honduras	2,388	18	35	21	741	80	263	3	X	X	8	60	11	39
Jamaica	317	13	442	12	250	15	37	(5)	X	X	8	60	0	31
Mexico	31,224	9	16,629	1	15,830	(10)	12,550	1	X	X	255	38	19	35
Nicaragua	1,651	(29)	10	11	695	25	303	(7)	X	X	7	62	13	15
Panama	1,396	(3)	5	(17)	246	17	158	21	X	X	8	56	7	23
Trinidad and Tobago	60	(20)	66	18	50	(17)	5	0	9	13	10	29	0	34
United States	98,872	(13)	13,015	(9)	55,327	(13)	5,580	9	X	X	1,383	29	81	69
SOUTH AMERICA	273,242	12	125,944	2	53,655	4	22,224	12	1,480	167	922	30		
Argentina	50,227	(7)	29,586	(13)	4,590	19	3,629	11	X	X	49	21	49	42
Bolivia	5,643	23	8,882	(18)	2,193	33	1,032	(3)	X	X	26	271	23	38
Brazil	150,034	24	31,903	16	33,058	(1)	9,520	16	1,479	167	555	22	44	58
Chile	3,400	(9)	7,150	7	1,377	24	565	16	X	X	30	54	23	36
Colombia	24,502	1	3,514	12	2,642	26	3,315	12	X	X	43	34	15	24
Ecuador	4,513	45	1,789	22	2,327	(33)	915	46	X	X	55	48	10	31
Guyana	225	28	207	9	59	(41)	3	0	X	X	13	(3)	0	3
Paraguay	7,894	26	521	9	2,541	152	390	10	X	X	18	51	0	2
Peru	4,035	2	13,936	(16)	2,411	13	1,370	1	X	X	60	59	18	35
Suriname	94	88	19	115	31	65	X	X	1	X	8	60	0	0
Uruguay	9,040	(20)	25,650	27	215	(25)	475	(4)	X	X	9	44	45	16
Venezuela	13,611	26	2,055	21	2,201	(6)	1,008	0	X	X	56	26	20	32
EUROPE	119,428	(10)	157,961	14	178,582	2	5,593	(21)	330	(24)	1,235	0		
Albania	578	(5)	2,397	14	187	(1)	178	46	2	0	5	36	0	0
Austria	2,543	0	344	52	3,680	(6)	51	23	X	X	13	(9)	62	66
Belgium {a}	3,310	7	160	41	6,524	28	21	(39)	X	X	35	20	55	38
Bulgaria	1,448	(19)	8,085	(27)	3,850	1	464	(5)	25	(49)	28	(30)	48	49
Czechoslovakia (former)	4,792	(4)	1,040	7	7,242	(5)	38	(15)	X	X	47	4	63	68
Denmark	2,216	(24)	132	148	9,798	1	34	(21)	X	X	15	0	86	85
Finland	1,314	(24)	64	(40)	1,332	(11)	46	38	X	X	5	(36)	76	62
France	21,104	(11)	11,997	(14)	12,330	7	364	(2)	X	X	200	9	68	61
Germany	12,207	X	1,967	X	18,961	X	328	X	X	X	76	X	X	57
Greece	625	(29)	15,066	18	1,096	11	252	(43)	1	(25)	27	(9)	53	55
Hungary	1,530	(21)	1,823	(41)	7,218	(13)	79	(36)	X	X	44	(29)	73	74
Iceland	73	24	700	(12)	19	76	70	35	X	X	X	X	0	0
Ireland	6,000	1	5,999	151	1,067	(3)	69	(25)	X	X	9	4	67	66
Italy	8,297	(5)	11,996	18	8,880	(0)	381	(22)	97	(3)	138	(0)	62	42
Netherlands	4,953	(5)	1,881	122	13,716	34	65	5	X	X	103	22	62	42
Norway	979	(2)	2,300	4	725	7	19	18	X	X	4	0	68	73
Poland	9,038	(25)	3,099	(23)	21,139	7	927	(47)	X	X	55	(25)	62	47
Portugal	1,361	0	6,556	22	2,558	(28)	276	(9)	X	X	18	2	52	49
Romania	5,342	(15)	15,466	(7)	11,543	(1)	706	16	180	(20)	114	20	53	63
Spain	5,038	6	27,641	55	16,829	51	470	(24)	X	X	51	(3)	66	64
Sweden	1,733	(11)	424	4	2,248	(17)	55	1	X	X	12	(10)	75	74
Switzerland	1,822	(8)	470	11	1,739	(18)	51	8	X	X	6	0	63	57
United Kingdom	11,796	(10)	29,586	36	7,427	(5)	180	13	X	X	122	7	59	50
Yugoslavia (former)	4,536	(17)	7,282	(1)	6,975	(12)	304	(49)	26	(54)	67	10	54	59
U.S.S.R. (former)	115,327	(0)	140,325	(6)	74,534	1	6,174	4	715	24	1,154	19	60	X
Armenia	583	(25)	1,133	(50)	267	19	X	X	X	X	10	(9)	X	X
Azerbaijan	1,833	2	5,400	(0)	167	(12)	37 b	131 b	X	X	29	40	X	X
Belarus	6,914	2	433	(26)	4,985	9	217 b	42 b	X	X	51	30	X	X
Estonia	757	(7)	141	(23)	946	(10)	9 b	93 b	X	X	7	0	X	X
Georgia	1,275	(19)	1,567	(25)	919	(5)	21 b	121 b	X	X	22	18	X	X
Kazakhstan	9,733	13	35,500	1	3,167	4	X	X	X	X	60	23	X	X
Kyrgyzstan	1,200	22	10,000	(1)	367	14	313 b	262 b	X	X	14	39	X	X
Latvia	1,431	0	175	(16)	1,401	(18)	31 b	(11) b	X	X	10	(6)	X	X
Lithuania	2,314	4	65	(4)	2,449	(4)	79 b	2 b	X	X	17	19	X	X
Moldova	1,074	(9)	1,192	1	1,735	(11)	47 b	176 b	X	X	25	42	X	X
Russian Federation	56,840	(2)	58,267	(11)	37,899	5	2,616 b	208 b	X	X	655	17	X	X
Tajikistan	1,400	13	3,367	11	167	7	52 b	346 b	X	X	8	21	X	X
Turkmenistan	833	29	5,500	22	300	70	19 b	338 b	X	X	8	44	X	X
Ukraine	24,506	(4)	8,219	(9)	19,067	(5)	741 b	(12) b	X	X	248	7	X	X
Uzbekistan	4,633	31	9,367	4	700	35	103 b	278 b	X	X	36	38	X	X
OCEANIA	32,277	(5)	217,183	5	4,711	11	487	(25)	X	X	74	26		
Australia	23,485	(7)	160,621	18	2,646	8	311	(36)	X	X	56	21	58	55
Fiji	159	4	121	41	14	(7)	43	10	X	X	3	80	0	0
New Zealand	8,205	2	56,357	(19)	404	(4)	94	18	X	X	10	45	48	49
Papua New Guinea	104	(18)	6	50	1,003	14	2	67	X	X	3	50	0	0
Solomon Islands	13	(44)	X	X	53	16	X	X	X	X	X	X	X	X

Sources: Food and Agriculture Organization of the United Nations and the U.S. Department of Agriculture.
Notes: a. Data for Belgium and Luxembourg are combined under Belgium. b. Horses only.
World and regional totals for livestock populations include data for countries not listed here.
0 = zero or less than half of the unit of measure; X = not available; negative numbers are shown in parentheses.
For additional information, see Sources and Technical Notes.

Table 18.4 Food Trade and Aid, 1979–91

	Average Annual Net Trade in Food						Average Annual Donations or Receipts of Food Aid					
	Cereals (000 metric tons)		Oils (metric tons)		Pulses (metric tons)		Cereals				Oils (metric tons)	Milk (metric tons)
							(000 metric tons)		Kg Per Capita			
	1979-81	1989-91	1979-81	1989-91	1979-81	1989-91	1978-80	1988-90	1978-80	1988-90	1987-89	1987-89
WORLD												
AFRICA	16,720	25,587	1,287,005	2,143,983	154,129	186,456	3,529	5,167	8	8	223,984	65,111
Algeria	3,036	6,273	255,939	464,186	88,150	135,803	14	18	1	1	941	460
Angola	341	314	34,952	54,628	41,221	31,994	13	100	2	11	3,336	2,297
Benin	64	118	(19,528)	(10,333)	207	233	7	13	2	3	987	463
Botswana	63	113	(156)	1,333	(413)	1,100	12	30	14	25	2,917	3,915
Burkina Faso	68	146	4,580	4,733	(1,792)	(2,000)	45	45	7	5	2,645	3,775
Burundi	17	17	1,899	1,264	0	0	9	4	2	1	222	90
Cameroon	132	258	(4,411)	(17,121)	(79)	(1)	6	3	1	0	X	52
Central African Rep	14	31	274	2,159	22	1	2	3	1	1	220	20
Chad	22	48	0	0	0	0	29	22	7	4	624	528
Congo	68	86	2,186	5,273	7	178	4	3	2	2	113	19
Cote d'Ivoire	465	567	(86,973)	(161,108)	254	1,367	1	15	0	1	51	68
Djibouti	27	58	113	4,525	1,824	921	4	9	15	22	269	255
Egypt	6,114	8,107	511,897	783,591	96,918	59,310	1,850	1,427	46	28	53,989	6,687
Equatorial Guinea	2	12	0	1,972	67	37	0	2	0	7	2	0
Ethiopia	285	650	3,234	35,700	(29,522)	7,405	117	646	3	13	20,207	8,912
Gabon	30	55	2,325	(2,628)	24	26	1	0	1	0	X	1
Gambia, The	45	93	(8,713)	1,837	0	0	11	13	17	15	569	614
Ghana	192	302	10,443	7,043	210	470	89	76	8	5	6,006	1,410
Guinea	137	203	3,154	11,179	0	(118)	30	31	7	6	297	405
Guinea-Bissau	35	55	261	1,083	64	73	19	12	25	13	451	251
Kenya	143	205	88,355	162,204	(8,773)	(18,793)	36	97	2	4	1,428	82
Lesotho	101	92	X	X	1,803	4,970	30	40	23	23	2,734	2,274
Liberia	102	133	(4,149)	(1,246)	146	1,423	2	37	1	15	135	21
Libya	708	1,992	60,715	84,902	14,635	6,667	0	0	0	0	0	0
Madagascar	207	98	17,209	18,996	(4,442)	(4,712)	9	62	1	5	9,966	1,553
Malawi	32	116	6,066	8,818	(7,235)	(5,638)	3	168	1	18	132	192
Mali	94	126	(5,887)	(4,197)	12	0	25	42	4	5	1,064	567
Mauritania	146	254	7,932	14,583	0	67	36	65	24	33	1,178	949
Mauritius	169	200	21,197	22,106	7,697	9,439	13	21	13	19	26	150
Morocco	2,047	1,639	172,110	189,398	(28,477)	(25,122)	137	265	7	11	49,385	3,213
Mozambique	343	473	9,177	60,793	(1,040)	19,333	136	469	12	33	12,764	4,173
Namibia	0	8	X	X	8,000	8,000	0	2	0	1	67	0
Niger	61	110	4,822	12,813	(22,824)	(23,273)	17	47	3	6	905	942
Nigeria	1,893	556	189,951	55,748	26,098	(73)	0	0	0	0	X	37
Rwanda	13	16	1,319	11,899	(810)	5,848	13	6	3	1	1,671	1,001
Senegal	477	683	(43,801)	(66,163)	428	1,012	96	74	18	10	839	1,438
Sierra Leone	96	157	(1,743)	4,114	17	0	16	44	5	11	1,275	894
Somalia	262	191	15,874	15,850	657	4,500	99	106	15	12	17,447	5,194
South Africa	(3,362)	(1,464)	18,325	142,480	1,192	(18,062)	X	X	X	X	X	0
Sudan	3	658	(13,791)	63,229	10,315	20,667	138	383	8	16	5,458	2,438
Swaziland	31	53	127	1,000	0	0	1	10	1	13	570	1,008
Tanzania	202	32	8,730	41,187	(37,765)	(41,028)	81	58	5	2	1,093	3,532
Togo	47	131	457	(379)	194	319	12	13	5	4	1,564	516
Tunisia	884	1,321	15,196	56,532	(13,594)	5,442	177	392	29	50	1,209	1,097
Uganda	34	(3)	0	17,567	333	(7,899)	6	27	0	2	4,938	1,216
Zaire	412	338	(23,804)	(3,676)	967	0	58	113	2	3	202	1,079
Zambia	325	109	11,453	15,862	492	(482)	77	72	14	9	11,751	297
Zimbabwe	(121)	(454)	8,893	17,670	(1,103)	(1,929)	0	12	0	1	192	144
ASIA	63,377	78,790	164,337	(1,011,870)	(55,359)	3,859	4,049	3,252	2	1	273,548	86,836
Afghanistan	91	249	1,163	6,333	(5,500)	0	105	204	7	13	360	0
Bangladesh	1,372	1,794	129,569	320,892	395	90,642	1,418	1,283	17	12	20,997	128
Bhutan	5	17	X	X	X	X	1	3	1	2	492	318
Cambodia	241	28	2,575	0	293	0	65	11	10	1	1,169	0
China	15,906	14,700	309,368	2,010,380	(15,726)	(588,047)	(32)	(0)	(0)	(0)	2,346	0
India	(380)	(344)	1,338,454	376,716	126,630	583,537	275	329	0	0	77,891	35,908
Indonesia	2,740	2,082	(358,598)	(1,344,124)	2,419	51,138	857	142	6	1	499	3,819
Iran, Islamic Rep	2,666	6,170	288,968	689,532	20,961	32,354	0	15	0	0	196	0
Iraq	2,694	3,125	166,906	257,967	28,667	51,689	3	33	0	2	0	X
Israel	1,671	1,769	4,113	26,442	11,677	20,783	29	2	8	0	X	48
Japan	23,677	26,860	400,073	549,997	198,088	180,899	(392)	(477)	(3)	(4)	(800)	0
Jordan	493	1,266	15,014	49,352	8,484	23,257	106	101	37	26	946	291
Korea, Dem People's Rep	272	750	15,170	12,250	X	X	0	0	0	0	X	X
Korea, Rep	5,880	9,886	195,779	394,466	10,551	11,755	391	0	10	0	X	X
Kuwait	286	408	6,928	21,547	8,884	8,490	0	0	0	0	X	X
Lao People's Dem Rep	107	48	X	X	0	0	27	22	9	5	35	0
Lebanon	574	489	21,265	51,643	40,333	17,500	75	41	28	15	6,315	3,088
Malaysia	1,415	2,517	(2,384,608)	(5,869,545)	38,119	66,973	0	4	0	0	X	X
Mongolia	124	34	1,200	1,224	X	X	X	X	X	X	X	0
Myanmar	(643)	(199)	28,800	99,147	(66,767)	(127,267)	11	0	0	0	X	0
Nepal	7	10	4,987	16,667	(6,615)	(7,080)	11	13	1	1	467	1,415
Oman	103	291	2,009	18,803	1,625	5,790	X	X	X	X	X	X
Pakistan	(101)	796	474,725	1,036,027	3,987	115,033	261	502	3	4	154,411	2,368
Philippines	796	1,998	(896,135)	(876,181)	3,192	35,768	95	224	2	4	1,030	24,398
Saudi Arabia	3,123	3,682	100,964	112,812	23,078	48,285	(12)	(61)	(1)	(4)	X	(200)
Singapore	709	534	12,196	141,291	9,778	21,958	0	0	0	0	X	X
Sri Lanka	849	1,024	(12,123)	15,550	16,835	38,497	244	288	17	17	55	6,851
Syrian Arab Rep	705	1,732	18,287	22,510	(65,567)	(66,530)	69	48	8	4	1,320	1,248
Thailand	(5,111)	(5,753)	51,769	16,631	(207,475)	(159,726)	4	92	0	2	2,144	68
Turkey	(631)	582	118,918	555,636	(274,384)	(522,694)	(1)	6	(0)	0	183	0
United Arab Emirates	279	342	23,313	57,440	8,377	23,043	X	X	X	X	X	X
Viet Nam	1,377	(1,197)	3,982	(20,926)	(1,189)	(569)	372	82	7	1	1,812	1,142
Yemen	X	X	X	X	X	X	35	115	4	10	X	X

Table 18.4

	Average Annual Net Trade in Food						Average Annual Donations or Receipts of Food Aid					
	Cereals		Oils		Pulses		Cereals				Oils	Milk
	(000 metric tons)		(metric tons)		(metric tons)		(000 metric tons)		Kg Per Capita		(metric tons)	(metric tons)
	1979-81	1989-91	1979-81	1989-91	1979-81	1989-91	1978-80	1988-90	1978-80	1988-90	1987-89	1987-89
NORTH & CENTRAL AMERICA	(118,727)	(103,525)	(2,003,346)	(89,930)	(403,729)	(637,648)	(6,347)	(5,942)	(19)	(15)	(445,819)	(121,891)
Belize	10	15	1,620	1,445	(31)	(47)	0	2	0	11	X	X
Canada	(19,309)	(22,099)	518,879	486,254	17,696	12,577	(783)	(1,064)	(33)	(40)	(59,359)	(9,417)
Costa Rica	113	333	165,680	443,792	(351)	17,733	1	126	0	43	137	86
Cuba	2,097	2,301	182,837	206,429	(45)	1,278	0	0	0	0	1,331	X
Dominican Rep	345	659	21,758	39,513	(19)	(68)	63	171	11	24	34,289	2,366
El Salvador	125	218	511,899	458,629	(39)	13,151	6	208	1	41	22,581	5,303
Guatemala	180	292	(972,441)	(515,474)	(138)	(148)	8	251	1	28	14,478	8,048
Haiti	191	300	49,265	108,353	768	77,751	56	127	11	20	5,213	4,535
Honduras	101	212	(161,457)	249,522	20	(13)	16	116	5	23	2,715	5,145
Jamaica	384	327	39,686	12,709	(110)	(41)	112	246	53	102	710	2,415
Mexico	5,905	6,640	(93,815)	264,676	(26,965)	(92,046)	0	221	0	3	4,117	16,009
Nicaragua	122	160	145,852	269,364	(8,777)	(15,912)	26	58	10	16	8,272	2,886
Panama	79	111	7,937	532	245	325	2	0	1	0	13	17
Trinidad and Tobago	237	254	22,224	14,618	0	(0)	0	0	0	0	X	X
United States	(109,579)	(93,537)	(1,308,006)	(1,236,522)	129	0	(5,855)	(6,417)	(26)	(26)	(480,326)	(162,344)
SOUTH AMERICA	(2,347)	(1,697)	(1,211,201)	(2,585,776)	(69,369)	6,492	240	558	1	2	20,210	27,569
Argentina	(14,293)	(9,525)	(732,540)	(2,396,984)	(163,441)	(149,255)	(33)	(16)	(1)	(0)	X	22
Bolivia	301	193	26,115	(2,468)	166	(3,802)	111	160	20	23	4,583	7,930
Brazil	6,052	3,857	(1,019,049)	(712,253)	34,977	82,087	3	18	0	0	0	7,231
Chile	1,201	281	71,873	68,432	(69,750)	(62,489)	28	11	3	1	8	1,629
Colombia	653	734	134,623	101,936	31,523	62,780	8	36	0	1	102	27
Ecuador	329	458	45,005	48,275	1,367	1,869	8	53	1	5	3,198	1,729
Guyana	(30)	4	6,063	547	3,389	4,000	1	49	2	62	2,575	741
Paraguay	60	(275)	(12,401)	(34,902)	61	(3,064)	11	2	4	0	22	369
Peru	1,273	1,399	43,407	57,404	3,524	9,647	101	245	6	12	9,690	7,872
Suriname	(51)	(25)	349	4,567	1,400	3,700	0	0	0	0	X	X
Uruguay	(128)	(422)	(6,574)	(8,635)	1,400	2,430	2	0	1	0	X	15
Venezuela	2,278	1,624	231,158	286,835	85,622	58,027	X	X	X	X	X	X
EUROPE	23,029	(23,479)	1,388,229	1,064,705	514,254	866,553	(1,075)	(2,397)	(2)	(5)	(91,578) a	(116,435) a
Albania	21	156	9,957	23,533	(300)	1,077	X	X	X	X	X	X
Austria	(166)	(795)	82,701	74,290	5,730	8,548	(0)	(22)	(0)	(3)	X	0
Belgium {b}	2,389	2,595	36,487	(130,591)	72,290	405,156	(49)	(33)	(5)	(3)	X	0
Bulgaria	385	476	(28,097)	(15,258)	63	(4,961)	X	X	X	X	X	X
Czechoslovakia (former)	1,735	72	41,450	17,462	6,533	(41,833)	X	X	X	X	X	X
Denmark	(490)	(2,516)	11,248	19,401	(2,695)	(235,166)	(31)	(36)	(6)	(7)	(353)	(0)
Finland	390	(554)	5,826	4,102	4,545	3,329	(25)	(18)	(5)	(4)	(6,328)	(2,405)
France	(17,883)	(28,826)	293,754	4,895	(54,285)	(1,096,591)	(161)	(224)	(3)	(4)	(2,467)	(384)
Germany	X	(1,003)	X	(12,649)	X	254,317	(144)	(282)	(2)	(4)	(6,905)	(3,208)
Greece	162	(729)	(23,170)	(59,752)	8,636	35,688	(0)	(6)	(0)	(1)	0	X
Hungary	(800)	(1,507)	(142,939)	(259,685)	(45,111)	(210,221)	0	0	0	0	X	X
Iceland	27	23	894	2,661	337	263	0	0	0	0	X	X
Ireland	347	(22)	21,440	12,843	7,875	31,411	(4)	(3)	(1)	(1)	0	0
Italy	5,771	4,599	355,280	485,963	108,044	434,065	(56)	(133)	(1)	(2)	(1,459)	(354)
Netherlands	3,487	3,141	133,941	1,149	186,920	802,256	(80)	(124)	(6)	(8)	(4,770)	(6,739)
Norway	679	373	259	14,579	6,039	4,594	(10)	(38)	(3)	(9)	(1,057)	0
Poland	7,391	1,353	133,685	46,920	109	(249,475)	0	528	0	14	910	1,755
Portugal	3,507	1,399	(8,109)	21,327	5,368	43,238	339	0	35	0	11	0
Romania	900	901	(99,383)	23,500	6,467	67	0	0	0	0	X	0
Spain	4,882	1,024	(315,027)	(162,265)	54,350	301,238	(0)	(33)	(0)	(1)	0	X
Sweden	(836)	(1,132)	45,901	53,051	4,008	13,381	(102)	(110)	(12)	(13)	(20,520)	0
Switzerland	1,211	530	43,380	30,076	12,660	11,856	(32)	(57)	(5)	(8)	(176)	(2,584)
United Kingdom	2,533	(3,548)	677,064	825,487	19,306	(109,704)	(82)	(144)	(1)	(3)	0	0
Yugoslavia (former)	988	(191)	50,124	38,094	5,775	8,341	0	0	0	0	X	X
U.S.S.R. (former)	30,979	35,497	389,371	718,479	(35,733)	(32,843)	X	X	X	X	X	X
Armenia	X	X	X	X	X	X	X	X	X	X	X	X
Azerbaijan	X	X	X	X	X	X	X	X	X	X	X	X
Belarus	X	X	X	X	X	X	X	X	X	X	X	X
Estonia	X	X	X	X	X	X	X	X	X	X	X	X
Georgia	X	X	X	X	X	X	X	X	X	X	X	X
Kazakhstan	X	X	X	X	X	X	X	X	X	X	X	X
Kyrgyzstan	X	X	X	X	X	X	X	X	X	X	X	X
Latvia	X	X	X	X	X	X	X	X	X	X	X	X
Lithuania	X	X	X	X	X	X	X	X	X	X	X	X
Moldova	X	X	X	X	X	X	X	X	X	X	X	X
Russian Federation	X	X	X	X	X	X	X	X	X	X	X	X
Tajikistan	X	X	X	X	X	X	X	X	X	X	X	X
Turkmenistan	X	X	X	X	X	X	X	X	X	X	X	X
Ukraine	X	X	X	X	X	X	X	X	X	X	X	X
Uzbekistan	X	X	X	X	X	X	X	X	X	X	X	X
OCEANIA	(13,863)	(13,600)	(315,687)	(358,894)	(43,125)	(411,875)	(287)	(336)	(13)	(13)	(1,594)	(1,392)
Australia	(14,161)	(14,275)	(128,010)	(91,377)	(5,394)	(372,197)	(299)	(338)	(21)	(20)	(1,511)	(1,185)
Fiji	82	100	(5,590)	2,312	3,686	5,663	9	2	14	2	0	0
New Zealand	(32)	177	(76,479)	(68,003)	(42,172)	(46,233)	X	X	X	X	(83)	(230)
Papua New Guinea	142	250	(67,886)	(167,697)	63	28	0	0	0	0	0	X
Solomon Islands	5	18	(15,111)	(21,341)	10	10	0	0	0	0	X	X

Sources: Food and Agriculture Organization of the United Nations and the United Nations Population Division.
Notes: a. Total includes European Community action. b. Data for Belgium and Luxembourg are combined under Belgium.
World and regional totals for net trade include some countries not listed here. Totals for food aid do not add because of rounding.
Imports and food aid receipts are shown as positive numbers; exports and food aid donations are shown as negative numbers in parentheses.
0 = zero or less than half of the unit of measure; X = not available; negative numbers are shown in parentheses.
For additional information, see Sources and Technical Notes.

Table 18.5 Agricultural Productivity, Research

	Agricultural Gross Domestic Product (AGDP) {a}				Agricultural Labor Force (percentage of total labor force)		Total Public Agricultural Research Expenditures (millions of 1980 I$)			Total Number of BSc-Equivalent Researchers (full-time equivalents)		
	Total (millions of I$) 1985	Per Capita (I$) 1985	Per Hectare of Arable Land (I$) 1985	Per Labor Unit (I$) 1985	1970	1990	1961-65	1971-75	1981-85	1961-65	1971-75	1981-85
WORLD					55	47						
AFRICA					74	63						
Algeria	1,153	53	154	891	47	24	7.75	13.52	21.33	49	117	305
Angola	449	51	132	168	78	70	5.76	4.31	4.33	29	37	28
Benin	X	X	X	X	81	61	3.34	5.09	2.30	9	22	47
Botswana	X	X	X	X	85	63	0.56	2.10	5.84	4	24	56
Burkina Faso	468	60	154	128	88	84	0.97	2.33	17.38	6	17	120
Burundi	493	104	372	211	94	91	0.69	1.53	4.41	11	20	55
Cameroon	953	95	137	373	83	61	2.04	2.96	15.45	43	97	176
Central African Rep	X	X	X	X	83	63	2.36	3.94	2.07	14	34	22
Chad	395	79	125	278	90	75	2.43	3.32	1.64	13	31	28
Congo	X	X	X	X	65	60	0.92	1.13	2.63	21	24	73
Cote d'Ivoire	1,581	159	442	655	77	56	10.20	25.54	28.83	68	179	201
Djibouti	X	X	X	X	X	X	X	X	X	X	X	X
Egypt	4,097	88	1,641	744	52	41	16.84	23.32	44.73	569	2,070	4,246
Equatorial Guinea	X	X	X	X	75	56	X	X	X	X	X	X
Ethiopia	2,428	56	174	167	85	75	2.45	5.24	11.82	10	53	136
Gabon	X	X	X	X	80	68	1.23	1.14	2.63	6	7	24
Gambia, The	X	X	X	X	86	81	0.41	0.65	2.82	4	7	62
Ghana	1,094	85	407	428	58	50	6.36	4.49	2.88	70	111	147
Guinea	418	84	576	242	85	74	2.26	3.06	8.77	23	28	177
Guinea-Bissau	X	X	X	X	84	79	0.46	0.47	0.77	4	4	8
Kenya	1,682	84	710	253	85	77	12.86	26.28	27.14	129	332	462
Lesotho	X	X	X	X	90	80	0.22	0.82	5.98	2	9	18
Liberia	X	X	X	X	77	70	0.51	0.58	5.24	7	17	33
Libya	X	X	X	X	29	14	8.69	17.07	20.11	97	103	127
Madagascar	1,174	115	386	324	84	77	5.80	11.27	6.63	58	71	82
Malawi	547	75	230	219	91	75	2.45	3.68	4.92	22	38	82
Mali	645	82	311	301	89	81	1.38	1.58	13.78	11	24	275
Mauritania	X	X	X	X	85	64	0.60	1.51	0.57	4	5	12
Mauritius	X	X	X	X	34	23	2.04	3.74	5.41	28	55	100
Morocco	1,692	77	201	623	58	37	10.32	17.47	25.16	117	111	217
Mozambique	680	50	220	110	86	82	6.45	6.95	7.94	32	25	77
Namibia	X	X	X	X	51	35	X	X	X	X	X	X
Niger	382	58	108	124	94	87	1.20	1.80	1.92	6	12	57
Nigeria	5,161	56	166	215	71	65	20.64	62.81	80.06	172	348	1,003
Rwanda	632	104	565	226	94	91	1.38	1.96	2.09	9	16	34
Senegal	471	74	200	210	83	78	7.95	13.61	14.75	60	63	174
Sierra Leone	X	X	X	X	76	62	1.78	2.27	1.44	20	27	46
Somalia	897	141	875	456	79	70	2.00	0.39	0.38	8	9	31
South Africa	3,786	120	288	2,132	33	14	X	X	X	X	X	X
Sudan	2,382	109	188	511	77	60	7.14	12.27	12.07	45	76	206
Swaziland	X	X	X	X	81	66	0.31	1.82	3.07	6	12	14
Tanzania	2,172	96	649	235	90	81	7.07	20.53	19.73	107	127	276
Togo	X	X	X	X	77	70	0.78	1.90	5.86	6	18	58
Tunisia	865	119	185	1,285	42	24	3.28	9.93	14.70	39	113	121
Uganda	1,729	111	262	294	89	81	6.41	7.47	12.51	71	148	185
Zaire	2,263	74	290	283	79	66	6.79	6.69	3.96	45	64	43
Zambia	X	X	X	X	77	69	2.29	3.87	4.01	25	76	110
Zimbabwe	844	102	309	361	77	68	8.28	14.61	16.62	107	133	166
ASIA					70	60						
Afghanistan	X	X	X	X	66	55	1.72	2.95	4.00	24	44	80
Bangladesh	5,052	50	553	244	81	69	21.76	28.24	68.42	296	635	927
Bhutan	X	X	X	X	94	91	X	X	X	X	X	X
Cambodia	X	X	X	X	78	70	X	X	X	X	X	X
China	X	X	X	X	78	67	486.65	874.84	1,712.68	7,469	11,781	36,335
India	56,256	73	333	282	72	66	116.12	253.79	450.02	2,939	5,666	8,389
Indonesia	13,458	80	638	399	66	48	40.65	73.90	141.11	415	449	1,349
Iran, Islamic Rep	4,325	91	290	1,043	44	28	23.30	94.02	82.26	322	563	493
Iraq	1,116	70	205	1,070	47	21	6.37	9.28	37.94	101	162	542
Israel	568	134	1,352	6,963	10	4	16.24	22.37	45.46	300	417	550
Japan	5,897	49	1,239	1,160	20	6	404.40	780.63	1,021.60	12,535	13,798	14,779
Jordan	X	X	X	X	28	6	1.20	1.52	1.47	20	27	57
Korea, Dem People's Rep	X	X	X	X	53	34	X	X	X	X	X	X
Korea, Rep	2,945	72	1,374	579	49	25	8.92	25.70	50.03	521	887	1,356
Kuwait	X	X	X	X	X	X	0.30	0.60	1.20	2	4	8
Lao People's Dem	X	X	X	X	79	72	1.45	1.45	1.45	29	29	29
Lebanon	X	X	X	X	20	9	2.99	4.85	2.93	41	120	67
Malaysia	2,632	168	539	1,170	54	32	14.02	71.24	110.85	151	295	811
Mongolia	X	X	X	X	48	30	X	X	X	X	X	X
Myanmar	X	X	X	X	59	47	1.49	3.35	11.96	21	55	267
Nepal	1,069	63	431	163	94	92	2.61	8.97	10.75	61	202	446
Oman	X	X	X	X	57	40	0.27	0.58	3.93	3	6	42
Pakistan	8,238	80	400	520	59	50	13.49	18.25	74.28	893	1,551	2,972
Philippines	6,510	118	824	666	55	47	17.61	41.93	28.62	375	972	1,965
Saudi Arabia	292	25	134	196	64	39	4.20	9.10	23.43	42	91	171
Singapore	X	X	X	X	3	1	1.10	1.50	2.82	7	10	19
Sri Lanka	1,414	88	754	455	55	52	6.74	12.83	21.40	74	148	391
Syrian Arab Rep	1,174	112	209	1,648	50	24	2.99	11.87	6.59	15	112	217
Thailand	7,352	143	370	408	80	64	38.99	55.49	77.80	308	585	1,676
Turkey	8,397	167	305	722	71	48	18.45	57.26	107.40	397	630	1,612
United Arab Emirates	X	X	X	X	14	3	0.30	0.70	1.25	3	6	12
Viet Nam	X	X	X	X	77	61	X	X	X	X	X	X
Yemen	X	X	X	X	X	X	X	X	X	X	X	X

Personnel, and Expenditures, 1961–90

Table 18.5

	Agricultural Gross Domestic Product (AGDP) {a}				Agricultural Labor Force (percentage of total labor force)		Total Public Agricultural Research Expenditures (millions of 1980 I$)			Total Number of BSc-Equivalent Researchers (full-time equivalents)		
	Total (millions of I$) 1985	Per Capita (I$) 1985	Per Hectare of Arable Land (I$) 1985	Per Labor Unit (I$) 1985	1970	1990	1961-65	1971-75	1981-85	1961-65	1971-75	1981-85
NORTH & CENTRAL AMERICA					14	11						
Belize	X	X	X	X	X	X	0.22	0.48	0.70	5	11	16
Canada	6,164	245	134	11,618	8	3	148.83	258.30	421.37	1,879	2,252	2,737
Costa Rica	482	183	922	1,937	43	24	2.19	3.44	2.78	51	60	114
Cuba	X	X	X	X	30	19	X	X	X	X	X	X
Dominican Rep *	810	126	567	1,010	55	36	0.56	1.59	3.95	8	12	136
El Salvador *	492	103	673	830	56	37	2.92	3.52	5.41	49	77	131
Guatemala *	828	104	451	678	61	51	2.00	6.04	7.34	22	63	160
Haiti *	525	98	582	297	74	64	0.86	0.80	1.65	39	42	32
Honduras *	512	117	288	672	65	55	1.37	2.29	2.57	21	56	65
Jamaica	X	X	X	X	33	27	2.48	4.86	2.39	44	79	48
Mexico	9,872	124	400	1,113	44	30	11.47	36.44	128.99	191	444	1,058
Nicaragua *	362	111	286	860	52	37	3.00	3.00	5.11	24	29	65
Panama	X	X	X	X	42	25	0.87	1.01	6.08	7	23	115
Trinidad and Tobago	X	X	X	X	19	7	X	X	X	X	X	X
United States	64,544	270	340	19,328	4	2	844.69	1,140.77	1,423.86	12,061	13,313	14,366
SOUTH AMERICA					38	23						
Argentina	11,434	377	420	9,024	16	10	47.59	67.62	61.70	520	867	1,062
Bolivia *	708	111	315	811	52	42	1.69	3.96	2.29	29	51	103
Brazil	25,101	185	480	1,832	45	24	60.25	173.39	292.27	657	2,181	3,794
Chile	1,355	112	312	2,256	23	13	11.08	27.17	26.87	134	228	271
Colombia	3,697	124	700	1,306	39	27	33.35	40.50	47.82	326	559	454
Ecuador *	1,261	135	497	1,294	51	30	3.36	16.24	13.32	34	138	211
Guyana	X	X	X	X	32	22	0.37	3.87	4.30	7	38	50
Paraguay	1,086	294	499	1,817	53	46	0.64	2.06	10.15	10	26	86
Peru *	1,520	78	411	659	47	35	6.14	19.39	20.34	121	217	262
Suriname	X	X	X	X	25	17	0.91	0.94	0.82	13	19	22
Uruguay	1,048	348	790	6,195	19	14	2.01	4.03	4.12	33	75	77
Venezuela	1,656	96	439	2,122	26	11	20.37	42.46	35.89	130	316	383
EUROPE					20	9						
Albania	X	X	X	X	66	48	X	X	X	X	X	X
Austria	1,566	207	1,027	6,155	15	6	6.28	12.86	18.35	145	222	285
Belgium	1,353 b	132 b	1,665 b	13,976 b	5 b	2 b	20.13	30.23	41.70	610	568	496
Bulgaria	X	X	X	X	35	12	X	X	X	X	X	X
Czechoslovakia (former)	X	X	X	X	17	9	X	X	X	X	X	X
Denmark	1,857	363	711	11,419	11	5	28.91	27.46	33.66	413	411	457
Finland	903	184	375	3,683	20	8	15.51	20.39	32.40	242	341	405
France	15,251	276	793	9,214	14	5	56.83	175.25	241.36	1,143	1,558	2,361
Germany	8,061 c	132 c	1,082 c	6,022 c	9	5	X	X	X	X	X	X
Greece	2,987	301	758	2,852	42	24	8.88	17.04	25.02	253	371	460
Hungary	3,164	297	598	4,180	25	12	X	X	X	X	X	X
Iceland	X	X	X	X	17	7	1.51	3.05	3.54	39	42	77
Ireland	2,039	576	1,976	9,655	26	14	18.11	25.04	24.72	276	345	400
Italy	13,543	237	1,118	6,473	19	7	46.46	67.71	181.30	995	1,200	2,327
Netherlands	4,206	290	4,716	15,973	7	4	56.69	154.33	189.66	832	1,249	1,630
Norway	471	113	549	3,476	12	5	21.09	37.49	57.82	410	551	759
Poland	X	X	X	X	39	21	X	X	X	X	X	X
Portugal	1,059	104	335	1,174	32	16	11.18	18.95	22.09	298	376	449
Romania	X	X	X	X	49	20	X	X	X	X	X	X
Spain	8,242	214	404	4,379	26	11	21.85	38.23	88.44	589	637	1,249
Sweden	1,213	145	415	6,136	8	4	22.54	46.43	54.27	415	650	1,013
Switzerland	1,064	165	2,583	6,515	8	4	11.63	21.34	18.87	130	189	286
United Kingdom	6,464	114	916	10,190	3	2	136.41	276.33	346.81	2,220	3,113	3,814
Yugoslavia (former)	3,927	170	505	1,415	50	22	X	X	X	X	X	X
U.S.S.R. (former)	X	X	X	X	26	13	X	X	X	X	X	X
Armenia	X	X	X	X	X	X	X	X	X	X	X	X
Azerbaijan	X	X	X	X	X	X	X	X	X	X	X	X
Belarus	X	X	X	X	X	X	X	X	X	X	X	X
Estonia	X	X	X	X	X	X	X	X	X	X	X	X
Georgia	X	X	X	X	X	X	X	X	X	X	X	X
Kazakhstan	X	X	X	X	X	X	X	X	X	X	X	X
Kyrgyzstan	X	X	X	X	X	X	X	X	X	X	X	X
Latvia	X	X	X	X	X	X	X	X	X	X	X	X
Lithuania	X	X	X	X	X	X	X	X	X	X	X	X
Moldova	X	X	X	X	X	X	X	X	X	X	X	X
Russian Federation	X	X	X	X	X	X	X	X	X	X	X	X
Tajikistan	X	X	X	X	X	X	X	X	X	X	X	X
Turkmenistan	X	X	X	X	X	X	X	X	X	X	X	X
Ukraine	X	X	X	X	X	X	X	X	X	X	X	X
Uzbekistan	X	X	X	X	X	X	X	X	X	X	X	X
OCEANIA					22	16						
Australia	8,758	545	185	20,240	8	5	131.63	229.44	236.08	2,118	3,519	4,579
Fiji	X	X	X	X	51	39	1.44	3.72	4.98	12	31	38
New Zealand	3,824	1,178	7,484	26,752	12	9	29.46	60.64	76.63	509	776	1,324
Papua New Guinea *	709	205	1,850	593	84	67	3.75	7.71	20.34	59	107	140
Solomon Islands *	X	X	X	X	X	X	0.48	0.63	0.58	7	8	11

Sources: The Food and Agriculture Organization of the United Nations and the International Service for National Agriculture Research
Notes: a. AGDP estimates are in international dollars (I$) based on purchasing power parities (PPPs); for further information concerning PPPs, see Technical Notes 15.1 and 18.5. b. Data are for Belgium and Luxembourg. c. Data are for the former Federal Republic of Germany.
* Low-income, food-deficit countries, see Technical Notes.
0 = zero or less than half of the unit of measure; X = not available; negative numbers are shown in parentheses.
For additional information, see Sources and Technical Notes.

Sources and Technical Notes

Table 18.1   Food and Agricultural Production, 1980–92

Source: Food and Agriculture Organization of the United Nations (FAO), *Agrostat-PC*, on diskette (FAO, Rome, July 1993).

Indexes of agricultural and food production portray the disposable output (after deduction for feed and seed) of a country's agriculture sector relative to the base period 1979–81. For a given year and country, the index is calculated as follows: the disposable average output of a commodity in terms of weight or volume during the period of interest is multiplied by the 1979–81 average national producer price per unit. The product of this equation represents the total value of the commodity for that period in terms of the 1979–81 price. The values of all crop and livestock products are totaled to an aggregated value of agricultural production in 1979–81 prices. The ratio of this aggregate for a given year to that for 1979–81 is multiplied by 100 to obtain the index number.

The multiplication of disposable outputs with the 1979–81 unit value eliminates inflationary or deflationary distortion. However, the base period's relative prices among the individual commodities are also preserved. Especially in economies with high inflation, price patterns among agricultural commodities can change dramatically over time. To overcome the latter problem, the FAO generally shifts the base period every five years.

The continental and world index numbers for a given year are calculated by totaling the disposable outputs of all relevant countries for each agricultural commodity. Each of these aggregates is multiplied by a respective 1979–81 average "international" producer price and summed in a total agricultural output value for that region or the world in terms of 1979–81 prices. The total agricultural output value for a given year is then divided by the "international" 1979–81 output value and multiplied by 100 to obtain the continental and world index values. This method avoids distortion caused by the use of international exchange rates.

The agricultural production index includes all crop and livestock products originating in each country. The food production index covers all edible agricultural products that contain nutrients. Coffee and tea have virtually no nutritive value and thus are excluded.

Crop yields (*average yields of cereals* and *average yields of roots and tubers*) are calculated from production and area data. *Average production of cereals* includes cereal production for feed and seed. Area refers to the area harvested. Cereals comprise all cereals harvested for dry grain, exclusive of crops cut for hay or harvested green. Roots and tubers cover all root crops grown principally for human consumption; root crops grown principally for feed are excluded.

Most of the data in Tables 18.1–18.5 are supplied by national agriculture ministries in response to annual FAO questionnaires or are derived from decennial agricultural censuses. The FAO compiles data from more than 200 country reports and from many other sources and enters them into a computerized data base. The FAO fills gaps in these data by preparing its own estimates. As better information becomes available, the FAO corrects its estimates and recalculates the entire time series when necessary.

Table 18.2   Agricultural Inputs, 1979–91

Source: Food and Agriculture Organization of the United Nations (FAO), *Agrostat-PC*, on diskette (FAO, Rome, July 1993). Per capita figures: United Nations Population Division, *Interpolated National Populations, 1950–2025 (The 1992 Revision)*, on diskette (United Nations, New York, 1993).

Crop land refers to land under temporary and permanent crops, temporary meadows, market and kitchen gardens, and temporarily fallow land. Permanent crop land is land under crops that does not need to be replanted after each harvest, such as cocoa, coffee, rubber, fruit trees, and vines. Human population data used to calculate *hectares per capita* are for 1991. For trends in crop land area, see Table 17.1.

Irrigated land as a percentage of crop land refers to areas purposely provided with water, including land flooded by river water for crop production or pasture improvement, whether this area is irrigated several times or only once during the year.

Average annual fertilizer use refers to application of nutrients in terms of nitrogen (N), phosphate (P_2O_5), and potash (K_2O). The fertilizer year is July 1–June 30; data refer to the year beginning in July.

Data on *pesticide consumption* were compiled by FAO. Data are expressed in net weight of active ingredients in the pesticides used. The active ingredients in a pesticide are the chemicals with pesticidal properties. In a pesticide formulation, active ingredients are often mixed with inert ingredients, which dilute or deliver the active ingredients. Inert ingredients can exert their own toxic effects in the environment.

Active ingredients vary widely in potency; information on pesticide ingredients is necessary to ensure accurate application and to minimize harmful environmental effects. For example, 1 metric ton of the modern synthetic pyrethroid insecticide permethrin is as potent a pesticide as 3–5 metric tons of a carbamate or an organophosphate or 10–30 metric tons of DDT. The data shown in this table do not describe the potency of the active ingredients used. As a result, two countries with similar levels of pesticide use may be treating different amounts of land and getting different results. Increasingly potent pesticides have been developed in recent years; thus,

a smaller amount of active ingredients used may not indicate a smaller amount of toxic materials introduced into the environment.

Tractors generally refer to wheel and crawler tractors used in agriculture. Garden tractors are excluded. *Harvesters* refer to harvesters and threshers.

Table 18.3   Livestock Populations and Grain Consumed as Feed, 1972–92

Sources: Livestock data: Food and Agriculture Organization of the United Nations (FAO), *Agrostat-PC*, on diskette (FAO, Rome, July 1993). Feed data: Economic Research Service, U.S. Department of Agriculture (USDA), *PS&D View '92*, on diskette (USDA, Washington, D.C., 1993).

Data on livestock include all animals in the country, regardless of place or purpose of their breeding. Data on livestock numbers are collected annually by the FAO; estimates are made by the FAO for countries that either do not report data or only partially report data. *Equines* include horses, mules, and asses. For some countries, data on *chickens* include all poultry. *Grain fed to livestock as percentage of total grain consumption* was calculated using USDA grain consumption and feed numbers. Grains include wheat, rice (milled weight), corn, barley, sorghum, millet, rye, oats, and mixed grains. Grain consumption is the total domestic use during the local marketing year of the individual country. It is the sum of feed, food, seed, and industrial uses.

Table 18.4   Food Trade and Aid, 1979–91

Sources: Trade and food aid data: Food and Agriculture Organization of the United Nations (FAO), *Agrostat-PC*, on diskette (FAO, Rome, July 1993). Population data: United Nations Population Division, *Interpolated National Populations, 1950–2025 (The 1992 Revision)*, on diskette (United Nations, New York, 1993).

Figures shown for food trade are *net imports or exports*: exports were subtracted from imports.

Two definitions of trade are used by countries reporting trade data. "Special trade" refers only to imports for domestic consumption and exports of domestic goods. "General trade" encompasses total imports and total exports, including reexports. In some cases, trade figures include goods purchased by a country that are reexported to a third country without ever entering the purchasing country. For information on the definition used by a particular country, see the *FAO Trade Yearbook 1992* (FAO, Rome, 1993).

Average annual donations or receipts of food aid are shown as either positive or negative numbers: receipts are shown as positive numbers and donations as negative numbers. For countries that are both recipients and donors of food aid, donations were subtracted from receipts.

Trade in *cereals* includes wheat and wheat flour, rice, barley, maize, rye, and oats. Trade in *oils* includes oils from soybeans, groundnuts (peanuts), olives, cottonseeds, sunflower seeds, rape/mustard seeds, linseeds, palms, coconuts, palm-kernels, castor beans, and maize, as well as animal oils, fats, and greases (including lard). Trade in *pulses* includes all kinds of dried leguminous vegetables, with the exception of vetches and lupins.

Food aid refers to the donation or concessional sale of food commodities. *Cereals* include wheat, rice, coarse grains, bulgur wheat, wheat flour, and the cereal component of blended foods. Cereal donations or receipts *(kilograms per capita)* are the result of dividing the three-year averages by the respective 1978–80 and 1988–90 three-year population averages, provided by the United Nations Population Division. *Oils* include vegetable oil and butter oil. *Milk* includes skimmed milk powder and other dairy products (mainly cheese).

Food aid data are reported by donor countries and international organizations.

Table 18.5 Agricultural Productivity, Research Personnel, and Expenditures, 1961–1990

Sources: Low-income, food-deficit countries: Idriss Jazairy, Mohiuddin Alamgir, and Theresa Panuccio, *The State of World Rural Poverty; An Inquiry into Its Causes and Consequences* (International Fund for Agricultural Development, New York, 1992); agricultural gross domestic product (AGDP) total, per capita, per hectare of arable land, and per labor unit: D.S. Prasada Rao, *Intercountry Comparisons of Agricultural Output and Productivity*, Food and Agricultural Organization of the United Nations (FAO) Economic and Social Development Paper 112 (FAO, Rome, 1993) and FAO *Quarterly Bulletin of Statistics*, Vol. 5, No. 4 (1992); labor force: FAO, *Agrostat-PC 1993*, on diskette (FAO, Rome, 1993); total number of BSc-equivalent researchers and total public agricultural research expenditures: P.G. Pardey and J. Roseboom, *ISNAR Agricultural Research Indicator Series: A Global Data Base on National Agricultural Research Systems* (Cambridge University Press, Cambridge, United Kingdom, 1989); P.G.

Pardey, J. Roseboom, and J.R. Anderson, *Agricultural Research Policy: International Quantitative Perspectives* (Cambridge University Press, Cambridge, United Kingdom, 1991); and S. Fan and P.G. Pardey, *Agricultural Research in China: Its Institutional Development and Impact* (International Service for National Agricultural Research, The Hague, 1992).

Low-income, food-deficit countries, as defined by FAO, are indicated with an asterisk. Low-income countries are those with a per capita income below the level used by the World Bank to determine eligibility for International Development Association assistance (i.e., GNP per capita of $635 or less in 1991). Food-deficit countries are those where food supplies are not sufficient to meet the population's demands; such countries neither produce enough food to meet population demand nor do they export enough commodities to pay for the imports needed to meet the demand. The Guidelines and Criteria for Food Aid agreed to by the Committee on Food Aid Policies and Programmes indicate that low-income, food-deficit countries should be given priority in the allocation of food aid.

The International Comparisons Project (ICP) discussed in Technical Note 15.1 is the most extensive effort to compare real gross domestic products (GDPs) using the expenditure approach. This approach results in purchasing power parities of currencies that are useful for comparing GDPs of different countries. However, since ICP parities are based on prices paid by end users, they include trade and marketing margins and therefore are not suitable for sectoral comparisons across countries. Any measure of agricultural output involves a valuation process and the value aggregate depends upon the prices used for valuation. Uniformity of valuation is essential for comparability across countries. To derive the value added figures for *agricultural gross domestic product*, farm-gate prices were used both for valuing agricultural production revenue (transport and marketing expenses were not included) and for purchasing prices of agricultural inputs used for production. Input prices include all distribution charges, transport costs, and taxes. By utilizing producer prices received and paid by farmers at the farm gate, a more accurate measure of revenues and expenditures components of the production account results.

The basket of goods used for calculating the purchasing power parities included 185 commodities. The result represented the number of currency units required to purchase a common basket of commodities.

For the 42 countries that had detailed information for nonagricultural inputs, the AGDP was calculated using the double deflation procedure (deflating the inputs and outputs). For the remaining 61 countries of the FAO study, the AGDP is extrapolated using a regression model based on the AGDP comparisons of the 42 countries for which there are data. For further information, refer to Intercountry Comparisons of Agricultural Output and Productivity (FAO, 1993).

Agricultural labor force refers to all economically active persons who furnish labor for the production of agricultural goods and services during the reference period, as a percentage of total labor force. For additional information, see the Technical Notes for Tables 16.1 and 17.2.

Number of BSc-equivalent researchers includes all researchers in a country's public, semipublic, and academic agricultural research institutes. National as well as expatriate researchers are included, with the proviso that they should hold at least a BSc degree. Agricultural research is defined here as all research in support of crop, livestock, forestry, and fisheries production. Explicitly not included are researchers working for international and commercial organizations. For institutes with a mandate broader than research (e.g., universities), research staff time has been expressed in full-time equivalents. However, no attempt has been made to eliminate the time spent by researchers on meetings, administration, vacation, sick leave, and so on.

Public agricultural *research expenditures* include the expenditures of the agricultural research institutes described above. For institutes with a broader mandate than research, only the research component has been included. Where possible, actual expenditures by the institutes are included, not the expenditures budgeted by funding agencies. The expenditure data include all salary, operating, and capital expenses. These data were collected in current local currency, deflated to base year 1980 using local, implicit GDP deflators, and then converted to international dollars using 1980 purchasing power parities (for more information, see Technical Note 15.1).

19. Forests and Rangelands

This chapter contains summary data from two new studies of forest resources—one covering tropical countries; the second, temperate developed countries—recently released by two United Nations agencies: the Food and Agriculture Organization (FAO) and the Economic Commission for Europe. These studies provide estimates of much of the world's forest cover in 1990, as well as estimates of forest loss over the preceding decade. Data on wood production and trade are presented at the end of this chapter.

Of the world's estimated 3.4 billion hectares of forests in 1990, tropical forests covered 1.76 billion hectares, while forests in industrialized countries extended over 1.43 billion hectares. (The 1980 estimate of temperate forest extent for developing countries, 0.2 billion hectares, has been included in the 1990 global total.) During 1981–90, tropical forests were lost at a rate of 0.8 percent (15.4 million hectares) a year. While most of the countries of the temperate developed regions experienced a slight increase in forest and other wooded land area during this period, no comparable data exist to provide a regional rate of forest change.

Table 19.1 provides country- and regional-level information on forest extent in 1980 and 1990, annual rates of deforestation and logging, plantation establishment, and protected area coverage in forest zones. Estimates of forest extent and deforestation in the tropics were standardized to common classifications and years using a model. For this reason, these data may not be as accurate as individual country inventories based on satellite imagery and more complete ground data (results of some of these latter inventories are provided in the Technical Notes to this table).

The former U.S.S.R., with 755 million hectares of forest, and Brazil, with 561 million hectares, accounted for 39 percent of the world's natural forest cover in 1990. Net annual deforestation during 1981–90 exceeded 2 percent in 10 tropical countries, all located in either Asia or the Americas. Brazil and Indonesia accounted for the largest extent of forest area lost annually, with deforestation levels of 3.7 million hectares and 1.2 million hectares on average per year, respectively (although annual deforestation rates were close to the global average–0.6 percent for Brazil and 1.0 percent for Indonesia).

Annual logging of closed tropical broadleaf forests during the 1980s averaged 5.6 million hectares, or 0.5 percent of the total broadleaf forest area. Eighty-four percent of this logging occurred in primary (undisturbed) forests.

Data on tropical forest extent and loss by ecosystem type are presented in Table 19.2, the first comprehensive data set of this nature available by country. Of the world's tropical forests in 1990, 41 percent were rainforests, 34 percent were moist deciduous forests, 14 percent were dry, very dry or desert forests, and 12 percent were hill or montane forests. Of these categories, the world's very dry forests declined at the slowest annual rate (0.5 percent) during 1981–90, followed by rainforests (0.6 percent), while hill and montane forests declined at the highest annual rate (1.1 percent). Jamaica lost 5.7 percent of this latter forest type per year during 1981–90, while 11 other countries lost at least 2 percent of their hill and montane forests annually during the 1980s. Forest loss in certain dry zones is also of concern: in Asia, almost 3 percent of forests in very dry areas were lost annually, while annual deforestation rates in the Americas were highest in desert areas, averaging 2 percent during 1981–90.

Logging is a contributing factor to forest degradation and, indirectly, to deforestation. Table 19.3 provides several measures of this activity at country, regional and global levels. Global roundwood production increased 19 percent between 1979–81 and 1989–91. This increase was highest in Africa, where production rose by one third during this period. Most of the roundwood cut in Africa (about 90 percent) is used for fuelwood and charcoal, as opposed to industrial purposes, such as for construction or paper production. Globally, about half of the roundwood produced in 1989–91 was used for heating and cooking.

Net trade in roundwood during this period was highest in Asia, almost 50 million cubic meters per year. This was largely a reflection of Japan's demand for wood; it was the world's largest net importer of roundwood during 1989–91. Net exporting regions, that is, all areas except Asia and Europe, experienced an increase in annual roundwood trade between 1979–81 and 1989–91, except for Africa, where trade volume dropped about 23 percent.

Table 19.1 Forests Resources, 1980–90

	Extent of Forest and Woodland (000 ha)				Annual Deforestation Total Forest			Annual Logging of Closed Broadleaf Forest, 1981-90			Plantations (000 ha)		Protected Forest (000 ha)
	1990		1980		1981-90		1981-85		% of	% That		Annual	
	Natural Forest	Other Wooded Land	Natural Forest	Other Wooded Land	Extent (000 ha)	(%)	Extent (000 ha)	Extent (000 ha)	Closed Forest	Is Primary Forest	Extent 1990	Change 1981-90	Protected Forest (000 ha)
WORLD													
AFRICA													
North Africa	X	X	5,490	3,775	X	X	58	X	X	X	X	X	X
Algeria	X	X	1,767	2,168	X	X	40	X	X	X	X	X	X
Egypt	X	X	X	X	X	X	X	X	X	X	X	X	X
Libya	X	X	190	446	X	X	X	X	X	X	X	X	X
Morocco	X	X	3,236	1,161	X	X	13	X	X	X	X	X	X
Tunisia	X	X	297	X	X	X	5	X	X	X	X	X	X
West Sahelian Africa	40,768	X	43,720	X	295	0.7	388	6	0.2	78	251	21	X
Burkina Faso	4,416	X	4,735	X	32	0.7	80	0	0.0	0	28	2	X
Cape Verde	6	X	6	X	0	0.0	X	X	X	X	14	1	X
Chad	11,434	X	12,320	X	89	0.7	80	0	0.0	81	6	0	X
Gambia, The	97	X	105	X	1	0.8	5	0	1.1	0	1	0	10 a
Guinea-Bissau	2,021	X	2,180	X	16	0.7	57	5	0.6	90	1	0	0 a
Mali	12,144	X	13,207	X	106	0.8	36	0	0.0	0	20	2	X
Mauritania	554	X	554	X	0	0.0	13	0	0.1	0	3	0	X
Niger	2,550	X	2,550	X	0	0.0	67	0	0.0	0	17	1	X
Senegal	7,544	X	8,063	X	52	0.6	50	0	0.0	5	160	15	85 a
East Sahelian Africa	65,450	X	71,395	X	595	0.8	695	4	0.1	65	762	32	X
Djibouti	22	X	22	X	0	0.0	X	X	X	X	0	0	X
Ethiopia	14,165	X	14,552	X	39	0.3	88	0	0.0	92	270	17	1,157 a
Kenya	1,187	X	1,256	X	7	0.5	39	2	0.6	86	168	2	X
Somalia	754	X	782	X	3	0.4	14	1	0.6	0	6	(1)	X
Sudan	42,976	X	47,793	X	482	1.0	504	0	0.0	0	290	13	X
Uganda	6,346	X	6,991	X	65	0.9	50	1	0.1	61	28	0	448 a
West Africa	55,607	X	61,520	X	591	1.0	1,199	312	2.0	47	445	14	1,166 a
Benin	4,947	X	5,644	X	70	1.2	67	0	0.3	57	20	1	0 a
Cote d'Ivoire	10,904	X	12,097	X	119	1.0	510	85	7.6	34	90	5	710 a
Ghana	9,555	X	10,930	X	138	1.3	72	11	0.7	19	75	2	95 a
Guinea	6,692	X	7,558	X	87	1.1	86	9	0.5	87	5	0	14 a
Liberia	4,633	X	4,887	X	25	0.5	46	79	1.7	87	8	0	131 a
Nigeria	15,634	X	16,821	X	119	0.7	400	127	2.3	31	216	5	216 a
Sierra Leone	1,889	X	2,011	X	12	0.6	6	1	0.2	0	8	0	1 a
Togo	1,353	X	1,571	X	22	1.4	12	1	0.3	47	24	2	0 a
Central Africa	204,112	X	215,503	X	1,140	0.5	575	571	0.4	90	175	11	11,195 a
Cameroon	20,350	X	21,569	X	122	0.6	110	333	4.5	89	23	2	1,127 a
Central African Rep	30,562	X	31,854	X	129	0.4	55	3	0.0	93	9	1	436 a
Congo	19,865	X	20,188	X	32	0.2	22	78	0.4	89	53	4	1,215 a
Equatorial Guinea	1,826	X	1,896	X	7	0.4	3	5	0.3	88	0	0	315 a
Gabon	18,235	X	19,398	X	116	0.6	15	126	0.7	93	30	1	1,790 a
Zaire	113,275	X	120,597	X	732	0.6	370	26	0.0	95	60	4	6,313 a
Tropical Southern Africa	145,868	X	159,322	X	1,345	0.8	700	9	0.1	38	1,057	47	X
Angola	23,074	X	24,812	X	174	0.7	94	1	0.0	5	171	1	X
Botswana	14,261	X	15,029	X	77	0.5	20	X	X	X	1	0	X
Burundi	233	X	247	X	1	0.6	1	0	0.0	0	132	11	38 a
Malawi	3,486	X	4,011	X	53	1.3	150	0	0.0	0	180	10	X
Mozambique	17,329	X	18,683	X	135	0.7	120	1	0.0	40	40	1	X
Namibia	12,569	X	13,000	X	43	0.3	30	X	X	X	0	0	X
Rwanda	164	X	168	X	0	0.2	5	1	0.4	5	125	6	15 a
Tanzania	33,555	X	37,936	X	438	1.2	130	2	0.2	77	220	12	7,701 a
Zambia	32,301	X	35,931	X	363	1.0	70	5	0.2	34	68	3	X
Zimbabwe	8,897	X	9,506	X	61	0.6	80	0	0.2	14	120	2	X
Temperate Southern Africa	X	X	1,421	2,803	X	X	X	X	X	X	X	X	X
South Africa	X	X	1,347 b	2,803	X	X	X	X	X	X	X	X	X
Swaziland	X	X	74	X	X	X	0	X	X	X	X	X	X
Insular Africa	15,782	X	17,128	X	135	0.8	157	20	0.3	31	310	4	X
Comoros	X	X	X	X	X	X	1	X	X	X	X	X	X
Madagascar	15,782	X	17,128	X	135	0.8	156	20	0.3	31	310	4	579 a
Mauritius	X	X	X	X	X	X	0	X	X	X	X	X	X
ASIA													
Temperate and Middle East Asia	X	X	186,084	57,314	X	X	20	X	X	X	X	X	X
Afghanistan	X	X	1,210	690	X	X	X	X	X	X	X	X	X
China	X	X	115,047	27,730	X	X	X	X	X	X	X	X	387 a
Cyprus	140	140	278 c	X	(0)	(0.1)	X	X	X	X	X	X	X
Iran, Islamic Rep	X	X	3,750	14,250	X	X	20	X	X	X	X	X	X
Iraq	X	X	1,230	300	X	X	X	X	X	X	X	X	X
Israel	102	22	X	X	X	X	X	X	X	X	X	X	X
Japan	24,158	560	24,766 c	X	5	0.0	X	X	X	X	X	155 d	X
Jordan	X	X	50	75	X	X	X	X	X	X	X	X	X
Korea, Dem People's Rep	X	X	4,800 b	4,200	X	X	X	X	X	X	X	X	X
Korea, Rep	X	X	4,887 b	X	X	X	X	X	X	X	X	X	X
Lebanon	X	X	20	45	X	X	X	X	X	X	X	X	X
Mongolia	X	X	9,528 b	4,335	X	X	X	X	X	X	X	X	X
Saudi Arabia	X	X	200	1,400	X	X	X	X	X	X	X	X	X
Syrian Arab Rep	X	X	150	239	X	X	X	X	X	X	X	X	X
Turkey	8,856	11,343	20,168 c	X	(3)	(0.0)	X	X	X	X	X	X	X
Yemen	X	X	X	4,050	X	X	X	X	X	X	X	X	X
South Asia	63,931	X	69,442	X	551	0.8	307	62	0.2	17	19,758	1,480	2,971 a
Bangladesh	769	X	1,145	X	38	3.3	8	15	2.5	7	335	18	74 a
Bhutan	2,809	X	2,973	X	16	0.6	1	2	0.2	79	5	0	X
India	51,729	X	55,119	X	339	0.6	147	42	0.1	18	18,900	1,441	2,266 a
Nepal	5,023	X	5,567	X	55	1.0	84	X	X	X	80	6	X
Pakistan	1,855	X	2,623	X	77	2.9	9	X	X	X	240	6	X
Sri Lanka	1,746	X	2,015	X	27	1.3	58	3	0.2	3	198	9	631 a

Table 19.1

	Extent of Forest and Woodland (000 ha)				Annual Deforestation Total Forest			Annual Logging of Closed Broadleaf Forest, 1981-90			Plantations (000 ha)		Protected
	1990		1980		1981-90		1981-85		% of	% That		Annual	Forest
	Natural Forest	Other Wooded Land	Natural Forest	Other Wooded Land	Extent (000 ha)	(%)	Extent (000 ha)	Extent (000 ha)	Closed Forest	Is Primary Forest	Extent 1990	Change 1981-90	(000 ha)
Continental South East Asia	75,240	X	88,377	X	1,314	1.5	709	304	0.5	76	3,197	140	7,703 a
Cambodia	12,163	X	13,477	X	131	1.0	30	3	0.0	88	0	0	2,035 a
Lao People's Dem Rep	13,173	X	14,467	X	129	0.9	130	9	0.1	94	6	0	X
Myanmar	28,856	X	32,862	X	401	1.2	105	198	0.7	90	335	28	564 a
Thailand	12,735	X	17,888	X	515	2.9	379	37	0.5	45	756	42	4,479 a
Viet Nam	8,312	X	9,683	X	137	1.4	65	58	1.2	45	2,100	70	625 a
Insular South East Asia	135,426	X	154,687	X	1,926	1.2	967	1,721	1.5	85	9,156	482	15,291 a
Indonesia	109,549	X	121,669	X	1,212	1.0	620	1,223	1.4	86	8,750	474	13,788 a
Malaysia	17,583	X	21,546	X	396	1.8	255	455	2.6	85	116	9	1,326 a
Philippines	7,831	X	10,991	X	316	2.9	92	41	0.5	62	290	(1)	178 a
Singapore	4	X	4	X	0	0.0	X	X	X	X	0	0	0 a
THE AMERICAS													
Temperate North America	456,737	292,552	X	X	X	X	X	X	X	X	X	X	X
Canada	247,164	206,136	X	X	X	X	X	X	X	X	X	231 d	X
United States	209,573	86,416	299,154 c	X	317	0.1	X	X	X	X	X	X	X
Central America and Mexico	68,096	X	79,216	X	1,112	1.4	1,022	90	0.4	65	273	17	X
Costa Rica	1,428	X	1,923	X	50	2.6	65	34	2.6	27	40	4	X
El Salvador	123	X	155	X	3	2.1	5	X	X	X	6	1	X
Guatemala	4,225	X	5,038	X	81	1.6	90	3	0.1	50	40	3	X
Honduras	4,605	X	5,720	X	112	1.9	90	2	0.1	19	4	0	X
Mexico	48,586	X	55,366	X	678	1.2	615	4	0.0	94	155	8	X
Nicaragua	6,013	X	7,254	X	124	1.7	121	45	0.9	92	20	2	X
Panama	3,117	X	3,761	X	64	1.7	36	3	0.1	71	9	1	X
Caribbean Subregion	47,115	X	48,333	X	122	0.3	26	42	0.1	73	442	23	X
Belize	1,996	X	2,046	X	5	0.2	9	3	0.2	5	3	0	X
Cuba	1,715	X	1,888	X	17	0.9	2	3	0.2	8	350	19	X
Dominican Rep	1,077	X	1,428	X	35	2.5	4	0	0.0	61	10	0	X
Guyana	18,416	X	18,597	X	18	0.1	3	9	0.0	91	12	1	X
Haiti	23	X	38	X	2	3.9	2	1	7.7	11	12	1	X
Jamaica	239	X	507	X	27	5.3	2	1	0.4	91	21	1	X
Suriname	14,768	X	14,895	X	13	0.1	3	11	0.1	94	12	0	X
Trinidad and Tobago	155	X	192	X	4	1.9	1	3	1.8	4	18	0	X
Nontropical South America	X	X	52,540 b	25,170	X	X	50	X	X	X	X	X	X
Argentina	X	X	44,500 b	16,500	X	X	X	X	X	X	X	X	X
Chile	X	X	7,550 b	8,550	X	X	50	X	X	X	X	X	X
Uruguay	X	X	490 b	120	X	X	X	X	X	X	X	X	X
Tropical South America	802,904	X	864,639	X	6,174	0.7	4,604	2,445	0.4	90	7,922	333	X
Bolivia	49,317	X	55,564	X	625	1.1	117	12	0.0	71	40	1	X
Brazil	561,107	X	597,816	X	3,671	0.6	2,530	1,982	0.5	93	7,000	279	X
Colombia	54,064	X	57,734	X	367	0.6	890	108	0.2	94	180	13	X
Ecuador	11,962	X	14,342	X	238	1.7	340	152	1.3	96	64	2	X
Paraguay	12,859	X	16,884	X	403	2.4	212	49	1.8	19	13	1	X
Peru	67,906	X	70,618	X	271	0.4	270	89	0.1	85	263	13	X
Venezuela	45,690	X	51,681	X	599	1.2	245	54	0.1	39	362	24	X
EUROPE													
Albania	1,046	403	1,448 c	X	(0)	(0.0)	X	X	X	X	X	3 e	X
Austria	3,877	X	3,735 c	X	(14)	(0.4)	X	X	X	X	X	16 e	X
Belgium	620	X	601 c	X	(2)	(0.3)	X	X	X	X	X	X	X
Bulgaria	3,386	298	3,605 c	X	(8)	(0.2)	X	X	X	X	X	45 e	156
Czechoslovakia (former)	4,491	X	4,471 c	X	(2)	(0.0)	X	X	X	X	X	59 e	198
Denmark	466	X	456 c	X	(1)	(0.2)	X	X	X	X	X	6 e	X
Finland	20,112	3,261	23,318 c	X	(6)	(0.0)	X	X	X	X	X	134 e	X
France	13,110	1,044	14,074 c	X	(8)	(0.1)	X	X	X	X	X	46 f	391
Germany	10,490	245	10,266 c	X	(47)	(0.5)	X	X	X	X	X	29 e,g	177
Greece	2,512	3,520	6,023 c	X	(1)	(0.0)	X	X	X	X	X	1 f	281
Hungary	1,675	X	1,593 c	X	(8)	(0.5)	X	X	X	X	X	19 e	290
Iceland	11	123	X	X	X	X	X	X	X	X	X	X	X
Ireland	396	33	381 c	X	(5)	(1.3)	X	X	X	X	X	7 e	5
Italy	6,750	1,800	X	X	X	X	X	X	X	X	X	9 f	X
Luxembourg	85	3	87 c	X	(0)	(0.1)	X	X	X	X	X	0 f	0
Netherlands	334	X	324 c	X	(1)	(0.3)	X	X	X	X	X	1 f	81
Norway	8,697	868	X	X	X	X	X	X	X	X	X	X	132 h
Poland	8,672	X	8,622 c	X	(5)	(0.1)	X	X	X	X	X	70 e	133
Portugal	2,755	347	2,964 c	X	(14)	(0.5)	X	X	X	X	X	23 e	X
Romania	6,190	75	6,263 c	X	(0)	(0.0)	X	X	X	X	X	1 e	X
Spain	8,388	17,234	25,613 c	X	(1)	(0.0)	X	X	X	X	X	44 e	19 h
Sweden	24,437	3,578	X	X	X	X	X	X	X	X	X	22 d	540
Switzerland	1,130	56	1,120 c	X	(7)	(0.6)	X	X	X	X	X	2 e	7
United Kingdom	2,207	173	2,138 c	X	(24)	(1.1)	X	X	X	X	X	35 e	158 h
Yugoslavia (former)	8,370	1,083	9,108 c	X	(35)	(0.4)	X	X	X	X	X	45 f	146
U.S.S.R. (former)	754,958	186,572	918,930 c	X	(2,260)	(0.2)	X	X	X	X	X	3,930 e	10,612
Belarus	6,016	240	5,983 c	X	(27)	(0.5)	X	X	X	X	X	64 e	X
Ukraine	9,213	26	8,999 c	X	(24)	(0.3)	X	X	X	X	X	72 e	121
OCEANIA													
Australia	39,837	105,776	145,607 c	X	(1)	(0.0)	X	X	X	X	X	X	9,310
Fiji	X	X	811	6	X	X	2	X	X	X	X	X	X
New Zealand	7,472	X	X	X	X	X	X	X	X	X	X	X	X
Papua New Guinea	36,000	X	37,130	X	113	0.3	23	57	0.2	93	43	2	916 a
Solomon Islands	X	X	2,440	40	X	X	1	X	X	X	X	X	X

Sources: Food and Agriculture Organization of the United Nations and the United Nations Economic Commission for Europe.
Notes: a. Protected areas within tropical moist forest regions only. b. Closed forest only. c. Includes woodlands. d. Artificial regeneration of forest only. e. Artificial regeneration and afforestation. f. Afforestation only. g. Former German Democratic Republic only. h. National parks only.
See Sources and Technical Notes for alternative estimates of forest extent and deforestation for some countries.
Subregional totals may include countries not listed.
0 = zero or less than half the unit of measure; numbers in parentheses indicate increase in forest area; X = not available.
For additional information, see Sources and Technical Notes.

Table 19.2 Tropical Forest Extent and Loss by Ecosystem

	Total Forest		Rain		Moist Deciduous		Hill and Montane		Dry Deciduous		Very Dry		Desert	
	1990 Extent (000 ha)	Percent Annual Change 1981-90	1990 Extent (000 ha)	Percent Annual Change 1981-90	1990 Extent (000 ha)	Percent Annual Change 1981-90	1990 Extent (000 ha)	Percent Annual Change 1981-90	1990 Extent (000 ha)	Percent Annual Change 1981-90	1990 Extent (000 ha)	Percent Annual Change 1981-90	1990 Extent (000 ha)	Percent Annual Change 1981-90
WORLD	1,756,299	(0.8)	713,790	(0.6)	591,779	(0.9)	201,417	(1.1)	178,579	(0.9)	59,742	(0.5)	8,086	(0.9)
AFRICA	527,586	(0.7)	86,411	(0.5)	251,348	(0.8)	35,256	(0.8)	92,527	(0.8)	58,660	(0.5)	3,385	(0.4)
West Sahelian Africa	40,768	(0.7)	0	0.0	14,437	(0.9)	0	0.0	13,029	(0.7)	13,285	(0.5)	17	0.0
Burkina Faso	4,416	(0.7)	0	0.0	2,112	(0.7)	0	0.0	1,533	(0.7)	771	(0.7)	0	0.0
Cape Verde	6	0.0	0	0.0	0	0.0	0	0.0	0	0.0	6	0.0	0	0.0
Chad	11,434	(0.7)	0	0.0	3,932	(1.1)	0	0.0	5,024	(0.5)	2,461	(0.5)	17	0.0
Gambia, The	97	(0.8)	0	0.0	79	(0.7)	0	0.0	18	(0.5)	0	0.0	0	0.0
Guinea-Bissau	2,021	(0.7)	0	0.0	2,021	(0.7)	0	0.0	0	0.0	0	0.0	0	0.0
Mali	12,144	(0.8)	0	0.0	3,706	(0.9)	0	0.0	4,548	(0.8)	3,891	(0.7)	0	0.0
Mauritania	554	0.0	0	0.0	0	0.0	0	0.0	0	0.0	554	0.0	0	0.0
Niger	2,550	0.0	0	0.0	0	0.0	0	0.0	190	0.0	2,359	0.0	0	0.0
Senegal	7,544	(0.6)	0	0.0	2,586	(0.7)	0	0.0	1,716	(0.7)	3,242	(0.6)	0	0.0
East Sahelian Africa	65,450	(0.8)	0	0.0	13,576	(1.4)	12,780	(0.6)	19,784	(0.8)	18,513	(0.5)	797	(0.3)
Djibouti	22	0.0	0	0.0	0	0.0	0	0.0	0	0.0	0	0.0	22	0.0
Ethiopia	14,165	(0.3)	0	0.0	0	0.0	6,173	(0.3)	2,008	(0.3)	5,346	(0.2)	639	(0.2)
Kenya	1,187	(0.5)	0	0.0	13	0.0	908	(0.6)	19	0.0	156	(0.2)	91	(0.9)
Somalia	754	(0.4)	0	0.0	0	0.0	0	0.0	0	0.0	754	(0.4)	0	0.0
Sudan	42,976	(1.0)	0	0.0	12,472	(1.5)	720	(1.4)	17,757	(0.9)	12,027	(0.6)	0	0.0
Uganda	6,346	(0.9)	0	0.0	1,091	(1.1)	4,980	(0.9)	0	0.0	231	(0.6)	45	(1.2)
West Africa	55,607	(1.0)	3,230	(0.5)	48,523	(1.0)	468	(0.9)	2,583	(0.8)	803	(0.2)	0	0.0
Benin	4,947	(1.2)	0	0.0	4,183	(1.2)	0	0.0	764	(1.5)	0	0.0	0	0.0
Cote d'Ivoire	10,904	(1.0)	0	0.0	10,831	(1.0)	73	(0.6)	0	0.0	0	0.0	0	0.0
Ghana	9,555	(1.3)	0	0.0	9,151	(1.3)	0	0.0	404	(0.8)	0	0.0	0	0.0
Guinea	6,692	(1.1)	385	(0.1)	6,180	(1.2)	128	(1.2)	0	0.0	0	0.0	0	0.0
Liberia	4,633	(0.5)	893	(0.6)	3,741	(0.5)	0	0.0	0	0.0	0	0.0	0	0.0
Nigeria	15,634	(0.7)	1,197	(0.6)	12,011	(0.8)	243	(0.9)	1,380	(0.4)	803	(0.2)	0	0.0
Sierra Leone	1,889	(0.6)	756	(0.6)	1,108	(0.6)	25	(0.7)	0	0.0	0	0.0	0	0.0
Togo	1,353	(1.4)	0	0.0	1,318	(1.4)	0	0.0	35	(0.5)	0	0.0	0	0.0
Central Africa	204,112	(0.5)	78,674	(0.5)	113,564	(0.5)	10,072	(0.8)	1,512	(0.6)	86	(0.2)	0	0.0
Cameroon	20,350	(0.6)	8,021	(0.4)	9,892	(0.6)	1,767	(0.7)	585	(0.8)	86	(0.2)	0	0.0
Central African Rep	30,562	(0.4)	616	(0.7)	28,357	(0.4)	772	(0.4)	816	(0.3)	0	0.0	0	0.0
Congo	19,865	(0.2)	7,667	(0.2)	12,198	(0.2)	0	0.0	0	0.0	0	0.0	0	0.0
Equatorial Guinea	1,826	(0.4)	822	(0.4)	930	(0.4)	14	(0.7)	0	0.0	0	0.0	0	0.0
Gabon	18,235	(0.6)	1,155	(0.6)	17,080	(0.6)	0	0.0	0	0.0	0	0.0	0	0.0
Zaire	113,275	(0.6)	60,437	(0.6)	45,209	(0.6)	7,518	(0.8)	111	(0.6)	0	0.0	0	0.0
Tropical Southern Africa	145,868	(0.8)	0	0.0	57,267	(1.1)	7,339	(0.9)	53,400	(0.8)	25,291	(0.5)	2,571	(0.4)
Angola	23,074	(0.7)	0	0.0	11,942	(0.7)	3,163	(0.7)	7,218	(0.7)	751	(0.7)	0	0.0
Botswana	14,261	(0.5)	0	0.0	0	0.0	0	0.0	2,940	(0.5)	10,816	(0.5)	504	(0.5)
Burundi	233	(0.6)	0	0.0	47	(0.8)	186	(0.5)	0	0.0	0	0.0	0	0.0
Malawi	3,486	(1.3)	0	0.0	2,948	(1.3)	373	(1.2)	166	(1.3)	0	0.0	0	0.0
Mozambique	17,329	(0.7)	0	0.0	6,526	(0.9)	13	(0.7)	10,163	(0.7)	627	(0.2)	0	0.0
Namibia	12,569	(0.3)	0	0.0	0	0.0	0	0.0	2,521	(0.3)	7,994	(0.3)	2,054	(0.3)
Rwanda	164	(0.2)	0	0.0	0	0.0	164	(0.2)	0	0.0	0	0.0	0	0.0
Tanzania	33,555	(1.2)	0	0.0	14,128	(1.4)	3,035	(1.1)	12,375	(1.0)	4,004	(0.9)	13	(0.7)
Zambia	32,301	(1.0)	0	0.0	21,676	(1.1)	337	(0.7)	10,288	(0.9)	0	0.0	0	0.0
Zimbabwe	8,897	(0.6)	0	0.0	0	0.0	69	(0.7)	7,729	(0.6)	1,099	(0.6)	0	0.0
Insular Africa	15,782	(0.8)	4,507	(0.6)	3,777	(1.0)	4,596	(0.8)	2,219	(0.8)	682	(0.9)	0	0.0
Madagascar	15,782	(0.8)	4,507	(0.6)	3,777	(1.0)	4,596	(0.8)	2,219	(0.8)	682	(0.9)	0	0.0
ASIA	274,597	(1.2)	148,027	(1.2)	41,797	(1.4)	41,122	(1.2)	40,691	(1.0)	37	(2.9)	2,901	(0.9)
South Asia	63,931	(0.8)	9,850	(0.8)	9,155	(0.6)	14,988	(0.9)	27,119	(0.8)	37	(2.9)	2,781	(1.0)
Bangladesh	769	(3.3)	572	(3.6)	197	(2.1)	0	0.0	0	0.0	0	0.0	0	0.0
Bhutan	2,809	(0.6)	176	(0.5)	0	0.0	2,230	(0.6)	0	0.0	0	0.0	403	(0.6)
India	51,729	(0.6)	8,246	(0.6)	7,042	(0.5)	8,917	(0.4)	26,242	(0.8)	0	0.0	1,283	(0.2)
Nepal	5,023	(1.0)	609	(0.6)	1,300	(0.6)	2,361	(1.2)	37	(0.5)	0	0.0	716	(1.1)
Pakistan	1,855	(2.9)	0	0.0	11	(3.1)	1,423	(2.9)	4	(3.3)	37	(2.9)	380	(2.9)
Sri Lanka	1,746	(1.3)	247	(0.6)	605	(1.4)	57	0.0	836	(1.5)	0	0.0	0	0.0
Continental South East Asia	75,240	(1.5)	23,719	(1.5)	27,192	(1.6)	10,786	(1.3)	13,499	(1.5)	0	0.0	43	(0.7)
Cambodia	12,163	(1.0)	1,689	(1.0)	3,610	(1.0)	93	(1.0)	6,771	(1.0)	0	0.0	0	0.0
Lao People's Dem Rep	13,173	(0.9)	3,960	(0.9)	4,542	(0.9)	2,405	(1.0)	2,267	(0.8)	0	0.0	0	0.0
Myanmar	28,856	(1.2)	12,094	(1.2)	10,427	(1.4)	5,942	(1.0)	351	(1.1)	0	0.0	43	(0.7)
Thailand	12,735	(2.9)	3,082	(3.3)	5,232	(2.7)	1,263	(2.7)	3,159	(2.8)	0	0.0	0	0.0
Viet Nam	8,312	(1.4)	2,894	(1.4)	3,382	(1.4)	1,084	(1.4)	952	(1.4)	0	0.0	0	0.0
Insular South East Asia	135,426	(1.2)	114,355	(1.2)	4,779	(1.6)	16,018	(1.4)	73	(0.9)	0	0.0	77	(0.4)
Brunei	458	(0.4)	458	(0.4)	0	0.0	0	0.0	0	0.0	0	0.0	0	0.0
Indonesia	109,549	(1.0)	93,827	(1.0)	3,366	(1.0)	12,083	(1.1)	73	(0.9)	0	0.0	77	(0.4)
Malaysia	17,583	(1.8)	16,339	(1.8)	0	0.0	1,244	(1.8)	0	0.0	0	0.0	0	0.0
Philippines	7,831	(2.9)	3,728	(3.1)	1,413	(2.7)	2,690	(2.6)	0	0.0	0	0.0	0	0.0
Singapore	4	0.0	4	0.0	0	0.0	0	0.0	0	0.0	0	0.0	0	0.0
OCEANIA	36,000	(0.3)	29,323	(0.3)	705	(0.3)	5,370	(0.3)	417	(0.3)	0	0.0	184	(0.3)
Pacific	36,000	(0.3)	29,323	(0.3)	705	(0.3)	5,370	(0.3)	417	(0.3)	0	0.0	184	(0.3)
Papua New Guinea	36,000	(0.3)	29,323	(0.3)	705	(0.3)	5,370	(0.3)	417	(0.3)	0	0.0	184	(0.3)

Type, 1981–90

Table 19.2

	Total Forest		Forest Ecosystem Type												
			Rain		Moist Deciduous		Hill and Montane		Dry Deciduous		Very Dry		Desert	
	1990 Extent (000 ha)	Percent Annual Change 1981-90	1990 Extent (000 ha)	Percent Annual Change 1981-90	1990 Extent (000 ha)	Percent Annual Change 1981-90	1990 Extent (000 ha)	Percent Annual Change 1981-90	1990 Extent (000 ha)	Percent Annual Change 1981-90	1990 Extent (000 ha)	Percent Annual Change 1981-90	1990 Extent (000 ha)	Percent Annual Change 1981-90
THE AMERICAS	918,115	(0.7)	450,162	(0.4)	297,929	(1.0)	119,669	(1.2)	44,944	(1.2)	1,045	(1.8)	1,616	(2.0)
Central America and Mexico	68,096	(1.4)	11,154	(1.8)	12,267	(1.5)	36,296	(1.4)	1,590	(1.6)	759	(1.8)	1,424	(2.0)
Costa Rica	1,428	(2.6)	625	(2.6)	0	0.0	802	(2.6)	0	0.0	0	0.0	0	0.0
El Salvador	123	(2.0)	33	(2.0)	12	(2.0)	79	(2.0)	0	0.0	0	0.0	0	0.0
Guatemala	4,225	(1.6)	2,542	(1.6)	731	0.0	953	(2.5)	0	0.0	0	0.0	0	0.0
Honduras	4,605	(2.0)	1,286	(2.0)	437	(2.0)	2,882	(1.9)	0	0.0	0	0.0	0	0.0
Mexico	48,586	(1.2)	2,441	(1.0)	11,110	(1.5)	31,261	(1.1)	1,590	(1.6)	759	(1.8)	1,424	(2.0)
Nicaragua	6,013	(1.7)	3,712	(1.7)	348	(1.7)	1,953	(1.7)	0	0.0	0	0.0	0	0.0
Panama	3,117	(1.7)	1,802	(1.6)	67	(0.1)	1,249	(2.0)	0	0.0	0	0.0	0	0.0
Caribbean Subregion	47,115	(0.3)	31,428	(0.1)	12,991	(0.5)	2,639	(0.8)	49	(2.0)	5	(1.7)	4	(2.0)
Antigua and Barbuda	10	0.0	0	0.0	10	0.0	0	0.0	0	0.0	0	0.0	0	0.0
Bahamas	186	(1.9)	0	0.0	124	(1.9)	6	(2.5)	47	(1.9)	5	(1.7)	4	(2.0)
Belize	1,996	(0.2)	1,741	0.0	238	(0.0)	16	0.0	0	0.0	0	0.0	0	0.0
Cuba	1,715	(0.9)	114	(0.9)	1,247	(0.9)	352	(0.9)	2	0.0	0	0.0	0	0.0
Dominica	44	(0.6)	44	(0.6)	0	0.0	0	0.0	0	0.0	0	0.0	0	0.0
Dominican Rep	1,077	(2.5)	341	(2.5)	273	(2.5)	463	(2.5)	0	0.0	0	0.0	0	0.0
French Guiana	7,997	(0.0)	7,993	(0.0)	3	0.0	0	0.0	0	0.0	0	0.0	0	0.0
Grenada	6	5.0	0	0.0	6	5.0	0	0.0	0	0.0	0	0.0	0	0.0
Guadeloupe	93	(0.3)	93	(0.3)	0	0.0	0	0.0	0	0.0	0	0.0	0	0.0
Guyana	18,416	(0.1)	11,671	0.0	5,078	(0.3)	1,668	(0.1)	0	0.0	0	0.0	0	0.0
Haiti	23	(3.9)	5	(3.8)	9	(4.0)	10	(3.8)	0	0.0	0	0.0	0	0.0
Jamaica	239	(5.3)	122	(5.3)	113	(5.3)	3	(5.7)	0	0.0	0	0.0	0	0.0
Martinique	43	(0.4)	43	(0.4)	0	0.0	0	0.0	0	0.0	0	0.0	0	0.0
Puerto Rico	321	1.5	49	1.7	151	1.5	121	1.5	0	0.0	0	0.0	0	0.0
Saint Kitts and Nevis	13	0.0	0	0.0	13	0.0	0	0.0	0	0.0	0	0.0	0	0.0
Saint Lucia	5	(3.8)	5	(3.8)	0	0.0	0	0.0	0	0.0	0	0.0	0	0.0
Saint Vincent	11	(2.1)	10	(1.7)	0	0.0	0	0.0	0	0.0	0	0.0	0	0.0
Suriname	14,768	(0.1)	9,042	0.0	5,726	(0.2)	0	0.0	0	0.0	0	0.0	0	0.0
Trinidad and Tobago	155	(1.9)	155	(1.9)	0	0.0	0	0.0	0	0.0	0	0.0	0	0.0
Tropical South America	802,904	(0.7)	406,162	(0.4)	272,235	(1.0)	80,734	(1.2)	43,304	(1.2)	282	(2.1)	188	(2.0)
Bolivia	49,317	(1.1)	0	0.0	35,582	(1.1)	6,385	(1.3)	7,346	(1.1)	0	0.0	4	(2.0)
Brazil	561,107	(0.6)	291,597	(0.3)	197,082	(0.8)	43,565	(1.3)	28,863	(1.0)	0	0.0	0	0.0
Colombia	54,064	(0.6)	47,455	(0.4)	4,101	(1.9)	2,490	(1.6)	18	(1.8)	0	0.0	0	0.0
Ecuador	11,962	(1.7)	7,150	(1.7)	1,669	(1.7)	3,100	(1.7)	44	(1.7)	0	0.0	0	0.0
Paraguay	12,859	(2.4)	0	0.0	6,037	(2.9)	27	(5.0)	6,794	(1.8)	0	0.0	0	0.0
Peru	67,906	(0.4)	40,358	(0.3)	12,299	(0.3)	14,777	(0.7)	19	(1.7)	269	(2.1)	184	(2.0)
Venezuela	45,690	(1.2)	19,602	(0.7)	15,465	(1.8)	10,390	(0.9)	222	(3.2)	12	(2.5)	0	0.0

Source: Food and Agriculture Organization of the United Nations.
Notes: 0 = zero or less than half the unit of measure; X = not available; numbers in parentheses indicate a decrease in forest area.
For additional information, see Sources and Technical Notes.

Table 19.3 Wood Production and Trade, 1979–91

| | Roundwood Production | | | | | | Processed Wood Production | | | | Paper Production | | Average Annual Net Trade in Roundwood {a} | |
| | Total | | Fuel and Charcoal | | Industrial Roundwood | | Sawnwood | | Panels | | | | | |
	(000 cubic meters) 1989-91	Percent Change Since 1979-81	(000 cubic meters) 1989-91	Percent Change Since 1979-81	(000 cubic meters) 1989-91	Percent Change Since 1979-81	(000 cubic meters) 1989-91	Percent Change Since 1979-81	(000 cubic meters) 1989-91	Percent Change Since 1979-81	(000 metric tons) 1989-91	Percent Change Since 1979-81	(000 cubic meters) 1979-81	1989-91
WORLD	3,462,348	19	1,801,216	23	1,661,131	15	490,392	10	125,245	22	238,056	40		
AFRICA	513,545	34	455,760	36	57,785	15	8,624	15	1,887	28	2,735	59	(5,286)	(4,098)
Algeria	2,163	33	1,902	33	261	30	13	0	50	0	101	13	98	137
Angola	6,440	25	5,529	30	910	2	5	(63)	11	(48)	0	(100)	0	(1)
Benin	5,046	34	4,777	34	269	36	14	56	X	X	X	X	X	X
Botswana	1,389	45	1,303	45	86	46	X	X	X	X	X	X	X	X
Burkina Faso	8,751	29	8,355	29	396	28	2	20	X	X	X	X	X	X
Burundi	4,215	33	4,166	32	50	41	3	167	X	X	X	X	X	X
Cameroon	14,225	48	11,170	51	3,055	37	574	33	80	12	5	0	(677)	(641)
Central African Rep	3,491	16	3,055	23	436	(16)	60	(14)	2	(68)	X	X	(128)	(50)
Chad	4,037	27	3,466	27	572	27	1	33	X	X	X	X	X	X
Congo	3,670	61	2,078	37	1,591	110	47	(26)	55	(26)	X	X	(225)	(796)
Cote d'Ivoire	12,635	7	9,756	46	2,879	(44)	761	17	246	62	X	X	(2,829)	(476)
Djibouti	X	X	X	X	X	X	X	X	X	X	X	X	0	0
Egypt	2,248	28	2,144	28	104	29	X	X	61	40	219	68	113	116
Equatorial Guinea	607	33	447	6	160	371	53	700	10	2,900	X	X	(25)	(123)
Ethiopia	42,536	27	40,807	27	1,729	18	23	(65)	12	(17)	9	8	X	X
Gabon	4,130	37	2,568	45	1,563	26	126	17	228	28	X	X	(1,119)	(1,077)
Gambia, The	930	3	909	2	21	110	1	0	X	X	X	X	0	0
Ghana	17,343	40	15,883	41	1,461	38	470	77	74	2	X	X	(119)	(205)
Guinea	3,870	22	3,454	29	415	(15)	70	(22)	0	(100)	X	X	(3)	(8)
Guinea-Bissau	567	3	422	0	145	14	16	0	X	X	X	X	0	(5)
Kenya	35,599	43	33,835	45	1,764	26	185	18	52	120	98	58	(20)	0
Lesotho	613	32	613	32	X	X	X	X	X	X	X	X	0	33
Liberia	6,056	31	4,890	27	1,166	52	411	143	5	(50)	X	X	(373)	(701)
Libya	643	2	536	0	107	16	31	0	X	X	6	20	100	30
Madagascar	8,099	32	7,292	37	807	0	234	(0)	5	400	7	67	X	X
Malawi	8,210	40	7,820	42	390	13	42	(9)	14	75	X	X	X	X
Mali	5,592	34	5,235	34	357	35	13	117	X	X	X	X	X	X
Mauritania	12	28	7	29	5	25	X	X	X	X	X	X	X	X
Mauritius	25	(41)	12	(49)	13	(29)	5	17	0	X	X	X	2	14
Morocco	2,221	43	1,383	30	838	70	83	(21)	156	83	113	23	230	312
Mozambique	16,037	22	15,022	23	1,015	6	24	(63)	4	38	1	(43)	(10)	(1)
Namibia	X	X	X	X	X	X	X	X	X	X	X	X	X	X
Niger	4,958	38	4,652	38	306	38	X	X	X	X	X	X	X	X
Nigeria	107,761	36	99,893	38	7,868	7	2,710	5	233	55	72	302	(15)	(6)
Rwanda	5,936	24	5,704	26	232	(16)	9	170	2	50	X	X	X	X
Senegal	4,787	35	4,185	35	602	33	20	79	X	X	X	X	38	29
Sierra Leone	3,082	24	2,949	27	133	(21)	11	(52)	X	X	X	X	0	0
Somalia	7,129	40	7,038	40	91	25	14	0	0	(100)	X	X	3	0
South Africa	19,709	5	7,078	(1)	12,631	9	1,867	14	367	(3)	1,903	58	(124)	(576)
Sudan	22,798	35	20,688	35	2,110	33	6	(23)	2	0	6	(32)	0	0
Swaziland	2,223	6	560	3	1,663	7	103	(11)	8	85	X	X	(189)	(14)
Tanzania	34,295	46	32,258	45	2,037	79	156	49	15	105	26	X	(4)	0
Togo	1,002	50	820	54	182	34	4	57	X	X	X	X	0	3
Tunisia	3,249	29	3,083	28	166	44	17	478	97	131	79	240	36	10
Uganda	15,149	43	13,193	43	1,956	40	28	18	3	200	3	X	0	0
Zaire	38,933	46	36,046	47	2,887	35	118	(2)	33	11	1	(50)	(57)	(101)
Zambia	13,195	49	12,477	48	718	55	101	140	39	883	3	X	7	0
Zimbabwe	7,893	23	6,269	20	1,624	34	190	6	26	(28)	85	48	1	(1)
ASIA	1,071,682	19	817,437	22	254,245	11	104,587	12	27,515	43	56,357	93	37,310	49,527
Afghanistan	6,480	3	4,940	4	1,540	2	400	0	1	0	X	X	0	0
Bangladesh	30,944	30	30,061	31	882	0	79	(55)	8	(35)	95	28	0	87
Bhutan	1,532	17	1,254	22	278	0	33	567	12	X	X	X	(7)	(4)
Cambodia	6,048	27	5,366	28	681	20	79	83	2	0	X	X	(6)	(56)
China	281,371	21	188,498	22	92,872	20	22,953	9	3,246	38	16,951	153	8,103	9,913
India	274,510	24	250,089	24	24,421	24	17,460	59	442	57	2,202	102	(2)	1,118
Indonesia	167,822	16	141,017	22	26,804	(6)	9,549	112	8,837	731·	1,432	513	(14,511)	(1,245)
Iran, Islamic Rep	6,745	1	2,453	6	4,292	(2)	201	24	275	200	196	151	118	68
Iraq	153	20	103	34	50	0	8	0	3	50	32	14	8	1
Israel	108	(9)	11	0	97	(10)	X	X	175	27	191	77	180	308
Japan	29,582	(12)	324	(44)	29,258	(11)	29,529	(19)	8,650	(14)	27,983	59	52,427	48,744
Jordan	9	29	5	67	4	0	X	X	X	X	14	133	4	5
Korea, Dem People's Rep	4,693	9	4,093	10	600	0	280	0	X	X	80	0	38	(47)
Korea, Rep	6,592	(24)	4,489	(30)	2,103	(6)	4,044	32	1,468	(23)	4,488	166	6,928	8,471
Kuwait	X	X	X	X	X	X	X	X	X	X	X	X	21	54
Lao People's Dem Rep	4,194	33	3,827	29	367	86	66	103	10	400	X	X	(15)	(20)
Lebanon	473	(1)	455	1	18	(36)	16	(58)	46	0	39	(14)	26	15
Malaysia	49,938	35	8,719	30	41,219	37	8,684	45	2,071	98	283	374	(16,138)	(20,125)
Mongolia	2,390	26	1,350	0	1,040	0	470	0	4	0	X	X	X	X
Myanmar	22,850	26	17,785	23	5,065	34	436	(35)	15	15	11	7	(195)	(669)
Nepal	18,244	28	17,661	29	583	4	470	114	X	X	9	367	(125)	(4)
Oman	X	X	X	X	X	X	X	X	X	X	X	X	8	12
Pakistan	26,183	51	23,963	44	2,220	248	1,331	2,181	81	64	195	207	46	48
Philippines	38,466	10	33,447	28	5,019	(43)	845	(42)	455	(37)	212	(34)	(1,593)	276
Saudi Arabia	X	X	X	X	X	X	X	X	X	X	X	X	178	123
Singapore	X	X	X	X	X	X	206	(37)	489	(32)	58	77	1,163	(187)
Sri Lanka	9,037	14	8,364	14	674	6	12	(53)	10	(14)	17	(12)	(120)	0
Syrian Arab Rep	56	21	15	(34)	42	70	9	4	27	1	13	333	56	18
Thailand	37,739	12	34,585	19	3,154	(32)	1,123	(16)	340	109	868	156	(75)	1,444
Turkey	15,681	(30)	9,796	(38)	5,885	(12)	4,925	6	781	62	841	76	(12)	789
United Arab Emirates	X	X	X	X	X	X	X	X	X	X	X	X	X	X
Viet Nam	28,970	28	24,154	24	4,816	54	782	63	40	109	67	67	33	(262)
Yemen	324	29	324	29	X	X	X	X	X	X	X	X	1	4

Table 19.3

| | Roundwood Production | | | | | | Processed Wood Production | | | | Paper Production | | Average Annual Net Trade in Roundwood {a} (000 cubic meters) | |
| | Total | | Fuel and Charcoal | | Industrial Roundwood | | Sawnwood | | Panels | | | | | |
	(000 cubic meters) 1989-91	Percent Change Since 1979-81	(000 cubic meters) 1989-91	Percent Change Since 1979-81	(000 cubic meters) 1989-91	Percent Change Since 1979-81	(000 cubic meters) 1989-91	Percent Change Since 1979-81	(000 cubic meters) 1989-91	Percent Change Since 1979-81	(000 metric tons) 1989-91	Percent Change Since 1979-81	1979-81	1989-91
NORTH & CENTRAL AMERICA	**749,939**	**20**	**147,280**	**14**	**602,659**	**22**	**165,276**	**25**	**39,043**	**15**	**91,174**	**25**	**(19,116)**	**(25,974)**
Bahamas	115	0	X	X	115	0	1	0	X	X	X	X	4	6
Barbados	X	X	X	X	X	X	X	X	X	X	X	X	X	X
Belize	188	58	126	59	62	54	14	(28)	X	X	X	X	(4)	(4)
Canada	179,004	15	6,834	40	172,170	15	55,397	29	6,277	29	16,527	22	(473)	1,179
Costa Rica	4,123	16	2,960	32	1,164	(11)	421	(11)	66	3	19	47	2	0
Cuba	3,134	(5)	2,523	(10)	611	19	130	21	149	2,383	136	87	0	6
Dominica	X	X	X	X	X	X	X	X	X	X	X	X	0	1
Dominican Rep	982	27	976	27	6	13	0	X	X	X	10	11	35	22
El Salvador	4,566	17	4,420	16	146	38	70	74	X	X	17	6	0	0
Guatemala	7,825	30	7,711	33	114	(42)	83	2	6	(31)	14	(53)	3	(13)
Haiti	5,841	20	5,602	21	239	0	14	0	X	X	X	X	2	0
Honduras	6,189	27	5,336	40	853	(21)	347	(40)	9	(22)	X	X	(23)	(88)
Jamaica	204	354	13	86	191	404	37	49	0	(100)	4	(60)	6	5
Martinique	12	9	10	0	2	100	1	X	X	X	X	X	0	0
Mexico	23,514	27	15,528	26	7,987	29	2,503	25	613	6	3,021	63	42	35
Nicaragua	4,077	29	3,197	40	880	0	222	(45)	7	(52)	X	X	6	(1)
Panama	1,872	3	1,708	2	164	11	49	24	7	(51)	25	(8)	5	2
Trinidad and Tobago	75	(12)	22	38	53	(24)	62	90	X	X	X	X	1	2
United States	508,200	22	90,300	8	417,900	26	105,923	24	31,909	13	71,401	25	(18,728)	(27,129)
SOUTH AMERICA	**343,918**	**24**	**238,304**	**22**	**105,614**	**28**	**26,091**	**19**	**4,211**	**23**	**7,688**	**43**	**(922)**	**(5,836)**
Argentina	10,819	10	4,332	(23)	6,487	53	1,446	53	386	8	924	28	11	(670)
Bolivia	1,595	11	1,339	32	256	(38)	94	(55)	4	(73)	2	133	X	X
Brazil	262,439	25	186,477	24	75,962	29	17,512	17	2,892	19	4,846	54	(97)	21
Chile	18,309	32	6,648	18	11,661	42	3,076	48	339	175	463	46	(793)	(5,162)
Colombia	19,384	16	16,711	23	2,673	(14)	777	(21)	130	22	505	40	0	0
Ecuador	9,233	23	6,666	20	2,567	29	1,591	75	145	69	47	82	X	X
Guyana	190	(3)	14	(4)	176	(3)	23	(66)	X	X	X	X	(30)	(10)
Paraguay	8,430	28	5,324	24	3,106	37	482	(21)	110	82	12	(5)	X	X
Peru	8,061	2	7,042	14	1,019	(40)	581	(4)	36	(52)	232	2	1	0
Suriname	147	(57)	18	(30)	129	(60)	43	(45)	7	(69)	X	X	(27)	(2)
Uruguay	3,729	31	2,907	16	822	150	212	113	9	(44)	66	31	5	0
Venezuela	1,328	9	759	31	569	(11)	235	(33)	152	18	589	16	48	0
EUROPE	**366,822**	**10**	**52,594**	**3**	**314,228**	**12**	**85,253**	**(3)**	**37,795**	**15**	**67,016**	**34**	**16,856**	**17,526**
Albania	2,307	(1)	1,573	(2)	733	2	321	61	15	22	38	375	X	X
Austria	16,865	18	2,740	94	14,125	9	7,217	10	1,762	30	2,905	80	2,709	3,855
Belgium {b}	5,182	94	572	72	4,610	96	1,201	79	2,374	33	1,200	38	2,552	2,186
Bulgaria	3,975	(11)	1,461	27	2,514	(24)	1,240	(19)	422	(25)	308	(23)	273	(33)
Czechoslovakia (former)	17,521	(7)	1,513	(15)	16,008	(6)	4,412	(10)	1,300	11	1,231	5	(3,154)	(565)
Denmark	2,223	6	446	70	1,777	(4)	861	6	300	(21)	340	38	(448)	(291)
Finland	41,589	(8)	3,253	(18)	38,336	(7)	7,083	(25)	1,273	(24)	8,620	45	1,971	5,614
France	44,946	16	10,440	0	34,506	22	10,868	15	3,268	6	7,082	37	(420)	(3,908)
Germany	59,236	43	4,412	3	54,823	48	14,597	17	9,813	20	13,125	48	1,281	(3,949)
Greece	2,424	(6)	1,471	2	953	27	377	1	413	5	333	10	343	541
Hungary	6,265	0	2,689	3	3,576	(1)	1,257	(3)	406	4	435	(2)	714	(353)
Iceland	X	X	X	X	X	X	X	X	X	X	X	X	20	1
Ireland	1,619	327	50	28	1,569	361	376	138	240	344	35	(49)	(177)	(242)
Italy	8,426	(3)	4,062	4	4,364	(9)	1,503	(41)	4,283	66	5,676	14	6,009	6,982
Malta	X	X	X	X	X	X	X	X	X	X	X	X	1	1
Netherlands	1,386	56	151	76	1,235	54	448	52	99	(40)	2,751	65	372	184
Norway	11,437	22	916	44	10,522	20	2,406	(1)	617	5	1,797	30	397	1,053
Poland	18,788	(9)	2,501	15	16,288	(12)	4,071	(44)	1,584	(18)	940	(23)	(1,048)	(601)
Portugal	10,929	29	598	11	10,331	30	1,687	(21)	1,096	138	795	66	(457)	180
Romania	15,789	(17)	2,455	(40)	13,334	(11)	2,739	(41)	1,288	(20)	538	(35)	200	17
Spain	17,477	39	2,257	60	15,221	36	2,981	21	2,408	28	3,489	36	987	2,227
Sweden	53,691	6	4,424	4	49,267	6	11,680	6	1,227	(34)	8,379	35	3,590	4,862
Switzerland	4,970	13	797	(10)	4,174	19	1,890	11	862	17	1,257	39	212	(214)
United Kingdom	6,485	56	270	93	6,215	55	2,217	32	1,710	152	4,783	26	148	65
Yugoslavia (former)	13,291	(3)	3,544	8	9,747	(6)	3,821	(10)	1,033	(20)	960	(11)	782	(87)
U.S.S.R. (former)	**375,400**	**5**	**81,100**	**2**	**294,300**	**6**	**95,100**	**(4)**	**13,083**	**24**	**10,348**	**18**	**(14,993)**	**(15,898)**
OCEANIA	**41,043**	**21**	**8,742**	**22**	**32,301**	**20**	**5,460**	**(4)**	**1,710**	**44**	**2,739**	**33**	**(8,299)**	**(10,825)**
Australia	19,630	18	2,890	90	16,740	11	3,022	(10)	976	18	1,970	42	(5,905)	(6,004)
Fiji	307	27	37	66	270	23	93	(9)	16	50	X	X	(5)	(175)
New Zealand	12,243	26	50	0	12,193	26	2,177	7	677	107	769	14	(1,362)	(2,916)
Papua New Guinea	8,202	19	5,533	3	2,669	75	117	(22)	40	89	X	X	(744)	(1,424)
Solomon Islands	449	12	138	35	311	4	16	(16)	0	(100)	X	X	(282)	(302)
Vanuatu	63	99	24	0	39	409	7	250	X	X	X	X	(5)	(6)

Source: Food and Agriculture Organization of the United Nations.
Notes: a. Imports of roundwood are shown as positive numbers; exports are represented by negative numbers (in parentheses). b. Data are for Belgium and Luxembourg.
World and regional totals include countries not listed.
0 = zero or less than half of the unit of measure; X = not available; negative numbers are shown in parentheses.
For additional information, see Sources and Technical Notes.

Sources and Technical Notes

Table 19.1 Forest Resources, 1980–90

Sources: Food and Agriculture Organization of the United Nations (FAO), Forest Resources Division, *Forest Resources Assessment 1990: Tropical Countries* (FAO, Rome, 1993); FAO, *An Interim Report on the State of the Forest Resources in the Developing Countries* (FAO, Rome, 1988); FAO, *Forest Resources 1980* (FAO, Rome, 1985); United Nations Economic Commission for Europe and FAO (UNECE), *The Forest Resources of the Temperate Zones. Volume I: General Forest Resource Information* (UNECE/FAO, Geneva, 1993); UNECE/FAO, *The Forest Resources of the Temperate Zones. Volume II: Benefits and Functions of the Forest* (UNECE/FAO, Geneva, 1992); deforestation data (1981–85) for Algeria, Chile, Islamic Republic of Iran, Morocco, and Tunisia: FAO, unpublished data (FAO, Rome, March 1988); protected area data for temperate countries: The World Conservation Union, formerly the International Union for Conservation of Nature and Natural Resources (IUCN), *The Conservation Atlas of Tropical Forests: Africa* (Simon & Schuster, New York, 1992), and IUCN, *The Conservation Atlas of Tropical Forests: Asia and the Pacific* (Macmillan Press Ltd, London, 1991).

The FAO and UNECE/FAO used slightly different definitions in their assessments, each adapting their definitions to the respective forest ecosystem (tropical and temperate). For this reason, data from tropical and temperate countries are not strictly comparable. The FAO defines a *natural forest* in tropical countries as either a closed forest where trees cover a high proportion of the ground and where grass does not form a continuous layer on the forest floor (this includes broadleaved forests, coniferous forests, and bamboo forests), or an open forest, which the FAO defines as mixed forest/grasslands with at least 10 percent tree cover and a continuous grass layer on the forest floor. A tropical forest encompasses all stands except plantations and includes stands that have been degraded to some degree by agriculture, fire, logging, or acid precipitation. For all regions, trees are distinguished from shrubs on the basis of height: a mature tree has a single well-defined stem and is taller than 7 meters; a mature shrub is usually less than 7 meters tall.

UNECE/FAO defines a forest as land where tree crowns cover more than 20 percent of the area. Also included are open forest formations; forest roads and firebreaks; small, temporarily cleared areas; young stands expected to achieve at least 20 percent crown cover upon maturity; and windbreaks and shelterbelts exceeding 0.5 hectare in size. Plantation area is included under temperate country estimates of natural forest extent.

The category *other wooded land* encompasses forest fallows (closed and open forests) and shrubs in tropical countries. In the temperate zone, other wooded land consists of open woodland and scrub, shrub, and brushland. The category also includes wooded areas used for rangeland, but excludes orchards, wood lots under 0.5 hectare and tree hedgerows.

Annual deforestation refers to the "clearing of forest lands for all forms of agricultural uses (shifting cultivation, permanent agriculture and ranching) and for other land uses such as settlements, other infrastructure and mining." In tropical countries, this entails clearing that reduces tree crown cover to less than 10 percent. As defined here, deforestation does not include other alterations, such as selective logging (unless the forest cover is permanently reduced to less than 10 percent), that can substantially affect forests, forest soil, wildlife and its habitat, and the global carbon cycle.

Logging of closed broadleaf forest provides averages of the total area of *primary* (undisturbed) and thus secondary (previously logged) forest logged each year. Note that many "primary" forests are essentially old secondary forests.

Plantations refer to forest stands established artificially by afforestation and reforestation for industrial and nonindustrial usage. Reforestation does not include regeneration of old tree crops (through either natural regeneration or forest management), although some countries may report regeneration as reforestation. Many trees are also planted for nonindustrial uses, such as village wood lots. Reforestation data often exclude this component.

Protected forests in tropical countries are protected areas such as national parks and reserves occurring within mapped moist forest zones. Because only fragments of forest remain within some of these areas, these data may overestimate the actual extent of protected forest. Totals for African countries do not include areas protected as forest reserves. Totals for Asian countries do not include protected areas under 5,000 hectares. Protected forests for temperate countries consist primarily of national parks and nature reserves found within forests and other wooded lands, although other protected area categories apply.

Data for tropical developing countries are based on the FAO's 1990 tropical forest resources assessment. The survey provides a consistent estimate of tropical forest extent and rates of forest area change between 1981 and 1990 by using a model to adjust baseline forest inventory data from each country to a common year (1990). Existing forest inventory data on national and subnational scales were carefully reviewed, adjusted to a common set of classifications and concepts, and finally combined in a data base. The FAO used a geographic information system to integrate statistical and map data for this purpose. The model used forest area adjustment functions that correlated the share of forest cover for each subnational unit to population density and growth, initial forest extent, and ecological zone. This relation is expressed through the differential equation $dY/dP = b_1 \times Y^{b_2} - b_3 \times Y$ where Y is the percentage of nonforest area, P is the natural log of (1 + population density), and b_1, b_2, and b_3 are the model parameters. The shape of the respective adjustment curves differed for each ecological zone; for example, there was a logistic function for the wet zones and an inverted j-function for the dry zones.

The reliability of these modeled estimates hinges partly on the quality of the primary data sources feeding into the model. The FAO assessed the quality and appropriateness of the national forestry inventories and their contribution to the reliability of the reported state and change assessments. The variation in quality, comprehensiveness, and timeliness of the forest information is tremendous, and acute information deficits in regards to forest resources can easily be highlighted. While good forest resources data are hard to find for Africa, better data are available for Latin America, and the best information obtainable is that for Asia. Only four countries in Africa, Côte d'Ivoire, the Gambia, Mali, and Rwanda, had survey data, useful as baselines, that was judged to be in the highest of three data reliability classes because of their dependence on high-resolution satellite data and extensive ground truthing. In regard to the data's appropriateness for change assessments, all African countries but two, Côte d'Ivoire and Rwanda, were judged as having no reliable multidate information (the lowest of three reliability classes); thus, forest change estimates for those countries were based exclusively on models. Medium-to-high quality data for change estimates were available for 8 of the 33 Latin American countries and for 13 of the 17 Asian countries, which had the highest percentage of countries in the high-reliability category.

While the forest change model allowed standardization of country data to a common baseline, a number of factors may have contributed to discrepancies in forest area and change estimates for specific countries: the 1990 baseline data are, on average, 10 years old; potential forest cover estimates for dry forests and the related adjustment function are of unknown reliability; for some countries, socioeconomic factors may have played a larger role in deforestation, for example, livestock projects in Central America and resettlement schemes in Indonesia. The FAO acknowledged these shortcomings implicitly and noted that their country estimates are "not intended to replace the original country information which remain a unique source of reference."

Because of the shortcomings of the FAO methodology, readers are encouraged to refer to those country inventories that use satellite data or extensive ground data for estimates of forest cover and deforestation. Data for several independent country assessments are presented below:

■ *Brazil*: Two recent satellite-imagery-based assessments of deforestation in the Brazilian Amazon have resulted in different deforestation rate estimates for this region. A study by the U.S. National Space and Aeronautics Administration (NASA) and the University of New Hampshire (UNH) compared forest cover in 1978 and 1988 and estimated forest loss at 1.5 million hectares per year during the intervening period. Brazil's National Institute for Space Research (INPE) and National Institute for Research in the Amazon (INPA) looked at deforestation during 1978, 1988, 1989, 1990, and 1991. Their deforestation estimate for 1978–88 is 2.2 million hectares per year, although unlike the NASA/UNH estimate, this figure includes forest areas inundated by hydroelectric projects. The difference, compared to the NASA/UNH estimate, is also attributable to differences in how 1978 imagery was interpreted and the fact that INPE/INPA's 1988 imagery was more detailed than that used by NASA/UNH. A tentative, revised INPE/INPA estimate of deforestation between 1978 and 1988 put annual deforestation at 2.03 million hectares (including areas inundated for hydroelectric projects). Deforestation in secondary forest areas and within Cerrado (dry scrub savannah) areas were not included in either of the INPE/INPA or NASA/UNH studies. The FAO data presented in this table include deforestation in all of Brazil including secondary forest areas and other forested areas. INPE/INPA found that deforestation in Brazilian Amazonia declined from 1988 through 1991. Deforestation in 1990–91 was 1.11 million hectares. **Sources:** Philip Fearnside, *Deforestation in Brazilian Amazonia: Comparison of Recent LANDSAT estimates* (INPA, Manaus, Brazil, September 1993), and David Skole and Compton Tucker, "Tropical Deforestation and Habitat Fragmentation in the Amazon: Satellite Data from 1978 to 1988," *Science* Vol. 260 (June 25, 1993), pp. 1905–1909.

■ *India*: A 1991 country-wide assessment using Landsat imagery covering 1987 to 1989, supplemented by ground surveys in 1990–91, estimated India's forest cover (mangrove forests and forests with a crown density of at least 10 percent) at 63.9 million hectares. Comparison with data from a 1989 forest assessment suggested a 28,000-hectare annual increase in forest area. This increase may have been partially due to technical changes in assessment techniques (e.g., better imagery, more accurate interpretation, and corrections in geographical area). **Source:** Ministry of Environment and Forest, *The State of the Forest Report 1991* (Ministry of Environment and Forest, Dehra Dun, India, undated).

■ *Mexico*: An inventory based on 1990 LANDSAT TM imagery estimated forest cover at 49.6 million hectares. Comparison with 1980 LANDSAT MSS imagery yields an annual deforestation estimate of 406,000 hectares. **Source:** Secretaria de Agricultura y Recursos Hidraulicos (SARH), *Mexico 1991–92 Inventario Nacional Forestal de Gran Vision: Reporte Principal* (SARH, Mexico City, Mexico, undated), and Victor Sosa

Cedillo, personal communication (Subsecretaria Forestal y de Fauna Silvestre, Mexico City, Mexico, September 1993).

The 1980 forest extent estimates for tropical countries presented in this table are taken from the 1990 assessment and therefore are not comparable with estimates for that year presented in previous editions of *World Resources*. Past estimates were taken from two earlier FAO studies on forest extent. The FAO's 1980 assessment covered 76 tropical developing countries and used subnational statistical data on population and socioeconomic variables, maps on vegetation and ecofloristic zones, forest survey data, and remote-sensing images to determine forest area. In many cases, the FAO adjusted data to fit common definitions and to correspond to the baseline year of 1980. The FAO *1988 Interim Report* expanded the country coverage of the 1980 assessment to 53 more developing countries (covering the whole developing world and overseas territories of industrialized countries), keeping 1980 as the reference year. In that document, the FAO evaluated the overall reliability of data on closed forest areas and deforestation rates for the original 76 developing countries. The 1990 assessment incorporated previously unavailable baseline inventory data to improve on 1980 country estimates.

The UNECE/FAO 1990 survey of temperate-zone countries covers all forests in the 32 countries of the ECE region (Europe, North America, and the former U.S.S.R.), as well as forests in Japan, Australia, and New Zealand. Data for this study were obtained mainly from official sources in response to a questionnaire, although estimates by experts in some countries; recent ECE and FAO publications, country reports, and official articles; and estimates by the professional staff conducting the study are also included. Most data refer to the period around 1990, although data for Belgium are based on 1980 figures, data for Iceland cover 1970–85, and estimates for several other countries are from the mid- to late 1980s.

Table 19.2 Tropical Forest Extent and Loss by Ecosystem Type, 1981–90

Source: Food and Agriculture Organization of the United Nations (FAO), Forest Resources Division, *Forest Resources Assessment 1990: Tropical Countries* (FAO, Rome, 1993).

Total forest consists of both closed forest where trees cover a high proportion of the ground and where grass does not form a continuous layer on the forest floor (this includes broadleaved forests, coniferous forests, and bamboo forests), or open forest, which the FAO defines as mixed forest/grasslands with at least 10 percent tree cover and a continuous grass layer.

The *forest ecosystem types* presented in this table were defined by the FAO on the basis of ecofloristic zone and vegetation maps. Ecofloristic zones are classified according

to the dominant vegetation expected within areas sharing common ecological parameters: rainfall, length of dry season, relative humidity, temperature, and soil types. By including data from vegetation maps that incorporate information on land use, the FAO was able to provide some measure of anthropogenic change that has occurred to the landscape. The FAO defines the following ecosystem types:

■ *Rainforests* consist of wet and very moist evergreen and semi-evergreen forests in regions where mean annual rainfall exceeds 2,000 millimeters.

■ *Moist deciduous forests* include moist semideciduous and deciduous forests, woodlands, and tree savannahs in regions where mean annual rainfall is between 1,000 and 2,000 millimeters.

■ *Hill and montane forests* range from premontane to alpine forests (wet, moist, and dry) in upland areas over 800 meters in elevation.

■ *Dry deciduous forests* consist of drought deciduous and evergreen forests, woodlands, and tree savannahs in regions where mean annual rainfall is between 500 and 1,000 millimeters.

■ *Very dry forests* include discontinuous thickets and tree/shrub savannahs in regions where mean annual rainfall is between 200 and 500 millimeters.

■ *Desert forests* consist of tree/shrub steppes in regions where mean annual rainfall is below 200 millimeters.

For details concerning the 1990 Forest Resources Assessment methodology, refer to the Technical Notes for Table 19.1.

Table 19.3 Wood Production and Trade, 1979–91

Source: Food and Agriculture Organization of the United Nations (FAO), *Agrostat-PC* on diskette (FAO, Rome, April 1993).

Total roundwood production refers to all wood in the rough, whether destined for industrial or fuelwood uses. All wood felled or harvested from forests and trees outside the forest, with or without bark, round, split, roughly squared, or other forms such as roots and stumps, is included.

Fuel and charcoal production covers all rough wood used for cooking, heating, and power production. Wood intended for charcoal production, pit kilns, and portable ovens is included.

Industrial roundwood production comprises all roundwood products other than fuelwood and charcoal: sawlogs, veneer logs, sleepers, pitprops, pulpwood, and other industrial products.

Processed wood production includes sawnwood and panels. *Sawnwood* is wood that has been sawn, planed, or shaped into products such as planks, beams, boards, rafters, or railroad ties. Wood flooring is excluded. Sawnwood generally is thicker than 5 millimeters. *Panels* include all wood-based panel commodities such as veneer sheets, plywood, particle board, and compressed or noncompressed fiberboard.

Paper production includes newsprint, printing and writing paper, and other paper and paperboard.

Average annual net trade in roundwood is the balance of imports minus exports. Trade in roundwood includes sawlogs and veneer logs, fuelwood, pulpwood, other industrial roundwood, and the roundwood equivalent of trade in charcoal, wood residues, and chips and particles. All trade data refer to both coniferous and nonconiferous wood. Imports are usually on a cost, insurance, and freight basis. Exports are generally on a free-on-board basis.

The FAO compiles forest products data from responses to annual questionnaires sent to national governments. Data from other sources, such as national statistical yearbooks, are also used. In some cases, the FAO prepares its own estimates. The FAO continually revises its data using new information; the latest figures are subject to revision.

Statistics on the production of fuelwood and charcoal are lacking for many countries. The FAO uses population data and country-specific, per capita consumption figures to estimate fuelwood and charcoal production. Consumption of nonconiferous fuelwood ranges from a low of 0.0016 cubic meter per capita per year in Jordan to a high of 0.9783 cubic meter per capita per year in Benin. Consumption was also estimated for coniferous fuelwood. For both coniferous and nonconiferous fuelwood, the per capita consumption estimates were multiplied by the number of people in the country to determine national totals.

20. Biodiversity

Biodiversity—the genetic variation within a species, and the diversity of species and the ecosystems they inhabit—is the focus of this chapter. Natural habitats and the species within them are critical for maintaining ecosystem functions such as the cycling of water, nutrients, and other materials necessary for human survival. The data presented here, therefore, provide an indication of the Earth's health. Wild species, although valuable in their own right, are also an important economic capital resource—they are a source of medicines, industrial products, food, fuel, and other goods. This chapter includes data on the trade in wild species.

The establishment of parks and reserves is a primary method used by governments to preserve habitats and species. Table 20.1 shows the number and total area of nationally protected systems, by country. Currently, 6 percent of the world's land area, excluding Antarctica, is either strictly or partially protected. A further 3 percent (359 million hectares) is managed as resource and anthropological reserves, where some extractive use is permitted. The 1992 Caracas Action Plan of the World Parks Congress (see Chapter 8, "Biodiversity"), sets a goal of protecting at least 10 percent of each of the world's major biomes. At the regional level, only North and Central America (11.7 percent) and Oceania (9.9 percent) meet this goal when total land area is considered, although the degree of protection afforded different ecosystems within these regions varies. The countries of the former U.S.S.R. protect the least amount of their land area; just over 1 percent. Table 20.1 also provides information on the size of protected areas. Only 11 percent of the world's protected areas cover at least 100,000 hectares. One quarter of Africa's and South America's protected areas are at least 100,000 hectares in size, while less than 5 percent of Europe's parks and reserves fall within this category.

Table 20.2 provides information on internationally protected systems, marine and coastal protected areas, and areas of low, medium, and high human disturbance. Biosphere reserves, world heritage sites, and wetlands of international importance are areas of particular conservation value, and thus are afforded global recognition. In addition, biosphere reserve design can embrace the concept of integrating human needs with biodiversity protection by permitting limited traditional land uses within designated reserve areas. As of June 1993, 312 biosphere sites had been designated globally, 170 of these in Europe and North and Central America.

Human disturbance provides one surrogate measure of the extent of remaining natural habitat. Less than half of the Earth's land surface, excluding Antarctica, is in areas currently subject to low human disturbance. This figure includes nonvegetated land such as deserts and rocky mountaintops. According to these data, South America has the largest area with low human disturbance (59 percent), while Europe has the smallest area (15 percent).

Table 20.3 shows direct measures of habitat extent and loss. These data are not necessarily comparable among countries due to differences in the definitions and methodologies used in compiling these estimates. This table identifies remaining habitats and habitat loss by six broad vegetational categories, ranging from moist forests to desert/scrub.

Tables 20.4 and 20.5 present information on numbers of known species, endemic species, and threatened species by country for six taxonomic groups. The number of species per 10,000 square kilometers gives readers a measure of relative species richness among countries of differing size. In general, tropical countries have far higher numbers of mammalian, bird, and higher plant species relative to their size than do temperate countries. Countries with high levels of endemism are conservation-priority areas, because, by definition, loss of endemic species from a country implies their extinction. Data on total and endemic species numbers for reptiles and amphibians are spottier than data presented for mammals, birds and higher plants, as these taxa have not been as thoroughly studied.

Table 20.6 contains information on Convention on International Trade in Endangered Species of Wild Flora and Fauna (CITES)-regulated trade. These data show that a handful of developed countries consistently ranked among the top 10 importers of live primates, cat skins, live birds and reptiles, and live cacti and orchids in 1990. The United States and Japan led this category, while the United Kingdom, Switzerland, Belgium, France, and Italy were also major importers. No clear patterns of a similar nature existed among exporting countries in 1990. China was the number one exporter of cat skins, reptile skins, and live orchids. Indonesia led in exports of live primates, and Senegal was the primary exporter of live birds. The Dominican Republic exported the largest number of live cacti.

Table 20.1 National Protection of Natural Areas, 1993

	All Protected Areas (IUCN categories I-V)			Totally Protected Areas (IUCN categories I-III)		Partially Protected Areas (IUCN categories IV-V)		Protected Areas (IUCN categories I-V) at Least 100,000 ha in Size			1 million ha in Size			Resource and Anthropological Reserves (IUCN categories VI-VIII)	
	Number	Area (000 ha)	Percent of Land Area	Number	Area (000 ha)	Number	Area (000 ha)	Number	Area (000 ha)	Number as % of Total	Number	Area (000 ha)	Number as % of Total	Number	Area (000 ha)
WORLD	8,619	792,266	5.9	2,546	464,447	6,073	327,818	964	682,714	11.2	130	441,300	1.5	3,868	358,848
AFRICA	704	138,893	4.6	260	91,218	444	47,675	180	127,703	25.6	34	81,275	4.8	1,562	74,636
Algeria	19	12,719	5.3	12	12,601	7	118	2	12,500	10.5	2	12,500	10.5	0	0
Angola	5	2,641	2.1	1	790	4	1,851	3	2,568	60.0	0	0	0.0	3	3,620
Benin	2	844	7.5	2	844	0	0	2	844	100.0	0	0	0.0	36	1,881
Botswana	9	10,225	17.6	4	8,987	5	1,238	8	10,217	88.9	3	8,837	33.3	6	456
Burkina Faso	12	2,662	9.7	3	489	9	2,173	5	2,355	41.7	1	1,600	8.3	47	970
Burundi	3	89	3.2	0	0	3	89	0	0	0.0	0	0	0.0	2	5
Cameroon	14	2,050	4.3	7	1,032	7	1,019	8	2,012	57.1	0	0	0.0	8	98
Central African Rep	13	6,106	9.8	5	3,188	8	2,918	12	6,020	92.3	3	3,820	23.1	28	966
Chad	7	2,980	2.3	2	414	5	2,566	6	2,930	85.7	1	2,060	14.3	7	480
Congo	10	1,177	3.4	1	127	9	1,051	3	901	30.0	0	0	0.0	0	0
Cote d'Ivoire	12	1,993	6.2	10	1,891	2	102	4	1,724	33.3	1	1,150	8.3	135	3,437
Djibouti	1	10	0.4	1	10	0	0	0	0	0.0	0	0	0.0	0	0
Egypt	13	800	0.8	4	57	9	744	1	480	7.7	0	0	0.0	0	0
Equatorial Guinea	0	0	0.0	0	0	0	0	0	0	0.0	0	0	0.0	0	0
Ethiopia	11	2,534	2.1	11	2,534	0	0	6	2,295	54.5	0	0	0.0	0	0
Gabon	6	1,045	3.9	1	15	5	1,030	2	880	33.3	0	0	0.0	4	650
Gambia, The	3	18	1.6	3	18	0	0	0	0	0.0	0	0	0.0	0	0
Ghana	8	1,075	4.5	6	1,062	2	12	3	1,011	37.5	0	0	0.0	214	2,555
Guinea	3	164	0.7	3	164	0	0	1	112	33.3	0	0	0.0	74	881
Guinea-Bissau	0	0	0.0	0	0	0	0	0	0	0.0	0	0	0.0	0	0
Kenya	36	3,470	6.0	31	3,411	5	59	6	2,777	16.7	1	1,175	2.8	115	2,725
Lesotho	1	7	0.2	0	0	1	7	0	0	0.0	0	0	0.0	0	0
Liberia	1	129	1.3	1	129	0	0	1	129	100.0	0	0	0.0	12	1,429
Libya	3	155	0.1	1	35	2	120	1	100	33.3	0	0	0.0	1	15
Madagascar	36	1,115	1.9	16	740	20	375	1	152	2.8	0	0	0.0	6	125
Malawi	9	1,059	8.9	5	696	4	362	3	725	33.3	0	0	0.0	60	704
Mali	11	4,012	3.2	1	350	10	3,662	6	3,788	54.5	2	2,950	18.2	5	1,735
Mauritania	4	1,746	1.7	3	1,496	1	250	3	1,733	75.0	1	1,173	25.0	0	0
Mauritius	0	0	0.0	0	0	0	0	0	0	0.0	0	0	0.0	0	0
Morocco	10	362	0.8	5	55	5	307	1	220	10.0	0	0	0.0	1	6
Mozambique	1	2	0.0	0	0	1	2	0	0	0.0	0	0	0.0	4	41
Namibia	11	10,371	12.6	6	8,978	5	1,393	6	10,285	54.5	3	8,804	27.3	5	784
Niger	6	9,697	7.7	2	1,501	4	8,196	4	9,543	66.7	2	9,017	33.3	0	0
Nigeria	20	3,062	3.3	7	2,317	13	745	9	2,714	45.0	0	0	0.0	4	717
Rwanda	2	327	12.4	2	327	0	0	1	312	50.0	0	0	0.0	4	150
Senegal	9	2,180	11.1	5	1,012	4	1,168	3	2,034	33.3	0	0	0.0	1	60
Sierra Leone	2	82	1.1	0	0	2	82	0	0	0.0	0	0	0.0	18	266
Somalia	1	180	0.3	0	0	1	180	1	180	100.0	0	0	0.0	1	334
South Africa	235	7,413	6.1	20	3,252	215	4,161	9	3,916	3.8	1	1,949	0.4	3	11
Sudan	16	9,383	3.7	9	8,514	7	869	7	9,116	43.8	4	7,480	25.0	11	2,867
Swaziland	4	46	2.6	0	0	4	46	0	0	0.0	0	0	0.0	1	14
Tanzania	28	13,000	13.8	11	3,910	17	9,090	18	12,577	64.3	3	7,771	10.7	54	11,895
Togo	11	647	11.4	3	357	8	290	3	503	27.3	0	0	0.0	39	269
Tunisia	6	44	0.3	6	44	0	0	0	0	0.0	0	0	0.0	11	131
Uganda	32	1,871	7.9	6	834	26	1,037	6	1,307	18.8	0	0	0.0	166	4,539
Zaire	8	9,917	4.2	8	9,917	0	0	8	9,917	100.0	4	7,285	50.0	12	3,708
Zambia	20	6,361	8.5	20	6,361	0	0	11	6,022	55.0	1	2,240	5.0	404	23,219
Zimbabwe	25	3,068	7.9	11	2,704	14	364	6	2,805	24.0	1	1,465	4.0	59	2,889
ASIA	2,181	121,161	4.4	422	36,146	1,759	85,015	190	89,996	8.7	18	48,532	0.8	1,149	30,629
Afghanistan	5	183	0.3	1	41	4	142	0	0	0.0	0	0	0.0	0	0
Bangladesh	8	97	0.7	0	0	8	97	0	0	0.0	0	0	0.0	1	12
Bhutan	5	906	19.3	1	66	4	840	1	790	20.0	0	0	0.0	3	46
Cambodia	0	0	0.0	0	0	0	0	0	0	0.0	0	0	0.0	0	0
China	434	30,767	3.2	3	98	431	30,669	49	24,423	11.3	8	15,398	1.8	1	130
India	331	13,160	4.0	60	3,725	271	9,435	18	5,414	5.4	0	0	0.0	1	71
Indonesia	186	19,339	10.2	108	13,910	78	5,428	41	15,938	22.0	4	6,668	2.2	528	13,657
Iran, Islamic Rep	62	7,979	4.8	26	2,986	36	4,994	17	6,282	27.4	1	1,295	1.6	0	0
Iraq	0	0	0.0	0	0	0	0	0	0	0.0	0	0	0.0	0	0
Israel	21	207	10.0	1	3	20	204	1	100	4.8	0	0	0.0	0	0
Japan	685	4,666	12.3	22	1,310	663	3,356	8	1,276	1.2	0	0	0.0	54	1,342
Jordan	8	100	1.1	1	1	7	99	0	0	0.0	0	0	0.0	0	0
Korea, Dem People's Rep	2	58	0.5	1	44	1	14	0	0	0.0	0	0	0.0	0	0
Korea, Rep	26	757	7.6	6	41	20	715	1	234	3.8	0	0	0.0	0	0
Kuwait	1	25	1.4	0	0	1	25	0	0	0.0	0	0	0.0	0	0
Lao People's Dem Rep	0	0	0.0	0	0	0	0	0	0	0.0	0	0	0.0	0	0
Lebanon	1	4	0.3	1	4	0	0	0	0	0.0	0	0	0.0	0	0
Malaysia	48	1,487	4.5	38	897	10	589	5	965	10.4	0	0	0.0	359	9,415
Mongolia	15	6,168	3.9	15	6,168	0	0	2	5,850	13.3	1	5,300	6.7	2	890
Myanmar	2	173	0.3	1	161	1	13	1	161	50.0	0	0	0.0	6	262
Nepal	12	1,109	7.9	8	1,014	4	94	4	791	33.3	0	0	0.0	2	216
Oman	2	54	0.3	0	0	2	54	0	0	0.0	0	0	0.0	4	2,782
Pakistan	53	3,655	4.6	6	882	47	2,773	11	2,688	20.8	0	0	0.0	0	0
Philippines	27	573	1.9	14	226	13	347	1	140	3.7	0	0	0.0	11	103
Saudi Arabia	9	21,197	9.9	2	260	7	20,937	8	21,137	88.9	4	19,871	44.4	0	0
Singapore	1	2	2.6	0	0	1	2	0	0	0.0	0	0	0.0	0	0
Sri Lanka	43	784	11.9	14	492	29	292	1	132	2.3	0	0	0.0	154	1,182
Syrian Arab Rep	0	0	0.0	0	0	0	0	0	0	0.0	0	0	0.0	0	0
Thailand	106	6,475	12.6	66	3,424	40	3,051	19	3,387	17.9	0	0	0.0	0	0
Turkey	18	239	0.3	12	158	6	82	0	0	0.0	0	0	0.0	14	211
United Arab Emirates	0	0	0.0	0	0	0	0	0	0	0.0	0	0	0.0	1	12
Viet Nam	59	897	2.7	7	142	52	755	1	182	1.7	0	0	0.0	1	150
Yemen	0	0	0.0	0	0	0	0	0	0	0.0	0	0	0.0	0	0

Table 20.1

	All Protected Areas (IUCN categories I-V)			Totally Protected Areas (IUCN categories I-III)		Partially Protected Areas (IUCN categories IV-V)		Protected Areas (IUCN categories I-V) at Least 100,000 ha in Size			1 million ha in Size			Resource and Anthropological Reserves (IUCN categories VI-VIII)	
	Number	Area (000 ha)	Percent of Land Area	Number	Area (000 ha)	Number	Area (000 ha)	Number	Area (000 ha)	as % of Total	Number	Area (000 ha)	as % of Total	Number	Area (000 ha)
NORTH & CENTRAL AMERICA {a}	1,752	263,250	11.7	606	170,353	1,146	92,897	197	244,217	11.2	37	192,468	2.1	243	16,147
Belize	10	291	12.7	5	156	5	135	2	210	20.0	0	0	0.0	15	410
Canada	411	49,448	5.0	132	26,812	279	22,636	59	44,638	14.4	12	30,981	2.9	27	5,989
Costa Rica	25	621	12.1	15	484	10	137	1	194	4.0	0	0	0.0	59	1,035
Cuba	57	894	8.1	18	157	39	737	1	179	1.8	0	0	0.0	5	742
Dominican Rep	18	1,048	21.5	8	564	10	484	3	643	16.7	0	0	0.0	0	0
El Salvador	5	19	0.9	1	6	4	14	0	0	0.0	0	0	0.0	0	0
Guatemala	17	833	7.6	11	779	6	54	3	697	17.6	0	0	0.0	10	843
Haiti	3	10	0.3	2	8	1	2	0	0	0.0	0	0	0.0	0	0
Honduras	38	543	4.8	15	401	23	142	1	113	2.6	0	0	0.0	8	1,233
Jamaica	1	2	0.1	1	2	0	0	0	0	0.0	0	0	0.0	46	93
Mexico	60	9,897	5.1	42	1,985	18	7,912	11	8,869	18.3	2	6,047	3.3	18	2,542
Nicaragua	21	952	7.3	5	323	16	629	2	798	9.5	0	0	0.0	10	865
Panama	15	1,328	17.2	14	1,326	1	2	4	1,185	26.7	0	0	0.0	10	1,435
Trinidad and Tobago	9	18	3.4	3	3	6	15	0	0	0.0	0	0	0.0	0	0
United States	937	98,456	10.5	290	38,659	647	59,796	108	88,442	11.5	21	57,191	2.2	2	899
SOUTH AMERICA	667	114,596	6.4	314	65,836	353	48,759	181	104,177	27.1	25	55,746	3.7	679	227,935
Argentina	100	9,336	3.4	37	3,937	63	5,399	18	7,805	18.0	2	2,640	2.0	19	3,829
Bolivia	26	9,250	8.4	8	3,774	18	5,476	15	8,928	57.7	4	5,684	15.4	17	15,371
Brazil	214	27,742	3.3	112	18,371	102	9,370	56	24,527	26.2	4	7,796	1.9	295	115,275
Chile	65	13,715	18.1	31	8,365	34	5,350	17	12,621	26.2	5	10,140	7.7	0	0
Colombia	79	9,391	8.2	35	8,991	44	400	18	8,230	22.8	2	2,372	2.5	268	72,443
Ecuador	15	11,136	39.3	9	3,105	6	8,031	7	10,972	46.7	1	7,990	6.7	52	2,918
Guyana	1	59	0.3	1	59	0	0	0	0	0.0	0	0	0.0	0	0
Paraguay	19	1,483	3.6	13	1,365	6	118	3	1,160	15.8	0	0	0.0	19	8,544
Peru	22	4,176	3.2	14	4,011	8	165	6	3,850	27.3	2	3,012	9.1	19	8,544
Suriname	13	736	4.5	2	87	11	649	3	460	23.1	0	0	0.0	1	68
Uruguay	8	32	0.2	2	15	6	17	0	0	0.0	0	0	0.0	3	15
Venezuela	104	27,534	30.2	49	13,750	55	13,784	38	25,624	36.5	5	16,112	4.8	4	9,364
EUROPE	2,177	45,533	9.3	298	8,513	1,879	37,020	99	20,414	4.5	1	1,903	0.0	143	4,035
Albania	13	45	1.5	6	23	7	22	0	0	0.0	0	0	0.0	0	0
Austria	187	2,118	25.3	1	1	186	2,117	1	105	0.5	0	0	0.0	0	0
Belgium	3	77	2.5	0	0	3	77	0	0	0.0	0	0	0.0	0	0
Bulgaria	50	261	2.4	28	168	22	94	0	0	0.0	0	0	0.0	0	0
Czechoslovakia (former)	65	2,059	16.1	13	290	52	1,769	2	224	3.1	0	0	0.0	0	0
Denmark	65	409	9.5	6	16	59	393	1	120	1.5	0	0	0.0	0	0
Finland	38	850	2.5	36	545	2	306	2	541	5.3	0	0	0.0	0	0
France	88	5,300	9.6	9	289	79	5,011	21	4,160	23.9	0	0	0.0	1	9
Germany	472	8,781	24.6	1	13	471	8,768	24	3,895	5.1	0	0	0.0	0	0
Greece	18	103	0.8	10	78	8	24	0	0	0.0	0	0	0.0	5	125
Hungary	54	577	6.2	5	159	49	418	0	0	0.0	0	0	0.0	0	0
Iceland	20	916	8.9	8	219	12	697	2	600	10.0	0	0	0.0	2	38
Ireland	6	39	0.6	4	34	2	4	0	0	0.0	0	0	0.0	0	0
Italy	143	2,008	6.7	7	295	136	1,713	2	268	1.4	0	0	0.0	0	0
Netherlands	67	353	9.4	26	230	41	122	1	155	1.5	0	0	0.0	0	0
Norway	81	1,609	5.0	52	1,265	29	344	5	830	6.2	0	0	0.0	0	0
Poland	80	2,242	7.2	16	150	64	2,092	5	706	6.3	0	0	0.0	124	3,584
Portugal	23	560	6.1	1	21	22	539	1	100	4.3	0	0	0.0	2	16
Romania	40	1,089	4.6	10	106	30	983	1	547	2.5	0	0	0.0	1	1
Spain	161	3,504	6.9	9	123	152	3,382	6	989	3.7	0	0	0.0	0	0
Sweden	193	2,960	6.6	14	495	179	2,466	6	1,476	3.1	0	0	0.0	0	0
Switzerland	112	753	18.2	1	17	111	736	0	0	0.0	0	0	0.0	0	0
United Kingdom	131	4,635	18.9	0	0	131	4,635	15	2,272	11.5	0	0	0.0	0	0
Yugoslavia (former)	61	788	3.1	30	484	31	304	0	0	0.0	0	0	0.0	6	224
U.S.S.R. (former)	218	24,330	1.1	164	23,789	54	541	40	20,022	18.3	4	5,768	1.8	1	400
Armenia	4	222	7.4	4	222	0	0	1	150	25.0	0	0	0.0	0	0
Azerbaijan	11	178	2.0	11	178	0	0	0	0	0.0	0	0	0.0	0	0
Belarus	4	237	1.1	2	138	2	99	0	0	0.0	0	0	0.0	0	0
Estonia	37	360	8.0	6	165	31	195	1	112	2.7	0	0	0.0	0	0
Georgia	15	187	2.7	15	187	0	0	0	0	0.0	0	0	0.0	0	0
Kazakhstan	8	835	0.3	8	835	0	0	2	460	25.0	0	0	0.0	0	0
Kyrgyzstan	5	197	1.0	5	197	0	0	1	117	20.0	0	0	0.0	0	0
Latvia	21	175	2.7	5	131	16	44	0	0	0.0	0	0	0.0	1	400
Lithuania	0	0	0.0	0	0	0	0	0	0	0.0	0	0	0.0	0	0
Moldova	0	0	0.0	0	0	0	0	0	0	0.0	0	0	0.0	0	0
Russian Federation	75	20,033	1.2	74	20,003	1	30	33	18,351	44.0	4	5,768	5.3	0	0
Tajikistan	3	86	0.6	3	86	0	0	0	0	0.0	0	0	0.0	0	0
Turkmenistan	8	1,111	2.3	8	1,111	0	0	2	832	25.0	0	0	0.0	0	0
Ukraine	17	465	0.8	13	292	4	173	0	0	0.0	0	0	0.0	0	0
Uzbekistan	10	245	0.5	10	245	0	0	0	0	0.0	0	0	0.0	0	0
OCEANIA	920	84,504	9.9	482	68,592	438	15,911	77	76,185	8.4	11	55,610	1.2	91	5,065
Australia	733	81,403	10.6	424	65,897	309	15,505	72	74,304	9.8	10	54,587	1.4	43	2,379
Fiji	4	6	0.3	3	6	1	0	0	0	0.0	0	0	0.0	0	0
New Zealand	124	2,901	10.7	36	2,582	88	319	5	1,881	4.0	1	1,023	0.8	19	1,639
Papua New Guinea	6	29	0.1	3	7	3	22	0	0	0.0	0	0	0.0	16	952
Solomon Islands	0	0	0.0	0	0	0	0	0	0	0.0	0	0	0.0	0	0

Source: World Conservation Monitoring Centre.
Notes: a. Regional totals include Greenland.
World totals exclude Antarctica. World and regional totals include some countries, territories, and islands not listed here.
0 = zero or less than half the unit of measure.
For additional information, see Sources and Technical Notes.

Table 20.2 International and Marine Protected Areas and

| | International Protection Systems {a} | | | | | | Marine and Coastal Protected Areas {b} | | Percentage of Total Land Area Classified as Regions of {c} | | |
| | Biosphere Reserves | | World Heritage Sites | | Wetlands of International Importance | | | | Low Human Disturbance | Medium Human Disturbance | High Human Disturbance |
	Number	Area (000 ha)	Number	Area (000 ha)	Number	Area (000 ha)	Number	Area (000 ha)			
WORLD	312	171,241	100	100,980	590	36,695	977	211,406	48	28	24
AFRICA	43	20,619	28	28,122	53	4,222	43	9,570	49	35	16
Algeria	2	7,276	1	300	2	5	1	2	83	10	7
Angola	--	--	0	0	--	--	2	62	53	29	18
Benin	1	880	0	0	0	0	0	0	13	64	24
Botswana	--	--	--	--	--	--	NA	NA	57	42	1
Burkina Faso	1	16	0	0	3	299	NA	NA	12	67	21
Burundi	--	--	0	0	--	--	NA	NA	0	3	97
Cameroon	3	850	1	526	--	--	1	160	15	51	33
Central African Rep	2	1,640	1	1,740	--	--	NA	NA	46	44	10
Chad	--	--	--	--	1	195	NA	NA	54	40	6
Congo	2	172	0	0	--	--	1	300	57	36	8
Cote d'Ivoire	2	1,480	3	1,485	--	--	1	30	23	38	39
Djibouti	--	--	--	--	--	--	0	0	0	100	0
Egypt	1	1	0	0	2	106	3	62	79	15	6
Equatorial Guinea	--	--	--	--	--	--	0	0	84	0	16
Ethiopia	--	--	1	22	--	--	1	200	2	93	5
Gabon	1	15	0	0	3	1,080	2	1,058	81	2	17
Gambia, The	--	--	0	0	--	--	0	0	X	X	X
Ghana	1	8	0	0	6	--	0	0	2	56	42
Guinea	2	133	1	13	5	225	0	0	34	41	24
Guinea-Bissau	--	--	--	--	1	39	0	0	0	36	64
Kenya	5	1,335	0	0	1	19	3	7	43	45	12
Lesotho	--	--	--	--	--	--	NA	NA	0	81	19
Liberia	--	--	--	--	--	--	0	0	27	17	57
Libya	--	--	0	0	--	--	0	0	90	9	1
Madagascar	1	140	1	152	--	--	1	2	15	4	81
Malawi	--	--	1	9	--	--	NA	NA	4	37	59
Mali	1	771	0	0	3	162	NA	NA	67	31	3
Mauritania	--	--	1	1,200	1	1,173	0	0	92	8	0
Mauritius	1	4	--	--	--	--	1	4	X	X	X
Morocco	--	--	0	0	4	11	2	13	1	9	90
Mozambique	--	--	0	0	--	--	0	0	35	43	22
Namibia	--	--	--	--	--	--	X	X	76	21	4
Niger	--	--	1	7,736	1	220	NA	NA	75	24	1
Nigeria	1	--	0	0	--	--	0	0	3	54	43
Rwanda	1	15	--	--	--	--	NA	NA	0	34	66
Senegal	3	1,094	2	929	4	100	4	81	1	48	52
Sierra Leone	--	--	--	--	--	--	0	0	0	31	69
Somalia	--	--	--	--	--	--	0	0	32	65	3
South Africa	--	--	--	--	12	228	13	152	27	33	40
Sudan	2	1,901	0	0	--	--	0	0	32	59	9
Swaziland	--	--	--	--	--	--	NA	NA	0	50	50
Tanzania	2	2,338	4	7,381	--	--	0	0	41	43	16
Togo	--	--	--	--	--	--	0	0	0	58	42
Tunisia	4	32	1	13	1	13	1	4	18	56	26
Uganda	1	220	0	0	1	15	0	0	45	15	40
Zaire	3	298	4	5,482	--	--	0	0	45	40	15
Zambia	--	--	1	4	2	333	NA	NA	82	9	9
Zimbabwe	--	--	2	1,095	--	--	NA	NA	18	55	27
ASIA	39	13,166	16	1,676	49	2,377	189	13,987	30	38	32
Afghanistan	--	--	0	0	--	--	NA	NA	17	75	8
Bangladesh	--	--	0	0	1	60	3	32	0	19	81
Bhutan	--	--	--	--	--	--	NA	NA	29	58	13
Cambodia	--	--	0	0	--	--	0	0	22	21	57
China	9	2,247	4	249	6	529	20	1,184	32	35	33
India	--	--	5	281	6	193	14	474	2	42	55
Indonesia	6	1,482	2	298	1	163	68	8,941	52	10	38
Iran, Islamic Rep	9	2,610	0	0	18	1,358	3	725	6	83	11
Iraq	--	--	0	0	--	--	0	0	25	57	17
Israel	--	--	--	--	--	--	1	31	0	64	36
Japan	4	116	0	0	4	10	30	637	0	40	61
Jordan	--	--	0	0	1	7	0	0	47	41	12
Korea, Dem People's Rep	1	132	--	--	--	--	0	0	0	35	65
Korea, Rep	1	37	0	0	--	--	3	285	0	18	82
Kuwait	--	--	--	--	--	--	0	0	33	54	13
Lao People's Dem Rep	--	--	0	0	--	--	NA	NA	28	6	66
Lebanon	--	--	0	0	--	--	0	0	0	13	87
Malaysia	--	--	0	0	--	--	9	52	41	19	40
Mongolia	1	5,300	0	0	--	--	NA	NA	60	35	6
Myanmar	--	--	--	--	--	--	0	0	7	47	45
Nepal	--	--	2	208	1	18	NA	NA	21	65	14
Oman	--	--	0	0	--	--	1	1	77	23	0
Pakistan	1	31	0	0	9	21	1	16	5	80	15
Philippines	2	1,174	0	0	--	--	5	31	3	10	87
Saudi Arabia	--	--	0	0	--	--	2	475	83	17	0
Singapore	--	--	--	--	--	--	0	0	X	X	X
Sri Lanka	2	9	1	9	1	6	6	303	0	60	40
Syrian Arab Rep	--	--	0	0	--	--	0	0	9	69	22
Thailand	3	26	1	622	--	--	10	625	8	19	73
Turkey	--	--	1	10	--	--	3	114	12	40	48
United Arab Emirates	--	--	--	--	--	--	0	0	90	10	0
Viet Nam	--	--	0	0	1	12	2	34	2	10	88
Yemen	--	--	0	0	--	--	0	0	34	66	0

Levels of Human Disturbance, 1993

Table 20.2

	Biosphere Reserves Number	Area (000 ha)	World Heritage Sites Number	Area (000 ha)	Wetlands of International Importance Number	Area (000 ha)	Marine and Coastal Protected Areas {b} Number	Area (000 ha)	Low Human Disturbance	Medium Human Disturbance	High Human Disturbance
NORTH & CENTRAL AMERICA {d}	71	98,150	22	21,541	64	15,515	214	135,781	56	21	23
Belize	--	--	0	0	--	--	X	X	36	0	64
Canada	6	1,050	6	14,710	30	13,016	48	7,106	92	5	2
Costa Rica	2	729	1	585	2	30	7	194	12	18	71
Cuba	4	324	0	0	--	--	6	227	2	14	84
Dominican Rep	--	--	0	0	--	--	7	270	18	16	65
El Salvador	--	--	0	0	--	--	0	0	0	50	50
Guatemala	2	1,236	1	58	1	48	3	13	25	12	62
Haiti	--	--	0	0	--	--	0	0	5	0	95
Honduras	1	500	1	500	--	--	1	350	32	4	63
Jamaica	--	--	0	0	--	--	0	0	0	25	75
Mexico	6	1,288	1	528	1	47	11	1,119	23	33	44
Nicaragua	--	--	0	0	--	--	1	4	32	13	56
Panama	1	597	2	804	1	81	6	898	99	0	1
Trinidad and Tobago	--	--	--	--	--	--	2	3	50	0	50
United States	44	22,335	10	4,357	11	1,192	107	54,317	25	36	39
SOUTH AMERICA	26	16,866	9	4,043	13	2,820	94	24,717	59	25	16
Argentina	5	2,410	2	655	3	82	7	1,499	37	47	17
Bolivia	3	435	0	0	1	5	NA	NA	78	18	4
Brazil	1	4,937	1	170	--	--	20	2,032	67	15	18
Chile	8	2,417	0	0	1	5	32	10,050	56	27	17
Colombia	3	2,514	0	0	--	--	9	615	69	11	20
Ecuador	2	1,446	2	1,038	2	90	5	8,975	47	12	41
Guyana	--	--	0	0	--	--	0	0	98	1	1
Paraguay	--	--	0	0	--	--	NA	NA	84	13	3
Peru	3	2,507	4	2,180	3	2,416	4	710	60	36	4
Suriname	--	--	--	--	1	12	5	128	91	3	6
Uruguay	1	200	0	0	1	200	1	3	0	76	24
Venezuela	--	--	0	0	1	10	11	704	0	79	21
EUROPE	99	6,765	11	661	353	4,248	180	7,700	15	18	67
Albania	--	--	0	0	--	--	5	28	0	28	72
Austria	4	28	--	--	7	103	NA	NA	0	39	61
Belgium	--	--	--	--	6	10	0	0	0	15	85
Bulgaria	17	25	2	41	4	2	0	0	0	37	63
Czechoslovakia (former)	9	563	0	0	8	17	NA	NA	1	28	72
Denmark	--	--	0	0	27	734	3	12	0	0	100
Finland	1	350	0	0	11	101	0	0	52	30	18
France	6	576	1	12	8	423	27	849	1	14	85
Germany	12	1,259	0	0	31	661	14	732	0	20	80
Greece	2	9	0	0	11	107	13	84	0	14	86
Hungary	5	129	0	0	13	110	0	0	1	7	93
Iceland	--	--	--	--	2	58	5	509	78	1	21
Ireland	2	9	0	0	21	13	0	0	0	0	100
Italy	3	4	0	0	46	57	18	211	0	16	84
Netherlands	1	260	--	--	15	313	10	54	0	2	98
Norway	1	1,555	0	0	14	16	12	3,508	66	21	13
Poland	4	161	1	5	5	7	4	73	0	13	87
Portugal	1	--	0	0	2	31	8	132	0	20	80
Romania	3	614	1	547	1	647	0	0	1	23	77
Spain	11	716	1	4	17	102	9	75	1	16	82
Sweden	1	97	0	0	30	383	5	12	57	17	26
Switzerland	1	17	0	0	8	7	NA	NA	0	35	65
United Kingdom	13	44	2	1	57	215	35	1,194	1	2	97
Yugoslavia (former)	2	350	3	51	7	131	12	227	1	24	76
U.S.S.R. (former)	22	10,930	1	88	13	2,993	22	4,925	57	16	28
Armenia	X	X	X	X	X	X	X	X	X	X	X
Azerbaijan	X	X	X	X	1	133	X	X	X	X	X
Belarus	1	76	1	88	X	X	X	X	X	X	X
Estonia	1	1,560	X	X	1	49	X	X	X	X	X
Georgia	X	X	X	X	X	X	X	X	X	X	X
Kazakhstan	X	X	X	X	3	1,238	X	X	X	X	X
Kyrgyzstan	1	24	X	X	X	X	X	X	X	X	X
Latvia	X	X	X	X	X	X	X	X	X	X	X
Lithuania	X	X	0	0	X	X	X	X	X	X	X
Moldova	X	X	X	X	X	X	X	X	X	X	X
Russian Federation	14	9,029	0	0	3	1,168	X	X	X	X	X
Tajikistan	X	X	0	0	1	6	X	X	X	X	X
Turkmenistan	1	35	X	X	1	189	X	X	X	X	X
Ukraine	3	160	0	0	3	211	X	X	X	X	X
Uzbekistan	1	48	X	X	X	X	X	X	X	X	X
OCEANIA	13	4,745	13	44,848	45	4,519	229	14,547	61	27	12
Australia	12	4,743	10	42,168	40	4,481	184	13,035	62	28	10
Fiji	--	--	0	0	--	--	1	4	X	X	X
New Zealand	--	--	2	2,677	5	38	32	1,386	27	4	69
Papua New Guinea	--	--	--	--	--	--	0	0	64	24	13
Solomon Islands	--	--	--	--	--	--	0	0	X	X	X

Sources: World Conservation Monitoring Centre and Conservation International.
Notes: a. Areas listed often include nationally protected systems. b. 1989 data. c. Classified by units of 40,000 square hectares (see Technical Notes for details).
d. Regional totals include Greenland.
World totals exclude Antarctica. World and regional totals include countries not listed here.
0 = zero or less than half the unit of measure; X = not available; NA = not applicable; -- = country is not a party to the convention.
For additional information, see Sources and Technical Notes.

Table 20.3 Habitat Extent and Loss, 1980s

	All Forests Current Extent (000 ha)	% Lost	Dry Forests Current Extent (000 ha)	% Lost	Moist Forests Current Extent (000 ha)	% Lost	Savannah/ Grassland Current Extent (000 ha)	% Lost	Desert/ Scrub Current Extent (000 ha)	% Lost	Wetlands/ Marsh Current Extent (000 ha)	% Lost	Mangroves Current Extent (000 ha)	% Lost
WORLD	X	X	X	X	X	X	X	X	X	X	X	X	X	X
AFRICA {a}	X	X	X	X	X	X	X	X	X	X	X	X	X	X
Algeria	X	X	X	X	X	X	X	X	X	X	730	X	0	0
Angola	51,428	45	40,261	45	11,167	48	24,590	17	456	20	X	X	110	50
Benin	4,448 b	62 b	4,406	55	42 b	97 b	0	0	0	0	0	0	7	X
Botswana	11,293	62	11,293	62	0	0	12,247	53	0	0	2,331	10	0	0
Burkina Faso	4,964	80	4,964	80	0	0	768	70	0	0	0	0	0	0
Burundi	117	91	114	91	3	95	246	80	0	0	14	X	0	0
Cameroon	18,468	59	2,949	69	15,519	56	376	72	0	0	16	80	486	40
Central African Rep	27,933	55	14,667	51	13,266	59	0	0	0	0	0	0	0	0
Chad {a}	5,848	80	5,848	80	0	0	11,958	72	0	0	66	90	0	0
Congo	17,442	49	0	0	17,442	49	0	0	0	0	290	X	2	0
Cote d'Ivoire	6,308 b	80 b	3,562	60	2,746 b	88 b	0	0	0	0	32	X	3	X
Djibouti	0	0	0	0	0	0	1,000	50	120	20	0	0	9	70
Egypt	X	X	X	X	X	X	X	X	X	X	809	X	X	X
Equatorial Guinea	1,285	50	0	0	1,285	50	0	0	0	0	0	0	12	60
Ethiopia	5,570	86	5,570	86	0	0	27,469	61	525	30	0	0	0	0
Gabon	17,245	35	0	0	17,245	35	0	0	0	0	0	0	115	50
Gambia, The	122 b	89 b	72	90	50 b	88 b	0	0	0	0	0	0	50	X
Ghana	4,254 b	82 b	2,670	71	1,584 b	89 b	0	0	0	0	853	X	2	X
Guinea	7,440	69	1,799	71	5,641	69	0	0	0	0	525	X	120	60
Guinea-Bissau	512	80	0	0	512	80	0	0	0	0	0	0	315	70
Kenya	2,274	71	2,130	67	144	90	27,682	43	0	0	0	0	93	70
Lesotho	851	67	851	67	0	0	141	70	0	0	0	0	0	0
Liberia	1,424	87	8	20	1,416	87	0	0	0	0	40	X	36	70
Libya	X	X	X	X	X	X	X	X	X	X	X	X	0	0
Madagascar	13,049	75	11,401	62	1,648	84	1,509	78	0	0	197	X	130	40
Malawi	3,977	56	3,977	56	0	0	0	0	0	0	112	60	0	0
Mali {a}	7,670	78	7,670	78	0	0	8,368	80	0	0	2,000	X	0	0
Mauritania {a}	6	90	6	90	0	0	4,610	88	0	0	0	0	0	0
Mauritius	11 c	X	X	X	X	X	X	X	X	X	X	X	0	X
Morocco	X	X	X	X	X	X	X	X	X	X	33	X	0	0
Mozambique	33,137	57	33,137	57	0	0	696	20	0	0	171	10	276	60
Namibia	15,020	52	15,020	52	0	0	14,741	59	14,570	0	225	10	0	0
Niger {a}	2,278	80	2,278	80	0	0	10,985	75	0	0	38	80	0	0
Nigeria	18,201 b	80 b	14,339	70	3,862 b	91 b	498	80	0	0	42	80	1,052	X
Rwanda	184	80	184	80	0	0	157	90	0	0	80	X	0	0
Senegal	2,455 b	82	2,250	80	205 b	93 b	1,120	80	0	0	2	X	185	X
Sierra Leone	554 b	92 b	48	40	506 b	93 b	0	0	0	0	0	0	102	X
Somalia	642	67	642	67	0	0	36,374	40	712	4	0	0	54	70
South Africa	20,444	46	20,444	46	0	0	32,257	62	880	0	0	0	45	50
Sudan {a}	15,367	74	15,162	73	205	91	36,007	68	0	0	11,170	X	0	0
Swaziland	772	56	772	56	0	0	0	0	0	0	0	0	0	0
Tanzania	36,137	40	35,867	39	270	80	14,352	49	0	0	1,545	X	212	60
Togo	1,758 b	69 b	1,622	57	136 b	92 b	0	0	0	0	0	0	0	X
Tunisia	X	X	X	X	X	X	X	X	X	X	868	X	0	0
Uganda	3,371	79	2,062	67	1,309	86	1,042	71	0	0	1,420	X	0	0
Zaire	83,255	57	9,135	54	74,120	57	5,405	30	0	0	215	50	125	50
Zambia	44,606	30	44,606	30	0	0	8,175	18	0	0	1,106	10	0	0
Zimbabwe	17,169	56	17,169	56	0	0	0	0	0	0	0	0	0	0
ASIA	X	X	X	X	X	X	X	X	X	X	X	X	X	X
Afghanistan	X	X	X	X	X	X	X	X	X	X	40	X	0	0
Bahrain	X	X	X	X	X	X	X	X	X	X	X	X	0	0
Bangladesh	482	96	0	0	482	96	0	0	0	0	68	96	291	73
Bhutan	2,298	33	700	30	1,598	35	0	0	0	0	7	X	0	0
Brunei	304	25	0	0	304	25	0	0	0	0	85	27	45	17
Cambodia	3,885	78	1,608	81	2,277	74	0	0	0	0	389	45	16	5
China	6,000 d	99	X	X	X	X	X	X	391,680	X	4,200	X	67	X
India	49,929	78	35,785	81	14,144	56	0	0	8,527	88	941	79	189	85
Indonesia	60,403	51	10,503	27	49,900	54	0	0	0	0	11,872	39	2,101	45
Iran, Islamic Rep	X	X	X	X	X	X	X	X	X	X	1,418	X	X	X
Iraq	X	X	X	X	X	X	X	X	X	X	1,921	X	X	X
Israel	X	X	X	X	X	X	X	X	X	X	170	X	X	X
Japan	1,204 e	X	X	X	X	X	X	X	X	X	250	X	0	0
Jordan	X	X	X	X	X	X	X	X	X	X	1	X	0	0
Korea, Dem People's Rep	X	X	X	X	X	X	0	0	0	0	136	X	0	X
Korea, Rep	X	X	X	X	X	X	X	X	X	X	84	X	X	X
Lao People's Dem Rep	6,897	68	3,794	67	3,103	75	0	0	0	0	0	0	0	0
Lebanon	X	X	X	X	X	X	X	X	X	X	X	85	0	0
Malaysia	18,008	42	2,852	19	15,155	45	0	0	0	0	2,214	35	731	32
Mongolia	X	X	X	X	X	X	X	X	X	X	1,708	X	0	0
Myanmar	24,131	64	12,000	68	12,130	65	1,203	74	29	93	49	98	171	58
Nepal	5,381	54	882	16	4,499	58	0	0	0	0	291	X	0	0
Oman	X	X	X	X	X	X	X	X	X	X	X	X	X	X
Pakistan	764	86	184	96	580	27	0	0	2,811	69	320	74	154	78
Philippines	<1,000 d	X	X	X	X	X	X	X	X	X	1,322	X	140	X
Saudi Arabia	X	X	X	X	X	X	120,000	X	<70,500	X	X	X	X	X
Singapore	0	~100	0	0	0	~100	X	X	X	X	0	X	2	76
Sri Lanka	610	86	446	76	163	94	0	0	495	75	512	X	120	X
Syrian Arab Rep	X	X	X	X	X	X	X	X	X	X	38	X	0	0
Thailand	13,107	73	8,330	78	4,777	57	0	0	0	0	83	96	19	87
Turkey	606 e	X	X	X	X	X	X	X	X	X	1,391	X	0	0
United Arab Emirates	X	X	X	X	X	X	X	X	X	X	X	X	3	X
Viet Nam	6,758	76	2,105	68	4,654	79	0	0	0	0	26	100	147	62

Table 20.3

	All Forests (Habitat Types)		Dry Forests		Moist Forests		Savannah/ Grassland		Desert/ Scrub		Wetlands/ Marsh		Mangroves	
	Current Extent (000 ha)	% Lost	Current Extent (000 ha)	% Lost	Current Extent (000 ha)	% Lost	Current Extent (000 ha)	% Lost	Current Extent (000 ha)	% Lost	Current Extent (000 ha)	% Lost	Current Extent (000 ha)	% Lost
NORTH & CENTRAL AMERICA	X	X	X	X	X	X	X	X	X	X	X	X	X	X
Antigua and Barbuda	X	X	1	X	X	X	X	X	5	X	X	X	2	X
Barbados	X	X	X	X	X	X	X	X	X	X	X	X	0	X
Belize	X	X	X	X	975 d	X	X	X	X	X	X	X	78	X
Canada	274,000 d	48	X	X	X	X	27,663	X	X	X	127,000	X	0	0
Costa Rica	X	X	X	X	1,540 d	X	X	X	X	X	82	X	35	X
Cuba	X	X	X	X	X	X	X	X	X	X	1,747	X	626	X
Dominican Rep	335 d	93	X	X	X	X	X	X	X	X	4,844	X	24	X
El Salvador	1	X	X	X	0 d	X	X	X	X	X	77	X	45	X
Grenada	1	X	X	X	X	X	X	X	X	X	0	0	X	X
Guadeloupe	17	X	2	X	15	X	X	X	X	X	X	X	6	X
Guatemala	4,500	60	X	X	X	X	X	X	X	X	220	X	16	X
Haiti	X	X	X	X	X	X	X	X	X	X	113	X	18	X
Honduras	X	X	X	X	1,930 d	X	X	X	X	X	649	X	117	X
Jamaica	77	X	X	X	X	X	X	X	X	X	14	X	20	X
Mexico	38,461	66	X	X	X	X	X	X	100,000	X	3,264	X	1,420	X
Nicaragua	X	X	X	X	2,700 d	X	X	X	X	X	2,053	X	60	X
Panama	X	X	X	X	2,150 d	X	X	X	X	X	647	X	298	X
Saint Lucia	7	X	X	X	X	X	X	X	X	X	X	X	0	X
Saint Vincent	2 d	X	X	X	X	X	X	X	X	X	X	X	X	X
Trinidad and Tobago	X	X	X	X	X	X	X	X	X	X	21	X	9	X
United States {f}	13,000 d	95-98	X	X	X	X	3,000	~99	X	X	42,240	53	281	X
SOUTH AMERICA	964,050	20	310,980	18	653,070 g	22	264,200	23	141,230	X	74,617	X	X	X
Argentina	74,220	2	64,540	2	9,680 g	1	75,540	24	93,190	X	6,169	X	X	X
Bolivia	75,430	14	34,510	23	40,920 g	6	8,770	50	2,130	X	2,419	X	0	0
Brazil	524,190	28	155,590	17	368,600 g	31	74,000	20	0	X	29,690	X	2,500	X
Chile	20,930	22	7,520	28	13,410 g	18	10,110	12	27,370	X	8,827	X	X	X
Colombia	73,880	3	11,630	11	62,250 g	2	25,550	20	0	X	1,928	X	501	X
Ecuador	15,470	4	3,370	11	12,100 g	1	4,190	24	570	X	993	X	182	X
French Guiana	8,040	3	60	0	7,980 g	3	20	0	0	X	X	X	6	X
Guyana	17,700	2	540	5	17,160 g	1	1,840	8	0	X	814	X	80	X
Paraguay	21,800	19	20,910	20	890 g	2	10,400	20	0	X	5,724	X	0	0
Peru	74,270	12	8,800	47	65,470 g	3	13,900	41	15,230	X	1,303	X	6	X
Suriname	12,900	7	50	38	12,850 g	7	120	25	0	X	1,625	X	115	X
Uruguay	300	0	90	0	210 g	0	15,410	7	0	X	625	X	X	X
Venezuela	44,940	10	3,390	54	41,550 g	2	24,330	25	2,720	X	14,501	X	674	X
EUROPE	X	X	X	X	X	X	X	X	X	X	X	X	X	X
Albania	X	X	X	X	X	X	X	X	X	X	33	X	0	0
Austria	194 e	X	X	X	X	X	X	X	X	X	29	X	0	0
Belgium	6 e	X	X	X	X	X	~1 h	X	X	X	7	X	0	0
Bulgaria	165 e	X	X	X	X	X	X	X	X	X	15	X	0	0
Czechoslovakia (former)	135 e	X	X	X	X	X	X	X	X	X	69	X	0	0
Denmark	17 e	X	X	X	X	X	X	X	X	X	716	X	0	0
Finland	15 i	X	X	X	X	X	X	X	X	X	300	X	0	0
France	131 e	~99	X	X	X	X	250 h	X	X	X	1,171	X	0	0
Germany	30 e	X	X	X	X	X	100 h	X	X	X	1,466	X	0	0
Greece	64 e	X	X	X	X	X	X	X	X	X	87	X	0	0
Hungary	267 e	X	X	X	X	X	200 h	X	X	X	94	X	0	0
Iceland	X	X	X	X	X	X	X	X	X	X	443	X	0	0
Ireland	3 e	X	X	X	X	X	700 h	X	X	X	115	X	0	0
Italy	1,215 e	X	X	X	X	X	200+ h	X	X	X	3,000	94	0	0
Malta	X	X	X	X	X	X	X	X	X	X	0	X	0	0
Netherlands	38 e	X	X	X	X	X	10 h	X	X	X	353	X	0	0
Norway	96 e	X	X	X	X	X	X	X	X	X	152	X	0	0
Poland	144 e	X	X	X	X	X	X	X	X	X	194	X	0	0
Portugal	X	X	X	X	X	X	755	X	X	X	85	X	0	0
Romania	193 e	X	X	X	X	X	X	X	X	X	483	X	0	0
Spain	582 e	X	X	X	X	X	1,452 h	X	X	X	445	X	0	0
Sweden	985 e	X	X	X	X	X	X	X	X	X	2,098	X	0	0
Switzerland	95 e	X	X	X	X	X	X	X	X	X	178	X	0	0
United Kingdom	200 j	X	X	X	X	X	5,298 k	X	X	X	446	X	0	0
Yugoslavia (former)	945 e	X	X	X	X	X	X	X	X	X	89	X	0	0
U.S.S.R. (former)	37,573	38	X	X	X	X	X	X	X	X	2,837	X	X	X
OCEANIA	X	X	X	X	X	X	X	X	X	X	X	X	X	X
Australia	13,000 d	95	X	X	X	X	75,900	X	87,600	58	17,000	~95	2,200	0
Fiji	750	X	X	X	X	X	X	X	X	X	X	X	42	7
New Zealand	5,000 d	77	18,807	69	X	X	6,500	~90	X	X	32,240	90	20	X
Papua New Guinea	X	X	350	X	23,600	X	2,800	X	X	X	5,000	X	200	X
Solomon Islands	X	X	X	X	X	X	X	X	X	X	X	X	64	X
Vanuatu	X	X	X	X	X	X	X	X	X	X	X	X	3	X

Sources: World Conservation Union, The Woods Hole Research Center, World Conservation Monitoring Centre, and other sources.

Notes: a. Data are for sub-Saharan region only. b. Includes mangroves. c. Protected private and crown forest lands. d. Primary forest extent. e. Forest area considered of high importance to nature conservation. f. Continental United States, excluding Alaska. g. Closed forest. h. Dry semi-natural grassland. i. Protected "primeval" forest. j. Ancient semi-natural woodlands, England only. k. Nonagricultural upland areas.
X = not available; 0 = zero or less than half the unit of measure; + = probably exceeds figure given; < = probably less than figure given; ~ = approximately.
For additional information, see Sources and Technical Notes.

Table 20.4 Globally Threatened Species: Mammals, Birds,

	Mammals				Birds				Higher Plants			
	Total Number of Known Species			Number of Species per 10,000 Square km {a}	Total Number of Known Species			Number of Species per 10,000 Square km {a}	Total Number of Known Species			Number of Species per 10,000 Square km {a}
	All Species	Endemic Species	Threatened Species		All Species	Endemic Species	Threatened Species		All Species	Endemic Species	Threatened Species	
WORLD	4,327 b	X	X	X	9,672	X	1,029	X	270,000	X	X	X
AFRICA	X	X	X	X	X	X	X	X	X	X	3,114	X
Algeria	92	2	12	15	192	1	15	32	3,164	250	147	520
Angola	276	4	14	56	872	12	12	177	5,185	1,260	23	1,055
Benin	188	0	11	85	630	0	1	283	2,201	0	3	990
Botswana	154	0	9	40	569	0	6	149	X	17	4	X
Burkina Faso	147	1	10	49	497	0	1	167	1,100	0	1	369
Burundi	107	0	4	76	633	0	5	452	2,500	X	0	1,783
Cameroon	297	10	27	83	848	11	17	237	8,260	156	76	2,310
Central African Rep	209	2	12	53	668	0	2	171	3,602	100	1	921
Chad	134	0	18	27	496	0	4	100	1,600	X	13	322
Congo	200	1	12	62	500	0	3	156	6,000	X	3	1,870
Cote d'Ivoire	230	2	18	73	683	0	9	217	3,660	62	68	1,163
Djibouti	X	0	6	X	311	0	3	236	641	2	3	486
Egypt	102	4	9	22	132	0	16	29	2,076	70	98	454
Equatorial Guinea	184	1	15	131	392	3	3	279	3,250	66	8	2,312
Ethiopia	255	26	25	52	836	26	14	171	6,603	600-1,400	44	1,352
Gabon	190	3	17	64	617	0	4	209	6,651	X	78	2,248
Gambia, The	108	0	7	104	489	0	1	470	974	0	0	935
Ghana	222	0	13	78	721	1	8	253	3,725	43	35	1,308
Guinea	190	1	17	66	529	0	6	184	3,000	88	36	1,043
Guinea-Bissau	108	0	5	71	376	0	2	246	1,000	12	0	655
Kenya	309	10	17	81	1,067	7	18	279	6,506	265	150	1,703
Lesotho	33	0	2	23	288	0	7	200	1,591	2	7	1,103
Liberia	193	1	18	91	590	2	10	278	2,200	103	1	1,037
Libya	76	4	12	14	80	0	9	15	1,825	134	58	331
Madagascar	105	67	50	27	250	97	28	65	9,505	5,000-8,000	166	2,479
Malawi	195	0	10	86	630	0	7	279	3,765	49	60	1,665
Mali	137	0	16	28	647	0	4	132	1,741	11	17	355
Mauritania	61	1	14	13	49	0	5	11	1,100	X	3	239
Mauritius	X	1	3	X	102	10	10	172	878	325-329	245	1,484
Morocco	105	5	9	30	209	0	14	60	3,675	600-650	197	1,049
Mozambique	179	2	10	42	666	0	11	157	5,692	219	92	1,340
Namibia	154	2	11	36	640	1	7	149	3,174	X	20	740
Niger	131	0	15	27	473	0	1	96	1,178	0	1	238
Nigeria	274	2	25	62	831	2	10	187	4,715	205	10	1,059
Rwanda	151	0	11	110	669	0	7	486	2,290	26	0	1,664
Senegal	155	1	11	58	625	0	5	234	2,086	26	34	780
Sierra Leone	147	0	13	77	614	0	7	320	2,090	74	12	1,091
Somalia	171	8	17	43	639	11	7	162	3,028	500	61	768
South Africa	247	27	25	51	774	7	13	159	23,420	X	1,001	4,797
Sudan	267	7	17	43	938	0	8	152	3,137	50	10	507
Swaziland	47	0	0	39	381	0	5	318	2,715	4	40	2,263
Tanzania	306	13	30	68	1,016	13	26	226	10,008	1,122	160	2,231
Togo	196	1	9	110	630	0	1	355	2,201	0	0	1,241
Tunisia	78	1	6	31	173	0	14	69	2,196	X	26	873
Uganda	315	4	16	111	989	3	12	349	5,406	30	13	1,905
Zaire	415	25	31	69	1,086	23	27	179	11,007	3,200	7	1,818
Zambia	229	3	10	55	732	0	10	176	4,747	211	7	1,141
Zimbabwe	196	2	9	58	635	0	6	189	4,440	95	95	1,325
ASIA	X	X	X	X	X	X	X	X	17,931	X	5,990	X
Afghanistan	123	0	13	31	456	0	13	115	4,000	800	5	1,008
Bangladesh	109	0	15	45	354	0	27	147	5,000	X	34	2,074
Bhutan	109	0	15	65	448	0	10	269	5,468	50-100	16	3,281
Cambodia	117	0	21	45	305	0	13	117	X	X	8	X
China	394	62	40	41	1,100	66	83	114	32,200	18,000	307	3,340
India	317	38	39	47	969	69	72	143	16,000	5,000	1,331	2,363
Indonesia	515	166	49	91	1,519	356	135	269	24,375	15,000	283	4,311
Iran, Islamic Rep	140	4	15	26	X	1	20	X	8,000	1,400	2	1,484
Iraq	81	1	9	23	145	1	17	42	2,937	190	3	844
Israel	X	2	8	X	169	0	15	133	2,317	155	47	1,820
Japan	90	29	5	27	250+	20	31	75+	5,565	2,000	713	1,679
Jordan	X	0	5	X	132	0	11	64	2,212	150	12	1,074
Korea, Dem People's Rep	X	0	5	X	X	0	25	X	2,898	107	13	1,274
Korea, Rep	49	0	6	23	X	0	22	X	2,898	224	78	1,360
Kuwait	X	0	5	X	27	0	7	22	282	0	1	233
Lao People's Dem Rep	173	0	23	61	481	1	18	169	X	X	6	X
Lebanon	52	0	4	51	124	0	15	122	3,000	330	6	2,961
Malaysia	264	14	23	83	501	4	35	158	15,500	2,700-4,500	490	4,890
Mongolia	X	6	9	X	X	0	13	X	2,272	229	1	429
Myanmar	300	8	23	75	~867	4	42	~216	7,000	1,071	35	1,742
Nepal	167	1	22	70	629	1	20	263	6,973	315	33	2,913
Oman	46	3	6	17	X	0	8	X	1,200	74-73	4	438
Pakistan	151	3	15	36	476	0	25	112	4,950	372	16	1,168
Philippines	166	91	12	54	395	172	39	129	8,931	3,500	198	2,907
Saudi Arabia	X	1	9	X	59	0	12	10	2,028	34	6	345
Singapore	57	1	4	143	118	0	5	295	2,168	2	15	5,427
Sri Lanka	86	12	7	46	221	21	8	119	3,314	879-900	224	1,781
Syrian Arab Rep	X	0	4	X	165	0	15	63	3,000	330	12	1,145
Thailand	251	6	26	68	616	2	34	168	12,625	X	0	3,442
Turkey	116	0	5	28	284	0	18	67	8,650	2,651-2,675	1,848	2,055
United Arab Emirates	X	0	4	X	X	0	7	X	347	0	0	172
Viet Nam	273	5	28	86	638	12	34	201	10,500	1,260	357	3,306
Yemen	X	1	6	X	X	8	9	X	1,415	58-77	152	382

and Higher Plants, 1990s

Table 20.4

	Mammals				Birds				Higher Plants			
	Total Number of Known Species			Number of Species per 10,000	Total Number of Known Species			Number of Species per 10,000	Total Number of Known Species			Number of Species per 10,000
	All Species	Endemic Species	Threatened Species	Square km {a}	All Species	Endemic Species	Threatened Species	Square km {a}	All Species	Endemic Species	Threatened Species	Square km {a}
NORTH & CENTRAL AMERICA	X	X	X	X	X	X	X	X	18,849	X	6,173	X
Bahamas	12	2	2	11	88	3	4	79	1,217	112-118	25	1,092
Barbados	6	0	1	17	24	0	1	68	572	34,034	1	1,616
Belize	125	0	8	95	528	0	4	401	2,894	150	48	2,200
Canada	139	4	5	14	426	3	6	44	3,270	147	700	335
Costa Rica	205	8	10	120	848	7	14	495	12,119	600-1,300	478	7,074
Cuba	31	15	11	14	159	22	15	72	6,514	3,224-3,233	851	2,945
Dominica	12	1	0	28	59	2	3	139	1,325	34,285	62	3,115
Dominican Rep	20	0	1	12	125	0	5	74	5,657	1,800	51	3,354
El Salvador	135	1	6	106	~450	0	2	~352	2,911	17	43	2,277
Guatemala	184	4	10	84	480	0	10	218	8,681	1,171	326	3,948
Haiti	20	0	1	14	X	0	4	X	5,242	1,445-1,800	13	3,743
Honduras	173	1	7	78	X	1	11	X	5,680	148	65	2,559
Jamaica	22	3	5	21	159	25	2	154	3,308	889-923	371	3,207
Martinique	9	1	0	19	53	1	3	110	1,287	24-36	12	2,666
Mexico	439	137	25	77	961	88	35	168	26,071	10,000-15,000	495	4,569
Nicaragua	X	2	8	X	X	0	7	X	7,590	30-50	101	3,256
Panama	~218	12	13	~111	~922	8	14	~470	9,915	1,222	588	5,054
Trinidad and Tobago	100	1	1	125	258	1	3	322	2,420	215-236	7	3,016
United States	346	94	27	36	650	70	43	68	19,473	4,036	2,279	2,036
SOUTH AMERICA	X	X	X	X	X	X	X	X	4,958	X	1,822	X
Argentina	258	47	23	40	X	21	53	X	9,372	1,000-1,200	156	1,465
Bolivia	280	19	21	59	1,257	17	34	267	17,367	4,000	43	3,683
Brazil	394	70	40	43	1,573	177	123	170	56,215	X	361	6,067
Chile	91	12	9	22	432	15	18	104	5,292	2,698	287	1,269
Colombia	359	26	25	75	1,721	59	69	361	51,220	1,500	393	10,735
Ecuador	271	25	21	90	1,435	37	64	476	19,362	4,000	233	6,421
Guyana	193	0	12	70	X	0	9	X	6,409	X	73	2,329
Paraguay	156	3	14	46	~650	0	34	~191	7,851	X	15	2,311
Peru	344	46	29	69	1,705	106	75	343	18,245	5,356	361	3,674
Suriname	187	2	11	74	X	0	6	X	5,018	X	72	1,997
Uruguay	81	0	5	31	X	0	11	X	2,278	40	14	882
Venezuela	288	11	19	65	1,308	45	34	295	21,073	8,000	112	4,752
EUROPE	X	X	X	X	X	X	X	X	7,777	X	2,561	X
Albania	68	0	2	48	215	0	14	152	3,031	24	88	2,139
Austria	83	0	2	41	227	0	13	113	3,100	35	54	1,537
Belgium	58	0	2	40	180	0	13	125	1,550	1	21	1,076
Bulgaria	81	0	3	37	242	0	15	109	3,572	320	196	1,615
Czechoslovakia (former)	81	0	2	35	227	0	18	98	2,590	62	155	1,117
Denmark	43	0	1	27	185	0	16	114	1,450	1	22	895
Finland	60	0	3	19	230	0	12	72	1,102	0	32	345
France	93	0	6	25	267	9	21	71	4,630	133	184	1,233
Germany	76	0	2	23	237	0	17	73	2,682	6	49	824
Greece	95	2	4	41	244	0	19	104	4,992	742	544	2,131
Hungary	72	0	2	34	203	0	16	97	2,214	38	84	1,061
Iceland	11	0	1	5	80	0	2	37	377	1	3	175
Ireland	25	0	0	13	141	0	10	74	950	0	18	499
Italy	90	2	3	29	254	0	19	83	5,598	712	255	1,820
Malta	22	0	0	69	28	0	13	87	914	5	106	2,846
Netherlands	55	0	2	36	187	0	13	121	1,221	0	16	791
Norway	54	0	3	17	235	0	8	75	1,715	1	50	544
Poland	85	0	4	27	224	0	16	72	2,450	3	98	787
Portugal	63	1	6	30	214	2	18	103	X	150	266	X
Romania	84	0	2	30	249	0	18	88	3,400	41	214	1,195
Spain	82	4	6	22	275	6	23	75	5,050	941	951	1,384
Sweden	60	0	1	17	249	0	14	71	1,750	1	29	498
Switzerland	75	0	2	47	201	0	15	126	3,030	1	38	1,898
United Kingdom	50	0	3	17	219	13	22	76	1,623	16	48	565
Yugoslavia (former)	95	2	3	33	245	0	17	84	5,351	137	224	1,836
U.S.S.R. (former)	276	55	20	22	X	13	38	X	1,916	X	597	150
OCEANIA	X	X	X	X	X	X	X	X	5,825	X	2,410	X
Australia	282	209	38	31	571	351	39	64	15,990	13,240	1,725	1,783
Fiji	4	1	1	3	87	25	5	71	1,628	760-812	24	1,334
New Zealand	X	4	1	X	285	74	26	96	2,377	1,942	234	800
Papua New Guinea	242	50	5	68	578	56	25	163	11,544	X	90	3,257
Solomon Islands	47	18	2	33	163	69	20	115	3,172	30	43	2,235
Vanuatu	12	2	1	11	84	10	3	79	870	150	25	815

Source: World Conservation Monitoring Centre.
Notes: a. Values are standardized using a species-area curve. b. Includes cetaceans.
Plant data are as of June 1993. Other taxa: total and endemic species data are as of 1992; threatened species data are as of 1990.
World and regional totals include countries not listed.
X = not available; ~ = approximately; + = probably greater than number given.
For additional information, see Sources and Technical Notes.

Table 20.5 Globally Threatened Species: Reptiles,

	Reptiles				Amphibians				
	Total Number of Known Species			Number of Species per 10,000 Square km {a}	Total Number of Known Species			Number of Species per 10,000 Square km {a}	Threatened Fish Species {b}
	All Species	Endemic Species	Threatened Species		All Species	Endemic Species	Threatened Species		
WORLD	4,771	X	169	X	4,014	X	57	X	713
AFRICA	X	X	X	X	X	X	X	X	X
Algeria	X	3	0	X	X	0	0	X	
Angola	X	18	2	X	X	23	0	X	1
Benin	X	1	2	X	X	0	0	X	0
Botswana	143	2	1	37	36	1	0	9	0
Burkina Faso	X	3	2	X	X	0	0	X	0
Burundi	X	X	1	X	X	2	0	X	0
Cameroon	X	19	2	X	X	65	1	X	11
Central African Rep	X	X	2	X	X	0	0	X	0
Chad	X	1	2	X	X	0	0	X	0
Congo	X	1	2	X	X	1	0	X	0
Cote d'Ivoire	X	2	1	X	X	2	1	X	0
Djibouti	X	X	0	X	X	0	0	X	0
Egypt	83	1	2	18	6	0	0	1	1
Equatorial Guinea	X	3	2	X	X	2	1	X	0
Ethiopia	X	6	1	X	X	30	0	X	0
Gabon	X	3	2	X	X	4	0	X	0
Gambia, The	X	1	2	X	X	0	0	X	0
Ghana	X	1	2	X	X	4	0	X	0
Guinea	X	3	1	X	X	3	1	X	0
Guinea-Bissau	X	2	2	X	X	1	0	X	0
Kenya	187	15	2	49	88	10	0	23	0
Lesotho	X	2	0	X	X	1	0	X	0
Liberia	62	2	2	29	38	4	0	18	0
Libya	X	1	1	X	X	0	0	X	0
Madagascar	252	231	10	66	144	142	0	38	0
Malawi	124	6	1	55	69	1	0	31	0
Mali	16	2	2	3	X	1	0	X	0
Mauritania	X	1	1	X	X	0	0	X	0
Mauritius	X	2	6	X	2	0	0	3	0
Morocco	X	8	0	X	X	2	0	X	1
Mozambique	X	5	1	X	62	2	0	15	1
Namibia	X	26	2	X	32	2	0	7	4
Niger	X	X	1	X	X	0	0	X	0
Nigeria	100+	7	2	22+	60+	1	0	13+	0
Rwanda	X	1	2	X	X	0	0	X	0
Senegal	X	1	2	X	X	1	0	X	0
Sierra Leone	X	1	2	X	X	2	0	X	0
Somalia	193	66	1	49	27	3	0	7	0
South Africa	299	81	3	61	95	36	1	19	28
Sudan	X	6	1	X	X	2	0	X	0
Swaziland	106	1	1	88	39	0	0	33	0
Tanzania	245	56	3	55	121	40	0	27	0
Togo	X	1	2	X	X	3	0	X	0
Tunisia	X	1	1	X	X	0	0	X	0
Uganda	119	2	1	42	44	0	0	16	0
Zaire	X	33	2	X	X	53	0	X	1
Zambia	X	2	2	X	83	1	0	20	0
Zimbabwe	153	2	1	46	120	3	0	36	0
ASIA	X	X	X	X	X	X	X	X	X
Afghanistan	103	4	1	26	6	1	1	2	0
Bangladesh	119	1	14	49	19	0	0	8	0
Bhutan	19	2	1	11	24	0	0	14	0
Cambodia	82	1	6	32	28	0	0	11	5
China	282	74	7	29	190	131	1	20	7
India	389	214	17	57	206	110	3	30	2
Indonesia	511	302	13	90	270	100	0	48	29
Iran, Islamic Rep	164	26	4	30	11	5	0	2	2
Iraq	81	1	0	23	6	0	0	2	2
Israel	X	1	1	X	X	1	1	X	0
Japan	63	27	0	19	52	36	1	16	3
Jordan	X	X	0	X	X	0	0	X	0
Korea, Dem People's Rep	19	1	0	8	13	0	0	6	0
Korea, Rep	18	3	0	8	13	1	0	6	0
Kuwait	29	0	0	24	2	0	0	2	0
Lao People's Dem Rep	66	1	5	23	37	1	0	13	5
Lebanon	X	2	1	X	X	0	0	X	0
Malaysia	268	69	12	85	158	39	0	50	6
Mongolia	X	X	0	X	X	0	0	X	0
Myanmar	203	48	10	51	75	9	0	19	2
Nepal	80	5	9	33	36	7	0	15	0
Oman	64	9	0	23	X	0	0	X	2
Pakistan	143	23	6	34	17	2	0	4	0
Philippines	193	158	6	63	63	44	0	21	21
Saudi Arabia	84	4	0	14	X	0	0	X	0
Singapore	X	X	1	X	X	0	0	X	1
Sri Lanka	144	75	3	77	39	21	0	21	12
Syrian Arab Rep	X	2	1	X	X	0	0	X	0
Thailand	298	35	9	81	107	16	0	29	13
Turkey	102	4	5	24	18	2	1	4	5
United Arab Emirates	37	1	0	18	X	0	0	X	0
Viet Nam	180	39	8	57	80	26	1	25	4
Yemen	77	22	0	21	X	1	0	X	0

Amphibians, and Fish, 1990s

Table 20.5

	Reptiles				Amphibians				
	Total Number of Known Species			Number of Species per 10,000 Square km {a}	Total Number of Known Species			Number of Species per 10,000 Square km {a}	Threatened Fish Species {b}
	All Species	Endemic Species	Threatened Species		All Species	Endemic Species	Threatened Species		
NORTH & CENTRAL AMERICA	X	X	X	X	X	X	X	X	X
Bahamas	24	16	3	22	5	0	0	4	0
Barbados	X	3	0	X	X	0	0	X	0
Belize	107	2	3	81	X	0	0	X	15
Canada	41	0	0	4	40	0	0	4	0
Costa Rica	214	36	2	125	162	33	0	95	0
Cuba	100	80	4	45	41	36	0	19	0
Dominica	13	2	0	31	2	0	0	5	0
Dominican Rep	X	22	4	X	X	15	0	X	0
El Salvador	73	4	1	57	23	0	0	18	0
Guatemala	231	20	4	105	88	26	0	40	0
Haiti	X	29	4	X	X	17	0	X	0
Honduras	152	12	3	68	56	9	0	25	0
Jamaica	X	26	3	X	X	18	0	X	0
Martinique	X	3	0	X	X	0	0	X	0
Mexico	717	368	16	126	284	169	4	50	98
Nicaragua	161	6	2	69	59	2	0	25	0
Panama	~226	25	2	~115	164	20	0	84	0
Trinidad and Tobago	X	2	0	X	X	2	0	X	0
United States	X	72	25	X	X	122	22	X	164
SOUTH AMERICA	X	X	X	X	X	X	X	X	X
Argentina	X	64	4	X	123	37	1	19	1
Bolivia	250	17	4	53	110	18	0	23	1
Brazil	468	178	11	51	502	296	0	54	9
Chile	78	33	0	19	39	26	0	9	1
Colombia	383	106	10	80	407	131	0	85	0
Ecuador	337	114	8	112	343	138	0	114	0
Guyana	X	2	3	X	X	10	0	X	1
Paraguay	120	3	4	35	85	4	0	25	0
Peru	298	95	6	60	241	91	1	49	1
Suriname	X	0	1	X	X	7	0	X	0
Uruguay	X	1	2	X	X	2	0	X	0
Venezuela	X	57	3	X	X	76	0	X	0
EUROPE	X	X	X	X	X	X	X	X	X
Albania	31	0	1	22	13	0	0	9	1
Austria	14	0	0	7	20	0	0	10	2
Belgium	8	0	0	6	17	0	0	12	1
Bulgaria	33	0	1	15	17	0	0	8	3
Czechoslovakia (former)	12	0	0	5	19	0	0	8	2
Denmark	5	0	0	3	14	0	0	9	0
Finland	5	0	0	2	5	0	0	2	1
France	32	0	2	9	32	3	1	9	3
Germany	12	0	0	4	20	0	0	6	3
Greece	51	4	3	22	15	1	0	6	6
Hungary	15	0	0	7	17	0	0	8	2
Iceland	0	0	0	X	0	0	0	X	1
Ireland	1	0	0	1	3	0	0	2	1
Italy	40	1	2	13	34	10	7	11	3
Malta	8	1	0	25	1	0	0	3	0
Netherlands	7	0	0	5	16	0	0	10	1
Norway	5	0	0	2	5	0	0	2	1
Poland	9	0	0	3	18	0	0	6	1
Portugal	29	2	0	14	17	0	1	8	0
Romania	25	0	1	9	19	0	0	7	4
Spain	53	13	5	15	25	2	3	7	2
Sweden	6	0	0	2	13	0	0	4	1
Switzerland	14	0	0	9	18	0	1	11	3
United Kingdom	8	0	0	3	7	0	0	2	1
Yugoslavia (former)	41	2	1	14	23	0	2	8	5
U.S.S.R. (former)	168	1	3	13	37	2	0	3	5
OCEANIA	X	X	X	X	X	X	X	X	X
Australia	700	608	9	78	180	156	3	20	16
Fiji	25	11	4	20	2	2	1	2	0
New Zealand	40	36	1	13	3	3	3	1	2
Papua New Guinea	249	81	1	70	183	100	0	52	0
Solomon Islands	57	10	3	40	15	9	0	11	0
Vanuatu	22	4	1	21	0	0	0	X	0

Source: World Conservation Monitoring Centre.
Notes: a. Values are standardized using a species-area curve. b. Does not include threatened Lake Victoria cichlid species.
Total and endemic species totals are as of 1992; threatened species data are as of 1990.
World and regional totals include countries not listed.
X = not available; ~ = approximately; + = probably greater than number given.
For additional information, see Sources and Technical Notes.

Table 20.6 Net Trade in Wildlife and Wildlife Products

	CITES Reporting Requirement Met {a} (percent)	Mammals Live Primates (number) Imports	Exports	Cat Skins (number) Imports	Exports	Birds Live Birds (number) Imports	Exports	Reptiles Reptile Skins {b} (number) Imports	Exports	Plants Live Cacti (number) Imports	Exports	Live Orchids (number) Imports	Exports
WORLD	X	26,631	26,631	44,810	44,810	933,672	933,672	9,132,623	9,132,623	919,499	919,499	1,293,692	1,293,692
AFRICA	X	50	6,820	150	358	8,985	673,758	3,380	493,557	0	101	0	20,128
Algeria	50	X	X	X	X	1	0	X	X	X	X	X	X
Angola {c}	NA	0	4	2	0	0	2	X	X	X	X	X	X
Benin	0	X	X	X	X	0	510	X	X	X	X	X	X
Botswana	86	X	X	122	0	0	1,974	0	380	X	X	X	X
Burkina Faso	0	X	X	X	X	0	0	X	X	X	X	X	X
Burundi	0	X	X	X	X	0	5	X	X	X	X	X	X
Cameroon	92	X	X	9	0	0	18,194	0	72,351	X	X	X	X
Central African Rep	50	X	X	X	X	0	1	0	1	X	X	X	X
Chad	0	X	X	X	X	0	2	0	13,180	X	X	X	X
Congo	100	0	3	0	2	0	45	0	546	X	X	0	20
Cote d'Ivoire {c}	NA	X	X	X	X	0	5,850	X	X	X	X	X	X
Djibouti	X	X	X	0	2	X	X	X	X	X	X	X	X
Egypt	0	31	0	X	X	1,000	0	0	16,949	X	X	X	X
Equatorial Guinea	X	X	X	X	X	X	X	X	X	X	X	X	X
Ethiopia	75	0	287	0	3	X	X	0	2,075	X	X	X	X
Gabon	67	14	0	13	0	0	29	X	X	X	X	0	123
Gambia, The	20	X	X	X	X	X	X	X	X	X	X	X	X
Ghana	81	0	457	X	X	0	6,015	0	21	X	X	0	723
Guinea	45	0	2	0	2	0	121,887	0	7,648	X	X	X	X
Guinea-Bissau	0	X	X	X	X	0	1	0	165	X	X	X	X
Kenya	54	0	1,929	0	100	0	11	0	2,201	X	X	0	3
Lesotho {c}	NA	X	X	X	X	X	X	X	X	X	X	X	X
Liberia	73	X	X	0	1	0	2,939	X	X	X	X	X	X
Libya {c}	NA	X	X	X	X	20	0	4	0	X	X	X	X
Madagascar	82	0	7	X	X	0	1,923	0	853	0	101	0	18,558
Malawi	70	X	X	0	2	X	X	0	1,070	X	X	0	22
Mali {c}	NA	X	X	0	1	0	89,033	0	240,695	X	X	X	X
Mauritania {c}	NA	X	X	X	X	X	X	1	0	X	X	X	X
Mauritius	88	0	1,929	X	X	76	0	12	0	X	X	0	26
Morocco	44	X	X	X	X	0	37	60	0	X	X	X	X
Mozambique	73	0	20	0	5	0	21,322	0	590	X	X	X	X
Namibia	0	X	X	0	16	53	0	1	0	X	X	X	X
Niger	41	2	0	X	X	46	0	0	1	X	X	X	X
Nigeria	18	X	X	0	1	0	15	0	52	X	X	0	12
Rwanda	27	X	X	X	X	X	X	X	X	X	X	X	X
Senegal	80	0	62	1	0	0	270,671	0	11,568	X	X	X	X
Sierra Leone {c}	NA	X	X	X	X	0	4,019	X	X	X	X	X	X
Somalia	17	X	X	X	X	0	1	X	X	X	X	X	X
South Africa	94	0	178	0	52	7,751	0	3,302	0	X	X	0	73
Sudan	44	X	X	2	0	37	0	0	95,288	X	X	X	X
Swaziland {c}	NA	X	X	1	0	X	X	X	X	X	X	X	X
Tanzania	75	0	1,455	0	27	0	122,761	0	1,556	X	X	X	X
Togo	69	0	484	X	X	0	4,643	0	10,393	X	X	X	X
Tunisia	100	X	X	X	X	1	0	X	X	X	X	X	X
Uganda	0	X	X	X	X	X	X	X	X	X	X	0	568
Zaire	69	0	3	X	X	0	711	0	1	X	X	X	X
Zambia	45	3	0	0	10	0	1	0	2,290	X	X	X	X
Zimbabwe	83	X	X	0	134	0	1,156	0	13,683	X	X	X	X
ASIA	X	5,836	15,722	32,295	21,707	27,327	94,024	1,559,233	6,480,976	0	302,055	239,099	1,208,212
Afghanistan	0	X	X	X	X	X	X	X	X	X	X	X	X
Bangladesh	80	X	X	X	X	25	0	X	X	X	X	X	X
Bhutan {c}	NA	X	X	X	X	X	X	X	X	X	X	X	X
Cambodia {c}	NA	X	X	X	X	X	X	0	1	X	X	X	X
China	100	0	1,447	0	21,700	2	0	0	2,195,483	0	82	0	681,503
India	100	3	0	1	0	0	31,470	0	295,002	X	X	46	0
Indonesia	92	0	10,909	0	2	0	58,271	0	1,305,988	X	X	0	5,265
Iran, Islamic Rep	31	X	X	X	X	X	X	0	4	X	X	X	X
Iraq {c}	NA	X	X	X	X	5	0	0	0	X	X	X	X
Israel	25	135	0	X	X	2,498	0	0	731	0	120	X	X
Japan	92	5,639	0	31,218	0	12,172	0	1,500,958	0	0	156,103	226,811	0
Jordan	31	X	X	X	X	0	1	X	X	X	X	X	X
Korea, Dem People's Rep {c}	NA	X	X	X	X	10	0	26	0	X	X	X	X
Korea, Rep {c}	NA	10	0	1,073	0	1,929	0	31,653	0	0	145,750	8,389	0
Kuwait {c}	NA	X	X	X	X	5	0	X	X	X	X	X	X
Lao People's Dem Rep {c}	NA	X	X	X	X	X	X	X	X	X	X	X	X
Lebanon {c}	NA	2	0	0	3	2	0	1	0	X	X	X	X
Malaysia	86	2	0	X	X	0	2,030	0	438,804	X	X	0	350
Mongolia {c}	NA	X	X	X	X	X	X	X	X	X	X	X	X
Myanmar {c}	NA	0	201	X	X	0	1,298	X	X	X	X	X	X
Nepal	76	X	X	X	X	X	X	X	X	X	X	X	X
Oman {c}	NA	X	X	X	X	11	0	X	X	X	X	X	X
Pakistan	94	2	0	X	X	0	53	X	X	X	X	X	X
Philippines	82	0	3,109	X	X	545	0	0	24,424	X	X	3,853	0
Saudi Arabia {c}	NA	2	0	2	0	947	0	102	0	X	X	X	X
Singapore	100	0	6	1	0	5,399	0	0	1,177,225	X	X	0	2,005
Sri Lanka	54	X	X	X	X	32	0	0	0	X	X	X	X
Syrian Arab Rep {c}	NA	X	X	X	X	X	X	4	0	X	X	X	X
Thailand	56	7	0	0	2	234	0	0	1,036,752	X	X	0	519,089
Turkey {c}	NA	X	X	X	X	898	0	26,489	0	X	X	X	X
United Arab Emirates	0	34	0	X	X	2,612	0	0	913	X	X	X	X
Viet Nam {c}	NA	0	50	X	X	0	900	0	5,649	X	X	X	X
Yemen {c}	NA	X	X	X	X	1	0	X	X	X	X	X	X

Reported by CITES, 1990

Table 20.6

	CITES Reporting Requirement Met {a} (percent)	Mammals Live Primates (number)		Cat Skins (number)		Birds Live Birds (number)		Reptiles Reptile Skins {b} (number)		Plants Live Cacti (number)		Live Orchids (number)	
		Imports	Exports	Imports	Exports	Imports	Exports	Imports	Exports	Imports	Exports	Imports	Exports
NORTH & CENTRAL AMERICA	X	10,254	534	0	20,396	169,298	9,830	1,757,970	10,055	915,950	616,659	418,501	23,419
Bahamas	23	X	X	X	X	61	0	X	X	X	X	X	X
Barbados	X	0	532	0	1	63	0	X	X	X	X	X	4,518
Belize	55	X	X	0	2	0	6	X	X	X	X	0	0
Canada	100	1,290	0	0	4,360	13,332	0	85,214	0	0	12,735	863	0
Costa Rica	76	1	0	0	2	14	0	X	X	0	3	45,973	0
Cuba	50	X	X	X	X	0	405	X	X	X	X	X	X
Dominica {c}	NA	X	X	X	X	X	X	X	X	X	X	X	X
Dominican Rep	80	X	X	X	X	78	0	X	X	0	552,904	135,239	0
El Salvador	20	X	X	0	3	0	6	X	X	X	X	0	8
Guatemala	83	X	X	0	8	65	0	X	X	X	X	0	754
Haiti {c}	NA	X	X	X	X	0	2	X	X	0	13,836	X	X
Honduras	29	X	X	0	8	0	2,463	0	2,003	0	82	0	5
Jamaica {c}	NA	X	X	X	X	0	2	X	X	0	8	0	2,670
Martinique {c}	NA	X	X	X	X	X	X	X	X	X	X	X	X
Mexico	100	325	0	0	56	498	0	206,461	0	0	37,091	0	15,180
Nicaragua	80	X	X	0	3	0	6,899	0	8,050	X	X	X	X
Panama	86	0	2	0	2	0	47	27,148	0	X	X	0	74
Trinidad and Tobago	67	X	X	X	X	236	0	0	2	X	X	0	210
United States	88	8,638	0	0	15,951	154,951	0	1,439,147	0	915,950	0	236,426	0
SOUTH AMERICA	X	26	2,894	0	39	748	152,970	1,894	2,113,514	0	251	0	35,385
Argentina	82	0	17	0	10	0	77,170	0	1,919,139	0	230	0	17
Bolivia	62	10	0	0	3	7	0	0	7,457	0	18	X	X
Brazil	41	0	75	0	3	494	0	0	240	X	X	0	28,055
Chile	65	16	0	X	X	247	0	X	X	X	X	X	X
Colombia	64	0	3	0	2	0	12	0	79,749	X	X	0	2
Ecuador	76	X	X	0	7	0	9	0	6	0	3	0	879
Guyana	53	0	2,606	X	X	0	18,399	X	X	X	X	X	X
Paraguay	60	X	X	0	4	X	X	X	X	X	X	0	4
Peru	59	0	192	0	6	0	23,737	0	1	X	X	0	867
Suriname	100	X	X	X	X	0	8,597	X	X	X	X	0	3
Uruguay	59	X	X	X	X	0	25,040	1,894	0	X	X	X	X
Venezuela	79	0	1	0	4	0	6	0	106,922	X	X	0	5,558
EUROPE	X	8,726	271	10,991	330	692,214	2,032	2,243,440	0	1,319	426	16,015	0
Albania {c}	NA	X	X	X	X	6	0	X	X	X	X	X	X
Austria	100	44	0	73	0	4,252	0	306,974	0	0	3	2,414	0
Belgium	100	762	0	102	0	91,484	0	1,131	0	14	0	2,504	0
Bulgaria	0	X	X	X	X	4	0	X	X	X	X	X	X
Czechoslovakia (former)	100	18	0	1	0	0	52	1	0	X	X	X	X
Denmark	100	63	0	1,284	0	9,060	0	603	0	6	0	684	0
Finland	75	2	0	0	66	0	1,012	5,560	0	X	X	X	X
France	100	2,061	0	68	0	27,374	0	597,750	0	18	0	215	0
Germany	100 d	126	0	2,010	264	116,849	0	X	X	X	X	X	X
Greece {c}	NA	2	0	1,521	0	681	0	X	X	X	X	X	X
Hungary	57	49	0	X	X	474	0	X	X	X	X	X	X
Iceland {c}	NA	X	X	X	X	8	0	X	X	X	X	X	X
Ireland {c}	NA	X	X	X	X	0	0	1	0	X	X	X	X
Italy	86	49	0	2,366	0	20,542	0	682,263	0	19	0	201	0
Malta	100	X	X	X	X	31	0	7,457	0	X	X	X	X
Netherlands	100	1,904	0	2	0	186,749	0	101	0	353	0	1,119	0
Norway	100	X	X	100	0	62	0	1	0	X	X	270	0
Poland	0	X	X	X	X	0	968	8	0	X	X	X	X
Portugal	55	22	0	1	0	62,165	0	481	0	X	X	43	0
Romania {c}	NA	1	0	X	X	X	X	X	X	X	X	X	X
Spain	100	5	0	1,061	0	40,736	0	315,911	0	0	423	379	0
Sweden	94	583	0	2	0	4,022	0	1	0	426	0	8	0
Switzerland	100	0	271	2,325	0	3,854	0	162,416	0	60	0	2,697	0
United Kingdom	100	1,394	0	75	0	121,364	0	162,781	0	423	0	5,481	0
Yugoslavia (former) {c}	NA	1,641	0	X	X	2,497	0	X	X	X	X	X	X
U.S.S.R. (former)	75	1,665	0	0	1,978	150	0	X	X	X	X	X	X
OCEANIA	X	45	0	8	0	0	425	615	34,430	0	0	2,669	6,400
Australia	88	45	0	7	0	0	39	601	0	X	X	2,669	0
Fiji {c}	NA	X	X	X	X	X	X	X	X	X	X	X	X
New Zealand	67	X	X	1	0	0	244	14	0	X	X	0	802
Papua New Guinea	75	X	X	X	X	X	X	0	34,430	X	X	0	5,575
Solomon Islands {c}	NA	X	X	X	X	0	127	X	X	X	X	X	X
Vanuatu	75	X	X	X	X	0	15	X	X	X	X	0	23

Source: World Conservation Monitoring Centre.
Notes: a. Includes all trade reported by members of the Convention on International Trade in Endangered Species of Wild Flora and Fauna (CITES) as of May 1993.
b. Reptile skins include skins of snakes, lizards, and crocodilians. c. Not a member of CITES as of May 1993. d. Data are for former Federal Republic of Germany.
World totals include countries not listed. Regional totals consist only of countries listed.
0 = zero or less than half the unit of measurement; X = not available; NA = not applicable.
For additional information, see Sources and Technical Notes.

Sources and Technical Notes

Table 20.1 National Protection of Natural Areas, 1993

Source: Protected Areas Data Unit of the World Conservation Monitoring Centre (WCMC), unpublished data (WCMC, Cambridge, U.K., June 1993).

All protected areas combine natural areas in five World Conservation Union, formerly the International Union for Conservation of Nature and Natural Resources (IUCN), management categories (areas at least 1,000 hectares). *Totally protected areas* are maintained in a natural state and are closed to extractive uses. They encompass the following three management categories:

■ Category I. Scientific reserves and strict nature reserves possess outstanding, representative ecosystems. Public access is generally limited, with only scientific research and educational use permitted.

■ Category II. National parks and provincial parks are relatively large areas of national or international significance not materially altered by humans. Visitors may use them for recreation and study.

■ Category III. Natural monuments and natural landmarks contain unique geological formations, special animals or plants, or unusual habitats.

Partially protected areas are areas that may be managed for specific uses, such as recreation or tourism, or areas that provide optimum conditions for certain species or communities of wildlife. Some extractive use within these areas is allowed. They encompass two management categories:

■ Category IV. Managed nature reserves and wildlife sanctuaries are protected for specific purposes, such as conservation of a significant plant or animal species.

■ Category V. Protected landscapes and seascapes may be entirely natural or may include cultural landscapes (e.g., scenically attractive agricultural areas).

Protected areas at least 100,000 hectares and *1 million hectares in size* refer to all IUCN category I–V protected areas that fall within these two classifications. The totals are for single sites, and it is likely that some sites are not contiguous blocks. These data do not account for agglomerations of protected areas that together might exceed 100,000 or 1 million hectares.

Resource and Anthropological Reserves encompass IUCN categories VI–VIII, and refer to areas where limited resource use is permitted, as described below:

■ Category VI. Resource reserves/interim conservation units are undeveloped regions where access is restricted to "ongoing ecologically sound activities." This category is established for areas where governments want to control development, or areas where protective legislation has been established, but not yet implemented.

■ Category VII. Natural biotic areas/anthropological reserves are areas where use is limited to traditional activities by local cultures.

■ Category VIII. Multiple-use management areas/managed resource areas are government-owned areas managed for recreation, grazing, and sustainable use of natural resources. A limited amount of land that has been settled and otherwise "altered by humans" may be included.

The values in Table 20.1 do not include locally or provincially protected sites, or privately owned areas.

Table 20.2 International and Marine Protected Areas and Levels of Human Disturbance, 1993

Sources: Protected Areas Data Unit of the World Conservation Monitoring Centre (WCMC), unpublished data (WCMC, Cambridge, U.K., June 1993); Lee Hannah, Conservation International (CI), *Human Disturbance Map* and unpublished data (CI, Washington, D.C., August 1993), with David Lohse of the University of California, Santa Barbara. Ali Lankerani and David Lieu digitized the base maps under the supervision of Charles Hutchison. The data presented in Table 20.2 were extracted from the map-based data using CI's geographic information system by Ali Lankerani under the supervision of John L. Carr.

International protected areas usually include sites that are listed under national protection systems (see Table 20.1).

Biosphere reserves are representative of terrestrial and coastal environments that have been internationally recognized under the Man and the Biosphere Programme of the United Nations Educational, Scientific, and Cultural Organization. They have been selected for their value to conservation and are intended to foster the scientific knowledge, skills, and human values necessary to support sustainable development. Each reserve must contain a diverse, natural ecosystem of a specific biogeographical province, large enough to be an effective conservation unit. For further details, refer to M. Udvardy, *A Classification of the Biogeographical Provinces of the World* (IUCN, Morges, Switzerland, 1975), and to *World Resources 1986,* Chapter 6. Each reserve also must include a minimally disturbed core area for conservation and research and may be surrounded by buffer zones where traditional land uses, experimental ecosystem research, and ecosystem rehabilitation may be permitted.

World heritage sites represent areas of "outstanding universal value" for their natural features, their cultural value, or for both natural and cultural values. The table includes only natural and mixed natural and cultural sites. Any party to the World Heritage Convention may nominate natural sites that contain examples of a major stage of the earth's evolutionary history; a significant ongoing geological process; a unique or superlative natural phenomenon, formation, or feature; or a habitat for a threatened species. Several countries share world heri-

tage sites. These sites, referred to as international heritage sites, are counted only once in continental and world totals.

Any party to the Convention on Wetlands of International Importance Especially as Waterfowl Habitat (Ramsar, Iran, 1971) that agrees to respect the site's integrity and to establish wetland reserves can designate *wetlands of international importance.*

Marine and coastal protected areas refer to all protected areas over 1,000 hectares with littoral, coral, island, marine, or estuarine components. The area given is the whole protected area.

Data on *human disturbance* have been extracted from map-based data taken from various global, country, and regional atlases; maps of human and livestock population densities, land use, and forest cover; desertification estimates; and other sources portraying human infrastructure, development, and vegetation cover. The CI map uses a minimum mapping area of 40,000 hectares and classifies areas as undisturbed, partially disturbed, and disturbed (areas of low, medium, and high disturbance, respectively, in this table) based on map units dominated by the following criteria:

■ Areas of *low human disturbance* are covered by natural vegetation and/or have a population density under 10 people per square kilometer or under 1 person per square kilometer in arid, semiarid, and tundra regions.

■ Areas of *medium human disturbance* are under shifting or extensive agriculture, and/or contain secondary, naturally regenerating vegetation; have a livestock density exceeding their carrying capacity; exhibit other evidence of human disturbance (eg., contain a logging concession); or otherwise do not fit into the other two disturbance categories.

■ Areas of *high human disturbance* are under permanent agricultural cultivation or urban settlement, and/or contain primary vegetation removed without evidence of regrowth; contain current vegetation differing from potential vegetation; have a record of desertification or other permanent degradation.

The underlying data vary considerably in quality, and readers should be aware that areas of low human disturbance are likely overrepresented due to dated or inaccurate information.

Table 20.3 Habitat Extent and Loss, 1980s

Sources: This table updates information presented in Table 20.4 in World Resources Institute (WRI), in collaboration with the United Nations Environment Programme and the United Nations Development Programme, *World Resources 1990–91* (Oxford University Press, New York, 1990), and readers should consult this report for data sources not listed below. Data from *World Resources 1990–91* were taken primarily from John T. and Kathy MacKinnon, *Review* of the Protected Areas in the Afrotropical Realm and Review of the Protected Areas System in the Indo-Malayan Realm (The World Conservation Union, formerly the International Union for Conservation of Nature and Natural Resources (IUCN), Gland, Switzerland, 1986). New data presented here for Namibia and Brunei were taken from these two volumes.

Sources of new data: South American habitats excepting mangroves: Thomas Stone, "South America's Vanishing Natural Vegetation," Cultural Survival Quarterly, Vol. 16, No. 3 (1992), pp. 67–70 and T. Stone, P. Schlesinger, G. M. Goodwell, and R. A. Houghton, "A Map of the Vegetation of South America Based on Satellite Imagery," Photogrammetric Engineering and Remote Sensing (in press); Mangrove data for North and Central America, South America (except Brazil), Bahrain, China, the Congo, Ghana, Japan, Mauritius, New Zealand, Papua New Guinea, Singapore, Solomon Islands, Sri Lanka, and current grasslands extent for Europe (except for Portugal and the United Kingdom): World Conservation Monitoring Centre, Global Biodiversity Status of the Earth's Living Resources (Chapman & Hall, London, 1992); forest and mangroves for Benin, Cote d'Ivoire, the Gambia, Ghana, Nigeria, Senegal, and Sierra Leone: IUCN, The Conservation Atlas of Tropical Forests: Africa (Simon & Schuster, New York, 1992); current forest extent for Japan, Turkey, and Europe (except Finland and the United Kingdom): United Nations Economic Commission for Europe and the Food and Agriculture Organization of the United Nations, The Forest Resources of the Temperate Zones, Volume II (U.N., New York, 1993); forest data for Belize, Costa Rica, El Salvador, Honduras, Nicaragua, and Panama: James Nations and Daniel Komer, "Central America's Tropical Rainforests: Positive Steps for Survival," Ambio, Vol. 7, No. 5 (1983), p. 232; forest data for Australia, Canada, China, and the United States: Worldwatch Institute, State of the World 1991 (W. W. Norton & Company, New York, 1991); Antigua and Barbuda's dry forests: Gregory Miller, Marty Fujita, and Loren Ford, An Assessment of Biological Diversity and Tropical Forestry for the Eastern Caribbean Islands (U.S. Agency for International Development, Washington, D.C., 1988); Australia's grasslands and desert/scrub: Wayne Fletcher, unpublished data (Biodiversity Section, Department of the Environment, Sport and Territories, Canberra, Australia, July 1993); the Dominican Republic's forests: Gary Hartshorn, Gustavo Antonini, Random DuBois, et al., The Dominican Republic Country Environmental Profile (JRB Associates, McLean, Virginia, 1981); Fiji's forests and mangroves: Stuart Chape and Dick Watling, United Nations Conference on Environment and Development Republic of Fiji National Report (Fiji Government, 1992); Finland's forests: Government of Finland, Environment and Development in Finland: National Report for the United Nations Conference on Environment and Development (U.N. New York, 1993); France's original forest extent: DocTer Insti-

tute for Environmental Studies, European Environmental Yearbook (DocTer International, London, 1991); Jamaica's forests: Susan Braatz, Draft Environmental Profile on Jamaica (U.S. Department of State, Washington, D.C., May 1982); Grenada's forests and wetlands: The Caribbean Conservation Association, Grenada Country Environmental Profile (The Caribbean Conservation Association, St. Michael, Barbados, 1991); Guadeloupe's forests: International Council for Bird Preservation (ICBP), Biodiversity and Conservation in the Caribbean: Profiles of Selected Islands (ICBP, Cambridge, U.K., 1988); Guatemala's forests: James Nations, Brian Houseal, Ismael Ponciano, et al., Biodiversity in Guatemala: Biological Diversity and Tropical Forests Assessment (WRI, Washington, D.C., 1988); Mauritius' forests: Ministry of Environment and Quality of Life, State of the Environment in Mauritius (Government of Mauritius, Port Louis, Mauritius, 1991); Department of Environment and Natural Resources, A Report on Philippine Environment and Development: Issues and Strategies (Quezon City, Philippines, 1991); Saint Lucia's forests: The Caribbean Conservation Association, St. Lucia Country Environmental Profile (The Caribbean Conservation Association, St. Michael, Barbados, 1991); Saint Vincent's forests: Richard Birdsey, Peter Weaver, and Calvin Nicholls, The Forest Resources of St. Vincent, West Indies (U.S. Department of Agriculture, New Orleans, Louisiana, 1986); Singapore's forests and original mangrove extent: IUCN, The Conservation Atlas of Tropical Forests: Asia and the Pacific (Macmillan Press Ltd., London, 1991); the United Kingdom's forests: Heather Ferguson, unpublished data (Nature Conservancy Council for England, Habitats Branch, Peterborough, U.K., April 1993) the United Kingdom's grasslands: Department of the Environment, The UK Environment (HMSO, London, 1992); the United States' wetlands: Thomas Dahl, Wetlands Losses in the United States 1780s to 1980s (U.S. Department of the Interior, Fish and Wildlife Service, Washington, D.C., 1990); Vanuatu's mangroves: Ministry of Home affairs, Vanuatu National Report for UNCED (Republic of Vanuatu, Port Vila, July 1991).

Habitat data presented here are not comparable when taken from different sources, as definitions of habitat and scales of measurement differ among sources. Ideally, habitat measurements should incorporate information on vegetation type, degree of naturalness, and degree of degradation. However, comprehensive information of this type is rarely available. Where possible, estimates of remaining primary vegetation are presented in this table (except where data were based on a region-wide study, permitting comparisons between countries). Except where otherwise defined below, habitat is variously defined as "wildland," "undisturbed vegetation," and "natural vegetation," depending on the source. Most mangrove data are total estimates of current mangrove cover, regardless of degree of degradation. Except where otherwise indicated, percent lost refers to

habitat lost since preagricultural times. Original habitat extent is estimated based on potential vegetation maps, which generally predict vegetation cover from the physical characteristics of a region, such as temperature and rainfall patterns.

The MacKinnon studies define habitat as natural vegetation and exclude large areas of degraded vegetation from country totals. The MacKinnons relied on field investigations, interviews and other personal communications, and published sources. The categories shown in Table 20.3 are aggregated from the MacKinnons' data. AFRICA—forests: areas under the forest categories below; dry forests: upland montane forest/nonforest, dry forest, and woodland; moist forests: lowland rainforest; savannah/grassland: salt-pan vegetation, brushland/thicket, shrubland, grassland, and halophytic; desert/scrub: desert; wetlands/marsh: wetland; mangroves: mangrove forest/swamp. ASIA—dry forests: subalpine, dry dipterocarp, mixed deciduous, submontane dry evergreen, forest on limestone, Himalayan dry temperate, subtropical dry evergreen, and tropical dry deciduous; moist forests: subtropical broadleaved hill, ironwood, lowland rain, tropical moist deciduous, montane wet temperate, tropical semievergreen, subtropical pine, tropical montane evergreen, moist lowland, tropical dry evergreen, heath, monsoon, tropical montane deciduous, and forest on ultrabasic; savannah/grassland: savannah forest; desert/scrub: tropical thorn forest, desert/semidesert, and tropical thorn scrub; wetlands/marsh: freshwater swamp, peat swamp, and seasonal marsh/seasonal salt marsh; mangroves: mangrove.

South American habitat data, where taken from Thomas Stone's study, is land cover as of 1988, and provides no indication of degree of degradation. Because of differences in scale and methodology, forest habitat estimates differ from forest cover data presented in Table 19.1 of this volume, and thus are not comparable. Thomas Stone used 1 kilometer resolution Advanced Very High Resolution Radiometer (AVHRR) satellite imagery of the continent as a basis for this work. Vegetation classes were interpreted from these data with the help of the United Nations Educational, Scientific, and Cultural Organization (UNESCO) vegetation map, national vegetation maps, and other atlases and relevant data at the country level. These maps were also the basis for determining lost habitat ("degraded" vegetation types). As the process of classifying anthropogenically modified landscapes was based, in part, on map spatial patterns, a considerable amount of this interpretation relied on researchers' subjective judgement. The Stone study incorporated a data quality rating process that ranked underlying data sources. The mean rank for the entire map of South America was .69 out of 1.0.

Forest habitat for Europe, where taken from The Forest Resources of the Temperate Zones Volume II, is public and privately owned forest area judged by country experts to be of high importance to nature conservation.

Most other sources use nomenclature similar to the habitat types shown in this table. In some cases, only a portion of a given vegetation type (e.g., peatlands, as opposed to wetlands) may be discussed. Some data were not used because they could not be disaggregated to specific countries. The determination of the extent of vegetation types in a country is difficult, and estimates vary significantly. Some data on current extent of habitat may include restorations, although the new vegetation may differ significantly from the original vegetation.

Wetlands/marsh: Many estimates of wetland extent are likely to be low. Some include only peatlands; others exclude peatlands, the inclusion of which could increase total wetlands area, especially in Finland, Ireland, Norway, Poland, and Sweden. Some wetland figures may include lakes, ponds, streams, and areas that are periodically flooded; others note only permanently inundated areas. *Mangroves:* These estimates refer specifically to mangrove forests or swamps. For further details, consult the Technical Notes to Table 20.4 in *World Resources 1990–91*, and the original sources.

Readers are invited to submit data to expand or improve this table.

Table 20.4 Globally Threatened Species: Mammals, Birds, and Higher Plants, 1990s

Sources: World Conservation Monitoring Centre (WCMC), *Global Biodiversity Status of the Earth's Living Resources* (Chapman and Hall, London, 1992), and unpublished data (WCMC, Cambridge, U.K., June 1993).

The *total number of known species* may include introductions in some instances. Data on mammals exclude cetaceans (whales and porpoises), except where otherwise indicated. Threatened bird species are listed for countries included within their breeding or wintering ranges. *Higher plants* refer to numbers of native vascular plant species. Total plant species numbers may differ from earlier estimates published in previous editions of *World Resources*, as totals are of full species only, rather than of species and subspecies. The number of *endemic species* refers to those species known to be found only within the country listed. Figures are not necessarily comparable among countries because taxonomic concepts and the extent of knowledge vary (for the latter reason, country totals of species and endemics may be underestimates). In general, numbers of mammals and birds are fairly well known, while plants have not been as well inventoried.

The World Conservation Union classifies threatened and endangered species in six categories:

■ Endangered. "Taxa in danger of extinction and whose survival is unlikely if the causal factors continue operating."
■ Vulnerable. "Taxa believed likely to move into the Endangered category in the near fu-

ture if the causal factors continue operating."
■ Rare. "Taxa with world populations that are not at present Endangered or Vulnerable, but are at risk."
■ Indeterminate. "Taxa known to be Endangered, Vulnerable, or Rare but where there is not enough information to say which of the three categories is appropriate."
■ Out of Danger. "Taxa formerly included in one of the above categories, but which are now considered relatively secure because effective conservation measures have been taken or the previous threat to their survival has been removed."
■ Insufficiently Known. "Taxa that are suspected but not definitely known to belong to any of the above categories."

The number of *threatened species* listed for all countries includes full species that are endangered, vulnerable, rare, indeterminate, and insufficiently known, but excludes introduced species or those known to be extinct.

Number of species per 10,000 square kilometers provides a relative estimate for comparing numbers of species among countries of differing size. Because the relationship between area and species number is nonlinear (i.e., as the area sampled increases, the number of new species located decreases), a species-area curve has been used to standardize these species numbers. The curve predicts how many species a country would have, given its current number of species, if it was a uniform 10,000 square kilometers in size. This number is calculated using the formula: $S = cA^z$, where S = the number of endangered species, A = area, and c and z are constants. The slope of the species-area curve is determined by the constant z, which is approximately 0.33 for large areas containing many habitats. This constant is based on data from previous studies of species-area relationships. In reality, the constant z would differ among regions and countries, because of differences in species' range size (which tend to be smaller in the tropics) and differences in varieties of habitats present. A tropical country with a broad variety of habitats would be expected to have a steeper species-area curve than a temperate, homogenous country because one would predict a greater number of both species and threatened species per unit area. Species-area curves are also steeper for islands than for mainland countries. At present, there are insufficient regional data to estimate separate slopes for each country.

Table 20.5 Globally Threatened Species: Reptiles, Amphibians, and Fish, 1990s

Sources: World Conservation Monitoring Centre (WCMC), *Global Biodiversity Status of the Earth's Living Resources* (Chapman and Hall, London, 1992), and unpublished data (WCMC, Cambridge, U.K., June 1993).

For definitions of *total species* and *endemic species*, refer to the Technical Notes for Table 20.4. Threatened marine turtles and ma-

rine fish are excluded from country totals. Endangered fish species numbers do not include approximately 250 haplochromine and 2 tilapiine species of Lake Victoria cichlids, since the ranges of these species are undetermined.

The number of species per 10,000 square kilometers provides a relative estimate for comparing numbers of species among countries of differing size. For details, refer to the Technical Notes for Table 20.4.

Table 20.6 Net Trade in Wildlife and Wildlife Products Reported by CITES, 1990

Source: World Conservation Monitoring Centre (WCMC), unpublished data (WCMC, Cambridge, U.K., June 1993).

Convention on International Trade in Endangered Species of Wild Flora and Fauna (CITES) members agree to prohibit commercial international trade in endangered species and to closely monitor trade in species that may become depleted by trade. Species are listed in the appendixes to CITES on the basis of their degree of rarity and of the threat posed by trade. Trade is prohibited for species in Appendix I (species threatened with extinction) and is regulated for species in Appendix II (species not yet threatened but that could become endangered if trade is not controlled). Parties to the Convention are required to submit annual reports, including trade records, to the CITES Secretariat in Switzerland. WCMC compiles these data from those reports. Figures refer primarily to legal trade, though illegal trade is included when known.

CITES reporting requirement met refers to the percentage of years for which a country has submitted an annual report to the CITES Secretariat since it became a party to the Convention, through 1991 (1992 for a few countries that had submitted reports for this year as of May 1993). Countries that had ratified the CITES treaty by May 1993 are listed as members.

Live primates include all species of monkeys, apes, and prosimians.

Cat skins include skins of all species of *Felidae*, excluding a small number of skins reported only by weight or length.

Live birds include parrots, macaws, cockatoos, and other species.

Reptile skins include whole skins, reported by number, of all crocodilians and many commonly traded lizard and snake species.

Live cacti include wild and artificially propagated *Cactaceae* plants.

Live orchids include wild and artificially propagated *Orchidaceae* plants.

This table shows net trade in wild and captive-bred species. The impact of international trade on a particular species can be greater than the numbers reported because of mortality (during capture or collection, transit, and quarantine), illegal trade, trade to or from countries that are not CITES members, and omission of domestic trade data.

21. Energy and Materials

The production and use of energy, the ever-increasing mining of subsoil wealth, and the generation of waste are important factors in national and global environmental quality and essential elements of modern industrial activity and the global economy. Countries vary in their production and use of energy and minerals and in their generation of waste. They also vary in their inherent energy and mineral wealth. This chapter presents data that will illustrate those differences as well as trends in resource use over time.

Vast changes have occurred in the production and consumption of energy over the last 20 years, well within the lifetimes of most of the users of this book. Table 21.1 provides data on regional and national production of both fossil fuels and primary electricity (i.e., non-fossil fuel generated) and changes in production over that period. World production of commercial energy has increased 35 percent, with the bulk of the growth in solid and gaseous fuels. The fastest growing sector, however, has been primary electricity, led by the creation of a nuclear power generation industry of global importance. Even hydroelectric power generation—the most mature of energy technologies—has more than doubled over the past two decades. Primary electricity as a whole—nuclear and hydroelectric power production coupled with the development of commercial geothermal, wind, and solar power industries—now makes up almost 10 percent of all commercial energy production.

The United States is the largest producer of energy, followed closely by the former U.S.S.R. Together they produce almost 40 percent of the world's supply. China, while third in rank, produces just 8.8 percent of the supply of global commercial energy. Africa and South America are the least favored regions, producing only 6.4 and 4.3 percent, respectively, of global commercial energy.

The United States is not only the largest producer of commercial energy, it is also the largest consumer. Table 21.2 details changes in consumption over the past 20 years, including the consumption of "traditional fuels." Per capita commercial energy consumption in the United States has actually declined 4 percent (although total consumption has increased 17 percent), and United States energy intensity (energy use per unit of economic output) has declined 17 percent. Still, the U.S. per capita consumption of 320 gigajoules is over 35 times that of India (9 gigajoules) and 14 times that of China (23 gigajoules). In turn, 19 countries, 16 of them in Africa, use less than 1.5 gigajoules of commercial energy per capita. These same countries obtain between 83 and 96 percent of their total energy from traditional fuels. The global share of traditional fuels is 6 percent and has increased 6 percent over the last 20 years.

Table 21.3 shows that known reserves of commercial energy are unequally distributed among the countries of the world. Again, the former U.S.S.R. and the United States lead the world in proved recoverable reserves of coal (both hard and soft). The countries of southwest Asia, surrounding the Persian Gulf, control 57 percent of proved recoverable petroleum reserves, of which Saudi Arabia alone is thought to control 26 percent. The former U.S.S.R. is estimated to control 42 percent of the world's proved recoverable reserves of natural gas, with the Persian Gulf states controlling an additional 25 percent. The United States and the former U.S.S.R. also lead the world in installed hydroelectric generation capacity, with 14 percent and 10 percent of the global total, respectively. Many countries, especially in Africa, have developed only a small fraction of their hydroelectric potential.

Table 21.4 shows world production, consumption, and reserves of major metals. The United States, the former U.S.S.R., Japan, and the countries of the European Community are the major consumers of metals to feed their resource-hungry industrial economies. The former U.S.S.R., the United States, and Australia, however, are also important producers of many of the world's metals. With the exception of tin and mercury, both the production and the consumption of metals have climbed continuously between 1977 and 1992. Interestingly, many estimates of world reserves, and therefore, world reserves life indexes, have also increased due to exploration effort, prices, commercial opportunities, and national priorities.

Table 21.5 shows estimates of the value of known metal reserves held by the various countries of the world. In aggregate, the same resource-rich countries are the leaders here. The former U.S.S.R. holds 24 percent of the wealth, followed, distantly, by Australia, the United States, Canada, and Brazil. The discovery of previously unknown reserves in underexplored countries could change this picture.

Our understanding of waste generation on a global scale is still poor. Table 21.6 details the amounts of some important categories of industrial waste generated in selected countries. Comparisons are perilous, but the United States appears to be the largest waste generator in most categories. In part, this is probably due to its well-developed reporting system.

Table 21.1 Commercial Energy Production, 1971–91

| | Total | | Solid | | Liquid | | Gas | | Primary Electricity {a} | | | | | |
| | | | | | | | | | Geothermal & Wind | | Hydro | | Nuclear | |
	Peta-joules 1991	Percent Change Since 1971	Peta-joules 1991	Percent Change Since 1971	Peta-joules 1991	Percent Change Since 1971	Peta-joules 1991	Percent Change Since 1971	Peta-joules 1991	Percent Change Since 1971	Peta-joules 1991	Percent Change Since 1971	Peta-joules 1991	Percent Change Since 1971
WORLD	334,890	35	93,689	42	132,992	9	76,275	39	1,261	650	8,049	76	22,669	1,817
AFRICA	21,335	70	4,119	162	14,368	44	2,598	184	13	X	192	101	46	X
Algeria	4,392	77	0	X	2,653	34	1,738	244	0	X	1	(9)	0	X
Angola	1,047	243	0	X	1,035	245	7	85	0	X	5	125	0	X
Benin	12	37	0	X	12	37	0	X	0	X	0	X	0	X
Botswana	0	X	0	X	0	X	0	X	0	X	0	X	0	X
Burkina Faso	0	X	0	X	0	X	0	X	0	X	X	X	X	X
Burundi	0	1,546	0	X	0	X	0	X	0	X	0	X	0	X
Cameroon	332	79	0	X	323	78	0	X	0	X	10	132	0	X
Central African Rep	0	77	0	X	0	X	0	X	0	X	0	77	0	X
Chad	0	X	0	X	0	X	0	X	0	X	0	X	0	X
Congo	331	84	0	X	329	83	0	200	0	X	2	771	0	X
Cote d'Ivoire	19	23	0	X	13	(11)	0	X	0	X	6	1,047	0	X
Djibouti	0	X	0	X	0	X	0	X	0	X	0	X	0	X
Egypt	2,320	73	0	X	1,981	59	303	307	0	X	36	96	0	X
Equatorial Guinea	0	(0)	0	X	0	X	0	X	0	X	0	(0)	0	X
Ethiopia	5	611	0	X	0	X	0	X	2	X	3	163	0	X
Gabon	733	127	0	X	727	127	4	43	0	X	3	X	0	X
Gambia, The	0	X	0	X	0	X	0	X	0	X	0	X	0	X
Ghana	22	68	0	X	0	X	0	X	0	X	22	110	0	X
Guinea	1	604	0	X	0	X	0	X	0	X	1	604	0	X
Guinea-Bissau	0	X	0	X	0	X	0	X	0	X	0	X	0	X
Kenya	21	2,475	0	X	0	X	0	X	11	X	10	717	0	X
Lesotho	0	X	0	X	0	X	0	X	0	X	0	X	0	X
Liberia	1	(40)	0	X	0	X	0	X	0	X	1	(40)	0	X
Libya	3,417	30	0	X	3,070	22	347	229	0	X	0	X	0	X
Madagascar	1	148	0	X	0	X	0	X	0	X	1	148	0	X
Malawi	3	429	0	X	0	X	0	X	0	X	3	429	0	X
Mali	1	561	0	X	0	X	0	X	0	X	1	561	0	X
Mauritania	0	X	0	X	0	X	0	X	0	X	0	X	0	X
Mauritius	0	47	0	X	0	X	0	X	0	X	0	47	0	X
Morocco	22	3	16	36	0	(37)	2	(59)	0	X	4	(22)	0	X
Mozambique	1	(87)	1	(88)	0	X	0	X	0	X	0	(79)	0	X
Namibia	0	X	0	X	0	X	0	X	0	X	0	X	0	X
Niger	5	X	5	X	0	X	0	X	0	X	0	X	0	X
Nigeria	4,145	30	3	(38)	3,949	33	185	(7)	0	X	8	41	0	X
Rwanda	1	90	0	X	0	X	0	X	0	X	1	108	0	X
Senegal	0	X	0	X	0	X	0	X	0	X	0	X	0	X
Sierra Leone	0	X	0	X	0	X	0	X	0	X	0	X	0	X
Somalia	0	X	0	X	0	X	0	X	0	X	0	X	0	X
South Africa {b}	3,964	173	3,916	170	0	X	0	X	0	X	2	454	46	X
Sudan	3	838	0	X	0	X	0	X	0	X	3	838	0	X
Swaziland	1	(82)	0	X	0	X	0	X	0	X	1	110	0	X
Tanzania	2	87	0	X	0	X	0	X	0	X	2	101	X	X
Togo	0	25	0	X	0	X	0	X	0	X	0	25	0	X
Tunisia	232	(5)	0	X	219	(3)	13	(31)	0	X	0	(10)	0	X
Uganda	3	(8)	0	X	0	X	0	X	0	X	3	(8)	0	X
Zaire	83	41	4	45	57	31	0	X	0	X	22	75	0	X
Zambia	37	58	9	(55)	0	X	0	X	0	X	28	751	X	X
Zimbabwe	177	95	164	132	0	X	0	X	0	X	13	(37)	0	X
ASIA	94,351	54	32,336	130	47,731	10	9,061	166	282	3,215	1,557	149	3,391	3,262
Afghanistan	99	(4)	4	20	0	(55)	92	(6)	0	X	2	72	0	X
Bangladesh	192	286	0	X	5	1,867	184	271	0	X	3	X	0	X
Bhutan	6	39,225	0	X	0	X	0	X	0	X	6	39,225	0	X
Cambodia	0	15	0	X	0	X	0	X	0	X	0	15	0	X
China	29,720	105	22,741	135	5,903	39	626	26	0	X	450	398	0	X
India	7,327	179	5,313	191	1,314	110	397	577	0	X	243	141	59	355
Indonesia	5,291	34	402	8,114	3,031	(8)	1,819	179	8	X	31	500	0	X
Iran, Islamic Rep	8,335	151	41	176	7,271	139	999	305	0	X	24	146	0	X
Iraq	606	(68)	0	X	560	(70)	46	241	0	X	1	55	0	X
Israel	1	(77)	0	X	0	(30)	1	(82)	0	X	0	X	0	X
Japan	3,099	135	208	(75)	31	73	88	(5)	64	652	380	18	2,329	2,565
Jordan	0	X	0	X	0	X	0	X	0	X	0	X	0	X
Korea, Dem People's Rep	2,464	151	2,350	150	0	X	0	X	0	X	114	174	0	X
Korea, Rep	916	186	284	(10)	0	X	0	X	0	X	18	283	614	X
Kuwait	436	(84)	0	X	417	(83)	18	(92)	0	X	0	X	0	X
Lao People's Dem Rep	3	9,150	0	X	0	X	0	X	0	X	3	9,150	0	X
Lebanon	2	(33)	0	X	0	X	0	X	0	X	2	(33)	0	X
Malaysia	1,950	266	5	X	1,303	148	626	17,548	0	X	16	326	0	X
Mongolia	88	179	88	179	0	X	0	X	0	X	0	X	0	X
Myanmar	84	4	2	425	39	(38)	39	137	0	X	4	141	0	X
Nepal	3	1,188	0	X	0	X	0	X	0	X	3	1,188	0	X
Oman	1,581	121	0	X	1,477	114	104	332	0	X	0	X	0	X
Pakistan	707	70	60	83	137	(36)	440	62	0	X	66	434	4	702
Philippines	258	2,401	25	2,409	7	(35)	0	X	207	X	19	166	0	X
Saudi Arabia	19,367	(9)	0	X	17,914	(15)	1,452	3,530	0	X	0	X	0	X
Singapore	0	X	0	X	0	X	0	X	0	X	0	X	0	X
Sri Lanka	11	274	0	X	0	X	0	X	0	X	11	274	0	X
Syrian Arab Rep	1,192	198	0	X	1,158	191	11	513	0	X	22	12,153	0	X
Thailand	523	1,741	161	2,363	137	4,348	209	1,727	0	X	17	124	0	X
Turkey	771	166	495	172	183	85	8	1,229	3	X	82	760	0	X
United Arab Emirates	5,968	74	0	X	5,036	63	932	173	0	X	0	X	0	X
Viet Nam	332	336	147	99	166	X	0	X	0	X	19	759	0	X
Yemen	391	X	X	X	391	X	0	X	X	X	X	X	X	X

Table 21.1

| | Total | | Solid | | Liquid | | Gas | | Primary Electricity {a} | | | | | |
| | | | | | | | | | Geothermal & Wind | | Hydro | | Nuclear | |
	Peta-joules 1991	Percent Change Since 1971	Peta-joules 1991	Percent Change Since 1971	Peta-joules 1991	Percent Change Since 1971	Peta-joules 1991	Percent Change Since 1971	Peta-joules 1991	Percent Change Since 1971	Peta-joules 1991	Percent Change Since 1971	Peta-joules 1991	Percent Change Since 1971
NORTH & CENTRAL AMERICA	88,467	33	23,923	85	28,800	(1)	25,054	9	784	3,705	2,280	40	7,642	1,572
Belize	0	X	0	X	0	X	0	X	0	X	0	X	0	X
Canada	11,851	73	1,620	387	3,819	22	4,374	59	0	X	1,111	92	926	2,030
Costa Rica	13	252	0	X	0	X	0	X	0	X	13	252	0	X
Cuba	35	198	0	X	33	209	1	141	0	X	0	(23)	0	X
Dominican Rep	3	1,169	0	X	0	X	0	X	0	X	3	1,169	0	X
El Salvador	21	1,931	0	X	0	X	0	X	15	X	6	238	0	X
Guatemala	15	46	0	X	7	(18)	0	X	0	X	8	473	0	X
Haiti	1	X	0	X	0	X	0	X	0	X	1	X	0	X
Honduras	3	266	0	X	0	X	0	X	0	X	3	266	0	X
Jamaica	0	3	0	X	0	X	0	X	0	X	0	3	0	X
Mexico	8,053	25	220	154	6,574	21	948	(8)	190	528,900	87	67	33	X
Nicaragua	12	3,144	0	X	0	X	0	X	11	X	1	38	0	X
Panama	7	280	0	X	0	X	0	X	0	X	7	399	0	X
Trinidad and Tobago	533	(2)	0	X	312	(24)	221	64	0	X	0	X	0	X
United States	67,936	29	22,084	77	18,055	(10)	19,509	2	568	2,660	1,038	5	6,683	1,516
SOUTH AMERICA	14,541	55	890	395	9,810	29	2,441	85	0	X	1,300	420	101	X
Argentina	2,145	47	7	(55)	1,108	1	886	160	0	X	59	964	85	X
Bolivia	164	15	0	X	52	3	107	19	0	X	5	87	0	X
Brazil	2,434	243	93	51	1,392	204	149	335	0	X	784	403	16	X
Chile	211	13	64	69	49	(51)	61	84	0	X	37	133	0	X
Colombia	1,807	238	642	923	904	203	161	7	0	X	100	315	0	X
Ecuador	684	51	0	X	662	47	4	66	0	X	18	1,050	0	X
Guyana	0	X	0	X	0	X	0	X	0	X	0	X	0	X
Paraguay	107	17,415	0	X	0	X	0	X	0	X	107	17,415	0	X
Peru	320	(28)	4	405	257	(36)	18	(27)	0	X	41	164	0	X
Suriname	14	257	0	X	10	X	0	X	0	X	4	4	0	X
Uruguay	22	316	0	X	0	X	0	X	X	X	22	316	X	X
Venezuela	6,633	22	79	7,388	5,377	13	1,054	63	X	X	123	536	X	X
EUROPE	44,335	11	15,285	(29)	9,341	48	8,689	(15)	127	32	1,732	25	9,177	1,544
Albania	83	(23)	27	173	25	(68)	22	32	X	X	9	264	0	X
Austria	244	6	23	(58)	56	(2)	48	(18)	0	X	118	95	0	X
Belgium	488	79	16	(94)	0	X	0	(70)	0	X	4	520	468	X
Bulgaria	360	(15)	205	(49)	2	(81)	0	(93)	0	X	9	12	144	X
Czechoslovakia (former)	1,780	11	1,484	(24)	6	57	19	(18)	0	X	11	17	260	X
Denmark	451	1,324	0	X	297	835	151	X	2	323	1	613	0	X
Finland	317	704	57	3,373	0	X	0	X	0	X	47	25	213	X
France	4,372	184	311	(65)	139	33	83	(70)	0	X	223	26	3,615	3,452
Germany	8,002	(15)	5,377	(35)	143	(33)	630	(17)	0	X	76	58	1,776	2,519
Greece	342	92	289	80	35	329	6	X	0	X	11	20	0	X
Hungary	591	(26)	176	(61)	103	(11)	161	(31)	0	X	1	102	150	X
Iceland	25	493	0	X	0	X	0	X	10	2,258	15	153	0	X
Ireland	139	6	46	(40)	0	X	89	71	0	X	3	82	0	X
Italy	1,165	42	10	(61)	181	191	695	29	115	19	164	(31)	0	X
Netherlands	3,041	(12)	0	X	157	131	2,847	(13)	0	3,400	0	X	36	722
Norway	5,438	139	10	(7)	3,925	300	1,105	4	0	X	398	75	0	X
Poland	3,872	(10)	3,744	(9)	7	(54)	110	(41)	0	X	12	77	0	X
Portugal	38	35	5	(20)	0	X	0	X	0	X	33	49	0	X
Romania	1,448	(41)	285	(23)	284	(42)	828	(48)	0	X	51	217	0	X
Spain	1,314	144	490	58	61	18	55	188,900	0	X	102	(32)	606	2,103
Sweden	1,072	468	1	241	0	(56)	0	X	0	X	229	22	841	85,584
Switzerland	371	205	0	X	0	X	0	X	0	X	120	17	250	1,250
United Kingdom	8,773	(4)	2,367	(36)	3,835	2	1,779	29	0	X	22	73	770	156
Yugoslavia (former)	626	(20)	363	(21)	86	(54)	60	(24)	X	X	69	22	48	X
U.S.S.R. (former)	64,994	15	12,719	(10)	21,708	(15)	27,412	69	1	X	846	86	2,313	3,375
Armenia	X	X	X	X	0 c	X	X	X	X	X	X	X	X	X
Azerbaijan	X	X	X	X	465 c	X	310 c	X	X	X	X	X	X	X
Belarus	X	X	X	X	76 c	X	X	X	X	X	X	X	X	X
Estonia	X	X	X	X	0 c	X	X	X	X	X	X	X	X	X
Georgia	X	X	X	X	8 c	X	X	X	X	X	X	X	X	X
Kazakhstan	X	X	X	X	957 c	X	244 c	X	X	X	X	X	X	X
Kyrgyzstan	X	X	X	X	8 c	X	4 c	X	X	X	X	X	X	X
Latvia	X	X	X	X	0 c	X	X	X	X	X	X	X	X	X
Lithuania	X	X	X	X	0 c	X	X	X	X	X	X	X	X	X
Moldova	X	X	X	X	0 c	X	X	X	X	X	X	X	X	X
Russian Federation	X	X	X	X	19,681 c	X	20,413 c	X	X	X	X	X	X	X
Tajikistan	X	X	X	X	8 c	X	7 c	X	X	X	X	X	X	X
Turkmenistan	X	X	X	X	213 c	X	3,024 c	X	X	X	X	X	X	X
Ukraine	X	X	X	X	191 c	X	X	X	X	X	X	X	X	X
Uzbekistan	X	X	X	X	107 c	X	1,405 c	X	X	X	X	X	X	X
OCEANIA	6,867	136	4,417	199	1,234	44	1,021	123	54	28	141	7	0	X
Australia	6,402	135	4,353	205	1,151	37	841	103	0	X	58	35	0	X
Fiji	1	X	0	X	0	X	0	X	0	X	1	X	0	X
New Zealand	460	154	64	26	84	354	180	309	54	28	79	(12)	0	X
Papua New Guinea	2	224	0	X	0	X	0	X	0	X	2	224	0	X
Solomon Islands	0	X	0	X	0	X	0	X	0	X	0	X	0	X

Source: United Nations Statistical Division.
Notes:
a. The production of primary electricity was assessed at the equivalent of 100 percent efficiency for wind and hydroelectric generation (at the heat value of electricity: 1 kilowatt hour = 3.6 million joules), at 33 percent efficiency for nuclear power generation, and at 10 percent efficiency for geothermal generation.
b. Data are for the South Africa Customs Union (Botswana, Lesotho, Namibia, South Africa, and Swaziland). c = estimated from other data, see Technical Notes.
1 petajoule = 1,000,000,000,000,000 joules = 947,800,000,000 Btus = 163,400 "U.N. standard" barrels of oil = 34,140 "U.N. standard" metric tons of coal.
World and regional totals include countries not listed.
0 = zero or less than half of the unit of measure; X = not available or indeterminate; negative numbers are shown in parentheses.
For additional information, see Sources and Technical Notes.

Table 21.2 Energy Consumption, 1971–91

| | Commercial Energy Consumption | | | | | | | | Traditional Fuels | | | | | |
| | Total | | Per Capita | | Per Constant 1987 $US of GNP | | Imports as Percentage of Consumption | | Total | | Per Capita | | Percentage of Total Consumption | |
	Peta-joules 1991	Percent Change Since 1971	Giga-joules 1991	Percent Change Since 1971	Mega-joules 1991	Percent Change Since 1971	1971	1991	Peta-joules 1991	Percent Change Since 1971	Mega-joules 1991	Percent Change Since 1971	1991	1971
WORLD	321,430	45	60	2	X	X	X	X	19,942	6	3,702	9	6	5
AFRICA	7,871	121	12	24	X	X	(286)	(166)	4,815	6	7,275	6	38	42
Algeria	785	431	31	193	12	126	(962)	(434)	19	6	744	(5)	2	7
Angola	27	7	3	(36)	X	X	(761)	(3,638)	56	(8)	5,887	(45)	68	71
Benin	7	57	1	(9)	4	(12)	105	(72)	48	76	10,113	2	88	87
Botswana	X	X	X	X	X	X	0	X	13	111	10,344	7	X	40
Burkina Faso	8	279	1	133	3	78	100	97	85	69	9,143	4	91	96
Burundi	4	240	1	113	3	65	95	90	44	65	7,696	4	92	96
Cameroon	36	145	3	40	4	3	86	(833)	114	78	9,642	2	76	82
Central African Rep	3	21	1	(26)	3	(5)	98	107	34	79	10,926	9	91	87
Chad	4	92	1	26	4	28	145	111	35	75	6,230	15	90	91
Congo	25	201	11	70	11	2	55	(1,217)	22	73	9,514	(2)	47	60
Cote d'Ivoire	79	145	6	13	9	63	102	96	103	131	8,270	7	57	58
Djibouti	5	210	11	25	X	X	1,482	444	0	X	0	X	0	0
Egypt	1,122	275	21	136	31	18	(120)	(93)	45	66	846	4	4	8
Equatorial Guinea	2	171	6	113	15	X	127	85	4	22	12,130	(4)	69	83
Ethiopia	40	86	1	13	7	26	108	102	414	94	8,059	18	91	91
Gabon	26	45	21	(37)	7	(11)	(1,297)	(2,683)	26	143	22,060	6	51	38
Gambia, The	3	279	3	105	11	69	96	92	9	36	10,112	(27)	75	89
Ghana	56	51	4	(14)	9	17	81	83	152	144	9,786	39	73	63
Guinea	15	32	2	(12)	7	X	100	102	35	51	5,948	0	71	68
Guinea-Bissau	3	220	3	75	18	107	100	106	4	15	4,200	(37)	58	79
Kenya	78	84	3	(10)	9	(31)	172	83	344	99	14,117	(3)	81	80
Lesotho	X	X	X	X	X	X	X	X	6	180	3,616	70	X	100
Liberia	5	(78)	2	(88)	X	X	96	99	49	66	18,228	(11)	91	58
Libya	597	1,692	127	687	X	X	(16,624)	(460)	5	29	1,114	(43)	1	11
Madagascar	15	8	1	(40)	6	8	119	102	76	67	6,121	(7)	83	76
Malawi	11	76	1	(18)	8	(16)	94	82	132	219	13,269	48	93	87
Mali	7	102	1	19	3	11	105	99	54	76	5,627	4	89	90
Mauritania	35	540	17	284	40	406	103	117	0	50	42	(10)	0	1
Mauritius	16	195	15	128	7	(8)	134	157	17	0	15,463	(22)	51	75
Morocco	290	232	11	103	13	36	101	103	14	160	534	59	5	6
Mozambique	14	(50)	1	(67)	7	X	148	110	147	63	10,166	8	91	76
Namibia	0	X	0	X	0	X	X	X	0	X	0	X	X	X
Niger	14	262	2	94	6	242	81	71	47	94	5,872	4	77	86
Nigeria	691	99	6	262	23	300	(3,053)	(480)	1,010	93	9,008	1	59	84
Rwanda	7	464	1	199	3	230	77	91	53	23	7,259	(35)	89	97
Senegal	32	122	4	26	7	35	417	142	49	78	6,567	1	61	66
Sierra Leone	9	(23)	2	(51)	15	(42)	128	159	30	65	6,961	5	77	61
Somalia	3	15	0	(37)	X	X	113	275	71	154	8,007	40	96	92
South Africa {a}	2,714	(23)	70	(55)	33	(58)	(1)	(47)	131	19	3,380	(29)	5	3
Sudan	47	(19)	2	(55)	3	(46)	121	111	220	99	8,490	9	82	65
Swaziland	1	(83)	1	(91)	1	(94)	0	0	18	115	23,986	20	96	66
Tanzania	29	12	1	(41)	9	(34)	129	102	330	157	12,259	35	92	83
Togo	8	89	2	8	6	11	104	104	10	150	2,838	43	56	49
Tunisia	203	346	25	183	19	67	(220)	(9)	31	60	3,744	2	13	30
Uganda	15	(25)	1	(58)	3	X	88	80	137	92	7,563	7	90	78
Zaire	73	62	2	(13)	X	X	86	(3)	365	79	9,452	(3)	83	82
Zambia	51	43	6	(27)	X	X	66	32	130	242	15,484	76	72	52
Zimbabwe	203	89	20	0	33	6	13	14	70	19	6,812	(37)	26	35
ASIA	80,374	238	25	129	X	X	(87)	(12)	8,996	62	2,833	10	10	19
Afghanistan	85	253	5	179	X	X	(318)	(12)	51	38	2,863	9	37	60
Bangladesh	262	3,945	2	2,281	13	X	0	32	277	X	2,375	X	51	0
Bhutan	3	2,474	2	1,600	9	X	57	(132)	12	84	7,443	22	82	98
Cambodia	6	174	1	125	5	X	133	106	54	22	6,295	0	90	95
China	27,345	66	23	21	69	(59)	(1)	(4)	2,018	58	1,724	15	7	7
India	8,011	107	9	36	25	(11)	15	18	2,824	65	3,273	8	26	31
Indonesia	1,914	337	10	187	20	24	(316)	(160)	1,465	60	7,803	5	43	68
Iran, Islamic Rep	2,906	258	48	75	18	128	(1,108)	(176)	29	105	477	1	1	2
Iraq	531	194	28	52	37	812	(1,846)	(22)	1	(8)	55	(52)	0	1
Israel	429	104	88	28	10	(14)	1	103	0	(20)	24	(50)	0	0
Japan	17,384	78	140	52	6	(25)	101	84	10	X	78	X	0	0
Jordan	125	557	30	274	21	X	135	103	0	50	21	(15)	0	0
Korea, Dem People's Rep	2,729	143	123	65	X	X	4	9	40	42	1,821	(4)	1	2
Korea, Rep	3,821	254	87	164	21	(35)	44	85	26	(85)	589	(89)	1	14
Kuwait	120	10	58	(58)	X	X	(5,938)	(246)	0	(43)	112	(78)	0	0
Lao People's Dem Rep	5	(11)	1	(43)	4	X	99	28	39	41	8,890	(10)	88	82
Lebanon	112	68	40	53	X	X	128	100	5	14	1,663	4	4	6
Malaysia	825	344	45	169	19	14	28	(138)	90	73	4,918	5	10	22
Mongolia	113	44	50	(17)	37	X	15	18	13	4	5,864	(40)	10	14
Myanmar	68	39	2	(10)	X	X	35	2	193	54	4,512	(0)	74	72
Nepal	15	318	1	145	4	100	74	69	206	96	10,247	15	93	97
Oman	168	4,378	106	1,805	19	909	(14,735)	(831)	0	X	0	X	0	0
Pakistan	1,032	1,629	8	861	24	457	0	35	296	X	2,439	X	22	0
Philippines	757	147	12	49	20	24	115	74	382	51	5,983	(9)	34	45
Saudi Arabia	3,121	3,279	203	1,217	29	959	(9,957)	(489)	1	800	34	251	0	0
Singapore	467	145	171	89	16	(46)	145	265	(2)	(439)	(653)	(361)	(0)	0
Sri Lanka	67	72	4	26	9	(28)	173	110	89	49	5,127	X	57	61
Syrian Arab Rep	412	393	32	150	29	53	(128)	(181)	0	X	9	X	0	0
Thailand	1,281	425	23	249	18	28	103	63	526	87	9,503	24	29	54
Turkey	1,736	147	30	56	23	(3)	34	58	96	(65)	1,674	(78)	5	28
United Arab Emirates	1,069	3,371	656	451	36	X	(6,894)	(451)	0	X	0	X	0	0
Viet Nam	248	(33)	4	(57)	5	X	63	(32)	251	61	3,684	3	50	30
Yemen	117	X	10	X	X	X	X	(208)	0	X	0	X	0	X

Table 21.2

| | Commercial Energy Consumption | | | | | | | | Traditional Fuels | | | | | |
| | Total | | Per Capita | | Per Constant 1987 $US of GNP | | Imports as Percentage of Consumption | | Total | | Per Capita | | Percentage of Total Consumption | |
	Peta-joules 1991	Percent Change Since 1971	Giga-joules 1991	Percent Change Since 1971	Mega-joules 1991	Percent Change Since 1971	1971	1991	Peta-joules 1991	Percent Change Since 1971	Mega-joules 1991	Percent Change Since 1971	1991	1971
NORTH & CENTRAL AMERICA	96,086	430	243	300	X	X	(29)	(13)	825	33	2,086	0	1	3
Belize	4	98	21	24	11	(30)	107	133	4	68	19,790	6	49	53
Canada	8,779	53	325	22	21	(18)	(11)	(38)	67	22	2,483	(2)	1	1
Costa Rica	51	127	16	30	10	10	93	79	35	(22)	11,326	(56)	41	67
Cuba	451	69	42	37	X	X	107	102	205	22	19,137	(1)	31	39
Dominican Rep	77	73	11	8	16	(16)	100	102	25	(22)	3,463	(52)	25	42
El Salvador	51	143	10	70	11	79	92	62	39	17	7,364	(18)	43	61
Guatemala	50	53	5	(13)	6	(18)	107	88	104	105	10,950	17	68	61
Haiti	10	105	2	43	5	62	107	95	57	37	8,555	(5)	85	89
Honduras	26	56	5	(20)	6	(25)	137	89	58	101	10,975	3	69	64
Jamaica	59	(22)	24	(40)	27	(10)	102	106	6	(40)	2,459	(53)	9	12
Mexico	4,834	201	56	81	31	38	3	(58)	248	62	2,874	(2)	5	9
Nicaragua	39	95	10	9	10	124	109	73	39	88	10,216	5	50	51
Panama	54	53	22	(2)	11	(8)	349	(20)	0	(100)	0	(100)	0	30
Trinidad and Tobago	296	169	237	111	72	161	(137)	(76)	3	(51)	2,249	(62)	1	5
United States	80,839	17	320	(4)	17	(27)	11	17	916	375	3,629	289	1	0
SOUTH AMERICA	9,493	1,304	32	818	X	X	(861)	(43)	2,748	36	9,180	(11)	22	75
Argentina	1,896	62	58	21	25	42	13	(3)	116	17	3,533	(13)	6	8
Bolivia	81	166	11	61	17	86	(152)	(104)	19	90	2,617	14	19	25
Brazil	3,551	135	23	52	13	2	58	43	2,021	31	13,328	(15)	36	51
Chile	464	38	35	0	20	(12)	51	63	84	78	6,246	29	15	12
Colombia	806	96	25	31	20	(13)	(51)	(109)	235	90	7,163	27	23	23
Ecuador	238	338	22	153	20	54	89	(183)	74	82	6,871	5	24	43
Guyana	12	(42)	15	(48)	44	(24)	101	101	4	(56)	5,452	(61)	27	33
Paraguay	33	264	7	100	7	23	90	(224)	55	62	12,511	(11)	63	79
Peru	287	22	13	(25)	14	(1)	35	(3)	88	9	3,984	(33)	23	26
Suriname	24	(9)	56	(21)	20	(23)	87	74	1	282	2,863	232	5	1
Uruguay	70	(3)	22	(12)	9	(29)	111	96	28	121	9,050	100	29	15
Venezuela	2,020	167	102	48	38	67	(928)	(219)	22	28	1,108	(29)	1	2
EUROPE	68,507	163	134	142	X	X	115	40	598	(19)	1,171	(25)	1	3
Albania	84	46	26	(3)	X	X	(9)	33	15	(3)	4,628	(35)	15	21
Austria	953	35	123	31	7	(22)	66	74	30	141	3,826	134	3	2
Belgium	2,019	38	202	33	13	(15)	105	89	6	10	561	7	0	0
Bulgaria	860	(16)	96	(20)	40	X	56	65	13	16	1,430	11	1	1
Czechoslovakia (former)	2,607	1	166	(7)	59	X	21	36	13	(36)	859	(42)	1	1
Denmark	767	(14)	149	(17)	7	(41)	93	49	5	2,271	945	2,184	1	0
Finland	1,002	63	201	51	11	(5)	98	67	30	(60)	5,967	(63)	3	11
France	9,123	71	160	53	9	4	93	57	101	(10)	1,774	(19)	1	2
Germany	14,928	5	187	2	X	X	41	49	46	7	573	4	0	0
Greece	943	44	93	25	19	(16)	48	70	13	(41)	1,302	(49)	1	3
Hungary	1,103	23	105	21	52	X	38	49	24	(13)	2,248	(15)	2	3
Iceland	49	91	192	54	9	(11)	86	53	0	X	0	X	0	0
Ireland	424	52	122	30	13	(24)	82	65	0	143	143	108	0	0
Italy	6,768	55	117	46	8	(12)	100	80	48	25	839	18	1	1
Netherlands	3,197	77	212	55	13	13	57	16	2	1,460	152	1,265	0	0
Norway	854	66	200	52	10	(12)	61	(527)	9	28	2,212	17	1	1
Poland	3,555	(24)	93	(35)	66	X	(9)	4	28	39	726	19	1	0
Portugal	567	192	57	167	13	46	118	107	6	(10)	570	(18)	1	3
Romania	2,063	(11)	89	(21)	72	X	(0)	32	19	(67)	832	(71)	1	2
Spain	3,507	74	90	53	10	(4)	72	73	18	(63)	472	(68)	1	2
Sweden	1,741	35	202	27	11	(3)	99	43	122	(7)	14,198	(13)	7	9
Switzerland	936	46	138	34	5	8	86	66	14	61	2,141	48	2	1
United Kingdom	9,065	20	157	17	13	(18)	60	6	4	4	72	0	0	0
Yugoslavia (former)	1,212	(5)	51	(18)	X	X	22	55	30	(57)	1,237	(63)	2	5
U.S.S.R. (former)	54,730	68	193	42	X	X	(13)	(15)	792	(6)	2,797	(21)	1	3
Armenia	X	X	X	X	X	X	X	X	X	X	X	X	X	X
Azerbaijan	X	X	X	X	X	X	X	X	X	X	X	X	X	X
Belarus	X	X	X	X	X	X	X	X	X	X	X	X	X	X
Estonia	X	X	X	X	X	X	X	X	X	X	X	X	X	X
Georgia	X	X	X	X	X	X	X	X	X	X	X	X	X	X
Kazakhstan	X	X	X	X	X	X	X	X	X	X	X	X	X	X
Kyrgyzystan	X	X	X	X	X	X	X	X	X	X	X	X	X	X
Latvia	X	X	X	X	X	X	X	X	X	X	X	X	X	X
Lithuania	X	X	X	X	X	X	X	X	X	X	X	X	X	X
Moldova	X	X	X	X	X	X	X	X	X	X	X	X	X	X
Russian Federation	X	X	X	X	X	X	X	X	X	X	X	X	X	X
Tajikistan	X	X	X	X	X	X	X	X	X	X	X	X	X	X
Turkmenistan	X	X	X	X	X	X	X	X	X	X	X	X	X	X
Ukraine	X	X	X	X	X	X	X	X	X	X	X	X	X	X
Uzbekistan	X	X	X	X	X	X	X	X	X	X	X	X	X	X
OCEANIA	4,367	183	161	106	X	X	7	(61)	185	33	6,837	(3)	4	8
Australia	3,722	55	215	14	17	(8)	(3)	(78)	109	36	6,287	0	3	3
Fiji	10	61	14	17	8	(12)	201	104	12	24	16,175	(10)	53	60
New Zealand	533	99	156	67	16	52	59	14	0	(90)	146	(92)	0	2
Papua New Guinea	33	170	8	69	11	93	106	99	60	41	15,083	(12)	65	78
Solomon Islands	2	197	6	49	11	X	109	117	3	129	9,740	15	62	68

Sources: United Nations Statistical Division and The World Bank.
Notes: Commercial energy consumption does not include bunkers (fuel for aircraft and ships in international transport) or additions to stocks.
Imports are net imports (gross imports minus exports) and may exceed consumption due to additions to stocks and use for bunkers.
a. Data are for the South African Customs Union (Botswana, Lesotho, Namibia, South Africa, and Swaziland).
1 petajoule = 1,000,000,000,000,000 joules = 947,800,000,000 Btus = 163,400 "U.N. standard" barrels of oil = 34,140 "U.N. standard" metric tons of coal.
1 gigajoule = 1,000,000,000 joules = 947,800 Btus; 1 megajoule = 1,000,000 joules = 947.8 Btus. World and regional totals include countries not listed.
0 = zero or less than half of the unit of measure; X = not available or indeterminate; negative numbers are shown in parentheses; GNP = gross national product.
For additional information, see Sources and Technical Notes.

Table 21.3 Reserves and Resources of Commercial Energy, 1990

	Anthracite and Bituminous Coals (million metric tons) 1990		Subbituminous and Lignite Coals (million metric tons) 1990		Crude Oil (million metric tons) 1990	Natural Gas (billion cubic meters) 1990	Uranium (metric tons)		Hydroelectric (megawatts)	
	Proved Reserves in Place	Proved Recoverable Reserves	Proved Reserves in Place	Proved Recoverable Reserves	Proved Recoverable Reserves	Proved Recoverable Reserves	Recoverable at Less Than $80 per kg 1990	Recoverable at Less Than $130 per kg 1990	Known Exploitable Potential	Installed Capacity 1990
WORLD	1,212,852	521,413	743,193	517,770	134,792	128,852	1,410,040	673,670	X	624,044
AFRICA	131,841	60,811	1,506	1,267	9,005	8,178	547,020	138,700	X	19,204
Algeria	X	43	X	X	1,800	3,300	26,000	X	287 b	286
Angola	X	X	X	X	250	51	X	X	100,000	412
Benin	X	X	X	X	3	X	X	X	500 b	0
Botswana	7,000	3,500	X	X	X	X	X	X	1 b	0 c
Burkina Faso	X	X	X	X	X	X	X	X	200 b	0
Burundi	X	X	X	X	X	X	X	X	1,366	32
Cameroon	X	X	X	X	55	110	X	X	115,000	530
Central African Rep	X	X	4	4	X	X	8,000	8,000	2,000 b	22
Chad	X	X	X	X	X	X	X	X	30 b	0
Congo	X	X	X	X	110	74	X	X	50,000	120
Cote d'Ivoire	X	X	X	X	14	100	X	X	14,000	895
Djibouti	X	X	X	X	X	X	X	X	X	0
Egypt	25	13	X	40	840	351	X	X	3,210 b	2,745
Equatorial Guinea	X	X	X	X	X	24	X	X	2,000 b	1
Ethiopia	X	X	X	X	X	25	X	X	162,000	230
Gabon	X	X	X	X	100	14	11,000	4,650	32,500	204
Gambia, The	X	X	X	X	X	X	X	X	X	0
Ghana	X	X	X	X	X	X	X	X	11,550	1,072
Guinea	X	X	X	X	X	X	X	X	26,000	47
Guinea-Bissau	X	X	X	X	X	X	X	X	300	0
Kenya	X	X	X	X	X	X	X	X	30,000	498
Lesotho	X	X	X	X	X	X	X	X	2,000	0 c
Liberia	X	X	X	X	X	X	X	X	11,000	81
Libya	X	X	X	X	3,150	1,218	X	X	X	0
Madagascar	1,000	X	85	X	X	2	X	X	23,061	106
Malawi	25	12	X	X	X	X	X	X	6,000	146
Mali	X	X	X	X	X	X	X	X	10,000	45
Mauritania	X	X	X	X	X	X	X	X	X	61
Mauritius	X	X	X	X	X	X	X	X	65 b	59
Morocco	134	45	44	X	X	2	X	X	4,000	626
Mozambique	X	240	X	X	X	65	X	X	72,000	2,078
Namibia	X	X	X	X	X	59	84,750	16,000	1,060	0 c
Niger	X	70	X	X	X	X	166,070	6,650	235 b	0
Nigeria	X	21	339	169	2,400	2,475	X	X	40,000	1,900
Rwanda	X	X	X	X	X	57	X	X	3,000	56
Senegal	X	X	X	X	X	X	X	X	500 b	0
Sierra Leone	X	X	X	X	X	X	X	X	6,800	2
Somalia	X	X	X	X	X	6	X	6,600	50 b	0
South Africa	121,218	55,333	X	X	X	51	247,600	96,800	X	593 c
Sudan	X	X	X	X	41	85	X	X	1,900	225
Swaziland	X	X	X	999	X	X	X	X	400	0 c
Tanzania	304	200	X	X	X	24	X	X	20,000	259
Togo	X	X	X	X	X	X	X	X	270 b	4
Tunisia	X	X	X	X	230	85	X	X	65 b	64
Uganda	X	X	X	X	X	X	X	X	10,200	155
Zaire	600	600	X	X	12	1	1,800	X	530,000	2,772
Zambia	X	X	69	55	X	X	1,800	X	309,009	2,245
Zimbabwe	1,535	734	965	X	X	X	X	X	19,281	633
ASIA	335,204	125,656	135,304	87,403	95,137	45,148	4,320	46,730	X	117,701
Afghanistan	112	66	X	X	X	100	X	X	25,000 b	292
Bangladesh	1,054	X	X	X	X	360	X	X	800 b	230
Bhutan	X	X	X	X	X	X	X	X	X	342
Cambodia	X	X	X	X	X	X	X	X	83,000	10
China {d}	177,600	62,200	108,800	52,300	3,264	1,127	X	X	2,168,304	30,100
India	129,154	60,648	2,100	1,900	810	730	X	X	205,000	18,864
Indonesia	X	962	X	31,101	726	1,804	4,320	X	709,000	1,950
Iran, Islamic Rep	3,754	193	2,295	X	12,700	17,000	X	X	56,000	1,804
Iraq	X	X	X	X	13,600	2,690	X	X	70,000	150
Israel	X	X	X	X	X	X	X	X	1,600	0
Japan	8,319	827	175	17	7	36	X	6,600	134,750	37,830
Jordan	X	X	X	X	3	11	X	X	87	7
Korea, Dem People's Rep	2,000	300	300	300	X	X	X	X	X	5,000
Korea, Rep	301	203	X	X	X	X	X	31,000	3,467	2,340
Kuwait	X	X	X	X	12,785	1,360	X	X	X	0
Lao People's Dem Rep	X	X	X	X	X	X	X	X	22,638	200
Lebanon	X	X	X	X	X	X	X	X	1,000	267
Malaysia	15	4	126	X	347	1,817	X	X	59,229	1,457
Mongolia	12,000	X	12,000	X	X	X	X	X	X	0
Myanmar	5	2	X	X	7	265	X	X	160,000	267
Nepal	X	X	X	X	X	X	X	X	144,000	235
Oman	X	X	X	X	580	280	X	X	X	0
Pakistan	X	X	X	524	28	728	X	X	85,000	2,897
Philippines	1	X	369	262	19	17	X	X	31,951	2,168
Saudi Arabia	X	X	X	X	35,650	5,497	X	X	X	0
Singapore	X	X	X	X	X	X	X	X	X	0
Sri Lanka	X	X	X	X	X	X	X	X	7,175	1,017
Syrian Arab Rep	X	X	X	X	240	181	X	X	4,500	910
Thailand	X	X	1,422	999	27	196	X	X	8,169	2,274
Turkey	590	162	7,705	6,986	52	44	X	9,130	216,000	6,765
United Arab Emirates	X	X	X	X	1,300	5,646	X	X	X	0
Viet Nam	300	150	12	X	X	3	X	X	6,490	325
Yemen	X	X	X	X	550	200	X	X	X	0

Table 21.3

	Anthracite and Bituminous Coals (million metric tons) 1990		Subbituminous and Lignite Coals (million metric tons) 1990		Crude Oil (million metric tons) 1990	Natural Gas (billion cubic meters) 1990	Uranium (metric tons)		Hydroelectric (megawatts)	
							Recoverable at Less Than $80 per kg 1990	Recoverable at Less Than $130 per kg 1990		
	Proved Reserves in Place	Proved Recoverable Reserves	Proved Reserves in Place	Proved Recoverable Reserves	Proved Recoverable Reserves	Proved Recoverable Reserves			Known Exploitable Potential	Installed Capacity 1990
NORTH & CENTRAL AMERICA	231,947	118,429	219,051	132,474	10,478	10,129	247,900	323,900	X	160,087
Belize	X	X	X	X	X	X	X	X	X	0
Canada	6,435	4,509	14,355	4,114	720	3,116	146,000	68,000	614,882	59,381
Costa Rica	X	X	27	X	X	X	X	X	37,000	754
Cuba	X	X	X	X	15	3	X	X	X	49
Dominican Rep	X	X	X	X	X	X	X	X	2,517	207
El Salvador	X	X	X	X	X	X	X	X	4,009	406
Guatemala	X	X	X	X	24	1	X	X	43,370	438
Haiti	X	X	13	X	X	X	X	X	430	70
Honduras	X	X	21	X	X	X	X	X	24,000	130
Jamaica	X	X	75	34	X	X	X	X	335	20
Mexico	1,569	1,252	732	468	6,079	2,025	X	1,700	80,000	7,837
Nicaragua	X	X	X	X	X	X	X	X	6,552	103
Panama	X	X	X	X	X	X	X	X	16,233	551
Trinidad and Tobago	X	X	X	X	80	252	X	X	X	0
United States	223,943	112,668	203,828	127,892	3,560	4,735	101,900	254,200	376,000	90,141
SOUTH AMERICA	6,225	5,648	15,312	4,062	9,872	4,695	83,530	29,190	X	80,375
Argentina	X	130	195	X	215	579	8,740	2,190	390,038	6,499
Bolivia	X	X	X	X	25	118	X	X	50,000	342
Brazil	X	X	10,176	2,359	395	115	73,000	27,000	1,116,900	45,558
Chile	79	31	4,500	1,150	41	131	X	X	162,262	2,290
Colombia	5,449	4,240	411	299	280	108	X	X	418,200	7,201
Ecuador	X	X	30	24	207	16	X	X	180,000	897
Guyana	X	X	X	X	X	X	X	X	63,100	2
Paraguay	X	X	X	X	X	X	X	X	39,630	5,790
Peru	X	960	X	100	52	200	1,790	X	412,000	2,396
Suriname	X	X	X	X	5	X	X	X	12,840	290
Uruguay	X	X	X	X	X	X	X	X	6,750	1,196
Venezuela	697	417	X	X	8,604	3,429	X	X	261,700	7,914
EUROPE	311,366	61,500	162,587	109,873	2,145	5,180	58,270	48,150	X	170,425
Albania	X	X	15	X	24	20	X	X	17,000	690
Austria	X	X	350	59	15	19	X	X	56,800	10,923
Belgium	715	410	X	X	X	X	X	X	500	1,401
Bulgaria	36	30	4,418	3,700	2	7	X	X	2,240	1,975
Czechoslovakia (former)	5,400	1,870	6,100	3,500	2	14	X	X	10,826	2,940
Denmark	X	X	63	X	103	115	X	X	14	12
Finland	X	X	X	X	X	X	X	1,500	22,600	2,621
France	745	178	135	32	19	53	23,800	15,700	101,976	24,747
Germany	44,000	23,919	102,000	56,150	62	347	600	4,000	27,000	8,944
Greece	X	X	5,312	3,000	4	1	300	X	16,000	2,408
Hungary	1,407	596	8,305	3,865	22	104	1,620	1,500	4,500	48
Iceland	X	X	X	X	X	X	X	X	64,000	756
Ireland	19	14	X	X	X	19	X	X	194	513
Italy	X	X	X	X	66	282	4,800	X	65,000	18,770
Netherlands	1,406	497	X	X	20	1,970	X	X	500	36
Norway	X	13	38	38	1,025	1,227	X	X	171,400	26,945
Poland	65,800	29,600	12,900	11,600	2	166	X	X	12,000	1,851
Portugal	8	3	38	33	X	X	7,300	1,400	30,500	3,360
Romania	1	1	3,199	3,117	157	150	X	X	40,000	5,583
Spain	1,750	850	950	600	3	16	17,850	21,150	69,100	16,050
Sweden	X	X	4	1	X	X	2,000	2,000	70,000	16,331
Switzerland	X	X	X	X	X	X	X	X	41,000	12,350
United Kingdom	190,000	3,300	1,000	500	535	545	X	X	5,600	4,171
Yugoslavia (former)	80	70	17,760	16,500	32	82	X	900	71	7,000
U.S.S.R. (former)	130,000	104,000	157,000	137,000	8,000 e	54,530	X	X	3,831,000	64,100
Armenia	X	X	X	X	X	X	X	X	X	X
Azerbaijan	X	X	X	X	163 f	538 f	X	X	X	X
Belarus	X	X	X	X	X	X	X	X	X	X
Estonia	X	X	X	X	X	X	X	X	X	X
Georgia	X	X	X	X	X	X	X	X	X	X
Kazakhstan	X	X	X	X	449 f	425 f	X	X	X	X
Kyrgyzstan	X	X	X	X	41 f	28 f	X	X	X	X
Latvia	X	X	X	X	X	X	X	X	X	X
Lithuania	X	X	X	X	X	X	X	X	X	X
Moldova	X	X	X	X	X	X	X	X	X	X
Russian Federation	X	X	X	X	5,132 f	40,692 f	X	X	X	X
Tajikistan	X	X	X	X	41 f	28 f	X	X	X	X
Turkmenistan	X	X	X	X	190 f	5,352 f	X	X	X	X
Ukraine	X	X	X	X	X	X	X	X	X	X
Uzbekistan	X	X	X	X	41 f	X	X	X	X	X
OCEANIA	66,269	45,369	52,433	45,690	204	991	469,000	60,000	X	12,152
Australia	66,220	45,340	50,600	45,600	155	493	469,000	60,000	25,248	7,268
Fiji	X	X	X	X	X	X	X	X	515	80
New Zealand	49	27	1,833	90	22	98	X	X	60,000	4,649
Papua New Guinea	X	X	X	X	27	400	X	X	98,000	155
Solomon Islands	X	X	X	X	X	X	X	X	37	0

Sources: World Energy Council, United Nations Statistical Division.
Notes: a. World total includes Greenland's 27,000 metric tons. b. Technical potential. c. South Africa includes other members of its customs union, Botswana, Lesotho, Swaziland, and Namibia. d. These estimates of China's coal reserves contrast sharply with previous estimates, see Chapter 10.
e. The 'Russian language newspaper "Ekonomika i Zhizn" (Economy and Life), February 1992, is quoted as reporting a new figure of 23,100 metric tons, 85 percent in the Russian Federation. f. Data estimate from other sources, see Technical Notes.
0 = zero or less than half of the unit of measures. X = not available.
For additional information, see Sources and Technical Notes.

Table 21.4 Production, Consumption, and Reserves of

	Annual Production (000 metric tons)					Annual Consumption (000 metric tons)			
	1977	1982	1987	1992		1977	1982	1987	1991
ALUMINUM {a}									
Australia	23,283.1	23,625.0	34,101.7	39,950.0	United States	4,756.0	3,649.5	4,539.0	4,137.2
Guinea	10,108.9	11,827.0	13,500.0	13,773.0	Japan	1,418.7	1,639.3	1,696.8	2,431.6
Jamaica	10,211.4	8,378.0	7,660.0	11,302.0	Germany {b}	1,127.3	1,235.2	1,420.7	1,360.9
Brazil	893.8	6,289.0	8,750.0	10,800.0	U.S.S.R. (former)	1,760.0	1,880.0	1,800.0	1,100.0
India	1,349.4	1,854.0	2,736.0	4,475.0	China	370.0	580.0	660.0	800.0
Russian Federation {c}	4,083.5	4,600.0	4,600.0	4,000.0	France	533.8	578.4	615.6	734.2
Suriname	4,292.2	4,205.0	2,581.0	3,250.0	Italy	382.0	420.0	547.5	670.0
China	1,070.8	1,500.0	2,400.0	3,000.0	India	187.6	219.7	326.0	420.0
Guyana	2,441.0	1,783.0	2,785.0	2,300.0	United Kingdom	418.1	326.3	383.6	412.4
Greece	2,664.2	2,853.0	2,472.0	2,100.0	Korea, Rep	79.5	97.1	207.9	383.5
Ten Countries Total	60,398.4	66,914.0	81,585.7	94,950.0	Ten Countries Total	11,033.0	10,625.5	12,197.1	12,449.8
World Total	73,595.3	79,335.0	93,968.2	103,625.0	World Total	14,383.3	14,139.1	17,055.2	17,194.1
Bauxite, World Reserves 1992 (000 metric tons)				23,000,000	World Reserves Life Index (years)				222
Bauxite, World Reserve Base 1992 (000 metric tons)				28,000,000	World Reserve Base Life Index (years)				270
CADMIUM									
Japan	3.2	2.0	2.5	3.0	Japan	0.8	1.1	2.3	6.4
United States	3.4	1.0	1.5	1.6	United States	4.1	4.1	4.2	3.3
Canada	1.4	0.9	1.5	1.5	Belgium	1.6	1.7	2.4	2.6
Belgium	1.1	1.0	1.3	1.5	U.S.S.R. (former)	2.4	2.3	2.5	1.8
China	0.1	0.3	0.7	1.2	France	1.2	1.0	1.4	1.4
Australia	0.7	1.0	0.9	1.0	United Kingdom	1.2	1.2	1.6	0.8
Kazakhstan	X	X	X	1.0	Germany {b}	2.3	1.9	1.5	0.7
Germany	1.2	1.0	1.1	0.9	China	X	0.3	0.4	0.5
Russian Federation {c}	2.5	2.9	3.0	0.8	India	0.1	0.2	0.2	0.4
Italy	0.4	0.5	0.3	0.6	Korea, Rep	X	0.2	0.4	0.4
Ten Countries Total	14.0	10.6	12.8	13.1	Ten Countries Total	13.8	14.0	16.8	18.4
World Total	17.2	16.4	19.1	18.8	World Total	16.2	16.4	19.2	20.2
World Reserves 1992 (000 metric tons)				540	World Reserves Life Index (years)				X d
World Reserve Base 1992 (000 metric tons)				970	World Reserve Base Life Index (years)				X d
COPPER									
Chile	1,056.5	1,242.2	1,412.9	1,940.0	United States	1,986.6	1,664.2	2,126.7	2,057.8
United States	1,364.8	1,147.0	1,243.6	1,760.5	Japan	1,127.1	1,243.0	1,276.6	1,613.2
Canada	780.9	612.4	794.1	764.2	Germany {b}	894.9	847.8	970.1	994.8
Zambia	656.2	574.5	463.2	440.0	U.S.S.R. (former)	1,290.0	1,320.0	1,270.0	880.0
Poland	284.8	376.0	438.0	387.0	China	346.0	398.0	470.0	590.0
China	99.8	175.0	250.0	375.0	France	326.1	419.0	399.0	481.2
Russian Federation {c}	853.0	560.0	630.0	375.0	Italy	326.0	342.0	420.0	470.7
Peru	350.1	353.8	417.6	368.1	Belgium	295.4	277.1	291.8	372.0
Kazakhstan	X	X	X	350.0	Korea, Rep	53.2	131.9	259.0	343.2
Australia	220.0	245.3	232.7	326.0	United Kingdom	512.2	355.4	327.7	269.4
Ten Countries Total	5,666.1	5,286.2	5,882.1	7,085.8	Ten Countries Total	7,157.5	6,998.4	7,810.9	8,072.3
World Total	7,716.4	7,622.3	8,306.3	9,289.6	World Total	9,059.9	9,033.1	10,413.6	10,714.0
World Reserves 1992 (000 metric tons)				310,000	World Reserves Life Index (years)				33
World Reserve Base 1992 (000 metric tons)				590,000	World Reserve Base Life Index (years)				64
LEAD									
Australia	432.2	455.3	489.1	548.0	United States	988.4	1,106.1	1,216.9	1,246.3
United States	573.5	530.3	318.7	407.5	U.S.S.R. (former)	620.0	810.0	775.0	600.0
China	135.0	160.0	252.0	385.0	Japan	245.8	354.0	378.0	422.2
Canada	281.0	341.2	413.7	342.5	Germany {b}	377.9	433.2	444.2	413.5
Kazakhstan	X	X	X	240.0	United Kingdom	241.0	271.9	287.5	263.7
Peru	166.1	197.6	204.0	193.2	Italy	206.1	243.0	244.0	259.0
Mexico	163.5	103.6	177.2	174.0	France	190.2	194.5	207.5	252.5
Sweden	88.1	8,038.0	90.4	106.2	China	200.0	215.0	256.0	250.0
South Africa	X	90.3	93.6	75.4	Korea, Rep	X	31.5	112.4	172.8
Russian Federation {c}	510.0	430.0	440.0	75.0	Spain	94.7	102.7	105.8	121.5
Ten Countries Total	2,349.4	10,346.3	2,478.7	2,546.8	Ten Countries Total	3,164.1	3,761.9	4,027.3	4,001.5
World Total	3,442.1	3,448.0	3,428.8	3,424.2	World Total	4,435.6	5,236.6	5,676.5	5,342.2
World Reserves 1992 (000 metric tons)				63,000	World Reserves Life Index (years)				18
World Reserve Base 1992 (000 metric tons)				130,000	World Reserve Base Life Index (years)				38
MERCURY									
China	0.7	0.7	0.7	0.9	United States	1.9	1.7	1.4	1.2 e
Mexico	0.5	0.3	0.1	0.7	Spain	0.2	1.0	0.8	X
Algeria	0.9	0.4	0.7	0.4	Algeria	0.6	0.1	0.7	X
Russian Federation {c}	2.0	2.2	2.3	0.4	United Kingdom	0.3	0.2	0.4	X
Ukraine	X	X	X	0.2	China	0.5	0.6	{f}	X
Kyrgyzstan	X	X	X	0.1	Brazil	0.2	0.1	0.3	X
Czechoslovakia	0.2	0.2	0.2	0.1	Germany {b}	0.2	0.1	0.2	X
Finland	0.0	0.1	0.1	0.1	Mexico	0.0	0.1	0.2	X
United States	1.0	0.9	0.0	0.1	Belgium	0.1	0.3	0.1	X
Slovenia	X	X	X	0.0	U.S.S.R. (former)	2.0	2.4	2.0	X
Ten Countries Total	5.3	4.7	4.2	2.9	Ten Countries Total	6.0	6.6	6.2	X
World Total	6.9	6.8	5.5	3.0	World Total	6.9	7.0	6.6	X
World Reserves 1992 (000 metric tons)				130	World Reserves Life Index (years)				43
World Reserve Base 1992 (000 metric tons)				240	World Reserve Base Life Index (years)				80

Selected Metals, 1977–92

Table 21.4

NICKEL

	Annual Production (000 metric tons)					Annual Consumption (000 metric tons)			
	1977	1982	1987	1992		1977	1982	1987	1991
Russian Federation {c}	144.3	165.2	272.0	215.0	Japan	97.3	106.7	153.9	180.1
Canada	235.4	88.6	189.1	192.1	U.S.S.R. (former)	125.0	138.0	135.0	150.0
New Caledonia	109.1	60.1	56.9	113.1	United States	140.9	125.2	146.3	126.9
Indonesia	14.0	45.9	57.8	78.1	Germany {b}	64.7	67.7	89.3	77.0
Australia	85.8	87.6	74.6	64.0	China	18.0	19.0	24.0	40.0
China	X	12.0	25.0	37.0	France	35.8	31.8	39.3	36.8
Cuba	37.0	36.1	33.8	32.2	Italy	22.6	24.0	28.8	31.5
South Africa	23.0	22.0	34.3	28.4	United Kingdom	30.5	22.5	33.1	29.5
Dominican Republic	24.2	5.4	32.5	25.0	Belgium	2.6	3.9	8.5	19.6
Botswana	12.1	17.8	25.9	23.5	Finland	2.8	8.7	14.9	18.0
Ten Countries Total	685.0	540.6	801.8	808.4	Ten Countries Total	540.2	547.5	673.1	709.4
World Total	772.8	621.6	892.5	921.9	World Total	643.2	648.3	837.7	882.0
World Reserves 1992 (000 metric tons)				47,000	World Reserves Life Index (years)				51
World Reserve Base 1992 (000 metric tons)				110,000	World Reserve Base Life Index (years)				119

TIN

	1977	1982	1987	1992		1977	1982	1987	1991
China	20.0	15.0	20.0	43.0	United States	47.6	46.3	37.0	37.1
Brazil	6.4	8.2	30.4	30.0	Japan	29.7	28.7	32.6	34.9
Indonesia	24.0	33.8	26.1	25.0	China	14.0	12.5	16.5	23.2
Bolivia	32.6	26.8	8.1	15.3	Germany {b}	17.6	16.8	19.8	19.2
Thailand	24.2	26.1	14.9	15.0	U.S.S.R. (former)	25.0	27.0	29.0	17.0
Malaysia	58.7	52.3	30.4	14.3	United Kingdom	14.9	10.4	9.8	10.3
Russian Federation {c}	33.0	21.0	16.0	10.0	France	9.8	8.2	7.4	8.2
Portugal	0.5	0.4	0.1	6.5	Netherlands	6.2	5.4	4.9	6.2
Australia	10.0	12.1	7.7	6.4	Brazil	4.8	4.9	7.9	6.2
Peru	0.3	1.7	5.3	6.0	Korea, Rep	0.8	2.1	5.8	5.9
Ten Countries Total	209.7	197.5	158.9	171.5	Ten Countries Total	170.4	162.3	170.7	168.2
World Total	231.4	219.5	181.3	179.5	World Total	232.5	215.4	229.1	218.2
World Reserves 1992 (000 metric tons)				8,000	World Reserves Life Index (years)				45
World Reserve Base 1992 (000 metric tons)				10,000	World Reserve Base Life Index (years)				56

ZINC

	1977	1982	1987	1992		1977	1982	1987	1991
Canada	1,300.6	1,036.1	1,481.5	1,311.9	United States	998.2	800.6	1,052.2	933.0
Australia	491.9	664.8	778.4	1,028.0	Japan	667.2	703.1	728.7	845.5
China	99.8	160.0	458.0	670.0	U.S.S.R. (former)	945.0	1,050.0	1,030.0	775.0
Peru	405.5	507.1	612.5	600.6	China	225.0	260.0	409.0	530.0
United States	408.0	326.5	232.9	551.6	Germany {b}	397.5	440.6	527.0	540.1
Mexico	265.5	242.3	271.5	279.0	France	257.7	263.9	252.7	289.1
Spain	93.0	167.0	273.0	201.8	Italy	197.0	202.0	245.0	283.0
Kazakhstan {c}	735.0	800.0	810.0	200.0	Korea, Rep	46.5	94.4	178.5	281.0
Korea, Dem People's Rep	149.7	140.0	220.0	200.0	Belgium	112.1	126.5	163.4	200.0
Ireland	116.3	167.2	177.0	194.1	Australia	80.2	74.2	82.0	196.6
Ten Countries Total	4,065.4	4,211.0	5,314.8	5,237.0	Ten Countries Total	3,926.4	4,015.3	4,668.5	4,873.3
World Total	6,064.4	6,125.0	7,231.9	7,136.5	World Total	5,773.5	5,933.4	6,887.7	6,992.8
World Reserves 1992 (000 metric tons)				140,000	World Reserves Life Index (years)				20
World Reserve Base 1992 (000 metric tons)				330,000	World Reserve Base Life Index (years)				46

IRON ORE

	1977	1982	1987	1992		1977	1982	1987	1991
China	62,992.1	107,320.0	161,430.0	194,000.0	China	125,812.0 g	110,772.0	173,528.0	209,593.0
Brazil	84,645.7	90,243.1	134,105.0	146,000.0	U.S.S.R. (former)	198,160.0 g	201,574.0	205,434.0	171,912.0
Australia	93,090.6	84,949.8	101,748.0	117,170.0	Japan	115,240.0 g	122,172.0	112,451.0	127,413.0
Russian Federation {c}	230,262.8	236,762.8	250,874.0	82,500.0	United States	111,901.0 g	47,505.0	58,747.0	64,810.0
Ukraine	X	X	X	75,700.0	Germany {b}	47,503.0 g	42,935.0	44,126.0	43,177.0
United States	54,872.0	34,875.0	47,648.0	55,593.0	Brazil	18,001.0 g	12,703.0	39,368.0	36,497.0
India	40,983.3	39,622.0	51,018.0	54,000.0	Korea, Rep	4,376.0 g	12,334.0	16,487.0	28,730.0
Canada	54,548.2	34,478.3	37,702.0	34,136.0	France	36,691.0 g	28,776.0	22,882.0	22,492.0
South Africa	25,652.6	23,785.4	22,008.0	28,226.0	United Kingdom	19,693.0 g	11,041.0	18,290.0	18,578.0
Venezuela	13,949.8	10,849.4	17,782.0	22,000.0	Belgium	24,200.0 g	18,613.0	18,382.0	19,420.0
Ten Countries Total	660,997.0	662,885.9	824,315.0	809,325.0	Ten Countries Total	701,577.0 g	608,425.0	709,695.0	742,622.0
World Total	830,708.7	819,234.0	949,440.0	929,754.0	World Total	891,288.0 g	818,067.0	880,515.0	959,609.0
World Reserves 1992 (000 metric tons)				150,000,000	World Reserves Life Index (years)				161
World Reserve Base 1992 (000 metric tons)				230,000,000	World Reserve Base Life Index (years)				247

STEEL, CRUDE

	1977	1982	1987	1992		1977	1982	1987	1991
Japan	102,433.8	99,576.2	98,513.0	98,131.0	U.S.S.R.	146,577.0	150,463.0	163,032.0	131,865.0
United States	113,732.3	67,674.2	80,877.0	84,322.0	Japan	63,205.0	69,504.0	75,751.0	99,149.0
China	27,223.2	37,170.6	56,000.0	80,000.0	United States	133,043.0	92,306.0	105,890.0	93,325.0
Russian Federation {c}	147,005.4	147,206.0	161,887.0	67,000.0	China	30,244.0	40,953.0	72,105.0	71,042.0
Ukraine	X	X	X	42,000.0	Germany {b}	43,779.0	37,891.0	38,113.0	39,088.0
Germany {b}	45,848.5	43,060.8	44,491.0	39,768.0	Italy	21,435.0	21,482.0	23,468.0	26,593.0
Korea, Rep	2,737.7	11,755.9	16,782.0	28,054.0	Korea, Rep	5,700.0	7,630.0	15,050.0	26,190.0
Italy	23,340.3	23,987.3	22,859.0	24,904.0	India	9,321.0	13,900.0	17,640.0	20,300.0
Brazil	11,055.4	13,003.6	22,231.0	24,000.0	France	19,616.0	17,197.0	14,820.0	16,588.0
India	9,923.8	10,717.8	12,883.0	18,000.0	United Kingdom	19,608.0	15,180.0	14,980.0	14,600.0
Ten Countries Total	483,300.4	454,152.5	516,523.0	506,179.0	Ten Countries Total	492,528.0	466,506.0	540,849.0	538,740.0
World Total	673,001.8	644,156.1	734,589.0	721,315.0	World Total	679,994.0	656,830.0	743,942.0	732,002.0

Sources: U.S. Bureau of Mines, World Bureau of Metal Statistics, and International Iron and Steel Institute.
Notes: a. Production refers to bauxite, consumption data to aluminum. b. Data are for both the Federal Republic of Germany and the German Democratic Republic. c. Years other than 1992 refer to the former U.S.S.R. in its entirety. d. A production/reserve ratio would be misleading because production data include secondary metal. e. Data refer to 1989. f. Calculated apparent consumption was less than zero as China exported more (from stocks) than it produced. g. Data refer to 1978.
World reserves life index equals world reserves estimated for 1990 divided by 1992 world production.
World reserve base life index equals the world reserve base estimated for 1990 divided by 1992 world production.
0 = zero or less than half the unit of measure; X = not available.
For additional information, see Sources and Technical Notes.

Table 21.5   Value of Reserves of Major Metals, 1989

	Copper	Lead	Tin	Zinc	Iron Ore	Manga-nese	Nickel	Chro-mium	Cobalt	Molyb-denum	Tung-sten	Vana-dium	Bauxite	Rutile	Ilmenite	Total Reserve Value	Reserves Value Index (%)
WORLD	731,880	43,389	43,002	119,161	2,024,987	114,575	272,920	87,340	25,143	41,454	16,804	68,908	536,764	43,363	20,660	4,190,350	100.00
AFRICA	95,760	2,482	1,052	7,444	76,951	70,244	29,711	70,067	13,538	0	120	14,065	201,346	2,867	3,969	589,615	14.07
Algeria	0	62	0	83	1,950	0	0	0	0	0	0	0	0	0	0	2,094	0.05
Angola	0	0	0	0	468	0	0	0	0	0	0	0	0	0	0	468	0.01
Botswana	980	0	0	0	X	0	3,538	0	15	0	0	0	0	0	0	4,534	0.11
Burkina Faso	0	0	0	0	X	0	0	0	0	0	0	0	0	0	0	0	0.00
Cameroon	0	0	X	0	0	0	0	0	0	0	0	0	15,096	0	0	15,096	0.36
Congo	46	12	0	17	0	0	0	0	0	0	0	0	0	0	0	74	0.00
Egypt	0	0	0	0	2,808	0	0	0	0	0	0	0	0	0	0	2,808	0.07
Ethiopia	0	0	0	0	X	0	0	0	0	0	0	0	0	0	0	0	0.00
Gabon	0	0	0	0	0	5,946	0	0	0	0	0	0	0	0	0	5,946	0.14
Ghana	0	0	0	0	0	52	0	0	0	0	0	0	17,685	0	0	17,737	0.42
Guinea	0	0	0	0	0	0	0	0	0	0	0	0	166,320	0	0	166,320	3.97
Kenya	0	6	0	0	0	0	0	0	0	0	0	0	0	0	0	6	0.00
Liberia	0	0	0	0	16,750	0	0	0	0	0	0	0	0	0	0	16,750	0.40
Libya	0	0	0	0	X	0	0	0	0	0	0	0	0	0	0	0	0.00
Madagascar	0	0	0	0	0	0	0	454	0	0	0	0	0	0	0	454	0.01
Mauritania	0	0	0	0	5,120	0	0	0	0	0	0	0	0	0	0	5,120	0.12
Morocco	570	616	0	132	726	X	0	0	X	0	0	0	0	0	0	2,044	0.05
Mozambique	X	0	0	0	0	0	0	0	0	0	0	0	44	51	232	328	0.01
Namibia	2,280	92	435	273	0	0	0	0	0	0	58	0	0	0	0	3,139	0.07
Niger	0	0	36	0	0	0	0	0	0	X	0	0	0	0	0	36	0.00
Nigeria	0	0	145	0	0	0	0	0	0	0	0	0	0	0	0	145	0.00
Sierra Leone	0	0	0	0	343	0	0	0	0	0	0	0	2,156	980	101	3,580	0.09
South Africa	4,560	1,232	218	2,484	47,750	64,246	25,402	63,763	455	0	0	14,065	0	1,836	3,636	229,647	5.48
Sudan	0	0	0	0	0	0	0	0	108	0	0	0	0	0	0	108	0.00
Tanzania	0	0	X	0	X	0	0	0	0	0	0	0	0	0	0	0	0.00
Tunisia	0	370	0	66	406	0	0	0	0	0	0	0	0	0	0	841	0.02
Uganda	0	X	X	0	0	0	0	0	15	0	7	0	0	0	0	22	0.00
Zaire	59,280	0	145	4,140	0	0	0	0	10,309	0	29	0	0	0	0	73,903	1.76
Zambia	27,360	92	X	248	0	0	0	0	2,729	0	0	0	0	0	0	30,430	0.73
Zimbabwe	684	0	73	0	630	0	771	5,742	15	0	25	0	44	0	0	7,985	0.19
ASIA	68,400	5,903	26,550	19,044	211,348	3,981	16,284	5,652	152	4,069	9,989	9,815	26,629	2,652	6,525	416,993	9.95
China	6,840	3,696	10,881	4,140	109,200	2,913	7,258	X	0	3,730	7,758	9,815	7,050	0	3,030	176,310	4.21
Cyprus	23	0	0	0	0	0	0	0	0	0	0	0	0	0	0	23	0.00
India	6,840	62	0	4,140	92,730	1,069	0	4,235	0	0	65	0	8,600	2,244	3,131	123,116	2.94
Indonesia	6,840	0	4,933	0	499	0	8,006	43	152	0	0	0	9,750	0	0	30,223	0.72
Iran	6,840	0	0	1,656	842	X	0	151	0	339	0	0	0	0	0	9,829	0.23
Iraq	0	0	0	0	X	0	0	0	0	0	0	0	0	0	0	0	0.00
Japan	2,280	493	653	3,312	406	0	0	X	0	0	102	X	0	0	0	7,245	0.17
Korea, Dem People's Rep	1,642	1,232	0	3,312	4,368	0	0	0	0	0	580	0	0	0	0	11,134	0.27
Korea, Rep	0	111	X	563	882	0	0	0	0	X	373	0	0	0	0	1,929	0.05
Laos	0	0	X	0	X	0	0	0	0	0	0	0	0	0	0	0	0.00
Malaysia	2,759	0	7,979	0	1,061	0	0	0	0	0	123	0	210	0	X	12,132	0.29
Mongolia	6,840	0	0	0	0	0	0	0	0	X	350	0	0	0	0	7,190	0.17
Myanmar	547	62	145	50	0	0	X	0	0	0	105	0	0	0	0	909	0.02
Oman	1,801	0	0	0	0	0	0	X	0	0	0	0	0	0	0	1,801	0.04
Pakistan	0	0	0	0	0	0	0	X	0	0	0	0	444	0	0	444	0.01
Philippines	22,800	0	0	33	0	0	1,021	605	0	0	0	0	0	0	0	24,459	0.58
Saudi Arabia	68	0	0	50	X	0	0	0	0	0	0	0	0	0	0	118	0.00
Sri Lanka	0	0	0	0	0	0	0	0	0	0	0	0	0	408	364	772	0.02
Thailand	0	246	1,959	828	X	X	0	X	0	0	208	0	0	0	0	3,241	0.08
Turkey	2,280	2	0	828	1,360	X	0	618	0	0	325	0	575	0	0	5,987	0.14
Vietnam	0	0	X	132	X	0	0	X	0	0	0	0	0	0	0	132	0.00
NORTH & CENTRAL AMERICA	184,680	13,170	580	38,916	389,330	653	128,274	151	8,224	24,481	2,881	2,035	62,617	153	3,515	859,660	20.52
Canada	27,360	4,312	435	17,388	189,520	0	81,285	0	341	3,391	1,885	0	0	0	2,727	328,644	7.84
Costa Rica	0	0	0	0	0	0	0	0	0	0	0	0	1,732	0	0	1,732	0.04
Cuba	X	0	0	0	X	0	45,360	151	7,883	0	0	0	0	0	0	53,394	1.27
Dominican Rep	0	0	0	0	0	0	1,293	0	0	0	0	0	255	0	0	1,548	0.04
Greenland	0	172	0	X	X	0	0	0	0	0	0	0	0	0	0	172	0.00
Haiti	0	0	0	0	0	0	0	0	0	0	0	0	222	0	0	222	0.01
Honduras	X	62	0	X	0	0	0	0	0	0	0	0	0	0	0	62	0.00
Jamaica	0	0	0	0	0	0	0	0	0	0	0	0	59,800	0	0	59,800	1.43
Mexico	31,920	1,848	X	4,968	2,970	653	0	0	0	610	43	0	0	0	0	43,012	1.03
Panama	0	0	0	0	X	0	0	0	0	0	0	0	0	0	0	0	0.00
United States	125,400	6,776	145	16,560	196,840	0	336	0	0	20,481	953	2,035	608	153	788	371,074	8.86
SOUTH AMERICA	214,320	1,696	10,032	8,218	244,797	2,108	3,060	497	76	9,493	620	0	148,341	33,660	162	677,080	16.16
Argentina	X	111	22	257	1,872	0	0	0	0	0	44	0	0	0	0	2,305	0.06
Bolivia	X	31	1,016	455	X	0	0	0	0	0	398	0	0	0	0	1,899	0.05
Brazil	2,280	308	8,705	1,656	195,000	2,108	1,665	497	76	0	125	0	78,400	33,660	162	324,640	7.75
Chile	193,800	12	0	52	6,292	X	0	0	0	8,476	0	0	0	0	0	208,632	4.98
Colombia	0	1	0	1	1,333	0	1,395	0	0	0	0	0	0	0	0	2,729	0.07
Ecuador	X	2	0	1	0	0	0	0	0	0	0	0	0	0	0	3	0.00
French Guiana	0	0	0	0	0	0	0	0	0	0	0	0	932	0	0	932	0.02
Guyana	0	0	0	0	0	0	0	0	0	0	0	0	47,530	0	0	47,530	1.13
Peru	18,240	1,232	290	5,796	4,660	0	0	0	0	1,017	54	0	0	0	0	31,289	0.75
Suriname	0	0	0	0	0	0	0	0	0	0	0	0	14,375	0	0	14,375	0.34
Venezuela	0	0	0	0	35,640	0	0	0	0	0	0	0	7,104	0	0	42,744	1.02

Table 21.5

	Copper	Lead	Tin	Zinc	Iron Ore	Manga-nese	Nickel	Chro-mium	Cobalt	Molyb-denum	Tung-sten	Vana-dium	Bauxite	Rutile	Ilmenite	Total Reserve Value	Reserves Value Index (%)
EUROPE	52,440	5,969	1,161	21,528	101,133	0	5,325	2,419	174	20	619	0	32,341	0	3,373	226,503	5.41
Albania	1,140	0	0	0	X	0	1,814	410	X	0	0	0	0	0	0	3,365	0.08
Austria	0	12	0	157	936	0	0	0	0	0	73	0	0	0	0	1,178	0.03
Bulgaria	3,420	1,232	0	687	936	X	0	0	0	20	0	0	0	0	0	6,296	0.15
Czechoslovakia (former)	0	25	X	75	936	0	0	0	0	0	22	0	0	0	0	1,057	0.03
Finland	2,280	6	0	828	842	0	798	1,922	174	0	0	0	0	0	141	6,993	0.17
France	X	62	0	828	22,770	0	0	0	0	0	60	0	1,110	0	0	24,830	0.59
Germany, Fed Rep (former)	X	62	0	828	998	0	0	0	0	0	0	0	44	0	0	1,932	0.05
German Dem Rep (former)	X	0	X	0	94	0	X	0	0	0	0	0	0	0	0	94	0.00
Greece	0	308	0	828	374	0	1,134	86	0	0	0	0	14,400	0	0	17,131	0.41
Hungary	0	0	0	0	406	X	0	0	0	0	0	0	3,240	0	0	3,646	0.09
Ireland	0	431	0	4,140	0	0	0	0	0	0	0	0	0	0	0	4,571	0.11
Italy	0	154	0	1,656	94	0	0	0	0	0	0	0	111	0	0	2,015	0.05
Norway	2,280	25	0	149	7,740	0	X	0	0	0	0	0	0	0	3,232	13,426	0.32
Poland	22,800	370	0	2,484	780	0	X	0	0	0	0	0	0	0	0	26,434	0.63
Portugal	6,840	0	508	1,656	X	0	0	0	0	0	196	0	0	0	0	9,200	0.22
Romania	X	308	0	530	780	X	0	0	0	0	0	0	1,110	0	0	2,728	0.07
Spain	2,280	1,047	X	4,140	4,002	0	0	0	0	0	157	0	111	0	0	11,737	0.28
Sweden	2,280	616	0	828	57,760	0	0	0	0	0	31	0	0	0	0	61,515	1.47
United Kingdom	X	80	653	437	58	0	0	0	0	0	81	0	0	0	0	1,309	0.03
Yugoslavia (former)	9,120	1,232	0	1,656	1,248	X	1,579	X	0	0	0	0	12,215	0	0	27,050	0.65
U.S.S.R. (former)	84,360	5,544	2,176	8,280	733,200	33,317	66,226	8,554	1,061	3,391	2,030	42,481	6,660	1,275	596	999,150	23.84
OCEANIA	31,920	8,624	1,451	15,732	268,228	4,271	24,041	0	1,918	0	546	513	58,830	2,756	2,520	421,350	10.06
Australia	15,960	8,624	1,451	15,732	263,160	4,271	12,701	0	174	0	539	513	57,720	2,756	2,520	386,121	9.21
New Caledonia	0	0	0	0	0	0	11,340	X	1,743	0	0	0	0	0	0	13,083	0.31
New Zealand	0	0	0	0	5,068	0	0	0	0	0	7	0	0	0	0	5,075	0.12
Papua New Guinea	15,960	0	0	0	0	0	0	0	0	0	0	0	0	0	0	15,960	0.38
Solomon Islands	0	0	0	0	0	0	0	0	0	0	0	0	1,110	0	0	1,110	0.03

Values of Reserves (million U.S. dollars)

Source: World Resources Institute.
Notes: 0 = zero or less than half the unit of measure; X = not available.
For additional information, see Sources and Technical Notes.

Table 21.6 Industrial Waste Generation in Selected Countries

	Year of Estimate	Waste Generated from Surface Treatment of Metals and Plastics (metric tons)	Biocide Production (metric tons)	Oil	Containing PCBs	Clinical and Pharmaceutical	Photographic Materials	Organic Solvents	Paints and Pigments	Resins and Latex
Austria	1990	14,731	450	60,300	81	8,254	1,400	27,253	15,000	X
Canada {a}	1985	186,200	4,500	367,000	120,000	X	X	262,000	72,700	74,000
Czechoslovakia (former)	1987	2,561,174	183	565,764	X	X	X	20,723	13,875	131,519
Finland	1987	1,813	361	35,684	1,789	97	547	7,384	5,787	2,123
France {b}	1990	X	X	409,000	17,000	X	X	285,000	X	X
Germany, Fed Rep	1987	219,527	X	859,456	10,537	X	X	454,489	225,525	867,015
Greece	1990	X	X	25,000	1,800	1,500	X	21,000	6,000	150
Hungary	1989	12,000	10,300	455,000	134	X	X	49,000	11,000	X
Ireland {c}	1991	7,000	5	1,000	X	X	X	12,500	X	45,000
Japan {d}	1985	8,877,000	X	3,672,000	X	X	X	X	X	2,894,000
Luxembourg	1990	22,200	5	3,900	480	356	29	284	540	X
Netherlands	1990	22,000	1,800	279,000	400	1,000	21,000	69,000	25,000	20,000
New Zealand	1990	3,030	1,100	18,151	4	2,770	451	3,690	29,381	12,892
Norway {e}	1988	8,000	400	55,000	2,000	X	6,000	9,000	16,000	X
Poland	1990	X	X	41,400	X	X	X	X	175,900	X
Portugal	1989	X	X	16,473	703	X	X	X	X	X
Spain	1990	X	X	320,000	2,200	X	X	5,400	X	X
United States {f}	1990	1,982,379	13,216	4,960,000	5,015,060	2,800,000	X	70,000,000	693,833	41,000,000

Source: Organisation for Economic Co-operation and Development.
Notes: a. Data for resins and latex are from 1987; PCB waste includes 6,500 tons in storage. b. Data for PCBs and organic solvents are from 1989.
c. Waste oil is only lubricating oil; data for organic solvents includes miscellaneous chemical wastes.
d. Waste oil includes waste solvents; waste surface treatment of metals is total waste metals;1 data for resins and latex refer to plastics and rubber.
e. Data for PCBs refer to 1987. f. Data are from 1989 through 1991; PCB data are from a survey and do not represent total PCB waste; organic solvents include all organic chemicals; resins and latex refer to plastics and rubber.
0 = zero or less than half the unit of measure; X = not available.
For additional information, see Sources and Technical Notes.

Sources and Technical Notes

Table 21.1 Commercial Energy Production, 1971–91

Sources: United Nations Statistical Division (UNSTAT) *U.N. Energy Tape* (UNSTAT, New York, May 1993). Oil and gas production data for the constituent republics of the former U.S.S.R.: A. Knonplyanik, "Russia Struggling To Revive Production, Rebuild Oil Industry" (*Oil & Gas Journal*, August 2, 1993), p. 43; Joseph P. Riva, Jr., "Large Oil Resource Awaits Exploitation in Former Soviet Union's Muslim Republics" (*Oil & Gas Journal*, January 4, 1993), p. 56; "Worldwide Production" (*Oil & Gas Journal*, December 28, 1992), p. 56.

Energy data are compiled by UNSTAT, primarily from responses to questionnaires sent to national governments, supplemented by official national statistical publications and by data from intergovernmental organizations. When official numbers are not available, UNSTAT prepares estimates based on professional and commercial literature. Data for the former U.S.S.R. were compiled by UNSTAT. Data for the new republics of the former U.S.S.R. were estimated by the compilers of this table using the sources cited above.

Total production of commercially traded fuels includes solid, liquid, and gaseous fuels and primary electricity production. *Solid* fuels include bituminous coal, lignite, peat, and oil shale burned directly. *Liquid* fuels include crude petroleum and liquid natural gas. *Gas* includes natural gas and other petroleum gases. *Primary electricity* is valued differently depending on its source. Wind, tide, wave, solar, and hydroelectric power generation is expressed at the energy value of electricity (1 kilowatt hour = 3.6 million joules). Nuclear and geothermal power generation is valued on a fossil-fuel-avoided basis rather than an energy-output basis. For example, a nuclear power plant that produces 1,000 kilowatt hours of electricity provides the equivalent heat of 0.123 metric ton of coal. However, more than 0.123 metric ton of coal would be required to produce 1,000 kilowatt hours of electricity. Much of the energy released from coal combustion (or from a nuclear or geothermal plant) in a power plant is used in the mechanical work of turning dynamos or is lost in waste heat, so less energy is embodied in the final electricity than in the initial coal. The efficiency of a thermal electric plant is the ratio between final electricity produced and initial energy supplied. Although this rating varies widely from country to country and from plant to plant, UNSTAT and other international energy organizations use a standard factor of 33 percent efficiency to estimate the fossil fuel value of electricity produced by nuclear power and 10 percent efficiency to estimate the fossil fuel value of geothermal energy. Electricity production data generally refer to gross production. Data for the Dominican Republic, Finland, France (including Monaco), Mexico, the United States, Zambia, and Zimbabwe refer to net production. Gross production is the amount of electricity produced by a generating station before consumption by station auxiliaries and transformer losses within the station are deducted. Net production is the amount of electricity remaining after these deductions. Typically, net production is 5–10 percent less than gross production. Energy production from pumped storage is not included in gross or net electricity generation.

Electricity production includes both public and self-producer power plants. Public power plants produce electricity for many users. They may be operated by private, cooperative, or governmental organizations. Self-producer power plants are operated by organizations or companies to produce electricity for internal applications, such as factory operations.

Fuelwood, charcoal, bagasse, animal and vegetal wastes, and all forms of solar energy are excluded from production figures, even when traded commercially.

One petajoule (10^{15} joules) is the same as 0.0009478 Quads (10^{15} British Thermal Units) and is the equivalent of 163,400 "U.N. standard" barrels of oil or 34,140 "U.N. standard" metric tons of coal. The heat content of various fuels has been converted to coal-equivalent and then petajoule-equivalent values using country- and year-specific conversion factors. For example, a metric ton of bituminous coal produced in Argentina has an energy value of 0.843 metric ton of standard coal equivalent (7 million kilocalories). A metric ton of bituminous coal produced in Turkey has a 1991 energy value of 0.925 metric ton of standard coal equivalent. The original national production data for bituminous coal were multiplied by these conversion factors and then by 29.3076×10^{-6} to yield petajoule equivalents. Other fuels were converted to coal-equivalent and petajoule-equivalent terms in a similar manner.

South Africa refers to the South Africa Customs Union: Botswana, Lesotho, Namibia, South Africa, and Swaziland.

For additional information refer to the United Nations *Energy Statistics Yearbook 1991*.

Table 21.2 Energy Consumption, 1971–91

Sources: United Nations Statistical Division (UNSTAT), *U.N. Energy Tape* (UNSTAT, New York, May 1993). Gross National Product (GNP): The World Bank, unpublished data (The World Bank, Washington, D.C., April 1993).

Commercial energy consumption refers to "apparent consumption" and is defined as domestic production plus net imports, minus net stock increases, minus aircraft and marine bunkers. *Total* consumption includes energy from solid, liquid, and gaseous fuels, plus primary electricity (see the definition in the Sources and Notes for Table 21.1). Energy consumption *per constant 1987 $US of GNP* is calculated using GNP data from The World Bank and is a measure of relative energy efficiency. Included under *imports as percentage of consumption* are imports minus exports. A negative value (in parentheses) indicates that exports are greater than imports.

Traditional fuels includes estimates of the consumption of fuelwood, charcoal, bagasse, and animal and vegetal wastes. Fuelwood and charcoal consumption data are estimated from population data and country-specific per capita consumption figures. These per capita estimates were prepared by the Food and Agriculture Organization of the United Nations (FAO) after an assessment of the available consumption data. Data were supplied by answers to questionnaires or by official publications from Bangladesh, Bhutan, Brazil, Central African Republic, Chile, Colombia, Costa Rica, Cuba, Cyprus, El Salvador, the Gambia, Japan, Kenya, the Democratic People's Republic of Korea, the Republic of Korea, Luxembourg, Malawi, Mauritius, Nepal, Panama, Portugal, Sri Lanka, Sweden, Thailand, former U.S.S.R., and Uruguay. FAO estimates of per capita consumption of non-coniferous fuelwood have ranged from 0.0016 cubic meter per capita per year in Jordan to 0.9783 cubic meter per capita per year in Benin.

Similar estimates were prepared for coniferous fuelwood and for charcoal. Although the energy values of fuelwood and charcoal vary widely, UNSTAT uses standard factors of 0.33 metric ton of coal equivalent per cubic meter of fuelwood and 0.986 metric ton of coal equivalent per metric ton of charcoal.

Bagasse production is based on sugar production data in the Sugar Yearbook of the International Sugar Organization. It is assumed that 3.26 metric tons of fuel bagasse at 50 percent moisture are produced per metric ton of extracted cane sugar. The energy of a metric ton of bagasse is valued at 0.264 metric ton of coal equivalent.

A petajoule is one quadrillion (10^{15}) joules. A gigajoule is one billion (10^9) joules. A megajoule is one million (10^6) joules.

Table 21.3 Reserves and Resources of Commercial Energy, 1990

Sources: World Energy Council (WEC), *1992 Survey of Energy Resources* (WEC, London, 1992). Hydroelectric technical potential: The World Bank, *A Survey of the Future Role of Hydroelectric Power in 100 Developing Countries* (The World Bank, Washington, D.C., 1984). Hydroelectric installed capacity: United Nations Statistical Division, *1990 Energy Statistics Yearbook* (UNSTAT, New York, 1992). Oil and gas resource data for the constituent republics of the former U.S.S.R.: Joseph P. Riva, Jr., "Large Oil Resource Awaits Exploitation in Former Soviet Union's Muslim Republics" (*Oil & Gas Journal*, January 4, 1993), p. 56.

Energy resource estimates are based on geological, economic, and technical criteria. Resources are first graded according to the degree of confidence in the extent and location of the resource, based on available geological information, and are then judged on the technical and economic feasibility of their exploitation.

Proved reserves in place are the total resource that is known to exist in specific locations and in specific quantities and qualities. *Proved recoverable reserves* are the fraction of proved reserves in place that can be extracted under present and expected local economic conditions with existing technology. Additional energy resources, comprising those that are not currently economic, are not shown in this table.

The coal, oil, and gas sectors of the energy industry each have their own categories for estimating reserves. WEC attempts to reconcile these categories to fit their cross-sectoral reserve concepts. Each country estimates its resource reserves using its own judgement and interpretation of commonly held concepts. Inter-country comparisons should be made with this caveat in mind. Reserve estimates are not final measured quantities. Those estimates change as exploration, exploitation, and technology advance and as economic conditions change. Data for the former U.S.S.R. were compiled by WEC. Data for some of the new republics of the former U.S.S.R. were estimated by the compilers of this table using the source cited above.

There is no internationally accepted standard for categorizing coals of different ranks, although WEC has used all the information available to do so. Anthracite makes up only a small fraction (3–4 percent) of *anthracite and bituminous coals*. Lignite makes up 57 percent (globally) of the proved reserves in place of *subbituminous and lignite coals* and 63 percent of global proved recoverable reserves.

Crude oil also includes liquids obtained by condensation or extraction from natural gas.

Uranium data refer to known uranium deposits of a size and quality that could be recovered within specified production cost ranges (under $80 per kilogram and $80–$130 per kilogram) using currently proven mining and processing technologies.

Hydroelectric known exploitable potential refers to that part of a country's annual gross theoretical capacity (the amount of energy that would be obtained if all flows were exploited with 100 percent efficiency) that could be exploited using current technology and under current and expected local economic conditions. This includes both large- and small-scale schemes. Hydroelectric *technical potential* refers to the annual energy potential of all sites where it is physically possible to construct dams, with no consideration of economic return or adverse effects of site development.

Installed capacity refers to the combined generating capacity of hydroelectric plants

installed in the country as of December 31, 1990.

Table 21.4 Production, Consumption, and Reserves of Selected Metals, 1977–92

Sources: Production data for 1977, 1982, and 1987: U.S. Bureau of Mines (U.S. BOM), *Minerals Yearbook 1977, 1983, 1989, and 1991* (U.S. Government Printing Office, Washington, D.C., 1980, 1984, 1991, and 1993). Production data for 1992: U.S. BOM, unpublished data (U.S. BOM, September 1993). Consumption data for aluminum, cadmium, copper, lead, nickel, tin, and zinc: World Bureau of Metal Statistics, *World Metal Statistics* (World Bureau of Metal Statistics, Ware, United Kingdom, December 1979, December 1980, December 1985, July 1990, August 1991, September 1991, October 1991, and December 1992). Consumption data for mercury: Roskill Information Services Ltd., *Roskill's Metals Databook, 5th Edition 1984* (Roskill, London, March 1984); Roskill Information Services Ltd., *Statistical Supplement to the Economics of Mercury, 4th Edition 1978* (Roskill, London, 1980); Roskill Information Services Ltd., *The Economics of Mercury, 7th Edition 1990* (Roskill, London, 1990); U.S. BOM, *Mineral Industry Surveys, Mercury in 1989* (U.S. Government Printing Office, Washington, D.C., 1989). Consumption data for iron ore and crude steel: International Iron and Steel Institute, *Steel Statistical Yearbook 1985 and 1992*. Reserves and reserve base data: U.S. BOM, *Mineral Commodity Summaries 1993* (U.S. Government Printing Office, Washington, D.C., 1993).

The U.S. BOM publishes production, trade, consumption, and other data on commodities for the United States as well as for all other countries of the world (depending on the availability of reliable data). These data are based on information from government mineral and statistical agencies, the United Nations, and U.S. and foreign technical and trade literature.

The World Bureau of Metal Statistics publishes consumption data on the metals presented, excluding mercury, iron, and steel. Data on the metals included were supplied by metal companies, government agencies, trade groups, and statistical bureaus. Obviously incorrect data have been revised, but most data were compiled and reported without adjustment or retrospective revisions.

The countries listed represent the top 10 producers of each material in 1992 and the top 10 consumers in 1991.

The *annual production* data are the metal content of the ore mined for *copper, lead, mercury, nickel, tin,* and *zinc. Aluminum* (bauxite) and *iron ore* production are expressed in gross weight of ore mined (marketable product). Iron ore production refers to iron ore, iron ore concentrates, and iron ore agglomerates (sinter and pellets). *Cadmium* production is the production of refined metal. *Crude steel* production is defined as the total of usable ingots, con-

tinuously cast semifinished products, and liquid steel for castings. The United Nations' definition of crude steel is the equivalent of the term "raw steel" as used by the United States.

Annual consumption of metal refers to the domestic use of refined metals, which include metals refined from either primary (raw) or secondary (recovered) materials. Metal used in a product that is then exported is considered to be consumed by the producing country rather than by the importing country. Data on *mercury* consumption must be viewed with caution; they include estimates on consumption of secondary materials, which are generally not reported. Consumption of *iron ore* is the quantity of iron ore used and is calculated as apparent consumption, the net of production plus imports minus exports. Such a consumption number makes no allowance for stock inventories. This can lead to discrepancies in the published consumption data evident in the latest report by the United Nations Conference on Trade and Development Intergovernmental Group of Experts on Iron Ore. For example, Brazil had a "reported consumption" (domestic and imported ores consumed in iron and steel plants, as well as ores consumed for nonmetallurgical uses) of 23.7 million metric tons in 1990, compared to 40 million metric tons of apparent consumption. Apparent consumption of iron ore was chosen in Table 21.5 because "reported consumption" data were only available for a limited number of countries and years. Because different countries report different grades of iron ore, consumption data are not strictly comparable among countries. Because world consumption of iron ore is roughly equal to world production, world production data were used for world consumption totals. Worldwide stock inventories are assumed to be negligible. *Crude steel* consumption is calculated as apparent consumption. The International Iron and Steel Institute converted imports and exports into crude steel equivalents by using a factor of $1.3/(1+0.175c)$, where c is the domestic proportion of crude steel that is continuously cast. Such an adjustment avoids distortion of the export or import share relative to domestic production.

The *world reserve base life index* and the *world reserves life index* are expressed in years remaining. They were computed by dividing the 1992 world reserve base and world reserves by the respective world production rate of 1992. The underlying assumption is constant world production at the 1992 level and capacity.

The reserve base is the portion of the mineral resource that meets grade, quality, thickness, and depth criteria defined by current mining and production practices. It includes both measured and indicated reserves and refers to those resources that are both currently economic and marginally economic, as well as some of those that are currently subeconomic.

Mineral reserves are those deposits whose quantity and grade have been determined by samples and measurements and can be profitably recovered at the time of the assessment. Changes in geologic information, technology, costs of extraction and production, and prices of mined product can affect the reserve estimates. Reserves do not signify that extraction facilities are in place and operative.

Table 21.5 Value of Reserves of Major Metals, 1989

Sources: Norbert Henninger, "Value of Mine Production and Reserves for Fifteen Metals" (unpublished paper, World Resources Institute, May 1992). This study was based on U.S. Bureau of Mines (U.S. BOM), *Mineral Commodity Summaries 1991* (U.S. BOM, Washington, D.C., 1991), U.S. BOM, *Minerals Yearbook 1989* (U.S. BOM, Washington, D.C., 1991), and numerous other sources including national mining statistics, statistical yearbooks, The United Nations Conference on Trade and Development international commodity statistics, and U.S. BOM value data. The framework for estimation follows the work of F. Callot, "Production et Consommation Mondiales de Minerais en 1983" (*Annales des Mines*, July-August-September 1985), pp. 5–124.

This table presents information on the relative value of the known reserves of 15 important metals. These metals are believed to represent about 4.1 percent of all subsoil mineral wealth (energy minerals such as coal, oil, and natural gas make up 90.8 percent; nonmetallic products, 2.3 percent; precious metals, about 2.7 percent; and other metals, less than 0.02 percent).

Mineral reserves are those deposits whose quantity and grade have been determined by samples and measurements and can be profitably recovered at the time of the assessment. Changes in geologic information, technology, costs of extraction and production, and prices of mined product can affect the reserve estimates. Reserves do not signify that extraction facilities are in place and operative.

This table extends work reported in *World Resources 1992–93* Table 21.6, which estimated each country's share of the global reserves of each of the 15 metals and constructed an index of the country's physical share of all 15 metals. This table presents estimates of the value of each country's reserves based on the values of its production of each metal. The total value of each metal was divided by its volume to calculate a unit value of the mined product. These unit values, multiplied by a country's reserves, yielded an estimate of the country's subsoil wealth.

Such an approach assumes that all materials in a reserve can be removed instantly at the current price. In reality, this is a function of installed mining capacity, and raw materials are removed over a long period of time. Production costs and commodity prices vary over the life of a mine, and the economic evaluation of the primary commodity is complicated by the presence of co-product and by-product elements.

These estimates of reserve value followed the principals applied by F. Callot:

■ For each substance, he used the value of the first commercially viable mine product. For minerals that undergo beneficiation and concentration, this is the value at the corresponding enrichment installation, and for minerals that are barely treated, this is the value of the shipped crude ore.

■ For six metals for which producing countries sometimes gave quite differing unit values, he preferred to use a markdown of the refined metal price. Thus, cobalt was assessed at 45 percent of its refined metal value in New York, copper at 80 percent of the average London and New York prices, tin at 85 percent of the average price in London, nickel from sulfite ore at 75 percent of the value in New York, and nickel from laterite ore at the export unit value of Caledonian ore. Lead was valued at 80 percent of the average price in New York, London, and Paris, zinc was valued at 50 percent of the European producer price.

■ For those countries that did not provide data on the value of mine production, he calculated a weighted average for those countries that did 5 provide value data and applied this value to the other countries.

■ For some minerals with missing data, he used the unit import value for Europe or the United States.

Value data in local currencies were converted to U.S. dollars using average annual exchange rates from The World Bank's *International Financial Statistics*. Despite an effort to include as many national sources as possible, especially for major producing countries, there remain still a number of holes in the data. In cases in which there were no national data on the value of mine production, unit export values (free on board) were used as a proxy for the major exporting countries. For all other countries with no country-specific data, a global average unit price was calculated, dividing the total value of all producing countries with national data by the total volume of all producing countries with national data.

The value of a country's production and reserve is the respective volume multiplied by the country's specific unit value or by the global average unit value.

Table 21.6 Industrial Waste in Selected Countries

Sources: Organisation for Economic Co-operation and Development (OECD), *Environmental Data Compendium 1993* (OECD, Paris, 1993). Waste definitions: *Basel Convention on the Control of Transboundary Movements of Hazardous Wastes and Their Disposal* (United Nations Environment Programme, 1989) Annex I; Roger Batstone, James E. Smith, Jr., and David Wilson, eds., *The Safe Disposal of Hazardous Wastes, Vol. I* (World Bank Technical Paper No. 93, Washington, D.C., 1989), pp. 19–23.

Industrial waste data are collected by various means and definitions might vary across countries. OECD generally collects data using questionnaires completed by government representatives. Comparisons should be made cautiously because definitions and the mix of hazardous materials in each category vary, since these data do not include all industrial or hazardous waste (some data are based only on surveys of particular segments of an industry), and these data do not represent potential toxicity.

Waste generated from the surface treatment of metals and plastics includes acids and alkalis (surface metal treatment is the largest source of acid wastes) as well as other toxics. *Waste generated from biocide production* comes from the manufacturing and use of insecticides, herbicides, and fungicides (not including those quantities applied correctly, but including spills, residues, etc.). *Waste Oil* includes used motor oil, contaminated fuel oils, wastes from industrial processes, and waste vegetable oils, among others. *Waste containing PCBs* includes waste from their manufacture, the scraping of equipment containing PCBs, and from certain hydraulic fluids, mining equipment, and aircraft. *Clinical and pharmaceutical* waste includes waste pharmaceuticals, laboratory chemical residues from their production and preparation, and clinical (infectious) waste from hospitals, medical centers, clinics, and research institutions. Wastes from the production and use of *photographic materials* includes waste chemicals from photographic processing. Waste *organic solvents* arise from dry cleaning and metal cleaning, chemical processes, as well as from the production of numerous manufactured products such as paints, toiletries, thinners, and degreasants. *Paint and pigments* waste includes waste from the manufacture and use of inks, dyes, pigments, paints, lacquers, and varnish. *Resins and latex* waste comes from the production, formulation, and use of resins, latex, plasticizers, glues, and other adhesives.

22. Water

Water is essential to life on Earth. People cluster along ocean, lake, and river shores because water courses provide natural transportation routes and disposal grounds, because water is essential for farming and industry, and because aquatic ecosystems are sources of fish and other wild protein. The data in this chapter document some of these human activities and their effects on the world's freshwater, coastal, and marine resources.

Fresh water is unequally distributed among the countries and people of the world. Although global renewable water resources average 7,420 cubic meters per capita per year, many countries have far more limited resources. In Egypt, for example, potential per capita internal renewable water resources total only 50 cubic meters, far below its per capita withdrawal of 1,028 cubic meters. Egyptians depend mainly on Nile River water flowing from other countries (see Table 22.1) to insure sufficient water for their survival. In contrast, Canada's supply of over 100,000 cubic meters of water per person per year ensures not only sufficient water for survival, but for ecosystem health, wildlife needs, recreational uses, and abundant hydroelectric power as well. Only a small fraction of the Nile's flow ever reaches the sea. When water does return to river flows, it has usually been altered either chemically or thermally. Globally, most water is used for agriculture (69 percent).

The large lakes of the world are surprisingly fragile reservoirs of both fresh water and biodiversity. As Table 22.2 demonstrates, many of the largest lakes are shared by more than one country—requiring competent international cooperation for their management. These natural reservoirs (which contain most of the world's surface stores of liquid fresh water) are unevenly distributed. North and Central America contain half of the world's large lakes, and Canada contains most of those.

Table 22.3 provides indicators of water quality for the industrialized countries that are members of the Organisation for Economic Co-operation and Development (OECD). Investment in water treatment facilities in these countries, illustrated by the percentage of people served by sewage treatment plants, has important positive impacts on public health and the health of aquatic and marine ecosystems. (See Table 16.4.)

Table 22.4 provides catch and potential yield estimates for the 17 marine areas of the world. Total marine fish catch in these areas increased 25 percent between 1979–81 and 1989–91. Most of these increases occurred in Pacific and Indian Ocean waters, masking declines in six other areas during this period. Total cephalopod catch (squid, octopuses, cuttlefish, and related species) has increased by two thirds since 1979–81.

Cephalopod catch appears to be near the total potential yield in 5 of the 14 fishing areas where potential estimates are available, while marine fish catch is within or exceeds potential yields in 7 of the 15 areas with estimates. Crustaceans are overfished in many of the world's fishing regions, although potential yields as presented here may be too low for this fishery.

As Table 22.5 indicates, almost one third of the world's marine catch during 1989–91 was taken by Japan, the countries of the former U.S.S.R, and China. Aquaculture offers one solution to the problem of overfishing of wild stock. Approximately 12 million metric tons of fish and shellfish were raised annually during 1989–91, 12 percent of the global marine and freshwater catches during this period. China alone accounted for 45 percent of this aquaculture production.

Data related to human activities within coastal areas—populations in cities within 60 kilometers of the shore, cargo shipping, and offshore oil and gas production—are presented in Table 22.6. Globally, offshore oil production increased 37 percent between 1982 and 1992. Asia is currently the largest offshore-oil-producing region, followed by Europe. Of the 10 countries with the biggest offshore oil reserves, 8 are located outside of the Middle East. These countries are Brazil, India, Mexico, Nigeria, Norway, the United Kingdom, the United States, and Venezuela.

Offshore gas production increased 23 percent between 1982 and 1992. North and Central America and Europe are the largest producing regions at present, whereas Asia has the largest reserves.

Table 22.7 presents data on populated oceanic islands between 50 and 17,000 square kilometers in size. Because islands are isolated and of limited area, their flora and fauna are particularly vulnerable to human activities. Information on total and endemic plant species, coral reefs and mangroves, and protected areas are presented here, along with measures of the size and isolation of each of these islands. Population density varies considerably: from 1,301 persons per square kilometer on Malta to nearly no people per square kilometer on other islands, particularly those found in waters near the Arctic and Antarctic.

Table 22.1 Freshwater Resources and Withdrawals

	Annual Internal Renewable Water Resources		Annual River Flows			Annual Withdrawals			Sectoral Withdrawals (percent) {b}		
	Total (cubic km)	1992 Per Capita (000 cubic meters)	From Other Countries (cubic km)	To Other Countries (cubic km)	Year of Data	Total (cubic km)	Percentage of Water Resources {a}	Per Capita (cubic meters)	Domestic	Industry	Agriculture
WORLD	40,673.00 c	7.42			1987 c	3,240.00	8	644	8	23	69
AFRICA	4,184.00 c	6.14			1987 c	144.00	3	245	7	5	88
Algeria	18.90	0.72	0.20	0.70	1980	3.00	16	160	22	4	74
Angola	158.00 c	15.98	X	X	1987 c	0.48	0	57	14	10	76
Benin	26.00	5.29	X	X	1987 c	0.11	0	26	28	14	58
Botswana	1.00	0.76	17.00	X	1980	0.09	1	100	5	10	85
Burkina Faso	28.00 c	2.94	X	X	1987 c	0.15	1	18	28	5	67
Burundi	3.60 c	0.62	X	X	1987 c	0.10	3	20	36	0	64
Cameroon	208.00	17.05	X	X	1987 c	0.40	0	38	46	19	35
Central African Rep	141.00 c	44.44	X	X	1987 c	0.07	0	25	21	5	74
Chad	38.40 c	6.57	X	X	1987 c	0.18	0	34	16	2	82
Congo	181.00 c	76.44	621.00	X	1987 c	0.04	0	20	62	27	11
Cote d'Ivoire	74.00	5.73	X	X	1987 c	0.71	1	66	22	11	67
Djibouti	0.30	0.64	0.00	X	1973 c	0.01	2	28	28	21	51
Egypt	2.60	0.05	55.50	0.00	1992	56.40	97	1,028	7	5	88
Equatorial Guinea	30.00 c	81.30	X	X	1987 c	0.01	0	15	81	13	6
Ethiopia	110.00	2.08	X	X	1987 c	2.21	2	49	11	3	86
Gabon	164.00 c	132.58	X	X	1987 c	0.06	0	57	72	22	6
Gambia, The	3.00	3.30	19.00	X	1982	0.02	0	29	7	2	91
Ghana	53.00	3.32	X	X	1970	0.30	1	35	35	13	52
Guinea	226.00 c	36.95	X	X	1987 c	0.74	0	140	10	3	87
Guinea-Bissau	31.00 c	30.82	X	X	1987 c	0.01	0	11	31	6	63
Kenya	14.80	0.59	X	X	1987 c	1.09	7	51	27	11	62
Lesotho	4.00 c	2.18	X	X	1987 c	0.05	1	31	22	22	56
Liberia	232.00 c	84.33	X	X	1987 c	0.13	0	56	27	13	60
Libya	0.70	0.14	0.00	0.00	1985 d	2.62	374	692	15	10	75
Madagascar	40.00	3.12	0.00	0.00	1984	16.30	41	1,642	1	0	99
Malawi	9.00 c	0.87	X	X	1987 c	0.16	2	20	34	17	49
Mali	62.00 c	6.31	X	X	1987 c	1.36	2	162	2	1	97
Mauritania	0.40	0.19	7.00	X	1978	0.73	10	495	12	4	84
Mauritius	2.20	2.00	0.00	0.00	1974	0.36	16	410	16	7	77
Morocco	30.00	1.14	0.00	0.30	1992	10.85	36	412	6	3	92
Mozambique	58.00 c	3.90	X	X	1987 c	0.76	1	55	24	10	66
Namibia	9.00 c	5.87	X	X	1987 c	0.14	2	104	6	12	82
Niger	14.00 c	1.70	30.00	X	1987 c	0.29	1	41	21	5	74
Nigeria	261.00 c	2.26	47.00	X	1987 c	3.63	1	37	31	15	54
Rwanda	6.30 c	0.84	X	X	1987 c	0.15	2	23	24	8	68
Senegal	23.20 c	3.00	12.00	X	1987 c	1.36	4	202	5	3	92
Sierra Leone	160.00 c	36.56	X	X	1987 c	0.37	0	96	7	4	89
Somalia	11.50	1.25	0.00	X	1987 c	0.81	7	99	3	0	97
South Africa	50.00	1.26	X	X	1990	14.67	29	386	12	36	52
Sudan	30.00	1.13	100.00	56.50	1977	18.60	14	1,093	1	0	99
Swaziland	6.96 c	8.79	X	X	1987 c	0.29	4	417	5	2	93
Tanzania	76.00 c	2.73	X	X	1970	0.48	1	35	21	5	74
Togo	11.50	3.06	X	X	1987 c	0.09	1	28	62	13	25
Tunisia	3.75	0.45	0.60	0.00	1985	2.30	53	317	13	7	80
Uganda	66.00	3.53	X	X	1970	0.20	0	20	32	8	60
Zaire	1,019.00 c	25.55	X	X	1987 c	0.70	0	21	58	25	17
Zambia	96.00 c	11.11	X	X	1970	0.36	0	86	63	11	26
Zimbabwe	23.00 c	2.17	X	X	1987 c	1.22	5	136	14	7	79
ASIA	10,485.00	3.24	X	X	1987 c	1,531.00	15	519	6	8	86
Afghanistan	50.00	2.62	X	X	1987 c	26.11	52	1,775	1	0	99
Bangladesh	1,357.00	11.38	1,000.00	X	1987 c	22.50	1	212	3	1	96
Bhutan	95.00 c	58.93	X	X	1987 c	0.02	0	14	36	10	54
Cambodia	88.10	10.04	410.00	X	1987 c	0.52	0	67	5	1	94
China	2,800.00	2.36	0.00	X	1980	460.00	16	462	6	7	87
India	1,850.00	2.10	235.00	X	1975	380.00	18	612	3	4	93
Indonesia	2,530.00	13.23	X	X	1987 c	16.59	1	95	13	11	76
Iran, Islamic Rep	117.50	1.91	X	X	1975	45.40	39	1,362	4	9	87
Iraq	34.00	1.76	66.00	X	1970	42.80	43	4,575	3	5	92
Israel	1.70	0.33	0.45	0.00	1989 g	1.85	86	410	16 e	5 e	79 e
Japan	547.00	4.39	0.00	0.00	1987	89.29	16	732	17	33	50
Jordan	1.02	0.24	0.40	X	1975	0.45	32	173	29	6	65
Korea, Dem People's Rep	67.00 c	2.96	X	X	1987 c	14.16	21	687	11	16	73
Korea, Rep	66.12	1.50	X	X	1992	27.60	42	625	19	35	46
Kuwait	0.00	0.00	0.00	X	1974 d	0.50	X	525	64	32	4
Lao People's Dem Rep	270.00	60.42	X	X	1987 c	0.99	0	259	8	10	82
Lebanon	4.80	1.69	0.00	0.86	1975	0.75	16	271	11	4	85
Malaysia	456.00	24.27	X	X	1975	9.42	2	768	23	30	47
Mongolia	24.60	10.65	X	X	1987 c	0.55	2	273	11	27	62
Myanmar	1,082.00	24.78	X	X	1987 c	3.96	0	101	7	3	90
Nepal	170.00	8.26	X	X	1987 c	2.68	2	148	4	1	95
Oman	2.00	1.22	0.00	X	1975 d	0.48	24	623	3	3	94
Pakistan	298.00	2.39	170.00	X	1975	153.40	33	2,053	1	1	98
Philippines	323.00	4.96	0.00	0.00	1975	29.50	9	686	18	21	61
Saudi Arabia	2.20	0.14	0.00	X	1975 d	3.60	164	497	45	8	47
Singapore	0.60	0.22	0.00	0.00	1975	0.19	32	84	45	51	4
Sri Lanka	43.20	2.45	0.00	0.00	1970	6.30	15	503	2	2	96
Syrian Arab Rep	7.60	0.57	27.90	30.00	1976 d	3.34	9	435	7	10	83
Thailand	110.00	1.96	69.00	X	1987 c	31.90	18	606	4	6	90
Turkey	186.10	3.19	7.00	69.00	1989	23.75	12	433	24 e	19 e	57 e
United Arab Emirates	0.30	0.18	0.00	X	1980 d	0.90	299	884	11	9	80
Viet Nam	376.00 c	5.41	X	X	1992 c	28.90	8	416	13	9	78
Yemen	2.50	0.20	X	X	1987 c	3.40	136	324	5	2	93

Table 22.1

	Annual Internal Renewable Water Resources		Annual River Flows		Annual Withdrawals				Sectoral Withdrawals (percent) {b}		
	Total (cubic km)	1992 Per Capita (000 cubic meters)	From Other Countries (cubic km)	To Other Countries (cubic km)	Year of Data	Total (cubic km)	Percentage of Water Resources {a}	Per Capita (cubic meters)	Domestic	Industry	Agriculture
NORTH & CENTRAL AMERICA	6,945.00 c	17.31	X	X	1987 c	697.00	10	1,861	9	42	49
Belize	16.00	80.81	X	X	1987 c	0.02	0	109	10	0	90
Canada	2,901.00	106.00	X	X	1988	43.89	2	1,688	18	70	12
Costa Rica	95.00	29.76	X	X	1970	1.35	1	780	4	7	89
Cuba	34.50	3.19	0.00	0.00	1975	8.10	23	870	9	2	89
Dominican Rep	20.00	2.68	X	X	1987 c	2.97	15	442	5	6	89
El Salvador	18.95	3.51	X	X	1975	1.00	5	245	7	4	89
Guatemala	116.00	11.90	X	X	1970	0.73	1	139	9	17	74
Haiti	11.00	1.63	X	X	1987 c	0.04	0	7	24	8	68
Honduras	63.42	11.61	8.00	8.00	1992	1.52	2	279	4	5	91
Jamaica	8.30	3.36	0.00	0.00	1975	0.32	4	159	7	7	86
Mexico	357.40	4.05	X	X	1975	54.20	15	921	6	8	86
Nicaragua	175.00	44.25	X	X	1975	0.89	1	367	25	21	54
Panama	144.00	57.26	X	X	1975	1.30	1	744	12	11	77
Trinidad and Tobago	5.10 c	4.03	0.00	0.00	1975	0.15	3	148	27	38	35
United States	2,478.00	9.71	X	X	1990	467.00	19	1,868	13	45	42
SOUTH AMERICA	10,377.00 c	34.08	X	X	1987 c	133.00	1	478	18	23	59
Argentina	694.00	20.97	300.00	X	1976	27.60	3	1,042	9	18	73
Bolivia	300.00 c	39.87	X	X	1987 c	1.24	0	186	10	5	85
Brazil	5,190.00	33.68	1,760.00	X	1990	36.47	1	245	22	19	59
Chile	468.00 c	34.41	X	X	1975	16.80	4	1,623	6	5	89
Colombia	1,070.00	32.01	X	X	1987 c	5.34	0	174	41	16	43
Ecuador	314.00	28.40	X	X	1987 c	5.56	2	567	7	3	90
Guyana	241.00 c	298.27	X	X	1992	1.46	1	1,812	1	0	99
Paraguay	94.00 c	20.80	220.00	X	1987 c	0.43	0	110	15	7	78
Peru	40.00	1.78	X	X	1987 c	6.10	15	301	19	9	72
Suriname	200.00 c	456.62	X	X	1987 c	0.46	0	1,156	6	5	89
Uruguay	59.00 c	18.85	65.00	X	1965	0.65	1	241	6	3	91
Venezuela	856.00	42.41	461.00	X	1970	4.10	0	387	43	11	46
EUROPE	2,321.00 c	4.53	X	X	1987 c	359.00	15	713	13	54	33
Albania	10.00	3.02	11.30	X	1970	0.20	1	94	6	18	76
Austria	56.30	7.24	34.00	X	1989	2.12	2	276	19	73	8
Belgium	8.40	0.84	4.10	X	1980	9.03	72	917	11	85	4
Bulgaria	18.00	2.01	187.00	X	1988 g	13.90	7	1,545	3	76	22
Czechoslovakia (former)	28.00	1.78	62.60	X	1988 g	5.59	6	359	14	81	5
Denmark	11.00	2.13	2.00	X	1988 f	1.17	9	228	30	27	43
Finland	110.00	21.96	3.00	X	1989	3.00	3	604	12	85	3
France	170.00	2.97	15.00	20.50	1988 f	43.67	24	778	16	69	15
Germany	96.00	1.20	75.00	X	1987 f	53.72	31	687	11	70	20
Greece	45.15	4.43	13.50	3.00	1980	6.95	12	721	8	29	63
Hungary	6.00	0.57	109.00	X	1985 g	6.35	6	596	9	55	36
Iceland	170.00	653.85	0.00	0.00	1987 c	0.09	0	364	31	63	6
Ireland	50.00	14.34	0.00	X	1979 f	0.79	2	235	16	74	10
Italy	179.40	3.10	7.60	0.00	1980 f	56.20	30	996	14	27	59
Netherlands	10.00	0.66	80.00	X	1986 f	14.47	16	994	5	61	34
Norway	405.00	94.45	8.00	X	1983	2.03	0	491	20	72	8
Poland	49.40	1.29	6.80	X	1988 g	14.49	26	383	13	76	11
Portugal	34.00	3.45	31.60	X	1980	10.50	16	1,075	15	37	48
Romania	37.00	1.59	171.00	X	1988 g	19.65	9	853	8	33	59
Spain	110.30	2.82	1.00	17.00	1986 f	45.85	41	1,188	12	26	62
Sweden	176.00	20.34	4.00	X	1989	3.00	2	352	36	55	9
Switzerland	42.50	6.24	7.50	X	1989	1.12	2	168	23	73	4
United Kingdom	120.00	2.08	0.00	X	1989	14.50	12	253	20	77	3
Yugoslavia (former)	150.00	6.26	115.00	200.00	1980	8.77	3	393	16	72	12
U.S.S.R. (former)	4,413.11	15.51	330.00	X	X	357.60	8	1,280	7	27	65
Armenia	6.19	1.77	2.08	5.22	1989	3.80	46	1,140	13	15	72
Azerbaijan	7.78	1.07	20.20	X	1989	15.80	56	2,215	4	22	74
Belarus	34.10	3.31	21.70	54.90	1989	3.00	5	292	32	49	19
Estonia	10.90	6.89	4.68	X	1989	3.30	21	2,085	5	92	3
Georgia	53.30	9.74	7.87	20.20	1989	4.00	7	733	21	37	42
Kazakhstan	69.40	4.07	56.00	32.00	1989	37.90	30	2,264	4	17	79
Kyrgyzstan	48.70	10.78	0.00	38.30	1989	11.70	24	2,663	3	7	90
Latvia	15.20	5.67	16.80	X	1989	0.70	2	261	42	44	14
Lithuania	12.80	3.41	10.40	X	1989	4.40	19	1,179	7	90	3
Moldova	1.31	0.30	11.40	12.00	1989	3.70	29	848	7	70	23
Russian Federation	4,043.00	27.13	227.00	54.00	1991	117.00	3	787	17	60	23
Tajikistan	47.40	8.48	47.90	86.90	1989	12.60	13	2,376	5	7	88
Turkmenistan	1.13	0.29	68.90	52.60	1989	22.80	33	6,216	1	8	91
Ukraine	52.40	1.00	34.40	X	1989	34.70	40	669	16	54	30
Uzbekistan	9.50	0.44	98.10	X	1989	82.20	76	4,007	4	12	84
OCEANIA	2,011.00 c	73.05	X	X	1987 c	23.00	1	905	64	2	34
Australia	343.00	19.49	0.00	0.00	1975	17.80	5	1,306	65	2	33
Fiji	28.55 c	38.63	0.00	0.00	1987 c	0.03	0	42	20	20	60
New Zealand	397.00	114.91	0.00	0.00	1985	1.90	0	585	46	10	44
Papua New Guinea	801.00 c	197.49	X	X	1987 c	0.10	0	28	29	22	49
Solomon Islands	44.70 c	130.70	0.00	0.00	1987 c	0.00	0	18	40	20	40

Sources: Bureau of Geological and Mining Research, National Geological Survey, France; Institute of Geography, National Academy of Sciences, U.S.S.R.; Eurostat; and the International Desalination Association.

Notes: a. Water resources include both internal renewable resources and river flows from other countries. b. Unless otherwise noted, sectoral withdrawal percentages are estimated for 1987. c. Estimated by the Institute of Geography, U.S.S.R. d. Withdrawal quantitites include desalination capacities as of June 1988. e. Sectoral percentages date from the year of other annual withdrawal data. f. Reported to Eurostat. g. Reported to the Economic Commission for Europe. Regional and world totals may include countries not listed. Total withdrawals may exceed 100 percent due to groundwater draw downs. 0 = zero or less than half the unit of measure; X = not available. For additional information, see Sources and Technical Notes.

Table 22.2 Major Lakes of the World

	Country	Surface Area (sq km)		Mean Depth (meters)	Maximum Depth (meters)	Volume (cubic km)	Shoreline Length (kilometers)	Catchment Area (sq km)	Population Density (per sq km)	Fish Catch (metric tons)	Lake Origin
AFRICA											
Victoria	Tanzania, Kenya, Uganda	68,460		40.0	84.0	2,750	3,440	184,000	170.0	120,000	T
Tanganyika	Tanzania, Zaire, Zambia, Burundi, Rwanda	32,900		574.0	1,471.0	17,800	1,900	263,000	X	X	T
Nyasa	Malawi, Mozambique. Tanzania	22,490		273.0	706.0	8,400	1,500	65,000	X	21,000	T
Chad	Chad, Niger, Nigeria	16,600	a	3.0	12.0	44	650	2,426,370	X	136,000	T
Turkana (Rudolf)	Kenya	8,660		29.0	73.0	251	684	X	X	X	T
Mobutusese Seko (Albert)	Uganda, Zaire	5,590		25.0	58.0	280	486	X	X	10,000	T
Bangweulu	Zambia	4,920	a	1.0	5.0	5	490	100,800	X	X	T
Kyoga	Uganda	4,430		6.0	X	27	1,830	75,000	X	138,000	T
Mweru	Zambia, Zaire	4,350		7.0	37.0	32	340	X	X	X	T?
Tana	Ethiopia	3,600		9.0	14.0	28	333	X	X	X	T?
Rukwa	Tanzania	2,716	a	1.0	1.0	2	343	77,340	X	X	T
Kivu	Zaire, Rwanda	2,370		240.0	480.0	569	556	X	X	X	T&V
Mai Ndombe	Zaire	2,325	a	5.0	10.0	12	444	X	X	X	T&F
Rutanzige (Edward)	Zaire, Uganda	2,150		35.0	112.0	78	280	12,096	51.7	7	T
Manzala	Egypt	1,360	b	1.0	1.0	1	375	X	X	X	C
Abaya	Ethiopia	1,160		7.0	13.0	8	225	17,300	X	X	T
Chilwa (Shirwa)	Malawi, Mozambique	1,040	a	1.0	2.7	2	196	7,500	51.1	21,342	T
Abe	Djibouti, Ethiopia	780		X	X	X	130	X	X	X	T
Aby Lagoon	Cote d'Ivoire	780	b	X	X	X	236	X	X	X	C
Faguibine	Mali	590		6.0	10.0	4	165	X	X	X	T?
Shamo (Chamo)	Ethiopia	551		6.0	13.0	3	105	X	X	X	T?
Upemba	Zaire	530		2.0	4.0	1	109	X	X	X	T?
Tumba	Zaire	500		2.0	5.0	1	203	X	X	X	T&F?
ASIA											
Caspian Sea	Iran, former U.S.S.R. {c}	374,000		209.0	1,025.0	78,200	6,000	3,625,000	X	X	T
Dongtinghu (Tungting)	China	6,000	a	6.7	30.8	18	402	259,430	381.0	70,000	F
Risaiyeh (Urmia)	Iran	5,800	a	8.0	16.0	45	478	5,200	X	X	T
Kukunor (Koko)	China	4,460		14.0	38.0	62	346	X	X	X	T?
Chanka (Khanka)	Russian Federation, China	4,190	a	5.0	11.0	19	352	X	X	X	T
Van	Turkey	3,740		55.0	145.0	206	493	15,500	X	X	T?
Ubsa Nor (Uvs)	Mongolia	3,350		1.0	1.0	3	322	X	X	X	T?
Poyanghu	China	3,350		8.0	20.0	27	1,307	X	X	X	F
Lob Nor (Lop)	China	3,100		2.0	5.0	5	1,054	X	X	X	T?
Hungtze	China	2,700		X	X	X	347	X	X	X	F
Chovsgol Nuur (Hovsgul)	Mongolia	2,620		138.0	267.0	381	414	4,940	1.3	300	T?
Namru Tso	China	2,500		X	X	X	288	X	X	X	T
Tonle Sap	Cambodia	2,450	a	4.0	12.0	10	382	81,200	X	X	F
Taihu	China	2,210		1.9	4.3	4	369	X	877.0	13,696	F
Helmand	Afghanistan, Iran	2,080	a	4.0	11.0	8	467	350,000	X	X	T?
Hammar	Iraq	1,940		1.0	2.0	2	417	X	X	X	T?
Ziling	China	1,860		3.0	8.0	6	231	X	X	X	T
Char Us Nuur (Har Us)	Mongolia	1,760		X	X	X	265	X	X	X	T?
Tuz	Turkey	1,640		1.0	1.0	1	246	11,400	X	X	T?
Dalai Nur (Hulun)	China	1,590		1.0	2.0	2	180	X	X	X	f
Tangra	China	1,400		X	X	X	186	X	X	X	T
Bagrax Hu (Baghrash)	China	1,380		X	X	X	201	X	X	X	T?
Chigis Nuur (Hyargas)	Mongolia	1,360		X	X	X	307	X	X	X	T?
Chilka	India	1,170	a	3.0	5.0	4	244	X	X	X	C
Toba	Indonesia	1,150		249.0	529.0	249	280	3,440	127.0	2,820	V&T
Luang	Cambodia	1,073	b	2.0	6.0	2	313	8,265	X	X	C
Ebi Nor	China	1,070		X	X	X	153	X	X	X	T?
Dead Sea	Israel, Jordan	1,020		184.0	433.0	188	212	32,000	X	X	T
Weishan	China	1,000		X	X	X	225	X	X	X	F
Chao	China	900		7.7	X	2	185	10,430	583.0	3,000	F
Laguna de Bay	Philippines	890		2.8	7.3	3	220	3,820	712.7	120,000	T
Pomo	China	880		X	X	X	151	X	X	X	T
Ulyungur Nor	China	830		X	X	X	169	X	X	X	T?
Terinam	China	810		X	X	X	165	X	X	X	T
Yamdrok	China	800		X	X	X	440	X	X	X	T
Namak	Iran	750		1.0	1.0	1	193	X	X	X	T?
Kaoyu (Gaoyu)	China	700		X	X	X	365	X	X	X	F
Biwa ko	Japan	688		41.0	104.0	28	235	3,174	345.7	3,246	T
Kyaring (Chalin)	China	670		X	X	X	153	X	X	X	T
Beysehir	Turkey	650		3.0	9.0	2	245	X	X	X	T
Ngoring	China	650		X	X	X	149	X	X	X	T?
Buyr Nuur	China, Mongolia	610		4.0	11.0	2	98	X	X	X	T
Pangong	China, India	600		16.0	43.0	10	161	X	X	X	T&G
Oling (Gyaring)	China	570		X	X	X	118	X	X	X	T?
Har	Mongolia	530		X	X	X	157	X	X	X	T?
Istada	Afghanistan	520		X	X	X	185	X	X	X	T?
Egridir (Hoyran Golu)	Turkey	520		6.0	13.0	3	134	X	X	X	T?
NORTH & CENTRAL AMERICA											
Superior	Canada, United States	82,100		148.0	406.0	12,221	4,768	124,838	X	4,184	G&T
Huron	Canada, United States	59,500		22.0	228.0	3,535	5,088	128,464	X	2,977	G
Michigan	United States	57,750		84.0	281.0	4,871	2,656	117,845	114.7	11,432	G
Great Bear	Canada	31,326		71.7	446.0	2,236	3,543	114,717	X	35	G
Great Slave	Canada	28,568		73.0	625.0	2,088	2,200	971,000	X	X	G
Erie	Canada, United States	25,657		17.7	64.0	458	1,369	78,769	175.8	23,000	G
Winnipeg	Canada	24,387		12.0	36.0	284	1,750	953,250	4.0	7,726	G
Ontario	Canada, United States	19,000		86.0	224.0	1,638	1,161	75,272	X	2,300	G
Nicaragua	Nicaragua	8,150		13.0	70.0	108	785	X	X	X	T&V
Athabaska	Canada	7,935		26.0	120.0	204	897	158,000	X	X	G
Reindeer	Canada	6,640		17.0	219.0	96	1,528	64,800	X	X	G
Netilling	Canada	5,530		X	X	X	1,004	X	X	X	G
Winnipegosis	Canada	5,375		3.0	12.0	16	957	X	X	X	G
Nipigon	Canada	4,848		63.0	165.0	31	720	X	X	X	G
Manitoba	Canada	4,625		3.0	4.0	17	810	X	X	X	G
Great Salt	United States	4,360		4.0	15.0	19	497	54,370	X	X	T
Woods, Lake of the	Canada, United States	4,350		8.0	21.0	35	1,133	X	X	X	G
Dubawnt	Canada	3,833		X	X	X	760	X	X	X	G
Amadjuak	Canada	3,115		X	X	X	688	X	X	X	G
Melville	Canada	3,069	b	97.0	256.0	298	528	X	X	X	G&C

Table 22.2

	Country	Surface Area (sq km)	Mean Depth (meters)	Maximum Depth (meters)	Volume (cubic km)	Shoreline Length (kilometers)	Catchment Area (sq km)	Population Density (per sq km)	Fish Catch (metric tons)	Lake Origin
NORTH & CENTRAL AMERICA (continued)										
Wollaston	Canada	2,690	17.0	97.0	40	1,026	23,300	X	X	G
Iliamna	United States	2,590	123.0	299.0	319	401	X	X	X	G?
Mistassini	Canada	2,335	75.0	193.0	175	770	18,100	X	X	G
Nueltin	Canada	2,279	X	X	X	430	X	X	X	G
South Indian	Canada	2,247	9.8	30.0	23	3,768	242,000	X	188	G
Michikamua	Canada	2,030	33.0	80.0	67	629	X	X	X	G
Baker	Canada	1,887	93.0	230.0	176	339	X	X	X	G
Okeechobee	United States	1,810	2.0	4.5	4	216	12,394	42.2	X	T
Martre	Canada	1,776	X	X	X	352	X	X	X	G
Seul	Canada	1,638	8.0	34.0	13	1,045	X	X	X	G
Pontchartrain	United States	1,620	2.0	5.0	3	227	X	X	X	F
Terminos	Mexico	1,550 b	1.0	1.0	1	383	X	X	X	C
Yathkyed	Canada	1,449	X	X	X	386	X	X	X	G
Cree	Canada	1,440	15.0	60.0	18	476	6,320	X	X	G
Claire	Canada	1,436	1.0	2.0	2	448	19,900	X	X	G
Ronge	Canada	1,413	13.0	38.0	18	830	14,763	X	X	G
Selawik	United States	1,400 b	X	X	X	223	X	X	X	C
Eau Claire	Canada	1,383	X	X	X	411	X	X	X	G
Moose	Canada	1,367	X	X	X	573	X	X	X	G
Cedar	Canada	1,353	X	X	X	438	339,000	X	X	G
Kasba	Canada	1,341	X	X	X	344	X	X	X	G
Bienville	Canada	1,249	X	X	X	446	15,600	X	X	G
Island	Canada	1,223	X	X	X	728	X	X	X	G
Saint Clair	Canada	1,210	4.0	7.0	5	272	17,900	X	X	G
Becharof	United States	1,190	37.0	92.0	44	227	X	X	X	G
Red	United States	1,170	6.0	9.0	7	200	X	X	X	G?
Lesser Slave	Canada	1,169	12.0	21.0	14	264	13,900	X	X	G?
Gods	Canada	1,151	X	X	X	397	25,900	X	X	G
Chapala	Mexico	1,140	9.0	13.0	10	208	4,755	X	X	T?
Laguna de Caratasca	Honduras	1,110 b	2.0	5.0	2	332	X	X	X	L
Champlain	United States	1,100	22.8	123.0	26	945	19,881	X	X	T
Aberdeen	Canada	1,100	X	X	X	368	X	X	X	G
Bras d'Or	Canada	1,099 b	28.0	70.0	31	597	X	X	X	C
Takiyuak	Canada	1,080	X	X	X	430	X	X	X	G
Mackay	Canada	1,061	X	X	X	592	X	X	X	G
Managua	Nicaragua	1,040	X	32.0	80	209	X	X	X	T
Saint Jean	Canada	1,003	11.4	63.1	12	170	71,947	18.1	X	G
Hottah	Canada	984	19.0	70.0	17	278	25,000	X	X	G
Garry	Canada	976	X	X	X	514	X	X	X	G
Contwoyto	Canada	958	X	X	X	553	X	X	X	G
Salton	United States	950	6.0	12.0	6	140	19,400	X	X	F&T
Rainy	Canada	940	10.0	49.0	9	747	X	X	X	G
Abitibi	Canada	931	X	X	X	364	X	X	X	C
Chiriqui	Panama	900 b	X	X	X	191	X	X	X	G
Aylmer	Canada	847	X	X	X	528	X	X	X	G
Eskimo North	Canada	838 b	X	X	X	382	838	X	X	C
Nipissing	Canada	833	8.0	22.0	7	245	X	X	X	G
Teshekpuk	United States	820	X	X	X	184	X	X	X	T?
Llanquihue	Canada	800	133.0	350.0	106	164	X	X	X	G?
Nonacho	Canada	784	X	X	X	716	X	X	X	G
Peter Pond	Canada	778	14.0	24.0	11	180	13,600	X	X	G
Atlin	Canada	774	86.0	283.0	67	306	6,530	X	X	G
Minto	Canada	761	X	X	X	343	5,540	X	X	G
Cross	Canada	755	8.0	27.0	6	491	X	X	X	G
Simcoe	Canada	744	15.0	41.0	12	184	2,840	76.0	X	G
Clinton Colden	Canada	737	X	X	X	409	X	X	X	G
Selwyn	Canada	717	X	X	X	406	X	X	X	G
Point	Canada	701	X	X	X	445	20,300	X	X	G
Guillaume	Canada	700 b	X	X	X	240	X	X	X	C&G
Ennadai	Canada	681	X	X	X	452	X	X	X	G
Wholdaia	Canada	678	X	X	X	519	X	X	X	G
Tulemalu	Canada	668	X	X	X	188	X	X	X	G
Big Trout	Canada	661	16.0	40.0	11	277	2,509	X	X	G
Playgreen	Canada	657	X	X	X	317	X	X	X	G
Dore	Canada	640	X	X	X	167	X	X	X	G
Kamilukuak	Canada	638	X	X	X	222	X	X	X	G
Gras	Canada	633	X	X	X	441	X	X	X	G?
Naknek	United States	630	X	X	X	163	X	X	X	G?
Eskimo South	Canada	628	X	X	X	346	X	X	X	G
Buffalo	Canada	612	X	X	X	166	X	X	X	G
Kaminak	Canada	600	X	X	X	495	X	X	X	G
Ashuanipi	Canada	597	X	X	X	399	X	X	X	G
Sakami	Canada	592	52.0	110.0	31	520	9,890	X	X	T
Izabal	Guatemala	590	12.0	20.0	8	175	8,200	X	X	G?
Ferguson	Canada	588	X	X	X	207	X	X	X	G?
Manouane	Canada	584	X	X	X	297	5,000	X	X	G?
Lower Seal	Canada	576	X	X	X	639	8,390	X	X	G
Tebesjuak	Canada	575	X	X	X	204	X	X	X	G
Tathlina	Canada	573	X	X	X	119	X	X	X	G
Winnibago	United States	560	5.0	7.0	3	121	X	X	X	G
Churchill	Canada	559	9.0	21.0	5	176	5,960	X	X	G
Artillery	Canada	551	X	X	X	234	25,900	X	X	G
Kaminuriak	Canada	550	X	X	X	456	X	X	X	G
Evans	Canada	547	6.0	13.0	3	285	15,800	X	X	G
Deschambault	Canada	542	6.0	22.0	3	346	7,360	X	X	G
Hazen	Canada	542	X	280.0	X	185	X	X	X	G?
Trout	Canada	540	X	X	X	168	X	X	X	G?
Mille Lacs	United States	540	5.0	11.0	3	99	X	X	X	G?
Grand	Canada	537	52.0	110.0	28	220	5,020	X	X	G?
Payne	Canada	533	X	X	X	408	8,260	X	X	G
Sandy	Canada	527	X	X	X	470	X	X	X	G
Princess Mary	Canada	524	X	X	X	181	X	X	X	G
Dauphin	Canada	519	X	X	X	111	X	X	X	G
Frobisher	Canada	516	5.0	19.0	2	377	5,180	X	X	G

Table 22.2 Major Lakes of the World (continued)

	Country	Surface Area (sq km)		Mean Depth (meters)	Maximum Depth (meters)	Volume (cubic km)	Shoreline Length (kilometers)	Catchment Area (sq km)	Population Density (per sq km)	Fish Catch (metric tons)	Lake Origin
NORTH & CENTRAL AMERICA (continued)											
Lobstick	Canada	511		X	X	X	246	5,440	X	X	G
Angikuni	Canada	510		X	X	X	274	X	X	X	G
Pyramid	United States	510	a	60.0	105.0	28	160	4,730	X	30	T
Snowbird	Canada	505		X	X	X	220	X	X	X	G
Goose	United States	503	a	3.0	7.0	2	101	X	X	X	T
South Henik	Canada	503		X	X	X	239	X	X	X	G
Tahoe	United States	500		313.0	505.0	375	120	841	93.0	X	T
Flathead	United States	500		50.0	113.0	24	302	17,800	X	X	G
Enriquillo	Dominican Republic	500		1.0	2.0	1	108	X	X	X	T
SOUTH AMERICA											
Maricaibo	Venezuela	13,010	b	22.0	60.0	280	592	90,200	X	X	T&C
Patos	Brazil	10,140	b	2.0	5.0	20	959	X	X	X	C
Titicaca	Peru, Bolivia	8,030		107.0	281.0	893	1,125	58,000	12.3	6,327	T
Mirim	Brazil	3,750		5.0	18.0	19	588	62,250	X	X	C
Buenos-Aires	Chile, Argentina	2,240		X	X	X	262	X	X	X	G
Chiquita	Argentina	1,850		X	X	X	255	X	X	X	T
Lago Argentina	Argentina	1,410		120.0	300.0	169	643	X	X	X	T
Poopo	Bolivia	1,340		1.0	3.0	2	223	X	X	X	T
Viedma	Argentina	1,090		X	X	X	241	X	X	X	G
San Martin	Argentina	1,010		68.0	170.0	68	520	X	X	X	G
Colhue Huapi	Argentina	800		2.0	4.0	2	203	X	X	X	T?
Fagnano	Argentina, Chile	590		211.0	449.0	125	221	X	X	X	G?
Nahuel Huapi	Argentina	550		206.0	438.0	113	359	X	X	X	G
EUROPE											
Vanern	Sweden	5,648		27.0	106.0	153	1,943	41,182	32.9	540	G&T
Saimaa	Finland	4,380		14.0	82.0	61	14,850	61,265	X	X	G&T
Vattern	Sweden	1,836		39.9	128.0	74	642	4,503	46.5	250	G&T
Malaren	Sweden	1,096		11.9	61.0	14	1,413	21,460	50.6	370	G&T
Payanne	Finland	1,090		17.0	98.0	18	2,250	25,400	16.0	1,200	G
Inari	Finland	1,050		14.4	96.0	15	2,776	14,575	0.5	137	T
Pielinen	Finland	960		9.9	60.0	9	610	12,823	5.7	644	G?
Oulu	Finland	928		8.0	35.0	7	581	X	X	X	G?
Oder (Stettiner Haff)	Germany, Poland	900	b	3.0	9.0	3	425	X	X	X	C
Skadarsko (Scutari)	Albania, former Yugoslavia	600	a	5.0	60.0	2	207	5,490	X	X	S
Balaton	Hungary	590		3.3	12.2	2	236	5,181	X	1,315	T
Lac de Geneve (Leman)	Switzerland, France	580		152.7	309.7	89	167	7,975	119.0	348	G
Bodensee (Constance)	Germany, Switzerland, Austria	540		90.0	252.0	49	255	10,900	138.0	1,280	G
U.S.S.R. (former)											
Caspian Sea	Iran, former U.S.S.R. {c}	374,000	d	209.0	1,025.0	78,200	6,000	3,625,000	X	X	T
Aral Sea	Kazakhstan, Uzbekistan	33,642	d	X	51.5	300	2,300	d 1,618,000	X	X	T
Baikal	Russian Federation	31,500		740.0	1,741.0	22,995	2,200	560,000	9.0	12,500	T
Balchas (Balkhash)	Kazakhstan	18,200	a	6.0	26.0	112	2,384	176,500	X	X	T
Ladoga (Ladozkoje)	Russian Federation	17,700		51.0	230.0	908	1,570	70,120	12.9	8,000	G&T
Onega (Onezskoje)	Russian Federation	9,700		30.0	120.0	280	1,139	51,540	9.7	2,100	G
Issyk-Kul	Kyrgyzystan	6,240		277.0	702.0	1,730	760	X	X	X	T
Taymyr (Tajmyr)	Russian Federation	4,560	a	3.0	26.0	13	880	X	X	X	G?
Peipus	Estonia	4,300		6.0	15.0	25	460	48,000	X	X	G?
Chanka (Khanka)	Russian Federation, China	4,190	a	5.0	11.0	19	352	X	X	X	T
Alakol	Kasakhstan	2,650		22.0	54.0	57	322	X	X	X	T
Chany	Russian Federation	2,500	a	2.0	10.0	5	423	X	X	X	T?
Il'men (Ilmen)	Russian Federation	2,100	a	6.0	11.0	12	239	58,000	X	X	G?
Zaysan	Kazakhstan	1,800		4.0	9.0	7	318	X	X	X	T?
Kurisches	Lithuania, Russian Federation	1,610	b	4.0	7.0	6	258	X	X	X	C
Tengiz	Kazakhstan	1,590		3.0	8.0	5	401	X	X	X	T?
Sevan	Armenia	1,360		28.0	83.0	38	255	X	X	X	T?
Beloye	Russian Federation	1,290		4.0	20.0	5	131	X	X	X	G
Vygozero	Russian Federation	1,250		6.0	24.0	7	212	X	X	X	G?
Top	Russian Federation	990		21.0	56.0	21	361	X	X	X	G
Seg	Russian Federation	910		37.0	97.0	34	160	X	X	X	G?
Imandra	Russian Federation	900		12.0	67.0	11	362	X	X	X	G
Seletyteniz	Kazakhstan	780		2.0	3.0	2	303	X	X	X	G?
Kulundinskoje	Russian Federation	758		2.0	5.0	1	171	X	X	X	T?
Sasykkol	Kazakhstan	740		2.0	5.0	2	322	X	X	X	T?
Pyaozero	Russian Federation	660		19.0	49.0	13	177	X	X	X	G?
Evoron (Zvoron)	Russian Federation	590	a	X	X	X	190	X	X	X	T?
Ubinskoje	Russian Federation	559		1.0	3.0	1	98	X	X	X	T?
OCEANIA											
Eyre	Australia	7,690	a	3.0	5.7	30	1,718	1,140,000	0.0	X	T
Torrens	Australia	5,780	a	1.0	1.0	5	730	70,000	X	X	T
Gairdner	Australia	4,770	a	1.0	1.0	4	550	11,400	X	X	G
Frome	Australia	2,410	a	1.0	1.0	2	263	85,500	X	X	T
Amadeus	Australia	880	a	X	X	X	523	X	X	X	T
Austin	Australia	829	a	X	X	X	258	20,000	X	X	T
Taupo	New Zealand	616		91.0	164.0	59	153	3,327	7.7	671	V&T
Alexandrina	Australia	580		3.0	5.0	2	299	1,072,000	X	X	C

Sources: Charles E. Herdendorf, International Lake Environment Committee, Peter Gleick, and The Water Encyclopedia.

Notes: Lake origins are geological processes classified as T = tectonic, V = volcanic, F = fluvial, C = coastal, and G = glacial.
A question mark (?) indicates the lake origin is uncertain. A lake might have its origin in more than one geological process.
a. Subject to large fluctuations in area. b. Tidal. c. Azerbaijan, Kazakhstam, Russian Federation, and Turkmenistan.
d. The area of the Aral Sea declined from 67,900 sq. km. in 1960 when its shoreline was 2300 km. It is now in two parts,
a large sea of 33,642 sq. km. and a small sea of 2,689 sq. km.
X = not available.
For additional information, see Sources and Technical Notes.

Table 22.3 Wastewater Treatment 1980–90

| | Waste Water Treatment (Percentage of Population Served) | | | | | | | | | | | |
| | Primary Treatment | | | Secondary Treatment | | | Tertiary Treatment | | | All Treatments | | |
	1980	1985	1990 {a}	1980	1985	1990 {a}	1980	1985	1990 {a}	1980	1985	1990 {a}
NORTH & CENTRAL AMERICA												
Canada	14.0	13.0	17.0	25.0	23.0	25.0	25.0	27.0	28.0	64.0	63.0	70.0
United States	17.0	15.0	X	28.0	31.0	X	25.0	28.0	X	70.0	74.0	X
ASIA												
Japan	X	X	X	30.0	36.0	42.0	X	X	X	30.0	36.0	42.0
Turkey	X	X	0.8	X	X	X	X	X	X	X	X	0.8
EUROPE												
Austria	10.0	7.0	5.0	25.0	53.0	60.0	3.0	5.0	7.0	38.0	65.0	72.0
Belgium	X	X	X	22.9	X	X	X	X	X	22.9	X	X
Czechoslovakia (former)	X	X	X	38.4	43.8	47.0	X	X	X	38.3	43.8	47.0
Denmark	X	18.0	8.0	X	66.0	69.0	X	7.0	21.0	X	91.0	98.0
Finland	2.0	0.1	0.0	15.0	10.0	0.1	48.0	62.0	76.0	65.0	72.1	76.1
France	X	X	X	X	X	X	X	X	X	61.5	64.0	68.3
Germany (former Fed Rep)	10.2	7.5	1.1	64.7	70.5	55.6	5.0	6.7	34.7	79.9	84.7	91.3
(former Dem Rep)	X	X	24.7	X	X	27.1	X	X	10.6	X	X	62.4
Greece	0.0	0.7	X	0.5	9.3	X	X	X	X	0.5	10.0	X
Hungary	7.0	8.0	9.0	12.0	17.0	22.0	X	X	X	19.0	25.0	31.0
Iceland	X	X	6.0	X	X	X	X	X	X	X	X	6.0
Ireland	0.2	X	X	11.0	X	X	X	X	X	11.2	X	X
Italy	X	X	X	X	X	X	X	X	X	30.0	X	60.7
Luxembourg	16.0	14.0	3.2	65.0	69.0	82.2	X	X	5.0	81.0	83.0	90.4
Netherlands	7.0	8.0	1.0	56.0	72.0	83.0	9.0	7.0	8.0	73.0	87.0	93.0
Norway	7.0	8.0	13.0	1.0	1.0	1.0	26.0	33.0	43.0	34.0	42.0	57.0
Poland	X	X	X	X	X	X	X	X	X	X	X	34.4
Portugal	X	X	9.4	X	X	11.4	X	X	0.1	2.3	3.5	20.9
Spain	8.8	13.2	11.0	9.1	15.8	38.0	X	X	4.0	17.9	29.0	53.0
Sweden	1.0	1.0	1.0	20.0	11.0	10.0	61.0	82.0	84.0	82.0	94.0	95.0
Switzerland	0.0	0.0	X	70.0	83.0	90.0	X	X	X	70.0	83.0	90.0
United Kingdom	6.0	6.0	8.0	51.0	52.0	65.0	25.0	25.0	14.0	82.0	83.0	87.0

Source: Organisation for Economic Co-operation and Development.
Notes: a. 1990 or the most recent year.
X = not available.
For additional information, see Sources and Technical Notes.

Table 22.4 Marine Fisheries, Yield and Estimated Potential

| | Marine Fish (million metric tons) | | | Cephalopods (million metric tons) | | | Crustaceans (million metric tons) | | | Total Marine Catch {a} (million metric tons) | | |
| | Average Annual Catch | | | Average Annual Catch | | | Average Annual Catch | | | Average Annual Catch | | |
	1979-81	1989-91	Potential	1979-81	1989-91	Potential	1979-81	1989-91 {b}	Potential	1979-81	1989-91 {b}	Potential
WORLD	55.88	69.85	62.29-86.91	1.51	2.54	4.09-6.09	3.08	3.72	2.44-3.23	60.47	76.11	68.82-96.23
ATLANTIC OCEAN	20.43	18.26	25.50-33.30 c	0.39	0.97	2.01-2.97	0.74	0.94	0.72-0.94	21.57	20.17	28.23-37.21
Northwest	1.92	2.06	3.40-4.30 d	0.13	0.04	X	0.17	0.28	0.14-0.18	2.22	2.38	
Northeast	10.93	8.32	10.10-12.30 d	0.03	0.05	0.60-1.00	0.17	0.24	0.15-0.19	11.13	8.60	
Western Central	1.32	1.27	3.20-5.10 d	0.01	0.02	0.40-0.60	0.25	0.25	0.29-0.35	1.58	1.55	
Eastern Central	2.76	3.61	2.90-3.70 d	0.15	0.20	0.18-0.22	0.05	0.06	0.02-0.04	2.97	3.88	
Southwest	1.15	1.40	2.60-3.80 d	0.07	0.65	0.80-1.10	0.08	0.09	0.09-0.13	1.30	2.14	
Southeast	2.35	1.59	2.50-3.10 d	0.01	0.01	0.03-0.05	0.02	0.01	0.03-0.05	2.38	1.62	
PACIFIC OCEAN	30.49	44.99	31.00-45.10 e	1.02	1.40	1.71-2.57	1.45	1.94	1.40-1.81	32.96	48.32	34.11-49.48
Northwest	15.68	19.71	13.50-16.50 d	0.77	0.89	0.70-0.90	0.71	1.25	0.36-0.44	17.17	21.85	
Northeast	1.54	2.49	2.60-3.20 d	0.01	0.04	0.06-0.10	0.19	0.17	0.22-0.26	1.73	2.70	
Western Central	4.24	6.38	5.80-7.80 d	0.13	0.20	0.13-0.19	0.42	0.40	0.43-0.53	4.78	6.98	
Eastern Central	1.58	1.37	2.20-3.00 d	0.03	0.08	0.40-0.80	0.08	0.07	0.32-0.48	1.69	1.51	
Southwest	0.35	0.89	1.20-2.00 d	0.09	0.14	0.10-0.14	0.01	0.01	0.01-0.02	0.45	1.04	
Southeast	7.09	14.14	3.70-10.20 d	0.00	0.05	0.32-0.44	0.05	0.05	0.06-0.08	7.14	14.24	
INDIAN OCEAN	3.44	5.37	4.70-7.10 f	0.05	0.09	0.32-0.48	0.41	0.46	0.29-0.43	3.89	5.93	5.31-8.01
Western	1.77	3.08	2.70-4.20 d	0.02	0.04	0.19-0.29	0.24	0.24	0.20-0.30	2.03	3.36	
Eastern	1.67	2.29	1.50-2.20 d	0.03	0.05	0.13-0.19	0.17	0.22	0.09-0.13	1.86	2.56	
MEDITERRANEAN AND BLACK SEA	1.40	1.17	1.09-1.41	0.05	0.07	0.05-0.07	0.03	0.05	0.03-0.05	1.48	1.29	1.17-1.53
ANTARCTIC	0.12	0.07	X	0.00	0.00	X	0.42	0.33	X	0.54	0.40	X
ARCTIC	0.00	0.00	X	0.00	0.00	X	0.00	0.00	X	0.00	0.00	X

Source: Food and Agriculture Organization of the United Nations.
Notes: a. Total marine catch includes marine fish, cephalopods, and crustaceans only. b. Excludes aquaculture production of crustaceans. c. Includes oceanic pelagic fish whose estimated potential is 0.8-1.0 million metric tons for the whole Atlantic Ocean. d. Does not include oceanic pelagic fish. e. Includes oceanic pelagic fish whose estimated potential is 2.0-2.4 million metric tons for the whole Pacific Ocean. f. Includes oceanic pelagic fish whose estimated potential is 0.5-0.7 million metric tons for the whole Indian Ocean.
0 = zero or less than half the unit of measure; X = not available.

Table 22.5 Marine and Freshwater Catches, Aquaculture, and

	Average Annual Marine Catch		Average Annual Freshwater Catch		Average Annual Aquaculture Production 1989-91 (000 metric tons)							Per Capita Annual Food Supply from Fish and Seafood	
	(000 metric tons) 1989-91	Percent Change Since 1979-81	(000 metric tons) 1989-91	Percent Change Since 1979-81	Fresh-water Fish	Diad-romous Fish	Marine Fish	Crus-taceans	Molluscs	Total Fish and Shellfish	Other [a]	Total 1988-90 (kg)	Percent Change Since 1978-80
WORLD	83,620.25	29	14,422.6	91	6,920.8	1,054.7	310.2	748.8	2,995.1	12,029.7	3,511.0	13.2	16.8
AFRICA	3,180.71	19	1,837.3	44	54.0	1.7	8.2	0.3	2.9	67.2	0.7	7.9	(2.9)
Algeria	89.88	89	0.4	X	0.2	0.0 b	0.0	0.0	0.0	0.3	X	4.8	114.9
Angola	90.05	(12)	7.7	(4)	X	X	X	X	X	X	X	23.3	99.1
Benin	8.94	142	29.5	(12)	0.1	X	X	X	X	0.1	X	9.6	(26.5)
Botswana	X	X	1.9	54	X	X	X	X	X	X	X	2.9	0.0
Burkina Faso	X	X	7.3	5	0.0	X	X	X	X	0.0	X	2.1	52.4
Burundi	X	X	17.4	38	0.0	X	X	X	X	0.0	X	2.2	(37.4)
Cameroon	57.10	(21)	20.7	3	0.2	X	X	X	X	0.2	X	13.4	18.2
Central African Rep	X	X	13.2	1	0.1	X	X	X	X	0.1	X	4.8	(19.0)
Chad	X	X	61.7	0	X	X	X	X	X	X	X	17.1	(4.5)
Congo	20.68	6	25.9	177	0.2	X	X	X	X	0.2	X	34.8	22.5
Cote d'Ivoire	68.88	(2)	27.4	55	0.2	X	X	X	X	0.2	X	15.7	(13.6)
Djibouti	0.38	30	0.0	X	X	X	X	X	X	X	X	3.3	312.5
Egypt	78.90	129	199.5	96	32.6	X	6.7	X	X	39.4	X	7.2	49.3
Equatorial Guinea	3.35	12	0.4	X	X	X	X	X	X	X	X	X	X
Ethiopia	1.77	382	2.8	(10)	0.0	X	X	X	X	0.0	X	0.1	0.0
Gabon	20.50	11	2.0	9	0.0	X	X	X	X	0.0	X	28.6	(24.9)
Gambia, The	17.82	76	2.6	(2)	X	X	X	0.1	X	0.1	X	13.7	42.2
Ghana	315.02	60	57.6	45	0.4	X	X	X	X	0.4	X	24.9	(3.4)
Guinea	32.33	70	3.2	179	0.0	X	X	X	X	0.0	X	7.9	29.5
Guinea-Bissau	5.07	42	0.2	1,400	X	X	X	X	X	X	X	3.5	0.0
Kenya	8.31	57	174.0	270	0.7	0.3	X	0.1	X	1.1	X	5.5	80.2
Lesotho	X	X	0.0	31	0.0	0.0	X	X	X	0.0	X	1.5	64.3
Liberia	6.30	(28)	4.0	0	0.0	X	X	X	X	0.0	X	13.8	(11.2)
Libya	7.81	(23)	0.0	X	0.1	X	X	X	X	0.1	X	3.5	(50.2)
Madagascar	71.08	320	30.0	(24)	0.2	0.0	X	0.0	X	0.2	X	8.0	27.0
Malawi	X	X	69.5	18	0.2	X	X	0.0	X	0.2	X	10.4	2.3
Mali	X	X	65.6	(20)	0.0	X	X	X	X	0.0	X	7.4	(34.5)
Mauritania	85.20	173	6.0	0	X	X	X	X	X	X	X	8.6	(21.6)
Mauritius	16.85	153	0.1	193	0.0	X	0.0	0.0	0.0	0.1	X	17.8	1.3
Morocco	558.02	67	1.6	159	0.0	0.0	X	X	0.1	0.2	X	7.8	23.2
Mozambique	33.77	9	0.3	(93)	0.0	X	X	X	X	0.0	X	3.0	(17.4)
Namibia	160.07	1,464	0.1	55	X	X	X	X	X	X	X	9.0	18.4
Niger	X	X	3.8	(57)	0.1	X	X	X	X	0.1	X	0.4	(66.7)
Nigeria	192.68	29	101.5	(11)	15.4	0.4 c	0.8	X	X	16.6	X	6.5	(48.4)
Rwanda	X	X	2.5	143	0.1	X	X	X	X	0.1	X	0.2	(25.0)
Senegal	282.90	37	17.2	15	0.0	X	X	0.0	0.0	0.0	X	21.3	(6.6)
Sierra Leone	36.59	(5)	15.3	9	0.0	X	X	X	X	0.0	X	13.6	(36.4)
Somalia	16.86	45	0.4	33	X	X	X	X	X	X	X	2.2	37.5
South Africa	635.66	(30)	2.3	100	0.5	1.0	0.0	X	2.5	4.0	0.3	10.1	7.9
Sudan	1.40	67	30.4	13	0.2	X	X	X	X	0.2	X	0.9	(36.4)
Swaziland	X	X	0.1	62	0.0	X	X	X	X	0.0	X	0.1	0.0
Tanzania	53.86	45	343.3	95	0.4	X	X	X	X	0.4	0.4	14.9	31.4
Togo	10.14	78	0.4	(40)	0.0	X	X	X	X	0.0	X	15.0	36.5
Tunisia	94.51	57	0.0	X	X	0.1 b	0.7	0.0	0.2	1.0	X	10.8	28.7
Uganda	X	X	237.4	39	0.0	X	X	X	X	0.0	X	13.3	(11.3)
Zaire	2.00	168	160.7	52	0.7	X	X	X	X	0.7	X	8.0	22.3
Zambia	X	X	65.7	42	1.1	X	X	X	X	1.1	X	8.2	(14.5)
Zimbabwe	X	X	24.0	82	0.1	0.1	X	0.0	X	0.2	X	1.9	(3.3)
ASIA	35,167.85	34	10,283.3	120	6,093.4	559.8	292.3	603.5	2,148.4	9,697.4	3,459.8	11.7	23.6
Afghanistan	X	X	1.5	0	X	X	X	X	X	X	X	0.1	0.0
Bangladesh	254.63	109	606.7	15	151.3	X	X	18.8	X	170.1	X	7.2	(4.0)
Bhutan	X	X	1.0	0	0.0	X	X	X	X	0.0	X	X	X
Cambodia	34.12	922	63.4	109	6.2	X	X	6.2	X	X	X	8.7	38.1
China	6,942.47	133	5,207.6	319	4,134.7	0.8	37.7	190.1	1,118.6	5,481.8	1,897.0	9.6	100.0
India	2,271.78	52	1,551.9	70	1,047.2	0.7	X	27.4	2.9	1,078.1	X	3.3	7.5
Indonesia	2,272.05	66	779.8	70	236.2	131.5	6.6	107.8	X	482.2	96.7	13.9	23.1
Iran, Islamic Rep	201.73	332	65.8	1,664	31.3	0.8	X	X	X	32.1	X	4.6	183.7
Iraq	3.83	(86)	10.9	(38)	5.0	X	X	X	X	5.0	X	1.0	(71.2)
Israel	6.77	(43)	15.9	9	13.4	0.4	1.0	0.0	X	14.8	X	21.8	28.7
Japan	10,072.51	(1)	203.2	(8)	23.8	95.6	228.4	2.7	436.6	787.2	577.5	71.7	11.5
Jordan	0.00	(95)	0.0	X	0.0	X	X	X	X	0.0	X	2.5	(13.8)
Korea, Dem People's Rep	1,613.43	21	103.3	44	10.7	1.1	X	11.0	51.7	74.5	127.1	42.6	32.6
Korea, Rep	2,695.71	24	31.8	(21)	10.5	2.9	2.8	0.4	329.2	345.8	468.2	47.6	21.2
Kuwait	4.71	35	0.0	X	X	X	0.0	X	X	0.0	X	11.8	29.6
Lao People's Dem Rep	X	X	20.0	0	3.4	X	X	X	X	3.4	X	5.0	(21.2)
Lebanon	1.61	(1)	0.1	(7)	X	0.1	X	X	X	0.1	X	0.7	5.0
Malaysia	596.27	(19)	14.9	161	6.7	2.5	0.7	2.1	42.3	54.3	X	27.5	(36.8)
Mongolia	X	X	0.2	(58)	X	X	X	X	X	X	X	1.1	(15.0)
Myanmar	594.62	39	154.3	2	6.1	X	X	0.0	X	6.1	X	15.3	5.0
Nepal	X	X	14.2	287	8.8	X	X	X	X	8.8	X	0.7	250.0
Oman	118.57	49	0.0	X	X	X	X	0.0	X	X	X	X	X
Pakistan	368.90	47	111.4	133	10.7	0.0	X	X	X	10.7	X	1.9	7.7
Philippines	1,622.51	40	579.0	40	84.0	214.5	4.6 b	52.1	29.9	385.0	281.2	33.5	6.5
Saudi Arabia	46.08	69	1.5	X	1.6	X	0.0	0.0	X	1.6	X	7.5	(3.8)
Singapore	12.94	(18)	0.1	(89)	X	0.2	0.4	0.3	1.0	1.9	X	28.4	(2.1)
Sri Lanka	157.98	(4)	31.6	41	4.5	X	X	0.7	X	5.2	X	14.6	10.3
Syrian Arab Rep	1.56	48	3.9	38	2.5	0.1	X	X	X	2.5	X	0.5	(75.8)
Thailand	2,613.91	48	236.6	60	90.5	1.4	1.1	120.9	75.3	289.3	0.0	19.6	3.5
Turkey	357.12	(8)	32.2	46	0.9	3.9	1.3	X	X	6.0	X	6.7	12.4
United Arab Emirates	92.86	42	0.0	X	0.0	X	0.0	0.0	X	0.0	X	24.4	27.9
Viet Nam	607.67	48	257.3	47	120.0	X	X	33.7	X	153.7	1.9	12.6	14.8
Yemen	78.22	10	0.7 b	X	X	X	X	X	X	X	X	5.3	(35.5)

Fish Consumption

Table 22.5

	Average Annual Marine Catch		Average Annual Freshwater Catch		Average Annual Aquaculture Production 1989-91 (000 metric tons)							Per Capita Annual Food Supply from Fish and Seafood	
	(000 metric tons) 1989-91	Percent Change Since 1979-81	(000 metric tons) 1989-91	Percent Change Since 1979-81	Fresh-water Fish	Diad-romous Fish	Marine Fish	Crus-taceans	Molluscs	Total Fish and Shellfish	Other {a}	Total 1988-90 (kg)	Percent Change Since 1978-80
NORTH & CENTRAL AMERICA	8,820.01	32	536.1	230	217.6	56.1	0.4	43.7	156.8	474.6	X	17.4	27.7
Antigua and Barbuda	2.30	95	0.0	X	X	X	X	X	X	X	X	38.5	0.3
Bahamas	8.27	85	0.0	X	0.0	X	0.0	0.0	X	0.0	X	24.9	50.6
Barbados	2.74	(29)	0.0	X	X	X	X	X	X	X	X	35.2	16.8
Belize	1.64	21	0.0	(97)	0.0	X	X	0.3	X	0.3	X	6.5	(6.2)
Bermuda	0.56	(77)	0.0	X	X	X	X	X	X	X	X	48.8	20.9
Canada	1,525.48	14	50.2	(2)	0.0	23.6	0.0	X	9.7	33.3	0.0	25.1	20.1
Costa Rica	16.60	(15)	1.0	257	0.5	0.0	X	0.4	0.0	1.0	X	4.0	(49.8)
Cuba	160.60	(0)	21.1	187	19.9	X	X	0.0	1.0	21.0	X	20.0	24.9
Dominica	0.61	(49)	0.0	X	X	X	X	X	X	X	X	16.5	(31.0)
Dominican Rep	18.07	124	1.6	(23)	0.2	0.0	X	0.1	0.0	0.4	X	4.7	(39.0)
El Salvador	6.69	(53)	4.0	167	0.0	X	0.3	0.2	X	0.5	X	1.8	(11.7)
Guatemala	3.60	(4)	2.1	352	0.2	X	X	0.7	X	0.9	X	0.5	(37.5)
Haiti	4.93	5	0.3	11	X	X	X	X	X	X	X	4.0	26.3
Honduras	17.63	170	0.2	66	0.2	X	X	3.4	X	3.6	X	3.3	120.0
Jamaica	7.23	(18)	3.3	7,363	2.4	X	X	0.0	0.0	2.5	X	18.7	(5.9)
Martinique	3.35	(30)	0.1	X	0.0	X	0.0	0.1	X	0.1	X	41.2	(0.2)
Mexico	1,253.83	2	179.5	1,400	6.9	1.2	X	3.7	44.8	56.7	X	10.1	24.1
Nicaragua	4.29	(35)	0.2	31	0.0	X	X	0.1	X	0.1	X	0.7	(33.3)
Panama	162.07	(8)	0.3	X	0.3	X	X	3.4	X	3.7	X	13.4	(11.3)
Saint Lucia	0.87	(10)	0.0	X	0.0	X	X	0.0	X	0.0	0.0	15.4	(25.3)
Trinidad and Tobago	8.42	109	0.0	X	X	X	X	X	X	X	X	7.4	(42.1)
United States	5,425.79	52	272.1	212	186.8	31.3	X	31.1	101.0	350.2	X	21.3	36.3
SOUTH AMERICA	14,958.25	88	332.4	25	22.1	31.6	0.1	97.2	4.5	155.5	43.9	8.2	(7.9)
Argentina	550.16	29	10.8	(5)	X	0.4	X	X	0.0	0.4	X	6.3	(8.3)
Bolivia	X	X	3.6	(18)	0.0	0.2	0.1	X	X	0.4	X	0.9	(63.9)
Brazil	606.25	(4)	211.4	24	18.0	0.6 c	X	2.3	0.1	21.0	X	6.0	(12.6)
Chile	5,879.99	100	4.2	6,859	X	27.7	X	X	4.2	31.9	43.9	22.9	11.3
Colombia	77.59	155	34.1	(29)	3.1	1.1	0.0	5.3	X	9.5	X	2.6	(33.6)
Ecuador	502.87	(15)	2.0	772	0.1	0.6	X	85.4	0.0	86.0	X	10.8	(8.0)
Guyana	36.86	14	0.8	7	0.0	X	X	0.0	X	0.1	X	43.0	7.7
Paraguay	X	X	12.2	271	0.1	X	X	X	X	0.1	X	2.4	132.3
Peru	6,858.88	128	32.1	119	0.5	1.3	X	3.8	0.1	5.7	X	23.2	(9.2)
Suriname	3.79	19	0.1	82	X	X	X	0.0	X	0.0	X	6.6	(65.5)
Uruguay	118.43	(5)	0.3	(20)	X	X	X	X	X	X	X	3.5	(49.5)
Venezuela	312.65	96	20.8	72	0.3	0.2	X	0.3	0.1	0.9	X	13.5	17.1
EUROPE	11,263.84	(8)	459.2	27	148.2	392.6	9.0	2.8	640.4	1,193.0	0.1	18.8	23.1
Albania	6.61	8	4.9	63	0.5	0.2	0.0	X	1.8	2.5	X	3.0	(12.6)
Austria	X	X	4.8	12	1.3	3.0	X	X	X	4.2	X	8.7	56.0
Belgium	39.82	(16)	0.8	X	0.3	0.5	X	X	X	0.7	X	19.8 d	4.9 d
Bulgaria	59.63	(37)	9.7	(20)	8.2	1.0	X	X	0.0	9.1	X	6.2	(11.0)
Czechoslovakia (former)	X	X	22.2	35	20.9	1.0	X	X	X	21.9	X	6.9	40.8
Denmark	1,712.71	(8)	33.1	76	X	39.0	X	X	X	39.0	X	19.1	0.5
Finland	86.31	3	8.5	(74)	0.0 b	18.8	X	X	X	18.8	X	31.2	7.6
France	828.15	9	45.2	88	8.4	38.1	0.4	0.0	216.4	263.3	0.1	30.6	28.4
Germany	313.17	(41)	51.7	64	19.8	24.5	0.0	X	23.0	67.4	X	12.0	12.5
Greece	133.67	41	10.0	8	0.3	2.2	2.0	X	3.7	8.2	X	18.2	14.5
Hungary	X	X	32.9	(7)	17.3	0.2	X	X	X	17.5	X	4.8	26.3
Iceland	1,354.38	(12)	0.7	41	X	2.5	X	X	X	2.5	X	93.0	9.4
Ireland	219.14	52	0.7	X	X	8.2	X	X	16.9	25.1	X	16.4	18.6
Italy	480.59	3	55.0	62	4.1	38.8	4.6	0.0	90.0	137.6	X	20.1	44.4
Malta	0.80	(28)	0.0	X	0.0	X	X	X	X	0.0	X	15.4	(11.7)
Netherlands	447.56	23	3.7	80	0.9	0.7	X	X	85.7	87.3	0.0	8.0	(23.2)
Norway	1,904.84	(25)	0.5	42	X	119.5	0.0	X	0.1	119.6	X	44.2	4.7
Poland	452.57	(24)	42.4	105	23.3	3.9	X	X	X	27.3	X	13.4	8.9
Portugal	324.19	26	2.1	X	X	2.0	0.2	0.0	4.5	6.7	X	57.8	111.7
Romania	107.29	(17)	51.8	(1)	34.3	X	X	0.0	X	34.3	X	8.2	18.3
Spain	1,423.61	10	29.7	1	0.4	17.5	1.7	2.7	193.0	215.3	X	37.7	20.6
Sweden	248.04	10	5.7	(47)	0.0	7.3	X	0.0	1.0	8.4	X	27.6	(1.7)
Switzerland	X	X	4.5	21	0.1	1.0	X	X	X	1.1	X	13.2	47.2
United Kingdom	802.58	(8)	18.2	449	0.1	49.3	X	0.0	3.5	52.9	X	18.7	16.1
Yugoslavia (former)	37.16	(1)	20.4	(16)	8.0	0.3	0.2	X	0.8	9.3	X	3.2	3.3
U.S.S.R. (former)	9,290.91	9	952.4	22	385.4	6.5	0.1 b	X	0.7	392.6	6.1	29.0	13.6
OCEANIA	938.19	109	21.8	96	0.2	6.4	0.0	1.3	41.3	49.3	0.5	21.6	32.2
Australia	205.72	54	4.1	188	0.0	4.1	0.0	0.8	8.7	13.6	X	16.8	28.9
Cook Islands	1.15	33	0.0	X	X	0.0	X	X	X	0.0	X	X	X
Fiji	28.76	30	4.2	476	0.0	X	0.0	0.0	0.0	0.0	0.1	40.4	26.0
Kiribati	30.82	176	0.0	X	0.0	0.0	X	X	X	0.0	0.4	77.2	13.6
New Caledonia	4.49	159	0.0	X	X	X	X	0.5	0.1	0.6	X	18.1	7.5
New Zealand	577.80	193	1.1	79	X	2.3	X	X	32.5	34.8	X	36.8	71.2
Niue	0.12	192	0.0	X	X	X	X	X	X	X	X	X	X
Papua New Guinea	11.79	(64)	12.3	47	0.0	0.0	X	X	0.0	0.0	X	22.0	21.5
Solomon Islands	60.36	68	0.0	X	X	X	X	0.0	X	0.0	X	56.8	(7.4)
Vanuatu	3.30	17	0.0	X	X	X	X	X	X	X	X	31.8	(28.7)

Source: Food and Agriculture Organization of the United Nations.
Notes: a. Includes production of aquatic plants and seaweeds, which are excluded from marine catch; their harvest is to be subtracted as appropriate.
b. Two years of data. c. One year of data. d. Data are for Belgium and Luxembourg.
Total of aquaculture production is included in the country totals for marine and freshwater catches.
World and regional totals include countries not listed and unallocated quantities.
0 = zero or less than half of the unit of measure; X = not available; negative numbers are shown in parentheses.
For additional information, see Sources and Technical Notes.

Table 22.6 Coastal Areas and Resources

	Length of Coastline (kilometers)	Maritime Area (thousand square kilometers) Shelf to 200-m Depth	Maritime Area (thousand square kilometers) Exclusive Economic Zone	Population in Coastal Urban Agglomerations (thousands) 1980	Population in Coastal Urban Agglomerations (thousands) 2000	Average Annual Volume of Goods Loaded and Unloaded 1988-90 (thousand metric tons) Petroleum Crude	Average Annual Volume of Goods Loaded and Unloaded 1988-90 (thousand metric tons) Petroleum Products	Average Annual Volume of Goods Loaded and Unloaded 1988-90 (thousand metric tons) Dry Cargo	Oil Annual Production (thousand metric tons) 1982	Oil Annual Production (thousand metric tons) 1992	Gas Annual Production (million cubic meters) 1982	Gas Annual Production (million cubic meters) 1992	Proven Reserves Oil (million metric tons) 1992	Proven Reserves Gas (billion cubic meters) 1992
WORLD	586,153	21,426.5	94,466.1	617,081	996,855	2,457,980	902,984	4,493,255	665,324	909,398	292,452	358,697	37,276	25,393
AFRICA	37,908	1,325.7	11,981.1	43,213	111,643	382,522	44,255	285,737	63,792	117,677	6,080	2,119	3,479	3,957
Algeria	1,183	13.7	137.2	3,493	7,613	29,110	24,409	15,266	0	0	0	0	0	0
Angola	1,600	66.9	605.7	1,132	3,603	18,438 a	376	2,749	4,365	19,422	0	486	241	57
Benin	121	X	27.1	585	2,527	31 a	429 b	743	0	0	0	0	117	0
Cameroon	402	10.6	15.4	854	2,802	8,098 a	1,264	3,704	0	7,470	0	52	76	110
Cape Verde	965	X	789.4	125	360	X	X	X	0	0	0	0	0	0
Comoros	340	X	249.0	89	240	X	X	115	0	0	0	0	0	0
Congo	169	8.9	24.7	217	571	6,172 a	246	3,519	4,316	7,022	0	72	150	76
Cote d'Ivoire	515	10.3	104.6	1,495	4,125	1,849	1,670	6,422	467	0	0	41	3	100
Djibouti	314	X	6.2	211	455	X	652	684	0	0	0	0	0	0
Egypt	2,450	37.4	173.5	4,246	8,020	146,855	4,204	25,351	28,386	0	755	0	367	142
Equatorial Guinea	296	X	283.2	181	392	X	X	165	0	996	0	0	1	3
Ethiopia	1,094	47.7	75.8	760	1,909	763 b	476	2,444	0	0	0	0	0	0
Gabon	885	46.0	213.6	155	498	10,341 a	217	607	5,105	11,952	81 c	0	190	11
Gambia, The	80	X	19.5	109	293	X	24 b	348	0	0	0	0	0	0
Ghana	539	20.9	218.1	1,336	3,139	1,149 b	243	2,922	65	598	76	0	4	0
Guinea	346	38.4	71.0	696	2,025	X	132 b	11,451	0	0	0	0	0	0
Guinea-Bissau	274	X	150.5	174	353	X	26 b	285	0	0	0	0	0	0
Kenya	536	14.4	118.0	489	2,020	2,173 b	109	5,401	0	0	0	0	0	0
Liberia	579	19.6	229.7	465	1,195	462 b	77 b	18,375	0	0	0	0	0	0
Libya	1,770	83.7	338.1	1,496	4,322	48,241 a	4,545	7,242	0	6,972	0	0	109	3
Madagascar	4,828	180.4	1,292.0	570	2,032	X	398	1,135	0	0	0	0	0	0
Mauritania	754	44.2	154.3	238	1,177	X	107 b	9,862	0	0	0	0	0	0
Mauritius	177	91.6	1,183.0	410	565	X	321 b	1,992	0	0	0	0	0	0
Morocco	1,835	62.1	278.1	5,543	11,472	4,910	140	28,990	0	0	0	0	0	0
Mozambique	2,470	104.3	562.0	1,109	5,240	515 b	121	5,098	0	0	0	0	0	0
Namibia	1,489	X	X	76	290	X	X	X	0	0	0	0	0	0
Nigeria	853	46.3	210.9	4,383	14,135	73,373 a	1,018	10,673	18,498	61,254	5,168	1,468	2,040	3,398
Reunion	201	X	X	279	479	X	203 b	845	0	0	0	0	0	0
Senegal	531	31.6	205.7	1,378	3,077	177 b	367 b	4,770	0	0	0	0	136	0
Seychelles	491	X	1,349.3	X	X	X	118 b	148	0	0	0	0	0	0
Sierra Leone	402	26.4	155.7	453	1,175	189 b	16 b	1,745	0	0	0	0	0	0
Somalia	3,025	60.7	782.8	1,186	3,308	498 b	48	969	0	0	0	0	0	0
South Africa	2,881	143.4	1,553.4	4,272	8,294	20,842 b	286 b	88,307	0	0	0	0	0	0
Sudan	853	22.3	91.6	356	1,193	1,294 b	87	3,460	0	0	0	0	0	0
Tanzania	1,424	41.2	223.2	1,750	6,945	688 b	742	2,532	0	0	0	0	0	28
Togo	56	1.0	2.1	324	983	X	124 b	1,458	0	0	0	0	0	0
Tunisia	1,143	50.8	85.7	2,476	4,540	4,330 a	937	13,762	1,520	1,245	0	0	34	0
Zaire	37	1.0	1.0	102	276	2,024	580 b	1,816	1,070	747	0	0	11	28
ASIA	163,609	6,768.6	20,258.5	281,828	487,093	947,243	306,454	1,392,641	229,432	309,308	19,492	73,691	18,784	6,805
Bahrain	161	5.1	5.1	279	582	X	12,658	4,452	0	0	0	0	13	0
Bangladesh	580	54.9	76.8	1,809	5,053	1,207 b	889	8,546	0	0	0	0	0	0
Brunei	161	X	X	X	X	8,579 a	5,174	1,266	6,026	7,470	8,786	7,442	137	212
Cambodia	443	X	55.6	50	287	X	X	109	0	0	0	0	14	99
China	14,500	869.8	1,355.8	38,936	66,510	30,909	4,993	120,377	0	2,241	0	496	560	120
Cyprus	648	6.5	99.4	291	457	545 b	4,586	4,586	0	0	0	0	0	0
Hong Kong	733	X	X	4,614	6,088	X	7,654	55,646	0	0	0	0	0	0
India	12,700	452.1	2,014.9	37,317	78,255	18,597	5,841	45,445	12,799	35,856	1,457	6,202	1,047	430
Indonesia	54,716	2,776.9	5,408.6	29,166	58,303	46,975	26,235	32,817	26,677	57,270	5,685	7,236	286	1,447
Iran, Islamic Rep	3,180	107.0	155.7	872	1,480	97,160 a	4,629	13,291	0	23,904	0	2,791	408	453
Iraq	58	0.7	0.7	X	X	X	X	X	0	0	0	0	0	0
Israel	273	4.5	23.3	2,826	4,110	6,463 b	1,412	15,593	0	0	0	0	0	0
Japan	13,685	480.5	3,861.1	78,349	88,798	189,707 b	81,238	499,734	43	697	286	72	1	0
Jordan	26	X	0.7	70	146	X	X	17,619	0	0	0	0	0	0
Korea, Dem People's Rep	2,495	X	129.6	5,973	14,233	3,258 b	1,034 b	1,812	0	0	0	0	0	0
Korea, Rep	2,413	244.6	X	16,911	29,292	35,995 b	9,678	152,628	0	0	0	0	0	0
Kuwait	499	12.0	12.0	1,190	2,660	41,372 a	17,319	8,288	0	0	0	0	0	0
Lebanon	225	4.5	22.6	2,016	3,135	23 b	205 b	1,058	0	0	0	0	0	0
Macao	40	X	X	X	X	X	316 b	4,354	0	0	0	0	0	0
Malaysia	4,675	373.5	475.6	3,997	9,158	22,229	14,164	53,703	15,050	35,308	0	18,606	530	1,529
Maldives	644	X	959.1	X	X	X	5 b	94	0	0	0	0	0	0
Myanmar	3,060	229.5	509.5	3,923	7,695	X	55	1,423	0	0	0	0	109	54
Oman	2,092	61.1	561.7	62	302	31,752 a	192 b	2,401	0	797	0	413	11	28
Pakistan	1,046	58.3	318.5	5,215	12,350	4,732 b	2,891	14,633	0	0	0	0	0	0
Philippines	22,540	178.4	1,786.0	17,736	37,181	9,690 b	1,222	26,966	822	1,245	0	0	39	57
Qatar	563	24.0	24.0	197	455	15,602 a	785	2,662	8,341	9,064	0	1,437	0	0
Saudi Arabia	2,510	77.9	186.2	1,954	4,201	141,697 a	38,104	44,591	119,122	78,684	0	6,099	7,888	1,331
Singapore	193	0.3	0.3	2,414	2,950	44,854	44,900	64,088	0	0	0	0	0	0
Sri Lanka	1,340	26.8	517.4	2,433	3,496	1,507 b	438	10,089	0	0	0	0	0	0
Syrian Arab Rep	193	X	10.3	266	853	16,233	3,287	6,070	0	0	0	0	0	0
Thailand	3,219	257.6	85.8	5,698	13,541	7,211 b	2,317	47,178	0	1,992	0	7,029	65	357
Turkey	7,200	50.4	236.6	9,928	17,028	84,837	8,130	40,205	0	0	0	0	0	7
United Arab Emirates	1,448	59.3	59.3	824	1,517	65,491 a	5,001	13,494	40,553	49,800	3,277	7,598	7,072	396
Viet Nam	3,444	327.9	722.1	5,585	14,317	X	347 b	1,461	0	4,980	0	8,269	544	283
Yemen	1,906	24.7 d	584.2	927	2,660	4,002	1,750	3,523	0	0	0	0	60	0
OCEANIA	52,488	2,514.1	14,171.4	13,413	18,117	14,395	12,046	286,622	17,773	24,950	7,370	19,950	313	935
Australia	25,760	2,269.2	4,496.3	10,568	13,902	10,974	8,328	260,610	17,337	24,153	5,685	16,952	258	538
Fiji	1,129	2.1	1,135.3	244	423	X	497	691	0	0	0	0	0	0
New Zealand	15,134	242.8	4,833.2	2,279	2,832	3,421	984	14,885	435	797	1,685	2,998	18	82
Papua New Guinea	5,152	X	2,366.6	322	960	X	897 b	3,339	0	0	0	0	37	314
Solomon Islands	5,313	X	1,340.0	X	X	X	34 b	601	0	0	0	0	0	0

Table 22.6

	Length of Coastline (kilometers)	Maritime Area (thousand square kilometers)		Population in Coastal Urban Agglomerations (thousands)		Average Annual Volume of Goods Loaded and Unloaded 1988-90 (thousand metric tons)			Offshore Oil and Gas Resources					
									Annual Production				Proven Reserves	
									Oil (thousand metric tons)		Gas (million cubic meters)		Oil (million metric tons)	Gas (billion cubic meters)
		Shelf to 200-m Depth	Exclusive Economic Zone	1980	2000	Petroleum Crude	Products	Dry Cargo	1982	1992	1982	1992	1992	1992
NORTH & CENTRAL AMERICA	183,950	5,632.2	18,759.1	88,896	121,410	370,382	151,238	800,718	143,613	128,384	156,517	120,641	6,659	3,674
Antigua and Barbuda	153	X	X	X	X	X	62 b	83	0	0	0	0	0	0
Bahamas	3,542	85.7	759.2	X	X	10,524	3,702	3,222	0	0	0	0	0	0
Barbados	97	0.3	167.3	100	146	107 b	51 b	573	0	0	0	0	0	0
Belize	386	X	X	X	X	X	106 b	306	0	0	0	0	0	0
Bermuda	103	X	X	X	X	X	363	254	0	0	0	0	0	0
Canada	90,908	2,903.4	2,939.4	3,066	3,852	16,623	8,981	201,526	0	498	0	0	162	298
Cayman Islands	160	X	X	X	X	1,357	36 b	117	0	0	0	0	0	0
Costa Rica	1,290	15.8	258.9	1,050	2,258	464 b	336 b	2,662	0	0	0	0	0	0
Cuba	3,735	X	362.8	6,628	8,942	5,850 b	3,821	14,244	0	0	0	0	0	0
Dominica	148	X	20.0	X	X	X	5 b	93	0	0	0	0	0	0
Dominican Rep	1,288	18.2	268.8	2,787	5,797	1,630 b	785 b	4,358	0	0	0	0	0	0
El Salvador	307	17.8	91.9	1,680	3,049	716	17 b	1,140	0	0	0	0	0	0
Greenland	44,087	X	X	X	X	X	187	392	0	0	0	0	0	0
Grenada	121	X	27.0	X	X	X	22 b	71	0	0	0	0	0	0
Guadeloupe	306	X	X	142	196	X	370 b	1,221	0	0	0	0	0	0
Guatemala	400	12.3	99.1	780	932	683	204	4,232	0	0	0	0	0	0
Haiti	1,771	10.6	160.5	1,216	2,845	X	11 b	838	0	0	0	0	0	0
Honduras	820	53.5	200.9	583	1,923	397 b	204	1,849	0	0	0	0	0	0
Jamaica	1,022	40.1	297.6	1,016	1,689	1,210 b	1,203	10,122	0	0	0	0	0	0
Martinique	290	2.4	X	217	279	231 b	282	876	0	0	0	0	0	0
Mexico	9,330	442.1	2,851.2	6,529	9,501	71,817 a	7,377	19,833	81,604	85,656	9,261	11,370	5,712	1,926
Nicaragua	910	72.7	159.8	1,166	2,837	495 b	183 b	1,280	0	0	0	0	0	0
Panama	2,490	57.3	306.5	989	1,749	1,192 b	441	1,939	0	0	0	0	0	0
Trinidad and Tobago	362	29.2	76.8	623	1,110	6,518	2,670	5,638	6,731	6,922	5,047	5,799	78	261
United States	19,924	1,870.7	9,711.4	60,324	74,305	237,010	112,707	519,921	55,278	35,308	142,208	103,471	707	1,189
SOUTH AMERICA	30,663	1,984.9	10,124.8	59,553	104,628	111,570	41,009	302,118	61,233	73,405	1,074	13,179	1,727	953
Argentina	4,989	796.4	1,164.5	12,273	16,643	260 a	3,336	32,367	0	0	0	0	31	57
Brazil	7,491	768.6	3,168.4	25,616	49,160	31,467 b	3,607	184,934	8,810	26,145	49	7,236	631	2
Chile	6,435	27.4	2,288.2	3,212	4,856	2,462 b	230	17,333	0	847	0	569	54	65
Colombia	2,414	67.9	603.2	2,926	3,926	9,442	6,901	15,231	0	0	1,024	0	10	40
Ecuador	2,237	47.0	1,159.0	1,529	3,877	7,423 a	1,280	3,472	0	0	0	0	5	20
French Guiana	378	X	X	X	X	X	137 b	273	0	0	0	0	0	0
Guyana	459	50.1	130.3	213	425	X	474 b	1,919	0	0	0	0	0	0
Peru	2,414	82.7	1,026.9	6,975	14,339	1,175 a	857	12,504	1,323	3,685	0	0	31	4
Suriname	386	X	101.2	140	216	X	615 b	6,185	0	0	0	0	0	0
Uruguay	660	56.6	119.3	1,511	1,862	975 b	9 b	1,123	0	0	0	0	0	0
Venezuela	2,800	88.1	363.8	5,158	9,324	58,367 a	23,564	26,768	51,101	42,728	0	5,375	966	765
EUROPE	69,643	1,951.5	14,680.9	111,806	129,989	562,016	296,790	1,302,488	132,799	181,272	87,263	117,209	5,152	5,024
Albania	418	5.5	12.3	622	1,140	X	71	1,673	0	0	0	0	67	0
Belgium	64	2.7	2.7	1,968	2,097	20,598	20,609	110,975	0	0	0	0	0	0
Bulgaria	354	12.3	32.9	857	1,182	10,659 b	871	15,311	0	0	0	0	0	0
Denmark	3,379	68.6	1,464.2	3,980	4,201	6,303	5,888	32,753	1,693	6,474	0	3,101	35	93
Finland	1,126	98.1	98.1	1,539	1,998	10,723	6,880	39,495	0	0	0	0	0	0
France	3,427	147.8 e	3,493.1	9,380	10,692	68,135	40,443	110,786	0	0	0	0	0	0
Germany	2,389	40.8 f	50.4	3,944	4,301	X	17,695	134,357	0	398	0	0	11	3
Greece	13,676	24.7	505.1	5,252	6,559	15,407	4,590	26,680	0	299	0	0	4	11
Iceland	4,988	133.8	866.9	186	231	X	557 b	2,407	0	0	0	0	0	0
Ireland	1,448	125.9	380.3	1,766	2,469	3,405	1,585	18,127	0	0	1,551	2,067	0	23
Italy	4,996	144.1	552.1	21,232	23,721	88,893	46,074	100,510	498	3,685	10,523	3,618	8	227
Malta	140	13.0	66.2	303	327	X	564	1,546	0	0	0	0	0	0
Netherlands	451	84.7	84.7	7,764	9,032	87,630	47,442	226,503	0	2,191	11,071	17,573	18	283
Norway	5,832	102.9	2,024.8	2,324	3,033	44,653	5,779	36,468	26,606	89,640	25,842	32,044	2,364	3,088
Poland	491	28.5	28.5	1,842	2,853	1,383 b	3,798	42,436	0	0	0	0	27	0
Portugal	1,693	39.1	1,774.2	2,352	3,499	7,750 b	2,833	16,601	0	0	0	0	0	0
Romania	225	24.4	31.9	573	866	16,192 b	6,947	21,831	0	697	0	0	18	0
Spain	4,964	170.5	1,219.4	13,903	17,925	47,932	22,958	89,717	1,413	697	0	920	1	7
Sweden	3,218	155.3	155.3	4,018	4,306	15,547	16,462	73,950	0	0	0	0	0	0
United Kingdom	12,429	492.2	1,785.3	26,765	27,790	86,127	41,179	176,820	102,588	77,190	38,277	57,886	2,598	1,289
Yugoslavia (former)	3,935	36.7	52.5	1,236	1,767	8,827	3,044	22,946	0	0	0	0	1	0
U.S.S.R. (former)	47,892	1,249.5	4,490.3	18,372	23,975	69,858	51,202	122,961	8,815	30,926	14,678	10,337	315	17
Azerbaijan	X	X	X	X	X	X	X	X	X	19,920	X	0	272	0
Estonia	1,393	X	X	X	X	X	X	X	X	0	X	0	0	0
Georgia	310	X	X	X	X	X	X	X	X	0	X	0	0	0
Kazakhstan	2,909	X	X	X	X	X	X	X	X	0	X	0	0	0
Latvia	531	X	X	X	X	X	X	X	X	0	X	0	0	0
Lithuania	108	X	X	X	X	X	X	X	X	0	X	0	0	0
Russian Federation	37,653	X	X	X	X	X	X	X	X	10,558	X	10,337	41	17
Turkmenistan	1,786	X	X	X	X	X	X	X	X	398	X	0	2	0
Ukraine	2,782	X	X	X	X	X	X	X	X	50	X	0	0	0
Uzbekistan	420	X	X	X	X	X	X	X	X	0	X	0	0	0

Sources: United Nations Statistical Office, United Nations Office for Ocean Affairs and the Law of the Sea, Offshore Magazine, and other sources.
Notes: a. Goods loaded. b. Goods unloaded. c. Data are for 1981. d. Excludes data from former People's Democratic Republic of Yemen. e. Includes overseas territory except French Polynesia and New Caledonia. f. Excludes data from former German Democratic Republic.
Some world and regional totals include countries not listed.
0 = zero or less than half the unit of measure; X = not available; billion = thousand million.
For additional information, see Sources and Technical Notes.

Table 22.7 Midsized Oceanic Islands

	Island Name	Total Area (000 ha)	Length of Shoreline (km)	Population Density {a} (persons/km2)	Distance to Nearest Continent (00 km)	Island Type	Percentage of Coastline Fringed by Coral	Percentage of Coastline Fringed by Mangrove	Protected Areas {a} Number	Protected Areas Area (000 ha) Terrestrial	Protected Areas Area (000 ha) Marine	Number of Plants Total	Number of Plants Endemic
Arctic Ocean													
Norway	Bear	18	X	0	4	X	X	X	X	X	X	X	X
Atlantic Ocean and Caribbean Sea													
Antigua and Barbuda	Antigua	28	112	283	7	V/C	99	X	2	5 b	X	X	X
	Barbuda	17	66	7	8	C	99	X	1	X	1	X	X
Bahamas	North Andros	344	730	2	2	L	X	X	X	X	X	X	X
	South Andros	145	305	2	3	L	X	X	2	X	X	X	X
	Cat	39	216	6	5	X	X	X	X	X	X	X	X
	Eleuthera	46	412	18	3	X	X	X	1	X	X	X	X
	Grand Bahama	110	336	30	1	X	X	X	2	0 b	X	X	X
	Great Abaco	115	559	6	3	X	X	X	1	1 b	X	X	X
	Great Exuma	20	142	18	5	X	X	X	X	X	X	X	X
	Great Inagua	162	227	1	8	X	X	X	X	X	X	X	X
	Long	54	292	6	5	X	X	X	2	X	X	X	X
	Mayaguana	29	127	2	8	X	X	X	X	X	X	X	X
	New Providence	23	82	595	3	X	X	X	6	X	X	X	X
	San Salvador	16	79	3	6	X	X	X	X	X	X	X	X
Barbados	Barbados	46	100	543	4	V	P	X	1	0	X	X	X
Canada	Prince Edward	578	1,313	21	0	CT	X	X	X	X	X	X	X
Dominica	Dominica	79	140	102	5	AV	P	P	3	7	0	1,000	8
Equatorial Guinea	Bioko	194	208	31	0	V	X	P	0	0	0	1,105	75
France	Basse Terre	88	139	114	6	V	P	P	1	18	4	X	1
	Grande Terre	64	135	313	6	C	P	P	X	X	X	X	X
	Martinique	117	299	282	4	V	28	P	5	71	0	X	X
	Saint Martin	9	59	114	8	V	X	X	X	X	X	X	X
Grenada	Grenada	32	117	285	2	AV	P	X	1	2	0	X	2
Jamaica	Jamaica	1,119	694	209	7	CT	P	P	3	0	0	3,582	912
Mexico	Cozumel	54	123	37	0	C	P	P	1	0	77	X	X
Netherlands	Aruba	18	76	367	0	X	X	X	2	0	0	X	X
	Bonaire	28	106	41	1	X	X	X	3	12 b	X	X	X
	Curacao	44	195	371	1	V	P	X	2	3 b	X	X	X
Portugal	Madeira	75	141	334	6	V	X	X	5	17	0	760	131
Saint Lucia	Saint Lucia	64	156	192	3	V/L	P	P	9	16	0	X	X
Saint Vincent	Saint Vincent	38	91	323	3	AV	P	P	0	0	0	X	12
Sao Tome & Principe	Principe	15	79	135	2	V	X	X	0	0	0	314	35
	Sao Tome	85	136	110	2	V	X	P	0	0	0	601	108
Spain	Fuerteventura	163	250	11	1	V/CT	X	X	13	0	0	X	17
United Kingdom	Anguilla	7	56	105	8	L	P	P	0	0	0	X	X
	Ascension	10	X	14	17	V	X	X	X	X	X	25	10
	East Falkland	704	1,669	0	8	CT	0	0	6	X	X	163	1
	Gough	7	38	0	28	V	0	0	1	7	X	63	36
	Grand Cayman	20	124	92	5	C	95	P	2	0	0	X	4
	Guernsey	7	X	820	0	CT	0	0	X	X	X	X	X
	Jersey	12	X	656	0	CT	0	0	X	X	X	X	X
	Isle of Man	57	128	113	3	CT	0	0	X	X	X	X	X
	Montserrat	12	49	94	7	V	P	P	1	0	X	X	2
	North Caicos	20	84	6	10	L	P	P	X	X	X	X	X
	Saint Helena	13	50	44	19	V	X	X	4	X	X	60	50
	Tortola	5	60	185	9	V	P	P	1	X	X	X	X
	Tristan da Cunha	10	40	3	28	AV	0	0	1	10	X	93	54
United States	Puerto Rico	910	585	379	7	CT	P	P	6	16	X	X	234
Mediterranean Sea													
Cyprus	Cyprus	923	650	74	1	CT	X	X	X	X	X	X	X
France	Corse	874	784	28	1	CT	X	X	X	X	X	X	X
Greece	Kriti	835	836	60	1	CT	X	X	10	X	X	X	X
	Rodhos	141	208	46	0	X	X	X	1	X	X	X	X
Malta	Gozo	7	43	383	2	L	X	X	X	X	X	X	X
	Malta	25	137	1,301	2	L	X	X	2	0	X	1,013	24
Yugoslavia	Cres	35	182	29	0	X	X	X	X	X	X	X	X
Indian Ocean													
Australia	Christmas	14	X	24	15	C	X	X	X	X	X	X	X
Bahrain	Bahrain	67	143	595	0	CT	X	X	X	X	X	X	X
Comoros	Anjouan	43	127	241	5	V	P	P	X	X	X	X	X
	Grande Comore	101	165	134	5	V	P	X	X	X	X	X	X
	Moheli	20	82	59	5	V	P	P	X	X	X	X	X
France	Amsterdam	9	51	0	30	V	X	X	1	9	X	X	X
	Possession	15	60	0	20	V	0	0	X	X	X	X	X
	Mayotte	37	170	127	5	V	P	P	X	X	X	X	X
	Reunion	254	207	204	12	V	P	X	4	0	X	720	176
Mauritius	Mauritius	187	217	539	18	V	99	P	13	5	8	850	300
	Rodrigues	11	60	325	22	V	P	X	2	X	X	145	49
Seychelles	Aldabra	13	104	0	6	AT	P	P	1	13	X	273	19
	Mahe	15	X	413	14	CT	P	P	3	X	X	X	X
South Africa	Marion	30	73	0	18	AV	0	0	1	3	X	24	X
Tanzania	Zanzibar	157	321	381	0	X	X	X	X	X	X	X	X
Southern Ocean													
Australia	Macquarie	12	80	0	18	V	0	0	1	13	X	40	3

Table 22.7

Island Name	Total Area (000 ha)	Length of Shoreline (km)	Population Density {a} (persons/km2)	Distance to Nearest Continent (00 km)	Island Type	Percentage of Coastline Fringed by		Protected Areas {a}	Area (000 ha)		Number of Plants	
						Coral	Mangrove	Number	Terrestrial	Marine	Total	Endemic
Pacific Ocean												
Chile — Easter	17	64	13	36	V	P	X	1	7	X	45	5
Cook Islands — Rarotonga	7	34	140	45	V	99	X	X	X	X	560	20
Fiji — Kadavu	45	237	17	27	V	70	P	1	0	X	X	X
Koro	11	48	23	29	V	75	X	X	X	X	X	X
Lakeba	6	32	36	30	V/C	99	P	X	X	X	X	X
Moala	6	52	19	28	V	80	P	X	X	X	X	X
France — Art	5	49	13	12	CT	P	X	X	X	X	X	6
Fatuhiva	8	X	4	73	V	P	X	X	X	X	X	3
Futuna	6	45	69	32	V	P	X	X	X	X	X	X
Huahine	8	62	31	60	V	99	X	X	X	X	X	X
Isle of Pines	14	71	8	12	CT/C	P	X	X	X	X	X	X
Lifou	115	221	6	9	C	P	X	X	X	X	X	X
Mare	66	140	6	9	C/V	P	X	X	X	X	X	X
Moorea	13	58	27	60	V	90	P	X	X	X	X	X
New Caledonia	1,665	1,249	8	12	CT/C	90	P	18	62	47	3,250	2,474
Ouvea	13	128	18	9	AT	P	P	X	X	X	X	X
Raiatea	17	82	28	60	V	99	X	X	X	X	X	2
Tahaa	9	60	36	60	V	99	X	X	X	X	X	X
Tahiti	107	178	89	60	V	90	X	X	X	X	X	1
Tahuata	7	54	7	73	V	P	X	X	X	X	X	X
Uvea	8	44	98	35	V	P	X	X	X	X	X	X
Japan — Okinawa	120	397	944	6	X	X	X	2	X	X	X	X
Kiribati — Kiritimati	32	X	4	51	AT	98	X	5	0	X	41	1
Micronesia — Babeldaob	37	144	9	25	V/CT	X	X	X	X	X	X	X
Kosrae	11	X	50	51	V	95	P	X	X	X	X	X
Pohnpei	33	X	61	45	V	90	P	1	X	X	249	8
Yap	11	93	50	25	V/CT	99	P	X	X	X	X	X
New Zealand — Campbell	11	90	0	22	V	0	0	1	11	X	137	X
Niue — Niue	26	66	12	33	C	P	X	1	X	X	175	X
Papua New Guinea — Bougainville	932	569	8	15	V	P	P	X	X	X	X	X
Buka	68	143	47	15	V	X	X	X	X	X	X	X
Fergusson	144	225	9	9	V	X	X	1	11	X	X	X
Goodenough	69	116	15	8	V	X	P	X	X	X	X	X
Kiriwina	27	126	48	10	C	X	X	X	X	X	X	X
Lavongai	123	172	6	13	V	X	X	X	X	X	X	X
Manus	194	361	5	11	V	X	X	1	6	X	X	X
Muyua	87	216	2	11	X	X	X	X	X	X	X	X
New Ireland	740	886	7	14	V	X	P	X	X	X	X	X
Normanby	104	X	10	9	V	X	X	1	X	X	X	X
Sudest	87	201	2	11	V	X	X	X	X	X	X	X
Solomon Islands — Choiseul	297	415	4	16	V	X	P	X	X	X	X	X
Guadalcanal	535	390	9	17	V	X	P	1	6	X	X	X
Malaita	384	548	16	18	V	X	P	X	X	X	X	X
Nendo	51	173	10	21	V	X	X	X	X	X	X	X
Nggela	39	X	18	18	X	X	X	X	X	X	X	X
Rennell	66	197	4	16	C	P	X	X	X	X	X	X
San Cristobal	319	426	4	18	V	P	X	X	X	X	X	X
Santa Isabel	366	893	3	17	V/C	P	P	X	X	X	X	X
Shortland	20	89	10	15	V/C	P	X	X	X	X	X	X
Ulawa	6	X	30	18	X	X	X	X	X	X	X	X
Utupua	7	X	4	22	X	P	X	X	X	X	X	X
Vanikolo	17	73	2	22	X	X	X	X	X	X	X	X
Vella Lavella	63	149	18	15	V/C	P	X	X	X	X	X	X
Tonga — Niuafo'ou	5	27	11	36	V	X	X	X	X	X	X	X
Tongatapu	26	136	193	30	C	P	P	X	X	X	X	X
Vava'u	10	99	91	36	C	P	X	X	X	X	X	X
United States — Guam	54	153	198	30	V/C	P	P	7	5	3	330	20
Rota	10	52	12	30	V/C	P	X	X	X	X	X	X
Saipan	12	69	101	28	V/C	P	P	X	X	X	X	X
Santa Rosa	21	70	0	0	CT	0	0	1	21	109	490	4
Tinian	10	51	10	28	C	P	X	X	X	X	X	X
Tutuila	14	101	211	39	V	P	P	2	2	0	X	2
Vanuatu — Ambae	40	95	19	12	V	P	X	X	X	X	X	X
Ambrym	68	126	12	12	V	X	X	X	X	X	X	X
Aneityum	16	54	3	11	V	P	X	X	X	X	X	X
Aore	6	X	6	12	C	X	X	2	X	X	X	X
Efate	90	190	28	12	V/C	P	X	X	X	X	X	X
Epi	44	133	7	12	V/C	X	X	X	X	X	X	X
Erromango	89	162	1	11	V/C	P	X	X	X	X	X	X
Espiritu Santo	396	456	6	12	V/C	P	P	X	X	X	X	X
Hiu	5	48	2	13	C	P	X	X	X	X	X	X
Maewo	30	136	6	13	V/C	X	X	X	X	X	X	X
Malakula	204	365	9	12	V/C	P	P	X	X	X	X	X
Malo	18	X	13	12	V/C	P	X	1	X	X	X	X
Pentecost	49	157	23	12	V/C	X	X	X	X	X	X	X
Santa Maria	33	76	2	13	V	X	X	X	X	X	X	X
Tanna	56	119	28	11	V/C	P	X	X	X	X	X	X
Vanua Lava	33	97	3	13	V	X	X	X	X	X	X	X

Sources: United Nations Environment Programme, Organization of American States and the United States Department of Interior.
Notes: Island types: V = volcanic; C = coral; L = limestone; CT = continental; AV = active volcano; AT = atoll.
a. Data from latest year available from source. b. Includes marine area.
0 = zero or less than half the unit of measure; P = present; X = not available.
For additional information, see Sources and Technical Notes.

Sources and Technical Notes

Table 22.1 Freshwater Resources and Withdrawals

Sources: Water resources and withdrawal data: J. Forkasiewicz and J. Margat, *Tableau Mondial de Données Nationales d'Economie de l'Eau, Ressources et Utilisation* (Departement Hydrogéologie, Orléans, France, 1980). Data for Algeria, Egypt, Libya, Morocco, Tunisia, Cyprus, Israel, Lebanon, Syrian Arab Republic, Turkey, Albania, France, Greece, Italy, Malta, Spain, and Yugoslavia: J. Margat, Bureau de Recherches Géologiques et Miniéres, Orléans, France, April 1988 (personal communication). Alexander V. Belyaev, Institute of Geography, U.S.S.R. National Academy of Sciences, Moscow, September 1989 and January 1990 (personal communication); withdrawal and sectoral use data for the United States: Wayne B. Solley, Robert R. Pierce, and Howard A. Perlman, "Estimated Use of Water in the United States, in 1990," *U.S. Geological Survey Circular*, No. 1081 (U.S. Geological Survey, Reston, Virginia, 1993); withdrawal data as footnoted: European Communities—Commission, *Environment Statistics 1989* (Office des Publications Officielles des Communautés Européennes, Luxembourg, 1990), p. 130; Economic Commission for Europe, *The Environment in Europe and North America* (United Nations, New York, 1992), pp. 15–23; desalination data as footnoted: O.K. Buros for the International Desalination Association, *The Desalting ABC's* (Saline Water Conversion Corporation, Riyadh, Saudi Arabia, 1990), p. 5; population: United Nations Population Division, *World Population Prospects (The 1992 Revision)* (United Nations, New York, 1993). Withdrawal data in this table were updated or confirmed for Brazil, Egypt, Guyana, Honduras, Japan, Morocco, the Republic of Korea, South Africa, and Viet Nam based on reports prepared by each country for the 1992 United Nations Conference on Environment and Development in Rio de Janeiro. In general, data are compiled from published documents (including national, United Nations, and professional literature) and from estimates of resources and consumption from models using other data, such as area under irrigated agriculture, livestock populations, and precipitation, when necessary.

Annual internal renewable water resources refers to the average annual flow of rivers and groundwater generated from endogenous precipitation. Caution should be used when comparing different countries because these estimates are based on differing sources and dates. These annual averages also disguise large seasonal, interannual, and long-term variations. When data for *annual river flows from* and *to other countries* are not shown, the internal renewable water resources figure *may* include these flows. *Per capita annual internal renewable water resources* data were calculated using 1992 population estimates.

Annual withdrawals as a *percentage of water resources* refer to *total* water withdrawals, not counting evaporative losses from storage basins, as a percentage of internal renewable water resources and river flows from other countries. Water withdrawals also include water from desalination plants in countries where that source is a significant part of all water withdrawals.

Per capita annual withdrawals were calculated using national population data for the year of data shown for withdrawals.

Sectoral withdrawals are classified as *domestic* (drinking water, homes, commercial establishments, public services [e.g., hospitals], and municipal use or provision); *industry* (including water withdrawn to cool thermoelectric plants); and *agriculture* (irrigation and livestock). Totals may not add because of rounding.

Table 22.2 Major Lakes of the World

Sources: Charles E. Herdendorf, *Inventory of the Morphometric and Limnologic Characteristics of the Large Lakes of the World* (Ohio State University Sea Grant Program Technical Bulletin OHSU-TB-17, Columbus, Ohio, 1984); Lake Biwa Research Institute and International Lake Environment Committee, *Data Book of World Lake Environments* (International Lake Environment Committee and United Nations Environment Programme, Otsu, Japan, 1988, 1989, 1990, 1991); Peter H. Gleick, ed., *Water in Crises: A Guide to the World's Fresh Water Resources* (Oxford University Press, New York, 1993); Frits van der Leeden, Fred L. Troise, and David Keith Todd, *The Water Encyclopedia—2nd ed.* (Lewis Publishers, Chelsea, Michigan, 1990), pp. 196–200; Aral Sea data, Michael H. Glantz, Alvin Z. Rubinstein, and Igor Zonn, "Tragedy in the Aral Sea Basin," *Global Environmental Change*, Vol. 3, No. 2 (June 1993), pp. 174–198.

Large lakes contain over 90 percent of the nonoceanic surface water supply. Lakes serve human transport needs, act as buffers that limit riverine floods, are storage basins for drinking, industrial, and irrigation water, provide important sources of protein, especially in developing countries, and are a rich reserve of biodiversity, especially fish. Major lakes of the world, as defined here, are over 500 square kilometers in area, although for some, this area might be obtained only occasionally. A disproportionate share of these 253 large lakes are found in North America, especially Canada, where glacial scouring created many suitable depressions in which lakes could form.

In general, lakes are identified by their most common name—although alternatives are sometimes included. Measurements of *surface area* are generally reported as the largest area for lakes subject to normal size variations. The surface area also normally includes the area of any islands within the lakes. The surface area of the Aral Sea,

which is declining in size, is reported for 1990. Calculations of *mean depth* and *volume* require detailed knowledge of the lake bottom and thus are often estimated. *Maximum depth* is more easily measured directly. Knowing the mean and maximum depths and water volume is important to an understanding of lake water movements and potential productivity. *Shoreline length* is usually measured from maps (for most of these data at 1:1,000,000 scale). The *catchment area* is the area of the drainage basin (excluding the area of the lake) that provides water to the lake. Data on the human *population density* within the catchment area are from a variety of years and should serve only as a nominal measure of relative magnitude. *Population density* is an important indicator of anthropogenic stresses on lake water quality and biological resources. The *fish catch* is generally the commercial catch, and while representing a variety of years, is derived from the most recent data available. These data too should serve only as nominal indicators of relative productivity and fishing effort. Each *lake origin* was due to specific geological processes that provide the chemical substrate for potential biological productivity.

Data in this table are judged to be the best available. While lakes might be thought of as stable units whose parameters (e.g., surface area) can be measured once and for all, this is not the case. In fact, different investigators come to different results—sometimes they are trivially different and sometimes not—when estimating such parameters as surface area.

Table 22.3 Wastewater Treatment

Source: Organisation for Economic Co-operation and Development (OECD), *OECD Environmental Data Compendium 1993* (OECD, Paris, 1993), p. 57.

OECD surveys its members and associates on a variety of environmental questions. Definitions can vary among countries. The *percentage of the population served* is the actual number connected to wastewater treatment plants. *Primary treatment* is the physical and mechanical processes that remove 20–30 percent of the biological oxygen demand (BOD) and effluents separate sludge. *Secondary treatment* is the additional use of biological treatments, using anaerobic or aerobic micro-organisms that remove 80–90 percent of BOD. *Tertiary treatment* is advanced added chemical or biological and chemical treatments that remove 95 percent or more of BOD. The years given are the most recent available. See the source for country details.

Table 22.4 Marine Fisheries Yield and Estimated Potential

Sources: Marine fishery production: Food and Agriculture Organization of the United Nations (FAO), *Fishstat PC* (FAO, Rome, 1993). Estimated fishery potential: M.A. Robinson, *Trends and Prospects in World Fisheries*, Fisheries Circular No. 772 (FAO, Fisheries Department, Rome, 1984).

FAO divides the world's oceans into 19 marine statistical areas and organizes *annual catch* data by 840 "species items," species groups separated at the family, genus, or species level. *Marine fish* include the following FAO species groupings: flounders, halibuts, soles, etc.; cods, hakes, haddocks, etc.; redfishes, basses, congers, etc.; jacks, mullets, sauries, etc.; tunas, bonitos, billfishes, etc.; herrings, sardines, anchovies, etc.; mackerels, snoeks, cutlassfishes, etc.; sharks, rays, chimeras, etc.; and miscellaneous marine fishes. *Cephalopods* include squids, cuttlefishes, octopuses, etc. *Crustaceans* are the total of the following categories: seaspiders, crabs, etc.; lobsters, spiny-rock lobsters, etc.; squat lobsters; shrimps, prawns, etc.; krill, planktonic crustaceans, etc.; and miscellaneous marine crustaceans. Years shown are three-year averages. *Total marine catch* differs from average marine catch in Table 22.5 because the following mollusc categories are not included: abalones, winkles, conchs, etc.; oysters; mussels; scallops; clams, cockles, arkshells, etc.; and miscellaneous marine molluscs. Please refer to the Technical Note for Table 22.5 for the definition of nominal fish catch and additional information on FAO's fishery data base. Fish catch data presented in this table include harvest from marine aquaculture production, except where otherwise indicated. Marine aquaculture provides an insignificant contribution to the total yields of marine fish and cephalopods.

Estimates of *potential* are FAO estimates of marine fisheries' biologically realizable potentials. These estimates refer to the maximum harvest that can be sustained by a fishery year after year, given average environmental conditions. An assumed level of incidental take (catching one species while fishing for another) is subtracted from estimates of potential. The figures exclude the potential harvest from marine aquaculture. Potential estimates should be treated with caution, as these figures can vary widely over time as the populations of individual stocks change in response to changing fishing patterns and climatic variation.

Individual countries are charged with collecting catch data and reporting it to FAO. The quality of these estimates vary, as many countries lack the resources to adequately monitor catch landings within their borders. In addition, fishers sometimes underreport their catches because they have not kept within harvest limits established to manage the fishery. In some cases, catch statistics are inflated to increase the importance of the fishing industry to the national economy.

Table 22.5 Marine and Freshwater Catches, Aquaculture, and Fish Consumption

Sources: Marine and freshwater catches and aquaculture production: Food and Agriculture Organization of the United Nations (FAO), *Fishstat PC* (FAO, Rome, 1993). Food supply from seafood: FAO, *Agrostat PC* (FAO, Rome, 1993).

Marine and *freshwater catch* data refer to marine and freshwater fish killed, caught, trapped, collected, bred, or cultivated for commercial, industrial, and subsistence use. Crustaceans, molluscs, and miscellaneous aquatic animals are included. Statistics for mariculture, aquaculture, and other kinds of fish farming are included in the country totals. Quantities taken in recreational activities are excluded. Figures are the national totals averaged over a three-year period; they include fish caught by a country's fleet anywhere in the world. Catches of freshwater species caught in low-salinity seas are included in the statistics of the appropriate marine area. Catches of diadromous (migratory between saltwater and freshwater) species are shown either in the marine or inland area where they were caught.

Data are represented as a nominal catch, which is the landings converted to a live-weight basis, that is, weight when caught.

Landings for some countries are identical to catches. Catch data are provided annually to the FAO Fisheries Department by national fishery offices and regional fishery commissions. Some countries' data are provisional for the latest year. If no data are submitted, FAO uses the previous year's figures or makes estimates based on other information. For details on data quality, please refer to the Technical Notes to Table 22.4.

Years are calendar years except for Antarctic fisheries data, which are for split years (July 1—June 30). Data for Antarctic fisheries are given for the calendar year in which the split year ends.

Aquaculture is defined by FAO as "the farming of aquatic organisms, including fish, molluscs, crustaceans, and aquatic plants. Farming implies some form of intervention in the rearing process to enhance production, such as regular stocking, feeding, and protection from predators, etc. [It] also implies ownership of the stock being cultivated. . . ." Aquatic organisms that are exploitable by the public as a common property resource are included in the harvest of fisheries.

FAO's global collection of aquaculture statistics by questionnaire was begun in 1984; today, these data are a regular feature of the annual FAO survey of world fishery statistics.

FAO's 840 species items are summarized in six categories. *Freshwater fish* include carps, barbels, tilapias, and others. *Diadromous fish* include, among others, sturgeons, river eels, salmons, trouts, and smelts. *Marine fish* include a variety of species groups such as flounders, halibuts, and redfishes.

Crustaceans include, among others, freshwater crustaceans, crabs, lobsters, shrimps, and prawns. *Molluscs* include freshwater molluscs, oysters, mussels, scallops, clams, and squids. *Other* includes frogs, turtles, and aquatic plants. Data on whales and other mammals are excluded from this table. For a detailed listing of species, please refer to the most recent *FAO Yearbook of Fishery Statistics* (FAO, Rome), which provides notes to data published in *Fishstat PC*.

Per capita annual food supply from fish and seafood is the quantity of both freshwater and marine fish and fish products available for human consumption. Data on aquatic plants and whale meat are excluded from the totals. The amount of fish and seafood actually consumed may be lower than the figures provided, depending on how much is lost during storage, preparation, and cooking and on how much is discarded.

Table 22.6 Coastal Areas and Resources

Sources: Length of coastline: United Nations Office for Ocean Affairs and the Law of the Sea, unpublished data (United Nations, New York, June 1989); U.S. Central Intelligence Agency, *The World Factbook 1992* (U.S. Government Printing Office, Washington, D.C., 1992). Shelf area to 200-meter depth: John P. Albers, M. Devereux Carter, Allen L. Clark, *et al.*, *Summary Petroleum and Selected Mineral Statistics for 120 Countries, Including Offshore Areas*, Geological Survey Professional Paper 817 (U.S. Government Printing Office, Washington, D.C., 1973). Exclusive economic zone: United Nations Office for Ocean Affairs and the Law of the Sea, unpublished data (United Nations, New York, June 1989); French Polynesia and New Caledonia: Anthony Bergin, "Fisheries Surveillance in the South Pacific", *Ocean & Shoreline Management*, Vol. 11 (1988), p. 468. Population in coastal urban agglomerations: United Nations Centre for Human Settlements (Habitat), unpublished data (United Nations, Nairobi, February 1990).

Average annual volume of goods loaded and unloaded: United Nations Statistical Office, *Monthly Bulletin of Statistics*, Vol. XLVII, No. 2 (February 1993). Offshore oil and gas resources: *Offshore Magazine* (PennWell Publishing Company, Tulsa, Oklahoma, June 20, 1983, and June 1993).

The United Nations Office for Ocean Affairs and the Law of the Sea compiles information concerning coastal claims from the following sources: the United Nations Legislative Series, official gazettes, communications to the Secretary General, legal journals, and other publications. National claims to maritime zones fall into five categories: (1) territorial sea, (2) contiguous zone, (3) exclusive economic zone (EEZ), (4) exclusive fishing zone, and (5) continental shelf. The extent of the continental *shelf to 200-meter depth* and the *exclusive economic zone* for those countries with marine coastline are presented in the table. Only the potential and not the actual established area of the EEZ is shown. As of June 1993, only 84 countries had established a full 200-mile EEZ.

Under currently recognized international principles, a nation may establish an EEZ out to 200 nautical miles to claim all the resources within the zone, including fish and all other living resources; minerals; and energy from wind, waves, and tides. Nations may also claim rights to regulate scientific exploration, protect the marine environment, and establish marine terminals and artificial islands. The EEZ data shown do not reflect the decisions of some countries, such as those in the European Community, to collectively manage fishing zones on EEZs in some areas. When countries' EEZs overlap—such as those of the United States and Cuba, which both have 200-mile EEZs, yet are only 90 miles apart—they must agree on a maritime boundary between them, often a halfway point.

The shelf area to the 200-meter isobath is one indicator of potential offshore oil and gas resources because of sedimentation from continental areas. Other indicators are geologic and geographic. Accessibility and water depth place economic constraints on exploration and production operations in water deeper than 200 meters. Significant deep-water operations currently take place in the North Sea and off the Brazilian coast.

Population in coastal urban agglomerations was calculated using maps in scales from 1:500,000 to 1:2,000,000. Coastal area is defined as a zone no more than 60 kilometers inland. Projected population for the year 2000 is based on the medium variant of the 1988 United Nations Population Division assessment. Definitions of urban agglomeration vary greatly among countries. (See the Technical Note for Table 17.2.) The most recent country-level estimates are for the years from 1970 to 1986. Hence, a direct comparison of urban agglomerations

among countries should be done with caution.

The United Nations Statistical Office based its estimates of *average annual volume of goods loaded and unloaded* in maritime transport mostly on information available in external trade statistics. *Petroleum products* exclude bunkers and those products not generally carried by tanker, namely, paraffin wax, petroleum coke, asphalt, and lubricating oil, which are included with the data for *dry cargo*.

Offshore Magazine annually queries national governments for statistics on *offshore oil and gas resources*. These data are supplemented with figures from oil- and gas-producing companies, expert sources, and published literature. National governments often have difficulty providing offshore gas production figures; these data are more frequently obtained from alternative sources. Figures for offshore *oil* and *gas* production in Middle Eastern countries are particularly difficult to obtain and, as a result, are less reliable.

Proven reserves of offshore crude oil and gas represent the fraction of total resources that can be recovered in the future, given present and expected economic conditions and existing technological limits.

Table 22.7 Midsized Oceanic Islands

Sources: United Nations Environment Programme (UNEP), unpublished data (UNEP, Nairobi, 1991); Arthur Dahl, *Island Directory*, UNEP Regional Seas Directories and Bibliographies No. 35 (UNEP, Nairobi, 1991); Organization of American States (OAS) and the U.S. Department of the Interior, *Inventory of Caribbean Marine and Coastal Protected Areas* (OAS and U.S. Department of the Interior, Washington, D.C., 1988).

Midsized oceanic islands are inhabited ocean islands at least 50 square kilometers and no more than 17,000 square kilometers in size. Islands for which population density data were not available have been eliminated from this table.

With the exception of protected area data for some Caribbean islands, all information presented in this table comes from the *Island Directory* compiled by Arthur Dahl and funded by UNEP. This directory synthesized what information was available on ocean islands under 17,000 square kilometers in size, which generally were not located in shallow water. Many sources were used in this compilation, therefore these data vary considerably in quality and timeliness (in some cases, the information dates from World War II or from expeditions made during the early 1900s).

Population density is taken for the latest year available, usually from 1960 to 1989. Consult the original source for details.

Terrestrial and *marine protected areas* consist generally of legally recognized partially and fully protected areas (categories I–V of the World Conservation Union, formerly the International Union for Conservation of Nature and Natural Resources [IUCN]), although in some instances areas that are effectively protected as reserves, though not legally recognized as such, and resource management areas (IUCN categories VI and above) are included. For a description of IUCN category definitions, refer to the Technical Notes to Table 20.1.

The *total number of plants* reflects only those native species known to occur on a given island. *Endemic plants* are those occurring only on that particular island.

23. Atmosphere and Climate

Human activities continue to pour immense quantities of trace gases into the atmosphere that may affect the climate, increase ultraviolet exposure, impair the health of forests and crops, corrode the beauty and structural integrity of the built environment, and threaten human health. This chapter provides information on the emissions and concentrations of trace gases needed to understand these threats.

The most important of the greenhouse gases emitted as a result of human activities, carbon dioxide (CO_2), results largely from the combustion of fossil fuels. Table 23.1 details CO_2 emissions by country, region, source, and in total, as well as those from the manufacture of cement. The United States is the largest emitter of CO_2 and is responsible for 22 percent of global national emissions from industrial sources. It is followed by the former U.S.S.R., China, India, and Germany. While large economies such as these emit large amounts of CO_2, their per capita emissions vary considerably. Annual per capita CO_2 emissions in the United States, for example, are 19.53 metric tons, compared to 0.81 metric tons in India. Emissions from bunker fuels used in international trade are significant (larger, for example, than the emissions attributable to gas flaring), but because trade always benefits at least two countries and often more (as well as the countries of the vessel's owners, the country of its registration, and others), attributing these emissions to individual countries is difficult.

CO_2 is also produced by other human activities. Deforestation in particular adds substantial quantities to the global CO_2 flux. Table 23.2 shows estimates of CO_2 emissions from that change in land use patterns (based on United Nations Food and Agricultural Organization data on average annual deforestation between 1981 and 1990). CO_2 resulting from deforestation adds about 15 percent to the total emissions from industrial processes. Human activities also cause significant emissions of another greenhouse gas, methane (CH_4). While large amounts of CH_4 are released from the life-sustaining processes of wet rice agriculture and the raising of livestock, substantial amounts are also emitted from more manageable industrial sources such as landfills, uncontrolled emissions from coal mines, and leaks from the production and distribution of petroleum and natural gas. Total emissions of chlorofluoro-

carbons (CFCs) were reduced in 1991, in great part because of the existence of a protocol to eliminate their emission. The United States and Japan are the largest users and emitters of CFCs.

Table 23.3 shows the atmospheric concentrations of important trace gases. With the exception of carbon monoxide (CO), these concentrations continue to increase, although the rates of growth have slowed for many in recent years. CO_2 concentrations are now 27 percent higher than their estimated preindustrial concentrations. CH_4 concentrations have increased almost 150 percent from preindustrial times. No natural sources of CFCs exist, thus current concentrations are totally attributable to human industrial activity.

Increases in CO_2 concentrations are clearly paralleled by increases in global CO_2 emissions. Table 23.4 provides estimates of these emissions. Since 1950, annual emissions have risen 278 percent. Most of this increase is due to the buildup in total industrial activity attributable to the growth of the world's population. Per capita CO_2 emissions have risen from 2.38 metric tons to 4.21 metric tons, an increase of only 77 percent.

Anthropogenic emissions of sulfur and nitrogen oxides, which are major contributors to acid rain precipitation, have had important effects on the health of natural and human-modified ecosystems. Emissions data of these combustion products are available for only a few countries (see Table 23.5). Due to international agreements for their control and changes in industrial processes (including the recent slowdown in industrial activity in Central and Eastern Europe), sulfur emissions have declined over the last 5–6 years almost everywhere. Changes in nitrogen emissions are less clear; some important sources recently increased while others declined, illustrating the difficulty of documenting and controlling such emissions.

Emissions of other common anthropogenic pollutants, especially those that affect human health (Table 23.6), are less easily characterized. CO emissions are estimated to have declined in the United States but to have increased in the United Kingdom. Existing data for emissions of particulate matter (implicated in respiratory difficulties and disease) suggest a general reduction over the last decade. Changes in the emissions of hydrocarbons (important ingredients of photochemical smog) are less clear cut.

Table 23.1 CO₂ Emissions from Industrial Processes, 1991

	Carbon Dioxide Emissions (000 metric tons)						Per Capita Carbon Dioxide Emissions (metric tons)	Bunker Fuels (000 Metric Tons)
	Solid	Liquid	Gas	Gas Flaring	Cement Manufacture	Total		
WORLD	8,581,088	9,493,424	3,751,936	256,480	593,568	22,672,832	4.21	{a}
AFRICA	273,606	255,487	63,028	54,335	25,138	671,600	1.03	10,102
Algeria	3,558	24,032	21,460	2,958	3,189	55,194	2.16	0
Angola	0	1,517	319	2,455	497	4,789	0.51	0
Benin	0	425	0	0	136	561	0.11	0
Botswana	2,154	0	0	0	0	2,154	1.69	0
Burkina Faso	0	557	0	0	0	557	0.07	0
Burundi	15	205	0	0	0	220	0.04	0
Cameroon	4	1,920	0	0	0	1,924	0.15	0
Central African Rep	0	209	0	0	0	209	0.07	0
Chad	0	253	0	0	0	253	0.04	0
Congo	4	1,788	4	169	51	2,015	0.88	0
Cote d'Ivoire	0	6,130	0	0	249	6,379	0.51	0
Djibouti	0	359	0	0	0	359	0.81	0
Egypt	2,623	56,664	14,905	0	7,475	81,667	1.54	0
Equatorial Guinea	0	121	0	0	0	121	0.33	0
Ethiopia	0	2,682	0	0	145	2,825	0.07	0
Gabon	0	2,349	194	3,389	56	5,987	5.02	0
Gambia, The	0	198	0	0	0	198	0.22	0
Ghana	7	3,111	0	0	337	3,455	0.22	0
Guinea	0	1,026	0	0	0	1,026	0.18	0
Guinea-Bissau	0	205	0	0	0	205	0.22	0
Kenya	355	3,745	0	0	746	4,847	0.18	0
Lesotho	X	X	X	X	X	X	X	X
Liberia	0	275	0	0	0	275	0.11	0
Libya	15	25,839	14,022	1,774	1,356	43,008	9.12	0
Madagascar	40	1,022	0	0	11	1,074	0.07	0
Malawi	29	561	0	0	38	630	0.07	0
Mali	0	425	0	0	10	436	0.04	0
Mauritania	15	2,645	0	0	45	2,704	1.28	0
Mauritius	176	1,041	0	0	0	1,216	1.14	0
Morocco	4,785	17,243	73	0	2,093	24,197	0.95	0
Mozambique	165	821	0	0	40	1,030	0.07	0
Namibia	X	X	X	X	X	X	X	X
Niger	421	594	0	0	14	1,030	0.15	0
Nigeria	169	37,329	9,120	43,569	1,745	91,930	0.81	0
Rwanda	0	407	0	2	30	436	0.07	0
Senegal	0	2,554	0	0	249	2,799	0.37	0
Sierra Leone	0	689	0	0	0	689	0.15	0
Somalia	0	524	0	0	0	524	0.07	0
South Africa	241,681	33,276	0	0	3,736	278,695	7.18	10,102
Sudan	0	3,320	0	0	84	3,404	0.15	0
Swaziland	330	0	0	0	0	330	0.44	0
Tanzania	15	1,993	0	0	149	2,158	0.07	0
Togo	0	524	0	0	199	722	0.18	0
Tunisia	359	9,801	2,931	20	1,695	14,810	1.80	0
Uganda	0	909	0	0	5	912	0.04	0
Zaire	931	3,081	0	0	224	4,236	0.11	0
Zambia	850	1,392	0	0	188	2,429	0.29	0
Zimbabwe	14,905	1,729	0	0	348	16,983	1.65	0
ASIA	3,314,509	2,546,227	415,410	112,820	282,563	6,671,525	2.11	50,332
Afghanistan	363	1,711	2,726	291	54	5,148	0.29	0
Bangladesh	311	5,910	9,057	0	165	15,444	0.15	0
Bhutan	48	81	0	0	0	128	0.07	0
Cambodia	0	462	0	0	0	462	0.04	0
China	2,024,074	365,118	30,778	0	123,411	2,543,380	2.20	0
India	496,545	151,583	19,540	10,968	24,915	703,550	0.81	2,689
Indonesia	17,829	91,728	28,213	24,648	8,049	170,468	0.92	0
Iran, Islamic Rep	4,976	144,409	44,353	21,148	7,475	222,361	3.70	0
Iraq {b}	4	487,341	2,246	28,203	2,491	520,281	27.86	0
Israel	10,871	23,200	48	0	1,447	35,566	7.29	0
Japan	320,944	619,476	106,278	0	44,449	1,091,147	8.79	21,141
Jordan	0	9,112	0	0	897	10,010	2.42	0
Korea, Dem People's Rep	221,628	13,469	0	0	8,137	243,235	10.96	0
Korea, Rep	96,554	143,940	7,214	0	16,943	264,647	6.05	0
Kuwait	0	7,801	909	2,980	149	11,842	5.68	0
Lao People's Dem Rep	4	249	0	0	0	253	0.07	0
Lebanon	0	7,907	0	0	452	8,361	3.00	0
Malaysia	6,141	41,345	7,280	2,690	3,736	61,196	3.33	0
Mongolia	7,581	2,045	0	0	199	9,823	4.36	0
Myanmar	187	2,572	1,916	99	183	4,961	0.11	0
Nepal	180	692	0	0	50	923	0.04	0
Oman	0	4,738	5,133	1,331	497	11,695	7.40	0
Pakistan	8,424	32,492	21,640	2,342	3,587	68,487	0.55	0
Philippines	6,298	36,050	0	0	2,242	44,587	0.70	0
Saudi Arabia	0	122,707	71,444	14,789	5,981	214,919	13.96	0
Singapore	44	40,154	0	0	1,096	41,293	15.06	26,502
Sri Lanka	7	3,961	0	0	199	4,166	0.26	0
Syrian Arab Rep	0	26,700	564	759	1,745	29,766	2.31	0
Thailand	15,510	66,113	10,274	0	8,996	100,896	1.83	0
Turkey	65,084	57,708	6,797	0	12,970	142,555	2.49	0
United Arab Emirates	0	17,965	38,996	1,000	1,501	59,459	36.49	0
Viet Nam	10,904	7,944	4	1,573	149	20,573	0.29	0
Yemen	0	9,545	0	0	398	9,940	0.81	0

Table 23.1

	Carbon Dioxide Emissions (000 metric tons)						Per Capita Carbon Dioxide Emissions (metric tons)	Bunker Fuels (000 Metric Tons)
	Solid	Liquid	Gas	Gas Flaring	Cement Manufacture	Total		
NORTH & CENTRAL AMERICA	1,920,511	2,527,207	1,240,792	18,369	57,488	5,764,359	13.59	71,950
Belize	0	264	0	0	0	264	1.36	0
Canada	94,696	178,078	127,866	4,507	5,481	410,628	15.21	4,532
Costa Rica	0	2,803	0	0	447	3,250	1.06	0
Cuba	700	32,346	59	0	1,295	34,398	3.22	0
Dominican Rep	0	5,763	0	0	497	6,262	0.84	0
El Salvador	0	2,213	0	0	319	2,532	0.48	0
Guatemala	0	3,228	0	0	847	4,074	0.44	0
Haiti	0	634	0	0	99	733	0.11	0
Honduras	0	1,619	0	0	325	1,946	0.37	0
Jamaica	0	4,411	0	0	260	4,672	1.91	0
Mexico	20,801	251,061	49,779	4,930	13,304	339,873	3.92	0
Nicaragua	0	2,004	0	0	70	2,074	0.55	0
Panama	476	2,854	117	0	149	3,594	1.47	0
Trinidad and Tobago	0	5,884	10,845	1,479	219	18,430	14.73	0
United States	1,803,838	2,034,044	1,052,125	7,453	34,174	4,931,630	19.53	67,418
SOUTH AMERICA	68,601	364,136	119,681	17,556	24,996	594,986	2.00	0
Argentina	2,719	59,818	47,284	4,029	1,994	115,848	3.55	0
Bolivia	0	3,386	1,279	915	273	5,855	0.81	0
Brazil	39,879	153,009	7,310	2,444	12,956	215,601	1.43	0
Chile	7,991	20,471	2,928	237	897	32,525	2.42	0
Colombia	16,158	29,418	7,929	809	3,189	57,503	1.76	0
Ecuador	0	15,187	216	1,282	1,096	17,785	1.65	0
Guyana	0	850	0	0	0	850	1.06	0
Paraguay	0	1,616	0	0	163	1,781	0.40	0
Peru	546	16,477	887	248	997	19,155	0.88	0
Suriname	0	1,993	0	0	25	2,019	4.69	0
Uruguay	0	4,210	0	0	249	4,459	1.43	0
Venezuela	1,308	57,701	51,849	7,591	3,158	121,604	6.16	0
EUROPE	1,696,520	1,600,516	663,866	29,041	123,816	4,113,771	8.20	118,758
Albania	2,832	2,008	1,059	0	348	6,247	1.91	0
Austria	16,330	31,342	10,171	0	2,491	60,331	7.80	0
Belgium	36,831	41,825	19,987	0	3,436	102,079	10.22	16,290
Bulgaria	29,579	14,909	9,508	0	2,676	56,675	6.30	0
Czechoslovakia	137,583	26,124	23,512	0	4,136	191,356	12.20	0
Denmark	31,968	24,941	4,683	464	997	63,054	12.24	4,617
Finland	20,848	24,934	5,467	0	798	52,047	10.41	0
France	81,022	217,920	62,215	0	12,956	374,113	6.56	17,400
Germany	507,548	307,926	132,091	1,137	20,930	969,630	12.13	0
Greece	29,616	36,204	315	3	6,727	72,866	7.18	0
Hungary	23,490	20,537	18,203	0	1,345	63,574	6.05	0
Iceland	234	1,513	0	0	56	1,803	7.00	0
Ireland	14,337	12,714	4,386	0	798	32,236	9.23	0
Italy	50,527	234,478	97,576	0	19,931	402,516	6.96	0
Netherlands	30,891	28,671	77,615	194	1,623	138,990	9.23	40,546
Norway	3,041	27,949	4,060	23,048	572	58,672	13.74	0
Poland	251,251	34,636	16,279	0	5,994	308,164	8.06	572
Portugal	10,516	28,290	0	0	2,984	41,792	4.25	3,495
Romania	37,944	44,148	49,457	0	6,478	138,027	5.94	0
Spain	79,304	113,895	12,813	126	13,741	219,877	5.64	16,884
Sweden	9,123	40,989	894	0	2,491	53,498	6.23	0
Switzerland	1,220	33,844	4,192	0	2,590	41,843	6.16	0
United Kingdom	251,402	216,084	99,745	3,944	5,981	577,157	10.00	18,954
Yugoslavia	39,080	34,636	9,640	126	3,738	87,225	3.66	0
U.S.S.R.	1,105,766	1,216,320	1,172,733	23,074	63,288	3,581,179	12.31	0
Armenia	X	X	X	X	X	X	X	X
Azerbaijan	X	X	X	X	X	X	X	X
Belarus	X	X	X	X	X	X	X	X
Estonia	X	X	X	X	X	X	X	X
Georgia	X	X	X	X	X	X	X	X
Kazakhstan	X	X	X	X	X	X	X	X
Kyrgyzstan	X	X	X	X	X	X	X	X
Latvia	X	X	X	X	X	X	X	X
Lithuania	X	X	X	X	X	X	X	X
Moldova	X	X	X	X	X	X	X	X
Russian Federation	X	X	X	X	X	X	X	X
Tajikistan	X	X	X	X	X	X	X	X
Turkmenistan	X	X	X	X	X	X	X	X
Ukraine	X	X	X	X	X	X	X	X
Uzbekistan	X	X	X	X	X	X	X	X
OCEANIA	154,562	89,321	41,103	0	3,783	288,767	11.24	6,295
Australia	149,557	76,644	32,258	0	3,363	261,818	15.10	6,295
Fiji	48	594	0	0	45	689	0.95	0
New Zealand	4,954	9,669	8,845	0	375	23,842	6.96	0
Papua New Guinea	4	2,253	0	0	0	2,257	0.59	0
Solomon Islands	0	161	0	0	0	161	0.48	0

Sources: Carbon Dioxide Information Analysis Center.
Notes: Estimates are of the carbon dioxide emitted, 3.664 times the carbon it contains.
a. Bunker fuels are included in world total of fuel type. b. Totals for Iraq include emissions from oil fires in Kuwait.
World and regional totals include countries not listed.
0 = zero or less than half of the unit measured; X = not available.
For additional information, see Sources and Technical Notes.

Table 23.2 Other Greenhouse Gas Emissions, 1991

	Carbon Dioxide Emissions from Land-Use Change (000 metric tons)	Methane from Anthropogenic Sources (000 metric tons)						Chlorofluoro-carbons (000 metric tons)
		Solid Waste	Coal Mining	Oil and Gas Production	Wet Rice Agriculture	Livestock	Total	
WORLD	3,400,000	40,000	40,000	26,000	72,000	76,000	250,000	400
AFRICA	640,000	1,400	1,600	1,000	2,600	9,600	16,000	12
Algeria	X	110	0	690	X	160	960	1
Angola	16,000	24	X	3	8	120	150	X
Benin	3,000	15	X	X	2	44	61	X
Botswana	3,200	3	X	X	X	110	110	X
Burkina Faso	3,400	7	X	X	12	200	220	X
Burundi	120	3	X	X	8	22	32	X
Cameroon	23,000	42	X	X	5	200	250	X
Central African Rep	23,000	12	X	X	3	98	110	X
Chad	7,100	14	X	X	21	210	250	X
Congo	12,000	8	X	0	2	4	14	X
Cote d'Ivoire	9,900	41	X	X	150	49	240	0
Djibouti	X	3	X	X	X	14	17	X
Egypt	X	130	X	120	310	290	850	2
Equatorial Guinea	2,600	1	X	X	X	0	1	X
Ethiopia	8,000	54	X	X	X	1,400	1,400	X
Gabon	47,000	5	X	2	X	2	9	0
Gambia, The	94	2	X	X	3	16	21	X
Ghana	15,000	21	X	X	8	62	91	1
Guinea	9,800	13	X	X	360	68	440	X
Guinea-Bissau	1,700	2	X	X	33	17	51	X
Kenya	360	49	X	X	8	600	660	0
Lesotho	X	X	X	X	X	X	X	X
Liberia	7,400	10	X	X	36	4	49	0
Libya	X	27	X	140	X	44	210	X
Madagascar	20,000	25	X	X	690	370	1,100	0
Malawi	10,000	9	X	X	17	34	61	X
Mali	8,400	15	X	X	64	250	330	X
Mauritania	(1)	8	X	X	2	140	150	X
Mauritius	X	4	X	X	X	2	5	X
Morocco	X	100	8	1	2	220	330	1
Mozambique	14,000	X	X	X	X	X	X	X
Namibia	X	X	X	X	X	X	X	X
Niger	X	13	2	X	6	120	140	X
Nigeria	10,000	2	0	77	330	700	1,100	0
Rwanda	71	5	X	0	2	28	35	0
Senegal	4,600	24	X	X	15	130	170	0
Sierra Leone	1,800	11	X	X	110	14	130	X
Somalia	360	23	X	X	1	630	660	X
South Africa	X	180	1,500	X	1	920	2,600	5
Sudan	38,000	47	X	X	1	1,100	1,100	X
Swaziland	X	2	0	X	X	27	29	X
Tanzania	21,000	79	0	X	200	520	790	X
Togo	2,100	8	X	X	8	27	42	0
Tunisia	X	37	X	5	X	72	110	0
Uganda	4,700	17	X	X	24	200	240	X
Zaire	280,000	120	1	X	150	75	340	X
Zambia	33,000	36	0	X	6	100	150	X
Zimbabwe	4,100	23	44	X	X	230	300	0
ASIA	920,000	8,200	17,000	3,200	67,000	25,000	120,000	100
Afghanistan	X	27	1	36	85	160	310	X
Bangladesh	6,800	160	X	73	5,000	960	6,200	X
Bhutan	4,100	1	X	X	21	15	37	X
Cambodia	34,000	X	X	X	X	X	X	X
China	X	880	14,000	250	19,000	5,400	40,000	8
India	21,000	2,300	1,800	160	19,000	12,000	35,000	3
Indonesia	330,000	480	82	720	5,100	650	7,100	1
Iran, Islamic Rep	X	260	7	400	280	640	1,600	2
Iraq	X	290	X	20	53	130	490	1
Israel	X	35	X	0	X	15	50	2
Japan	X	1,900	97	35	1,400	280	3,600	64
Jordan	X	23	X	X	X	12	35	1
Korea, Dem People's Rep	X	110	820	X	310	53	1,300	X
Korea, Rep	X	260	260	X	640	80	1,200	4
Kuwait	X	41	X	8	X	2	51	0
Lao People's Dem Rep	36,000	7	X	X	190	86	280	X
Lebanon	X	19	X	X	X	6	25	X
Malaysia	110,000	65	0	250	290	39	640	2
Mongolia	X	10	5	X	X	260	280	X
Myanmar	120,000	86	0	15	3,000	440	3,600	X
Nepal	7,600	16	X	X	560	400	980	X
Oman	X	4	X	41	X	14	59	X
Pakistan	9,700	41	2	170	1,100	1,900	3,200	4
Philippines	110,000	220	X	X	1,500	220	1,900	1
Saudi Arabia	X	240	X	580	X	77	890	2
Singapore	X	61	X	X	X	0	62	0
Sri Lanka	3,700	24	X	X	460	110	600	0
Syrian Arab Rep	X	54	X	5	X	110	160	0
Thailand	91,000	110	9	83	5,300	440	6,000	2
Turkey	X	290	23	3	25	740	1,100	1
United Arab Emirates	X	26	X	370	X	13	410	1
Viet Nam	33,000	120	75	0	3,400	270	3,900	X
Yemen	X	9	X	X	X	X	9	X

Table 23.2

	Carbon Dioxide Emissions from Land-Use Change (000 metric tons)	Methane from Anthropogenic Sources (000 metric tons)						Chlorofluoro-carbons (000 metric tons)
		Solid Waste	Coal Mining	Oil and Gas Production	Wet Rice Agriculture	Livestock	Total	
NORTH & CENTRAL AMERICA	190,000	10,000	9,800	6,500	980	8,800	36,000	100
Belize	840	X	X	X	0	2	2	X
Canada	X	1,200	630	800	X	740	3,300	8
Costa Rica	12,000	12	X	X	8	64	84	0
Cuba	2,800	65	X	0	110	190	370	0
Dominican Rep	4,800	36	X	X	39	88	160	0
El Salvador	290	20	X	X	3	45	67	0
Guatemala	20,000	31	X	X	4	78	110	1
Haiti	(57)	16	X	X	9	66	91	X
Honduras	17,000	19	X	X	4	89	110	0
Jamaica	7,000	11	X	X	X	13	24	0
Mexico	50,000	540	130	380	16	1,300	2,400	3
Nicaragua	32,000	20	X	X	19	64	100	0
Panama	21,000	11	X	X	13	52	75	0
Trinidad and Tobago	1,100	7	X	87	1	3	98	0
United States	22,000	8,400	9,100	5,300	750	6,000	29,000	90
SOUTH AMERICA	1,600,000	1,900	270	970	820	14,000	18,000	10
Argentina	X	230	0	350	19	3,000	3,600	2
Bolivia	140,000	32	X	43	18	250	340	0
Brazil	970,000	1,100	3	59	330	8,300	9,800	4
Chile	X	93	19	24	6	160	310	0
Colombia	100,000	140	220	64	260	910	1,600	1
Ecuador	68,000	50	X	2	43	170	270	0
Guyana	6,500	2	X	X	14	9	26	X
Paraguay	28,000	17	X	X	3	300	320	0
Peru	94,000	130	2	7	42	230	400	0
Suriname	4,800	2	X	X	37	3	42	0
Uruguay	X	22	X	X	23	440	490	0
Venezuela	170,000	150	20	420	23	490	1,100	1
EUROPE	X	15,000	3,400	2,600	240	7,700	29,000	120
Albania	X	16	X	9	1	38	64	X
Austria	X	87	X	13	X	150	250	2
Belgium	X	190	12	0	X	X	200	3
Bulgaria	X	8,500	1	0	4	160	8,700	1
Czechoslovakia	X	170	240	7	X	290	710	3
Denmark	X	26	X	41	X	140	210	2
Finland	X	58	X	X	X	78	140	1
France	X	290	94	23	17	1,300	1,700	17
Germany	X	1,300	730	250	X	770	3,000	23
Greece	X	120	X	2	8	130	270	3
Hungary	X	94	100	64	6	120	380	2
Iceland	X	5	X	X	X	11	15	0
Ireland	X	42	0	24	X	360	420	1
Italy	X	610	0	190	110	600	1,500	17
Netherlands	X	250	X	770	X	310	1,300	4
Norway	X	75	0	300	X	72	450	1
Poland	X	380	890	43	X	630	1,900	4
Portugal	X	10	3	X	22	130	160	3
Romania	X	170	29	330	15	510	1,100	1
Spain	X	590	240	15	50	520	1,400	11
Sweden	X	70	0	X	X	100	170	2
Switzerland	X	18	X	0	X	110	130	2
United Kingdom	X	1,300	1,100	480	X	910	3,800	17
Yugoslavia	X	190	2	24	6	240	460	3
U.S.S.R.	X	2,600	6,300	11,000	320	7,900	28,000	44
Armenia	X	X	X	X	X	X	X	X
Azerbaijan	X	X	X	X	X	X	X	X
Belarus	X	X	X	X	X	X	X	X
Estonia	X	X	X	X	X	X	X	X
Georgia	X	X	X	X	X	X	X	X
Kazakhstan	X	X	X	X	X	X	X	X
Kyrgyzstan	X	X	X	X	X	X	X	X
Latvia	X	X	X	X	X	X	X	X
Lithuania	X	X	X	X	X	X	X	X
Moldova	X	X	X	X	X	X	X	X
Russian Federation	X	X	X	X	X	X	X	X
Tajikistan	X	X	X	X	X	X	X	X
Turkmenistan	X	X	X	X	X	X	X	X
Ukraine	X	X	X	X	X	X	X	X
Uzbekistan	X	X	X	X	X	X	X	X
OCEANIA	29,000	630	1,500	400	66	3,000	5,600	6
Australia	X	570	1,400	330	60	2,100	4,500	5
Fiji	X	2	X	X	6	7	15	0
New Zealand	X	56	19	71	X	910	1,100	1
Papua New Guinea	29,000	5	X	X	X	5	10	X
Solomon Islands	X	X	X	X	X	1	1	X

Source: World Resources Institute.
Notes: Estimates are of the carbon dioxide emitted, 3.664 times the carbon it contains.
Deforestation and biomass data used to estimate emissions from land use change are taken from United Nations Food and Agriculture Organization estimates.
Several countries dispute these estimates. See Chapter 19, "Forests and Rangelands," for further details.
0 = zero or less than half of the unit of measure; X = not available.
For additional information, see Sources and Technical Notes.

Table 23.3 Atmospheric Concentrations of Greenhouse and Ozone-Depleting Gases, 1959–92

Year	Carbon Dioxide (CO2) ppm	Carbon tetra-chloride (CCl4) ppt	Methyl chloro-form (CH3CCl3) ppt	CFC-11 (CCl3F) ppt	CFC-12 (CCl2F2) ppt	CFC-22 (CHClF2) ppt	CFC-113 (C2Cl3F3) ppt	Total Gaseous Chlorine ppt	Nitrous Oxide (N2O) ppb	Methane (CH4) ppb	Carbon Monoxide (CO) ppb
Preindustrial	280.0 a	0	0	0	0	0	0	0	285.0 a	700 a	X
1964	X	X	X	X	X	X	X	X	X	X	X
1965	319.9	X	X	X	X	X	X	X	X	1,386	X
1966	321.2	X	X	X	X	X	X	X	X	1,338	X
1967	322.0	X	X	X	X	X	X	X	X	1,480	X
1968	322.8	X	X	X	X	X	X	X	X	1,373	X
1969	323.9	X	X	X	X	X	X	X	X	1,385	X
1970	325.3	X	X	X	X	X	X	X	X	1,431	X
1971	326.2	X	X	X	X	X	X	X	X	1,436	X
1972	327.3	X	X	X	X	X	X	X	X	1,500	X
1973	329.5	X	X	X	X	X	X	X	X	1,624	X
1974	330.1	X	X	X	X	X	X	X	X	1,596	X
1975	331.0	104	70	120	X	X	X	1,386	291.4	1,541	X
1976	332.0	106	78	133	X	X	X	1,491	293.3	1,490	X
1977	333.7	115	86	148	X	X	X	1,640	294.6	1,471	X
1978	335.3	123	94	159	X	X	X	1,783	296.4	1,531	X
1979	336.7	116	112	167	X	46	X	1,913	296.3	1,545	X
1980	338.5	121	126	177	X	52	X	2,065	297.6	1,554	X
1981	339.8	122	127	180	209	59	X	2,113	298.5	1,569	71.7
1982	341.0	121	133	189	224	64	X	2,186	301.0	1,591	72.5
1983	342.6	126	144	198	239	71	24	2,393	300.9	1,615	70.2
1984	344.3	130	150	207	254	76	27	2,498	300.4	1,629	73.1
1985	345.7	130	158	218	269	85	31	2,609	301.5	1,643	75.5
1986	347.0	127	169	227	287	98	35	2,722	302.5	1,656	75.5
1987	348.8	X	X	239	303	X	X	X	304.5	1,667	76.9
1988	351.4	126 b	166 b	251	323	109 b	44 b	2,843	306.3	1,692	74.4
1989	352.8	126 b	172 b	260	339	X	51 b	2,834	X	1,705	71.5
1990	354.0	127 b	182 b	267	359	X	53 b	2,970	X	1,717	69.4
1991	355.4	X	X	272	375	X	X	X	X	1,728	67.2
1992	356.2	X	X	274 c	384	X	X	X	X	X	68.8

Sources: Charles D. Keeling of Scripps Institution of Oceanography for carbon dioxide and Oregon Graduate Center for other gases.
Notes: a. Approximately. b. Preliminary data; previous years are not calibrated to the same standard. c. Average for the first seven months. All estimates are by volume; ppm = parts per million; ppb = parts per billion; and ppt = parts per trillion. X = not available. For additional information, see Sources and Technical Notes.

Table 23.4 World CO2 Emissions from Fossil Fuel Consumption and Cement Manufacture, 1950–91

Year	Carbon Dioxide Emissions (millions of metric tons)						Per Capita Emissions (metric tons)
	Total	Solid Fuels	Liquid Fuels	Gas Fuels	Gas Flaring	Cement Manufacture	
1955	7,511	4,452	2,290	550	114	110	2.71
1956	8,006	4,694	2,488	590	117	117	2.86
1957	8,347	4,825	2,616	652	128	125	2.93
1958	8,566	4,924	2,682	703	128	132	2.93
1959	9,054	5,093	2,895	784	132	147	3.04
1960	9,475	5,199	3,114	861	143	158	3.15
1961	9,534	4,968	3,316	931	154	165	3.11
1962	9,922	4,976	3,594	1,015	161	180	3.15
1963	10,461	5,144	3,858	1,099	172	187	3.26
1964	11,051	5,283	4,170	1,202	187	209	3.37
1965	11,556	5,379	4,474	1,286	202	216	3.48
1966	12,142	5,441	4,855	1,392	220	231	3.55
1967	12,531	5,331	5,218	1,502	242	238	3.59
1968	13,176	5,335	5,687	1,630	267	256	3.70
1969	13,956	5,474	6,134	1,784	293	271	3.85
1970	14,964	5,730	6,734	1,891	319	286	4.03
1971	15,517	5,730	7,130	2,030	322	308	4.10
1972	16,133	5,789	7,530	2,136	344	326	4.18
1973	17,005	5,818	8,207	2,228	403	348	4.32
1974	17,034	5,807	8,222	2,264	392	352	4.25
1975	16,935	6,152	7,808	2,283	341	348	4.14
1976	17,913	6,291	8,475	2,371	399	377	4.32
1977	18,423	6,522	8,757	2,367	381	396	4.36
1978	18,598	6,581	8,731	2,470	392	425	4.32
1979	19,632	6,932	9,285	2,616	366	436	4.51
1980	19,390	7,145	8,819	2,660	326	440	4.36
1981	18,763	7,042	8,317	2,697	264	443	4.14
1982	18,617	7,273	7,973	2,678	253	443	4.03
1983	18,584	7,295	7,918	2,686	231	458	3.96
1984	19,188	7,632	8,006	2,876	209	469	4.03
1985	19,833	8,204	7,951	2,997	202	480	4.10
1986	20,522	8,427	8,339	3,059	194	502	4.14
1987	20,984	8,614	8,380	3,287	176	524	4.18
1988	21,812	8,841	8,772	3,444	202	557	4.25
1989	22,233	8,991	8,900	3,576	194	572	4.29
1990	22,343	8,768	9,094	3,679	227	575	4.21
1991	22,673	8,581	9,493	3,752	256	594	4.21

Source: Carbon Dioxide Information Analysis Center.
Notes: Mass of carbon dioxide. Totals differ from the sum of other columns because of rounding. For additional information, see Sources and Technical Notes.

Table 23.5 Sulfur and Nitrogen Emissions, 1970–91

	Sulfur Emissions (000 metric tons of SO2)						Nitrogen Emissions (000 metric tons of NO2)					
	1970	1975	1980	1985	1990	1991	1970	1975	1980	1985	1990	1991
Albania	X	X	(50)	(50)	(50)	X	X	X	(9)	(9)	(9)	X
Austria	X	X	397	195	90	84	X	X	246	245	222	216
Belgium	X	X	828	452	420	X	X	X	442	281	300	X
Bulgaria	X	X	1,034	1,094	1,030	X	X	X	150	150	150	X
Canada	6,677	5,319	4,643	3,692	3,326	3,306	1,364	1,756	1,959	1,958	1,923	X
Czechoslovakia (former)	2,600	2,900	3,100	3,150	2,564	X	X	X	1,204	1,127	960 b	X
Denmark	574	420	449	341	181	X	X	197	270	296	283	X
Finland	515	535	584	382	260	194	X	160	264	252	280	286
France	2,966	3,328	3,348	1,451	1,200	1,314	1,322	1,608	1,646	1,400	1,487	1,507
German Dem Rep	X	4,114	4,323	5,389	4,758	X	X	583	593	637	629	X
Germany, Fed Rep	3,743	3,334	3,194	2,396	939	X	2,345	2,530	2,944	2,928	2,605	X
Greece	X	X	400	500	500	X	X	X	217	X	150	X
Hungary	X	X	1,633	1,404	1,010	X	X	X	273	263	238	X
Iceland	X	6	9	7	8	7	X	15	14	21	28	27
Ireland	X	186	220	135	187	X	X	X	73	91	128	X
Italy	2,830	3,331	3,211	2,241	2,406	X	1,410	1,507	1,585	1,630	1,996 b	X
Japan	4,973	2,586	1,263	835 a	876 b	X	1,651	1,782	1,400	1,176 a	1,301 b	X
Luxembourg	X	X	24	17	10	X	X	X	23	22	15	X
Netherlands	807	427	502	259	208	204	456	481	571	564	552	550
Norway	171	137	141	91	54	46	159	179	186	216	230	218
Poland	X	X	4,100	4,300	3,216	2,995	X	X	X	1,500	1,280	1,205
Portugal	116	178	266	199	211	X	72	104	165	96	142	X
Romania	X	X	1,800	1,800	1,800	X	X	X	X	(390)	(390)	X
Spain	X	3,003	3,377	2,191	2,190	X	X	625	946	849	X	X
Sweden	930	690	489	261	128	106	302	308	424	X	396	389
Switzerland	125	109	126	96	63	61	149	162	196	214 c	184	175
Turkey	X	X	276	322	398	X	X	X	X	(175)	(175)	X
United Kingdom	6,424	5,368	4,898	3,724	3,780	3,565	2,293	2,245	2,365	2,392	2,779	2,747
United States	28,420	25,510	23,780	21,670	21,060	20,730	18,960	20,330	23,560	19,390	19,380	18,760
U.S.S.R. (former) {d}	X	X	12,800	11,110	8,930	X	X	X	3,167	3,369	4,407	X
Belarus	X	X	740	690	584	X	X	X	244	220	271	X
Ukraine	X	X	3,850	3,464	2,782	X	X	X	X	1,059	1,097	X
Yugoslavia (former)	X	X	1,176	1,500	1,480	X	X	X	350	400	420	X

Sources: Co-operative Programme for Monitoring and Evaluation of the Long-Range Transmission of Air Pollutants in Europe (EMEP); the Organisation for Economic Co-operation and Development; and the United Nations Economic Commission for Europe.
Notes: a. 1986 data. b. 1989 data. c. 1984 data. d. European part of the U.S.S.R. under the purview of EMEP.
X = not available. Emissions in parentheses were estimated by EMEP.
For additional information, see Sources and Technical Notes.

Table 23.6 Common Anthropogenic Pollutants, 1980–91

	Carbon Monoxide (000 metric tons)				Particulate Matter (000 metric tons)				Hydrocarbons (000 metric tons)			
	1980	1985	1990	1991	1980	1985	1990	1991	1980	1985	1990	1991
Albania	X	X	X	X	X	X	X	X	(30)	(30)	X	X
Austria	1,636	1,648	1,573	1,503	79	58	39	38	374	412	430	419
Belgium	839	X	X	X	X	X	X	X	374	374	X	X
Bulgaria	X	X	X	X	X	X	X	X	2,594	2,594	X	X
Canada	10,273	10,781	X	X	1,907	1,709	X	X	2,099	2,315	2,256	X
Czechoslovakia (former)	X	1,239	1,291	X	1,350	1,372	940	X	X	197	304	X
Denmark	X	X	X	X	X	X	X	X	197	146	174 a	X
Finland	660	X	484	X	X	X	X	X	163	181	229	X
France	9,316	8,399	7,580	7,338	427	303	276	287	1,975	1,877	X	X
German Dem Rep	3,409	3,664	3,803	X	2,498	2,364	1,825	X	886	942	1,144	X
Germany, Fed Rep	12,006	8,894	8,177	X	692	574	450	X	2,754	2,624	2,545	X
Greece	X	X	X	X	X	X	X	X	(260)	(260)	X	X
Hungary	1,730	1,800	X	X	576	492	343 a	X	(270)	(270)	X	X
Iceland	29	33	44	45	X	X	X	X	5	6	8	10
Ireland	497	456	454	X	94	117	105	X	101	91	97	X
Italy	5,487	6,919	6,590 a	X	433	445	501 a	X	696	1,771	1,912 a	X
Japan	X	X	X	X	X	X	X	X	X	X	X	X
Luxembourg	X	240	X	X	X	3	X	X	11	20	X	X
Netherlands	1,518	1,304	1,040	993	158	88	72	71	560	514	464	447
Norway	885	958	951	909	24	21	21	21	169	215	249	253
Poland	3,403	2,545	2,524	2,263	X	X	1,950	1,680	700	700	1,280	X
Portugal	533	X	X	X	119	X	X	X	92	134	168	X
Romania	X	X	X	X	X	X	X	X	(440)	(440)	X	X
Spain	3,780	X	X	X	X	814	X	X	760	785	X	X
Sweden	1,450	X	X	X	170	X	X	X	410	446	440 b	X
Switzerland	711	624 c	431	406	28	22 c	20	X	311	339 c	297	290
Turkey	X	X	X	X	X	X	X	X	(700)	(700)	X	X
United Kingdom	5,034	5,554	6,701	6,735	560	545	473	498	2,442	2,497	2,600	2,596
United States	99,970	83,120	67,740	62,100	9,060	7,850	7,400	7,410	21,750	19,800	17,580	16,880
U.S.S.R. (former) {d}	X	X	X	X	X	X	X	X	7,000	6,639	10,411	X
Belarus	X	X	X	X	X	X	X	X	549	516	508	X
Ukraine	X	X	X	X	X	X	X	X	X	1626	1369	X
Yugoslavia (former)	X	X	X	X	X	X	X	X	(600)	(600)	X	X

Sources: Co-operative Programme for Monitoring and Evaluation of the Long-Range Transmission of Air Pollutants in Europe (EMEP); the Organisation for Economic Co-operation and Development; and the United Nations Economic Commission for Europe.
Notes: a. 1989 data. b: 1988 data. c. 1984 data. d. European part of the U.S.S.R. under the purview of EMEP.
X = not available. Emissions in parentheses were estimated by EMEP.
For additional information, see Sources and Technical Notes.

Sources and Technical Notes

Table 23.1 CO₂ Emissions from Industrial Processes, 1991

Source: Carbon Dioxide Information Analysis Center (CDIAC), Environmental Sciences Division, Oak Ridge National Laboratory, "1991 Estimates of CO₂ Emissions from Fossil Fuel Burning and Cement Manufacturing Based on the United Nations Energy Statistics and the U.S. Bureau of Mines Cement Manufacturing Data," ORNL/CDIAC-25, NDP-030 (an accessible numerical data base) (Oak Ridge, Tennessee, September 1993).

This table includes data on industrial additions to the carbon dioxide flux from *solid* fuels, *liquid* fuels, *gas* fuels, *gas flaring*, and *cement manufacture*. CDIAC annually calculates emissions of CO₂ from the burning of fossil fuels and the manufacture of cement for most of the countries of the world. Estimates of total and per capita national emissions do not include *bunker fuels* used in international transport because of the difficulty of apportioning these fuels among the countries benefiting from that transport. Emissions from bunker fuels are shown separately for the country where the fuel was delivered.

CDIAC calculates emissions from data on the net apparent consumption of fossil fuels (based on the World Energy Data Set maintained by the United Nations Statistical Division) and from data on world cement manufacture (based on the Cement Manufacturing Data Set maintained by the U.S. Bureau of Mines). Emissions are calculated using global average fuel chemistry and usage. For 1991, CDIAC independently calculated emissions that resulted from the sabotage of Kuwaiti oil wells and used United Nations energy data on gas flaring from those wells to estimate total emissions from those fires. These emissions have been assigned to Iraq as the culpable party.

Although estimates of world emissions are probably within 10 percent of actual emissions, individual country estimates may depart more severely from reality. CDIAC points out that the time trends from a consistent and uniform time series "should be more accurate than the individual values." Each year, CDIAC recalculates the entire time series from 1950 to the present, incorporating their most recent understanding and the latest corrections to the data base. As a result, the estimated CO₂ emissions data set has become more consistent, and probably more accurate, each year.

Emissions of CO₂ are often calculated and reported in terms of their content of elemental carbon. CDIAC reports them that way. For this table, CDIAC's figures were converted to the actual mass of CO₂ by multiplying the carbon mass by 3.664 (the ratio of the mass of carbon to that of CO₂).

Solid, liquid, and *gas* fuels are primarily, but not exclusively, coals, petroleum products, and natural gas. *Gas flaring* is the practice of burning off gas released in the process of petroleum extraction, a practice that is declining. During *cement manufacture,* cement is calcined to produce calcium oxide. In the process, 0.498 metric ton of CO₂ is released for each metric ton of cement produced. *Total* emissions consist of the sum of the CO₂ produced during the consumption of solid, liquid, and gas fuels, and from gas flaring and the manufacture of cement.

Combustion of different fossil fuels releases CO₂ at different rates for the same level of energy production. Burning oil releases about 1.5 times the amount of CO₂ released from burning natural gas; burning coal releases about twice as much CO₂ as natural gas.

It was assumed that approximately 1 percent of the coal used by industry and power plants was not burned and that an additional few percent were converted to nonoxidizing uses. Other oxidative reactions of coal are assumed to be of negligible importance in carbon budget modeling. CO₂ emissions from gas flaring and cement production make up about 3 percent of the CO₂ emitted by fossil fuel combustion.

These data from CDIAC are the only complete global data set of CO₂ emissions. Individual country estimates are based on more detailed information and a country-specific methodology, could differ. An experts meeting convened by the Organisation for Economic Co-operation and Development in February 1991 yielded the recommendation that when countries calculate their own emissions of CO₂, they use a more detailed method when these data are available. Such data are available for only a few countries, and resulting inventories, if any, are not readily available. CDIAC's method has the advantage of calculating CO₂ emissions from a single common data set available for all countries.

Table 23.2 Other Greenhouse Gas Emissions, 1991

Sources: Land-use change: United Nations Food and Agriculture Organization (FAO), *Forest Resources Assessment 1990: Tropical Countries* (FAO, Forestry Paper 112, Rome, 1993).

Methane (CH₄) emitted from municipal solid waste: Jean Lerner, National Aeronautics and Space Administration Goddard Space Flight Center, Institute for Space Studies, May 1989 (personal communication); H.G. Bingemer and P.J. Crutzen, "The Production of CH₄ from Solid Wastes," *Journal of Geophysical Research,* Vol. 92, No. D2 (1987), pp. 2181–2187.

CH₄ produced from coal mining: D.W. Barns and J.A. Edmonds, *An Evaluation of the Relationship Between the Production and Use of Energy and Atmospheric Methane Emissions,* Carbon Dioxide Research Program, No. TR047 (U.S. Department of Energy, Office of Energy Research, 1990); World En-

ergy Council (WEC), *1991 Survey of Energy Resources* (WEC, London, 1992).

CH₄ resulting from oil and gas production and distribution: D.W. Barns and J.A. Edmonds, *An Evaluation of the Relationship Between the Production and Use of Energy and Atmospheric Methane Emissions* (U.S. Department of Energy, Office of Energy Research, Carbon Dioxide Research Program, No. TR047, April 1990); Carbon Dioxide Information Analysis Center (CDIAC), Environmental Sciences Division, Oak Ridge National Laboratory, "1991 Estimates of CO₂ Emissions from Fossil Fuel Burning and Cement Manufacturing Based on the United Nations Energy Statistics and the U.S. Bureau of Mines Cement Manufacturing Data," ORNL/CDIAC-25, NDP-030 (an accessible numerical data base) (Oak Ridge, Tennessee, September 1993); American Gas Association (AGA), "Natural Gas and Climate Change: The Greenhouse Effect," Issue Brief 1989-7 (AGA, Washington, D.C., June 14, 1989); A.A. Makarov and I.A. Basmakov, *The Soviet Union: A Strategy of Energy Development with Minimum Emission of Greenhouse Gases* (Pacific Northwest Laboratory, Richland, Washington, 1990); and S. Hobart, David Spottiswoode, James Ball, *et al., Methane Leakage from Natural Gas Operations* (The Alphatania Group, London, 1989).

CH₄ emitted from wet rice agriculture: FAO, *Agrostat PC* (FAO, Rome, 1993); and Elaine Mathews, Inez Fung, and Jean Lerner, "Methane Emission from Rice Cultivation: Geographic and Seasonal Distribution of Cultivated Areas and Emissions," *Global Biogeochemical Cycles,* Vol. 5, No. 1 (March 1991), pp. 3–24.

CH₄ produced from livestock: Jean Lerner, Elaine Mathews, and Inez Fung, "Methane Emissions from Animals: A Global High-Resolution Data Base," *Global Biogeochemical Cycles,* Vol. 2, No. 2 (June 1988), pp. 139–156; and FAO, *Agrostat PC* (FAO, Rome, 1993).

Chlorofluorocarbon (CFC) emissions: WRI estimate based on information from the U.S. Environmental Protection Agency, Stratospheric Protection Program, Office of Program Development and Office of Air and Radiation, *Appendices to Regulatory Impact Analysis: Protection of Stratospheric Ozone* (Washington, D.C., August 1988), Vol. 2, Part 2, Appendix K, pp. K-2-4–K-2-6; Alliance for Responsible CFC Use, unpublished data (Alliance for Responsible CFC Use, Arlington, Virginia, 1989); United Nations Environment Programme (UNEP), *Environmental Data Report* (Basil Blackwell Ltd., Oxford, 1991), pp. 26–27; and UNEP, *Report of the Secretariat on the Reporting of Data by the Parties in Accordance with Article 7 of the Montreal Protocol* (UNEP, Nairobi, 1991).

CO₂, CH₄, CFC-11, and CFC-12 are the four most important greenhouse gases. This table provides estimates of annual emissions of CO₂ from land use change (i.e., deforestation), CH₄ emissions by source, and current annual emissions of CFC-11 and CFC-12 combined. Nitrous oxide, tropospheric ozone, and other CFCs are also important to the greenhouse effect but have not been well studied and are more difficult to estimate, especially at the national level. Tropospheric ozone has an average lifetime measured in hours and is a product of chemical processes involving the precursors CH_4, carbon monoxide, nitrogen oxides, and nonmethane hydrocarbons in the presence of sunlight. Nitrous oxide emissions by country have proven difficult to estimate, in part because significant emissions are poorly understood. Production estimates and emission parameters from CFCs other than CFC-11 and CFC-12 are not available.

The Organisation for Economic Co-operation and Development (OECD) hosted an experts meeting in February 1991 on greenhouse emissions (its final report was published in August 1991, *Estimation of Greenhouse Gas Emissions and Sinks* (OECD, Paris)) to discuss methodologies that countries could use to estimate their own inventories of greenhouse gases (other than CFCs) and to point out areas requiring further research. Although these discussions illuminated and defined the methods used here, the final published recommendations were directed toward informing governments on what data they could collect and what kind of basic country-specific (and even ecosystem-specific) research is required if they are to "assess their contribution to greenhouse gas emissions in an international context." The final OECD report included additional suggested data sets and methods not fully discussed or validated during the meeting (e.g., a suggested source of deforestation data).

The emissions estimates in this table can be controversial but are believed to be both accurate estimates of the relative magnitudes of emissions and the best estimates possible, given the available data sets. WRI welcomes independent estimates of anthropogenic emissions of greenhouse gases from the countries of the world. The methods used here were chosen to maximize the use of the available international data so as to be comparable among countries. The international data set on any subject is limited, and so these estimates are also limited. Until most of the countries of the world publish their own independent estimates—based on common methods and scientifically valid parameters—global comparisons will require the use of the methods of the least common data set. Common methods and parameters were used among countries unless differing, but explicit and published, parameters were available that covered all countries. For example, estimates of CH_4 resulting from coal mining were based on published data on the differing CH_4 content of the various types of coal produced in each country. More complex calculations—which might have been possible for one or two data-rich countries—are inappropriate for the world as a whole and were not attempted even for those few

countries that might have sufficient (and uncontroversial) data.

A recently published alternative accounting of national greenhouse gas emissions for 1988 (Susan Subak, Paul Raskin, and David Von Hippel, *National Greenhouse Gas Accounts: Current Anthropogenic Sources and Sinks* (Stockholm Environment Institute, Boston, 1992)) generally produced results similar to those reported in past editions of the present volume and generally followed similar methodologies. WRI adopted their methodological refinement for estimating methane emissions from solid wastes.

Carbon dioxide emissions from land-use change are based on FAO estimates of deforestation and forest biomass for the world's tropical countries. The burning of biomass, per se, does not necessarily contribute to the CO_2 flux. Fire is a natural phenomenon, and as long as burning and growth are in balance, there is no net movement of carbon from biomass to the atmosphere. Deforestation, however, is defined as the conversion of land from forest to other uses. Carbon released in this process will not be replaced.

The carbon density used to estimate CO_2 emissions was 45 percent of biomass, and biomass estimates were taken from average forest densities for whole countries as reported by the FAO. These CO_2 emission estimates explicitly include shifting cultivation and the diversion of forest fallow to permanent clearing. They are also consistent and global in scope. They are the most complete estimates to date but are subject to modification should better data become available. Nevertheless, individual countries question these FAO estimates. See Sources and Technical Notes for Table 19.1 for further information.

Although, in principle, emissions from land-use change should also include the emissions of other gases resulting from the burning of forest land, as well as emissions from the burning of grassland, the conversion of grassland to crop land, the creation of wetlands, and the burning of crop and animal residues, the international data sets needed to estimate these emissions do not exist (OECD experts meeting). Except for CO_2 emissions resulting from deforestation, then, emissions from biomass burning in general are not available. Grass or trees that grow back after a fire merely recycle the available carbon and do not contribute CO_2 to long-term greenhouse warming.

WRI subtracted elemental carbon permanently sequestered in the soil (an estimated 5 percent of the biomass carbon) and also subtracted the weight of carbon contained in sawlogs and veneer logs (FAO, *Agrostat PC* (FAO, Rome, 1993)) produced in each tropical country from CO_2 releases calculated from land-use change. Carbon was estimated as making up 45 percent of the weight of these wood products. This step was taken to approximate the amount of carbon removed from the global carbon cycle by the production of durable wooden goods. This is only an estimate because portions of other forest products are also sequestered (e.g., books in libraries, pit

props, and utility poles), and portions of saw and veneer logs are consumed (e.g., wastewood and discarded plywood sheets used in concrete form building). This should lead to a small underestimate of total CO_2 emissions because it includes logs from areas not counted as having been deforested. The methods for estimating CO_2 emissions from land-use change, suggested at the OECD experts meeting, requires data and research into processes that do not yet exist. The method used here parallels that found in the work of R.A. Houghton, R.D. Boone, J.R. Fruci, *et al.*, "The Flux of Carbon from Terrestrial Ecosystems to the Atmosphere in 1980 Due to Changes in Land Use: Geographic Distribution of the Global Flux," *Tellus*, Vol. 39B, Nos. 1–2 (1987), pp. 122–139, which was peer reviewed.

Choices must be made regarding the exact parameters to use in these calculations, but the deforestation and carbon density measures used here are the best general parameters available. The parameters used for this calculation were based on consistent definitions and common data sources. Even if slightly lower values were used for deforestation and biomass per area, the magnitude of carbon emissions would remain about the same. These estimates are thus a good first approximation to current (i.e., circa 1991) carbon emissions that result from land-use changes. There is some suggestion that northern temperate and boreal forest areas are net sinks for atmospheric carbon, although this, too, is controversial.

CH_4 emissions from municipal *solid waste* were calculated by multiplying the 1991 population by per capita emission coefficients developed for each country by H.G. Bingemer and P.J. Crutzen in "The Production of CH_4 from Solid Wastes," *Journal of Geophysical Research,* Vol. 92, No. D2 (1987), pp. 2181–2187, and by S.D. Piccot, A. Chadha, J. De Waters, *et al.* in "Evaluation of Significant Anthropogenic Sources of Radiatively Important Trace Gases" (Office of Research and Development, U.S. Environmental Protection Agency, Washington, D.C., 1990), cited in OECD, *Estimation of Greenhouse Gas Emissions and Sinks* (OECD, Paris, August 1991), taking into account the proportion of solid waste landfilled and its degradable organic carbon content. R.J. Cicerone and R.S. Oremland in "Biogeochemical Aspects of Atmospheric Methane" *Global Biogeochemical Cycles*, Vol. 2, No. 4 (December 1988), pp. 299–327, suggest a likely range for annual world CH_4 emissions from landfills at 30–70 million metric tons. The method used here parallels that recommended at the OECD experts meeting.

CH_4 emissions from *coal mining* were estimated using information on the average CH_4 content of the anthracite and bituminous coals, subbituminous coals, and lignite mined (WEC) around the world. This data set is updated only every three years; thus the most recent year for which data are available is 1990. Less detailed data sets are available but are inadequate to the task. This estimate assumed that 100 percent of the CH_4 in extracted coal was emitted, although this is a slight exaggeration. CH_4 is often emitted from mines in larger quantities than would be expected, based on the amount of CH_4 contained only in the coal removed—although in the long run, the CH_4 in an extractable deposit of coal will be emitted, on average, at the rate that it is mined. CH_4 trapped within the rock is released by mining, and it is one of the hazards of underground coal mining. Cicerone and Oremland (*Aspects of Atmospheric Methane*) show a likely range of 25–45 million metric tons of CH_4 emitted annually in the course of mining coal. No international data set exists that would allow internationally comparable estimates using the methodology suggested by the OECD in its report on the experts meeting.

Substantial quantities of CH_4 are released to the atmosphere during oil and gas production and distribution. The amount of CH_4 vented in the course of oil production is estimated at 25 percent of the amount that is flared (Gregg Marland, Carbon Dioxide Information and Analysis Center (CDIAC), 1990 (personal communication)). The estimates of CO_2 emissions from gas flaring in Table 23.1 also include gas that is vented (see also Barns and Edmonds, p. 3.9). CH_4 emissions from natural gas production were estimated at 0.5 percent of production (Barns and Edmonds, pp. 3.2–3.3). Recent estimates show that CH_4 leakage from distribution systems is no more than 1 percent in the United States (AGA, "Natural Gas and Climate Change: The Greenhouse Effect") and no more than 1.7 percent in the former U.S.S.R. (Makarov and Basmakov, *The Soviet Union: A Strategy of Energy Development with Minimum Emission of Greenhouse Gases*), although careful surveys have not been done. There is reason to believe that pipeline leaks in the former U.S.S.R. are grossly understated—although the former U.S.S.R.'s natural gas volume is sometimes mistakenly overstated—but other estimates are nonexistent. For these estimates, the U.S. experience was extended to Western Europe, Canada was counted at half the U.S. rate, and the Soviet estimate was used for Central Europe and the developing world because their situations were thought to be similar (S. Hobart *et al.*, *Methane Leakage from Natural Gas Operations*). Cicerone and Oremland (*Aspects of Atmospheric Methane*) suggest a likely range of 25 million to 50 million metric tons of CH_4 emitted because of leaks associated with natural gas drilling, venting, and transmission. The OECD experts meeting developed a general conceptual model on how to estimate emissions from these production and distribution systems, but it was unable to identify data on the factors leading to emissions or any individual data source to use for this purpose.

CH_4 emissions from the practice of *wet rice agriculture* were calculated using the area of rice production (as reported by the FAO, *Agrostat PC* (FAO, Rome, 1993)) minus those areas devoted to dry (upland) and deepwater (floating) rice production in each country or, in the case of China and In-

dia, in each province (Dana G. Dalrymple, *Development and Spread of High-Yielding Rice Varieties in Developing Countries*, Bureau of Science and Technology, U.S. Agency for International Development, Washington, D.C., 1986; and Robert E. Huke, *Rice Area by Type of Culture: South, Southeast, and East Asia*, International Rice Research Institute, Los Baños, Laguna, Philippines, 1982). This estimate follows the method suggested in the OECD experts meeting report and calculates the number of days of rice cultivation and the percentage of total rice area in each crop cycle by country or, in the case of China and India, by province (Elaine Mathews, Inez Fung, and Jean Lerner, "Methane Emissions from Rice Cultivation: Geographic and Seasonal Distribution of Cultivated Areas and Emissions," *Global Biogeochemical Cycles*, Vol. 5, No. 1 (March 1991), pp. 3–24).

There are many different studies of CH_4 emissions from wet rice agriculture. In the past, many of these studies had been criticized because they had been undertaken on temperate rices grown in North America or Europe. Recently published studies, based on similar rigorous methods, from subtropical China have dispelled some of that criticism. Studies using similar methodologies are expected soon from Indonesia and India. The OECD experts meeting report recommended using a range of emissions found in a study in China (0.19–0.69 grams of CH_4 per m^2 per day, H. Schütz, W. Seiler, and H. Rennenberg, presented by H. Rennenberg at the International Conference on Soils and the Greenhouse Effect, August 14–18, 1989, Wageningen, the Netherlands, reported at the OECD experts meeting). The estimate used here was based on the midpoint of that range (0.44 grams of CH_4 per m^2 per day), assuming that this range is an unbiased estimate of the normally distributed range of CH_4 emissions. Alternate estimates are possible.

A two-year study in the subtropical rice bowl of China (Szechuan province) produced an estimated median flux (from some 3,000 flux estimates) of about 1.2 grams of CH_4 per m^2 per day and a mean flux of 1.39 grams of CH_4 per m^2 per day (M.A.K. Khalil, R.A. Rasmussen, Ming-Xing Wang, and Lixin Ren, "Methane Emissions from Rice Fields in China," *Environmental Science and Technology*, Vol. 25, No. 5 (1991), pp. 979–981). Studies in Europe and North America seem to support the range suggested at the OECD experts meeting. See the sources for more information. In general, estimates of CH_4 flux are based on a technique that captures the CH_4 produced anaerobically before the growth of the rice plant as well as the bulk of the CH_4 that is transported through the rice plant throughout the growing period. Growing periods, the type of rice cultivar, fertilizer, temperature, and possibly the use of pesticides could influence methanogenesis. In the tropics, using modern varieties of rice, sufficient fertilizer, and adequate water, two or even three crops per year are possible.

The cultivation of rice uses common techniques in both temperate and tropical

climes, even if the cultivars are not interchangeable. The preparation of the impoundments wherein wet rice is grown—the creation of a hardpan overlain by soft anaerobic muck—creates similar environmental and chemical regimes wherever it occurs. Nonetheless, variations in water quality, soils, ambient temperature, precision of water control, and the presence of cultivated algae or fish could also affect the total CH_4 flux.

Wet rice agriculture is practiced under four main water regimes: irrigated (52.8 percent of the world's total rice area), rainfed (similar to irrigated, 22.6 percent of the total), deep water (often dry in the early part of the season, may be planted to floating rice, 8.2 percent of the world's rice area), and tidal (3.4 percent of the total). Cicerone and Oremland (*Aspects of Atmospheric Methane*) suggest a likely range of 60 million to 170 million metric tons of CH_4 emissions due to wet rice agriculture.

CH_4 emissions from domestic *livestock* were calculated using FAO statistics on animal populations and published estimates of CH_4 emissions from each type of animal raised. The animals studied included cattle and dairy cows, water buffalo, sheep, goats, camels, pigs, and caribou. P.J. Crutzen, I. Aselmann, and W. Seiler ("Methane Production by Domestic Animals, Wild Ruminants, Other Herbivorous Fauna, and Humans," *Tellus*, Vol. 38B (1986), pp. 271–284) estimated CH_4 production by animals on the basis of energy intake under several different management methods for several different feeding regimes. These different emission coefficients were then assigned to each country, based on that country's animal husbandry practices and the nature and quality of feed available. Cicerone and Oremland's *Aspects of Atmospheric Methane* shows a likely range of 65 million to 100 million metric tons of CH_4 emissions from enteric fermentation in domestic animals. Alternate methods of estimation, such as a complex modeling method suggested in the OECD experts meeting report, are not yet possible because of the lack of basic data.

The only other major anthropogenic sources of CH_4 unaccounted for here are emissions consequent to the burning of biomass. Extensive biomass burning, especially in the tropics, is believed to release large amounts of CH_4. Cicerone and Oremland (*Aspects of Atmospheric Methane*) put the likely range of those emissions at 50 million to 100 million metric tons. The OECD experts meeting elaborated on the absence of data that would be necessary for countries to estimate CH_4 emissions from biomass burning.

Other natural sources of CH_4 include wetlands, methane hydrate destabilization in permafrost, termites, freshwater lakes, oceans, and enteric emissions from other animals. Natural sources account for an estimated 25 percent of all CH_4 emissions. Cicerone and Oremland (*Aspects of Atmospheric Methane*) estimate likely ranges of CH_4 emissions at 100 million to 200 million metric tons from natural wetlands, 10 million to 100 million metric tons from termites, 5 million to 25 million metric tons from the oceans, 1 million to 25 million metric tons from freshwater, and possible releases of 5 million metric tons (potentially rising to 100 million metric tons if temperatures increase in the high arctic) from methane hydrate destabilization.

WRI has estimated total *chlorofluorocarbon* use (CFC-11 and CFC-12) for many countries. It used data on 1986 per capita production and use from 47 countries and the European Community (EC) to estimate consumption in other similar countries, and updated these estimates using consumption data for 15 countries plus the EC in 1989. This estimate was based in part on the general level of total CFC (including CFC-113 and CFC-22) consumption (i.e., less than 0.3 kg, 0.3–0.5 kg, and over 0.5 kg, from the Alliance for Responsible CFC Use) and other relevant information. These data are, therefore, a mix of reported and estimated numbers. Consumption data for the EC, as reported by the EC and UNEP, were allocated to each member country in proportion to its share of the total EC population. Thus all EC members are tied and among the highest per capita consumers of CFCs. (The EC could have reported consumption by country but chose not to.)

Table 23.3 Atmospheric Concentrations of Greenhouse and Ozone-Depleting Gases, 1959–92

Sources: Carbon dioxide: C.D. Keeling, R.B. Bacastow, A.F. Carter, *et al.*, "A Three-Dimensional Model of Atmospheric CO_2 Transport Based on Observed Winds: 1. Observational Data and Preliminary Analysis," *Aspects of Climate Variability in the Pacific and the Western Americas,* American Geophysical Union (AGU) Monograph No. 55 (AGU, Washington, D.C., 1989), pp. 165–236; and C.D. Keeling, Scripps Institution of Oceanography, La Jolla, California, 1993 (personal communication). Other gases: R.A. Rasmussen and M.A.K. Khalil, "Atmospheric Trace Gases: Trends and Distributions Over the Last Decade," *Science,* Vol. 232, pp. 1623–1624. Concentrations of CCl_3F (CFC-11): M.A.K. Khalil and R.A. Rasmussen, "The Environmental History and Probable Future of Fluorocarbon-11" (submitted to *Journal of Geophysical Research,* 1993). Concentrations after 1985 of CCl_4, CH_3CCl_3, and N_2O: M.A.K. Khalil and R.A. Rasmussen, unpublished data (Oregon Graduate Center, Beaverton, September 1989). Concentrations of CCl_2F_2 (CFC-12) from 1981 to 1992: M.A.K. Khalil and R.A. Rasmussen, unpublished data (Oregon Graduate Center, Beaverton, September 1993). $C_2Cl_3F_3$ (CFC-113): M.A.K. Khalil and R.A. Rasmussen, unpublished data (Oregon Graduate Center, Beaverton, September 1989). Concentrations of CO from 1981 to 1992: M.A.K. Khalil and R.A. Rasmussen, unpublished data (Oregon Graduate Center, Beaverton, September 1993), submitted for publication to *Nature.* CH_4 data, 1979–88: M.A.K. Khalil and R.A. Rasmussen, "Atmospheric Methane: Re-

cent Global Trends," 1989 (draft paper used with permission). CH_4 data, 1962–78: M.A.K. Khalil, R.A. Rasmussen, and M.J. Shearer, "Trends of Atmospheric Methane During the 1960s and 70s," *Journal of Geophysical Research,* Vol. 94, No. D15 (1989), pp. 18,279–18,288. Recent data, 1987–91: M.A.K. Khalil, 1993 (personal communication).

The trace gases listed here affect atmospheric ozone or contribute to the greenhouse effect, or both.

Carbon dioxide (CO_2) accounts for about half the increase in the greenhouse effect and is emitted to the atmosphere by natural and anthropogenic processes. See the Technical Notes for Tables 23.1 and 23.2 for further details.

Atmospheric CO_2 concentrations are monitored at many sites worldwide; the data presented here are from Mauna Loa, Hawaii (19.53° N, 155.58° W). Trends at Mauna Loa reflect global trends, although CO_2 concentrations differ significantly among monitoring sites at any given time. For example, the average annual concentration at the South Pole in 1988 was 2.4 parts per million (ppm) lower than at Mauna Loa.

Annual means disguise large daily and seasonal variations in CO_2 concentrations. The seasonal variation is caused by photosynthetic plants storing larger amounts of carbon from CO_2 during the summer than during the winter. Some annual mean figures were derived from interpolated data.

Data are revised to correct for drift in instrument calibration, hardware changes, and perturbations to "background" conditions. Details concerning data collection, revisions, and analysis are contained in C.D. Keeling, *et al.,* "Measurement of the Concentration of Carbon Dioxide at Mauna Loa Observatory, Hawaii," *Carbon Dioxide Review: 1982,* W.C. Clark, ed. (Oxford University Press, New York, 1982).

Calibration is necessary for all instruments used to measure trace gases. Although collected at the same site by the same investigators, trace gas concentrations before 1986 have not been recalibrated as have measurements from 1986 to 1990, which themselves should be considered preliminary. *Carbon tetrachloride (CCl_4)* is an intermediate product in the production of CFC-11 and CFC-12. It is also used in other chemical and pharmaceutical applications and for grain fumigation. Compared with other gases, CCl_4 makes a small contribution to the greenhouse effect and to stratospheric ozone depletion.

Methyl chloroform (CH_3CCl_3) is used primarily as an industrial degreasing agent and as a solvent for paints and adhesives. Its contribution to the greenhouse effect and to stratospheric ozone depletion is also small.

CFC-11 (CCl_3F), CFC-12 (CCl_2F_2), CFC-22 ($CHClF_2$), and *CFC-113 ($C_2Cl_3F_3$)* are potent depletors of stratospheric ozone. Together, their cumulative effect may equal one fourth of the greenhouse contribution of CO_2.

Total gaseous chlorine is calculated by multiplying the number of chlorine atoms in each of the chlorine-containing gases (car-

bon tetrachloride, methyl chloroform, and the CFCs) by the concentration of that gas.

Nitrous oxide (N_2O) is emitted by aerobic decomposition of organic matter in oceans and soils, by bacteria, by combustion of fossil fuels and biomass (fuelwood and cleared forests), by the use of nitrogen fertilizers, and through other processes. N_2O is an important depletor of stratospheric ozone; present levels may contribute one twelfth the amount contributed by CO_2 toward the greenhouse effect.

Methane (CH_4) is emitted through the release of natural gas and as one of the products of anaerobic respiration. Sources of anaerobic respiration include the soils of moist forests, wetlands, bogs, tundra, and lakes. Emission sources associated with human activities include livestock management (enteric fermentation in ruminants), anaerobic respiration in the soils associated with wet rice agriculture, and combustion of fossil fuels and biomass (fuelwood and cleared forests). CH_4 acts to increase ozone in the troposphere and lower stratosphere; its cumulative greenhouse effect is currently thought to be one third that of CO_2, but on a molecule-for-molecule basis, its effect, ignoring any feedback or involvement in atmospheric processes, is 11–30 times that of CO_2.

Carbon monoxide (CO) is emitted by motor traffic, other fossil fuel combustion, slash-and-burn agriculture, and chemical processes in the atmosphere such as the oxidation of CH_4. Increasing levels of CO can lead to an increase in tropospheric ozone and a buildup of other trace gases, particularly CH_4, in the atmosphere.

Data for all gases except CO_2, CFC-11, CFC-12, CH_4, and CO are from values monitored at Cape Meares, Oregon (45° N, 124° W). Although gas concentrations at any given time vary among monitoring sites, the data reported here reflect global trends. Data for CO, CFC-11, CFC-12, and CH_4 were taken from six sites spanning the Arctic to the Antarctic and are averaged to reflect global concentrations and trends.

Table 23.4 World CO_2 Emissions from Fossil Fuel Consumption and Cement Manufacture, 1950–91

Source: Carbon Dioxide Information Analysis Center (CDIAC), Environmental Sciences Division, Oak Ridge National Laboratory (CDIAC, unpublished data, Oak Ridge, Tennessee, September 1993).

CDIAC calculates world emissions from data on the global production of fossil fuels (based on the World Energy Data Set maintained by the United Nations Statistical Office) and from data on world cement manufacturing (based on the Cement Manufacturing Data Set maintained by the U.S. Bureau of Mines). Emissions are calculated using global average fuel chemistry and usage. These data account for all fuels including "bunker fuels" not accounted for in Table 23.1. For further information, see the Technical Notes for Table 23.1.

Table 23.5 Sulfur and Nitrogen Emissions, 1970–91

Source: Hilde Sandnes and Helge Styves, *Calculated Budgets for Airborne Acidifying Components in Europe 1985, 1987, 1988, 1989, 1990, and 1991* (Co-operative Programme for Monitoring and Evaluation of the Long-Range Transmission of Air Pollutants in Europe (EMEP), The Norwegian Meteorological Institute, Oslo, Technical Report No. 97, 1992), pp. 11–14; Economic Commission for Europe (ECE), *Impacts of Long-Range Transboundary Air Pollution*, ECE Air Pollution Studies 8 (United Nations, New York, 1992), pp. 4–5; and Organisation for Economic Co-operation and Development (OECD), *OECD Environmental Data Compendium 1993* (OECD, Paris, 1993), pp. 17–23.

Emissions of *sulfur* in the form of sulfur oxides and of *nitrogen* in the form of its various oxides together contribute to acid rain and adversely affect agriculture, forests, aquatic habitats, and the weathering of building materials. Sulfate and nitrate aerosols impair visibility. These data on anthropogenic sources should be used carefully. Because different methods and procedures may have been used in each country, the best comparative data may be time trends within a country.

Sulfur dioxide (SO_2) is created by natural as well as anthropogenic activities. High concentrations of SO_2 have important health effects, and there is particular concern for the health of young children, the elderly, and people with existing respiratory illness (e.g., asthma). SO_2 in the presence of moisture contributes to acid precipitation as sulfuric acid.

Anthropogenic sources of nitrogen oxides come mainly from industrial sources and contribute to photochemical smog and the production of tropospheric ozone—an important greenhouse gas. All oxides of nitrogen also contribute to acid precipitation, in the form of nitric acid.

This table combines data from EMEP, ECE, and OECD to compile as complete a picture as possible of sulfur and nitrogen emissions. EMEP is an activity of the 1979 Convention on Long-Range Transboundary Air Pollution. Data on sulfur and nitrogen emissions are submitted to EMEP and ECE by parties to the 1985 protocol on SO_2 emissions and the 1988 protocol on nitrogen oxide emissions. Parties to these protocols should submit preliminary estimates of sulfur and nitrogen emissions by May of the year following and final estimates within a year after that. In the event of missing official data, EMEP interpolates between years with official data. If this is not possible, EMEP uses its own—or others'—emissions estimates.

OECD polls its members on emissions with questionnaires that are completed by the relevant national statistical service or designee. OECD does not have any independent estimation capability.

EMEP and ECE report emissions in terms of the elemental content of sulfur, whereas OECD reports emissions in terms of tons of sulfur oxides. EMEP's and ECE's emission estimates were converted to their weight in SO_2. EMEP and OECD report nitrogen emissions in terms of NO_2.

Please consult the sources for further information.

Table 23.6 Common Anthropogenic Pollutants, 1980–91

Source: Organisation for Economic Co-operation and Development (OECD), *OECD Environmental Data Compendium 1993* (OECD, Paris, 1993), pp. 25–30; and Economic Commission for Europe (ECE), *Impacts of Long-Range Transboundary Air Pollution*, ECE Air Pollution Studies 8 (United Nations, New York, 1992), p. 7.

This table reports OECD data for carbon monoxide (CO) and particulate matter emissions and combines data from both the Co-operative Programme for Monitoring and Evaluation of the Long-Range Transmission of Air Pollution in Europe (EMEP) and OECD data to describe the emissions of hydrocarbons. See the Sources and Technical Notes to Table 23.5 for additional information. Differences in definitions can limit the comparability of these estimates.

Carbon monoxide is formed both naturally and from industrial processes, including the incomplete combustion of fossil and other carbon-bearing fuels. Emissions from automobiles are the most important source of CO, especially in urban environments. CO interferes with oxygen uptake in the blood, producing chronic anoxia leading to illness or, in the case of massive and acute poisoning, even death. CO scavenges hydroxyl radicals that would otherwise contribute to the removal of methane—a potent greenhouse gas—from the atmosphere.

The health effects of *particulate matter (PM)* are in part dependent on the biological and chemical makeup and activity of the particles. Heavy metal particles or hydrocarbons condensed onto dust particles can be especially toxic. PM arises from numerous anthropogenic and natural sources. Among the anthropogenic sources are combustion, industrial and agricultural practices, and the formation of sulfates from sulfur dioxide emissions.

In the presence of sunlight, *hydrocarbons* are, along with oxides of nitrogen, responsible for photochemical smog. Anthropogenic emissions of hydrocarbons arise, in part, from the incomplete combustion of fuels or the evaporation of fuels, lubricants, and solvents as well as the incomplete burning of biomass. These data combine hydrocarbon emission data from OECD with volatile organic compound data from EMEP. EMEP uses OECD hydrocarbon data as volatile organic compound data for selected countries.

24. Policies and Institutions

Individual sovereign nations have come together to form structures of international governance, and to form agreements for common action and acceptable modes of behavior. This chapter details some of the environmentally relevant international agreements they have made, some of the available information sources on national, regional, and global environmental topics, and a description of the system of international governance, including the budgets of most its largest institutions.

International cooperation on the environment continues to grow. In June 1992, delegates to the United Nations Conference on Environment and Development (UNCED) approved three documents: the Rio Declaration on Environment and Development, Agenda 21 (a comprehensive plan to guide national and international action toward sustainable development), and a statement of 15 principles for the sustainable management of forests. In addition, two international treaties were signed; the Convention on Biological Diversity which went into force December 29, 1993, and the Convention on Climate Change, which by December 13, 1993, had been ratified by 44 of the required 50 countries.

Tables 24.1 and 24.2 present information on current country participation in key international conventions and regional agreements aimed at protecting the environment. In Africa, for example, realization of the dangers of uncontrolled toxic wastes has led to a convention on hazardous waste movement and management that was signed in 1991 in Bamako, Mali, by 17 countries and is in the ratification process. Another regional agreement in Europe and North America, the Convention on Environmental Impact Assessment in a Transboundary Context, which would help prevent, mitigate, and monitor significant transboundary environmental impacts, was signed in 1991 in Helsinki by 26 countries and two republics of the former U.S.S.R. In an effort to control levels of air pollutants from industrial sources, 27 industrialized nations (26 listed here, plus Liechtenstein) and two republics of the former U.S.S.R. have ratified the 1979 Geneva Convention on Long-Range Transboundary Air Pollution.

Examples of international conventions which appear in Table 24.1 and 24.2 are the Convention on the Law of the Sea, which will enter into force on November 16, 1994, and two conventions on nuclear accident notification and assistance created in response to the Chernobyl nuclear accident in April 1986.

Table 24.3 lists published sources of national environmental and natural resource information. These reports provide comprehensive assessments of natural resource and environmental conditions at the country level and often document trends and suggest policies for resource management. An increasing number of countries are preparing country and regional natural resource and environmental assessments, strategies, action plans, and compendiums of environmental statistics. In addition, almost all the nations of the world in preparation for UNCED, drafted reports that reflect national experiences and perspectives on environment and development.

Environmental information is increasingly being requested by foreign aid donors, development planners, resource policymakers, and finance ministers. This information is often an adjunct to action plans (e.g., the Tropical Forestry Action Plan, the National Conservation Strategy) or describes a sector or special issue (Biological Diversity Profile). The World Bank, for example, has increased its support of national environmental assessments and action plans for developing nations (particularly in Africa) that are produced by, or in cooperation with, governments. However, more resources are needed to help countries develop their own capacity for monitoring and assessing environmental problems.

Table 24.4 lists sources of global and regional environmental information. The Organisation of Economic Co-operation and Development state of the environment report and the Asian and Pacific state of the environment report are examples of the increasing number of regional environmental assessments. Large gaps remain in environmental information on the former U.S.S.R., the newly independent Baltic republics, Central Europe, and Africa.

Figure 24.5 provides a diagram of the United Nations system, including its specialized agencies and the associated institutions of the World Bank and the International Monetary Fund. Accompanying the description of the system are estimated expenditures for 1992–93.

Table 24.1 Participation in Major Global Conventions—

	Wildlife and Habitat						Oceans		
	Antarctic Treaty and Convention 1959 & 1980	Wetlands (Ramsar) 1971	World Heritage 1972	Endangered Species (CITES) 1973	Migratory Species 1979	Biodiversity 1992	Ocean Dumping 1972	Ship Pollution (MARPOL) 1978	Law of the Sea {a} 1982
WORLD									
AFRICA									
Algeria		CP	CP	CP		S		CP	S
Angola			CP			S			CP
Benin			CP	CP	CP	S			S
Botswana			CP	CP		S			CP
Burkina Faso		CP	CP	CP	CP	CP			S
Burundi			CP	CP		S			S
Cameroon			CP	CP	CP	S			CP
Central African Rep			CP	CP	S	S			S
Chad		CP		CP	S	S	S		S
Congo			CP	CP		S			S
Cote d'Ivoire			CP		S	S	CP	CP	CP
Djibouti				CP		S		CP	CP
Egypt		CP	CP	CP	CP	S		CP	CP
Equatorial Guinea									S
Ethiopia			CP	CP		S			S
Gabon		CP	CP	CP		S	CP	CP	S
Gambia, The			CP	CP		S		CP	CP
Ghana		CP	CP	CP	CP	S		CP	CP
Guinea		CP	CP	CP		CP			CP
Guinea-Bissau		CP		CP		S			CP
Kenya		CP	CP	CP		S	CP	CP	CP
Lesotho		CP		S		S	S		S
Liberia				CP		S	S	CP	S
Libya			CP			S	CP		S
Madagascar			CP	CP	S	S			S
Malawi			CP	CP		S			S
Mali		CP	CP	CP	CP	S			CP
Mauritania		CP	CP			S			S
Mauritius				CP		S			S
Morocco		CP	CP	CP	S	S	CP		S
Mozambique			CP	CP		S			S
Namibia				CP		S			CP
Niger		CP	CP	CP	CP	S			S
Nigeria			CP	CP	CP	S	CP		CP
Rwanda				CP		S			S
Senegal		CP	CP	CP	CP	S	S		CP
Sierra Leone									S
Somalia				CP	CP		S		CP
South Africa	CP, MLR	CP		CP	CP	S	CP	CP	S
Sudan			CP	CP		S			CP
Swaziland						S			S
Tanzania			CP	CP		S			CP
Togo				CP	S	S	S	CP	CP
Tunisia		CP	CP	CP	CP	CP	CP	CP	CP
Uganda		CP	CP	CP	S	CP			CP
Zaire			CP	CP	CP	S	CP		CP
Zambia		CP	CP	CP		CP			CP
Zimbabwe			CP	CP		S			S
ASIA									
Afghanistan			CP	CP		S	CP		S
Bangladesh		CP	CP	CP		S			S
Bhutan						S			S
Cambodia			CP	S			S		S
China	CP	CP	CP	CP		CP	CP	CP	S
India	CP, MLR	CP	CP	CP	CP	CP		CP	S
Indonesia			CP	CP		S		CP	CP
Iran, Islamic Rep		CP	CP	CP		S			S
Iraq			CP			S			CP
Israel				CP	CP			CP	
Japan	CP, MLR	CP	CP	CP		CP	CP	CP	S
Jordan		CP	CP	CP		CP	CP		
Korea, Dem People's Rep	CP					S		CP	S
Korea, Rep	CP, MLR		CP	CP		S		CP	S
Kuwait				S		S	S		CP
Lao People's Dem Rep			CP						S
Lebanon			CP						S
Malaysia			CP	CP		S	S	CP	S
Mongolia			CP			CP			S
Myanmar						S		CP	S
Nepal		CP	CP	CP		S	S		S
Oman			CP			S	CP	CP	CP
Pakistan		CP	CP	CP	CP	S			S
Philippines			CP	CP	S	CP	CP		CP
Singapore						S		CP	
Saudi Arabia			CP	CP		CP			S
Sri Lanka		CP	CP	CP	CP	S			S
Syrian Arab Rep			CP			S		CP	
Thailand			CP	CP		S		CP	S
Turkey			CP			S		CP	
United Arab Emirates				CP		S	CP		S
Viet Nam		CP	CP	S		S		CP	S
Yemen			CP			S			S

Wildlife, Habitat, and Oceans, 1993

Table 24.1

	Wildlife and Habitat						Oceans		
	Antarctic Treaty and Convention 1959 & 1980	Wetlands (Ramsar) 1971	World Heritage 1972	Endangered Species (CITES) 1973	Migratory Species 1979	Biodiversity 1992	Ocean Dumping 1972	Ship Pollution (MARPOL) 1978	Law of the Sea {a} 1982
NORTH & CENTRAL AMERICA									
Belize			CP	CP		S			CP
Canada	CP, MLR	CP	CP	CP		CP	CP	CP	S
Costa Rica		CP	CP	CP		S	CP		CP
Cuba	CP		CP	CP		S	CP	CP	CP
Dominican Rep			CP	CP		S	CP		S
El Salvador			CP	CP		S			S
Guatemala	CP	CP	CP	CP		S	CP		S
Haiti			CP			S	CP		S
Honduras			CP	CP		S	CP		S
Jamaica			CP		S	S	CP	CP	CP
Mexico		CP	CP	CP		CP	CP	CP	CP
Nicaragua			CP	CP		S			S
Panama		CP	CP	CP	CP	S	CP	CP	S
Trinidad and Tobago		CP		CP		S			CP
United States	CP, MLR	CP	CP	CP		S	CP	CP	
SOUTH AMERICA									
Argentina	CP, MLR	CP	CP	CP		S	CP		S
Bolivia		CP	CP	CP		S	S		S
Brazil	CP, MLR		CP	CP		S	CP	CP	CP
Chile	CP, MLR	CP	CP	CP	CP	S	CP		S
Colombia	CP		CP	CP		S	S	CP	S
Ecuador	CP	CP	CP	CP		CP		CP	
Guyana			CP	CP		S			S
Paraguay		S	CP	CP		S			CP
Peru	CP, MLR	CP	CP	CP		CP		CP	
Suriname		CP		CP	CP	S	CP	CP	S
Uruguay	CP, MLR	CP	CP	CP	CP	CP	S	CP	CP
Venezuela		CP	CP	CP		S	S		
EUROPE									
Albania			CP						
Austria	CP	CP	CP	CP		S		CP	S
Belgium	CP, MLR	CP	CP	CP	CP	S	CP	CP	S
Bulgaria	CP, MLR	CP	CP	CP		S		CP	S
Czechoslovakia (former)		CP b	CP b	CP b		S b		CP	S
Denmark	CP	CP	CP	CP	CP	S	CP	CP	S
Finland	CP, MLR	CP	CP	CP	CP	S	CP	CP	S
France	CP, MLR	CP	CP	CP	CP	S	CP	CP	S
Germany	CP, MLR	CP	CP	CP	CP	S	CP	CP	
Greece	CP, MLR	CP	CP	CP	S	S	CP	CP	S
Hungary	CP	CP	CP	CP	CP	S	CP	CP	S
Iceland		CP				S	CP	CP	CP
Ireland		CP	CP	S	CP	S	CP		S
Italy	CP, MLR	CP	CP	CP	CP	S	CP	CP	S
Netherlands	CP, MLR	CP	CP	CP	CP	S	CP	CP	S
Norway	CP, MLR	CP	CP	CP	CP	CP	CP	CP	S
Poland	CP, MLR	CP	CP	CP		S	CP	CP	S
Portugal		CP	CP	CP	CP	S	CP	CP	S
Romania	CP	CP	CP			S			S
Spain	CP, MLR	CP	CP	CP	CP	S	CP	CP	S
Sweden	CP, MLR	CP	CP	CP	CP	S	CP	CP	S
Switzerland	CP	CP	CP	CP		S	CP	CP	S
United Kingdom	CP, MLR	CP	CP	CP	CP	S	CP	CP	
Yugoslavia (former)		CP c	CP d			S e	CP c	CP c	CP
U.S.S.R. (former)									
Armenia		CP				CP			
Azerbaijan		CP				S			
Belarus			CP	CP		CP	CP		CP
Estonia		CP		CP		S			CP
Georgia		CP	CP						
Kazakhstan		CP				S			
Kyrgyzstan		CP							
Latvia						S			
Lithuania		CP	CP			S			CP
Moldova		CP				S			
Russian Federation	CP, MLR	CP	CP	CP		S	CP	CP	S
Tajikistan		CP	S						
Turkmenistan						S			
Ukraine			CP			S	CP		
Uzbekistan		CP	CP						
OCEANIA									
Australia	CP, MLR	CP	CP	CP	CP	CP	CP	CP	S
Fiji		CP				CP			CP
New Zealand	CP, MLR	CP	CP	CP		CP	CP	CP	S
Papua New Guinea	CP		CP	CP		CP	CP		S
Solomon Islands			CP			S			S

Sources: Environmental Law Information System of the World Conservation Union Environmental Law Centre and the United Nations Environment Programme.
Notes: a. Convention will enter into force November 16, 1994. b. Both the Czech and Slovak Republics. c. Croatia, Slovenia, and Yugoslavia. d. Croatia and Yugoslavia; Slovenia is a signatory only. e. The constituent republics of the former Yugoslavia inherited the status of signatories.
CP = contracting party (has ratified or taken equivalent action); S = signatory (has signed but not ratified); MLR = contracting party to the Convention on the Conservation of Antarctic Marine Living Resources.
Some small countries (signatories or contracting parties to the conventions and protocols listed) are not included in this table.
For formal titles of the conventions and protocols listed, and for additional information, see Sources and Technical Notes.

Table 24.2 Participation in Major Global Conventions—

	Global Conventions							Regional Agreements {b}	
	Atmosphere			Hazardous Substances					
	Ozone Layer 1985	CFC Control 1987	Climate Change {a} 1992	Biological and Toxin Weapons 1972	Nuclear Accident Notification 1986	Nuclear Accident Assistance 1986	Hazardous Waste Movement {a} 1989	UNEP Regional Seas	Other Regional Agreements
WORLD									
AFRICA									
Algeria	CP	CP	CP		S	S		M+	AFC
Angola			S						
Benin	CP	CP	S	CP				WCA*	AFC*, HW*
Botswana	CP	CP	S	CP					AFC*
Burkina Faso	CP	CP	CP	CP					HW*
Burundi			S	S					AFC*, HW*
Cameroon	CP	CP	S	S	S	S		WCA	AFC, HW*
Central African Rep	CP		S	S					AFC, HW*
Chad	CP		S						AFC*, HW*
Congo		S	S	CP				WCA	AFC
Cote d'Ivoire	CP	CP	S	S	S	S		WCA	AFC, HW*
Djibouti			S						AFC, HW*
Egypt	CP	CP	S	S	CP	CP		M+, RS	AFC, HW*
Equatorial Guinea	CP			CP					
Ethiopia			S	CP					AFC*
Gabon			S	S				WCA	AFC*
Gambia, The	CP	CP	S	S				WCA	AFC*
Ghana	CP	CP	S	CP				WCA	AFC
Guinea	CP	CP	CP	CP				WCA	AFC*, HW*
Guinea-Bissau			S	CP					HW*
Kenya	CP	CP	S	CP				EA+	AFC
Lesotho			S	CP					AFC*, HW*
Liberia			S					WCA*	AFC
Libya	CP	CP	S	CP		CP		M+	AFC*, HW*
Madagascar			S	S				EA*	AFC
Malawi	CP	CP	S	S					AFC
Mali			S	S	S	S			AFC, HW*
Mauritania			S					WCA*	AFC*
Mauritius			S	CP					AFC*
Morocco	S	S	S	S	S	S		M+	AFC
Mozambique			S						AFC
Namibia			S						
Niger	CP		S	CP	S	S		WCA	AFC, HW*
Nigeria	CP	CP	S	CP	CP	CP	CP	WCA	AFC
Rwanda			S	CP					AFC, HW*
Senegal		CP	S	CP	S	S	CP	WCA	AFC, EC, HW*
Sierra Leone		S	S	CP	S	S			AFC*
Somalia			S	S				EA*, RS	AFC*, HW*
South Africa	CP	CP	S	CP	CP	CP		RS	
Sudan	CP	CP	S		S	S		RS	AFC
Swaziland	CP	CP	S						AFC, HW*
Tanzania	CP	CP	S	S			CP		AFC, HW*
Togo	CP	CP	S	CP				WCA	AFC, HW*
Tunisia	CP	CP	CP	CP	CP	CP		M+	AFC, HW
Uganda	CP	CP	CP						AFC
Zaire			S	CP	S	S			AFC
Zambia	CP	CP	CP						AFC
Zimbabwe	CP	CP	CP	CP	S	S			HW
ASIA									
Afghanistan			S	CP	S	S	S		
Bangladesh	CP	CP	S	CP	CP	CP	CP		
Bhutan			S	CP					
Cambodia				CP					
China	CP	CP	CP	CP	CP	CP	CP		
India	CP	CP	CP	CP	CP	CP	CP		
Indonesia	CP	CP	S	CP	S	S			ASC
Iran, Islamic Rep	CP	CP	S	CP	S	S	CP	K+	
Iraq				CP	CP	CP		K+	
Israel	CP	CP	S		CP	CP	S	M+	
Japan	CP	CP	CP	CP	CP	CP			
Jordan	CP	CP	CP	CP	CP	CP	CP	RS	
Korea, Dem People's Rep			S	CP	S	S			
Korea, Rep	CP		S	CP	CP	CP			
Kuwait	CP			CP			S	K+	
Lao People's Dem Rep				CP					
Lebanon	CP		S	CP	S	S	S	M+	
Malaysia	CP	CP	S	CP	CP	CP			ASC
Mongolia			CP	CP	CP	CP			
Myanmar			S	S					
Nepal			S	S					
Oman			S	CP				K+	
Pakistan	CP	CP	S	CP		CP			
Philippines	CP	CP	S	CP			S		ASC
Saudi Arabia	CP	CP		CP	CP	CP	CP	K+, RS	
Singapore	CP	CP	S	CP					ASC
Sri Lanka	CP	CP	S	CP	CP	CP	CP		
Syrian Arab Rep	CP	CP	S		S	S	CP	M+	
Thailand	CP	CP	S	CP	CP	CP	S		ASC
Turkey	CP	CP		CP	S	S	S	M+, BS	EC, LR
United Arab Emirates	CP	CP		S	CP	CP	S	K+	
Viet Nam			S	CP	CP	CP			RS
Yemen			S					RS	

Atmosphere and Hazardous Substances, 1993 — Table 24.2

| | Global Conventions | | | | | | | Regional Agreements {b} | |
| | Atmosphere | | | Hazardous Substances | | | | | |
	Ozone Layer 1985	CFC Control 1987	Climate Change {a} 1992	Biological and Toxin Weapons 1972	Nuclear Accident Notification 1986	Nuclear Accident Assistance 1986	Hazardous Waste Movement {a} 1989	UNEP Regional Seas	Other Regional Agreements
NORTH & CENTRAL AMERICA									
Belize			S	CP					
Canada	CP	CP	CP	CP	CP	S	CP		LR+, EIA*
Costa Rica	CP	CP	S	CP	CP	S			
Cuba	CP	CP	S	CP	S	CP		C	
Dominican Rep	CP	CP	S	CP					
El Salvador	CP		S	CP			CP		
Guatemala	CP	CP	S	CP	CP	CP	S	C	
Haiti			S	S			S		
Honduras			S	CP				C*	
Jamaica	CP	CP	S	CP				C	
Mexico	CP	CP	CP	CP	CP	CP	CP	C	
Nicaragua	CP	CP	S	CP				C*	
Panama	CP	CP	S	CP	S	S	CP	SEP+, C	
Trinidad and Tobago	CP	CP	S					C	
United States	CP	CP	CP	CP	CP	CP	S	C, SP*	LR+, EIA*
SOUTH AMERICA									
Argentina	CP	CP	S	CP	CP	CP	CP		
Bolivia			S	CP			S		AMC
Brazil	CP	CP	S	CP	CP	CP	CP		AMC
Chile	CP	CP	S	CP	S	S	CP	SEP+	
Colombia	CP		S				S	SEP+, C	AMC
Ecuador	CP	CP	CP	CP			CP	SEP+	AMC
Guyana			S	S					AMC
Paraguay	CP	CP	S	CP	S	S			
Peru	CP	CP	CP	CP				SEP+	AMC
Suriname			S	CP					AMC
Uruguay	CP	CP	S	CP	CP	CP	CP	C	
Venezuela	CP	CP	S	CP			S		AMC
EUROPE									
Albania				CP				M+	EIA*
Austria	CP	CP	S	CP	CP	CP	CP		EC, LR+, EIA*
Belgium	CP	CP	S	CP	S	S	S		EC, LR+, EIA*
Bulgaria	CP	CP	S	CP	CP	CP		BS	EC, LR+, EIA*
Czechoslovakia (former)			CP	c	CP	d	CP	d		LR+, EIA*
Denmark	CP	CP	S	CP	CP	S	S		EC, LR+, EIA*
Finland	CP	CP	S	CP	CP	CP	CP		EC, LR+, EIA*
France	CP	CP	S	CP	CP	CP	CP	M+,C,EA+,SP+	EC, SPC, LR+, EIA*
Germany	CP	CP	S	CP	CP	CP	S		EC, LR+, EIA*
Greece	CP	CP	S	CP	CP	CP	S	M+	EC, LR, EIA*
Hungary	CP	CP	S	CP	CP	CP	CP		EC, LR+, EIA*
Iceland	CP	CP	CP	CP	CP	S			LR, EIA*
Ireland	CP	CP	S	CP	CP	CP	S		EC, LR, EIA*
Italy	CP	CP	S	CP	CP	CP	S	M+	EC, LR+, EIA*
Netherlands	CP	CP	S	CP	CP	CP	CP	C {e}	EC, LR+, EIA*
Norway	CP	CP	CP	CP	CP	CP	CP		EC, LR, EIA*
Poland	CP	CP	S	CP	CP	CP	CP		LR+, EIA*
Portugal	CP	CP	S	CP	S	S	S		EC, LR, EIA*
Romania	CP	CP	S	CP	CP	CP	CP	BS	LR+, EIA*
Spain	CP	CP	S	CP	CP	CP	S	M+	EC, LR+, EIA*
Sweden	CP	CP	CP	CP	CP	CP	CP		EC, LR+, EIA
Switzerland	CP	CP	S	CP	CP	CP	CP		EC, LR+
United Kingdom	CP	CP	S	CP	CP	CP	S	C {f}, SP*	EC, LR+, EIA*
Yugoslavia (former)	CP g	CP g	S h	CP i	CP g	CP g		M+	LR
U.S.S.R. (former)									LR+
Armenia			CP						
Azerbaijan			S						
Belarus	CP	CP	S	CP	CP	CP			LR+, EIA*
Estonia			S				CP		
Georgia								BS	
Kazakhstan			S						
Kyrgyzstan									
Latvia			S		CP	CP	CP		
Lithuania			S						
Moldova			S						
Russian Federation	CP	CP	S	CP	CP	CP	CP	BS	LR+, EIA*
Tajikistan									
Turkmenistan									
Ukraine	CP	CP	S	CP	CP	CP		BS	LR+, EIA*
Uzbekistan	CP	CP	CP						
OCEANIA									
Australia	CP	CP	CP	CP	CP	CP	CP	SP+	SPC
Fiji	CP	CP	CP	CP				SP+	SPC
New Zealand	CP	CP	CP	CP	CP	CP	S	SP+	
Papua New Guinea	CP	CP	CP	CP				SP+	SPC*
Solomon Islands	CP	CP	S	CP				SP+	

Sources: Environmental Law Information System of the World Conservation Union Environmental Law Centre and the United Nations Environment Programme (UNEP).

Notes: a. Convention not yet in force. b. Regional agreement letter codes (M, ML, etc.) indicate ratification of specific regional agreements. c. Czech Republic; the Slovak Republic is a signatory. d. Slovak Republic. e. Ratified on behalf of Aruba and the Netherlands Antilles Federation. f. Ratified on behalf of the British Virgin Islands, Cayman Islands, and the Turks and Caicos Islands. g. Croatia, Slovenia, and Yugoslavia. h. The constituent republics of the former Yugoslavia inherited the status of signatories. i. Slovenia and Yugoslavia. CP = contracting party (has ratified or taken equivalent action); S = signatory; + = has signed or ratified at least two protocols to this convention. * = signatory to regional agreement. UNEP Regional Seas agreements: BS = Black Sea convention; M = Mediterranean convention; WCA = West and Central African convention; EA = East African convention; RS = Red Sea and Gulf of Aden convention; C = Caribbean convention; SEP = South-East Pacific convention; SP = South Pacific convention; K = Kuwait convention. Other Regional Agreements: AFC = African conservation convention; HW = African hazardous waste convention; EC = European conservation convention; LR = transboundary air pollution convention; EIA = environmental impact assessment convention; AMC = Amazonian cooperation treaty; ASC = ASEAN conservation agreement; SPC = South Pacific conservation convention. Some small countries are not included in this table. For formal titles of the conventions and protocols listed, and for additional information, see Sources and Technical Notes.

Table 24.3 Sources of Environmental and Natural Resource

	INFOTERRA Member	National State of the Environment Report	UNCED National Reports	Country Environmental Profile	Environmental Synopses	Biological Diversity Profile	National Conservation Strategy	Environmental Action Plan	Tropical Forestry Action Plan
AFRICA									
Algeria	Yes		1991						
Angola	Yes		1991		IP				
Benin	Yes		1991		IP			IP	
Botswana	Yes	1990	1992			1991	1990		
Burkina Faso	Yes		1991	1980, 1982	IP			IP	FSR IP
Burundi	Yes		1991	1981	IP			1991	
Cameroon	Yes		1992	1981					TFAP 1988,1989
Central African Rep	Yes		1991		IP				FSR IP
Chad	Yes		1991				1990		
Congo	Yes		1992		IP			IP	FSR IP
Cote d'Ivoire	Yes	1992	1991		IP	1991		IP	FSR IP
Djibouti	No		1991		IP				
Egypt	Yes		1991	1980					
Equatorial Guinea	No		1991		IP				FSR IP
Ethiopia	Yes	IP	1992		IP	1991	1990		FSR IP
Gabon	Yes		1991		IP			IP	FSR IP
Gambia, The	Yes		1991	1981				IP	FSR IP
Ghana	Yes		1991	1980	1992	1988		1991	FSR 1988
Guinea	Yes		1991	1983		1988		IP	TFAP 1988
Guinea-Bissau	Yes		1991			1991	IP	IP	FSR IP
Kenya	Yes	1987	1991			1988	IP		FSR 1987,TFAP IP
Lesotho	Yes		1992	1982	IP			1989	FSR IP
Liberia	Yes			1980	IP				
Libya	Yes								
Madagascar	Yes	1987				1991	1984	1988	FSR IP
Malawi	Yes		1992	1982	IP		IP		
Mali	Yes		1991	1980, 1989					FSR IP
Mauritania	Yes		1991	1979, 1981	IP		1987		FSR IP
Mauritius	Yes		1991		IP			1990	
Morocco	Yes	IP	1992	1980					
Mozambique	Yes		1991		IP				
Namibia	No	1991	IP		IP				
Niger	Yes		1991	1980	IP				FSR IP
Nigeria	Yes	1991	1991		IP	1988	1986	IP	FSR IP
Rwanda	Yes		1991	1981, 1987	IP			1991	FSR IP
Senegal	Yes		1991	1980		1991			FSR IP
Sierra Leone	No		1991				1985		TFAP 1990
Somalia	Yes			1979	IP		1990		FSR 1990
South Africa	No	1989	1991				1980		
Sudan	Yes		1991	1989					FSR 1986
Swaziland	No		1991	1980	IP				
Tanzania	Yes		1991			1988	1986		TFAP 1989
Togo	Yes		1992		IP		1985	IP	FSR IP
Tunisia	Yes		1992	1980				IP	
Uganda	Yes		1991	1982	1992	1988	1983	IP	
Zaire	Yes		1991	1981	IP	1988	1984		TFAP 1988,1990
Zambia	Yes	1988	1992	1982			1985		FSR IP
Zimbabwe	Yes	1988	1991	1982	1992		1987		FSR IP
ASIA									
Afghanistan	No		1992						
Bangladesh	Yes	1987	1991	1980			1987, 1991	IP	MPFD IP
Bhutan	Yes		1991				IP	IP	MPFD IP
Cambodia	No			1989					
China	Yes		1991				1990	IP	
India	Yes	1988,1991,1991	1992	1980		1989	IP	IP	TFAP IP
Indonesia	Yes	1991	1991	1987	IP		IP	IP	TFAP 1991
Iran, Islamic Rep	Yes		1992						
Iraq	Yes		1992						
Israel	Yes	1979,1988,1992	1992						
Japan	Yes	1991	1991						
Jordan	Yes	1989	1992	1979			IP		
Korea, Dem People's Rep	Yes		1991						
Korea, Rep	Yes		1991						
Kuwait	Yes								
Lao People's Dem Rep	No		1992						TFAP 1990
Lebanon	Yes		1991						
Malaysia	Yes	1990,1991	1992		IP	1988 (2 docs)	1988,1989,1991		TFAP 1992
Mongolia	Yes		1991						
Myanmar	No		1992	1982		1989			MPFD 1991
Nepal	Yes	IP	1992	1979			1987	IP	MPFD 1988
Oman	Yes	IP	1992	1981			IP		
Pakistan	Yes	1986	1991	1986, 1988	1992	1991	1991		MPFD IP
Philippines	Yes		1991	1980		1988	IP	1988	MPFD 1990
Saudi Arabia	Yes		1992						
Singapore	Yes	1989,1990	1991	1988			1990		
Sri Lanka	Yes	1989	1991	1988	1992		1988	1991	MPFD 1986
Syrian Arab Rep	Yes	IP	1992	1981					
Thailand	Yes	IP	1992	1987			IP		MPFD IP
Turkey	Yes	1989	1991						
United Arab Emirates	Yes								
Viet Nam	Yes		1991				1985	IP	TFAP 1991
Yemen	Yes		1991	1982					

Sources of National Environmental Information {a}

Information, 1993

Table 24.3

		Sources of National Environmental Information {a}							Tropical
	INFOTERRA Member	National State of the Environment Report	UNCED National Reports	Country Environmental Profile	Environmental Synopses	Biological Diversity Profile	National Conservation Strategy	Environmental Action Plan	Forestry Action Plan
NORTH & CENTRAL AMERICA									
Belize	Yes		1992	1984	IP		IP		TFAP 1989
Canada	Yes	1986, IP	1991				1986		
Costa Rica	Yes	1988	1991	1982			1990		TFAP 1990
Cuba	Yes		1991						TFAP 1991
Dominican Rep	No		1991	1981	IP				TFAP 1990
El Salvador	Yes		1992	1985				IP	
Guatemala	Yes		1992	1984			IP		TFAP 1991
Haiti	Yes	IP	1992	1985				IP	FSR IP
Honduras	Yes		1991	1982, 1989				IP	TFAP 1988
Jamaica	Yes	IP	1992	1987	IP				TFAP 1990
Mexico	Yes	1986-1990 (7 docs)	1992			1988			TFAP 1991
Nicaragua	No		1992	1981			IP	IP	FSR IP
Panama	Yes	1985	1991	1980					TFAP 1990
Trinidad and Tobago	No		1992				IP		FSR IP
United States	Yes	1989,1990,1991	1992						
SOUTH AMERICA									
Argentina	Yes	IP	1991						TFAP 1988
Bolivia	Yes		1992	1986	IP			IP	TFAP 1989
Brazil	Yes		1991			1988			
Chile	Yes	1990	1992	1990					FSR IP
Colombia	Yes		1992	1990	IP	1988	IP		TFAP 1989
Ecuador	Yes	IP	1991	1987		1988	IP	IP	TFAP 1990
Guyana	Yes		1992	1982					TFAP 1989
Paraguay	Yes		1991	1985				IP	
Peru	Yes		1992	1986	IP	1988	IP		TFAP 1988
Suriname			1992						FSR IP
Uruguay	Yes	1992	1991						
Venezuela	Yes	1990,1992	1992						FSR IP
EUROPE									
Austria	Yes	1988,1989,1991	1992						
Belgium	Yes	1979	1992						
Bulgaria	Yes		1992						
Czechoslovakia (former)	Yes	1990 b	1991						
Denmark	Yes	1982	1991						
Finland	Yes	1988, IP	1992						
France	Yes	1990,1993	1991				IP		
Germany	Yes	1989,1990	1992						
Greece	Yes	1983	1991						
Hungary	Yes	1990	1991						
Iceland	Yes	1986	1992						
Ireland	Yes	1985	1992						
Italy	Yes	1989	1991				ND		
Netherlands	Yes	1989,1990	1991						
Norway	Yes	1993	1992				IP		
Poland	Yes	1989,1990	1991						
Portugal	Yes	1989	1991						
Romania	Yes		1992						
Spain	Yes	1977	1991				IP		
Sweden	Yes	1984,1990,1993	1992						
Switzerland	Yes	1989	1992					IP	
United Kingdom	Yes	1990,1992	1992				1983, 1990		
Yugoslavia (former)	Yes	1987	1991	c			IP		
U.S.S.R. (former)	Yes	1988	1991						
Armenia			1992						
Azerbaijan			1992						
Belarus			1992						
Estonia									
Georgia									
Kazakhstan			1992						
Kyrgyzstan									
Latvia			1992						
Lithuania			1992						
Moldova									
Russian Federation			1992						
Tajikistan									
Turkmenistan									
Ukraine			1991						
Uzbekistan									
OCEANIA									
Australia	Yes	1987,1988,1992	1991				1988		
Fiji	Yes		1992		IP	1989	IP		FSR 1990
New Zealand	Yes	1988	1991				1985		
Papua New Guinea	Yes		1992		IP				TFAP 1990
Solomon Islands	No		1991		IP				

Sources: World Resources Institute, International Institute for Environment and Development, World Conservation Union, U.S. Agency for International Development, World Conservation Monitoring Centre, and the United Nations Environment Programme.

Notes: a. Publication date of most recent edition; multiple dates indicate different reports. b. Produced by and about the Czech Republic. c. Yugoslavia 1991 and Croatia 1992.
INFOTERRA: member of INFOTERRA, the global environmental information system; FSR = Forestry Sector Review; TFAP = Tropical Forestry Action Plan;
MPFD = Master Plan for Forestry Development; IP = in preparation; ND = published, no date.
For additional information, see Sources and Technical Notes.

Table 24.4 Sources of Published Global and Regional Environmental Information

World:

Lester R. Brown, *et al.*, *State of the World 1994* (W.W. Norton, New York, 1994). {a}*

Food and Agriculture Organization of the United Nations (FAO), *State of Food and Agriculture* (FAO, Rome, 1992) {a}

Global Environment Monitoring System, *Global Freshwater Quality: A First Assessment* (World Health Organization and United Nations Environment Programme, Oxford, U.K., 1989).

United Nations Children's Fund, *The State of the World's Children 1993* (Oxford University Press, New York, 1993). {a}

United Nations Conference on Environment and Development (UNCED), *Nations of the Earth Report, Vols. 1–3* (UNCED, Geneva, 1992).

United Nations (U.N.), Department of International Economic and Social Affairs, *Prospects of World Urbanization 1990* (U. N., New York, 1991). {a}

United Nations Development Programme, *Human Development Report 1993* (Oxford University Press, New York, 1993). {a}

United Nations Educational, Scientific, and Cultural Organization (UNESCO), *Sustainable Development and Environmental Management of Small Islands* (UNESCO, Paris, 1990).

United Nations Environment Programme, *1993 Environmental Data Report* (Basil Blackwell, Oxford, U.K., 1993). {b}

United Nations Environment Programme (UNEP), *Saving Our Planet, Challenges and Hopes* (UNEP, Nairobi, Kenya, 1992).

United Nations Environment Programme (UNEP), *State of the Environment: 1972-1992* (UNEP, Nairobi, Kenya, 1992).

United Nations Environment Programme (UNEP) and United Nations Children's Fund (UNICEF), *The State of the Environment 1990: Children and the Environment* (UNEP and UNICEF, Nairobi, Kenya, and New York, 1990).

United Nations Environment Program (UNEP), *The World Environment 1972–82: A Report* (UNEP, Nairobi, Kenya, 1982).

United Nations (U.N.) Population Division, *World Population Prospects 1992* (U.N., New York, 1993).

United Nations Population Fund (UNFPA), *The State of the World's Population 1993; The Individual and the World: Population, Migration and Development in the 1990s* (UNFPA, New York, 1993).

The World Bank, *World Development Report 1993; Investing in Health* (Oxford University Press, New York, 1993). {a}

World Commission on Environment and Development, *Our Common Future* (Oxford University Press, Oxford, U.K., 1987).

World Conservation Monitoring Centre, *Global Biodiversity: Status of the Earth's Living Resources* (Chapman & Hall, London, 1992).

World Conservation Union, formerly the International Union for Conservation of Nature and Natural Resources (IUCN), United Nations Environment Programme, and World Wide Fund for Nature, *Caring for the Earth: A Strategy for Sustainable Living* (IUCN, Gland, Switzerland, 1991).

World Health Organization (WHO), *World Health Statistics Annual* (WHO, Geneva, 1993). {a}

World Health Organization (WHO), *Our Planet, Our Health: Report of the WHO Commission on Health and the Environment* (WHO, Geneva, 1992).

World Resources Institute (WRI), World Conservation Union, formerly the International Union for Conservation of Nature and Natural Resources (IUCN), and the United Nations Environment Programme (UNEP), *Global Biodiversity Strategy* (WRI, IUCN, and UNEP, Washington, D.C., 1992).

World Resources Institute, in collaboration with the United Nations Environment Programme and the United Nations Development Programme, *World Resources 1994-95* (Oxford University Press, New York, 1994). {b}

All Regions:

United Nations Environment Programme (UNEP), *Regional Seas Programme Studies and Reports* (UNEP, Nairobi, Kenya). Regional series include West and Central Africa, Eastern Africa, Wider Caribbean, Mediterranean, Kuwait Action Plan, Red Sea and Gulf of Aden, East Asian Seas, South Asian Seas, South East Pacific, South Pacific, and South West Atlantic Regions.

Africa:

Food and Agriculture Organization of United Nations (FAO), *Natural Resources and the Human Environment for Food and Agriculture in Africa* (FAO, Rome, 1986).

L.O. Lewis and L. Berry, *African Environments and Resources* (Unwin Hyman, Boston, 1988).

United Nations Development Programme and the World Bank, *African Development Indicators* (The World Bank, Washington, D.C., 1992).

The World Bank, *Sub-Saharan Africa: From Crisis to Sustainable Growth* (The World Bank, Washington, D.C., 1989).

World Conservation Union, formerly the International Union for Conservation of Nature and Natural Resources (IUCN), *Biodiversity in Sub-Saharan Africa and Its Islands: Conservation, Management and Sustainable Use* (IUCN, Gland, Switzerland, 1990).

World Conservation Union, formerly the International Union for Conservation of Nature and Natural Resources (IUCN), *IUCN Sahel Studies, 1989* (IUCN, Gland, Switzerland, 1989).

Latin America:

Sheldon Annis, *et al.*, *Poverty, Natural Resources, and Public Policy in Central America* (Transaction, Oxford, U.K., 1992).

Eric Cardich, ed., *Conservando el Patrimonio Natural de la Region Neotropical* (World Conservation Union, Gland, Switzerland, 1986).

Inter-American Development Bank (IDB), *Natural Resources in Latin America* (IDB, Washington, D.C., 1983).

Latin American and Caribbean Commission on Development and Environment, *Our Own Agenda* (Inter-American Development Bank and United Nations Environment Programme, Washington, D.C., 1990).

Jeffrey Leonard, *Natural Resources and Economic Development in Central America: A Regional Environmental Profile* (Transaction, Oxford, U.K., 1987).

Jorge Morello, *Perfil Ecologico de Sudamerica* (Instituto de Cooperacion Iberoamericana, Barcelona, 1984).

Programa de las Naciones Unidas para el Medio Ambiente, Agencia Española de Cooperación International, y Ministerio de Obras Públicas y Urbanismo (MOPU), *Desarrollo y Medio Ambiente en America Latina y el Caribe* (MOPU, Madrid, 1990).

United Nations Economic Commission for Latin America and the Caribbean (UNECLAC), *Sustainable Development: Changing Production Patterns, Social Equity and the Environment* (UNECLAC, Chile, 1991).

Asia and Oceania:

Asian Development Bank (ADB), *Economic Policies for Sustainable Development* (ADB, Manila, 1990).

Mark N. Collins, Jeffrey A. Sayer, and Timothy C. Whitmore, *The Conservation Atlas of Tropical Forests: Asia and the Pacific* (World Conservation Union, Gland, Switzerland, 1991).

A.L. Dahl and L.L. Baumgart, *The State of the Environment in the South Pacific* (United Nations Environment Programme, Geneva, 1983).

United Nations Economic and Social Commission for Asia and the Pacific (UNESCAP), *State of the Environment in Asia and the Pacific 1990* (UNESCAP, Bangkok, 1990).

Europe, North America, and Other Developed Countries:

Commission of the European Communities (CEC), *The State of the Environment in the European Community 1992* (CEC, Luxembourg, 1992).

DocTer Institute for Environmental Studies, Milan, *European Environmental Yearbook 1991* (DocTer International U.K., London, 1991). {a}

European Community (EC), *The European Community and the Environment* (EC, Luxembourg, 1987).

Eurostat, *Environment Statistics 1989* (Eurostat, Luxembourg, 1990).

Stanley P. Johnson and Guy Corcelle, *The Environmental Policy of the European Communities* (Graham and Trotman/Kluwer, London, 1989).

Organisation for Economic Co-operation and Development (OECD), *Environmental Indicators* (OECD, Paris, 1991).

Organisation for Economic Co-operation and Development (OECD), *OECD Environmental Data Compendium 1993* (OECD, Paris, 1993).

Organisation for Economic Co-operation and Development (OECD), *The State of the Environment 1993* (OECD, Paris, 1993).

United Nations (U.N.) Statistical Commission and United Nations Economic Commission for Europe, *The Environment in Europe and North America: Annotated Statistics 1992* (U.N., New York, 1992).

Source: Compiled by the World Resources Institute.

Notes: * forthcoming; {a} annual series; {b} biennial series. For additional information, see Sources and Technical Notes.

Schematic 24.5 The United Nations System

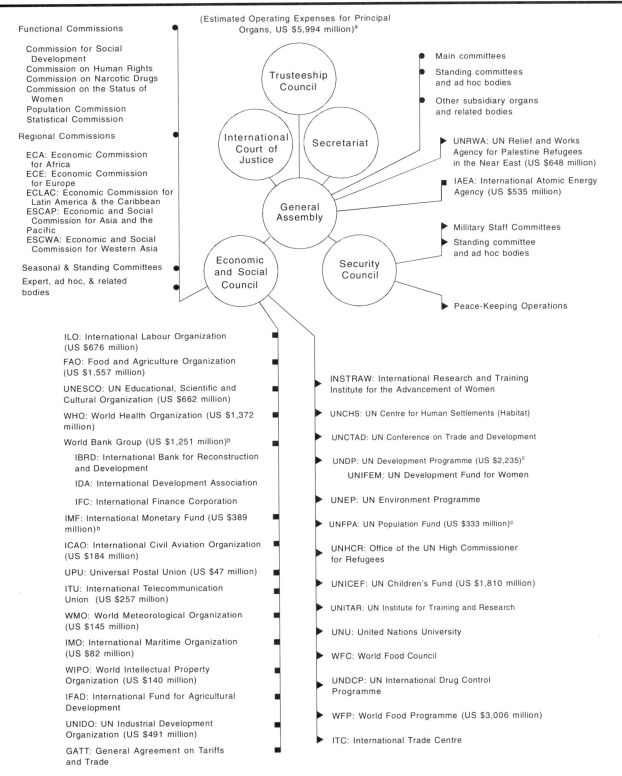

(Estimated Operating Expenses for Principal Organs, US $5,994 million)[a]

Functional Commissions

Commission for Social
Development
Commission on Human Rights
Commission on Narcotic Drugs
Commission on the Status of
Women
Population Commission
Statistical Commission

Regional Commissions

ECA: Economic Commission
for Africa
ECE: Economic Commission
for Europe
ECLAC: Economic Commission for
Latin America & the Caribbean
ESCAP: Economic and Social
Commission for Asia and the
Pacific
ESCWA: Economic and Social
Commission for Western Asia

Seasonal & Standing Committees

Expert, ad hoc, & related
bodies

Trusteeship Council

International Court of Justice

Secretariat

General Assembly

Economic and Social Council

Security Council

Main committees

Standing committees
and ad hoc bodies

Other subsidiary organs
and related bodies

UNRWA: UN Relief and Works
Agency for Palestine Refugees
in the Near East (US $648 million)

IAEA: International Atomic Energy
Agency (US $535 million)

Military Staff Committees

Standing committee
and ad hoc bodies

Peace-Keeping Operations

ILO: International Labour Organization
(US $676 million)

FAO: Food and Agriculture Organization
(US $1,557 million)

UNESCO: UN Educational, Scientific and
Cultural Organization (US $662 million)

WHO: World Health Organization (US $1,372
million)

World Bank Group (US $1,251 million)[b]

IBRD: International Bank for Reconstruction
and Development

IDA: International Development Association

IFC: International Finance Corporation

IMF: International Monetary Fund (US $389
million)[b]

ICAO: International Civil Aviation Organization
(US $184 million)

UPU: Universal Postal Union (US $47 million)

ITU: International Telecommunication
Union (US $257 million)

WMO: World Meteorological Organization
(US $145 million)

IMO: International Maritime Organization
(US $82 million)

WIPO: World Intellectual Property
Organization (US $140 million)

IFAD: International Fund for Agricultural
Development

UNIDO: UN Industrial Development
Organization (US $491 million)

GATT: General Agreement on Tariffs
and Trade

INSTRAW: International Research and Training
Institute for the Advancement of Women

UNCHS: UN Centre for Human Settlements (Habitat)

UNCTAD: UN Conference on Trade and Development

UNDP: UN Development Programme (US $2,235)[c]

UNIFEM: UN Development Fund for Women

UNEP: UN Environment Programme

UNFPA: UN Population Fund (US $333 million)[c]

UNHCR: Office of the UN High Commissioner
for Refugees

UNICEF: UN Children's Fund (US $1,810 million)

UNITAR: UN Institute for Training and Research

UNU: United Nations University

WFC: World Food Council

UNDCP: UN International Drug Control
Programme

WFP: World Food Programme (US $3,006 million)

ITC: International Trade Centre

Sources: United Nations (U.N.), *UN Chronicle* (U.N., New York, June 1993) and United Nations (U.N.) Economic and Social Council, *Programmes and Resources of the United Nations System for the Biennium 1992–1993: Report of the Administrative Committee on Coordination* (U.N., New York, 1993), p. 6

Notes: Numbers in parenthesis are total estimated expenditures for 1992–93 from all sources of funds by main program sector for the 18 organizations. ○ Principal organs of the U.N. ▲ U.N. Programmes and Organs (representative list only). ■ Specialized agencies and other autonomous organizations within the system. ● Other commissions, committees and ad hoc and related bodies. * Administrative Expenses only. a. Activities funded by reporting organizations and executed by other reporting organizations are included in the figures for the executing organizations. b. Administrative expenses for 1993 only. c. The figures cover resources expended by them or made available to other organizations of the United Nations System and to other executing agents.

Sources and Technical Notes

Table 24.1 Participation in Major Global Conventions— Wildlife, Habitat, and Oceans, 1993

Sources: United Nations Environment Programme (UNEP) Ocean and Coastal Areas Programme Activity Center, unpublished data (UNEP, Nairobi, Kenya, November 1993); Environmental Law Information System of the World Conservation Union, formerly the International Union for Conservation of Nature and Natural Resources (IUCN) Environmental Law Centre, unpublished data (IUCN, Bonn, October 1993).

A country becomes a signatory of a treaty when a person given authority by the national government signs it. Unless otherwise provided in the treaty, a signatory is under no duty to perform the obligations stipulated before the treaty comes into force for the country. The authorized signature indicates a commitment to undertake domestic action to ratify, accept, approve, or accede to the treaty. A country is a contracting party when the treaty comes into force in that country. Typically, this occurs when the country has ratified the treaty or otherwise adopted the treaty's provisions as national law and when a prescribed number of countries indicate consent to be bound by the treaty and register instruments of ratification, acceptance, approval, or accession with the treaty's depositary (which may be a national government, a U.N. organization, or another international organization; some treaties have multiple depositaries). The complete titles of the conventions and treaties summarized in Table 24.1 and their places and dates of adoption are as follows:

■ *Antarctic treaty and convention*: The Antarctic Treaty (Washington, D.C., 1959) is to ensure that Antarctica is used for peaceful purposes, such as, for international cooperation in scientific research, and that it does not become the scene or object of international discord. The Convention on the Conservation of Antarctic Marine Living Resources (Canberra, 1980) is to safeguard the environment and protect the integrity of the marine ecosystems surrounding Antarctica.

■ *Wetlands (Ramsar)*: The Convention on Wetlands of International Importance Especially as Waterfowl Habitat (Ramsar, Iran, 1971) is designed to stem the progressive encroachment on and loss of wetlands. The Convention recognizes the fundamental ecological functions of wetlands and their economic, cultural, scientific, and recreational value, by establishing a List of Wetlands of International Importance and by providing that parties will establish wetland nature reserves and consider their international responsibilities for migratory waterfowl.

■ *World heritage*: The Convention Concerning the Protection of the World Cultural and Natural Heritage (Paris, 1972) establishes a system of collective protection of cultural and natural heritage sites of outstanding universal value, organized on a permanent basis and in accordance with modern scientific methods.

■ *Endangered species (CITES)*: The Convention on International Trade in Endangered Species of Wild Fauna and Flora (Washington, D.C., 1973) protects endangered species from overexploitation by controlling trade in live or dead animals and in animal parts through a system of permits.

■ *Migratory species*: The Convention on the Conservation of Migratory Species of Wild Animals (Bonn, 1979) promotes international agreements to protect wild animal species that migrate across international borders.

■ *Biodiversity*: The Convention on Biological Diversity (Nairobi, Kenya 1992) protects biological resources and includes regulation of biotechnology firms, access to and ownership of genetic material, and compensation to developing countries for extraction of their genetic materials. (See Chapter 8, "Biodiversity," Focus On the Convention on Biological Diversity.)

■ *Ocean dumping*: The Convention on the Prevention of Marine Pollution by Dumping of Wastes and Other Matter (London, Mexico City, Moscow, and Washington, D.C., 1972) controls pollution of the seas by prohibiting the dumping of certain materials and regulating ocean disposal of others, encourages regional agreements, and undertakes the establishment of a mechanism for assessing liability and settling disputes.

■ *Ship pollution (MARPOL)*: The Protocol of 1978 Relating to the International Convention for the Prevention of Pollution from Ships, 1973 (London, 1978), is a modification of the 1973 convention to eliminate international pollution by oil and other harmful substances and to minimize accidental discharge of such substances.

■ *Law of the sea*: The United Nations Convention on the Law of the Sea (Montego Bay, Jamaica, 1982) establishes a comprehensive legal regime for the seas and oceans, establishes rules for environmental standards and enforcement provisions, and develops international rules and national legislation to prevent and control marine pollution. The United Nations Convention on the Law of the Sea will enter into force on November 16, 1994.

The European Community has signed the Convention on the Conservation of Antarctic Marine Living Resources, the Convention on the Conservation of Migratory Species of Wild Animals, the Convention on Biological Diversity, and the United Nations Convention on the Law of the Sea.

Information on the number of Natural World Heritage Sites and Wetlands of International Importance is contained in Chapter 20, "Biodiversity," Table 20.2. For information on treaty terms, refer to the sources.

Table 24.2 Participation in Major Global Conventions– Atmosphere and Hazardous Substances, 1993

Sources: United Nations Environment Programme (UNEP), Ocean and Coastal Areas Programme Activity Center, unpublished data (UNEP, Nairobi, Kenya, November 1993); Environmental Law Information System of the World Conservation Union, formerly the International Union for Conservation of Nature and Natural Resources (IUCN) Environmental Law Centre, unpublished data (IUCN, Bonn, October 1993).

See the Technical Note for Table 24.1 for general information on the meaning of conventions, signing, and ratification.

The complete titles of the conventions and treaties summarized in Table 24.2 and places and dates of adoption follow:

■ *Ozone layer*: The Vienna Convention for the Protection of the Ozone Layer (Vienna, 1985) is designed to protect human health and the environment by promoting research on the effects of ozone layer modification and on alternative substances and technologies, by monitoring the ozone layer, and by taking measures to control activities that produce adverse effects.

■ *CFC control*: The Protocol on Substances That Deplete the Ozone Layer (Montreal, 1987) requires nations to cut consumption of five chlorofluorocarbons and three halons by 20 percent of their 1986 level by 1994 and by 50 percent of their 1986 level by 1999, with allowances for increases in consumption by developing countries.

■ *Climate change*: The Convention on Climate Change (New York, 1993) aims to stabilize atmospheric concentrations of greenhouse gases at levels that will prevent human activities from interfering dangerously with the global climate system.

As of mid-October 1992, 158 countries had signed the Convention, including the European Community. For the Convention to become law, it must be ratified by national legislatures of 50 countries (as of December 13, 1993, 44 countries had ratified the convention).

■ *Biological and toxin weapons*: The Convention on the Prohibition of the Development, Production, and Stockpiling of Bacteriological (Biological) and Toxin Weapons, and on Their Destruction (London, Moscow, and Washington, D.C., 1972) prohibits acquisition and retention of biological agents and toxins that are not justified for peaceful purposes and of the means of delivering them for hostile purposes or armed conflict.

■ *Nuclear accident notification*: The Convention on Early Notification of a Nuclear Accident (Vienna, 1986) provides relevant information about nuclear accidents as early as possible so that transboundary radiological consequences can be minimized.

■ *Nuclear accident assistance*: The Convention on Assistance in the Case of a Nuclear Accident or Radiological Emergency (Vienna, 1986) facilitates the prompt provision of assistance in the event of a nuclear accident or radiological emergency.

■ *Hazardous waste movement*: The Basel Convention on the Control of Transboundary Movements of Hazardous Wastes and their Disposal (Basel, 1989) sets up obligations to reduce transboundary movement of wastes, to minimize the amount and toxicity of hazardous wastes generated and to ensure their environmentally sound management, and to assist developing countries in environmentally sound management of hazardous wastes.

■ The *UNEP Regional Seas Programme*, initiated by UNEP in 1974, has developed regional action plans for controlling marine pollution and managing marine and coastal resources. The action plans usually include regional environmental assessments, environmental management and legislation, and institutional and financial arrangements. The regional conventions and associated protocols that are a part of these action plans are included in the table and address region-specific marine-related environmental issues.

Some of the symbols used to indicate participation in a Regional Sea convention denote several related conventions and protocols. An asterisk (*) follows the convention abbreviation if a country has signed but not ratified the regional convention. A plus sign (+) follows the convention abbreviation if a country has signed or ratified at least two of the associated protocols to the regional convention. The abbreviations and full titles of Regional Seas conventions, their dates of adoption, and associated protocols mentioned in the table are listed below.

■ BS: Convention for the Protection of the Black Sea (1992).

■ M: Convention for the Protection of the Mediterranean Sea Against Pollution (1976). Associated protocols: Protocol for the Prevention of Pollution of the Mediterranean Sea by Dumping from Ships and Aircraft (1976); Protocol Concerning Co-operation in Combating Pollution of the Mediterranean Sea by Oil and Other Harmful Substances in Cases of Emergency (1976); Protocol for the Protection of the Mediterranean Sea Against Pollution from Land-based Sources (1980); and Protocol Concerning Mediterranean Specially Protected Areas (1982).

■ WCA: Convention for Co-operation in the Protection and Development of the Marine and Coastal Environment of the West and Central African Region (1981). Associated protocol: Protocol Concerning Co-operation in Combating Pollution in Cases of Emergency (1981).

■ EA: Convention for the Protection, Management and Development of the Marine and Coastal Environment of the Eastern African Region (1985). Associated protocols: Protocol Concerning Protected Areas and Wild Fauna and Flora in the Eastern African Region (1985); and Protocol Concerning Co-operation in Combating Marine

Pollution in Cases of Emergency in the Eastern African Region (1985).

■ RS: Regional Convention for the Conservation of the Red Sea and Gulf of Aden Environment (1982). Associated protocol: Protocol Concerning Regional Co-operation in Combating Pollution by Oil and Other Harmful Substances in Cases of Emergency (1982).

■ C: Convention for the Protection and Development of the Marine Environment of the Wider Caribbean Region (1983). Associated protocols: Protocol Concerning Co-operation in Combating Oil Spills in the Wider Caribbean Region (1983); and Protocol Concerning Specially Protected Areas and Wildlife to the Convention for the Protection and Development of the Marine Environment of the Wider Caribbean Region (1990).

■ SEP: Convention for the Protection of the Marine Environment and Coastal Area of the South-East Pacific (1981). Associated protocols: Agreement on Regional Co-operation in Combating Pollution of the South-East Pacific by Hydrocarbons or Other Harmful Substances in Cases of Emergency (1981); Supplementary Protocol to the Agreement on Regional Co-operation in Combating Pollution of the South-East Pacific by Hydrocarbons or Other Harmful Substances in Cases of Emergency (1983); Protocol for the Protection of the South-East Pacific Against Pollution from Land-Based Sources (1983); and Protocol for the Conservation and Management of Protected Marine and Coastal Areas of the South-East Pacific Against Radioactive Contamination (1989).

■ SP: Convention for the Protection of the Natural Resources and Environment of the South Pacific Region (1986). Associated protocols: Protocol Concerning Co-operation in Combating Pollution Emergencies in the South Pacific Region (1986); and Protocol for the Prevention of Pollution of the South Pacific Region by Dumping (1986).

■ K: Kuwait Regional Convention for Co-operation on the Protection of the Marine Environment from Pollution (1978). Associated protocols: Protocol Concerning Regional Co-operation in Combating Pollution by Oil and Other Harmful Substances in Cases of Emergency (1978); Protocol concerning Marine Pollution Resulting from Exploration and Exploitation of the Continental Shelf (1989); and Protocol for the Protection of the Marine Environment Against Pollution from Land-Based Sources (1990).

■ *Other regional agreements* include a variety of agreements addressing region-specific environmental issues. The abbreviations and full titles of the agreements and their date and place of adoption are listed below.

■ AFC: African Convention on the Conservation of Nature and Natural Resources (Algiers, 1968).

■ HW: Bamako Convention on the Ban of the Import into Africa and the Control of Transboundary Movements of Hazardous Wastes Within Africa (1991).

■ EC: Convention on the Conservation of European Wildlife and Natural Habitats (Bern, 1979).

■ LR: Convention on Long-Range Transboundary Air Pollution (Geneva, 1979); Protocol to the 1979 Convention on Long-Range Transboundary Air Pollution on Long-Term Financing of the Co-operative Programme for Monitoring and Evaluation of the Long-Range Transmission of Air Pollutants in Europe (Geneva, 1984); Protocol to the 1979 Convention on Long-Range Transboundary Air Pollution on the Reduction of Sulphur Emissions or Their Transboundary Fluxes by at Least 30 Percent (Helsinki, 1985); Protocol to the 1979 Convention on Long-Range Transboundary Air Pollution Concerning the Control of Emissions of Nitrogen or Their Transboundary Fluxes (Sofia, 1988).

■ EIA: Convention on Environmental Impact Assessment in a Transboundary Context (Espoo, Finland, 1991).

■ AMC: Treaty for Amazonian Cooperation (Brasilia, 1978).

■ ASC: ASEAN Agreement on the Conservation of Nature and Natural Resources (Kuala Lumpur, 1985). Please note, this agreement is not yet in force.

■ SPC: Convention on Conservation of Nature in the South Pacific (Apia, Western Samoa, 1976).

The European Community has signed the Vienna Convention for the Protection of the Ozone Layer, the Protocol on Substances That Deplete the Ozone Layer, the Convention on the Control of Transboundary Movements of Hazardous Wastes and Their Disposal, and the Convention on Climate Change. It has also signed conventions on three regional seas with associated protocols on the conservation of wildlife, on environmental impact assessments, and on long-range transboundary air pollution.

The Eastern African and South Pacific Regional Seas conventions and their protocols have not yet entered into force. For information on treaty terms, refer to the sources.

Table 24.3   Sources of Environmental and Natural Resource Information, 1993

Source: Compiled by the World Resources Institute (WRI) (unpublished data, 1993), the International Institute for Environment and Development, the World Conservation Union, formerly the International Union for Conservation of Nature and Natural Resources (IUCN), and the World Resources Institute, *1993 Directory of Country Environmental Studies* (WRI, Washington, D.C., 1992).

INFOTERRA, the global environmental information system, is a network of national information centers established by the United Nations Environment Programme (UNEP) for the exchange of environmental information. Each member country compiles a register of institutions willing to share expertise in environmentally related areas, such as atmosphere and climate, energy, food and agriculture, plant and animal wildlife, and pollution. An international directory is developed from the national registers; the national offices use the directory to select experts who can answer the queries. In 1991, the network processed 24,500 queries, and in 1992, the total rose to 29,097.

National State of the Environment Reports are published by government agencies, multilateral organizations, universities, and nongovernmental organizations (NGOs). They analyze the condition and management of a country's natural resources and document its progress or failure in sustaining its natural resource base. UNEP supports the development of state-of-the- environment reports in several countries. Their goal is to help developing countries improve their knowledge of their environment and thus formulate more environmentally sound national strategies. UNEP provides consultants on a short-term basis and helps prepare and publish the final report.

UNCED National Reports were prepared by countries of the United Nations Conference on Environment and Development. They identify how national economic and other activities can stay within the constraints imposed by the need to conserve natural resources. Some consider issues of equity, justice, and fairness.

Country Environmental Profiles are sponsored by the U.S. Agency for International Development. These profiles assess a country's natural resource potential in relation to its economic growth and development. The environmental profile program helps to establish an information base that can be used in planning and policy development.

Environmental Synopses were prepared by the International Institute for Environment and Development for the European Community, and the Australian International Development Assistance Bureau. They are 25-page overviews of the state of a country's environment and the institutional context in which environmental problems are managed, and analyses of pollution and degradation processes.

Biological Diversity Profiles are published by the Habitats Data Unit of the World Conservation Monitoring Centre and the Tropical Forest Programme of IUCN, in support of the conservation of biological diversity. The profiles provide basic background on species diversity, major ecosystems and habitat types, protected area systems, and legislative and administrative support; they identify the status of sites of critical importance for biological diversity and ecosystem conservation; and they provide a concise report on the values, threats, and conservation needs of these sites for decisionmakers and development agencies.

National Conservation Strategy (NCS) reports involve a consideration of the current and future needs and aspirations of a people, the institutional capacities of a country, the prevailing technical conditions in it, and the status of its natural resources. On the basis of review, analysis, and assignment of priorities, an NCS is intended to define the best possible allocation of human and financial resources to achieve the goals of sustainable development. Host governments

bear the main responsibility for implementing NCSs and must take the lead in their preparation. For more information on the status of NCSs, see past issues of the *IUCN Bulletin Supplement.*

Environmental Action Plans (EAPs) are sponsored by the World Bank and prepared by its staff and consultants in close collaboration with governments, various international organizations, NGOs, and other donors. These plans are detailed studies that culminate in the implementation of environmental projects and policies. Some EAPs provide a framework for integrating environmental considerations into a nation's overall economic and social development programs. The EAPs also make recommendations for specific actions, outlining the environmental policies, investment strategies, legislation, and institutional arrangements required.

Tropical Forestry Action Plan (TFAP) is a global strategy developed by the Food and Agriculture Organization of the United Nations, the United Nations Development Program, the World Bank, and the World Resources Institute, with the cooperation of some 40 bilateral donors, international organizations, and nongovernmental organizations. It provides a framework for concerted national and international action to manage, protect, and restore forest resources in the tropics.

Table 24.4 Sources of Published Global and Regional Environmental Information, 1993

Source: Compiled by the World Resources Institute. The bibliography of Sources of Published Global and Regional Environmental Information includes general statistical and analytical publications. It includes neither specialized reports nor journal articles.

Schematic 24.5 The United Nations System

Sources: United Nations (U.N.), *UN Chronicle* (U.N., New York, 1993); United Nations Economic and Social Council, *Programmes and Resources of the United Nations System for the Biennium 1992–1993: Report of the Administrative Committee on Coordination* (U.N., New York, 1993); International Monetary Fund (IMF), *Annual Report, 1993* (IMF, Washington, D.C., 1993); The World Bank, *Annual Report 1993* (The World Bank, Washington, D.C., 1993).

The United Nations is a vehicle that member governments can use to forge agreements among themselves to solve the world's problems and to carry out the specific social, humanitarian, or peacekeeping tasks they charge it with. Its limits are imposed by its member governments.

The Extended U.N. Family of Organizations. Many people wrongly assume that the United Nations controls the *specialized agencies* that make up the U.N. system, such as the Food and Agriculture Organization and

the United Nations Industrial Development Organization. It does not. The United Nations Charter provides for the establishment of independent, specialized agencies to promote higher standards of living, full employment, economic and social progress, and respect for human rights—in effect, to create the conditions of stability and well-being necessary for peace. Although these agencies enter into a legal "relationship agreement" with the United Nations, each has a separate legal charter and its own intergovernmental decision-making body, secretariat, and budget. Economic and Social Council coordinates the activities of this "system," but—like the General Assembly—it can only *recommend* actions to the agencies (and to member states), require regular reports from them, and examine their administrative budgets.

A 1944 conference in Bretton Woods, New Hampshire, founded the two principal international organizations dealing with financial matters—the World Bank and the International Monetary Fund (IMF). These organizations are generally considered part of the U.N. family, though more removed from it than are the specialized agencies that make up the system. In the United Nations, the one-nation/one-vote system means that the major industrialized countries can easily be outvoted by developing nation majorities, except in the Security Council. The weighted voting procedures in the Bretton Woods institutions give predominant power to the major shareholders—the industrialized nations.

Total *estimated expenditures* are for 1992–93 and are from all sources of funds by main program sector. The 18 organizations listed include the United Nations, the United Nations Children's Fund (UNICEF), the United Nations Development Programme (UNDP), the United Nations Population Fund (UNFPA), the United Nations Relief and Works Agency for Palestine Refugees in the Near East (UNRWA), the World Food Programme (WFP), 11 technical specialized agencies, and the International Atomic Energy Agency (IAEA).

The United Nations includes in addition to the various offices and departments, subsidiary or semi-autonomous entities and organs and organizations such as the United Nations Conference on Trade and Development (UNCTAD), the United Nations Environment Programme (UNEP), the United Nations Institute for Training and Research (UNITAR), the United Nations University (UNU), the Regional Commissions, the United Nations High Commissioner for Refugees (UNHCR), the United Nations International Drug Control Programme (UNDCP) and the International Trade Centre (ITC[UNCTAD/GATT]).

Budgets for the World Bank and the IMF are administrative budgets only and do not include the flux of loans, grants, payments, and other monies that they handle for the community of nations.

Index

Page numbers in italics refer to tables or figures.

This index does not include page numbers for specific country data shown in Part IV tables. See Table of Contents for list of table titles. Most tables include data for 152 countries.

Index

WORLD RESOURCES DATABASE INDEX

The *World Resources* electronic database is IBM-PC compatible. Most variables are presented in annual or five-year time series for up to 152 countries. The data can be searched by variable, by country, or by country grouping. An asterisk (*) indicates non-typical data files. The program is able to export the data in WK1, ASC, PRN, and DBF formats. Created by DSC Data Services, Inc. of Stamford, Connecticut, it also has the capacity to graph, create tables, and print. Data sources and technical notes are included. **To order,** call 410-516-6963 or write to: WRI Publications, P.O. Box 4852, Hampden Station, Baltimore, MD USA 21211.

Basic Economic Indicators

Gross national product (GNP), (current U.S.$); Atlas methodology, 1970–92
GNP per capita (current dollars); Atlas methodology, 1970–92
Gross domestic product (GDP), (current U.S.$)
GDP per capita (current dollars)
GDP (international dollars)
GDP per capita (international dollars)
Average annual growth rate of GNP, 1980–91
Average annual growth rate of GDP, 1980–91
GDP (current local currency), 1970–92
Distribution of GDP (current local currency)
    Agricultural share, 1971–91
    Industrial share, 1971–91
    Services share, 1971–91
Conversion factors (current local to U.S. currency), 1970–92
Official development assistance (ODA), (current U.S.$), 1982–91
Total external debt (current U.S.$), 1970–91
Disbursed long-term public debt (current U.S.$), 1970–91
Total debt service (current U.S.$), 1970–91
Total exports of goods and services (current U.S.$), 1970–91
Current borrowing (current U.S.$), 1970–91
Selected world commodity indexes and prices (constant 1990 U.S.$), 1975–92 *
International trade flows (current U.S.$):*
    (Standard International Trade Classification [SITC] categories 0 and 1), 1965–90*
    SITC categories 2 and 4, 1965–90*
    SITC category 3, 1965–90*
    SITC category 5 through 9, 1965–90*
    total trade, 1965–90*
Defense expenditures in U.S. dollars, 1985 and 1991
Numbers in armed forces, 1985 and 1991
Estimated reservists, 1991
Location of refugees and asylum seekers, 1992
Export of arms in U.S. dollars

Population and Human Development

Total population, 1950–2025
Population growth rate, 1950–2025
Total economically active population, 1950–2005
Crude birth rate, 1950–2025
Life expectancy—both sexes, 1950–2025
Life expectancy—females, 1950–2025
Life expectancy—males, 1950–2025
Total fertility rate, 1950–2025
Total population over age 65, 1950–2025
Total population under age 15, 1950–2025
Crude death rates, 1950–2025
Infant mortality, 1950–2025
Under-five mortality rate, 1960–91
Maternal mortality rate
Child malnutrition—wasting
Child malnutrition—stunting
Per capita average calories available (% of need)
Percent share of household consumption expenditure for food
Safe drinking water—urban (1980 and 1990)
Safe drinking water—rural (1980 and 1990)
Sanitation services—urban (1980 and 1990)
Sanitation services—rural (1980 and 1990)

Health services availability
    all
    urban
    rural
Percentage of total central government expenditure for health
Adult female literacy (1970 and 1990)
Adult male literacy (1970 and 1990)
Gross primary school enrollment—female
Gross primary school enrollment—male
Births attended by trained personnel
Oral rehydration therapy use
Low birth-weight infants
Percent of 1-year-olds immunized against:
    TB
    DPT
    polio
    measles
Females as a percentage of males—life expectancy
Females as a percentage of males—literacy
Females as a percentage of total labor force
Mean years of school for females age 25 and above
Mean years of school for males age 25 and above
Couples using contraception
Average age of first marriage—female
Average age of first marriage—male
Year women received vote
Females per 100 males—urban
Females per 100 males—rural
Households headed by women

Land Cover and Settlements

Land area, 1970–93
Population density, 1970–91
Domesticated land as a percentage of land area
Cropland area, 1970–91
Permanent pasture area, 1970–91
Forest and woodland area, 1970–91
Other land area, 1970–91
Total urban population, 1950–2025
Total rural population, 1950–2025
Average annual population change—urban, 1965–95
Average annual population change—rural, 1965–95
Number of cities with at least 750,000 inhabitants
Percentage of population residing in cities with at least 750,000 inhabitants, 1950–2000
Number of people residing in cities with at least 750,000 inhabitants, 1950–2000
Persons per vehicle
Total labor force
Percentage of labor force in:
    agriculture
    industry
    services
Percent unemployed—male
Percent unemployed—female
Name of megacity*
    size (1,000 ha)*
    population*
    annual population growth rate*
    percentage of household income spent on food*
    persons per room*
    percent of households with running water*
    percent of households with electricity*
    telephones per 100 people*
    motor vehicle registrations*

Food and Agriculture

Index of agricultural production, total, 1961–92
Index of agricultural production, per capita, 1960–92
Index of food production, total, 1960–92
Index of food production, per capita, 1960–92
Production of cereals, 1961–92
Area harvested for cereals, 1961–92
Production of roots and tubers, 1961–92
Area harvested for roots and tubers, 1961–92
Total cropland area, 1961–92
Total irrigated land, 1961–92
Total fertilizers consumed, 1961–92
Pesticide consumption
Total tractors in use, 1961–92
Total harvesters in use, 1961–92
Total number of cattle, 1961–92
Total number of sheep, 1961–92
Total number of goats, 1961–92

Total number of pigs, 1961–92
Total number of horses, 1961–92
Total number of mules, 1961–92
Total number of asses, 1961–92
Total number of buffaloes, 1961–92
Total number of camels, 1961–92
Total number of chickens, 1961–92
Grain fed to livestock, 1970–92
Total cereal imports, 1961–91
Total cereal exports, 1961–91
Total pulse imports, 1961–91
Total pulse exports, 1961–91
Total edible oil imports, 1961–91
Total edible oil exports, 1961–91
Total cereal donations, 1977–89
Total cereal receipts, 1977–89
Total edible oil donations, 1977–89
Total edible oil receipts, 1977–89
Total milk donations, 1977–89
Total milk receipts, 1977–89
Agricultural gross domestic product (AGDP)—total
AGDP per capita
AGDP per hectare of arable land
AGDP per labor unit
Agricultural labor force (% of total)
Total public agricultural research expenditures, 1961–85
Total number of BSc equivalent researchers, 1961–85

Forests and Rangelands

Extent of natural forest, 1980 and 1990
Extent of other wooded land, 1980 and 1990
Annual deforestation total forest—extent
Annual deforestation total forest—percent
Annual logging of closed broadleaf forest:
    extent
    percent of closed forest
    percent of which is primary forest
Plantations—extent
Plantations—annual change
Protected forest
Rain forest—extent, 1980 and 1990
Rain forest—percent annual change
Moist deciduous forest—extent, 1980 and 1990
Moist deciduous forest—percent annual change
Hill and montane forest—extent, 1980 and 1990
Hill and montane forest—percent annual change
Dry deciduous forest—extent, 1980 and 1990
Dry deciduous forest—percent annual change
Very dry forest—extent, 1980 and 1990
Very dry forest—percent annual change
Desert forest—extent, 1980 and 1990
Desert forest—percent annual change
Roundwood production, total, 1961–91
Fuel and charcoal, production, 1961–91
Industrial roundwood, production, 1961–91
Sawnwood, production, 1961–91
Panels, production, 1961–91
Paper, production, 1961–91
Exports, roundwood, 1961–91
Imports, roundwood, 1961–91

Biodiversity

Number of IUCN category (cat.) I-V protected areas
Total area under IUCN cat. I-V protection
Percent of land area under IUCN cat. I–V protection
Number of IUCN cat. I-III protected areas
Total area under IUCN cat. I-III protection
Number of IUCN cat. IV and V protected areas
Total area under IUCN cat. IV and V protection
Protected areas under IUCN cat. I–V of at least 100,000 ha in size:
    number
    total area
    percent of total
Protected areas under IUCN cat. I–V of at least 1 million ha in size:
    number
    total area
    percent of total
Resource and anthropological reserves (IUCN cat. VI–VIII):
    number
    total area
Biosphere reserves—number

Biosphere reserves—total area
World heritage sites—number
World heritage sites—total area
Wetlands of international importance—number
Wetlands of international importance—total area
Marine and coastal protected areas—number
Marine and coastal protected areas—total area
Percent of total land area classified as regions of low
    human disturbance
Percent of total land area classified as regions of me-
    dium human disturbance
Percent of total land area classified as regions of
    high human disturbance
Habitat types:
    current extent of all forests
    percentage lost of all forests
    current extent of dry forests
    percentage lost of dry forests
    current extent of moist forests
    percentage lost of moist forests
    current extent of savannah/grassland
    percentage lost of savannah/grassland
    current extent of desert/scrub
    percentage lost of desert/scrub
    current extent of wetlands/marsh
    percentage lost of wetlands/marsh
    current extent of mangroves
    percentage lost of mangroves
Number of mammal species:
    all
    endemic
    threatened
    per 10,000 square km
Number of bird species:
    all
    endemic
    threatened
    per 10,000 square km
Number of higher plant species:
    all
    endemic
    threatened
    per 10,000 square km
Number of reptile species:
    all
    endemic
    threatened
    per 10,000 square km
Number of amphibian species:
    all
    endemic
    threatened
    per 10,000 square km
Number of threatened fish species
Percent of CITES reporting requirement met
Number of live primates imported
Number of live primates exported
Number of cat skins imported
Number of cat skins exported
Number of live birds imported
Number of live birds exported
Number of reptile skins imported
Number of reptile skins exported
Number of live cacti imported
Number of live cacti exported
Number of live orchids imported
Number of live orchids exported

Energy and Materials
Commercial energy production:
    total, 1970–91
    solid fuel, 1979–91
    liquid fuel, 1970–91
    gaseous fuel, 1970–91
    geothermal and wind, 1970–91
    hydro, 1970–91
    nuclear, 1970–91
    total, 1970–91
    per capita, 1970–91
    per constant 1987 U.S. dollars of GNP, 1970–91
Imports as percentage of consumption, 1970–91
Traditional fuels consumption, total 1970–91
Traditional fuels consumption per capita, 1970–91
Traditional fuels as percentage of total require-
    ments, 1970–91
Anthracite and bituminous coals—reserves in place
Anthracite, bituminous coal reserves—recoverable
Subbituminous and lignite coals—reserves in place

Subbituminous and lignite coals—recoverable
    reserves
Crude oil—recoverable reserves
Natural gas—recoverable reserves
Uranium—recoverable at less than $80 U.S. per kg
Uranium—recoverable at less than $130 U.S. per kg
Hydroelectric—known exploitable potential
Hydroelectric—installed capacity
Production, bauxite
Consumption, aluminum
Production, cadmium
Consumption, cadmium
Production, copper
Consumption, copper
Production, lead
Consumption, lead
Production, mercury
Consumption, mercury
Production, nickel
Consumption, nickel
Production, tin
Consumption, tin
Production, zinc
Consumption, zinc
Production, iron ore
Consumption, iron ore
Production, steel crude
Consumption, steel crude
Reserves (million U.S.$)
    copper
    lead
    tin
    zinc
    iron ore
    manganese
    nickel
    chromium
    cobalt
    molybdenum
    tungsten
    vanadium
    bauxite
    rutile
    Ilmenite
Total reserve value
Metal reserves index
Waste generated (metric tons)
    from surface treatment of metals and plastics
    from biocide production (metric tons)
Waste-oil (metric tons)
Waste-containing PCBs (metric tons)
Waste-clinical and pharmaceutical (metric tons)
Waste from production and use of (metric tons)
    photographic materials
    organic solvents
    paints and pigments
    resins and latex

Water
Annual internal renewable water resources—total
Annual internal renewable water resources—per
    capita
Annual river flows from other countries
Annual river flows to other countries
Year of data: annual withdrawal
Annual withdrawal—total
Annual withdrawal—percent of water resources
Annual withdrawal per capita
Sectoral withdrawal—domestic
Sectoral withdrawal—industry
Sectoral withdrawal—agriculture
Location of major lakes*
    surface area (square km)*
    mean depth (meters)*
    maximum depth (meters)*
    volume (cubic km)*
    shoreline length (kilometers)*
    catchment area (square km)*
    population density (per square km)*
    fish catch (metric tons)*
    origin*
Percent of population served by primary waste
    water treatment (OECD countries)
Percent of population served by secondary waste
    water treatment (OECD countries)
Percent of population served by tertiary waste water
    treatment (OECD countries)

Percent of population served by all waste water
    treatment (OECD countries)
Annual marine catch, by region, 1970–91
Annual freshwater catch, 1970–91
Annual aquaculture production:
    freshwater fish, 1984–91
    diadromous fish, 1984–91
    marine fish, 1984–91
    crustaceans, 1984–91
    molluscs, 1984–91
    total fish and shellfish, 1984–91
    other, 1984–91
Per capita annual food supply from fish and fishery
    products
Length of coastline
Maritime area—shelf to 200 meter depth
Maritime area—exclusive economic zone
Percent of urban population in large coastal cities
Goods loaded—crude petroleum
Goods unloaded—crude petroleum
Goods loaded—petroleum products
Goods unloaded—petroleum products
Goods loaded—dry cargo
Goods unloaded—dry cargo
Offshore annual production—oil (1982 and 1992)
Offshore annual production—gas (1982 and 1992)
Offshore proven reserves—oil
Offshore proven reserves—gas
Name of mid-sized oceanic islands*
    total area*
    length of shoreline*
    population density*
    distance to nearest continent*
    type of island*
    percent of coastline fringed by coral*
    percent of coastline fringed by mangrove*
    protected areas—number*
    protected areas—terrestrial*
    protected areas—marine*
    number of plants—total*
    number of plants—endemic*

Atmosphere and Climate
Carbon dioxide emissions from industrial sources:
    solid fuels, 1970–91
    liquid fuels, 1970–91
    gas fuels, 1970–91
    gas flaring, 1970–91
    cement manufacture, 1970–91
    total, 1970–91
    per capita, 1970–91
Carbon dioxide emissions from bunker fuels
Carbon dioxide emissions from land-use change
Methane emissions from:
    solid waste
    coal mining
    oil and gas production
    wet rice agriculture
    from livestock
    Total
Total emissions of chlorofluorocarbons
Atmospheric concentrations of greenhouse and
    ozone depleting gases:
    carbon dioxide, 1965–92
    carbon tetrachloride, 1975–90
    methyl chloroform, 1975–90
    CFC-11, 1975–92
    CFC-12, 1981–92
    CFC-22, 1979–88
    CFC-113, 1983–90
    total gaseous chlorine, 1975–90
    nitrous oxide, 1975–88
    methane, 1965–91
    carbon monoxide, 1981–92
World carbon dioxide emissions from fossil fuels:
    total, 1955–91
    solid fuels, 1955–91
    liquid fuels, 1955–91
    gas fuels, 1955–91
    gas flaring, 1955–91
    cement manufacture, 1955–91
    per capita, 1955–91
Sulfur emissions, 1970–91
Nitrogen emissions, 1970–91
Common anthropogenic pollutants:
    carbon monoxide, 1980–91
    particulate matter, 1980–91
    hydrocarbons, 1980–91

The World Resources Institute (WRI) is a research and policy institute helping governments, the private sector, environmental and development organizations, and others address a fundamental question: How can societies meet human needs and nurture economic growth without destroying the natural resources and environmental integrity that make prosperity possible?

Through its policy studies, WRI aims to generate accurate information about global resources and environmental conditions, analyze emerging issues, and develop creative yet workable policy responses. In seeking to deepen public understanding, it publishes a variety of reports and papers; undertakes briefings, seminars, and conferences; and offers material for use in the press and on the air.

In developing countries, WRI provides technical support, policy analysis, and other services for governments and nongovernmental organizations that are trying to manage natural resources sustainably.

A central task of WRI is to build bridges between scholarship and action, bringing the insights of scientific research, economic analysis, and practical experience to the attention of policymakers and other leaders around the world.

WRI's projects are now directed at two principal concerns:
■ The effects of natural resources deterioration on economic development and on the alleviation of poverty and hunger in developing countries; and
■ The new generation of globally important environmental and resource problems that threaten the economic and environmental interests of all the nations of the world.

WRI is an independent, not-for-profit corporation that receives its financial support from private foundations and corporations, governmental and intergovernmental institutions, and interested individuals.

WRI is currently carrying out policy research in five major areas: Climate, Energy, and Pollution; Biological Resources and Institutions; Economics and Population; Technology and the Environment; and Resource and Environmental Information. In collaboration with several other research organizations, WRI is also involved in the "2050 Project," an ambitious effort to envision a sustainable world in the year 2050 and to identify the policy changes needed to reach that goal.

In developing countries, WRI's Center for International Development and Environment provides policy advice, technical assistance and other supporting services to governments, nongovernmental organizations and local groups charged with managing natural resources and economic development.

United Nations Environment Programme

P.O. Box 30552
Nairobi, Kenya

Executive Director
Elizabeth Dowdeswell

Deputy Executive Director
Nay Htun

Regional and Liaison Offices

Latin America and the Caribbean:
UNEP Regional Office for Latin America and Caribbean
Boulevard de los Virreyes No. 155
Lomas Virreyes
1100 Mexico City
P.O. Box 10-793
Mexico

West Asia:
UNEP Regional Office for West Asia
1083 Road No. 425
Jufair 342
P.O. Box 10880
Manama, Bahrain

Asia and the Pacific:
UNEP Regional Office for Asia and the Pacific
United Nations Building
Rajadamnern Avenue
Bangkok 10200 Thailand

Europe:
UNEP Regional Office for Europe
Geneva Executive Centre
Case Postale 356
15 Chemin des Anemones
121 Chatelaine
Geneva, Switzerland

Africa:
UNEP Regional Office for Africa
UNEP Headquarters
P.O. Box 30552
Nairobi, Kenya

New York:
UNEP Regional Office for North America
The United Nations Plaza
Room DC2-0803
New York, N.Y. 10017 U.S.A.

Washington:
UNEP Liaison Office
Ground Floor
1889 F Street, N.W.
Washington, D.C. 20006 U.S.A.

Cairo:
UNEP Arab League Liaison Office
31 Abdel Moneim Riad
Dokki, P.O. Box 212
Cairo, Egypt

Outposed PAC Offices:
International Register for Potentially Toxic Chemicals
Programme Activity Centre (IRPTC/PAC)
Palais des Nations
CH-1211 Geneva 10
Switzerland

UNEP Industry and Environment Programme Activity Centre
(IE/PAC)
Tour Mirabeau
39-43 Quai Andre Citroen, F-75739 Paris Cedex 15
France

The United Nations Environment Programme (UNEP) was established in 1972 and given by the United Nations General Assembly a broad and challenging mandate to stimulate, co-ordinate, and provide policy guidance for sound environmental action throughout the world. Initial impetus for UNEP's formation came out of the largely nongovernmental and antipollution lobby in industrialized countries. This interest in pollutants remains, but right from the early years, as perceptions of environmental problems broadened to encompass those arising from the misuse and abuse of renewable natural resources, the promotion of environmentally sound or sustainable development became a main purpose of UNEP.

From the global headquarters in Nairobi, Kenya, and seven regional and liaison offices worldwide, UNEP's staff of some 200 scientists, lawyers, administrators, and information specialists carry out UNEP's program, which is laid down and revised every two years by a Governing Council of representatives from its 58 member states. These members are elected on a staggered basis for four years by the United Nations General Assembly.

Broadly, this program aims to stimulate research into major environmental problems, promote environmentally sound management at both national and international levels by encouraging the application of research results, and make such actions and findings known to the public—from scientists and policymakers to industrialists and schoolchildren.

By the terms of its mandate, UNEP runs its program in cooperation with numerous other United Nations agencies, governments, intergovernmental organizations, and nongovernmental organizations. Its main concerns are climate change, pollution, water resources, desertification control, forests, oceans, and regional seas' biological diversity, human settlements, renewable sources of energy, environmentally sound management of industry, toxic chemicals, and international environmental lawmaking.

The essential base for environmentally sound management is provided by UNEP's work on the monitoring and assessment of the state and trends of the global environment. This is carried out in conjunction with agency partners, through the Global Environment Monitoring System (GEMS). The Global Resource Information Database (GRID) stores and analyzes geographically referenced environmental and resource data, and provides the essential link between monitoring and assessment and sound environmental management by putting information in forms useful to planners and managers. GEMS, the Geneva-based International Register of Potentially Toxic Chemicals, and INFOTERRA provide both the international community and individual countries and organizations with the vital environmental information they need to take action. For its part, UNEP's Industry and Environment Office in Paris (IE/PAC) brings industry and government together for environmentally sound industrial development through technical cooperation and information transfer.

The United Nations Development Programme (UNDP) is the world's largest multilateral source of grant funding for development cooperation. It was created in 1965 through a merger of two predecessor programs for United Nations technical cooperation. Its funds, which total $1.5 billion for 1991, come from the yearly voluntary contributions of member states of the United Nations or its affiliated agencies. A 48-nation Governing Council composed of both developed and developing countries approves major programs and policy decisions.

Through a network of offices in 130 developing countries, and in cooperation with over 30 international and regional agencies, UNDP works with 170 governments to promote higher standards of living, faster economic growth, and environmentally sound development. Currently, it is providing financial and technical support for over 6,000 projects designed to build governments' management capacities, train human resources, and transfer technology. These projects cover such fields as agriculture, forestry, land reclamation, water supply, environmental sanitation, energy, meteorology, industry, education, transport, communications, public administration, health, housing, trade, and development finance. Currently, projects valued at approximately $500 million are targeted on activities concerned with environmental aspects of development.

All UNDP-supported activities emphasize the permanent enhancement of self-reliant, sustainable development. Projects are therefore designed to:

■ Survey, assess, and promote the effective management of natural resources; industrial, commercial, and export potentials; and other development assets.
■ Stimulate capital investments to help realize these possibilities.
■ Train people in a wide range of vocational and professional skills.
■ Transfer appropriate technologies that respect and enhance the environment and stimulate the growth of local technological capabilities.
■ Foster economic and social development, with particular emphasis on meeting the needs of the poorest segments of the population.

In each developing country, UNDP also plays the chief coordinating role for operational development activities undertaken by the whole United Nations system. Globally, UNDP has been assigned numerous coordinating roles—from administering special-purpose funds such as those entrusted to the United Nations Sudano-Sahelian Office, to chairing the interagency steering committee of the International Drinking Water and Supply and Sanitation Decade. It also focuses on bringing women more fully into the process, fostering participatory grassroots development, and encouraging entrepreneurship.

United Nations Development Programme
1 U.N. Plaza
New York, New York 10017 U.S.A.

Administrator
James Gustave Speth

Associate Administrator
Luis María Gómez

Bureau for Programmes and Policies
Assistant Administrator and Director
Gus Edgren

Regional Bureau for Asia and the Pacific
Officer-in-Charge
Elena Martinez

Regional Bureau for Arab States and Europe
Assistant Administrator and Director
Ali A. Attiga

Regional Bureau for Latin America and the Caribbean
Assistant Administrator and Director
Fernando Zumbado

Regional Bureau for Africa
Assistant Administrator and Director
Ellen Johnson Sirleaf

Bureau for External Relations
Director
Jean-Jacques Graisse